2018 Football Preview

By: Warren Sharp
@SharpFootball

of

SharpFootballAnalysis.com
SharpFootballStats.com
sharp@sharpfootballanalysis.com

Evan Silva
Executive Editor

Associate Editors:
Julie Rone
Matthew Freedman
Bryan Mears
Chris Raybon
Jose Martinez

Logo designs courtesy of Addison Foote of addisonfoote.com

Foreword

Football is America's true passion. Every single week during the NFL season, over 250 million viewers tune in. To put that in perspective, there are only 320 million or so people in the United States. Sure, some people watch more than one game, but, regardless, it's hard to deny football's importance in the American culture.

What does that mean? With that many people represented, every kind of football fan you can think of is in that viewer pool. That would represent all ages of people, men and women, all races, gamblers, fantasy players, hometown fans, all career fields, and just about anything else you can think of. Warren Sharp's Football Preview is the only book that will have something for everyone. It has illustrations and graphics for the visual person. It covers the analytical part of the game in many ways differently than I have seen. It has trends for people who like to bet the games, as well as philosophical thoughts on things that have happened in the past and how they might affect the future of the game.

Do you care about only one team? There is enough information on each and every part of your team that will more than satisfy you. Here is a warning, though: After reading the book, you will probably be angry at the front office and have a few things to say yourself. There are things in here that those front office people should be reading and applying to their franchises!

This book breaks down each team by every category imaginable and describes exactly what they did in every situation. If you coach any level of football, from youth to the NFL, you will assuredly receive valuable information.

Now I am not trying to sell you the book. What I am trying to say is that what makes the book so great is Warren thinks about the game in so many ways and sheds light on it from so many view points; it makes you want to keep reading and learning more. The analysis, the information, the conclusions drawn -- that's what everyone wants in a book, isn't it? You won't want to put it down.

It's time to be selfish. I want someone to understand the game like I do. I want someone to view the game as I do.

I see numbers everywhere in football. They are accurate. They tell a story. They can help coaches and players, especially quarterbacks and offensive coordinators, make decisions. What I love about the book is that I learn something every time I read it. That's almost embarrassing for me to say because I think I love the game of football and study as much as anyone. I get to coach the game for a living, and, in doing so, I also try to study the game from every angle. I want to know why teams do what they do, as well as what they SHOULD be doing according to the numbers. Warren shows me that I still have a ton to learn.

I started using analytics on the beginning levels early on in my coaching in 2003 when there wasn't much out there. My use of analytics translated into a very different brand of football than what you watch on Sundays in the fall.

My teams rarely punt (eight times in the last 11 years). We onside kick almost all the time (we have used about 15 different types of kicks). We frequently get more people to touch the ball on a single play than most teams would consider. And we throw the ball down the field more than anyone. It's all based on sound thinking, analytics, and things I have learned along my lifelong journey in the game.

Other coaches will tell you they use analytics, and on some level, I guess they do. It is very basic, though. They are just looking at situations, formations, down and distance, and then simply building out percentages based on history of what a team has done in those situations. Those who are slightly more analytics-savvy apply the same thing to themselves as a "self-scout." So, yes, they all use analytics, but I would honestly guess the clear majority do not go beyond that.

Over the past 15 years, I have been looking for several edges to come from my study of analytics.

One thing I was looking for, and continue to look for, is something that will raise my teams' chances to win the game without getting any better at all on the field or without increasing the talent level.

I guess in a sense, I want my team to simply be as efficient as possible. The applications of efficiency are way too numerous to go into, but I will give you a few examples.

For instance, the taking of a penalty in the following situation: Assume my team is on defense and it is first-and-10. The opposing team runs a play but has an illegal formation penalty post-snap. The play gains zero yards. I wanted to know based on our defense and the other team's offense whether we should accept the penalty and have first-and-15 or decline it and have second-and-10. Every decision like that either gives your team a better chance at that moment or a worse chance to win the game.

I wanted us to have a better chance to win the game based on that decision *WITHOUT OUR TEAM GETTING ANY BETTER*, just like I mentioned above. I wanted to do the same thing with not only decisions, but my own type of team goals.

Some coaches value data points, like completion percentage, and try to hold the opposing team to less than 20% on third-down conversions. Unlike arbitrary goals based on theories, I wanted to do things that I KNEW affect games and has been proven over an immensely large sample size.

So I used analytics to decide our goals. Some apply to all teams, some only to us.

For example: we want to have more explosive plays which gain over 20 yards than the other team. A more common goal is we also want to have fewer turnovers. Data shows if you win those battles, you'll win the game over 80% of the time.

We added things like having at least one onside kick per game. I believe we are 110-3 when we recover one onside kick. We are 48-0 when we recover two in a game.

We also want our defensive ends to "set the edge." We give up an unusually high rate of plays over 20 yards when we don't, and, again, 20-plus yard plays are incredibly important.

I learned how important the first *PLAY OF A SERIES* -- not first down -- is regarding a team scoring on that drive. (I wrote in all caps because most coaches and many fans think the goal should simply be four yards on first down, which is NOT true.) If a team gains over four yards, the chance of scoring is about 40% higher on that drive alone. That is a crazy stat. We got better as a team immediately by knowing those stats and building our strategy around them.

I started using analytics to look at formations. We focus on throwing out of the most efficient formations and less out of those which are inefficient.

I use analytics to determine player efficiency on certain run schemes. I employ sets with multiple running backs, and ensure my RBs are deployed so that they have different skills: Some are good at outside zone, some inside, some quick trap, some long trap.

By the way, in 2015 the Eagles should have done that with DeMarco Murray. He was terrible at outside zone but fantastic between the tackles. Everyone thought he was terrible and lost his abilities to be successful. It wasn't Murray, the Eagles were using him for the wrong things, mostly because they were afraid they'd show a tendency if they took it away. In Tennessee in 2016 he gained 1,287 rushing yards at 4.4 YPC and scored 9 rushing TDs, proving his 2015 season wasn't bad because of his demise, but rather his coaching.

I obviously use analytics to make decisions on field position: when to punt, when not to, and when to onside kick.

I have since deviated from my early rules, as I saw the butterfly effects throughout the game when we always onside kicked. When I did it every time, teams would plan for it, although there's value in that as well. When they're spending extra practice time scheming to prepare for our onside kicks, they don't have as much time to spend to fix their own problems, working against my schemes, etc.

NFL coaches seem to be very risk-adverse. It seems they would rather lose traditionally than increase their odds of winning non-traditionally.

Perhaps it is because of the ego factor.

Out of all sports, NFL coaches, as well as star players, are the "face" of the team. I can recognize the face of the head coach of the Minnesota Vikings but couldn't pick the face of the head coach of the Minnesota Twins out of a lineup of three people. Everyone knows what Jason Garrett looks like but not the manager of the Texas Rangers or Dallas Stars. That alone puts pressure on coaches.

The ego might factor in because of that recognition and their desire to win on coaching, not analytics. Maybe they are afraid that if they are known as an analytics coach, the public will think "anyone" can win that way and it's not due to their own good coaching.

I think that's short-sighted, because winning trumps all else.

When I started coaching at my current high school, they had been to the State Semifinals only two times in the history of the school. During the 15 years I have been the Head Coach, we have been to the semifinals 12 times, the Championship game nine times, and we've won seven State Championships.

I am proud to say that I have learned and applied many things during these last few years that I took from Warren Sharp's book.

I knew Warren knew his craft well when we were talking and he recited what he thought was my own personal football philosophy based on his study of my decision making. I have had so many people who want to talk with me about my thoughts and why my teams play the game so differently. EVERYONE THINKS they have it figured out, but they usually have only a small part of it figured out. Warren summed it up in one sentence and was right on the money.

I knew right then he has a gift when it comes to taking in information and interpreting it in a way that is real and not manipulated.

I have had the blessing of meeting many people who are extremely successful in the business, sports, and coaching world. The common denominator among them is that they have a true passion for what they do. WARREN HAS THAT PASSION! And Warren's "Football Preview" is a huge success for anyone that reads it! No matter how deep your love of football goes -- whether you like the charts, graphics, and numbers, or if you just love the many ways to view the details of the game -- I can't wait for you to dig in to this year's preview.

Kevin Kelley,
Head Football Coach - Pulaski Academy
7-time State Champions

COLUMNS

DEDICATION

TO my wife & children TO the decision makers in NFL front offices who exhaust every means to gain an edge because they care about winning TO anyone who spreads the word about this book, my websites and my passion for analyzing football TO anyone who reviews this book on Amazon and buys an accompanying electronic pdf copy, allowing this effort to continue into 2019 TO all who join in 2018 as clients of SharpFootballAnalysis.com and TO those who use SharpFootballStats.com regularly for more intelligent analysis

ACKNOWLEDGMENTS

TO Evan Silva, a great friend and incredible football mind, who suggested I let him edit this year's book and then made it far better than I ever could have hoped

TEAM CHAPTERS

The Age of Enlightenment: Analytics in the NFL

By Joe Banner
20 Year NFL President & CEO
Philadelphia Eagles
Cleveland Browns

Most institutions, to their detriment, are driven by "we have always done it that way" as a guiding principle. It is this commitment to conventional wisdom that has left businesses, charities, government and even sports on a path to unnecessarily slow evolution.

Surprisingly, this is actually more of an issue in sports than most areas. Specifically, within all types of sport, football proves over and over it is almost pre-historic when it comes to intelligent evolution. Football is devout in its commitment to remain in the past, clinging to the days of unenlightened information.

Analytics try to pierce the dark veil of unintelligence. But some view analytics as a dirty word. Analytics are really nothing more than added information to increase the chances of good decision making.

But some people, stuck in yesterday, actually have tried to demonize the word. Others have embraced the value of added information as being a good thing.

The two teams in this year's Super Bowl have been two of the best franchises in the NFL and have been embracing enhanced information, aka analytics, for over 20 years.

Almost 25 years ago I started what was the first (or one of the first) analytics departments in the NFL. The thinking was really simple. I realized that coaches generally ran whatever system and scheme they had been taught when they first got into coaching, period. There was no way that that made sense.

My hope was that added information would enlighten decision making beyond the "we have always done it that way".

Even the most basic person, with or without a football background, should realize the value in a pass play when hearing that a solid run averages 4.5 yards while a solid pass averages 7.2 yards.

But it took 50 years and a few new rules to be introduced (for player safety) for teams to be more pass oriented than run oriented.

Almost 80% of games are won by the team that leads at the half, but very few coaches scheme, call plays or build rosters as if they know that.

Bill Walsh knew this 40 years ago. He used that knowledge to win three Super Bowls in a decade. Ray Rhodes told me how Bill pressed him to rest his best pass rushers in the first half to make sure they didn't blow the lead he would get them by the half. That visionary strategy worked out pretty well.

Warren's preview exemplifies the use of analytics and information in a way that should be interesting to any fan.

It is more in depth than many teams in the NFL are using today. Every GM and coach would serve themselves well to read the analysis of their team. They would both learn something and immediately appreciate the benefit of the information.

Some still live in a world where they don't know what they don't know. This has become a crowded field, but no one presents it better, and breaks down what it means better than Warren.

QR Code Audio and Video

One of my favorite things to do is to share as much educational information as possible. Unfortunately, every printed page in this book comes with a cost. But embedded audio is free. Download any QR Reader or QR Scanner as an app on your phone. Below I've recorded audio that goes division by division, and talks 2018 prospects as well as elements I want to make sure you don't miss in the team chapter.

Scan the code above to watch a short video of me talking about the 2018 Football Preview and what I hope you'll take from it.

This upcoming season is going to be extremely compelling and I'm optimistic it will be tremendous. I can't wait for you to dive into the audio below and the team chapters so you can learn from my 4 months of research on these teams and what I think they'll do in 2018!

AFCN

NFCN

AFCE

NFCE

AFCS

NFCS

AFCW

NFCW

Improving Efficiency in Pro Football

By Warren Sharp

Time is fleeting. Any parent knows this. Their children grow up too quickly right before their eyes. Any aging adult knows this. The body does not continue to respond like it once did. There is an illusion that time is limitless. But time is life's most precious commodity.

The pessimist says that from the moment we are born, we're slowly dying with each minute that passes. I'm not a pessimist. But I am a realist. And with the way NFL coaches operate and the decisions they make, the truth is that from the moment a coach is hired, he's slowly approaching the end of his career as each minute passes. I'm not just talking about aging, but job security as well.

I literally watch every minute of every NFL game. I study the statistics long after the games have ended. During the football season I sleep very little and instead, devote my time to understanding the game of football. When I watch an NFL game, I'm looking for the following: Will the edges I thought existed in the matchups come to fruition, and will the team with the edges capitalize on them? Most of my week during the season is spent on uncovering these edges. With a strong understanding of teams' strengths and weaknesses, I'm looking to predict mismatches when players, units and teams go head-to-head.

I've had a good deal of success with my predictions regarding the outcome of games (which is why I bet significant sums). And while a lot of my success comes from understanding the teams—their edges and mismatches—an equal amount comes from knowing the coaches well enough to predict whether they will or will not take advantage of mismatches.

Over the years, it has become increasingly painful for me to watch the inefficiency on the football field. Mostly, teams don't even know it exists because they don't study their mistakes in great enough detail. And then someone like me comes along and points out how terribly inefficient they actually were.

In this annual, you'll see countless examples of me identifying inefficiencies that exist on nearly every team. Some are so infuriating they will make your jaw drop, as they did mine. My good friend Evan Silva told me as he was editing a team's chapter, that he grew enraged by what he was reading (not in reference to my writing ability.) He was literally moved to anger by the inefficiency of a particular coaching staff and how often they were misusing their team's assets.

I graduated nearly two decades ago with a degree in Civil Engineering from a top-10 engineering school. As I worked to obtain my Professional Engineer license, I became well-trained in problem solving. I learned to identify problems or inefficiencies, and then work to solve them expeditiously.

What follows is a primer on inefficiencies that exist in today's NFL. I could (and might) write an entire book dedicated solely to this subject. Here, I attempt to not only identify a specific inefficiency, but to illustrate why it is a problem and how teams can fix it. I include quotes from military visionaries including Sun Tzu, Napoleon Bonaparte, Carl von Clausewitz and others, which help to convey efficiency problems in a non-football sense.

My dream is to turn on the TV on a Sunday in the near future and to not witness rampant inefficiency. I want to see well-played games featuring well-made decisions, where the only errors are from an execution standpoint. It is hard enough to get 11 players on the field to work in unison against 11 opponents and have them play mistake-free football. But when they are put at big disadvantage beforehand--due to poor planning or poor decision making--it's a disservice to the players and a disappointment for the fans.

Hopefully more teams will choose to incorporate these strategies. We will all be better for it. Time for teams is fleeting and the value of NFL franchises is staggering. Most are worth at least $2 billion. Just this spring, the small-market Carolina Panthers sold for $2.3 billion. The average value of NFL teams compared to NBA, MLB and NHL franchises is substantially greater. As of 2016, the average NFL team was worth 88% more than the average NBA team, 95% more than the average MLB team, and 353% more than the average NHL team.

Yet the NFL is well behind the other leagues in investment and employment of analytics. Why NFL teams choose not to study and incorporate analytics to improve their performance is something I will never understand.

Pass on first down (and do so especially with a young quarterback)

Warfare is like hunting. Wild animals are taken by scouting, by nets, by lying in wait, by stalking, by circling around, and by other such stratagems rather than by sheer force. In waging war we should proceed in the same way, whether the enemy be many or few. To try simply to overpower the enemy in the open, hand to hand and face to face, even though you might appear to win, is an enterprise which is very risky and can result in serious harm. Apart from extreme emergency, it is ridiculous to try to gain a victory which is so costly and brings only empty glory. - Byzantine Emperor Maurikios, A.D. 539–602

This one was from last summer's book. The old "establish the run" oligarchy has seeped into the bloodstream of most NFL offenses. Teams legitimately believe it is physically and psychologically important for them to run the ball early to create a perception of "we are here to do the bullying today." However, the data proves this to be a flawed tactic. Trying to overpower the opponent in the run game early on, when all the edges in the passing game get placed on the shelf for use at another time, is a fool's errand.

Over the last two years, first down passes have been more successful (53%) than first down rushes (45%). Removing two-minute situations and isolating one-score scenarios, passing is 9% more successful and leads to a gain of 3.2 more yards per play on average (7.2 vs 4.0). Yet teams run the ball 54% of the time on these neutral 1st and 10 situations. And it's even more predictable in the first quarter.

On average, teams ran the ball 57% of the time in first quarter 1st-and-10s over the past two years. However, data shows this to be the worst time to run, as rushes produce a 44% success rate compared to a 55% success rate from passes. In the typical, predictable NFL, leave it to teams to do something *more* when it's even less efficient to do it. In the first quarter of games, it's the least efficient time to run the ball on 1st and 10, yet teams run it the most. Isolating even further: inside a team's own 40-yard line in the first quarter, running plays on first down produce a 43% success rate—14% worse than passes—but teams call for these plays 57% of the time. A great example of the inefficiency can be seen on a team like the Buccaneers. Seemingly unwilling to "throw Jameis Winston to the wolves" the Bucs called 67% run plays on first down in the 1st quarter for the last two years, the highest rate in the NFL. These run plays were successful just 43% of the time and produced only 3.6 YPC. Meanwhile, passes were successful 67% of the time (+24%) and teams gained 7.5 YPA. Winston's first down passer rating was 95.9 in the first quarter. After seeing this strategy fail in 2016, the Buccaneers continued it in 2017, apparently unaware of the analytics that showed how disastrous its impact was on the offense. In 2017, rushes gained just 3.3 YPC while passes gained 10.8 YPA and were 31% more successful, with Winston delivering a 117-passer rating. Yet the team still went 63% run.

For a second straight year, I have to repeat: don't run on first down in the first half to "establish the run". Pass instead to gain more yardage and see more success, By doing so, allow your offense to gain a first down on first down, or face a shorter second down. We need to change the philosophy of "establish the run" to "establish the lead" and that comes by passing early and allowing teams to run late. Both in the game and on a particular series, the goal is to stay on or ahead of schedule in ever down possible.

Don't run the ball on 2nd-and-10 after a first down incompletion

However desperate the situation and circumstances, don't despair. When there is everything to fear, be unafraid. When surrounded by dangers, fear none of them. When without resources, depend on resourcefulness. When surprised, take the enemy itself by surprise. —Sun-Tzu, The Art of War (fourth century B.C.)

This is another antiquated thought process that needs to be eradicated from the NFL. Offensive coordinators are so fearful of going pass-pass-pass-punt that they justify one of the worst play calls just to be viewed as more traditional, more like their colleagues. Following a 1st-and-10 incompletion, teams will be faced with 2nd-and-10. Especially for "drive starters", inside a team's own 40-yard-line these coordinators grow fearful. They see a desperate situation and revert back to comfortable, historically proper decision making. Even though they know their odds of converting a 3rd and long are slim, they are far too optimistic that a run play on 2nd-and-10 will put them in 3rd and manageable. Using my predictive play model and the last 2 years of data, I've calculated that following a 1st-and-10 incompletion, 54% of the time teams run the ball on 2nd-and-10. These plays produce a dismal 28% success rate. Meanwhile, 2nd-and-10 passes following an incompletion produce a 50% success rate and average 7.8 YPA. It's one thing to run the ball if you're in fringe FG range, but here we are talking about inside a team's own 40-yard line.

I also removed 4th quarter plays to eliminate game theory and running out the clock.

One of the worst offenders last season was the Buffalo Bills. They ran the ball 82% of the time on 2nd-and-10 in this situation. These run plays produced a 13% success rate and gained just 3.4 YPC. Pass plays produced a 40% success rate and gained 5.5 YPA. With a terrible receiving corps, the now-fired Rick Dennison thought running would be safer and more successful. He was wrong.

One of the teams that understood this the best was the New England Patriots. They ran the ball on just 32% of 2nd-and-10s in this situation, opting to pass the ball 68% of the time. Pass plays edged out run plays with a success rate advantage of 64% compared to 33%, and produced an average yardage edge of 10.8 YPA to 3.4 YPC.

If the Patriots are doing one thing to an extreme (passing) and the Bills are doing the opposite (rushing) you can guess who is analytically correct. But it's not even a "QB" have or have not issue. Even a team like the Cardinals, with a terrible QB situation, had a +30% success edge for passes and a +1.8 yds/play edge. Teams need to stop running in these situations and simply make good, +EV decisions as often as possible.

Target the middle of the field on pass plays more often

If battle cannot be avoided, get them to fight on your terms. Aim at their weaknesses; make the war expensive for them and cheap for you. Fighting with perfect economy, you can outlast even the most powerful foe. – The 33 Strategies of War, Robert Greene, 2007

Often, Napoleon and the French were faced by two or a series of enemy armies. In many such situations, the Napoleonic attack would attack where the enemy army boundaries converged, as he believed this area was vulnerable. He would blitzkrieg this area, shielded by cavalry, and fall like a thunderbolt. Typically, this would prove successful, and then his army, newly massed at a central position, would force the enemy to operate on the exterior and be more cut off from one another.

The middle of the field has become weaker over the years as NFL rules have evolved. It is particularly more noticeable on early downs. It is more vulnerable to all positions, particularly the short middle of the field (within 15 yards of the line of scrimmage). Comparing short middle passes to short left and right passes, every single position sees a +8% increase in pass success rate over the last 2 years, with an average boost from 53% to the perimeter up to 61% to the middle of the field. The YPA is greater as well, with all passes to this area gaining 7.5 YPA while to the short left they gain 6.1 YPA, and the short right 5.8 YPA.

Yet teams target this area on just 19% of all early down passes. If an early down pass is thrown short (within 15 yards of the line of scrimmage), it travels to the perimeter 77% of the time and to the middle just 23% of the time. Teams need to attack this area of the field much more often due to the massive efficiency boost. The team that has targeted this area the most is the Baltimore Ravens. Frankly, it is the only reason Joe Flacco is still a starter in the league. His passes

www.sharp football analysis.com

The Forefront of Inventing & Incorporating Custom Advanced Analytics & Metrics into Football Handicapping

<u>Lifetime NFL Record</u>
Totals: 479-312 (61%)
Sides (Personal Plays): 583-436 (57%)

Lifetime NFL Playoffs Record: 130-74 (64%)
Lifetime Super Bowl Record: 17-8 (68%)

<u>Lifetime College Football Record</u>
Totals: 688-564 (55%)

<u>Transparent Record Keeping</u>
All client plays publicly displayed minutes after the start of the game

<u>NFL's Most Consistent Results</u>
12 Years, 12 Winning Seasons
Emphasizing sound money management, +EV betting opportunities & beating the market

<u>Specializing in NFL Totals</u>
<u>By Year:</u>
2017: 62%
2016: 65%
2015: 68%
2014: 61%
<u>Lifetime (12 yrs): 61%</u>

<u>Respected Analysis</u>
Numerous betting syndicates acquire recommendations & Warren's work is well known by current and former linemakers

<u>Line Value</u>
Using timed release system, when Warren releases a play to clients, the market reacts giving clients consistent, significant & measurable line value

"I noticed Warren was moving some lines around on Wednesdays after he put his stuff up on his site, and he was winning. Instantly, when Warren gives out his play, the books move toward his line. Very rarely will you get a better number than his. He's a consistent winner."

- Professional Bettor & Las Vegas Legend **Bill "Krackman" Krackomberger**

<u>As currently seen in:</u>

"Warren's synopsis on game totals is vastly superior utilizing his mathematical formulas, to any preview I have ever seen. His success is two-fold, beating the closing number by up to 3 pts and winning at a clip needed to secure a hefty profit. Getting in early ensures some fantastic middling opportunities."

- **Richie Baccellieri**, former Director of Race and Sports in Las Vegas at Caesars Palace, MGM Grand and The Palms

Warren Sharp of <u>sharpfootballanalysis.com</u> is an industry pioneer at the forefront of incorporating advanced analytics and metrics into football handicapping after spending years constructing, testing, betting and perfecting computer models written to beat NFL and college football totals.

<u>Hear Pro Bettor Bill "Krackman" Krackomberger:</u>

A licensed Professional Engineer by trade, Warren now works as a quantitative analyst for multiple professional sports betting syndicates in Las Vegas and has parlayed a long-term winning record into selections for clients which move the Vegas line and beat the closing number with regularity.

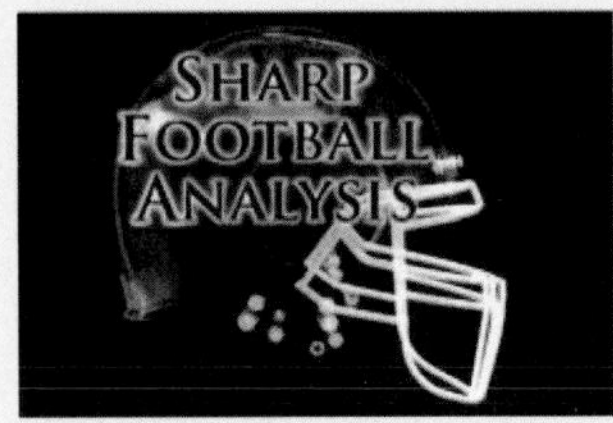

Get all the detailed weekly analysis, write-ups and recommendations now, pay only after the 2018 season! Details at www . sharp football analysis . com

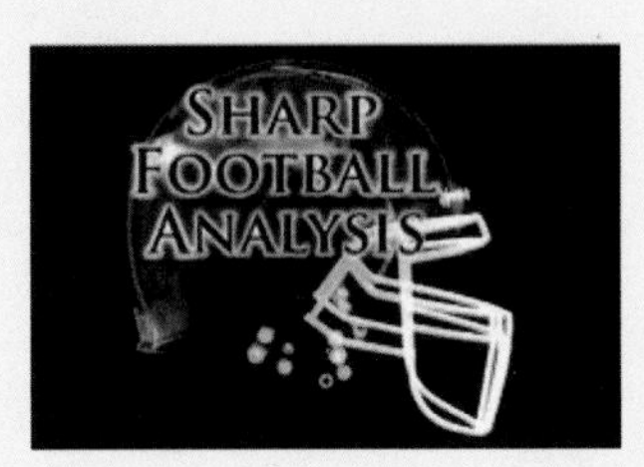

to the short left produced a 41% success rate and 4.4 YPA, and to the short right a 46% success rate and 4.6 YPA. The only edge the passing offense has with Flacco is to exploit the weakness of the defense over the short middle, and his production there is a 62% success rate and 7.9 YPA. The Ravens targeted this area 32% of all early down passes—most in the league and 19% above average.

Target running backs in the passing game, especially on early downs

The Emperor [Napoleon Bonaparte] disliked having to force a full-scale, fully arrayed frontal battle. Instead, whenever possible... he marched his main army by the quickest possible "safe" route, hidden by the cavalry screen and natural obstacles, to place himself on the rear or flank of his opponent. Thereafter, Napoleon advanced relentlessly toward the foe's army. The enemy army would be both taken by surprise and almost certainly demoralized by the sudden apparition of the enemy army in its rear. – The Campaigns of Napoleon, David G. Chandler, 1966

How often do we hear the term "third down back?" Why are such players used? There is little likelihood these players are the best pass blockers that could be used. Teams that use third down backs sacrifice pass protection to achieve the main goal—an outlet receiver if downfield weapons are covered or if the pass rush comes too quickly for routes to develop. But passes to RBs on third down are garbage attempts. Passes to RBs on third down gain first downs 32% of the time, which is 10% less than passes to WRs and 11% less than passes to TEs over the past two years.

The time to target RBs in the passing game is not when they are at their worst. It's when they are at their best. That time is on early downs, and particularly on 1st-and-10.

On 1st-and-10, RB targets produce a 58% success rate, which was 2% more successful than WR targets (56%) over the past two years. Yet they are targeted just 19% of the time as opposed to 59% for WRs. In fact, RBs (58%) and TEs (60%) are more successful targets on first and 10 than WRs (56%).

The strategy behind RB passes is a brilliant one. It gets the ball into one of the team's best all-around athletes, who is capable of speed, power, and vision in open space. It takes advantage of the upside of any pass play, which is different for run plays. Instead of starting in front of 11 defenders running downhill at the ball carrier, trying to get through your own line and past the 11 defenders, on pass plays the defensive line is ostensibly eliminated from the play. And very few LBs are running downhill to attempt a tackle. Instead, these players are racing to cut off a RB at the perimeter, and are therefore more subject to missed tackles.

Like Napoleon's strategy, these plays avoid a fully arrayed frontal battle and allow for a quick attack along the flank of the defense. These plays also demoralize one of the best weapons a defense has—its pass rush. It's very unlikely a QB will be sacked by a pass rush on a RB pass, but by virtue of the drop back, the pass rush is invited. This further weakens and wears out the pass rush. And with little hope of getting there, it creates doubt in their minds about setting up an inherent edge in future downfield pass plays to WR or TE targets.

RB passes provide de facto life extension to any RB, preventing the likelihood of their own linemen falling onto their lower extremities or collisions with heavy defensive linemen. It gets natural runners out in space, with a head start on the defense and fewer tacklers within range to tackle. Channeling more touches to RBs via receptions as opposed to carries will increase their life span, decrease the number of collisions they experience, leaving them fresher for longer in a game and, in turn, over the course of a long season.

Another thing first down passing to RBs does is it reduces turnovers. Quarterbacks throw just 1 interception every 108 pass attempts when targeting RBs in these situations (0.9%) whereas they record 1 interception every 41 pass attempts to wide receivers (2.4%).

When offenses like the Patriots and Saints are among the league leaders in RB pass rate on 1st-and-10, other teams should realize there is value to be found there. One of the most frustrating offenses has been the Seattle Seahawks. During the last two years, the Seahawks targeted RBs least of any team in the NFL on early downs (14% v NFL avg. 21%). What Seattle missed out on was huge. The few times they did throw to their running backs, they ranked 2nd best in the NFL in YPA (7.5 v NFL avg. 6.0) and 3rd best in success rate (58% v NFL avg. 49%). On 1st-and-10 passes, Seattle was +10% more successful when targeting RBs as opposed to WRs, yet passed to RBs just 14% compared to 60% to WRs.

Additional suggestions on usage of expensive RBs

This relates to RBs who occupy high cap hits or were high draft picks. In addition to getting a large percentage of their total touches via receptions rather than rushes, I would avoid overusing them in the second half with large leads, except in the red zone. I would reinsert them in the red zone as red zone rushing, as will be discussed shortly, leads to easy points and absolutely boosts team morale and unity, when an offensive line is run blocking for a lead back who is recording a high rushing touchdown total. Additionally, it will always keep that back mentally in the game, supportive of his position group to provide him with such touches, but yet saves his body from the wear and tear of unnecessary punishment between the 20s unless the offense needs him.

Pass more from 2-WR sets (12 or 21 personnel) and target TEs more

According to Machiavelli, human beings naturally tend to think in terms of patterns. They like to see events conforming to their expectations by fitting into a pattern or scheme, for schemes, whatever their actual content, comfort us by suggesting that the chaos of life is predictable. This mental habit offers excellent ground for deception, using a strategy that Machiavelli calls "acclimatization"—deliberately creating some pattern to make your enemies believe that your next action will follow true to form. Having lulled them into complacency, you now have room to work against their expectations, break the pattern, and take them by surprise. – The 33 Strategies of War, Robert Greene, 2007

As recently as 2011, the first full season after rules were modified to protect quarterbacks and defenseless receivers, the usage of 11 personnel was only 40%. By 2016, it was 60%. Last year saw a slight tick down to 59%. But while it

affords a lot of options, 11 personnel is not the most optimal or efficient personnel grouping to pass out of.
On pass plays, 69% of the time offenses use 11 personnel, but these plays deliver a 44% success rate. Meanwhile, 12 and 21 personnel deliver 49% and 48% respectively.

Passing to TEs from 12 or 21 personnel nets:

- 1st down: 58% success rate, 8.1 YPA, 92 passer rating
- 2nd down: 50% success rate, 7.4 YPA, 102 passer rating
- 3rd down: 50% success rate, 7.5 YPA, 103 passer rating

Compare that to WRs from 11 personnel, which dwarf the TE targets by a scale of almost 8:1:

- 1st down: 54% success rate, 7.6 YPA, 88 passer rating
- 2nd down: 49% success rate, 7.4 YPA, 87 passer rating
- 3rd down: 41% success rate, 7.4 YPA, 79 passer rating

Tight ends provide a huge efficiency edge, and teams need to work to target these players more often.

Teams that led the NFL in usage of 12 personnel on pass plays last year included the Eagles, Chiefs, and Ravens. Teams that led the NFL in usage of 21 personnel on pass plays last year included the Patriots, 49ers, and Bears. While there are a couple of poor offenses thrown in there, the fact is brilliant offensive minds including Kyle Shanahan, Bill Belichick/Josh McDaniels (impossible to separate the two), Andy Reid and Doug Pederson were all in the mix. All of those teams made the playoffs.

Both 12 and 21 personnel allow for significant multiplicity in the NFL. Having the ability to use an extra pass protector while still sending out both a TE and a RB in a pass route is something that 11 personnel doesn't afford. TEs and RBs in the receiving game are massive skeleton keys.

League-wide over the last 2 years, both TE and RB targets on first down had better success rates (59% and 56% respectively) than WR targets (55%). Getting both players out in routes while still protecting the QB is a huge benefit to the offense.
I'm not suggesting going away from 11 personnel entirely. But there is not as decided advantage that offenses should be passing the ball 69% of the time from 11 personnel, only 15% from 12 personnel, and 5% from 21 personnel.

Rushing is not dead Part 1: run the ball more often on 3rd and short (and 4th downs)

RB runs on 3rd & 1 produce a 70% success rate, and teams wisely run the ball 71% of the time, as passing success (58%) is substantially worse. But on third down and 2-4 yards-to-go, the success rate of RB runs is 51%--the exact same as the success rate of passes. Yet teams go 80% pass. And while just 20% of the plays are runs, only 14% are actually RB runs.

All teams fall into this trap, whether good or bad, with or without good quarterbacks or run games. Two teams that run the ball more than average are the Chiefs and the Broncos. The last two years, the Chiefs went 72% pass and 28% run in 3rd and 2-4 yards-to-go, but their passes were successful just 49% of the time, as compared to a 63% success rate on RB-runs. The Chiefs, a team with a QB they trust, still pass the ball nearly 3 times more often, but with substantially worse success. A team without a trusted QB is the Broncos. Denver still went 76% pass and only 24% run on third downs, but their passes produced just a 45% success rate while the success rate of RB-runs was 69%.
With or without a QB they trust, with or without a run game you trust, teams need to be more open to running the ball beyond just 3rd-and-1. They need to be willing to exhaust every edge possible in order to produce success against their opponents, including bucking the trend that only 14% of all 3rd and 2-4 yards-to-go are RB runs. Especially when it is shown that league- wide, RB run conversions are equally as likely as any pass attempt.

The last point to make here is that teams should also be open to preparing their QB to run the ball if the situation warrants it. QB rushes on 3rd and 2-4 are successful 70% of the time. Some of these are designed QB runs, but many come on broken plays. Not all QBs are adept at these rushes, but rushes are substantially more successful than pass attempts (51%). Therefore, if the defense dictates it, QBs should be encouraged to scramble for the 2-4 yards. If the defense is cutting that off, then obviously the pass would provide the best avenue.

Rushing is not dead Part 2: run the ball more often in the red zone

Like the suggestion to run the ball more on 3rd and short, this suggestion comes from the 2017 Football Preview, but with updated numbers over the last two years. Most teams get far too pass happy in the red zone, when rushing is quite efficient. Eliminating third down as a reactionary down, early downs in the red zone the last two years were 52% run, 48% pass. Yet early down run plays are substantially more successful (47% vs 42%).

Excluding goal line rushing (as will be discussed shortly), running the ball out of 3+ WR sets was successful on early downs 46% of the time. Running from 2 WR sets was successful 43% of the time. Running from 1 WR sets was successful 42% of the time. And running from 0 WR sets is successful 18% of the time. Clearly the evidence suggests spreading the defense to run is optimal, rather than loading up heavy personnel and tipping your hand that your team is going to run the ball.
Early down red zone pass plays produced a success rate of just 41%, worse than all but running from 0 WR sets. But of all early down red zone plays, only 25% of them were runs using 3+ WRs (46% success rate). Teams must run attempt to stay balanced between runs and passes in the red zone, and when running, don't tip plays by using traditional run personnel groupings.

Make smarter decisions on the goal line as it relates to personnel

When the stakes are the highest, much is to be gained, but much can also be lost. Near the goal line, teams need to be ultra-precise and sure in their play-calling. But far too many teams use subpar decision making and tactics.

From 1-2 yards out of the end zone, one of the worst strategies is to line up in 3+ WR sets and pass the ball on first down. These plays have a 46% TD rate. Compare other first down options, such as running from 3 WR sets at a 51% TD rate or passing from max-2 WR sets at a 51% TD rate.

But when you move beyond first down, passing efficiency drops severely, while rushing increases. This is backwards in the NFL. On first down, teams went 71% run the past two years, and when those plays didn't score a TD, they were far more pass heavy, at nearly a 50/50 rate on 3rd or 4th down. Run plays inside the 2 on 2nd-4th down converted TDs at a 55% rate, whereas passes converted nearly 10% less often (46%).

And when teams ran on 2nd-4th down, they rarely chose to do so from 11 personnel (3 WRs), but these runs scored TDs 63% of the time. They used 11 personnel runs only 22% of all goal line rushes. The most frequent package is 23, which they used 28% of the time, and this produced TDs just under 50% of the time (49.6%). If we isolate only RB runs, we still see a +13% edge in TD rate for the usage of 11 personnel as opposed to the heavy 23 personnel. Teams should look to pass on first down from max-2 WR sets and run from 11 personnel on 2nd-4th down.

Don't fear using receiving backs as rushers in the red zone

Along the lines of that which is mentioned above, and using your own chess pieces to exert pressure on the maximum number of squares, here is one that would likely fool many intelligent coaches. In the red zone, the obvious thought when running the ball is power in such a confined area. Many coaches prefer passing, but when they run, they often are looking to do so with their heavy packages and their bruising big bodies, such as LeGarrette Blount. But take a guess as to the 3 RBs with the highest success rate inside the red zone last year (first 3 quarters only): Christian McCaffrey (67%), Alvin Kamara (65%) and Jerick McKinnon (64%). All 3 are receiving backs.

The reason I caution their use in the 4th quarter is, thanks to all their passing game usage and rushing in other areas of the field, some of their power is lost by the 4th quarter. That said, the overarching principle is to not be afraid of using unconventional players in unconventional ways if the defense isn't playing to stop them. They often will have more success than the players a coach perceives as "best suited" if the defense is going to adjust differently to defend said player when he is in the lineup.

Run frequently on 2nd-and-short, and use tempo when doing so

While commentators will often suggest "shot" plays on 2nd-and-short, they don't know that 2nd-and-short is the easiest time an offense has to convert a first down of any down and distance. Additionally, "shot" plays have an extremely high turnover rate and there is a chance for a sack as well.

There is a reason why a great passing offense like the Patriots called run plays 71% of the time (above average) on 2nd-and-short the last two years. They converted these runs into first downs 82% of the time. Another great passing offense, led by Drew Brees, ran the ball even more often (72%) and converted first downs 80% of the time. Both of these teams took the ball out of the hands of their future Hall of Fame quarterbacks and ran the ball instead.

What is gained by huddling? Make a habit of getting to the line of scrimmage faster

The greatest power you could have in life would come neither from limitless resources nor even consummate skill in strategy. It would come from clear knowledge of those around you – the ability to read people like a book. You could anticipate your enemies' malice, pierce their strategies, and take defensive action. Armed with that knowledge, you could make them tumble into traps and destroy them. This kind of knowledge has been a military goal since the dawn of history. – The 33 Strategies of War, Robert Greene, 2007

Before hand signals, before more focus on verbiage, I understood why teams would try to huddle more often. But now I see it and it makes less and less sense each year. What is gained by huddling? When a team huddles, the defense can let its guard down for 10+ seconds while fresh personnel enter and fatigued personnel exit. Why should an offense ever invite such goodwill?

Moving quickly to the line of scrimmage allows the intelligence gathering phase to begin. It allows an offense to gather knowledge on what the defense is going to do. I certainly am not in favor of going tempo at all times. But simply getting to the line of scrimmage quickly affords the option of using tempo, should it be desired. There are a myriad of benefits to avoiding the huddle. It prevents substitutions and prevents the defense from relaxing. It lessens the defense's ability to communicate. It affords the quarterback more time to survey the defense at the line of scrimmage. It allows longer for the play caller to survey the defense and communicate ideas or thoughts to the quarterback. With more time, there is more opportunity to use pre-snap motion in an attempt to further force the defense to show its hand.

Standing at the line of scrimmage is a position of power and control. Offenses should not give that up by huddling. It is both a psychological and physical edge. Coaches should work on quick play call verbiage that can be made at the line. In hostile territory, the linemen and RBs should still be able to hear the QB while the receivers can operate off hand signals. There is very little to be gained by huddling in the modern NFL, and teams should avoid it as much as possible.

Use cadence and pre-snap motion to gather free information on a defense before you snap the ball

The target of your strategies should be less the army you face than the mind of the man or woman who runs it. If you understand how that mind works, you have the key to deceiving and controlling it. A friendly front will let you watch them closely and mine them for information. – The 33 Strategies of War, Robert Greene, 2007

I view cadence and pre-snap motion in a similar way. They are opportunities to gather free information and knowledge regarding the defense. Why ignore them? Most defenses are inevitably shown some tip of the hand when an offense uses pre-snap motion. If not, what is lost? With cadence, you have the added benefit of getting free yardage in addition to free information, should the defense jump off sides. And again, even if they do not jump off sides, what is lost? On the contrary, there is an added benefit, and that is the defense may be less expeditious when the real snap is called for. Quarterbacks absolutely should take more advantage of cadence, and OCs should take more advantage of pre-snap motion.

Use post-snap motion (via play action) to disguise your intent and confuse the opponent

Since no creature can survive without the ability to see or sense what is going on around it, you must make it hard for your enemies to know what is going on around them, including what you are doing. Disturb their focus and you weaken their strategic powers. People's perceptions are filtered through their emotions; they tend to interpret the world according to what they want to see. Feed their expectations, manufacture a reality to match their desires, and they will fool themselves. The best deceptions are based on ambiguity, mixing fact and fiction so that the one cannot be disentangled from the other. Control people's perceptions of reality and you control them. – The 33 Strategies of War, Robert Greene, 2007

Good run team or bad, it matters not. Linebackers are trained to read and react. If they read run, they will react as they have been coached. I have studied play action usage since 2012 and found that the 5 worst rushing teams based on efficiency all have quarterbacks that rank inside the top-10 in YPA improvement when using play action. They all also have a well above average jump in passer rating when using play action. Rushing efficiently is not a prerequisite for play action to work.

Play action creates voids in the defense. Attacking those voids is highly desirable. But much like cadence, there are many subtle benefits to using play action. It manufactures a reality for the defense, and creates an ambiguous situation. Do they attack or do they sit back? Frequent play action volume doesn't just help the pass game, but the run game as well. Linebackers, tired of biting on play action, are less likely to crash as quickly to fill their gaps with frequent play action usage.

Many coaches are using play action for their lesser experienced QBs, to help them open up the defense ever so slightly. When creative offensive coaches like Sean McVay (with Jared Goff), Doug Pederson (with Carson Wentz) and Bill O'Brien (with Deshaun Watson) all rank inside the top-5 for play action usage, using it on over 25% of all pass attempts, it should signal something. And when Tom Brady and the Patriots use it 7th most often in the league, there is more than "something" to it. The year Cam Newton took the NFL by storm and went to the Super Bowl (2015) he used play action on nearly 30% of his attempts. Over the last two years he's struggled comparatively, and has used play action just 19% and 17% of attempts.

During the last 5 years, when teams used play action, the average increase in passer rating was 11 points, to 98 up from 87. YPA increased from 6.9 to 8.3. TD rate increased from 4.3% to 5.4% while interception rate decreased from 2.4% down to 2.3%.

Stop playing prevent defense in one-score games

A teacher, wishing to test a theory of his concerning the power of that condition we would call "desperation," challenged a servant found guilty and punished with a death sentence to a duel. Knowing full well the irrevocability of his sentence, the doomed servant was beyond caring one way or the other, and the ensuing duel proved that even a skilled fencer and teacher of the art could find himself in great difficulty when confronted by a man who, because of his acceptance of imminent death, could go to the limit (and even beyond) in his strategy, without a single hesitation or distracting consideration. The servant, in fact, fought like a man possessed, forcing the teacher to retreat until his back was almost to the wall. At last the teacher had to cut him down in a final effort, wherein the teacher's own desperation brought about the fullest coordination of his courage, skill, and determination. SECRETS OF THE SAMURAI, OSCAR RATTI AND ADELE WESTBROOK, 1973

The notion of your back being up against a wall is often called being on "death ground". It is when people are placed in such situations that they often act and perform superior to what they might otherwise. The same is often true in preventive defense. With the way modern NFL offenses are performing—thanks to better strategies and more favorable rules—scoring points on a defensive play is easier now than it has ever been. Defenses must play smart, but there are better ways to win games than to play loose and hope the offense takes too long to score.

Practice return TDs and unless it will end the game, encourage aggressiveness in return attempts

A rapid, powerful transition to the attack—the glinting sword of vengeance—is the most brilliant moment of the defense. - Carl von Clausewitz, 1780–1831

Defenses with at least one interception or fumble return TD win almost 75% of their games, and if they don't allow one on offense, it's 78%. If it's the better teams (defined as the favorite to win the game), they ensure an 89% chance of winning. Such plays are devastating both on the scoreboard and psychologically to opposing coaches, players, and tactics. Scoring touchdowns is difficult in the NFL. In a 60-minute game, teams average less than 2.5 offensive TDs per game. To be able to score 7 points via your defense, within seconds, provides a massive edge.

Do not go fast, with a hurry up offense frequently without specific purpose

We live in a world in which speed is prized above almost all else, and acting faster than the other side has itself become the primary goal. But most often people are merely in a hurry, acting and reacting frantically to events, all of which makes them prone to error and wasting time in the long run. In order to separate yourself from the pack, to harness a speed that has devastating force, you must be organized and strategic. – The 33 Strategies of War, Robert Greene, 2007

There is a time and place for everything. Using hurry-up offense strategically should be the goal in certain plays and situations, rather than entire series. The goal should be to ensure +EV situations at all times. Otherwise, if there is not a distinct edge to be gained, why go fast on a particular play? It prevents proper survey of the defense, eliminates pre-snap motion, and limits audibles. We aren't discussing going no huddle, we're specifically discussing up-tempo and hurry-up offense. It should be used sparingly, and its usage should come as a shock to the defense on a particular play or sequence, rather than something they can plan for in advance.

Create conflict using route concepts against defenders not accustomed to handling situations

There were three oxen who always grazed together. A lion had his designs upon them and wanted to eat them, but he could never get at one of them because they were always together. So he set them against each other with slanderous talk and managed to get them separated, whereupon they were isolated and he was able to eat them one after the other. Fables, Aesop, sixth century B.C.

Attack LBs using mesh concepts. With mesh concepts and the MLB's instruction to "pass off" the WRs on the crossing route to the OLB, it can cause conflict for OLBs. If he continues to sag, the crossing route will be wide open. His responsibility is no longer to the outside WR running behind him on a deeper route, but to the slot WR who is crossing his face. As the OLB moves to cover the crossing route, he leaves a void in front of the single high safety, who is deep and on his heels. These are not pick routes. Mesh concepts which create traffic and distract the LBs while creating conflict with their responsibilities. The Giants used this often, despite having most of their WRs injured in week 14, and put up 29 points on the Super Bowl Champion Eagles defense.

Use RPOs more to make the offense "right" and the defense "wrong" on every play

Give your enemy dilemmas, not problems. Most of your opponents are likely to be clever and resourceful; if your maneuvers simply present them with a problem, they will inevitably solve it. But a dilemma is different: whatever they do, however they respond – retreat, advance, stay still – they are in trouble. Make every option bad. Try constantly to put them in positions that seem alluring but are traps. – The 33 Strategies of War, Robert Greene, 2007

Run-Pass-Options (RPOs) are a tremendous weapon that more teams need to use. Pairing a run concept with a passing play allows the offense to always be right because the QB is reading the defense. The QB is counting the number of defenders in the box and reading the leverage and alignment of the DB on the receiver. More teams need to utilize these concepts. Less time is allowed on the practice field but that means more time should be afforded in the film room to study new strategies and implement them. RPOs work because they involve a decision which is made post-snap, allowing the offense to gather information as to the defense's strategy mid-play, and attack the weakness.

Make plays look like one another, create disguises

No one is so brave that he is not disturbed by something unexpected. – Julius Caesar (100-44 B.C.)

In a competitive world, deception is a vital weapon that can give you a constant advantage. You can use it to distract your opponents, send them on goose chases, waste valuable time and resources in defending attacks that never come. But more than likely, your concept of deception is wrong. It does not entail elaborate illusions or showy distractions. People are too sophisticated to fall for such things. Deception should mirror reality. It can be elaborate, as the British deception around D-Day was, but the effect should be of reality only subtly, slightly altered, not completely transformed. – The 33 Strategies of War, Robert Greene, 2007

Kyle Shanahan loves to shift or motion to disguise the formation. He also loves to use plays that look identical. Far too often, teams implement beautiful game scripts, see success, and then don't go back to those plays. Teams need to go back to use strategies that worked earlier in the game, and they also need to have plays to use that look nearly identical to those plays. This will allow them to not only gain the benefit of a great play that worked earlier, they can deceive the defense with one of the plays that gashed them. Then, when the defense over commits to stopping that result, a totally different play is actually run.

Be multiple, be creative, and be ever evolving on offense

It is the goal of a good chess player to ensure that each of his pieces can exert pressure upon a maximum number of squares, rather than being bottled up in a corner, surrounded by other pieces. – The Art of Maneuver, Robert Leonhard, 1991

Offensive coordinators need to realize that they can dictate so much more to a defense than they currently do. They can make defenses account for each player on the field, and they can even move lesser caliber players (pawns) into positions of power offensively by forcing stronger defenders to switch onto those players, freeing up mismatches with superior offensive players against subpar defenders.

Kyle Shanahan once said "all plays are designed with the goal of making the defense defend everybody. Each play should get the defense to think about and account for the run, the pass, the screen game, play action bootlegs and drop backs. With the weapons they have spread around, it challenges the defense tremendously." There is no doubt this plan has been highly successful for them this year. It is also highly unusual in the NFL, though it should not be. Implementing this strategy immediately out of the gates, at full throttle, really stresses the defense. It comes as a shock to their system and there is no time for adjustments until halftime.

Look to build halftime leads and force your opponent to change tactics

War is such that the supreme consideration is speed. This is to take advantage of what is beyond the reach of the enemy, to go by way of routes where he least expects you, and to attack where he has made no preparations. - Sun-Tzu, fourth century B.C.

Striking first, before your opponents have time to think or prepare, will make them emotional, unbalanced, and prone to error. When you follow with another swift and sudden maneuver, you will induce further panic and confusion. This strategy works best with a setup, a lull—your unexpected action catches your enemy off guard. When you strike, hit with unrelenting force. – The 33 Strategies of War, Robert Greene, 2007

There is a common thought in NFL circles to "not lose the game early". It is thought that a game is not won early, but can be lost early. At its core, this makes no sense. A coach believes his team will lose the game if they turn the ball over early and fall into a deficit of perhaps 10 points. Would that not inherently mean that an early 10-point lead would lead to victory? Alas, the coaches think of only the negative, rather than reality.

Reality is that building halftime leads is paramount. While I've argued that teams need to ignore the mantra "establish the run" and adopt "establish the lead", the question is how to get there? The way is through aggressiveness and creativity. If you can attack the defense where it is weak or at a time when it is unexpected, you can cause confusion. That confusion will lead later in the game to indecision, reduction in confidence, and a defense that can be picked apart at will. The opportunity is there at the beginning of the game to be aggressive and creative. When this strategy builds a halftime lead, the opposing team will be forced to change strategies in the second half and adopt desperate measures.

When strategies aren't working, extending the stalemate is a fool's errand – adapt the offense

Whenever you and your opponent become stagnant, you must immediately employ a different method of dealing with him in order to overcome him. – The Book of Five Rings, Miyamoto Musashi, 1584-1645

All too often, we see offenses that meet an opponent they cannot produce against. Their strategies are not working, and the opponent is able to neutralize every effort. And yet how often do we see these coaches adopt a defeatist strategy and simply continue to repeat the same plays in hopes that eventually, they will break through? Players sense this as well. Being on the field, getting stalemated constantly, and hearing the same plays called into the huddle breeds frustration. Coaches need to be quicker to adapt, quicker to assess what is or is not working, and rely on their extensive study to try new strategies they should have prepared as back up.

Be prepared to overcome mistakes, adjust and adapt to whatever situation lies before you

Military tactics are like unto water; for water in its natural course runs away from high places and hastens downwards. So in war, the way is to avoid what is strong and to strike at what is weak. Water shapes its course according to the nature of the ground over which it flows; the soldier works out his victory in relation to the foe whom he is facing. Therefore, just as water retains no constant shape, so in warfare there are no constant conditions. He who can modify his tactics in relation to his opponent and thereby succeed in winning, may be called a heaven-born captain. – Sun Tzu (fourth century B.C.)

Coaches need to do a better job of incorporating contingencies into their plan of attack. If the opposing defense does something to stifle us, how do we respond? And if we respond but part of our plan doesn't work, how do we recover to gain the upper hand? Anticipate a variety of possibilities and always have ready solutions during the game. Such technical planning allows for quick adjustments during the game because the possibilities were foreseen in the planning stage.

Always have multiple backup plans

Everything which the enemy least expects will succeed the best. – Frederick the Great, 1712-86

All too often, there is a limitation in the creativity of an offense. We see nice scripting over the first 15 plays but a lull sets in near the start of the second quarter. We see another burst of scoring to close the half in two-minute situations, but the second half is often played without imagination and somewhat robotically. Sometimes this is even viewed as acceptable. "We have a 10-point lead, so what if we punted our last 3 drives." When the defense is thwarting your attack, the OC must realize that offenses are getting better while defenses are falling further behind. This is due in part to rule changes. A 7-point halftime lead in the 1990s translated into a 79%-win rate. Since the passing rule changes of 2010, that win rate has dropped to 74%. It's important to continue to score on your opponent, and to adapt strategies whenever needed to continue this production.

Devote more time to studying your own tendencies and then break them in the second half

People expect your behavior to conform to known patterns and conventions. Your task as a strategist is to upset their expectations. Surprise them and chaos and unpredictability—which they try desperately to keep at bay—enter their world, and in the ensuing mental disturbance, their defenses are down and they are vulnerable. First, do something ordinary and conventional to fix their image of you, then hit them with the extraordinary. According to Machiavelli, human beings naturally tend to think in terms of patterns. They like to see events conforming to their expectations by fitting into a pattern or scheme, for schemes, whatever their actual content, comfort us by suggesting that the chaos of life is predictable. This mental habit offers excellent ground for deception, using a strategy that Machiavelli calls "acclimatization"—deliberately creating some pattern to make your enemies believe that your next action will follow true to form. Having lulled them into complacency, you now have room to work against their expectations, break the pattern, and take them by surprise. – The 33 Strategies of War, Robert Greene, 2007

An excellent way to overcome friction is by breaking tendencies. To do this, you have to understand what your own tendencies are. Most offenses spend time studying the defense they will face and defenses study offensive tendencies. But not enough offenses study their own tendencies and specifically design plays to break them in the second half, once a defense has adjusted enough to their style. The best time to employ these tendency breakers is either at the very beginning of the game or early in the second half. But I prefer to use them in the second half because that is when traditional play caller fatigue sets in. A lot of other means for creativity is available early in the game, so I would reserve tendency breakers for the second half.

Always take something away from your opponent – both offensively and defensively

When the vanes are removed from an arrow, even though the shaft and tip remain it is difficult for the arrow to penetrate deeply – Ming dynasty strategist Chieh Hsüan (early seventeenth century A.D.)

Take away something from your opponent, but not necessarily the most difficult thing for you to take or their predominant strength. If a defense is strong at stopping the run, pass the ball often on them and take away a key element they rely on for victory. If a defense has a strong man-to-man coverage defensive back who plays on the outside, use your best receiver out of the slot, forcing the defender to either play where they are not comfortable or stay on the outside and allow your best receiver to play against a subpar defender. If a defense has a strong pass rush that frequently can overpower your offensive line, invite pressure and throw quickly to RBs in the flat or align in typical passing formations but call run plays to attack the edge defenders on the ground.

Avoid play caller fatigue

When Napoleon was asked what principles of war he followed, he replied that he followed none. His genius was his ability to respond to circumstances, to make the most of what he was given—he was the supreme opportunist. – The 33 Strategies of War, Robert Greene, 2007

Far too often we see a pattern in the NFL. Once the game script wears out, offenses grow predictable. By the time the second half rolls around, far too often teams are simply going with plays they are accustomed to using in those situations. The problem is, defenses know this. They know what the offense likes to do. If the efficacy of such plays is slowing down, play callers need to employ n creativity. Play callers need to always see the defense as a puzzle to solve. Opportunity is there every single play. Stay creative, stay aggressive, and take advantage of that opportunity.

Improve decision making in times of crisis

Presence of mind is the ability to detach yourself from all that, to see the whole battlefield, the whole picture, with clarity. All great generals have this quality. Our minds seem rather strong when we're following our routines. But place any of us in an adverse situation and our rationality vanishes; we react to pressure by growing fearful, impatient, confused. Only with great effort can we reason our way through these periods and respond rationally. Your mind is weaker than your emotions. But you become aware of this weakness only in moments of adversity – precisely the time when you need strength. – The 33 Strategies of War, Robert Greene, 2007

How often do we hear about play callers choking? Never. It isn't discussed. But it's a real problem in the NFL. All too often, in the heat of battle, when it matters most, play callers choke. They don't call in the right play. They waste too much time deciding what to do and then call in the wrong play. My advice for teams is to get their coaches to military-style crisis management classes ASAP. It is only through mental practice, and placing yourself in stressful situations, that the ability to overcome them can be trained and improved. If I was running a team, I would ensure my coaches became masters of this and were able to calmly make rational decisions even in the most pressure-packed moments.

Players respond to aggressive, passionate coaching

Everything which the enemy least expects will succeed the best. – Frederick the Great, 1712-86

When a coach creates an aggressive game plan with aggressive play calls, they and their players know the coach is transferring trust onto them. Executing aggressive, creative plays often is not easy. Going for it on fourth down when most teams might punt puts a burden on the offensive execution. But when a coach makes that call, he expresses belief in the players. And as a player, the best edges you can have are the belief that plays are being called which maximize your ability to win. A coach that expressly trusts you and believes you are good enough to execute and make him look smart. We saw it last year with the Eagles as they won the Super Bowl. They incorporated analytics and aggressive play calling. The players bought into it. The team played passionately and had fun winning.

Never transmit uncertainty or doubt

Any army is like a horse, in that it reflects the temper and the spirit of its rider. If there is an uneasiness and an uncertainty, it transmits itself through the reins, and the horse feels uneasy and uncertain. Lone Star Preacher, Colonel John W. Thomason, Jr., 1941

The optimal way to gain confidence is to be overly prepared—to know you have the ability as a coach to adapt as the game conditions require and have plenty of good plays in reserve for all four quarters of a game. Calling bad plays that players know won't work, and repeating them multiple times in a game shows you doubt their ability to do anything more complicated with higher risk/reward. That transmits doubt. When up against a better opponent, put in the study time to figure out the optimal way to attack that opponent based on your own team. Then, execute a creative strategy which is borne from confidence. Win or lose, it is the superior approach.

Make every player feel important

In war it is not men, but the man, that counts. Napoleon Bonaparte, 1769–1821

Make every single player feel valuable. Challenge each player in order to get the most out of him. Each player will be required to execute a complicated and aggressive game plan. Once players feel empowered and they see the benefits of their actions on the game, they will take more ownership of their performance and look to improve it every single day.

Why the Professionals Use & Trust Warren Sharp

When I was told about and introduced to Warren Sharp I was beyond skeptical. After working with some of the most successful syndicate groups for 15+ years I knew the NFL was practically unbeatable. After all, I worked 60+ hour work weeks breaking down and analyzing lines and looked forward to my Sunday's off. Needless to say that's not the way it is anymore on Sundays due to Warren. His NFL and especially his totals are second to none. Also, nobody can break down a NFL game like Warren and I don't know how anyone bets without his analysis and selections.

I am now proud to say he is now one of my best friends and I do not fail to mention him when I am a guest on a radio or tv show. I also give him a live podcast each and every Sunday live from Las Vegas which is available free to his customers. He has proved to me and the gambling public that you CAN beat the NFL.

Warren's Football Preview is amazing. It touches on everything you could hope to find, and many things you never thought you'd find, in a preview. It's not often that a football mind like Warren lays out his thoughts as extensively, in such an organized manner for easy reading and comprehension. I don't see how anyone could afford to pass this book up if they plan to make money on football this fall. It's that good.

- Bill Krackomberger, winning professional gambler, seen on ESPN, CNN, Fox Sports and dozens of publications and newspapers around the country

Warren's dedication and acumen for analyzing football is clearly evident in the work he produces. This book is completely unlike anything I've read in a preview before, but that's what I've come to expect from Warren. His ability to approach the game logically, analytically and in a predictive manner sets him apart from the crowd. Between the narratives, articles and graphics, I have no doubt after reading this preview you will be far more prepared for your fantasy drafts and just football in general. If you're a NFL fan of any kind, I cannot recommend this preview enough.

- Evan Silva, Rotoworld.com Senior Football Editor, @evansilva

A truly indispensable resource to kick off your handicapping process for the upcoming NFL season, Warren Sharp's analytics-based Football Preview makes up for mainstream media's shortcomings by providing smart and advanced schedule analysis, insightful context to roster construction, and team and player projections, all certain to give you a leg up on both sportsbooks and your fantasy competition alike.

- Gill Alexander, Host of "A Numbers Game" - Vegas Stats & Information Network (VSiN), @beatingthebook

Been at this for 38 years in print, and have enjoyed every minute, win or lose. The NFL has given me problems forever. A few games over .500, a few games under .500, nothing exceptional, and mostly paying my guy every week. Until last season when one of the most INFLUENTIAL whales in the wagering world put me on to Warren Sharp. Read Sharp's 2016 Football Preview from cover to cover, and wound up posting a Ridiculous 137-110-8 record picking every game in the NFL. And even tastier, 12-3-1 in my weekly best bets Coincidence? NAH. It was Sharp's amazing angles and deep dives into stats I didn't even know existed. And when you see his records, it's STRAIGHT UP HONEST. How do I know? I had access to Sharp's picks every week, and his percentages tickled and exceeded the 60% range. As most know who have read my columns for the past 37 years, I have NEVER recommended any handicapper. Most are SCAMDICAPPERS that get you to pay for recycled GARBAGE. Sharp's stats, amazing graphics and advanced metrics are FREAKIN' GROUND BREAKING. Get Sharp, stay Sharp, live Sharp. You will be AMAZED!!!

- Benjamin Eckstein, AmericasLine.com, nationally syndicated sportswriter in the New York Daily News and part of Ecks & Bacon

Analytics plays a bigger role in sports betting than ever before. Information travels at a speed nobody would have thought possible a decade ago. With so many analytical options available to both the bettor and the odds maker the choices we make for analytics have never been more important. When it comes to the NFL there is no one I trust and use more than Warren Sharp. Warren has an amazing grasp of the analytics that matter in the sports betting world and how to implement those in a practical and easy to read format. I would highly recommend that anyone involved in the sports betting industry try implementing Warren's analyses into their NFL work.

- Matthew Holt, COO of CG Analytics, @MatthewHoltVP

Warren's synopsis on game totals is vastly superior utilizing his mathematical formulas, to any preview I have ever seen. His success is two-fold, beating the closing number by up to 3 pts and winning at a clip needed to secure a hefty profit. Getting in early ensures some fantastic middling opportunities.

- Richie Baccellieri, former Director of Race and Sports in Las Vegas at Caesars Palace, MGM Grand and The Palms

I can't speak highly enough about Warren to give him the credit he deserves. He's the hardest working guy I know in the business, more importantly, his attention to detail is unparalleled. I don't think we've ever had a phone conversation less than an hour due to the amazing wealth of knowledge he rolls off with ease. I hold him in great regard. I appreciate his dedication and talent.

- @lasvegascris, winning professional gambler

Superior Data-Driven Measurement of 2018 Strength of Schedule

By Warren Sharp

"What's the point of strength of schedule?" they said. "Don't use it, it's a waste of time." They didn't want to entertain drafting Leonard Fournette, the oft-injured rookie out of LSU who would be playing with Blake Bortles on a bad Jaguars team which hadn't won more than five games since 2010 and would likely face negative game-script situations. In 2012-2016, only two Jaguars running backs produced seasons with more than three rushing TDs, and only three ran for over 500 yards. In 2016, T.J. Yeldon and Chris Ivory combined for just 904 yards and four TDs. Linemakers projected six wins for the Jags and a fourth-place finish. "Who cares about strength of schedule? I want nothing to do with a rookie in this terrible Jacksonville backfield."

In this space last year, my non-traditional method of calculating strength of schedule forecast the Jaguars with the NFL's easiest slate. What does an easy schedule mean? Ideally, better game scripts. And more opportunities to run the ball because instead of trailing by double digits in the second half like the pre-2017 Jaguars were accustomed to, they would have more fourth-quarter leads to hold onto via the run game.

50% of Fournette's rushes gained two yards or fewer, which ranked 25th out of 28 NFL backs with at least 175 attempts. Only 26% of his runs gained five yards or more (27th). Fournette averaged just 3.88 yards per carry, and his 43% success rate ranked 17th of 28 qualifiers. But thanks to improved game script, Fournette ranked 7th in rushing attempts (268) and finished as the fantasy RB8. This is just one anecdote to show why schedule strength matters.

The current method used to analyze schedule strength is the least efficient possible, looking at only prior-year win-loss records without context and applying them to current-year opponents. Measuring 2018 strength of schedule based on 2017 records is lazy and inaccurate. But like most things in the NFL, it is an accepted method from the past, and there is reluctance to shift away from established thought processes. I've built my foundation on questioning tradition and employing more efficient means of making NFL decisions.

At SharpFootballAnalysis.com, I attack the NFL from an analytical perspective and often use contrarian thinking to find edges. I also developed a free-to-use stats website (SharpFootballStats.com) which uses advanced analytics and visual graphs to allow users to customize, visualize, process, and retain information.

This article will focus on 2018 SOS using 2018 Vegas projected win totals. My method starts by taking three of the largest, most reputable Vegas sportsbooks (Westgate, South Point, CG Technology) to build a model creating a consensus line which factors in juice. Ignoring juice is a massive mistake. For example, ignoring juice on a team with a win total set at 7.0 but juice on the over of -150 would be misleading. My juice-adjusted win totals are

2018 Strength of Schedule

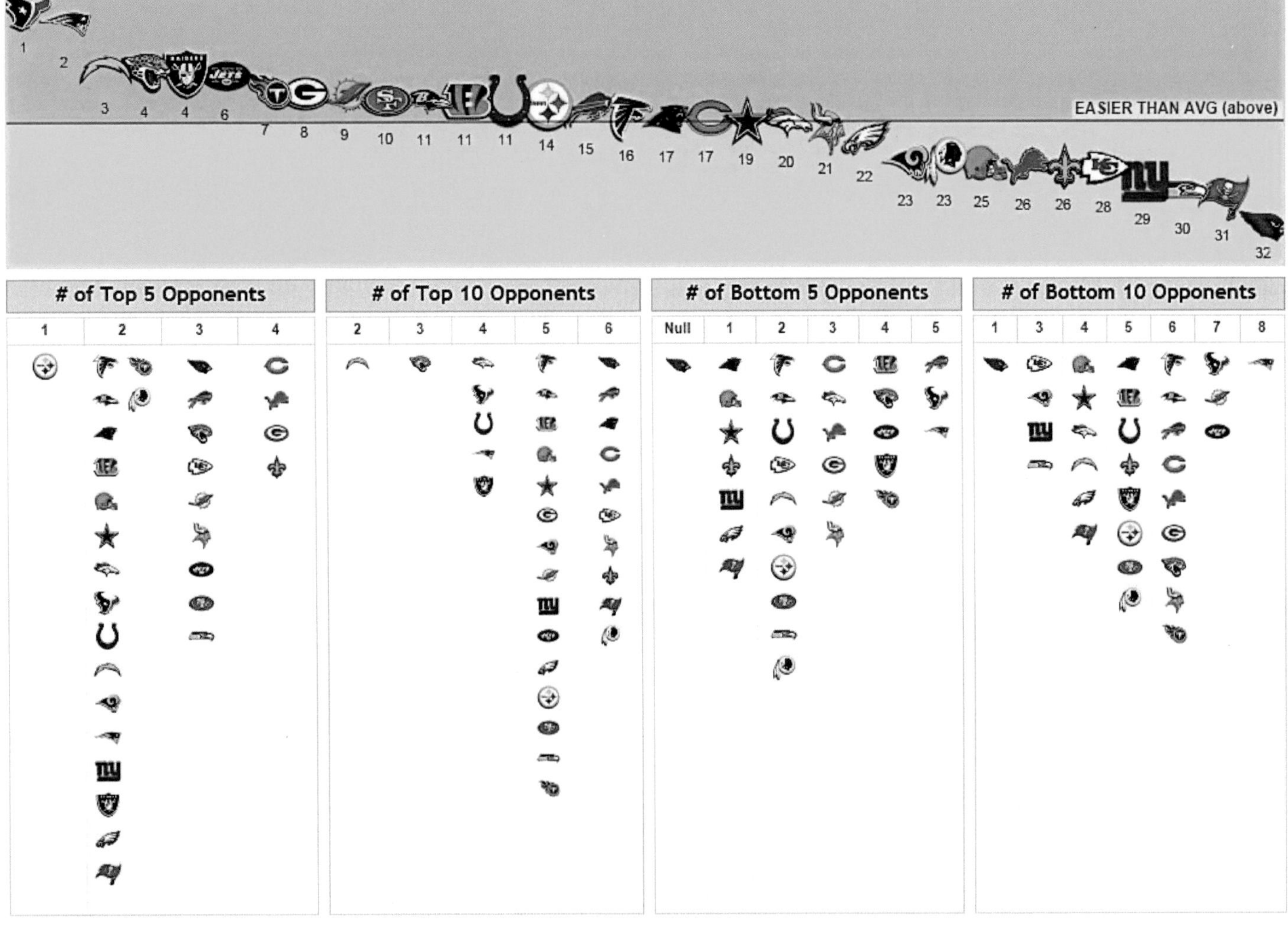

a superior means of calculating opponent strength.

The other edge in calculating SOS in this manner is that I can update the data over the course of spring and summer. As bigger-money bets are made, linemakers adjusted the juice and sometimes the win totals themselves. Sportsbooks and sharp bettors tell us how their opinion of each team is evolving.

And lastly, as to why strength of schedule in general is essential for fantasy as well as for the betting market, the answer is because of game script. The NFL is almost 60% pass, 40% run over the course of all teams and all 4 quarters of a game. Third down is a reactionary down, based on distance to go. So, scrapping that momentarily and looking only at the early downs: all game long early downs are 54% pass, 46% run. But across the entire game, that inverts itself for the team with the lead: they are 56% run, 44% pass. Specifically, on early downs in the second half, the team with the lead (of any size) is 64% run, 36% pass. Even with a one-score lead (one to eight points), these teams are 60% run to 40% pass. Meanwhile, the team trailing is 66% pass, 34% run. Thus, understanding which team is likely to be leading or trailing is a massive factor in fantasy production. The tougher the opponents, the less likely a team is to be leading. The below analysis should help tremendously to project fantasy fortunes in 2017.

I'll run through all 32 teams, starting with the toughest schedule (32) and moving to the easiest (1).

32. Arizona Cardinals

Arizona's 2018 home-road splits will be fascinating. They play just one top-ten opponent at home (Rams) and a league-high five top-ten opponents on the road. The back half of Arizona's schedule features four top-ten opponents in a five-week span. The Cardinals are the only team to not face a single bottom-five opponent this year. On a more specific note, Arizona plays a brutal schedule of pass-rush defenses to start the season. With Sam Bradford's fragility behind an undermanned offensive line, Josh Rosen figures to start sooner rather than later.

31. Tampa Bay Buccaneers

The Bucs are one of the few teams that might be thankful for an early bye. They play the NFL's most difficult schedule in September, including three top-ten teams (Saints, Eagles, Steelers) in consecutive weeks. Tampa Bay draws a reasonable midseason slate before closing its final six games without a single below-average opponent. More specifically, the Bucs face one of the league's most difficult schedules of pass defenses. So if they struggle on the scoreboard against this brutal schedule, the Bucs won't necessarily be able to rally back in these games via the pass.

30. Seattle Seahawks

Seattle moves from 2017's second-softest projected schedule to 2018's third toughest. The Seahawks' SOS is highlighted by a ridiculously tough final nine games featuring two top-five opponents, two top-ten teams, and four more games against teams ranked 11th-16th. Seattle's schedule does begin favorably with two bottom-five opponents (Bears, Cardinals) in the first month. But three of the Seahawks' first four games are on the road, and they have a slightly early bye (Week 7), limiting their rest and recovery ahead of the grueling Weeks 9-16 stretch.

29. New York Giants

New GM Dave Gettleman pushed in his chips on Eli Manning this year. Some have suggested Eli must start hot for that strategy to pay off, but it will be easier said than done. No team plays a tougher Weeks 1-7 schedule than the Giants, who face four top-ten teams in their first seven games (Eagles, Saints, Falcons, Jaguars) as well as the Panthers and Texans. Collectively, the G-Men draw the second-most-difficult schedule of pass defenses in the league. The second half of the season is considerably easier, including five bottom-ten opponents in Weeks 8-16.

28. Kansas City Chiefs

Pat Mahomes won't be eased into the 2018 season against the difficult pass defenses of the Chargers and Steelers – both on the road – in Weeks 1-2. After that, Kansas City's toughest two-week test comes in Weeks 5-6 against the Jaguars and Patriots. Overall, the Chiefs face the NFL's fewest bottom-ten opponents (two) and a league-high six top-ten opponents. Their defense should face an above-average schedule, but the defenses Kansas City's offense faces are especially difficult, collectively ranking second toughest in the league.

27. New Orleans Saints

Presuming they take care of business in early games they're favored to win, the Saints should be in good position entering their Week 6 bye. They face four bottom-ten teams in the first five weeks. From Week 8 onward, however, New Orleans draws four top-ten teams in a five-week span (Vikings, Rams, Eagles, Falcons) and overall has the NFL's most difficult schedule in the season's second half. The offenses they draw during this stretch are cumulatively the toughest any defense will face, and Drew Brees will have his work cut out against a very tough slate of defenses, as well. The Saints play three primetime games in four weeks between Weeks 12-15, and two are on the road. (New Orleans is 0-3 in on-the-road primetime games since 2016.)

26. Detroit Lions

Detroit's lone saving grace from facing a downright brutal schedule is the AFC East, giving the Lions games against the Jets, Dolphins, and Bills. Because apart from a game against the lowly Cardinals in Week 14, there is nothing remotely easy about this slate. No team in the NFL plays more top-ten (6) or top-five (4) opponents than Detroit. And if they are lucky enough to be fighting for playoff position, they must overcome late-December trips to Buffalo and Green Bay, no easy task for a dome team. From Weeks 8-16, Detroit faces a nasty gauntlet of defenses – toughest in the NFL – highlighted by the league's toughest slate of pass defenses in that span.

25. Cleveland Browns

Last year's Browns went winless against an average schedule, but you'd be wrong to think that they can't have success against the NFL's eighth-toughest 2018 slate. And that's because the roster suddenly has plenty of talent. But the reason Cleveland's schedule is so tough is that they don't play any easy teams except for the Jets at home in Week 3. The Browns' next-weakest opponent is the Bucs in Week 7, although that game is on the road. And beyond that, no other team on the Browns' schedule is worse than in-state rival Cincinnati. The good news is Cleveland gets four of its toughest non-division opponents at home (Falcons, Chargers, Chiefs, Panthers). Gregg Williams' defense had better ramp up quickly, because through the first ten weeks, the Browns play by far the NFL's most difficult schedule of opposing offenses. While the Browns are again pegged as the league's worst team, I can picture them pulling off more upsets than expected with a revamped talent base.

24. Washington Redskins

Seeming to face difficult schedules annually, the Skins again draw a tough 2018 road including a league-high six top-ten opponents. Washington does face the bottom-five Cardinals and Colts to start off, but has the NFL's earliest bye (Week 4) and plays eight opponents ranked in the top 14 in their ensuing ten games. From Weeks 3-17, the Skins face the toughest schedule in the NFL. And all three of their primetime games are on the road.

23. Los Angeles Rams

The Rams have the NFL's fifth-highest win total, but unlike the Patriots, Steelers, Eagles, and Vikings, Los Angeles must get it done against a difficult slate. The good news is the Rams draw their three toughest opponents (Philly, Minnesota, Green Bay) at home. Probably the most dangerous spot for the Rams will be a Week 7 road game at San Francisco – their third road game in a row – followed by the Packers at home, then back on the road to face the Saints. While this schedule is tough, it should at very least battle test the Rams enough to adjust before meeting these familiar NFC opponents in the postseason.

22. Philadelphia Eagles

All of the highly-rated NFC teams for 2018 were really good last year. Many of them won their divisions, setting up stellar battles thanks to the way the schedule is made. The Eagles draw the Falcons, Vikings, Saints, and Rams, leaving only the Packers as a top NFC foe off Philadelphia's schedule. The Eagles do play the seventh-easiest slate in September before embarking on the fifth-toughest schedule the rest of the way. The Eagles' only non-top-half opponents from October onward are the in-division Redskins and Giants. It is notable that from Weeks 8-17, the Eagles face the easiest schedule of opposing run defenses.

21. Minnesota Vikings

Chalk it up to playing in the NFC – a far superior conference to the AFC – but yet again we have a very good NFC team with a tough slate. But, frankly, I'd rather play the Rams or Eagles' schedule than the Vikings. And that is because they must face so many of their toughest opponents on the road, such as Philadelphia, the L.A. Rams, Green Bay, and New England. The Vikings' at-home schedule is quite favorable, however, specifically games against the Dolphins, Cardinals, and Bills.

20. Denver Broncos

The Broncos face a sneaky-tough schedule with a fair share of layups (Jets, Cardinals, Browns) but a ton of mid-tier opponents that are expected to have success against Denver based on the Broncos' own win-total projections. Denver is only favored at home once by the standard three-point home-field advantage (vs. Browns), and on the road the Broncos are underdogs by over three points in five of their eight lined games. Denver does draw the NFL's seventh-easiest schedule of opposing pass defenses, which is good news for new quarterback Case Keenum.

19. Dallas Cowboys

Expect the Cowboys to ride Ezekiel Elliott as hard as possible; not only are Dez Bryant and Jason Witten gone, but the Cowboys face the NFL's fifth-toughest schedule of pass defenses. In Weeks 1-14, Dallas faces the league's fourth-toughest overall slate. It's a schedule that features just one bottom-ten opponent and zero bottom-five foes. Making matters worse is that the Cowboys' defense faces the fourth-toughest slate of pass offenses. The teams they face struggled to run the ball last year, however, which could keep Dallas in games if their opponents have leads but fail to run out the clock.

18. Carolina Panthers

The Panthers won't like the front or back ends of their schedule, but from Weeks 3-14 they play the NFL's third-softest slate. Carolina's Week 4 bye comes a bit early but may be useful for a team learning a new offensive scheme under Norv Turner. The Panthers project to face the NFL's third-toughest schedule in the final three weeks (Falcons, Saints twice), but at least two of them are at home in Carolina. The Panthers paired C.J. Anderson with Christian McCaffrey and face the NFL's third-easiest schedule of run defenses this year.

17. Chicago Bears

Like the Panthers, the Bears' offense might be able to capitalize on its early (Week 5) bye. Chicago has the NFL's second-softest schedule through Week 10. They play five bottom-five teams during that span, although they are favored in just three of those games because the Bears are also viewed as a bottom-five team. Note that Chicago plays the NFL's fourth-softest schedule of opposing defenses, including the fifth-easiest schedule of pass defenses after heavily upgrading their passing game in the offseason.

16. Atlanta Falcons

Of all the top NFC teams we expect to vie for home-field advantage, only the Packers have an easier road than the Falcons. Following a revenge game against the Super Bowl champion Eagles in Week 1, Atlanta plays five of its next six games at home, then enters a bye. Between Weeks 3-9, the Falcons face the NFL's second-easiest run-defense schedule. And given their likely game script in these meetings – and how so many are at home – look for the Falcons' running backs to start the season faster than expected.

15. Buffalo Bills

The Bills face the NFL's toughest schedule in Weeks 1-6, including road games at the Vikings, Packers, Texans, and Ravens. Buffalo also faces the NFL's second-toughest schedule of run defenses, which will put more onto A.J. McCarron or Josh Allen's plate. The only reason the Bills' schedule isn't rated tougher in these rankings is because they play the Jets and Dolphins twice apiece. But make no mistake, this is a difficult slate that starts off especially tough.

14. Pittsburgh Steelers

Pittsburgh is the only team in football to play just one top-five opponent all year based on win totals. And thanks to a couple of games against the Browns (5.5-game win total), the Steelers' schedule isn't overly imposing. Pittsburgh has the good fortune of hosting the Falcons, Chiefs, and Ravens at Heinz Field before a Week 7 bye. But from Weeks 9-17, the Steelers draw the NFL's fourth-toughest slate featuring strong AFC teams in the Jaguars, Chargers, and Patriots, and then the Saints in New Orleans. From Week 11 onward, the Steelers do face the league's fourth-easiest schedule of run defenses.

13. Cincinnati Bengals

Unlike the Steelers – who face the Browns twice early in the season – Cincinnati doesn't face Cleveland until late in the year. And unlike the Steelers facing tough non-division teams like the Falcons and Chiefs early in the year at home, the Bengals must face them early in the year on the road. Throw in a trip to the Panthers and the only thing preventing the Bengals from having a tougher first seven weeks than Pittsburgh are games against the bottom-five Colts and Dolphins. Cincinnati does face the NFL's eighth-easiest schedule of pass defenses this year.

12. Baltimore Ravens

While the Ravens face an easy slate in the first half of the season, their opponents are seventh best against the run in that span. But the Ravens' rushing offense could kick into high gear after their bye. They have the league's easiest schedule of run defenses in the final six weeks.

11. Indianapolis Colts

Although Indy plays in an improving AFC South and draws the Eagles and Patriots in the first five weeks, the Colts nearly have one of the league's ten softest schedules. Indianapolis does face both Super Bowl 52 participants on the road, games in which Frank Reich's team will likely be a double-digit underdog. Yet this gives the Colts more home games against easier competition, which is what you want if you're pulling for a higher win-total ceiling. The Colts also face the NFL's fifth-softest schedule of defenses, including the league's easiest slate of run defenses (and rush defense correlates better year to year than pass defense). Indy's season still hinges on Andrew Luck's health. Sportsbooks currently appear to be operating as if Luck won't play; the Colts are favored in only three games with a weak 6.0-game win total. The Colts played the NFL's third-toughest pass-defense schedule last year and still led entering the fourth quarter in 9-of-16 games. Terrible, predictable coaching caused them to win just four of those games.

10. San Francisco 49ers

It was a great time for Jimmy Garoppolo to arrive in San Francisco. The Cardinals are in rebuild mode. The Seahawks aren't close to the team they were two years ago. The 49ers' 2018 schedule is extremely segmented, however. They open as underdogs in five of their first seven games, facing the NFL's third-toughest schedule with four games against top-ten teams in that stretch. But from Week 8 onward, the 49ers have the NFL's second-softest slate and face the league's fourth-easiest schedule of opposing offenses. This translates to positive game-script city with the Niners set up to get a ton of production from their Jerick McKinnon-infused run game.

9. Miami Dolphins

All of the AFC teams' schedules are softened merely by playing in the soft AFC East. For the Dolphins, it means four games against the Jets and Bills. A big plus for the Fins is that they face the NFL's easiest schedule of pass defenses in Weeks 1-12. Miami no longer has target monster Jarvis Landry, of course, which means plenty of opportunity for DeVante Parker, Kenny Stills, Albert Wilson, and perhaps rookie TE Mike Gesicki. The Dolphins also face a difficult run-defense slate during that stretch, enhancing their need to rely on the Landry-less passing game.

8. Green Bay Packers

Depending on which way you read this article – top down or skipping ahead to see who faces the easiest slate – this will either be the final or first NFC team you read about. Indeed, the NFL's seven easiest schedules all belong to AFC clubs, illustrating the NFC's vast superiority. Not only is the Packers' schedule navigable, but it's distributed nicely. In the first six weeks, Green Bay draws just one top-ten team (Vikings) and it's at Lambeau. The Packers have a Week 7 bye before facing the Rams. The do draw New England the following week, but it's a Sunday night game, giving the Packers a little extra rest. From Week 9 onward, Green Bay's slate is the second softest in football with four bottom-ten opponents, including three bottom-five clubs.

7. Tennessee Titans

The Titans' schedule is harder than its average makes it appear; they simply benefit from facing four bottom-ten opponents. Tennessee's slate does set up relatively nicely pre-bye; they draw difficult foes Philadelphia, Houston, and Baltimore at home with a road game at the Chargers, where home-field edge is minimal. If the Titans can navigate those four games, they'll be in prime position to rev up entering the playoffs with the NFL's softest schedule from Weeks 11-17, including four bottom-ten opponents in a seven-week span. One note is that entering their bye, the Titans face a gauntlet of top pass defenses (Jags, Ravens, Eagles, Chargers, Bills) in five consecutive weeks. Post-bye, the strength of opposing pass defenses dips markedly, however. Tennessee's passing game is set up to start slowly and finish fast.

6. New York Jets

Unlike Baker Mayfield, Josh Allen, or Josh Rosen, if Sam Darnold wins the Jets' starting job in training camp, he will face a soft slate to begin the year. The Jets have the NFL's easiest schedule in Weeks 1-6, including the league's tenth-softest slate of pass defenses. They play just one top-ten team (Jacksonville) and three bottom-five teams (Miami, Cleveland, Indy) during that stretch. And through Week 10, Gang Green still has the easiest schedule in the league, and no team plays more bottom-ten opponents (six) or bottom-five clubs (four) than the Jets. It's not until after the Jets' Week 11 bye that they face a difficult run (three top-ten teams). Ultimately, the Jets may be better off starting Darnold early than waiting for the bye.

5. Oakland Raiders

After a tough opener against the Rams, the Raiders' schedule turns progressively easier in September with games against the Broncos, Dolphins, and Browns. But from Week 9 onward, Oakland draws the NFL's fifth-toughest schedule of defenses. After a decade away from the sidelines, it will be fascinating to watch Jon Gruden's club handle those opponents.

4. Jacksonville Jaguars

The Jaguars drew the NFL's softest 2017 slate and it paid off for Leonard Fournette. This year, the Jags' schedule divides at their Week 9 bye. Before the open date, the Jaguars face the league's 12th-hardest schedule featuring both Super Bowl 52 participants. After the bye, the Jaguars face the league's second-softest slate with four bottom-ten foes and just one top-ten team. Jacksonville's offense is projected to face the easiest 2018 schedule, so Fournette should be in store for another volume-heavy campaign.

3. Los Angeles Chargers

The Chargers benefit from being the NFL's only team to play just two top-ten opponents: the Rams and Steelers. (Both are road games, however.) The Bolts do not have an overly easy schedule filled with tremendously bad teams – they face only four bottom-ten foes all year – but the schedule is stocked with winnable games. Given the Chargers' lack of a real home-field advantage, this note may be overrated, but the Bolts play four tough opponents at home in the first seven weeks (Chiefs, 49ers, Titans, Raiders). The back half of L.A.'s slate features more difficult road games and good run defenses. It will be critical for the Chargers to avoid the predictable and highly inefficient first-down runs they were so confusingly committed to in 2017.

2. New England Patriots

Any schedule is going to be easy when you face the Jets, Bills, and Dolphins for six of your 16 games. The Patriots' toughest tests come at the beginning and end of their season, facing the Jaguars and Steelers in Weeks 2 and 15, respectively, and both games are on the road. No team plays more bottom-ten opponents (8) than New England. The Pats get the rest of their tough draws at home (Packers, Vikings, Texans, Chiefs). But New England is currently favored by 4.5 points or more in all four of those contests.

1. Houston Texans

The AFC South is not remotely the pushover it once was, and the division will get even harder if Andrew Luck returns. But fortunately for the Texans, their toughest opponents are broken up nicely over the course of their schedule. Houston faces New England in Week 1, hosts the Bills before facing the Jaguars, and draws the Jets before the Eagles. Overall, it's the softest schedule in the league, and massively so from Weeks 3-15 with winnable-to-cupcake dates against the Giants, Colts (twice), Cowboys, Bills, Dolphins, Broncos, Redskins, Browns, and Jets. In a higher-scoring offense quarterbacked by Deshaun Watson, figuring out which Texans running back will lead the team in touches could be an underrated edge in 2018 fantasy football.

Players I Might Be Higher on Than You

By Warren Sharp

After writing all 32 team chapters for this 2018 Preview, several players stood out as offering more upside than what's currently envisioned in the fantasy football community. Not all will beat their Average Draft Position (ADP). But you should be able to use this information in combination with other resources to improve your decision-making process entering your draft. Each player's ADP is next to their name.

Alex Collins (RB19, Pick 3.11)

Collins finished as last year's RB16 despite not even being on the Ravens' roster in Week 1, and not starting until Week 10. OC Marty Mornhinweg showed he's willing to go run heavy; Baltimore finished seventh in the league in rushing attempts. The Ravens won nine games despite going 2-5 in one-score games, a statistic that typically regresses to the mean. Collins went from averaging 15 snaps per game in Weeks 2-7 to averaging 32 from Week 8 onward. The Ravens faced the NFL's seventh-toughest run-defense schedule during that stretch, yet Collins registered a sturdy 53% Success Rate while handling 150 of the Ravens' 235 carries.

From Weeks 1-17, Collins' 50% rushing Success Rate ranked fourth among 32 qualified backs behind only Ezekiel Elliott, Dion Lewis, and Todd Gurley. Whereas Collins faced one of the NFL's toughest schedules, Elliott and Lewis each drew easier-than-average slates. Collins' 4.6 yards-per-carry average ranked fifth among those 32 qualified backs. I project this year's Ravens to draw the NFL's tenth-softest run-defense slate.

Christian McCaffrey (RB14, Pick 2.08)

There is a perception that C.J. Anderson's addition hurts McCaffrey's fantasy outlook. But as a rookie, McCaffrey finished RB10 in PPR leagues despite logging just 34% of Carolina's running back carries and only 19% of the Panthers' red-zone rushes.

I believe Anderson will have a shorter leash than predecessor Jonathan Stewart, and that McCaffrey will log more carries than last year. Although McCaffrey's smallish frame suggests he isn't an ideal red-zone rusher, he led the team in red-zone rushing Success Rate (44%) last year. McCaffrey did tend to wear down in games; his red-zone rushing through three quarters was 67% -- by far best on the team – but his fourth-quarter red-zone rushing Success Rate was just 14%.

This year, Carolina faces the NFL's second-softest run-defense schedule. The Panthers also play nine games against defenses that ranked among the league's worst in short-yardage situations last year. It should mean fewer punts, more first downs, more plays, and more points.

McCaffrey still does most of his damage in the passing game. Last year's Panthers wisely funneled 28% of their early-down passes to running backs – well above league average – and their Success Rate on running back targets was greater than any other position. McCaffrey delivered a 70% Success Rate on first-down targets. While the downside is more passing-game weapons introduced and a healthier Greg Olsen, I think McCaffrey maintains upside at his ADP and would prefer him over someone like Derrick Henry in the same range. I even see a legitimate argument for McCaffrey over LeSean McCoy.

Rex Burkhead (RB35, Pick 7.09)

(Editor's Note: Burkhead-lover Evan Silva signs off wholeheartedly on this one.)

Once the Patriots selected Georgia's Sony Michel in the first round, his ADP skyrocketed from the double-digit rounds to round five as RB25 overall. Burkhead dropped from the RB20s range to RB35. Key to Burkhead's fantasy outlook is Dion Lewis' departure. Lewis left behind 39 red-zone carries, and if Mike Gillislee gets cut he'll vacate 25 more. That's 64 open red-zone carries in New England. Burkhead's 2017 rushes produced a 54% Success Rate. In the red zone, Burkhead's 56% Success Rate was far superior to Gillislee (44%) and James White (40%).

After the 2017 season, the Patriots extended Burkhead's contract at three years and $10 million. With Rob Gronkowski healthy last season – just the second time since 2011 – the Patriots passed at a high frequency in scoring position, but those passes were too inefficient.

Smart teams like the Patriots examine data to improve their decision making. I expect we'll see them run the ball more in scoring position, with Burkhead in the goal-line role.

Jack Doyle (TE12, Pick 11.08)

The Colts' addition of Eric Ebron has scared fantasy analysts away from Doyle, but I expect him to remain a huge part of new coach Frank Reich's offense. Doyle led Indianapolis in 2017 red-zone targets, and only Doyle and T.Y. Hilton drew 50 or more targets overall. Doyle played an incredible 95% of Indy's offensive snaps, by far most on the team.

Doyle's 59% Success Rate on targets within 15 yards of the line of scrimmage was bested only by Rob Gronkowski and Hunter Henry last year. Zach Ertz – Reich's tight end in Philadelphia – was the NFL's only tight end to draw more targets within 15 yards of the line of scrimmage than Doyle. Ebron's Success Rate on such routes was just 41%.

Doyle's 2017 touchdown upside was limited in a low-scoring offense, but his 80 receptions and 108 targets were near league highs among tight ends. And Doyle's season must be contextualized. The Colts added 15-game quarterback starter Jacoby Brissett one week before Week 1. Brissett began starting in Week 2. And he had no familiarity in then-OC Rob Chudzinski's antiquated offense. Indianapolis faced the NFL's third-toughest pass-defense schedule. And yet Doyle still registered TE7 (PPR) and TE9 (non-PPR) fantasy finishes.

Both Brissett and Andrew Luck have shown confidence in Doyle inside and outside the red zone, and Doyle's career 77% catch rate illustrates why. He's a reliable target. That catch rate is best in the NFL among non-running backs with at least 200 targets in league history. I think Reich will use Doyle in many of the same ways he used Zach Ertz. And because the Colts lack high-end wide receiver talent beyond T.Y. Hilton, I think they will continue to lean on Doyle.

Chris Hogan (WR28, Pick 6.10)

The Patriots are scheduled to face the NFL's fourth-softest slate of pass defenses. Gone are two of their top-three targets from 2017 in Brandin Cooks (133 targets) and Danny Amendola (119, including playoffs).

Hogan drew only 75 targets because he played in just 9-of-16 regular season games. But he scored seven receiving TDs – second most on the Pats – and was highly efficient on shorter routes, logging a 126.5 passer rating when targeted within 15 yards of the line of scrimmage. The year before, Hogan led the entire NFL in yards per target (20.7) on deep passes with a massive 61% Success Rate and 144.8 passer rating when thrown to deep.

The Patriots have one of the league's most-creative offensive coaching staffs and, of course, Tom Brady. With so much available opportunity, Hogan deserves much more respect in drafts.

DJ Moore (WR49, Pick 11.06)

I won't argue if you roll with Devin Funchess at his seventh-round ADP, but my preference is to wait four more rounds for Moore. This year's Panthers do face a brutal pass-defense schedule, but they are likely to be involved in shootout games against division foes Atlanta, New Orleans, and Tampa Bay.

Moore tested as a 92nd-percentile SPARQ athlete before the draft and was the first receiver taken. New OC Norv Turner last worked in Minnesota, where Adam Thielen quickly developed from a nobody into one of the league's best and most versatile wide receivers. Moore also offers versatility with an ability to win both outside and in the slot. As soon as Moore was drafted, Cam Newton texted coach Ron Rivera to thank him for the pick. Moore can be an immediate factor.

Paul Richardson (WR60, Pick 14.07)

The Redskins lost Terrelle Pryor, Ryan Grant, and Niles Paul. Their lone wide receiver addition was Richardson. Washington moves from the NFL's fourth-hardest pass-defense schedule down to No. 20, representing the second-biggest change of all teams.

Jamison Crowder will continue to patrol the slot, even after he produced an underwhelming 43% Success Rate in 2017. Josh Doctson (40%) was even worse at 6.4 yards per target. The Skins play a ton of 11 personnel, creating opportunity for Richardson in three-receiver sets. Over the last two years, Richardson ranked No. 2 in passer rating when targeted on early-down deep passes (127) and averaged 16.3 yards per target.

New QB Alex Smith has no established rapport with any Washington receiver. So Richardson is just as familiar to Smith as Crowder, Doctson, and Jordan Reed. Smith's 2017 propensity to take deeper shots bodes well for Richardson's chances of outscoring his late-round ADP.

Larry Fitzgerald (WR21, Pick 5.04)

Fitzgerald recorded a 2017 target share of 27% as Arizona's slot receiver and de-facto tight end. Based on my analysis of new OC Mike McCoy's offense, I expect fewer four-plus wide receiver groupings than retired Bruce Arians ran, and more focused targeting of the team's top receivers. I also believe complementary WRs Brice Butler and Christian Kirk can exceed box-score expectations.

But the Cardinals will need to rely heavily on Fitzgerald again. In St. Louis (Danny Amendola), Philadelphia (Jordan Matthews), and Minnesota (Stefon Diggs), Sam Bradford has shown a consistent affinity for targeting slot receivers. Fitzgerald ran over 60% of his 2017 routes in the slot. And with a weakened defense, the NFL's toughest schedule, and a lower projected win total, the Cardinals' pass attempts are likely to rise.

The Cards' offensive line is also worrisomely weak, necessitating shorter throws to compensate for pass-protection deficiencies. Arizona's defense draws the NFL's second-toughest schedule of offenses, so they will need to keep pace on the scoreboard. Fitzgerald was quietly last year's overall WR4 in PPR leagues and has 100-plus catches in three straight years.

Pierre Garcon (WR34, Pick 8.03)

Garcon has been underdiscussed in San Francisco after he suffered a year-ending neck injury eight games into 2017. Jimmy Garoppolo has generated all the headlines. And Garcon is barely being drafted as a WR3.

Before Garoppolo's acquisition, Garcon had a quiet first half to 2017. He didn't score a single TD. The 49ers faced the league's toughest pass-defense schedule. And Garcon's quarterbacks were terrible. But it's easy to forget Garcon was on pace for 80 catches and 1,000 yards.

Garcon's biggest concern is his recovery from last year's neck injury. His zero-touchdown season was unsurprising considering the 49ers' offense. Even when Garoppolo took over for the final five games, backup TE Garrett Celek led the team with four TDs, and no other 49er exceeded two. Garcon still delivered a 56% Early-Down Success Rate and had 23 catches of ten-plus yards. This year's 49ers face the league's 14th-toughest pass-defense schedule, good for the third-biggest year-to-year drop among NFL teams. And they have a full year of Jimmy G.

Support this Project

Each year, I start work on this book at the end of February. Just over four long months later, I deliver the finished product. It's not made for the money, it's made to educate the fans and hopefully make the on-field product we love so much better. In addition to this book, I offer a free-to-use visualized data for NFL stats: SharpFootballStats.com. Between this annual and the website, you'll have plenty to dive into and analyze. But your support ensures we'll be able to continue running that site freely and providing key analysis to help you and the teams. Here's what you can do to support our efforts:

1. Rate & review this book on Amazon (even if you bought the PDF)
2. If you bought from Amazon, consider getting the PDF copy as well from SharpFootballAnalysis.com or SharpFootballStats.com
    - Amazon sales generate less than $1 per copy
3. Follow Warren, @SharpFootball on Twitter
4. Purchase a 2018 Football Subscription from SharpFootballAnalysis.com
    - And pay nothing until the end of the 2018 season
    - You'll receive all my in-depth in season analysis & weekly game predictions
5. Tweet out a picture of your book, and share your feedback on Twitter
    - I'll try to retweet everyone who shares feedback & helps spread the word
6. Subscribe, rate & review the Sharp Football Analysis Podcast on iTunes
7. Visit & explore SharpFootballStats.com
8. Join the Mailing List at SharpFootballStats.com

Layout and Definitions

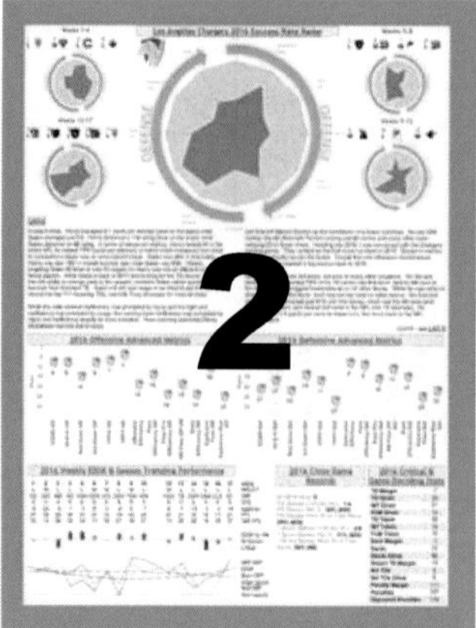

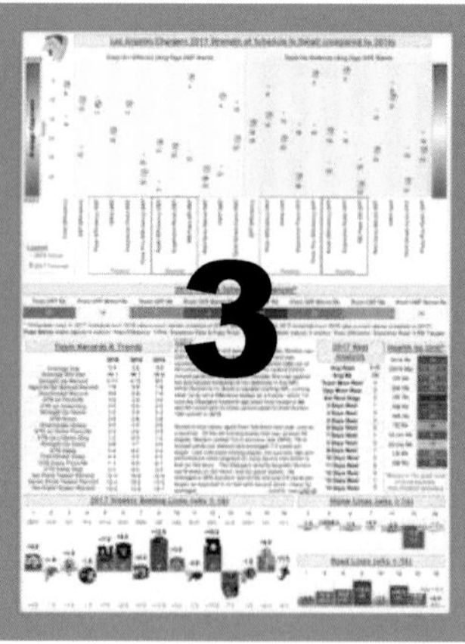

PAGE 1: Schedule listed according to strength of opponent based on win totals // Asterisk next to draft round indicates compensatory selection // Projected starting roster shaded based on current year (2017) cap hit to see where team is spending for its starters // Positional spending shows 2017 rank as "Rank" and 2016 rank as "2016 Rk" // Average line listed is based on weeks 1-16 lines which were opened by CG Technology

PAGE 2: Radars posted based on success rates only. These radars will be posted on Sharp Football Stats and updated in-season for 2017 on a weekly basis // Weekly EDSR and Season Trending Performance measures total EDSR per week, combining offense and defense together. A green vertical bar indicates the team "won" the EDSR battle that week. A red vertical bar indicates they lost. The longer the bar, the more lopsided the result. The trend chart represents offense (blue) and defense (red). When blue is high, the offense was efficient in EDSR. When the red bar is low, the defense was efficient in EDSR. EDSR stands for Early Down Success Rate, and measures efficiency on early downs only and ability to bypass 3rd down on offense, or force opponent into 3rd downs on defense.

PAGE 3: Strength of Schedule in Detail – the red "dot" is the true final result in 2016 based on the real schedule played. The logo is the 2017 forecast rank based on the real schedule the team will play // Schedule Variances indicate if the schedule became easier or harder than last year's schedule, and by how much. Extremes are most notable (a team ranking 31st or 32nd saw their schedule become much easier. A team ranking 1st or 2nd saw their schedule become much harder this year // Health by Unit are league rankings (1-32) based on Football Outsiders (Scott Kacsmar's) work.

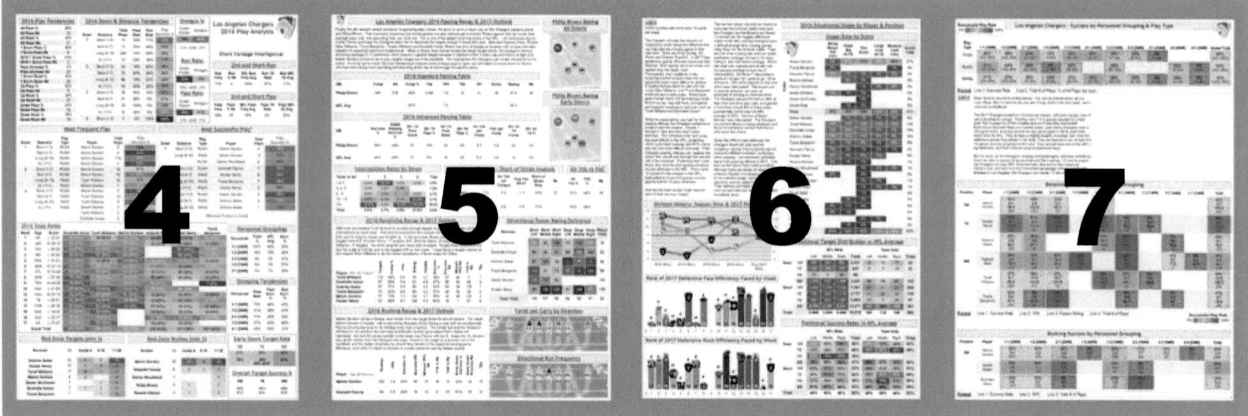

PAGE 4: Most metrics should be self explanatory // Frequent play vs successful play looks at play frequency and compares to when a team saw the most success for a particular down & distance // Snap rates include players who recorded 300+ snaps, with cutoff if too many on a certain team hit that mark // Target rates are only for early downs, target success looks at every down

PAGE 5: YPA = yards per attempt // Success rate is defined as a play which gained the minimum required yardage based on down and distance. Cutoffs are 40% of yards to go on 1st down, 60% of yards to go on 2nd down and 100% of yards to go on 3rd or 4th down // 20+ and 30+ yard pass gains are not air yards, but pass plays which totaled gains of 20 or 30 yards // Air Yds = distance ball traveled in the air per attempt // YAC = yards gained after the catch // TOARS = Target and Output-Adjusted Receiving Success – the higher the number the better the performance delivered // Missed YPA = yardage on unsuccessful plays which fell short of that required yardage cutoff. The fewer Missed YPA, the closer a player was to turning the unsuccessful play into a successful one.

PAGE 6: Usage Rate By Score examines percentage of a team's total plays in that given score margin are delivered to that player // Positional target distribution and success rates look at where a team was throwing and how successful they were, based on field location (left/mid/right) and depth (short = within 15 yards of line of scrimmage, deep = greater than that) and position // Weekly schedule for offensive players based on defensive strengths for the run and pass is found in the bottom left.

PAGE 7: Team success rate by personnel grouping and play type. Shares success rate & personnel grouping usage (frequency) // Also lists individual players, first receiving, then rushing, and lists data including success rate, yards per play, passer rating and total number of plays

Arizona Cardinals

2018 Coaches

Head Coach:
Steve Wilks (CAR DC) (1st yr)
Offensive Coordinator:
Mike McCoy (DEN OC) (1st yr)
Defensive Coordinator:
Al Holcomb (CAR LB) (1st yr)

EASY HARD

2018 Forecast

Wins	Div Rank
5.5	#4

Past Records

2017: 8-8
2016: 7-8-1
2015: 13-3

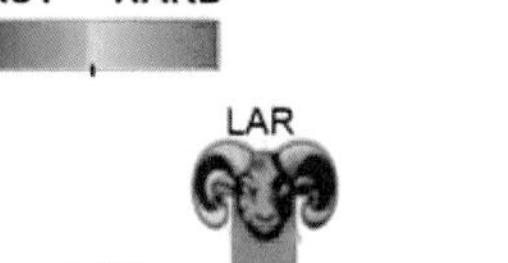

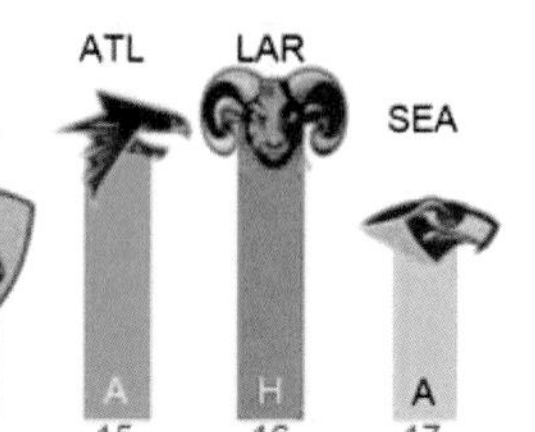

Week	1	2	3	4	5	6	7	8	9	10	11	12	13	14	15	16	17
Opponent	WSH	LAR	CHI	SEA	SF	MIN	DEN	SF		KC	OAK	LAC	GB	DET	ATL	LAR	SEA
H/A	H	A	H	H	A	A	H	H		A	H	A	A	H	A	H	A

TNF

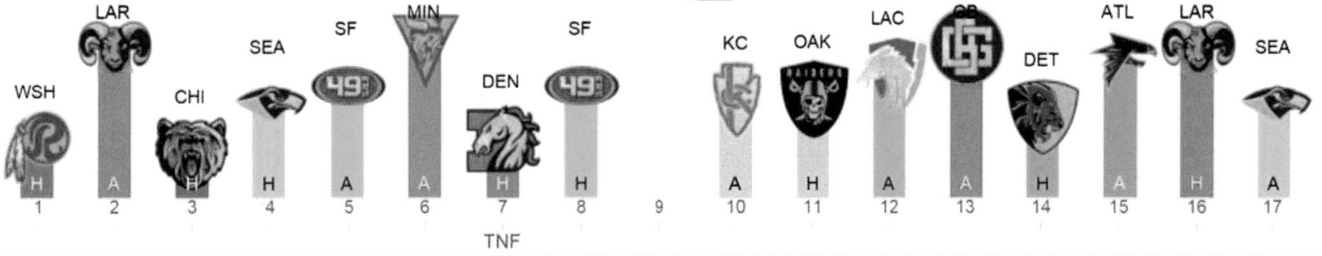

Key Players Lost

TXN	Player (POS)
Cut	Mathieu, Tyrann S
	Peterson, Adrian RB
	Tuerk, Max C
Declared Free Agent	Bethel, Justin CB
	Boone, Alex G
	Branch, Tyvon S
	Brown, Jaron WR
	Brown, John WR
	Dansby, Karlos LB
	Gabbert, Blaine QB
	Golden, Brittan WR
	Martin, Kareem LB
	Niklas, Troy TE
	Rucker, Frostee DT
	Stanton, Drew QB
	Watford, Earl T
	Williams, Kerwynn RB
	Williams, Tramon CB
Retired	Palmer, Carson QB

Average Line	# Games Favored	# Games Underdog
4.4	3	11

2018 Arizona Cardinals Overview

I loved Bruce Arians.

He won two Super Bowls in Pittsburgh, but was fired by Mike Tomlin after 2011 because Arians wouldn't compromise his aggressive, vertical-passing-game philosophy enough for Tomlin. Arians joined the 2012 Colts, coached up Andrew Luck as a rookie, and stood in as head coach while Chuck Pagano battled leukemia. Arians earned AP Coach of the Year, directing Indy to a 9-3 record. Arians was rewarded with the Cardinals' head-coaching job in 2012. Arizona went three straight years without a winning record before his arrival. Arians led the Cardinals to 10, 11, and 13 wins, advancing to the NFC Championship game in 2015 with another AP Coach of the Year award.

Here's what I wrote about Arians in my 2016 preview: "The best part about his tenure has been his ability to do what he wants without reproach or being talked out of it by ownership. That has allowed the team to quickly assimilate his personality and style. Aggressive. Leaving no arrow in the quiver. Both offensively and defensively."

Arians employed a "no risk it, no biscuit" approach. Arians loved his players, and was particularly upset about getting fired in Pittsburgh because he loved working with Ben Roethlisberger, whom Arians openly called "a second son to me."

Arians' strategy didn't stop working in Arizona, but his players couldn't stay healthy. The 2016 Cardinals offensive line was the sixth-most injured in football, and pass-protection deficiencies derailed Arizona's deep-passing style. The '16 Cards were also unfortunate, going 3-5 in one-score games and 0-7 when trailing at halftime, including 0-5 when down by five or fewer points.

Last year was more of the same. Arizona was the NFL's fifth-most-injured team, including the league's fourth-most-injured offensive line. They lost David Johnson for the season in Week 1. They lost Carson Palmer in Week 7. John Brown was never healthy.

(cont'd - see ARI2)

Key Free Agents/ Trades Added

Benwikere, Bene CB
Bradford, Sam QB
Butler, Brice WR
Djeri, Moubarak DE
Glennon, Mike QB
Pugh, Justin G
Sandland, Beau TE
Smith, Andre T
Williams, Bryce TE
Williams, Marcus CB

Drafted Players

Rd	Pk	Player (College)
1	10	QB - Josh Rosen (UCLA)
2	47	WR - Christian Kirk (Texas A&M)
3*	97	C - Mason Cole (Michigan)
4*	134	RB - Chase Edmonds (Fordham)
6	182	CB - Chris Campbell (Penn State)
7*	254	OT - Korey Cunningham (Cincinnati)

Regular Season Wins: Past & Current Proj

	Wins
Forecast 2018 Wins	5.5
2017 Wins	8
Forecast 2017 Wins	10
2016 Wins	7
2015 Wins	13
2014 Wins	11

1 3 5 7 9 11 13 15

Lineup & Cap Hits

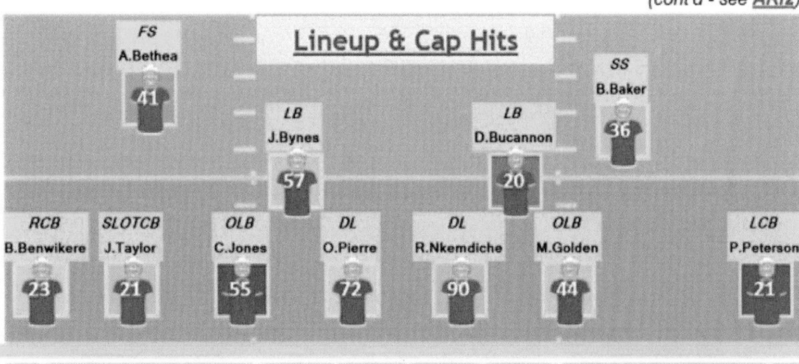

2018 Unit Spending

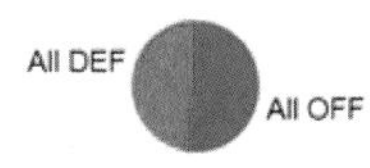

All DEF
All OFF

Positional Spending

	Rank	Total	2017 Rk
All OFF	26	$81.11M	5
QB	22	$16.30M	1
OL	31	$24.30M	11
RB	26	$4.86M	31
WR	12	$25.32M	8
TE	13	$10.32M	25
All DEF	26	$72.82M	19
DL	32	$10.07M	31
LB	2	$35.61M	11
CB	17	$19.02M	11
S	25	$8.12M	4

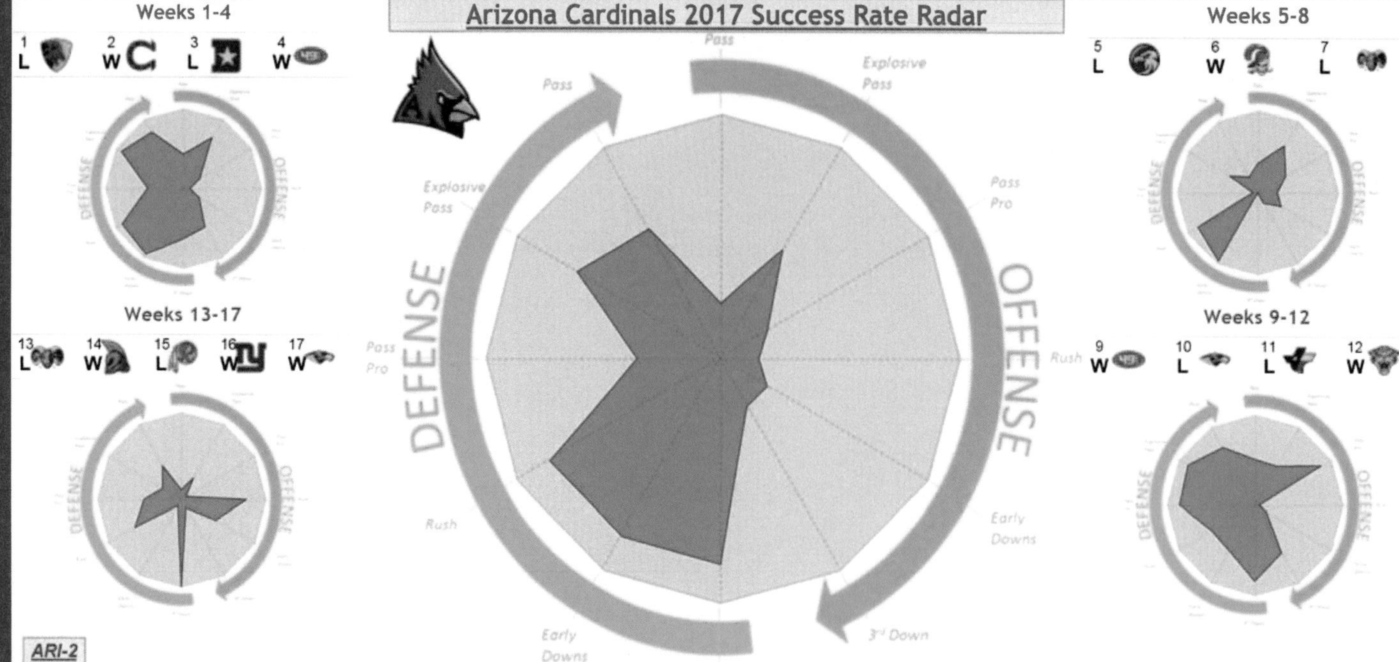

ARI-2

Without Johnson, the Cardinals couldn't run the ball. They ranked dead last in the NFL in both rushing efficiency and explosive runs. And they got zero production from tight ends. Jermaine Gresham drew just 46 targets, ranking sixth on the team. His 54% Success Rate led the team, however, and Gresham's 87 passer rating when targeted ranked third. Old faithful Larry Fitzgerald was the Cardinals' volume monster, recording a team-best 27% target share. Runner-up Jaron Brown managed a 12% target share.

Despite a disastrous offensive line, Arizona used four-plus wide receivers on a shocking 271 pass plays. No other team came close. The runner-up Giants went four wide or more on just 144 snaps. Third-place Jacksonville went four wide or more on 107 plays. The NFL average is 31 snaps of four-plus wide receivers. The Cardinals had 649 passing snaps, going four wide or more on 42% of those plays. And Arizona was not staring at weekly deficits; their record was 8-8. Even when games were within one score, the Cards went four-plus wide on 35% of passing-down snaps.

They ran 83 snaps of five-receiver "00" personnel. As the NFL ** totaled ** 125 snaps of 00 personnel, Arizona accounted for 66% of five-wide plays across the league.

The Cardinals' efficiency varied, of course, depending on whether Carson Palmer was healthy. Palmer produced a 54% Success Rate, 8.7 yards per attempt, and 111 passer rating in two-tight end formations. But Arians only used two tight ends on 17% of Palmer's throws. In three-receiver 11 personnel, Palmer's Success Rate plummeted to 47% with a 7.2 YPA and 81 passer rating. Yet Arians used 11 personnel on 85% of Palmer's attempts. Plans didn't change much for Blaine Gabbert and Drew Stanton. Arians had the team in three-receiver formations on 83% of his backup quarterbacks' passing snaps. They went four wide on 41% of attempts. By far, the backups' most successful passes occurred on early downs to running backs and tight ends in 11 personnel. Those plays netted a 73% Success Rate, 9.3 YPA, and 111 passer rating.

(cont'd - see ARI-3)

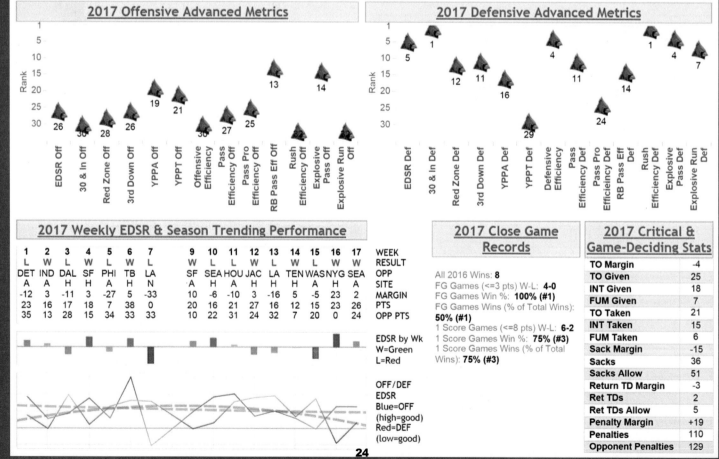

2017 Offensive Advanced Metrics

	Rank
EDSR Off	26
30 & In Off	30
Red Zone Off	28
3rd Down Off	26
YPPA Off	19
YPPT Off	21
Offensive Efficiency	30
Pass Efficiency Off	27
Pass Pro Efficiency Off	25
RB Pass Eff Off	13
Rush Efficiency Off	32
Explosive Pass Off	14
Explosive Run Off	32

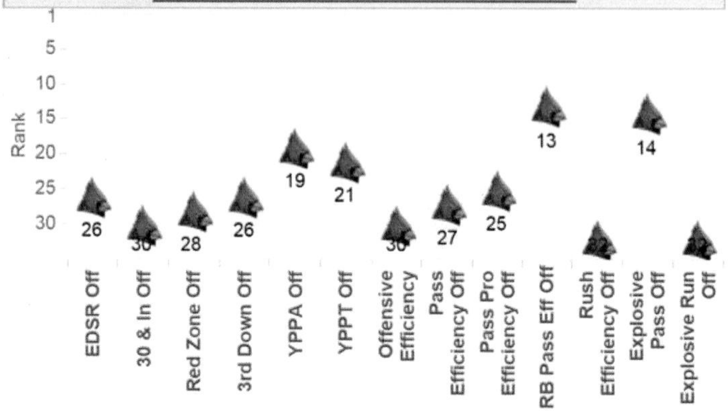

2017 Defensive Advanced Metrics

	Rank
EDSR Def	5
30 & In Def	1
Red Zone Def	12
3rd Down Def	11
YPPA Def	16
YPPT Def	29
Defensive Efficiency	4
Pass Efficiency Def	11
Pass Pro Efficieincy Def	24
RB Pass Eff Def	14
Rush Efficiency Def	1
Explosive Pass Def	4
Explosive Run Def	7

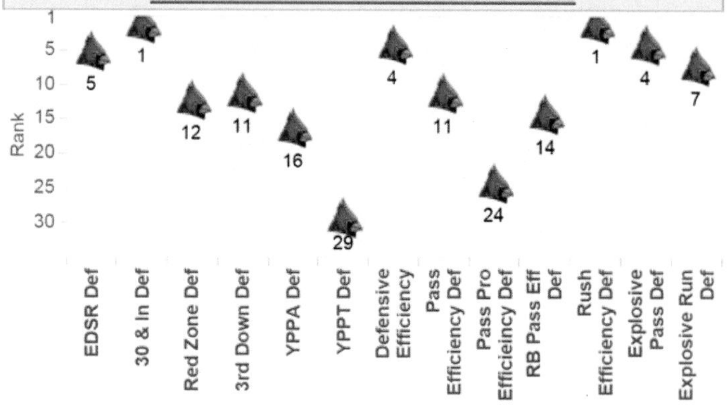

2017 Weekly EDSR & Season Trending Performance

WEEK	1	2	3	4	5	6	7	9	10	11	12	13	14	15	16	17
RESULT	L	W	L	W	L	W	L	W	L	L	W	L	W	L	W	W
OPP	DET	IND	DAL	SF	PHI	TB	LA	SF	SEA	HOU	JAC	LA	TEN	WAS	NYG	SEA
SITE	A	A	H	H	A	H	N	A	H	A	H	H	H	A	H	A
MARGIN	-12	3	-11	3	-27	5	-33	10	-6	-10	3	-16	5	-5	23	2
PTS	23	16	17	18	7	38	0	20	16	21	27	16	12	15	23	26
OPP PTS	35	13	28	15	34	33	33	10	22	31	24	32	7	20	0	24

EDSR by Wk
W=Green
L=Red

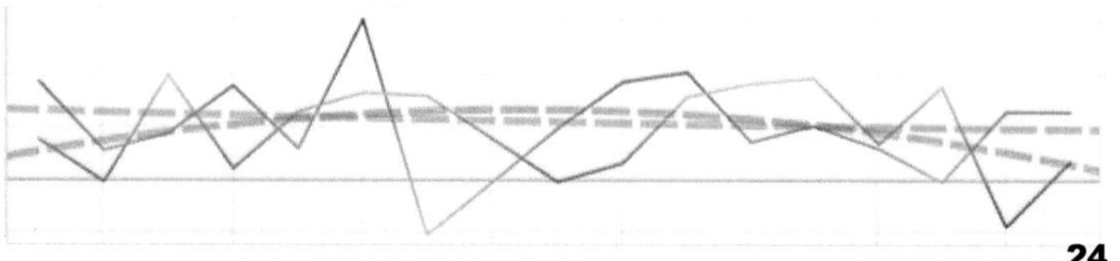

OFF/DEF EDSR
Blue=OFF (high=good)
Red=DEF (low=good)

2017 Close Game Records

All 2016 Wins: **8**
FG Games (<=3 pts) W-L: **4-0**
FG Games Win %: **100% (#1)**
FG Games Wins (% of Total Wins): **50% (#1)**
1 Score Games (<=8 pts) W-L: **6-2**
1 Score Games Win %: **75% (#3)**
1 Score Games Wins (% of Total Wins): **75% (#3)**

2017 Critical & Game-Deciding Stats

TO Margin	-4
TO Given	25
INT Given	18
FUM Given	7
TO Taken	21
INT Taken	15
FUM Taken	6
Sack Margin	-15
Sacks	36
Sacks Allow	51
Return TD Margin	-3
Ret TDs	2
Ret TDs Allow	5
Penalty Margin	+19
Penalties	110
Opponent Penalties	129

Arizona Cardinals 2018 Strength of Schedule In Detail (compared to 2017)

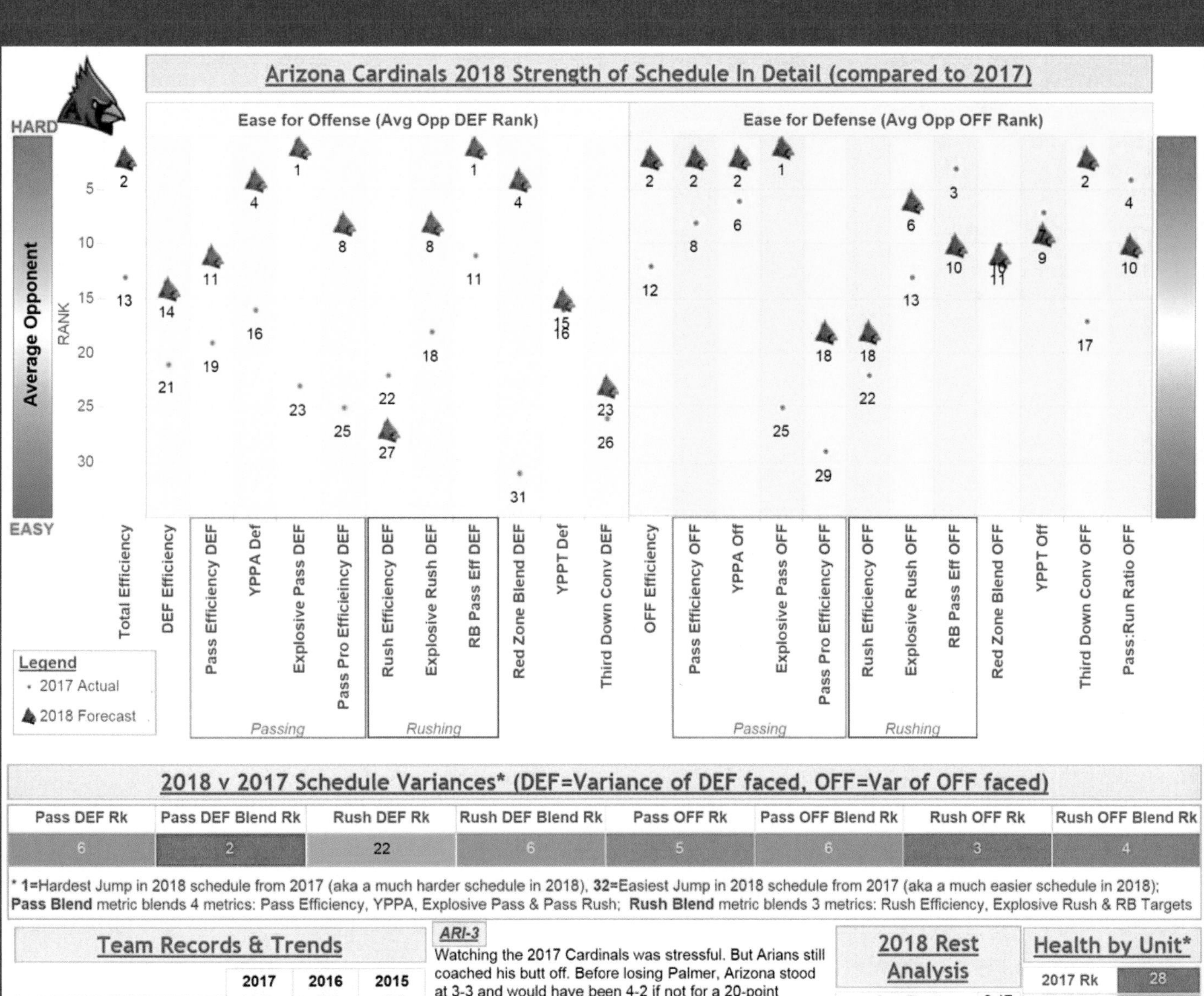

2018 v 2017 Schedule Variances* (DEF=Variance of DEF faced, OFF=Var of OFF faced)

Pass DEF Rk	Pass DEF Blend Rk	Rush DEF Rk	Rush DEF Blend Rk	Pass OFF Rk	Pass OFF Blend Rk	Rush OFF Rk	Rush OFF Blend Rk
6	2	22	6	5	6	3	4

* **1**=Hardest Jump in 2018 schedule from 2017 (aka a much harder schedule in 2018), **32**=Easiest Jump in 2018 schedule from 2017 (aka a much easier schedule in 2018); **Pass Blend** metric blends 4 metrics: Pass Efficiency, YPPA, Explosive Pass & Pass Rush; **Rush Blend** metric blends 3 metrics: Rush Efficiency, Explosive Rush & RB Targets

Team Records & Trends

	2017	2016	2015
Average line	1.9	-3.1	-5.1
Average O/U line	42.7	45.7	46.4
Straight Up Record	8-8	7-8	13-3
Against the Spread Record	6-9	6-10	9-7
Over/Under Record	6-10	10-6	9-7
ATS as Favorite	2-3	5-7	8-7
ATS as Underdog	4-6	1-3	1-0
Straight Up Home	5-3	4-3	6-2
ATS Home	4-3	3-5	3-5
Over/Under Home	3-5	2-6	4-4
ATS as Home Favorite	1-1	3-5	3-5
ATS as a Home Dog	3-2	0-0	0-0
Straight Up Away	3-4	3-5	7-1
ATS Away	2-5	3-5	6-2
Over/Under Away	3-4	8-0	5-3
ATS Away Favorite	1-2	2-2	5-2
ATS Away Dog	1-3	1-3	1-0
Six Point Teaser Record	10-6	9-7	12-4
Seven Point Teaser Record	10-6	9-6	13-3
Ten Point Teaser Record	13-3	11-5	14-2

ARI-3

Watching the 2017 Cardinals was stressful. But Arians still coached his butt off. Before losing Palmer, Arizona stood at 3-3 and would have been 4-2 if not for a 20-point fourth-quarter meltdown against Detroit in Week 1.

The rest of the way, the Cardinals played with the NFL's most-injured roster and Gabbert or Stanton at quarterback. They still led entering fourth quarters in five of their final nine games. In only one game were the Cards down by more than five points entering the fourth quarter (Rams). Arizona beat playoff teams Tennessee and Jacksonville.

These games weren't fun to watch, however. It was bad football, but Arians kept his team competitive. On a personal level, I reached out to a Cardinals scout before Gabbert's start against the Titans. While Gabbert had just been pasted at home 32-16 by the Rams, Tennessee won six of its previous seven. I implored the Cardinals scout to pass on early downs, and especially on first downs to running backs. The Titans' defense was terrible against early-down running back passes. The Cardinals were three-point underdogs. They went nowhere in the first half. *(cont'd - see ARI-4)*

2018 Rest Analysis

Avg Rest	6.47
Avg Rk	3
Team More Rest	4
Opp More Rest	0
Net Rest Edge	4
3 Days Rest	1
4 Days Rest	0
5 Days Rest	0
6 Days Rest	12
7 Days Rest	0
8 Days Rest	0
9 Days Rest	1
10 Days Rest	0
11 Days Rest	0
12 Days Rest	0
13 Days Rest	1
14 Days Rest	0

Health by Unit*

2017 Rk	28
2016 Rk	19
Off Rk	32
Def Rk	13
QB Rk	28
RB Rk	32
WR Rk	20
TE Rk	23
Oline Rk	29
Dline Rk	15
LB Rk	27
DB Rk	14

**Based on the great work of Scott Kacsmar from Football Outsiders*

2018 Weekly Betting Lines (wks 1-16)

1	2	3	4	5	6	7	8	10	11	12	13	14	15	16
WSH	LAR	CHI	SEA	SF	MIN	DEN	SF	KC	OAK	LAC	GB	DET	ATL	LAR
H	A	H	H	A	A	H	H	A	H	A	A	H	A	H
-1	10.5	-1	0	7	10.5	1.5	1.5	6.5	1	9	11	-1	7.5	3.5

Avg = 4.4

Home Lines (wks 1-16)

1	3	4	7	8	11	14	16
WSH	CHI	SEA	DEN	SF	OAK	DET	
-1	-1	0	1.5	1.5	1	-1	3.5

Avg = 0.6

Road Lines (wks 1-16)

2	5	6	10	12	13	15
LAR	SF	MIN	KC	LAC	GB	ATL
10.5	7	10.5	6.5	9	11	7.5

Avg = 8.9

Arizona Cardinals 2017 Play Analysis

2017 Play Tendencies

All Pass %	61%
All Pass Rk	8
All Rush %	39%
All Rush Rk	25
1 Score Pass %	60%
1 Score Pass Rk	5
2016 1 Score Pass %	62%
2016 1 Score Pass Rk	6
2017 Pass Increase %	-2%
Pass Increase Rk	18
1 Score Rush %	40%
1 Score Rush Rk	27
Up Pass %	50%
Up Pass Rk	13
Up Rush %	50%
Up Rush Rk	20
Down Pass %	68%
Down Pass Rk	8
Down Rush %	32%
Down Rush Rk	25

2017 Down & Distance Tendencies

Down	Distance	Total Plays	Pass Rate	Run Rate	Play Success %
1	Short (1-3)	3	33%	67%	33%
	Med (4-7)	3	33%	67%	33%
	Long (8-10)	317	46%	54%	46%
	XL (11+)	13	85%	15%	38%
2	Short (1-3)	31	19%	81%	61%
	Med (4-7)	79	56%	44%	39%
	Long (8-10)	93	61%	39%	38%
	XL (11+)	45	73%	27%	29%
3	Short (1-3)	34	76%	24%	50%
	Med (4-7)	58	93%	7%	45%
	Long (8-10)	35	100%	0%	29%
	XL (11+)	33	94%	6%	18%
4	Short (1-3)	4	25%	75%	75%
	Long (8-10)	1	100%	0%	0%

Shotgun %:

Under Center	Shotgun
56%	44%
37% AVG	*63%*

Run Rate:

Under Center	Shotgun
62%	6%
68% AVG	*23%*

Pass Rate:

Under Center	Shotgun
38%	94%
32% AVG	*77%*

Short Yardage Intelligence:

2nd and Short Run

Run Freq	Run Rk	NFL Run Freq Avg	Run 1D Rate	Run NFL 1D Avg
63%	24	67%	71%	69%

2nd and Short Pass

Pass Freq	Pass Rk	NFL Pass Freq Avg	Pass 1D Rate	Pass NFL 1D Avg
37%	9	33%	70%	53%

Most Frequent Play

Down	Distance	Play Type	Player	Total Plays	Play Success %
1	Long (8-10)	RUSH	Adrian Peterson	61	44%
	XL (11+)	PASS	J.J. Nelson	3	67%
2	Short (1-3)	RUSH	Adrian Peterson	10	60%
			Kerwynn Williams	10	70%
	Med (4-7)	RUSH	Kerwynn Williams	15	33%
	Long (8-10)	PASS	Larry Fitzgerald	19	47%
	XL (11+)	PASS	Larry Fitzgerald	9	22%
3	Short (1-3)	PASS	Larry Fitzgerald	7	43%
	Med (4-7)	PASS	Larry Fitzgerald	17	71%
	Long (8-10)	PASS	Larry Fitzgerald	8	25%
			John Brown	8	25%
	XL (11+)	PASS	J.J. Nelson	6	17%
			Andre Ellington	6	0%

Most Successful Play*

Down	Distance	Play Type	Player	Total Plays	Play Success %
1	Long (8-10)	PASS	Andre Ellington	9	78%
2	Short (1-3)	RUSH	Kerwynn Williams	10	70%
	Med (4-7)	PASS	Larry Fitzgerald	12	42%
	Long (8-10)	PASS	Larry Fitzgerald	19	47%
	XL (11+)	PASS	Larry Fitzgerald	9	22%
3	Short (1-3)	PASS	Jaron Brown	5	80%
	Med (4-7)	PASS	Larry Fitzgerald	17	71%
	Long (8-10)	PASS	Jaron Brown	5	40%
	XL (11+)	PASS	J.J. Nelson	6	17%

**Minimum 5 plays to qualify*

2017 Snap Rates

Wk	Opp	Score	Larry Fitzgerald	Jaron Brown	Jermaine Gresham	J.J. Nelson	Troy Niklas	John Brown	Andre Ellington	David Johnson
1	DET	L 35-23	74 (99%)	118 (79%)	55 (73%)	33 (44%)	21 (28%)		20 (27%)	46 (61%)
2	IND	W 16-13	62 (94%)	50 (76%)		50 (76%)	30 (45%)		30 (45%)	
3	DAL	L 28-17	77 (95%)	76 (94%)	55 (68%)	52 (64%)	19 (23%)		49 (60%)	
4	SF	W 18-15	82 (95%)	82 (95%)	73 (85%)	24 (28%)	21 (24%)	53 (62%)	46 (53%)	
5	PHI	L 34-7	57 (95%)	82 (68%)	40 (67%)	32 (53%)	18 (30%)		31 (52%)	
6	TB	W 38-33	58 (89%)	81 (62%)	61 (94%)	12 (18%)	35 (54%)		13 (20%)	
7	LA	L 33-0	46 (94%)	42 (86%)	30 (61%)	28 (57%)	17 (35%)	31 (63%)		
9	SF	W 20-10	68 (88%)	40 (52%)	70 (91%)	27 (35%)	44 (57%)	46 (60%)	14 (18%)	
10	SEA	L 22-16	80 (100%)	52 (65%)	72 (90%)	29 (36%)	15 (19%)	68 (85%)	43 (54%)	
11	HOU	L 31-21	57 (98%)	31 (53%)	45 (78%)	29 (50%)	17 (29%)	41 (71%)		
12	JAC	W 27-24	72 (99%)	55 (75%)	50 (68%)	38 (52%)	27 (37%)			
13	LA	L 32-16	63 (98%)	46 (72%)	33 (52%)	50 (78%)	25 (39%)			
14	TEN	W 12-7	62 (95%)	55 (85%)	49 (75%)	40 (62%)	19 (29%)			
15	WAS	L 20-15	84 (99%)	68 (80%)		59 (69%)	79 (93%)			
16	NYG	W 23-0	60 (88%)	89 (65%)	67 (99%)	10 (15%)				
17	SEA	W 26-24	71 (100%)	58 (82%)	52 (73%)	26 (37%)	30 (42%)	42 (59%)		
	Grand Total		1,073 (95%)	1,025 (73%)	752 (77%)	539 (48%)	417 (39%)	281 (67%)	246 (41%)	46 (61%)

Personnel Groupings

Personnel	Team %	NFL Avg	Succ. %
1-1 [3WR]	40%	59%	40%
1-2 [2WR]	25%	19%	46%
1-0 [4WR]	12%	2%	46%
0-0 [5WR]	8%	0%	41%
0-1 [4WR]	8%	1%	38%
1-3 [1WR]	4%	5%	35%

Grouping Tendencies

Personnel	Pass Rate	Pass Succ. %	Run Succ. %
1-1 [3WR]	58%	41%	40%
1-2 [2WR]	37%	45%	46%
1-0 [4WR]	90%	46%	42%
0-0 [5WR]	98%	41%	50%
0-1 [4WR]	98%	37%	50%
1-3 [1WR]	28%	36%	34%

Red Zone Targets (min 3)

Receiver	All	Inside 5	6-10	11-20
Larry Fitzgerald	20	3	3	14
Jaron Brown	11	1	2	8
Jermaine Gresham	11	3	2	6
John Brown	6			6
D.J. Foster	5	2		3
Andre Ellington	4	1	1	2
J.J. Nelson	3	1	1	1
Brittan Golden	2	1		1
David Johnson	1	1		

Red Zone Rushes (min 3)

Rusher	All	Inside 5	6-10	11-20
Kerwynn Williams	19	2	3	14
Adrian Peterson	16	3	3	10
Elijhaa Penny	6	3	2	1
David Johnson	3	1		2
Andre Ellington	2	1		1

Early Down Target Rate

RB	TE	WR
22%	18%	60%
23%	*21% NFL AVG*	*56%*

Overall Target Success %

RB	TE	WR
45% #12	46% #24	45% #26

Arizona Cardinals 2017 Passing Recap & 2018 Outlook

Combine competing inside the division with Jimmy Garoppolo, Jared Goff, and Russell Wilson with the NFL's toughest overall schedule, and it would be a major surprise if the 2018 Cardinals vied for a playoff spot. Arizona should focus on transitioning to Josh Rosen at a best-possible time. The Cards open the season against three of the NFL's top-ten pass rushes from 2017. If Sam Bradford starts in Week 1, I don't envision Rosen taking over (barring injury) until Week 7.

I would strongly advise against transitioning during the Cardinals' Week 9 bye. Arizona plays three of its next four games on the road, all against playoff contenders. I would prefer Rosen make back-to-back home-game starts against the Broncos and 49ers leading into the bye. And I can't imagine it taking much longer than Week 7 for Rosen to be ready. McCoy's offense isn't overly complex and is adaptable to its personnel. McCoy plays to the strengths of his players.

Carson Palmer Rating All Downs

71 91 92
96
84 86

Carson Palmer Rating Early Downs

74 66 102
102
94 91

2017 Standard Passing Table

QB	Comp	Att	Comp %	Yds	YPA	TDs	INT	Sacks	Rating	Rk
Carson Palmer	164	267	61%	1,979	7.4	9	7	22	85	29
Blaine Gabbert	95	172	55%	1,068	6.2	6	6	21	71	49
NFL Avg			62%		7.0				87.5	

2017 Advanced Passing Table

QB	Success %	EDSR Passing Success %	20+ Yd Pass Gains	20+ Yd Pass %	30+ Yd Pass Gains	30+ Yd Pass %	Avg. Air Yds per Comp	Avg. YAC per Comp	20+ Air Yd Comp	20+ Air Yd %
Carson Palmer	44%	48%	28	10.5%	8	3.0%	6.9	4.9	9	5%
Blaine Gabbert	39%	44%	17	9.9%	2	1.2%	7.1	4.3	3	3%
NFL Avg	44%	48%	27.7	8.8%	10.3	3.3%	6.0	4.7	11.7	6%

Interception Rates by Down

Yards to Go	1	2	3	4	Total
1 & 2	0.0%	0.0%	0.0%	0.0%	0.0%
3, 4, 5	0.0%	0.0%	5.9%		3.3%
6 - 9		0.0%	0.0%	0.0%	0.0%
10 - 14	3.8%	0.0%	6.3%		3.2%
15+	0.0%	7.1%	0.0%		3.0%
Total	3.5%	1.2%	2.4%	0.0%	2.4%

3rd Down Passing - Short of Sticks Analysis

QB	Avg. Yds to Go	Avg. YIA (of Comp)	Avg Yds Short	Short of Sticks Rate	Short Rk
Carson Palmer	8.3	7.4	-0.8	55%	17
NFL Avg	7.8	6.7	-1.1	60%	

Air Yds vs YAC

	Air Yds %	YAC %	Rk
Carson Palmer	61%	39%	17
NFL Avg	58%	42%	

2017 Receiving Recap & 2018 Outlook

McCoy passes almost strictly out of 11- and 12-personnel groupings. And he doesn't rotate receivers. With Jermaine Gresham unlikely to play early in the year due to a torn Achilles', a large part of forecasting Arizona's passing game comes down to converted Texas A&M wide receiver Ricky Seals-Jones at tight end. McCoy's offenses featured tight ends with Julius Thomas and Antonio Gates in their prime, but ignored tight ends with the 2017 Broncos due to weak talent. McCoy won't force what isn't there. With Fitzgerald already playing a de-facto tight end role in the slot, I'd bet one of the other wide receivers will massively beat expectations.

Player *Min 50 Targets*	Targets	Comp %	YPA	Rating	TOARS	Success %	Success Rk	Missed YPA Rk	YAS % Rk	TDs
Larry Fitzgerald	161	68%	7.2	98	5.5	50%	57	67	76	6
Jaron Brown	69	45%	6.9	82	3.9	39%	116	122	44	4
John Brown	55	38%	5.4	60	3.2	33%	130	128	98	3
J.J. Nelson	61	48%	8.3	53	3.3	43%	98	96	48	2
Andre Ellington	59	66%	6.3	76	3.7	46%	84	130	113	0

Directional Passer Rating Delivered

Receiver	Short Left	Short Middle	Short Right	Deep Left	Deep Middle	Deep Right	Player Total
Larry Fitzgerald	93	96	98	138	103	73	98
Jaron Brown	51	58	119	50	90	122	82
J.J. Nelson	112	110	2	43	74	12	53
John Brown	55	120	78	40	42	64	60
Andre Ellington	98	36	83				74
Jermaine Gresham	118	66	128		18		87
D.J. Foster	38	95	56				58
David Johnson	38	115	56	119			50
Team Total	82	81	86	66	90	67	79

2017 Rushing Recap & 2017 Outlook

David Johnson's biggest edge under Arians was his receiving usage. McCoy's 2017 Broncos passed to running backs on early downs 2% below league average last year, and these targets ranked 30th in Success Rate. (The 2017 Cardinals posted a 57% Success Rate even without Johnson.) In 2016, McCoy's Chargers were league average in running back target frequency but had better efficiency (11th in Success Rate, 6th in yards per target). Johnson especially killed it on third-down receptions, where the Cardinals passed to backs on 27% of third-down plays. McCoy's Chargers and Broncos teams passed to backs on just 21% and 13% of third downs. Coaching tendencies suggest Johnson will struggle to hit his Arians target rates under McCoy.

Player *Min 50 Rushes*	Rushes	YPC	Success %	Success Rk	Missed YPA Rk	YTS % Rk	YAS % Rk	Early Down Success %	Early Down Success Rk	TDs
Adrian Peterson	156	3.5	40%	63	41	15	49	40%	57	2
Kerwynn Williams	120	3.6	43%	41	27	21	62	43%	43	1

Yards per Carry by Direction

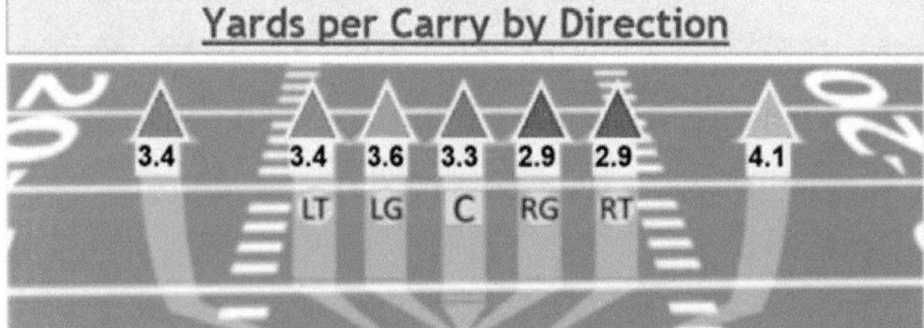

Directional Run Frequency

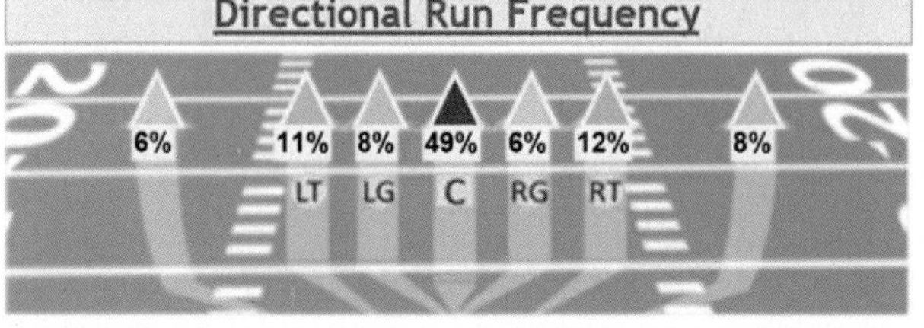

They trailed 7-0 after two quarters with an abysmal 33% Success Rate on first-half plays, gaining just five first downs. Gabbert averaged 1.8 yards per attempt. The Cardinals didn't once pass to a running back on first down, and their lead back averaged just 3.0 yards per carry with a 33% Success Rate on first-down runs. "What were they waiting for?" I thought.

Beginning late in the third quarter, the Cardinals targeted running backs repeatedly on first down. On first-down running back targets, Gabbert posted a 100% Success Rate, 16.5 yards per attempt, and a 119 passer rating. To all other players on first down, Gabbert managed a 67% Success Rate and 4.7 yards per attempt. The Cardinals' longest pass plays came on first down to running backs. Arizona eked out an ugly 12-7 win, and a running back pass put them in field goal range to take a 9-7 lead in the fourth quarter.

The Cardinals had to think outside the box with an injury-ruined team. They didn't have an 8-8 roster, but went 4-0 in games decided by a field goal or less, and 6-2 in one-score outcomes. The Cardinals lost the turnover battle -4. They went -15 in sack margin and -3 in return-TD margin. Gabbert posted a putrid 6.4 YPA and 72 passer rating. Stanton's YPA was 5.6 with a 66 rating. Luck was involved, but so was a lot of good coaching. I was sad to see Arians go.

(cont'd - see ARI-5)

Evan Silva's Fantasy Corner

The Cardinals selected Christian Kirk 47th overall after he dominated the SEC at ages 19-21 for 229 catches and seven return touchdowns (6 PR, 1 KR) in three seasons. The football analytics community has shown collegiate return-game dominance to be a positive indicator for skill-position players like Antonio Brown, T.Y. Hilton, and Cooper Kupp. Although Kirk managed below-par 31st-percentile SPARQ athleticism before the draft, he blazed 4.45 at the Combine and profiles as a cross between Kupp and Nelson Agholor in the slot. Kirk will likely begin his career running primarily outside routes before Fitzgerald retires after this season. As Arizona is missing the NFL's third-most Air Yards from last year's roster, Kirk fell into an abundance of opportunity with a good chance to be the Cardinals' immediate No. 3 pass option behind Fitzgerald and David Johnson. Kirk is a last-round sleeper in fantasy drafts.

Division History: Season Wins & 2018 Projection

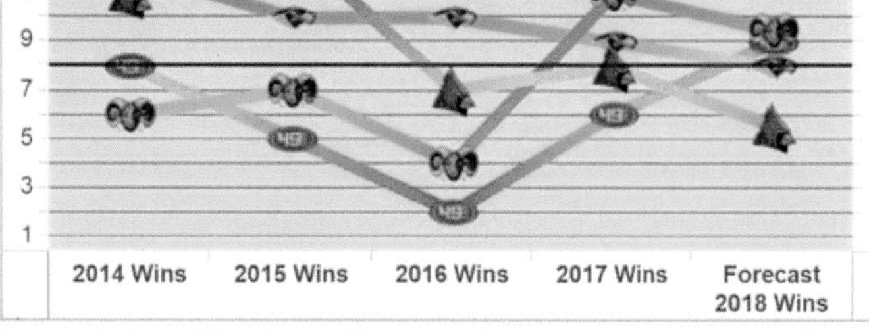

Rank of 2018 Defensive Pass Efficiency Faced by Week

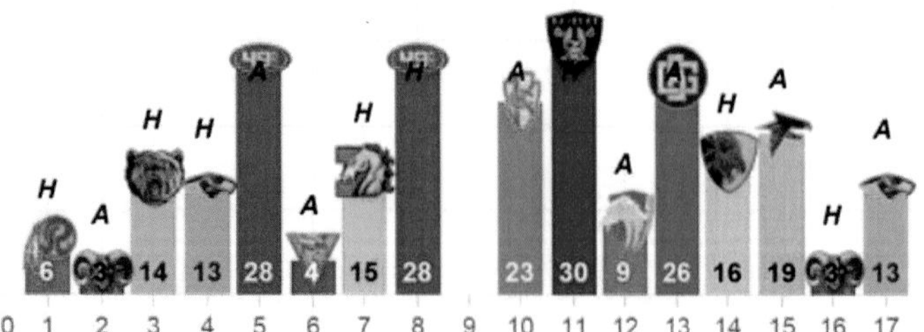

Rank of 2018 Defensive Rush Efficiency Faced by Week

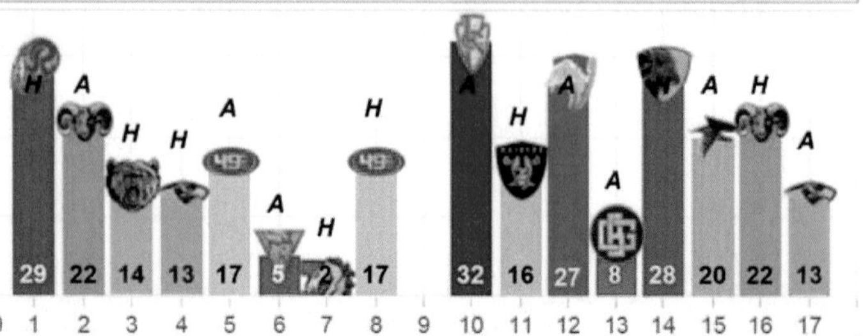

2017 Situational Usage by Player & Position

Usage Rate by Score

		Being Blown Out (14+)	Down Big (9-13)	One Score	Large Lead (9-13)	Blowout Lead (14+)	Grand Total
RUSH	Adrian Peterson	3%	3%	14%	31%	22%	13%
	Kerwynn Williams	11%	13%	12%	17%	20%	13%
	Andre Ellington	1%	2%	2%			2%
	J.J. Nelson			0%		2%	0%
	John Brown			0%			0%
	Chris Johnson	8%	4%	5%			5%
	Elijhaa Penny	2%		3%	3%	11%	3%
	D.J. Foster		2%	0%	1%		1%
	David Johnson			2%	1%		1%
	Chad Williams			0%			0%
	Bronson Hill					2%	0%
	Total	25%	23%	40%	53%	58%	38%
PASS	Larry Fitzgerald	18%	17%	16%	15%	24%	17%
	Adrian Peterson	1%	1%	2%	1%		2%
	Kerwynn Williams	4%	3%	1%	1%		2%
	Jaron Brown	8%	13%	7%	1%	4%	7%
	Andre Ellington	12%	8%	5%		2%	5%
	J.J. Nelson	10%	10%	6%	4%	4%	6%
	John Brown	11%	5%	5%	11%	4%	6%
	Chris Johnson	1%		1%			1%
	Jermaine Gresham	3%	7%	5%	4%		5%
	Elijhaa Penny			0%	3%	2%	1%
	D.J. Foster	3%	3%	3%	1%		3%
	Ricky Seals-Jones	2%	4%	3%	1%		3%
	Troy Niklas	1%	2%	3%	1%		2%
	David Johnson			1%	1%		1%
	Brittan Golden		3%	1%			1%
	Chad Williams		2%	1%			1%
	Ifeanyi Momah		2%				0%
	Gabe Holmes			0%			0%
	Total	75%	77%	60%	47%	42%	62%

Positional Target Distribution vs NFL Average

		NFL Wide				Team Only			
		Left	Middle	Right	**Total**	Left	Middle	Right	**Total**
Deep	WR	941	488	951	**2,380**	45	21	36	**102**
	TE	192	147	188	**527**		3		**3**
	RB	38	9	42	**89**	1			**1**
	All	**1,171**	**644**	**1,181**	**2,996**	**46**	**24**	**36**	**106**
Short	WR	2,771	1,612	2,696	**7,079**	91	59	94	**244**
	TE	852	818	1,159	**2,829**	11	21	11	**43**
	RB	1,293	800	1,260	**3,353**	28	23	35	**86**
	All	**4,916**	**3,230**	**5,115**	**13,261**	**130**	**103**	**140**	**373**
Total		**6,087**	**3,874**	**6,296**	**16,257**	**176**	**127**	**176**	**479**

Positional Success Rates vs NFL Average

		NFL Wide				Team Only			
		Left	Middle	Right	**Total**	Left	Middle	Right	**Total**
Deep	WR	37%	45%	38%	**39%**	33%	48%	39%	**38%**
	TE	38%	53%	45%	**45%**		33%		**33%**
	RB	34%	56%	38%	**38%**	100%			**100%**
	All	**37%**	**47%**	**39%**	**40%**	**35%**	**46%**	**39%**	**39%**
Short	WR	52%	58%	50%	**53%**	43%	51%	50%	**48%**
	TE	51%	56%	49%	**52%**	45%	52%	73%	**56%**
	RB	44%	51%	43%	**45%**	54%	48%	34%	**44%**
	All	**50%**	**56%**	**48%**	**50%**	**45%**	**50%**	**48%**	**48%**
Total		**47%**	**54%**	**46%**	**49%**	**43%**	**50%**	**46%**	**46%**

Successful Play Rate
0% 100%

Arizona Cardinals - Success by Personnel Grouping & Play Type

Play Type	1-1 [3WR]	1-2 [2WR]	2-1 [2WR]	1-0 [4WR]	1-3 [1WR]	0-1 [4WR]	2-0 [3WR]	2-2 [1WR]	0-0 [5WR]	0-2 [3WR]	3-1 [1WR]	2-3 [0WR]	Grand Total
PASS	41% (249, 38%)	45% (96, 15%)		46% (110, 17%)	36% (11, 2%)	37% (78, 12%)	22% (9, 1%)	0% (2, 0%)	41% (83, 13%)	36% (11, 2%)			41% (649, 100%)
RUSH	40% (177, 43%)	46% (167, 41%)	0% (1, 0%)	42% (12, 3%)	34% (29, 7%)	50% (2, 0%)	100% (1, 0%)	0% (2, 0%)	50% (2, 0%)		0% (1, 0%)	40% (5, 1%)	41% (410, 100%)
TOTAL	40% (426, 40%)	46% (263, 25%)	0% (1, 0%)	46% (122, 12%)	35% (40, 4%)	38% (80, 8%)	30% (10, 1%)	0% (4, 0%)	41% (85, 8%)	36% (11, 1%)	0% (1, 0%)	40% (5, 0%)	41% (1,059, 100%)

Format Line 1: Success Rate Line 2: Total # of Plays, % of All Plays (by type)

ARI-5 The 2018 Cardinals have a completely new quarterback room headlined by Sam Bradford and No. 10 overall pick Josh Rosen. New OC Mike McCoy designed an offense for Tim Tebow's 2011 Broncos to make the playoffs, oversaw Peyton Manning's prolific Denver years, and engineered Philip Rivers' late-career renaissance in San Diego. In McCoy's 2013 offense, Rivers completed a career-high 69.5% of his passes at 8.5 yards per attempt. Rivers hasn't topped 7.9 YPA since.

Bradford and Rosen are in good hands. And the Cardinals should turn to Rosen sooner rather than later. Bradford signed what amounts to a one-year deal with the Cardinals, who aren't going anywhere in 2018. To compete in a division featuring Jimmy Garoppolo, Russell Wilson, and Jared Goff, the Cardinals must develop their own young-stud quarterback. And Rosen can't do that from the bench. The offensive line must stay healthy. Both LG Mike Iupati (lost Week 1) and LT D.J. Humphries (lost Week 5) return after missing most of last season. The right side was overhauled with RG Justin Pugh and RT Andre Smith, but the Cardinals still have short-armed A.Q. Shipley at center. The hope is in better quarterback play, pass protection and the return is that of do-it-all running back David Johnson.

This year's Cardinals are a difficult team to forecast. The coaching staff and quarterback rooms are new. Johnson is back. Personnel groupings are sure to change. Whereas Arians skewed to three- and four-receiver sets, McCoy's history is primarily with 11 personnel and some 12 mixed in. McCoy's 2017 Broncos passed in three-receiver 11 personnel on 77% of snaps – well above the 69% league average – and threw from two-tight end sets 13% of the time. McCoy's 2016 Chargers and 2017 Broncos offenses passed from four-plus-wideout formations on just six combined snaps. Arians attempted 366 combined throws from such packages during that time. Under McCoy, this should mean less involvement from auxiliary receivers and more focused targeting of Arizona's Nos. 1-3 wideouts.

Arizona's Win Total is 5.5, a mark they'll struggle to beat against the NFL's toughest schedule. The 2018 Cardinals draw just one top-ten opponent at home (Rams) and a league-high five top-ten opponents on the road. I can already envision myself backing this year's Cardinals against the spread at home multiple times after a tough road loss that improves our line value. The back half of Arizona's schedule features four top-ten opponents in a five-week span. The Cardinals are the only team to not face a single bottom-five opponent all year.

Receiving Success by Personnel Grouping

Position	Player	1-1 [3WR]	1-2 [2WR]	1-0 [4WR]	1-3 [1WR]	0-1 [4WR]	2-0 [3WR]	2-2 [1WR]	0-0 [5WR]	0-2 [3WR]	Total
RB	Andre Ellington	47% 4.4 51.0 (19)	33% 6.7 85.4 (3)	53% 7.9 99.5 (17)		50% 10.0 85.4 (2)	0% 0.0 39.6 (1)		38% 5.0 64.6 (8)		46% 5.9 73.5 (50)
TE	Jermaine Gresham	52% 7.2 80.0 (21)	67% 8.9 103.7 (9)	50% 4.0 60.4 (2)		38% 5.5 87.5 (8)			60% 6.4 93.3 (5)	100% 6.0 91.7 (1)	54% 7.0 87.4 (46)
	Ricky Seals-Jones	50% 14.0 135.4 (2)	13% 1.9 39.6 (8)	100% 18.5 118.8 (2)	50% 7.8 76.0 (4)	50% 8.3 78.5 (6)		0% 2.0 56.3 (2)	50% 3.5 58.3 (2)	50% 14.5 135.4 (2)	39% 7.2 88.5 (28)
WR	Larry Fitzgerald	49% 7.2 102.8 (73)	62% 7.8 88.9 (26)	68% 7.0 109.0 (25)		36% 6.3 85.0 (22)	100% 24.0 118.8 (1)		54% 7.2 89.6 (13)	0% 0.0 39.6 (1)	53% 7.2 98.3 (161)
	Jaron Brown	41% 8.2 85.7 (27)	33% 10.0 111.1 (6)	29% 5.4 54.2 (14)		50% 4.2 75.0 (6)	25% 2.3 39.6 (4)		45% 6.1 95.6 (11)	100% 19.0 118.8 (1)	39% 6.9 81.6 (69)
	J.J. Nelson	30% 5.9 12.1 (20)	75% 17.8 116.7 (4)	47% 9.2 88.7 (19)		44% 7.0 28.7 (9)			38% 9.6 83.9 (8)	0% 0.0 39.6 (1)	41% 8.3 52.9 (61)

Format Line 1: Success Rate Line 2: YPA Line 3: Passer Rating Line 4: Total # of Plays

Successful Play Rate
0% 100%

Rushing Success by Personnel Grouping

Position	Player	1-1 [3WR]	1-2 [2WR]	2-1 [2WR]	1-0 [4WR]	1-3 [1WR]	2-3 [0WR]	Total
RB	Adrian Peterson	38% 3.9 (53)	43% 3.6 (61)			29% 1.3 (14)	100% 1.0 (1)	40% 3.5 (129)
	Kerwynn Williams	34% 2.8 (50)	52% 4.1 (61)		50% 5.5 (2)	29% 2.9 (7)		43% 3.6 (120)
	Chris Johnson	30% 2.8 (23)	37% 2.3 (19)	0% 1.0 (1)		0% 2.0 (2)		31% 2.5 (45)

Format Line 1: Success Rate Line 2: YPC Line 3: Total # of Plays

2018 Coaches

Head Coach:
Dan Quinn (4th yr)
Offensive Coordinator:
Steve Sarkisian (2nd yr)
Defensive Coordinator:
Marquand Manuel (2nd yr)

Atlanta Falcons

2018 Forecast

Wins	Div Rank
9	#2

Past Records

2017: 10-6
2016: 11-5
2015: 8-8

EASY HARD

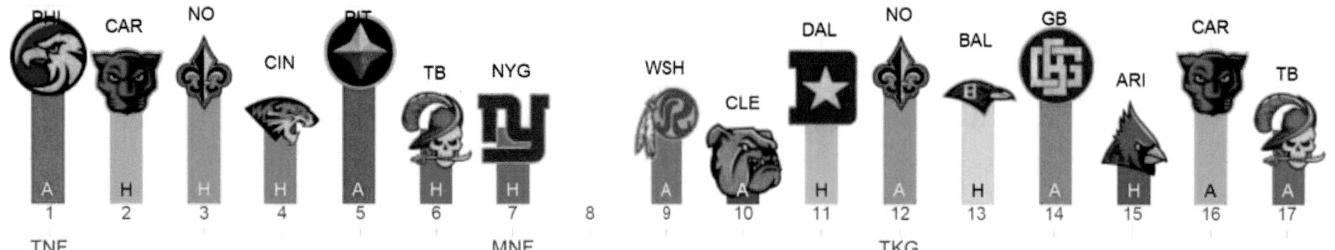

Key Players Lost

TXN	Player (POS)
Cut	Ifedi, Martin DE
	Shelby, Derrick DE
	Toilolo, Levine TE
	Tupou, Tani DT
Declared Free Agent	Clayborn, Adrian DE
	Coleman, Derrick RB
	Gabriel, Taylor WR
	Ishmael, Kemal S
	Neasman, Sharrod S
	Poe, Dontari DT
	Reynolds, LaRoy LB
	Roberts, Andre WR
	Rubin, Ahtyba DT
	Tripp, Jordan LB
	Upshaw, Courtney DT
	Ward, Terron RB
	Weatherspoon, Sean LB
	Williams, Nick WR

Average Line	# Games Favored	# Games Underdog
-1.9	10	5

2018 Atlanta Falcons Overview

The 2017 spotlight shined brightly on Steve Sarkisian as Super Bowl coordinator Kyle Shanahan's replacement. And there was no way around the comparison, especially when Sarkisian's plan was to simply utilize the same offensive concepts Shanahan left behind. The Falcons kept Shanahan's outside-zone running scheme, used a lot of play action, and tried to maintain run-pass balance.

Sarkisian says he's more comfortable in year two. He said last year, "learning the system that was in place and learning the players that were in place" caused Atlanta's 2017 offensive drop off. And drop off it did.

Shanahan's 2016 Falcons averaged 19 first-half points per game, second most in NFL history behind only the 2007 Patriots. And Shanahan accomplished this feat against the NFL's second-toughest schedule of defense. The 2016 Falcons finished No. 1 in Early-Down Success Rate, efficiency, passing efficiency, and explosive pass efficiency. They averaged 33.8 points per game and an eight-point halftime lead. Last year's Falcons averaged 12 first-half points despite facing the league's 11th-softest defensive slate. Sark's unit ranked No. 5 in EDSR, No. 9 in offensive efficiency, No. 10 in passing efficiency, and No. 4 in explosive pass efficiency. They averaged 22.1 points per game with an average halftime lead of 2.5. It was a massive regression.

A whopping 16 of the Falcons' 19 games in 2016 (84%) went over the lined Vegas total, even in a year when 12 of their games were lined at or above 50 points. And all 12 of those went over the total. But just four of Atlanta's 18 games last year (22%) exceeded the total, falling flat relative to linemakers' projections. Sark's Falcons fell below the total in seven straight games to close out the year.

The 2017 Falcons offense was hardly a dud, but it barely left the ground compared to 2016. And it left us in the analytics community scratching our heads to figure out what went wrong. The personnel was essentially the same, and Atlanta faced a much easier schedule.

(cont'd - see ATL2)

Key Free Agents/ Trades Added

Bethel, Justin CB
Fusco, Brandon G
Graham, Tyson S
Paulsen, Logan TE
Smith, Garrison DT
Zimmer, Justin DT

Drafted Players

Rd	Pk	Player (College)
1	26	WR - Calvin Ridley (Alabama)
2	58	CB - Isaiah Oliver (Colorado)
3	90	DT - Deadrin Senat (South Florida)
4	126	RB - Ito Smith (Southern Miss)
6	194	WR - Russell Gage (LSU)
	200	S - Foyesade Oluokun (Yale)

Regular Season Wins: Past & Current Proj

Lineup & Cap Hits

FS R.Allen 37
SS K.Neal 22
LB D.Campbell 59
LB D.Jones 45
RCB R.Alford 23
SLOTCB B.Poole 34
DE T.McKinley 98
DE T.McClain 99
DT G.Jarrett 97
DE V.Beasley 44
LCB D.Trufant 21

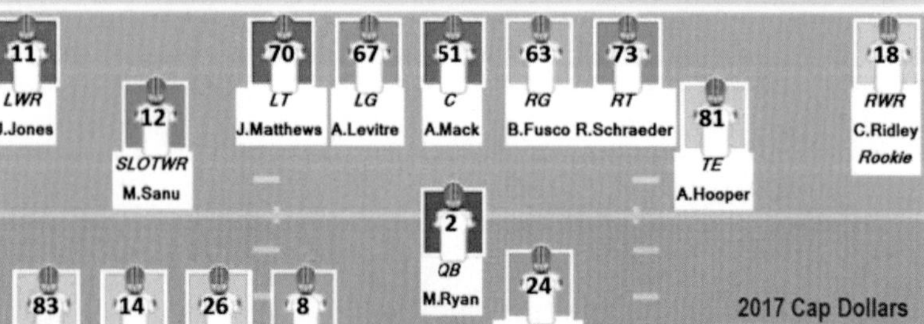

2018 Unit Spending

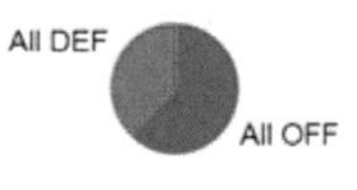

Positional Spending

	Rank	Total	2017 Rk
All OFF	3	$109.28M	3
QB	14	$23.24M	2
OL	1	$47.32M	14
RB	14	$8.28M	28
WR	8	$26.83M	2
TE	31	$3.61M	27
All DEF	31	$65.42M	24
DL	26	$18.58M	12
LB	30	$9.90M	30
CB	5	$28.18M	16
S	22	$8.76M	25

Atlanta Falcons 2017 Success Rate Radar

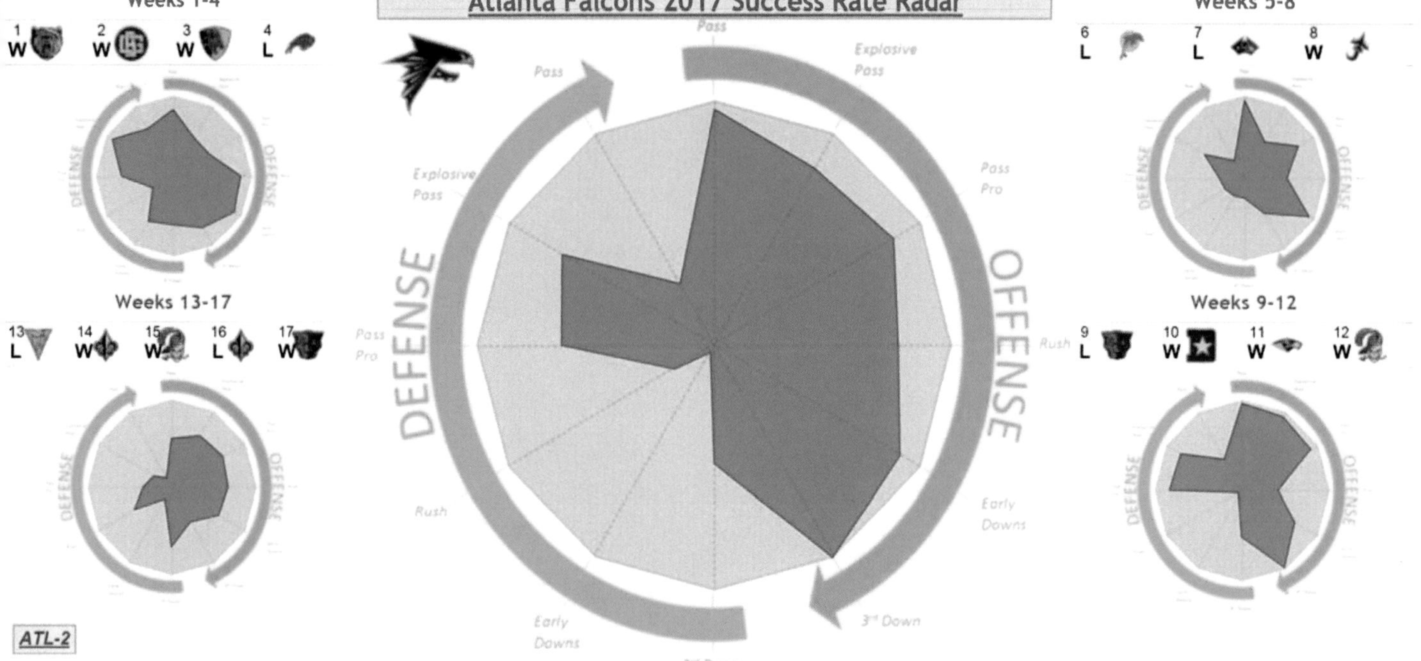

ATL-2

After their Week 7 loss to the Patriots, I believe the Falcons' mindset changed. Trailing 20-0 with 14:36 left in the fourth quarter, Atlanta had the ball at New England's one-yard line on fourth down. Sarkisian called a Taylor Gabriel jet sweep that never stood a chance. Gabriel was tackled at the six, and the Patriots took over on downs. The horrendous play call blew up all over Twitter.

The next morning, I set out to understand what Sarkisian had done to this offense. I shared my findings on a live Periscope video I do each week before Monday Night Football kicks off, presenting immediate analytics-based reactions to Sunday's games. The Falcons were 3-3 at the time, and I noticed some glaring issues.

Through Week 7, Julio Jones' first-down targets dipped from 29% under Shanahan to 24% under Sarkisian. And Sark wasn't going deep much on first down. Only 18% of Matt Ryan's first-down targets traveled 15-plus yards downfield. Shanahan went deep on 26% of Ryan's first-down attempts.

The impact of more conservative first-down play calling and less targeting of Julio showed up in Ryan's first-down stats. After recording a league-best 121 first-down passer rating with Shanahan in 2016, Ryan's rating plummeted to 86.4 under Sarkisian. Ryan's first-down yards per attempt fell from 10.8 in 2016 to 7.9 last year.

Target location was also problematic. Sark called first-down targets to Julio in the short-right area of the field on 35% of attempts and went deep on only 30% of Jones' targets. Sarkisian targeted Julio on the right side of the field 50% of the time, but just 20% on the left. In 2016, Shanahan moved Julio around. Jones drew 20% of his targets to the short left, 17% in the short middle, and 17% to the short right. And 45% of Jones' Shanahan-coordinated targets went deep. Shanahan's difference between left- and right-side Julio targets was only 4%, compared to Sarkisian's massive 30% split.

..

(cont'd - see ATL-3)

2017 Offensive Advanced Metrics

2017 Defensive Advanced Metrics

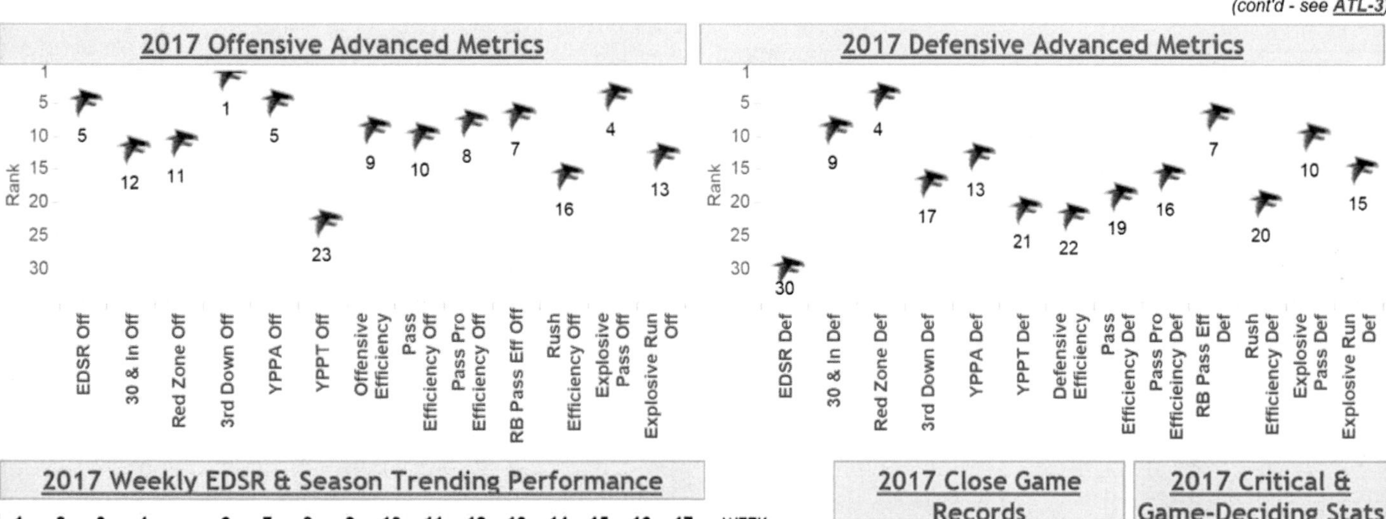

2017 Weekly EDSR & Season Trending Performance

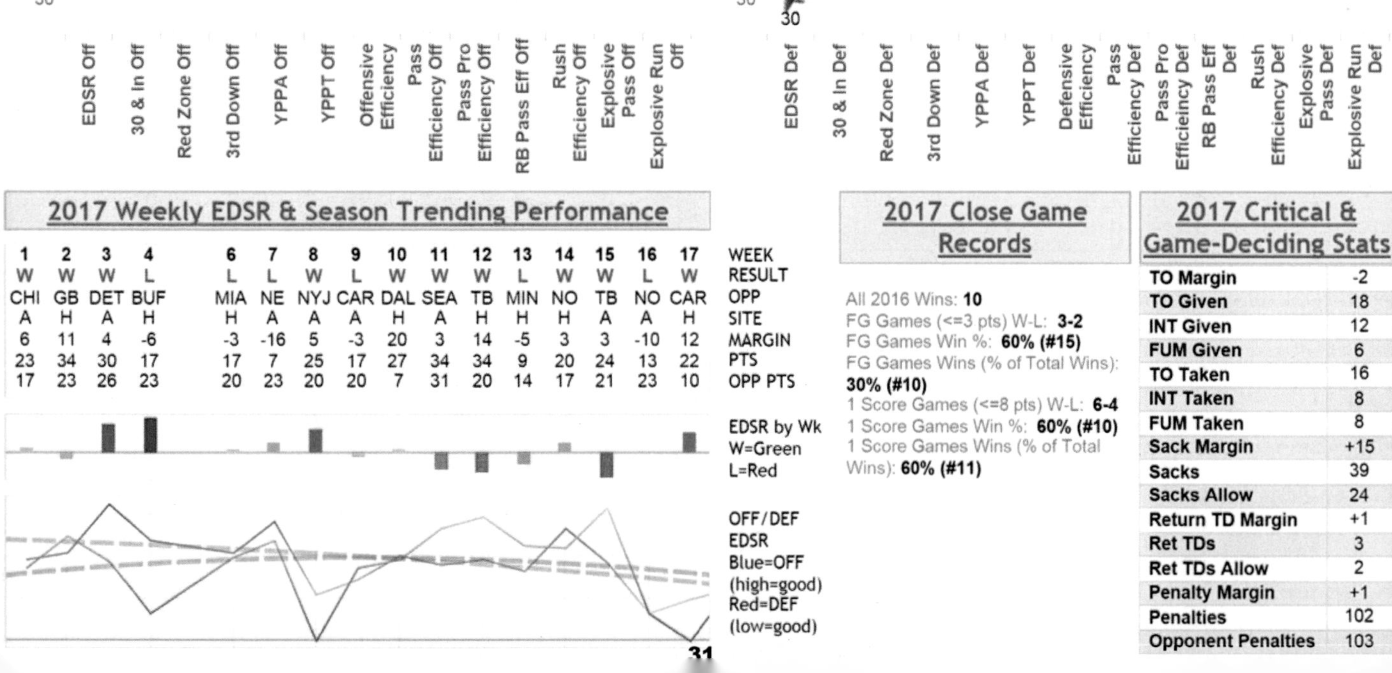

1	2	3	4	6	7	8	9	10	11	12	13	14	15	16	17	WEEK
W	W	W	L	L	L	W	L	W	W	W	L	W	W	L	W	RESULT
CHI	GB	DET	BUF	MIA	NE	NYJ	CAR	DAL	SEA	TB	MIN	NO	TB	NO	CAR	OPP
A	H	A	H	H	A	A	A	H	A	H	H	H	A	A	H	SITE
6	11	4	-6	-3	-16	5	-3	20	3	14	-5	3	3	-10	12	MARGIN
23	34	30	17	17	7	25	17	27	34	34	9	20	24	13	22	PTS
17	23	26	23	20	23	20	20	7	31	20	14	17	21	23	10	OPP PTS

2017 Close Game Records

All 2016 Wins: **10**
FG Games (<=3 pts) W-L: **3-2**
FG Games Win %: **60% (#15)**
FG Games Wins (% of Total Wins): **30% (#10)**
1 Score Games (<=8 pts) W-L: **6-4**
1 Score Games Win %: **60% (#10)**
1 Score Games Wins (% of Total Wins): **60% (#11)**

2017 Critical & Game-Deciding Stats

TO Margin	-2
TO Given	18
INT Given	12
FUM Given	6
TO Taken	16
INT Taken	8
FUM Taken	8
Sack Margin	+15
Sacks	39
Sacks Allow	24
Return TD Margin	+1
Ret TDs	3
Ret TDs Allow	2
Penalty Margin	+1
Penalties	102
Opponent Penalties	103

Atlanta Falcons 2018 Strength of Schedule In Detail (compared to 2017)

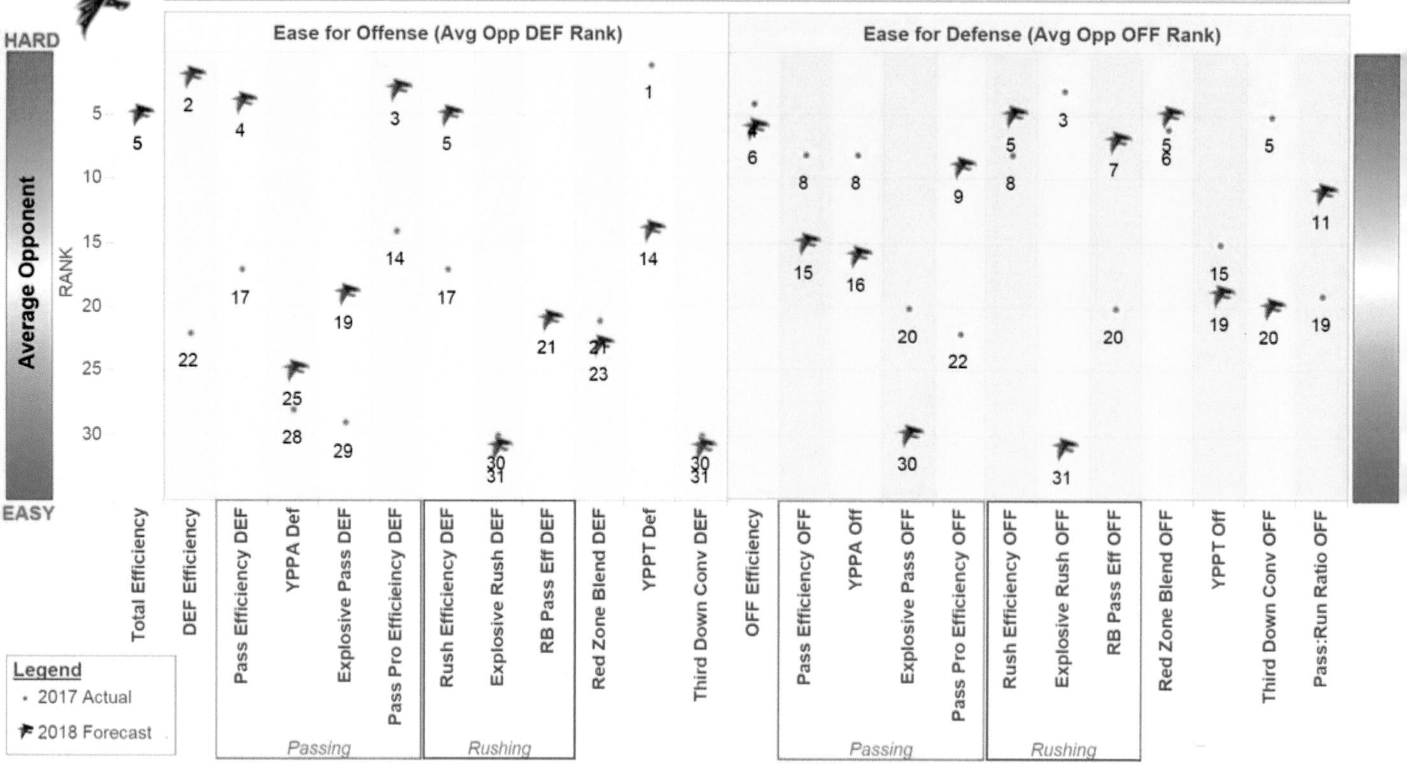

Average Opponent (RANK): HARD (1) to EASY (32)

Legend: · 2017 Actual; falcon = 2018 Forecast

Ease for Offense (Avg Opp DEF Rank)

Metric	Group	Values shown (2017 Actual / 2018 Forecast)
Total Efficiency		5
DEF Efficiency		22 / 2
Pass Efficiency DEF	Passing	17 / 4
YPPA Def	Passing	28 / 25
Explosive Pass DEF	Passing	29 / 19
Pass Pro Efficiency DEF	Passing	14 / 3
Rush Efficiency DEF	Rushing	17 / 5
Explosive Rush DEF	Rushing	30, 31
RB Pass Eff DEF	Rushing	21
Red Zone Blend DEF		21 / 23
YPPT Def		1 / 14
Third Down Conv DEF		30, 31

Ease for Defense (Avg Opp OFF Rank)

Metric	Group	Values shown (2017 Actual / 2018 Forecast)
OFF Efficiency		6
Pass Efficiency OFF	Passing	8 / 15
YPPA Off	Passing	8 / 16
Explosive Pass OFF	Passing	20 / 30
Pass Pro Efficiency OFF	Passing	22 / 9
Rush Efficiency OFF	Rushing	8 / 5
Explosive Rush OFF	Rushing	3 / 31
RB Pass Eff OFF	Rushing	20 / 7
Red Zone Blend OFF		5, 6
YPPT Off		15 / 19
Third Down Conv OFF		5 / 20
Pass:Run Ratio OFF		19 / 11

2018 v 2017 Schedule Variances* (DEF=Variance of DEF faced, OFF=Var of OFF faced)

Pass DEF Rk	Pass DEF Blend Rk	Rush DEF Rk	Rush DEF Blend Rk	Pass OFF Rk	Pass OFF Blend Rk	Rush OFF Rk	Rush OFF Blend Rk
4	7	6	9	4	23	31	17

* **1**=Hardest Jump in 2018 schedule from 2017 (aka a much harder schedule in 2018), **32**=Easiest Jump in 2018 schedule from 2017 (aka a much easier schedule in 2018); **Pass Blend** metric blends 4 metrics: Pass Efficiency, YPPA, Explosive Pass & Pass Rush; **Rush Blend** metric blends 3 metrics: Rush Efficiency, Explosive Rush & RB Targets

Team Records & Trends

	2017	2016	2015
Average line	-3.7	-2.1	-1.5
Average O/U line	48.6	49.8	47.8
Straight Up Record	10-6	11-5	8-8
Against the Spread Record	7-9	10-6	6-10
Over/Under Record	4-11	13-3	2-13
ATS as Favorite	6-7	5-5	2-8
ATS as Underdog	1-2	5-1	4-2
Straight Up Home	5-3	5-3	4-4
ATS Home	5-3	3-5	3-5
Over/Under Home	2-6	8-0	1-7
ATS as Home Favorite	5-3	2-5	1-5
ATS as a Home Dog	0-0	1-0	2-0
Straight Up Away	5-3	6-2	4-4
ATS Away	2-6	7-1	3-5
Over/Under Away	2-5	5-3	1-6
ATS Away Favorite	1-4	3-0	1-3
ATS Away Dog	1-2	4-1	2-2
Six Point Teaser Record	12-4	13-3	9-7
Seven Point Teaser Record	12-3	13-3	9-6
Ten Point Teaser Record	13-3	16-0	12-3

ATL-3

Whereas the 2016 Falcons generated 20-plus-yard "explosive" gains on a league-high 16% of their first-down passes, just 8% of Sarkisian's first-down throws went for 20-plus yards. The Falcons fell from No. 1 in in explosive first-down passes to No. 26.

The Falcons also ignored Julio in scoring position early in the season. He drew just two red-zone targets through Week 7. Diminutive situational receiver Taylor Gabriel had six, five producing a 0% Success Rate. On a positive note, the run game was more productive under Sarkisian in the first six games, and the Falcons ran slightly more often.

The Falcons needed more early-down urgency to keep defenses on their heels. The field had gotten too compressed. The 2016 Falcons' goal was to Blitzkrieg opponents early in games, racing out to large halftime leads and forcing opponents into desperation. But Sark's lack of first-down urgency created more "four-quarter" than "two-quarter" games, and Atlanta's defense wasn't good enough to win late when less-desperate offenses had full playbooks at their disposal.

(cont'd - see ATL-4)

2018 Rest Analysis

Avg Rest	6.67
Avg Rk	1
Team More Rest	4
Opp More Rest	2
Net Rest Edge	2
3 Days Rest	1
4 Days Rest	0
5 Days Rest	0
6 Days Rest	10
7 Days Rest	1
8 Days Rest	0
9 Days Rest	2
10 Days Rest	0
11 Days Rest	0
12 Days Rest	1
13 Days Rest	0
14 Days Rest	0

Health by Unit*

2017 Rk	2
2016 Rk	6
Off Rk	3
Def Rk	3
QB Rk	1
RB Rk	22
WR Rk	6
TE Rk	10
Oline Rk	3
Dline Rk	2
LB Rk	4
DB Rk	1

Based on the great work of Scott Kacsmar from Football Outsiders

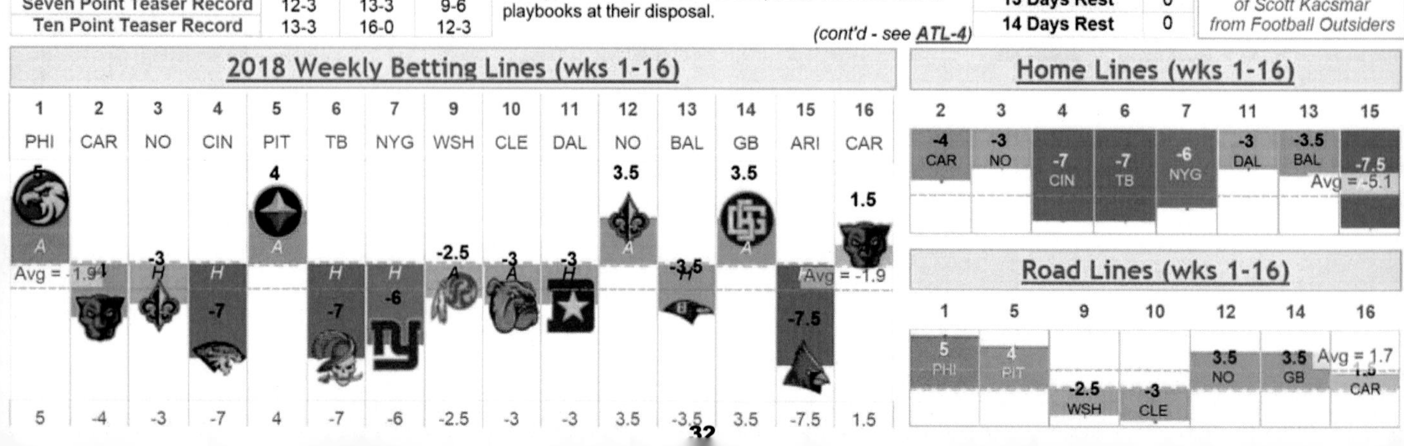

Atlanta Falcons 2017 Play Analysis

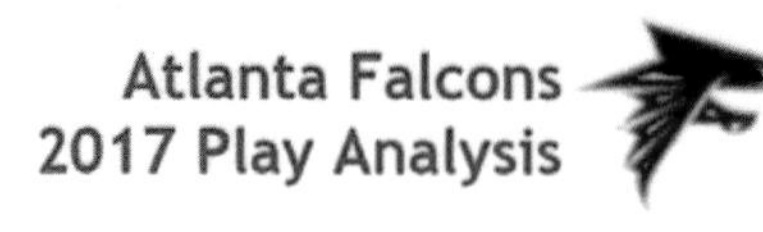

2017 Play Tendencies

All Pass %	56%
All Pass Rk	21
All Rush %	44%
All Rush Rk	12
1 Score Pass %	55%
1 Score Pass Rk	21
2016 1 Score Pass %	61%
2016 1 Score Pass Rk	8
2017 Pass Increase %	-6%
Pass Increase Rk	28
1 Score Rush %	45%
1 Score Rush Rk	12
Up Pass %	53%
Up Pass Rk	6
Up Rush %	47%
Up Rush Rk	27
Down Pass %	62%
Down Pass Rk	27
Down Rush %	38%
Down Rush Rk	6

2017 Down & Distance Tendencies

Down	Distance	Total Plays	Pass Rate	Run Rate	Play Success %
1	Short (1-3)	9	22%	78%	67%
	Med (4-7)	12	50%	50%	67%
	Long (8-10)	350	49%	51%	53%
	XL (11+)	15	40%	60%	20%
2	Short (1-3)	49	35%	65%	67%
	Med (4-7)	75	52%	48%	48%
	Long (8-10)	102	53%	47%	43%
	XL (11+)	37	84%	16%	32%
	35	1	100%	0%	0%
3	Short (1-3)	44	45%	55%	66%
	Med (4-7)	62	92%	8%	48%
	Long (8-10)	36	94%	6%	28%
	XL (11+)	22	95%	5%	18%
4	Short (1-3)	3	33%	67%	67%
	Med (4-7)	2	50%	50%	50%

Shotgun %:

Under Center	Shotgun
59%	41%
37%	*63%*

37% AVG 63%

Run Rate:

Under Center	Shotgun
64%	15%

68% AVG 23%

Pass Rate:

Under Center	Shotgun
36%	85%

32% AVG 77%

Short Yardage Intelligence:

2nd and Short Run

Run Freq	Run Rk	NFL Run Freq Avg	Run 1D Rate	Run NFL 1D Avg
66%	18	67%	65%	69%

2nd and Short Pass

Pass Freq	Pass Rk	NFL Pass Freq Avg	Pass 1D Rate	Pass NFL 1D Avg
34%	15	33%	56%	53%

Most Frequent Play

Down	Distance	Play Type	Player	Total Plays	Play Success %
1	Short (1-3)	RUSH	Devonta Freeman	5	60%
	Med (4-7)	RUSH	Devonta Freeman	3	100%
	Long (8-10)	RUSH	Devonta Freeman	86	55%
	XL (11+)	RUSH	Devonta Freeman	5	0%
2	Short (1-3)	RUSH	Devonta Freeman	19	74%
	Med (4-7)	RUSH	Tevin Coleman	18	33%
	Long (8-10)	RUSH	Devonta Freeman	23	26%
	XL (11+)	PASS	Julio Jones	11	45%
3	Short (1-3)	RUSH	Devonta Freeman	9	89%
			Tevin Coleman	9	56%
	Med (4-7)	PASS	Julio Jones	15	60%
	Long (8-10)	PASS	Mohamed Sanu	7	57%
	XL (11+)	PASS	Julio Jones	5	40%

Most Successful Play*

Down	Distance	Play Type	Player	Total Plays	Play Success %
1	Short (1-3)	RUSH	Devonta Freeman	5	60%
	Long (8-10)	PASS	Levine Toilolo	10	90%
	XL (11+)	RUSH	Devonta Freeman	5	0%
2	Short (1-3)	RUSH	Devonta Freeman	19	74%
	Med (4-7)	PASS	Devonta Freeman	5	80%
	Long (8-10)	PASS	Taylor Gabriel	6	83%
	XL (11+)	PASS	Julio Jones	11	45%
3	Short (1-3)	RUSH	Devonta Freeman	9	89%
	Med (4-7)	PASS	Julio Jones	15	60%
	Long (8-10)	PASS	Mohamed Sanu	7	57%
	XL (11+)	PASS	Julio Jones	5	40%

**Minimum 5 plays to qualify*

2017 Snap Rates

Wk	Opp	Score	Austin Hooper	Julio Jones	Mohamed Sanu	Devonta Freeman	Taylor Gabriel	Levine Toilolo	Tevin Coleman
1	CHI	W 23-17	47 (80%)	48 (81%)	48 (81%)	36 (61%)	31 (53%)	29 (49%)	24 (41%)
2	GB	W 34-23	41 (71%)	48 (83%)	48 (83%)	38 (66%)	27 (47%)	28 (48%)	22 (38%)
3	DET	W 30-26	49 (72%)	58 (85%)	57 (84%)	41 (60%)	36 (53%)	35 (51%)	28 (41%)
4	BUF	L 23-17	59 (79%)	15 (20%)	31 (41%)	49 (65%)	60 (80%)	29 (39%)	27 (36%)
6	MIA	L 20-17	52 (91%)	45 (79%)		42 (74%)	48 (84%)	15 (26%)	18 (32%)
7	NE	L 23-7	52 (91%)	50 (88%)	51 (89%)	41 (72%)	35 (61%)	19 (33%)	20 (35%)
8	NYJ	W 25-20	50 (76%)	59 (89%)	60 (91%)	40 (61%)	31 (47%)	31 (47%)	29 (44%)
9	CAR	L 20-17	50 (83%)	43 (72%)	43 (72%)	41 (68%)	38 (63%)	28 (47%)	19 (32%)
10	DAL	W 27-7	54 (83%)	43 (66%)	48 (74%)	2 (3%)	27 (42%)	30 (46%)	44 (68%)
11	SEA	W 34-31	39 (63%)	50 (81%)	47 (76%)		34 (55%)	31 (50%)	42 (68%)
12	TB	W 34-20	44 (69%)	46 (72%)	52 (81%)		42 (66%)	29 (45%)	44 (69%)
13	MIN	L 14-9	34 (64%)	42 (79%)	45 (85%)	39 (74%)	27 (51%)	25 (47%)	20 (38%)
14	NO	W 20-17	50 (68%)	54 (73%)	54 (73%)	51 (69%)	31 (42%)	43 (58%)	24 (32%)
15	TB	W 24-21	54 (76%)	54 (76%)	52 (73%)	51 (72%)	32 (45%)	40 (56%)	
16	NO	L 23-13	56 (86%)	57 (88%)	59 (91%)	43 (66%)	32 (49%)	13 (20%)	23 (35%)
17	CAR	W 22-10	58 (81%)	54 (75%)	61 (85%)	38 (53%)	9 (13%)		41 (57%)
Grand Total			789 (77%)	766 (75%)	756 (79%)	552 (62%)	540 (53%)	425 (44%)	425 (44%)

Personnel Groupings

Personnel	Team %	NFL Avg	Succ. %
1-1 [3WR]	50%	59%	48%
1-2 [2WR]	21%	19%	53%
2-1 [2WR]	16%	7%	48%
2-0 [3WR]	4%	1%	49%
1-0 [4WR]	3%	2%	45%
2-2 [1WR]	3%	4%	32%

Grouping Tendencies

Personnel	Pass Rate	Pass Succ. %	Run Succ. %
1-1 [3WR]	68%	47%	50%
1-2 [2WR]	43%	64%	45%
2-1 [2WR]	43%	49%	47%
2-0 [3WR]	49%	50%	47%
1-0 [4WR]	91%	43%	67%
2-2 [1WR]	16%	60%	27%

Red Zone Targets (min 3)

Receiver	All	Inside 5	6-10	11-20
Julio Jones	25	6	11	8
Mohamed Sanu	13	2	5	6
Austin Hooper	12	4	2	6
Devonta Freeman	9		2	7
Justin Hardy	7	2	1	4
Taylor Gabriel	7		3	4
Tevin Coleman	5	1		4
Levine Toilolo	3		2	1
Andre Roberts	1			1

Red Zone Rushes (min 3)

Rusher	All	Inside 5	6-10	11-20
Devonta Freeman	40	16	9	15
Tevin Coleman	28	8	6	14
Matt Ryan	5	1	1	3
Terron Ward	5			5

Early Down Target Rate

	RB	TE	WR
	21%	14%	65%
NFL AVG	*23%*	*21%*	*56%*

Overall Target Success %

RB	TE	WR
51%	55%	53%
#5	#6	#4

Atlanta Falcons 2017 Passing Recap & 2018 Outlook

I'll give Sarkisian the benefit of the doubt entering his second offseason to find a comfort zone with his personnel. The first-round addition of Calvin Ridley will bolster Atlanta's three-receiver sets. But Atlanta's biggest area in need of offensive improvement is red-zone efficiency. On first-, second-, and third-down passes, Matt Ryan never exceeded a 40% Success Rate in his first year under Sark. Ryan's 2016 Success Rates were 48% on first down, 41% on second, and a tremendous 58% on third-down plays. Ryan's 2016 Success Rate of 60% when targeting tight ends in the red zone was especially dominant with balanced red-zone play calling that threw defenses off. Ryan targeted tight ends in the red zone 15 times, wide receivers in the red zone 15 times, and running backs on eight occasions. Sarkisian focused too heavily on red-zone passes to wide receivers. 24 red-zone targets went to wideouts with just a 38% Success Rate. Tight ends drew only three red-zone targets, and running backs saw six. Sarkisian needs to add variety to his red-zone distribution. Note that Julio was targeted just four times on third-down red-zone plays under Shanahan in 2016. In 2017, Julio saw eight such targets but produced a lowly 13% Success Rate.

Matt Ryan Rating All Downs

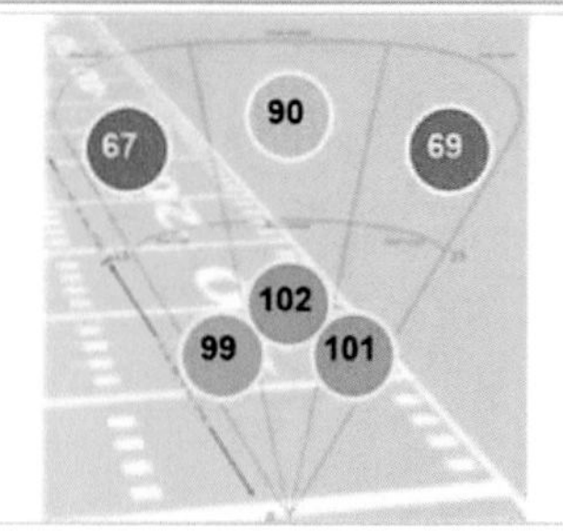

2017 Standard Passing Table

QB	Comp	Att	Comp %	Yds	YPA	TDs	INT	Sacks	Rating	Rk
Matt Ryan	385	594	65%	4,523	7.6	22	12	30	92	19
NFL Avg			62%		7.0				87.5	

Matt Ryan Rating Early Downs

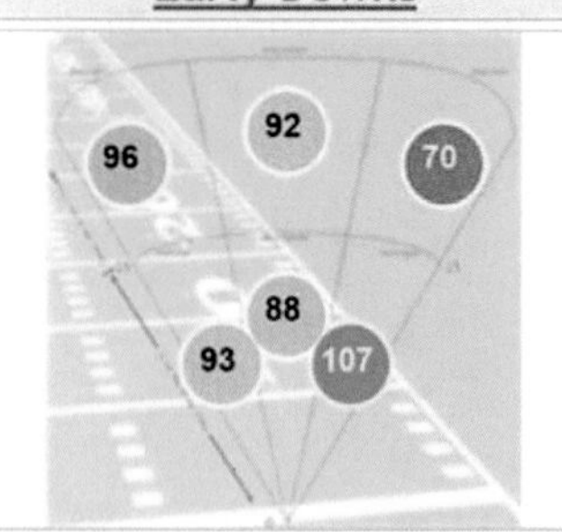

2017 Advanced Passing Table

QB	Success %	EDSR Passing Success %	20+ Yd Pass Gains	20+ Yd Pass %	30+ Yd Pass Gains	30+ Yd Pass %	Avg. Air Yds per Comp	Avg. YAC per Comp	20+ Air Yd Comp	20+ Air Yd %
Matt Ryan	49%	54%	59	9.9%	15	2.5%	6.4	4.9	19	5%
NFL Avg	44%	48%	27.7	8.8%	10.3	3.3%	6.0	4.7	11.7	6%

Interception Rates by Down

Yards to Go	1	2	3	4	Total
1 & 2	0.0%	6.3%	0.0%	0.0%	2.9%
3, 4, 5	0.0%	0.0%	0.0%	0.0%	0.0%
6 - 9	0.0%	0.0%	2.7%	0.0%	1.4%
10 - 14	2.7%	1.3%	2.9%	0.0%	2.4%
15+	0.0%	0.0%	7.7%		2.9%
Total	2.5%	1.0%	2.2%	0.0%	1.9%

3rd Down Passing - Short of Sticks Analysis

QB	Avg. Yds to Go	Avg. YIA (of Comp)	Avg Yds Short	Short of Sticks Rate	Short Rk
Matt Ryan	7.7	6.6	-1.2	64%	23
NFL Avg	7.8	6.7	-1.1	60%	

Air Yds vs YAC

Air Yds %	YAC %	Rk
53%	47%	31
58%	42%	

2017 Receiving Recap & 2018 Outlook

Calvin Ridley's addition should boost Atlanta's passing efficiency in three-receiver 11-personnel. Shanahan's 11-personnel passes averaged 7.7 yards per attempt with a 48% Success Rate and 115 rating. Sarkisian's 11-personnel passes managed 7.1 YPA, a 47% Success Rate, and a 90 rating. Former third receiver Taylor Gabriel was highly successful in 11-personnel packages, but terrible in 12 and 21. Ridley is the lone new face in Atlanta's passing game, so Sarkisian's improved familiarity with the rest of his personnel should improve his understanding of their strengths and weaknesses.

Player *Min 50 Targets*	Targets	Comp %	YPA	Rating	TOARS	Success %	Success Rk	Missed YPA Rk	YAS % Rk	TDs
Julio Jones	174	61%	9.4	93	5.5	55%	24	32	14	4
Mohamed Sanu	109	68%	7.6	98	4.9	59%	9	26	82	5
Austin Hooper	71	75%	7.7	93	4.2	52%	45	23	102	3
Devonta Freeman	54	78%	6.4	106	4.0	54%	33	42	118	2
Taylor Gabriel	54	65%	7.1	84	3.6	44%	93	107	69	1

Directional Passer Rating Delivered

Receiver	Short Left	Short Middle	Short Right	Deep Left	Deep Middle	Deep Right	Player Total
Julio Jones	92	82	104	83	102	82	93
Mohamed Sanu	104	110	88	72	110	73	98
Austin Hooper	111	101	85	49	96		93
Devonta Freeman	116	93	97		119		106
Taylor Gabriel	105	119	95	40	0	40	84
Tevin Coleman	93	72	147	96	40		109
Justin Hardy	90	149	129	40	119	96	121
Levine Toilolo	108	97	93	135			122
Andre Roberts	40	40	117				40
Team Total	101	103	104	80	79	73	97

2017 Rushing Recap & 2017 Outlook

Sark's running game was very close to being even more successful than Shanahan's, but produced fewer yards per carry due to a shortage of explosive runs. Devonta Freeman was the NFL's most explosive rusher in 2016. He fell to 26th in 2017, battling multiple concussions and late-season knee injuries. The Falcons' conservative early-season early-down play calling was also to blame. Creative, aggressive passing games force defenses to prepare and play differently, resulting in more favorable run-game looks. I did like that Sark called more run plays from spread formations inside the five-yard line than Shanahan did.

Yards per Carry by Direction

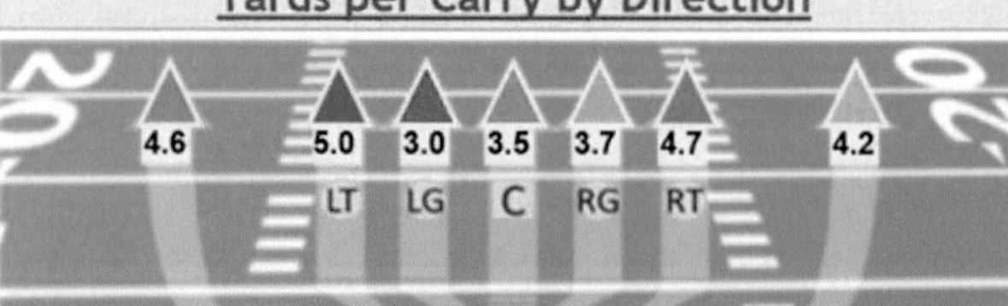

Player *Min 50 Rushes*	Rushes	YPC	Success %	Success Rk	Missed YPA Rk	YTS % Rk	YAS % Rk	Early Down Success %	Early Down Success Rk	TDs
Devonta Freeman	224	4.2	49%	19	24	55	26	47%	25	9
Tevin Coleman	180	4.2	43%	41	39	52	16	44%	36	5

Directional Run Frequency

19% | 15% | 12% | 12% | 11% | 16% | 16%

LT | LG | C | RG | RT

I concluded that until Sarkisian optimized his first-down play calling, Atlanta's problems would remain.

In addition to my October 23 Sharp Football Show, I released a Twitter thread on these topics. Over their next five games, the Falcons did every single thing I suggested Sarkisian should do.

Sark's 18% deep passing rate on first down skyrocketed to 40% over the next month. Julio's target rate soared from 24% to 44%. After throwing deep to Julio on just 30% of his first-down targets in Weeks 1-7, the Falcons went deep to Julio on 67% of his first-down targets for the next five weeks.

And there were ripple effects. On first down, Atlanta morphed into the NFL's most-explosive passing offense with a league-high 22% of their first-down throws gaining 20-plus yards. And over those next five games, the Falcons went 4-1 after starting 3-3.

The Falcons didn't have a Week 7 or 8 bye to reconsider Sarkisian's play calling. I have not confirmed that Sarkisian received my published research. But it sure looks like he did. I don't think the Falcons would have otherwise decided, "We're not throwing deep to Julio enough on first downs." I do like to think somehow, some way, my data analysis helped this offense get on track.

(cont'd - see ATL-5)

Evan Silva's Fantasy Corner

Although 2017 was considered a down season for 2016's NFL MVP, Matt Ryan's efficiency metrics like completion rate (64.7%) and yards per attempt (7.7) aligned with his career norms, and Ryan engineered an Atlanta offense that ranked third in the NFL in both yards per play and yards per drive. The Falcons dipped from first in points per game (33.8) to 15th in 2017 (22.1), however, and Ryan's touchdown rate (TDs/pass attempts) was sawed from an otherworldly 7.1% to 3.8%. Had Ryan's TD rate simply matched his career average (4.6%), he would have thrown 4.3 more touchdown passes. Ryan entered his magical 2016 season as a positive-touchdown-regression candidate after managing a career-worst 3.4% TD rate in his first year under then-OC Kyle Shanahan. Ryan enters season two under current OC Steve Sarkisian as a positive-touchdown-regression candidate again. Now carrying the Average Draft Position of a fantasy backup, Ryan will be one of my highest-owned quarterbacks in leagues of all types this year.

Division History: Season Wins & 2018 Projection

2014 Wins | 2015 Wins | 2016 Wins | 2017 Wins | Forecast 2018 Wins

Rank of 2018 Defensive Pass Efficiency Faced by Week

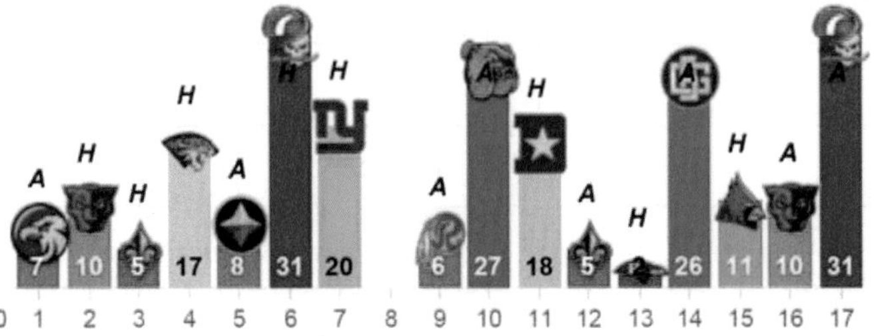

Rank of 2018 Defensive Rush Efficiency Faced by Week

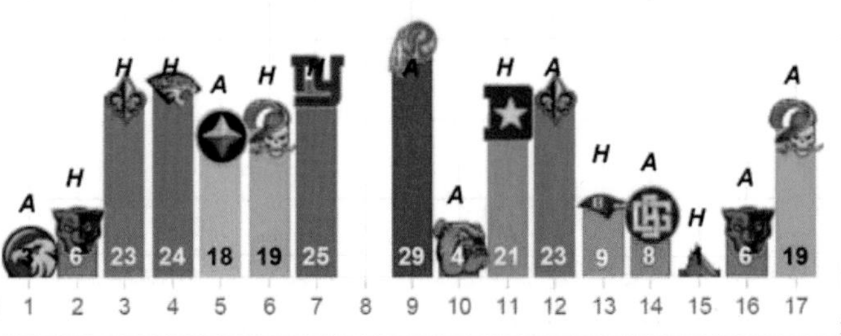

2017 Situational Usage by Player & Position

Usage Rate by Score

		Being Blown Out (14+)	Down Big (9-13)	One Score	Large Lead (9-13)	Blowout Lead (14+)	Grand Total
RUSH	Devonta Freeman	18%	23%	22%	24%	17%	22%
	Tevin Coleman	6%	9%	18%	18%	27%	17%
	Julio Jones			0%			0%
	Mohamed Sanu			0%			0%
	Taylor Gabriel	4%		1%	1%		1%
	Terron Ward			3%	1%	15%	3%
	Derrick Coleman					4%	0%
	Total	27%	31%	44%	45%	63%	44%
PASS	Devonta Freeman	6%	9%	5%	8%	4%	5%
	Tevin Coleman	8%	9%	4%	4%	2%	4%
	Julio Jones	24%	23%	17%	13%	15%	17%
	Mohamed Sanu	14%	14%	10%	12%	8%	11%
	Austin Hooper	6%	3%	7%	9%	4%	7%
	Taylor Gabriel	8%	6%	5%	7%		5%
	Terron Ward			0%		2%	0%
	Justin Hardy	6%	6%	3%		2%	3%
	Levine Toilolo			2%			2%
	Derrick Coleman	2%		1%			1%
	Marvin Hall			1%	1%		1%
	Nick Williams			1%			0%
	Andre Roberts			0%	1%		0%
	Total	73%	69%	56%	55%	38%	56%

Positional Target Distribution vs NFL Average

		NFL Wide				Team Only			
		Left	Middle	Right	**Total**	Left	Middle	Right	**Total**
Deep	WR	943	497	953	**2,393**	43	12	34	**89**
	TE	186	146	188	**520**	6	4		**10**
	RB	37	7	42	**86**	2	2		**4**
	All	**1,166**	**650**	**1,183**	**2,999**	**51**	**18**	**34**	**103**
Short	WR	2,745	1,610	2,685	**7,040**	117	61	105	**283**
	TE	841	818	1,136	**2,795**	22	21	34	**77**
	RB	1,287	794	1,265	**3,346**	34	29	30	**93**
	All	**4,873**	**3,222**	**5,086**	**13,181**	**173**	**111**	**169**	**453**
Total		**6,039**	**3,872**	**6,269**	**16,180**	**224**	**129**	**203**	**556**

Positional Success Rates vs NFL Average

		NFL Wide				Team Only			
		Left	Middle	Right	**Total**	Left	Middle	Right	**Total**
Deep	WR	37%	45%	38%	**39%**	33%	58%	38%	**38%**
	TE	38%	53%	45%	**45%**	33%	50%		**40%**
	RB	35%	57%	38%	**38%**	50%	50%		**50%**
	All	**37%**	**47%**	**39%**	**40%**	**33%**	**56%**	**38%**	**39%**
Short	WR	51%	57%	50%	**52%**	56%	62%	61%	**59%**
	TE	51%	56%	49%	**51%**	41%	71%	59%	**57%**
	RB	45%	51%	42%	**45%**	29%	55%	80%	**54%**
	All	**50%**	**55%**	**48%**	**50%**	**49%**	**62%**	**64%**	**58%**
Total		**47%**	**54%**	**46%**	**48%**	**45%**	**61%**	**60%**	**54%**

Successful Play Rate
0% ▬ 100%

Atlanta Falcons - Success by Personnel Grouping & Play Type

Play Type	1-1 [3WR]	1-2 [2WR]	2-1 [2WR]	1-0 [4WR]	1-3 [1WR]	0-1 [4WR]	2-0 [3WR]	2-2 [1WR]	0-0 [5WR]	2-3 [0WR]	3-2 [0WR]	Grand Total
PASS	47% (335, 60%)	64% (89, 16%)	49% (67, 12%)	43% (30, 5%)	50% (6, 1%)	50% (2, 0%)	50% (18, 3%)	60% (5, 1%)	0% (1, 0%)	0% (1, 0%)		50% (554, 100%)
RUSH	50% (156, 36%)	45% (116, 27%)	47% (90, 21%)	67% (3, 1%)	62% (13, 3%)	100% (1, 0%)	47% (19, 4%)	27% (26, 6%)		60% (5, 1%)	0% (1, 0%)	47% (430, 100%)
TOTAL	48% (491, 50%)	53% (205, 21%)	48% (157, 16%)	45% (33, 3%)	58% (19, 2%)	67% (3, 0%)	49% (37, 4%)	32% (31, 3%)	0% (1, 0%)	50% (6, 1%)	0% (1, 0%)	49% (984, 100%)

Format Line 1: Success Rate Line 2: Total # of Plays, % of All Plays (by type)

ATL-5 And they finished strong. The Falcons won eight of their next 11. They upset the Rams 26-13 in the playoffs on the road. Outdoors in Philly in the NFC Championship game, the Falcons had the ball down by just five points with 1:19 left at the Eagles' nine-yard line. Unfortunately, Atlanta failed to score a touchdown and went home for the winter.

I genuinely believe Sarkisian improved as his first year as Falcons offensive coordinator progressed. Atlanta didn't light up the scoreboard, but the team played six of its final seven games against top-ten pass defenses, including four top-five groups.

Apart from new RG Brandon Fusco and rookie WR Calvin Ridley, this year's Falcons offensive starters are identical to 2017. Their biggest 2018 problem may not be Sarkisian, but a pass-defense schedule that's much tougher than last year's. The Falcons should be able to lean on their run game, however, and Atlanta figures to find itself back in the playoffs if Sarkisian solves his offense's red-zone woes.

Receiving Success by Personnel Grouping

Position	Player	1-1 [3WR]	1-2 [2WR]	2-1 [2WR]	1-0 [4WR]	1-3 [1WR]	0-1 [4WR]	2-0 [3WR]	2-2 [1WR]	0-0 [5WR]	Total
RB	Devonta Freeman	54% 7.4 107.1 (28)	57% 4.0 66.4 (7)	60% 5.4 89.2 (5)		0% 2.0 79.2 (1)		83% 9.0 104.2 (6)			57% 6.7 101.1 (47)
	Tevin Coleman	62% 9.2 123.6 (21)	38% 5.9 78.6 (8)	33% 5.0 50.7 (3)	0% 2.0 79.2 (1)	100% 20.0 118.8 (1)		20% 4.4 70.4 (5)			49% 7.7 106.7 (39)
TE	Austin Hooper	43% 8.5 90.2 (46)	64% 7.9 69.9 (14)	0% 0.0 39.6 (1)		100% 20.0 118.8 (1)			67% 0.7 109.7 (3)		49% 8.1 94.8 (65)
WR	Julio Jones	44% 8.2 77.5 (81)	79% 14.6 118.8 (24)	59% 9.4 90.5 (27)	67% 11.1 103.9 (9)	0% 0.0 39.6 (2)	100% 17.0 118.8 (1)	67% 9.3 96.5 (3)	100% 29.0 118.8 (1)		55% 9.8 90.6 (148)
	Mohamed Sanu	57% 6.6 97.2 (69)	73% 11.1 112.9 (11)	86% 11.1 113.1 (7)	57% 6.9 90.2 (7)		0% 0.0 39.6 (1)	0% 0.0 39.6 (1)			59% 7.3 99.4 (96)
	Taylor Gabriel	50% 7.8 92.6 (36)	25% 3.8 40.6 (4)	29% 4.0 43.8 (7)	0% 3.0 56.3 (2)			100% 40.0 158.3 (1)		0% 7.0 95.8 (1)	43% 7.4 85.3 (51)

Format Line 1: Success Rate Line 2: YPA Line 3: Passer Rating Line 4: Total # of Plays

Successful Play Rate
0% ▬ 100%

Rushing Success by Personnel Grouping

Position	Player	1-1 [3WR]	1-2 [2WR]	2-1 [2WR]	1-0 [4WR]	1-3 [1WR]	2-0 [3WR]	2-2 [1WR]	2-3 [0WR]	3-2 [0WR]	Total
QB	Matt Ryan	100% 8.6 (10)	50% 6.0 (4)	17% 2.2 (6)	50% 7.5 (2)		50% 6.5 (2)	0% -1.0 (6)	0% -1.0 (1)	0% -1.0 (1)	47% 4.5 (32)
RB	Devonta Freeman	51% 4.4 (69)	52% 5.0 (61)	51% 4.3 (45)	100% 4.0 (1)	86% 3.6 (7)	50% 5.3 (6)	0% 0.0 (5)	50% 0.5 (2)		52% 4.4 (196)
	Tevin Coleman	41% 3.7 (63)	35% 4.1 (37)	41% 5.3 (32)		0% 1.0 (3)	50% 4.7 (10)	44% 2.6 (9)	100% 1.0 (2)		40% 4.0 (156)

Format Line 1: Success Rate Line 2: YPC Line 3: Total # of Plays

2018 Coaches

Head Coach:
John Harbaugh (11th yr)
Offensive Coordinator:
Marty Morinwheg (3rd yr)
Defensive Coordinator:
Don Martingale (BAL LB) (1st yr)

Baltimore Ravens

2018 Forecast

Wins	Div Rank
8	#2

Past Records

2017: 9-7
2016: 8-8
2015: 5-11

EASY HARD

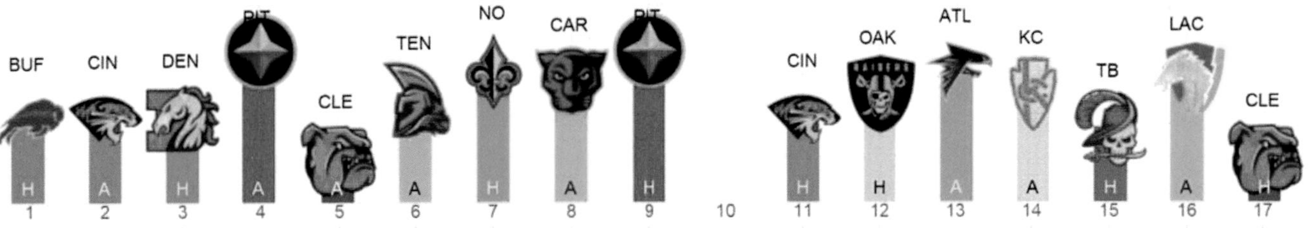

Key Players Lost

TXN	Player (POS)
Cut	Crockett, John RB
	Kublanow, Brandon C
	Maclin, Jeremy WR
	Nembot, Stephane T
	Webb, Lardarius S
	Woodhead, Danny RB
Declared Free Agent	Bowanko, Luke C
	Boykin, Brandon CB
	Campanaro, Michael WR
	Gillmore, Crockett TE
	Howard, Austin T
	Jensen, Ryan C
	Johnson, Steven LB
	Mallett, Ryan QB
	Wallace, Mike WR
	Watson, Benjamin TE
	West, Terrance RB
Retired	Woodhead, Danny RB

Average Line	# Games Favored	# Games Underdog
-0.6	6	6

2018 Baltimore Ravens Overview

The 2016 Ravens went 8-8 but sported the NFL's highest pass rate. Joe Flacco passed on 67% of offensive plays, far and away most in the league. This pass-heavy imbalance was incredibly odd because Baltimore was a .500 team that didn't have to rally back from deficits each week. I hoped the 2017 Ravens would become more balanced, and knew they needed more talent in the backfield. That didn't seem possible, until Seattle's loss became Baltimore's gain.

On September 3 – mere days before Week 1 – the Seahawks cut Alex Collins. Collins averaged a respectable 4.03 yards per carry and caught 11-of-11 targets as a 2016 rookie. Collins led Seattle with a 75% rushing Success Rate in the first half of games and produced an 88% receiving Success Rate. But the Seahawks rarely threw to backs on early downs, so they probably didn't value Collins' pass-catching production enough. Collins rolled over his productivity into obvious passing situations, delivering a team-best 63% Success Rate on third-down targets. And Collins averaged 5.9 yards per carry on third-down runs.

In the first three quarters of games, Collins led the 2016 Seahawks in combined run-catch Success Rate (58%), superior to C.J. Prosise (51%), Christine Michael (49%), Thomas Rawls (46%), and C.J. Spiller (30%). Most likely, Collins' underutilization came about because Seahawks coaches didn't study the analytics as much as they should have.

So the Seahawks signed Eddie Lacy, re-signed Rawls, drafted Chris Carson, and returned Prosise as the four backs on their 53-man roster. And after cutting Collins, they didn't even sign him to their practice squad. The Ravens did sign Collins to their practice squad and added him to the active roster on September 16.

Truly gifted talent evaluators are rare, but Ravens GM Ozzie Newsome is one. Rather than analytics, though, Newsome likely used his own evaluation methods to arrive at the decision to pluck Collins off the scrapheap. And that's part of the beauty of analytics. You could either have access to one of the league's top evaluators, or access to these advanced metrics and arrive at the same decision: Taking a cheap, no-risk flyer on 23-year-old Collins was smart.

(cont'd - see BAL2)

Key Free Agents/ Trades Added

Brown, John WR
Crabtree, Michael WR
Griffin III, Robert QB
Nacua, Kai CB
Snead IV, Willie WR

Drafted Players

Rd	Pk	Player (College)
1	25	TE - Hayden Hurst (South Ca..
	32	QB - Lamar Jackson (Louisvil..
3	83	OT - Orlando Brown (Oklaho..
	86	TE - Mark Andrews (Oklaho..
4	118	CB - Anthony Averett (Alaba..
	122	LB - Kenny Young (UCLA)
	132	WR - Jaleel Scott (New Mexi..
5	162	WR - Jordan Lasley (UCLA)
6	190	S - DeShon Elliott (Texas)
6*	212	OT - Greg Senat (Wagner)
	215	C - Bradley Bozeman (Alaba..
7	238	DE - Zach Sieler (Ferris State)

Regular Season Wins: Past & Current Proj

Lineup & Cap Hits

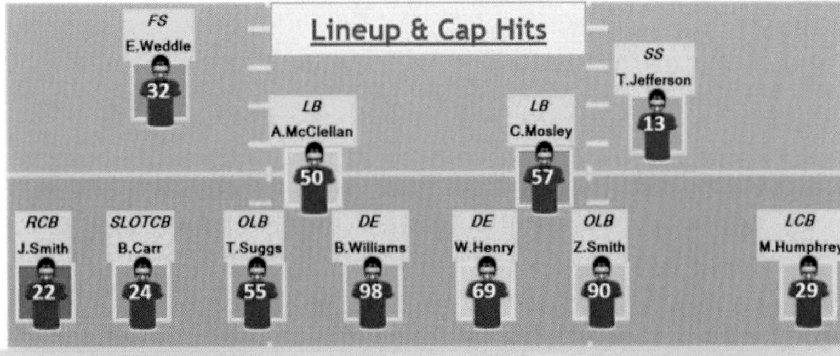

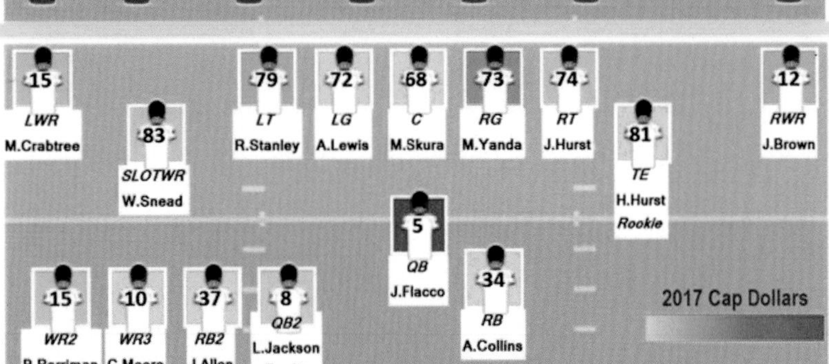

2018 Unit Spending

Positional Spending

	Rank	Total	2017 Rk
All OFF	29	$79.54M	19
QB	2	$28.05M	4
OL	30	$25.31M	28
RB	29	$3.61M	21
WR	22	$18.24M	20
TE	27	$4.34M	20
All DEF	12	$85.72M	28
DL	31	$12.58M	32
LB	7	$26.75M	16
CB	3	$29.27M	10
S	7	$17.11M	7

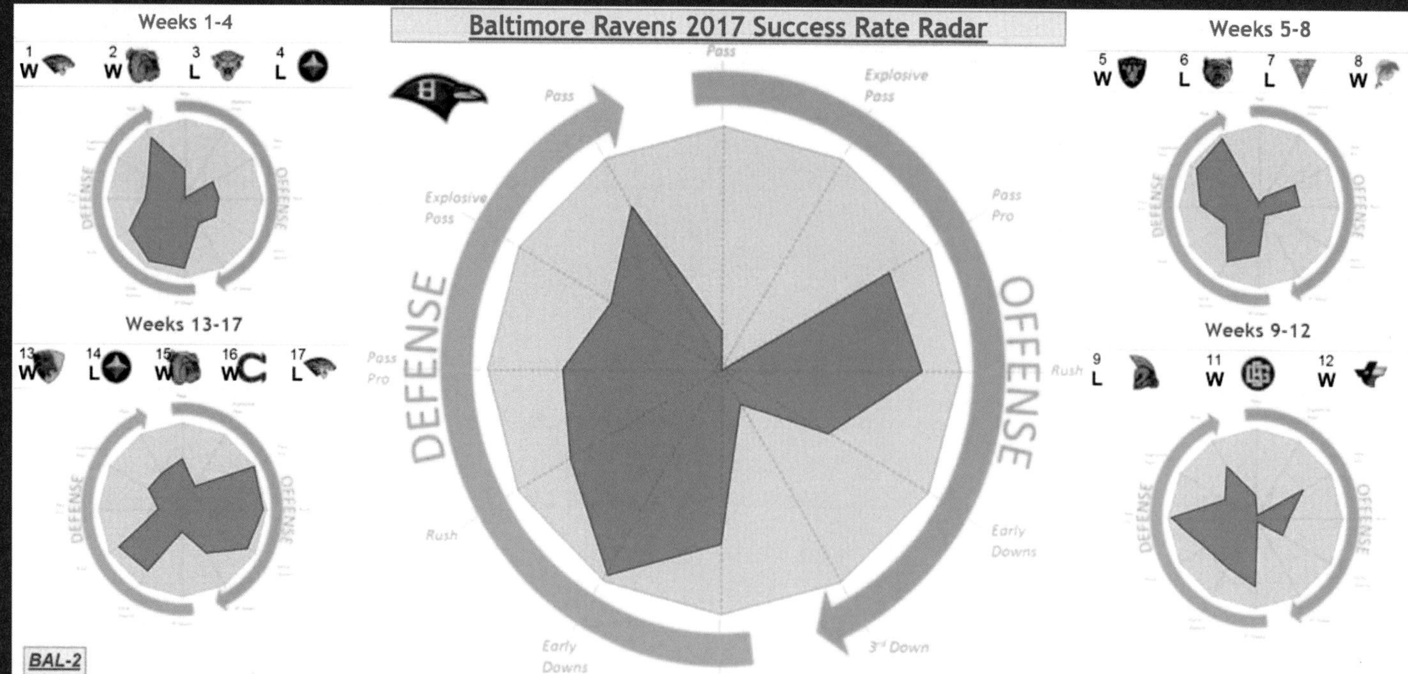

BAL-2

Especially when the Ravens' backfield consisted of Buck Allen, Terrance West, and 32-year-old Danny Woodhead. Analytics is a tool to incorporate into analysis, and even if you generally dislike numbers – most often resulting from fear or misunderstanding – they are a great safety net for decision-making consultation.

It still took time for the Ravens to realize how valuable Collins so quickly became. Through the first seven weeks of the season, the Ravens faced the NFL's 13th-toughest schedule of run defenses. Allen managed 3.7 yards per carry and a 37% Success Rate on 82 carries in that span. (Allen did shine on third downs with a 59% Success Rate and 5.1 YPC.) Collins didn't play on third downs, but he recorded 6.0 yards per carry and a 45% Success Rate on early down-runs in Weeks 1-7.

The tide turned in Week 8 against the Dolphins, when Collins torched Miami for 6.1 yards per carry and a 59% Success Rate compared to Allen's 3.0 YPC with 43% Success. Collins took over from that point forward, averaging 4.1 YPC with a 53% Success Rate on 150 attempts despite facing the NFL's seventh-toughest run-defense schedule from Week 8 on.

Overall, Collins' 50% rushing Success Rate ranked fourth among 32 running backs with at least 150 carries, trailing only Todd Gurley, Ezekiel Elliott, and Dion Lewis. And Collins faced the league's eighth-hardest run-defense schedule. Elliott and Lewis both faced easier-than-average slates. Collins' 4.6 yards-per-carry average ranked fifth among those 32 backs.

It was tremendous efficiency relative to Collins' situation. He wasn't playing with Tom Brady, Bill Belichick, Sean McVay, or the Cowboys' offensive line. Collins tore it up with Joe Flacco, Marty Mornhinweg, and the league's most-injured line blocking for him. And their tight end corps – a big factor in run blocking – was sixth-most injured across the league.

(cont'd - see BAL-3)

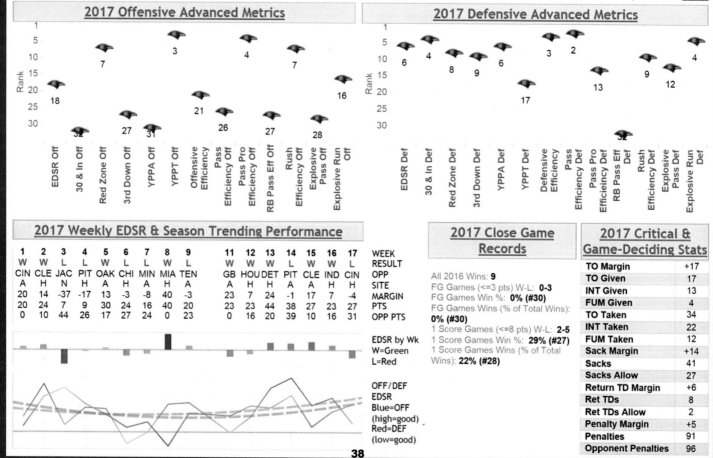

2017 Offensive Advanced Metrics

Metric	Rank
EDSR Off	18
30 & In Off	32
Red Zone Off	7
3rd Down Off	27
YPPA Off	31
YPPT Off	3
Offensive Efficiency	21
Pass Efficiency Off	26
Pass Pro Efficiency Off	4
RB Pass Eff Off	27
Rush Efficiency Off	7
Explosive Pass Off	28
Explosive Run Off	16

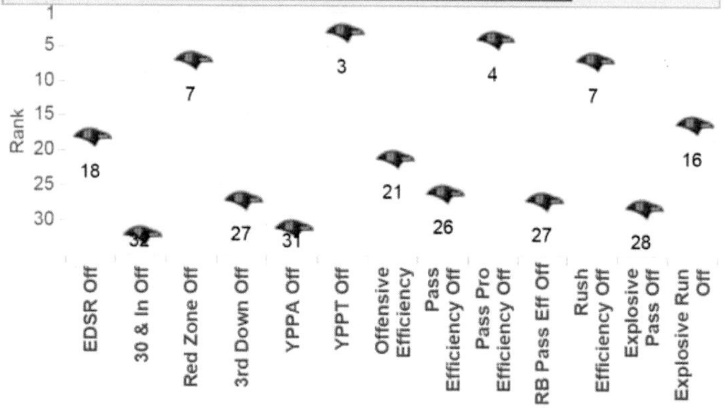

2017 Defensive Advanced Metrics

Metric	Rank
EDSR Def	6
30 & In Def	4
Red Zone Def	8
3rd Down Def	9
YPPA Def	6
YPPT Def	17
Defensive Efficiency	3
Pass Efficiency Def	2
Pass Pro Efficiency Def	13
RB Pass Eff Def	32
Rush Efficiency Def	9
Explosive Pass Def	12
Explosive Run Def	4

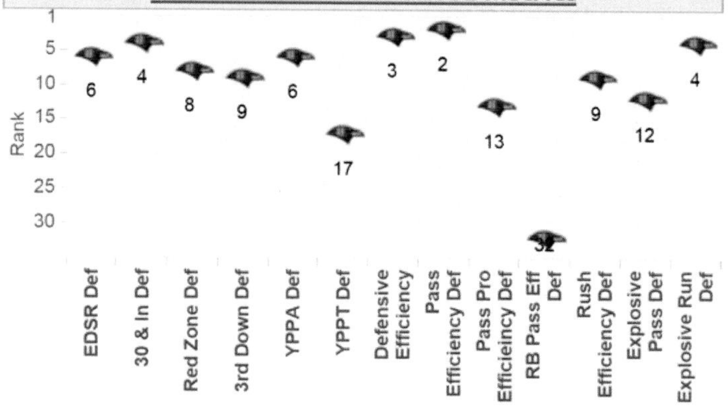

2017 Weekly EDSR & Season Trending Performance

1	2	3	4	5	6	7	8	9	11	12	13	14	15	16	17	WEEK
W	W	L	L	W	L	L	W	L	W	W	W	L	W	W	L	RESULT
CIN	CLE	JAC	PIT	OAK	CHI	MIN	MIA	TEN	GB	HOU	DET	PIT	CLE	IND	CIN	OPP
A	H	N	H	A	H	A	H	A	A	H	H	A	A	H	H	SITE
20	14	-37	-17	13	-3	-8	40	-3	23	7	24	-1	17	7	-4	MARGIN
20	24	7	9	30	24	16	40	20	23	23	44	38	27	23	27	PTS
0	10	44	26	17	27	24	0	23	0	16	20	39	10	16	31	OPP PTS

EDSR by Wk
W=Green
L=Red

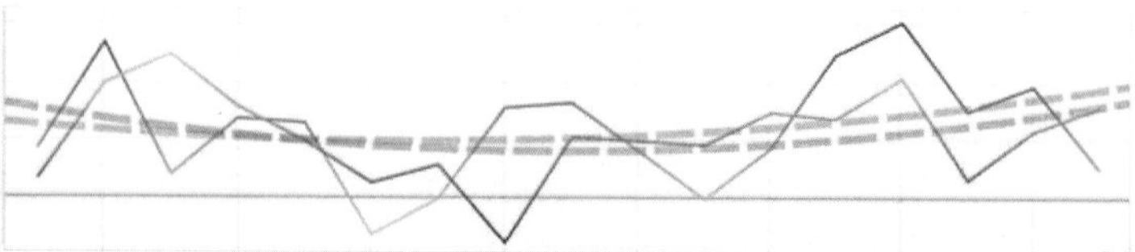

OFF/DEF
EDSR
Blue=OFF
(high=good)
Red=DEF
(low=good)

2017 Close Game Records

All 2016 Wins: **9**
FG Games (<=3 pts) W-L: **0-3**
FG Games Win %: **0% (#30)**
FG Games Wins (% of Total Wins): **0% (#30)**
1 Score Games (<=8 pts) W-L: **2-5**
1 Score Games Win %: **29% (#27)**
1 Score Games Wins (% of Total Wins): **22% (#28)**

2017 Critical & Game-Deciding Stats

TO Margin	+17
TO Given	17
INT Given	13
FUM Given	4
TO Taken	34
INT Taken	22
FUM Taken	12
Sack Margin	+14
Sacks	41
Sacks Allow	27
Return TD Margin	+6
Ret TDs	8
Ret TDs Allow	2
Penalty Margin	+5
Penalties	91
Opponent Penalties	96

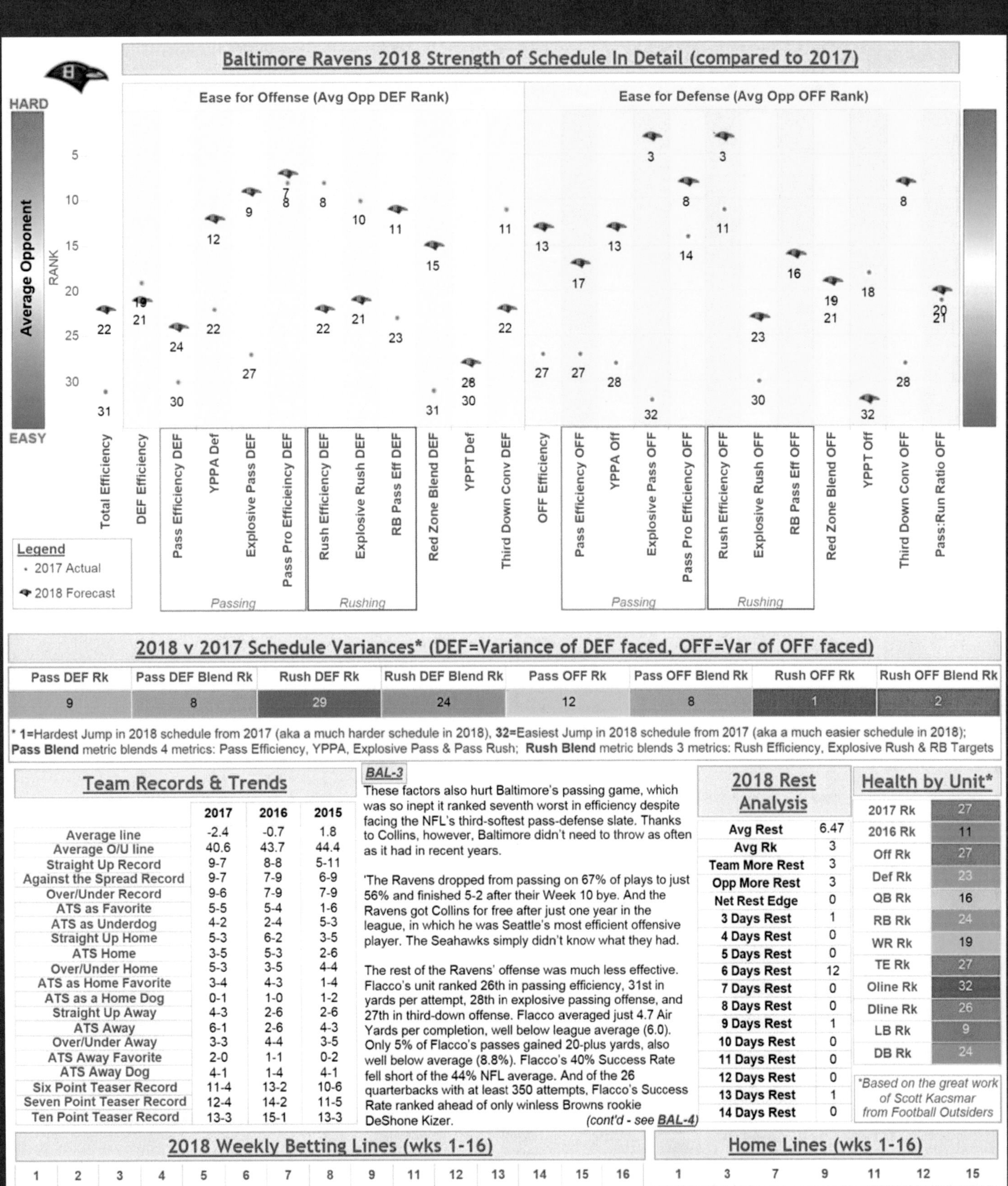

Baltimore Ravens 2018 Strength of Schedule In Detail (compared to 2017)

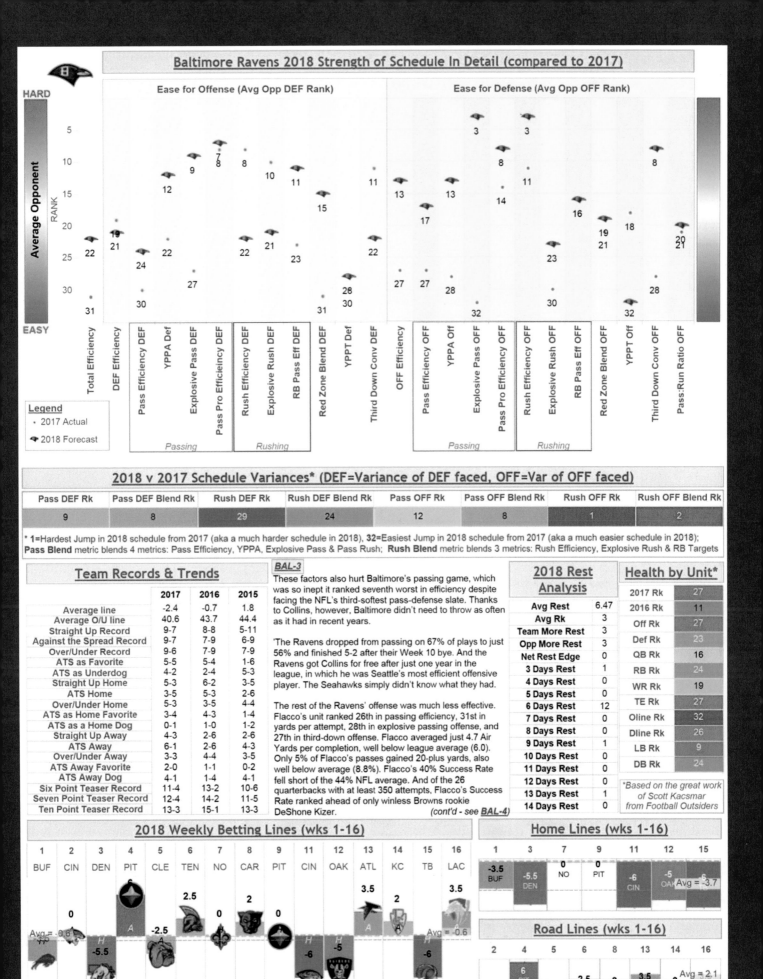

2018 v 2017 Schedule Variances* (DEF=Variance of DEF faced, OFF=Var of OFF faced)

Pass DEF Rk	Pass DEF Blend Rk	Rush DEF Rk	Rush DEF Blend Rk	Pass OFF Rk	Pass OFF Blend Rk	Rush OFF Rk	Rush OFF Blend Rk
9	8	29	24	12	8	1	2

* **1**=Hardest Jump in 2018 schedule from 2017 (aka a much harder schedule in 2018), **32**=Easiest Jump in 2018 schedule from 2017 (aka a much easier schedule in 2018); **Pass Blend** metric blends 4 metrics: Pass Efficiency, YPPA, Explosive Pass & Pass Rush; **Rush Blend** metric blends 3 metrics: Rush Efficiency, Explosive Rush & RB Targets

Team Records & Trends

	2017	2016	2015
Average line	-2.4	-0.7	1.8
Average O/U line	40.6	43.7	44.4
Straight Up Record	9-7	8-8	5-11
Against the Spread Record	9-7	7-9	6-9
Over/Under Record	9-6	7-9	7-9
ATS as Favorite	5-5	5-4	1-6
ATS as Underdog	4-2	2-4	5-3
Straight Up Home	5-3	6-2	3-5
ATS Home	3-5	5-3	2-6
Over/Under Home	5-3	3-5	4-4
ATS as Home Favorite	3-4	4-3	1-4
ATS as a Home Dog	0-1	1-0	1-2
Straight Up Away	4-3	2-6	2-6
ATS Away	6-1	2-6	4-3
Over/Under Away	3-3	4-4	3-5
ATS Away Favorite	2-0	1-1	0-2
ATS Away Dog	4-1	1-4	4-1
Six Point Teaser Record	11-4	13-2	10-6
Seven Point Teaser Record	12-4	14-2	11-5
Ten Point Teaser Record	13-3	15-1	13-3

BAL-3

These factors also hurt Baltimore's passing game, which was so inept it ranked seventh worst in efficiency despite facing the NFL's third-softest pass-defense slate. Thanks to Collins, however, Baltimore didn't need to throw as often as it had in recent years.

'The Ravens dropped from passing on 67% of plays to just 56% and finished 5-2 after their Week 10 bye. And the Ravens got Collins for free after just one year in the league, in which he was Seattle's most efficient offensive player. The Seahawks simply didn't know what they had.

The rest of the Ravens' offense was much less effective. Flacco's unit ranked 26th in passing efficiency, 31st in yards per attempt, 28th in explosive passing offense, and 27th in third-down offense. Flacco averaged just 4.7 Air Yards per completion, well below league average (6.0). Only 5% of Flacco's passes gained 20-plus yards, also well below average (8.8%). Flacco's 40% Success Rate fell short of the 44% NFL average. And of the 26 quarterbacks with at least 350 attempts, Flacco's Success Rate ranked ahead of only winless Browns rookie DeShone Kizer. *(cont'd - see **BAL-4**)*

2018 Rest Analysis

Avg Rest	6.47
Avg Rk	3
Team More Rest	3
Opp More Rest	3
Net Rest Edge	0
3 Days Rest	1
4 Days Rest	0
5 Days Rest	0
6 Days Rest	12
7 Days Rest	0
8 Days Rest	0
9 Days Rest	1
10 Days Rest	0
11 Days Rest	0
12 Days Rest	0
13 Days Rest	1
14 Days Rest	0

Health by Unit*

2017 Rk	27
2016 Rk	11
Off Rk	27
Def Rk	23
QB Rk	16
RB Rk	24
WR Rk	19
TE Rk	27
Oline Rk	32
Dline Rk	26
LB Rk	9
DB Rk	24

**Based on the great work of Scott Kacsmar from Football Outsiders*

2018 Weekly Betting Lines (wks 1-16)

1	2	3	4	5	6	7	8	9	11	12	13	14	15	16
BUF	CIN	DEN	PIT	CLE	TEN	NO	CAR	PIT	CIN	OAK	ATL	KC	TB	LAC
H	A	H	A	A	A	H	A	H	H	H	A	A	H	A
-3.5	0	-5.5	6	-2.5	2.5	0	2	0	-6	-5	3.5	2	-6	3.5

Avg = -0.6

Home Lines (wks 1-16)

1	3	7	9	11	12	15
BUF	DEN	NO	PIT	CIN	OAK	TB
-3.5	-5.5	0	0	-6	-5	-6

Avg = -3.7

Road Lines (wks 1-16)

2	4	5	6	8	13	14	16
CIN	PIT	CLE	TEN	CAR	ATL	KC	LAC
0	6	-2.5	2.5	2	3.5	2	3.5

Avg = 2.1

Baltimore Ravens 2017 Play Analysis

2017 Play Tendencies

All Pass %	56%
All Pass Rk	20
All Rush %	44%
All Rush Rk	13
1 Score Pass %	58%
1 Score Pass Rk	15
2016 1 Score Pass %	63%
2016 1 Score Pass Rk	2
2017 Pass Increase %	-6%
Pass Increase Rk	25
1 Score Rush %	42%
1 Score Rush Rk	18
Up Pass %	47%
Up Pass Rk	23
Up Rush %	53%
Up Rush Rk	10
Down Pass %	68%
Down Pass Rk	9
Down Rush %	32%
Down Rush Rk	24

2017 Down & Distance Tendencies

Down	Distance	Total Plays	Pass Rate	Run Rate	Play Success %
1	Short (1-3)	6	50%	50%	83%
	Med (4-7)	10	50%	50%	70%
	Long (8-10)	311	50%	50%	47%
	XL (11+)	8	63%	38%	13%
2	Short (1-3)	42	43%	57%	62%
	Med (4-7)	66	44%	56%	53%
	Long (8-10)	103	60%	40%	37%
	XL (11+)	38	84%	16%	24%
3	Short (1-3)	38	53%	47%	53%
	Med (4-7)	61	95%	5%	38%
	Long (8-10)	34	91%	9%	12%
	XL (11+)	24	88%	13%	8%
4	Short (1-3)	6	0%	100%	83%
	Med (4-7)	2	100%	0%	100%

Shotgun %:

Under Center	Shotgun
52%	48%
37% AVG	*63%*

Run Rate:

Under Center	Shotgun
63%	22%
68% AVG	*23%*

Pass Rate:

Under Center	Shotgun
37%	78%
32% AVG	*77%*

Short Yardage Intelligence:

2nd and Short Run

Run Freq	Run Rk	NFL Run Freq Avg	Run 1D Rate	Run NFL 1D Avg
69%	14	67%	83%	69%

2nd and Short Pass

Pass Freq	Pass Rk	NFL Pass Freq Avg	Pass 1D Rate	Pass NFL 1D Avg
31%	19	33%	46%	53%

Most Frequent Play

Down	Distance	Play Type	Player	Total Plays	Play Success %
1	Short (1-3)	RUSH	Javorius Allen	2	50%
	Med (4-7)	PASS	Chris Moore	2	50%
		RUSH	Alex Collins	2	50%
	Long (8-10)	RUSH	Alex Collins	85	47%
	XL (11+)	RUSH	Javorius Allen	2	0%
2	Short (1-3)	RUSH	Alex Collins	9	89%
			Javorius Allen	9	67%
	Med (4-7)	RUSH	Alex Collins	22	68%
	Long (8-10)	RUSH	Alex Collins	20	30%
	XL (11+)	PASS	Ben Watson	6	83%
3	Short (1-3)	RUSH	Alex Collins	7	43%
	Med (4-7)	PASS	Mike Wallace	10	50%
	Long (8-10)	PASS	Mike Wallace	5	20%

Most Successful Play*

Down	Distance	Play Type	Player	Total Plays	Play Success %
1	Long (8-10)	PASS	Nick Boyle	10	80%
2	Short (1-3)	RUSH	Alex Collins	9	89%
	Med (4-7)	RUSH	Alex Collins	22	68%
	Long (8-10)	PASS	Mike Wallace	19	63%
	XL (11+)	PASS	Ben Watson	6	83%
3	Short (1-3)	RUSH	Javorius Allen	6	83%
	Med (4-7)	PASS	Jeremy Maclin	8	63%
	Long (8-10)	PASS	Mike Wallace	5	20%
			Jeremy Maclin	5	20%

**Minimum 5 plays to qualify*

2017 Snap Rates

Wk	Opp	Score	Mike Wallace	Ben Watson	Nick Boyle	Jeremy Maclin	Javorius Allen	Breshad Perriman	Alex Collins	Chris Moore	Maxx Williams	Terrance West
1	CIN	W 20-0	47 (71%)	40 (61%)	45 (68%)	48 (73%)	33 (50%)	42 (64%)			17 (26%)	27 (41%)
2	CLE	W 24-10	48 (71%)	51 (75%)	42 (62%)	43 (63%)	43 (63%)	42 (62%)	8 (12%)		28 (41%)	15 (22%)
3	JAC	L 44-7	50 (86%)	40 (69%)	40 (69%)	36 (62%)	34 (59%)	35 (60%)	10 (17%)	7 (12%)		10 (17%)
4	PIT	L 26-9	52 (75%)	43 (62%)	49 (71%)	47 (68%)	40 (58%)	49 (71%)	17 (25%)			10 (14%)
5	OAK	W 30-17	34 (52%)	59 (89%)	44 (67%)	46 (70%)	47 (71%)	38 (58%)	16 (24%)			3 (5%)
6	CHI	L 27-24	70 (96%)	51 (70%)	44 (60%)		47 (64%)	20 (27%)	22 (30%)	34 (47%)	9 (12%)	
7	MIN	L 24-16	5 (8%)	52 (80%)	47 (72%)		41 (63%)		16 (25%)	59 (91%)		
8	MIA	W 40-0		32 (49%)	55 (85%)	37 (57%)	31 (48%)	49 (75%)	32 (49%)	17 (26%)		
9	TEN	L 23-20	58 (77%)	70 (93%)		60 (80%)	35 (47%)	35 (47%)	28 (37%)	30 (40%)	32 (43%)	
11	GB	W 23-0	41 (69%)	26 (44%)	43 (73%)	44 (75%)	10 (17%)		38 (64%)	33 (56%)	34 (58%)	
12	HOU	W 23-16	50 (75%)	41 (61%)	47 (70%)	49 (73%)	15 (22%)	16 (24%)	31 (46%)	23 (34%)	28 (42%)	
13	DET	W 44-20	47 (73%)	30 (47%)	43 (67%)	46 (72%)	13 (20%)		33 (52%)	32 (50%)	30 (47%)	
14	PIT	L 39-38	40 (63%)	33 (52%)	41 (64%)	50 (78%)	13 (20%)		29 (45%)	24 (38%)	33 (52%)	
15	CLE	W 27-10	49 (63%)	42 (54%)	51 (65%)	5 (6%)	26 (33%)	31 (40%)	30 (38%)	43 (55%)	36 (46%)	
16	IND	W 23-16	58 (79%)	48 (66%)	49 (67%)		15 (21%)	30 (41%)	39 (53%)	44 (60%)	38 (52%)	
17	CIN	L 31-27	65 (86%)	45 (59%)	56 (74%)		23 (30%)		29 (38%)	30 (39%)	30 (39%)	
	Grand Total		714 (70%)	703 (64%)	696 (69%)	511 (65%)	466 (43%)	387 (52%)	378 (37%)	376 (46%)	315 (42%)	65 (20%)

Personnel Groupings

Personnel	Team %	NFL Avg	Succ. %
1-1 [3WR]	41%	59%	37%
1-2 [2WR]	34%	19%	45%
2-2 [1WR]	11%	4%	59%
1-3 [1WR]	7%	5%	44%
2-1 [2WR]	3%	7%	52%

Grouping Tendencies

Personnel	Pass Rate	Pass Succ. %	Run Succ. %
1-1 [3WR]	73%	35%	42%
1-2 [2WR]	53%	46%	44%
2-2 [1WR]	13%	47%	60%
1-3 [1WR]	38%	50%	40%
2-1 [2WR]	45%	46%	56%

Red Zone Targets (min 3)

Receiver	All	Inside 5	6-10	11-20
Ben Watson	13	3	4	6
Mike Wallace	12	1	3	8
Nick Boyle	11	2	2	7
Danny Woodhead	8		1	7
Chris Moore	6		2	4
Javorius Allen	6	2	2	2
Jeremy Maclin	4	2	1	1
Breshad Perriman	3		1	2

Red Zone Rushes (min 3)

Rusher	All	Inside 5	6-10	11-20
Javorius Allen	32	9	8	15
Alex Collins	27	5	7	15
Joe Flacco	10	2	1	7
Terrance West	5	2	2	1
Danny Woodhead	3		1	2

Early Down Target Rate

RB	TE	WR
28%	25%	47%
23%	*21% NFL AVG*	*56%*

Overall Target Success %

RB	TE	WR
39% #29	51% #14	42% #31

Baltimore Ravens 2017 Passing Recap & 2018 Outlook

Since the Ravens gave Flacco that initial extension, he ranks 33rd in yards per attempt (6.5) and 31st in passer rating (82.5) among 34 quarterbacks with at least 1,000 attempts. He hasn't been good for quite some time. So Newsome traded back into round one for Louisville's Lamar Jackson at the No. 32 pick, landing Jackson with a fifth-year team option given only to first-round players. The fifth-year option can act as a "bye," giving teams an extra season to evaluate first-round picks. Next year, the Ravens can cut Flacco and save over $10 million in cap space, in addition to over $20 million in cap room in 2020. And in OC Marty Mornhinweg (Michael Vick) and assistant HC Greg Roman (Tyrod Taylor, Colin Kaepernick), the Ravens have two coaches on staff with histories crafting offenses for dual-threat quarterbacks like Jackson. Mornhinweg helped turn Vick from a 54% passer at 6.7 yards per attempt into a 63% quarterback at 8.1 YPA. Roman and Kaepernick's zone-read offense took them to the Super Bowl, and Taylor's career-best season (2015) came on Roman's watch.

Joe Flacco Rating All Downs

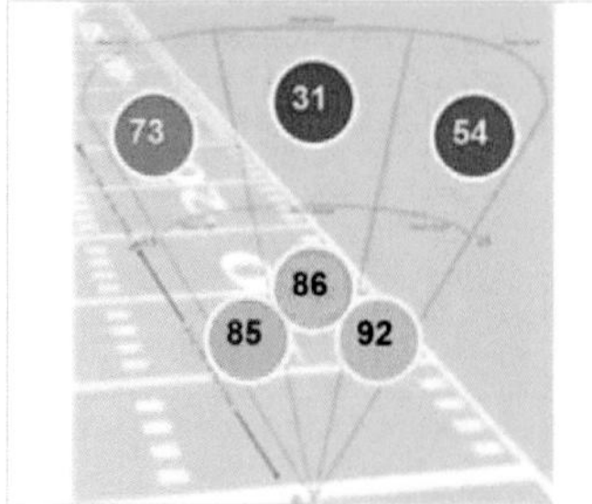

Joe Flacco Rating Early Downs

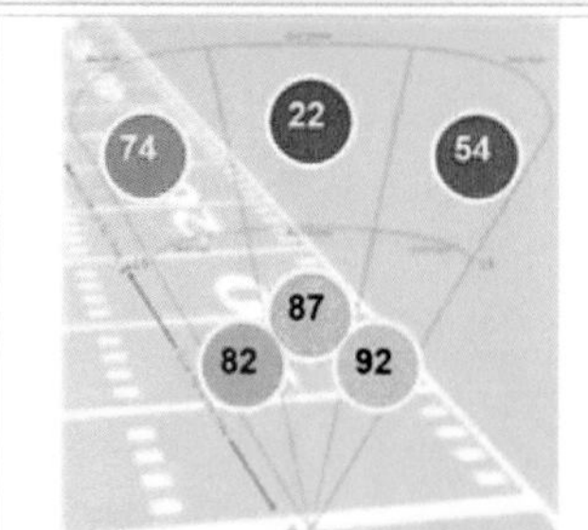

2017 Standard Passing Table

QB	Comp	Att	Comp %	Yds	YPA	TDs	INT	Sacks	Rating	Rk
Joe Flacco	349	546	64%	3,131	5.7	16	13	27	79	36
NFL Avg			62%		7.0				87.5	

2017 Advanced Passing Table

QB	Success %	EDSR Passing Success %	20+ Yd Pass Gains	20+ Yd Pass %	30+ Yd Pass Gains	30+ Yd Pass %	Avg. Air Yds per Comp	Avg. YAC per Comp	20+ Air Yd Comp	20+ Air Yd %
Joe Flacco	40%	45%	28	5.1%	11	2.0%	4.7	4.1	14	4%
NFL Avg	44%	48%	27.7	8.8%	10.3	3.3%	6.0	4.7	11.7	6%

Interception Rates by Down

Yards to Go	1	2	3	4	Total
1 & 2	0.0%	0.0%	0.0%		0.0%
3, 4, 5	0.0%	3.3%	3.8%	0.0%	3.4%
6 - 9	0.0%	1.5%	0.0%		0.8%
10 - 14	3.1%	3.1%	0.0%	33.3%	3.1%
15+	0.0%	0.0%	0.0%		0.0%
Total	2.8%	2.1%	1.2%	20.0%	2.3%

3rd Down Passing - Short of Sticks Analysis

QB	Avg. Yds to Go	Avg. YIA (of Comp)	Avg Yds Short	Short of Sticks Rate	Short Rk
Joe Flacco	7.2	5.1	-2.1	69%	31
NFL Avg	7.8	6.7	-1.1	60%	

Air Yds vs YAC

Air Yds %	YAC %	Rk
55%	45%	28
58%	42%	

2017 Receiving Recap & 2018 Outlook

The Ravens' brand-new pass-catcher corps extends to tight end, where rookies Hayden Hurst and Mark Andrews replace Ben Watson and failed 2015 second-round pick Maxx Williams. The more-versatile Hurst was picked 25th out of South Carolina. Andrews, more a one-dimensional receiving threat, was selected at No. 86 from Oklahoma. Flacco's most-efficient target during his decade as the Ravens' starter is Dennis Pitta, who logged a 68% catch rate and 98 rating when targeted. Michael Crabtree can upgrade Baltimore's red-zone passing game, Snead is a reliable slot target, and a healthy Brown is one of the NFL's most underrated vertical threats.

Player *Min 50 Targets*	Targets	Comp %	YPA	Rating	TOARS	Success %	Success Rk	Missed YPA Rk	YAS % Rk	TDs
Mike Wallace	92	57%	8.1	88	4.5	49%	68	74	18	4
Ben Watson	79	77%	6.6	100	4.4	53%	39	8	119	4
Jeremy Maclin	72	56%	6.1	76	3.9	39%	117	95	91	3
Javorius Allen	60	77%	4.2	94	3.8	37%	122	72	129	2

Directional Passer Rating Delivered

Receiver	Short Left	Short Middle	Short Right	Deep Left	Deep Middle	Deep Right	Player Total
Mike Wallace	93	82	92	75	46	124	88
Ben Watson	99	90	108	149	77	46	100
Jeremy Maclin	77	96	80	21	24	106	76
Javorius Allen	75	85	110				94
Danny Woodhead	92	87	85	0			77
Chris Moore	99	76	98	90		45	73
Nick Boyle	76	99	83			40	88
Alex Collins	67	68	85				77
Breshad Perriman	45	67	42	40	0	0	16
Michael Campanaro	70	96	69			40	84
Maxx Williams	119	83	123			40	105
Bobby Rainey	79		73				74
Terrance West		50	40				28
Team Total	84	86	94	70	26	54	81

2017 Rushing Recap & 2017 Outlook

In fantasy football, Alex Collins' Average Draft Position is RB20 as the 40th overall player off the board. It's too low. Collins finished 2017 at RB16 despite not even being on the Ravens' roster until Week 2, and not becoming Baltimore's starter until Week 10. Mornhinweg showed last year that he won't pass just to pass. The Ravens finished 9-7 despite going 2-5 in one-score games. They project to have a softer 2018 schedule – increasing the probability of more run-friendly game scripts – and Baltimore's run-defense slate goes from eighth toughest to tenth easiest.

Yards per Carry by Direction

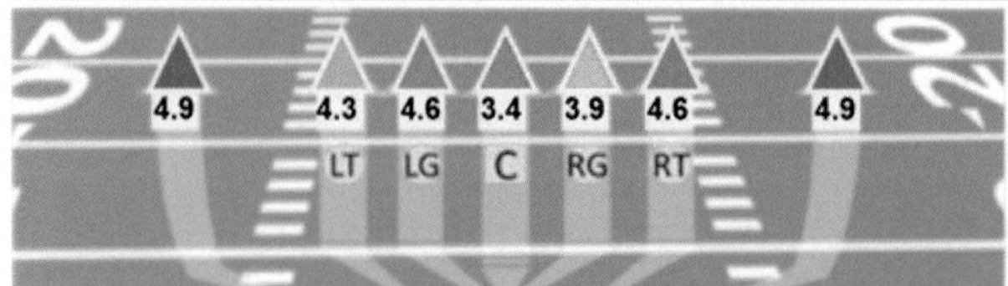

Player *Min 50 Rushes*	Rushes	YPC	Success %	Success Rk	Missed YPA Rk	YTS % Rk	YAS % Rk	Early Down Success %	Early Down Success Rk	TDs
Alex Collins	212	4.6	50%	15	34	42	13	50%	14	6
Javorius Allen	153	3.9	47%	27	40	30	56	45%	33	4

Directional Run Frequency

7% 11% 21% 15% 30% 8% 7%

LT LG C RG RT

Yet, somehow, no quarterback hit the cap for more 2017 money than Flacco. For all the credit Newsome deserves, Flacco's contract is an eyesore. The Ravens went 63-30 with a 9-4 postseason record during Flacco's rookie deal. Since Flacco's initial extension, Baltimore is 41-41 and 1-1 in the playoffs.

That initial six-year deal was severely backloaded. Flacco's cap costs in the first three years never exceeded $14.8 million. The cap hit doubled to $28.55 million in 2016 and reached $31.15 millon in 2017. So the Ravens tore up the initial deal after year three and signed Flacco to a three-year extension for $66.4 million. In 2016, his cap charge reduced to $22.55 million. In 2017, a still-league-high $24.55 million. And this year it is $24.75 million, fourth highest among quarterbacks. In the five years from 2013-2016, Flacco received two separate contracts totaling $73 million guaranteed with $69 million in signing bonuses. Not bad for one of the league's least-productive passers.

Newsome has made a habit of bringing in free agent wide receivers, either to cover for Flacco's annual underachievement or Newsome's own inability to successfully draft receivers. In either case, the list is incredible over the last ten years: Steve Smith, Jeremy Maclin, Mike Wallace, Anquan Boldin, T.J. Houshmandzadeh, and Derrick Mason.

(cont'd - see BAL-5)

Evan Silva's Fantasy Corner

Michael Crabtree landed a three-year, $21 million deal from the Ravens one day after getting cut by the Raiders, who viewed 33-year-old Jordy Nelson as an upgrade on 31-year-old Crabtree. Nevertheless, Crabtree is the heavy favorite to lead Baltimore in targets, and most valuably in the red zone, where he converted 13-of-49 (26.5%) targets into TDs compared to Amari Cooper's 5-of-31 (16.1%) mark over three years in Oakland. Target competitors John Brown (5'10/179) and Willie Snead (5'11/195) are unlikely to command nearly as many scoring-position looks. On sheer volume projection, Crabtree can be an undervalued fantasy WR2 if Joe Flacco keeps his job over Lamar Jackson. The Ravens have finished top 11 in pass attempts for three straight years, but that volume would likely plummet with a dual-threat rookie at QB.

Division History: Season Wins & 2018 Projection

2014 Wins | 2015 Wins | 2016 Wins | 2017 Wins | Forecast 2018 Wins

Rank of 2018 Defensive Pass Efficiency Faced by Week

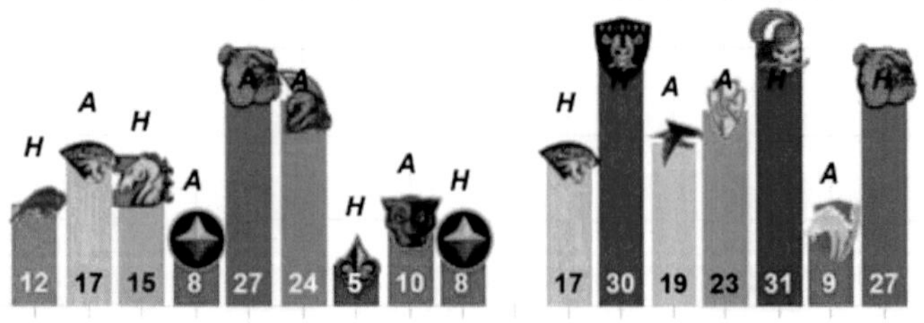

Rank of 2018 Defensive Rush Efficiency Faced by Week

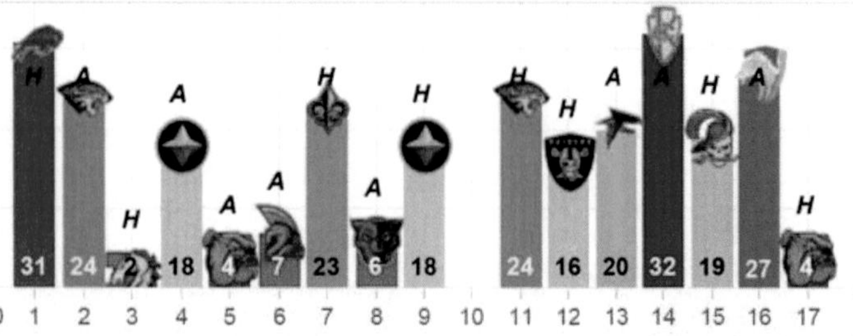

2017 Situational Usage by Player & Position

Usage Rate by Score

		Being Blown Out (14+)	Down Big (9-13)	One Score	Large Lead (9-13)	Blowout Lead (14+)	Grand Total
RUSH	Alex Collins	17%	11%	24%	29%	16%	21%
	Javorius Allen	10%	7%	11%	26%	38%	15%
	Mike Wallace			0%			0%
	Danny Woodhead			2%	1%	1%	1%
	Terrance West	4%	2%	3%	1%	10%	4%
	Chris Moore		1%	0%			0%
	Michael Campanaro	1%	1%	0%		1%	1%
	Maxx Williams			0%		1%	0%
	Bobby Rainey			0%			0%
	Vince Mayle			0%			0%
	Total	32%	23%	42%	57%	67%	43%
PASS	Alex Collins	1%	3%	5%	3%	2%	4%
	Javorius Allen	14%	12%	4%	6%	5%	6%
	Mike Wallace	11%	11%	11%	2%	3%	9%
	Ben Watson	6%	14%	8%	8%	2%	8%
	Jeremy Maclin	2%	11%	7%	9%	6%	7%
	Danny Woodhead	1%		6%	2%	2%	4%
	Terrance West			0%	1%	1%	0%
	Chris Moore	6%	8%	4%		2%	4%
	Nick Boyle	9%	1%	3%	7%	2%	4%
	Breshad Perriman	4%	2%	4%	1%	5%	4%
	Michael Campanaro	7%	4%	2%		2%	3%
	Maxx Williams		2%	2%	3%	2%	2%
	Bobby Rainey	1%	5%				1%
	Chris Matthews	3%	2%	0%			1%
	Griff Whalen	1%	2%	0%			1%
	Patrick Ricard	1%		0%	1%		0%
	Vince Mayle		1%				0%
	Total	68%	77%	58%	43%	33%	57%

Positional Target Distribution vs NFL Average

		NFL Wide				Team Only			
		Left	Middle	Right	Total	Left	Middle	Right	Total
Deep	WR	968	496	948	2,412	18	13	39	70
	TE	189	148	184	521	3	2	4	9
	RB	38	9	42	89	1			1
	All	1,195	653	1,174	3,022	22	15	43	80
Short	WR	2,819	1,582	2,728	7,129	43	89	62	194
	TE	847	789	1,111	2,747	16	50	59	125
	RB	1,292	766	1,236	3,294	29	57	59	145
	All	4,958	3,137	5,075	13,170	88	196	180	464
Total		6,153	3,790	6,249	16,192	110	211	223	544

Positional Success Rates vs NFL Average

		NFL Wide				Team Only			
		Left	Middle	Right	Total	Left	Middle	Right	Total
Deep	WR	37%	45%	38%	39%	33%	38%	28%	31%
	TE	38%	53%	46%	45%	67%	50%	25%	44%
	RB	37%	56%	38%	39%	0%			0%
	All	37%	47%	39%	40%	36%	40%	28%	33%
Short	WR	52%	58%	50%	53%	40%	51%	44%	46%
	TE	51%	56%	49%	52%	50%	62%	42%	51%
	RB	44%	52%	43%	46%	38%	40%	39%	39%
	All	50%	56%	48%	51%	41%	51%	42%	45%
Total		47%	54%	47%	49%	40%	50%	39%	43%

Successful Play Rate
0% – 100%

Baltimore Ravens - Success by Personnel Grouping & Play Type

Play Type	1-1 [3WR]	1-2 [2WR]	2-1 [2WR]	1-0 [4WR]	1-3 [1WR]	0-1 [4WR]	2-0 [3WR]	2-2 [1WR]	0-2 [3WR]	0-3 [2WR]	2-3 [0WR]	Grand Total
PASS	35% (312, 53%)	46% (191, 32%)	46% (13, 2%)	33% (12, 2%)	50% (30, 5%)	60% (5, 1%)	75% (4, 1%)	47% (15, 3%)	57% (7, 1%)	100% (1, 0%)	50% (4, 1%)	41% (594, 100%)
RUSH	42% (115, 25%)	44% (167, 36%)	56% (16, 3%)	50% (2, 0%)	40% (48, 10%)	100% (1, 0%)		60% (101, 22%)			60% (10, 2%)	47% (460, 100%)
TOTAL	37% (427, 41%)	45% (358, 34%)	52% (29, 3%)	36% (14, 1%)	44% (78, 7%)	67% (6, 1%)	75% (4, 0%)	59% (116, 11%)	57% (7, 1%)	100% (1, 0%)	57% (14, 1%)	44% (1,054, 100%)

Format Line 1: Success Rate Line 2: Total # of Plays, % of All Plays (by type)

BAL-5 This offseason, that list grew to Michael Crabtree, John Brown, and Willie Snead. Every offseason, the mantra is "this could be the year" based on Baltimore's alleged weapons upgrades. Ever year, Flacco fails to deliver.

Defensively, the Ravens are again poised to field one of the best units in football presuming CB Jimmy Smith returns from his December 3 Achilles' tear. The 2017 Ravens were a top 5-10 defense by most advanced metrics, and the league's best defense against wide receivers. But they were one of the worst at stopping running back passes and allowed a 102 passer rating and 51% Success Rate on targets to tight ends, both near league bottom. I took these numbers into account when advising readers to use Marcedes Lewis in DFS last Week 3 in London. (Lewis scored three TDs.)

Baltimore faces an easier-than-average schedule this year, featuring a far-softer slate of run defenses. If the Ravens keep feeding Collins, and the new pass-catching faces help improve Flacco's efficiency, this team will be set up for a better season than its projected 8.0-game Win Total.

Receiving Success by Personnel Grouping

Position	Player	1-1 [3WR]	1-2 [2WR]	2-1 [2WR]	1-0 [4WR]	1-3 [1WR]	0-1 [4WR]	2-0 [3WR]	2-2 [1WR]	0-2 [3WR]	0-3 [2WR]	2-3 [0WR]	Total
RB	Javorius Allen	42% 4.0 81.3 (36)	32% 4.4 102.6 (19)		0% 3.0 79.2 (1)	33% 3.3 43.8 (3)			100% 9.0 143.8 (1)				38% 4.2 94.4 (60)
TE	Ben Watson	48% 5.8 96.8 (33)	50% 7.2 73.5 (36)			80% 10.4 110.0 (5)			67% 6.0 122.2 (3)			100% 1.5 118.8 (2)	53% 6.6 100.3 (79)
WR	Mike Wallace	43% 4.9 81.0 (47)	52% 12.2 68.3 (27)	100% 40.0 118.8 (1)	100% 17.0 118.8 (1)	57% 6.9 78.3 (7)	0% 0.0 39.6 (2)	0% 0.0 39.6 (1)	100% 23.5 118.8 (2)	100% 12.0 156.3 (3)	100% 1.0 118.8 (1)		50% 8.1 88.5 (92)
	Jeremy Maclin	30% 5.0 60.5 (40)	55% 8.5 109.5 (22)	0% 0.0 39.6 (2)	50% 4.0 60.4 (4)	100% 6.0 91.7 (1)		100% 22.0 118.8 (1)		0% 4.0 60.4 (2)			39% 6.1 76.2 (72)
	Chris Moore	42% 6.9 82.2 (26)	30% 4.0 37.5 (10)		0% 12.0 116.7 (1)			100% 16.0 118.8 (1)					39% 6.5 73.1 (38)
	Breshad Perriman	18% 2.0 20.6 (22)	33% 3.7 14.8 (9)		0% 0.0 39.6 (3)				0% 0.0 39.6 (1)				20% 2.2 15.8 (35)

Format Line 1: Success Rate Line 2: YPA Line 3: Passer Rating Line 4: Total # of Plays

Successful Play Rate
0% – 100%

Rushing Success by Personnel Grouping

Position	Player	1-1 [3WR]	1-2 [2WR]	2-1 [2WR]	1-0 [4WR]	1-3 [1WR]	2-2 [1WR]	2-3 [0WR]	Total
RB	Alex Collins	38% 4.7 (47)	49% 4.9 (97)	60% 3.6 (5)		53% 3.7 (17)	65% 4.7 (43)	33% 0.0 (3)	50% 4.6 (212)
	Javorius Allen	43% 4.9 (42)	28% 2.4 (36)	50% 3.9 (8)	50% 10.5 (2)	46% 4.9 (13)	64% 3.8 (47)	60% 0.4 (5)	47% 3.9 (153)
	Terrance West	40% 4.0 (5)	50% 3.3 (24)	100% 11.0 (1)		50% 4.8 (4)	50% 1.8 (4)	100% 2.0 (1)	51% 3.6 (39)

Format Line 1: Success Rate Line 2: YPC Line 3: Total # of Plays

2018 Coaches

Head Coach:
Sean McDermott (2nd yr)
Offensive Coordinator:
Brian Daboll (Alabama QB) (1st yr)
Defensive Coordinator:
Leslie Frazier (2nd yr)

Buffalo Bills

2018 Forecast

Wins	Div Rank
6.5	#2

Past Records

2017: 9-7
2016: 7-9
2015: 8-8

EASY HARD

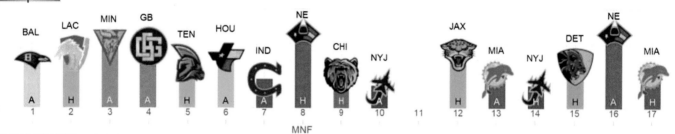

Week	1	2	3	4	5	6	7	8	9	10	11	12	13	14	15	16	17
Opponent	BAL	LAC	MIN	GB	TEN	HOU	IND	NE	CHI	NYJ		JAX	MIA	NYJ	DET	NE	MIA
H/A	A	H	A	A	H	A	A	H	H	A		H	A	H	H	A	H

MNF (week 8)

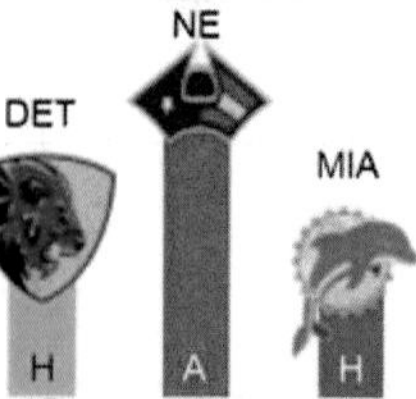

Key Players Lost

TXN	Player (POS)
Cut	Davis, Ryan DE
Declared Free Agent	Anderson, Colt S
	Brown, Preston LB
	Gaines, E.J. CB
	Henderson, Seantrel T
	Humber, Ramon LB
	Johnson, Leonard CB
	Jones, Taiwan RB
	Matthews, Jordan WR
	Tate, Brandon WR
	Thomas, Shamarko S
	Thompson, Deonte WR
	Thornton, Cedric DT
	Tolbert, Mike RB
	Webb III, Joe QB
	Wright, Shareece CB
Retired	Ihedigbo, James S
	Incognito, Richie G
	Jackson, Fred RB
	Wood, Eric C

Average Line	# Games Favored	# Games Underdog
3.2	2	11

2018 Buffalo Bills Overview

A recurring dream.

Alex Trebeck turns to me onstage and presents the clue. "This team should have spent 2017 abiding to the precept 'destroy and rebuild'." My thumb uncontrollably smashes the buzzer.

"Who are the Buffalo Bills?"

It's hard. No one wants to lose. But because the Bills half-stepped their rebuild and backed into a 9-7 record with an unwanted Wild Card berth, quarterback-needy Buffalo earned itself the No. 21 pick in one of the strongest QB drafts in recent years.

Costs to maneuver atop the quarterback-rich 2018 draft were aplenty.

The 2017 Bills traded out of No. 10 (bypassing Pat Mahomes and Deshaun Watson) for an extra 2018 first-rounder (No. 22) from the Chiefs. Armed with Nos. 21 and 22 selections, Buffalo furthered its first-round position by sending LT Cordy Glenn to Cincinnati, turning No. 21 into 12. Still out of prime quarterback position, the Bills doled out two second-round picks (Nos. 53 and 56) to climb from No. 12 to 7, where GM Brandon Beane selected Wyoming QB Josh Allen. Buffalo's second first-round trade up cost the No. 65 pick to climb from No. 22 to 16, where the Bills drafted 19-year-old Virginia Tech LB Tremaine Edmunds.

The 2017 Bills earned 6.3 Pythagorean Wins. Had Buffalo logged 6.3 actual wins, Beane's club would have drafted between pick Nos. 9 and 12. Thus, the Bills could have kept Glenn plus pick Nos. 53 and 56 had they executed their intended year-one rebuilding strategy.

While Bills fans won't want to hear their lone playoff trip in two decades was undeserved, facts and statistics show the 2017 Bills went 0-6 in regulation when tying or losing the turnover battle, and an otherworldly 8-2 when winning the turnover battle with 5-of-8 wins decided by one score. The Bills beat the Dolphins twice and were waxed by the Patriots, yet finished 9-7 and (bad?) lucked into the playoffs.

(cont'd - see BUF2)

Key Free Agents/ Trades Added

Bodine, Russell C
Bush, Rafael S
Davis, Vontae CB
Gaines, Phillip CB
Ivory, Chris RB
Kerley, Jeremy WR
Lotulelei, Star DT
McCarron, AJ QB
Newhouse, Marshall T
Odighizuwa, Owamagbe DE

Drafted Players

Rd	Pk	Player (College)
1	7	QB - Josh Allen (Wyoming)
	16	LB - Tremaine Edmunds (Virginia Tech)
3	96	DT - Harrison Phillips (Stanford)
4	121	CB - Taron Johnson (Weber State)
5	154	CB - Siran Neal (Jacksonville State)
	166	G - Wyatt Teller (Virginia Tech)
6	187	WR - Ray-Ray McCloud (Clemson)
7*	255	WR - Austin Proehl (North Carolina)

Regular Season Wins: Past & Current Proj

Lineup & Cap Hits

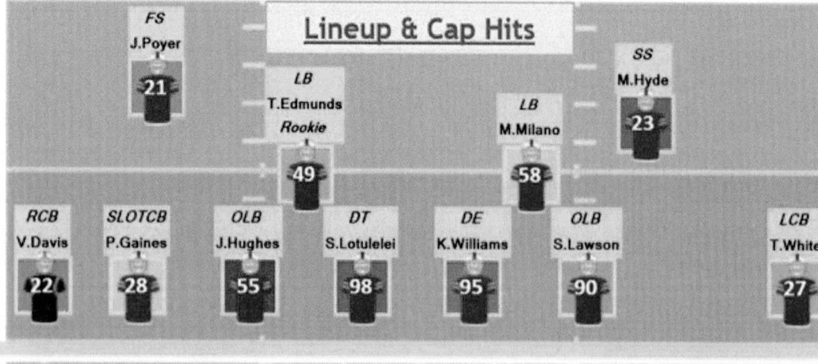

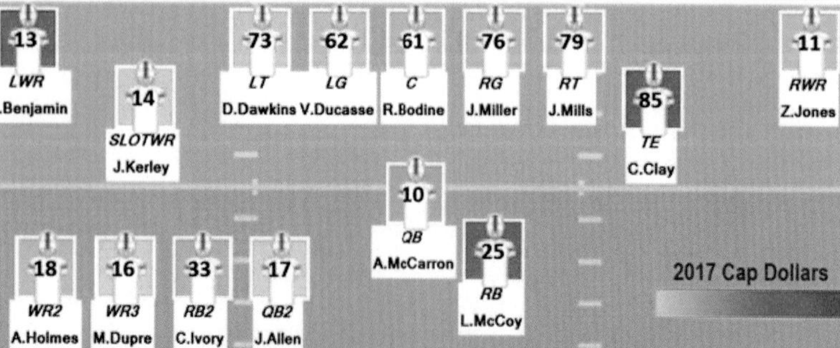

2018 Unit Spending

Positional Spending

	Rank	Total	2017 Rk
All OFF	31	$73.67M	10
QB	31	$4.09M	21
OL	29	$26.11M	5
RB	2	$13.97M	8
WR	24	$17.49M	28
TE	9	$12.00M	7
All DEF	27	$71.78M	26
DL	10	$35.96M	5
LB	29	$10.90M	32
CB	26	$10.18M	32
S	10	$14.75M	21

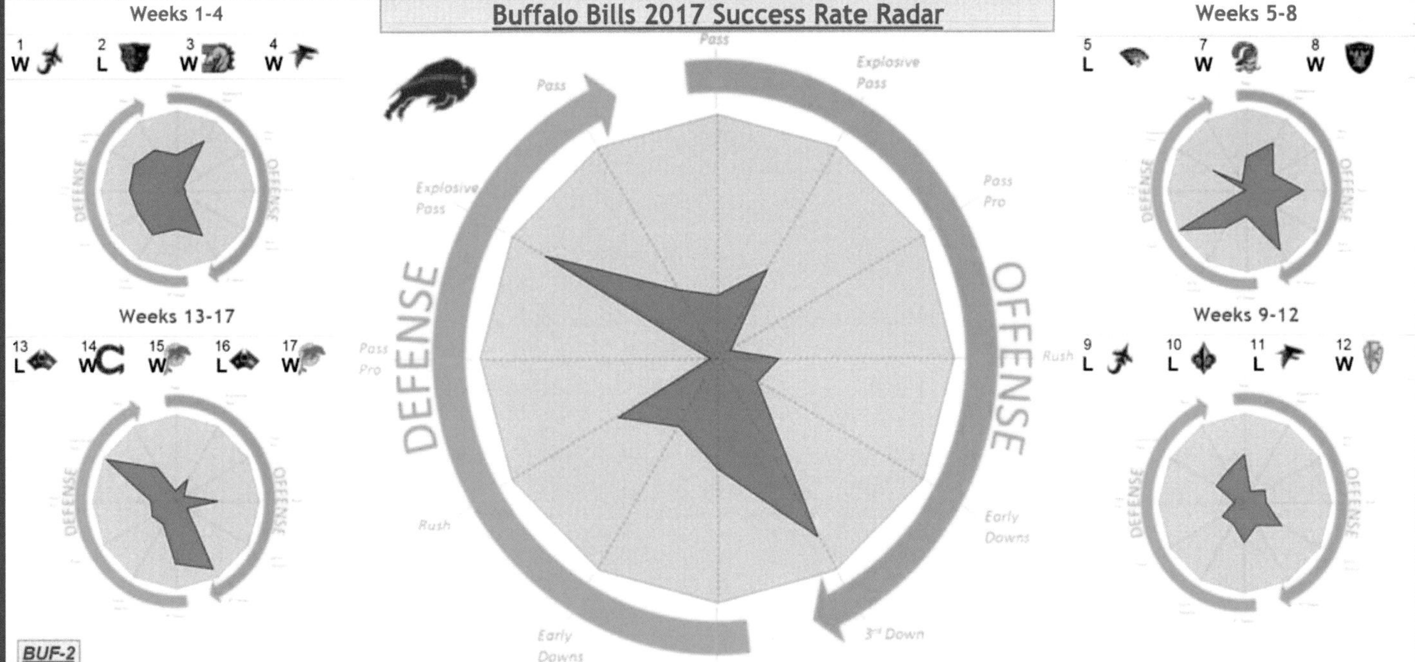

BUF-2

The Bills' metrics were horrendous. Their offense ranked dead last in Early Down Success Rate -- my most reliable team-efficiency analytic – and their defense finished 27th in EDSR. On page two of this chapter, the graphic shows the offense ranked average or worse in 11-of-13 metrics. Defensively, Buffalo won its EDSR battle in 3-of-16 games – with wins against the Jets and Dolphins twice, all by narrow margins.

Buffalo flopped even against the easiest schedule of opposing defenses in the league, including the NFL's softest pass-defense slate.

Last year's Bills went 6-2 in one-score games and 3-9 in games decided by more than one score, showing an inability to contend with higher-scoring opposition.

The 2017 Bills were a wolf in sheep's clothing. So instead of viewing them as a "playoff team," we have to ask: Has this team done anything to improve on mediocrity? I don't think so.

It starts up front with an offensive line that was below average in 2017 and is much worse this year. Gone are LT Cordy Glenn (Bengals), C Eric Wood (retirement), and LG Richie Incognito (???). Replacing Wood at center is Russell Bodine, behind whom 2017's Bengals ran just 11.5% of the time (league average behind-center runs is 29%) because Bodine was so often overpowered. On left-guard and behind-center runs, last year's Bills averaged crisp clips of 5.9 yards per carry (Incognito) and 5.2 (Wood). The downgrades show financially; Buffalo dipped from the NFL's fifth-most-expensive offensive line to fifth cheapest.

In 2016, LeSean McCoy faced the NFL's toughest run-defense schedule, yet dominated for a career-high 5.4 yards per carry. McCoy managed a career-worst 3.97 YPC against last year's seventh-softest run-defense slate. Perhaps the coordinator change from Rick Dennison to ex-Alabama OC Brian Daboll will help. On 2nd-and-10 plays, Dennison called runs at a whopping 81% clip. These predictable run calls produced a lame 12% Success Rate and 3.2 YPC.

(cont'd - see BUF-3)

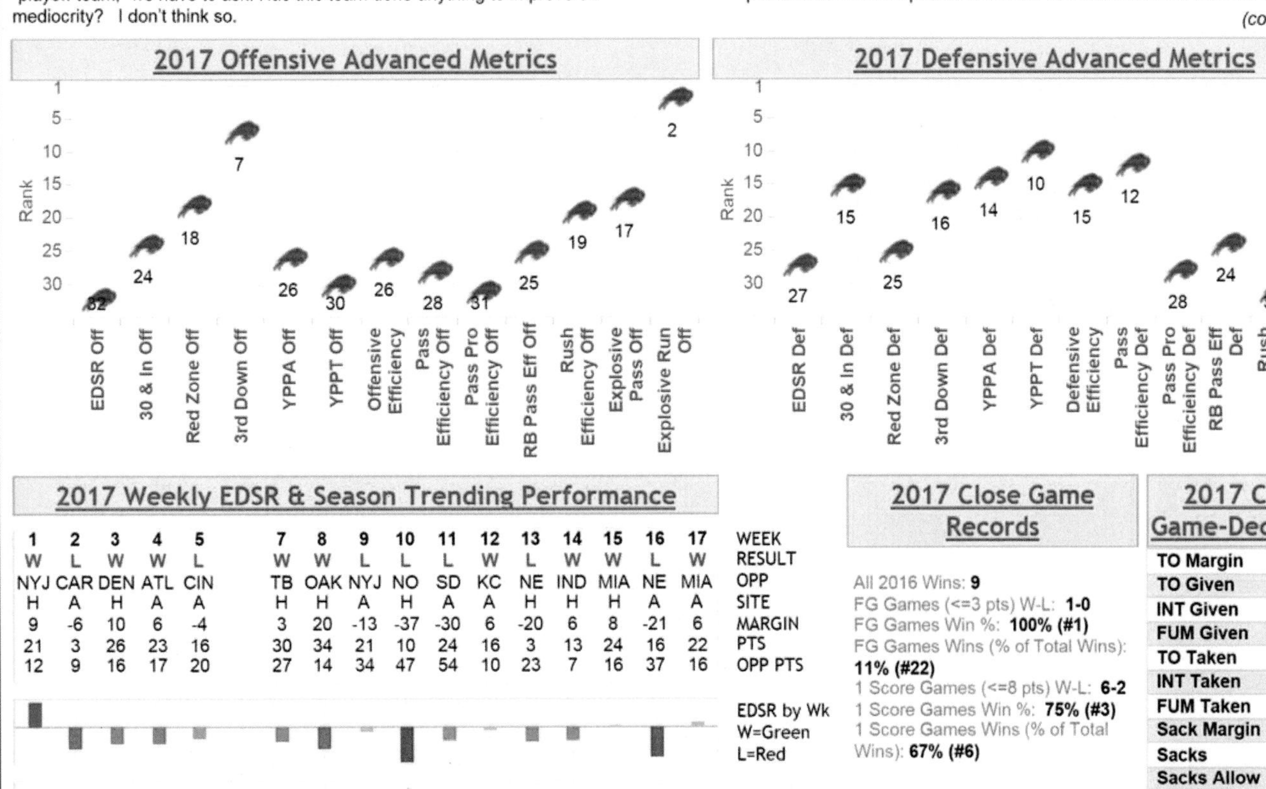

2017 Weekly EDSR & Season Trending Performance

1	2	3	4	5	7	8	9	10	11	12	13	14	15	16	17	WEEK
W	L	W	W	L	W	W	L	L	L	W	L	W	W	L	W	RESULT
NYJ	CAR	DEN	ATL	CIN	TB	OAK	NYJ	NO	SD	KC	NE	IND	MIA	NE	MIA	OPP
H	A	H	A	A	H	H	A	H	A	A	H	H	H	A	A	SITE
9	-6	10	6	-4	3	20	-13	-37	-30	6	-20	6	8	-21	6	MARGIN
21	3	26	23	16	30	34	21	10	24	16	3	13	24	16	22	PTS
12	9	16	17	20	27	14	34	47	54	10	23	7	16	37	16	OPP PTS

EDSR by Wk
W=Green
L=Red

OFF/DEF
EDSR
Blue=OFF
(high=good)
Red=DEF
(low=good)

2017 Close Game Records

All 2016 Wins: **9**
FG Games (<=3 pts) W-L: **1-0**
FG Games Win %: **100% (#1)**
FG Games Wins (% of Total Wins): **11% (#22)**
1 Score Games (<=8 pts) W-L: **6-2**
1 Score Games Win %: **75% (#3)**
1 Score Games Wins (% of Total Wins): **67% (#6)**

2017 Critical & Game-Deciding Stats

TO Margin	+9
TO Given	16
INT Given	10
FUM Given	6
TO Taken	25
INT Taken	18
FUM Taken	7
Sack Margin	-20
Sacks	27
Sacks Allow	47
Return TD Margin	+1
Ret TDs	3
Ret TDs Allow	2
Penalty Margin	-1
Penalties	98
Opponent Penalties	97

Buffalo Bills 2018 Strength of Schedule In Detail (compared to 2017)

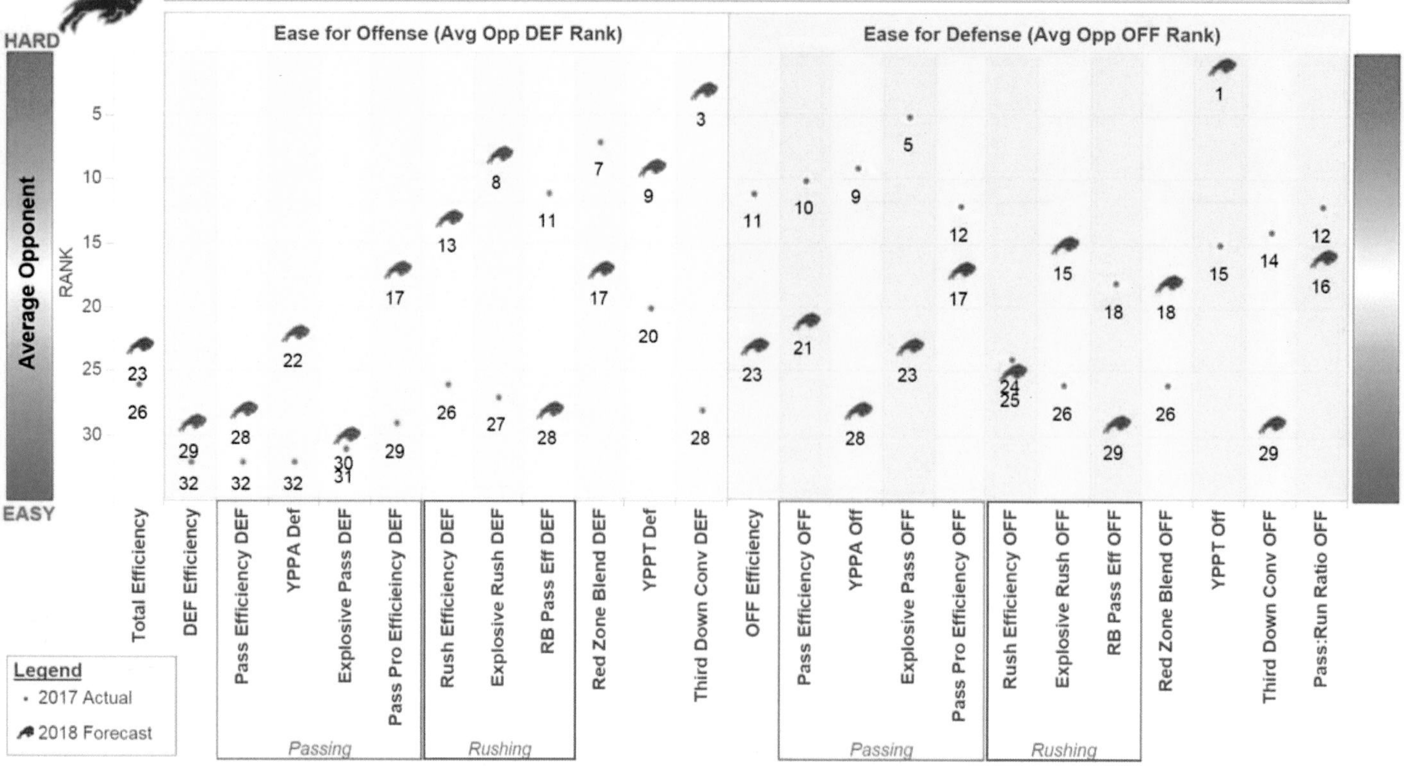

Average Opponent RANK (HARD 5 … 30 EASY)

Legend: • 2017 Actual; 2018 Forecast

Ease for Offense (Avg Opp DEF Rank)

Metric	Group	2018 Forecast	2017 Actual
Total Efficiency		23	26
DEF Efficiency		29	32
Pass Efficiency DEF	Passing	28	32
YPPA Def	Passing	22	32
Explosive Pass DEF	Passing	30	31
Pass Pro Efficieincy DEF	Passing	17	29
Rush Efficiency DEF	Rushing	13	26
Explosive Rush DEF	Rushing	8	27
RB Pass Eff DEF	Rushing	28	11
Red Zone Blend DEF		17	7
YPPT Def		9	20
Third Down Conv DEF		3	28

Ease for Defense (Avg Opp OFF Rank)

Metric	Group	2018 Forecast	2017 Actual
OFF Efficiency		23	11
Pass Efficiency OFF	Passing	21	10
YPPA Off	Passing	28	9
Explosive Pass OFF	Passing	23	5
Pass Pro Efficiency OFF	Passing	17	12
Rush Efficiency OFF	Rushing	25	24
Explosive Rush OFF	Rushing	15	26
RB Pass Eff OFF	Rushing	29	18
Red Zone Blend OFF		18	26
YPPT Off		1	15
Third Down Conv OFF		29	14
Pass:Run Ratio OFF		16	12

2018 v 2017 Schedule Variances* (DEF=Variance of DEF faced, OFF=Var of OFF faced)

Pass DEF Rk	Pass DEF Blend Rk	Rush DEF Rk	Rush DEF Blend Rk	Pass OFF Rk	Pass OFF Blend Rk	Rush OFF Rk	Rush OFF Blend Rk
13	10	3	6	23	15	31	32

* **1**=Hardest Jump in 2018 schedule from 2017 (aka a much harder schedule in 2018), **32**=Easiest Jump in 2018 schedule from 2017 (aka a much easier schedule in 2018); **Pass Blend** metric blends 4 metrics: Pass Efficiency, YPPA, Explosive Pass & Pass Rush; **Rush Blend** metric blends 3 metrics: Rush Efficiency, Explosive Rush & RB Targets

Team Records & Trends

	2017	2016	2015
Average line	2.0	-0.4	-0.2
Average O/U line	43.4	44.7	43.7
Straight Up Record	9-7	7-9	8-8
Against the Spread Record	9-6	6-9	7-8
Over/Under Record	8-8	12-4	8-8
ATS as Favorite	5-1	2-4	3-4
ATS as Underdog	4-5	3-4	4-3
Straight Up Home	6-2	4-4	5-3
ATS Home	5-2	3-5	5-3
Over/Under Home	5-3	8-0	4-4
ATS as Home Favorite	4-0	2-2	3-1
ATS as a Home Dog	1-2	1-2	2-1
Straight Up Away	3-5	3-5	3-5
ATS Away	4-4	3-4	2-5
Over/Under Away	3-5	4-4	4-4
ATS Away Favorite	1-1	0-2	0-3
ATS Away Dog	3-3	2-2	2-2
Six Point Teaser Record	11-5	11-4	11-5
Seven Point Teaser Record	11-5	12-4	12-4
Ten Point Teaser Record	12-4	13-3	13-2

BUF-3

While I'm not extremely high on Daboll's hire, I do think the inclusion of college concepts could provide an edge. But Buffalo must be careful how it "practices" these concepts in preseason games. The Bills will be tested early by the NFL's toughest first-half schedule.

Ex-quarterback Tyrod Taylor was not above scrutiny, but he played a big role in Buffalo's 9-7 finish simply by limiting turnovers. Most of the Bills' wins came in close games or games in which Buffalo got fortunate in the turnover battle; interceptions and lost fumbles would be catastrophic to Sean McDermott's conservative team. Taylor averaged just 7.0 turnovers per year in 2015-2017 and recorded a 1.29% interception rate, second best in the league during that span behind only Tom Brady.

*(cont'd - see **BUF-4**)*

2018 Rest Analysis

Avg Rest	6.47
Avg Rk	3
Team More Rest	1
Opp More Rest	1
Net Rest Edge	0
3 Days Rest	0
4 Days Rest	0
5 Days Rest	1
6 Days Rest	12
7 Days Rest	1
8 Days Rest	0
9 Days Rest	0
10 Days Rest	0
11 Days Rest	0
12 Days Rest	0
13 Days Rest	1
14 Days Rest	0

Health by Unit*

2017 Rk	9
2016 Rk	27
Off Rk	13
Def Rk	8
QB Rk	18
RB Rk	12
WR Rk	25
TE Rk	25
Oline Rk	10
Dline Rk	19
LB Rk	6
DB Rk	9

*Based on the great work of Scott Kacsmar from Football Outsiders

2018 Weekly Betting Lines (wks 1-16)

Week	1	2	3	4	5	6	7	8	9	10	12	13	14	15	16
Opp	BAL	LAC	MIN	GB	TEN	HOU	IND	NE	CHI	NYJ	JAX	MIA	NYJ	DET	NE
Site	A	H	A	A		A	A	H			H	A	A		A
Line	3.5	1	10	9.5	0	6	2	4.5	-1.5	1	4.5	1	-4	0	10.5

Avg = 3.2

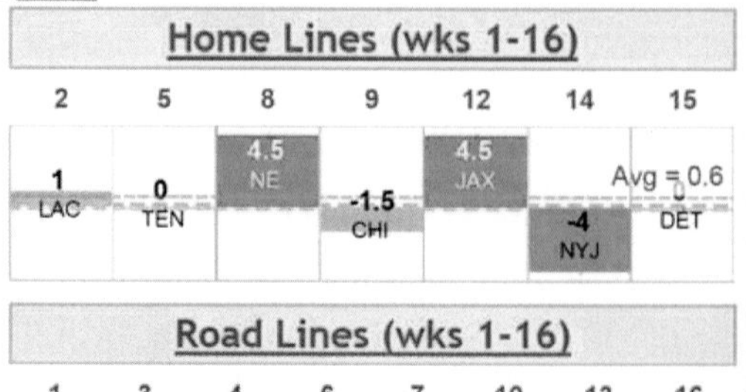

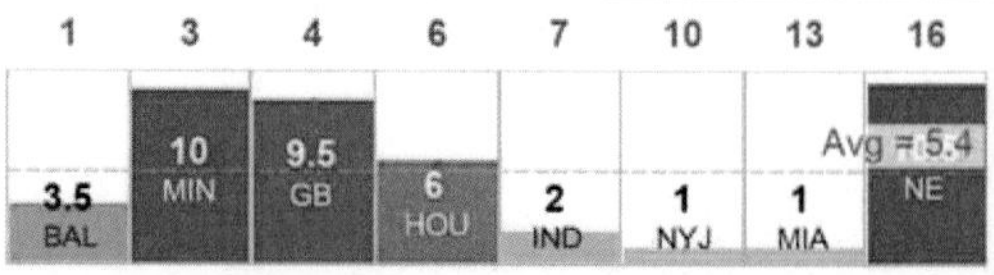

Buffalo Bills 2017 Play Analysis

2017 Play Tendencies

All Pass %	52%
All Pass Rk	31
All Rush %	48%
All Rush Rk	2
1 Score Pass %	50%
1 Score Pass Rk	31
2016 1 Score Pass %	49%
2016 1 Score Pass Rk	31
2017 Pass Increase %	1%
Pass Increase Rk	10
1 Score Rush %	50%
1 Score Rush Rk	2
Up Pass %	39%
Up Pass Rk	32
Up Rush %	61%
Up Rush Rk	1
Down Pass %	64%
Down Pass Rk	24
Down Rush %	36%
Down Rush Rk	9

2017 Down & Distance Tendencies

Down	Distance	Total Plays	Pass Rate	Run Rate	Play Success %
1	Short (1-3)	8	13%	88%	38%
	Med (4-7)	7	57%	43%	43%
	Long (8-10)	316	45%	55%	46%
	XL (11+)	10	30%	70%	10%
2	Short (1-3)	38	42%	58%	55%
	Med (4-7)	73	44%	56%	48%
	Long (8-10)	102	44%	56%	30%
	XL (11+)	56	68%	32%	29%
3	Short (1-3)	50	44%	56%	72%
	Med (4-7)	64	77%	23%	48%
	Long (8-10)	37	81%	19%	43%
	XL (11+)	43	84%	16%	16%
4	Short (1-3)	3	67%	33%	0%
	Med (4-7)	3	100%	0%	0%

Shotgun %:

Under Center	Shotgun
53%	47%
37%	*63%*

AVG

Run Rate:

Under Center	Shotgun
70%	18%
68%	*23%*

AVG

Pass Rate:

Under Center	Shotgun
30%	82%
32%	*77%*

AVG

Short Yardage Intelligence:

2nd and Short Run

Run Freq	Run Rk	NFL Run Freq Avg	Run 1D Rate	Run NFL 1D Avg
66%	21	67%	58%	69%

2nd and Short Pass

Pass Freq	Pass Rk	NFL Pass Freq Avg	Pass 1D Rate	Pass NFL 1D Avg
34%	11	33%	30%	53%

Most Frequent Play

Down	Distance	Play Type	Player	Total Plays	Play Success %
1	Short (1-3)	RUSH	Mike Tolbert	4	25%
	Med (4-7)	RUSH	LeSean McCoy	3	67%
	Long (8-10)	RUSH	LeSean McCoy	121	44%
	XL (11+)	RUSH	LeSean McCoy	3	0%
2	Short (1-3)	RUSH	LeSean McCoy	15	60%
	Med (4-7)	RUSH	LeSean McCoy	29	59%
	Long (8-10)	RUSH	LeSean McCoy	34	29%
	XL (11+)	RUSH	LeSean McCoy	11	18%
3	Short (1-3)	RUSH	LeSean McCoy	14	79%
	Med (4-7)	PASS	Charles Clay	7	71%
		RUSH	Tyrod Taylor	7	86%
	Long (8-10)	PASS	Deonte Thompson	5	40%
		RUSH	Tyrod Taylor	5	60%
	XL (11+)	PASS	LeSean McCoy	9	11%

Most Successful Play*

Down	Distance	Play Type	Player	Total Plays	Play Success %
1	Long (8-10)	RUSH	Tyrod Taylor	14	79%
2	Short (1-3)	RUSH	LeSean McCoy	15	60%
	Med (4-7)	RUSH	LeSean McCoy	29	59%
	Long (8-10)	PASS	LeSean McCoy	12	33%
	XL (11+)	PASS	Kelvin Benjamin	5	100%
3	Short (1-3)	PASS	LeSean McCoy	5	80%
	Med (4-7)	RUSH	Tyrod Taylor	7	86%
	Long (8-10)	RUSH	Tyrod Taylor	5	60%
	XL (11+)	PASS	Charles Clay	5	20%

**Minimum 5 plays to qualify*

2017 Snap Rates

Wk	Opp	Score	Zay Jones	LeSean McCoy	Charles Clay	Nick O'Leary	Jordan Matthews	Andre Holmes	Patrick DiMarco	Kelvin Benjamin
1	NYJ	W 21-12	66 (86%)	54 (70%)	65 (84%)	43 (56%)	67 (87%)	39 (51%)	20 (26%)	
2	CAR	L 9-3	49 (91%)	40 (74%)	45 (83%)	20 (37%)	50 (93%)	34 (63%)	13 (24%)	
3	DEN	W 26-16	55 (85%)	43 (66%)	52 (80%)	34 (52%)	50 (77%)	22 (34%)	15 (23%)	
4	ATL	W 23-17	44 (73%)	43 (72%)	48 (80%)	32 (53%)	39 (65%)	27 (45%)	30 (50%)	
5	CIN	L 20-16	66 (94%)	54 (77%)	13 (19%)	59 (84%)		31 (44%)	16 (23%)	
7	TB	W 30-27	55 (81%)	57 (84%)		54 (79%)	55 (81%)	27 (40%)	16 (24%)	
8	OAK	W 34-14	55 (80%)	50 (72%)		54 (78%)	48 (70%)	21 (30%)	28 (41%)	
9	NYJ	L 34-21	40 (53%)	55 (73%)		58 (77%)	71 (95%)	35 (47%)	6 (8%)	
10	NO	L 47-10		24 (50%)	29 (60%)	19 (40%)	36 (75%)	9 (19%)	14 (29%)	41 (85%)
11	LAC	L 54-24	53 (82%)	42 (65%)	35 (54%)	34 (52%)		39 (60%)	8 (12%)	2 (3%)
12	KC	W 16-10	57 (81%)	49 (70%)	45 (64%)	30 (43%)	42 (60%)	14 (20%)	17 (24%)	
13	NE	L 23-3	65 (97%)	41 (61%)	44 (66%)		51 (76%)	13 (19%)	5 (7%)	
14	IND	W 13-7	41 (61%)	50 (75%)	58 (87%)	32 (48%)		15 (22%)	16 (24%)	41 (61%)
15	MIA	W 24-16	44 (70%)	41 (65%)	48 (76%)	27 (43%)		14 (22%)	24 (38%)	37 (59%)
16	NE	L 37-16	53 (76%)	50 (71%)	51 (73%)	22 (31%)			13 (19%)	52 (74%)
17	MIA	W 22-16	50 (75%)	29 (43%)	44 (66%)	31 (46%)			22 (33%)	45 (67%)
	Grand Total		793 (79%)	722 (68%)	577 (69%)	549 (55%)	509 (78%)	340 (37%)	263 (25%)	218 (58%)

Personnel Groupings

Personnel	Team %	NFL Avg	Succ. %
1-1 [3WR]	55%	59%	42%
1-2 [2WR]	19%	19%	42%
2-1 [2WR]	15%	7%	43%
2-2 [1WR]	9%	4%	39%

Grouping Tendencies

Personnel	Pass Rate	Pass Succ. %	Run Succ. %
1-1 [3WR]	66%	40%	46%
1-2 [2WR]	49%	50%	34%
2-1 [2WR]	29%	41%	44%
2-2 [1WR]	13%	25%	42%

Red Zone Targets (min 3)

Receiver	All	Inside 5	6-10	11-20
LeSean McCoy	16	1	6	9
Charles Clay	11	3	3	5
Zay Jones	11	2	3	6
Andre Holmes	5	2	1	2
Kelvin Benjamin	5	2	1	2
Jordan Matthews	4	2	1	1
Nick O'Leary	4	1	1	2

Red Zone Rushes (min 3)

Rusher	All	Inside 5	6-10	11-20
LeSean McCoy	36	12	9	15
Tyrod Taylor	17	6	5	6
Mike Tolbert	8	4		4

Early Down Target Rate

RB	TE	WR
29%	24%	47%
23%	*21%* *NFL AVG*	*56%*

Overall Target Success %

RB	TE	WR
43% #21	52% #10	44% #29

Buffalo Bills 2017 Passing Recap & 2018 Outlook

Assuming Allen out-snaps McCarron, the Bills will require adequate rushing production under a new playcaller. Allen's Wyoming Cougars produced an adjusted run rate of 54.1%, one of the highest in the country. Wyoming's rushing efficiency was terrible, but the Cougars still ran the ball far more frequently than you'd expect with a future top-ten NFL pick at quarterback. Wyoming's run-first strategy confounded me, and I wondered whether it was worth reading into regarding Cougars coaches on Allen, or a poorly-designed scheme that ignored analytical self scouting. Tyrod Taylor's 2017 numbers were bad, as shown below. Taylor's poor Early-Down Passing Success Rate was especially worrisome because run-first teams should find leverage when passing. This may speak to Taylor's supporting cast over his own deficiencies. Daboll should explore increasing his team's short passing (under 15 yards) to the middle of the field, where the 2017 Bills produced a 59% Success Rate and 7.6 yards per pass attempt. (Their Success Rate was 42% at 6.1 YPA to all other areas.). Last year's Bills targeted the short middle on just 20% of attempts, equaling league average.

Tyrod Taylor Rating All Downs

99 50 75
97
98 74

2017 Standard Passing Table

QB	Comp	Att	Comp %	Yds	YPA	TDs	INT	Sacks	Rating	Rk
Tyrod Taylor	280	457	61%	2,933	6.4	14	5	48	86	27
Nathan Peterman	25	52	48%	266	5.1	2	6	1	37	58
NFL Avg			62%		7.0				87.5	

Tyrod Taylor Rating Early Downs

89 58 90
91
93 71

2017 Advanced Passing Table

QB	Success %	EDSR Passing Success %	20+ Yd Pass Gains	20+ Yd Pass %	30+ Yd Pass Gains	30+ Yd Pass %	Avg. Air Yds per Comp	Avg. YAC per Comp	20+ Air Yd Comp	20+ Air Yd %
Tyrod Taylor	41%	43%	36	7.9%	14	3.1%	5.6	4.5	15	5%
Nathan Peterman	38%	49%	3	5.8%	0	0.0%	6.6	3.1	0	0%
NFL Avg	44%	48%	27.7	8.8%	10.3	3.3%	6.0	4.7	11.7	6%

Interception Rates by Down

Yards to Go	1	2	3	4	Total
1 & 2	0.0%	0.0%	0.0%	0.0%	0.0%
3, 4, 5	0.0%	0.0%	0.0%	0.0%	0.0%
6 - 9	33.3%	0.0%	2.0%	0.0%	2.0%
10 - 14	0.6%	0.0%	2.3%	0.0%	0.7%
15+	0.0%	0.0%	5.6%		2.3%
Total	1.1%	0.0%	1.9%	0.0%	1.0%

3rd Down Passing - Short of Sticks Analysis

QB	Avg. Yds to Go	Avg. YIA (of Comp)	Avg Yds Short	Short of Sticks Rate	Short Rk
Tyrod Taylor	8.4	5.8	-2.6	68%	37
NFL Avg	7.8	6.7	-1.1	60%	

Air Yds vs YAC

Air Yds %	YAC %	Rk
57%	43%	24
58%	42%	

2017 Receiving Recap & 2018 Outlook

When your top-two receivers play running back and tight end, you know your wide receivers aren't a strength. Buffalo's top offseason addition was journeyman slot receiver Jeremy Kerley. Knee-hobbled Kelvin Benjamin does have size to reel in off-target passes. Albeit in a small sample, Benjamin excelled when targeted to the deep right section of the field for last year's Bills, catching 11-of-13 deep-right targets for an 86% Success Rate and 141.0 passer rating.

Player *Min 50 Targets*	Targets	Comp %	YPA	Rating	TOARS	Success %	Success Rk	Missed YPA Rk	YAS % Rk	TDs
LeSean McCoy	85	76%	5.8	93	4.4	46%	83	116	126	2
Charles Clay	79	66%	7.3	80	4.2	50%	58	85	57	2
Zay Jones	78	37%	4.3	54	3.6	34%	129	129	70	2

Directional Passer Rating Delivered

Receiver	Short Left	Short Middle	Short Right	Deep Left	Deep Middle	Deep Right	Player Total
LeSean McCoy	94	94	74	119		92	93
Charles Clay	82	93	58	96		102	80
Zay Jones	78	113	47	54	40	10	54
Deonte Thompson	87	1	37	56		92	55
Nick O'Leary	119	82	99	73	40	144	110
Jordan Matthews	120	117	81	40		119	102
Kelvin Benjamin	80	119	121	119	119	45	95
Andre Holmes	129	94	100	40	40	65	111
Mike Tolbert	65	97	79				87
Patrick DiMarco	56	96	17				30
Team Total	94	95	66	70	42	73	81

2017 Rushing Recap & 2017 Outlook

Even as one of the NFL's best backs, LeSean McCoy's 2017 drop in production was concerning against a soft run-defense schedule with increased volume. If you remove blowout-game productivity versus the Chargers, Saints, and Patriots, McCoy managed 3.5 yards per carry and a 39% Success Rate in 13 games.

Player *Min 50 Rushes*	Rushes	YPC	Success %	Success Rk	Missed YPA Rk	YTS % Rk	YAS % Rk	Early Down Success %	Early Down Success Rk	TDs
LeSean McCoy	306	4.0	42%	50	64	45	8	41%	55	6
Mike Tolbert	70	3.7	37%	67	59	60	73	38%	66	1

Yards per Carry by Direction

4.1 | 3.4 | 5.0 | 3.5 | 3.1 | 3.9 | 6.0

LT LG C RG RT

Directional Run Frequency

10% | 11% | 15% | 27% | 15% | 14% | 7%

LT LG C RG RT

Atop the list of Tyrod replacements is No. 7 overall pick Josh Allen. Over the last five years, the NFL's average interception rate for rookie quarterbacks is 2.95%, more than doubling Taylor's pick rate in three seasons as a starter. Even if veteran bridge A.J. McCarron and Allen combine for a league-average INT rate, this year's Bills interception rate would nearly double to 2.54%.

Color me skeptical about the 2018 Bills. McDermott's team overshot its 2017 metrics thanks to turnover margin and stumbled into the playoffs with a 4-6 finish. They parted with several high picks in two first-round trades up and in 2018 will field the NFL's least-talented pass-catcher corps.

(cont'd - see BUF-5)

Evan Silva's Fantasy Corner

Even as one of the NFL's best backs, LeSean McCoy's 2017 drop in production was concerning against a soft run-defense schedule with increased volume. If you remove blowout-game productivity versus the Chargers, Saints, and Patriots, McCoy managed 3.5 yards per carry and a 39% Success Rate in 13 games.

Division History: Season Wins & 2018 Projection

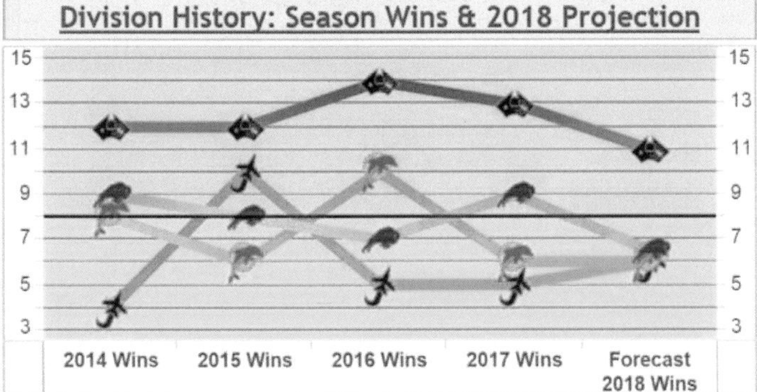

Rank of 2018 Defensive Pass Efficiency Faced by Week

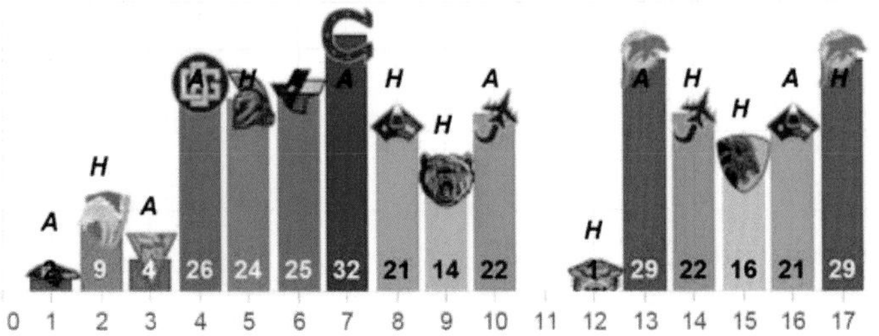

Rank of 2018 Defensive Rush Efficiency Faced by Week

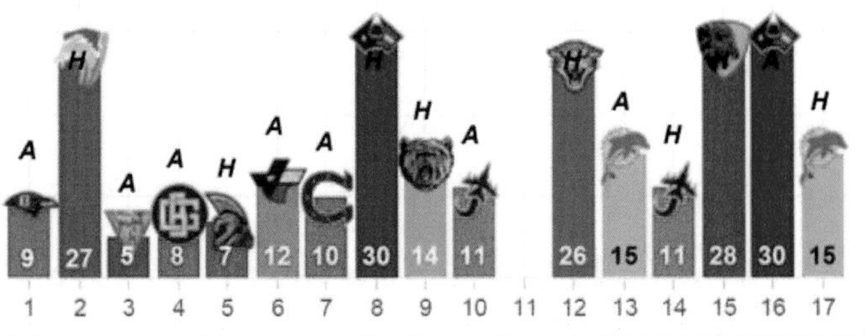

2017 Situational Usage by Player & Position

Usage Rate by Score

		Being Blown Out (14+)	Down Big (9-13)	One Score	Large Lead (9-13)	Blowout Lead (14+)	Grand Total
RUSH	LeSean McCoy	12%	27%	36%	49%	30%	34%
	Mike Tolbert	2%		8%	8%	22%	8%
	Deonte Thompson			0%			0%
	Travaris Cadet	4%	13%	2%	3%	4%	2%
	Patrick DiMarco	1%		0%			0%
	Marcus Murphy			0%	4%	7%	1%
	Kaelin Clay			0%			0%
	Total	18%	40%	47%	63%	63%	46%
PASS	LeSean McCoy	5%	7%	11%	1%		9%
	Mike Tolbert	4%		2%	4%		2%
	Charles Clay	6%	7%	9%	10%	11%	9%
	Zay Jones	12%	7%	8%	8%	11%	9%
	Deonte Thompson	21%	13%	4%	3%	4%	6%
	Nick O'Leary	9%	7%	4%	1%		4%
	Travaris Cadet	5%		1%			2%
	Jordan Matthews	6%	13%	4%	1%		4%
	Kelvin Benjamin	4%		3%	3%	4%	3%
	Andre Holmes	4%		3%	1%		3%
	Brandon Tate	5%		1%	1%	4%	2%
	Patrick DiMarco	2%	7%	1%	1%	4%	1%
	Marcus Murphy				3%		0%
	Kaelin Clay			1%			1%
	Taiwan Jones			0%			0%
	Total	82%	60%	53%	37%	37%	54%

Positional Target Distribution vs NFL Average

		NFL Wide				Team Only			
		Left	Middle	Right	**Total**	Left	Middle	Right	**Total**
Deep	WR	975	507	964	**2,446**	11	2	23	**36**
	TE	185	149	176	**510**	7	1	12	**20**
	RB	38	8	39	**85**	1	1	3	**5**
	All	**1,198**	**664**	**1,179**	**3,041**	**19**	**4**	**38**	**61**
Short	WR	2,822	1,653	2,740	**7,215**	40	18	50	**108**
	TE	830	816	1,129	**2,775**	33	23	41	**97**
	RB	1,272	782	1,260	**3,314**	49	41	35	**125**
	All	**4,924**	**3,251**	**5,129**	**13,304**	**122**	**82**	**126**	**330**
Total		**6,122**	**3,915**	**6,308**	**16,345**	**141**	**86**	**164**	**391**

Positional Success Rates vs NFL Average

		NFL Wide				Team Only			
		Left	Middle	Right	**Total**	Left	Middle	Right	**Total**
Deep	WR	37%	45%	38%	**39%**	45%	50%	30%	**36%**
	TE	38%	53%	44%	**45%**	43%	0%	58%	**50%**
	RB	34%	63%	38%	**39%**	100%	0%	33%	**40%**
	All	**37%**	**47%**	**39%**	**40%**	**47%**	**25%**	**39%**	**41%**
Short	WR	52%	57%	50%	**52%**	58%	67%	48%	**55%**
	TE	50%	56%	49%	**52%**	61%	61%	41%	**53%**
	RB	45%	51%	43%	**45%**	27%	56%	49%	**42%**
	All	**50%**	**55%**	**48%**	**50%**	**46%**	**60%**	**46%**	**49%**
Total		**47%**	**54%**	**46%**	**48%**	**46%**	**58%**	**45%**	**48%**

Successful Play Rate
0% 100%

Buffalo Bills - Success by Personnel Grouping & Play Type

Play Type	1-1 [3WR]	1-2 [2WR]	2-1 [2WR]	1-0 [4WR]	1-3 [1WR]	0-1 [4WR]	2-0 [3WR]	2-2 [1WR]	2-3 [0WR]	Grand Total
PASS	40% (368, 70%)	50% (92, 18%)	41% (44, 8%)		40% (5, 1%)	0% (2, 0%)		25% (12, 2%)		41% (523, 100%)
RUSH	46% (188, 39%)	34% (96, 20%)	44% (109, 22%)	100% (1, 0%)	20% (10, 2%)	0% (1, 0%)	0% (1, 0%)	42% (77, 16%)	50% (4, 1%)	42% (487, 100%)
TOTAL	42% (556, 55%)	42% (188, 19%)	43% (153, 15%)	100% (1, 0%)	27% (15, 1%)	0% (3, 0%)	0% (1, 0%)	39% (89, 9%)	50% (4, 0%)	42% (1,010, 100%)

Format Line 1: Success Rate Line 2: Total # of Plays, % of All Plays (by type)

BUF-5

Receiving Success by Personnel Grouping

Position	Player	1-1 [3WR]	1-2 [2WR]	2-1 [2WR]	1-3 [1WR]	0-1 [4WR]	2-2 [1WR]	Total
RB	LeSean McCoy	46% 5.8 93.7 (52)	41% 6.2 92.6 (17)	40% 5.4 74.6 (5)	0% 1.5 56.3 (2)		0% 9.0 104.2 (1)	43% 5.8 93.4 (77)
TE	Charles Clay	46% 5.1 63.4 (48)	68% 11.6 132.5 (19)	75% 21.0 118.8 (4)		0% 0.0 0.0 (1)	50% 4.0 60.4 (2)	53% 7.5 80.8 (74)
	Nick O'Leary	47% 8.1 105.8 (19)	88% 11.8 155.2 (8)	50% 9.5 83.3 (2)	100% 31.0 118.8 (1)		50% 12.5 95.8 (2)	59% 10.1 122.1 (32)
WR	Zay Jones	33% 4.1 54.9 (42)	38% 4.0 54.3 (21)	30% 6.1 52.5 (10)		0% 0.0 39.6 (1)		34% 4.3 53.7 (74)
	Jordan Matthews	50% 6.0 81.9 (32)	100% 22.3 158.3 (4)					56% 7.8 101.9 (36)
	Kelvin Benjamin	57% 7.3 100.1 (21)	67% 14.3 109.7 (3)	33% 6.7 57.6 (3)				56% 8.0 97.3 (27)

Format Line 1: Success Rate Line 2: YPA Line 3: Passer Rating Line 4: Total # of Plays

Successful Play Rate
0% 100%

Rushing Success by Personnel Grouping

Position	Player	1-1 [3WR]	1-2 [2WR]	2-1 [2WR]	1-3 [1WR]	0-1 [4WR]	2-0 [3WR]	2-2 [1WR]	2-3 [0WR]	Total
QB	Tyrod Taylor	53% 6.5 (57)	50% 5.8 (4)	80% 7.0 (5)	0% 3.0 (1)	0% 6.0 (1)		6% -0.8 (16)		44% 5.1 (84)
RB	LeSean McCoy	47% 5.0 (87)	37% 2.8 (65)	39% 3.7 (79)	25% 2.3 (8)			53% 4.9 (45)	33% -0.3 (3)	43% 4.0 (287)
	Mike Tolbert	14% 3.0 (14)	32% 3.6 (22)	59% 5.9 (17)	0% -2.0 (1)		0% 1.0 (1)	55% 2.4 (11)		38% 3.7 (66)

Format Line 1: Success Rate Line 2: YPC Line 3: Total # of Plays

2018 Coaches

Head Coach:
Ron Rivera (7th yr)

Offensive Coordinator:
Norv Turner (MIN OC) (1st yr)

Defensive Coordinator:
Eric Washington (CAR DL) (1st yr)

Carolina Panthers

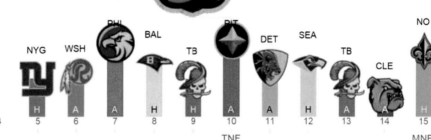

2018 Forecast

Wins	Div Rank
9	#3

Past Records

2017: 11-5
2016: 6-10
2015: 15-1

EASY HARD

Week	1	2	3	4	5	6	7	8	9	10	11	12	13	14	15	16	17
Opponent	DAL	ATL	CIN		NYG	WSH	PHI	BAL	TB	PIT	DET	SEA	TB	CLE	NO	ATL	NO
Site	H	A	H		H	A	A	H	H	A	A	H	A	A	H	H	A
										TNF					MNF		

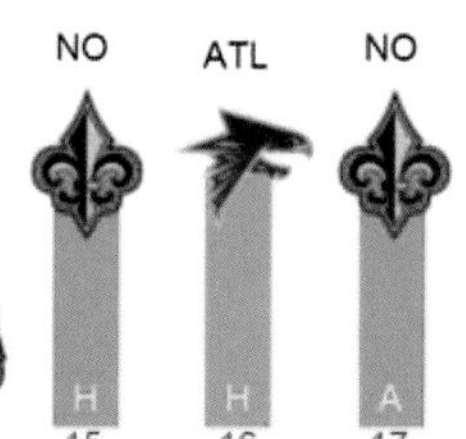

Key Players Lost

TXN	Player (POS)
Cut	Coleman, Kurt S
	Johnson, Charles DE
	Stewart, Jonathan RB
	Theus, John T
	Williams, Teddy CB
Declared Free Agent	Anderson, Derek QB
	Bersin, Brenton WR
	Byrd, Jairus S
	Clay, Kaelin WR
	Dickson, Ed TE
	France, Dan T
	Gachkar, Andrew LB
	Gunter, LaDarius CB
	Johnson, Charles WR
	Lotulelei, Star DT
	Norwell, Andrew G
	Silatolu, Amini T
	Simonson, Scott TE
	Yankey, David G

Average Line	# Games Favored	# Games Underdog
-0.6	9	6

2018 Carolina Panthers Overview

I projected Cam Newton for 2017 improvement primarily because of Carolina's soft schedule. The 2016 Panthers faced the NFL's sixth-toughest pass-defense slate. Entering 2017, I projected Carolina's slate as third softest. At season's end, Newton's actual pass-defense SOS was eighth easiest. And Newton was more productive as a result. But the Panthers need even more from him in 2018.

Newton's 2017 increase in completion rate can be attributed to more short passes to Christian McCaffrey, who led all NFL running backs in targets. But Cam also increased his rate of explosive completions (20-plus-yard gains) to 9.6%. The Panthers' approach was less risky with fewer Air Yards, but their performance more efficient. Their Success Rate on early-down passes jumped from 43% to 48%.

Last year, I suggested Cam embrace a "live to fight another day" mentality after interceptions. In 2016, Newton threw 64% of his INTs on early downs, with over 33% on early downs with less than ten yards to go. I attributed some of that poor decision making to playing behind the NFL's fifth-most injured offensive line, which ranked 19th in pass protection. The Panthers made offensive line changes entering 2017 and played a much softer pass-rush schedule. I predicted they would face the NFL's ninth-easiest pass-rush schedule and they wound up facing the third softest.

On early downs, Cam's "live to fight another day" mentality improved. After throwing over a third of his 2016 interceptions on early downs with less than ten yards to go, Newton threw just one interception in these situations in 2017. Only 25% of Cam's picks came on early downs, dramatically improving on his prior-year 64% rate. But when the "another day" came on third-down plays, Newton lost his composure. He threw 12 interceptions on third down, accounting for 75% of his picks.

Up by seven points against the Eagles in the second quarter of Week 6, Newton threw an INT on his own 14-yard line on third-and-five. In the third quarter with the score tied, Cam threw another interception on his own 18-yard line on third-and-12.

(cont'd - see CAR2)

Key Free Agents/ Trades Added

Anderson, C.J. RB
Banner, Zach T
Cockrell, Ross CB
Heinicke, Taylor QB
Hood, Elijah RB
Poe, Dontari DT
Searcy, Da'Norris S
Sirles, Jeremiah G
Smith, Torrey WR
Wright, Jarius WR

Drafted Players

Rd	Pk	Player (College)
1	24	WR - D. J. Moore (Maryland)
2	55	CB - Donte Jackson (LSU)
3	85	CB - Rashaan Gaulden (Tennessee)
4	101	TE - Ian Thomas (Indiana)
4*	136	DE - Marquis Haynes (Ole Miss)
5	161	LB - Jermaine Carter Jr. (Maryland)
7	234	ILB - Andre Smith (North Carolina)
	242	DT - Kendrick Norton (Miami (FL))

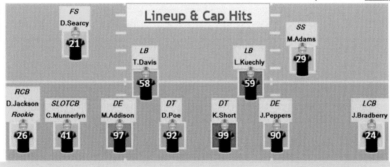

Regular Season Wins: Past & Current Proj

	Wins
Forecast 2018 Wins	9
2017 Wins	11
Forecast 2017 Wins	10.5
2016 Wins	6
2015 Wins	15
2014 Wins	7

1 3 5 7 9 11 13 15

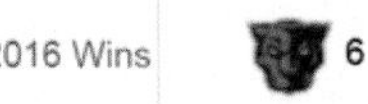

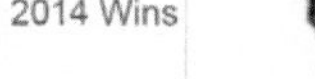
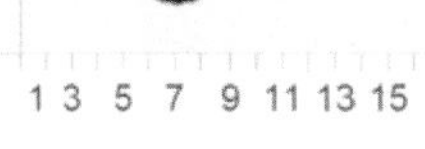

Lineup & Cap Hits

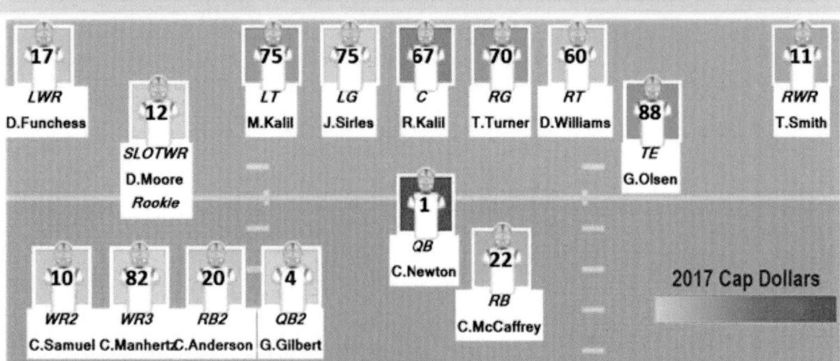

2018 Unit Spending

Positional Spending

	Rank	Total	2017 Rk
All OFF	18	$91.27M	7
QB	13	$23.24M	8
OL	17	$34.75M	17
RB	10	$9.22M	5
WR	31	$13.78M	29
TE	14	$10.28M	2
All DEF	8	$91.70M	15
DL	5	$46.39M	9
LB	10	$25.45M	9
CB	24	$11.76M	31
S	26	$8.11M	22

Carolina Panthers 2017 Success Rate Radar

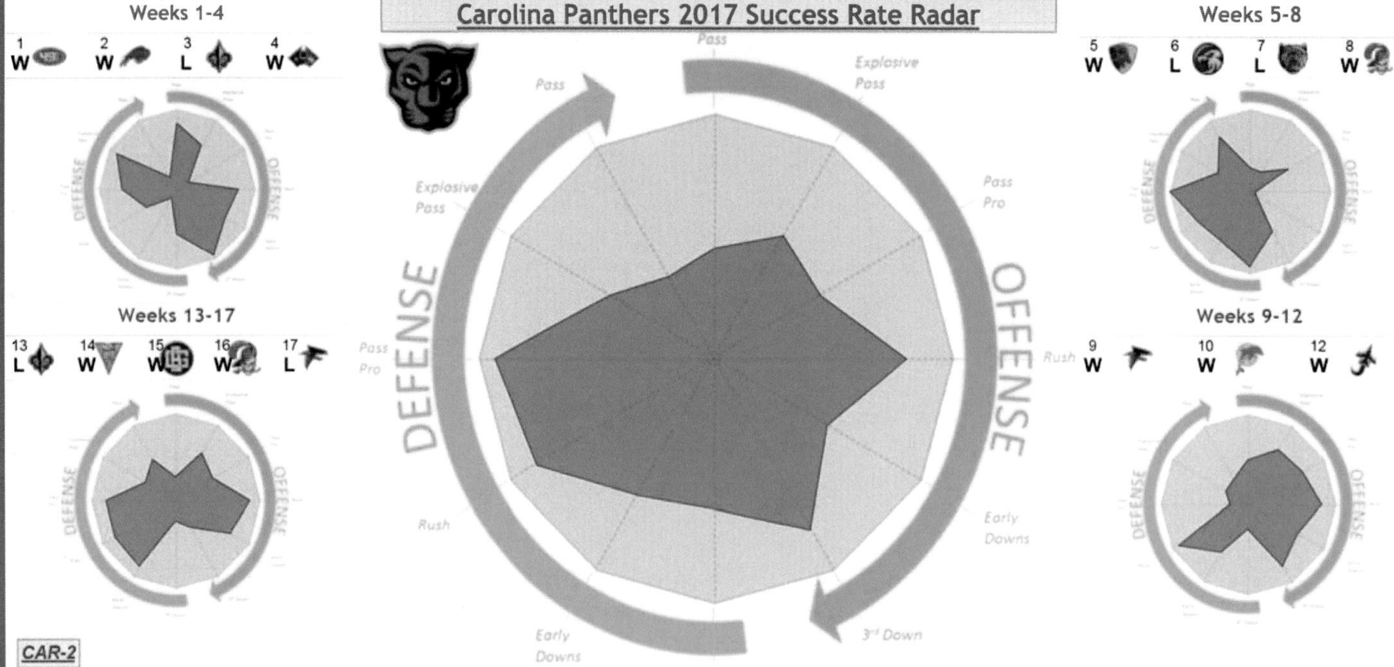

CAR-2

These picks gave Philadelphia starting field position inside the Panthers' 20-yard line, and the Eagles scored touchdowns on both drives. In the fourth quarter of that same game, Newton was picked off at the Eagles' 41-yard line on third-and-ten. The Panthers lost to the Super Bowl champions by only five points.

Facing the Bears the very next week, Newton threw a second-quarter interception on third-and-ten with the Panthers in field-goal range and trailing by seven points. That pick was returned 76 yards to the house. In the fourth quarter on Carolina's 36-yard line, Newton got picked off on third-and-ten. The Panthers lost by 14 despite Chicago's offense scoring just three points.

In Week 17 against Atlanta, Newton threw three interceptions in a 12-point loss. All three picks came in the second half. The first occurred with Carolina trailing by three points on second-and-seven at the Panthers' 27-yard line, leading to a Falcons field goal.

The second came with Carolina down by nine on first-and-ten at the Panthers' 25, yielding another Atlanta field goal. The third came on third-and-goal at the Falcons' 19-yard line with Carolina down by 12. Despite reducing his early-down turnovers, Cam's interception rate was far worse than 2016 thanks to those back-breaking interceptions.

If you own last year's Football Preview, you'll see the Panthers' "Critical and Game Deciding Stats" look similar from 2016 to 2017. Turnover margin was within one, sack margin within three, and penalty margin within three. But the Panthers improved their record in one-score games from 2-6 to 8-1. In games decided by a field goal or less, Carolina went 4-0. The swing did not result from being better in Critical and Game Deciding Stats. On top of basic variance, the Panthers' improvements in efficiency helped produce their 11-win campaign. Last year's Panthers suffered only five truly negative performances in Early-Down Success Rate and lost only two of the five.

(cont'd - see CAR-3)

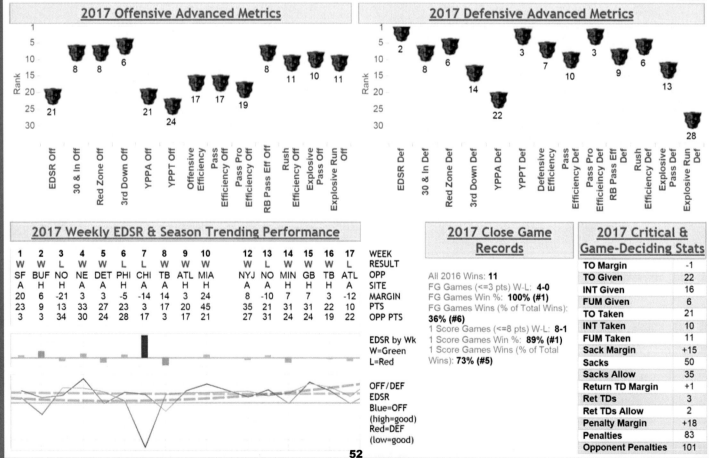

2017 Offensive Advanced Metrics

Metric	Rank
EDSR Off	21
30 & In Off	8
Red Zone Off	8
3rd Down Off	6
YPPA Off	21
YPPT Off	24
Offensive Efficiency	17
Pass Efficiency Off	17
Pass Pro Efficiency Off	19
RB Pass Eff Off	8
Rush Efficiency Off	11
Explosive Pass Off	10
Explosive Run Off	11

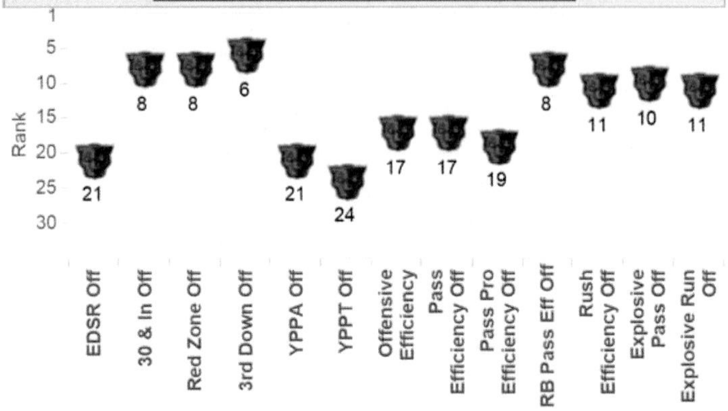

2017 Defensive Advanced Metrics

Metric	Rank
EDSR Def	2
30 & In Def	8
Red Zone Def	6
3rd Down Def	14
YPPA Def	22
YPPT Def	3
Defensive Efficiency	7
Pass Efficiency Def	10
Pass Pro Efficieincy Def	3
RB Pass Eff Def	9
Rush Efficiency Def	6
Explosive Pass Def	13
Explosive Run Def	28

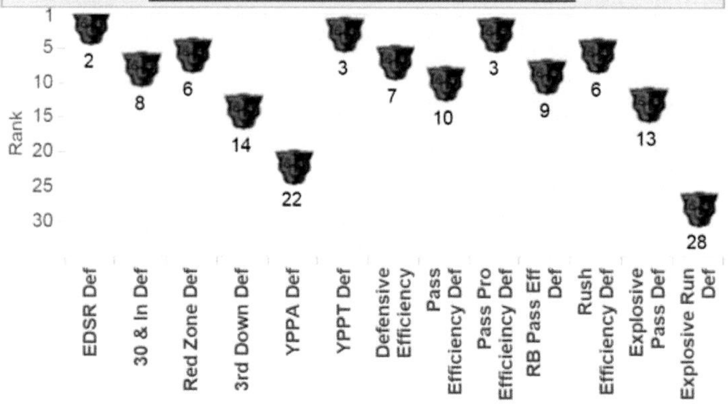

2017 Weekly EDSR & Season Trending Performance

1	2	3	4	5	6	7	8	9	10		12	13	14	15	16	17	WEEK
W	W	L	W	W	L	L	W	W	W		W	L	W	W	W	L	RESULT
SF	BUF	NO	NE	DET	PHI	CHI	TB	ATL	MIA		NYJ	NO	MIN	GB	TB	ATL	OPP
A	H	H	A	A	H	A	A	H	H		A	A	H	H	H	A	SITE
20	6	-21	3	3	-5	-14	14	3	24		8	-10	7	7	3	-12	MARGIN
23	9	13	33	27	23	3	17	20	45		35	21	31	31	22	10	PTS
3	3	34	30	24	28	17	3	17	21		27	31	24	24	19	22	OPP PTS

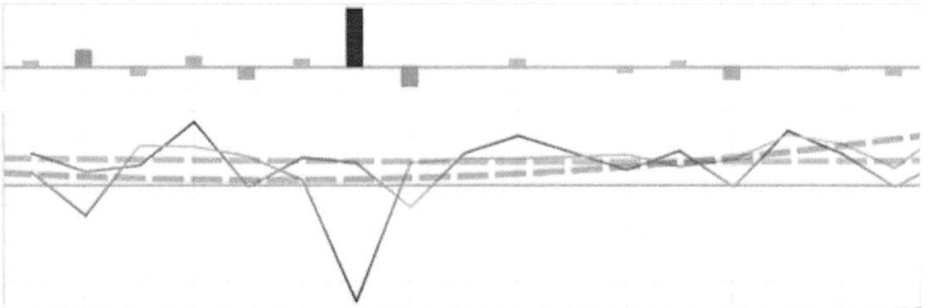

EDSR by Wk
W=Green
L=Red

OFF/DEF EDSR
Blue=OFF (high=good)
Red=DEF (low=good)

2017 Close Game Records

All 2016 Wins: **11**
FG Games (<=3 pts) W-L: **4-0**
FG Games Win %: **100% (#1)**
FG Games Wins (% of Total Wins): **36% (#6)**
1 Score Games (<=8 pts) W-L: **8-1**
1 Score Games Win %: **89% (#1)**
1 Score Games Wins (% of Total Wins): **73% (#5)**

2017 Critical & Game-Deciding Stats

TO Margin	-1
TO Given	22
INT Given	16
FUM Given	6
TO Taken	21
INT Taken	10
FUM Taken	11
Sack Margin	+15
Sacks	50
Sacks Allow	35
Return TD Margin	+1
Ret TDs	3
Ret TDs Allow	2
Penalty Margin	+18
Penalties	83
Opponent Penalties	101

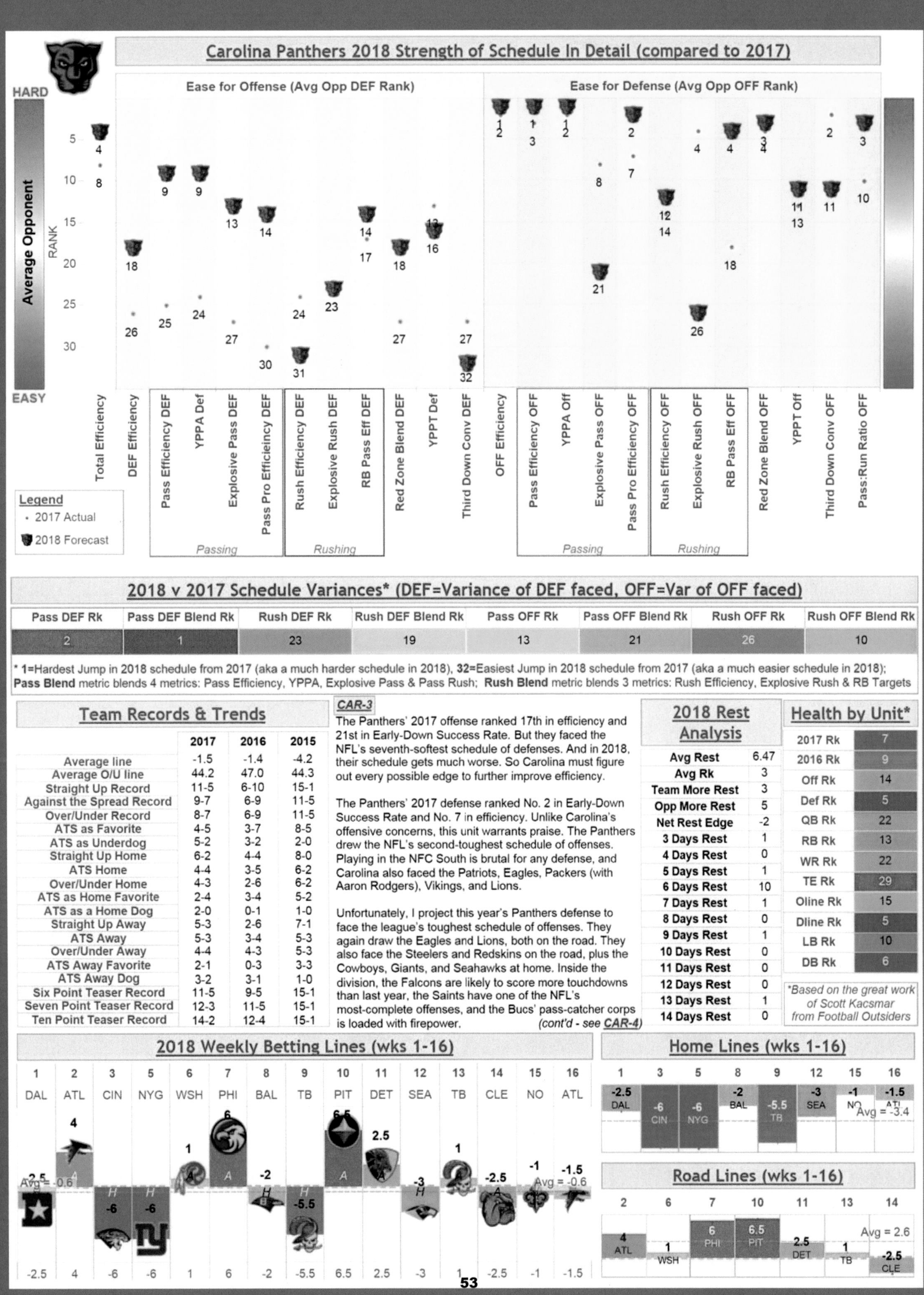

Carolina Panthers 2018 Strength of Schedule In Detail (compared to 2017)

2018 v 2017 Schedule Variances* (DEF=Variance of DEF faced, OFF=Var of OFF faced)

Pass DEF Rk	Pass DEF Blend Rk	Rush DEF Rk	Rush DEF Blend Rk	Pass OFF Rk	Pass OFF Blend Rk	Rush OFF Rk	Rush OFF Blend Rk
2	1	23	19	13	21	26	10

* **1**=Hardest Jump in 2018 schedule from 2017 (aka a much harder schedule in 2018), **32**=Easiest Jump in 2018 schedule from 2017 (aka a much easier schedule in 2018); **Pass Blend** metric blends 4 metrics: Pass Efficiency, YPPA, Explosive Pass & Pass Rush; **Rush Blend** metric blends 3 metrics: Rush Efficiency, Explosive Rush & RB Targets

Team Records & Trends

	2017	2016	2015
Average line	-1.5	-1.4	-4.2
Average O/U line	44.2	47.0	44.3
Straight Up Record	11-5	6-10	15-1
Against the Spread Record	9-7	6-9	11-5
Over/Under Record	8-7	6-9	11-5
ATS as Favorite	4-5	3-7	8-5
ATS as Underdog	5-2	3-2	2-0
Straight Up Home	6-2	4-4	8-0
ATS Home	4-4	3-5	6-2
Over/Under Home	4-3	2-6	6-2
ATS as Home Favorite	2-4	3-4	5-2
ATS as a Home Dog	2-0	0-1	1-0
Straight Up Away	5-3	2-6	7-1
ATS Away	5-3	3-4	5-3
Over/Under Away	4-4	4-3	5-3
ATS Away Favorite	2-1	0-3	3-3
ATS Away Dog	3-2	3-1	1-0
Six Point Teaser Record	11-5	9-5	15-1
Seven Point Teaser Record	12-3	11-5	15-1
Ten Point Teaser Record	14-2	12-4	15-1

CAR-3

The Panthers' 2017 offense ranked 17th in efficiency and 21st in Early-Down Success Rate. But they faced the NFL's seventh-softest schedule of defenses. And in 2018, their schedule gets much worse. So Carolina must figure out every possible edge to further improve efficiency.

The Panthers' 2017 defense ranked No. 2 in Early-Down Success Rate and No. 7 in efficiency. Unlike Carolina's offensive concerns, this unit warrants praise. The Panthers drew the NFL's second-toughest schedule of offenses. Playing in the NFC South is brutal for any defense, and Carolina also faced the Patriots, Eagles, Packers (with Aaron Rodgers), Vikings, and Lions.

Unfortunately, I project this year's Panthers defense to face the league's toughest schedule of offenses. They again draw the Eagles and Lions, both on the road. They also face the Steelers and Redskins on the road, plus the Cowboys, Giants, and Seahawks at home. Inside the division, the Falcons are likely to score more touchdowns than last year, the Saints have one of the NFL's most-complete offenses, and the Bucs' pass-catcher corps is loaded with firepower. *(cont'd - see CAR-4)*

2018 Rest Analysis

Avg Rest	6.47
Avg Rk	3
Team More Rest	3
Opp More Rest	5
Net Rest Edge	-2
3 Days Rest	1
4 Days Rest	0
5 Days Rest	1
6 Days Rest	10
7 Days Rest	1
8 Days Rest	0
9 Days Rest	1
10 Days Rest	0
11 Days Rest	0
12 Days Rest	0
13 Days Rest	1
14 Days Rest	0

Health by Unit*

2017 Rk	7
2016 Rk	9
Off Rk	14
Def Rk	5
QB Rk	22
RB Rk	13
WR Rk	22
TE Rk	29
Oline Rk	15
Dline Rk	5
LB Rk	10
DB Rk	6

**Based on the great work of Scott Kacsmar from Football Outsiders*

2018 Weekly Betting Lines (wks 1-16)

1	2	3	5	6	7	8	9	10	11	12	13	14	15	16
DAL	ATL	CIN	NYG	WSH	PHI	BAL	TB	PIT	DET	SEA	TB	CLE	NO	ATL
-2.5	4	-6	-6	1	6	-2	-5.5	6.5	2.5	-3	1	-2.5	-1	-1.5

Avg = -0.6

Home Lines (wks 1-16)

1	3	5	8	9	12	15	16
DAL	CIN	NYG	BAL	TB	SEA	NO	ATL
-2.5	-6	-6	-2	-5.5	-3	-1	-1.5

Avg = -3.4

Road Lines (wks 1-16)

2	6	7	10	11	13	14
ATL	WSH	PHI	PIT	DET	TB	CLE
4	1	6	6.5	2.5	1	-2.5

Avg = 2.6

Carolina Panthers 2017 Play Analysis

2017 Play Tendencies

All Pass %	52%
All Pass Rk	29
All Rush %	48%
All Rush Rk	4
1 Score Pass %	53%
1 Score Pass Rk	27
2016 1 Score Pass %	56%
2016 1 Score Pass Rk	24
2017 Pass Increase %	-3%
Pass Increase Rk	21
1 Score Rush %	47%
1 Score Rush Rk	6
Up Pass %	47%
Up Pass Rk	21
Up Rush %	53%
Up Rush Rk	12
Down Pass %	59%
Down Pass Rk	32
Down Rush %	41%
Down Rush Rk	1

2017 Down & Distance Tendencies

Down	Distance	Total Plays	Pass Rate	Run Rate	Play Success %
1	Short (1-3)	4	25%	75%	25%
	Med (4-7)	12	33%	67%	58%
	Long (8-10)	343	46%	54%	48%
	XL (11+)	10	50%	50%	30%
2	Short (1-3)	38	21%	79%	66%
	Med (4-7)	80	45%	55%	43%
	Long (8-10)	103	52%	48%	40%
	XL (11+)	44	73%	27%	34%
3	Short (1-3)	49	53%	47%	63%
	Med (4-7)	53	81%	19%	45%
	Long (8-10)	39	92%	8%	33%
	XL (11+)	34	94%	6%	24%
4	Short (1-3)	5	20%	80%	80%
	Med (4-7)	1	100%	0%	0%
	XL (11+)	1	100%	0%	0%

Shotgun %:

Under Center	Shotgun
28%	72%
37%	*63%*

37% AVG 63%

Run Rate:

Under Center	Shotgun
78%	26%

68% AVG 23%

Pass Rate:

Under Center	Shotgun
22%	74%

32% AVG 77%

Short Yardage Intelligence:

2nd and Short Run

Run Freq	Run Rk	NFL Run Freq Avg	Run 1D Rate	Run NFL 1D Avg
81%	3	67%	68%	69%

2nd and Short Pass

Pass Freq	Pass Rk	NFL Pass Freq Avg	Pass 1D Rate	Pass NFL 1D Avg
19%	30	33%	63%	53%

Most Frequent Play

Down	Distance	Play Type	Player	Total Plays	Play Success %
1	Short (1-3)	RUSH	Jonathan Stewart	2	0%
	Med (4-7)	RUSH	Christian McCaffrey	3	100%
			Cam Newton	3	0%
	Long (8-10)	RUSH	Jonathan Stewart	89	38%
	XL (11+)	PASS	Christian McCaffrey	3	33%
2	Short (1-3)	RUSH	Jonathan Stewart	16	69%
	Med (4-7)	RUSH	Jonathan Stewart	20	35%
	Long (8-10)	RUSH	Cam Newton	17	59%
	XL (11+)	PASS	Devin Funchess	11	64%
3	Short (1-3)	RUSH	Jonathan Stewart	10	60%
			Cam Newton	10	90%
	Med (4-7)	PASS	Devin Funchess	13	54%
	Long (8-10)	PASS	Devin Funchess	12	33%
	XL (11+)	PASS	Christian McCaffrey	7	43%

Most Successful Play*

Down	Distance	Play Type	Player	Total Plays	Play Success %
1	Long (8-10)	PASS	Christian McCaffrey	37	62%
2	Short (1-3)	RUSH	Christian McCaffrey	7	71%
	Med (4-7)	PASS	Christian McCaffrey	6	67%
	Long (8-10)	PASS	Kelvin Benjamin	5	80%
	XL (11+)	PASS	Devin Funchess	11	64%
3	Short (1-3)	RUSH	Cam Newton	10	90%
	Med (4-7)	RUSH	Cam Newton	10	80%
	Long (8-10)	PASS	Devin Funchess	12	33%
	XL (11+)	PASS	Christian McCaffrey	7	43%

**Minimum 5 plays to qualify*

2017 Snap Rates

Wk	Opp	Score	Ed Dickson	Devin Funchess	Christian McCaffrey	Russell Shepard	Jonathan Stewart	Kelvin Benjamin	Greg Olsen	Chris Manhertz
1	SF	W 23-3	40 (60%)	45 (67%)	47 (70%)	20 (30%)	29 (43%)	43 (64%)	67 (100%)	12 (18%)
2	BUF	W 9-3	56 (81%)	57 (83%)	44 (64%)	33 (48%)	26 (38%)	44 (64%)	25 (36%)	14 (20%)
3	NO	L 34-13	59 (100%)	50 (85%)	41 (69%)	38 (64%)	26 (44%)	7 (12%)		15 (25%)
4	NE	W 33-30	62 (98%)	58 (92%)	48 (76%)	35 (56%)	28 (44%)	57 (90%)		15 (24%)
5	DET	W 27-24	66 (100%)	41 (62%)	37 (56%)	38 (58%)	40 (61%)	50 (76%)		29 (44%)
6	PHI	L 28-23	82 (100%)	69 (84%)	61 (74%)	52 (63%)	27 (33%)	67 (82%)		20 (24%)
7	CHI	L 17-3	72 (100%)	56 (78%)	53 (74%)	37 (51%)	28 (39%)	61 (85%)		27 (38%)
8	TB	W 17-3	65 (100%)	43 (66%)	38 (58%)	30 (46%)	28 (43%)	47 (72%)		26 (40%)
9	ATL	W 20-17	64 (98%)	48 (74%)	53 (82%)	38 (58%)	21 (32%)			5 (8%)
10	MIA	W 45-21	73 (95%)	59 (77%)	45 (58%)	44 (57%)	25 (32%)			27 (35%)
12	NYJ	W 35-27	63 (88%)	60 (83%)	50 (69%)	30 (42%)	27 (38%)		24 (33%)	29 (40%)
13	NO	L 31-21	56 (98%)	47 (82%)	40 (70%)	32 (56%)	22 (39%)			20 (35%)
14	MIN	W 31-24	33 (52%)	45 (70%)	43 (67%)	23 (36%)	26 (41%)		59 (92%)	20 (31%)
15	GB	W 31-24	34 (45%)	64 (85%)	53 (71%)	23 (31%)	30 (40%)		73 (97%)	15 (20%)
16	TB	W 22-19	22 (33%)	58 (88%)	53 (80%)		25 (38%)		62 (94%)	7 (11%)
17	ATL	L 22-10	29 (48%)	53 (87%)	52 (85%)	8 (13%)			57 (93%)	8 (13%)
Grand Total			876 (81%)	853 (79%)	758 (70%)	481 (47%)	408 (40%)	376 (68%)	367 (78%)	289 (27%)

Personnel Groupings

Personnel	Team %	NFL Avg	Succ. %
1-1 [3WR]	47%	59%	45%
1-2 [2WR]	22%	19%	49%
2-1 [2WR]	13%	7%	40%
1-3 [1WR]	10%	5%	45%
2-2 [1WR]	5%	4%	50%

Grouping Tendencies

Personnel	Pass Rate	Pass Succ. %	Run Succ. %
1-1 [3WR]	66%	44%	46%
1-2 [2WR]	50%	50%	48%
2-1 [2WR]	53%	36%	43%
1-3 [1WR]	9%	44%	45%
2-2 [1WR]	21%	18%	59%

Red Zone Targets (min 3)

Receiver	All	Inside 5	6-10	11-20
Devin Funchess	16	1	4	11
Christian McCaffrey	13	4	4	5
Greg Olsen	9		4	5
Kelvin Benjamin	6	2	1	3
Ed Dickson	5	1	1	3
Russell Shepard	4		1	3
Brenton Bersin	2		1	1
Jonathan Stewart	1		1	

Red Zone Rushes (min 3)

Rusher	All	Inside 5	6-10	11-20
Jonathan Stewart	33	16	5	12
Cam Newton	28	5	8	15
Christian McCaffrey	16	2	3	11
Cameron Artis-Payne	7	2		5

Early Down Target Rate

	RB	TE	WR
Team	28%	20%	52%
NFL AVG	*23%*	*21%*	*56%*

Overall Target Success %

RB	TE	WR
50% #9	47% #22	47% #20

Carolina Panthers 2017 Passing Recap & 2018 Outlook

I've called Cam Newton a "frontrunner" before, and that remained the case in 2017. When Cam starts hot and gets rolling early, we see his fun-loving nature. He'll run over you, laugh, then throw a 45-yard touchdown pass on the next play. But when pressure gets to him or he throws an early pick, Newton tends to get too down on himself, and it's hard to right the ship. Although the Panthers have historically been a run-first team that tries to punch the ball down opponents' throats and plays great defense, they need to figure out more optimal ways to build leads. They can resume run-heavy offense after gaining those leads. But it's a first-half race to a lead, and Carolina's most-efficient means is for Newton to pass early and more often than he has in the past. Early-down passes followed by later-down runs will be optimal for the Panthers. Carolina is one of the NFL's best third-and-short running teams. But over the past two years, they went 55% pass on third and 1-3 yards to go despite converting third-and-short run plays at the NFL's seventh-highest Success Rate (73%) and third-and-short passes at the league's second-worst clip (38%).

Cam Newton Rating All Downs

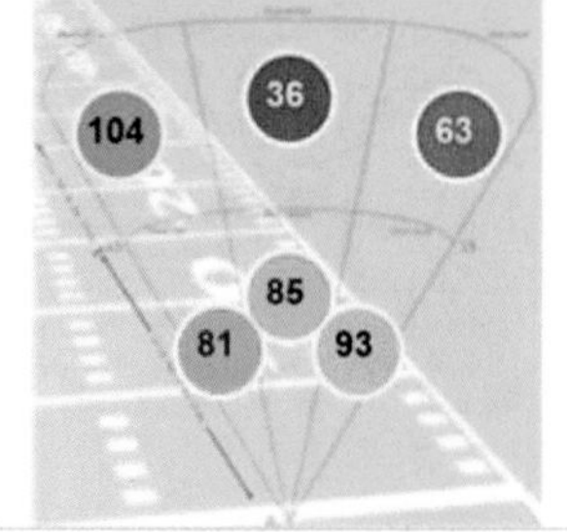

Cam Newton Rating Early Downs

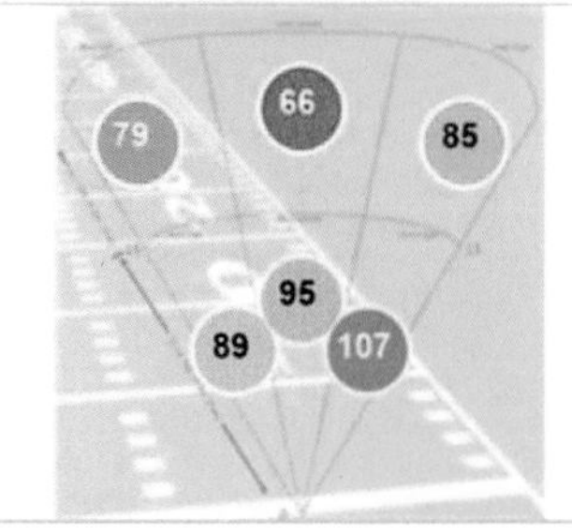

2017 Standard Passing Table

QB	Comp	Att	Comp %	Yds	YPA	TDs	INT	Sacks	Rating	Rk
Cam Newton	315	533	59%	3,643	6.8	24	16	38	82	30
NFL Avg			62%		7.0				87.5	

2017 Advanced Passing Table

QB	Success %	EDSR Passing Success %	20+ Yd Pass Gains	20+ Yd Pass %	30+ Yd Pass Gains	30+ Yd Pass %	Avg. Air Yds per Comp	Avg. YAC per Comp	20+ Air Yd Comp	20+ Air Yd %
Cam Newton	44%	48%	51	9.6%	15	2.8%	5.7	5.1	17	5%
NFL Avg	44%	48%	27.7	8.8%	10.3	3.3%	6.0	4.7	11.7	6%

Interception Rates by Down

Yards to Go	1	2	3	4	Total
1 & 2	0.0%	0.0%	0.0%	0.0%	0.0%
3, 4, 5	0.0%	0.0%	8.7%	0.0%	5.9%
6 - 9	0.0%	1.5%	4.0%	0.0%	2.5%
10 - 14	1.5%	0.0%	8.9%	0.0%	2.2%
15+	0.0%	0.0%	10.5%	0.0%	5.1%
Total	1.4%	0.6%	6.7%	0.0%	2.8%

3rd Down Passing - Short of Sticks Analysis

QB	Avg. Yds to Go	Avg. YIA (of Comp)	Avg Yds Short	Short of Sticks Rate	Short Rk
Cam Newton	7.9	7.0	-0.9	60%	19
NFL Avg	7.8	6.7	-1.1	60%	

Air Yds vs YAC

Air Yds %	YAC %	Rk
54%	46%	30
58%	42%	

2017 Receiving Recap & 2018 Outlook

The Panthers have reason for pass-catcher optimism after being ravaged by injuries in 2017. They traded Kelvin Benjamin to Buffalo midyear and lost Greg Olsen for nine games. Olsen replacement Ed Dickson was terrible in the red zone and delivered an abysmal 75 passer rating when targeted within 15 yards of the line of scrimmage. With Olsen healthy and a wideout tandem of Devin Funchess and first-round pick D.J. Moore, the Panthers should have a more stable corps for 12 and 21 personnel. Add McCaffrey, and this can be one of the NFL's most-diverse passing attacks.

Player *Min 50 Targets*	Targets	Comp %	YPA	Rating	TOARS	Success %	Success Rk	Missed YPA Rk	YAS % Rk	TDs
Christian McCaffrey	121	71%	6.2	93	5.0	52%	46	60	97	6
Devin Funchess	120	56%	7.7	89	4.9	49%	69	98	60	8
Kelvin Benjamin	80	61%	8.8	92	4.4	57%	17	21	66	3
Greg Olsen	50	50%	6.0	74	3.3	42%	105	111	43	2

Directional Passer Rating Delivered

Receiver	Short Left	Short Middle	Short Right	Deep Left	Deep Middle	Deep Right	Player Total
Christian McCaffrey	101	75	96	119		40	93
Devin Funchess	106	99	74	53	93	103	89
Kelvin Benjamin	61	100	85	106	119	82	90
Ed Dickson	74	77	74	104	104	89	89
Greg Olsen	64	82	102	40	14	92	74
Russell Shepard	52	110	63	135	40	0	64
Curtis Samuel	66	104	85	40	40	62	69
Jonathan Stewart	0		124				55
Fozzy Whittaker	140		92				139
Team Total	83	89	88	101	69	70	85

2017 Rushing Recap & 2017 Outlook

Whereas NFL Twitter was shocked the Broncos cut C.J. Anderson, I wasn't all that surprised. Anderson's fantasy upside may improve in Carolina, but his productivity in Denver was far from stellar. The 2017 Broncos faced the NFL's easiest run-defense schedule over the last two years, yet Anderson ranked fourth worst in Success Rate (41%) among 27 running backs to log 275-plus carries. He was 20th or worst in Missed YPA and YAS%. Anderson averaged just 3.4 yards per carry on first-down runs, the worst rate on the Broncos. Denver's poor line and quarterback play were certainly partly to blame, but Anderson's history of inefficiency furthers my belief Carolina must pass more on early downs rather than hand the ball off to their backs.

Player *Min 50 Rushes*	Rushes	YPC	Success %	Success Rk	Missed YPA Rk	YTS % Rk	YAS % Rk	Early Down Success %	Early Down Success Rk	TDs
Jonathan Stewart	209	3.5	43%	46	35	36	41	41%	53	6
Christian McCaffrey	123	3.7	44%	38	36	11	66	43%	43	2

Yards per Carry by Direction

Directional Run Frequency

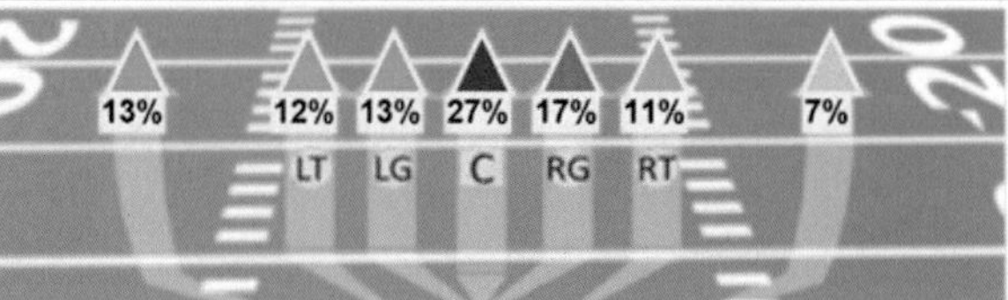

CAR-4

Starting hot has long been critical to Cam's success. The 2015 Super Bowl Panthers went 14-0 in games they led at halftime. Last year's Panthers went 10-0 when leading at halftime. Over the last five years, Carolina is 45-8 with a halftime lead but just 9-24-1 when tied or losing at the half. Newton's 85%-win rate when leading at the half is far above league average (77%).

When the Panthers are trailing at halftime, they still come back to win 35% of the time when Cam exceeds 30 pass attempts. But when Newton is limited to 30 or fewer throws and Carolina trails at halftime, the Panthers' win rate plummets to 10%. Most quarterbacks – including Tom Brady – have worse records when they are forced to throw more. But this involves a large element of causation. Teams pass more when losing, especially in the second half.

One way to maximize efficiency is to get Newton to pass more on early downs, and earlier in games. Excluding the fourth quarter last year, the Panthers ran at the NFL's fifth-highest clip on early downs (53%). On first down, Carolina ran at league-average frequency (54%) but had a higher first-down passing Success Rate (50%) than rushing (46%). On first-down passes in the first half, Newton's Success Rate was 49%. But on first-and-ten passes to tight ends and running backs, Newton's 62% Success Rate ranked fourth best in the league. His first-and-ten throws to tight ends and backs averaged a crisp 7.2 yards per attempt.

(cont'd - see CAR-5)

Evan Silva's Fantasy Corner

Devin Funchess broke out as a third-year pro, logging WR19 (non-PPR) and WR21 (PPR) finishes, buoyed by Kelvin Benjamin's in-season trade and Greg Olsen's foot fracture, which cost Olsen nine games. In five games sans Benjamin and Olsen, Funchess averaged 7.8 targets for 81.0 yards with four TDs. In four games after Olsen returned, Funchess averaged 5.5 targets for 39.3 yards with two scores. Although Funchess has never created separation, Newton is one of the NFL's most-willing quarterbacks to throw into tight coverage. Funchess is above average in contested situations and running after the catch, and he commands red-zone targets at 6-foot-4, 232. Olsen's return and Carolina's first-round pick of Moore add risk, but Funchess offers TD upside and room for further growth in his contract year.

Division History: Season Wins & 2018 Projection

2014 Wins | 2015 Wins | 2016 Wins | 2017 Wins | Forecast 2018 Wins

Rank of 2018 Defensive Pass Efficiency Faced by Week

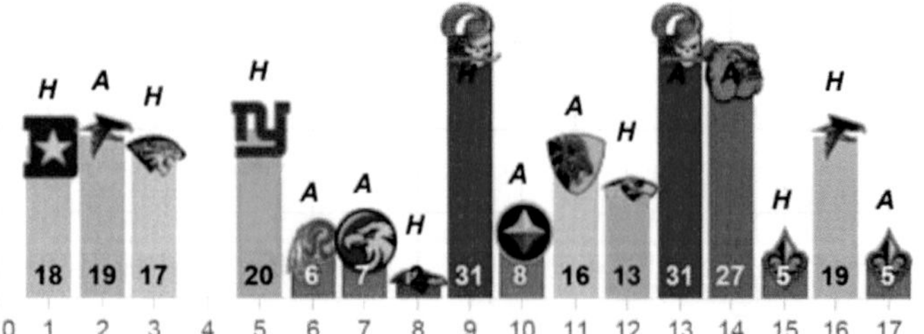

Rank of 2018 Defensive Rush Efficiency Faced by Week

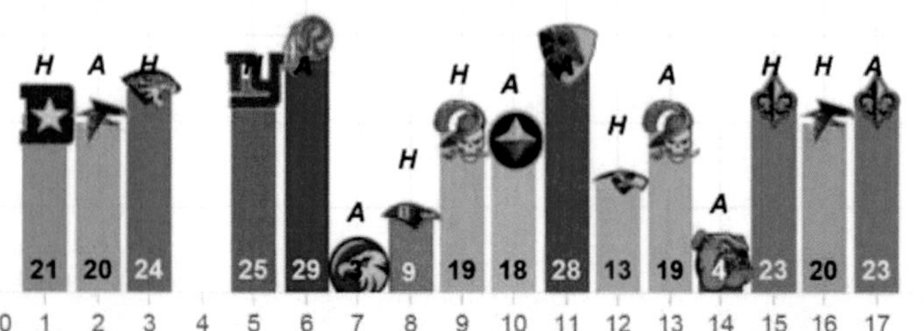

2017 Situational Usage by Player & Position

Usage Rate by Score

		Being Blown Out (14+)	Down Big (9-13)	One Score	Large Lead (9-13)	Blowout Lead (14+)	Grand Total
RUSH	Christian McCaffrey	9%	18%	14%	17%	14%	14%
	Jonathan Stewart	15%	15%	23%	30%	43%	23%
	Russell Shepard			0%			0%
	Curtis Samuel			1%			0%
	Kaelin Clay			0%			0%
	Cameron Artis-Payne			2%	2%	10%	2%
	Damiere Byrd			0%			0%
	Fozzy Whittaker	2%		1%			1%
	Total	26%	33%	41%	49%	67%	41%
PASS	Christian McCaffrey	21%	14%	13%	11%	10%	13%
	Jonathan Stewart	1%		2%	2%	2%	2%
	Devin Funchess	21%	15%	13%	11%	10%	13%
	Kelvin Benjamin	2%	2%	7%	2%		6%
	Ed Dickson	7%	8%	6%	6%		6%
	Greg Olsen		15%	6%	6%	2%	6%
	Russell Shepard	10%	5%	3%		6%	4%
	Curtis Samuel	5%	3%	2%	4%	3%	3%
	Kaelin Clay		2%	3%		2%	2%
	Cameron Artis-Payne			0%			0%
	Damiere Byrd	2%		2%	6%		2%
	Brenton Bersin	3%	5%	2%			2%
	Fozzy Whittaker			1%	2%		1%
	Chris Manhertz	1%		0%			0%
	Total	74%	67%	59%	51%	33%	59%

Positional Target Distribution vs NFL Average

		NFL Wide				Team Only			
		Left	Middle	Right	**Total**	Left	Middle	Right	**Total**
Deep	WR	955	500	961	**2,416**	31	9	26	**66**
	TE	185	142	179	**506**	7	8	9	**24**
	RB	38	9	40	**87**	1		2	**3**
	All	**1,178**	**651**	**1,180**	**3,009**	**39**	**17**	**37**	**93**
Short	WR	2,780	1,642	2,735	**7,157**	82	29	55	**166**
	TE	838	823	1,135	**2,796**	25	16	35	**76**
	RB	1,259	798	1,243	**3,300**	62	25	52	**139**
	All	**4,877**	**3,263**	**5,113**	**13,253**	**169**	**70**	**142**	**381**
Total		**6,055**	**3,914**	**6,293**	**16,262**	**208**	**87**	**179**	**474**

Positional Success Rates vs NFL Average

		NFL Wide				Team Only			
		Left	Middle	Right	**Total**	Left	Middle	Right	**Total**
Deep	WR	37%	45%	38%	**39%**	39%	44%	35%	**38%**
	TE	38%	53%	46%	**45%**	43%	50%	33%	**42%**
	RB	34%	56%	40%	**39%**	100%		0%	**33%**
	All	**37%**	**47%**	**39%**	**40%**	**41%**	**47%**	**32%**	**39%**
Short	WR	52%	57%	50%	**52%**	48%	66%	49%	**51%**
	TE	51%	56%	49%	**52%**	48%	63%	46%	**50%**
	RB	44%	51%	42%	**45%**	50%	44%	54%	**50%**
	All	**50%**	**56%**	**48%**	**50%**	**49%**	**57%**	**50%**	**51%**
Total		**47%**	**54%**	**46%**	**48%**	**47%**	**55%**	**46%**	**48%**

Successful Play Rate
0% 100%

Carolina Panthers - Success by Personnel Grouping & Play Type

Play Type	1-1 [3WR]	1-2 [2WR]	2-1 [2WR]	1-0 [4WR]	1-3 [1WR]	2-0 [3WR]	2-2 [1WR]	3-1 [1WR]	2-3 [0WR]	1-4 [0WR]	Grand Total
PASS	44% (323, 60%)	50% (115, 21%)	36% (69, 13%)	25% (4, 1%)	44% (9, 2%)	0% (1, 0%)	18% (11, 2%)		75% (4, 1%)		43% (536, 100%)
RUSH	46% (164, 33%)	48% (115, 23%)	43% (60, 12%)	100% (1, 0%)	45% (92, 19%)	100% (1, 0%)	59% (41, 8%)	0% (2, 0%)	50% (2, 0%)	58% (12, 2%)	47% (490, 100%)
TOTAL	45% (487, 47%)	49% (230, 22%)	40% (129, 13%)	40% (5, 0%)	45% (101, 10%)	50% (2, 0%)	50% (52, 5%)	0% (2, 0%)	67% (6, 1%)	58% (12, 1%)	45% (1,026, 100%)

Format Line 1: Success Rate Line 2: Total # of Plays, % of All Plays (by type)

CAR-5 The 2017 Panthers leaned on three personnel groupings when passing: 11, 12, and 21. On first down, 93% of their passes came from those three formations. It was 96% on second down and 97% on third. Carolina used 11 personnel on 50% of their passes on first and second down, but ratcheted that up to 73% on third down. Cam's efficiency decreases dramatically from first to third down. On first down in 12 personnel, Newton posted a 60% Success Rate and 7.3 yards per attempt. But on third down in 12, his Success Rate fell to 29% and 5.5 YPA. It was the second-worst third-down Success Rate in the league from 12 personnel. From 21 personnel on first down, Newton's Success Rate was 60% with 10.2 yards per attempt. But on third down, Cam managed a 14% Success Rate and 3.1 YPA. It was the NFL's worst third-down passing Success Rate in 21 personnel. The story was similar in 2016, especially in 11 personnel. Over the last two years, Newton has averaged a 54% Success Rate from 11 personnel on first down but a 41% Success Rate on third-down passes in 11. On early downs in the first half, the 2017 Panthers' strengths were passing to primary receivers Devin Funchess, Kelvin Benjamin, and Curtis Samuel from 11 personnel, and passing to tight ends Greg Olsen and Ed Dickson in 12 or 21. Newton's efficiency to tight ends in 11 was very bad (20%).

I've long banged the drum for early-down running back passes and was eager to see McCaffrey targeted on early downs. He was the Panthers' most-targeted player on first downs in the first half of games, and those targets delivered a sparkling 70% Success Rate. Non-first-down passes to McCaffrey in the first half managed a 53% Success Rate. On first-down plays in the second half, McCaffrey still delivered a 55% Success Rate when targeted. But non-first-down targets to McCaffrey in the second half plummeted to a 37% Success Rate. The Panthers must continue to use McCaffrey's first-down mismatch ability to increase Cam's early-down passing efficiency. But they cannot continue to funnel as much receiving volume to McCaffrey on later downs if it's going to be that unproductive. McCaffrey led the Panthers with 35 targets in the second half on later downs, which wound up being detrimental to the team. Coach Rivera said it doesn't matter how you get to the playoffs; just getting there gives you a Super Bowl chance. While not wrong, seven of the last ten Super Bowl winners had a first-round playoff bye and homefield advantage in conference championship games. The Panthers are at disadvantage due to their early bye (week 4). If Newton gets started fast in games and the Panthers build halftime leads, they will be difficult opponent in 2018.

Receiving Success by Personnel Grouping

Position	Player	1-1 [3WR]	1-2 [2WR]	2-1 [2WR]	1-0 [4WR]	1-3 [1WR]	2-2 [1WR]	2-3 [0WR]	Total
RB	Christian McCaffrey	57% 6.4 91.3 (68)	35% 4.3 38.0 (23)	41% 5.6 109.6 (17)	100% 19.0 118.8 (1)		0% 0.0 39.6 (2)	100% 1.5 118.8 (2)	50% 5.8 88.8 (113)
TE	Ed Dickson	47% 5.1 76.0 (19)	71% 9.8 118.2 (21)	33% 21.3 42.4 (3)		33% 4.7 49.3 (3)	0% 0.0 39.6 (1)	100% 57.0 118.8 (1)	56% 9.1 90.4 (48)
	Greg Olsen	20% 3.0 42.4 (15)	50% 5.1 35.4 (14)	33% 5.8 68.1 (6)		67% 13.0 149.3 (3)			37% 5.0 58.1 (38)
WR	Devin Funchess	49% 7.4 91.0 (79)	53% 8.9 87.6 (19)	40% 8.1 69.2 (10)	0% 0.0 39.6 (1)	50% 2.0 95.8 (2)	0% 0.0 39.6 (1)		48% 7.5 89.1 (112)
	Kelvin Benjamin	59% 11.0 107.7 (32)	57% 7.3 62.2 (14)	40% 4.4 53.8 (5)					57% 9.3 89.9 (51)
	Curtis Samuel	35% 3.3 65.8 (20)	100% 23.0 118.8 (1)	40% 5.2 57.1 (5)					38% 4.4 68.6 (26)

Format Line 1: Success Rate Line 2: YPA Line 3: Passer Rating Line 4: Total # of Plays

Successful Play Rate
0% 100%

Rushing Success by Personnel Grouping

Position	Player	1-1 [3WR]	1-2 [2WR]	2-1 [2WR]	1-0 [4WR]	1-3 [1WR]	2-0 [3WR]	2-2 [1WR]	3-1 [1WR]	2-3 [0WR]	1-4 [0WR]	Total
QB	Cam Newton	53% 6.7 (64)	61% 4.4 (28)	64% 5.1 (14)	100% 8.0 (1)	25% 3.3 (24)		60% 8.0 (5)			67% 1.0 (3)	52% 5.4 (139)
RB	Jonathan Stewart	35% 3.8 (17)	38% 2.8 (60)	25% 2.4 (32)		52% 4.1 (54)		64% 5.6 (25)		50% 1.0 (2)	63% 0.6 (8)	44% 3.4 (198)
	Christian McCaffrey	40% 3.8 (73)	50% 3.4 (18)	64% 3.9 (11)		60% 3.9 (10)	100% 6.0 (1)	50% 1.0 (2)	0% 2.5 (2)			45% 3.7 (117)

Format Line 1: Success Rate Line 2: YPC Line 3: Total # of Plays

Chicago Bears

2018 Coaches

Head Coach:
Matt Nagy (KC OC) (1st yr)
Offensive Coordinator:
Mark Helfrich (Oregon HC) (1st yr)
Defensive Coordinator:
Vic Fangio (4th yr)

2018 Forecast

Wins	Div Rank
6.5	#4

Past Records

2017: 5-11
2016: 3-13
2015: 6-10

EASY HARD

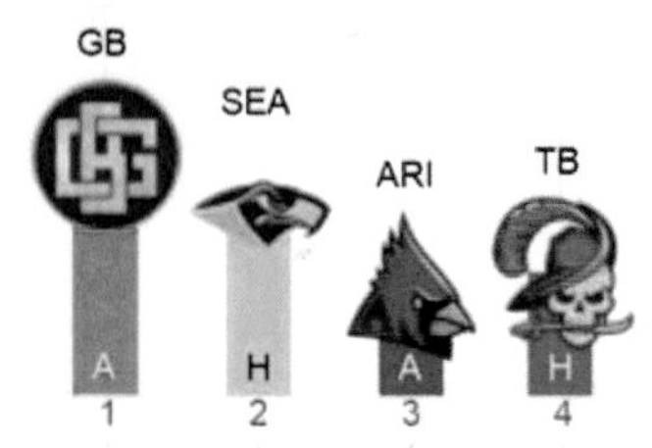

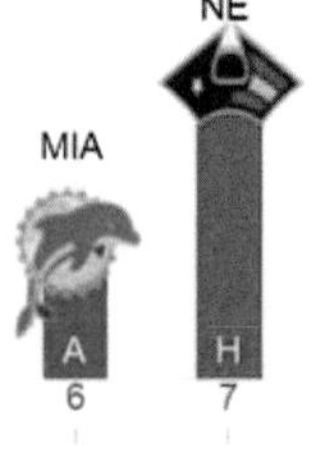
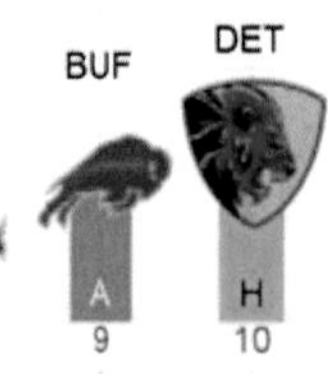

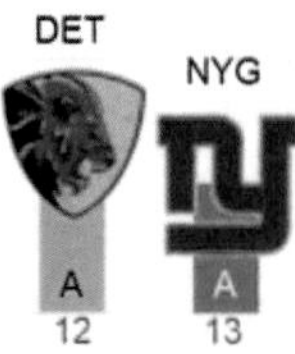

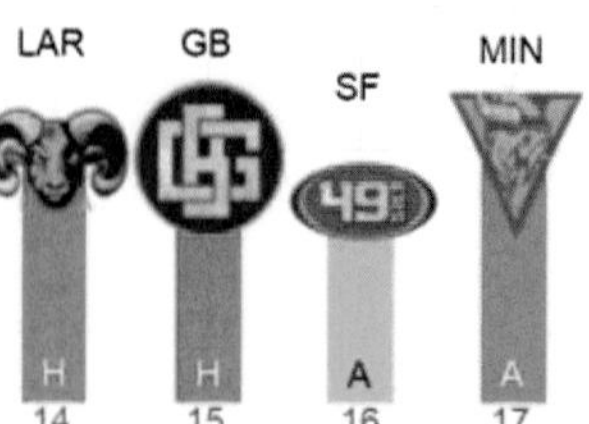

Week	1	2	3	4	5	6	7	8	9	10	11	12	13	14	15	16	17
Opponent	GB	SEA	ARI	TB		MIA	NE	NYJ	BUF	DET	MIN	DET	NYG	LAR	GB	SF	MIN
H/A	A	H	A	H		A	H	H	A	H	H	A	A	H	H	A	A
	SNF	MNF										TKG					

Key Players Lost

TXN	Player (POS)
Cut	Cooper, Marcus CB
	Demps, Quintin S
	Freeman, Jerrell LB
	Glennon, Mike QB
	McPhee, Pernell LB
	Wheaton, Markus WR
	Young, Willie LB
Declared Free Agent	Acho, Sam LB
	Amukamara, Prince CB
	Compton, Tom G
	Houston, Lamarr LB
	Inman, Dontrelle WR
	McManis, Sherrick CB
	Miller, Zach TE
	Scales, Patrick TE
	Sitton, Josh G
	Sowell, Bradley T
	Unrein, Mitch DE
	Wright, Kendall WR
Retired	Freeman, Jerrell LB

Average Line	# Games Favored	# Games Underdog
2.2	3	11

2018 Chicago Bears Overview

Sophomore slump? More like sophomore jump. In 2012-2016, eight quarterbacks were drafted in the top-15 picks. From production and efficiency standpoints, we've seen these baby-faced rookies enter their second full offseasons, put on their first pair of Reebok Pumps, and dunk on the league. 7-of-8 quarterbacks drafted in the top 15 improved rather than regressed, and most translated that improvement into W-L jumps for their teams. Robert Griffin III – ruined by knee injuries – was the only quarterback drafted in the top 15 to not improve in his second year. Only Andrew Luck had a winning record as a rookie. But six of the remaining seven went .500 or better as sophomores. The seven non-RG3 quarterbacks produced a combined record of 37-59 (39%) as rookies, then 63-44 (59%) in year two.

Modern football is driven by passing offenses, which are driven by quarterbacks. So it makes sense that that these teams' primary means of improvement came from quarterback improvement. Collectively, the eight quarterbacks drafted with top-15 picks in 2012-2016 combined for a 59% completion rate, 6.8 YPA, 108:94 TD-to-INT ratio, and 78 rating. They improved to 60% completions, 7.2 YPA, 197:85 TD-to-INT, and 91 rating as sophomores. No slumps. Just a bunch of jumps.

Last year, Jared Goff moved from 55% completions with a 5.3 YPA and 64 rating to 62% completions, 8.0 YPA, and 101 rating. Carson Wentz improved his TD-to-INT ratio from 16:14 to 33:7, upping his YPA from 6.2 to 7.5 and his rating from 79 to 102. Two years ago, Jameis Winston's rating, completion rate, and TD rate all improved and his team went from 6-10 to 9-7 in Winston's second season. That same year, Marcus Mariota's Titans went from 3-9 to 8-7 in his starts, and his passer rating improved from 92 to 96, promulgated by better TD-to-INT rates.

In Blake Bortles' second year (2015), Bortles improved his TD-to-INT ratio from 11:17 to 35:18, his YPA from 6.1 to 7.3, and his rating from 70 to 88. Andrew Luck improved his rookie completion rate from 54% to 60% and his passer rating from 77 to 87.

These year-two quarterback trends bode well for Mitchell Trubisky. Last year, Trubisky logged a 59% completion rate, 6.6 YPA, 7:7 TD-to-INT ratio, and 78 rating. His 59% completions were

(cont'd - see CHI2)

Key Free Agents/ Trades Added

Bray, Tyler QB
Burton, Trey TE
Daniel, Chase QB
Fowler, Bennie WR
Gabriel, Taylor WR
Lynch, Aaron LB
Robinson II, Allen WR
Watford, Earl T
Williams, Nick DE

Drafted Players

Rd	Pk	Player (College)
1	8	LB - Roquan Smith (Georgia)
2	39	C - James Daniels (Iowa)
	51	WR - Anthony Miller (Memphis)
4	115	LB - Joel Iyiegbuniwe (Western Kentucky)
5	145	DT - Bilal Nichols (Delaware)
6	181	DE - Kylie Fitts (Utah)
7	224	WR - Javon Wims (Georgia)

Regular Season Wins: Past & Current Proj

	Wins
Forecast 2018 Wins	6.5
2017 Wins	5
Forecast 2017 Wins	7.5
2016 Wins	3
2015 Wins	6
2014 Wins	5

1 3 5 7 9 11 13 15

Lineup & Cap Hits

FS A.Amos 38
LB D.Trevathan 59
LB R.Smith *Rookie* 58
SS E.Jackson 39
RCB K.Fuller 23
SLOTCB B.Callahan 37
OLB A.Lynch 59
RE J.Bullard 90
LE A.Hicks 96
OLB L.Floyd 94
LCB P.Amukamara 20

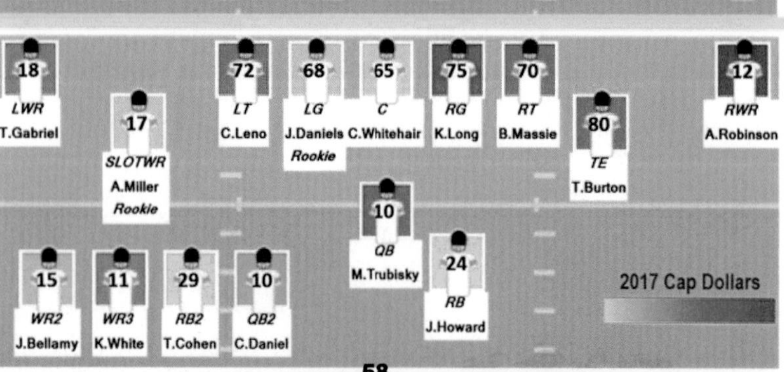

2018 Unit Spending

All DEF
All OFF

Positional Spending

	Rank	Total	2017 Rk
All OFF	17	$91.40M	20
QB	24	$11.39M	19
OL	21	$31.39M	10
RB	30	$3.48M	30
WR	3	$28.99M	21
TE	3	$16.14M	11
All DEF	29	$67.97M	12
DL	27	$16.87M	30
LB	12	$23.32M	3
CB	11	$22.47M	13
S	32	$5.32M	24

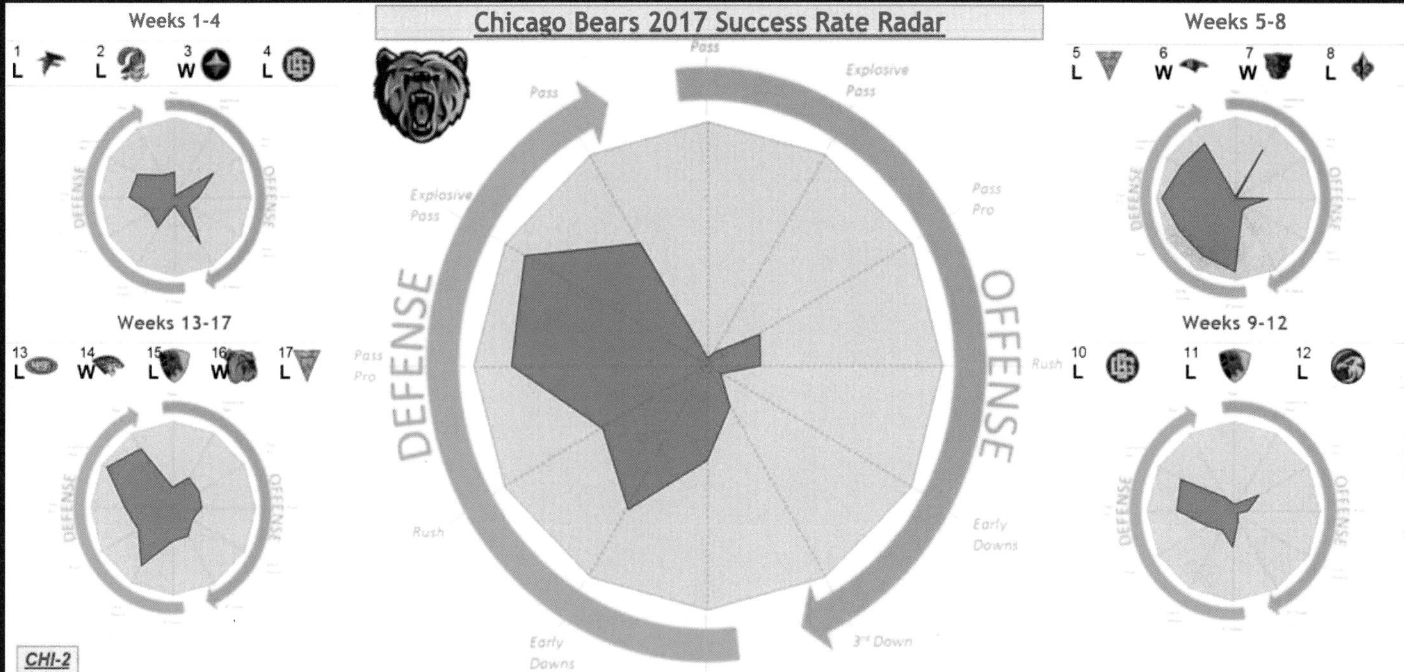

CHI-2

identical to the top-15 draft pick cohort's combined rookie percentage. Trubisky's 6.6 YPA was similar to the group's 6.8 rookie YPA, and their 78 ratings are identical. Trubisky's rookie year isn't seen as superlative, but his total efficiency is right in line with top-15 quarterback norms.

Much as Jared Goff upgraded from Jeff Fisher to Sean McVay, Trubisky stands to benefit from shedding crusty John Fox and Dowell Loggains for spread-game proponents Matt Nagy and Mark Helfrich. Nagy's offense will employ more shotgun and Run-Pass Option (RPO) than Loggains' archconservative scheme. The Bears added former Chiefs QBs Chase Daniel and Tyler Bray to further instruct Trubisky as peers in the quarterback room. Nagy will call plays, mimicking Goff's setup with McVay.

As seen with McVay and Kyle Shanahan, young, offensive-minded coaches tend to take an ultra-aggressive approach with creativity and an immense focus that their first-year system looks good, and works. We should expect similar focus from Nagy on a Bears team whose front office invested heavily in pass-catching upgrades. Nagy's non-conventional, "outside the box" ideas helped Alex Smith's deep passing via spread concepts. OC Helfrich is very familiar with spread-option offenses after working with Chip Kelly at Oregon, and can provide ideas apart from simply greater usage of RPOs.

There are even some similarities between Nagy's Chiefs scheme and Trubisky's introductory offense last year. The Chiefs used three-receiver 11 personnel only 53% of the time, ninth lowest in the league. The Bears used 11 on only 41% of Trubisky's snaps. However, when Nagy took over Kansas City's playcalling from Andy Reid, the Chiefs' 11-personnel usage climbed to 63%. Nagy's next-most-often-used personnel grouping was one-back, two-tight end 12 personnel (24%). The Bears prepared for more two-tight end sets by pairing Trey Burton with 2017 second-round pick Adam Shaheen. Trubisky's highest rookie-year efficiency marks came from two-tight end sets.

(cont'd - see CHI-3)

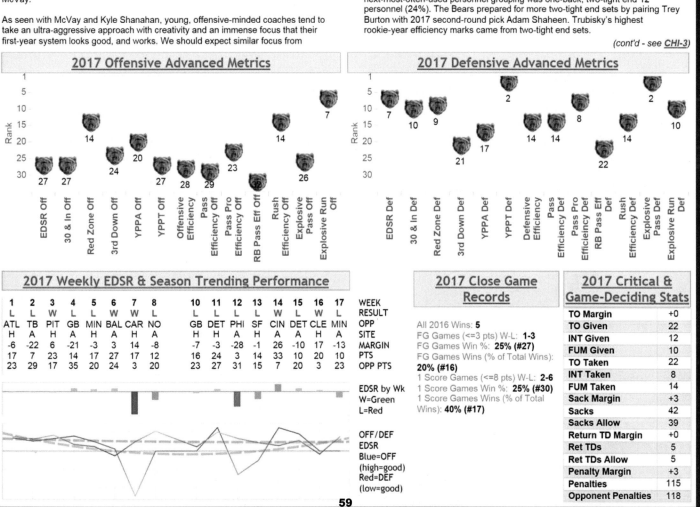

2017 Offensive Advanced Metrics

Metric	Rank
EDSR Off	27
30 & In Off	27
Red Zone Off	14
3rd Down Off	24
YPPA Off	20
YPPT Off	27
Offensive Efficiency	28
Pass Efficiency Off	29
Pass Pro Efficiency Off	23
RB Pass Eff Off	32
Rush Efficiency Off	14
Explosive Pass Off	26
Explosive Run Off	7

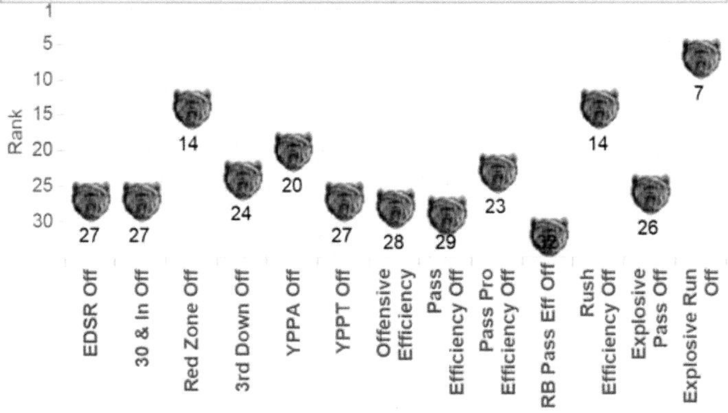

2017 Defensive Advanced Metrics

Metric	Rank
EDSR Def	7
30 & In Def	10
Red Zone Def	9
3rd Down Def	21
YPPA Def	17
YPPT Def	2
Defensive Efficiency	14
Pass Efficiency Def	14
Pass Pro Efficieincy Def	8
RB Pass Eff Def	22
Rush Efficiency Def	14
Explosive Pass Def	2
Explosive Run Def	10

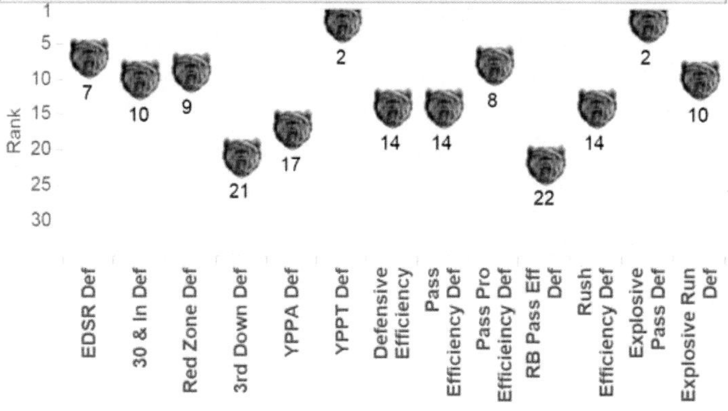

2017 Weekly EDSR & Season Trending Performance

WEEK	1	2	3	4	5	6	7	8	10	11	12	13	14	15	16	17
RESULT	L	L	W	L	L	W	W	L	L	L	L	L	W	L	W	L
OPP	ATL	TB	PIT	GB	MIN	BAL	CAR	NO	GB	DET	PHI	SF	CIN	DET	CLE	MIN
SITE	H	A	H	A	H	A	H	A	H	H	A	H	A	A	H	A
MARGIN	-6	-22	6	-21	-3	3	14	-8	-7	-3	-28	-1	26	-10	17	-13
PTS	17	7	23	14	17	27	17	12	16	24	3	14	33	10	20	10
OPP PTS	23	29	17	35	20	24	3	20	23	27	31	15	7	20	3	23

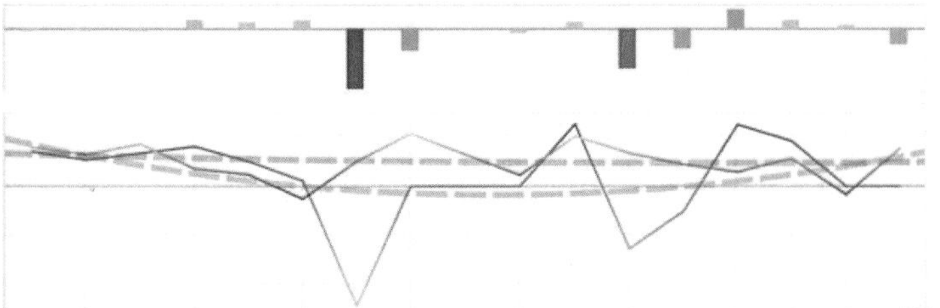

EDSR by Wk
W=Green
L=Red

OFF/DEF EDSR
Blue=OFF (high=good)
Red=DEF (low=good)

2017 Close Game Records

All 2016 Wins: **5**
FG Games (<=3 pts) W-L: **1-3**
FG Games Win %: **25% (#27)**
FG Games Wins (% of Total Wins): **20% (#16)**
1 Score Games (<=8 pts) W-L: **2-6**
1 Score Games Win %: **25% (#30)**
1 Score Games Wins (% of Total Wins): **40% (#17)**

2017 Critical & Game-Deciding Stats

TO Margin	+0
TO Given	22
INT Given	12
FUM Given	10
TO Taken	22
INT Taken	8
FUM Taken	14
Sack Margin	+3
Sacks	42
Sacks Allow	39
Return TD Margin	+0
Ret TDs	5
Ret TDs Allow	5
Penalty Margin	+3
Penalties	115
Opponent Penalties	118

Chicago Bears 2018 Strength of Schedule In Detail (compared to 2017)

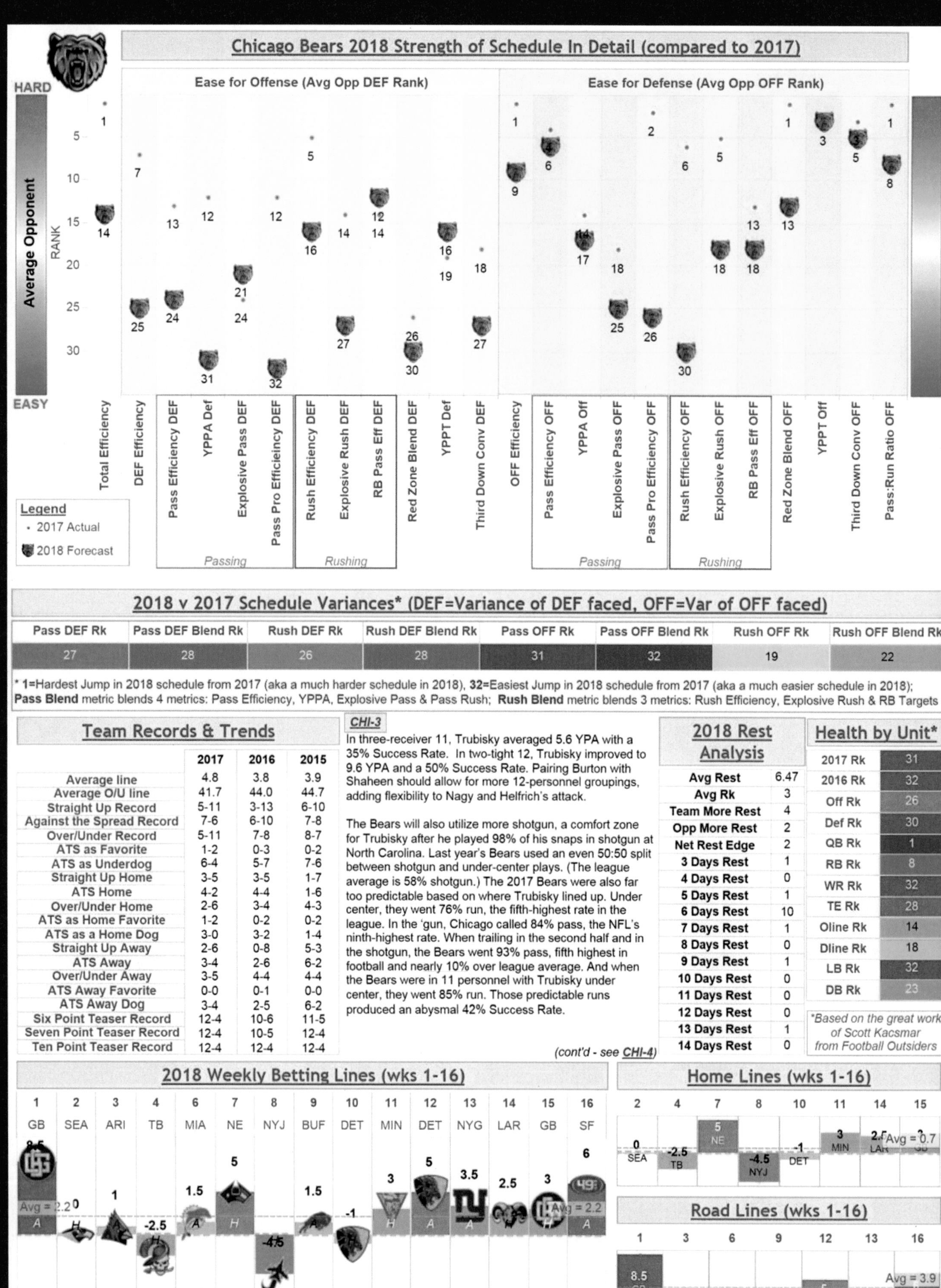

2018 v 2017 Schedule Variances* (DEF=Variance of DEF faced, OFF=Var of OFF faced)

Pass DEF Rk	Pass DEF Blend Rk	Rush DEF Rk	Rush DEF Blend Rk	Pass OFF Rk	Pass OFF Blend Rk	Rush OFF Rk	Rush OFF Blend Rk
27	28	26	28	31	32	19	22

* **1**=Hardest Jump in 2018 schedule from 2017 (aka a much harder schedule in 2018), **32**=Easiest Jump in 2018 schedule from 2017 (aka a much easier schedule in 2018); **Pass Blend** metric blends 4 metrics: Pass Efficiency, YPPA, Explosive Pass & Pass Rush; **Rush Blend** metric blends 3 metrics: Rush Efficiency, Explosive Rush & RB Targets

Team Records & Trends

	2017	2016	2015
Average line	4.8	3.8	3.9
Average O/U line	41.7	44.0	44.7
Straight Up Record	5-11	3-13	6-10
Against the Spread Record	7-6	6-10	7-8
Over/Under Record	5-11	7-8	8-7
ATS as Favorite	1-2	0-3	0-2
ATS as Underdog	6-4	5-7	7-6
Straight Up Home	3-5	3-5	1-7
ATS Home	4-2	4-4	1-6
Over/Under Home	2-6	3-4	4-3
ATS as Home Favorite	1-2	0-2	0-2
ATS as a Home Dog	3-0	3-2	1-4
Straight Up Away	2-6	0-8	5-3
ATS Away	3-4	2-6	6-2
Over/Under Away	3-5	4-4	4-4
ATS Away Favorite	0-0	0-1	0-0
ATS Away Dog	3-4	2-5	6-2
Six Point Teaser Record	12-4	10-6	11-5
Seven Point Teaser Record	12-4	10-5	12-4
Ten Point Teaser Record	12-4	12-4	12-4

CHI-3

In three-receiver 11, Trubisky averaged 5.6 YPA with a 35% Success Rate. In two-tight 12, Trubisky improved to 9.6 YPA and a 50% Success Rate. Pairing Burton with Shaheen should allow for more 12-personnel groupings, adding flexibility to Nagy and Helfrich's attack.

The Bears will also utilize more shotgun, a comfort zone for Trubisky after he played 98% of his snaps in shotgun at North Carolina. Last year's Bears used an even 50:50 split between shotgun and under-center plays. (The league average is 58% shotgun.) The 2017 Bears were also far too predictable based on where Trubisky lined up. Under center, they went 76% run, the fifth-highest rate in the league. In the 'gun, Chicago called 84% pass, the NFL's ninth-highest rate. When trailing in the second half and in the shotgun, the Bears went 93% pass, fifth highest in football and nearly 10% over league average. And when the Bears were in 11 personnel with Trubisky under center, they went 85% run. Those predictable runs produced an abysmal 42% Success Rate.

(cont'd - see CHI-4)

2018 Rest Analysis

Avg Rest	6.47
Avg Rk	3
Team More Rest	4
Opp More Rest	2
Net Rest Edge	2
3 Days Rest	1
4 Days Rest	0
5 Days Rest	1
6 Days Rest	10
7 Days Rest	1
8 Days Rest	0
9 Days Rest	1
10 Days Rest	0
11 Days Rest	0
12 Days Rest	0
13 Days Rest	1
14 Days Rest	0

Health by Unit*

2017 Rk	31
2016 Rk	32
Off Rk	26
Def Rk	30
QB Rk	1
RB Rk	8
WR Rk	32
TE Rk	28
Oline Rk	14
Dline Rk	18
LB Rk	32
DB Rk	23

**Based on the great work of Scott Kacsmar from Football Outsiders*

2018 Weekly Betting Lines (wks 1-16)

1	2	3	4	6	7	8	9	10	11	12	13	14	15	16
GB	SEA	ARI	TB	MIA	NE	NYJ	BUF	DET	MIN	DET	NYG	LAR	GB	SF
A	H	A	H	A	H	H	A	H	H	A	A	H	H	A
8.5	0	1	-2.5	1.5	5	-4.5	1.5	-1	3	5	3.5	2.5	3	6

Avg = 2.2

Home Lines (wks 1-16)

2	4	7	8	10	11	14	15
SEA	TB	NE	NYJ	DET	MIN	LAR	GB
0	-2.5	5	-4.5	-1	3	2.5	3

Avg = 0.7

Road Lines (wks 1-16)

1	3	6	9	12	13	16
GB	ARI	MIA	BUF	DET	NYG	SF
8.5	1	1.5	1.5	5	3.5	6

Avg = 3.9

Chicago Bears 2017 Play Analysis

2017 Play Tendencies

All Pass %	55%
All Pass Rk	26
All Rush %	45%
All Rush Rk	7
1 Score Pass %	49%
1 Score Pass Rk	32
2016 1 Score Pass %	59%
2016 1 Score Pass Rk	16
2017 Pass Increase %	-10%
Pass Increase Rk	32
1 Score Rush %	51%
1 Score Rush Rk	1
Up Pass %	41%
Up Pass Rk	30
Up Rush %	59%
Up Rush Rk	3
Down Pass %	65%
Down Pass Rk	18
Down Rush %	35%
Down Rush Rk	15

2017 Down & Distance Tendencies

Down	Distance	Total Plays	Pass Rate	Run Rate	Play Success %
1	Short (1-3)	1	100%	0%	100%
	Med (4-7)	10	0%	100%	70%
	Long (8-10)	261	33%	67%	43%
	XL (11+)	12	67%	33%	25%
2	Short (1-3)	24	21%	79%	58%
	Med (4-7)	52	25%	75%	52%
	Long (8-10)	72	47%	53%	33%
	XL (11+)	66	83%	17%	20%
3	Short (1-3)	32	50%	50%	59%
	Med (4-7)	35	91%	9%	46%
	Long (8-10)	30	87%	13%	37%
	XL (11+)	49	82%	18%	14%
4	Short (1-3)	2	50%	50%	100%
	Med (4-7)	1	100%	0%	100%

Shotgun %:

Under Center	Shotgun
50%	50%
37%	*AVG 63%*

Run Rate:

Under Center	Shotgun
76%	13%
68%	*AVG 23%*

Pass Rate:

Under Center	Shotgun
24%	87%
32%	*AVG 77%*

Short Yardage Intelligence:

2nd and Short Run

Run Freq	Run Rk	NFL Run Freq Avg	Run 1D Rate	Run NFL 1D Avg
71%	10	67%	53%	69%

2nd and Short Pass

Pass Freq	Pass Rk	NFL Pass Freq Avg	Pass 1D Rate	Pass NFL 1D Avg
29%	22	33%	50%	53%

Most Frequent Play

Down	Distance	Play Type	Player	Total Plays	Play Success %
1	Med (4-7)	RUSH	Jordan Howard	7	57%
	Long (8-10)	RUSH	Jordan Howard	127	40%
	XL (11+)	PASS	Kendall Wright	2	50%
			Dion Sims	2	50%
		RUSH	Jordan Howard	2	50%
2	Short (1-3)	RUSH	Jordan Howard	13	69%
	Med (4-7)	RUSH	Jordan Howard	28	50%
	Long (8-10)	RUSH	Jordan Howard	26	27%
	XL (11+)	PASS	Kendall Wright	13	38%
3	Short (1-3)	RUSH	Jordan Howard	12	75%
	Med (4-7)	PASS	Kendall Wright	9	56%
	Long (8-10)	PASS	Kendall Wright	4	50%
	XL (11+)	RUSH	Mitchell Trubisky	6	17%

Most Successful Play*

Down	Distance	Play Type	Player	Total Plays	Play Success %
1	Med (4-7)	RUSH	Jordan Howard	7	57%
	Long (8-10)	PASS	Dontrelle Inman	7	86%
2	Short (1-3)	RUSH	Jordan Howard	13	69%
	Med (4-7)	RUSH	Jordan Howard	28	50%
	Long (8-10)	PASS	Tarik Cohen	8	50%
	XL (11+)	PASS	Kendall Wright	13	38%
3	Short (1-3)	RUSH	Jordan Howard	12	75%
	Med (4-7)	PASS	Kendall Wright	9	56%
	XL (11+)	PASS	Benny Cunningham	5	20%

**Minimum 5 plays to qualify*

2017 Snap Rates

Wk	Opp	Score	Kendall Wright	Dion Sims	Jordan Howard	Josh Bellamy	Dontrelle Inman	Tarik Cohen	Zach Miller	Daniel Brown
1	ATL	L 23-17	39 (58%)	48 (72%)	38 (57%)	33 (49%)		28 (42%)	40 (60%)	
2	TB	L 29-7	55 (86%)	30 (47%)	31 (48%)	59 (92%)		40 (63%)	48 (75%)	
3	PIT	W 23-17	35 (54%)	50 (77%)	41 (63%)	19 (29%)		28 (43%)	32 (49%)	
4	GB	L 35-14	37 (54%)	37 (54%)	35 (51%)	36 (53%)		18 (26%)	48 (71%)	
5	MIN	L 20-17	33 (54%)	47 (77%)	34 (56%)	7 (11%)		17 (28%)	42 (69%)	
6	BAL	W 27-24	25 (31%)	69 (86%)	54 (68%)	2 (3%)		26 (33%)	55 (69%)	
7	CAR	W 17-3	8 (21%)	29 (76%)	34 (89%)	3 (8%)		7 (18%)	25 (66%)	
8	NO	L 20-12	38 (57%)	40 (60%)	48 (72%)	2 (3%)		19 (28%)	24 (36%)	16 (24%)
10	GB	L 23-16	46 (77%)		29 (48%)	40 (67%)	57 (95%)	13 (22%)		38 (63%)
11	DET	L 27-24	39 (62%)		31 (49%)	25 (40%)	53 (84%)	31 (49%)		32 (51%)
12	PHI	L 31-3	42 (76%)	20 (36%)	23 (42%)		51 (93%)	19 (35%)		30 (55%)
13	SF	L 15-14	20 (54%)	25 (68%)	22 (59%)	30 (81%)	35 (95%)	17 (46%)		11 (30%)
14	CIN	W 33-7	47 (62%)	49 (64%)	44 (58%)	48 (63%)	67 (88%)	37 (49%)		19 (25%)
15	DET	L 20-10	46 (67%)	42 (61%)	33 (48%)	53 (77%)	47 (68%)	25 (36%)		35 (51%)
16	CLE	W 20-3	32 (52%)	44 (71%)	43 (69%)	40 (65%)	59 (95%)	18 (29%)		38 (61%)
17	MIN	L 23-10	38 (68%)	48 (86%)	36 (64%)	40 (71%)	46 (82%)	19 (34%)		22 (39%)
Grand Total			580 (58%)	578 (67%)	576 (59%)	437 (47%)	415 (88%)	362 (36%)	314 (62%)	241 (44%)

Personnel Groupings

Personnel	Team %	NFL Avg	Succ. %
1-1 [3WR]	42%	59%	37%
2-1 [2WR]	23%	7%	42%
1-2 [2WR]	22%	19%	42%
1-3 [1WR]	6%	5%	46%
2-2 [1WR]	5%	4%	34%

Grouping Tendencies

Personnel	Pass Rate	Pass Succ. %	Run Succ. %
1-1 [3WR]	77%	35%	40%
2-1 [2WR]	49%	39%	45%
1-2 [2WR]	39%	43%	41%
1-3 [1WR]	13%	57%	45%
2-2 [1WR]	17%	13%	38%

Red Zone Targets (min 3)

Receiver	All	Inside 5	6-10	11-20
Tarik Cohen	10	3		7
Kendall Wright	7	1	1	5
Adam Shaheen	6	3	2	1
Dontrelle Inman	6	2	4	
Zach Miller	5	1	1	3
Benny Cunningham	4	1	3	
Deonte Thompson	4			4
Josh Bellamy	3	1	1	1
Dion Sims	2		1	1
Jordan Howard	2	1	1	

Red Zone Rushes (min 3)

Rusher	All	Inside 5	6-10	11-20
Jordan Howard	32	9	8	15
Tarik Cohen	9	1	5	3
Mitchell Trubisky	8	4	1	3

Early Down Target Rate

RB	TE	WR
29%	20%	51%
23%	*21% NFL AVG*	*56%*

Overall Target Success %

RB	TE	WR
32% #32	48% #21	44% #28

Chicago Bears 2017 Passing Recap & 2018 Outlook

A fascinating element of Mitchell Trubisky's rookie campaign was his dominance on throws in the middle of the field but extreme struggles to the left and right. (Review passing-cone vizzes to the right and directional-passer rating viz below.) On all downs when targeting the middle of the field, Trubisky's 105 rating ranked No. 7 among 32 qualified quarterbacks, and his Success Rate (61%) ranked No. 2. On early downs only, Trubisky's 114 rating ranked third of 32 with a league-best 69% Success Rate.

On all other passes, however, Trubisky ranked 39th in rating (64) and dead last in Success Rate (34%). On all downs throwing to the left and right, Trubisky's 71 rating ranked 35th, and he finished dead last in Success Rate (34%). While Trubisky's receivers were admittedly bad, Trubisky's passer rating remained 34% when targeting tight ends and backs. The middle of the field is the most efficient area of the field to target, and that especially holds true for Trubisky. But most of his 2017 throws were still to the outside.

Mitchell Trubisky Rating All Downs

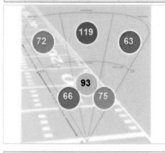

72 119 63
93
66 75

Mitchell Trubisky Rating Early Downs

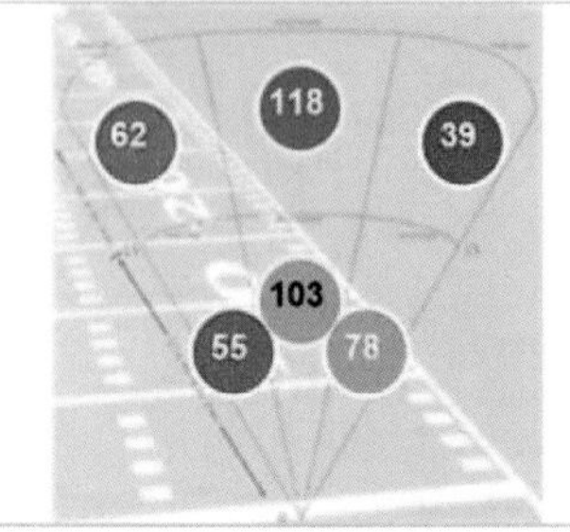

2017 Standard Passing Table

QB	Comp	Att	Comp %	Yds	YPA	TDs	INT	Sacks	Rating	Rk
Mitchell Trubisky	196	330	59%	2,189	6.6	7	7	31	77	37
Mike Glennon	93	140	66%	833	6.0	4	5	8	77	38
NFL Avg			62%		7.0				87.5	

2017 Advanced Passing Table

QB	Success %	EDSR Passing Success %	20+ Yd Pass Gains	20+ Yd Pass %	30+ Yd Pass Gains	30+ Yd Pass %	Avg. Air Yds per Comp	Avg. YAC per Comp	20+ Air Yd Comp	20+ Air Yd %
Mitchell Trubisky	36%	39%	24	7.3%	7	2.1%	6.0	5.1	8	4%
Mike Glennon	41%	42%	4	2.9%	0	0.0%	5.2	3.4	1	1%
NFL Avg	44%	48%	27.7	8.8%	10.3	3.3%	6.0	4.7	11.7	6%

Interception Rates by Down

Yards to Go	1	2	3	4	Total
1 & 2	0.0%	0.0%	0.0%	0.0%	0.0%
3, 4, 5		0.0%	4.5%	0.0%	3.4%
6 - 9	0.0%	3.7%	0.0%	50.0%	2.9%
10 - 14	2.7%	0.0%	0.0%	0.0%	1.5%
15+	0.0%	3.7%	0.0%		1.9%
Total	2.4%	1.8%	0.8%	14.3%	1.9%

3rd Down Passing - Short of Sticks Analysis

QB	Avg. Yds to Go	Avg. YIA (of Comp)	Avg Yds Short	Short of Sticks Rate	Short Rk
Mitchell Trubisky	8.8	6.2	-2.6	66%	39
NFL Avg	7.8	6.7	-1.1	60%	

Air Yds vs YAC

Air Yds %	YAC %	Rk
49%	51%	38
58%	42%	

2017 Receiving Recap & 2018 Outlook

Only one 2017 Bears wide receiver exceeded 50 targets. Only one other team (Colts) met that mark. Whereas Indianapolis has T.Y. Hilton, Chicago's top 2017 wideout was Kendall Wright, who is no longer with the team. Last year's Bears receiver corps was also the most injured in the league. Best, the Bears go from facing the league's seventh-toughest schedule of defenses to one of the ten softest. And Chicago faces the second-largest decrease in pass-defense strength of schedule.

Player *Min 50 Targets*	Targets	Comp %	YPA	Rating	TOARS	Success %	Success Rk	Missed YPA Rk	YAS % Rk	TDs
Kendall Wright	91	65%	6.7	83	4.4	47%	75	63	124	1
Tarik Cohen	71	75%	5.0	90	3.9	27%	131	104	130	1

Directional Passer Rating Delivered

Receiver	Short Left	Short Middle	Short Right	Deep Left	Deep Middle	Deep Right	Player Total
Kendall Wright	80	107	73	7	117	65	83
Tarik Cohen	78	90	96	40	119	40	90
Josh Bellamy	3	93	90	122	97	40	78
Dontrelle Inman	27	82	66	95	119	117	72
Zach Miller	80	93	20	119	119	109	73
Jordan Howard	72	65	88				78
Dion Sims	68	91	15			118	68
Benny Cunningham	96	135	130				130
Daniel Brown	99	113	28	40	119	40	62
Deonte Thompson	113	35	95	40		85	77
Kevin White	40	92	79				56
Team Total	70	95	74	56	117	107	82

2017 Rushing Recap & 2017 Outlook

If there is one running game from 2017 that I loved most, it was the Bears. Everyone knew the rest of the top-ten fantasy running backs like Le'Veon Bell, Todd Gurley, LeSean McCoy, Leonard Fournette, and Ezekiel Elliott. The running back no one talks about is Jordan Howard, who faced the NFL's fifth-toughest run-defense schedule in a predictable offense that ran the ball seventh most in the league, including most in the league in one-score games. The fact that Chicago's rushing offense still ranked top half in efficiency and No. 7 in explosiveness bodes well for the Bears' 2018 run-game fortunes against a far softer slate. Combine Howard with versatile Cohen's second-year potential under a creative new staff, and this backfield is ready for liftoff.

Player *Min 50 Rushes*	Rushes	YPC	Success %	Success Rk	Missed YPA Rk	YTS % Rk	YAS % Rk	Early Down Success %	Early Down Success Rk	TDs
Jordan Howard	277	4.0	42%	53	60	53	12	41%	56	9
Tarik Cohen	86	4.4	47%	31	74	40	3	49%	16	2

Yards per Carry by Direction

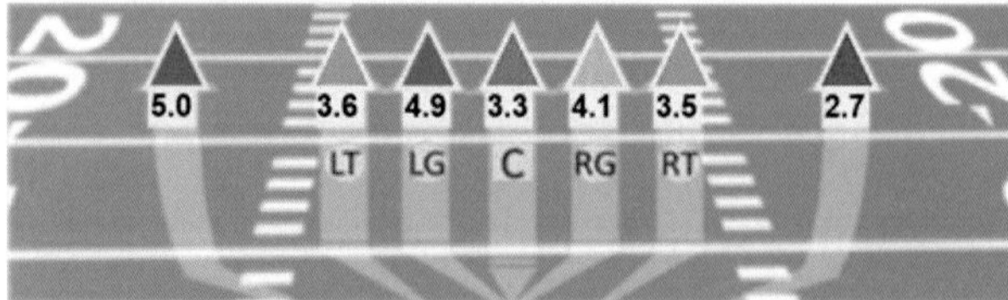

Directional Run Frequency

23% 13% 19% 7% 14% 9% 15%
LT LG C RG RT

CHI-4

Nagy's 2017 Chiefs ran shotgun on 72% of plays, far above Chicago's 50:50 split. And they weren't nearly as predictable. In shotgun, Kansas City went 73% pass, well below NFL average (79%). So while the Chiefs went shotgun and passed frequently from that formation, they used tendencies that required defenses to honor the run more than average. (The stone-age 2017 Bears took an opposite approach.)

Shotgun formations can also help Jordan Howard. On shotgun runs, Howard averaged 6.4 yards per carry with a 52% Success Rate the past two years. Under center, Howard dipped to 4.0 YPC with 43% Success. Last year's Bears also faced the NFL's fifth-most difficult schedule of run defenses. (In fantasy, Howard still finished RB10.). I project an easier run-defense schedule this year. And with an improved passing game, Howard's efficiency should improve.

The final piece for a Trubisky jump is an influx of weapons. The Bears signed Allen Robinson and Taylor Gabriel in free agency. Anthony Miller was drafted in the second round to man the slot. At tight end, Burton now teams with Shaheen. Nagy spoke at OTAs of how second-year RB/WR Tarik Cohen makes him "giddy" and compared Cohen to Tyreek Hill. Coming off a dynamic, 53-catch rookie season, Cohen is capable of being employed in unique ways.

(cont'd - see CHI-5)

Evan Silva's Fantasy Corner

The Bears traded this year's No. 105 pick and next year's second-rounder to move up for Anthony Miller at No. 51 and will play him in the slot between Allen Robinson and Taylor Gabriel. A Sterling Shepard-level talent who drew some Antonio Brown comparisons before the draft, Miller was an otherworldly producer his final two seasons at Memphis, especially dominating on the interior as a sudden-footed route technician with superb short-area quickness (6.65 three-cone time) and unusually large hands (10 5/8"). As Robinson hasn't actually played well since the 2015 season and Gabriel isn't a high-volume receiver, it's not crazy to call Miller a sleeper to lead Chicago in targets. Miller has a target-hot skill set, and Trubisky's go-to guys the past two seasons (Kendall Wright, Ryan Switzer) operated in the slot.

Division History: Season Wins & 2018 Projection

2014 Wins | 2015 Wins | 2016 Wins | 2017 Wins | Forecast 2018 Wins

Rank of 2018 Defensive Pass Efficiency Faced by Week

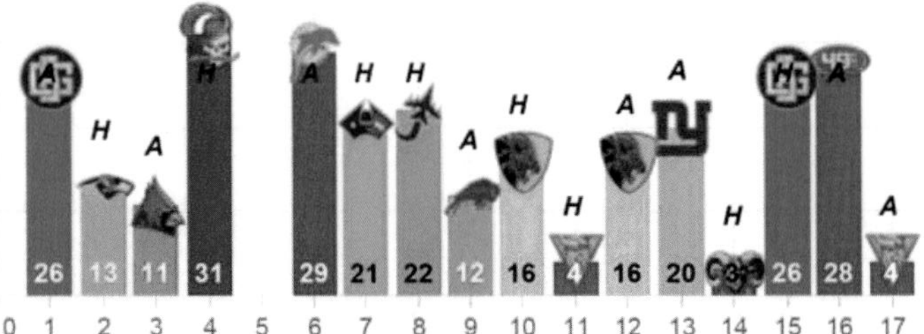

Rank of 2018 Defensive Rush Efficiency Faced by Week

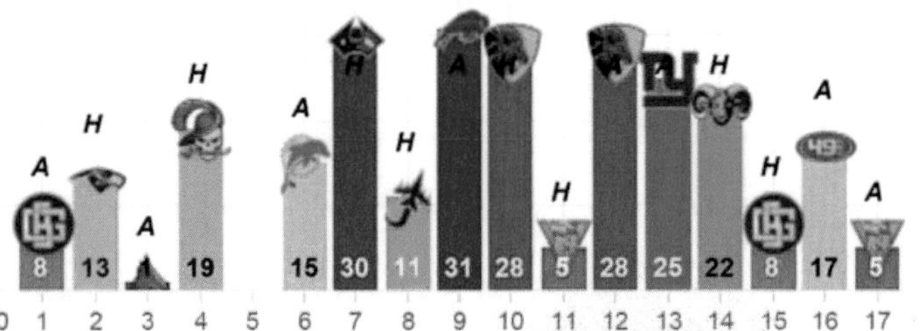

2017 Situational Usage by Player & Position

Usage Rate by Score

		Being Blown Out (14+)	Down Big (9-13)	One Score	Large Lead (9-13)	Blowout Lead (14+)	Grand Total
RUSH	Jordan Howard	16%	21%	38%	38%	59%	33%
	Tarik Cohen	7%	6%	11%	14%	18%	10%
	Josh Bellamy	1%					0%
	Benny Cunningham	3%	1%	0%			1%
	Mike Burton	1%		0%	3%		0%
	Total	27%	28%	51%	55%	77%	45%
PASS	Jordan Howard	5%	4%	4%	3%		4%
	Tarik Cohen	8%	13%	8%	14%		8%
	Kendall Wright	14%	17%	9%	10%	5%	11%
	Josh Bellamy	10%	7%	4%	3%	2%	5%
	Dontrelle Inman	8%	6%	3%	3%	5%	5%
	Benny Cunningham	2%	3%	4%	3%		3%
	Zach Miller	5%	3%	4%	3%	5%	4%
	Dion Sims	1%	6%	4%		2%	3%
	Daniel Brown	2%	4%	2%			2%
	Deonte Thompson	8%		1%			2%
	Markus Wheaton	4%	2%	2%			2%
	Tre McBride	3%	4%	1%			2%
	Adam Shaheen			3%	3%		2%
	Mike Burton		1%	0%		2%	0%
	Tanner Gentry	2%		0%		2%	1%
	Kevin White		1%	1%			0%
	Total	73%	72%	49%	45%	23%	55%

Positional Target Distribution vs NFL Average

		NFL Wide				Team Only			
		Left	Middle	Right	**Total**	Left	Middle	Right	**Total**
Deep	WR	973	496	973	**2,442**	13	13	14	**40**
	TE	190	148	177	**515**	2	2	11	**15**
	RB	36	8	41	**85**	3	1	1	**5**
	All	**1,199**	**652**	**1,191**	**3,042**	**18**	**16**	**26**	**60**
Short	WR	2,820	1,622	2,722	**7,164**	42	49	68	**159**
	TE	845	821	1,137	**2,803**	18	18	33	**69**
	RB	1,275	798	1,242	**3,315**	46	25	53	**124**
	All	**4,940**	**3,241**	**5,101**	**13,282**	**106**	**92**	**154**	**352**
Total		**6,139**	**3,893**	**6,292**	**16,324**	**124**	**108**	**180**	**412**

Positional Success Rates vs NFL Average

		NFL Wide				Team Only			
		Left	Middle	Right	**Total**	Left	Middle	Right	**Total**
Deep	WR	37%	45%	38%	**39%**	31%	69%	43%	**48%**
	TE	38%	52%	46%	**45%**	50%	100%	36%	**47%**
	RB	39%	50%	39%	**40%**	0%	100%	0%	**20%**
	All	**37%**	**46%**	**39%**	**40%**	**28%**	**75%**	**38%**	**45%**
Short	WR	52%	57%	50%	**52%**	38%	65%	38%	**47%**
	TE	51%	56%	50%	**52%**	50%	56%	33%	**43%**
	RB	44%	52%	43%	**46%**	39%	24%	30%	**32%**
	All	**50%**	**56%**	**48%**	**51%**	**41%**	**52%**	**34%**	**41%**
Total		**47%**	**54%**	**47%**	**49%**	**39%**	**56%**	**35%**	**42%**

Successful Play Rate
0% ▭ 100%

Chicago Bears - Success by Personnel Grouping & Play Type

Play Type	1-1 [3WR]	1-2 [2WR]	2-1 [2WR]	1-0 [4WR]	1-3 [1WR]	2-0 [3WR]	2-2 [1WR]	0-2 [3WR]	3-1 [1WR]	2-3 [0WR]	3-0 [2WR]	3-2 [0WR]	Grand Total
PASS	35% (302, 59%)	43% (79, 15%)	39% (104, 20%)	0% (2, 0%)	57% (7, 1%)		13% (8, 2%)	100% (1, 0%)	50% (4, 1%)	75% (4, 1%)		0% (1, 0%)	38% (512, 100%)
RUSH	40% (89, 21%)	41% (123, 29%)	45% (110, 26%)		45% (49, 12%)	100% (1, 0%)	38% (39, 9%)		0% (3, 1%)	17% (6, 1%)	100% (1, 0%)	100% (1, 0%)	42% (422, 100%)
TOTAL	37% (391, 42%)	42% (202, 22%)	42% (214, 23%)	0% (2, 0%)	46% (56, 6%)	100% (1, 0%)	34% (47, 5%)	100% (1, 0%)	29% (7, 1%)	40% (10, 1%)	100% (1, 0%)	50% (2, 0%)	40% (934, 100%)

Format Line 1: Success Rate Line 2: Total # of Plays, % of All Plays (by type)

CHI-5 Vic Fangio's 2017 Bears defense was forced to contend with playing opposite the NFL's fifth-least-efficient offense while facing the league's most-difficult schedule of opposing offenses. Chicago played just four offenses that ranked 17th or worse (Panthers, Ravens, Bengals, Browns) and went 4-0 in those games. Otherwise, the Bears faced a murderer's row of top-ten offenses: Falcons, Steelers, Saints, Eagles, Vikings twice, and one Packers game against Aaron Rodgers. Fangio's side of the ball still ranked seventh best in Early-Down Success Rate defense and was top ten in numerous other key metrics. Although the Bears went 2-6 in one-score games, they allowed over 23 points (league average) in just one of those eight contests. Intelligently, the Bears retained Fangio amid Fox's dismissal and drafted ILB Roquan Smith in the first round. With an improved offense, softer schedule, and better injury luck – last year's Bears defense was third-most injured in the NFL – Fangio's unit is likely to look even better.

In addition to facing the NFL's most-difficult schedule of opposing offenses, the Bears drew the league's hardest schedule overall. They were the league's second-most-injured team. They went an unlucky 2-6 in one-score games. They lost the EDSR battle in only 5-of-16 games, and those were to four playoff opponents (Eagles, Vikings, Saints, Panthers) plus Jimmy Garoppolo's 49ers in Week 13.

While nothing comes easy in the NFL – and the Bears are favored in just 11 games in 2018 – it's realistic to picture this team making a jump similar to the ones so commonplace for teams led by sophomore quarterbacks. I think the Bears have a great shot to exceed projections linemakers currently hold for them.

Receiving Success by Personnel Grouping

Position	Player	1-1 [3WR]	1-2 [2WR]	2-1 [2WR]	1-0 [4WR]	1-3 [1WR]	2-2 [1WR]	0-2 [3WR]	3-1 [1WR]	3-2 [0WR]	Total
RB	Tarik Cohen	25% 4.4 85.0 (32)	57% 5.3 88.7 (7)	26% 3.0 73.2 (27)			0% 3.5 81.3 (2)		100% 45.5 118.8 (2)	0% 0.0 39.6 (1)	30% 5.0 89.9 (71)
	Jordan Howard	19% 4.5 83.3 (16)	17% 2.5 56.3 (6)	29% 5.3 88.7 (7)		100% 6.0 91.7 (1)	0% -5.0 79.2 (1)		0% 0.0 39.6 (1)		22% 3.9 78.3 (32)
TE	Zach Miller	50% 6.8 40.8 (20)	36% 4.2 49.8 (11)		0% 8.0 100.0 (1)	100% 20.5 158.3 (2)	0% 5.0 87.5 (1)				46% 6.7 73.0 (35)
WR	Kendall Wright	45% 6.3 81.4 (66)	60% 7.2 82.1 (10)	54% 9.1 97.6 (13)			0% 0.0 39.6 (1)	100% 7.0 95.8 (1)			48% 6.7 83.3 (91)
	Josh Bellamy	45% 7.4 76.1 (29)	71% 15.1 153.3 (7)	30% 5.5 18.8 (10)							46% 8.2 77.8 (46)
	Dontrelle Inman	50% 7.8 97.0 (24)	57% 9.1 48.2 (7)	44% 9.2 86.8 (9)							50% 8.4 72.3 (40)

Format Line 1: Success Rate Line 2: YPA Line 3: Passer Rating Line 4: Total # of Plays

Successful Play Rate
0% ▭ 100%

Rushing Success by Personnel Grouping

Position	Player	1-1 [3WR]	1-2 [2WR]	2-1 [2WR]	1-3 [1WR]	2-0 [3WR]	2-2 [1WR]	3-1 [1WR]	2-3 [0WR]	3-0 [2WR]	3-2 [0WR]	Total
QB	Mitchell Trubisky	44% 10.1 (18)	33% 5.0 (9)	43% 3.6 (7)	20% -0.4 (5)		0% 0.0 (1)		0% -1.0 (1)			37% 6.0 (41)
RB	Jordan Howard	47% 5.5 (36)	41% 3.8 (82)	46% 4.3 (83)	41% 3.3 (34)		35% 3.9 (34)	0% 0.0 (3)	25% -0.3 (4)		100% 5.0 (1)	42% 4.0 (277)
	Tarik Cohen	36% 3.1 (28)	44% 3.7 (27)	44% 5.8 (18)	70% 6.9 (10)	100% 10.0 (1)	100% 8.0 (1)			100% 3.0 (1)		47% 4.4 (86)

Format Line 1: Success Rate Line 2: YPC Line 3: Total # of Plays

2018 Coaches

Head Coach:
Marvin Lewis (16th yr)
Offensive Coordinator:
Bill Lazor (2nd yr)
Defensive Coordinator:
Teryl Austin (DET DC) (1st yr)

Cincinnati Bengals

2018 Forecast

Wins	Div Rank
7	#3

Past Records

2017: 7-9
2016: 6-9-1
2015: 12-4

EASY HARD

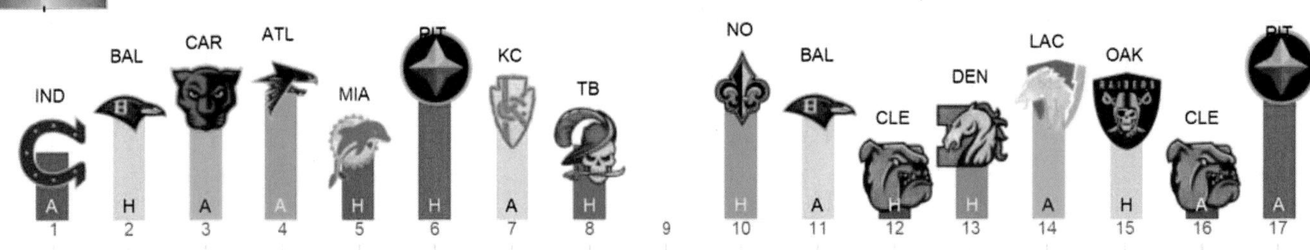

Key Players Lost

TXN	Player (POS)
Cut	Bradford, Carl LB
	Harris, Connor LB
Declared Free Agent	Bodine, Russell C
	Eifert, Tyler TE
	Hill, Jeremy RB
	Huber, Kevin P
	Jones, Adam CB
	McCarron, AJ QB
	Minter, Kevin LB
	Peerman, Cedric RB
	Sims, Pat DT
	Smith, Andre T
	Smith, Chris DE
	Winston, Eric T

Average Line	# Games Favored	# Games Underdog
2.2	3	11

2018 Cincinnati Bengals Overview

How slow of a start is too slow for Marvin Lewis? How about five days, which is how long it took Lewis to fire OC Ken Zampese after the start of last season. Trounced by the Ravens 20-0 in Week 1, the Bengals quickly racked up their second loss by falling 13-9 to the Texans on Thursday Night Football in Week 2. Cincinnati didn't score a touchdown in either game.

Still, something had to be boiling beneath the surface. 2016 was Zampese's first year as Bengals offensive coordinator. Cincinnati went 6-9-1, but Zampese's offense ranked 11th in efficiency and 11th in Early-Down Success Rate. The Bengals went 1-6 in one-score games and ranked 26th in pass protection, however, while Zampese's offense faced the NFL's sixth-toughest schedule of defenses. Zampese was on thin ice. And last year's touchdown-less, 0-2 start was the final straw.

By turning the page to QBs coach Bill Lazor, Lewis was hoping for something he believed Zampese couldn't offer. Logic says Lewis no longer liked the plays Zampese was calling. He wanted better plays, better flow, better player usage, and better production leading to wins.

But Lewis didn't get any of that. Lazor was Zampese 2.0. The Bengals' 2016 and 2017 offenses both used 11 personnel on 71% of plays. They both used 12 personnel 20% of the time. The Bengals passed in 11 personnel at a 67% rate in 2016, and a 68% rate in 2017. The two teams passed on first and ten at 47% and 48% clips. The Bengals used 11 personnel on 83% of pass plays in 2016, and 82% of pass plays in 2017. Both offenses went 11 on 89% of third downs.

Also much like Zampese, Lazor's 2017 offense faced a tough schedule; Lazor's Bengals played the NFL's second-hardest slate of defenses. A big part of Cincinnati's struggles was offensive line play. Their 2016 line was second healthiest and ninth-most expensive in the league, but ranked seventh worst in pass-blocking efficiency and allowed 41 sacks. The 2017 Bengals let LT Andrew Whitworth and RG Kevin Zeitler walk. Cincinnati's offensive line went from ninth-most expensive to second cheapest.

(cont'd - see CIN2)

Key Free Agents/ Trades Added

- Baker, Chris DT
- Barkley, Matt QB
- Brown, Preston LB
- Glenn, Cordy T
- Hart, Bobby T
- White, Ka'Raun WR

Drafted Players

Rd	Pk	Player (College)
1	21	C - Billy Price (Ohio State)
2	54	S - Jessie Bates III (Wake Fo..
3	77	DE - Sam Hubbard (Ohio Sta..
	78	LB - Malik Jefferson (Texas)
4	112	RB - Mark Walton (Miami (FL))
5	151	CB - Davontae Harris (Illinois..
	158	DE - Andrew Brown (Virginia)
5*	170	CB - Darius Phillips (Western..
7	249	QB - Logan Woodside (Toled..
7*	252	G - Rod Taylor (Ole Miss)
	253	WR - Auden Tate (Florida St..

Regular Season Wins: Past & Current Proj

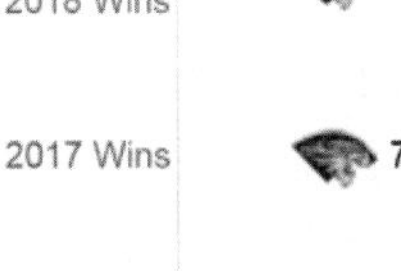

Lineup & Cap Hits

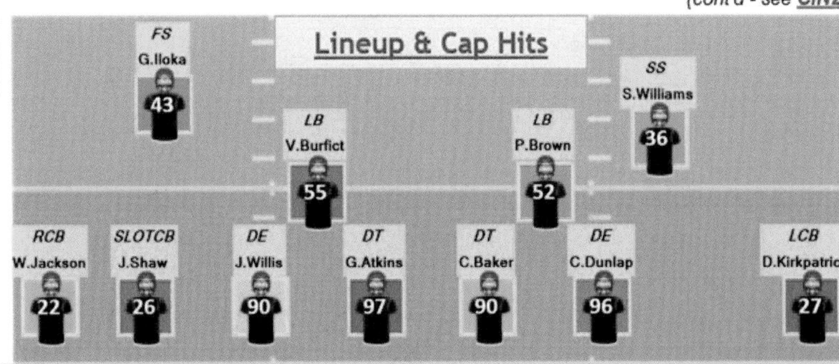

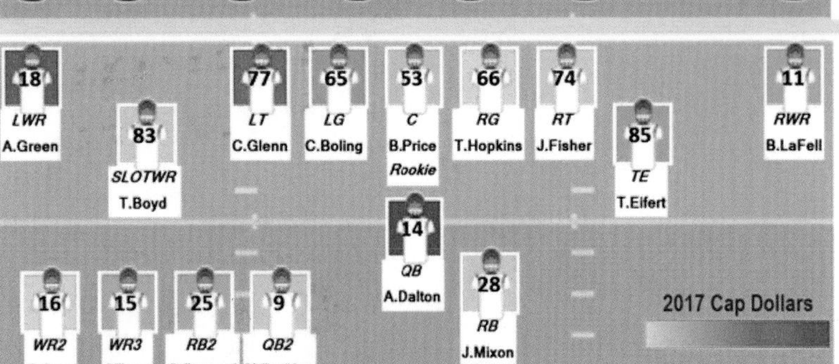

2018 Unit Spending

All DEF
All OFF

Positional Spending

	Rank	Total	2017 Rk
All OFF	13	$97.46M	18
QB	19	$18.95M	18
OL	22	$30.70M	31
RB	9	$9.25M	13
WR	7	$27.22M	6
TE	11	$11.34M	14
All DEF	10	$90.12M	8
DL	13	$30.70M	11
LB	16	$21.04M	19
CB	6	$25.60M	5
S	14	$12.78M	19

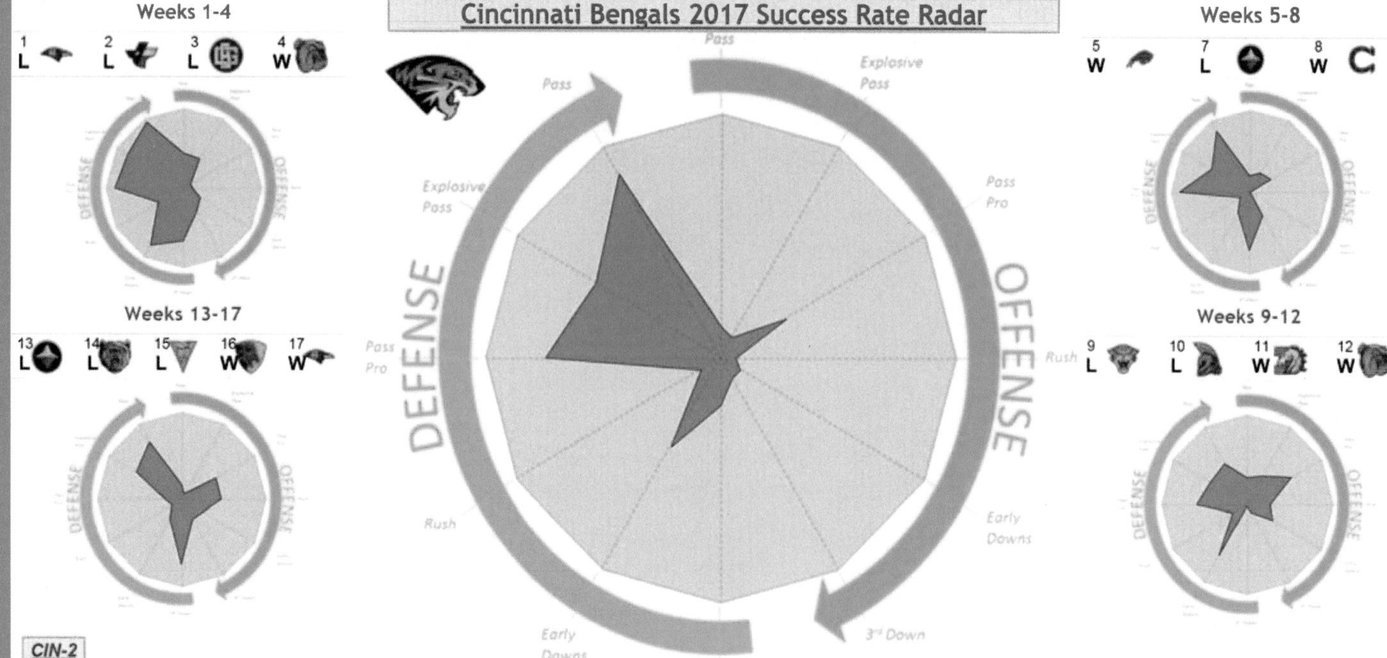

CIN-2

But the only offensive lineman the 2017 Bengals drafted was a backup center in the fifth round. So the line was predictably terrible. Dalton took 39 sacks, and Cincinnati ranked 20th in pass-protection efficiency. Lazor's offense did incorporate more running back passes, which take less time to develop and reduce quarterback hits.

Center is a highly underrated position. The league average Success Rate on run plays behind center is 46%. The Bengals managed a 41% Success Rate behind C Russell Bodine over the last two years. They logged even to above-average Success Rates behind all other offensive line positions. They were even worse running behind center on early downs, managing a 39% Success Rate which ranked 7% below league average. While the NFL average is 29% runs behind center, the Bengals ran behind Bodine on only 11.5% of carries in an effort to decrease his impact on games.

The 2018 Bengals replaced Bodine with Ohio State's Billy Price in the first round. They traded for LT Cordy Glenn. Bodine's departure for Buffalo is addition by subtraction. And the Bengals face a softer 2018 slate after drawing last year's third-toughest schedule of pass rushes.

The Bengals' wide receiver corps returns intact, which isn't necessarily a good thing after pedestrian Brandon LaFell led the team in wideout snaps two straight years. A.J. Green is a bona-fide No. 1, but Cincinnati has problems at third receiver and tight end. 2017 first-round pick John Ross' rookie year was a disaster, earning fewer than 30 snaps. Tyler Boyd had a falling out with the coaching staff and missed three games with an MCL injury. The Bengals were forced to lean on guys like Alex Erickson and Josh Malone in three-receiver sets.

(cont'd - see CIN-3)

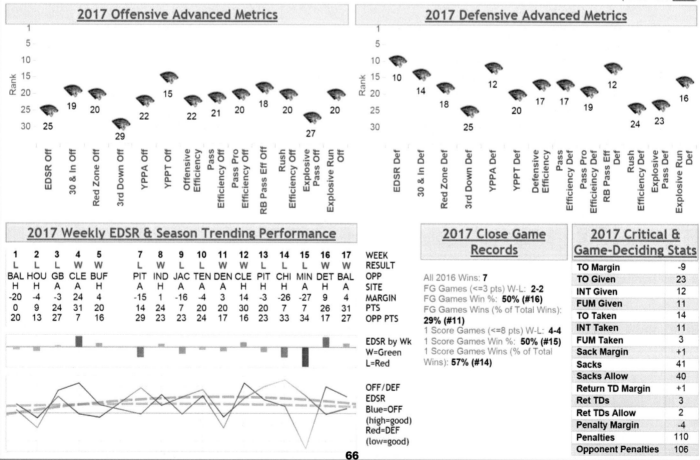

2017 Offensive Advanced Metrics

Metric	Rank
EDSR Off	25
30 & In Off	19
Red Zone Off	20
3rd Down Off	29
YPPA Off	22
YPPT Off	15
Offensive Efficiency	22
Pass Efficiency Off	21
Pass Pro Efficiency Off	20
RB Pass Eff Off	18
Rush Efficiency Off	20
Explosive Pass Off	27
Explosive Run Off	20

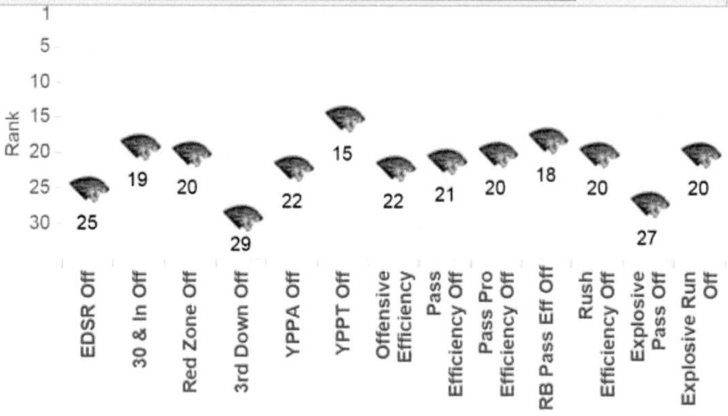

2017 Defensive Advanced Metrics

Metric	Rank
EDSR Def	10
30 & In Def	14
Red Zone Def	18
3rd Down Def	25
YPPA Def	12
YPPT Def	20
Defensive Efficiency	17
Pass Efficiency Def	17
Pass Pro Efficiency Def	19
RB Pass Eff Def	12
Rush Efficiency Def	24
Explosive Pass Def	23
Explosive Run Def	16

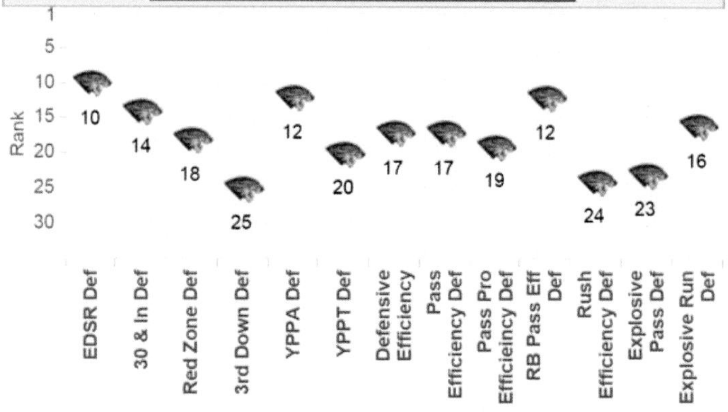

2017 Weekly EDSR & Season Trending Performance

WEEK	1	2	3	4	5	7	8	9	10	11	12	13	14	15	16	17
RESULT	L	L	L	W	W	L	W	L	L	W	W	L	L	L	W	W
OPP	BAL	HOU	GB	CLE	BUF	PIT	IND	JAC	TEN	DEN	CLE	PIT	CHI	MIN	DET	BAL
SITE	H	H	A	A	H	A	H	A	A	A	H	H	H	A	H	A
MARGIN	-20	-4	-3	24	4	-15	1	-16	-4	3	14	-3	-26	-27	9	4
PTS	0	9	24	31	20	14	24	7	20	20	30	20	7	7	26	31
OPP PTS	20	13	27	7	16	29	23	23	24	17	16	23	33	34	17	27

EDSR by Wk
W=Green
L=Red

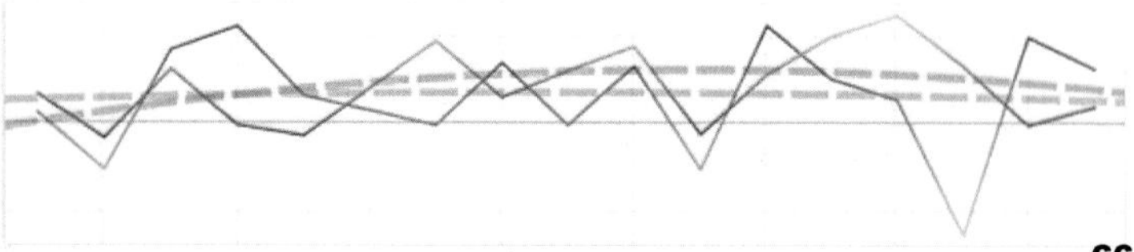

OFF/DEF EDSR
Blue=OFF (high=good)
Red=DEF (low=good)

2017 Close Game Records

All 2016 Wins: **7**
FG Games (<=3 pts) W-L: **2-2**
FG Games Win %: **50% (#16)**
FG Games Wins (% of Total Wins): **29% (#11)**
1 Score Games (<=8 pts) W-L: **4-4**
1 Score Games Win %: **50% (#15)**
1 Score Games Wins (% of Total Wins): **57% (#14)**

2017 Critical & Game-Deciding Stats

TO Margin	-9
TO Given	23
INT Given	12
FUM Given	11
TO Taken	14
INT Taken	11
FUM Taken	3
Sack Margin	+1
Sacks	41
Sacks Allow	40
Return TD Margin	+1
Ret TDs	3
Ret TDs Allow	2
Penalty Margin	-4
Penalties	110
Opponent Penalties	106

Cincinnati Bengals 2018 Strength of Schedule In Detail (compared to 2017)

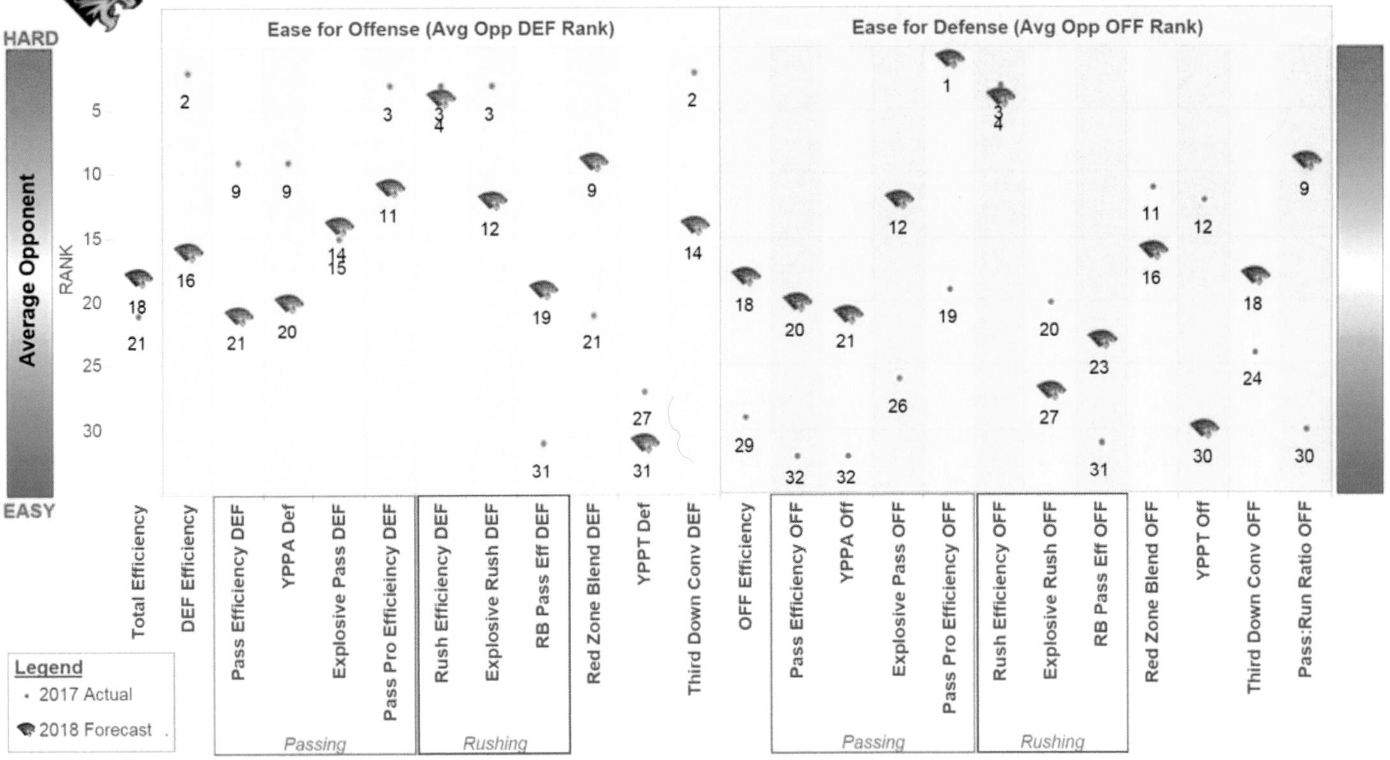

HARD — Average Opponent (RANK) — EASY

Ease for Offense (Avg Opp DEF Rank)

Metric	2017 Actual	2018 Forecast
Total Efficiency	21	18
DEF Efficiency	2	16
Pass Efficiency DEF (Passing)	9	21
YPPA Def (Passing)	9	20
Explosive Pass DEF (Passing)	15	14
Pass Pro Efficiency DEF (Passing)	3	11
Rush Efficiency DEF (Rushing)	3	4
Explosive Rush DEF (Rushing)	3	12
RB Pass Eff DEF (Rushing)	31	19
Red Zone Blend DEF	21	9
YPPT Def	27	31
Third Down Conv DEF	2	14

Ease for Defense (Avg Opp OFF Rank)

Metric	2017 Actual	2018 Forecast
OFF Efficiency	29	18
Pass Efficiency OFF (Passing)	32	20
YPPA Off (Passing)	32	21
Explosive Pass OFF (Passing)	26	12
Pass Pro Efficiency OFF (Passing)	19	1
Rush Efficiency OFF (Rushing)	3	4
Explosive Rush OFF (Rushing)	20	27
RB Pass Eff OFF (Rushing)	31	23
Red Zone Blend OFF	11	16
YPPT Off	12	30
Third Down Conv OFF	24	18
Pass:Run Ratio OFF	30	9

Legend: • 2017 Actual; 2018 Forecast

2018 v 2017 Schedule Variances* (DEF=Variance of DEF faced, OFF=Var of OFF faced)

Pass DEF Rk	Pass DEF Blend Rk	Rush DEF Rk	Rush DEF Blend Rk	Pass OFF Rk	Pass OFF Blend Rk	Rush OFF Rk	Rush OFF Blend Rk
29	26	18	17	3	13	9	3

* **1**=Hardest Jump in 2018 schedule from 2017 (aka a much harder schedule in 2018), **32**=Easiest Jump in 2018 schedule from 2017 (aka a much easier schedule in 2018); **Pass Blend** metric blends 4 metrics: Pass Efficiency, YPPA, Explosive Pass & Pass Rush; **Rush Blend** metric blends 3 metrics: Rush Efficiency, Explosive Rush & RB Targets

Team Records & Trends

	2017	2016	2015
Average line	1.0	-1.0	-4.1
Average O/U line	40.9	44.7	44.6
Straight Up Record	7-9	6-9	12-4
Against the Spread Record	9-7	5-9	12-3
Over/Under Record	7-8	6-10	7-9
ATS as Favorite	3-4	4-4	8-3
ATS as Underdog	6-3	0-4	3-0
Straight Up Home	4-4	4-3	6-2
ATS Home	4-4	4-3	4-3
Over/Under Home	3-4	3-4	3-5
ATS as Home Favorite	2-4	3-2	4-3
ATS as a Home Dog	2-0	0-1	0-0
Straight Up Away	3-5	2-6	6-2
ATS Away	5-3	1-5	8-0
Over/Under Away	4-4	2-6	4-4
ATS Away Favorite	1-0	1-1	4-0
ATS Away Dog	4-3	0-3	3-0
Six Point Teaser Record	9-7	12-4	14-2
Seven Point Teaser Record	9-7	13-3	14-2
Ten Point Teaser Record	12-3	13-2	14-2

CIN-3

Injuries have derailed Tyler Eifert's career. Over the past three years, Eifert is tied for sixth in the NFL in red-zone touchdowns (16) despite playing 23-of-48 games. He is No. 2 in red-zone TDs among tight ends. But Eifert played in less than 40% of available games over the past four seasons. After claiming to be 100% in March, Eifert is now considered questionable for training camp after an offseason setback.

No. 2 TE Tyler Kroft's best ability is availability. Primarily used in 11-personnel packages, Kroft delivered a mediocre 46% Success Rate and averaged 6.1 yards per target. Kroft was most valuable on decoy patterns. In 12 and 13 personnel, Kroft scored five TDs on just 12 targets with a 58% Success Rate and 138 passer rating when targeted.

Cincinnati's 2018 rushing offense fell off against the NFL's third-toughest schedule of run defenses, coupled with Bodine's poor play. And their creativity lacked under Lazor.

(cont'd - see CIN-4)

2018 Rest Analysis

Avg Rest	6.47
Avg Rk	3
Team More Rest	2
Opp More Rest	3
Net Rest Edge	-1
3 Days Rest	1
4 Days Rest	0
5 Days Rest	0
6 Days Rest	12
7 Days Rest	0
8 Days Rest	0
9 Days Rest	1
10 Days Rest	0
11 Days Rest	0
12 Days Rest	0
13 Days Rest	1
14 Days Rest	0

Health by Unit*

2017 Rk	20
2016 Rk	3
Off Rk	22
Def Rk	19
QB Rk	9
RB Rk	25
WR Rk	11
TE Rk	31
Oline Rk	19
Dline Rk	14
LB Rk	26
DB Rk	19

Based on the great work of Scott Kacsmar from Football Outsiders

2018 Weekly Betting Lines (wks 1-16)

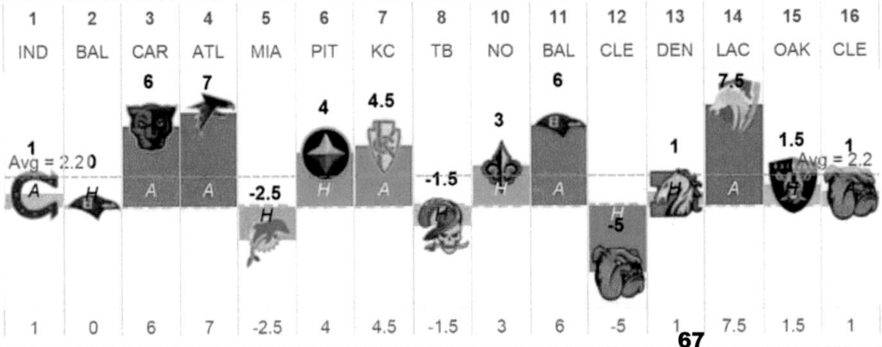

Week	1	2	3	4	5	6	7	8	10	11	12	13	14	15	16
Opponent	IND	BAL	CAR	ATL	MIA	PIT	KC	TB	NO	BAL	CLE	DEN	LAC	OAK	CLE
Site	A	H	A	A	H	H	A	H	H	A	H	H	A	A	H
Line	1	0	6	7	-2.5	4	4.5	-1.5	3	6	-5	1	7.5	1.5	1

Avg = 2.20

Home Lines (wks 1-16)

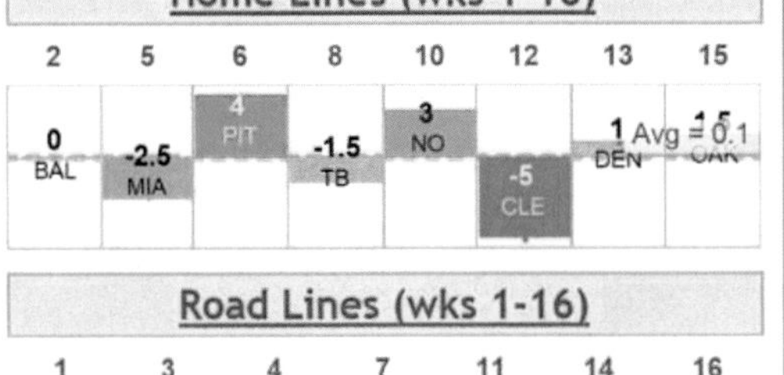

Road Lines (wks 1-16)

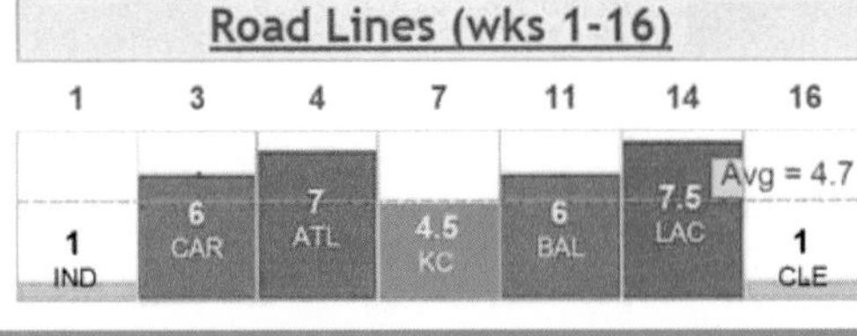

Cincinnati Bengals 2017 Play Analysis

2017 Play Tendencies

All Pass %	59%
All Pass Rk	11
All Rush %	41%
All Rush Rk	22
1 Score Pass %	57%
1 Score Pass Rk	16
2016 1 Score Pass %	59%
2016 1 Score Pass Rk	18
2017 Pass Increase %	-1%
Pass Increase Rk	15
1 Score Rush %	43%
1 Score Rush Rk	17
Up Pass %	54%
Up Pass Rk	3
Up Rush %	46%
Up Rush Rk	30
Down Pass %	65%
Down Pass Rk	21
Down Rush %	35%
Down Rush Rk	12

2017 Down & Distance Tendencies

Down	Distance	Total Plays	Pass Rate	Run Rate	Play Success %
1	Short (1-3)	5	60%	40%	60%
	Med (4-7)	4	75%	25%	25%
	Long (8-10)	292	46%	54%	48%
	XL (11+)	11	55%	45%	18%
2	Short (1-3)	32	38%	63%	50%
	Med (4-7)	75	61%	39%	36%
	Long (8-10)	89	60%	40%	42%
	XL (11+)	31	84%	16%	32%
3	Short (1-3)	34	59%	41%	47%
	Med (4-7)	58	88%	12%	36%
	Long (8-10)	35	94%	6%	49%
	XL (11+)	21	86%	14%	19%
4	Short (1-3)	3	33%	67%	67%

Shotgun %:

Under Center	Shotgun
36%	64%
37%	*63%*

AVG

Run Rate:

Under Center	Shotgun
66%	27%
68%	*23%*

AVG

Pass Rate:

Under Center	Shotgun
34%	73%
32%	*77%*

AVG

Short Yardage Intelligence:

2nd and Short Run

Run Freq	Run Rk	NFL Run Freq Avg	Run 1D Rate	Run NFL 1D Avg
66%	21	67%	42%	69%

2nd and Short Pass

Pass Freq	Pass Rk	NFL Pass Freq Avg	Pass 1D Rate	Pass NFL 1D Avg
34%	11	33%	70%	53%

Most Frequent Play

Down	Distance	Play Type	Player	Total Plays	Play Success %
1	Short (1-3)	PASS	Tyler Kroft	2	100%
		RUSH	Joe Mixon	2	50%
	Long (8-10)	RUSH	Joe Mixon	72	43%
	XL (11+)	PASS	Joe Mixon	2	50%
		RUSH	Joe Mixon	2	0%
2	Short (1-3)	RUSH	Joe Mixon	14	57%
	Med (4-7)	RUSH	Joe Mixon	15	40%
	Long (8-10)	RUSH	Joe Mixon	17	24%
	XL (11+)	PASS	Tyler Kroft	6	50%
3	Short (1-3)	RUSH	Giovani Bernard	7	57%
	Med (4-7)	PASS	A.J. Green	11	27%
	Long (8-10)	PASS	A.J. Green	8	63%
	XL (11+)	PASS	Giovani Bernard	5	0%

Most Successful Play*

Down	Distance	Play Type	Player	Total Plays	Play Success %
1	Long (8-10)	PASS	Tyler Kroft	10	80%
2	Short (1-3)	RUSH	Joe Mixon	14	57%
	Med (4-7)	RUSH	Giovani Bernard	9	67%
	Long (8-10)	PASS	A.J. Green	12	58%
	XL (11+)	PASS	Brandon LaFell	5	60%
3	Short (1-3)	RUSH	Giovani Bernard	7	57%
	Med (4-7)	PASS	Brandon LaFell	10	60%
	Long (8-10)	PASS	A.J. Green	8	63%
	XL (11+)	PASS	Giovani Bernard	5	0%

**Minimum 5 plays to qualify*

2017 Snap Rates

Wk	Opp	Score	Brandon LaFell	A.J. Green	Giovani Bernard	Joe Mixon	Tyler Boyd	C.J. Uzomah	Ryan Hewitt	Tyler Eifert	Jeremy Hill	Cody Core
1	BAL	L 20-0	57 (93%)	55 (90%)	29 (48%)	22 (36%)	42 (69%)		7 (11%)	54 (89%)	10 (16%)	10 (16%)
2	HOU	L 13-9	57 (89%)	62 (97%)	33 (52%)	16 (25%)			9 (14%)	50 (78%)	15 (23%)	7 (11%)
3	GB	L 27-24	56 (92%)	57 (93%)	13 (21%)	34 (56%)	30 (49%)	17 (28%)	4 (7%)		14 (23%)	5 (8%)
4	CLE	W 31-7	56 (88%)	55 (86%)	21 (33%)	31 (48%)	37 (58%)	24 (38%)	7 (11%)		12 (19%)	8 (13%)
5	BUF	W 20-16	61 (92%)	57 (86%)	22 (33%)	36 (55%)	5 (8%)	17 (26%)			11 (17%)	12 (18%)
7	PIT	L 29-14	46 (90%)	44 (86%)	23 (45%)	22 (43%)		13 (25%)			8 (16%)	21 (41%)
8	IND	W 24-23	51 (91%)	53 (95%)	14 (25%)	35 (63%)		10 (18%)			7 (13%)	
9	JAC	L 23-7	38 (97%)	15 (38%)	11 (28%)	28 (72%)		11 (28%)	6 (15%)			2 (5%)
10	TEN	L 24-20	48 (94%)	49 (96%)	20 (39%)	31 (61%)		8 (16%)	5 (10%)			
11	DEN	W 20-17	38 (69%)	48 (87%)	20 (36%)	36 (65%)	22 (40%)	18 (33%)	14 (25%)			1 (2%)
12	CLE	W 30-16	45 (74%)	56 (92%)	15 (25%)	46 (75%)	15 (25%)	17 (28%)	14 (23%)			
13	PIT	L 23-20	57 (89%)	62 (97%)	44 (69%)	17 (27%)	15 (23%)	9 (14%)	13 (20%)			
14	CHI	L 33-7	52 (96%)	43 (80%)	46 (85%)		30 (56%)	14 (26%)	4 (7%)			
15	MIN	L 34-7	50 (91%)	45 (82%)	49 (89%)			23 (42%)	9 (16%)			
16	DET	W 26-17	76 (88%)	81 (94%)	72 (84%)	7 (8%)	50 (58%)	23 (27%)	10 (12%)			
17	BAL	W 31-27	75 (95%)	75 (95%)	54 (68%)	25 (32%)	60 (76%)	12 (15%)	4 (5%)			
	Grand Total		863 (89%)	857 (87%)	486 (49%)	386 (48%)	306 (46%)	216 (26%)	106 (14%)	104 (83%)	77 (18%)	66 (14%)

Personnel Groupings

Personnel	Team %	NFL Avg	Succ. %
1-1 [3WR]	71%	59%	39%
1-2 [2WR]	20%	19%	40%
1-3 [1WR]	7%	5%	35%

Grouping Tendencies

Personnel	Pass Rate	Pass Succ. %	Run Succ. %
1-1 [3WR]	68%	39%	41%
1-2 [2WR]	42%	42%	39%
1-3 [1WR]	16%	60%	30%

Red Zone Targets (min 3)

Receiver	All	Inside 5	6-10	11-20
A.J. Green	16	1	7	8
Tyler Kroft	12	7		5
Brandon LaFell	11		4	7
Giovani Bernard	5		1	4
C.J. Uzomah	2	1	1	
Tyler Boyd	2		2	
Tyler Eifert	1			1

Red Zone Rushes (min 3)

Rusher	All	Inside 5	6-10	11-20
Joe Mixon	25	7	11	7
Giovani Bernard	10	1	1	8
Jeremy Hill	9		1	8
Andy Dalton	7		2	5

Early Down Target Rate

RB	TE	WR
23%	17%	60%
23%	*21%*	*56%*

NFL AVG

Overall Target Success %

RB	TE	WR
42%	51%	45%
#24	#15	#27

Cincinnati Bengals 2017 Passing Recap & 2018 Outlook

Andy Dalton experienced huge 2017 regression, even after he missed A.J. Green for nearly half of 2016. Dalton's YPA dipped from 7.5 (above average) to 6.7 (below average), his completion rate from 65% to 60%, and Dalton's passer rating fell from 92 to 87. Dalton's advanced metrics were equally concerning. His Early-Down Success Rate dropped from 52% to 45%. Passes that gained 20-plus yards dropped from 10% to 6.7%. Air Yards per completion went from 6.7 to 5.4.

The Success Rate of Dalton's wide receivers dipped from ninth best in the NFL (52%) to 27th (45%). Dalton's deep passing to wideouts particularly stumbled. The hope is Cincinnati's deep-pass efficiency will increase as pass protection improves, but the truth is they have limited receiving talent behind Green. So the burden falls on Lazor to scheme better play designs with less predictability to defeat coverage.

Andy Dalton Rating All Downs

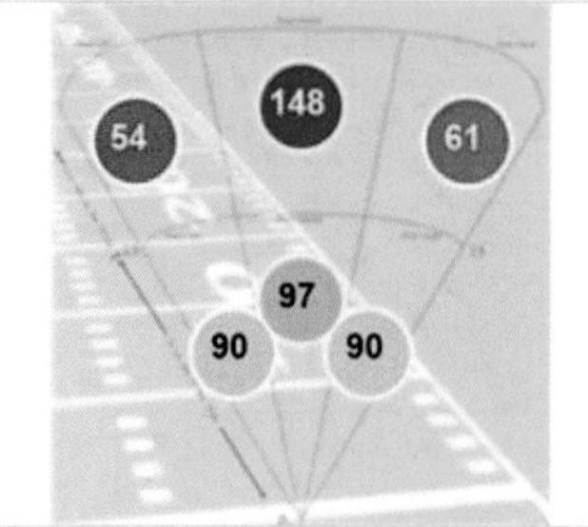

Andy Dalton Rating Early Downs

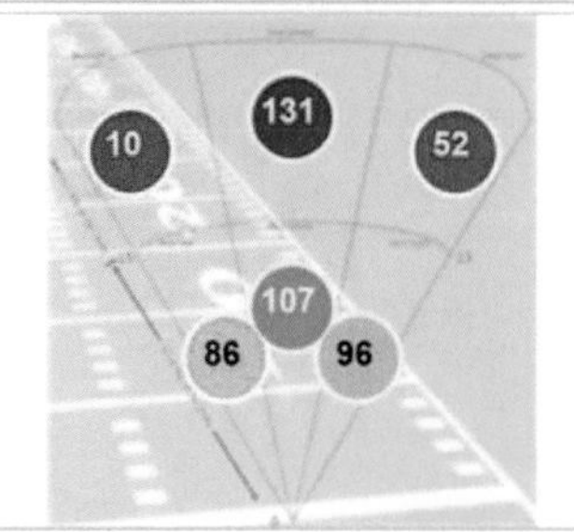

2017 Standard Passing Table

QB	Comp	Att	Comp %	Yds	YPA	TDs	INT	Sacks	Rating	Rk
Andy Dalton	297	496	60%	3,309	6.7	25	12	39	87	22
NFL Avg			62%		7.0				87.5	

2017 Advanced Passing Table

QB	Success %	EDSR Passing Success %	20+ Yd Pass Gains	20+ Yd Pass %	30+ Yd Pass Gains	30+ Yd Pass %	Avg. Air Yds per Comp	Avg. YAC per Comp	20+ Air Yd Comp	20+ Air Yd %
Andy Dalton	41%	45%	33	6.7%	14	2.8%	5.4	5.7	12	4%
NFL Avg	44%	48%	27.7	8.8%	10.3	3.3%	6.0	4.7	11.7	6%

Interception Rates by Down

Yards to Go	1	2	3	4	Total
1 & 2	0.0%	10.0%	0.0%	0.0%	4.0%
3, 4, 5	0.0%	0.0%	7.1%	0.0%	4.3%
6 - 9	0.0%	1.3%	4.5%	0.0%	2.7%
10 - 14	2.2%	0.0%	0.0%	0.0%	1.6%
15+	0.0%	0.0%	0.0%	0.0%	0.0%
Total	2.1%	1.2%	3.7%	0.0%	2.2%

3rd Down Passing - Short of Sticks Analysis

QB	Avg. Yds to Go	Avg. YIA (of Comp)	Avg Yds Short	Short of Sticks Rate	Short Rk
Andy Dalton	7.8	6.7	-1.1	54%	21
NFL Avg	7.8	6.7	-1.1	60%	

Air Yds vs YAC

Air Yds %	YAC %	Rk
60%	40%	19
58%	42%	

2017 Receiving Recap & 2018 Outlook

The drop-off behind A.J. Green is an overarching Bengals problem, and Cincinnati's lack of alternative threats hurt Green's 2017 efficiency. Among wide receivers with 100-plus targets, Green's 75 passer rating when thrown to ranked 31st of 33. His 44% Success Rate was 32nd of 33. And his 52% catch rate tied for dead last. reen should likewise benefit from an improved offensive line. But even if Green plays better, the Bengals need another pass catcher (or two) to make defenses pay for rolling coverage to Green's side. Lazor can also help by moving Green around more to dictate coverage matchups. Green ran just 14% of his 2017 routes in the slot.

Player *Min 50 Targets*	Targets	Comp %	YPA	Rating	TOARS	Success %	Success Rk	Missed YPA Rk	YAS % Rk	TDs
A.J. Green	143	52%	7.5	75	4.9	44%	95	29	40	8
Brandon LaFell	89	58%	6.2	78	4.2	42%	106	75	94	3
Tyler Kroft	62	68%	6.5	123	4.3	48%	71	59	112	7
Giovani Bernard	61	70%	6.2	98	3.8	34%	127	131	114	2

Directional Passer Rating Delivered

Receiver	Short Left	Short Middle	Short Right	Deep Left	Deep Middle	Deep Right	Player Total
A.J. Green	80	91	79	34	106	61	75
Brandon LaFell	86	65	69	65	135	88	78
Tyler Kroft	119	133	125	40	110	40	123
Giovani Bernard	100	94	96				98
Joe Mixon	103	105	93				102
Tyler Boyd	45	128	86	40	158	40	96
Alex Erickson	117	57	105	135		96	106
C.J. Uzomah	93	149	66	40			105
Tyler Eifert	40	108	83			119	105
Cody Core	40			40		40	40
Jeremy Hill			83				83
Team Total	90	98	92	55	149	64	91

2017 Rushing Recap & 2017 Outlook

Although Giovani Bernard's 2017 yards-per-carry average was substantially better than Joe Mixon's, Gio's explosiveness (YAS%) was worse. The difference came in missed yards-per-attempt rate, meaning production on unsuccessful plays. One 2017 improvement was the Bengals' increase in early-down running back passes. They targeted backs on 22% of early-down attempts, up from 19% in 2016. Bengals early-down running back passes generated 8.1 yards per attempt, which ranked third best in the NFL and was significantly better than their early-down targets to tight ends (7.2 YPA) and wide receivers (6.6). Cincinnati's 50% Success Rate on early-down running back passes was 5% better than their wide receiver targets.

Player *Min 50 Rushes*	Rushes	YPC	Success %	Success Rk	Missed YPA Rk	YTS % Rk	YAS % Rk	Early Down Success %	Early Down Success Rk	TDs
Joe Mixon	178	3.5	40%	58	58	28	37	40%	60	4
Giovani Bernard	105	4.4	40%	60	38	46	57	40%	58	2

Yards per Carry by Direction

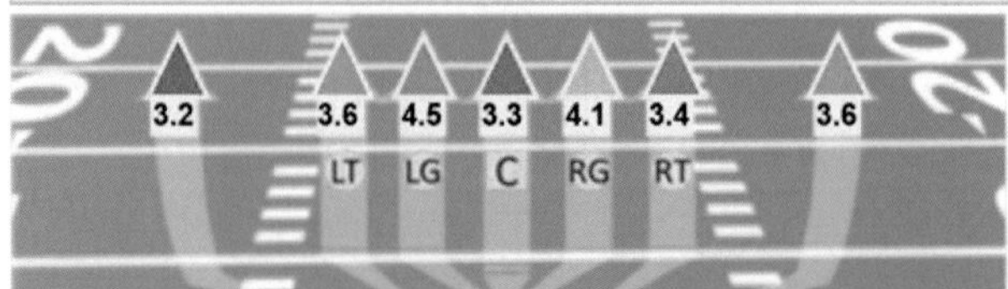

Directional Run Frequency

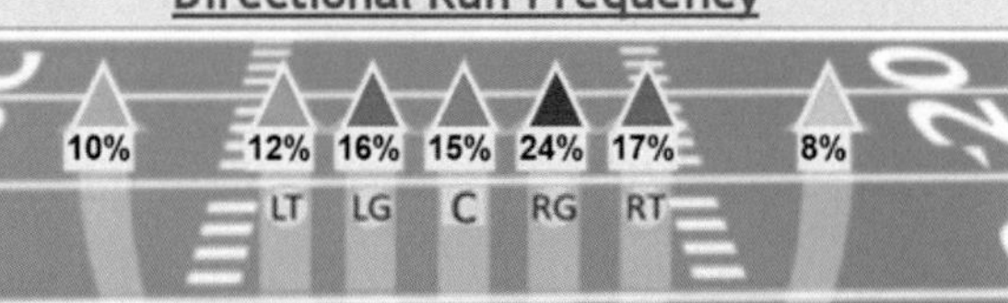

The Bengals ran out of three main groupings: 11, 12, and 13. In three-receiver 11 personnel, the Bengals ran 35% of the time. In two-tight end 12, they went 61% run. In three-tight end 13 personnel, Cincinnati ran on 87% of plays. Their usage in second halves of games was incredibly predictable. They ran 92% of the time from 13 personnel in the second half with an abysmal 23% Success Rate. They went 100% run from 13 personnel on all second-, third-, and fourth-down plays. These runs managed an even-worse 21% Success Rate and 2.1 yards per carry. Dalton ran the ball on 50% of these 13-personnel plays and had a 0% Success Rate.

Aside from becoming less predictable, the Bengals need to work on their overall play-calling habits and focus on efficiency. After a first-and-ten incompletion, all teams must pass the ball more often. But Cincinnati went run on 60% of second-and-ten plays, well above league average (54%). The NFL average for second-and-ten passes is 8.0 yards per attempt. But the Bengals averaged 2.7 yards per attempt. Dalton completed a league-worst 50% of his throws on second-and-ten plays. His 30% Success Rate ranked 35th of 37 qualified quarterbacks.

I'm positive the Bengals would improve both their run and pass efficiency if they worked more to optimize their play-calling strategy. They face an easier schedule of defenses.

(cont'd - see CIN-5)

Evan Silva's Fantasy Corner

Joe Mixon was mainly the lead part of the Bengals' 2017 backfield committee, logging over 50% of offensive snaps in just 7-of-14 appearances. Mixon did top 50% in five straight games during Weeks 8-12, then missed two with a concussion. His efficiency was poor behind an offensive line that finished 23rd in yards created before contact per attempt (PFF) and 24th in Football Outsiders' Adjusted Line Yards. The Bengals also faced the NFL's third-toughest schedule of run defenses. Mixon's 3.52 yards per carry, 41% Success Rate (37th among 47 qualified backs), and below-average Game Speed (Next Gen Stats) were still red flags. It's notable that Cincinnati's 2017 ranking of 29th in rushing attempts was very out of character for a Marvin Lewis-coached team; Lewis' offenses ranked top ten in rushing attempts in each of the previous four years. The Bengals are also headed for positive rushing-TD regression after scoring just six last year, third fewest in the league. Ultimately, Mixon' breakout potential hinges on holding off Giovani Bernard for featured work. For what it's worth, director of player personnel Duke Tobin said at the Combine Mixon will be the Bengals' "bellcow".

Division History: Season Wins & 2018 Projection

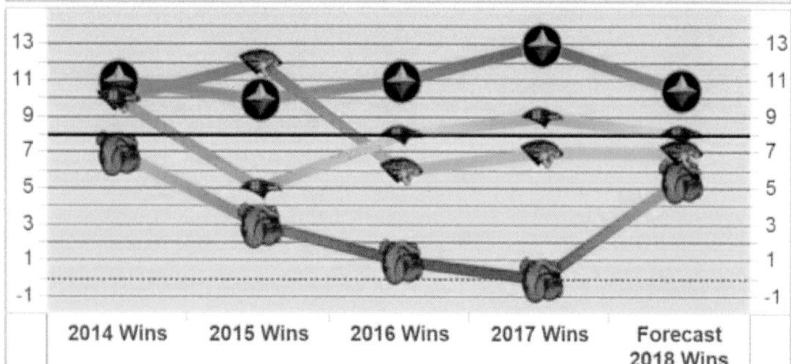

Rank of 2018 Defensive Pass Efficiency Faced by Week

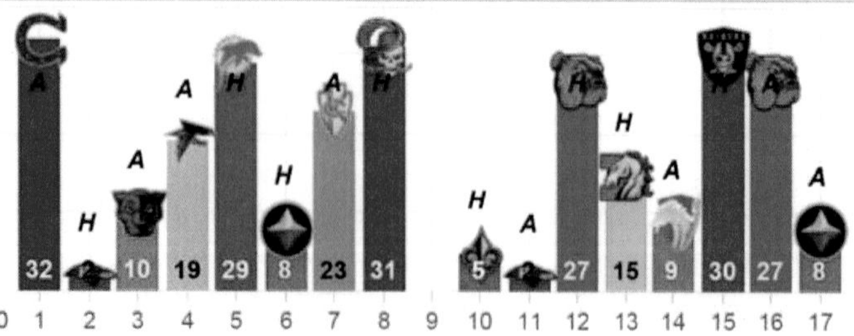

Rank of 2018 Defensive Rush Efficiency Faced by Week

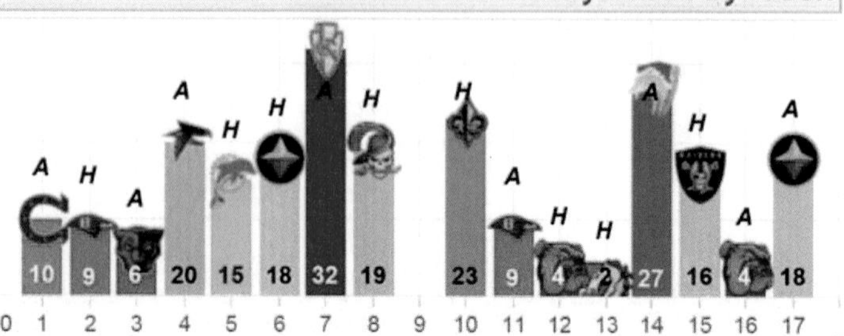

2017 Situational Usage by Player & Position

Usage Rate by Score

		Being Blown Out (14+)	Down Big (9-13)	One Score	Large Lead (9-13)	Blowout Lead (14+)	Grand Total
RUSH	Joe Mixon	6%	16%	23%	20%	38%	21%
	Giovani Bernard	15%	20%	12%	16%	8%	13%
	Jeremy Hill	2%		5%		4%	4%
	Alex Erickson			1%			1%
	Josh Malone			0%			0%
	Brian Hill	6%		1%			1%
	John Ross			0%			0%
	Total	29%	36%	43%	37%	50%	41%
PASS	Joe Mixon	3%	16%	4%	4%		4%
	Giovani Bernard	15%	8%	6%	2%	10%	7%
	A.J. Green	16%	8%	17%	27%	17%	17%
	Brandon LaFell	10%	4%	12%	10%	6%	11%
	Tyler Kroft	5%	8%	7%	12%	8%	7%
	Jeremy Hill	1%		0%		2%	0%
	Tyler Boyd	6%	4%	3%	6%	2%	4%
	Alex Erickson	2%		2%	2%		2%
	Josh Malone	5%	8%	1%		2%	2%
	C.J. Uzomah	5%	4%	1%		2%	2%
	Brian Hill	1%		0%			0%
	Tyler Eifert			1%			1%
	Cody Core	1%	4%	0%			0%
	John Ross			0%			0%
	Ryan Hewitt			0%		2%	0%
	Cethan Carter			0%			0%
	Total	71%	64%	57%	63%	50%	59%

Positional Target Distribution vs NFL Average

		NFL Wide				Team Only			
		Left	Middle	Right	Total	Left	Middle	Right	Total
Deep	WR	962	497	958	2,417	24	12	29	65
	TE	189	147	185	521	3	3	3	9
	RB	39	9	42	90				
	All	1,190	653	1,185	3,028	27	15	32	74
Short	WR	2,795	1,608	2,701	7,104	67	63	89	219
	TE	838	816	1,145	2,799	25	23	25	73
	RB	1,287	797	1,256	3,340	34	26	39	99
	All	4,920	3,221	5,102	13,243	126	112	153	391
Total		6,110	3,874	6,287	16,271	153	127	185	465

Positional Success Rates vs NFL Average

		NFL Wide				Team Only			
		Left	Middle	Right	Total	Left	Middle	Right	Total
Deep	WR	37%	45%	38%	39%	17%	67%	28%	31%
	TE	39%	52%	45%	45%	0%	67%	33%	33%
	RB	36%	56%	38%	39%				
	All	37%	47%	39%	40%	15%	67%	28%	31%
Short	WR	52%	58%	50%	52%	49%	48%	52%	50%
	TE	51%	56%	49%	52%	44%	61%	52%	52%
	RB	44%	51%	43%	45%	35%	54%	38%	41%
	All	50%	56%	48%	50%	44%	52%	48%	48%
Total		47%	54%	46%	49%	39%	54%	45%	45%

Successful Play Rate
0% 100%

Cincinnati Bengals - Success by Personnel Grouping & Play Type

Play Type	1-1 [3WR]	1-2 [2WR]	2-1 [2WR]	1-0 [4WR]	1-3 [1WR]	0-1 [4WR]	2-0 [3WR]	0-2 [3WR]	1-4 [0WR]	Grand Total
PASS	39% (450, 82%)	42% (77, 14%)	100% (1, 0%)	0% (3, 1%)	60% (10, 2%)	75% (4, 1%)	67% (3, 1%)	0% (1, 0%)	100% (1, 0%)	40% (550, 100%)
RUSH	41% (212, 56%)	39% (108, 29%)		50% (4, 1%)	30% (53, 14%)					39% (377, 100%)
TOTAL	39% (662, 71%)	40% (185, 20%)	100% (1, 0%)	29% (7, 1%)	35% (63, 7%)	75% (4, 0%)	67% (3, 0%)	0% (1, 0%)	100% (1, 0%)	39% (927, 100%)

Format Line 1: Success Rate Line 2: Total # of Plays, % of All Plays (by type)

CIN-5 And they need their offense to play better because their defense draws a much tougher schedule of opposing offenses, specifically featuring the NFL's third-highest jump in pass-offense degree of difficulty.

Last year's Bengals faced the league's easiest pass-offense slate but were only average (17th) in passer rating allowed. Every single Bengals win came against a quarterback-challenged team except their Week 16 late-December victory outdoors against the dome-team Lions. Cincinnati's other wins came against DeShone Kizer (twice), Jacoby Brissett (by one point), Brock Osweiler (by three), and Joe Flacco (four-point miracle comeback).

The Bengals need more out of Lazor, more creativity, less 11- and 12-personnel groupings, less predictability in those groupings, and possibly more two-back 21 personnel.

Dalton's pass protection should improve behind an upgrade offensive line. Losing Bodine and facing an easier schedule should help spark Cincinnati's rushing attack.

If their run game improves and 4.2 burner John Ross earns a role, the Bengals should get more from their deep passing game. Dalton's 21% Success Rate to the deep left or right last year was by far worst in the NFL. His passer rating was 58 on such attempts. In the last two drafts, the Bengals made an attempt to get younger with tremendous quantity (11 picks each year). I don't think they are good enough on either side of the ball for a legitimate Super Bowl run, but they do have enough talent to outproduce last year's results.

Receiving Success by Personnel Grouping

Position	Player	1-1 [3WR]	1-2 [2WR]	2-1 [2WR]	1-0 [4WR]	1-3 [1WR]	0-1 [4WR]	2-0 [3WR]	0-2 [3WR]	Total
RB	Giovani Bernard	34% 6.3 99.0 (59)	50% 4.0 60.4 (2)							34% 6.2 97.8 (61)
	Joe Mixon	52% 6.7 94.8 (27)	50% 16.2 109.7 (6)					100% 8.0 100.0 (1)		53% 8.4 101.8 (34)
TE	Tyler Kroft	46% 6.1 96.0 (50)	38% 11.6 142.2 (8)			100% 1.0 118.8 (4)				48% 6.5 123.3 (62)
WR	A.J. Green	43% 7.4 82.3 (115)	48% 8.4 62.4 (23)			50% 7.0 72.9 (4)			0% 0.0 0.0 (1)	44% 7.5 75.4 (143)
	Brandon LaFell	39% 5.9 71.3 (71)	43% 6.1 99.1 (14)	100% 9.0 104.2 (1)			100% 27.0 118.8 (1)	50% 3.0 79.2 (2)		42% 6.2 78.3 (89)
	Tyler Boyd	57% 7.2 97.5 (28)	100% 9.0 104.2 (1)		0% 0.0 39.6 (1)		50% 7.5 97.9 (2)			56% 7.0 96.5 (32)

Format Line 1: Success Rate Line 2: YPA Line 3: Passer Rating Line 4: Total # of Plays

Successful Play Rate
0% 100%

Rushing Success by Personnel Grouping

Position	Player	1-1 [3WR]	1-2 [2WR]	1-0 [4WR]	1-3 [1WR]	Total
QB	Andy Dalton	46% 6.4 (13)	75% 5.3 (4)	100% 11.0 (1)	5% -0.8 (20)	29% 2.6 (38)
RB	Joe Mixon	43% 4.2 (105)	31% 2.3 (48)	50% 0.0 (2)	48% 3.3 (23)	40% 3.5 (178)
	Giovani Bernard	38% 4.3 (68)	44% 5.0 (27)	0% 4.0 (1)	44% 2.7 (9)	40% 4.4 (105)

Format Line 1: Success Rate Line 2: YPC Line 3: Total # of Plays

Cleveland Browns

2018 Coaches

Head Coach:
Hue Jackson (3rd yr)
Offensive Coordinator:
Todd Haley (PIT OC) (1st yr)
Defensive Coordinator:
Gregg Williams (2nd yr)

2018 Forecast

Wins	Div Rank
5.5	#4

Past Records

2017: 0-16
2016: 1-15
2015: 3-13

EASY HARD

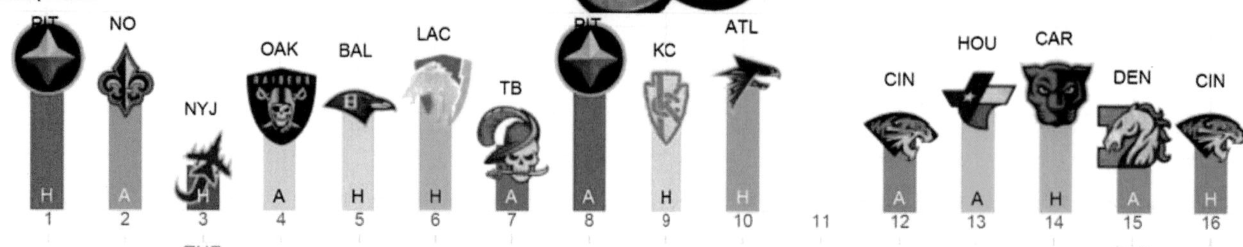

Key Players Lost

TXN	Player (POS)
Cut	Alexander, Dominique LB
	Bevins, Collin DT
	Coates, Sammie WR
	Escobar, Gavin TE
	Hartfield, Trevon CB
	Jackson, Darius RB
	McCourty, Jason CB
	Nacua, Kai CB
	Porter, Reggie CB
	Stave, Joel QB
	White, Corey CB
	Williams, Kasen WR
Declared Free Agent	Barker, Chris G
	Crowell, Isaiah RB
Retired	Thomas, Joe T

Average Line	# Games Favored	# Games Underdog
4.8	2	13

2018 Cleveland Browns Overview

What is the recipe for 0-16? In a large blender, add second-round rookie quarterback DeShone Kizer fresh out of the oven with heaping helpings of Hue Jackson and Gregg Williams. Blend thoroughly until mixed. Pour into a bucket and let marinate in the Factory of Sadness. Add a splash of Kevin Hogan. Garnish with a sprig of Cody Kessler. Serve at room temperature. After consumption, absolve coaches of all blame and pin all losses on the players for not being good enough.

I hate inefficient football. But more than that, I hate dishonesty. So I was bothered when owner Jimmy Haslam, new GM John Dorsey, and Jackson said last year's Browns roster lacked "real players" from ex-EVP Sashi Brown's tenure. For Jackson, it was a copout to deflect from his winless coaching.

Haslam, Dorsey, and Jackson want the story of the 2017 Browns to be a roster so poorly assembled that a winless season was inevitable regardless of coaching. So, Browns coaches took a summer plunge into Lake Erie to "cleanse the stench" of Sashi's administration.

I don't tell stories. I do share facts and truths. The 2017 Browns weren't Bad News Bears meets the NFL. The Browns were a team more talented than several in the league, certainly enough to win multiple games. They could have been merely below average. They'll be remembered for 0-16 due to bad coaching and decision making in training camp, practice, and games.

The Browns trailed at halftime by more than seven points in only five games. Playing in 11 one-score games at halftime -- up or down by no fewer than seven points – should not have resulted in 0-11. Cleveland trailed by between one and seven points at halftime in nine games. Over the last 25 years, only 16 teams played at least eight games in which they were down by one score at halftime. Those 16 teams played 131 games. Their combined record was 50-81 (38%), a far cry from winless. From Week 8 onward, the Browns scored a grand total of ten fourth-quarter points. In 7-of-9 games from Week 8 on, Cleveland didn't score a single fourth-quarter point.

(cont'd - see CLE2)

Key Free Agents/ Trades Added

Carrie, TJ CB
Gaines, E.J. CB
Hubbard, Chris C
Hyde, Carlos RB
Landry, Jarvis WR
Mitchell, Terrance CB
Randall, Damarious CB
Smith, Chris DE
Stephenson, Donald T
Taylor, Tyrod QB

Drafted Players

Rd	Pk	Player (College)
1	1	QB - Baker Mayfield (Oklahoma)
	4	CB - Denzel Ward (Ohio State)
2	33	G - Austin Corbett (Nevada)
	35	RB - Nick Chubb (Georgia)
3	67	DE - Chad Thomas (Miami (FL))
4	105	WR - Antonio Callaway (Florida)
5	150	LB - Genard Avery (Memphis)
6	175	WR - Damion Ratley (Texas A&M)
	188	CB - Simeon Thomas (Louisiana)

Regular Season Wins: Past & Current Proj

Forecast 2018 Wins  5.5

2017 Wins 0

Forecast 2017 Wins  4.5

2016 Wins  1

2015 Wins 3

2014 Wins 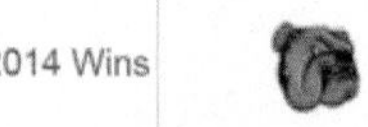 7

1 3 5 7 9 11 13 15

Lineup & Cap Hits

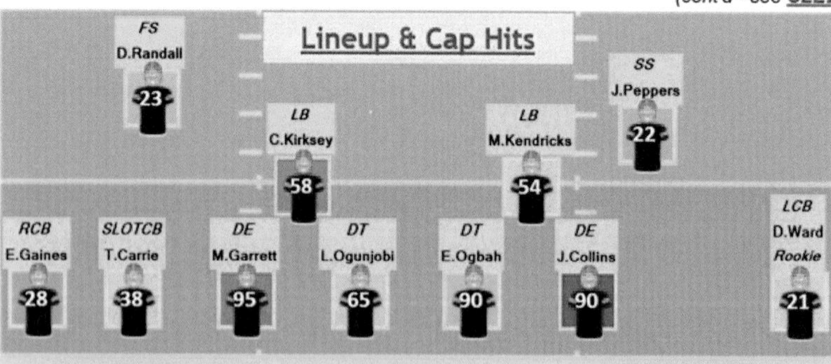

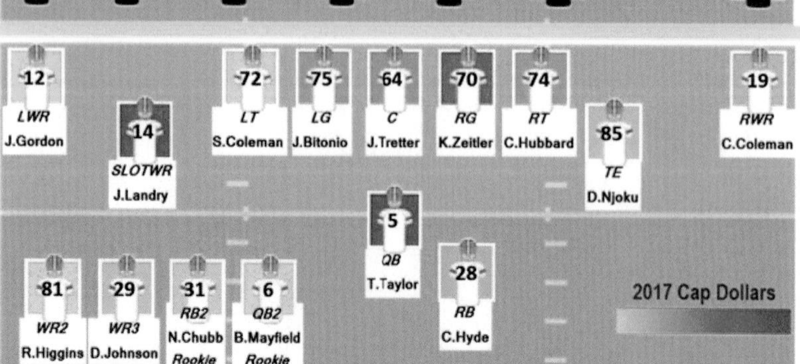

2018 Unit Spending

Positional Spending

	Rank	Total	2017 Rk
All OFF	10	$100.92M	8
QB	18	$19.46M	17
OL	5	$41.14M	1
RB	17	$7.64M	22
WR	9	$25.71M	26
TE	20	$6.97M	32
All DEF	30	$65.78M	25
DL	21	$20.89M	21
LB	15	$21.84M	15
CB	20	$16.77M	6
S	31	$6.29M	31

Cleveland Browns 2017 Success Rate Radar

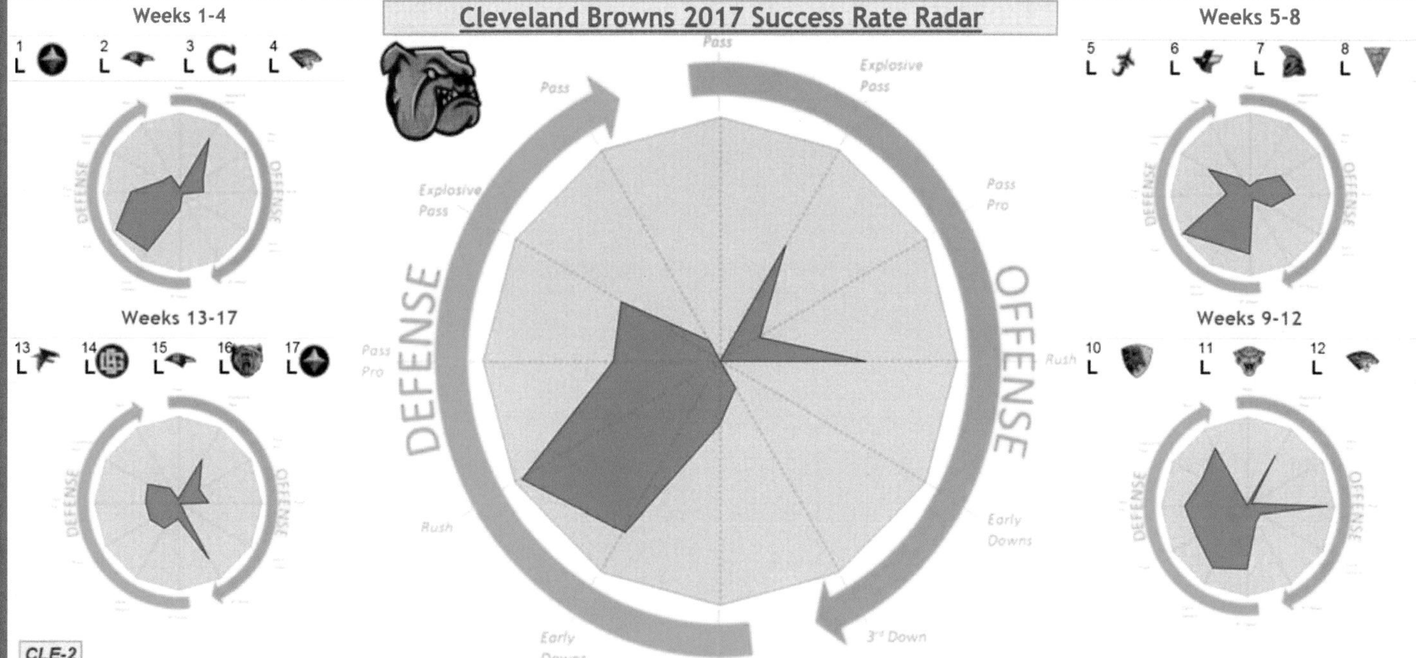

CLE-2

The Browns trailed the Vikings by seven entering the fourth quarter of Week 8 in London. Minnesota outscored Cleveland 10-0 in the fourth, and the final score looked like a blowout. 'The Browns were tied with the Lions entering the fourth quarter in Week 10. Detroit outscored Cleveland 14-0 in the fourth quarter, and the final score looked like a blowout. The very next week, the Browns trailed the Jaguars by three points entering the fourth quarter. Jacksonville outscored Cleveland 9-0 to win by 12. The Browns led the Packers 21-7 entering the fourth quarter in Week 13. Green Bay outscored Cleveland 14-0 in the fourth quarter and won in overtime. In Week 17 against the Steelers' backups, Cleveland trailed by four entering the fourth quarter, and lost by four.

The 2017 Browns stayed competitive with two teams that made conference championship games. How truly terrible was this team? The Browns lost four games decided by a field goal or less, and six by one score. Jackson's team lost the turnover battle by 28. They had 41 giveaways. Teams that lose the turnover battle lose 80% of their games, and Cleveland lost the turnover battle in all 16.

They lost the sack battle by 16 and the return-touchdown battle by five. These are critical metrics indicative of a team that won't win much. But winning zero games takes a special kind of bad. At the bottom of page two in this chapter, you will see a listing of weekly Early-Down Success Rates. A green bar indicates the team won the EDSR battle. A red bar means they lost. EDSR is one of the most correlated stats to winning that exists. The Browns' won the EDSR battle in seven games.

There was no excuse for this team to finish 0-16. The Browns went winless because of incompetent coaching asking too much from players and egregiously -EV in-game decisions. When naming Kizer his starter after training camp, Jackson said the green rookie "demonstrated the characteristics I was looking for, had a great training camp, played really well in some preseason games. It felt right, it looked right, it was the right decision for our organization. It was the process of me seeing this young man and spending as much time as I do with the quarterbacks. … We think he has 'it.'"

(cont'd - see CLE-3)

2017 Offensive Advanced Metrics

2017 Defensive Advanced Metrics

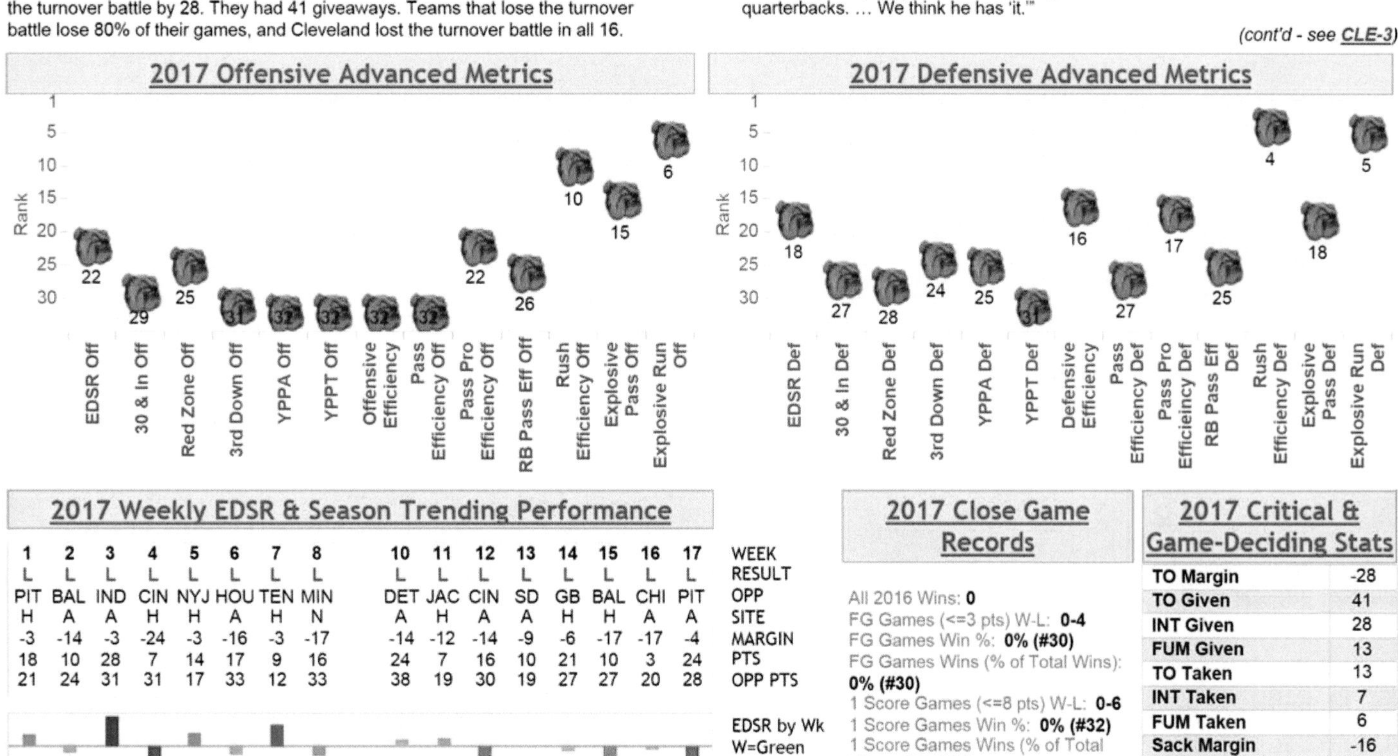

2017 Weekly EDSR & Season Trending Performance

WEEK	1	2	3	4	5	6	7	8	10	11	12	13	14	15	16	17
RESULT	L	L	L	L	L	L	L	L	L	L	L	L	L	L	L	L
OPP	PIT	BAL	IND	CIN	NYJ	HOU	TEN	MIN	DET	JAC	CIN	SD	GB	BAL	CHI	PIT
SITE	H	A	A	H	H	A	H	N	A	H	A	A	H	H	A	A
MARGIN	-3	-14	-3	-24	-3	-16	-3	-17	-14	-12	-14	-9	-6	-17	-17	-4
PTS	18	10	28	7	14	17	9	16	24	7	16	10	21	10	3	24
OPP PTS	21	24	31	31	17	33	12	33	38	19	30	19	27	27	20	28

EDSR by Wk
W=Green
L=Red

OFF/DEF
EDSR
Blue=OFF
(high=good)
Red=DEF
(low=good)

2017 Close Game Records

All 2016 Wins: **0**
FG Games (<=3 pts) W-L: **0-4**
FG Games Win %: **0% (#30)**
FG Games Wins (% of Total Wins): **0% (#30)**
1 Score Games (<=8 pts) W-L: **0-6**
1 Score Games Win %: **0% (#32)**
1 Score Games Wins (% of Total Wins): **0% (#32)**

2017 Critical & Game-Deciding Stats

TO Margin	-28
TO Given	41
INT Given	28
FUM Given	13
TO Taken	13
INT Taken	7
FUM Taken	6
Sack Margin	-16
Sacks	34
Sacks Allow	50
Return TD Margin	-5
Ret TDs	1
Ret TDs Allow	6
Penalty Margin	-9
Penalties	110
Opponent Penalties	101

Cleveland Browns 2018 Strength of Schedule In Detail (compared to 2017)

Ease for Offense (Avg Opp DEF Rank) | Ease for Defense (Avg Opp OFF Rank)

HARD / EASY — Average Opponent RANK

Metric	2017 Actual	2018 Forecast
Total Efficiency	9	7
DEF Efficiency	5	10
Pass Efficiency DEF	3	8
YPPA Def	1	3
Explosive Pass DEF	20	17
Pass Pro Efficieincy DEF	2	6
Rush Efficiency DEF	12	19
Explosive Rush DEF	6	12
RB Pass Eff DEF	27	8
Red Zone Blend DEF	11	3
YPPT Def	14	23
Third Down Conv DEF	3	4
OFF Efficiency	19	4
Pass Efficiency OFF	23	6
YPPA Off	25	14
Explosive Pass OFF	31	20
Pass Pro Efficiency OFF	4	4
Rush Efficiency OFF	12	7
Explosive Rush OFF	28	29
RB Pass Eff OFF	23	12
Red Zone Blend OFF	9	12
YPPT Off	1	17
Third Down Conv OFF	25	12
Pass:Run Ratio OFF	2	2

Passing | Rushing | Passing | Rushing

Legend
- 2017 Actual
- 2018 Forecast

2018 v 2017 Schedule Variances* (DEF=Variance of DEF faced, OFF=Var of OFF faced)

Pass DEF Rk	Pass DEF Blend Rk	Rush DEF Rk	Rush DEF Blend Rk	Pass OFF Rk	Pass OFF Blend Rk	Rush OFF Rk	Rush OFF Blend Rk
22	18	23	13	20	16	4	1

* **1**=Hardest Jump in 2018 schedule from 2017 (aka a much harder schedule in 2018), **32**=Easiest Jump in 2018 schedule from 2017 (aka a much easier schedule in 2018); **Pass Blend** metric blends 4 metrics: Pass Efficiency, YPPA, Explosive Pass & Pass Rush; **Rush Blend** metric blends 3 metrics: Rush Efficiency, Explosive Rush & RB Targets

Team Records & Trends

	2017	2016	2015
Average line	6.8	7.1	5.5
Average O/U line	41.3	44.5	43.3
Straight Up Record	0-16	1-15	3-13
Against the Spread Record	4-12	5-11	6-10
Over/Under Record	7-9	8-8	7-8
ATS as Favorite	0-1	0-0	1-2
ATS as Underdog	4-10	5-11	4-8
Straight Up Home	0-7	1-7	2-6
ATS Home	2-5	2-6	3-5
Over/Under Home	1-6	2-6	4-3
ATS as Home Favorite	0-0	0-0	1-2
ATS as a Home Dog	2-4	2-6	1-3
Straight Up Away	0-8	0-8	1-7
ATS Away	2-6	3-5	3-5
Over/Under Away	5-3	6-2	3-5
ATS Away Favorite	0-1	0-0	0-0
ATS Away Dog	2-5	3-5	3-5
Six Point Teaser Record	9-4	8-8	8-8
Seven Point Teaser Record	13-3	9-6	8-8
Ten Point Teaser Record	13-2	13-3	11-5

CLE-3

"At the quarterback position, you're going to make mistakes," Jackson cautioned. "We just have to coach him through it and get him to the other side."

Yet after four games, Jackson changed his tune. With the Browns trailing the Jets 3-0 in Week 5, Jackson ignored his "coach him through it" mantra and benched Kizer for Kevin Hogan at halftime.

Rarely do coaches commit to starting rookie quarterbacks, then bench them in their fifth career start. And Hue stuck with Hogan for Week 6. After Hogan managed 140 yards on 37 attempts and three interceptions in a blowout loss to the Texans, Hogan wasn't heard from again.

Jackson turned back to Kizer in Week 7, then did the unthinkable. He benched Kizer yet again in the third quarter of a three-point game, inserting Cody Kessler. Three straight weeks, three unnecessary blows to the psyche of 21-year-old Kizer. For Jackson, it didn't matter that Kizer faced 2017's third-toughest schedule of pass defenses, including top-ten pass defenses in seven games. *(cont'd - see CLE-4)*

2018 Rest Analysis

Avg Rest	6.47
Avg Rk	3
Team More Rest	4
Opp More Rest	1
Net Rest Edge	3
3 Days Rest	1
4 Days Rest	0
5 Days Rest	1
6 Days Rest	10
7 Days Rest	1
8 Days Rest	0
9 Days Rest	1
10 Days Rest	0
11 Days Rest	0
12 Days Rest	0
13 Days Rest	1
14 Days Rest	0

Health by Unit*

2017 Rk	12
2016 Rk	23
Off Rk	7
Def Rk	14
QB Rk	13
RB Rk	10
WR Rk	21
TE Rk	9
Oline Rk	13
Dline Rk	23
LB Rk	17
DB Rk	15

**Based on the great work of Scott Kacsmar from Football Outsiders*

2018 Weekly Betting Lines (wks 1-16)

Week	1	2	3	4	5	6	7	8	9	10	12	13	14	15	16
Opp	PIT	NO	NYJ	OAK	BAL	LAC	TB	PIT	KC	ATL	CIN	HOU	CAR	DEN	CIN
H/A	H	A	H	A	H	H	A	A	H	H	A	A		A	
Line	7	10	-2.5	7.5	2.5	4	5.5	10.5	3	3	5	10	2.5	5.5	-1

Avg = 4.8

Home Lines (wks 1-16)

Week	1	3	5	6	9	10	14	16
Opp	PIT	NYJ	BAL	LAC	KC	ATL	CAR	CIN
Line	7	-2.5	2.5	4	3	3	2.5	-1

Avg = 2.3

Road Lines (wks 1-16)

Week	2	4	7	8	12	13	15
Opp	NO	OAK	TB	PIT	CIN	HOU	DEN
Line	10	7.5	5.5	10.5	5	10	5.5

Avg = 7.7

Cleveland Browns 2017 Play Analysis

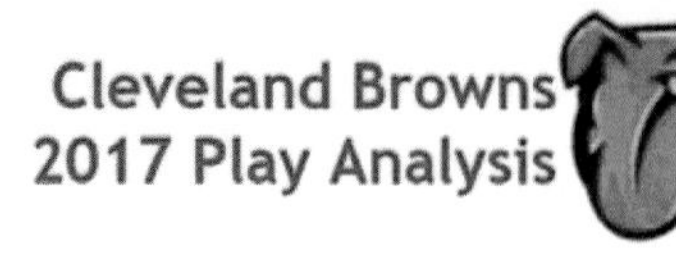

2017 Play Tendencies

All Pass %	62%
All Pass Rk	5
All Rush %	38%
All Rush Rk	28
1 Score Pass %	52%
1 Score Pass Rk	28
2016 1 Score Pass %	61%
2016 1 Score Pass Rk	12
2017 Pass Increase %	-9%
Pass Increase Rk	29
1 Score Rush %	48%
1 Score Rush Rk	5
Up Pass %	50%
Up Pass Rk	14
Up Rush %	50%
Up Rush Rk	19
Down Pass %	66%
Down Pass Rk	14
Down Rush %	34%
Down Rush Rk	19

2017 Down & Distance Tendencies

Down	Distance	Total Plays	Pass Rate	Run Rate	Play Success %
1	Short (1-3)	5	60%	40%	40%
	Med (4-7)	9	11%	89%	89%
	Long (8-10)	288	44%	56%	42%
	XL (11+)	15	53%	47%	33%
2	Short (1-3)	41	46%	54%	61%
	Med (4-7)	68	49%	51%	47%
	Long (8-10)	84	65%	35%	33%
	XL (11+)	49	73%	27%	20%
3	Short (1-3)	39	51%	49%	67%
	Med (4-7)	36	83%	17%	39%
	Long (8-10)	33	91%	9%	18%
	XL (11+)	47	85%	15%	21%
4	Short (1-3)	5	20%	80%	60%

Shotgun %:

Under Center	Shotgun
29%	71%
37%	*63%*

AVG

Run Rate:

Under Center	Shotgun
67%	21%
68%	*23%*

AVG

Pass Rate:

Under Center	Shotgun
33%	79%
32%	*77%*

AVG

Short Yardage Intelligence:

2nd and Short Run

Run Freq	Run Rk	NFL Run Freq Avg	Run 1D Rate	Run NFL 1D Avg
56%	27	67%	73%	69%

2nd and Short Pass

Pass Freq	Pass Rk	NFL Pass Freq Avg	Pass 1D Rate	Pass NFL 1D Avg
44%	6	33%	47%	53%

Most Frequent Play

Down	Distance	Play Type	Player	Total Plays	Play Success %
1	Short (1-3)	PASS	David Njoku	2	50%
		RUSH	Isaiah Crowell	2	50%
	Med (4-7)	RUSH	Isaiah Crowell	5	80%
	Long (8-10)	RUSH	Isaiah Crowell	107	37%
	XL (11+)	RUSH	Isaiah Crowell	4	50%
2	Short (1-3)	RUSH	Duke Johnson	9	67%
	Med (4-7)	RUSH	Isaiah Crowell	24	42%
	Long (8-10)	RUSH	Isaiah Crowell	22	32%
	XL (11+)	PASS	Isaiah Crowell	7	0%
3	Short (1-3)	RUSH	DeShone Kizer	8	88%
	Med (4-7)	PASS	Duke Johnson	6	67%
	Long (8-10)	PASS	Rashard Higgins	7	0%
	XL (11+)	PASS	Duke Johnson	9	0%

Most Successful Play*

Down	Distance	Play Type	Player	Total Plays	Play Success %
1	Med (4-7)	RUSH	Isaiah Crowell	5	80%
	Long (8-10)	PASS	Duke Johnson	15	80%
2	Short (1-3)	RUSH	Isaiah Crowell	7	71%
	Med (4-7)	RUSH	Duke Johnson	5	60%
	Long (8-10)	PASS	David Njoku	8	63%
	XL (11+)	PASS	Corey Coleman	5	40%
3	Short (1-3)	RUSH	DeShone Kizer	8	88%
	Med (4-7)	PASS	Duke Johnson	6	67%
	Long (8-10)	PASS	Rashard Higgins	7	0%
	XL (11+)	PASS	Corey Coleman	6	50%

**Minimum 5 plays to qualify*

2017 Snap Rates

Wk	Opp	Score	Rashard Higgins	Ricardo Louis	Duke Johnson	Isaiah Crowell	Seth DeValve	David Njoku	Corey Coleman	Randall Telfer	Sammie Coates
1	PIT	L 21-18		16 (24%)	50 (76%)	52 (79%)	31 (47%)	29 (44%)	53 (80%)	18 (27%)	
2	BAL	L 24-10	51 (72%)	32 (45%)	37 (52%)	32 (45%)	31 (44%)	34 (48%)	38 (54%)	19 (27%)	26 (37%)
3	IND	L 31-28	52 (68%)	57 (74%)	40 (52%)	41 (53%)	43 (56%)	30 (39%)		19 (25%)	
4	CIN	L 31-7	53 (82%)	56 (86%)	36 (55%)	22 (34%)	33 (51%)	33 (51%)		11 (17%)	
5	NYJ	L 17-14	37 (49%)	58 (76%)	40 (53%)	34 (45%)	36 (47%)	35 (46%)		31 (41%)	11 (14%)
6	HOU	L 33-17	45 (67%)	52 (78%)	30 (45%)	32 (48%)	36 (54%)	26 (39%)		17 (25%)	11 (16%)
7	TEN	L 12-9	48 (66%)	65 (89%)	36 (49%)	39 (53%)	37 (51%)	28 (38%)		24 (33%)	6 (8%)
8	MIN	L 33-16	39 (66%)	52 (88%)	22 (37%)	33 (56%)	32 (54%)	24 (41%)		17 (29%)	4 (7%)
10	DET	L 38-24	44 (54%)	60 (74%)	48 (59%)	36 (44%)	42 (52%)	46 (57%)		20 (25%)	17 (21%)
11	JAC	L 19-7	38 (69%)	33 (60%)	27 (49%)	24 (44%)	33 (60%)	21 (38%)	51 (93%)	15 (27%)	
12	CIN	L 30-16	50 (71%)	45 (64%)	38 (54%)	32 (46%)	24 (34%)	41 (59%)	63 (90%)	21 (30%)	
13	LAC	L 19-10	36 (57%)	13 (21%)	34 (54%)	32 (51%)	36 (57%)	34 (54%)	51 (81%)	12 (19%)	
14	GB	L 27-21	28 (48%)	4 (7%)	25 (43%)	36 (62%)	26 (45%)	34 (59%)	39 (67%)	28 (48%)	
15	BAL	L 27-10	52 (81%)	9 (14%)	43 (67%)	22 (34%)	29 (45%)	32 (50%)	49 (77%)	11 (17%)	6 (9%)
16	CHI	L 20-3	43 (73%)	9 (15%)	29 (49%)	31 (53%)	28 (47%)	30 (51%)	52 (88%)	13 (22%)	4 (7%)
17	PIT	L 28-24	45 (69%)	11 (17%)	30 (46%)	34 (52%)	35 (54%)	24 (37%)	52 (80%)	20 (31%)	8 (12%)
Grand Total			661 (66%)	572 (52%)	565 (53%)	532 (50%)	532 (50%)	501 (47%)	448 (79%)	296 (28%)	93 (15%)

Personnel Groupings

Personnel	Team %	NFL Avg	Succ. %
1-1 [3WR]	69%	59%	39%
1-2 [2WR]	12%	19%	44%
2-1 [2WR]	10%	7%	34%
2-2 [1WR]	4%	4%	39%
1-3 [1WR]	3%	5%	33%

Grouping Tendencies

Personnel	Pass Rate	Pass Succ. %	Run Succ. %
1-1 [3WR]	70%	34%	50%
1-2 [2WR]	51%	37%	51%
2-1 [2WR]	37%	30%	37%
2-2 [1WR]	21%	25%	43%
1-3 [1WR]	44%	58%	13%

Red Zone Targets (min 3)

Receiver	All	Inside 5	6-10	11-20
David Njoku	9	5	1	3
Corey Coleman	7	2		5
Duke Johnson	5		2	3
Seth DeValve	5	3		2
Kenny Britt	4		1	3
Rashard Higgins	4	1	1	2
Ricardo Louis	4	2	1	1
Isaiah Crowell	3	1	2	

Red Zone Rushes (min 3)

Rusher	All	Inside 5	6-10	11-20
Isaiah Crowell	22	5	9	8
DeShone Kizer	17	8	1	8
Duke Johnson	12	3	2	7

Early Down Target Rate

RB	TE	WR
26%	11%	63%
23%	*21%*	*56%*

NFL AVG

Overall Target Success %

RB	TE	WR
41% #25	41% #32	36% #32

Cleveland Browns 2017 Passing Recap & 2018 Outlook

Tyrod Taylor was an underrated acquisition. Taylor posted top-seven interception rates all three seasons in Buffalo, including last year's league-best 0.95% clip. Taylor threw just 16 picks across 1,236 pass attempts in Buffalo, good for a 1.29% INT rate that ranks second to only Tom Brady over the past three seasons. Kizer posted a 4.6% interception rate last year, and Hogan (6.7%) was even worse. Simply cutting down on last year's league-high 28 picks will go a long way toward increasing Cleveland's win probability.

Jackson told reporters last year that the only way to develop a quarterback was to let him play. Yet Jackson did such a poor job managing Kizer that it's a reach to expect he'll know the right time to replace Taylor with No. 1 overall pick Baker Mayfield. Once Hue turns to the rookie, he needs to go all in. And new OC Todd Haley must adapt his offense to Mayfield's skill set, something Jackson refused to do for Kizer.

DeShone Kizer Rating All Downs

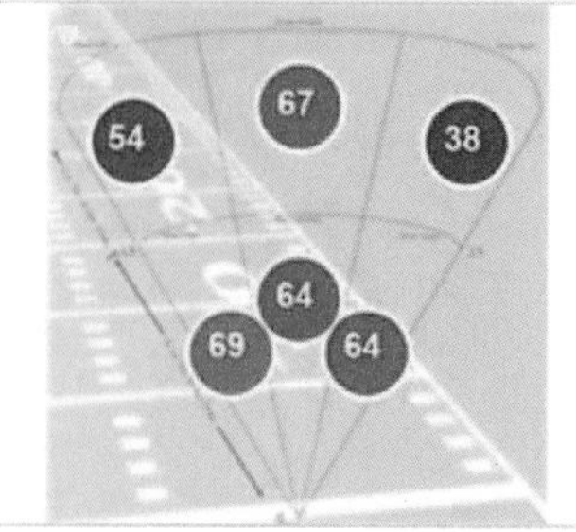

DeShone Kizer Rating Early Downs

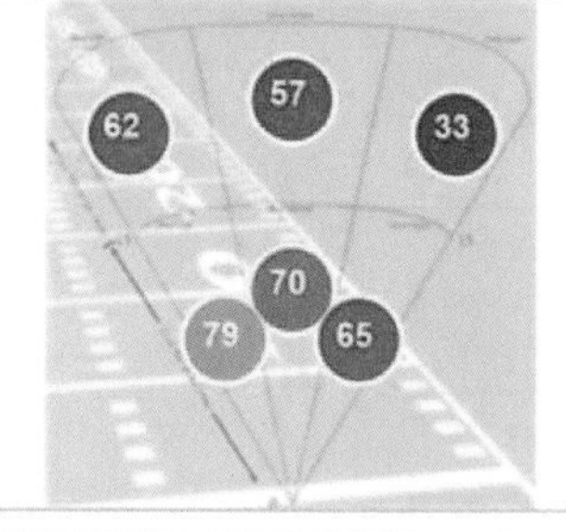

2017 Standard Passing Table

QB	Comp	Att	Comp %	Yds	YPA	TDs	INT	Sacks	Rating	Rk
DeShone Kizer	254	475	53%	2,898	6.1	11	22	38	61	54
Kevin Hogan	46	75	61%	517	6.9	4	5	6	72	47
NFL Avg			62%		7.0				87.5	

2017 Advanced Passing Table

QB	Success %	EDSR Passing Success %	20+ Yd Pass Gains	20+ Yd Pass %	30+ Yd Pass Gains	30+ Yd Pass %	Avg. Air Yds per Comp	Avg. YAC per Comp	20+ Air Yd Comp	20+ Air Yd %
DeShone Kizer	34%	35%	43	9.0%	17	3.6%	5.7	5.5	24	9%
Kevin Hogan	41%	48%	8	10.7%	4	5.3%	6.7	5.0	5	11%
NFL Avg	44%	48%	27.7	8.8%	10.3	3.3%	6.0	4.7	11.7	6%

Interception Rates by Down

Yards to Go	1	2	3	4	Total
1 & 2	0.0%	0.0%	7.7%	0.0%	3.1%
3, 4, 5	50.0%	4.8%	12.9%	0.0%	10.5%
6 - 9	0.0%	1.9%	5.1%	0.0%	3.2%
10 - 14	4.1%	3.1%	2.6%	20.0%	3.9%
15+	0.0%	4.3%	0.0%		2.0%
Total	4.3%	2.9%	5.6%	7.7%	4.3%

3rd Down Passing - Short of Sticks Analysis

QB	Avg. Yds to Go	Avg. YIA (of Comp)	Avg Yds Short	Short of Sticks Rate	Short Rk
DeShone Kizer	8.8	7.0	-1.7	63%	26
NFL Avg	7.8	6.7	-1.1	60%	

Air Yds vs YAC

Air Yds %	YAC %	Rk
56%	44%	27
58%	42%	

2017 Receiving Recap & 2018 Outlook

Wide receiver is arguably the Browns' strongest position group. Jarvis Landry has a limited set of skills, but he is excellent in his role. Of the 33 players who drew at least 20 targets inside the 15-yard line last season, Landry's 72% Success Rate ranked No. 1. Coming in cold after his multi-year suspension, athletic freak Josh Gordon averaged a team-best 18.6 yards per reception in five starts. Duke Johnson is a great receiving back. Second-year TE David Njoku is another elite athlete who inexplicably played just 46.9% of Cleveland's 2017 offensive snaps. This year, Jackson promises Njoku will be on the field full time.

Player *Min 50 Targets*	Targets	Comp %	YPA	Rating	TOARS	Success %	Success Rk	Missed YPA Rk	YAS % Rk	TDs
Duke Johnson	93	80%	7.5	95	4.6	49%	63	81	101	3
Ricardo Louis	61	44%	5.9	50	3.3	36%	124	126	16	0
Seth DeValve	58	57%	6.8	55	3.3	38%	118	110	103	1
David Njoku	60	53%	6.4	82	3.7	35%	126	108	62	4
Corey Coleman	57	40%	5.4	40	3.0	38%	120	125	81	2
Rashard Higgins	50	54%	6.2	47	2.9	34%	128	89	105	2

Directional Passer Rating Delivered

Receiver	Short Left	Short Middle	Short Right	Deep Left	Deep Middle	Deep Right	Player Total
Duke Johnson	96	98	90		119	55	95
Ricardo Louis	72	43	46	60	40	38	50
David Njoku	99	108	60	43	117	135	82
Seth DeValve	113	5	67	119	0	50	55
Corey Coleman	56	40	49	3	32	79	40
Rashard Higgins	62	62	92	69	80	0	47
Josh Gordon	71	94	53	110		44	67
Isaiah Crowell	79	65	66				66
Kenny Britt	62		95	82	96	0	63
Sammie Coates	79	40	37	119		40	36
Team Total	83	55	68	62	62	36	65

2017 Rushing Recap & 2017 Outlook

The Browns replaced Isaiah Crowell with free agent pickup Carlos Hyde and No. 35 pick Nick Chubb. Crowell posted a career-high 4.8 yards-per-carry average in 2016, but I cautioned in last year's preview that Crowell's YPC was deceiving. His Success Rate was 39% -- 62nd in the league – and his per-carry average was the byproduct of a handful of long runs. Crowell's 2017 Success Rate was 40%, which ranked 61st at the position. Last year's Browns had great success running to the left side, but legendary LT Joe Thomas' retirement will hurt them there. Chubb and newly-extended passing-game specialist Johnson are clearly the future of Cleveland's backfield. Hyde figures to be a one-year rental based on his contract.

Player *Min 50 Rushes*	Rushes	YPC	Success %	Success Rk	Missed YPA Rk	YTS % Rk	YAS % Rk	Early Down Success %	Early Down Success Rk	TDs
Isaiah Crowell	206	4.1	40%	61	55	64	25	39%	64	2
Duke Johnson	82	4.2	54%	8	16	59	11	50%	14	4

Yards per Carry by Direction

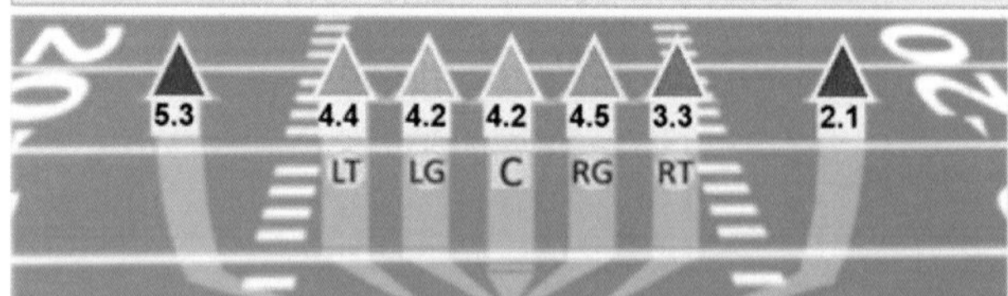

Directional Run Frequency

9%
7%
21%
18%
26%
12%
7%
LT
LG
C
RG
RT

CLE-4

And it didn't matter that the Browns' only player to top 400 receiving yards was running back Duke Johnson. Cleveland's most productive wide receiver was Ricardo Louis.

This Jackson quote after he benched Kizer in Week 5 stood out as particularly haunting when I reviewed old press conferences for this chapter:

"It's still about winning," Jackson claimed. "That's first and foremost. If it was just about development, I would have just left him in. It's not about that. It's about winning. I told you guys, we go into every game trying to win. That is our goal. That is our job. That is my job. I'm not here just to get players better."

I can't recall a more-damning statement from a coach. When you start a rookie quarterback, you have to focus on the long game with a goal of developing him into a franchise solution. But for Jackson, it was "all about winning," not development. "Winning is my job," Jackson said. And despite going 1-31 in two years as Browns coach, Jackson somehow kept Haslam's blessing and his job.

Jackson's incompetence wasn't the sole reason for Cleveland's winless year. Also to blame was DC Gregg Williams' callous arrogance. Through two weeks, Williams was outwardly proud of aligning first-round safety Jabril Peppers up to 25 yards deep of the line of scrimmage in Williams' "angel" role.

(cont'd - see CLE-5)

Evan Silva's Fantasy Corner

Jarvis Landry thrived on volume the last three years in Miami, averaging 9.5 targets per game but only 10.5 yards per reception with one season above 5 TDs among four. New GM John Dorsey landed Landry with the No. 123 pick ex-EVP Sashi Brown acquired for now-Cardinals P Andy Lee. Dorsey then signed Landry to a five-year, $75.5 million deal that made him the NFL's fifth-highest-paid receiver. Cleveland's commitment to Landry is large, but his fit is suspect with "bridge" QB Tyrod Taylor, whose teams ranked 31st, 32nd, and 31st in pass attempts in three years as Buffalo's starter. No Bills player exceeded 60 catches in a season during that three-year stretch. I expect Landry to break that trend with a 75-85-catch season, but Landry's volume dependency would still place him in precarious fantasy position. It's likely that the sooner the Browns bench Taylor for Baker Mayfield, the stronger Landry's statistical outlook will be.

Division History: Season Wins & 2018 Projection

2014 Wins | 2015 Wins | 2016 Wins | 2017 Wins | Forecast 2018 Wins

Rank of 2018 Defensive Pass Efficiency Faced by Week

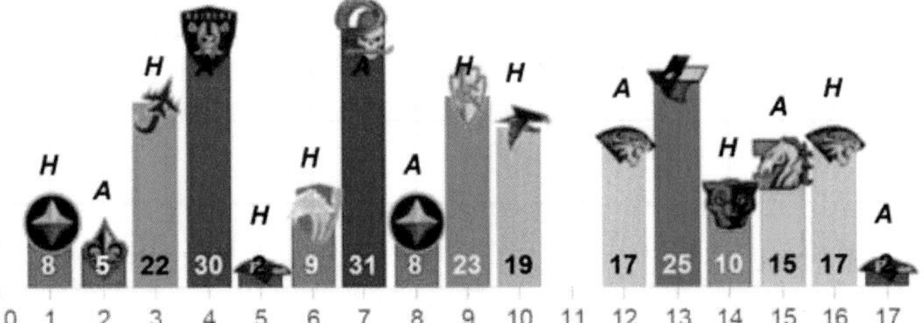

Rank of 2018 Defensive Rush Efficiency Faced by Week

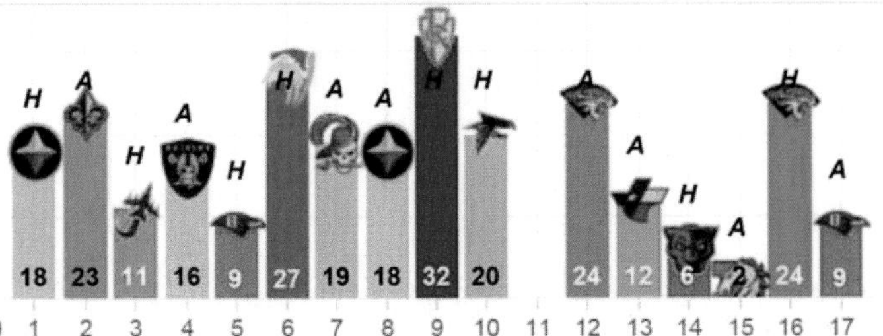

2017 Situational Usage by Player & Position

Usage Rate by Score

		Being Blown Out (14+)	Down Big (9-13)	One Score	Grand Total
RUSH	Isaiah Crowell	9%	10%	32%	24%
	Duke Johnson	6%	5%	12%	10%
	David Njoku			0%	0%
	Rashard Higgins	0%			0%
	Bryce Treggs			0%	0%
	Matt Dayes	1%	1%	0%	1%
	Total	17%	16%	45%	34%
PASS	Isaiah Crowell	7%	3%	4%	5%
	Duke Johnson	14%	13%	9%	11%
	David Njoku	8%	7%	6%	7%
	Ricardo Louis	11%	12%	4%	7%
	Seth DeValve	8%	11%	6%	7%
	Corey Coleman	6%	11%	6%	7%
	Rashard Higgins	10%	4%	4%	6%
	Josh Gordon	3%	9%	5%	5%
	Kenny Britt	5%	6%	4%	4%
	Bryce Treggs	2%		3%	2%
	Kasen Williams	4%	2%	1%	2%
	Sammie Coates	3%	2%	0%	1%
	Matt Dayes	0%	2%	0%	1%
	Dan Vitale	0%		1%	1%
	Randall Telfer	0%		1%	0%
	Jordan Leslie	0%			0%
	Marquez Williams	0%			0%
	Total	83%	84%	55%	66%

Positional Target Distribution vs NFL Average

		NFL Wide				Team Only			
		Left	Middle	Right	Total	Left	Middle	Right	Total
Deep	WR	958	489	932	2,379	28	20	55	103
	TE	180	146	184	510	12	4	4	20
	RB	39	8	38	85		1	4	5
	All	1,177	643	1,154	2,974	40	25	63	128
Short	WR	2,789	1,636	2,683	7,108	73	35	107	215
	TE	851	833	1,148	2,832	12	6	22	40
	RB	1,279	783	1,247	3,309	42	40	48	130
	All	4,919	3,252	5,078	13,249	127	81	177	385
Total		6,096	3,895	6,232	16,223	167	106	240	513

Positional Success Rates vs NFL Average

		NFL Wide				Team Only			
		Left	Middle	Right	Total	Left	Middle	Right	Total
Deep	WR	37%	46%	38%	39%	39%	35%	29%	33%
	TE	39%	52%	45%	45%	25%	75%	50%	40%
	RB	36%	50%	39%	39%		100%	25%	40%
	All	37%	47%	39%	40%	35%	44%	30%	34%
Short	WR	52%	58%	51%	53%	38%	31%	38%	37%
	TE	51%	56%	50%	52%	50%	83%	18%	38%
	RB	44%	51%	43%	45%	40%	53%	35%	42%
	All	50%	56%	49%	51%	40%	46%	35%	39%
Total		47%	54%	47%	49%	39%	45%	34%	38%

Successful Play Rate
0% — 100%

Cleveland Browns - Success by Personnel Grouping & Play Type

Play Type	1-1 [3WR]	1-2 [2WR]	2-1 [2WR]	1-0 [4WR]	1-3 [1WR]	0-1 [4WR]	2-0 [3WR]	2-2 [1WR]	0-0 [5WR]	0-3 [2WR]	2-3 [0WR]	3-2 [0WR]	Grand Total
PASS	34% (484, 78%)	37% (60, 10%)	30% (37, 6%)	38% (8, 1%)	58% (12, 2%)	100% (1, 0%)	0% (5, 1%)	25% (8, 1%)	25% (4, 1%)	0% (1, 0%)	33% (3, 0%)		34% (624, 100%)
RUSH	50% (206, 54%)	51% (57, 15%)	37% (63, 16%)	50% (2, 1%)	13% (15, 4%)		0% (2, 1%)	43% (30, 8%)			43% (7, 2%)	100% (2, 1%)	46% (384, 100%)
TOTAL	39% (690, 68%)	44% (117, 12%)	34% (100, 10%)	40% (10, 1%)	33% (27, 3%)	100% (1, 0%)	0% (7, 1%)	39% (38, 4%)	25% (4, 0%)	0% (1, 0%)	40% (10, 1%)	100% (2, 0%)	39% (1,008, 100%)

Format Line 1: Success Rate Line 2: Total # of Plays, % of All Plays (by type)

CLE-5 "There have only been four passes thrown further than 20 yards against us this year," Williams bragged to reporters after two games. "Two have been interceptions. One was an incompletion. And one was caught." In that press conference, Williams mocked a reporter and accused him of not being good at his job. (Ironic.) Over the final 14 games, Williams' defense was gashed for league highs allowed on deep passes in completion rate (50%) and Success Rate (50%). Cleveland was skewered for the NFL's second-worst passer rating (121) on deep passes. This was despite the Browns facing the league's fourth-easiest schedule of explosive passing offenses.

Williams' "angel" strategy is designed to limit big plays, but it was the worst in the league at doing so. A byproduct of the "angel" is it opens up a ton of holes underneath. The 2017 Browns also ranked dead last in passer rating allowed on short passes. Williams' defense was even bad enough to rank sixth worst all time in completion rate allowed (68.6%) versus the tenth-softest schedule of passing offenses. The Browns allowed an 85% completion rate and 8.9 yards per attempt to Landry Jones. To Brett Hundley, Cleveland served up a 76% completion rate, 111 passer rating, three touchdowns, and no picks.

Last year's Browns had a top-five run defense in Success Rate allowed. But because they gave up easy completions so regularly, their defense was easily carved up. Even offensive coordinators with bad quarterbacks could confidently dial up pass plays. I can only imagine how deflating it must have been to Browns players. Because of your defensive scheme, you're either hemorrhaging chunk plays or suffering death by a thousand cuts on short completions that essentially went unguarded.

Jackson pounded the table to draft Kizer, trained him through minicamp, training camp, and the full preseason, then gave him the Week 1 starting job. Weeks later, Jackson benched him, criticized Kizer publicly, and traded him 11 months after drafting him. Where is the accountability? Williams complained he didn't have good enough players to win, yet deployed a defensive strategy that was easy to beat with the pass. These two coaches had more influence on Cleveland's 2017 results than any players. After a busy offseason, the 2018 Browns have a rejuvenated roster with upside. Their ceiling is higher than last year. But coaching matters in the NFL. Jackson and Williams do have improved players now. And I hope for the sake of players and fans, these coaches also improve and bring wins to the city of Cleveland.

Receiving Success by Personnel Grouping

Position	Player	1-1 [3WR]	1-2 [2WR]	2-1 [2WR]	1-0 [4WR]	1-3 [1WR]	2-0 [3WR]	2-2 [1WR]	0-0 [5WR]	0-3 [2WR]	2-3 [0WR]	Total
RB	Duke Johnson	48% 8.1 87.7 (73)	50% 4.3 84.4 (8)	33% 2.5 109.7 (6)	100% 11.0 112.5 (2)	67% 11.0 152.1 (3)				0% 0.0 39.6 (1)		48% 7.5 95.0 (93)
TE	David Njoku	37% 6.4 61.6 (43)	33% 7.8 108.6 (9)	0% 0.0 39.6 (1)		33% 1.7 70.1 (3)		67% 12.0 147.2 (3)			100% 1.0 118.8 (1)	38% 6.4 81.7 (60)
WR	Ricardo Louis	35% 6.1 48.2 (52)	100% 6.0 91.7 (1)	50% 8.3 78.1 (4)	33% 1.0 42.4 (3)			0% 0.0 39.6 (1)				36% 5.9 49.7 (61)
	Seth DeValve	41% 6.8 68.0 (51)	100% 35.0 118.8 (1)	100% 8.0 100.0 (1)	0% 0.0 0.0 (1)	0% 0.0 0.0 (1)	0% 0.0 79.2 (1)	0% 5.0 87.5 (1)	0% 0.0 39.6 (1)			40% 6.8 54.9 (58)
	Corey Coleman	35% 5.5 27.1 (43)	33% 5.8 53.9 (9)	25% 3.0 56.3 (4)					100% 3.0 118.8 (1)			35% 5.4 40.5 (57)
	Josh Gordon	35% 5.6 44.4 (31)	33% 6.2 55.6 (6)	67% 30.7 109.7 (3)		67% 10.3 140.3 (3)						40% 7.8 67.5 (43)

Format Line 1: Success Rate Line 2: YPA Line 3: Passer Rating Line 4: Total # of Plays

Successful Play Rate
0% — 100%

Rushing Success by Personnel Grouping

Position	Player	1-1 [3WR]	1-2 [2WR]	2-1 [2WR]	1-0 [4WR]	1-3 [1WR]	2-0 [3WR]	2-2 [1WR]	2-3 [0WR]	3-2 [0WR]	Total
QB	DeShone Kizer	47% 5.8 (53)	86% 6.3 (7)	33% 5.1 (9)		0% 0.5 (2)		75% 5.0 (4)	100% 1.0 (2)		51% 5.4 (77)
RB	Isaiah Crowell	42% 4.2 (88)	44% 3.8 (36)	35% 3.2 (46)	50% 3.5 (2)	20% 3.3 (10)		42% 8.1 (19)	0% 0.0 (3)	100% 3.5 (2)	40% 4.1 (206)
	Duke Johnson	60% 5.6 (52)	46% 2.6 (13)	50% 2.8 (8)		0% -2.0 (1)	0% 1.0 (2)	50% 0.3 (4)	50% 0.5 (2)		54% 4.2 (82)

Format Line 1: Success Rate Line 2: YPC Line 3: Total # of Plays

Dallas Cowboys

2018 Coaches

Head Coach:
Jason Garrett (8th yr)
Offensive Coordinator:
Scott Linehan (5th yr)
Defensive Coordinator:
Rod Marinelli (5th yr)

EASY HARD

2018 Forecast

Wins	Div Rank
8.5	#2

Past Records

2017: 9-7
2016: 13-3
2015: 4-12

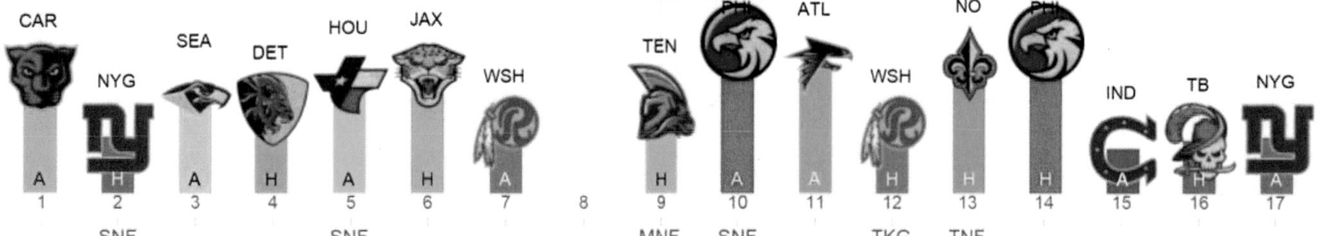

Key Players Lost

TXN	Player (POS)
Cut	Brown, Brian WR
	Bryant, Dez WR
	Mayowa, Benson DE
	Scandrick, Orlando CB
	Vellano, Joe DT
Declared Free Agent	Bell, Byron T
	Benwikere, Bene CB
	Butler, Brice WR
	Cooper, Jonathan G
	Dysert, Zac QB
	Hitchens, Anthony LB
	Ladouceur, L.P. LB
	Looney, Joe C
	Morris, Alfred RB
	Paea, Stephen DT
	Smith, Keith RB
Retired	Hanna, James TE
	McCown, Luke QB
	Witten, Jason TE

Average Line	# Games Favored	# Games Underdog
-1.0	8	6

2018 Dallas Cowboys Overview

Flip to page six of this chapter for a history of the NFC East. No division in football is less predictable year to year. Worst to firsts are common and happened in each of the last three years. This pattern would indicate the 2017 fourth-place Giants have just as good a shot to win the NFC East as their competition. As a 9-7 team from 2017 that narrowly missed the playoffs, the Cowboys should ask, "Why not us?"

Of the Cowboys' nine 2017 wins, five came against the NFC East. Their lone division loss was to the Eagles, who stomped Dallas 37-9. The Cowboys beat a Week 17 Eagles team resting starters, and swept the Giants and Redskins. As Dallas swept the G-Men and Skins just once in the previous 12 years, repeating is unlikely.

In their remaining ten non-division games, the Cowboys went 4-6. They were fortunate to face the AFC West and NFC West in historically bad years for both divisions. The Cowboys drew San Francisco pre-Jimmy Garoppolo, then the Seahawks in Week 16 after Pete Carroll's defense was ruined by injury. And the Cardinals were awful. Dallas split its NFC West games 2-2, losing to the Rams and Seahawks. In the AFC West, the Cowboys were blown out 42-17 by a bad Broncos team and embarrassed at home 28-6 on Thanksgiving by the Chargers. Dallas narrowly beat a bad Raiders team by three and overcame a second-half deficit to pull off a win over the Chiefs. The Cowboys were swept by the Packers and Falcons.

The 2018 Cowboys play the vast majority of their games in the NFC, by far the NFL's toughest conference. Dallas' only non-NFC games come against the AFC South, which has become the AFC's most complete division and gets stronger if Andrew Luck gets healthy by Week 15. The Cowboys also draw the NFC South, arguably the toughest division in football.

The Cowboys' post-Dez Bryant and Jason Witten passing game is in flux, but moving on from both was overdue from a financial standpoint. The timing was terrible. Dez was cut on April 13, well after the heart of free agency. As such, Dallas could not replace him with a high-end veteran and resorted to drafting Michael Gallup in the third round. Witten retired the day after the draft.

(cont'd - see DAL2)

Key Free Agents/ Trades Added

Austin, Tavon WR
Daly, Scott C
Ealy, Kony DE
Fleming, Cameron T
Hurns, Allen WR
Maher, Brett K
Martin, Marcus C
Thomas, Joe LB
Thompson, Deonte WR
Ward, Jihad DE

Drafted Players

Rd	Pk	Player (College)
1	19	LB - Leighton Vander Esch (Boise State)
2	50	G - Connor Williams (Texas)
3	81	WR - Michael Gallup (Colorado State)
4	116	DE - Dorance Armstrong (Kansas)
4*	137	TE - Dalton Schultz (Stanford)
5*	171	QB - Mike White (Western Kentucky)
6	193	LB - Chris Covington (Indiana)
6*	208	WR - Cedrick Wilson Jr. (Boise State)
7	236	RB - Bo Scarbrough (Alabama)

Regular Season Wins: Past & Current Proj

	Wins
Forecast 2018 Wins	8.5
2017 Wins	9
Forecast 2017 Wins	9
2016 Wins	13
2015 Wins	4
2014 Wins	12

1 3 5 7 9 11 13 15

Lineup & Cap Hits

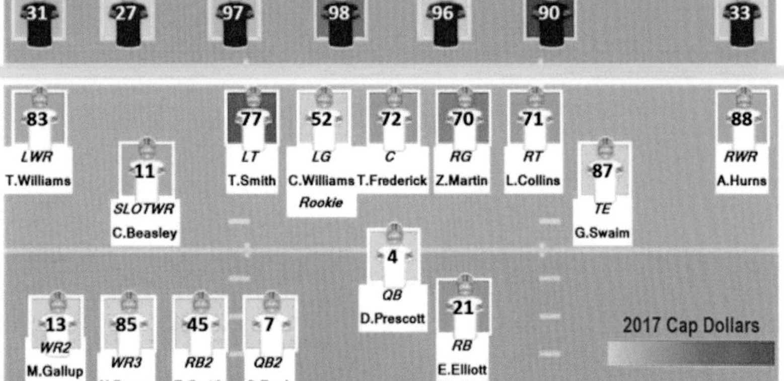

2018 Unit Spending

All DEF
All OFF

Positional Spending

	Rank	Total	2017 Rk
All OFF	25	$81.18M	17
QB	32	$2.78M	32
OL	3	$43.99M	25
RB	7	$9.68M	11
WR	18	$21.40M	3
TE	32	$3.33M	1
All DEF	23	$73.56M	30
DL	6	$40.87M	13
LB	21	$19.16M	20
CB	32	$4.81M	25
S	23	$8.73M	29

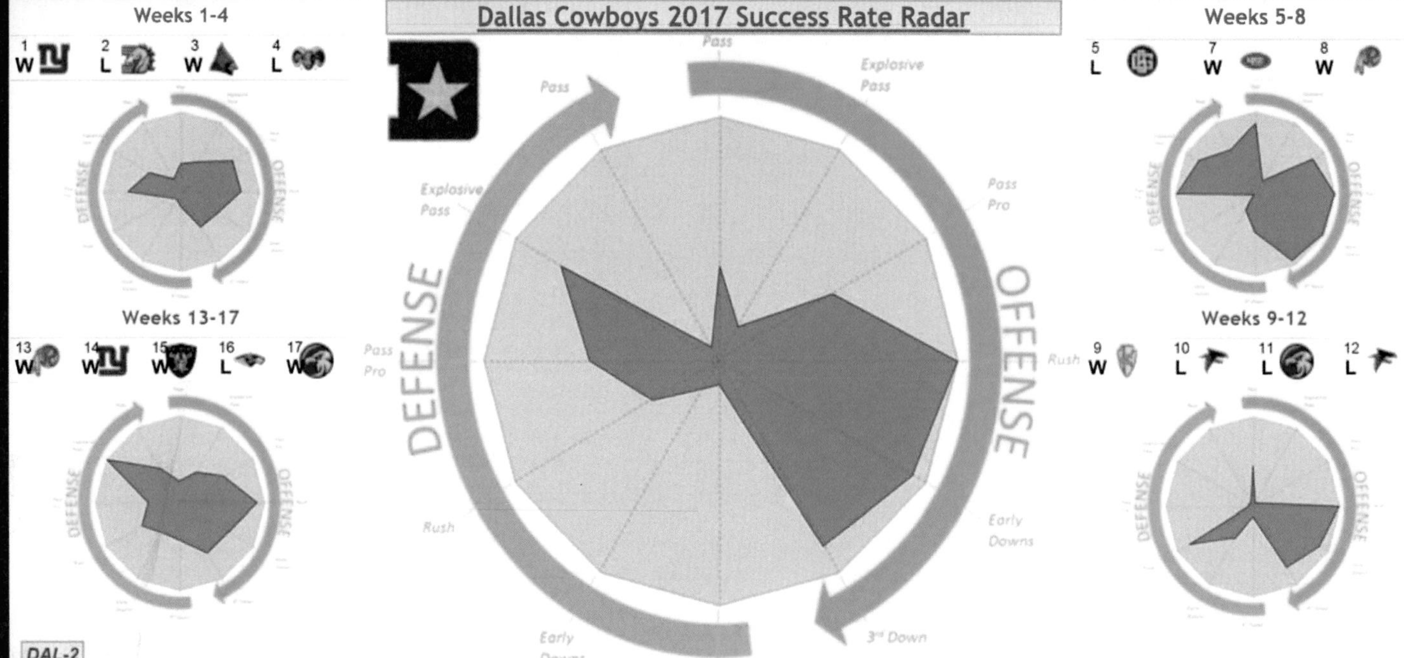

DAL-2

Witten played 99% of the Cowboys' 2017 offensive snaps. Bryant played 84%. No other Dallas non-quarterback skill-position player reached 65%. Witten and Bryant combined for 33 red-zone targets. No other Cowboy topped seven. There is a massive production void in this pass-catcher corps.

I supported these moves, but the decisions should have happened earlier. And I don't mean this past February or March. In 2016, Bryant had the fourth-highest cap hit among NFL receivers. In 2017, Dez's cost was second highest. It was going to be third highest in 2018. Before Witten retired, his combined 2017-2018 cap costs totaled over $19 million, second most of any tight end. Neither player's production was worth his price, and that had been the case for years. Witten was a reliable safety valve for young quarterback Dak Prescott, but he offered minimal playmaking ability for a passing game that was desperate for it, especially as Dez slowed down.

So unless they lure a first-ballot Hall of Famer and convince him to be substantially underpaid, an NFL team's best option is to draft a first-round quarterback with a fifth-year option. As Prescott was a fourth-round pick, the Cowboys lack a fifth-year luxury. Dallas needed to spend the last two years crafting a Super Bowl-caliber roster by 2019, Dak's contract year. Prescott hits the cap for just $725,000 this season, making him QB61. (It's $5,000 more than the Texans are paying backups Joe Webb and Brandon Weeden.) But apart from building a strong offensive line, it's hard to imagine a team has ever done less to surround a rookie-deal quarterback with talent. VP of Football Operations Stephen Jones has already skipped ahead with Prescott, publicly stating the Cowboys will pay Dak a "$100 million contract" after this season.

Dallas is set up to struggle on both sides of the ball in the passing game. Offensively, they have the worst receiver corps in the league and rarely throw to Ezekiel Elliott.

(cont'd - see DAL-3)

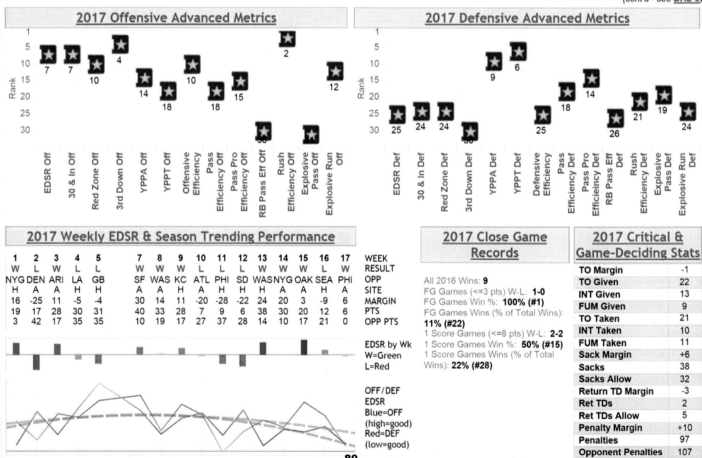

2017 Offensive Advanced Metrics

Metric	Rank
EDSR Off	7
30 & In Off	7
Red Zone Off	10
3rd Down Off	4
YPPA Off	14
YPPT Off	18
Offensive Efficiency	10
Pass Efficiency Off	18
Pass Pro Efficiency Off	15
RB Pass Eff Off	30
Rush Efficiency Off	2
Explosive Pass Off	[illegible]
Explosive Run Off	12

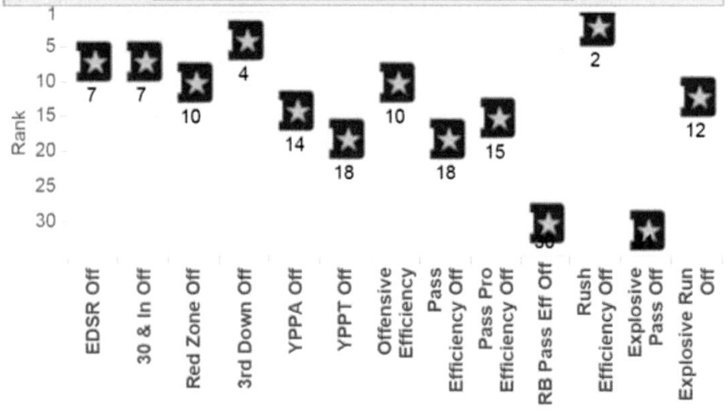

2017 Defensive Advanced Metrics

Metric	Rank
EDSR Def	25
30 & In Def	24
Red Zone Def	24
3rd Down Def	30
YPPA Def	9
YPPT Def	6
Defensive Efficiency	25
Pass Efficiency Def	18
Pass Pro Efficiency Def	14
RB Pass Eff Def	26
Rush Efficiency Def	21
Explosive Pass Def	19
Explosive Run Def	24

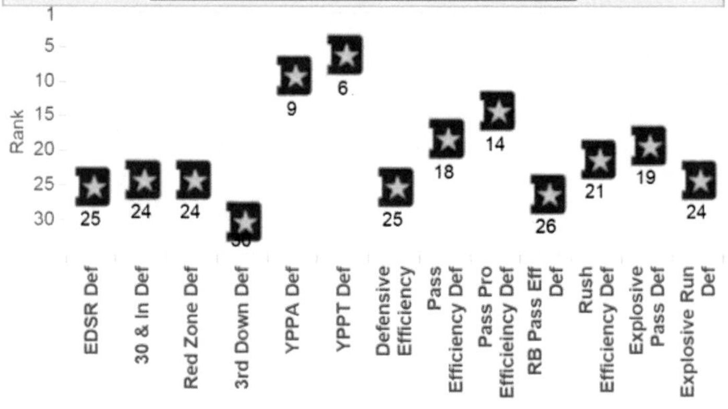

2017 Weekly EDSR & Season Trending Performance

WEEK	1	2	3	4	5	7	8	9	10	11	12	13	14	15	16	17
RESULT	W	L	W	L	L	W	W	W	L	L	L	W	W	W	L	W
OPP	NYG	DEN	ARI	LA	GB	SF	WAS	KC	ATL	PHI	SD	WAS	NYG	OAK	SEA	PHI
SITE	H	A	A	H	H	A	A	H	A	H	H	H	A	A	H	A
MARGIN	16	-25	11	-5	-4	30	14	11	-20	-28	-22	24	20	3	-9	6
PTS	19	17	28	30	31	40	33	28	7	9	6	38	30	20	12	6
OPP PTS	3	42	17	35	35	10	19	17	27	37	28	14	10	17	21	0

EDSR by Wk
W=Green
L=Red

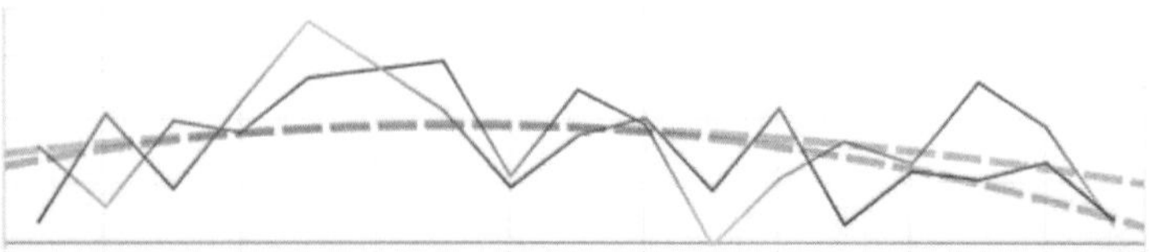

OFF/DEF
EDSR
Blue=OFF
(high=good)
Red=DEF
(low=good)

2017 Close Game Records

All 2016 Wins: **9**
FG Games (<=3 pts) W-L: **1-0**
FG Games Win %: **100% (#1)**
FG Games Wins (% of Total Wins): **11% (#22)**
1 Score Games (<=8 pts) W-L: **2-2**
1 Score Games Win %: **50% (#15)**
1 Score Games Wins (% of Total Wins): **22% (#28)**

2017 Critical & Game-Deciding Stats

TO Margin	-1
TO Given	22
INT Given	13
FUM Given	9
TO Taken	21
INT Taken	10
FUM Taken	11
Sack Margin	+6
Sacks	38
Sacks Allow	32
Return TD Margin	-3
Ret TDs	2
Ret TDs Allow	5
Penalty Margin	+10
Penalties	97
Opponent Penalties	107

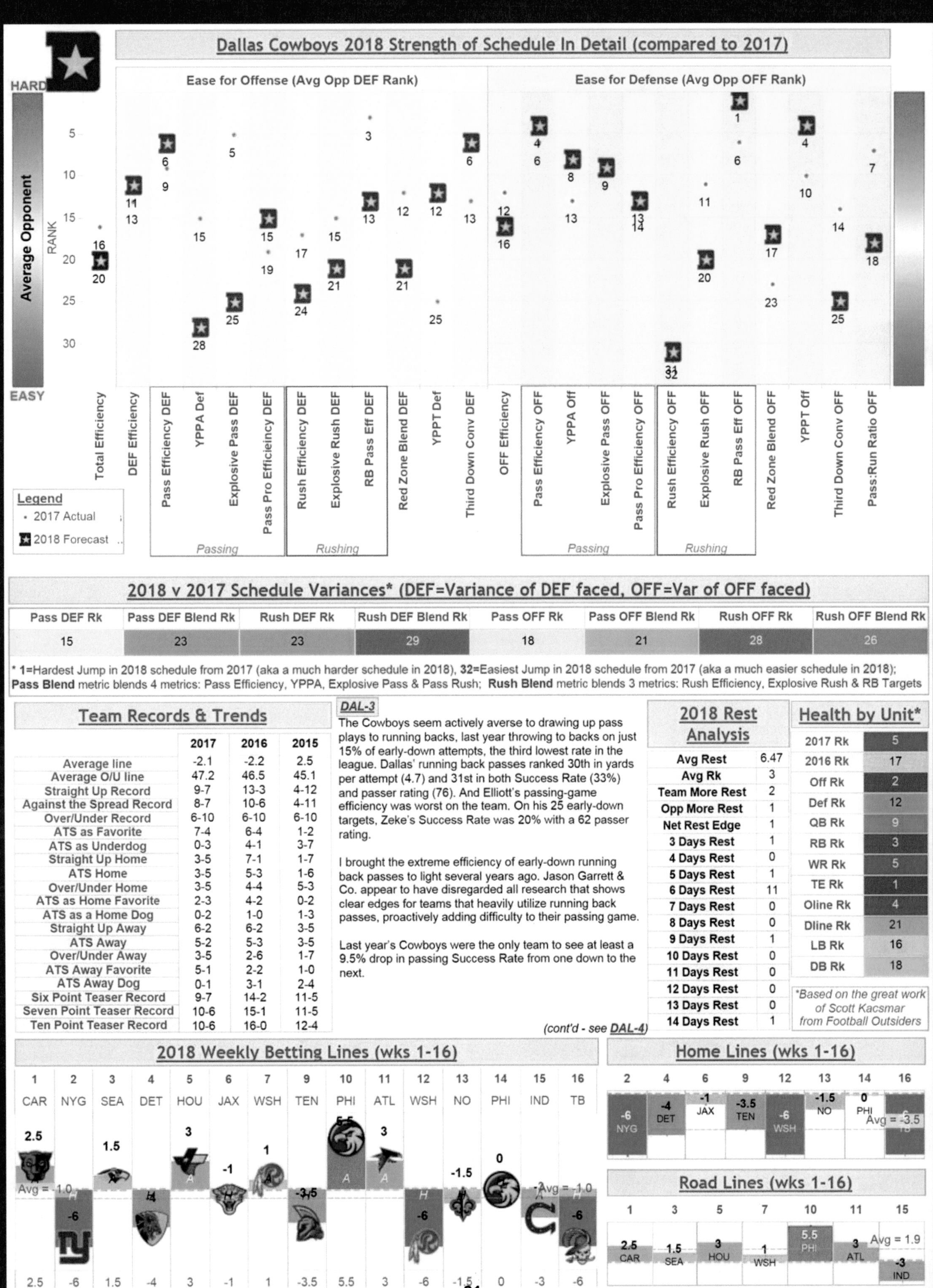

Dallas Cowboys 2018 Strength of Schedule In Detail (compared to 2017)

2018 v 2017 Schedule Variances* (DEF=Variance of DEF faced, OFF=Var of OFF faced)

Pass DEF Rk	Pass DEF Blend Rk	Rush DEF Rk	Rush DEF Blend Rk	Pass OFF Rk	Pass OFF Blend Rk	Rush OFF Rk	Rush OFF Blend Rk
15	23	23	29	18	21	28	26

* **1**=Hardest Jump in 2018 schedule from 2017 (aka a much harder schedule in 2018), **32**=Easiest Jump in 2018 schedule from 2017 (aka a much easier schedule in 2018); **Pass Blend** metric blends 4 metrics: Pass Efficiency, YPPA, Explosive Pass & Pass Rush; **Rush Blend** metric blends 3 metrics: Rush Efficiency, Explosive Rush & RB Targets

Team Records & Trends

	2017	2016	2015
Average line	-2.1	-2.2	2.5
Average O/U line	47.2	46.5	45.1
Straight Up Record	9-7	13-3	4-12
Against the Spread Record	8-7	10-6	4-11
Over/Under Record	6-10	6-10	6-10
ATS as Favorite	7-4	6-4	1-2
ATS as Underdog	0-3	4-1	3-7
Straight Up Home	3-5	7-1	1-7
ATS Home	3-5	5-3	1-6
Over/Under Home	3-5	4-4	5-3
ATS as Home Favorite	2-3	4-2	0-2
ATS as a Home Dog	0-2	1-0	1-3
Straight Up Away	6-2	6-2	3-5
ATS Away	5-2	5-3	3-5
Over/Under Away	3-5	2-6	1-7
ATS Away Favorite	5-1	2-2	1-0
ATS Away Dog	0-1	3-1	2-4
Six Point Teaser Record	9-7	14-2	11-5
Seven Point Teaser Record	10-6	15-1	11-5
Ten Point Teaser Record	10-6	16-0	12-4

DAL-3

The Cowboys seem actively averse to drawing up pass plays to running backs, last year throwing to backs on just 15% of early-down attempts, the third lowest rate in the league. Dallas' running back passes ranked 30th in yards per attempt (4.7) and 31st in both Success Rate (33%) and passer rating (76). And Elliott's passing-game efficiency was worst on the team. On his 25 early-down targets, Zeke's Success Rate was 20% with a 62 passer rating.

I brought the extreme efficiency of early-down running back passes to light several years ago. Jason Garrett & Co. appear to have disregarded all research that shows clear edges for teams that heavily utilize running back passes, proactively adding difficulty to their passing game.

Last year's Cowboys were the only team to see at least a 9.5% drop in passing Success Rate from one down to the next.

*(cont'd - see **DAL-4**)*

2018 Rest Analysis

Avg Rest	6.47
Avg Rk	3
Team More Rest	2
Opp More Rest	1
Net Rest Edge	1
3 Days Rest	1
4 Days Rest	0
5 Days Rest	1
6 Days Rest	11
7 Days Rest	0
8 Days Rest	0
9 Days Rest	1
10 Days Rest	0
11 Days Rest	0
12 Days Rest	0
13 Days Rest	0
14 Days Rest	1

Health by Unit*

2017 Rk	5
2016 Rk	17
Off Rk	2
Def Rk	12
QB Rk	9
RB Rk	3
WR Rk	5
TE Rk	1
Oline Rk	4
Dline Rk	21
LB Rk	16
DB Rk	18

**Based on the great work of Scott Kacsmar from Football Outsiders*

2018 Weekly Betting Lines (wks 1-16)

Week	1	2	3	4	5	6	7	9	10	11	12	13	14	15	16
Opp	CAR	NYG	SEA	DET	HOU	JAX	WSH	TEN	PHI	ATL	WSH	NO	PHI	IND	TB
Line	2.5	-6	1.5	-4	3	-1	1	-3.5	5.5	3	-6	-1.5	0	-3	-6

Home Lines (wks 1-16)

Week	2	4	6	9	12	13	14	16
Opp	NYG	DET	JAX	TEN	WSH	NO	PHI	TB
Line	-6	-4	-1	-3.5	-6	-1.5	0	-6

Avg = -3.5

Road Lines (wks 1-16)

Week	1	3	5	7	10	11	15
Opp	CAR	SEA	HOU	WSH	PHI	ATL	IND
Line	2.5	1.5	3	1	5.5	3	-3

Avg = 1.9

Dallas Cowboys 2017 Play Analysis

2017 Play Tendencies

All Pass %	52%
All Pass Rk	30
All Rush %	48%
All Rush Rk	3
1 Score Pass %	51%
1 Score Pass Rk	30
2016 1 Score Pass %	53%
2016 1 Score Pass Rk	28
2017 Pass Increase %	-2%
Pass Increase Rk	19
1 Score Rush %	49%
1 Score Rush Rk	3
Up Pass %	44%
Up Pass Rk	26
Up Rush %	56%
Up Rush Rk	7
Down Pass %	63%
Down Pass Rk	25
Down Rush %	37%
Down Rush Rk	8

2017 Down & Distance Tendencies

Down	Distance	Total Plays	Pass Rate	Run Rate	Play Success %
1	Short (1-3)	6	33%	67%	67%
	Med (4-7)	9	11%	89%	56%
	Long (8-10)	287	37%	63%	52%
	XL (11+)	13	62%	38%	31%
2	Short (1-3)	41	37%	63%	66%
	Med (4-7)	97	55%	45%	54%
	Long (8-10)	74	55%	45%	34%
	XL (11+)	34	68%	32%	29%
3	Short (1-3)	36	50%	50%	64%
	Med (4-7)	55	93%	7%	45%
	Long (8-10)	28	93%	7%	14%
	XL (11+)	26	100%	0%	15%
4	Short (1-3)	7	14%	86%	71%
	Med (4-7)	2	100%	0%	50%
	XL (11+)	1	0%	100%	100%

Shotgun %:

Under Center	Shotgun
50%	50%
37%	*63%*

37% AVG 63%

Run Rate:

Under Center	Shotgun
76%	17%

68% AVG 23%

Pass Rate:

Under Center	Shotgun
24%	83%

32% AVG 77%

Short Yardage Intelligence:

2nd and Short Run

Run Freq	Run Rk	NFL Run Freq Avg	Run 1D Rate	Run NFL 1D Avg
70%	12	67%	79%	69%

2nd and Short Pass

Pass Freq	Pass Rk	NFL Pass Freq Avg	Pass 1D Rate	Pass NFL 1D Avg
30%	21	33%	42%	53%

Most Frequent Play

Down	Distance	Play Type	Player	Total Plays	Play Success %
1	Short (1-3)	RUSH	Ezekiel Elliott	3	67%
	Med (4-7)	RUSH	Ezekiel Elliott	7	57%
	Long (8-10)	RUSH	Ezekiel Elliott	92	51%
	XL (11+)	PASS	Dez Bryant	4	25%
2	Short (1-3)	RUSH	Ezekiel Elliott	14	86%
	Med (4-7)	RUSH	Ezekiel Elliott	22	45%
	Long (8-10)	PASS	Terrance Williams	13	46%
	XL (11+)	PASS	Terrance Williams	8	38%
3	Short (1-3)	RUSH	Ezekiel Elliott	7	71%
	Med (4-7)	PASS	Dez Bryant	14	43%
	Long (8-10)	PASS	Jason Witten	7	0%
	XL (11+)	PASS	Dez Bryant	6	17%

Most Successful Play*

Down	Distance	Play Type	Player	Total Plays	Play Success %
1	Med (4-7)	RUSH	Ezekiel Elliott	7	57%
	Long (8-10)	PASS	Terrance Williams	16	81%
2	Short (1-3)	RUSH	Ezekiel Elliott	14	86%
	Med (4-7)	PASS	Jason Witten	7	100%
		RUSH	Dak Prescott	6	100%
	Long (8-10)	RUSH	Dak Prescott	10	50%
	XL (11+)	PASS	Terrance Williams	8	38%
3	Short (1-3)	RUSH	Dak Prescott	5	100%
	Med (4-7)	PASS	Terrance Williams	5	60%
	Long (8-10)	PASS	Dez Bryant	6	17%
	XL (11+)	PASS	Dez Bryant	6	17%
4	Short (1-3)	RUSH	Ezekiel Elliott	5	80%

**Minimum 5 plays to qualify*

2017 Snap Rates

Wk	Opp	Score	Jason Witten	Dez Bryant	Terrance Williams	Ezekiel Elliott	Cole Beasley	Brice Butler	Alfred Morris	Geoff Swaim
1	NYG	W 19-3	74 (100%)	67 (91%)	38 (51%)	60 (81%)	52 (70%)	35 (47%)	8 (11%)	9 (12%)
2	DEN	L 42-17	71 (100%)	66 (93%)	49 (69%)	66 (93%)	57 (80%)	22 (31%)	1 (1%)	
3	ARI	W 28-17	47 (100%)	41 (87%)	33 (70%)	43 (91%)	25 (53%)	7 (15%)		7 (15%)
4	LA	L 35-30	71 (100%)	58 (82%)	47 (66%)	64 (90%)	31 (44%)	22 (31%)	3 (4%)	4 (6%)
5	GB	L 35-31	73 (99%)	66 (89%)	55 (74%)	64 (86%)	37 (50%)	22 (30%)	5 (7%)	9 (12%)
7	SF	W 40-10	64 (85%)	54 (72%)	41 (55%)	50 (67%)	34 (45%)	23 (31%)	9 (12%)	22 (29%)
8	WAS	W 33-19	68 (100%)	60 (88%)	41 (60%)	58 (85%)	27 (40%)	18 (26%)	6 (9%)	17 (25%)
9	KC	W 28-17	66 (99%)	46 (69%)	55 (82%)	62 (93%)	45 (67%)	27 (40%)	1 (1%)	10 (15%)
10	ATL	L 27-7	62 (98%)	51 (81%)	45 (71%)		41 (65%)	22 (35%)	22 (35%)	
11	PHI	L 37-9	60 (95%)	54 (86%)	40 (63%)		32 (51%)	18 (29%)	25 (40%)	10 (16%)
12	LAC	L 28-6	55 (100%)	49 (89%)	32 (58%)		43 (78%)	16 (29%)	20 (36%)	7 (13%)
13	WAS	W 38-14	68 (100%)	57 (84%)	47 (69%)		38 (56%)	12 (18%)	36 (53%)	10 (15%)
14	NYG	W 30-10	63 (100%)	49 (78%)	35 (56%)		29 (46%)		33 (52%)	22 (35%)
15	OAK	W 20-17	65 (100%)	58 (89%)	41 (63%)		41 (63%)		27 (42%)	12 (18%)
16	SEA	L 21-12	76 (100%)	64 (84%)	59 (78%)	68 (89%)	45 (59%)			21 (28%)
17	PHI	W 6-0	68 (100%)	54 (79%)	34 (50%)	59 (87%)		19 (28%)	8 (12%)	13 (19%)
	Grand Total		1,051 (99%)	894 (84%)	692 (65%)	594 (86%)	577 (58%)	263 (30%)	204 (23%)	173 (18%)

Personnel Groupings

Personnel	Team %	NFL Avg	Succ. %
1-1 [3WR]	62%	59%	47%
1-2 [2WR]	14%	19%	48%
1-3 [1WR]	9%	5%	57%
2-2 [1WR]	6%	4%	56%
2-1 [2WR]	5%	7%	55%
0-1 [4WR]	3%	1%	36%

Grouping Tendencies

Personnel	Pass Rate	Pass Succ. %	Run Succ. %
1-1 [3WR]	64%	43%	55%
1-2 [2WR]	42%	47%	49%
1-3 [1WR]	24%	50%	59%
2-2 [1WR]	11%	50%	57%
2-1 [2WR]	33%	29%	68%
0-1 [4WR]	79%	27%	67%

Red Zone Targets (min 3)

Receiver	All	Inside 5	6-10	11-20
Dez Bryant	20	5	5	10
Jason Witten	13		3	10
Cole Beasley	7	2	4	1
Terrance Williams	6	3		3
Rod Smith	5			5
Brice Butler	4		2	2
Ezekiel Elliott	3		1	2

Red Zone Rushes (min 3)

Rusher	All	Inside 5	6-10	11-20
Ezekiel Elliott	40	12	8	20
Alfred Morris	21	5	2	14
Rod Smith	14	5	3	6
Dak Prescott	12	3	5	4

Early Down Target Rate

RB	TE	WR
16%	21%	63%
23%	*21%* *NFL AVG*	*56%*

Overall Target Success %

RB	TE	WR
36% #31	56% #4	46% #23

Dallas Cowboys 2017 Passing Recap & 2018 Outlook

How much of Prescott's 2017 struggles came from Dallas facing the NFL's ninth-toughest pass-defense schedule? And how hurt was Dak by his reliance on aging Dez and Witten? We'll have a better idea this year. But the Cowboys' 2018 pass-defense slate is even harder. Perhaps the most frustrating element of Dallas' 2017 passing game was Jason Garrett's deep-passing usage of Bryant and refusal to play Brice Butler. Whereas Bryant produced a 41 passer rating and 26% when targeted deep, Butler's deep-target rating was 100 with a 40% Success Rate. Bryant was targeted on 46% of Dak's deep passes; Butler saw only 14%. Both Dez and Butler are now gone. For the run game to function at peak efficiency, the Cowboys must develop their downfield passing game. And their two most-heavily-targeted receivers on deep passes (Bryant and Terrance Williams) were horribly inefficient on such plays. (Williams' 57 deep-target rating and 40% Success Rate were only slightly better than Bryant's.) All in all, Prescott's deep-passer rating to wide receivers ranked 32nd in the league.

Dak Prescott Rating All Downs

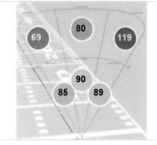

69
80
119
90
85
89

2017 Standard Passing Table

QB	Comp	Att	Comp %	Yds	YPA	TDs	INT	Sacks	Rating	Rk
Dak Prescott	307	489	63%	3,307	6.8	22	13	32	87	23
NFL Avg			62%		7.0				87.5	

Dak Prescott Rating Early Downs

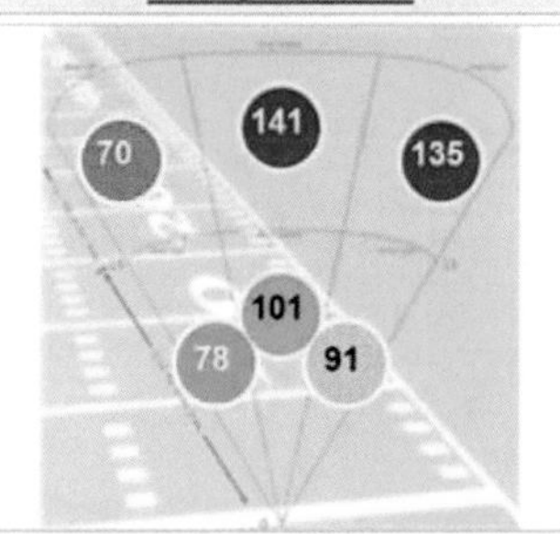

2017 Advanced Passing Table

QB	Success %	EDSR Passing Success %	20+ Yd Pass Gains	20+ Yd Pass %	30+ Yd Pass Gains	30+ Yd Pass %	Avg. Air Yds per Comp	Avg. YAC per Comp	20+ Air Yd Comp	20+ Air Yd %
Dak Prescott	43%	47%	33	6.7%	19	3.9%	6.4	4.4	15	5%
NFL Avg	44%	48%	27.7	8.8%	10.3	3.3%	6.0	4.7	11.7	6%

Interception Rates by Down

Yards to Go	1	2	3	4	Total
1 & 2	0.0%	0.0%	0.0%	0.0%	0.0%
3, 4, 5	0.0%	0.0%	0.0%	0.0%	0.0%
6 - 9	0.0%	3.0%	3.5%	50.0%	3.8%
10 - 14	1.3%	4.1%	3.1%	50.0%	2.5%
15+	9.1%	0.0%	8.3%		5.4%
Total	1.8%	2.2%	2.5%	22.2%	2.5%

3rd Down Passing - Short of Sticks Analysis

QB	Avg. Yds to Go	Avg. YIA (of Comp)	Avg Yds Short	Short of Sticks Rate	Short Rk
Dak Prescott	7.5	5.3	-2.3	61%	33
NFL Avg	7.8	6.7	-1.1	60%	

Air Yds vs YAC

Air Yds %	YAC %	Rk
49%	51%	36
58%	42%	

2017 Receiving Recap & 2018 Outlook

Out are the worst Cowboys receiver of 2017 (Dez Bryant), best (Brice Butler), and most reliable (Jason Witten). In are a ton of question markes. One likely starter is Terrance Williams, who delivered just a 73 passer rating and 53% Success Rate last year. Williams, however, was arrested in late May. The Cowboys signed Allen Hurns, who experienced a run-first offense similar to Dallas' with the Jaguars. Ankle and hamstring injuries cost Hurns 11 games over the past two years. And Hurns played over 70% of his snaps in the slot, which is Cole Beasley's position. Hurns will likely run more outside routes than he's used to in Dallas' 11 personnel.

Player *Min 50 Targets*	Targets	Comp %	YPA	Rating	TOARS	Success %	Success Rk	Missed YPA Rk	YAS % Rk	TDs
Dez Bryant	131	52%	6.4	71	4.7	40%	110	84	45	6
Jason Witten	87	72%	6.4	108	4.7	59%	10	16	128	5
Terrance Williams	78	68%	7.3	73	4.1	53%	38	12	80	0
Cole Beasley	63	57%	5.0	72	3.7	43%	99	102	107	4

Directional Passer Rating Delivered

Receiver	Short Left	Short Middle	Short Right	Deep Left	Deep Middle	Deep Right	Player Total
Dez Bryant	89	72	86	47	8	63	71
Jason Witten	84	126	80	135	158	158	108
Terrance Williams	95	43	76	103	56	68	73
Cole Beasley	49	93	89			53	72
Ezekiel Elliott	83	50	119				93
Brice Butler	135	40	158	46	96	158	130
Rod Smith	85	158	83		119		118
Team Total	84	91	90	61	80	113	87

2017 Rushing Recap & 2017 Outlook

Workhorse Ezekiel Elliott recorded a 57% Success Rate in 2017, even though his yards-per-carry average (4.06) was bested by both Alfred Morris (4.76) and Rod Smith (4.22). All three backs had high early-down Success Rates, which speaks the dominant quality of Dallas' offensive line. The Cowboys face an easier-than-average run-defense slate this year. Over the past two seasons, Elliott's 57% rushing Success Rate leads the NFL among backs with at least 125 attempts. Elliott maintains that 57% Success Rate on early-down runs, also best in the league. Zeke provides the floor for this offense. It's up to Dak to raise the ceiling.

Yards per Carry by Direction

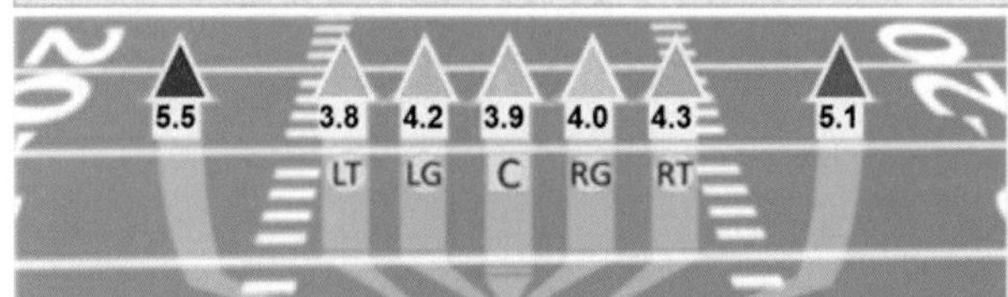

Player *Min 50 Rushes*	Rushes	YPC	Success %	Success Rk	Missed YPA Rk	YTS % Rk	YAS % Rk	Early Down Success %	Early Down Success Rk	TDs
Ezekiel Elliott	242	4.1	57%	2	8	10	46	56%	4	7
Alfred Morris	115	4.8	51%	12	25	32	19	52%	11	1
Rod Smith	55	4.2	60%	1	10	9	34	57%	3	4

Directional Run Frequency

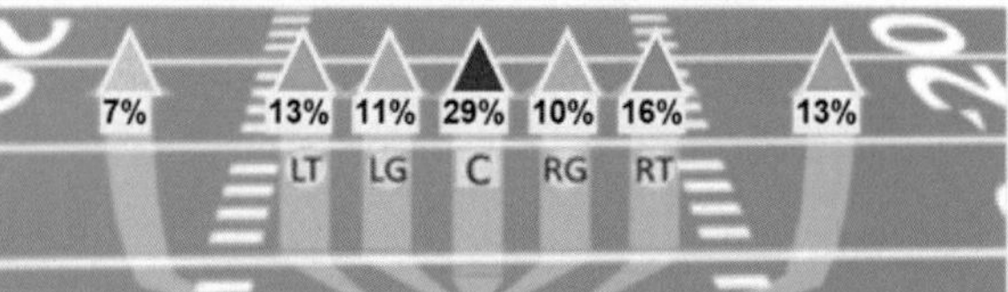

DAL-4

To non-running backs, first-down passes from Prescott recorded a 54% Success Rate. Third-down passes were successful only 35% of the time. This was atypical: the NFL average sees just a 5% drop from first- to second-down passing Success Rate, and an 8% drop from second to third. Prescott was successful on first down, but the 2016-2017 Cowboys ran the ball on 61% of first-down plays in games that were within one score. On first-and-ten plays the past two years, no team ran more than Dallas.

By definition, a successful first-and-10 play gains four-plus yards. On second-down passes, the Cowboys were very successful. The passed 43% of the time on second down with 1-6 yards to go, producing a 50% Success Rate and 96.5 rating. But they struggled when their first-down plays were unsuccessful (gained fewer than four yards). When needing 7-10 yards on second down, the Cowboys passed out of 11 personnel on 62% of snaps, and Prescott managed a 29% Success Rate with 4.5 yards per attempt and a 51.6 rating. League averages are a 45% Success Rate with 6.6 YPA and an 87 rating.

After failed first-down runs, the 2016 Cowboys recorded a 62% passing Success Rate at 8.9 yards per attempt. Last year's Cowboys dipped to 37% Success and only 6.8 YPA on such second-down passes. This year's Cowboys will have to try to return to 2016 form with worse receiving options in their preferred 11 personnel packages.

(cont'd - see DAL-5)

Evan Silva's Fantasy Corner

Ezekiel Elliott led the league in rushing yards per game in each of his first two seasons, averaging 24.9 touches with 25 TDs in 25 appearances. Elliott's impact has been far less in the passing game, where his 2.3 career targets-per-game average is dwarfed by Le'Veon Bell (6.4), Alvin Kamara (6.3), David Johnson (5.6), and Todd Gurley (3.9; 5.8 last year) among this year's consensus top-five fantasy backs. Whether due to his own deficiencies or coaching-staff scheming, Elliott's receiving production is his biggest box-score drawback. More promising is the healthy return of 4-of-5 offensive-line starters and addition of second-round LG Connor Williams at the front five's weakest link. Elliott's six-game suspension is also in the rearview mirror. He's my No. 5 back among the previously mentioned top five.

Division History: Season Wins & 2018 Projection

2014 Wins | 2015 Wins | 2016 Wins | 2017 Wins | Forecast 2018 Wins

Rank of 2018 Defensive Pass Efficiency Faced by Week

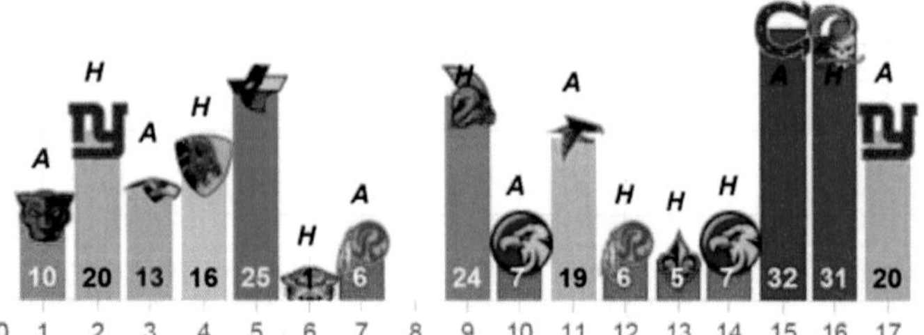

Rank of 2018 Defensive Rush Efficiency Faced by Week

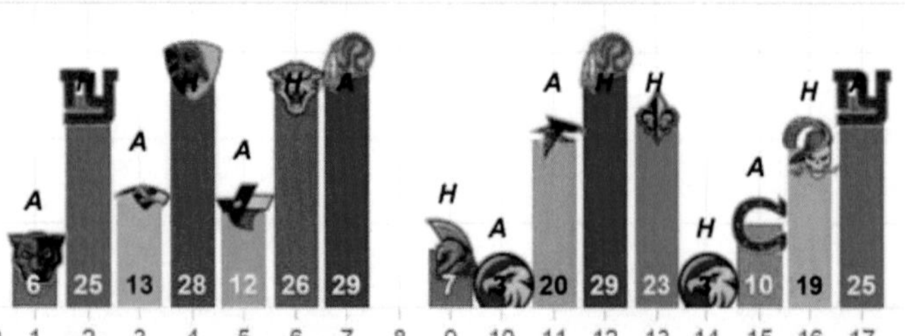

2017 Situational Usage by Player & Position

Usage Rate by Score

		Being Blown Out (14+)	Down Big (9-13)	One Score	Large Lead (9-13)	Blowout Lead (14+)	Grand Total
RUSH	Ezekiel Elliott	5%	7%	30%	25%	38%	27%
	Dez Bryant			0%			0%
	Alfred Morris	3%	29%	12%	23%	3%	13%
	Terrance Williams			0%			0%
	Rod Smith	12%		4%	5%	30%	6%
	Ryan Switzer			1%			0%
	Darren McFadden	1%					0%
	Total	22%	36%	48%	53%	70%	47%
PASS	Ezekiel Elliott	3%	14%	4%	5%	3%	4%
	Dez Bryant	20%	11%	15%	11%	10%	14%
	Alfred Morris	1%		1%	3%		1%
	Jason Witten	19%	18%	8%	11%	5%	10%
	Terrance Williams	11%		9%	9%	3%	9%
	Rod Smith	5%	4%	2%	1%	3%	3%
	Cole Beasley	12%	14%	6%	7%	3%	7%
	Brice Butler	4%		3%	1%		3%
	Ryan Switzer			1%		3%	1%
	James Hanna	2%		1%			1%
	Noah Brown			1%			1%
	Keith Smith		4%	1%			1%
	Geoff Swaim			0%		3%	0%
	Total	78%	64%	52%	47%	30%	53%

Positional Target Distribution vs NFL Average

		NFL Wide				Team Only			
		Left	Middle	Right	Total	Left	Middle	Right	Total
Deep	WR	961	498	959	**2,418**	25	11	28	**64**
	TE	190	148	186	**524**	2	2	2	**6**
	RB	39	8	42	**89**		1		**1**
	All	**1,190**	**654**	**1,187**	**3,031**	**27**	**14**	**30**	**71**
Short	WR	2,769	1,616	2,707	**7,092**	93	55	83	**231**
	TE	830	819	1,142	**2,791**	33	20	28	**81**
	RB	1,300	812	1,267	**3,379**	21	11	28	**60**
	All	**4,899**	**3,247**	**5,116**	**13,262**	**147**	**86**	**139**	**372**
Total		**6,089**	**3,901**	**6,303**	**16,293**	**174**	**100**	**169**	**443**

Positional Success Rates vs NFL Average

		NFL Wide				Team Only			
		Left	Middle	Right	Total	Left	Middle	Right	Total
Deep	WR	37%	45%	38%	**39%**	32%	36%	39%	**36%**
	TE	38%	52%	45%	**44%**	50%	100%	100%	**83%**
	RB	36%	50%	38%	**38%**		100%		**100%**
	All	**37%**	**47%**	**39%**	**40%**	**33%**	**50%**	**43%**	**41%**
Short	WR	52%	58%	50%	**52%**	47%	53%	47%	**48%**
	TE	50%	56%	49%	**52%**	52%	60%	54%	**54%**
	RB	44%	51%	43%	**46%**	38%	55%	18%	**32%**
	All	**50%**	**56%**	**48%**	**51%**	**47%**	**55%**	**42%**	**47%**
Total		**47%**	**54%**	**46%**	**49%**	**45%**	**54%**	**43%**	**46%**

Successful Play Rate
0% – 100%

Dallas Cowboys - Success by Personnel Grouping & Play Type

Play Type	1-1 [3WR]	1-2 [2WR]	2-1 [2WR]	1-3 [1WR]	0-1 [4WR]	2-2 [1WR]	0-0 [5WR]	0-2 [3WR]	3-1 [1WR]	2-3 [0WR]	Grand Total
PASS	43% (394, 75%)	47% (60, 11%)	29% (17, 3%)	50% (22, 4%)	27% (22, 4%)	50% (6, 1%)		67% (3, 1%)			43% (524, 100%)
RUSH	55% (225, 47%)	49% (82, 17%)	68% (34, 7%)	59% (69, 14%)	67% (6, 1%)	57% (51, 11%)	0% (1, 0%)	100% (1, 0%)	100% (2, 0%)	75% (8, 2%)	56% (481, 100%)
TOTAL	47% (619, 62%)	48% (142, 14%)	55% (51, 5%)	57% (91, 9%)	36% (28, 3%)	56% (57, 6%)	0% (1, 0%)	75% (4, 0%)	100% (2, 0%)	75% (8, 1%)	49% (1,005, 100%)

Format Line 1: Success Rate Line 2: Total # of Plays, % of All Plays (by type)

DAL-5 The 2018 Cowboys are also likely to struggle to defend the pass. Their secondary is in flux at both safety and cornerback, and they play one of the NFL's toughest schedules of passing games. Dallas draws two of the league's best mobile quarterbacks in two of its first three games: Cam Newton (Week 1) and Russell Wilson (Week 3), both on the road. The Cowboys face traditional pocket passers Eli Manning in Weeks 2 and 4. Dallas draws athletic Carson Wentz and Alex Smith twice apiece, plus Drew Brees, Matt Ryan, Deshaun Watson, and possibly Andrew Luck in Week 15.

Passing is substantially more correlated to wins than rushing. So if the Cowboys are set up to struggle to both pass and defend the pass, what is their upside in 2018? They should get a full 16-game season of Ezekiel Elliott and boast a great offensive line. The linebacker corps can be strong if Sean Lee finally stays healthy, first-round pick Leighton Vander Esch proves NFL ready, and Jaylon Smith takes another step. Their defense does face one of the NFL's softest rushing-offense schedules, jampacked with bottom-five run games from 2017.

If the Cowboys are going to take a step forward offensively, they must diversify their offense and use more running back passes, and more Prescott runs. If they hesitate, 2018 will likely produce another middling record and seventh postseason watching from the couch in the last nine years.

Receiving Success by Personnel Grouping

Position	Player	1-1 [3WR]	1-2 [2WR]	2-1 [2WR]	1-3 [1WR]	0-1 [4WR]	2-2 [1WR]	0-2 [3WR]	Total
RB	Ezekiel Elliott	30% 8.2 108.3 (30)	0% 0.0 47.9 (5)	0% 1.3 42.4 (3)					24% 6.6 93.0 (38)
TE	Jason Witten	56% 6.1 101.3 (71)	75% 13.0 158.3 (4)		60% 7.6 123.3 (5)	43% 5.6 84.8 (7)			56% 6.4 108.4 (87)
WR	Dez Bryant	39% 5.7 64.6 (90)	53% 9.0 93.5 (17)	50% 5.0 64.6 (4)	44% 5.2 79.4 (9)	29% 9.0 87.2 (7)	33% 11.0 75.7 (3)	100% 12.0 116.7 (1)	41% 6.4 71.4 (131)
	Terrance Williams	56% 7.7 85.5 (57)	50% 7.4 92.6 (14)	0% 0.0 0.0 (2)	100% 5.0 87.5 (1)	0% 0.0 0.0 (2)	100% 8.0 100.0 (1)	100% 10.0 108.3 (1)	54% 7.3 73.0 (78)
	Cole Beasley	45% 5.3 72.8 (58)	0% 3.0 79.2 (1)			25% 1.5 56.3 (4)			43% 5.0 71.8 (63)
	Brice Butler	50% 13.0 119.8 (16)	80% 22.2 158.3 (5)	0% 0.0 39.6 (1)	0% 0.0 39.6 (1)				52% 13.9 130.0 (23)

Format Line 1: Success Rate Line 2: YPA Line 3: Passer Rating Line 4: Total # of Plays

Successful Play Rate
0% – 100%

Rushing Success by Personnel Grouping

Position	Player	1-1 [3WR]	1-2 [2WR]	2-1 [2WR]	1-3 [1WR]	0-1 [4WR]	2-2 [1WR]	0-0 [5WR]	0-2 [3WR]	3-1 [1WR]	2-3 [0WR]	3-2 [0WR]	Total
QB	Dak Prescott	68% 7.4 (38)	67% 6.0 (3)	100% 12.0 (1)	100% 2.0 (1)	80% 8.6 (5)	17% -0.2 (6)	0% 3.0 (1)	100% 1.0 (1)			0% -1.0 (1)	63% 6.3 (57)
RB	Ezekiel Elliott	56% 4.2 (103)	50% 3.3 (52)	65% 5.6 (26)	56% 3.6 (34)		61% 4.5 (23)			100% 6.0 (1)	100% 1.3 (3)		57% 4.1 (242)
	Alfred Morris	51% 4.0 (47)	45% 6.1 (22)	60% 3.4 (5)	54% 5.0 (28)		50% 6.3 (10)			100% 5.0 (1)	50% 0.5 (2)		51% 4.8 (115)

Format Line 1: Success Rate Line 2: YPC Line 3: Total # of Plays

Denver Broncos

2018 Coaches

Head Coach:
Vance Joseph (2nd yr)
Offensive Coordinator:
Bill Musgrave (2nd yr)
Defensive Coordinator:
Joe Woods (2nd yr)

EASY HARD

2018 Forecast

Wins	Div Rank
7	#3

Past Records

2017: 5-11
2016: 9-7
2015: 12-4

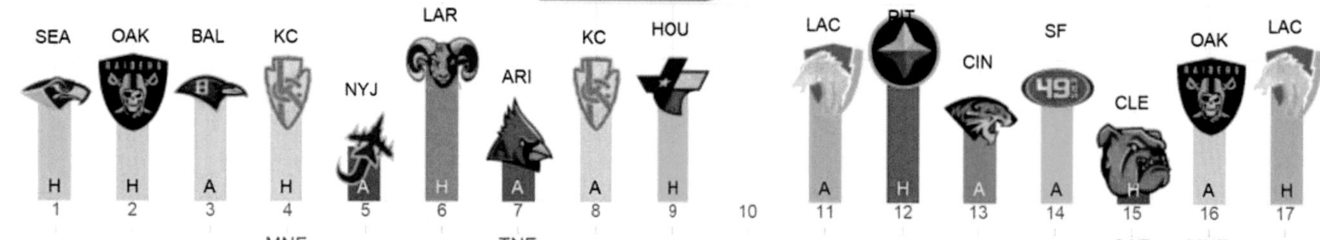

Key Players Lost

TXN	Player (POS)
Cut	Anderson, C.J. RB
	Bertolet, Taylor K
	Thomas, Jhaustin DE
Declared Free Agent	Barbre, Allen G
	Charles, Jamaal RB
	Crick, Jared DE
	Davis, Todd LB
	Fowler, Bennie WR
	Green, Virgil TE
	Latimer, Cody WR
	Nelson, Corey LB
	Osweiler, Brock QB
	Stephenson, Donald T
	Turner, Billy G
	Winn, Billy DE

Average Line	# Games Favored	# Games Underdog
1.0	7	7

2018 Denver Broncos Overview

One definition of progress is an onward movement. By that definition, Trevor Siemian made 2017 progress. A better definition of progress is "gradual betterment," and by that definition, Siemian did the opposite last year.

Through the first four games, Siemian didn't embarrass himself. He posted a 46% Success Rate, 7.0 yards per attempt, and 89 passer rating. The Broncos entered their bye week at 3-1. Headlines read, "Trevor Siemian beginning to earn more praise from national media," and "Broncos' Siemian earning respect – and wins – in Denver."

That's when Siemian began to slip. In Siemian's first three games after the bye, his Success Rate dropped from 46% to 35%, his YPA from 7.0 to 6.5, and his passer rating from 89 to 64. Much resulted from his abysmal third-down performance, where Siemian's Success Rate was 18% with a 5.3 YPA and 24 passer rating. In the red zone, Siemian averaged 3.1 YPA with an 18% Success Rate.

The Broncos lost all three post-bye games by double digits, and coach Vance Joseph started Brock Osweiler in Week 9. By Week 11, Siemian was demoted all the way to third string. After Osweiler went 0-3 in Weeks 9-11, the Broncos turned to first-round bust Paxton Lynch. Lynch injured his ankle, and Siemian reentered the lineup. Three games later, Siemian got yanked in Indianapolis after a dreadful start.

When you lack productivity at quarterback, you struggle on early downs. When you struggle on early downs, you must convert third downs. But bad quarterbacks don't win on third downs. And bad quarterbacks don't win in the red zone. When you don't have a productive quarterback, it's hard to win games. And that was the story of the 2017 Broncos.

Quarterback play wasn't the sole reason for Denver's 5-11 season, however. The Broncos were terrible in two metrics most correlated to victory: turnover margin and sack margin. After going plus-two in both turnover and sack margin in 2016, last year's Broncos went -17 in turnover margin and -20 in sack margin.

(cont'd - see DEN2)

Key Free Agents/ Trades Added

Bell, Kenny WR
Bertolet, Taylor K
Brock, Tramaine CB
Cravens, Su'a S
Keenum, Case QB
King, Marquette P
Knappe, Andreas T
McDonald, Clinton DT
Veldheer, Jared T
Williams, DeShawn DT

Drafted Players

Rd	Pk	Player (College)
1	5	DE - Bradley Chubb (NC State)
2	40	WR - Courtland Sutton (SMU)
3	71	RB - Royce Freeman (Oregon)
3*	99	CB - Isaac Yiadom (Boston College)
4	106	LB - Josey Jewell (Iowa)
	113	WR - DaeSean Hamilton (Penn State)
5	156	TE - Troy Fumagalli (Wisconsin)
6	183	G - Sam Jones (Arizona State)
6*	217	LB - Keishawn Bierria (Washington)
7	226	RB - David Williams (Arkansas)

Regular Season Wins: Past & Current Proj

Forecast 2018 Wins  7

2017 Wins  5

Forecast 2017 Wins  9.5

2016 Wins  9

2015 Wins  12

2014 Wins 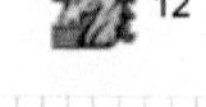 12

1 3 5 7 9 11 13 15

Lineup & Cap Hits

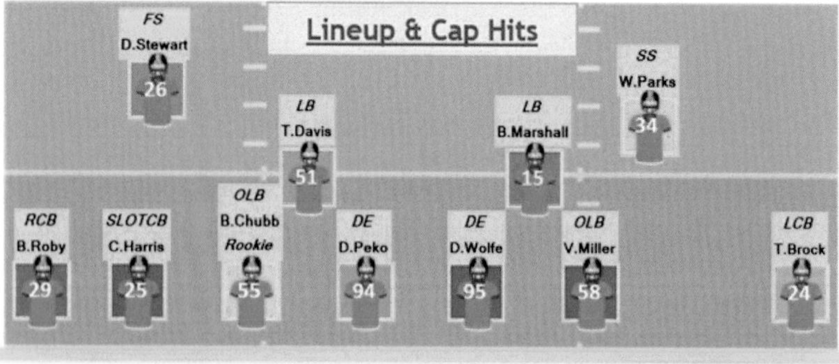

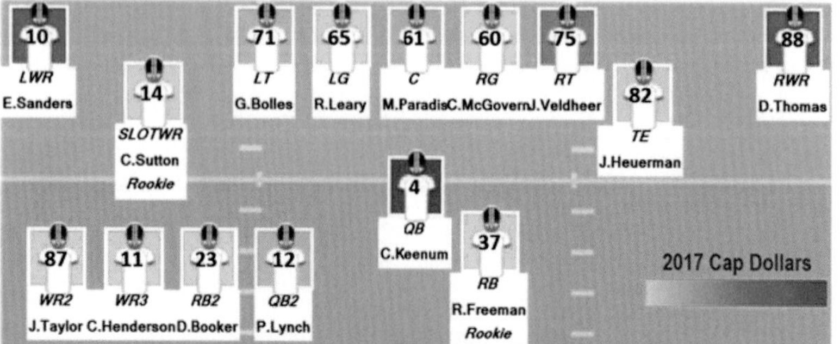

2018 Unit Spending

Positional Spending

	Rank	Total	2017 Rk
All OFF	15	$91.80M	29
QB	20	$18.08M	30
OL	10	$37.50M	20
RB	32	$2.79M	18
WR	2	$29.79M	4
TE	30	$3.65M	24
All DEF	7	$92.80M	1
DL	19	$23.99M	25
LB	4	$33.58M	4
CB	7	$25.13M	3
S	19	$10.09M	5

Denver Broncos 2017 Success Rate Radar

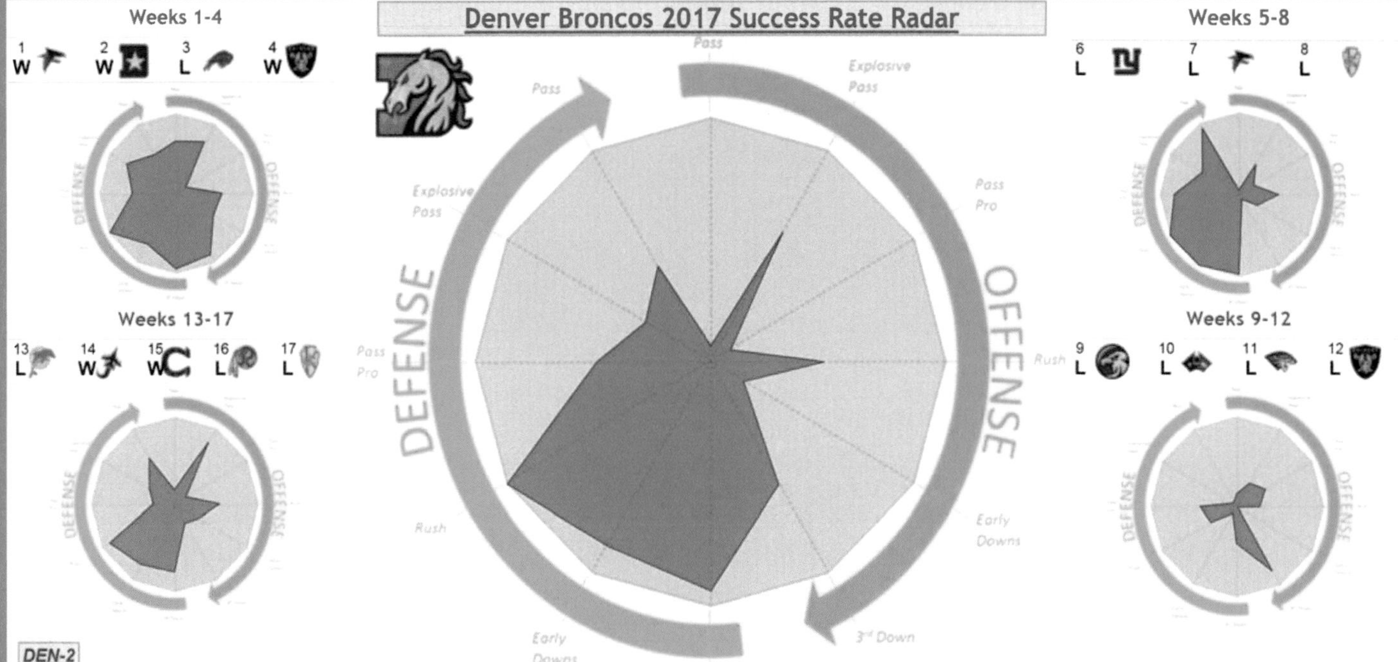

DEN-2

The offensive line got worse. And their No. 2-ranked pass rush from 2016 fell to No. 11 despite facing an easier schedule of opposing offenses.

Denver must improve its pass protection and pass rush. An average quarterback will look bad when unprotected. And when an average quarterback gets hit and rattled, he loses confidence in the players around him and often in himself.

The 2017 Broncos had a major offensive split between fired OC Mike McCoy and promoted OC Bill Musgrave, who took over on November 20. Under McCoy, the Broncos used 11 personnel on 70% of plays, 12 personnel on 14%, and 21 personnel on 7%. Musgrave went 55% 11 personnel, 17% 12 personnel, 10% 21 personnel, and 10% 22 personnel. This was partly due to Emmanuel Sanders playing his final game in Week 15. But even in Weeks 12-15, Demaryius Thomas dominated targets under Musgrave with 28 to Sanders' 19. It seemed evident that Musgrave was more concerned with pass protection than McCoy, who so frequently used three-receiver packages to throw the ball around the yard at the expense of Siemian absorbing hits. It was also a return to Denver's previous-year ways. The 2016 Broncos went 53% 11 personnel, 19% 21 personnel, and 10% 12 personnel.

But rather than upgrade their offensive line this offseason, the Broncos focused on adding to their defense. Their lone O-Line upgrade was RT Jared Veldheer, who struggled badly in Arizona. With blocker Virgil Green gone to the Chargers, the Broncos will turn to some combination of Jeff Heuerman, Jake Butt, and rookie Troy Fumagalli at tight end.

The wideout corps replaced pedestrian veterans Bennie Fowler and Cody Latimer with rookies Courtland Sutton (SMU) and DaeSean Hamilton (Penn State) behind Thomas and Sanders. Sutton is expected to play outside in 11 personnel, bookending Thomas with Sanders in the slot. Sutton profiles as a possession receiver who can win at the catch point and create yards after the catch.

(cont'd - see DEN-3)

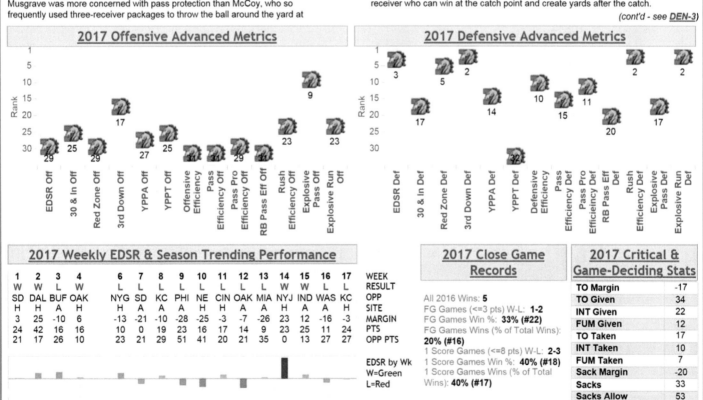

2017 Offensive Advanced Metrics

Metric	Rank
EDSR Off	29
30 & In Off	25
Red Zone Off	29
3rd Down Off	17
YPPA Off	27
YPPT Off	25
Offensive Efficiency	31
Pass Efficiency Off	31
Pass Pro Efficiency Off	29
RB Pass Eff Off	31
Rush Efficiency Off	23
Explosive Pass Off	9
Explosive Run Off	23

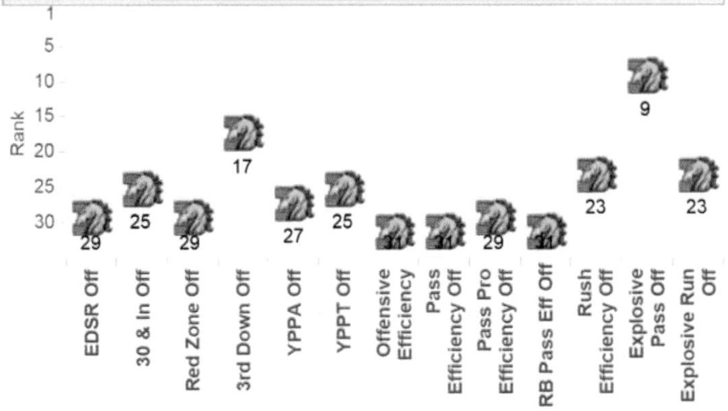

2017 Defensive Advanced Metrics

Metric	Rank
EDSR Def	3
30 & In Def	17
Red Zone Def	5
3rd Down Def	2
YPPA Def	14
YPPT Def	32
Defensive Efficiency	10
Pass Efficiency Def	15
Pass Pro Efficieincy Def	11
RB Pass Eff Def	20
Rush Efficiency Def	2
Explosive Pass Def	17
Explosive Run Def	2

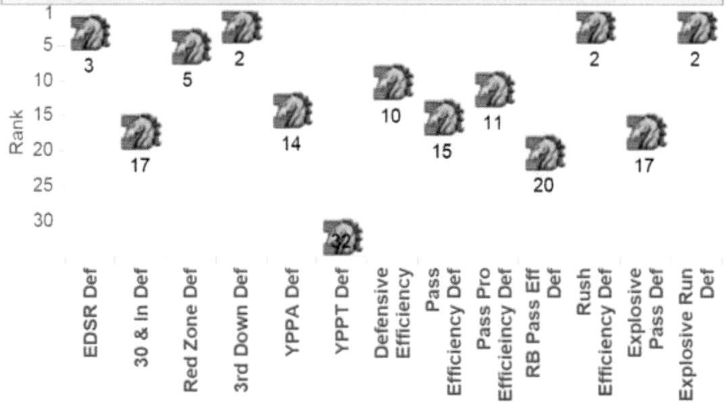

2017 Weekly EDSR & Season Trending Performance

WEEK	1	2	3	4	6	7	8	9	10	11	12	13	14	15	16	17
RESULT	W	W	L	W	L	L	L	L	L	L	L	L	W	W	L	L
OPP	SD	DAL	BUF	OAK	NYG	SD	KC	PHI	NE	CIN	OAK	MIA	NYJ	IND	WAS	KC
SITE	H	H	A	H	H	A	A	A	H	H	A	A	H	A	A	H
MARGIN	3	25	-10	6	-13	-21	-10	-28	-25	-3	-7	-26	23	12	-16	-3
PTS	24	42	16	16	10	0	19	23	16	17	14	9	23	25	11	24
OPP PTS	21	17	26	10	23	21	29	51	41	20	21	35	0	13	27	27

EDSR by Wk
W=Green
L=Red

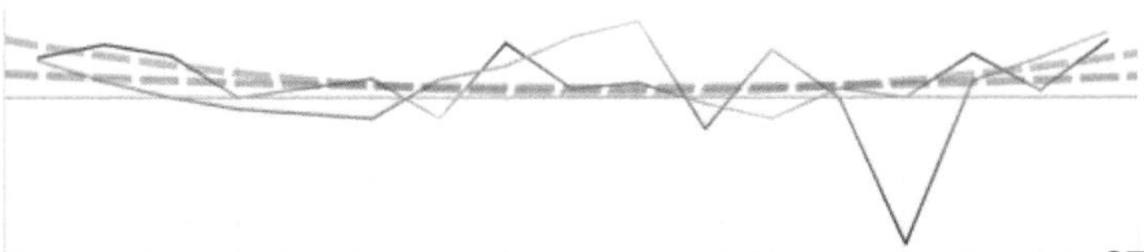

OFF/DEF
EDSR
Blue=OFF
(high=good)
Red=DEF
(low=good)

2017 Close Game Records

All 2016 Wins: **5**
FG Games (<=3 pts) W-L: **1-2**
FG Games Win %: **33% (#22)**
FG Games Wins (% of Total Wins): **20% (#16)**
1 Score Games (<=8 pts) W-L: **2-3**
1 Score Games Win %: **40% (#18)**
1 Score Games Wins (% of Total Wins): **40% (#17)**

2017 Critical & Game-Deciding Stats

TO Margin	-17
TO Given	34
INT Given	22
FUM Given	12
TO Taken	17
INT Taken	10
FUM Taken	7
Sack Margin	-20
Sacks	33
Sacks Allow	53
Return TD Margin	-2
Ret TDs	4
Ret TDs Allow	6
Penalty Margin	-24
Penalties	113
Opponent Penalties	89

Denver Broncos 2018 Strength of Schedule In Detail (compared to 2017)

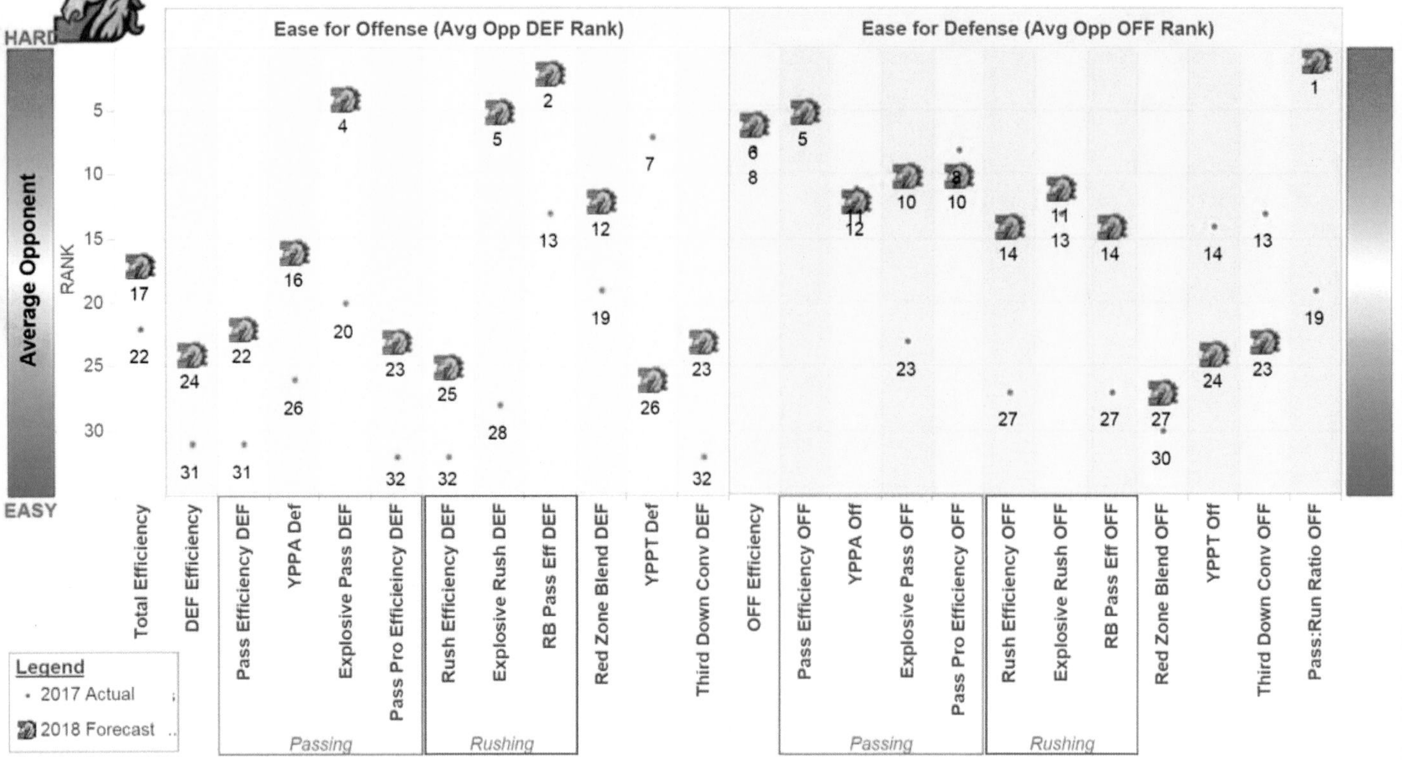

HARD / EASY — Average Opponent RANK

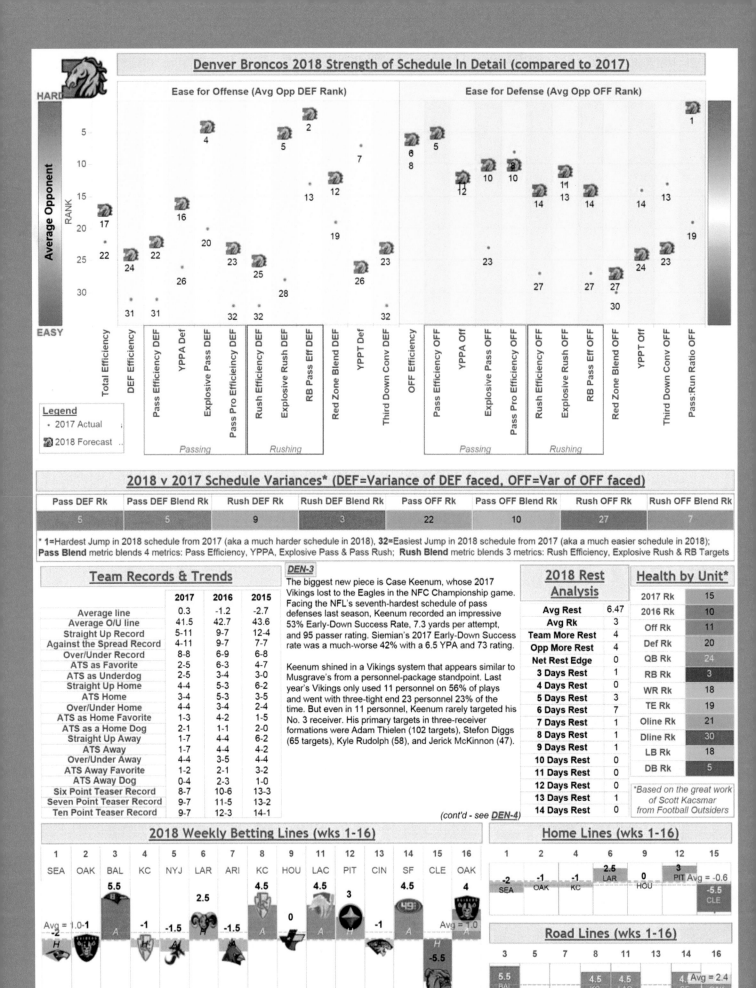

Ease for Offense (Avg Opp DEF Rank)

Metric	2017 Actual	2018 Forecast
Total Efficiency	22	17
DEF Efficiency	31	24
Pass Efficiency DEF (Passing)	31	22
YPPA Def (Passing)	26	16
Explosive Pass DEF (Passing)	20	4
Pass Pro Efficiency DEF (Passing)	32	23
Rush Efficiency DEF (Rushing)	32	25
Explosive Rush DEF (Rushing)	28	5
RB Pass Eff DEF (Rushing)	13	2
Red Zone Blend DEF	19	12
YPPT Def	7	26
Third Down Conv DEF	32	23

Ease for Defense (Avg Opp OFF Rank)

Metric	2017 Actual	2018 Forecast
OFF Efficiency	8	6
Pass Efficiency OFF (Passing)		5
YPPA Off (Passing)	12	11
Explosive Pass OFF (Passing)	23	10
Pass Pro Efficiency OFF (Passing)	8	10
Rush Efficiency OFF (Rushing)	27	14
Explosive Rush OFF (Rushing)	13	11
RB Pass Eff OFF (Rushing)	27	14
Red Zone Blend OFF	30	27
YPPT Off	14	24
Third Down Conv OFF	13	23
Pass:Run Ratio OFF	19	1

Legend
- 2017 Actual
- 2018 Forecast

2018 v 2017 Schedule Variances* (DEF=Variance of DEF faced, OFF=Var of OFF faced)

Pass DEF Rk	Pass DEF Blend Rk	Rush DEF Rk	Rush DEF Blend Rk	Pass OFF Rk	Pass OFF Blend Rk	Rush OFF Rk	Rush OFF Blend Rk
5	5	9	3	22	10	27	7

* **1**=Hardest Jump in 2018 schedule from 2017 (aka a much harder schedule in 2018), **32**=Easiest Jump in 2018 schedule from 2017 (aka a much easier schedule in 2018); **Pass Blend** metric blends 4 metrics: Pass Efficiency, YPPA, Explosive Pass & Pass Rush; **Rush Blend** metric blends 3 metrics: Rush Efficiency, Explosive Rush & RB Targets

Team Records & Trends

	2017	2016	2015
Average line	0.3	-1.2	-2.7
Average O/U line	41.5	42.7	43.6
Straight Up Record	5-11	9-7	12-4
Against the Spread Record	4-11	9-7	7-7
Over/Under Record	8-8	6-9	6-8
ATS as Favorite	2-5	6-3	4-7
ATS as Underdog	2-5	3-4	3-0
Straight Up Home	4-4	5-3	6-2
ATS Home	3-4	5-3	3-5
Over/Under Home	4-4	3-4	2-4
ATS as Home Favorite	1-3	4-2	1-5
ATS as a Home Dog	2-1	1-1	2-0
Straight Up Away	1-7	4-4	6-2
ATS Away	1-7	4-4	4-2
Over/Under Away	4-4	3-5	4-4
ATS Away Favorite	1-2	2-1	3-2
ATS Away Dog	0-4	2-3	1-0
Six Point Teaser Record	8-7	10-6	13-3
Seven Point Teaser Record	9-7	11-5	13-2
Ten Point Teaser Record	9-7	12-3	14-1

DEN-3

The biggest new piece is Case Keenum, whose 2017 Vikings lost to the Eagles in the NFC Championship game. Facing the NFL's seventh-hardest schedule of pass defenses last season, Keenum recorded an impressive 53% Early-Down Success Rate, 7.3 yards per attempt, and 95 passer rating. Siemian's 2017 Early-Down Success rate was a much-worse 42% with a 6.5 YPA and 73 rating.

Keenum shined in a Vikings system that appears similar to Musgrave's from a personnel-package standpoint. Last year's Vikings only used 11 personnel on 56% of plays and went with three-tight end 23 personnel 23% of the time. But even in 11 personnel, Keenum rarely targeted his No. 3 receiver. His primary targets in three-receiver formations were Adam Thielen (102 targets), Stefon Diggs (65 targets), Kyle Rudolph (58), and Jerick McKinnon (47).

(cont'd - see DEN-4)

2018 Rest Analysis

Avg Rest	6.47
Avg Rk	3
Team More Rest	4
Opp More Rest	4
Net Rest Edge	0
3 Days Rest	1
4 Days Rest	0
5 Days Rest	3
6 Days Rest	7
7 Days Rest	1
8 Days Rest	1
9 Days Rest	1
10 Days Rest	0
11 Days Rest	0
12 Days Rest	0
13 Days Rest	1
14 Days Rest	0

Health by Unit*

2017 Rk	15
2016 Rk	10
Off Rk	11
Def Rk	20
QB Rk	24
RB Rk	3
WR Rk	18
TE Rk	19
Oline Rk	21
Dline Rk	30
LB Rk	18
DB Rk	5

*Based on the great work of Scott Kacsmar from Football Outsiders

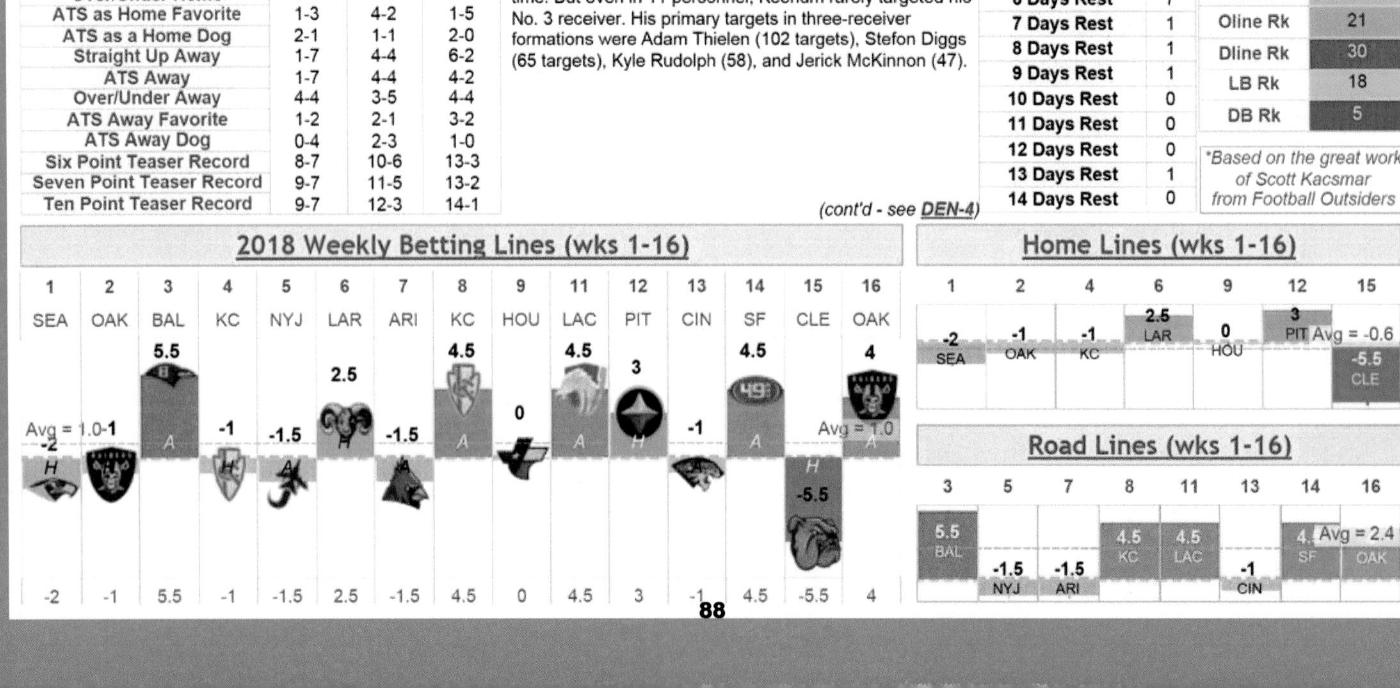

Denver Broncos 2017 Play Analysis

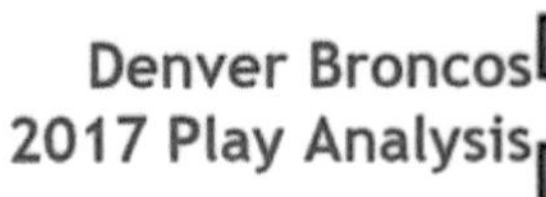

2017 Play Tendencies

All Pass %	58%
All Pass Rk	17
All Rush %	42%
All Rush Rk	16
1 Score Pass %	53%
1 Score Pass Rk	26
2016 1 Score Pass %	58%
2016 1 Score Pass Rk	20
2017 Pass Increase %	-4%
Pass Increase Rk	24
1 Score Rush %	47%
1 Score Rush Rk	7
Up Pass %	41%
Up Pass Rk	31
Up Rush %	59%
Up Rush Rk	2
Down Pass %	65%
Down Pass Rk	17
Down Rush %	35%
Down Rush Rk	16

2017 Down & Distance Tendencies

Down	Distance	Total Plays	Pass Rate	Run Rate	Play Success %
1	Short (1-3)	4	0%	100%	0%
	Med (4-7)	7	71%	29%	29%
	Long (8-10)	312	46%	54%	46%
	XL (11+)	15	47%	53%	33%
2	Short (1-3)	29	10%	90%	55%
	Med (4-7)	90	49%	51%	43%
	Long (8-10)	110	58%	42%	39%
	XL (11+)	39	69%	31%	23%
3	Short (1-3)	44	48%	52%	70%
	Med (4-7)	66	92%	8%	42%
	Long (8-10)	41	85%	15%	29%
	XL (11+)	31	77%	23%	6%
4	Short (1-3)	4	50%	50%	75%
	XL (11+)	2	50%	50%	0%

Shotgun %:

Under Center	Shotgun
37%	63%
37% AVG	*63%*

Run Rate:

Under Center	Shotgun
74%	24%
68% AVG	*23%*

Pass Rate:

Under Center	Shotgun
26%	76%
32% AVG	*77%*

Short Yardage Intelligence:

2nd and Short Run

Run Freq	Run Rk	NFL Run Freq Avg	Run 1D Rate	Run NFL 1D Avg
68%	15	67%	71%	69%

2nd and Short Pass

Pass Freq	Pass Rk	NFL Pass Freq Avg	Pass 1D Rate	Pass NFL 1D Avg
32%	18	33%	40%	53%

Most Frequent Play

Down	Distance	Play Type	Player	Total Plays	Play Success %
1	Short (1-3)	RUSH	C.J. Anderson	2	0%
	Med (4-7)	PASS	Emmanuel Sanders	3	33%
	Long (8-10)	RUSH	C.J. Anderson	100	45%
	XL (11+)	RUSH	C.J. Anderson	5	0%
2	Short (1-3)	RUSH	C.J. Anderson	19	63%
	Med (4-7)	RUSH	C.J. Anderson	24	42%
	Long (8-10)	RUSH	C.J. Anderson	28	32%
	XL (11+)	PASS	Demaryius Thomas	6	17%
			Emmanuel Sanders	6	67%
		RUSH	C.J. Anderson	6	17%
3	Short (1-3)	PASS	Emmanuel Sanders	9	44%
	Med (4-7)	PASS	Demaryius Thomas	16	44%
	Long (8-10)	PASS	Demaryius Thomas	10	30%
	XL (11+)	PASS	Jamaal Charles	5	20%

Most Successful Play*

Down	Distance	Play Type	Player	Total Plays	Play Success %
1	Long (8-10)	PASS	Bennie Fowler	8	75%
	XL (11+)	RUSH	C.J. Anderson	5	0%
2	Short (1-3)	RUSH	C.J. Anderson	19	63%
	Med (4-7)	RUSH	Jamaal Charles	6	50%
			Devontae Booker	10	50%
	Long (8-10)	RUSH	Jamaal Charles	6	67%
	XL (11+)	PASS	Emmanuel Sanders	6	67%
3	Short (1-3)	RUSH	Devontae Booker	8	88%
	Med (4-7)	PASS	Emmanuel Sanders	8	63%
	Long (8-10)	PASS	Emmanuel Sanders	6	67%
	XL (11+)	PASS	Jamaal Charles	5	20%

**Minimum 5 plays to qualify*

2017 Snap Rates

Wk	Opp	Score	Demaryius Thomas	Emmanuel Sanders	C.J. Anderson	Bennie Fowler	Virgil Green	Cody Latimer	Jeff Heuerman	Devontae Booker
1	LAC	W 24-21	60 (87%)	53 (77%)	48 (70%)	38 (55%)	45 (65%)	12 (17%)	17 (25%)	
2	DAL	W 42-17	68 (88%)	69 (90%)	56 (73%)	23 (30%)	46 (60%)	14 (18%)	22 (29%)	
3	BUF	L 26-16	61 (87%)	62 (89%)	49 (70%)	49 (70%)	37 (53%)	11 (16%)	15 (21%)	
4	OAK	W 16-10	56 (88%)	48 (75%)	44 (69%)	34 (53%)	42 (66%)		17 (27%)	8 (13%)
6	NYG	L 23-10	57 (70%)	50 (62%)	38 (47%)	61 (75%)	35 (43%)		17 (21%)	23 (28%)
7	LAC	L 21-0	50 (78%)		38 (59%)	53 (83%)	28 (44%)		15 (23%)	11 (17%)
8	KC	L 29-19	59 (81%)		33 (45%)	40 (55%)	31 (42%)	37 (51%)	22 (30%)	25 (34%)
9	PHI	L 51-23	53 (83%)	29 (45%)	23 (36%)	25 (39%)	21 (33%)	48 (75%)	24 (38%)	22 (34%)
10	NE	L 41-16	50 (79%)	55 (87%)	24 (38%)	18 (29%)	30 (48%)	47 (75%)	32 (51%)	23 (37%)
11	CIN	L 20-17	71 (88%)	76 (94%)	29 (36%)	24 (30%)	41 (51%)	49 (60%)		49 (60%)
12	OAK	L 21-14	48 (81%)	50 (85%)	19 (32%)	17 (29%)	30 (51%)	36 (61%)		26 (44%)
13	MIA	L 35-9	57 (79%)	57 (79%)	40 (56%)	19 (26%)	21 (29%)	45 (63%)	17 (24%)	11 (15%)
14	NYJ	W 23-0	45 (64%)	47 (67%)	41 (59%)	22 (31%)	44 (63%)	31 (44%)	25 (36%)	27 (39%)
15	IND	W 25-13	54 (68%)	39 (49%)	54 (68%)	39 (49%)	36 (46%)	44 (56%)	25 (32%)	23 (29%)
16	WAS	L 27-11	62 (84%)		42 (57%)	56 (76%)	26 (35%)		37 (50%)	30 (41%)
17	KC	L 27-24	35 (54%)		34 (52%)	58 (89%)	21 (32%)		38 (58%)	14 (22%)
Grand Total			886 (79%)	635 (75%)	612 (54%)	576 (51%)	534 (47%)	374 (49%)	323 (33%)	292 (32%)

Personnel Groupings

Personnel	Team %	NFL Avg	Succ. %
1-1 [3WR]	65%	59%	41%
1-2 [2WR]	15%	19%	47%
2-1 [2WR]	7%	7%	44%
2-2 [1WR]	6%	4%	41%
1-3 [1WR]	4%	5%	29%

Grouping Tendencies

Personnel	Pass Rate	Pass Succ. %	Run Succ. %
1-1 [3WR]	67%	37%	49%
1-2 [2WR]	51%	49%	45%
2-1 [2WR]	31%	56%	38%
2-2 [1WR]	11%	43%	41%
1-3 [1WR]	29%	18%	33%

Red Zone Targets (min 3)

Receiver	All	Inside 5	6-10	11-20
Demaryius Thomas	17	1	7	9
Emmanuel Sanders	10	2	3	5
Bennie Fowler	9	2	3	4
C.J. Anderson	7		2	5
A.J. Derby	6			6
Devontae Booker	5			5
Virgil Green	4	2		2
Jamaal Charles	3			3

Red Zone Rushes (min 3)

Rusher	All	Inside 5	6-10	11-20
C.J. Anderson	25	11	2	12
Devontae Booker	17	1	3	13
Jamaal Charles	13	3	1	9
Trevor Siemian	4	1	2	1

Early Down Target Rate

RB	TE	WR
21%	17%	62%
23%	*21% NFL AVG*	*56%*

Overall Target Success %

RB	TE	WR
37% #30	45% #26	45% #24

Denver Broncos 2017 Passing Recap & 2018 Outlook

Demaryius Thomas and Emmanuel Sanders should remain productive in Musgrave's offense, but tight end is a position of weakness. On 35 targets over the past two years, Jeff Heuerman has managed a 40% Success Rate and 74 passer rating when thrown to. It could have been more of a Siemian problem than Heuerman problem, of course. The other big hope with the quarterback change is Denver's ability to stretch a defense. Keenum isn't an ideal deep-ball passer, but he is much more dangerous than his predecessor. Of 32 quarterbacks with 40 or more deep-ball attempts in 2017, Siemian ranked dead last in passer rating (43), 31st in Success Rate (32%), and 30th in YPA (8.7). Keenum ranked No. 8 in rating (97), No. 6 in Success Rate (44%), and No. 12 in YPA (11.7). Going deep effectively allows offenses to bypass downs, prevents punts, sets up points, and gives the team's defense better starting field position. I hope Musgrave encourages more no-huddle plays and more deep passing in 2018.

Trevor Siemian Rating All Downs

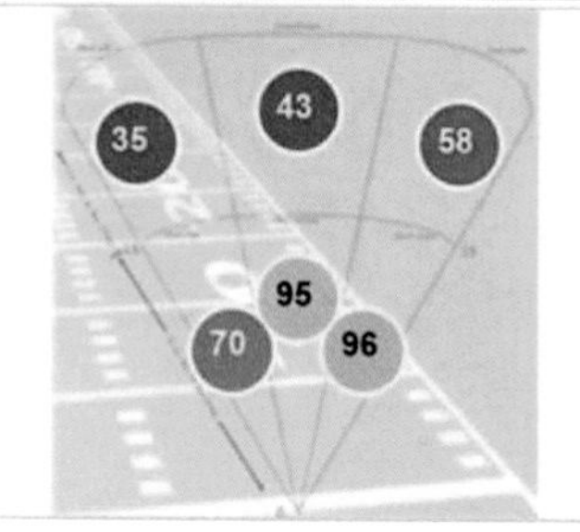

Trevor Siemian Rating Early Downs

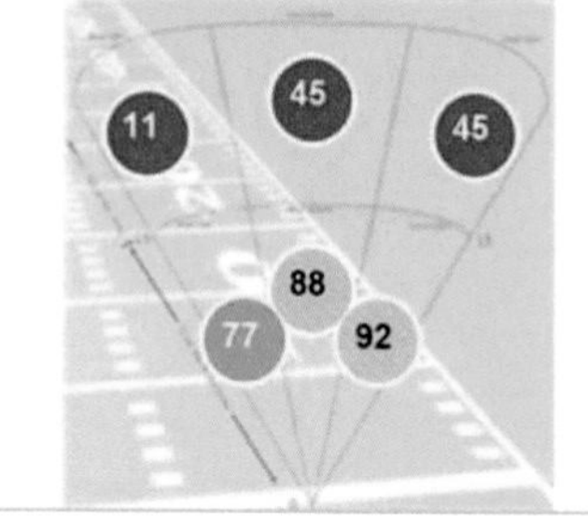

2017 Standard Passing Table

QB	Comp	Att	Comp %	Yds	YPA	TDs	INT	Sacks	Rating	Rk
Trevor Siemian	206	349	59%	2,285	6.5	12	14	33	73	42
Brock Osweiler	96	172	56%	1,088	6.3	5	5	11	73	43
NFL Avg			62%		7.0				87.5	

2017 Advanced Passing Table

QB	Success %	EDSR Passing Success %	20+ Yd Pass Gains	20+ Yd Pass %	30+ Yd Pass Gains	30+ Yd Pass %	Avg. Air Yds per Comp	Avg. YAC per Comp	20+ Air Yd Comp	20+ Air Yd %
Trevor Siemian	39%	42%	37	10.6%	5	1.4%	6.6	4.5	12	6%
Brock Osweiler	37%	38%	14	8.1%	5	2.9%	6.3	5.2	7	7%
NFL Avg	44%	48%	27.7	8.8%	10.3	3.3%	6.0	4.7	11.7	6%

Interception Rates by Down

Yards to Go	1	2	3	4	Total
1 & 2		20.0%	0.0%	0.0%	6.7%
3, 4, 5	0.0%	0.0%	3.2%	0.0%	2.2%
6 - 9	0.0%	2.4%	0.0%	50.0%	2.3%
10 - 14	2.9%	4.4%	11.1%	0.0%	4.3%
15+	0.0%	8.3%	0.0%	0.0%	4.2%
Total	2.7%	4.4%	3.6%	12.5%	3.7%

3rd Down Passing - Short of Sticks Analysis

QB	Avg. Yds to Go	Avg. YIA (of Comp)	Avg Yds Short	Short of Sticks Rate	Short Rk
Trevor Siemian	7.4	7.8	0.0	56%	8
NFL Avg	7.8	6.7	-1.1	60%	

Air Yds vs YAC

Air Yds %	YAC %	Rk
65%	35%	7
58%	42%	

2017 Receiving Recap & 2018 Outlook

The Broncos' biggest offensive question marks are tight end and third receiver. The ceiling will be higher on Thomas and Sanders with a new quarterback whose red-zone efficiency has been far superior to Siemian's. Siemian did improve his red-zone passer rating from 2016 to 2017, but only by throwing fewer interceptions. His Success Rate dropped from 34% to 26% on red-zone passes, ranking No. 35 among 38 qualified quarterbacks. Last year's most-targeted wide receiver on deep attempts was Thomas, but his production was poor. Sanders battled a high ankle sprain for most of last season and should be back healthy.

Player *Min 50 Targets*	Targets	Comp %	YPA	Rating	TOARS	Success %	Success Rk	Missed YPA Rk	YAS % Rk	TDs
Demaryius Thomas	140	59%	6.8	65	4.8	50%	58	45	78	5
Emmanuel Sanders	92	51%	6.0	73	4.2	42%	103	79	47	2
Bennie Fowler	56	52%	6.3	52	3.2	44%	93	105	106	3

Directional Passer Rating Delivered

Receiver	Short Left	Short Middle	Short Right	Deep Left	Deep Middle	Deep Right	Player Total
Demaryius Thomas	80	69	88	39	48	44	65
Emmanuel Sanders	68	83	77	102	40	48	73
Bennie Fowler	34	97	71	28	90	81	52
C.J. Anderson	94	142	56				92
Devontae Booker	82	95	102			83	97
A.J. Derby	121	102	119	51	40		105
Cody Latimer	79	113	6	158		131	100
Jamaal Charles	84	82	82				86
Virgil Green	45	74	135		94	96	88
Jordan Taylor	103	72	60			19	46
Jeff Heuerman	8	155	40		158	0	74
Team Total	72	98	79	71	80	39	75

2017 Rushing Recap & 2017 Outlook

The Broncos cut C.J. Anderson in hopes Booker and/or Freeman improve rushing productivity. Although Booker's yards-per-carry average wasn't high, his Success Rate and Early-Down Success Rates were much more respectable. Anderson's inefficiency was very underdiscussed. Of 27 running backs to log at least 275 carries the past two years, Anderson ranked fourth worst in Success Rate (41%) and 20th or worse in both average yards gained on unsuccessful plays (Missed YPA) and explosiveness rate. It's still hard to feel confident in any of the Broncos' current backs given a probable committee and how poorly last year's running game produced.

Player *Min 50 Rushes*	Rushes	YPC	Success %	Success Rk	Missed YPA Rk	YTS % Rk	YAS % Rk	Early Down Success %	Early Down Success Rk	TDs
C.J. Anderson	245	4.1	42%	51	44	47	50	41%	52	3
Devontae Booker	79	3.8	47%	28	49	5	74	45%	35	1
Jamaal Charles	69	4.4	48%	25	15	41	61	46%	30	1

Yards per Carry by Direction

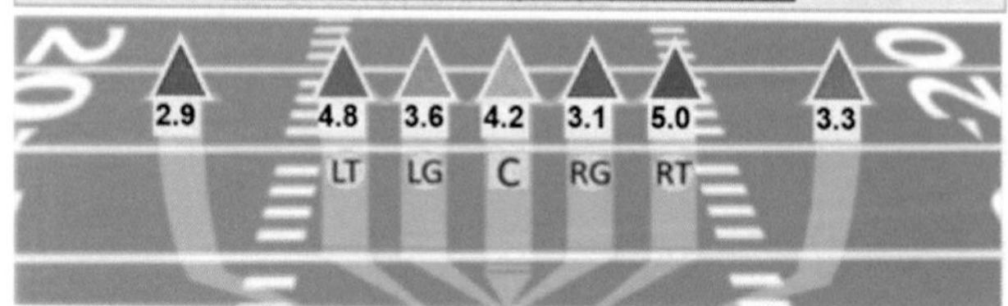

Directional Run Frequency

6%
12%
9%
40%
14%
13%
6%
LT
LG
C
RG
RT

This should create a smooth transition to Denver, where Thomas and Sanders both project for a ton of usage in both 11- and 12-personnel packages. Keenum was even better throwing out of 12 personnel in Minnesota with a 57% Success Rate and 102 passer rating. In 11, Keenum's Success Rate was 51% with a 95 rating.

So what will we get from Musgrave in 2018? In his own words, a system that is "great for our players, especially our quarterbacks." It means an offense more tailored to player strengths. For quarterbacks, it should mean more concise, one-word play calls that give Denver's offense multiple ways to go no-huddle. Musgrave's stated goal is to simplify the offense so players can "cut it loose and play."

Last year's Broncos passing game was so bad that if you turn to page four of this chapter, you'll see Denver's most successful play in non-third-and-long situations was actually a run. Siemian's passing cones on page five were abysmal. Keenum received boosts from Pat Shurmur and a talented Vikings supporting cast. His biggest downgrade will come at tight end, moving on from Rudolph to Heuerman, Butt, and Fumagalli. If Musgrave doesn't get enough out of Denver's younger players, expect this offense to funnel even more targets to proven producers Thomas and Sanders.

(cont'd - see DEN-5)

Evan Silva's Fantasy Corner

Emmanuel Sanders' 2017 season combined Siemian and Lynch's putrid quarterbacking with a high right ankle sprain Sanders suffered in Week 6. The injury noticeably bothered him the rest of the way, and Sanders aggravated it in Week 15, ending his season. He did not require post-season surgery. Now healthy, Sanders is ticketed for more slot work between perimeter wideouts Thomas and Sutton. Keenum's go-to receiver in Minnesota was Adam Thielen, who ran over half of his pass patterns in the slot and was targeted by Keenum on 25% of his slot routes, the highest rate in the league. For unclear reasons, Thomas' ADP is several rounds above Sanders'. I think Sanders can outscore Thomas this year.

Division History: Season Wins & 2018 Projection

2014 Wins	2015 Wins	2016 Wins	2017 Wins	Forecast 2018 Wins

Rank of 2018 Defensive Pass Efficiency Faced by Week

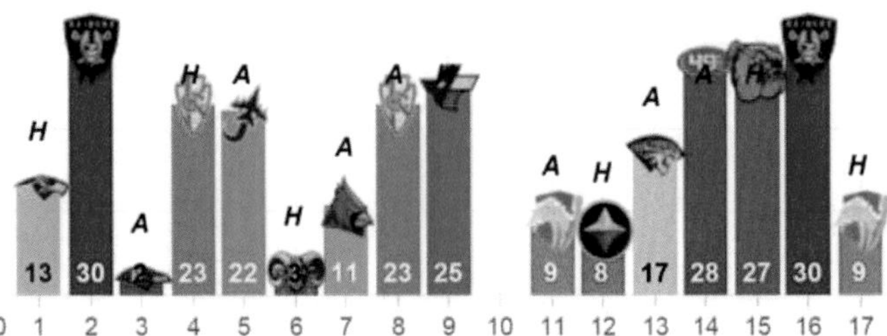

Rank of 2018 Defensive Rush Efficiency Faced by Week

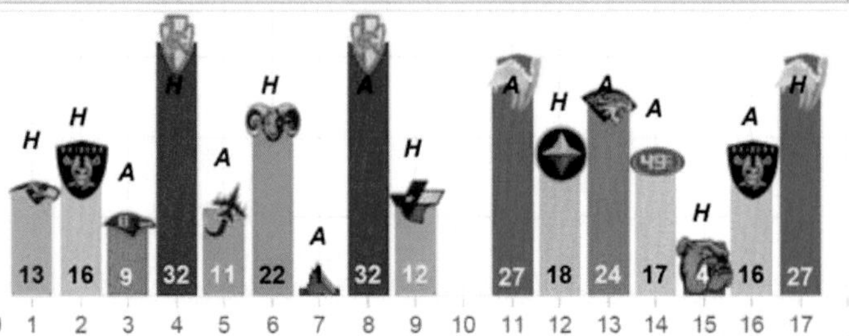

2017 Situational Usage by Player & Position

Usage Rate by Score

		Being Blown Out (14+)	Down Big (9-13)	One Score	Large Lead (9-13)	Blowout Lead (14+)	Grand Total
RUSH	C.J. Anderson	13%	19%	30%	41%	43%	26%
	Devontae Booker	8%	5%	8%	13%	7%	8%
	Jamaal Charles	8%	2%	7%	9%	15%	7%
	Isaiah McKenzie			0%			0%
	Andy Janovich	1%	1%	0%	1%		1%
	De'Angelo Henderson	1%		1%			1%
	Total	31%	27%	46%	63%	65%	42%
PASS	C.J. Anderson	5%	2%	4%	6%	2%	4%
	Demaryius Thomas	13%	28%	14%	9%	17%	15%
	Devontae Booker	7%	5%	3%	2%		4%
	Jamaal Charles	3%	5%	3%	1%		3%
	Emmanuel Sanders	9%	9%	11%	6%	7%	10%
	Bennie Fowler	8%	8%	6%		2%	6%
	A.J. Derby	4%	3%	2%	3%	4%	3%
	Cody Latimer	5%	1%	3%	2%	2%	3%
	Virgil Green	2%	5%	3%	1%		2%
	Jordan Taylor	4%	1%	2%			2%
	Jeff Heuerman	3%		1%	3%		2%
	Isaiah McKenzie	2%	2%	1%	2%		1%
	Austin Traylor	1%	2%	2%			1%
	Andy Janovich	1%		0%			1%
	De'Angelo Henderson		1%	0%			0%
	Hunter Sharp			0%			0%
	Total	69%	73%	54%	37%	35%	58%

Positional Target Distribution vs NFL Average

		NFL Wide				Team Only			
		Left	Middle	Right	Total	Left	Middle	Right	Total
Deep	WR	949	502	954	2,405	37	7	33	77
	TE	188	146	185	519	4	4	3	11
	RB	39	9	40	88			2	2
	All	1,176	657	1,179	3,012	41	11	38	90
Short	WR	2,738	1,626	2,697	7,061	124	45	93	262
	TE	840	825	1,147	2,812	23	14	23	60
	RB	1,278	799	1,258	3,335	43	24	37	104
	All	4,856	3,250	5,102	13,208	190	83	153	426
Total		6,032	3,907	6,281	16,220	231	94	191	516

Positional Success Rates vs NFL Average

		NFL Wide				Team Only			
		Left	Middle	Right	Total	Left	Middle	Right	Total
Deep	WR	36%	45%	38%	39%	46%	29%	30%	38%
	TE	39%	53%	45%	45%	0%	50%	33%	27%
	RB	36%	56%	38%	39%			50%	50%
	All	37%	47%	39%	40%	41%	36%	32%	37%
Short	WR	52%	58%	50%	52%	49%	56%	46%	49%
	TE	51%	56%	49%	52%	39%	57%	43%	45%
	RB	45%	51%	43%	46%	30%	46%	32%	35%
	All	50%	56%	48%	51%	44%	53%	42%	45%
Total		47%	54%	47%	49%	43%	51%	40%	44%

Successful Play Rate
0% — 100%

Denver Broncos - Success by Personnel Grouping & Play Type

Play Type	1-1 [3WR]	1-2 [2WR]	2-1 [2WR]	1-0 [4WR]	1-3 [1WR]	0-1 [4WR]	2-0 [3WR]	2-2 [1WR]	0-0 [5WR]	2-3 [0WR]	Grand Total
PASS	37% (474, 77%)	49% (83, 13%)	56% (25, 4%)	50% (6, 1%)	18% (11, 2%)	0% (1, 0%)	22% (9, 1%)	43% (7, 1%)	0% (1, 0%)	50% (2, 0%)	39% (619, 100%)
RUSH	49% (230, 50%)	45% (80, 18%)	38% (55, 12%)		33% (27, 6%)		0% (3, 1%)	41% (56, 12%)		0% (5, 1%)	44% (456, 100%)
TOTAL	41% (704, 65%)	47% (163, 15%)	44% (80, 7%)	50% (6, 1%)	29% (38, 4%)	0% (1, 0%)	17% (12, 1%)	41% (63, 6%)	0% (1, 0%)	14% (7, 1%)	41% (1,075, 100%)

Format Line 1: Success Rate Line 2: Total # of Plays, % of All Plays (by type)

DEN-5 The running game will also look different with C.J Anderson and Jamaal Charles moving on. Devontae Booker, third-round rookie Royce Freeman, and De'Angelo Henderson will vie for running back snaps. After drafting him, GM John Elway referred to Freeman as a "bellcow type. First and second down. A thumper." There certainly is a chance Freeman could take over this role, but he'll need to hold up in pass protection. And that's always a challenge for rookie backs.

The Broncos made major defensive and special teams upgrades in No. 5 overall pick Bradley Chubb and P Marquette King. Imagine how booming King's punts will look in Denver's thin air as opposed to sea level in Oakland. The Broncos will replace Aqib Talib internally with Bradley Roby opposite Chris Harris at cornerback.

The AFC West has no slam-dunk favorite. If the Broncos' offense can produce enough to keep Denver's defense rested, both sides of the ball will become more efficient. It's hard to imagine the Broncos being better than the Chargers or Chiefs this year, but so much hinges on quarterback play.

And Denver's quarterback play has been putrid for years. It's still probably a long shot, but if Musgrave maximizes the offensive talent and Keenum maintains his 2017 level of play, the defense is good enough to keep Denver in contention in the division.

Receiving Success by Personnel Grouping

Position	Player	1-1 [3WR]	1-2 [2WR]	2-1 [2WR]	1-0 [4WR]	1-3 [1WR]	2-0 [3WR]	2-2 [1WR]	2-3 [0WR]	Total
RB	C.J. Anderson	25% 5.5 95.4 (32)	67% 7.8 99.3 (6)			0% 0.0 39.6 (1)		0% 0.0 39.6 (1)		30% 5.6 92.1 (40)
	Devontae Booker	46% 7.5 97.8 (28)	75% 14.3 116.7 (4)	0% 3.0 79.2 (1)		0% 3.0 79.2 (1)	33% 1.0 70.1 (3)	0% 0.0 79.2 (1)		45% 7.2 96.8 (38)
TE	Virgil Green	54% 9.5 92.8 (13)	33% 2.7 109.7 (6)	100% 26.0 118.8 (2)					0% 0.0 0.0 (1)	50% 8.7 87.5 (22)
WR	Demaryius Thomas	43% 6.1 72.1 (101)	52% 6.8 38.0 (23)	73% 13.8 76.9 (11)	50% 3.0 56.3 (2)	100% 8.0 100.0 (1)		50% 4.0 60.4 (2)		47% 6.8 64.9 (140)
	Emmanuel Sanders	37% 5.4 64.9 (70)	63% 10.8 119.8 (16)	0% 0.0 39.6 (4)	100% 3.5 81.3 (2)					41% 6.0 72.5 (92)
	Bennie Fowler	41% 5.9 49.2 (51)	67% 10.3 100.7 (3)	100% 18.0 118.8 (1)	0% 0.0 39.6 (1)					43% 6.3 51.9 (56)

Format Line 1: Success Rate Line 2: YPA Line 3: Passer Rating Line 4: Total # of Plays

Successful Play Rate
0% — 100%

Rushing Success by Personnel Grouping

Position	Player	1-1 [3WR]	1-2 [2WR]	2-1 [2WR]	1-3 [1WR]	2-0 [3WR]	2-2 [1WR]	2-3 [0WR]	Total
RB	C.J. Anderson	46% 4.9 (104)	48% 3.8 (44)	34% 2.9 (38)	35% 4.3 (20)	0% -2.0 (1)	43% 4.0 (35)	0% 0.0 (3)	42% 4.1 (245)
	Devontae Booker	56% 4.4 (43)	30% 2.8 (20)	33% 3.8 (6)	100% 4.5 (2)		43% 3.3 (7)	0% 0.0 (1)	47% 3.8 (79)
	Jamaal Charles	49% 4.4 (45)	64% 3.6 (11)	50% 7.9 (8)	0% 2.5 (2)		0% 0.0 (2)	0% -2.0 (1)	48% 4.4 (69)

Format Line 1: Success Rate Line 2: YPC Line 3: Total # of Plays

Detroit Lions

2018 Coaches

Head Coach:
Matt Patricia (NE DC) (1st yr)
Offensive Coordinator:
Jim Bob Cooter (3rd yr)
Defensive Coordinator:
Paul Pasqualoni (Boston College DL) (1st yr)

2018 Forecast

Wins	Div Rank
8	#3

Past Records

2017: 9-7
2016: 9-7
2015: 7-9

EASY HARD

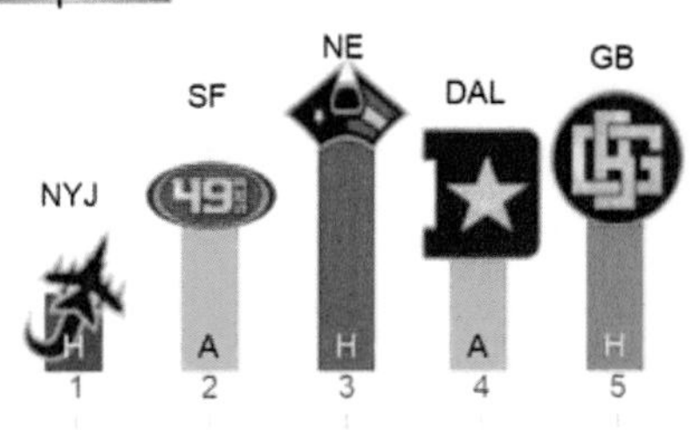

6

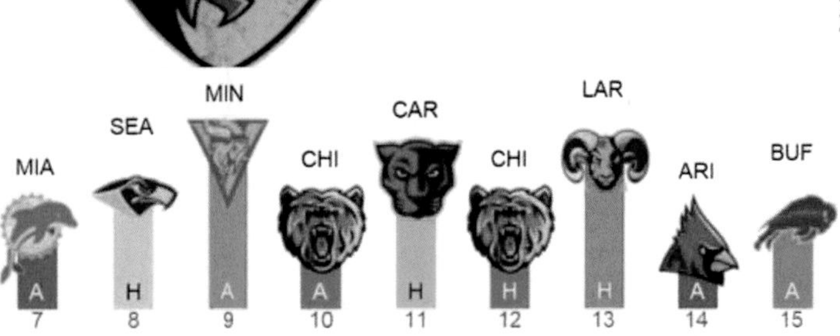

Key Players Lost

TXN	Player (POS)
Cut	Ebron, Eric TE
Declared Free Agent	Barclay, Don G
	Carey, Don S
	Coe, Rodney DT
	Copeland, Brandon LB
	Fells, Darren TE
	Freeney, Dwight DE
	Hayden, DJ CB
	Hill, Jordan DT
	James, Mike RB
	Kerin, Zac G
	Ngata, Haloti DT
	Redfern, Kasey P
	Robinson, Greg T
	Swanson, Travis C
	Whitehead, Tahir LB
	Worrilow, Paul LB
	Zenner, Zach RB

Average Line	# Games Favored	# Games Underdog
1.1	4	10

2018 Detroit Lions Overview

Treading water is tiresome, and the Lions were treading water under Jim Caldwell. The team was never terrible, making the playoffs in 2-of-4 years with three winning records. But they didn't show enough personal growth to suggest Detroit was trending toward a Super Bowl contender.

The 2016 Lions won nine games, but 8-of-9 were by one score. They ranked No. 27 in team efficiency. Last year's Lions posted a plus-ten turnover margin, and only five teams won the weekly turnover battle more than Detroit.

The Lions' team efficiency did improve from No. 32 in 2016 to No. 19 last year. The big driver was their pass-defense improvement, leaping from dead last to No. 16. Detroit faced the NFL's ninth-softest schedule of pass defenses, however. The Lions' biggest accomplishment was 32 takeaways, third most in the league.

But it was time for a change. And Detroit's hopes are now pinned on ex-Patriots DC Matt Patricia, who smartly retained OC Jim Bob Cooter. Cooter has developed a tremendous rapport with Matthew Stafford, together fielding fringe top-ten passing offenses in each of the last three years. Cooter's passing game is dynamic and exciting. And in 2017, it was particularly explosive following Detroit's Week 7 bye.

The Lions entered their open date with a 3-3 record. In those six games, 87% of Detroit's passes were thrown within 15 yards of the line of scrimmage. Over the next six weeks, however, Stafford's deep-passing rate spiked from 13% to 24%.

Cooter also changed the Lions' deep-passing tendencies. In the first six games, Stafford went deep on only 10% of first-down attempts and 11% of second-down passes. He threw deep on 20% of third-down plays. In their first post-bye game against the Steelers, Stafford threw deep on a whopping 50% of first-down attempts in the first half. Stafford's Success Rate on such throws was a magnificent 67% with a 110 passer rating. This aggressiveness gave Detroit a first-half lead over Pittsburgh, which went on to finish 13-3. But the Lions threw deep on just one second-half first down, completing it for 23 yards. Detroit blew the halftime lead and lost.

(cont'd - see DET2)

Key Free Agents/ Trades Added

Blount, LeGarrette RB
Freeny, Jonathan LB
Johnson, Wesley C
Jones, Christian LB
Kennard, Devon LB
Shead, Deshawn CB
Toilolo, Levine TE
Wiggins, Kenny G
Williams, Sylvester NT
Willson, Luke TE

Drafted Players

Rd	Pk	Player (College)
1	20	C - Frank Ragnow (Arkansas)
2	43	RB - Kerryon Johnson (Auburn)
3	82	S - Tracy Walker (Louisiana)
4	114	DE - Da'Shawn Hand (Alabama)
5	153	OT - Tyrell Crosby (Oregon)
7	237	FB - Nick Bawden (San Diego State)

Regular Season Wins: Past & Current Proj

	Wins
Forecast 2018 Wins	8
2017 Wins	9
Forecast 2017 Wins	7
2016 Wins	9
2015 Wins	7
2014 Wins	11

1 3 5 7 9 11 13 15

Lineup & Cap Hits

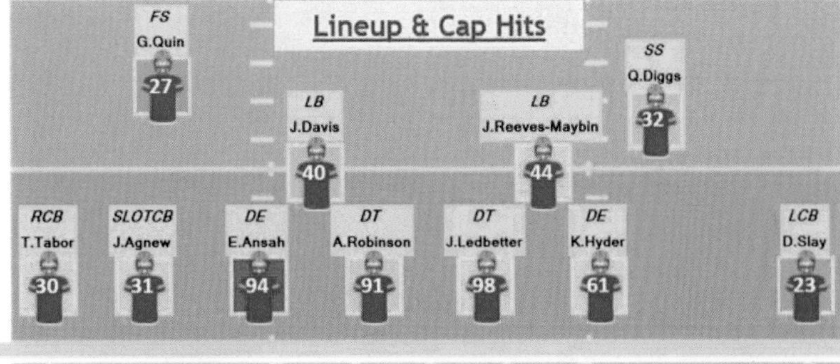

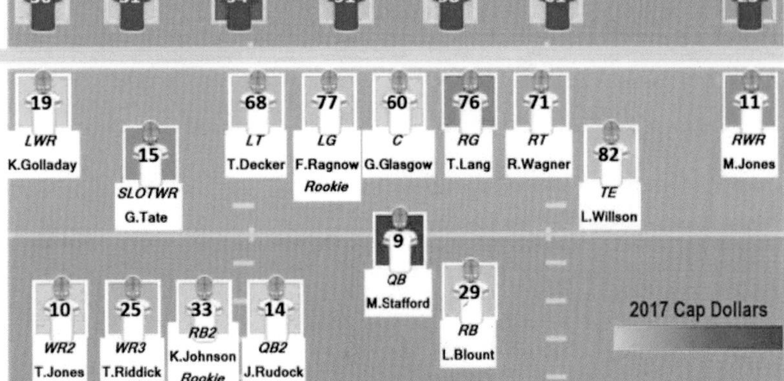

2018 Unit Spending

All DEF
All OFF

Positional Spending

	Rank	Total	2017 Rk
All OFF	11	$100.05M	15
QB	3	$27.85M	7
OL	23	$30.30M	22
RB	5	$10.22M	23
WR	11	$25.35M	12
TE	21	$6.33M	21
All DEF	20	$76.47M	13
DL	11	$31.18M	10
LB	28	$14.08M	27
CB	18	$18.73M	9
S	15	$12.49M	17

DET-2

In Weeks 8-13, the Lions went deep on 25% of first-down attempts and 25% of pass attempts overall. Stafford led the NFL with an 18.9 yards-per-attempt average on first-down deep throws. His 54% Success Rate ranked No. 2, and his 111 deep-ball passer rating ranked No. 6. His post-bye deep-ball YPA was an absurd 21.3. And Stafford did it against the NFL's sixth-toughest schedule of pass defenses.

The 2018 Lions need to throw more deep first-down passes. The easiest down to have passing success is first down, and Detroit's upgraded running game should further assist. Stafford's yards-per-attempt average and Success Rate was better on first than second or third down last year. Defenses are coached to play based on league tendencies and opponent expectations. On first and ten, most teams are not throwing 15-plus yards downfield unless they are trying to mount comebacks. So defenses play to defend the run. If you are a team like the Lions facing the NFL's sixth-toughest schedule of pass defenses, you need to attack those strong pass defenses when they least expect it. Or at least make them prepare for first-down shot plays.

The Lions' receiver corps is extremely talented. 2017 third-round pick Kenny Golladay exploded onto the scene for two touchdowns in Week 1, then injured his hamstring and missed five games in Weeks 4-9. He was eased into Week 10, split time with T.J. Jones, then regained hold of that third receiver spot. Once Golladay reentered the lineup for good, both he and Marvin Jones' efficiency spiked in 11 personnel. And the Lions used three receivers on 74% of plays, well above league average. They passed out of 11 on 84% of snaps, third most in the NFL.

But the Lions were too predictable based on personnel groupings. Outside of 11 personnel (74%) and 12 (17%), Detroit almost always ran the ball.

(cont'd - see DET-3)

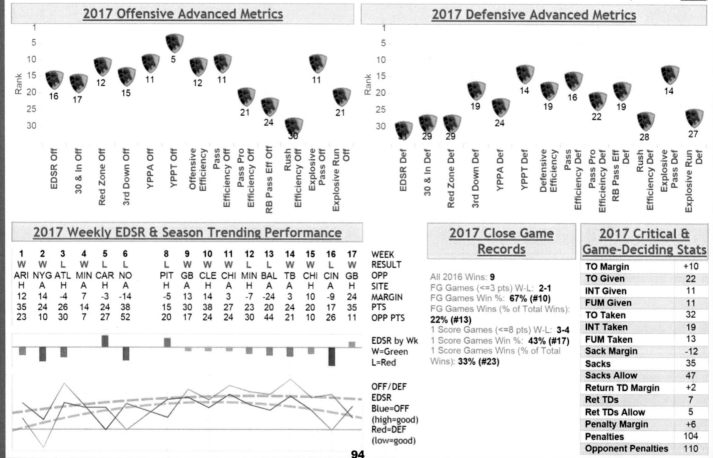

2017 Offensive Advanced Metrics

Metric	Rank
EDSR Off	16
30 & In Off	17
Red Zone Off	12
3rd Down Off	15
YPPA Off	11
YPPT Off	5
Offensive Efficiency	12
Pass Efficiency Off	11
Pass Pro Efficiency Off	21
RB Pass Eff Off	24
Rush Efficiency Off	30
Explosive Pass Off	11
Explosive Run Off	21

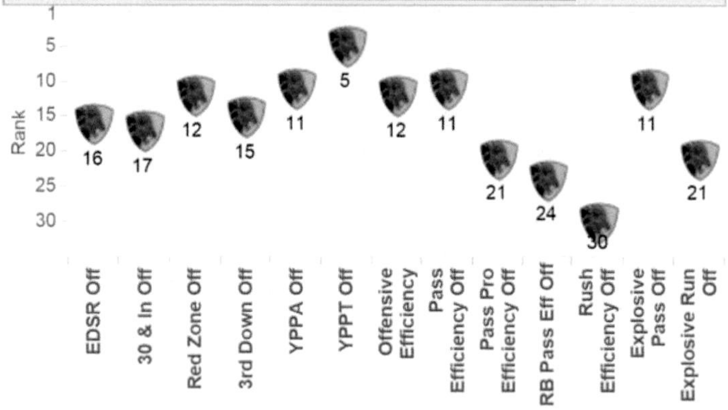

2017 Defensive Advanced Metrics

Metric	Rank
EDSR Def	31
30 & In Def	29
Red Zone Def	29
3rd Down Def	19
YPPA Def	24
YPPT Def	14
Defensive Efficiency	19
Pass Efficiency Def	16
Pass Pro Efficiency Def	22
RB Pass Eff Def	19
Rush Efficiency Def	28
Explosive Pass Def	14
Explosive Run Def	27

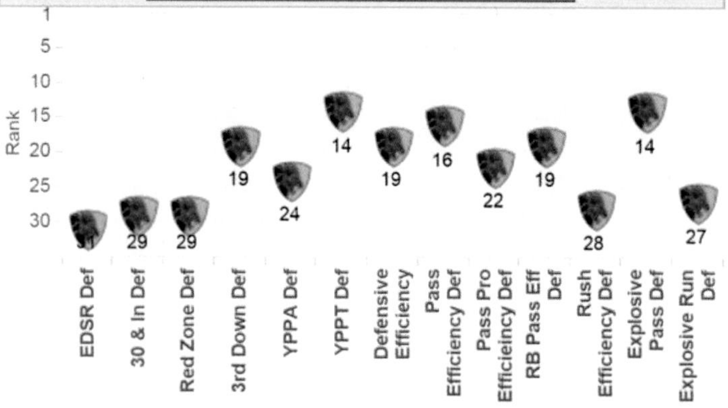

2017 Weekly EDSR & Season Trending Performance

WEEK	1	2	3	4	5	6	8	9	10	11	12	13	14	15	16	17
RESULT	W	W	L	W	L	L	L	W	W	W	L	L	W	W	L	W
OPP	ARI	NYG	ATL	MIN	CAR	NO	PIT	GB	CLE	CHI	MIN	BAL	TB	CHI	CIN	GB
SITE	H	A	H	A	H	A	H	A	H	A	H	A	A	H	A	H
MARGIN	12	14	-4	7	-3	-14	-5	13	14	3	-7	-24	3	10	-9	24
PTS	35	24	26	14	24	38	15	30	38	27	23	20	24	20	17	35
OPP PTS	23	10	30	7	27	52	20	17	24	24	30	44	21	10	26	11

EDSR by Wk
W=Green
L=Red

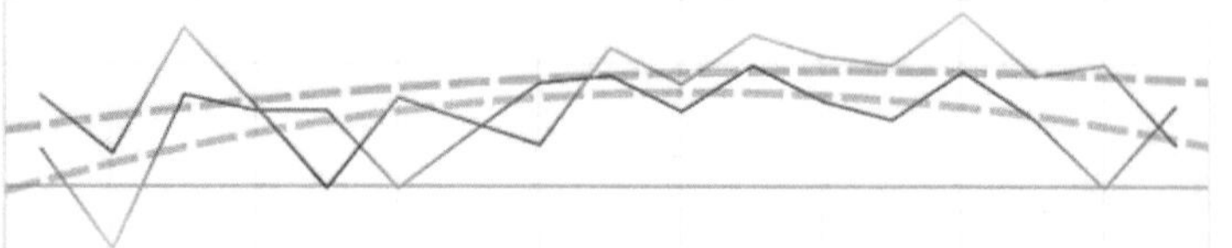

OFF/DEF
EDSR
Blue=OFF
(high=good)
Red=DEF
(low=good)

2017 Close Game Records

All 2016 Wins: **9**
FG Games (<=3 pts) W-L: **2-1**
FG Games Win %: **67% (#10)**
FG Games Wins (% of Total Wins): **22% (#13)**
1 Score Games (<=8 pts) W-L: **3-4**
1 Score Games Win %: **43% (#17)**
1 Score Games Wins (% of Total Wins): **33% (#23)**

2017 Critical & Game-Deciding Stats

TO Margin	+10
TO Given	22
INT Given	11
FUM Given	11
TO Taken	32
INT Taken	19
FUM Taken	13
Sack Margin	-12
Sacks	35
Sacks Allow	47
Return TD Margin	+2
Ret TDs	7
Ret TDs Allow	5
Penalty Margin	+6
Penalties	104
Opponent Penalties	110

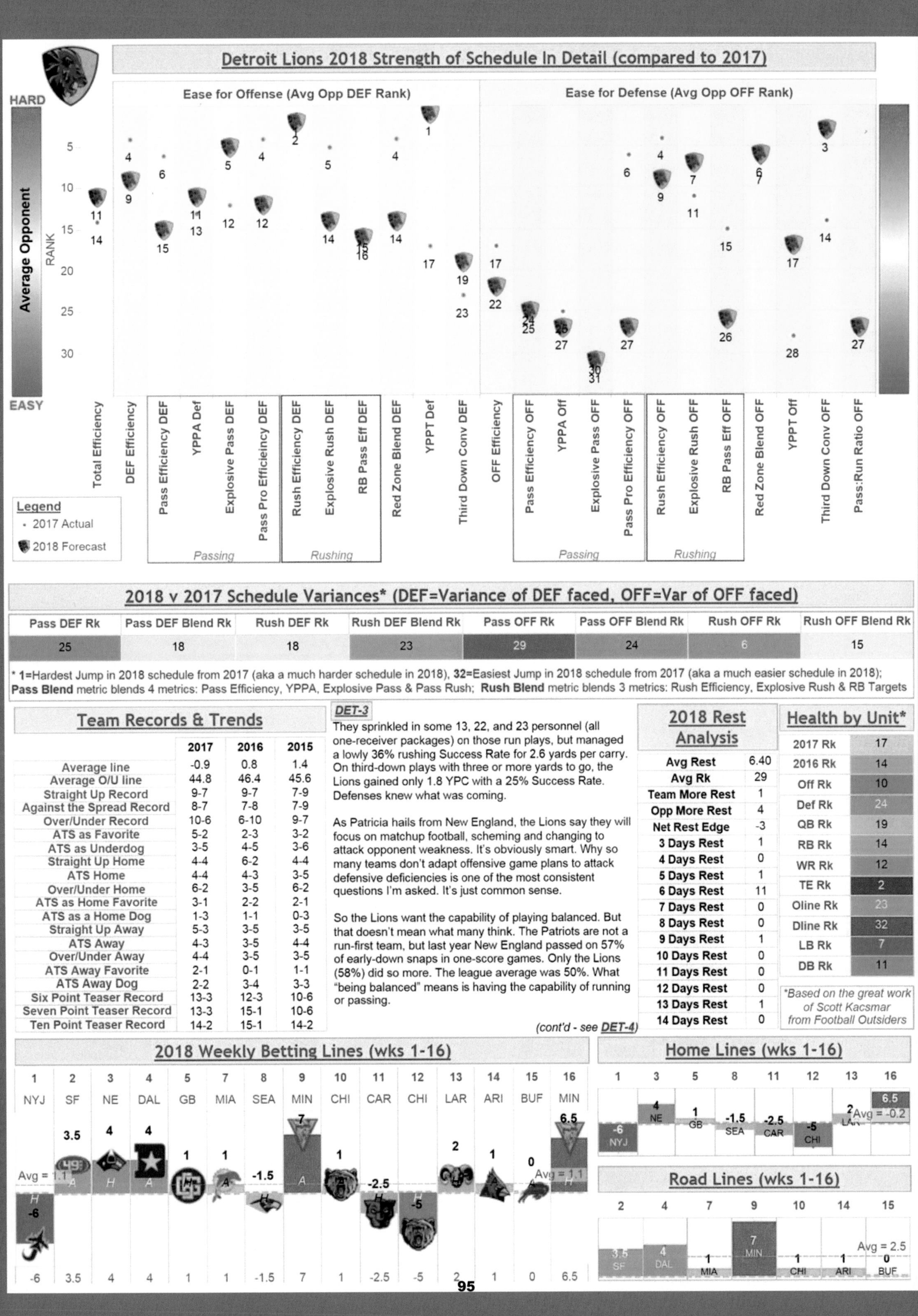

2018 v 2017 Schedule Variances* (DEF=Variance of DEF faced, OFF=Var of OFF faced)

Pass DEF Rk	Pass DEF Blend Rk	Rush DEF Rk	Rush DEF Blend Rk	Pass OFF Rk	Pass OFF Blend Rk	Rush OFF Rk	Rush OFF Blend Rk
25	18	18	23	29	24	6	15

* **1**=Hardest Jump in 2018 schedule from 2017 (aka a much harder schedule in 2018), **32**=Easiest Jump in 2018 schedule from 2017 (aka a much easier schedule in 2018); **Pass Blend** metric blends 4 metrics: Pass Efficiency, YPPA, Explosive Pass & Pass Rush; **Rush Blend** metric blends 3 metrics: Rush Efficiency, Explosive Rush & RB Targets

Team Records & Trends

	2017	2016	2015
Average line	-0.9	0.8	1.4
Average O/U line	44.8	46.4	45.6
Straight Up Record	9-7	9-7	7-9
Against the Spread Record	8-7	7-8	7-9
Over/Under Record	10-6	6-10	9-7
ATS as Favorite	5-2	2-3	3-2
ATS as Underdog	3-5	4-5	3-6
Straight Up Home	4-4	6-2	4-4
ATS Home	4-4	4-3	3-5
Over/Under Home	6-2	3-5	6-2
ATS as Home Favorite	3-1	2-2	2-1
ATS as a Home Dog	1-3	1-1	0-3
Straight Up Away	5-3	3-5	3-5
ATS Away	4-3	3-5	4-4
Over/Under Away	4-4	3-5	3-5
ATS Away Favorite	2-1	0-1	1-1
ATS Away Dog	2-2	3-4	3-3
Six Point Teaser Record	13-3	12-3	10-6
Seven Point Teaser Record	13-3	15-1	10-6
Ten Point Teaser Record	14-2	15-1	14-2

DET-3

They sprinkled in some 13, 22, and 23 personnel (all one-receiver packages) on those run plays, but managed a lowly 36% rushing Success Rate for 2.6 yards per carry. On third-down plays with three or more yards to go, the Lions gained only 1.8 YPC with a 25% Success Rate. Defenses knew what was coming.

As Patricia hails from New England, the Lions say they will focus on matchup football, scheming and changing to attack opponent weakness. It's obviously smart. Why so many teams don't adapt offensive game plans to attack defensive deficiencies is one of the most consistent questions I'm asked. It's just common sense.

So the Lions want the capability of playing balanced. But that doesn't mean what many think. The Patriots are not a run-first team, but last year New England passed on 57% of early-down snaps in one-score games. Only the Lions (58%) did so more. The league average was 50%. What "being balanced" means is having the capability of running or passing.

*(cont'd - see **DET-4**)*

2018 Rest Analysis

Avg Rest	6.40
Avg Rk	29
Team More Rest	1
Opp More Rest	4
Net Rest Edge	-3
3 Days Rest	1
4 Days Rest	0
5 Days Rest	1
6 Days Rest	11
7 Days Rest	0
8 Days Rest	0
9 Days Rest	1
10 Days Rest	0
11 Days Rest	0
12 Days Rest	0
13 Days Rest	1
14 Days Rest	0

Health by Unit*

2017 Rk	17
2016 Rk	14
Off Rk	10
Def Rk	24
QB Rk	19
RB Rk	14
WR Rk	12
TE Rk	2
Oline Rk	23
Dline Rk	32
LB Rk	7
DB Rk	11

**Based on the great work of Scott Kacsmar from Football Outsiders*

2018 Weekly Betting Lines (wks 1-16)

1	2	3	4	5	7	8	9	10	11	12	13	14	15	16
NYJ	SF	NE	DAL	GB	MIA	SEA	MIN	CHI	CAR	CHI	LAR	ARI	BUF	MIN
-6	3.5	4	4	1	1	-1.5	7	1	-2.5	-5	2	1	0	6.5

Avg = 1.1

Home Lines (wks 1-16)

1	3	5	8	11	12	13	16
NYJ	NE	GB	SEA	CAR	CHI	LAR	MIN
-6	4	1	-1.5	-2.5	-5	2	6.5

Avg = -0.2

Road Lines (wks 1-16)

2	4	7	9	10	14	15
SF	DAL	MIA	MIN	CHI	ARI	BUF
3.5	4	1	7	1	1	0

Avg = 2.5

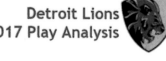

Detroit Lions 2017 Play Analysis

2017 Play Tendencies

All Pass %	63%
All Pass Rk	2
All Rush %	37%
All Rush Rk	31
1 Score Pass %	64%
1 Score Pass Rk	1
2016 1 Score Pass %	62%
2016 1 Score Pass Rk	5
2017 Pass Increase %	1%
Pass Increase Rk	11
1 Score Rush %	36%
1 Score Rush Rk	32
Up Pass %	51%
Up Pass Rk	12
Up Rush %	49%
Up Rush Rk	21
Down Pass %	70%
Down Pass Rk	5
Down Rush %	30%
Down Rush Rk	28

2017 Down & Distance Tendencies

Down	Distance	Total Plays	Pass Rate	Run Rate	Play Success %
1	Short (1-3)	4	50%	50%	75%
	Med (4-7)	9	33%	67%	67%
	Long (8-10)	300	46%	54%	45%
	XL (11+)	14	64%	36%	21%
2	Short (1-3)	31	52%	48%	77%
	Med (4-7)	68	66%	34%	56%
	Long (8-10)	87	76%	24%	38%
	XL (11+)	56	80%	20%	29%
3	Short (1-3)	41	78%	22%	51%
	Med (4-7)	41	98%	2%	51%
	Long (8-10)	33	88%	12%	36%
	XL (11+)	38	82%	18%	18%
4	Short (1-3)	2	50%	50%	0%
	Med (4-7)	1	100%	0%	0%
	XL (11+)	1	0%	100%	0%

Shotgun %:

Under Center	Shotgun
24%	76%
37%	*63%*

37% AVG 63%

Run Rate:

Under Center	Shotgun
73%	26%

68% AVG 23%

Pass Rate:

Under Center	Shotgun
27%	74%

32% AVG 77%

Short Yardage Intelligence:

2nd and Short Run

Run Freq	Run Rk	NFL Run Freq Avg	Run 1D Rate	Run NFL 1D Avg
53%	30	67%	72%	69%

2nd and Short Pass

Pass Freq	Pass Rk	NFL Pass Freq Avg	Pass 1D Rate	Pass NFL 1D Avg
47%	3	33%	50%	53%

Most Frequent Play

Down	Distance	Play Type	Player	Total Plays	Play Success %
1	Med (4-7)	PASS	Marvin Jones	2	50%
		RUSH	Ameer Abdullah	2	0%
			Theo Riddick	2	100%
	Long (8-10)	RUSH	Ameer Abdullah	91	31%
	XL (11+)	RUSH	Ameer Abdullah	4	0%
2	Short (1-3)	RUSH	Ameer Abdullah	9	78%
	Med (4-7)	RUSH	Ameer Abdullah	11	45%
	Long (8-10)	RUSH	Ameer Abdullah	15	13%
	XL (11+)	PASS	Theo Riddick	10	20%
			Eric Ebron	10	10%
3	Short (1-3)	PASS	Golden Tate	9	67%
	Med (4-7)	PASS	Eric Ebron	10	70%
	Long (8-10)	PASS	Marvin Jones	8	50%
	XL (11+)	PASS	Golden Tate	6	0%
			Marvin Jones	6	67%

Most Successful Play*

Down	Distance	Play Type	Player	Total Plays	Play Success %
1	Long (8-10)	PASS	T.J. Jones	9	89%
2	Short (1-3)	RUSH	Ameer Abdullah	9	78%
	Med (4-7)	PASS	Ameer Abdullah	5	80%
	Long (8-10)	PASS	Marvin Jones	13	62%
			Golden Tate	13	62%
	XL (11+)	PASS	Marvin Jones	7	86%
3	Short (1-3)	PASS	Golden Tate	9	67%
	Med (4-7)	PASS	Eric Ebron	10	70%
	Long (8-10)	PASS	Marvin Jones	8	50%
	XL (11+)	PASS	Marvin Jones	6	67%

**Minimum 5 plays to qualify*

2017 Snap Rates

Wk	Opp	Score	Marvin Jones	Golden Tate	Darren Fells	Eric Ebron	Kenny Golladay	Theo Riddick	T.J. Jones	Ameer Abdullah
1	ARI	W 35-23	69 (97%)	63 (89%)	32 (45%)	51 (72%)	44 (62%)	21 (30%)	19 (27%)	36 (51%)
2	NYG	W 24-10	56 (90%)	43 (69%)	41 (66%)	40 (65%)	34 (55%)	27 (44%)	15 (24%)	28 (45%)
3	ATL	L 30-26	68 (97%)	63 (90%)	29 (41%)	45 (64%)	45 (64%)	34 (49%)	15 (21%)	29 (41%)
4	MIN	W 14-7	64 (91%)	52 (74%)	51 (73%)	31 (44%)		18 (26%)	46 (66%)	33 (47%)
5	CAR	L 27-24	58 (95%)	55 (90%)	35 (57%)	34 (56%)		30 (49%)	40 (66%)	22 (36%)
6	NO	L 52-38	80 (99%)	46 (57%)	46 (57%)	41 (51%)		35 (43%)	58 (72%)	34 (42%)
8	PIT	L 20-15	68 (96%)	44 (62%)	46 (65%)	34 (48%)		30 (42%)	52 (73%)	32 (45%)
9	GB	W 30-17	65 (96%)	35 (51%)	43 (63%)	36 (53%)		25 (37%)	52 (76%)	30 (44%)
10	CLE	W 38-24	50 (96%)	35 (67%)	27 (52%)	34 (65%)	11 (21%)	17 (33%)	29 (56%)	31 (60%)
11	CHI	W 27-24	62 (98%)	48 (76%)	30 (48%)	28 (44%)	35 (56%)	30 (48%)	29 (46%)	29 (46%)
12	MIN	L 30-23	59 (100%)	51 (86%)	27 (46%)	29 (49%)	40 (68%)	26 (44%)	15 (25%)	29 (49%)
13	BAL	L 44-20	59 (94%)	51 (81%)	31 (49%)	29 (46%)	48 (76%)	40 (63%)	9 (14%)	
14	TB	W 24-21	67 (99%)	56 (82%)	30 (44%)	39 (57%)	58 (85%)	48 (71%)	10 (15%)	
15	CHI	W 20-10	62 (98%)	47 (75%)	24 (38%)	27 (43%)	50 (79%)	33 (52%)	13 (21%)	8 (13%)
16	CIN	L 26-17	64 (100%)	52 (81%)	28 (44%)	28 (44%)	61 (95%)	40 (63%)		11 (17%)
17	GB	W 35-11	55 (95%)	48 (83%)	31 (53%)	24 (41%)	51 (88%)	18 (31%)		20 (34%)
	Grand Total		1,006 (96%)	789 (76%)	551 (53%)	550 (53%)	477 (68%)	472 (45%)	402 (43%)	372 (41%)

Personnel Groupings

Personnel	Team %	NFL Avg	Succ. %
1-1 [3WR]	74%	59%	41%
1-2 [2WR]	17%	19%	48%
1-3 [1WR]	4%	5%	34%

Grouping Tendencies

Personnel	Pass Rate	Pass Succ. %	Run Succ. %
1-1 [3WR]	71%	44%	35%
1-2 [2WR]	40%	54%	43%
1-3 [1WR]	29%	30%	36%

Red Zone Targets (min 3)

Receiver	All	Inside 5	6-10	11-20
Marvin Jones	15	5	3	7
Eric Ebron	12	2	5	5
Ameer Abdullah	9	1	1	7
Theo Riddick	9	1	2	6
Darren Fells	8	3		5
Golden Tate	8	2		6
T.J. Jones	6	2		4
Kenny Golladay	5	2	1	2

Red Zone Rushes (min 3)

Rusher	All	Inside 5	6-10	11-20
Ameer Abdullah	20	5	3	12
Dwayne Washington	9	5	3	1
Theo Riddick	9	3	2	4
Tion Green	5	2	2	1
Matthew Stafford	3	1		2
Zach Zenner	2	1		1

Early Down Target Rate

RB	TE	WR
23%	20%	58%
23%	*21%*	*56%*
	NFL AVG	

Overall Target Success %

RB	TE	WR
43%	45%	53%
#16	#28	#6

Detroit Lions 2017 Passing Recap & 2018 Outlook

Stafford must improve his early-down passing. The 2017 Lions were successful on just 48% of early-down pass attempts, a 3% decrease from 2016 and right around league average. Stafford was above average or better in virtually every other category, including yards per attempt, Air Yards, percentage of 20- and 30-plus-yard completions, and Success Rate. But in part because Stafford struggled on early downs, and in part because of a terrible running game, the Lions averaged a massive 8.1 yards to go on third-down plays, the fourth-worst mark in the league. The Lions' 39% conversation rate on third-and-long plays was still impressive. But even with Brett Hundley at quarterback, the division-rival Packers averaged only 6.3 yards to go on third-down plays, a massive advantage. Unfortunately, the Lions remain deficient at tight end even after subtracting Ebron. The tight end position produces the NFL's highest receiving Success Rate, so lacking a quality weapon there can be detrimental. Yet given the efficiency of Detroit's wide receivers and underrated passing-game specialist Theo Riddick, the Lions can't afford to force targets to a sub-par tight end corps.

Matthew Stafford Rating All Downs

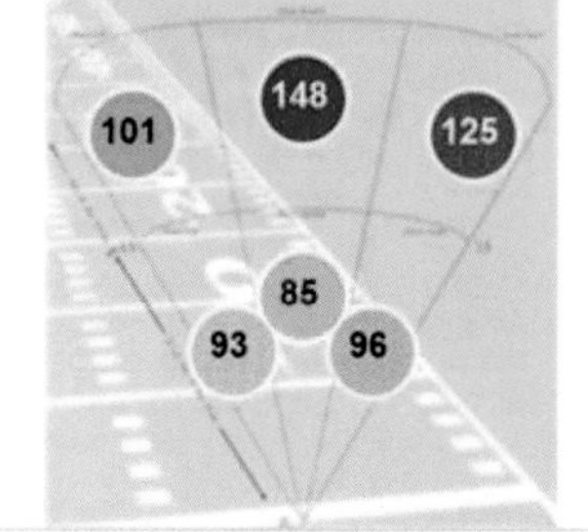

Matthew Stafford Rating Early Downs

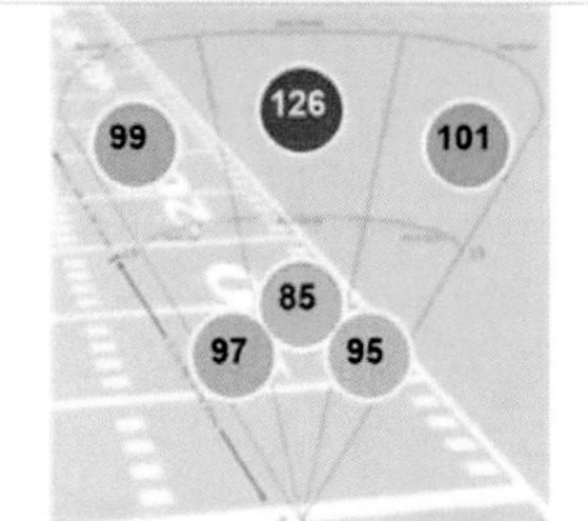

2017 Standard Passing Table

QB	Comp	Att	Comp %	Yds	YPA	TDs	INT	Sacks	Rating	Rk
Matthew Stafford	367	562	65%	4,407	7.8	28	10	46	98	8
NFL Avg			62%		7.0				87.5	

2017 Advanced Passing Table

QB	Success %	EDSR Passing Success %	20+ Yd Pass Gains	20+ Yd Pass %	30+ Yd Pass Gains	30+ Yd Pass %	Avg. Air Yds per Comp	Avg. YAC per Comp	20+ Air Yd Comp	20+ Air Yd %
Matthew Stafford	45%	48%	61	10.8%	27	4.8%	6.4	5.6	30	8%
NFL Avg	44%	48%	27.7	8.8%	10.3	3.3%	6.0	4.7	11.7	6%

Interception Rates by Down

Yards to Go	1	2	3	4	Total
1 & 2	0.0%	0.0%	0.0%	0.0%	0.0%
3, 4, 5	0.0%	3.2%	2.9%	0.0%	2.7%
6 - 9	0.0%	3.1%	0.0%	50.0%	2.6%
10 - 14	1.1%	2.2%	0.0%		1.3%
15+	0.0%	4.2%	0.0%	0.0%	1.8%
Total	1.0%	2.6%	0.6%	20.0%	1.6%

3rd Down Passing - Short of Sticks Analysis

QB	Avg. Yds to Go	Avg. YIA (of Comp)	Avg Yds Short	Short of Sticks Rate	Short Rk
Matthew Stafford	8.1	8.3	0.0	54%	9
NFL Avg	7.8	6.7	-1.1	60%	

Air Yds vs YAC

	Air Yds %	YAC %	Rk
Matthew Stafford	61%	39%	16
NFL Avg	58%	42%	

2017 Receiving Recap & 2018 Outlook

I expect the Lions' 11-personnel usage to grow because I don't envision new TE Luke Willson matching Ebron's 86 targets. (Wilson drew 89 targets in five years with Seattle.) So the Lions will need more receiving options on the field, inherently meaning more three-wide formations. And this will give Golladay more opportunities. Even as Golladay struggled with hamstring injuries as a rookie, his 9.9 yards-per-target average ranked second on the team. His 104 passer rating also ranked second. Marvin Jones is incredible, and I love the flexibility of lining up Jones and Golladay outside with Golden Tate in the slot.

Player *Min 50 Targets*	Targets	Comp %	YPA	Rating	TOARS	Success %	Success Rk	Missed YPA Rk	YAS % Rk	TDs
Golden Tate	120	77%	8.4	101	5.1	55%	29	43	75	5
Marvin Jones	107	57%	10.3	109	5.0	56%	22	52	26	9
Eric Ebron	86	62%	6.7	92	4.3	40%	111	123	61	4
Theo Riddick	71	75%	6.3	94	4.1	41%	108	117	63	2

Directional Passer Rating Delivered

Receiver	Short Left	Short Middle	Short Right	Deep Left	Deep Middle	Deep Right	Player Total
Golden Tate	91	82	108	127	119	45	101
Marvin Jones	83	90	76	62	104	140	109
Eric Ebron	90	83	77	135	96	135	92
Theo Riddick	87	103	91				94
T.J. Jones	69	68	103	110	119	106	94
Kenny Golladay	117	78	90	75	156	46	104
Ameer Abdullah	92	59	98	90			90
Darren Fells	138	61	105		129		123
Zach Zenner			40				40
Team Total	94	84	92	102	148	125	100

2017 Rushing Recap & 2017 Outlook

More short-yardage conversions would mean more first downs and more opportunities to run the ball again. It would also mean more red-zone trips, where rushing is typically very efficient. Last year's Lions were successful on 48% of red-zone runs, the NFL's 12th-best mark. At all other areas of the field, Detroit managed a league-worst 35% rushing Success Rate. Yet due to understandably limited confidence in their running-game unit, the Lions passed in the red zone at the league's second-highest rate (63%). And yet their red-zone passes produced a putrid 31% Success Rate, the NFL's sixth-worst mark. If this year's Lions can establish improved run-game efficiency, I hope they put it to use with more confidence on red-zone plays.

Player *Min 50 Rushes*	Rushes	YPC	Success %	Success Rk	Missed YPA Rk	YTS % Rk	YAS % Rk	Early Down Success %	Early Down Success Rk	TDs
Ameer Abdullah	165	3.3	35%	71	68	48	27	34%	70	4
Theo Riddick	84	3.4	39%	64	73	13	63	42%	47	3

Yards per Carry by Direction

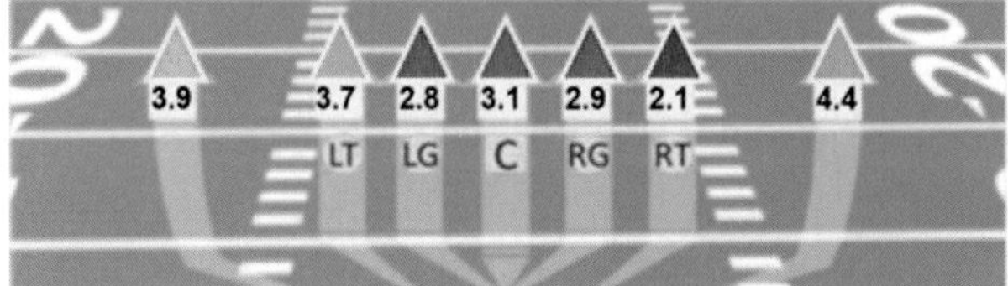

Directional Run Frequency

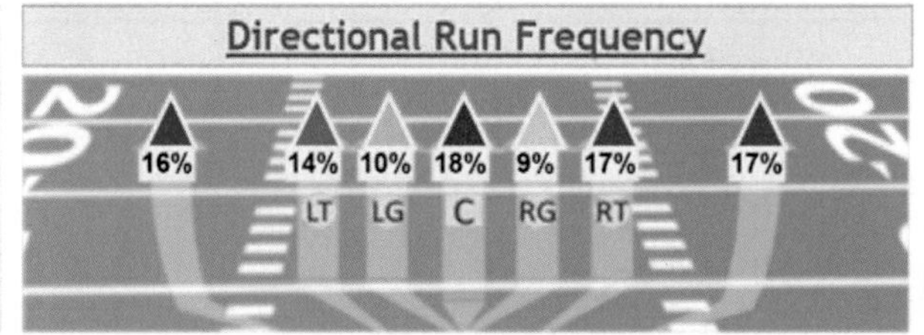

But usage is dictated by game situations and opponent strengths and weaknesses. Inevitably, the Lions will face teams with a great run defense and mediocre pass defense, and they will pass early and often. In other games, the Lions' best approach will be to run early. And if they grab a lead, to run late as well.

Since 2013, the Lions' rushing offense has been the worst in the NFL. They've never ranked better than 25th. Beginning with most recent, Detroit finished third worst, eighth worst, sixth worst, fourth worst, and sixth worst in rushing efficiency over the last half decade. In 2016-2017, the Lions finished dead last in first-down conversions on third- and fourth-and-short plays. It screwed their play balance. No NFL team passed more on those plays than Detroit. Yet rushing is far more likely to convert first downs in these situations. As a result of terrible rushing and higher-volume passing, the 2016-2017 Lions converted a league-low 49% of third- and fourth-and-short plays. It was an even-worse 44% last year. These conversions are layups for successful rushing teams. But for Detroit, they meant more punts, fewer points, and less time of possession.

So Patricia and GM Bob Quinn set out to improve their run game this offseason. They drafted first-round LG Frank Ragnow, traded up for second-round RB Kerryon Johnson, and selected fullback Nick Bawden in the seventh.

(cont'd - see DET-5)

Evan Silva's Fantasy Corner

The Lions were smitten enough with Kerryon Johnson to trade up for him at the No. 43 pick, where they selected Johnson over Derrius Guice. Johnson was a plus-sized (6'0/213) workhorse at Auburn, earning 2017 SEC Offensive Player of the Year with 1,585 yards from scrimmage and 20 TDs. Johnson only caught 32 passes in three college seasons, but he looked smooth in the passing game on tape. Johnson blazed an above-par 4.52 forty at Auburn's Pro Day and tested as a 63rd-percentile SPARQ athlete, good for top ten in this year's running back class. Johnson's main fantasy concern is the presence of Theo Riddick to siphon passing-down work and LeGarrette Blount at the goal line. Johnson could conceivably exceed 200 touches as a rookie but still provide low weekly ceilings due to shortages of catches and TDs.

Division History: Season Wins & 2018 Projection

2014 Wins | 2015 Wins | 2016 Wins | 2017 Wins | Forecast 2018 Wins

Rank of 2018 Defensive Pass Efficiency Faced by Week

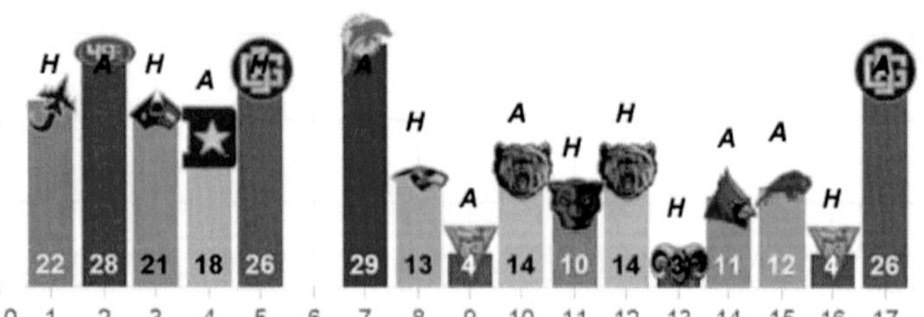

Rank of 2018 Defensive Rush Efficiency Faced by Week

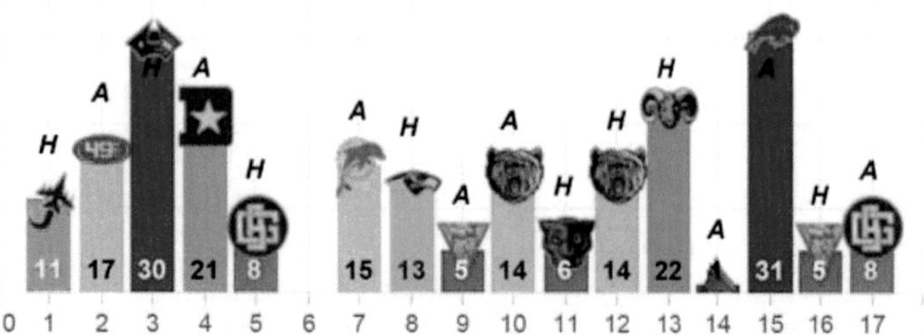

2017 Situational Usage by Player & Position

Usage Rate by Score

		Being Blown Out (14+)	Down Big (9-13)	One Score	Large Lead (9-13)	Blowout Lead (14+)	Grand Total
RUSH	Ameer Abdullah	13%	20%	19%	12%	28%	18%
	Theo Riddick	4%	11%	10%	9%	13%	9%
	Golden Tate	2%		1%			1%
	Kenny Golladay			0%			0%
	Tion Green	5%	3%	3%	9%	16%	5%
	Dwayne Washington		2%	2%	6%	8%	2%
	Zach Zenner	3%	1%	2%			2%
	Total	27%	37%	36%	36%	64%	37%
PASS	Ameer Abdullah	6%	4%	4%	6%	2%	4%
	Theo Riddick	12%	9%	8%	9%		8%
	Golden Tate	10%	16%	14%	15%	8%	13%
	Marvin Jones	17%	10%	11%	18%	11%	12%
	Eric Ebron	6%	6%	12%	12%	3%	10%
	Kenny Golladay	2%	6%	6%	3%	3%	5%
	T.J. Jones	8%	4%	6%		5%	5%
	Tion Green					3%	0%
	Darren Fells	6%	4%	2%		2%	3%
	Dwayne Washington			0%			0%
	Zach Zenner	1%					0%
	Jared Abbrederis	4%	2%				1%
	Michael Roberts	1%		1%			1%
	Total	73%	63%	64%	64%	36%	63%

Positional Target Distribution vs NFL Average

		NFL Wide				Team Only			
		Left	Middle	Right	**Total**	Left	Middle	Right	**Total**
Deep	WR	957	493	949	**2,399**	29	16	38	**83**
	TE	188	146	186	**520**	4	4	2	**10**
	RB	37	9	42	**88**	2			**2**
	All	**1,182**	**648**	**1,177**	**3,007**	**35**	**20**	**40**	**95**
Short	WR	2,777	1,610	2,695	**7,082**	85	61	95	**241**
	TE	830	818	1,122	**2,770**	33	21	48	**102**
	RB	1,281	798	1,255	**3,334**	40	25	40	**105**
	All	**4,888**	**3,226**	**5,072**	**13,186**	**158**	**107**	**183**	**448**
Total		**6,070**	**3,874**	**6,249**	**16,193**	**193**	**127**	**223**	**543**

Positional Success Rates vs NFL Average

		NFL Wide				Team Only			
		Left	Middle	Right	**Total**	Left	Middle	Right	**Total**
Deep	WR	37%	44%	37%	**38%**	45%	69%	50%	**52%**
	TE	38%	53%	45%	**45%**	50%	50%	50%	**50%**
	RB	35%	56%	38%	**39%**	50%			**50%**
	All	**37%**	**46%**	**39%**	**40%**	**46%**	**65%**	**50%**	**52%**
Short	WR	51%	57%	50%	**52%**	56%	57%	48%	**54%**
	TE	50%	57%	49%	**52%**	58%	33%	40%	**44%**
	RB	44%	51%	43%	**45%**	40%	60%	33%	**42%**
	All	**49%**	**56%**	**48%**	**50%**	**53%**	**53%**	**43%**	**49%**
Total		**47%**	**54%**	**46%**	**48%**	**51%**	**55%**	**44%**	**49%**

Successful Play Rate
0% 100%

Detroit Lions - Success by Personnel Grouping & Play Type

Play Type	1-1 [3WR]	1-2 [2WR]	2-1 [2WR]	1-0 [4WR]	1-3 [1WR]	0-1 [4WR]	2-0 [3WR]	2-2 [1WR]	0-2 [3WR]	2-3 [0WR]	Grand Total
PASS	44% (518, 84%)	54% (68, 11%)	83% (6, 1%)	25% (4, 1%)	30% (10, 2%)	25% (4, 1%)	100% (1, 0%)	100% (2, 0%)	0% (3, 0%)	100% (1, 0%)	45% (617, 100%)
RUSH	35% (211, 58%)	43% (102, 28%)	0% (1, 0%)	0% (1, 0%)	36% (25, 7%)			64% (11, 3%)		8% (12, 3%)	37% (363, 100%)
TOTAL	41% (729, 74%)	48% (170, 17%)	71% (7, 1%)	20% (5, 1%)	34% (35, 4%)	25% (4, 0%)	100% (1, 0%)	69% (13, 1%)	0% (3, 0%)	15% (13, 1%)	42% (980, 100%)

Format Line 1: Success Rate Line 2: Total # of Plays, % of All Plays (by type)

DET-5 Bawden tore his ACL at June minicamp, but this was all part of a coherent plan.

The 2017 Lions failed to convert a fourth-and-short play in the third quarter against the Steelers, losing by five points. They failed to convert a fourth-and-short against the Panthers, losing by three. All told, Detroit failed on 22 third-and-short attempts. Four of them came against the Falcons, losing by four. Three more occurred against Carolina, two against the Steelers, and one against the Vikings, losing by seven. Detroit failed on four third-and-short tries against the Bengals, losing by nine. Most of these were one-score losses where a single third- or fourth-and-short conversion could have turned that loss into a win.

I doubt the 2018 Lions will record another 32-takeaway season, and their defensive talent hasn't improved enough to survive a big dip in turnover margin.

But I'm more optimistic about this year's Lions than I was about last year's team. I'm hopeful Patricia's schemes will boost the defense, and I think Cooter has better weapons. Moving on from Eric Ebron's 40% Success Rate was addition by subtraction. The NFC North is arguably the NFL's strongest division, however, and Detroit's 2018 strength of schedule is seventh toughest in the league.

Receiving Success by Personnel Grouping

Position	Player	1-1 [3WR]	1-2 [2WR]	2-1 [2WR]	1-0 [4WR]	1-3 [1WR]	0-1 [4WR]	2-2 [1WR]	0-2 [3WR]	Total
RB	Theo Riddick	42% 6.5 102.8 (60)	50% 6.4 41.1 (8)	50% 1.5 79.2 (2)			0% -1.0 79.2 (1)			42% 6.3 93.9 (71)
TE	Eric Ebron	42% 6.5 93.9 (71)	43% 7.7 81.8 (7)	100% 21.0 118.8 (1)		25% 3.0 56.3 (4)		100% 13.0 118.8 (1)	0% 4.5 62.5 (2)	42% 6.7 91.9 (86)
WR	Golden Tate	52% 8.3 98.5 (105)	80% 10.9 112.1 (10)	100% 4.0 83.3 (1)	0% 5.0 87.5 (1)		0% 5.0 87.5 (2)	100% 6.0 91.7 (1)		54% 8.4 100.8 (120)
	Marvin Jones	53% 10.5 114.8 (88)	59% 10.6 90.6 (17)			0% 0.0 39.6 (2)				53% 10.3 108.8 (107)
	T.J. Jones	50% 7.8 91.5 (44)	67% 11.7 106.3 (3)	100% 6.0 91.7 (1)	100% 14.0 118.8 (1)					53% 8.1 93.8 (49)
	Kenny Golladay	48% 9.0 89.7 (40)	57% 15.9 158.3 (7)				100% 5.0 87.5 (1)			50% 9.9 104.3 (48)

Format Line 1: Success Rate Line 2: YPA Line 3: Passer Rating Line 4: Total # of Plays

Successful Play Rate
0% 100%

Rushing Success by Personnel Grouping

Position	Player	1-1 [3WR]	1-2 [2WR]	1-0 [4WR]	1-3 [1WR]	2-2 [1WR]	2-3 [0WR]	Total
RB	Ameer Abdullah	26% 2.9 (99)	48% 4.1 (54)	0% -2.0 (1)	44% 5.1 (9)	50% 1.5 (2)		35% 3.3 (165)
	Theo Riddick	37% 3.4 (57)	58% 4.3 (19)		13% 1.1 (8)			39% 3.4 (84)
	Tion Green	45% 2.9 (22)	27% 4.3 (15)			100% 9.0 (4)	0% 0.0 (1)	43% 3.9 (42)

Format Line 1: Success Rate Line 2: YPC Line 3: Total # of Plays

Green Bay Packers

2018 Coaches

Head Coach:
Mike McCarthy (13th yr)
Offensive Coordinator:
Joe Philbin (IND Asst HC) (1st yr)
Defensive Coordinator:
Mike Pettine (CLE HC) (1st yr)

EASY HARD

2018 Forecast

Wins	Div Rank
10	#2

Past Records

2017: 7-9
2016: 10-6
2015: 10-6

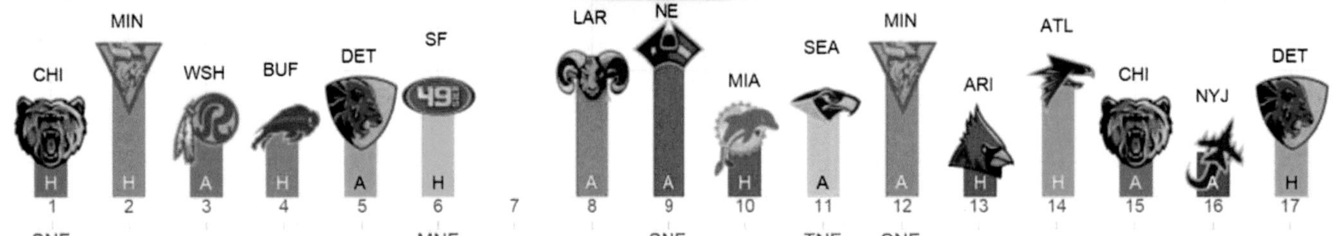

Key Players Lost

TXN	Player (POS)
Cut	Callahan, Joe QB
	Nelson, Jordy WR
	Talley, David LB
	Vogel, Justin P
Declared Free Agent	Brooks, Ahmad LB
	Burnett, Morgan S
	Dial, Quinton DT
	Evans, Jahri G
	Goode, Brett C
	House, Davon CB
	Janis, Jeff WR
	John, Ulrick T
	Pepper, Taybor C
	Rodgers, Richard TE
	Schum, Jacob P
	Thomas, Joe LB
	Waters, Herb CB

Average Line	# Games Favored	# Games Underdog
-3.4	12	3

2018 Green Bay Packers Overview

Imagine if the Packers used analytics to improve their efficiency.

It's hard to knock what has generally worked, and I won't hold Brett Hundley's stats against this offense. Even with Hundley quarterbacking, the 2017 Packers were better in many respects than most might recall. But how much does Green Bay depend on Aaron Rodgers' brilliance as opposed to designing an offense to exploit NFL edges? Rodgers has been insanely good, yet the Packers have made it to the NFC Championship game twice in seven years. And they haven't returned to the Super Bowl since winning the Lombardi Trophy in 2010.

Green Bay has made the playoffs every year since Rodgers replaced Brett Favre in 2008 save his first season and last year (injury). But three of the Packers' last four postseason trips did not come in their best years. They were fortunate the NFC North was terrible in 2013, when Green Bay eked out a Wild Card berth at 8-7-1. The 2015 Packers went 10-6 as a Wild Card team. The 2016 Packers had the third-worst record of 12 playoff teams and went on a Rodgers-fueled run that fell short due to injuries, ending in a 44-21 loss to the Falcons.

In their last two playoff trips, the Packers were a legitimate top-ten team based on total efficiency. They ranked tenth in 2015 and seventh in 2016. Yet Green Bay is stumbling to 10-6 records and failing to win the division. With the NFC North getting much more competitive, the Packers can't afford to rely solely on Rodgers if a Super Bowl return is their priority.

The obvious fix is on defense. Over the past two years in Rodgers starts, the Packers went 14-2 against teams with offenses ranked outside the top 12, but 2-8 against teams with offenses that ranked inside the top 12. In games played start to finish, Rodgers went 9-1 against defenses that ranked in the top half of the league, including 4-0 against teams with top-five defenses. Rodgers can beat any good defense in any given game.

(cont'd - see GB2)

Key Free Agents/ Trades Added

Bouagnon, Joel RB
Fuller, Kyle CB
Graham, Jimmy TE
Kizer, DeShone QB
Wilkerson, Muhammad DE
Williams, Tramon CB

Drafted Players

Rd	Pk	Player (College)
1	18	CB - Jaire Alexander (Louisvi..
2	45	CB - Josh Jackson (Iowa)
3	88	LB - Oren Burks (Vanderbilt)
4*	133	WR - J'Mon Moore (Missouri)
5	138	G - Cole Madison (Washingt..
5*	172	P - JK Scott (Alabama)
	174	WR - Marquez Valdes-Scantl..
6*	207	WR - Equanimeous St. Brow..
	232	DE - James Looney (Californi..
7	239	LS - Hunter Bradley (Mississi..
	248	OLB - Kendall Donnerson (S..

Regular Season Wins: Past & Current Proj

Lineup & Cap Hits

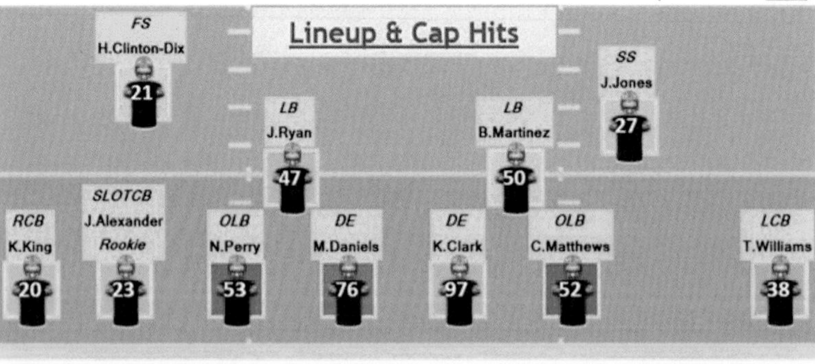

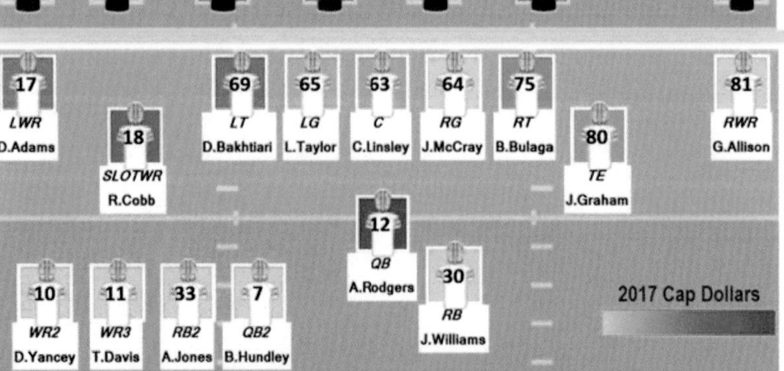

2018 Unit Spending

Positional Spending

	Rank	Total	2017 Rk
All OFF	6	$102.43M	6
QB	16	$22.49M	11
OL	13	$36.34M	18
RB	31	$3.24M	32
WR	4	$28.21M	1
TE	8	$12.16M	19
All DEF	21	$73.94M	22
DL	22	$20.25M	20
LB	5	$31.02M	6
CB	21	$12.98M	26
S	20	$9.69M	13

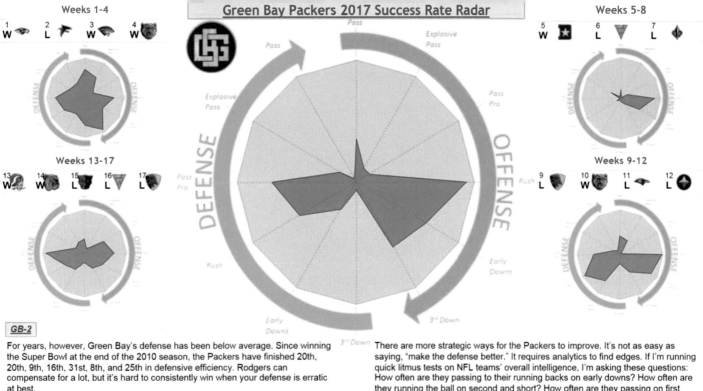

Green Bay Packers 2017 Success Rate Radar

Weeks 1-4

1 W 2 L 3 W 4 W

Weeks 5-8

5 W 6 L 7 L

Weeks 13-17

13 W 14 W 15 L 16 L 17 L

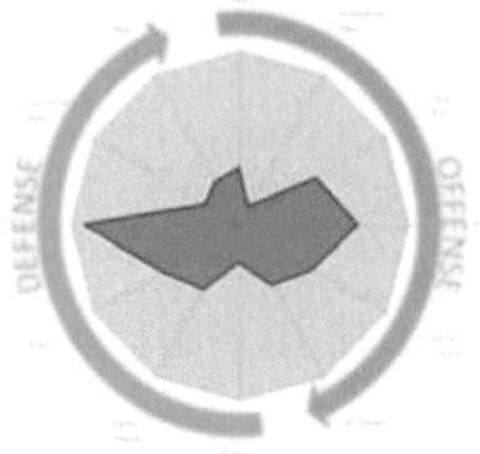

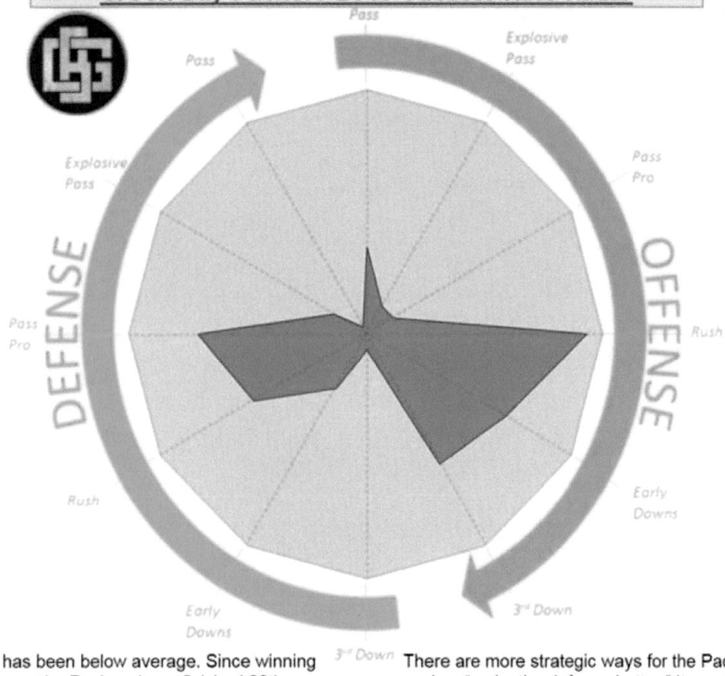

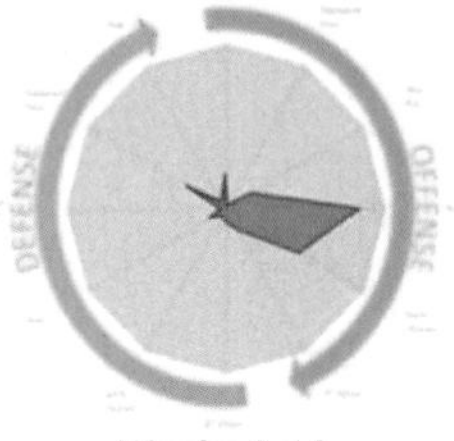

Weeks 9-12

9 L 10 W 11 L 12 L

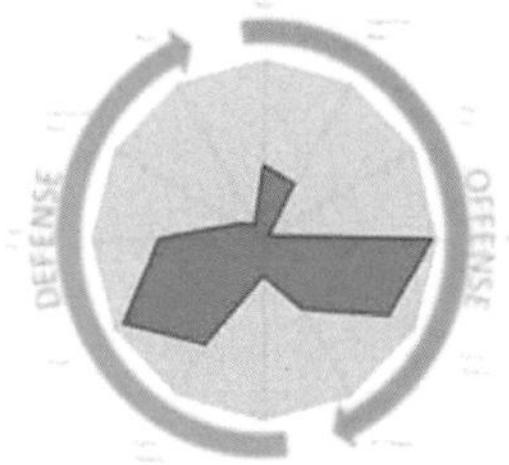

DEFENSE OFFENSE

Pass, Explosive Pass, Pass Pro, Rush, Early Downs, 3rd Down

GB-2

For years, however, Green Bay's defense has been below average. Since winning the Super Bowl at the end of the 2010 season, the Packers have finished 20th, 20th, 9th, 16th, 31st, 8th, and 25th in defensive efficiency. Rodgers can compensate for a lot, but it's hard to consistently win when your defense is erratic at best.

Internally, Green Bay hopes new DC Mike Pettine and two rare free-agent acquisitions (CB Tramon Williams and DE Muhammad Wilkerson) will turn around a defense that got stale under ex-DC Dom Capers. The Packers also used their first three draft picks on defense. Each of the last two years, Capers' unit ranked 20th or worse in defensive efficiency, Early-Down Success Rate, yards per attempt against, and third-down conversion rate allowed. My projections show the Packers' defense will face an easier schedule of opposing running games, but one of the league's toughest pass-offense slates.

There are more strategic ways for the Packers to improve. It's not as easy as saying, "make the defense better." It requires analytics to find edges. If I'm running quick litmus tests on NFL teams' overall intelligence, I'm asking these questions: How often are they passing to their running backs on early downs? How often are they running the ball on second and short? How often are they passing on first down inside the five-yard line with three wide receivers rather than base personnel? How often are they passing on first down in first halves of games?

All of these data points tell a story of a team's mindset and whether they've studied mathematical advantages that offer league-wide opportunities to increase efficiency.

The Packers are frustrating on all fronts.

(cont'd - see GB-3)

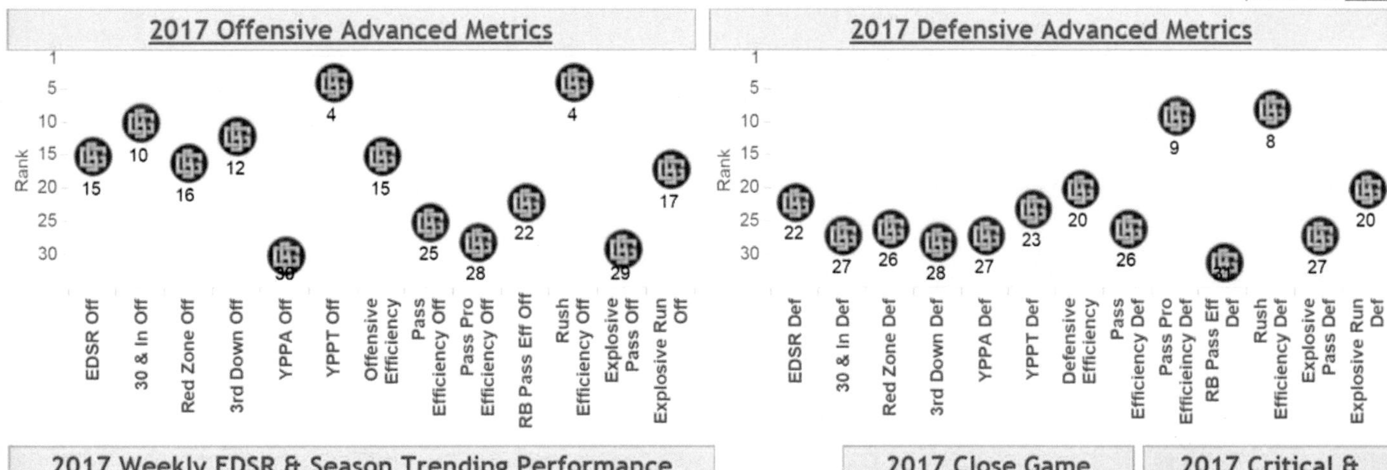

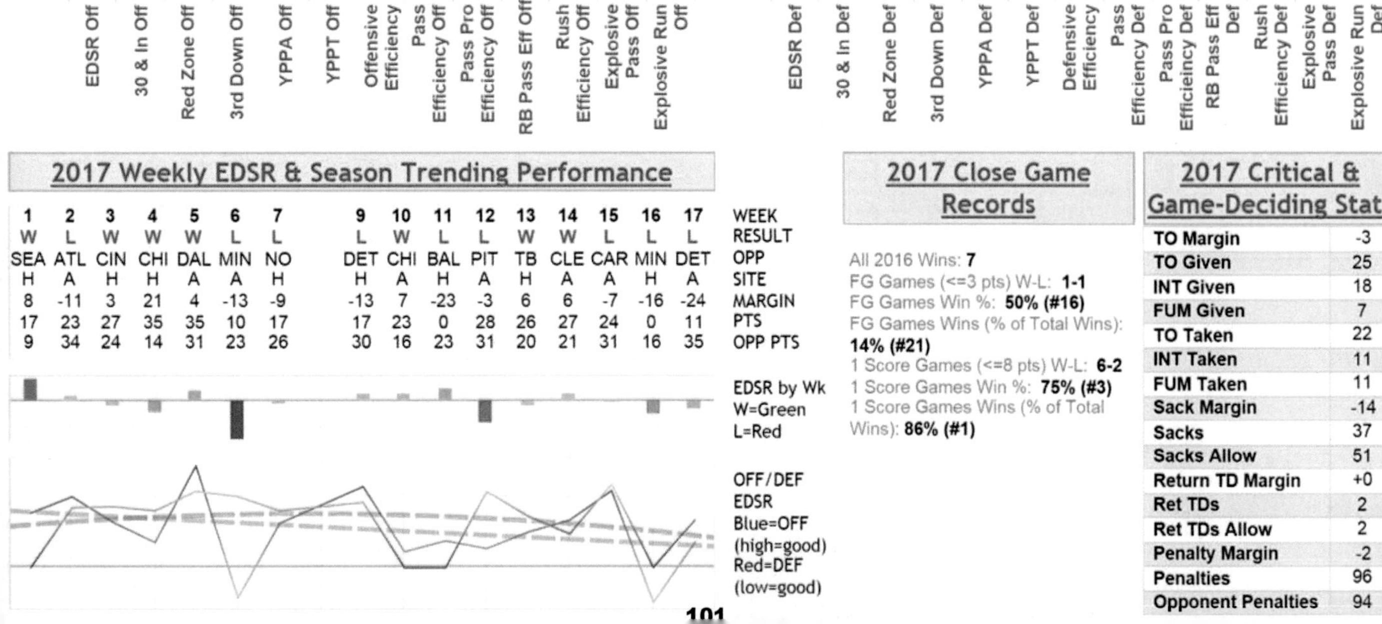

2017 Weekly EDSR & Season Trending Performance

WEEK	1	2	3	4	5	6	7	9	10	11	12	13	14	15	16	17
RESULT	W	L	W	W	W	L	L	L	W	L	L	W	W	L	L	L
OPP	SEA	ATL	CIN	CHI	DAL	MIN	NO	DET	CHI	BAL	PIT	TB	CLE	CAR	MIN	DET
SITE	H	A	H	H	A	A	H	H	A	H	A	H	A	A	H	A
MARGIN	8	-11	3	21	4	-13	-9	-13	7	-23	-3	6	6	-7	-16	-24
PTS	17	23	27	35	35	10	17	17	23	0	28	26	27	24	0	11
OPP PTS	9	34	24	14	31	23	26	30	16	23	31	20	21	31	16	35

2017 Close Game Records

All 2016 Wins: **7**
FG Games (<=3 pts) W-L: **1-1**
FG Games Win %: **50% (#16)**
FG Games Wins (% of Total Wins): **14% (#21)**
1 Score Games (<=8 pts) W-L: **6-2**
1 Score Games Win %: **75% (#3)**
1 Score Games Wins (% of Total Wins): **86% (#1)**

2017 Critical & Game-Deciding Stats

TO Margin	-3
TO Given	25
INT Given	18
FUM Given	7
TO Taken	22
INT Taken	11
FUM Taken	11
Sack Margin	-14
Sacks	37
Sacks Allow	51
Return TD Margin	+0
Ret TDs	2
Ret TDs Allow	2
Penalty Margin	-2
Penalties	96
Opponent Penalties	94

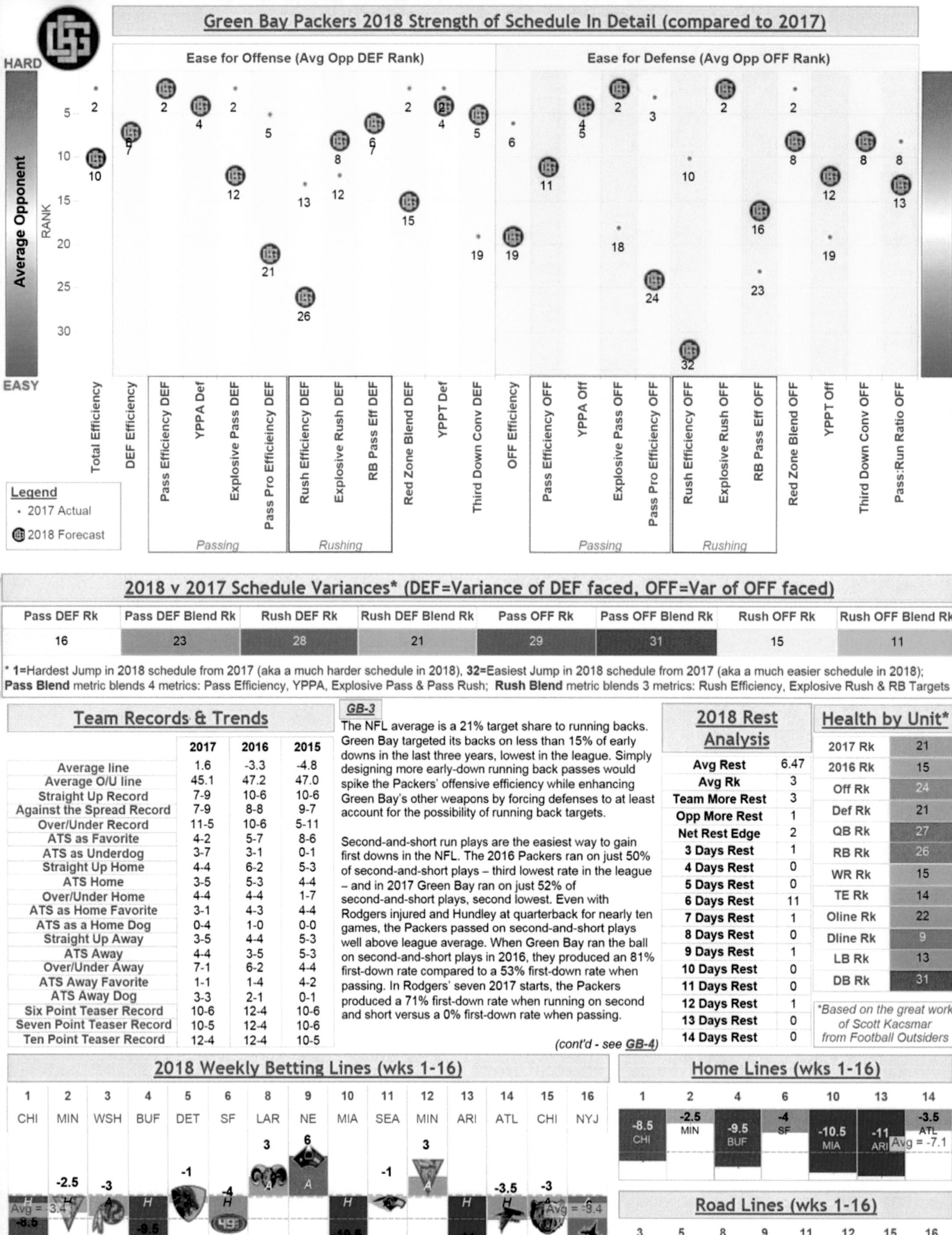

2018 v 2017 Schedule Variances* (DEF=Variance of DEF faced, OFF=Var of OFF faced)

Pass DEF Rk	Pass DEF Blend Rk	Rush DEF Rk	Rush DEF Blend Rk	Pass OFF Rk	Pass OFF Blend Rk	Rush OFF Rk	Rush OFF Blend Rk
16	23	28	21	29	31	15	11

* **1**=Hardest Jump in 2018 schedule from 2017 (aka a much harder schedule in 2018), **32**=Easiest Jump in 2018 schedule from 2017 (aka a much easier schedule in 2018); **Pass Blend** metric blends 4 metrics: Pass Efficiency, YPPA, Explosive Pass & Pass Rush; **Rush Blend** metric blends 3 metrics: Rush Efficiency, Explosive Rush & RB Targets

Team Records & Trends

	2017	2016	2015
Average line	1.6	-3.3	-4.8
Average O/U line	45.1	47.2	47.0
Straight Up Record	7-9	10-6	10-6
Against the Spread Record	7-9	8-8	9-7
Over/Under Record	11-5	10-6	5-11
ATS as Favorite	4-2	5-7	8-6
ATS as Underdog	3-7	3-1	0-1
Straight Up Home	4-4	6-2	5-3
ATS Home	3-5	5-3	4-4
Over/Under Home	4-4	4-4	1-7
ATS as Home Favorite	3-1	4-3	4-4
ATS as a Home Dog	0-4	1-0	0-0
Straight Up Away	3-5	4-4	5-3
ATS Away	4-4	3-5	5-3
Over/Under Away	7-1	6-2	4-4
ATS Away Favorite	1-1	1-4	4-2
ATS Away Dog	3-3	2-1	0-1
Six Point Teaser Record	10-6	12-4	10-6
Seven Point Teaser Record	10-5	12-4	10-6
Ten Point Teaser Record	12-4	12-4	10-5

GB-3

The NFL average is a 21% target share to running backs. Green Bay targeted its backs on less than 15% of early downs in the last three years, lowest in the league. Simply designing more early-down running back passes would spike the Packers' offensive efficiency while enhancing Green Bay's other weapons by forcing defenses to at least account for the possibility of running back targets.

Second-and-short run plays are the easiest way to gain first downs in the NFL. The 2016 Packers ran on just 50% of second-and-short plays – third lowest rate in the league – and in 2017 Green Bay ran on just 52% of second-and-short plays, second lowest. Even with Rodgers injured and Hundley at quarterback for nearly ten games, the Packers passed on second-and-short plays well above league average. When Green Bay ran the ball on second-and-short plays in 2016, they produced an 81% first-down rate compared to a 53% first-down rate when passing. In Rodgers' seven 2017 starts, the Packers produced a 71% first-down rate when running on second and short versus a 0% first-down rate when passing.

(cont'd - see GB-4)

2018 Rest Analysis

Avg Rest	6.47
Avg Rk	3
Team More Rest	3
Opp More Rest	1
Net Rest Edge	2
3 Days Rest	1
4 Days Rest	0
5 Days Rest	0
6 Days Rest	11
7 Days Rest	1
8 Days Rest	0
9 Days Rest	1
10 Days Rest	0
11 Days Rest	0
12 Days Rest	1
13 Days Rest	0
14 Days Rest	0

Health by Unit*

2017 Rk	21
2016 Rk	15
Off Rk	24
Def Rk	21
QB Rk	27
RB Rk	26
WR Rk	15
TE Rk	14
Oline Rk	22
Dline Rk	9
LB Rk	13
DB Rk	31

*Based on the great work of Scott Kacsmar from Football Outsiders

2018 Weekly Betting Lines (wks 1-16)

1	2	3	4	5	6	8	9	10	11	12	13	14	15	16
CHI	MIN	WSH	BUF	DET	SF	LAR	NE	MIA	SEA	MIN	ARI	ATL	CHI	NYJ
-8.5	-2.5	-3	-9.5	-1	-4	3	6	-10.5	-1	3	-11	-3.5	-3	-6

Avg = -3.4

Home Lines (wks 1-16)

1	2	4	6	10	13	14
CHI	MIN	BUF	SF	MIA	ARI	ATL
-8.5	-2.5	-9.5	-4	-10.5	-11	-3.5

Avg = -7.1

Road Lines (wks 1-16)

3	5	8	9	11	12	15	16
WSH	DET	LAR	NE	SEA	MIN	CHI	NYJ
-3	-1	3	6	-1	3	-3	-6

Avg = -0.3

Green Bay Packers 2017 Play Analysis

2017 Play Tendencies

All Pass %	61%
All Pass Rk	7
All Rush %	39%
All Rush Rk	26
1 Score Pass %	55%
1 Score Pass Rk	22
2016 1 Score Pass %	64%
2016 1 Score Pass Rk	1
2017 Pass Increase %	-9%
Pass Increase Rk	30
1 Score Rush %	45%
1 Score Rush Rk	11
Up Pass %	53%
Up Pass Rk	5
Up Rush %	47%
Up Rush Rk	28
Down Pass %	66%
Down Pass Rk	16
Down Rush %	34%
Down Rush Rk	17

2017 Down & Distance Tendencies

Down	Distance	Total Plays	Pass Rate	Run Rate	Play Success %
1	Short (1-3)	6	17%	83%	50%
	Med (4-7)	7	43%	57%	71%
	Long (8-10)	282	49%	51%	49%
	XL (11+)	10	70%	30%	30%
2	Short (1-3)	42	43%	57%	52%
	Med (4-7)	72	51%	49%	50%
	Long (8-10)	94	57%	43%	33%
	XL (11+)	29	83%	17%	17%
3	Short (1-3)	50	56%	44%	64%
	Med (4-7)	58	86%	14%	38%
	Long (8-10)	22	95%	5%	23%
	XL (11+)	23	87%	13%	13%
4	Short (1-3)	10	30%	70%	70%
	Med (4-7)	3	100%	0%	33%

Shotgun %:

Under Center	Shotgun
37%	63%
37% AVG	*63%*

Run Rate:

Under Center	Shotgun
63%	22%
68% AVG	*23%*

Pass Rate:

Under Center	Shotgun
37%	78%
32% AVG	*77%*

Short Yardage Intelligence:

2nd and Short Run

Run Freq	Run Rk	NFL Run Freq Avg	Run 1D Rate	Run NFL 1D Avg
52%	31	67%	50%	69%

2nd and Short Pass

Pass Freq	Pass Rk	NFL Pass Freq Avg	Pass 1D Rate	Pass NFL 1D Avg
48%	2	33%	55%	53%

Most Frequent Play

Down	Distance	Play Type	Player	Total Plays	Play Success %
1	Short (1-3)	RUSH	Aaron Jones	2	50%
			Ty Montgomery	2	50%
	Long (8-10)	RUSH	Jamaal Williams	59	39%
	XL (11+)	PASS	Aaron Jones	2	0%
2	Short (1-3)	RUSH	Jamaal Williams	10	70%
	Med (4-7)	RUSH	Jamaal Williams	16	56%
	Long (8-10)	RUSH	Jamaal Williams	13	38%
	XL (11+)	PASS	Randall Cobb	8	25%
3	Short (1-3)	RUSH	Jamaal Williams	9	56%
	Med (4-7)	PASS	Randall Cobb	10	50%
	Long (8-10)	PASS	Randall Cobb	4	25%
	XL (11+)	PASS	Davante Adams	5	20%

Most Successful Play*

Down	Distance	Play Type	Player	Total Plays	Play Success %
1	Long (8-10)	PASS	Randall Cobb	16	75%
2	Short (1-3)	RUSH	Jamaal Williams	10	70%
	Med (4-7)	RUSH	Aaron Jones	6	83%
	Long (8-10)	RUSH	Brett Hundley	5	60%
	XL (11+)	PASS	Randall Cobb	8	25%
3	Short (1-3)	PASS	Jordy Nelson	5	100%
	Med (4-7)	PASS	Davante Adams	5	60%
	XL (11+)	PASS	Davante Adams	5	20%

**Minimum 5 plays to qualify*

2017 Snap Rates

Wk	Opp	Score	Jordy Nelson	Davante Adams	Randall Cobb	Lance Kendricks	Jamaal Williams	Richard Rodgers	Ty Montgomery
1	SEA	W 17-9	76 (93%)	67 (82%)	63 (77%)	21 (26%)	8 (10%)	5 (6%)	74 (90%)
2	ATL	L 34-23	7 (9%)	71 (93%)	54 (71%)	13 (17%)	11 (14%)	10 (13%)	65 (86%)
3	CIN	W 27-24	67 (96%)	67 (96%)		19 (27%)	5 (7%)	10 (14%)	65 (93%)
4	CHI	W 35-14	51 (93%)	40 (73%)	34 (62%)	17 (31%)	12 (22%)	10 (18%)	5 (9%)
5	DAL	W 35-31	49 (82%)	56 (93%)	47 (78%)	18 (30%)	2 (3%)	6 (10%)	
6	MIN	L 23-10	61 (92%)	65 (98%)	53 (80%)	6 (9%)		11 (17%)	20 (30%)
7	NO	L 26-17	51 (93%)	48 (87%)	37 (67%)	14 (25%)		6 (11%)	7 (13%)
9	DET	L 30-17	49 (83%)	56 (95%)	49 (83%)	29 (49%)	9 (15%)	33 (56%)	24 (41%)
10	CHI	W 23-16	64 (97%)	54 (82%)	37 (56%)	46 (70%)	35 (53%)	32 (48%)	14 (21%)
11	BAL	L 23-0	62 (93%)	64 (96%)	48 (72%)	38 (57%)	59 (88%)	37 (55%)	
12	PIT	L 31-28	52 (95%)	48 (87%)	38 (69%)	29 (53%)	45 (82%)	37 (67%)	
13	TB	W 26-20	50 (91%)	49 (89%)	41 (75%)	30 (55%)	48 (87%)	29 (53%)	
14	CLE	W 27-21	70 (92%)	64 (84%)	57 (75%)	49 (64%)	50 (66%)	40 (53%)	
15	CAR	L 31-24	70 (100%)	27 (39%)	68 (97%)	22 (31%)	43 (61%)	38 (54%)	
16	MIN	L 16-0	27 (40%)		61 (91%)	58 (87%)	62 (93%)	2 (3%)	
17	DET	L 35-11			58 (85%)	58 (85%)	56 (82%)		
Grand Total			806 (83%)	776 (85%)	745 (76%)	467 (45%)	445 (49%)	306 (32%)	274 (48%)

Personnel Groupings

Personnel	Team %	NFL Avg	Succ. %
1-1 [3WR]	60%	59%	47%
1-2 [2WR]	11%	19%	52%
2-1 [2WR]	7%	7%	41%
0-1 [4WR]	7%	1%	47%
1-0 [4WR]	4%	2%	44%
2-2 [1WR]	4%	4%	38%
2-0 [3WR]	4%	1%	36%

Grouping Tendencies

Personnel	Pass Rate	Pass Succ. %	Run Succ. %
1-1 [3WR]	66%	42%	57%
1-2 [2WR]	44%	58%	47%
2-1 [2WR]	51%	31%	51%
0-1 [4WR]	92%	46%	60%
1-0 [4WR]	79%	41%	56%
2-2 [1WR]	13%	60%	35%
2-0 [3WR]	39%	43%	32%

Red Zone Targets (min 3)

Receiver	All	Inside 5	6-10	11-20
Davante Adams	23	3	3	17
Jordy Nelson	12	5	3	4
Randall Cobb	6	2	1	3
Geronimo Allison	5	1	1	3
Lance Kendricks	5	1	2	2
Ty Montgomery	4	1	1	2
Martellus Bennett	3	1	2	
Aaron Ripkowski	1			1

Red Zone Rushes (min 3)

Rusher	All	Inside 5	6-10	11-20
Jamaal Williams	21	8	2	11
Aaron Jones	11	2	2	7
Ty Montgomery	10	5	1	4
Brett Hundley	8	1	2	5
Aaron Ripkowski	2			2
Aaron Rodgers	2		1	1
Randall Cobb	2			2

Early Down Target Rate

	RB	TE	WR
	21%	17%	62%
NFL AVG	*23%*	*21%*	*56%*

Overall Target Success %

RB	TE	WR
40% #26	44% #29	50% #9

Green Bay Packers 2017 Passing Recap & 2018 Outlook

No quarterback is worth more to sportsbook linemakers than Aaron Rodgers. Last year, Rodgers played six full games, and Brett Hundley either started or finished ten. Yet Rodgers threw seven more touchdown passes with six fewer interceptions and only 161 fewer yards. The biggest changes are at tight end, where Green Bay signed Jimmy Graham and Marcedes Lewis. Last year, Rodgers targeted tight ends on 23% of attempts, but 81% of those targets came in three-receiver 11 personnel. In 2016, Rodgers targeted tight ends in three-receiver sets on 88% of throws. Those numbers are well above the 66% NFL average.

Rodgers attempted 91% of his throws in 11 personnel the past two years, so the chances we see new formations to specifically feed Green Bay's new tight ends seem small. Expect the same formations with new pieces. Graham was at his Seahawks best in two-tight end 12 personnel (57% Success Rate) but still had great numbers in 11. And Graham dominated in three-receiver sets in scoring position, leading the league in red-zone targets with a 49% Success Rate and 110 passer rating when targeted.

Aaron Rodgers Rating All Downs

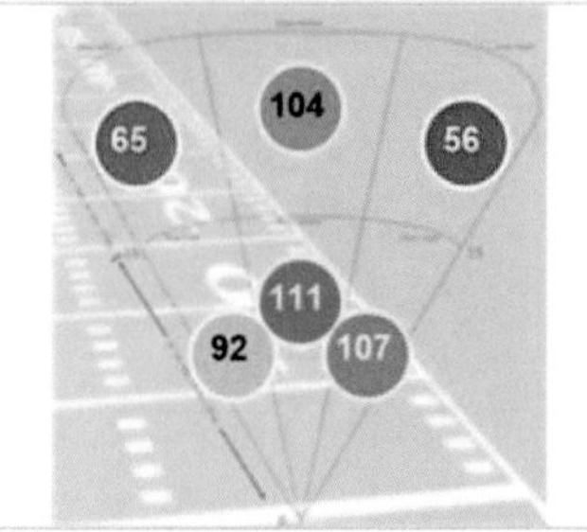

Aaron Rodgers Rating Early Downs

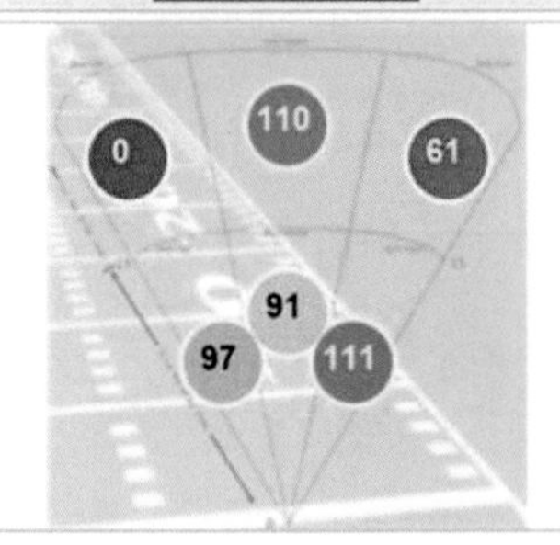

2017 Standard Passing Table

QB	Comp	Att	Comp %	Yds	YPA	TDs	INT	Sacks	Rating	Rk
Brett Hundley	192	316	61%	1,836	5.8	9	12	29	71	50
Aaron Rodgers	154	238	65%	1,675	7.0	16	6	22	97	11
NFL Avg			62%		7.0				87.5	

2017 Advanced Passing Table

QB	Success %	EDSR Passing Success %	20+ Yd Pass Gains	20+ Yd Pass %	30+ Yd Pass Gains	30+ Yd Pass %	Avg. Air Yds per Comp	Avg. YAC per Comp	20+ Air Yd Comp	20+ Air Yd %
Aaron Rodgers	47%	49%	21	8.8%	9	3.8%	5.3	5.5	11	7%
Brett Hundley	40%	46%	17	5.4%	8	2.5%	3.8	5.5	8	4%
NFL Avg	44%	48%	27.7	8.8%	10.3	3.3%	6.0	4.7	11.7	6%

Interception Rates by Down

Yards to Go	1	2	3	4	Total
1 & 2	0.0%	0.0%	0.0%	0.0%	0.0%
3, 4, 5	0.0%	4.8%	0.0%	0.0%	2.4%
6 - 9	0.0%	3.4%	5.3%	0.0%	4.0%
10 - 14	1.1%	4.0%	7.7%	0.0%	2.2%
15+	0.0%	0.0%	0.0%		0.0%
Total	1.0%	3.4%	3.3%	0.0%	2.3%

3rd Down Passing - Short of Sticks Analysis

QB	Avg. Yds to Go	Avg. YIA (of Comp)	Avg Yds Short	Short of Sticks Rate	Short Rk
Aaron Rodgers	6.7	9.6	0.0	31%	2
NFL Avg	7.8	6.7	-1.1	60%	

Air Yds vs YAC

Air Yds %	YAC %	Rk
69%	31%	3
58%	42%	

2017 Receiving Recap & 2018 Outlook

Rodgers' rapport with Jordy Nelson isn't easily replaced. And while it's easy to say Nelson was slowing down, last year he produced a 64% Success Rate and 8.2 yards per target from Rodgers, good for Nos. 2 and 22 in the NFL. In 2016, Nelson logged a 59% Success Rate (No. 4) and 8.2 yards per target (No. 11). The Packers once again face one of the five toughest pass-defense schedules in the league, including third toughest in Weeks 1-5. Part of Rodgers' brilliance is throwing beyond the sticks on third down. He ranked No. 2 each of the last two years in depth of completion beyond the sticks, providing a better chance to make first downs.

Player *Min 50 Targets*	Targets	Comp %	YPA	Rating	TOARS	Success %	Success Rk	Missed YPA Rk	YAS % Rk	TDs
Davante Adams	118	63%	7.5	110	5.2	54%	35	36	54	10
Randall Cobb	92	72%	7.1	97	4.6	48%	72	80	65	4
Jordy Nelson	88	60%	5.5	69	4.2	54%	34	57	31	6

Directional Passer Rating Delivered

Receiver	Short Left	Short Middle	Short Right	Deep Left	Deep Middle	Deep Right	Player Total
Davante Adams	123	110	96	45		142	110
Randall Cobb	72	152	93	135	0	43	97
Jordy Nelson	61	121	84	40	88	3	69
Geronimo Allison	57	90	39	82		14	46
Martellus Bennett	56	89	97		0	119	69
Lance Kendricks	92	21	42	94	119	42	39
Jamaal Williams	81	116	96			135	103
Ty Montgomery	91	126	77				98
Richard Rodgers	102	40	81		158	96	107
Aaron Ripkowski	79	72	75				77
Team Total	85	107	80	72	96	77	85

2017 Rushing Recap & 2017 Outlook

If only the Packers passed to their running backs at even a league-average clip, the winner of the Jamaal Williams-Aaron Jones-Ty Montgomery camp battle would offer massive fantasy football potential. Green Bay draws one of the softest run-defense schedules in the league. Part of the problem is that the Packers are such a pass-heavy team. In Rodgers' last full season (2016), Green Bay passed on a league-high 66% of offensive snaps. They passed 67% of the time in the red zone, third most. They passed on 66% of snaps in one-score games, most in the NFL. And over 20% of their run plays were from Rodgers. Even amid all of those concerns, Jones looks like a great value at his RB37/eighth-round ADP.

Player *Min 50 Rushes*	Rushes	YPC	Success %	Success Rk	Missed YPA Rk	YTS % Rk	YAS % Rk	Early Down Success %	Early Down Success Rk	TDs
Jamaal Williams	153	3.6	48%	22	7	19	68	47%	27	4
Aaron Jones	80	5.6	53%	11	5	72	6	51%	12	4
Ty Montgomery	71	3.8	49%	18	1	18	59	48%	17	3

Yards per Carry by Direction

4.3 5.0 3.2 4.4 4.3 3.9 3.1

LT LG C RG RT

Directional Run Frequency

14% 14% 16% 23% 15% 12% 7%

LT LG C RG RT

When the 2016-2017 Packers used two wide receivers or fewer on first-down plays inside the five-yard line, they had a 100% Success Rate and 100% TD rate, nearly double the league averages of 53% and 51%. The NFL uses groupings of two receivers or fewer on 45% of first-down snaps inside the five, and they are much more successful than passing with three or more receivers on near-goal-line plays. But the Packers used three or more receivers on over 90% of their first-down snaps inside the five, producing a 58% Success Rate and 58% TD rate.

These are just a few easy tweaks that could significantly enhance the Packers' offensive efficiency.

Fixing the "little things" is especially important in a loaded NFC. Of the nine teams with better than 20-to-1 odds to win the Super Bowl, seven play in the NFC. Of the seven highest Win Total teams, five play in the NFC. If the Packers are going to have a shot this year, they can't let Rodgers do it all himself again. They need Pettine to rescue the defense and Mike McCarthy to make more analytically-sound decisions on offense.

(cont'd - see GB-5)

Evan Silva's Fantasy Corner

Jamaal Williams and Aaron Jones both made strong rookie-year cases to lead Green Bay's 2018 backfield. Williams did so through reliability and workhorse demonstration with zero fumbles, the top pass-blocking grade among Packers backs, and 20.4 touches per game over the final eight weeks, during which Williams was the RB8 in PPR leagues. Whereas Williams is a throwback grinder, Jones showed more explosiveness with a 5.53 YPC average to Williams' 3.63 and Game Speed vastly superior to both Williams and Ty Montgomery. Jones battled a recurring MCL injury, struggled as both a blocker and receiver, and was caught operating a vehicle with marijuana in his system last October. Jones' ceiling is likely higher, but Williams' bankable attributes endear him to Mike McCarthy's staff. Even if Williams looks like a safer bet to operate as Green Bay's lead back, Jones' playmaking ability makes him an upside pick.

Division History: Season Wins & 2018 Projection

Rank of 2018 Defensive Pass Efficiency Faced by Week

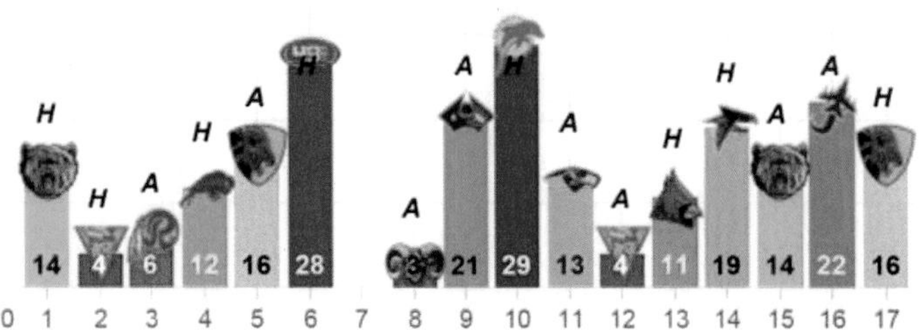

Rank of 2018 Defensive Rush Efficiency Faced by Week

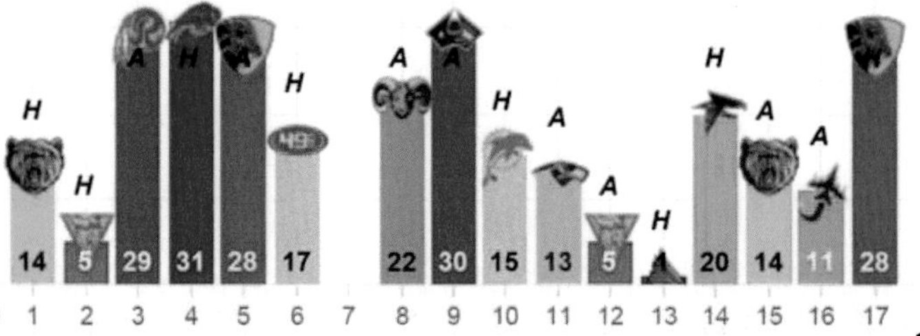

2017 Situational Usage by Player & Position

Usage Rate by Score

		Being Blown Out (14+)	Down Big (9-13)	One Score	Blowout Lead (14+)	Grand Total
RUSH	Jamaal Williams	11%	17%	20%	8%	17%
	Ty Montgomery	9%	2%	10%		8%
	Randall Cobb		1%	1%		1%
	Aaron Jones	4%	8%	9%	35%	9%
	Aaron Ripkowski			1%	3%	1%
	Trevor Davis			0%		0%
	Devante Mays	1%		0%		0%
	Total	25%	26%	42%	46%	37%
PASS	Jamaal Williams	4%	4%	4%	3%	4%
	Davante Adams	11%	13%	15%	8%	13%
	Ty Montgomery	4%	2%	4%		4%
	Randall Cobb	16%	10%	10%	3%	10%
	Aaron Jones	3%	2%	2%		2%
	Jordy Nelson	7%	11%	10%	19%	10%
	Geronimo Allison	6%	9%	3%		4%
	Martellus Bennett	4%	5%	3%	14%	4%
	Lance Kendricks	5%	8%	3%	3%	4%
	Richard Rodgers	5%	1%	2%		2%
	Aaron Ripkowski		2%	1%	5%	1%
	Michael Clark	3%	5%	1%		2%
	Trevor Davis	1%	2%	1%		1%
	Devante Mays	2%				0%
	Jeff Janis	1%	2%	0%		1%
	Emanuel Byrd	1%				0%
	Joe Kerridge	1%				0%
	Total	75%	74%	58%	54%	63%

Positional Target Distribution vs NFL Average

		NFL Wide				Team Only			
		Left	Middle	Right	Total	Left	Middle	Right	Total
Deep	WR	963	503	958	2,424	23	6	29	58
	TE	190	146	182	518	2	4	6	12
	RB	39	9	40	88			2	2
	All	1,192	658	1,180	3,030	25	10	37	72
Short	WR	2,744	1,617	2,683	7,044	118	54	107	279
	TE	837	820	1,135	2,792	26	19	35	80
	RB	1,296	804	1,266	3,366	25	19	29	73
	All	4,877	3,241	5,084	13,202	169	92	171	432
Total		6,069	3,899	6,264	16,232	194	102	208	504

Positional Success Rates vs NFL Average

		NFL Wide				Team Only			
		Left	Middle	Right	Total	Left	Middle	Right	Total
Deep	WR	37%	45%	38%	39%	22%	33%	34%	29%
	TE	38%	52%	45%	44%	50%	75%	50%	58%
	RB	36%	56%	38%	39%			50%	50%
	All	37%	47%	39%	40%	24%	50%	38%	35%
Short	WR	51%	57%	50%	52%	57%	67%	50%	56%
	TE	51%	56%	49%	52%	35%	47%	43%	41%
	RB	44%	51%	43%	45%	44%	63%	45%	49%
	All	49%	55%	48%	50%	51%	62%	47%	52%
Total		47%	54%	46%	48%	48%	61%	46%	50%

Successful Play Rate
0% 100%

Green Bay Packers - Success by Personnel Grouping & Play Type

Play Type	1-1 [3WR]	1-2 [2WR]	2-1 [2WR]	1-0 [4WR]	1-3 [1WR]	0-1 [4WR]	2-0 [3WR]	2-2 [1WR]	0-0 [5WR]	0-2 [3WR]	2-3 [0WR]	3-2 [0WR]	Grand Total
PASS	42% (396, 65%)	58% (48, 8%)	31% (36, 6%)	41% (34, 6%)	33% (3, 0%)	46% (61, 10%)	43% (14, 2%)	60% (5, 1%)	38% (8, 1%)	33% (6, 1%)	50% (2, 0%)		43% (613, 100%)
RUSH	57% (206, 53%)	47% (62, 16%)	51% (35, 9%)	56% (9, 2%)	25% (4, 1%)	60% (5, 1%)	32% (22, 6%)	35% (34, 9%)	50% (2, 1%)	0% (1, 0%)	40% (5, 1%)	0% (1, 0%)	51% (386, 100%)
TOTAL	47% (602, 60%)	52% (110, 11%)	41% (71, 7%)	44% (43, 4%)	29% (7, 1%)	47% (66, 7%)	36% (36, 4%)	38% (39, 4%)	40% (10, 1%)	29% (7, 1%)	43% (7, 1%)	0% (1, 0%)	46% (999, 100%)

Format Line 1: Success Rate Line 2: Total # of Plays, % of All Plays (by type)

GB-5 The 2017 Packers went 4-2 in Rodgers' six full games, but three of those wins were by one score. And Green Bay was losing at halftime in all of them. The NFC margin for error is razor thin, and the playoffs will likely come down to a single win or loss. It would be a shame for Green Bay to miss the postseason by not overturning every stone in search of an edge.

Receiving Success by Personnel Grouping

Position	Player	1-1 [3WR]	1-2 [2WR]	2-1 [2WR]	1-0 [4WR]	1-3 [1WR]	0-1 [4WR]	2-0 [3WR]	2-2 [1WR]	0-0 [5WR]	0-2 [3WR]	2-3 [0WR]	Total
RB	Jamaal Williams	44% 7.9 102.9 (27)	100% 9.3 105.2 (4)	100% 7.0 95.8 (1)	100% 5.0 87.5 (1)						0% 0.0 39.6 (1)		53% 7.7 102.8 (34)
	Ty Montgomery	45% 4.7 96.7 (20)	0% 2.0 79.2 (1)	0% 3.0 79.2 (1)	100% 15.0 118.8 (3)		100% 13.5 118.8 (2)	0% -2.0 79.2 (1)	0% 0.0 39.6 (1)	0% 0.0 39.6 (1)	0% 4.0 83.3 (1)		45% 5.6 97.9 (31)
TE	Lance Kendricks	38% 4.9 22.6 (21)	33% 12.5 81.9 (6)	0% 0.0 39.6 (1)		0% 0.0 79.2 (1)	50% 3.8 40.6 (4)				100% 9.0 104.2 (1)	100% 1.0 118.8 (1)	40% 5.8 39.0 (35)
WR	Davante Adams	51% 7.9 121.5 (76)	78% 7.8 99.1 (9)	57% 12.4 113.4 (7)	60% 4.8 72.1 (5)		67% 6.2 105.7 (15)	0% 0.0 39.6 (2)		50% 3.5 58.3 (2)	0% 2.5 56.3 (2)		54% 7.5 110.3 (118)
	Randall Cobb	52% 7.4 96.4 (67)	100% 23.5 158.3 (2)	0% 0.3 39.6 (4)	25% 5.5 66.7 (4)		45% 5.0 117.8 (11)	50% 11.5 52.1 (2)		0% 4.0 60.4 (2)			48% 7.1 96.9 (92)
	Jordy Nelson	48% 5.3 58.3 (44)	56% 7.6 85.9 (16)	40% 3.7 11.3 (10)	43% 3.9 105.4 (7)		50% 2.8 56.3 (4)	75% 7.8 96.9 (4)	100% 4.0 83.3 (1)	100% 8.0 139.6 (2)			51% 5.5 69.4 (88)

Format Line 1: Success Rate Line 2: YPA Line 3: Passer Rating Line 4: Total # of Plays

Successful Play Rate
0% 100%

Rushing Success by Personnel Grouping

Position	Player	1-1 [3WR]	1-2 [2WR]	2-1 [2WR]	1-0 [4WR]	1-3 [1WR]	2-0 [3WR]	2-2 [1WR]	2-3 [0WR]	Total
RB	Jamaal Williams	54% 3.9 (89)	42% 3.5 (24)	54% 4.8 (13)	50% 3.5 (2)		17% 2.8 (12)	46% 1.5 (13)		48% 3.6 (153)
	Aaron Jones	55% 6.0 (40)	57% 7.9 (14)	56% 3.6 (9)	100% 6.0 (1)	100% 21.0 (1)	0% 1.3 (3)	40% 3.1 (10)	50% 0.5 (2)	53% 5.6 (80)
	Ty Montgomery	58% 3.8 (31)	39% 3.5 (18)	75% 14.3 (4)	50% 4.0 (2)	0% 1.0 (3)	80% 4.0 (5)	20% 0.4 (5)	33% 0.3 (3)	49% 3.8 (71)

Format Line 1: Success Rate Line 2: YPC Line 3: Total # of Plays

Houston Texans

2018 Coaches

Head Coach:
Bill O'Brien (5th yr)
Offensive Coordinator:
(O'Brien calls plays) (5th yr)
Defensive Coordinator:
Romeo Crennel (6th yr)

2018 Forecast

Wins	Div Rank
8.5	#1

Past Records

2017: 4-12
2016: 9-7
2015: 9-7

EASY HARD

Week	1	2	3	4	5	6	7	8	9	10	11	12	13	14	15	16	17
Opponent	NE	TEN	NYG	IND	DAL	BUF	JAX	MIA	DEN		WSH	TEN	CLE	IND	NYJ	PHI	JAX
Site	A	A	H	A	H	H	A	H	A		A	H	H	H	A	A	H
					SNF			TNF				MNF			SAT		

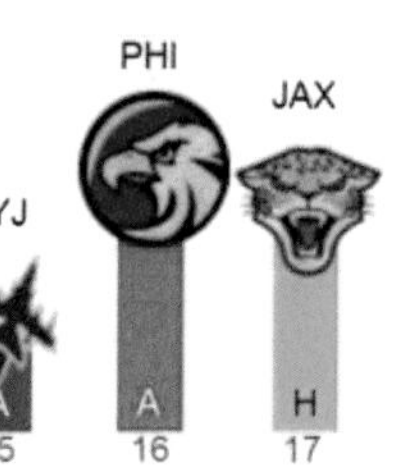

Key Players Lost

TXN	Player (POS)
Cut	Austell, Erik C
	Cushing, Brian LB
Declared Free Agent	Blackson, Angelo DE
	Blue, Alfred RB
	Clark, Chris T
	Ellington, Bruce WR
	Giacomini, Breno T
	Gilchrist, Kennan LB
	Gilchrist, Marcus S
	Heeney, Ben LB
	Jenkins, Jelani LB
	Johnson, Josh QB
	Joseph, Johnathan CB
	Peters, Brian LB
	Savage, Tom QB
	Su'a-Filo, Xavier G
	Todman, Jordan RB
	Williams, Marcus CB
Retired	Fiedorowicz, C.J. TE

Average Line	# Games Favored	# Games Underdog
-2.1	9	4

2018 Houston Texans Overview

Last October 23, I released my largest NFL total recommendation of the year. It was "over 43" on Texans-Seahawks, to be played on October 29. Within seconds on the 23rd, offshore books like Pinnacle, Cris, and "per head" shops adjusted their juice (the vig or "tax" which is paid by the bettor, most typically 10 cents on the dollar aka a risk of $110 to win $100). Within one minute, Pinnacle moved the total to 43.5. Within two minutes, Pinnacle went to 44. In four minutes, their adjusted total was 45. "Per head" shops acted even faster, adjusting to 44 within one minute of my release. The line closed at 45. I told clients I still liked the over, even at 45. My model strongly believed sportsbooks had gotten this one wrong.

My recommendations move lines. It can happen within seconds of my release, which is why my clients are notified ahead of time to be ready to place bets before line movement occurs. At first, only juice adjusts. Then, it's a half- or full-point move. But we almost always beat the closing number, often by 2-3 points. I earned the respect of linemakers by proving myself with a 60.5% hit rate on NFL totals in over 12 years in this profession. Over the last four seasons, my win rates on NFL totals are 61% (2014), 68% (2015), 65% (2016), and 62% (2017).

On this particular game's first drive, the Texans drove 75 yards in five plays for a touchdown. The in-game line soared to 50.5. The Seahawks answered with a 78-yard pick six. 14 points in the first five minutes, and the in-game line spiked to 55.5. Houston's third drive went 82 yards for a touchdown in four minutes. The Seahawks answered with another touchdown marching 75 yards in under four minutes. All told, 28 points were scored in the first 13 minutes of the game. The in-game market ballooned as high as 71.5 on the adjusted total. And it was arguably the most-exciting game of the 2017 regular season. The score was 21-21 at halftime, and the game ended as a 41-38 thriller won by Seattle.

On Thursday, November 2, it was reported Deshaun Watson tore his right ACL in practice. Watson tore his left ACL in 2014 at Clemson. Injuries are part of the game, but no injury hurt me personally more than Watson's last season. I'm not a fan of any team.

(cont'd - see HOU2)

Key Free Agents/ Trades Added

Bademosi, Johnson CB
Coates, Sammie WR
Colvin, Aaron CB
Crockett, Montay WR
Fulton, Zach C
Henderson, Seantrel T
Kelemete, Senio G
Mathieu, Tyrann S
Weeden, Brandon QB

Drafted Players

Rd	Pk	Player (College)
3	68	S - Justin Reid (Stanford)
	80	OT - Martinas Rankin (Mississippi State)
3*	98	TE - Jordan Akins (UCF)
4	103	WR - Keke Coutee (Texas Tech)
6	177	DE - Duke Ejiofor (Wake Forest)
6*	211	TE - Jordan Thomas (Mississippi State)
	214	LB - Peter Kalambayi (Stanford)
7	222	CB - Jermaine Kelly (San Jose State)

Regular Season Wins: Past & Current Proj

	Wins
Forecast 2018 Wins	8.5
2017 Wins	4
Forecast 2017 Wins	8.5
2016 Wins	9
2015 Wins	9
2014 Wins	9

1 3 5 7 9 11 13 15

 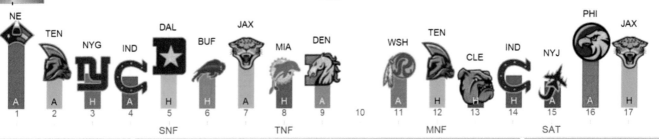

Lineup & Cap Hits

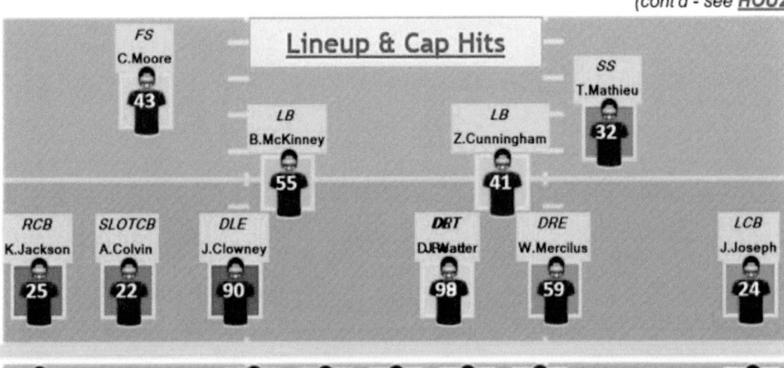

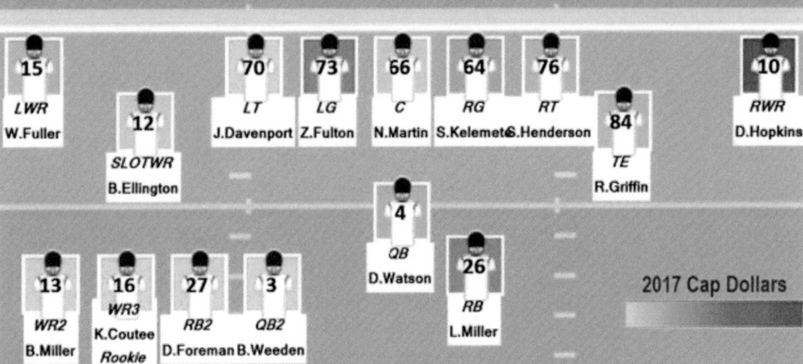

2018 Unit Spending

Positional Spending

	Rank	Total	2017 Rk
All OFF	32	$73.64M	31
QB	30	$5.14M	29
OL	25	$29.65M	12
RB	4	$10.54M	12
WR	16	$22.29M	24
TE	23	$6.02M	23
All DEF	6	$93.71M	17
DL	20	$22.60M	15
LB	8	$26.64M	13
CB	1	$31.01M	12
S	11	$13.45M	28

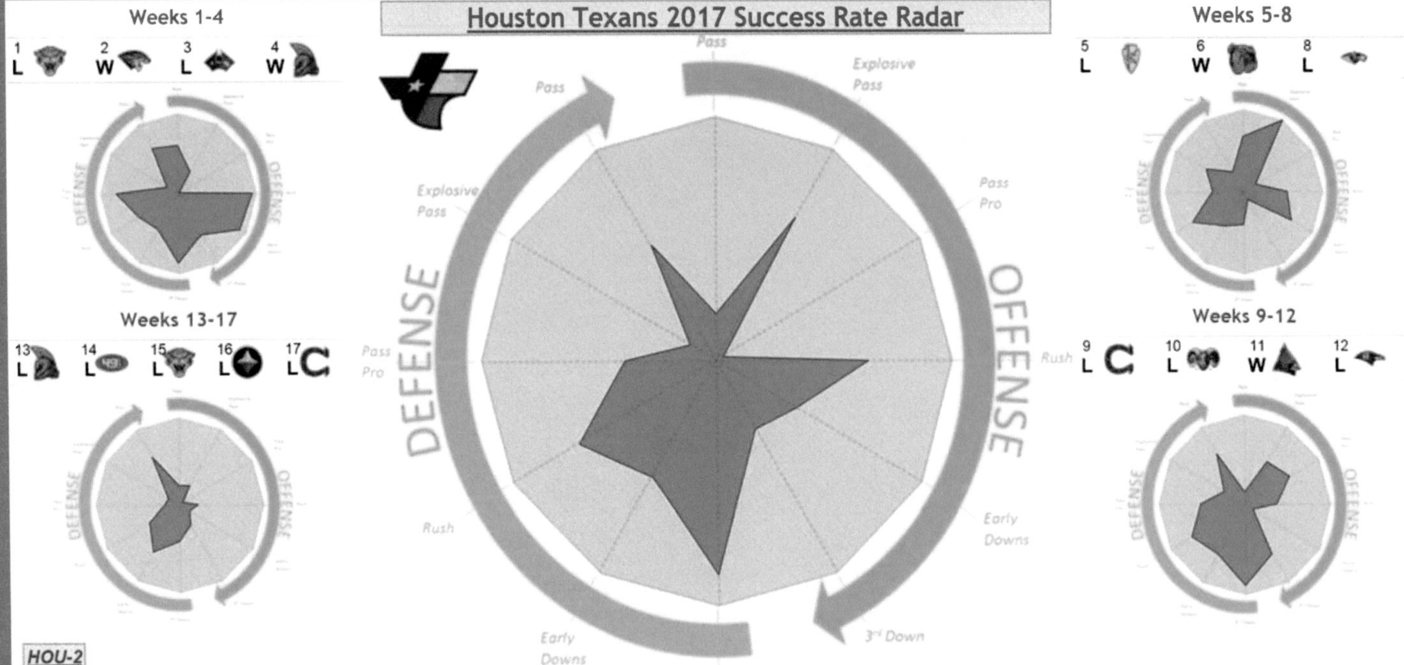

HOU-2

I'm a fan of efficiency. I root for players to be used optimally because it makes game watching more enjoyable. And I love watching, studying, and analyzing football, live and in real time as well as film study the ensuing week.

Watson didn't even start Week 1. His first start came on Week 2 Thursday Night Football in Cincinnati. And he looked extremely raw, but Houston pulled out a 13-9 win as a five-point underdog. Watson covered the spread in 5-of-6 starts, and the Texans scored 33 or more points five times with Watson at quarterback. Houston averaged 13 points per game in non-Watson starts, going 1-9 and 2-8 against the spread. Without Watson, the 2017 Texans were a disaster.

We can study Watson's limited performance for takeaways, but season-long stats are of no use.

This year's offensive line will feature second-year Bucknell alumnus Julien Davenport at left tackle and 2018 free agent addition Seantrel Henderson at right tackle. Anchoring the interior is third-year C Nick Martin, who struggled badly in 14 starts last year. Former Saints utilityman Senio Kelemete is penciled in at right guard. Another free agent pickup, Zach Fulton from Kansas City, is slated to start at left guard.

Why overhaul the line? Because last year's was terrible, ranking third worst in pass protection. And I believe Watson's ACL tear was actually suffered in that Seattle game on a hit to his lower-right leg. Watson was pressured on a league-high 48% of his dropbacks last season. For perspective, Drew Brees faced pressure just 23% of the time. The NFL's second-most-pressured quarterback was Tom Savage, Watson's 2017 Texans teammate. That line was an unmitigated disaster.

(cont'd - see **HOU-3**)

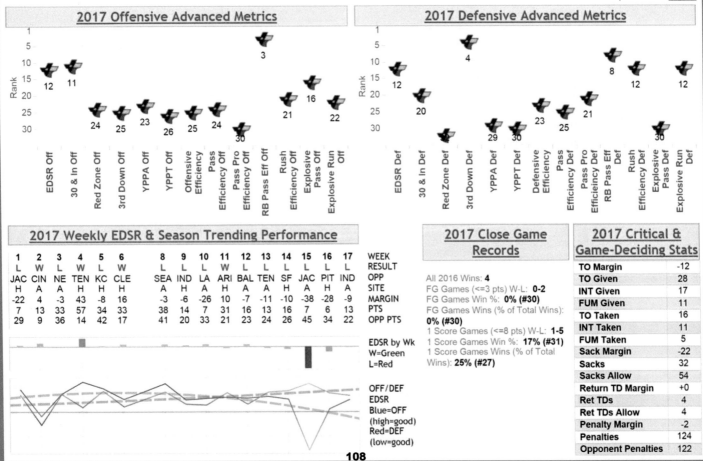

2017 Offensive Advanced Metrics

Metric	Rank
EDSR Off	12
30 & In Off	11
Red Zone Off	24
3rd Down Off	25
YPPA Off	23
YPPT Off	26
Offensive Efficiency	25
Pass Efficiency Off	24
Pass Pro Efficiency Off	30
RB Pass Eff Off	3
Rush Efficiency Off	21
Explosive Pass Off	16
Explosive Run Off	22

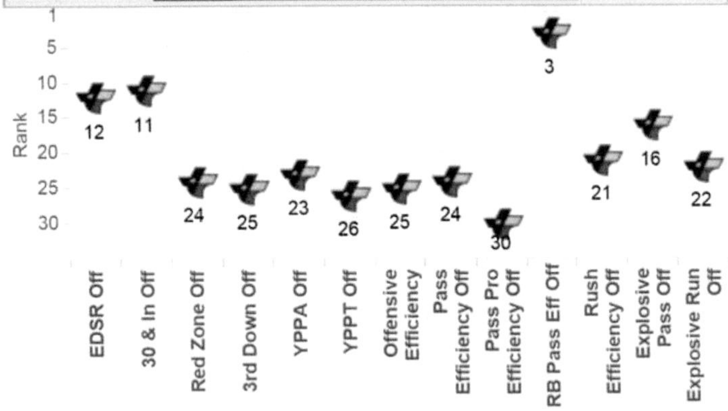

2017 Defensive Advanced Metrics

Metric	Rank
EDSR Def	12
30 & In Def	20
Red Zone Def	
3rd Down Def	4
YPPA Def	29
YPPT Def	30
Defensive Efficiency	23
Pass Efficiency Def	25
Pass Pro Effieicncy Def	21
RB Pass Eff Def	8
Rush Efficiency Def	12
Explosive Pass Def	30
Explosive Run Def	12

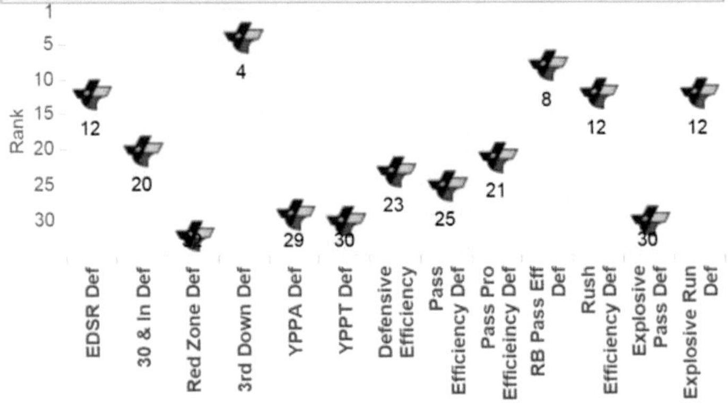

2017 Weekly EDSR & Season Trending Performance

WEEK	1	2	3	4	5	6	8	9	10	11	12	13	14	15	16	17
RESULT	L	W	L	W	L	W	L	L	L	W	L	L	L	L	L	L
OPP	JAC	CIN	NE	TEN	KC	CLE	SEA	IND	LA	ARI	BAL	TEN	SF	JAC	PIT	IND
SITE	H	A	A	H	H	H	A	H	A	H	A	A	H	A	H	A
MARGIN	-22	4	-3	43	-8	16	-3	-6	-26	10	-7	-11	-10	-38	-28	-9
PTS	7	13	33	57	34	33	38	14	7	31	16	13	16	7	6	13
OPP PTS	29	9	36	14	42	17	41	20	33	21	23	24	26	45	34	22

EDSR by Wk
W=Green
L=Red

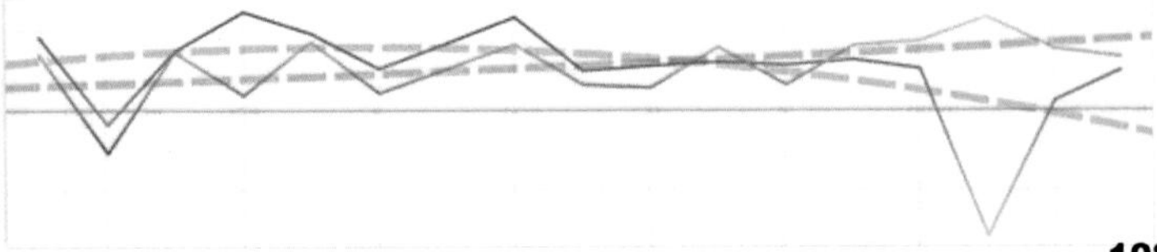

OFF/DEF
EDSR
Blue=OFF
(high=good)
Red=DEF
(low=good)

2017 Close Game Records

All 2016 Wins: **4**
FG Games (<=3 pts) W-L: **0-2**
FG Games Win %: **0% (#30)**
FG Games Wins (% of Total Wins): **0% (#30)**
1 Score Games (<=8 pts) W-L: **1-5**
1 Score Games Win %: **17% (#31)**
1 Score Games Wins (% of Total Wins): **25% (#27)**

2017 Critical & Game-Deciding Stats

TO Margin	-12
TO Given	28
INT Given	17
FUM Given	11
TO Taken	16
INT Taken	11
FUM Taken	5
Sack Margin	-22
Sacks	32
Sacks Allow	54
Return TD Margin	+0
Ret TDs	4
Ret TDs Allow	4
Penalty Margin	-2
Penalties	124
Opponent Penalties	122

Houston Texans 2018 Strength of Schedule In Detail (compared to 2017)

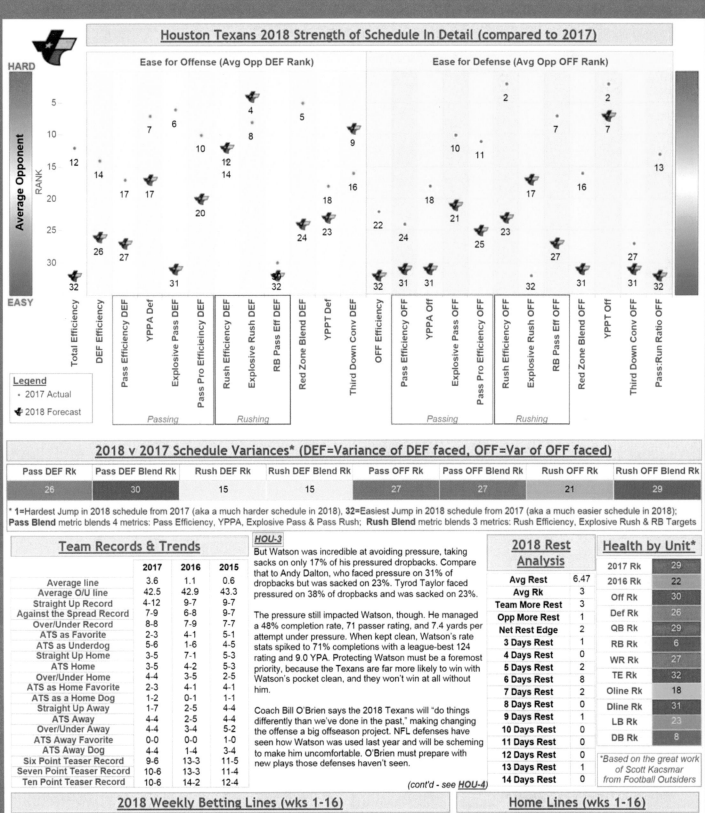

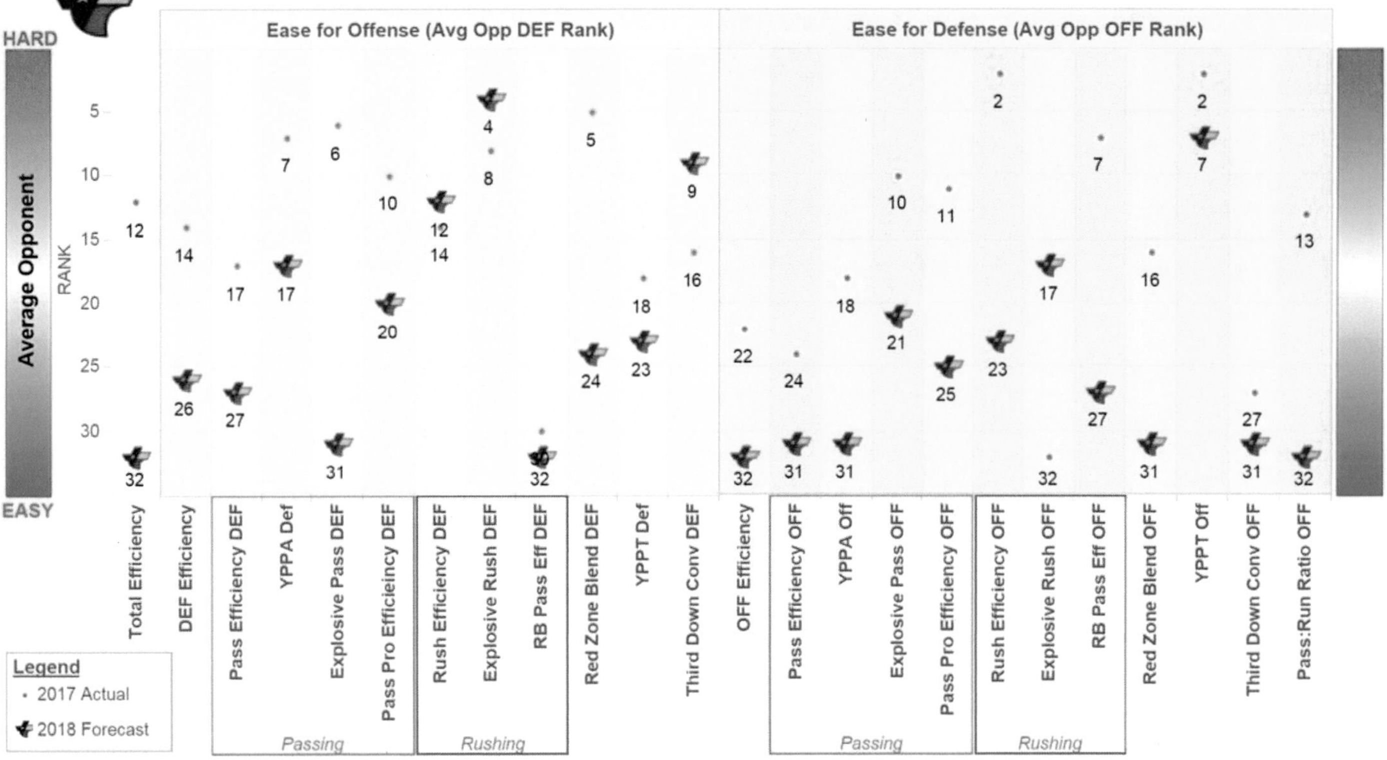

HARD — Average Opponent — EASY (RANK)

Ease for Offense (Avg Opp DEF Rank)

Metric	Group	2017 Actual	2018 Forecast
Total Efficiency		12	32
DEF Efficiency		14	26
Pass Efficiency DEF	Passing	17	27
YPPA Def	Passing	7	17
Explosive Pass DEF	Passing	6	31
Pass Pro Efficieincy DEF	Passing	10	20
Rush Efficiency DEF	Rushing	14	12
Explosive Rush DEF	Rushing	8	4
RB Pass Eff DEF	Rushing	30	32
Red Zone Blend DEF		5	24
YPPT Def		18	23
Third Down Conv DEF		16	9

Ease for Defense (Avg Opp OFF Rank)

Metric	Group	2017 Actual	2018 Forecast
OFF Efficiency		22	32
Pass Efficiency OFF	Passing	24	31
YPPA Off	Passing	18	31
Explosive Pass OFF	Passing	10	21
Pass Pro Efficiency OFF	Passing	11	25
Rush Efficiency OFF	Rushing	2	23
Explosive Rush OFF	Rushing	32	17
RB Pass Eff OFF	Rushing	7	27
Red Zone Blend OFF		16	31
YPPT Off		2	7
Third Down Conv OFF		27	31
Pass:Run Ratio OFF		13	32

Legend
- 2017 Actual
- 2018 Forecast

2018 v 2017 Schedule Variances* (DEF=Variance of DEF faced, OFF=Var of OFF faced)

Pass DEF Rk	Pass DEF Blend Rk	Rush DEF Rk	Rush DEF Blend Rk	Pass OFF Rk	Pass OFF Blend Rk	Rush OFF Rk	Rush OFF Blend Rk
26	30	15	15	27	27	21	29

* **1**=Hardest Jump in 2018 schedule from 2017 (aka a much harder schedule in 2018), **32**=Easiest Jump in 2018 schedule from 2017 (aka a much easier schedule in 2018); **Pass Blend** metric blends 4 metrics: Pass Efficiency, YPPA, Explosive Pass & Pass Rush; **Rush Blend** metric blends 3 metrics: Rush Efficiency, Explosive Rush & RB Targets

Team Records & Trends

	2017	2016	2015
Average line	3.6	1.1	0.6
Average O/U line	42.5	42.9	43.3
Straight Up Record	4-12	9-7	9-7
Against the Spread Record	7-9	6-8	9-7
Over/Under Record	8-8	7-9	7-7
ATS as Favorite	2-3	4-1	5-1
ATS as Underdog	5-6	1-6	4-5
Straight Up Home	3-5	7-1	5-3
ATS Home	3-5	4-2	5-3
Over/Under Home	4-4	3-5	2-5
ATS as Home Favorite	2-3	4-1	4-1
ATS as a Home Dog	1-2	0-1	1-1
Straight Up Away	1-7	2-5	4-4
ATS Away	4-4	2-5	4-4
Over/Under Away	4-4	3-4	5-2
ATS Away Favorite	0-0	0-0	1-0
ATS Away Dog	4-4	1-4	3-4
Six Point Teaser Record	9-6	13-3	11-5
Seven Point Teaser Record	10-6	13-3	11-4
Ten Point Teaser Record	10-6	14-2	12-4

HOU-3

But Watson was incredible at avoiding pressure, taking sacks on only 17% of his pressured dropbacks. Compare that to Andy Dalton, who faced pressure on 31% of dropbacks but was sacked on 23%. Tyrod Taylor faced pressured on 38% of dropbacks and was sacked on 23%.

The pressure still impacted Watson, though. He managed a 48% completion rate, 71 passer rating, and 7.4 yards per attempt under pressure. When kept clean, Watson's rate stats spiked to 71% completions with a league-best 124 rating and 9.0 YPA. Protecting Watson must be a foremost priority, because the Texans are far more likely to win with Watson's pocket clean, and they won't win at all without him.

Coach Bill O'Brien says the 2018 Texans will "do things differently than we've done in the past," making changing the offense a big offseason project. NFL defenses have seen how Watson was used last year and will be scheming to make him uncomfortable. O'Brien must prepare with new plays those defenses haven't seen.

(cont'd - see ***HOU-4***)

2018 Rest Analysis

Avg Rest	6.47
Avg Rk	3
Team More Rest	3
Opp More Rest	1
Net Rest Edge	2
3 Days Rest	1
4 Days Rest	0
5 Days Rest	2
6 Days Rest	8
7 Days Rest	2
8 Days Rest	0
9 Days Rest	1
10 Days Rest	0
11 Days Rest	0
12 Days Rest	0
13 Days Rest	1
14 Days Rest	0

Health by Unit*

2017 Rk	29
2016 Rk	22
Off Rk	30
Def Rk	26
QB Rk	29
RB Rk	6
WR Rk	27
TE Rk	32
Oline Rk	18
Dline Rk	31
LB Rk	23
DB Rk	8

*Based on the great work of Scott Kacsmar from Football Outsiders

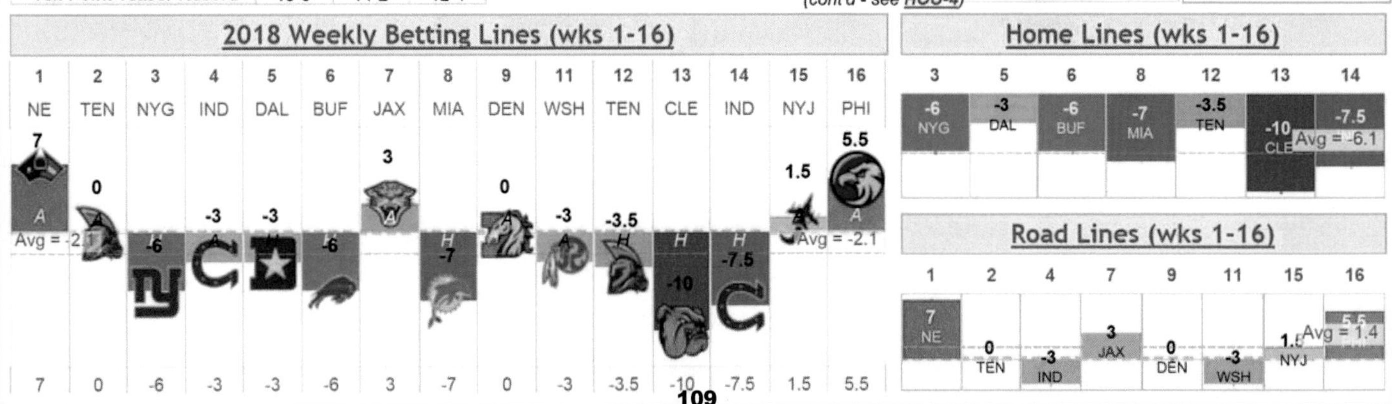

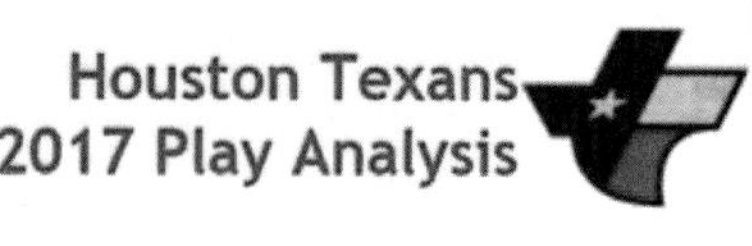

Houston Texans 2017 Play Analysis

2017 Play Tendencies

All Pass %	56%
All Pass Rk	19
All Rush %	44%
All Rush Rk	14
1 Score Pass %	57%
1 Score Pass Rk	18
2016 1 Score Pass %	53%
2016 1 Score Pass Rk	27
2017 Pass Increase %	4%
Pass Increase Rk	5
1 Score Rush %	43%
1 Score Rush Rk	15
Up Pass %	49%
Up Pass Rk	17
Up Rush %	51%
Up Rush Rk	16
Down Pass %	61%
Down Pass Rk	29
Down Rush %	39%
Down Rush Rk	4

2017 Down & Distance Tendencies

Down	Distance	Total Plays	Pass Rate	Run Rate	Play Success %
1	Short (1-3)	4	0%	100%	75%
	Med (4-7)	7	71%	29%	57%
	Long (8-10)	319	35%	65%	46%
	XL (11+)	7	71%	29%	0%
2	Short (1-3)	39	28%	72%	74%
	Med (4-7)	84	54%	46%	44%
	Long (8-10)	96	71%	29%	35%
	XL (11+)	47	85%	15%	28%
3	Short (1-3)	37	65%	35%	65%
	Med (4-7)	55	87%	13%	38%
	Long (8-10)	35	89%	11%	31%
	XL (11+)	30	90%	10%	23%
4	Short (1-3)	5	60%	40%	60%

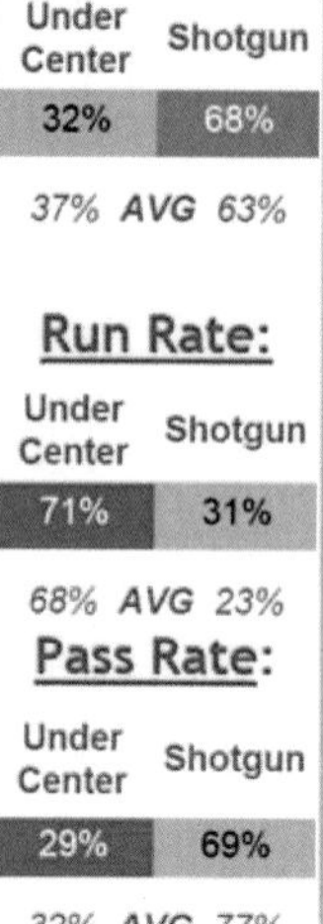

Shotgun %:

Under Center	Shotgun
32%	68%
37%	*63%*

AVG

Run Rate:

Under Center	Shotgun
71%	31%
68%	*23%*

AVG

Pass Rate:

Under Center	Shotgun
29%	69%
32%	*77%*

AVG

Short Yardage Intelligence:

2nd and Short Run

Run Freq	Run Rk	NFL Run Freq Avg	Run 1D Rate	Run NFL 1D Avg
69%	13	67%	80%	69%

2nd and Short Pass

Pass Freq	Pass Rk	NFL Pass Freq Avg	Pass 1D Rate	Pass NFL 1D Avg
31%	20	33%	55%	53%

Most Frequent Play

Down	Distance	Play Type	Player	Total Plays	Play Success %
1	Short (1-3)	RUSH	Deshaun Watson	2	100%
	Med (4-7)	PASS	DeAndre Hopkins	3	67%
	Long (8-10)	RUSH	Lamar Miller	117	43%
	XL (11+)	PASS	DeAndre Hopkins	2	0%
2	Short (1-3)	RUSH	Lamar Miller	17	82%
	Med (4-7)	PASS	DeAndre Hopkins	18	44%
	Long (8-10)	PASS	DeAndre Hopkins	19	68%
	XL (11+)	PASS	DeAndre Hopkins	10	30%
3	Short (1-3)	PASS	DeAndre Hopkins	7	86%
	Med (4-7)	PASS	DeAndre Hopkins	9	22%
	Long (8-10)	PASS	DeAndre Hopkins	12	33%
	XL (11+)	PASS	DeAndre Hopkins	10	30%

Most Successful Play*

Down	Distance	Play Type	Player	Total Plays	Play Success %
1	Long (8-10)	RUSH	Deshaun Watson	10	70%
2	Short (1-3)	RUSH	Lamar Miller	17	82%
	Med (4-7)	RUSH	Lamar Miller	17	59%
	Long (8-10)	PASS	DeAndre Hopkins	19	68%
	XL (11+)	PASS	Lamar Miller	6	33%
			Ryan Griffin	6	33%
3	Short (1-3)	PASS	DeAndre Hopkins	7	86%
	Med (4-7)	PASS	Bruce Ellington	7	43%
	Long (8-10)	PASS	DeAndre Hopkins	12	33%
	XL (11+)	PASS	DeAndre Hopkins	10	30%

**Minimum 5 plays to qualify*

2017 Snap Rates

Wk	Opp	Score	DeAndre Hopkins	Lamar Miller	Bruce Ellington	Will Fuller	Stephen Anderson	Braxton Miller	Ryan Griffin	C.J. Fiedorowicz
1	JAC	L 29-7	79 (100%)	64 (81%)	46 (58%)		57 (72%)	63 (80%)	10 (13%)	24 (30%)
2	CIN	W 13-9	66 (100%)	49 (74%)				63 (95%)		
3	NE	L 36-33	71 (100%)	50 (70%)	70 (99%)		31 (44%)	37 (52%)	61 (86%)	
4	TEN	W 57-14	78 (93%)	57 (68%)	66 (79%)	67 (80%)	11 (13%)		81 (96%)	
5	KC	L 42-34	64 (100%)	56 (88%)	55 (86%)	59 (92%)	16 (25%)		52 (81%)	
6	CLE	W 33-17	63 (95%)	44 (67%)	45 (68%)	54 (82%)	22 (33%)	7 (11%)	57 (86%)	
8	SEA	L 41-38	71 (100%)	62 (87%)	57 (80%)	63 (89%)	11 (15%)	3 (4%)	65 (92%)	
9	IND	L 20-14	71 (100%)	52 (73%)	63 (89%)	71 (100%)	40 (56%)		22 (31%)	
10	LA	L 33-7	69 (99%)	41 (59%)	43 (61%)	33 (47%)	35 (50%)	20 (29%)		63 (90%)
11	ARI	W 31-21	65 (93%)	52 (74%)	68 (97%)		11 (16%)	61 (87%)		60 (86%)
12	BAL	L 23-16	69 (100%)	48 (70%)	63 (91%)		7 (10%)	54 (78%)		66 (96%)
13	TEN	L 24-13	81 (100%)	65 (80%)	16 (20%)		68 (84%)	30 (37%)		17 (21%)
14	SF	L 26-16	67 (100%)	49 (73%)		67 (100%)	48 (72%)			
15	JAC	L 45-7	57 (92%)	31 (50%)		55 (89%)	34 (55%)			
16	PIT	L 34-6	56 (100%)	21 (38%)		54 (96%)	26 (46%)	34 (61%)		
17	IND	L 22-13		17 (31%)		5 (9%)	22 (40%)	55 (100%)		
Grand Total			1,027 (98%)	758 (68%)	592 (75%)	528 (78%)	439 (42%)	427 (58%)	348 (69%)	230 (65%)

Personnel Groupings

Personnel	Team %	NFL Avg	Succ. %
1-1 [3WR]	64%	59%	41%
1-2 [2WR]	17%	19%	46%
2-1 [2WR]	10%	7%	52%
2-0 [3WR]	7%	1%	46%

Grouping Tendencies

Personnel	Pass Rate	Pass Succ. %	Run Succ. %
1-1 [3WR]	66%	39%	45%
1-2 [2WR]	39%	51%	43%
2-1 [2WR]	39%	49%	54%
2-0 [3WR]	50%	44%	47%

Red Zone Targets (min 3)

Receiver	All	Inside 5	6-10	11-20
DeAndre Hopkins	19	6	4	9
Stephen Anderson	8	2	3	3
Bruce Ellington	7		2	5
Lamar Miller	5	1	2	2
Will Fuller	5	1	2	2
Braxton Miller	4	3	1	
C.J. Fiedorowicz	3		1	2
Ryan Griffin	3			3
Alfred Blue	2	1		1

Red Zone Rushes (min 3)

Rusher	All	Inside 5	6-10	11-20
Lamar Miller	21	6	5	10
D'Onta Foreman	11	2	2	7
Alfred Blue	7	3	1	3
Andre Ellington	2	1		1

Early Down Target Rate

RB	TE	WR
18%	21%	62%
23%	*21% NFL AVG*	*56%*

Overall Target Success %

RB	TE	WR
55% #1	43% #30	45% #25

Houston Texans 2017 Passing Recap & 2018 Outlook

Even in only six starts, the energy Deshaun Watson brought to the city of Houston was tangible. But he was still very raw, evidenced by his 124 passer rating when kept clean but 71 rating when pressured. He provided explosiveness in his starts: 14% of Watson's throws gained 20-plus yards, well above league average (8.8%). He averaged 7.9 Air Yards per completion, also well above the NFL average of 6.0. Watson must improve his deep passing to the left, however. As a rookie, he accounted for nearly twice as much yardage on right-side deep throws. And his variance on right-versus-left deep attempts was a rating of 115 versus 15. Watson also must improve his third-down passing. His third-down completions averaged 4.7 Air Yards, which ranked 42nd among quarterbacks and far below league average (7.9).

Deshaun Watson Rating All Downs

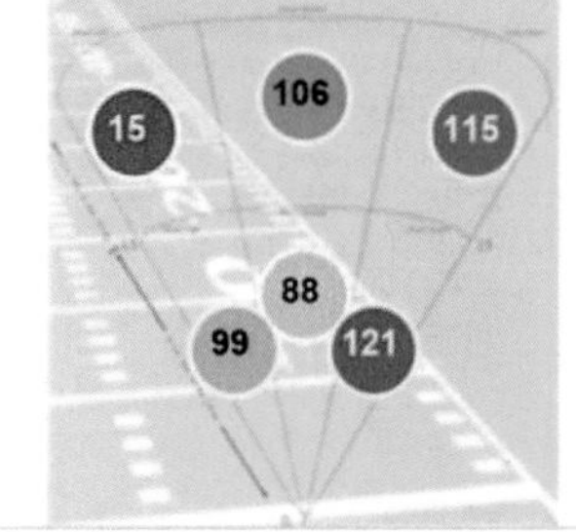

2017 Standard Passing Table

QB	Comp	Att	Comp %	Yds	YPA	TDs	INT	Sacks	Rating	Rk
Deshaun Watson	126	204	62%	1,699	8.3	19	8	19	103	5
Tom Savage	125	223	56%	1,412	6.3	5	6	21	71	48
NFL Avg			62%		7.0				87.5	

Deshaun Watson Rating Early Downs

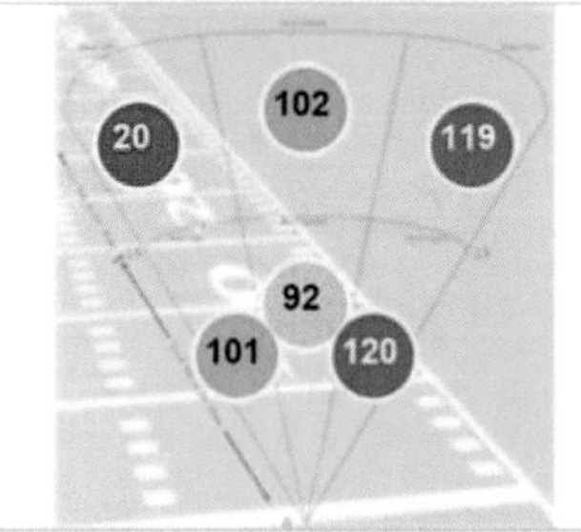

2017 Advanced Passing Table

QB	Success %	EDSR Passing Success %	20+ Yd Pass Gains	20+ Yd Pass %	30+ Yd Pass Gains	30+ Yd Pass %	Avg. Air Yds per Comp	Avg. YAC per Comp	20+ Air Yd Comp	20+ Air Yd %
Deshaun Watson	47%	50%	28	13.7%	13	6.4%	7.8	5.3	18	14%
Tom Savage	40%	41%	18	8.1%	7	3.1%	6.9	3.8	11	9%
NFL Avg	44%	48%	27.7	8.8%	10.3	3.3%	6.0	4.7	11.7	6%

Interception Rates by Down

Yards to Go	1	2	3	4	Total
1 & 2	0.0%	0.0%	0.0%	0.0%	**0.0%**
3, 4, 5	0.0%	11.1%	0.0%	0.0%	**4.0%**
6 - 9		3.3%	0.0%		**2.1%**
10 - 14	2.7%	3.2%	8.3%		**3.4%**
15+	0.0%	18.2%	0.0%		**10.0%**
Total	**2.5%**	**5.6%**	**2.0%**	**0.0%**	**3.6%**

3rd Down Passing - Short of Sticks Analysis

QB	Avg. Yds to Go	Avg. YIA (of Comp)	Avg Yds Short	Short of Sticks Rate	Short Rk
Deshaun Watson	7.9	4.7	-3.2	60%	42
NFL Avg	7.8	6.7	-1.1	60%	

Air Yds vs YAC

Air Yds %	YAC %	Rk
52%	48%	34
58%	42%	

2017 Receiving Recap & 2018 Outlook

Hopkins and Watson showed tremendous 2018 chemistry. Hopkins scored a league-high 13 receiving touchdowns, and getting Hopkins the ball has been a clear priority for O'Brien and his quarterbacks. But I'm most intrigued by TE Stephen Anderson, who quietly posted the highest Success Rate of any player targeted by Watson in 2017. Anderson is currently behind superior blocker Ryan Griffin on the depth chart. But Anderson is a far more athletic catch-first tight end who played wide receiver at Cal.

Player *Min 50 Targets*	Targets	Comp %	YPA	Rating	TOARS	Success %	Success Rk	Missed YPA Rk	YAS % Rk	TDs
DeAndre Hopkins	174	55%	7.9	92	5.5	51%	54	92	25	13
Bruce Ellington	56	52%	5.9	67	3.4	37%	123	109	29	2
Will Fuller	50	56%	8.5	99	3.7	46%	84	50	8	7

Directional Passer Rating Delivered

Receiver	Short Left	Short Middle	Short Right	Deep Left	Deep Middle	Deep Right	Player Total
DeAndre Hopkins	106	53	99	90	121	31	92
Bruce Ellington	94	46	65	42	104	40	67
Stephen Anderson	49	5	48	96	40	119	51
Will Fuller	108	19	105	0	135	100	99
Lamar Miller	91	128	138	40			119
Braxton Miller	60	127	81	40	119	40	91
Ryan Griffin	92	72	119	40		56	82
C.J. Fiedorowicz	44	48	94		0	40	40
Alfred Blue	78	104	86				92
Andre Ellington	88	110	81		40	96	91
Chris Thompson	113	83	113			119	119
Team Total	93	68	92	53	94	87	84

2017 Rushing Recap & 2017 Outlook

We think we know what Lamar Miller is at this stage of his career. We don't know what D'Onta Foreman will become, especially after tearing his Achilles'. We do know Foreman flashed explosiveness on third downs as both a rusher and receiver, and Miller was a terrible third-down back. But I am an opponent of the "third-down back" designation, because it prevents offenses from moving quickly by forcing substitutions and telegraphs tendencies to the defense. If Foreman gets healthy, I'd like to see what he could do as a potential three-down player. But there have been whispers he could begin the season on reserve/PUP. For an exciting offense and team that should improve its win total, it's depressing this backfield has so much uncertainty.

Player *Min 50 Rushes*	Rushes	YPC	Success %	Success Rk	Missed YPA Rk	YTS % Rk	YAS % Rk	Early Down Success %	Early Down Success Rk	TDs
Lamar Miller	238	3.7	45%	34	20	24	52	46%	31	3
D'Onta Foreman	78	4.2	44%	40	21	70	28	42%	50	2
Alfred Blue	71	3.7	42%	52	23	49	53	42%	51	1

Yards per Carry by Direction

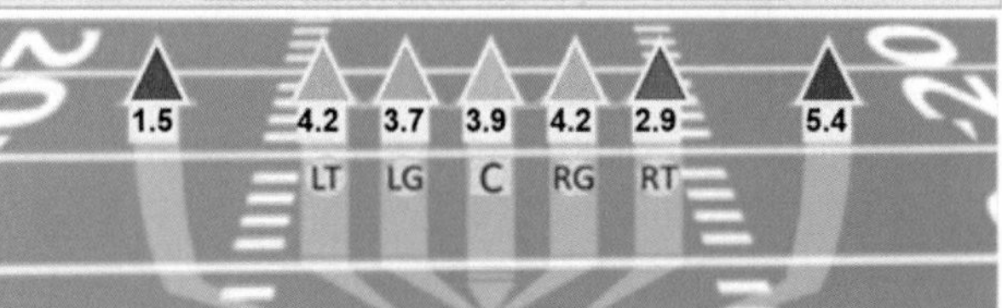

Directional Run Frequency

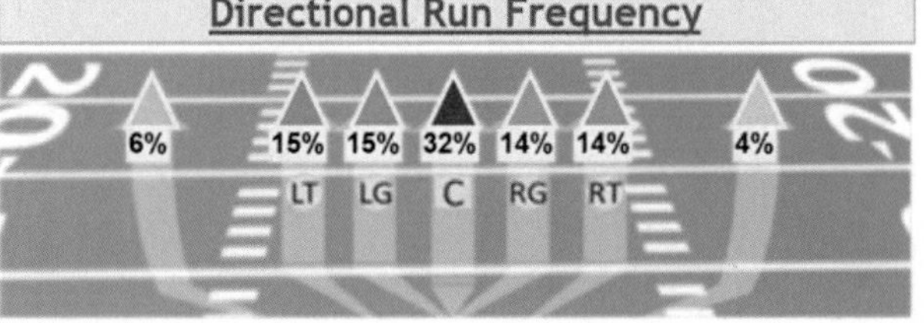

Entering 2017, the Texans had to design a specific offense for statuesque Week 1 starter Tom Savage. Watson made his first NFL start in Week 2 on a short week, giving O'Brien minimal time to change systems to maximize Watson's strengths. We should see a more creative offense in 2018, although it's still predicated on the health of Watson's knee.

Last year's Texans were the NFL's fourth-most-injured team with the second-most-injured defensive line. Houston lost DE J.J. Watt (tibial plateau fracture) and OLB Whitney Mercilus (torn pectoral) for the year in the same Week 5 game. And they had already lost many of their best defensive players that offseason or due to suspension, including CB A.J. Bouye, NT Vince Wilfork, and LB Brian Cushing. If the Texans get back Watt and Mercilus at 100% with FS Tyrann Mathieu and CB Aaron Colvin added in free agency, this defense should look much better. Last year's unit ranked 23rd in defensive efficiency, dead last in the red zone, and third worst in explosive passing allowed. When a team is -22 in sack margin and -12 in turnover margin, they aren't going to win many games. The Texans won four.

The Texans' schedule should help. I project it as the softest slate in the league, including the NFL's easiest schedule of both opposing offenses and opposing defenses.

(cont'd - see HOU-5)

Evan Silva's Fantasy Corner

Lamar Miller disappointed for the second straight season in Houston last year, averaging a career-low 3.73 yards per carry with a concerning drop in Game Speed. Miller looked in danger of losing significant work to rookie D'Onta Foreman before Foreman tore his Achilles' in Week 11, then got out-carried by Alfred Blue 46 to 27 in Weeks 15-17. Miller did top 1,200 yards from scrimmage for the fourth straight season and finished a respectable 21st among 47 qualified backs in Football Outsiders' rushing Success Rate. Foreman's Week 1 availability is questionable at best, and Houston made no notable offseason running back additions. This year's Texans face the NFL's softest schedule, which should translate to more run-friendly game scripts in combination with J.J. Watt and Whitney Mercilus' returns. Last year, Miller averaged nearly five more fantasy points per game in Watson's six starts. Miller remains at risk of falling into a committee, but his situation is favorable enough to make Miller a potential value pick at his fifth-/sixth-round ADP. The Texans have finished top 12 in both rush attempts and offensive plays all four years under Bill O'Brien.

Division History: Season Wins & 2018 Projection

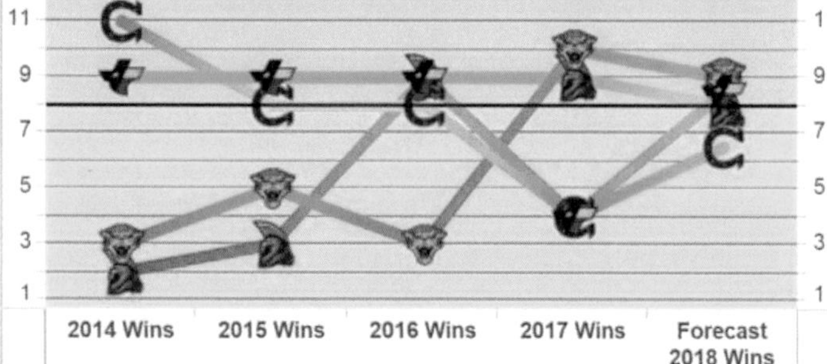

Rank of 2018 Defensive Pass Efficiency Faced by Week

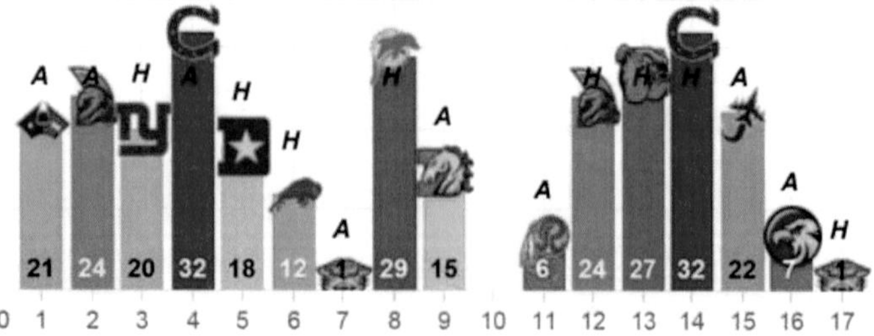

Rank of 2018 Defensive Rush Efficiency Faced by Week

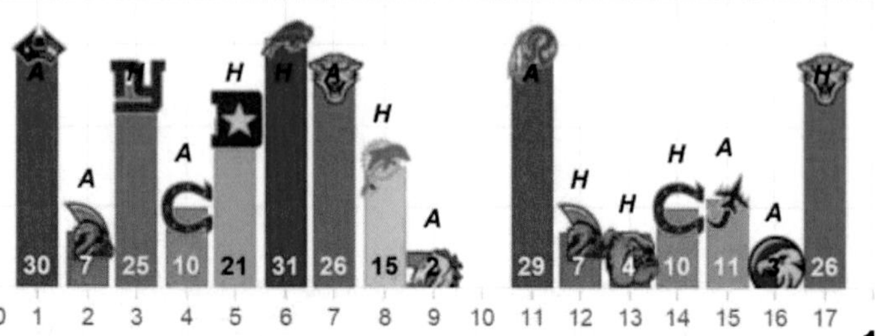

2017 Situational Usage by Player & Position

Usage Rate by Score

		Being Blown Out (14+)	Down Big (9-13)	One Score	Large Lead (9-13)	Blowout Lead (14+)	Grand Total
RUSH	Lamar Miller	21%	15%	28%	43%	24%	26%
	D'Onta Foreman	1%	13%	7%	14%	24%	8%
	Alfred Blue	17%	8%	6%		4%	8%
	Bruce Ellington			0%		1%	0%
	Will Fuller	1%				1%	0%
	Braxton Miller			0%			0%
	Tyler Ervin	1%		0%			0%
	Andre Ellington			1%			1%
	Total	41%	36%	43%	57%	54%	44%
PASS	Lamar Miller	5%	7%	4%		9%	5%
	DeAndre Hopkins	27%	21%	18%	14%	13%	19%
	D'Onta Foreman	1%		1%			1%
	Alfred Blue	1%	2%	1%			1%
	Bruce Ellington	5%	3%	7%	7%	4%	6%
	Stephen Anderson	7%	5%	6%	7%	1%	6%
	Will Fuller	6%	10%	4%		10%	5%
	Braxton Miller	1%	3%	4%	7%	1%	3%
	Ryan Griffin	1%	2%	3%	7%	6%	3%
	C.J. Fiedorowicz	1%	5%	3%			3%
	Tyler Ervin	3%		1%			1%
	Andre Ellington			1%			1%
	DeAndrew White	1%	3%	1%			1%
	Chris Thompson			1%			1%
	Cobi Hamilton	1%	3%	0%			1%
	Jay Prosch			0%		1%	0%
	Ryan Malleck	1%					0%
	Total	59%	64%	57%	43%	46%	56%

Positional Target Distribution vs NFL Average

		NFL Wide				Team Only			
		Left	Middle	Right	**Total**	Left	Middle	Right	**Total**
Deep	WR	943	490	952	**2,385**	43	19	35	**97**
	TE	188	147	177	**512**	4	3	11	**18**
	RB	38	8	40	**86**	1	1	2	**4**
	All	**1,169**	**645**	**1,169**	**2,983**	**48**	**23**	**48**	**119**
Short	WR	2,751	1,629	2,719	**7,099**	111	42	71	**224**
	TE	842	812	1,134	**2,788**	21	27	36	**84**
	RB	1,301	808	1,271	**3,380**	20	15	24	**59**
	All	**4,894**	**3,249**	**5,124**	**13,267**	**152**	**84**	**131**	**367**
Total		**6,063**	**3,894**	**6,293**	**16,250**	**200**	**107**	**179**	**486**

Positional Success Rates vs NFL Average

		NFL Wide				Team Only			
		Left	Middle	Right	**Total**	Left	Middle	Right	**Total**
Deep	WR	37%	45%	38%	**39%**	33%	53%	31%	**36%**
	TE	38%	54%	45%	**45%**	25%	0%	55%	**39%**
	RB	37%	63%	38%	**40%**	0%	0%	50%	**25%**
	All	**37%**	**47%**	**39%**	**40%**	**31%**	**43%**	**38%**	**36%**
Short	WR	51%	58%	50%	**52%**	55%	43%	46%	**50%**
	TE	51%	57%	49%	**52%**	43%	41%	47%	**44%**
	RB	44%	51%	43%	**45%**	50%	73%	58%	**59%**
	All	**49%**	**56%**	**48%**	**50%**	**53%**	**48%**	**49%**	**50%**
Total		**47%**	**54%**	**46%**	**49%**	**48%**	**47%**	**46%**	**47%**

Successful Play Rate
0% [color scale] 100%

Houston Texans - Success by Personnel Grouping & Play Type

Play Type	1-1 [3WR]	1-2 [2WR]	2-1 [2WR]	1-0 [4WR]	1-3 [1WR]	0-1 [4WR]	2-0 [3WR]	2-2 [1WR]	0-0 [5WR]	0-2 [3WR]	1-4 [0WR]	Grand Total
PASS	39% (431, 74%)	51% (68, 12%)	49% (39, 7%)	100% (1, 0%)	33% (3, 1%)	50% (2, 0%)	44% (34, 6%)		0% (1, 0%)			41% (579, 100%)
RUSH	45% (224, 50%)	43% (107, 24%)	54% (61, 14%)	33% (3, 1%)	20% (5, 1%)		47% (34, 8%)	36% (11, 2%)		100% (2, 0%)	100% (1, 0%)	46% (448, 100%)
TOTAL	41% (655, 64%)	46% (175, 17%)	52% (100, 10%)	50% (4, 0%)	25% (8, 1%)	50% (2, 0%)	46% (68, 7%)	36% (11, 1%)	0% (1, 0%)	100% (2, 0%)	100% (1, 0%)	43% (1,027, 100%)

Format Line 1: Success Rate Line 2: Total # of Plays, % of All Plays (by type)

HOU-5 Strength of schedule gives us a big edge because most mainstream analysts don't calculate it properly, or aren't aware of its advantages. But when a team is projected to face a soft slate, the running game stands to experience a bump. In the Texans' case, which running back will capitalize?

Last year, Lamar Miller dominated early-down work. Rookie D'Onta Foreman tore his Achilles' in Week 11, and his status for 2018 is up in the air. Playing with Watson in Weeks 2-8, Miller managed 3.5 yards per carry with a 47% Success Rate. Foreman averaged 4.2 YPC with a 45% Success Rate. Foreman showed more burst and explosiveness, but Miller produced more positive yardage on plays that were not graded as successful. Miller's Early-Down Success Rate was 51% to Foreman's 44%, and Miller's YPC was better as well. But on third down, Foreman's Success Rate (50%) and yards per carry (10.0) were far superior to Miller's (0%, 0.3 YPC). Both backs posted solid receiving Success Rates at 58% for Miller and 75% for Foreman. Foreman showed more passing-game explosiveness, as well. But neither back was a true bellcow. If they don't improve in 2018, the Texans' running game will be limited. And Houston will have more trouble holding onto second-half leads.

The passing offense is in much better shape, paced by superstar DeAndre Hopkins. In Watson's starts, Hopkins led all NFL wide receivers with a 58% Success Rate. Will Fuller's Success Rate was 50% with an explosive 12.7 yards per target. Even slot receiver Bruce Ellington produced an above-par 48% Success Rate and 8.0 yards per target. The Texans are hurting at tight end after C.J. Fiedorowicz's concussion-induced retirement, but I want to see them give Stephen Anderson more opportunities. Anderson struggles as a run blocker, but his 2017 receiving Success Rate (73%) and yards per target (12.1) were elite for the position.

The 2018 Texans are a fascinating team to project. We can optimistically forecast all of last year's injured players to return healthy and produce a great season. But the AFC South has fast become one of the NFL's toughest divisions. In 2013, AFC South teams combined for just 12 non-division wins. In 2014 and 2015, they won 13. They won 17 in 2016, and 13 last year. The Titans, Texans, and Jaguars all have 2018 Win Totals of 8.0 games or more. Jacksonville nearly made the Super Bowl last year. So Houston could greatly improve but still miss the postseason. If O'Brien's offensive plan comes together, however, the Texans can emerge as a sleeper to win the AFC South.

Receiving Success by Personnel Grouping

Position	Player	1-1 [3WR]	1-2 [2WR]	2-1 [2WR]	1-0 [4WR]	1-3 [1WR]	0-1 [4WR]	2-0 [3WR]	0-0 [5WR]	Total
RB	Lamar Miller	53% 6.7 127.9 (30)	50% 9.8 84.4 (4)	100% 11.8 115.6 (4)	100% 12.0 116.7 (1)			33% 4.7 77.1 (6)		56% 7.3 119.2 (45)
TE	Stephen Anderson	33% 6.1 70.4 (39)	67% 7.9 60.0 (9)	33% 6.0 15.3 (3)			100% 14.0 118.8 (1)		0% 0.0 39.6 (1)	40% 6.5 51.0 (53)
WR	DeAndre Hopkins	45% 7.0 80.5 (130)	59% 9.5 110.2 (17)	85% 14.2 144.4 (13)		100% 6.0 131.3 (1)		54% 9.2 85.4 (13)		51% 7.9 91.6 (174)
	Bruce Ellington	34% 4.9 47.1 (44)	67% 13.5 149.3 (6)	0% 2.5 56.3 (2)			0% 0.0 39.6 (1)	33% 9.7 109.7 (3)		36% 5.9 66.8 (56)
	Will Fuller	42% 9.5 104.0 (33)	73% 8.1 88.8 (11)	0% 0.0 39.6 (3)				33% 6.7 97.2 (3)		46% 8.5 98.6 (50)
	Braxton Miller	32% 6.9 83.9 (22)	25% -0.8 116.7 (4)	100% 8.0 100.0 (1)				50% 2.5 56.3 (2)		34% 5.6 91.5 (29)

Format Line 1: Success Rate Line 2: YPA Line 3: Passer Rating Line 4: Total # of Plays

Successful Play Rate
0% [color scale] 100%

Rushing Success by Personnel Grouping

Position	Player	1-1 [3WR]	1-2 [2WR]	2-1 [2WR]	1-0 [4WR]	1-3 [1WR]	2-0 [3WR]	2-2 [1WR]	1-4 [0WR]	Total
QB	Deshaun Watson	55% 6.5 (22)	75% 3.8 (4)	0% 5.0 (1)	100% 9.0 (1)		71% 13.6 (7)		100% 1.0 (1)	61% 7.5 (36)
RB	Lamar Miller	43% 4.1 (115)	46% 3.6 (54)	54% 3.3 (46)	0% 2.0 (1)	33% 0.0 (3)	40% 4.2 (15)	25% 3.3 (4)		45% 3.7 (238)
	D'Onta Foreman	48% 5.4 (42)	42% 3.2 (26)	50% 3.3 (4)		0% 0.5 (2)	33% 2.7 (3)	0% -2.0 (1)		44% 4.2 (78)

Format Line 1: Success Rate Line 2: YPC Line 3: Total # of Plays

Indianapolis Colts

2018 Coaches

Head Coach:
Frank Reich (PHI OC) (1st yr)
Offensive Coordinator:
Nick Sirianni (LAC WR) (1st yr)
Defensive Coordinator:
Matt Eberflus (DAL LB) (1st yr)

EASY **HARD**

2018 Forecast

Wins	Div Rank
6.5	#4

Past Records

2017: 4-12
2016: 8-8
2015: 8-8

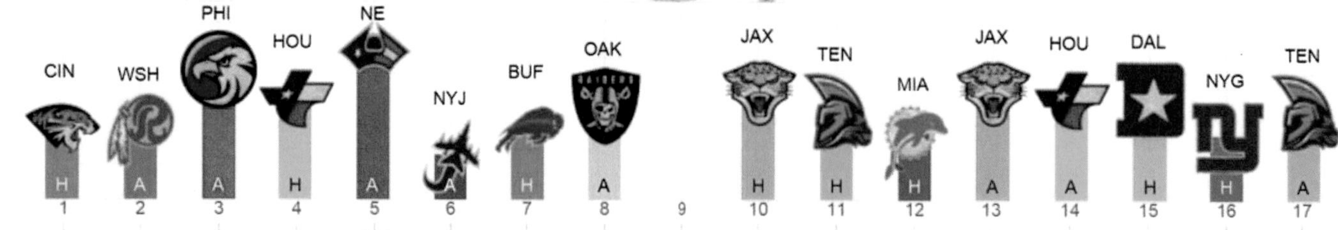

Key Players Lost

TXN	Player (POS)
Cut	Hankins, Johnathan DT
	Jones, Matt RB
Declared Free Agent	Aiken, Kamar WR
	Bostic, Jon LB
	Butler, Darius S
	Desir, Pierre CB
	Gore, Frank RB
	Melvin, Rashaan CB
	Mewhort, Jack T
	Michael, Christine RB
	Mingo, Barkevious LB
	Moncrief, Donte WR
	Person, Mike C
	Tolzien, Scott QB
	Williams, Brandon TE
Retired	Adams, Rodney WR
	Cromartie, Antonio CB
	Freeney, Dwight DE

Average Line	# Games Favored	# Games Underdog
3.4	3	11

2018 Indianapolis Colts Overview

Andrew Luck has never won MVP or a Super Bowl. But the three-time Pro Bowler is by far the most important member of the Colts. Indianapolis is 46-29 with Luck in the lineup, and 10-16 without him. The Colts have never posted a losing season with Luck under center.

In 2017, disaster struck. Luck first injured his throwing shoulder on September 27 of 2015. He missed the first game of his career the following week. According to those who studied his mechanics, Luck's throwing motion began to regress after his Week 6 return. A few weeks later, Luck suffered a kidney laceration and partially torn abdominal muscle, ending his season.

Playing all of 2016 with a torn labrum, Luck still wasn't the reason the Colts fell to 8-8. His Air Yards per completion (8.6) were well above league average (6.8), and Luck posted a career-best 7.8 yards per attempt. He fell just shy (96.3) of his career-best 96.4 passer rating. The supporting cast ex-GM Ryan Grigson assembled was terrible. Chuck Pagano's defense finished No. 32 against the run and No. 29 overall. The offensive line allowed 41 sacks. Luck kept fighting with a 66% completion rate, 8.2 YPA, 108 rating, and 17:13 TD-to-INT ratio in second halves of games. When the Colts trailed with four minutes or less, Luck improved to 71% completions at 10.0 yards per attempt and a 5:0 TD-to-INT ratio. The 2016 Colts lost 5-of-7 games by one score. All with Luck playing through a torn labrum in his throwing shoulder. Linemakers treated Luck as one of the NFL's two-most-valuable players alongside Aaron Rodgers. Just how great was Luck? As a favorite in his career, Luck has covered the spread in 58% of starts. It's a tick below Rodgers (59%) and above Tom Brady, Drew Brees, Ben Roethlisberger, Russell Wilson, Matt Ryan, and Peyton Manning. As an underdog, Luck is an even-more-remarkable 65% against the spread.

Luck underwent shoulder surgery after the 2016 season, and his rehab lasted longer than expected. The Colts were still run by over-the-hill Pagano with plays called by overmatched OC Rob Chudzinski. In early August, "doubts" emerged about Luck's Week 1 availability. By mid-August, owner Jim Irsay admitted Luck's Week 1 status was "in question." Two weeks before the Colts left for their opener in Los Angeles, Pagano declared there was "no timetable" for Luck's return. It wasn't until August 31 that Irsay admitted Luck was unlikely to play Week 1.

(cont'd - see IND2)

Key Free Agents/ Trades Added

Acker, Kenneth CB
Autry, Denico DE
Ebron, Eric TE
Goode, Najee LB
Grant, Ryan WR
Slauson, Matt C
Telfer, Randall TE

Drafted Players

Rd	Pk	Player (College)
1	6	G - Quenton Nelson (Notre D..
2	36	LB - Darius Leonard (South ..
	37	G - Braden Smith (Auburn)
	52	DE - Kemoko Turay (Rutgers)
	64	DE - Tyquan Lewis (Ohio Sta..
4	104	RB - Nyheim Hines (NC State)
5	159	WR - Daurice Fountain (Nort..
	169	RB - Jordan Wilkins (Ole Miss)
6	185	WR - Deon Cain (Clemson)
7	221	LB - Matthew Adams (Housto..
	235	LB - Zaire Franklin (Syracuse)

Regular Season Wins: Past & Current Proj

Lineup & Cap Hits

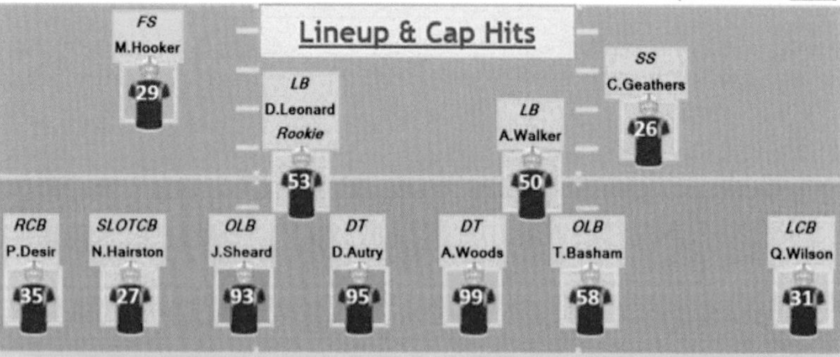

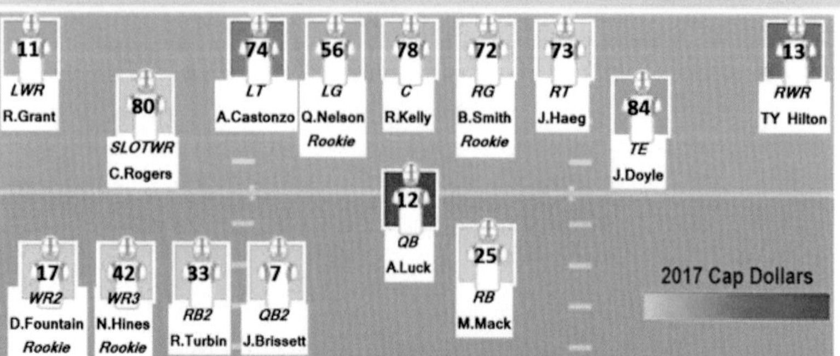

2018 Unit Spending

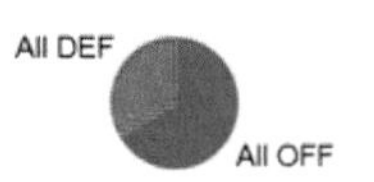

Positional Spending

	Rank	Total	2017 Rk
All OFF	5	$102.77M	13
QB	8	$26.20M	10
OL	19	$33.75M	26
RB	27	$4.23M	16
WR	13	$23.99M	14
TE	5	$14.59M	9
All DEF	32	$51.82M	18
DL	25	$19.06M	18
LB	22	$18.45M	7
CB	30	$7.25M	18
S	29	$7.07M	26

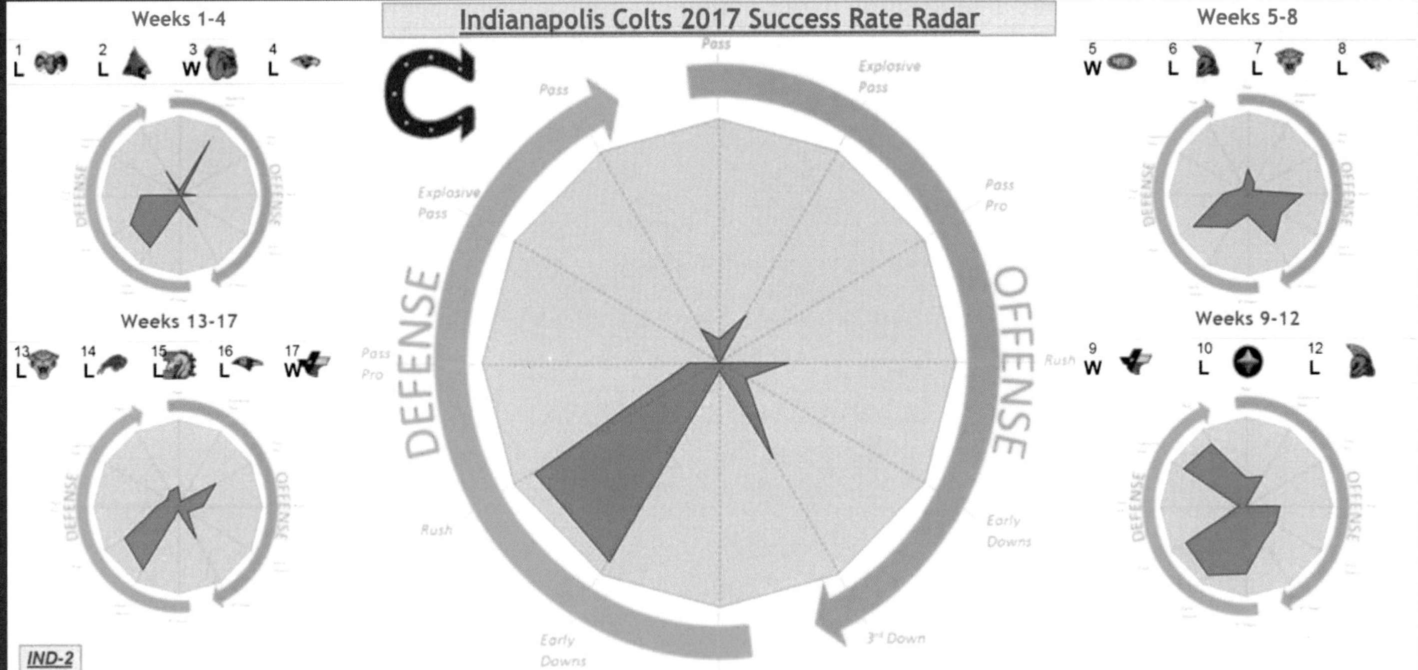

IND-2

Realizing how embarrassing the Colts would be quarterbacked by then-backup Scott Tolzien, GM Chris Ballard acquired Jacoby Brissett from the Patriots for Grigson's first-round WR bust Phillip Dorsett on September 2. Tolzien's Colts were destroyed by the Rams 46-9 on September 10. Brissett took over on September 17 and didn't look back, starting 15 games after getting less than two weeks to learn Chudzinski's system.

The Colts finished 4-12 against a stacked deck. They lost a top-two quarterback in value against the spread. They started a quarterback who was a third-stringer on another team, acquiring him days before the season. Brissett played behind the league's fifth-most-injured offensive line. Overall, Pagano's Colts were the fifth-most-injured team in the NFL. Pagano and Chudzinski were lame ducks. And their offense faced the league's fifth-most-difficult schedule of defenses.

4-12 doesn't tell the story of last year's Colts. The story is better told by way of horrendous decision making. A coaching staff that didn't pay attention to details. Coaches who didn't study details because they don't have analytical consultants concerned with play-calling optimization and tendencies.

The 2017 Colts trailed at halftime in only six games. They led at halftime nine times. Yet they went 2-7 in games with a halftime lead. Last year's Colts are the only team in the last 27 seasons to lose at least seven games they led at halftime. Indianapolis' leads didn't mysteriously evaporate in the third quarter, however. The Colts led through three quarters in nine games. Which means the 2017 Colts are the only team in the last 20 years to hold fourth-quarter leads in at least nine games, but finish no better than 4-12.

The Colts led entering the fourth quarter in eight of their first 11 games. Only the Super Bowl champion Eagles and runner-up Patriots led in more fourth quarters during that stretch. The Colts won just three of these games. They lost five by blowing fourth-quarter leads to drop to 3-8 on the season.

*(cont'd - see **IND-3**)*

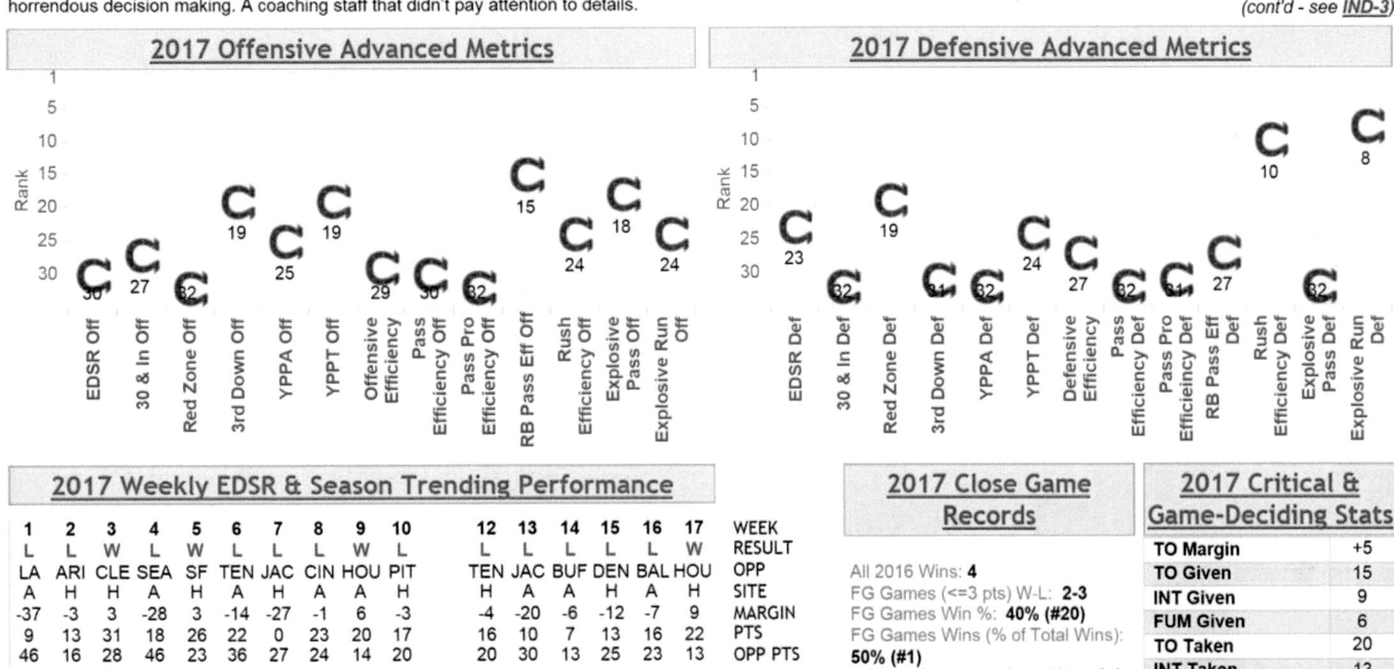

2017 Weekly EDSR & Season Trending Performance

1	2	3	4	5	6	7	8	9	10	12	13	14	15	16	17	WEEK
L	L	W	L	W	L	L	L	W	L	L	L	L	L	L	W	RESULT
LA	ARI	CLE	SEA	SF	TEN	JAC	CIN	HOU	PIT	TEN	JAC	BUF	DEN	BAL	HOU	OPP
A	H	H	A	H	A	H	A	A	H	H	A	A	H	A	H	SITE
-37	-3	3	-28	3	-14	-27	-1	6	-3	-4	-20	-6	-12	-7	9	MARGIN
9	13	31	18	26	22	0	23	20	17	16	10	7	13	16	22	PTS
46	16	28	46	23	36	27	24	14	20	20	30	13	25	23	13	OPP PTS

EDSR by Wk
W=Green
L=Red

OFF/DEF
EDSR
Blue=OFF
(high=good)
Red=DEF
(low=good)

2017 Close Game Records

All 2016 Wins: **4**
FG Games (<=3 pts) W-L: **2-3**
FG Games Win %: **40% (#20)**
FG Games Wins (% of Total Wins): **50% (#1)**
1 Score Games (<=8 pts) W-L: **3-6**
1 Score Games Win %: **33% (#24)**
1 Score Games Wins (% of Total Wins): **75% (#3)**

2017 Critical & Game-Deciding Stats

TO Margin	+5
TO Given	15
INT Given	9
FUM Given	6
TO Taken	20
INT Taken	13
FUM Taken	7
Sack Margin	-29
Sacks	26
Sacks Allow	55
Return TD Margin	-5
Ret TDs	1
Ret TDs Allow	6
Penalty Margin	+10
Penalties	92
Opponent Penalties	102

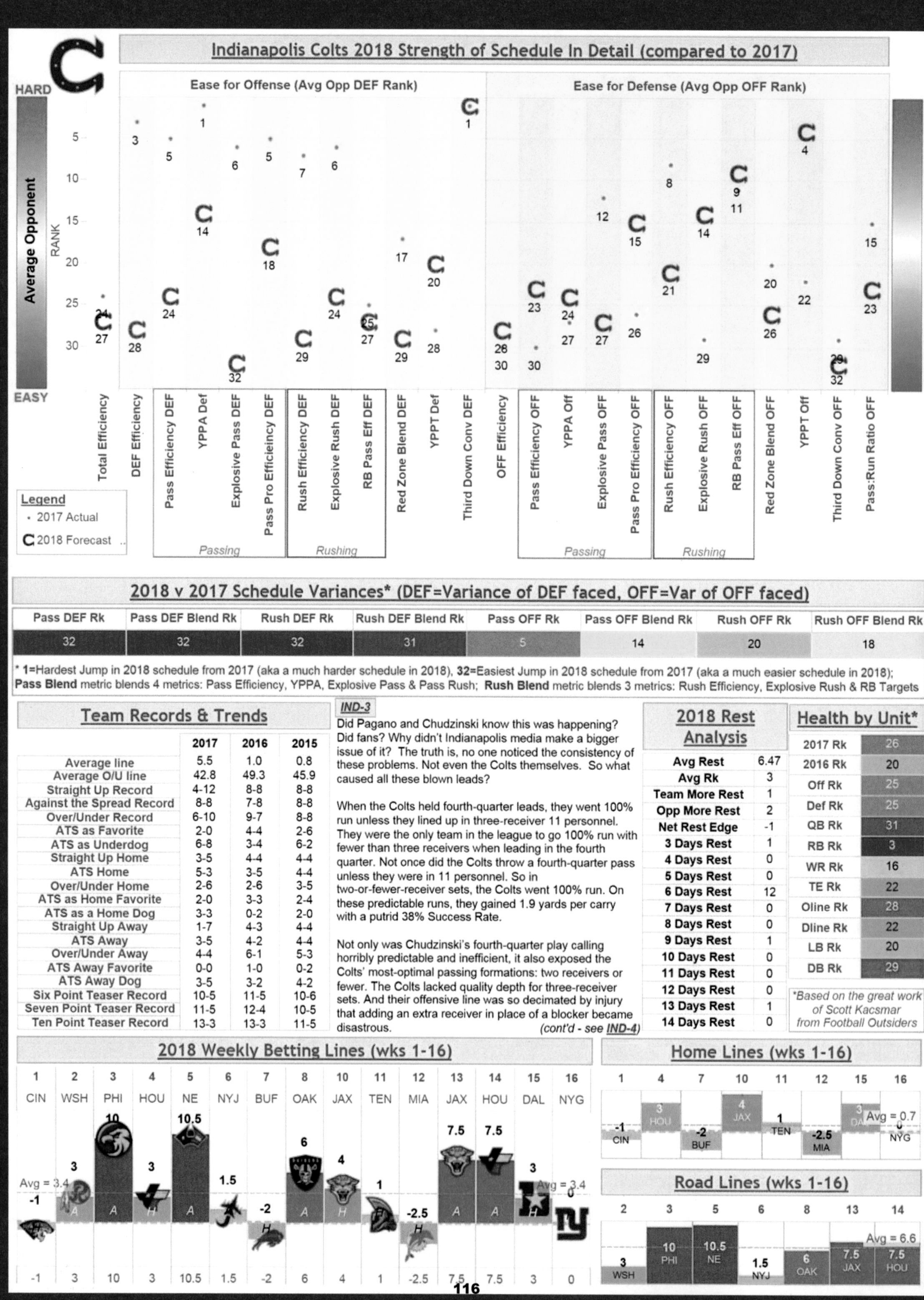

2018 v 2017 Schedule Variances* (DEF=Variance of DEF faced, OFF=Var of OFF faced)

Pass DEF Rk	Pass DEF Blend Rk	Rush DEF Rk	Rush DEF Blend Rk	Pass OFF Rk	Pass OFF Blend Rk	Rush OFF Rk	Rush OFF Blend Rk
32	32	32	31	5	14	20	18

* **1**=Hardest Jump in 2018 schedule from 2017 (aka a much harder schedule in 2018), **32**=Easiest Jump in 2018 schedule from 2017 (aka a much easier schedule in 2018); **Pass Blend** metric blends 4 metrics: Pass Efficiency, YPPA, Explosive Pass & Pass Rush; **Rush Blend** metric blends 3 metrics: Rush Efficiency, Explosive Rush & RB Targets

Team Records & Trends

	2017	2016	2015
Average line	5.5	1.0	0.8
Average O/U line	42.8	49.3	45.9
Straight Up Record	4-12	8-8	8-8
Against the Spread Record	8-8	7-8	8-8
Over/Under Record	6-10	9-7	8-8
ATS as Favorite	2-0	4-4	2-6
ATS as Underdog	6-8	3-4	6-2
Straight Up Home	3-5	4-4	4-4
ATS Home	5-3	3-5	4-4
Over/Under Home	2-6	2-6	3-5
ATS as Home Favorite	2-0	3-3	2-4
ATS as a Home Dog	3-3	0-2	2-0
Straight Up Away	1-7	4-3	4-4
ATS Away	3-5	4-2	4-4
Over/Under Away	4-4	6-1	5-3
ATS Away Favorite	0-0	1-0	0-2
ATS Away Dog	3-5	3-2	4-2
Six Point Teaser Record	10-5	11-5	10-6
Seven Point Teaser Record	11-5	12-4	10-5
Ten Point Teaser Record	13-3	13-3	11-5

IND-3

Did Pagano and Chudzinski know this was happening? Did fans? Why didn't Indianapolis media make a bigger issue of it? The truth is, no one noticed the consistency of these problems. Not even the Colts themselves. So what caused all these blown leads?

When the Colts held fourth-quarter leads, they went 100% run unless they lined up in three-receiver 11 personnel. They were the only team in the league to go 100% run with fewer than three receivers when leading in the fourth quarter. Not once did the Colts throw a fourth-quarter pass unless they were in 11 personnel. So in two-or-fewer-receiver sets, the Colts went 100% run. On these predictable runs, they gained 1.9 yards per carry with a putrid 38% Success Rate.

Not only was Chudzinski's fourth-quarter play calling horribly predictable and inefficient, it also exposed the Colts' most-optimal passing formations: two receivers or fewer. The Colts lacked quality depth for three-receiver sets. And their offensive line was so decimated by injury that adding an extra receiver in place of a blocker became disastrous. *(cont'd - see **IND-4**)*

2018 Rest Analysis

Avg Rest	6.47
Avg Rk	3
Team More Rest	1
Opp More Rest	2
Net Rest Edge	-1
3 Days Rest	1
4 Days Rest	0
5 Days Rest	0
6 Days Rest	12
7 Days Rest	0
8 Days Rest	0
9 Days Rest	1
10 Days Rest	0
11 Days Rest	0
12 Days Rest	0
13 Days Rest	1
14 Days Rest	0

Health by Unit*

2017 Rk	26
2016 Rk	20
Off Rk	25
Def Rk	25
QB Rk	31
RB Rk	3
WR Rk	16
TE Rk	22
Oline Rk	28
Dline Rk	22
LB Rk	20
DB Rk	29

**Based on the great work of Scott Kacsmar from Football Outsiders*

2018 Weekly Betting Lines (wks 1-16)

1	2	3	4	5	6	7	8	10	11	12	13	14	15	16
CIN	WSH	PHI	HOU	NE	NYJ	BUF	OAK	JAX	TEN	MIA	JAX	HOU	DAL	NYG
-1	3	10	3	10.5	1.5	-2	6	4	1	-2.5	7.5	7.5	3	0
	A	A	H	A		H	A	H		H	A	A	H	

Home Lines (wks 1-16)

1	4	7	10	11	12	15	16
CIN	HOU	BUF	JAX	TEN	MIA	DAL	NYG
-1	3	-2	4	1	-2.5	3	0

Road Lines (wks 1-16)

2	3	5	6	8	13	14
WSH	PHI	NE	NYJ	OAK	JAX	HOU
3	10	10.5	1.5	6	7.5	7.5

Indianapolis Colts 2017 Play Analysis

2017 Play Tendencies

All Pass %	54%
All Pass Rk	27
All Rush %	46%
All Rush Rk	6
1 Score Pass %	52%
1 Score Pass Rk	29
2016 1 Score Pass %	61%
2016 1 Score Pass Rk	9
2017 Pass Increase %	-9%
Pass Increase Rk	31
1 Score Rush %	48%
1 Score Rush Rk	4
Up Pass %	48%
Up Pass Rk	19
Up Rush %	52%
Up Rush Rk	14
Down Pass %	59%
Down Pass Rk	31
Down Rush %	41%
Down Rush Rk	2

2017 Down & Distance Tendencies

Down	Distance	Total Plays	Pass Rate	Run Rate	Play Success %
1	Short (1-3)	3	33%	67%	33%
	Med (4-7)	9	44%	56%	22%
	Long (8-10)	297	41%	59%	44%
	XL (11+)	9	67%	33%	44%
2	Short (1-3)	34	12%	88%	68%
	Med (4-7)	84	52%	48%	46%
	Long (8-10)	86	62%	38%	36%
	XL (11+)	47	74%	26%	21%
3	Short (1-3)	43	42%	58%	70%
	Med (4-7)	63	81%	19%	46%
	Long (8-10)	30	87%	13%	20%
	XL (11+)	32	75%	25%	16%
4	Short (1-3)	3	33%	67%	67%
	Med (4-7)	1	100%	0%	0%

Shotgun %:

Under Center	Shotgun
45%	55%
37%	*63%*

37% AVG 63%

Run Rate:

Under Center	Shotgun
77%	19%

68% AVG 23%

Pass Rate:

Under Center	Shotgun
23%	81%

32% AVG 77%

Short Yardage Intelligence:

2nd and Short Run

Run Freq	Run Rk	NFL Run Freq Avg	Run 1D Rate	Run NFL 1D Avg
88%	2	67%	62%	69%

2nd and Short Pass

Pass Freq	Pass Rk	NFL Pass Freq Avg	Pass 1D Rate	Pass NFL 1D Avg
13%	31	33%	0%	53%

Most Frequent Play

Down	Distance	Play Type	Player	Total Plays	Play Success %
1	Med (4-7)	RUSH	Frank Gore	2	50%
			Marlon Mack	2	0%
	Long (8-10)	RUSH	Frank Gore	114	46%
	XL (11+)	PASS	Marlon Mack	3	33%
2	Short (1-3)	RUSH	Frank Gore	19	68%
	Med (4-7)	RUSH	Frank Gore	25	56%
	Long (8-10)	RUSH	Frank Gore	21	14%
	XL (11+)	PASS	Jack Doyle	8	50%
3	Short (1-3)	RUSH	Frank Gore	11	91%
	Med (4-7)	PASS	Ty Hilton	21	43%
	Long (8-10)	PASS	Ty Hilton	7	14%
	XL (11+)	RUSH	Jacoby Brissett	6	0%

Most Successful Play*

Down	Distance	Play Type	Player	Total Plays	Play Success %
1	Long (8-10)	PASS	Brandon Williams	5	80%
2	Short (1-3)	RUSH	Marlon Mack	10	70%
	Med (4-7)	PASS	Donte Moncrief	7	57%
	Long (8-10)	PASS	Jack Doyle	12	75%
	XL (11+)	PASS	Jack Doyle	8	50%
3	Short (1-3)	RUSH	Robert Turbin	7	100%
	Med (4-7)	PASS	Jack Doyle	6	83%
	Long (8-10)	PASS	Donte Moncrief	5	40%
	XL (11+)	RUSH	Jacoby Brissett	6	0%

**Minimum 5 plays to qualify*

2017 Snap Rates

Wk	Opp	Score	Ty Hilton	Jack Doyle	Donte Moncrief	Kamar Aiken	Frank Gore	Chester Rogers	Marlon Mack	Brandon Williams	Robert Turbin
1	LA	L 46-9	44 (88%)	46 (92%)	45 (90%)	26 (52%)	19 (38%)		17 (34%)	19 (38%)	14 (28%)
2	ARI	L 16-13	64 (90%)	70 (99%)	53 (75%)	63 (89%)	32 (45%)		11 (15%)	13 (18%)	28 (39%)
3	CLE	W 31-28	64 (97%)	66 (100%)	57 (86%)	5 (8%)	41 (62%)			16 (24%)	21 (32%)
4	SEA	L 46-18	51 (85%)	48 (80%)	43 (72%)	51 (85%)	35 (58%)			17 (28%)	19 (32%)
5	SF	W 26-23	67 (88%)		53 (70%)	67 (88%)	39 (51%)		17 (22%)	50 (66%)	21 (28%)
6	TEN	L 36-22	54 (93%)	58 (100%)	43 (74%)	51 (88%)	23 (40%)	6 (10%)	14 (24%)	13 (22%)	21 (36%)
7	JAC	L 27-0	57 (85%)	54 (81%)	52 (78%)	43 (64%)	22 (33%)	34 (51%)	32 (48%)	10 (15%)	
8	CIN	L 24-23	67 (91%)	71 (96%)	56 (76%)	47 (64%)	36 (49%)	26 (35%)	39 (53%)	21 (28%)	
9	HOU	W 20-14	60 (91%)	62 (94%)	50 (76%)	46 (70%)	40 (61%)	15 (23%)	27 (41%)	21 (32%)	
10	PIT	L 20-17	49 (83%)	58 (98%)	51 (86%)		34 (58%)	42 (71%)	25 (42%)	20 (34%)	
12	TEN	L 20-16	62 (98%)	61 (97%)	60 (95%)	7 (11%)	41 (65%)	40 (63%)	20 (32%)	24 (38%)	
13	JAC	L 30-10	67 (97%)	64 (93%)	50 (72%)	21 (30%)	22 (32%)	54 (78%)	30 (43%)	17 (25%)	
14	BUF	L 13-7	48 (68%)	71 (100%)		42 (59%)	54 (76%)	66 (93%)	17 (24%)	45 (63%)	
15	DEN	L 25-13	51 (94%)	54 (100%)		34 (63%)	28 (52%)	53 (98%)	24 (44%)	8 (15%)	
16	BAL	L 23-16	62 (100%)	62 (100%)		53 (85%)	46 (74%)	58 (94%)	15 (24%)		
17	HOU	W 22-13	58 (91%)	64 (100%)		32 (50%)	43 (67%)	51 (80%)	22 (34%)		
	Grand Total		925 (90%)	909 (95%)	613 (79%)	588 (60%)	555 (54%)	445 (63%)	310 (34%)	294 (32%)	124 (32%)

Personnel Groupings

Personnel	Team %	NFL Avg	Succ. %
1-1 [3WR]	66%	59%	41%
1-2 [2WR]	28%	19%	39%
1-3 [1WR]	4%	5%	40%

Grouping Tendencies

Personnel	Pass Rate	Pass Succ. %	Run Succ. %
1-1 [3WR]	65%	38%	46%
1-2 [2WR]	36%	43%	37%
1-3 [1WR]	14%	33%	42%

Red Zone Targets (min 3)

Receiver	All	Inside 5	6-10	11-20
Jack Doyle	10	2	4	4
Ty Hilton	10	2	1	7
Donte Moncrief	7	2	2	3
Kamar Aiken	4	1		3
Frank Gore	3			3
Chester Rogers	2			2
Ross Travis	1			1

Red Zone Rushes (min 3)

Rusher	All	Inside 5	6-10	11-20
Frank Gore	24	2	3	19
Marlon Mack	18	4	3	11
Jacoby Brissett	15	3	5	7
Robert Turbin	6	4		2

Early Down Target Rate

	RB	TE	WR
	21%	35%	45%
NFL AVG	*23%*	*21%*	*56%*

Overall Target Success %

RB	TE	WR
43%	52%	42%
#18	#9	#30

Indianapolis Colts 2017 Passing Recap & 2018 Outlook

The 2017 Colts offense was exceedingly inefficient, much of it due to play calling. Jacoby Brissett ranked 14th among 43 qualified quarterbacks in deep passer rating. But specifically on early-down deep attempts, Brissett's 107 rating ranked ninth best in the league. Chudzinski's propensity for taking deep shots from under-center looks does produce superior efficiency across the league, but it also forces quarterbacks to take more time in the pocket for deep routes to develop. And that was difficult to accomplish with offensive line play as bad as Brissett's. League wide, nearly 75% of deep passes come with quarterbacks in the shotgun. Brissett produced the NFL's fourth-best passer rating on early-down deep passes from shotgun. But Brissett made nearly 50% of his early-down deep throws from under center and managed a 95 rating on those attempts with a far-worse 36% Success Rate. Reich-quarterbacked Carson Wentz delivered 79% of his deep attempts from shotgun. Brissett also needs to improve at pushing throws past the sticks on third down. On average, his third-down passes fell short of the sticks by 2.4 yards. In Philly, well-coached Wentz averaged 1.3 yards past the sticks on third-down throws, second best in the league.

Jacoby Brissett Rating All Downs

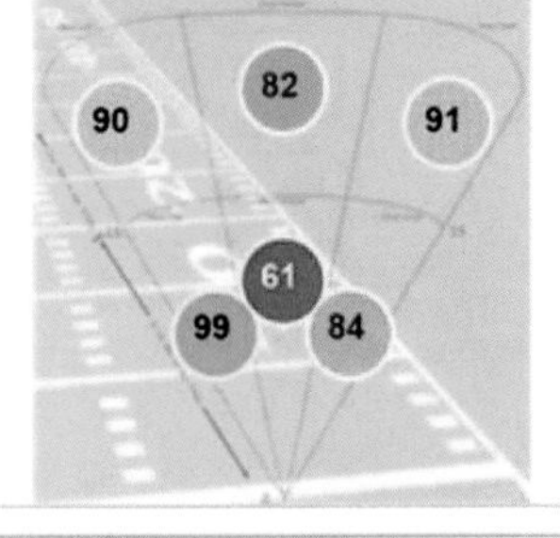

Jacoby Brissett Rating Early Downs

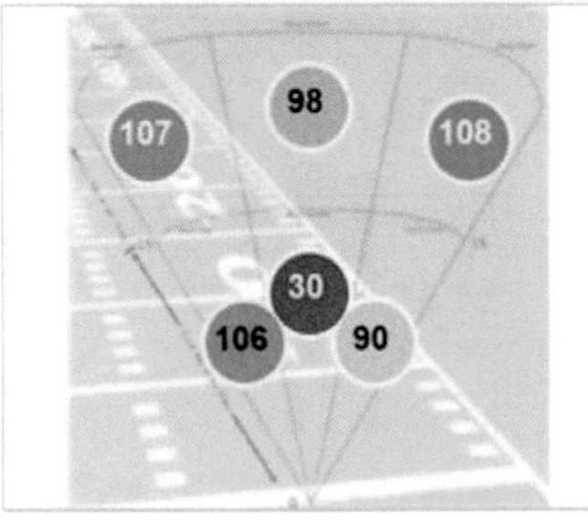

2017 Standard Passing Table

QB	Comp	Att	Comp %	Yds	YPA	TDs	INT	Sacks	Rating	Rk
Jacoby Brissett	276	469	59%	3,098	6.6	13	7	51	82	32
NFL Avg			62%		7.0				87.5	

2017 Advanced Passing Table

QB	Success %	EDSR Passing Success %	20+ Yd Pass Gains	20+ Yd Pass %	30+ Yd Pass Gains	30+ Yd Pass %	Avg. Air Yds per Comp	Avg. YAC per Comp	20+ Air Yd Comp	20+ Air Yd %
Jacoby Brissett	40%	42%	32	6.8%	14	3.0%	5.6	5.6	13	5%
NFL Avg	44%	48%	27.7	8.8%	10.3	3.3%	6.0	4.7	11.7	6%

Interception Rates by Down

Yards to Go	1	2	3	4	Total
1 & 2	0.0%	33.3%	0.0%	0.0%	4.0%
3, 4, 5	0.0%	0.0%	3.2%	0.0%	1.7%
6 - 9	25.0%	1.3%	1.6%	0.0%	2.1%
10 - 14	1.3%	0.0%	0.0%	0.0%	0.8%
15+	0.0%	0.0%	0.0%		0.0%
Total	1.8%	1.1%	1.3%	0.0%	1.3%

3rd Down Passing - Short of Sticks Analysis

QB	Avg. Yds to Go	Avg. YIA (of Comp)	Avg Yds Short	Short of Sticks Rate	Short Rk
Jacoby Brissett	7.8	5.5	-2.4	57%	34
NFL Avg	7.8	6.7	-1.1	60%	

Air Yds vs YAC

	Air Yds %	YAC %	Rk
Jacoby Brissett	48%	52%	42
NFL Avg	58%	42%	

2017 Receiving Recap & 2018 Outlook

Jack Doyle was one of 2017's most underrated tight ends. He lacked astronomical touchdown upside because the Colts didn't score many points and faced a brutal schedule of defenses, but Doyle's 80 receptions and 108 targets were near the top of the league. Reich's 2017 Eagles used Zach Ertz in so many ways similar to how Reich can use Doyle and I see him exceeding his fantasy Average Draft Position. Because of Reich and an improved offensive line, I am cautiously optimistic Doyle and T.Y. Hilton can handle this passing-game's heavy lifting. And I am intrigued by RBs Marlon Mack, Nyheim Hines, and Jordan Wilkins' receiving ability.

Player *Min 50 Targets*	Targets	Comp %	YPA	Rating	TOARS	Success %	Success Rk	Missed YPA Rk	YAS % Rk	TDs
Jack Doyle	108	74%	6.4	95	4.9	57%	15	7	125	4
Ty Hilton	109	52%	8.9	83	4.6	44%	96	99	20	4

Directional Passer Rating Delivered

Receiver	Short Left	Short Middle	Short Right	Deep Left	Deep Middle	Deep Right	Player Total
Ty Hilton	47	138	91	45	117	96	83
Jack Doyle	129	79	96	40	40	40	95
Donte Moncrief	102	40	49	149	40	40	97
Kamar Aiken	23	20	40	40	40	49	24
Frank Gore	130	81	87				101
Chester Rogers	89	0	92	90	119	135	84
Marlon Mack	126	40	91				94
Brandon Williams	119	87	90	40	119		95
Robert Turbin	83	88	83				88
Josh Ferguson	89					40	81
Team Total	91	67	87	96	82	91	85

2017 Rushing Recap & 2017 Outlook

Less rushing predictably would work wonders. Last year's Colts' most-frequent first-down play was a Frank Gore run, which was successful just 46% of the time. Their favorite second-down plays were also runs by Gore. I anticipate far more diversity from the 2018 Colts. Both Gore and Marlon Mack delivered sub-3.9 yards per carry on early-down runs. Gore received 24 red-zone carries. Robert Turbin was second in line for scoring-position work with six red-zone runs.

Player *Min 50 Rushes*	Rushes	YPC	Success %	Success Rk	Missed YPA Rk	YTS % Rk	YAS % Rk	Early Down Success %	Early Down Success Rk	TDs
Frank Gore	261	3.7	44%	35	31	26	64	42%	46	3
Marlon Mack	93	3.8	41%	55	70	56	2	39%	61	3

Yards per Carry by Direction

	LT	LG	C	RG	RT	
4.1	3.2	3.2	3.4	4.0	3.2	6.5

Directional Run Frequency

	LT	LG	C	RG	RT	
5%	13%	11%	39%	13%	11%	7%

IND-4

In fourth quarters on the season, the Colts' passing game delivered a 52% Success Rate, 91 rating, and 7.8 yards per attempt in formations of two receivers or fewer. In three-plus-receiver sets, the Colts' Success Rate plummeted to 33% with a 46 passer rating and 6.9 YPA.

Chudzinski intentionally ran the ball incredibly predictably in fourth quarters, gaining 1.9 yards per carry with a 38% Success Rate. And Chudzinski intentionally passed the ball only out of his offense's worst formations (three-plus receivers) for a 33% fourth-quarter Success Rate and 46 rating.

Despite an incredibly adverse environment, Brissett kept the Colts competitive enough to earn fourth-quarter leads in 60% of his 15 starts. Brissett's only games without fourth-quarter leads came against playoff-bound Jacksonville and Buffalo, as well as top-ten defensive teams Baltimore, Denver, and Seattle. But these fourth-quarter leads were lost due to horrifically predictable play calling. (In 2017, NFL teams that held fourth-quarter leads won 88% of games.)

Any yearly team outlook must start with where we left off in 2017: The impact of coaching. And the Colts made substantial offseason upgrades. Replacing Pagano is ex-Eagles OC Frank Reich, who understood Philadelphia's success with analytics and has vowed to bring strategies that challenge conventional NFL wisdom to Indianapolis.

(cont'd - see IND-5)

Evan Silva's Fantasy Corner

T.Y. Hilton showed his floor last year on WR25 (PPR) and WR24 (non-PPR) fantasy finishes with Jacoby Brissett at quarterback, failing to eclipse 1,000 yards after leading the NFL in receiving yards (1,448) with Andrew Luck in 2016. Even in a down season, Hilton's Game Speed was elite in Josh Hermsmeyer's Next Gen Stats research. Hilton's size (5'10/183) prevents him from being discussed among the league's elite receivers, but Hilton has shown an ability to win at all areas of the field. Hilton should remain a viable-if-unsteady WR2/3 if Brissett is the Colts' starter. T.Y. will offer WR1 upside if Luck gets right. In his career, Hilton averages 15.1 fantasy points per game when Luck plays versus 11.3 points when Luck doesn't. Another positive is Indy's bereft receiver corps besides him, setting up Hilton for heavy volume.

Division History: Season Wins & 2018 Projection

2014 Wins | 2015 Wins | 2016 Wins | 2017 Wins | Forecast 2018 Wins

Rank of 2018 Defensive Pass Efficiency Faced by Week

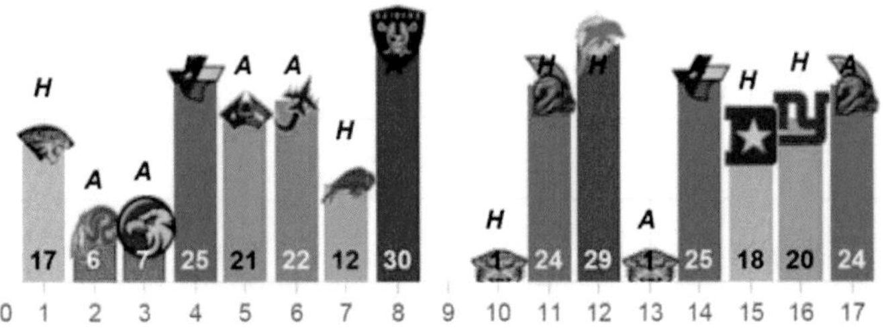

Rank of 2018 Defensive Rush Efficiency Faced by Week

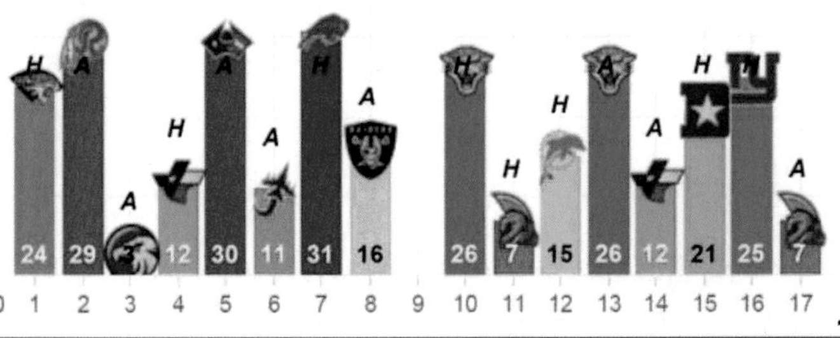

2017 Situational Usage by Player & Position

Usage Rate by Score

		Being Blown Out (14+)	Down Big (9-13)	One Score	Large Lead (9-13)	Blowout Lead (14+)	Grand Total
RUSH	Frank Gore	12%	25%	33%	32%	48%	30%
	Marlon Mack	15%	12%	11%	5%		11%
	Chester Rogers		2%	0%			0%
	Robert Turbin	2%		3%	9%	7%	3%
	Josh Ferguson	1%					0%
	Matt Jones	3%				4%	1%
	Total	32%	39%	47%	45%	59%	45%
PASS	Frank Gore	2%	2%	5%	5%	4%	4%
	Marlon Mack	7%	3%	3%	5%		4%
	Ty Hilton	11%	15%	13%	9%	7%	13%
	Jack Doyle	12%	17%	12%	14%	7%	13%
	Donte Moncrief	9%	8%	4%	14%	7%	5%
	Kamar Aiken	7%	3%	5%			5%
	Chester Rogers	5%	10%	4%	5%		4%
	Robert Turbin	1%		1%		7%	1%
	Brandon Williams	3%		2%	5%		2%
	Darrell Daniels	4%		1%		4%	2%
	Josh Ferguson	3%		0%			0%
	Ross Travis		2%	1%			1%
	Quan Bray	3%				4%	0%
	K.J. Brent			0%			0%
	Matt Hazel	1%					0%
	Total	68%	61%	53%	55%	41%	55%

Positional Target Distribution vs NFL Average

		NFL Wide				Team Only			
		Left	Middle	Right	**Total**	Left	Middle	Right	**Total**
Deep	WR	964	500	961	**2,425**	22	9	26	**57**
	TE	190	147	187	**524**	2	3	1	**6**
	RB	39	9	41	**89**			1	**1**
	All	**1,193**	**656**	**1,189**	**3,038**	**24**	**12**	**28**	**64**
Short	WR	2,784	1,631	2,728	**7,143**	78	40	62	**180**
	TE	839	801	1,113	**2,753**	24	38	57	**119**
	RB	1,289	806	1,259	**3,354**	32	17	36	**85**
	All	**4,912**	**3,238**	**5,100**	**13,250**	**134**	**95**	**155**	**384**
Total		**6,105**	**3,894**	**6,289**	**16,288**	**158**	**107**	**183**	**448**

Positional Success Rates vs NFL Average

		NFL Wide				Team Only			
		Left	Middle	Right	**Total**	Left	Middle	Right	**Total**
Deep	WR	37%	45%	38%	**39%**	32%	44%	42%	**39%**
	TE	38%	53%	45%	**45%**	0%	33%	0%	**17%**
	RB	36%	56%	39%	**39%**			0%	**0%**
	All	**37%**	**47%**	**39%**	**40%**	**29%**	**42%**	**39%**	**36%**
Short	WR	52%	58%	50%	**53%**	50%	33%	40%	**43%**
	TE	50%	56%	49%	**51%**	63%	55%	58%	**58%**
	RB	44%	52%	43%	**45%**	56%	24%	42%	**44%**
	All	**49%**	**56%**	**48%**	**50%**	**54%**	**40%**	**47%**	**48%**
Total		**47%**	**55%**	**46%**	**49%**	**50%**	**40%**	**46%**	**46%**

Successful Play Rate
0% [color scale] 100%

Indianapolis Colts - Success by Personnel Grouping & Play Type

Play Type	1-1 [3WR]	1-2 [2WR]	2-1 [2WR]	1-3 [1WR]	0-1 [4WR]	2-0 [3WR]	0-2 [3WR]	Grand Total
PASS	38% (424, 78%)	43% (100, 18%)	75% (4, 1%)	33% (6, 1%)		100% (1, 0%)	14% (7, 1%)	39% (542, 100%)
RUSH	46% (232, 51%)	37% (181, 40%)	100% (1, 0%)	42% (36, 8%)	100% (1, 0%)		100% (1, 0%)	42% (452, 100%)
TOTAL	41% (656, 66%)	39% (281, 28%)	80% (5, 1%)	40% (42, 4%)	100% (1, 0%)	100% (1, 0%)	25% (8, 1%)	41% (994, 100%)

Format Line 1: Success Rate Line 2: Total # of Plays, % of All Plays (by type)

IND-5 Reich and OC Nick Sirianni plan to run an "aggressive, up-tempo offense." New DC Matt Eberlus was last linebackers coach in Dallas, where he oversaw incredible Cowboys LB Sean Lee.

It's hard to confidently accept the Colts' promise Luck will be ready for the season. But we can have increased confidence in fallback option Brissett with a learning year under his belt and a full offseason of starter's reps under improved coaching. The Colts shored up their interior offensive line by using first- and second-round picks on guards Quenton Nelson (Notre Dame) and Braden Smith (Auburn).

Although their skill-position players don't move the needle beyond Luck and T.Y. Hilton, the best part about Indy's offense is its multiplicity. Reich's Eagles ran 12- and 13-tight end heavy personnel well above league average. Last year's Colts used Jack Doyle on 95% of snaps, by far most on the team. And I expect Doyle to remain a major factor, even with Eric Ebron aboard for two-tight end sets. Doyle led last year's Colts in red-zone targets, and his 59% Success Rate on targets within 15 yards of the line of scrimmage ranked third among tight ends.

Only Zach Ertz was targeted more often than Doyle on passes within 15 yards of the line. Reich, of course, was Ertz's OC. (Note that Ebron's Success Rate on routes inside 15 yards was just 41% with Matthew Stafford last year.)

The 2018 Colts also benefit from an easier schedule. Last year, Indy faced the league's third-toughest slate of opposing defenses. This year, they face one of the easiest. The Colts also draw the league's best Schedule Variance from both pass and run defenses faced when comparing 2017 to 2018's forecast. All that said, linemakers are decidedly down on the Colts.

Indianapolis is favored in just 3-of-16 games, and none of those is even by the equivalent of a three-point home-field advantage. Assuming home field is worth three points (it's actually slightly less), the Colts are viewed as superior to just 1-of-16 opponents: the Jets. I'm quite bullish on Indianapolis to exceed its Vegas projections, and put my money where my mouth is.

And I never even discussed the Colts' upside if Luck returns at peak performance. All my current projections pessimistically assume Brissett will be under center.

Receiving Success by Personnel Grouping

Position	Player	1-1 [3WR]	1-2 [2WR]	2-1 [2WR]	1-3 [1WR]	2-0 [3WR]	0-2 [3WR]	Total
RB	Frank Gore	41% 7.2 108.2 (29)	38% 3.6 69.3 (8)			100% 7.0 95.8 (1)		42% 6.4 101.3 (38)
	Marlon Mack	36% 6.1 87.1 (28)	100% 11.5 114.6 (4)	100% 8.0 100.0 (1)				45% 6.8 93.6 (33)
TE	Jack Doyle	54% 6.4 91.8 (87)	75% 7.7 119.5 (16)		50% 3.5 58.3 (2)		33% 2.3 42.4 (3)	56% 6.4 95.1 (108)
WR	Ty Hilton	40% 8.5 79.2 (82)	54% 10.0 95.7 (24)	100% 15.0 118.8 (2)			0% 0.0 39.6 (1)	44% 8.9 83.4 (109)
	Donte Moncrief	56% 8.3 103.8 (41)	20% 10.0 68.8 (5)				0% 0.0 39.6 (1)	51% 8.3 97.0 (47)
	Kamar Aiken	20% 2.7 20.8 (40)	50% 6.8 71.9 (4)					23% 3.0 24.1 (44)

Format Line 1: Success Rate Line 2: YPA Line 3: Passer Rating Line 4: Total # of Plays

Successful Play Rate
0% [color scale] 100%

Rushing Success by Personnel Grouping

Position	Player	1-1 [3WR]	1-2 [2WR]	2-1 [2WR]	1-3 [1WR]	0-1 [4WR]	0-2 [3WR]	Total
QB	Jacoby Brissett	34% 4.9 (44)	27% 2.9 (11)		14% 0.1 (7)	100% 5.0 (1)	100% 7.0 (1)	33% 4.1 (64)
RB	Frank Gore	50% 4.0 (121)	37% 3.2 (122)	100% 3.0 (1)	59% 4.5 (17)			44% 3.7 (261)
	Marlon Mack	49% 4.1 (49)	35% 4.0 (40)		0% -1.8 (4)			41% 3.8 (93)

Format Line 1: Success Rate Line 2: YPC Line 3: Total # of Plays

Jacksonville Jaguars

2018 Coaches

Head Coach:
Doug Marrone (2nd yr)
Offensive Coordinator:
Nathaniel Hackett (3rd yr)
Defensive Coordinator:
Todd Wash (3rd yr)

2018 Forecast

Wins	Div Rank
9	#2

Past Records

2017: 10-6
2016: 3-13
2015: 5-11

EASY HARD

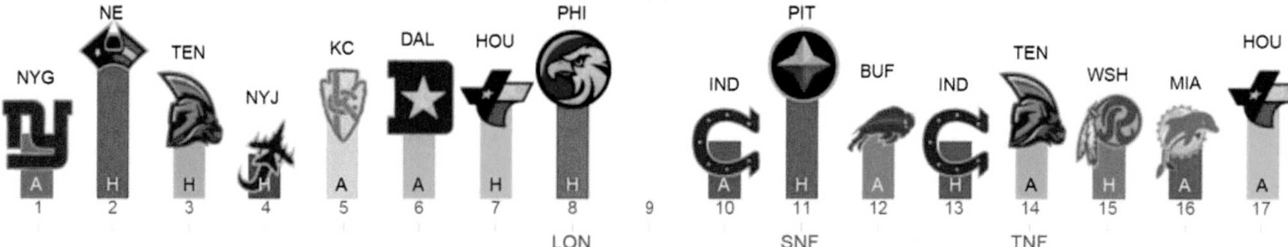

Key Players Lost

TXN	Player (POS)
Cut	Crockett, Montay WR
	Harper, Jarrod S
	Hurns, Allen WR
	Ivory, Chris RB
	Lewis, Marcedes TE
	Mathers, I'Tavius RB
	Nortman, Brad P
	Pinkard, Larry WR
	Strong, Jaelen WR
Declared Free Agent	Benn, Arrelious WR
	Colvin, Aaron CB
	Gaffney, Tyler RB
	Henne, Chad QB
	Lee, Marqise WR
	McCray, Lerentee LB
	Omameh, Patrick G
	Overton, Matt LB
	Rivera, Mychal TE
	Robinson II, Allen WR
Retired	Posluszny, Paul LB

Average Line	# Games Favored	# Games Underdog
-2.8	9	5

2018 Jacksonville Jaguars Overview

Bad NFL teams may look at the 2017 Jaguars and think, "that could be us. All we need is to draft a great running back." Jacksonville went nine full seasons without a winning record. They hadn't won more than five games since 2010. In 2017, the Jags drafted Leonard Fournette No. 4 overall and went to the AFC Championship game. And they led that game by ten points over the Patriots with ten minutes left.

You know "football guys" think this way. Was it a combination of "taking pressure off" Blake Bortles and better run efficiency? Was it an improved defense combined with more-efficient rushing? How do you determine the driver? Fournette, Bortles, the defense, or something else?

The Jaguars' passing efficiency improved from 22nd in 2016 to 15th last year. Bortles did face a much-easer schedule of pass defenses. His Success Rate improved by 2%, and his Early-Down Success Rate grew by 3%. And just like in 2016, 50% of Bortles' yards came from Air Yards, and the other 50% from yards after the catch. Bortles made slight enhancements in TD and INT rate. His deep passer rating was better but still needs work.

These are all steps in the right direction, but none indicate Bortles was the primary reason for Jacksonville's turnaround.

The 2017 Jaguars had terrible injury luck at wide receiver. Their receiver corps was third-most injured in the NFL. No. 1 wideout Allen Robinson tore his ACL three snaps into Week 1. Dynamic fourth-round pick Dede Westbrook underwent core muscle surgery in September and didn't see the field until Week 11. Allen Hurns injured his ankle and missed Weeks 11-16. Marqise Lee missed the final three weeks of the regular season. Undrafted rookie Keelan Cole led the receiver corps in snaps.

Gone are Robinson, Hurns, and TE Marcedes Lewis. Jacksonville added inconsistent Donte Moncrief, who also battled injuries as a Colt. Lee, Westbrook, and Cole return healthy, and LSU deep threat D.J. Chark arrived in the second round of the draft.

(cont'd - see JAC2)

Key Free Agents/ Trades Added

Carey, Don S
Davis, Cody S
Hayden, DJ CB
McDougle, Dexter CB
Moncrief, Donte WR
Norwell, Andrew G
Paul, Niles TE
Seferian-Jenkins, Austin TE

Drafted Players

Rd	Pk	Player (College)
1	29	DT - Taven Bryan (Florida)
2	61	WR - DJ Chark (LSU)
3	93	S - Ronnie Harrison (Alabama)
4	129	OT - Will Richardson (NC State)
6	203	QB - Tanner Lee (Nebraska)
7	230	OLB - Leon Jacobs (Wisconsin)
	247	P - Logan Cooke (Mississippi State)

Regular Season Wins: Past & Current Proj

Lineup & Cap Hits

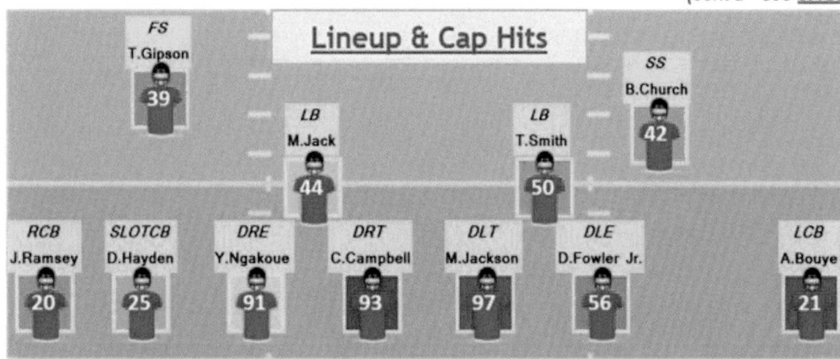

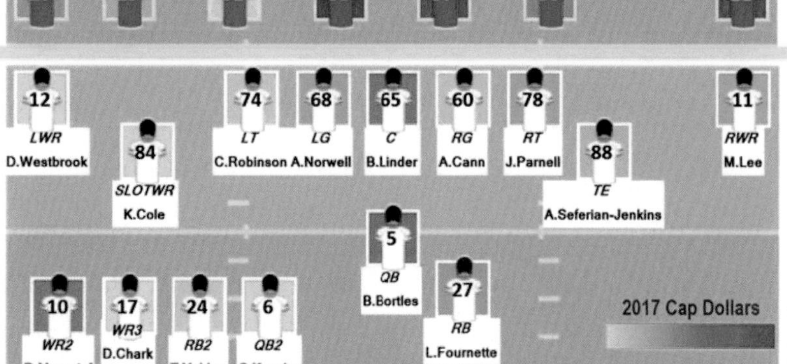

2018 Unit Spending

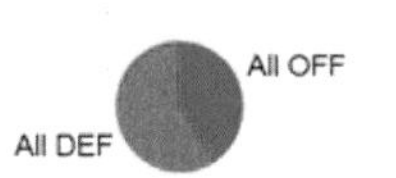

Positional Spending

	Rank	Total	2017 Rk
All OFF	27	$81.04M	26
QB	25	$11.27M	22
OL	26	$29.42M	19
RB	3	$12.00M	2
WR	20	$20.52M	22
TE	19	$7.82M	22
All DEF	1	$122.64M	5
DL	1	$60.19M	4
LB	27	$14.84M	24
CB	4	$29.22M	20
S	5	$18.39M	3

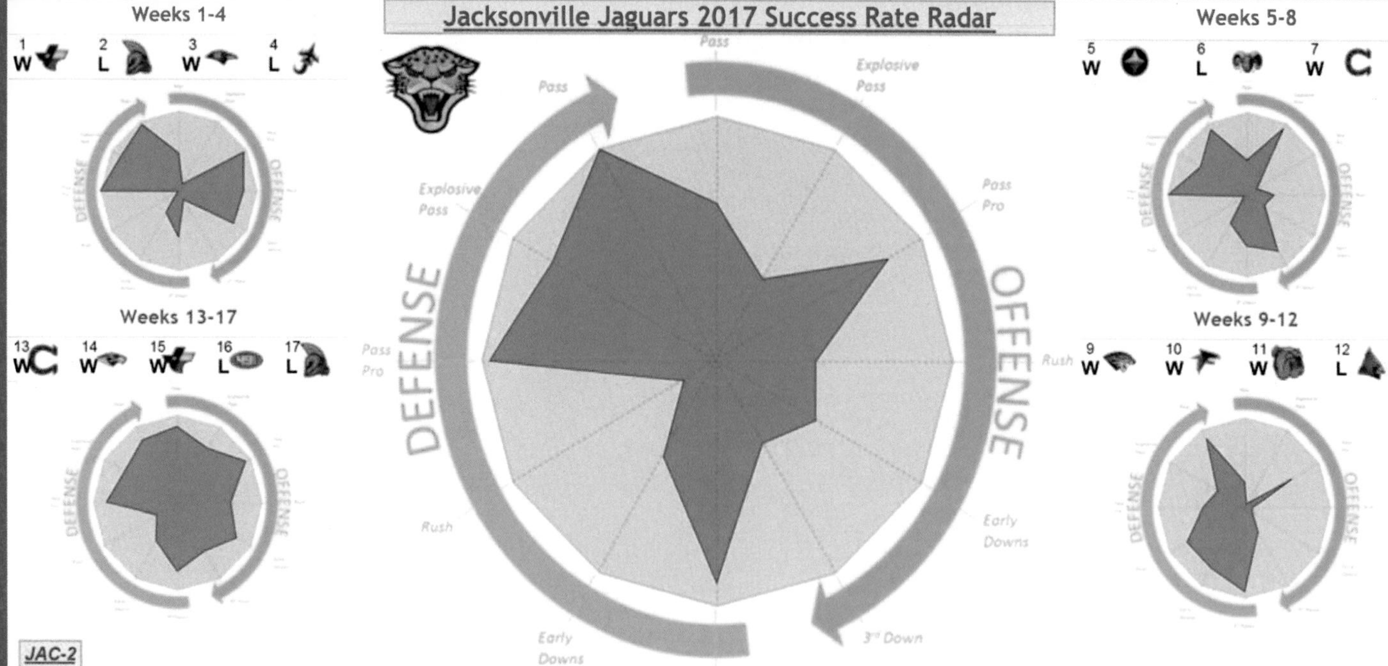

JAC-2

Teams that win the turnover margin win 80% of games. The 2016 Jaguars finished -16 in turnover margin. Last year's Jags were +10 in turnover margin. The difference was takeaways.Last year's Jags were +10 in turnover margin. The difference was takeaways. The 2017 Jaguars defense created 33 takeaways, versus 13 the year before. Their interceptions spiked from seven to 21. Last year's Jags recorded 14-of-21 interceptions in second halves of games, including ten when leading on the scoreboard.

The other big element to turnover margin is fumble luck. When a ball is stripped, recovery of the ball is a 50-50 proposition. An NFL football bounces in funny ways. And teams usually regress to the mean from bad fumble-luck years to good ones. The 2016 Jaguars had horrible fumble luck, recovering 39% of loose balls to rank dead last in the NFL. The 2017 Jags recovered 58% of fumbles, seventh best in the league. That 19% swing was highest in the league. Teams that win sack margin win 71% of games. The 2016 Jaguars were -1 in sack margin. Last year's Jags were +31. "Sacksonville" was real.

When the 2017 Jaguars won sack margin by +2, they went 8-1. They went 1-2 when losing the sack battle by -2 or worse.

And strength of schedule played a big role. Before last season, I projected Jacksonville to face the NFL's softest slate. They indeed wound up facing the easiest cumulative opponents. And when you face easy schedules, you get better game scripts, which mean more opportunities to run the ball. Whereas the pre-2017 Jaguars so often trailed by double digits in second halves of games, last year's team held onto fourth-quarter leads with an improved rushing attack.

Pull any team out of a hat. If you give them an average schedule and replay that season against the league's easiest slate, this random team will generate bigger second-half leads, more rushing attempts, fewer interceptions, and fewer sacks taken. Their defense will face more pass attempts and generate more interceptions and sacks.

(cont'd - see JAC-3)

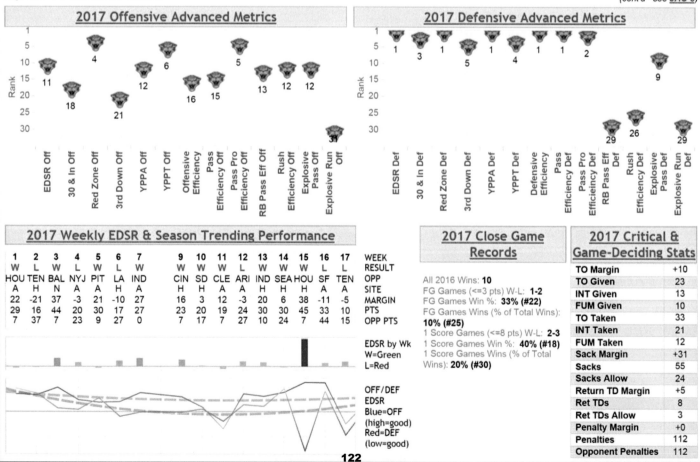

2017 Offensive Advanced Metrics

Metric	Rank
EDSR Off	11
30 & In Off	18
Red Zone Off	4
3rd Down Off	21
YPPA Off	12
YPPT Off	6
Offensive Efficiency	16
Pass Efficiency Off	15
Pass Pro Efficiency Off	5
RB Pass Eff Off	13
Rush Efficiency Off	12
Explosive Pass Off	12
Explosive Run Off	31

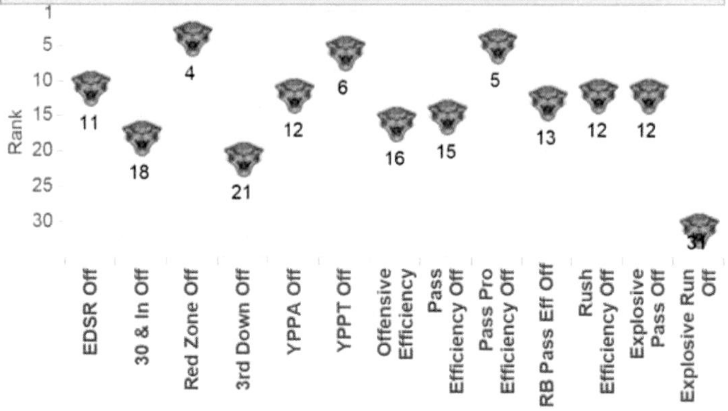

2017 Defensive Advanced Metrics

Metric	Rank
EDSR Def	1
30 & In Def	3
Red Zone Def	1
3rd Down Def	5
YPPA Def	1
YPPT Def	4
Defensive Efficiency	1
Pass Efficiency Def	1
Pass Pro Efficieincy Def	2
RB Pass Eff Def	29
Rush Efficiency Def	26
Explosive Pass Def	9
Explosive Run Def	29

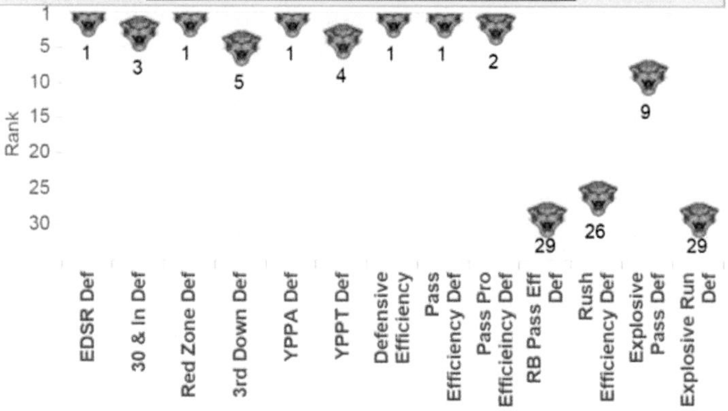

2017 Weekly EDSR & Season Trending Performance

WEEK	1	2	3	4	5	6	7	9	10	11	12	13	14	15	16	17
RESULT	W	L	W	L	W	L	W	W	W	W	L	W	W	W	L	L
OPP	HOU	TEN	BAL	NYJ	PIT	LA	IND	CIN	SD	CLE	ARI	IND	SEA	HOU	SF	TEN
SITE	A	H	N	A	A	H	A	H	H	A	A	H	H	H	A	A
MARGIN	22	-21	37	-3	21	-10	27	16	3	12	-3	20	6	38	-11	-5
PTS	29	16	44	20	30	17	27	23	20	19	24	30	30	45	33	10
OPP PTS	7	37	7	23	9	27	0	7	17	7	27	10	24	7	44	15

EDSR by Wk
W=Green
L=Red

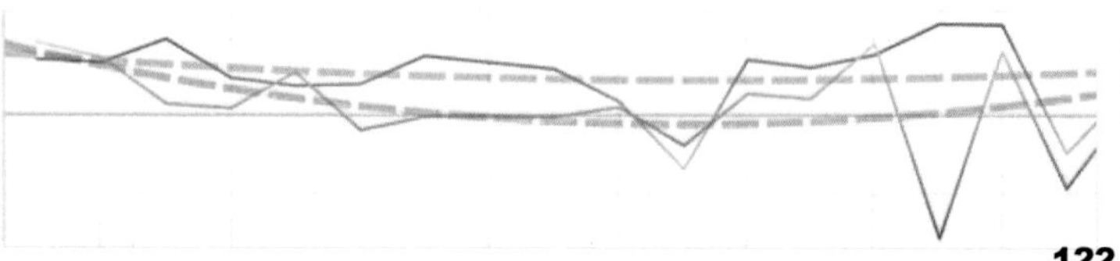

OFF/DEF
EDSR
Blue=OFF
(high=good)
Red=DEF
(low=good)

2017 Close Game Records

All 2016 Wins: **10**
FG Games (<=3 pts) W-L: **1-2**
FG Games Win %: **33% (#22)**
FG Games Wins (% of Total Wins): **10% (#25)**
1 Score Games (<=8 pts) W-L: **2-3**
1 Score Games Win %: **40% (#18)**
1 Score Games Wins (% of Total Wins): **20% (#30)**

2017 Critical & Game-Deciding Stats

TO Margin	+10
TO Given	23
INT Given	13
FUM Given	10
TO Taken	33
INT Taken	21
FUM Taken	12
Sack Margin	+31
Sacks	55
Sacks Allow	24
Return TD Margin	+5
Ret TDs	8
Ret TDs Allow	3
Penalty Margin	+0
Penalties	112
Opponent Penalties	112

Jacksonville Jaguars 2018 Strength of Schedule In Detail (compared to 2017)

Average Opponent RANK (HARD 1 – EASY 32)

Ease for Offense (Avg Opp DEF Rank) | Ease for Defense (Avg Opp OFF Rank)

Legend: • 2017 Actual; 2018 Forecast (icon)

Metric	Group	Values shown
Total Efficiency		30, 32
DEF Efficiency		18, 32
Pass Efficiency DEF	Passing	29, 32
YPPA Def	Passing	20, 32
Explosive Pass DEF	Passing	26, 29
Pass Pro Efficieincy DEF	Passing	24, 31
Rush Efficiency DEF	Rushing	2, 20
Explosive Rush DEF	Rushing	1, 17
RB Pass Eff DEF	Rushing	18, 20
Red Zone Blend DEF		30, 32
YPPT Def		26, 32
Third Down Conv DEF		9
OFF Efficiency		27, 30
Pass Efficiency OFF	Passing	26, 28
YPPA Off	Passing	23, 28
Explosive Pass OFF	Passing	21, 24
Pass Pro Efficiency OFF	Passing	28, 32
Rush Efficiency OFF	Rushing	19, 21
Explosive Rush OFF	Rushing	23, 32
RB Pass Eff OFF	Rushing	6, 10
Red Zone Blend OFF		32
YPPT Off		12, 26
Third Down Conv OFF		24, 30
Pass:Run Ratio OFF		11, 23

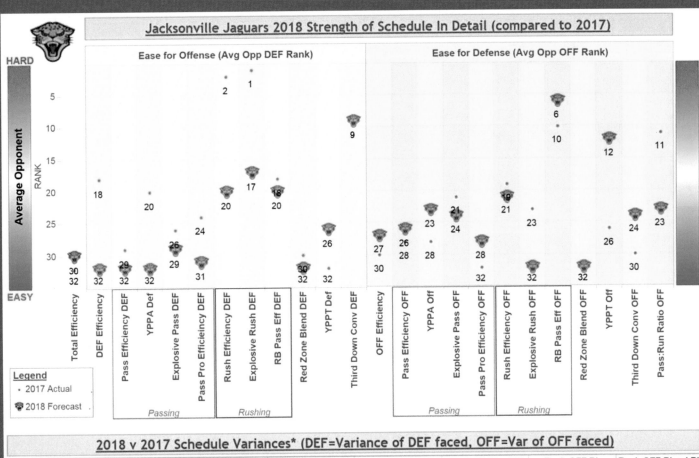

2018 v 2017 Schedule Variances* (DEF=Variance of DEF faced, OFF=Var of OFF faced)

Pass DEF Rk	Pass DEF Blend Rk	Rush DEF Rk	Rush DEF Blend Rk	Pass OFF Rk	Pass OFF Blend Rk	Rush OFF Rk	Rush OFF Blend Rk
19	22	30	30	14	19	9	12

* **1**=Hardest Jump in 2018 schedule from 2017 (aka a much harder schedule in 2018), **32**=Easiest Jump in 2018 schedule from 2017 (aka a much easier schedule in 2018); **Pass Blend** metric blends 4 metrics: Pass Efficiency, YPPA, Explosive Pass & Pass Rush; **Rush Blend** metric blends 3 metrics: Rush Efficiency, Explosive Rush & RB Targets

Team Records & Trends

	2017	2016	2015
Average line	-2.4	3.4	2.6
Average O/U line	40.3	44.7	44.9
Straight Up Record	10-6	3-13	5-11
Against the Spread Record	9-7	8-8	7-9
Over/Under Record	8-8	10-6	10-6
ATS as Favorite	6-5	0-1	2-3
ATS as Underdog	3-2	8-6	5-6
Straight Up Home	5-2	1-6	4-4
ATS Home	4-3	2-5	4-4
Over/Under Home	4-3	5-2	5-3
ATS as Home Favorite	4-2	0-1	2-3
ATS as a Home Dog	0-1	2-3	2-1
Straight Up Away	4-4	1-7	1-7
ATS Away	4-4	5-3	3-5
Over/Under Away	3-5	4-4	5-3
ATS Away Favorite	2-3	0-0	0-0
ATS Away Dog	2-1	5-3	3-5
Six Point Teaser Record	11-4	12-3	9-7
Seven Point Teaser Record	12-4	13-3	9-7
Ten Point Teaser Record	13-3	13-3	12-4

JAC-3

Good things are again in store for this year's Jaguars. I project them to face the NFL's fourth-softest schedule, including an easier run-defense slate than Fournette drew last year. Fournette's 2018 volume projection is enormous, and what we care most about in fantasy football.

Entering last season, the Jags were favored in just four games. But after they dominated the Steelers 30-9 in Pittsburgh as a seven-point underdog in Week 5, Jacksonville was favored in ten straight games. Projected to win just six games entering last season, the Jags wound up winning ten.

This year's Jaguars are projected for nine wins and are favored in 9-of-15 contests through Week 15. And that is positive for Fournette's volume projection.

(cont'd - see JAC-4)

2018 Rest Analysis

Avg Rest	6.47
Avg Rk	3
Team More Rest	2
Opp More Rest	3
Net Rest Edge	-1
3 Days Rest	1
4 Days Rest	0
5 Days Rest	0
6 Days Rest	12
7 Days Rest	0
8 Days Rest	0
9 Days Rest	1
10 Days Rest	0
11 Days Rest	0
12 Days Rest	0
13 Days Rest	1
14 Days Rest	0

Health by Unit*

2017 Rk	6
2016 Rk	16
Off Rk	15
Def Rk	2
QB Rk	21
RB Rk	17
WR Rk	30
TE Rk	4
Oline Rk	7
Dline Rk	3
LB Rk	3
DB Rk	3

*Based on the great work of Scott Kacsmar from Football Outsiders

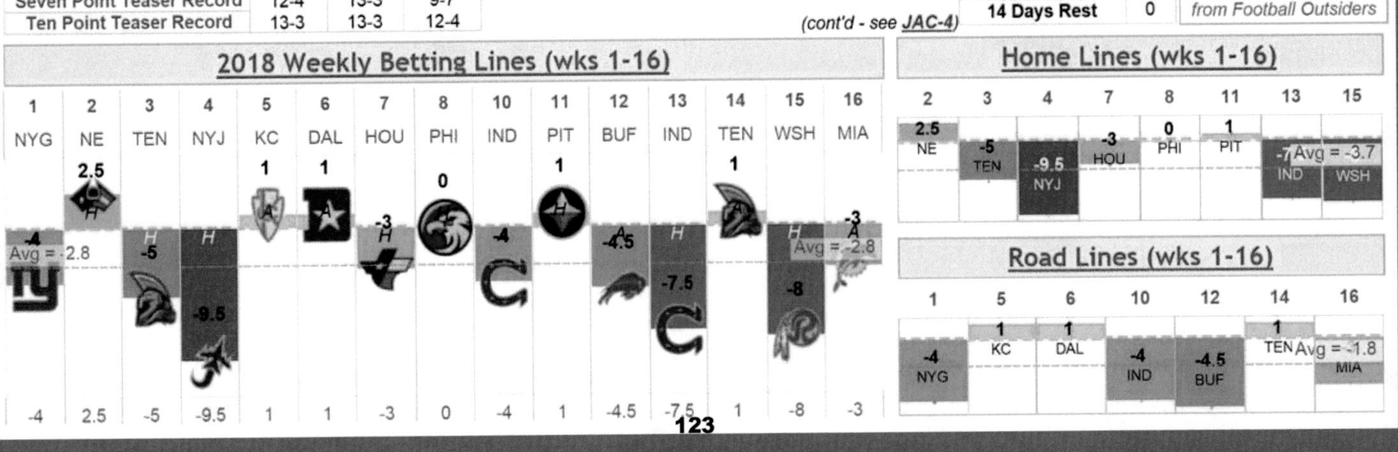

Jacksonville Jaguars 2017 Play Analysis

2017 Play Tendencies

All Pass %	51%
All Pass Rk	32
All Rush %	49%
All Rush Rk	1
1 Score Pass %	54%
1 Score Pass Rk	24
2016 1 Score Pass %	57%
2016 1 Score Pass Rk	22
2017 Pass Increase %	-3%
Pass Increase Rk	20
1 Score Rush %	46%
1 Score Rush Rk	9
Up Pass %	43%
Up Pass Rk	29
Up Rush %	57%
Up Rush Rk	4
Down Pass %	65%
Down Pass Rk	22
Down Rush %	35%
Down Rush Rk	11

2017 Down & Distance Tendencies

Down	Distance	Total Plays	Pass Rate	Run Rate	Play Success %
1	Short (1-3)	7	14%	86%	57%
	Med (4-7)	14	50%	50%	64%
	Long (8-10)	380	41%	59%	49%
	XL (11+)	23	30%	70%	35%
2	Short (1-3)	42	31%	69%	64%
	Med (4-7)	104	53%	47%	52%
	Long (8-10)	129	48%	52%	37%
	XL (11+)	46	65%	35%	30%
3	Short (1-3)	55	47%	53%	69%
	Med (4-7)	70	97%	3%	36%
	Long (8-10)	40	88%	13%	43%
	XL (11+)	35	86%	14%	9%
4	Short (1-3)	7	14%	86%	100%
	Med (4-7)	4	75%	25%	75%

Shotgun %:

Under Center	Shotgun
46%	54%
37% AVG	63%

Run Rate:

Under Center	Shotgun
72%	27%
68% AVG	23%

Pass Rate:

Under Center	Shotgun
28%	73%
32% AVG	77%

Short Yardage Intelligence:

2nd and Short Run

Run Freq	Run Rk	NFL Run Freq Avg	Run 1D Rate	Run NFL 1D Avg
68%	16	67%	70%	69%

2nd and Short Pass

Pass Freq	Pass Rk	NFL Pass Freq Avg	Pass 1D Rate	Pass NFL 1D Avg
32%	17	33%	64%	53%

Most Frequent Play

Down	Distance	Play Type	Player	Total Plays	Play Success %
1	Short (1-3)	RUSH	Leonard Fournette	3	67%
			Chris Ivory	3	33%
	Med (4-7)	RUSH	Leonard Fournette	3	67%
			Chris Ivory	3	67%
	Long (8-10)	RUSH	Leonard Fournette	137	47%
	XL (11+)	RUSH	Leonard Fournette	9	33%
2	Short (1-3)	RUSH	Leonard Fournette	21	86%
	Med (4-7)	RUSH	Leonard Fournette	29	38%
	Long (8-10)	RUSH	Leonard Fournette	36	25%
	XL (11+)	RUSH	Leonard Fournette	9	22%
3	Short (1-3)	RUSH	Leonard Fournette	13	69%
	Med (4-7)	PASS	Marqise Lee	21	43%
	Long (8-10)	PASS	Keelan Cole	7	43%
	XL (11+)	PASS	Marqise Lee	6	0%

Most Successful Play*

Down	Distance	Play Type	Player	Total Plays	Play Success %
1	Long (8-10)	PASS	Allen Hurns	15	67%
	XL (11+)	RUSH	Leonard Fournette	9	33%
2	Short (1-3)	RUSH	Leonard Fournette	21	86%
	Med (4-7)	PASS	Keelan Cole	9	78%
	Long (8-10)	RUSH	Blake Bortles	8	63%
	XL (11+)	PASS	Keelan Cole	5	80%
3	Short (1-3)	RUSH	Chris Ivory	7	86%
	Med (4-7)	PASS	Leonard Fournette	5	60%
	Long (8-10)	PASS	Allen Hurns	6	83%
	XL (11+)	PASS	Marqise Lee	6	0%

*Minimum 5 plays to qualify

2017 Snap Rates

Wk	Opp	Score	Marcedes Lewis	Keelan Cole	Marqise Lee	Leonard Fournette	Allen Hurns	Dede Westbrook	Chris Ivory	T.J. Yeldon	Allen Robinson
1	HOU	W 29-7	64 (100%)	19 (30%)	53 (83%)	39 (61%)	51 (80%)		26 (41%)		3 (5%)
2	TEN	L 37-16	54 (81%)	44 (66%)	58 (87%)	40 (60%)	59 (88%)		27 (40%)		
3	BAL	W 44-7	39 (53%)	37 (51%)	49 (67%)	37 (51%)	44 (60%)		25 (34%)		
4	NYJ	L 23-20	69 (88%)	46 (59%)	57 (73%)	39 (50%)	60 (77%)		34 (44%)		
5	PIT	W 30-9	45 (83%)	27 (50%)	34 (63%)	39 (72%)	39 (72%)		15 (28%)		
6	LA	L 27-17	52 (75%)	41 (59%)	55 (80%)	40 (58%)	56 (81%)		28 (41%)		
7	IND	W 27-0	57 (84%)	41 (60%)	47 (69%)		50 (74%)		38 (56%)	23 (34%)	
9	CIN	W 23-7	62 (78%)	49 (61%)	66 (83%)		71 (89%)		39 (49%)	35 (44%)	
10	LAC	W 20-17	77 (92%)	69 (82%)	71 (85%)	45 (54%)	60 (71%)		8 (10%)	31 (37%)	
11	CLE	W 19-7	67 (86%)	45 (58%)	63 (81%)	52 (67%)		35 (45%)	6 (8%)	20 (26%)	
12	ARI	L 27-24	56 (88%)	58 (91%)	58 (91%)	28 (44%)		45 (70%)	2 (3%)	34 (53%)	
13	IND	W 30-10	58 (88%)	49 (74%)	58 (88%)	57 (86%)		54 (82%)	9 (14%)	6 (9%)	
14	SEA	W 30-24	62 (94%)	40 (61%)	58 (88%)	50 (76%)		50 (76%)	12 (18%)	4 (6%)	
15	HOU	W 45-7	38 (53%)	53 (74%)	11 (15%)			57 (79%)	31 (43%)	29 (40%)	
16	SF	L 44-33	44 (49%)	77 (86%)		50 (56%)		87 (97%)		40 (44%)	
17	TEN	L 15-10	53 (88%)	60 (100%)		52 (87%)	47 (78%)	57 (95%)		8 (13%)	
Grand Total			897 (80%)	755 (66%)	738 (75%)	568 (63%)	537 (77%)	385 (78%)	300 (30%)	230 (31%)	3 (5%)

Personnel Groupings

Personnel	Team %	NFL Avg	Succ. %
1-1 [3WR]	46%	59%	46%
1-2 [2WR]	27%	19%	47%
1-3 [1WR]	11%	5%	37%
1-0 [4WR]	10%	2%	35%
2-1 [2WR]	3%	7%	61%

Grouping Tendencies

Personnel	Pass Rate	Pass Succ. %	Run Succ. %
1-1 [3WR]	66%	43%	50%
1-2 [2WR]	32%	57%	42%
1-3 [1WR]	7%	25%	37%
1-0 [4WR]	86%	38%	20%
2-1 [2WR]	36%	60%	61%

Red Zone Targets (min 3)

Receiver	All	Inside 5	6-10	11-20
Marcedes Lewis	11	5	1	5
Marqise Lee	8	5	2	1
Allen Hurns	7	1	2	4
James O'Shaughnessy	7		3	4
Jaydon Mickens	5	1		4
Keelan Cole	5		3	2
Chris Ivory	4		3	1
Dede Westbrook	4	1		3
T.J. Yeldon	3			3

Red Zone Rushes (min 3)

Rusher	All	Inside 5	6-10	11-20
Leonard Fournette	44	17	9	18
Chris Ivory	23	10	1	12
Blake Bortles	17	1	4	12
T.J. Yeldon	11	4	1	6
Corey Grant	2		1	1

Early Down Target Rate

RB	TE	WR
28%	17%	55%
23%	21% NFL AVG	56%

Overall Target Success %

RB	TE	WR
48% #11	47% #23	48% #13

Jacksonville Jaguars 2017 Passing Recap & 2018 Outlook

Blake Bortles dealt with a ton of 2017 injuries at receiver, but he showed improvement from 2016. To help him, the Jaguars need to spend more time analyzing his Success Rates in specific personnel groupings. In three-receiver 11 personnel, Jacksonville passed 68% of the time but managed a 74 passer rating. In two-wide sets, Bortles' Success Rate spiked to 62% with 9.4 yards per attempt and a 122 rating. Jacksonville's running game was also far more successful in two-receiver packages. But the Jags used two-receiver sets on only 18% of pass plays.

The Jaguars need to stop putting Bortles in obvious passing formations. They need to let him throw more on early downs, especially in 12 or 21 personnel.

Blake Bortles Rating All Downs

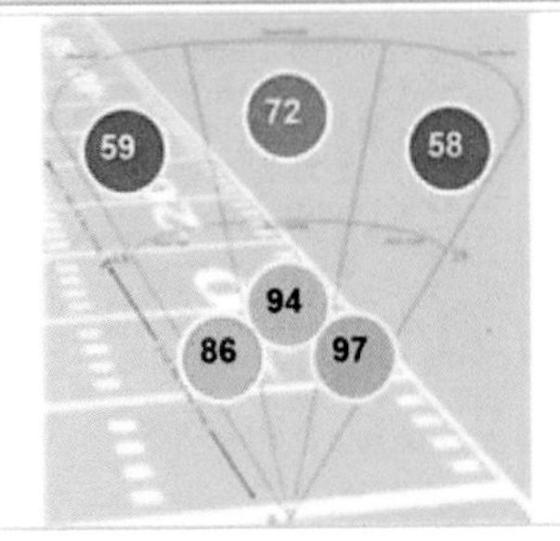

Blake Bortles Rating Early Downs

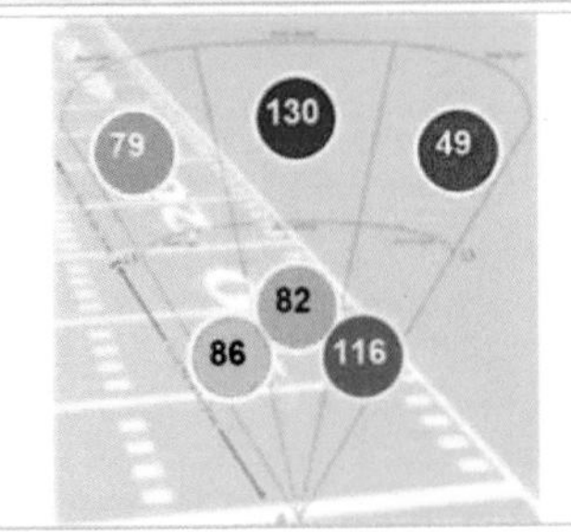

2017 Standard Passing Table

QB	Comp	Att	Comp %	Yds	YPA	TDs	INT	Sacks	Rating	Rk
Blake Bortles	364	608	60%	4,281	7.0	24	13	29	86	26
NFL Avg			62%		7.0				87.5	

2017 Advanced Passing Table

QB	Success %	EDSR Passing Success %	20+ Yd Pass Gains	20+ Yd Pass %	30+ Yd Pass Gains	30+ Yd Pass %	Avg. Air Yds per Comp	Avg. YAC per Comp	20+ Air Yd Comp	20+ Air Yd %
Blake Bortles	45%	50%	52	8.6%	17	2.8%	5.4	5.2	17	5%
NFL Avg	44%	48%	27.7	8.8%	10.3	3.3%	6.0	4.7	11.7	6%

Interception Rates by Down

Yards to Go	1	2	3	4	Total
1 & 2	0.0%	0.0%	0.0%	0.0%	0.0%
3, 4, 5	0.0%	5.9%	0.0%	0.0%	2.0%
6 - 9	0.0%	1.2%	5.2%	0.0%	3.1%
10 - 14	1.0%	0.0%	2.4%		1.0%
15+	0.0%	10.5%	6.7%	0.0%	6.7%
Total	0.9%	2.5%	2.9%	0.0%	2.0%

3rd Down Passing - Short of Sticks Analysis

QB	Avg. Yds to Go	Avg. YIA (of Comp)	Avg Yds Short	Short of Sticks Rate	Short Rk
Blake Bortles	7.6	5.1	-2.5	74%	36
NFL Avg	7.8	6.7	-1.1	60%	

Air Yds vs YAC

Air Yds %	YAC %	Rk
50%	50%	35
58%	42%	

2017 Receiving Recap & 2018 Outlook

The Jaguars need to take a longer look at Keelan Cole. Last year, he ranked No. 2 in the NFL in yards per target on early downs (12.2) with a 56% Success Rate and 101 passer rating when targeted. Yet Jacksonville mostly used Cole in three-receiver sets and rarely targeted him on early downs. On early downs in two-receiver formations, Cole delivered an incredible 70% Success Rate, 22.0 yards per target, and 119 passer rating when thrown to.

Player *Min 50 Targets*	Targets	Comp %	YPA	Rating	TOARS	Success %	Success Rk	Missed YPA Rk	YAS % Rk	TDs
Marqise Lee	111	57%	6.9	76	4.6	47%	79	115	77	3
Keelan Cole	89	51%	9.3	80	4.3	43%	101	83	1	3
Allen Hurns	66	70%	8.7	88	4.1	61%	5	5	55	2
Dede Westbrook	65	52%	6.5	72	3.7	38%	121	106	23	1
Leonard Fournette	60	72%	5.8	91	3.9	54%	35	34	104	1
Marcedes Lewis	55	51%	6.2	99	3.8	46%	84	118	13	6

Directional Passer Rating Delivered

Receiver	Short Left	Short Middle	Short Right	Deep Left	Deep Middle	Deep Right	Player Total
Marqise Lee	93	111	88	43	18	71	76
Keelan Cole	100	53	89	96	89	21	80
Allen Hurns	68	133	75	39	100	71	88
Dede Westbrook	61	73	50	76	71	117	72
Leonard Fournette	93	55	109	40			91
Marcedes Lewis	55	72	103	40	111	96	99
T.J. Yeldon	94	92	89	40			90
Chris Ivory	65	93	146				99
James O'Shaughnessy	54	108	71			0	59
Ben Koyack	85	123	54		119		119
Jaelen Strong		146	83				144
Allen Robinson	119						119
Team Total	83	91	95	55	72	57	85

2017 Rushing Recap & 2017 Outlook

50% of Fournette's 2017 carries gained two yards or fewer, which ranked 25th of 28 running backs with at least 175 attempts. Only 26% of Fournette's runs gained five yards or more (27th). Fournette averaged just 3.88 yards per carry, and his 43% Success Rate ranked 17th among 28 qualified backs. But thanks to improved game scripts, Fournette finished seventh in the NFL in carries (268) and as the fantasy RB8. This is just one example showing why strength of schedule matters. Fortunately, Fournette draws another favorable slate in 2018. And the Jaguars would be wise to not grind their franchise back into obvious running situations.

Player *Min 50 Rushes*	Rushes	YPC	Success %	Success Rk	Missed YPA Rk	YTS % Rk	YAS % Rk	Early Down Success %	Early Down Success Rk	TDs
Leonard Fournette	338	3.8	43%	44	42	34	44	42%	48	13
Chris Ivory	113	3.4	38%	66	51	43	70	36%	67	1
T.J. Yeldon	59	5.1	44%	37	30	51	65	48%	21	3

Yards per Carry by Direction

Directional Run Frequency

10% 7% 10% 44% 12% 8% 8%

LT LG C RG RT

The 2017 Jaguars built more halftime leads than the 2016 Jags, and their great defense shut down opponents in second halves. In first halves of games, only 38% of opponent passes against the Jaguars were successful (No. 2 in NFL). In second halves, Jacksonville's defense yielded just a 39% Success Rate on passes. The Jags still lost to Josh McCown, Blaine Gabbert, Marcus Mariiota twice, Jared Goff, and Jimmy Garoppolo. Fournette helped the team, but he was not the driver for Jacksonville's ten-win season and AFC Championship game berth.

In last year's Football Preview, I wrote the following: "The play calling was beyond bad in terms of predictability, and likely cost the Jaguars several wins. I would like to say things got better once (OC Nathaniel Hackett) took over (in Week 7), but they were actually worse. In Weeks 11, 12, 13, 15, and 17, the Jaguars led in the second half but lost every single game. If fewer than three receivers were in on any play, they went 100% run with a 29% Success Rate. When three receivers were on the field, the Jaguars went 65% pass including 78% after first down for a 29% passing Success Rate." I sent a copy of that preview to the Jaguars, urging them to review it. I followed up with an article noting that the combination of predictable formations and play calls and utterly painful prevent pass defense in second halves of games when leading cost Jacksonville five games in which they grabbed second-half leads. In January's AFC Championship game, the Jaguars had the ball with a ten-point lead in the fourth quarter, yet lost to the Patriots.

(cont'd - see JAC-5)

Evan Silva's Fantasy Corner

Leonard Fournette battled chronic ankle problems as a 2016 junior at LSU. They recurred in an August 13 practice last year, costing him the rest of the preseason. Fournette destroyed the league for 122.0 total yards per game and seven TDs in the first six weeks, only to aggravate the ankle in Week 6 against the Rams. Fournette missed nearly a month, then dipped to 3.22 YPC in Jacksonville's final seven games, then 3.46 YPC in the playoffs. On the season, Fournette ranked 26th of 47 backs in Football Outsiders' rushing Success Rate. Nevertheless, Fournette handled 381 touches in a 16-game season (including playoffs) and totaled 1,628 yards from scrimmage with 14 TDs. On a run-first, ball-control team with an elite defense and offensive line upgraded by LG Andrew Norwell and again facing a soft schedule, Fournette's sheer volume and touchdown upsides are immense as Jacksonville's offensive centerpiece.

Division History: Season Wins & 2018 Projection

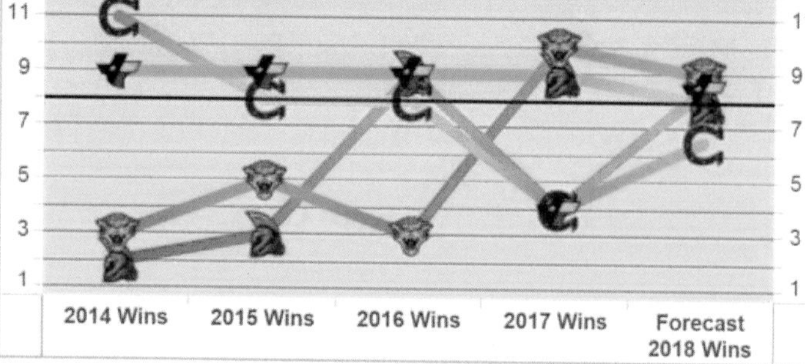

Rank of 2018 Defensive Pass Efficiency Faced by Week

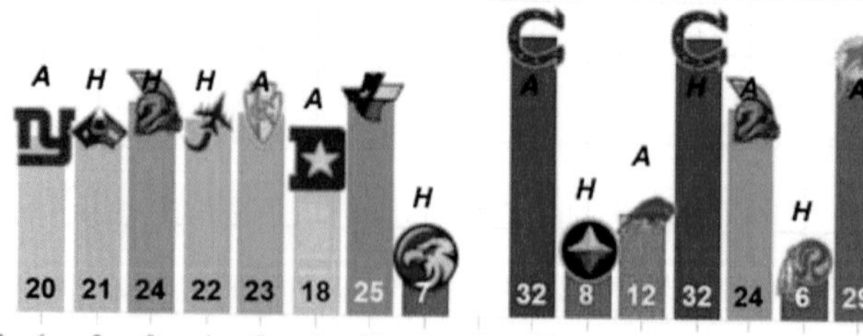

Rank of 2018 Defensive Rush Efficiency Faced by Week

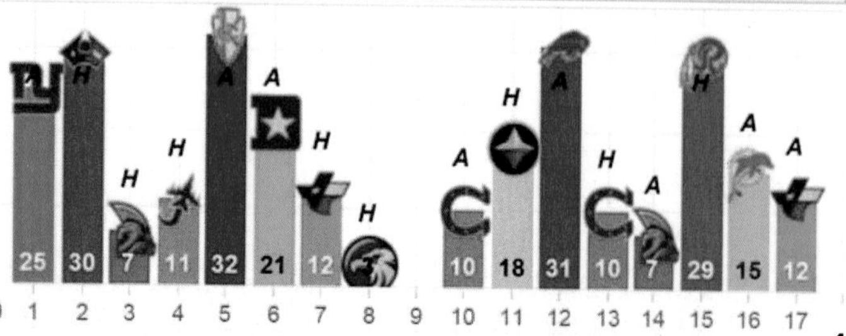

2017 Situational Usage by Player & Position

Usage Rate by Score

		Being Blown Out (14+)	Down Big (9-13)	One Score	Large Lead (9-13)	Blowout Lead (14+)	Grand Total
RUSH	Leonard Fournette	14%	32%	32%	42%	19%	29%
	Chris Ivory		1%	8%	13%	19%	10%
	Marqise Lee			0%			0%
	T.J. Yeldon	7%	1%	4%	6%	10%	5%
	Corey Grant			1%	3%	10%	3%
	Tommy Bohanon			0%		1%	0%
	Total	21%	35%	46%	64%	59%	48%
PASS	Leonard Fournette	2%	5%	6%	4%	2%	5%
	Chris Ivory	5%	9%	2%	1%	1%	3%
	Marqise Lee	12%	5%	11%	10%	6%	10%
	T.J. Yeldon	14%	3%	4%		4%	4%
	Keelan Cole	9%	12%	8%	3%	7%	8%
	Allen Hurns	14%	4%	5%	9%	6%	6%
	Dede Westbrook	7%	9%	6%	4%	2%	6%
	Marcedes Lewis		3%	6%	1%	2%	5%
	Corey Grant		1%	1%		1%	1%
	James O'Shaughnes..	7%	8%	2%		2%	2%
	Tommy Bohanon			1%	1%	2%	1%
	Jaydon Mickens	5%		1%		2%	1%
	Ben Koyack		3%	1%		1%	1%
	Jaelen Strong	5%	1%	0%			0%
	Arrelious Benn			0%		0%	0%
	Allen Robinson			0%			0%
	Larry Pinkard			0%			0%
	Maxwell McCaffrey			0%			0%
	Total	79%	65%	54%	36%	41%	52%

Positional Target Distribution vs NFL Average

		NFL Wide				Team Only			
		Left	Middle	Right	Total	Left	Middle	Right	Total
Deep	WR	947	481	958	2,386	39	28	29	96
	TE	189	146	185	520	3	4	3	10
	RB	36	9	42	87	3			3
	All	1,172	636	1,185	2,993	45	32	32	109
Short	WR	2,785	1,593	2,705	7,083	77	78	85	240
	TE	839	813	1,138	2,790	24	26	32	82
	RB	1,281	778	1,247	3,306	40	45	48	133
	All	4,905	3,184	5,090	13,179	141	149	165	455
Total		6,077	3,820	6,275	16,172	186	181	197	564

Positional Success Rates vs NFL Average

		NFL Wide				Team Only			
		Left	Middle	Right	Total	Left	Middle	Right	Total
Deep	WR	37%	45%	38%	39%	33%	43%	38%	38%
	TE	39%	53%	45%	45%	0%	50%	33%	30%
	RB	39%	56%	38%	40%	0%			0%
	All	37%	47%	39%	40%	29%	44%	38%	36%
Short	WR	52%	57%	50%	52%	51%	62%	47%	53%
	TE	51%	56%	49%	52%	33%	62%	50%	49%
	RB	44%	51%	43%	45%	50%	44%	48%	47%
	All	50%	56%	48%	50%	48%	56%	48%	51%
Total		47%	54%	46%	48%	43%	54%	46%	48%

Successful Play Rate
0% 100%

Jacksonville Jaguars - Success by Personnel Grouping & Play Type

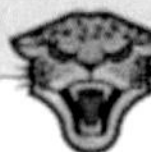

Play Type	1-1 [3WR]	1-2 [2WR]	2-1 [2WR]	1-0 [4WR]	1-3 [1WR]	0-1 [4WR]	2-0 [3WR]	2-2 [1WR]	0-0 [5WR]	0-2 [3WR]	0-3 [2WR]	2-3 [0WR]	Grand Total
PASS	43% (326, 59%)	57% (92, 17%)	60% (10, 2%)	38% (95, 17%)	25% (8, 1%)	50% (8, 1%)	0% (1, 0%)	100% (1, 0%)	50% (4, 1%)	50% (4, 1%)	0% (1, 0%)	100% (1, 0%)	45% (551, 100%)
RUSH	50% (167, 32%)	42% (199, 38%)	61% (18, 3%)	20% (15, 3%)	37% (107, 20%)			44% (16, 3%)				50% (4, 1%)	44% (526, 100%)
TOTAL	46% (493, 46%)	47% (291, 27%)	61% (28, 3%)	35% (110, 10%)	37% (115, 11%)	50% (8, 1%)	0% (1, 0%)	47% (17, 2%)	50% (4, 0%)	50% (4, 0%)	0% (1, 0%)	60% (5, 0%)	44% (1,077, 100%)

Format Line 1: Success Rate Line 2: Total # of Plays, % of All Plays (by type)

JAC-5 When leading, every single Jaguars first-down play was a run from shotgun. Those runs averaged 0.75 yards per carry. On every single second down, the Jaguars threw a long pass downfield with average Air Yards of 23.0. On third and long with a stopped clock, every single play was a pass, and only one was complete. In their most important game of the season, Jacksonville's predictability and poor play selection cost them.

From the 2018 Jaguars, I'd like to see more no-huddle offense. Bortles posted league highs in completion rate (78%) and Success Rate (64%) on no-huddle plays in 2017. His completion rate dipped to 41st (59%) when huddling with a 44% Success Rate (25th).

I'd also like to see more passing volume. Last year, Jacksonville's most frequent plays on second-and-extra-long (11-plus yards), second-and-long (8-10 yards), and second-and-medium (4-7 yards) were all Fournette runs. His Success Rates on those runs were 22%, 25%, and 38%. Backup running backs can produce those rates. The Jaguars must save Fournette for first down, second and third and short to medium, and in the red zone.

Nearly 50% of Fournette's runs went against eight-plus-man boxes. Looking only at first-half plays, last year's Jaguars went 57% run on first down and were one of the run-heaviest teams in the league. Fournette produced a poor 45% Success Rate on first-down carries, gaining 3.8 yards per rush. On first-half first-down passes, however, Bortles averaged 8.0 yards per attempt with a 54% Success Rate and league-best 118 passer rating.

If the defense you're facing is playing the run, you must pass the ball. It is simply more efficient. On top of all this is beating down the No. 4 overall draft pick and shortening his career by pounding him into first-down brick walls.

The Jaguars should be very good this year. I'd love to see them give the Patriots another run for the AFC crown. But they won't get there with predictable play calling, or by using Fournette like they did last season. They do benefit from another easy schedule and should repeat as a playoff team. But they need to throw the ball more often than they did last year and let their backup running backs absorb more fourth-quarter carries in blowout games to save Fournette.

Receiving Success by Personnel Grouping

Position	Player	1-1 [3WR]	1-2 [2WR]	2-1 [2WR]	1-0 [4WR]	1-3 [1WR]	0-1 [4WR]	2-2 [1WR]	0-0 [5WR]	0-2 [3WR]	0-3 [2WR]	Total
RB	Leonard Fournette	56% 7.2 96.5 (25)	77% 7.3 122.8 (13)	75% 6.0 89.6 (4)	0% 0.4 39.6 (5)	0% 2.0 79.2 (1)						56% 6.3 97.7 (48)
	T.J. Yeldon	42% 5.1 80.9 (26)	100% 20.0 118.8 (1)		46% 5.1 87.3 (13)		0% 6.0 91.7 (1)					44% 5.5 85.8 (41)
TE	Marcedes Lewis	52% 6.0 70.7 (21)	56% 8.1 122.1 (16)		25% 9.3 65.6 (4)	33% 3.3 83.3 (3)	0% 0.0 39.6 (1)	100% 16.0 118.8 (1)	0% 0.0 39.6 (1)		0% 0.0 39.6 (1)	48% 6.6 97.4 (48)
WR	Marqise Lee	37% 5.2 59.7 (49)	63% 8.8 113.5 (19)	100% 18.5 118.8 (2)	52% 9.5 81.6 (23)		100% 8.0 100.0 (1)			50% 6.5 70.8 (2)		48% 7.3 78.6 (96)
	Keelan Cole	39% 7.5 61.8 (56)	60% 18.2 112.5 (10)	100% 42.0 118.8 (1)	45% 5.0 91.1 (11)		50% 6.0 68.8 (2)		67% 11.7 106.3 (3)			45% 9.0 78.8 (83)
	Allen Hurns	65% 10.2 94.2 (37)	63% 8.9 101.6 (8)	0% 0.0 39.6 (1)	50% 3.6 58.9 (8)					50% 3.0 56.3 (2)		61% 8.6 85.7 (56)

Format Line 1: Success Rate Line 2: YPA Line 3: Passer Rating Line 4: Total # of Plays

Successful Play Rate
0% 100%

Rushing Success by Personnel Grouping

Position	Player	1-1 [3WR]	1-2 [2WR]	2-1 [2WR]	1-0 [4WR]	1-3 [1WR]	2-2 [1WR]	2-3 [0WR]	Total
QB	Blake Bortles	73% 11.0 (22)	69% 4.7 (13)		17% 5.0 (6)	15% -0.5 (13)	0% -1.0 (2)		50% 5.8 (56)
RB	Leonard Fournette	48% 3.4 (77)	37% 3.6 (112)	69% 5.9 (13)	0% 0.5 (2)	48% 5.2 (52)	44% 2.7 (9)	67% 1.0 (3)	44% 3.9 (268)
	Chris Ivory	50% 5.2 (30)	37% 3.4 (43)	40% 5.0 (5)	50% 2.8 (4)	19% 1.3 (26)	50% 2.5 (4)		38% 3.4 (112)

Format Line 1: Success Rate Line 2: YPC Line 3: Total # of Plays

Kansas City Chiefs

2018 Coaches

Head Coach:
Andy Reid (6th yr)
Offensive Coordinator:
Eric Bieniemy (KC RB) (1st yr)
Defensive Coordinator:
Bob Sutton (6th yr)

2018 Forecast

Wins	Div Rank
8.5	#4

Past Records

2017: 10-6
2016: 12-4
2015: 11-5

EASY HARD

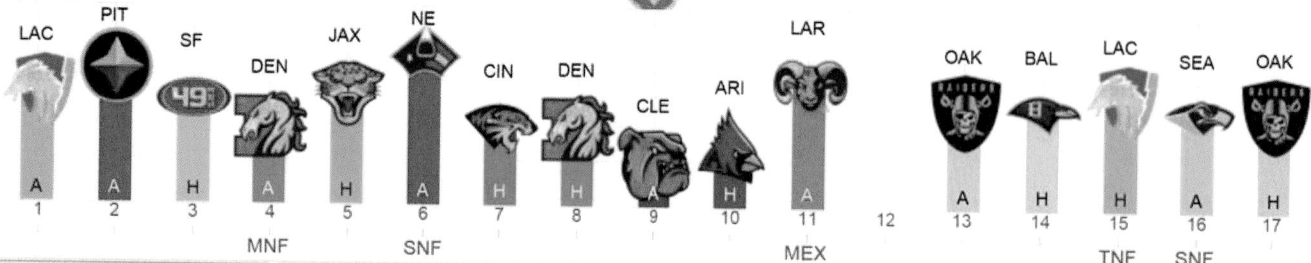

Key Players Lost

TXN	Player (POS)
Cut	Charles, Stefan DT
	Hali, Tamba LB
	Parker, Ron S
	Revis, Darrelle CB
	Seymour, DeVondre T
Declared Free Agent	Charles, Stefan DT
	Colquitt, Dustin P
	Gaines, Phillip CB
	Jenkins, Jarvis DE
	Johnson, Derrick LB
	Logan, Bennie DT
	Mitchell, Terrance CB
	Spiller, C.J. RB
	Terrell, Steven S
	Thomas, De'Anthony WR
	Wilson, Albert WR

Average Line	# Games Favored	# Games Underdog
0.1	8	7

Regular Season Wins: Past & Current Proj

Forecast 2018 Wins: 8.5
2017 Wins: 10
Forecast 2017 Wins: 9.5
2016 Wins: 12
2015 Wins: 11
2014 Wins: 9

1 3 5 7 9 11 13 15

2018 Kansas City Chiefs Overview

The Red Machine keeps on rolling, captained by Big Red himself. I have immense respect for Andy Reid because he's figured out a winning formula: the Chiefs don't beat themselves.

The 2016 and 2017 Chiefs each won the turnover battle in 10-of-16 games, combining for the best mark in the NFL over the last two years. And Kansas City went 18-2 when winning the turnover battle. Since Reid took over as head coach in 2014, the Chiefs have won the turnover battle in 46 games. The next-best team during that span is five games worse (41, Seahawks).

Winning the turnover battle is the surest path to NFL victories. Teams win nearly 80% of games when they win the turnover battle. But modeling the turnover battle for sports betting is easier said than done. Some teams cover the spread more than others, but so much of the turnover battle involves game script. Teams that trail late in games are likelier to force passes into coverage, raising interception and sack-fumble probabilities. Late-game turnovers don't "cause" teams to lose games, but they are highly correlated to losing.

Quarterback play has immense impact on turnovers. And from that standpoint, Alex Smith has been among the NFL's best. Before arriving in K.C., Smith threw ten or more interceptions in 3-of-6 seasons as a starter, despite starting 16 games only twice. His INT rate was 2.9%. In five years under Reid, Smith's INT rate was more than chopped in half (1.35%).

Smith's 1.35% INT rate is second best in the NFL over the last half decade. Tom Brady's pick rate is 1.3%. Tyrod Taylor's is third best at 1.37%. Last year's Bills were a mediocre or worse team, but they made the playoffs on the back of a solid defense and Taylor's league-best 0.95% interception rate. Of Buffalo's nine wins, seven came when Taylor did not throw an interception. In 2015-2017, the Bills went 20-11 when Taylor was not picked off. They went 4-11 when Taylor threw one interception, and 0-1 when he threw more than one.

(cont'd - see KC2)

Lineup & Cap Hits

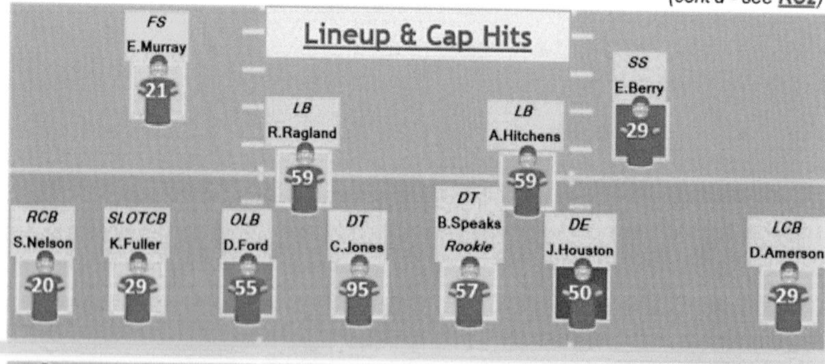

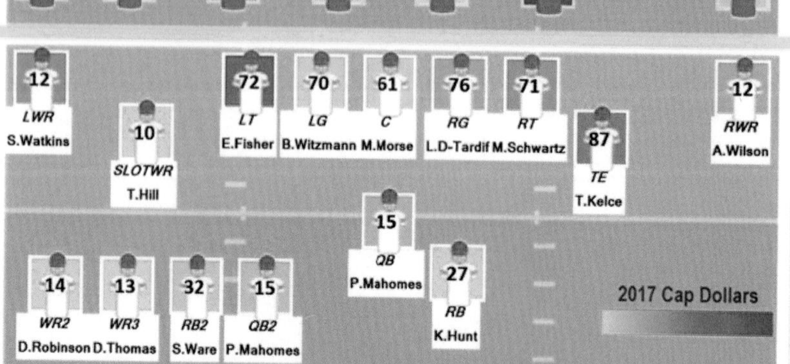

Key Free Agents/ Trades Added

Amerson, David CB
Fuller, Kendall CB
Golden, Robert S
Henne, Chad QB
Hitchens, Anthony LB
Smith, Terrance LB
Spiller, C.J. RB
Thomas, De'Anthony WR
Watkins, Sammy WR
Williams, Xavier NT

Drafted Players

Rd	Pk	Player (College)
2	46	DE - Breeland Speaks (Ole Miss)
3	75	DT - Derrick Nnadi (Florida State)
3*	100	LB - Dorian O'Daniel (Clemson)
4	124	S - Armani Watts (Texas A&M)
6	196	CB - Tremon Smith (Central Arkansas)
	198	DT - Kahlil McKenzie (Tennessee)

2018 Unit Spending

All DEF
All OFF

Positional Spending

	Rank	Total	2017 Rk
All OFF	22	$82.93M	28
QB	29	$7.44M	16
OL	14	$35.96M	9
RB	15	$8.17M	26
WR	27	$16.18M	32
TE	4	$15.18M	17
All DEF	11	$86.38M	6
DL	28	$16.00M	22
LB	1	$40.24M	1
CB	28	$8.74M	27
S	4	$21.40M	6

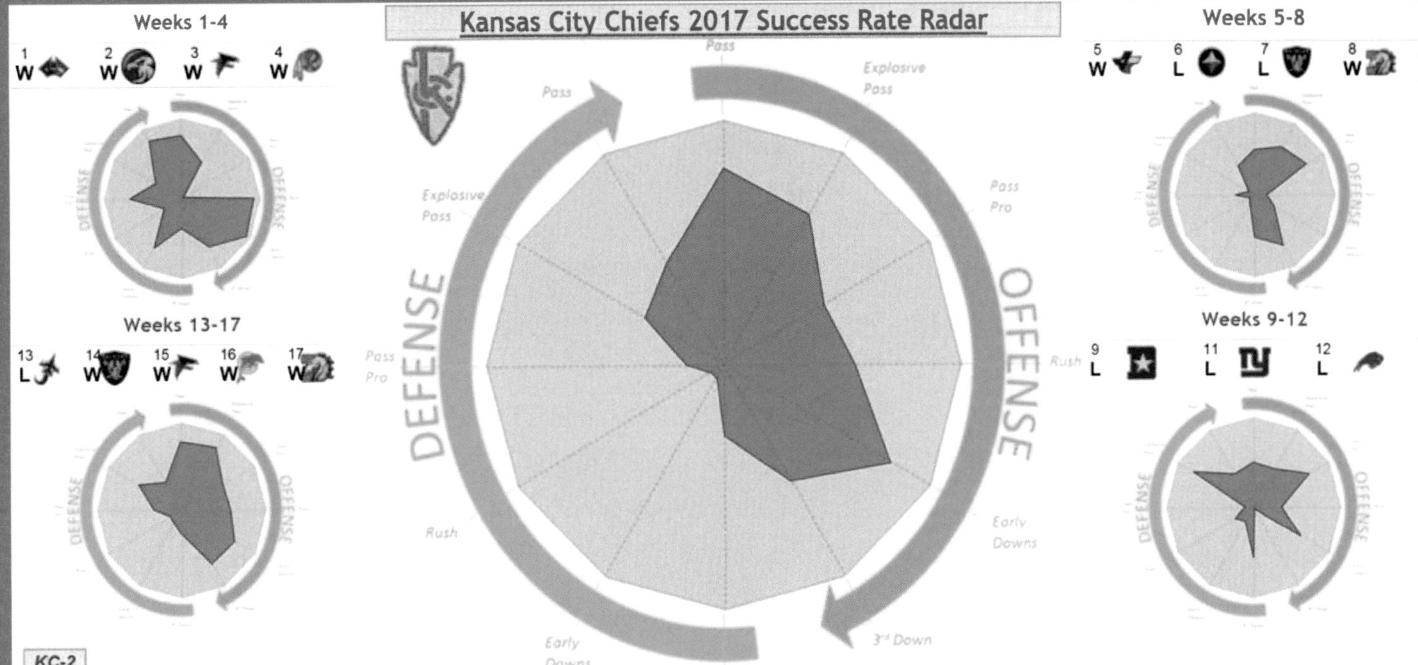

KC-2

The Chiefs are better than last year's Bills and more equipped to overcome turnovers. But there was still a massive drop-off when Smith threw picks. The Chiefs went 38-14 whenever Smith avoided INTs. They won only 48% of games when he threw one interception, and 33% when Smith threw more than one.

When the 2017 Chiefs tied or lost the turnover battle, they went 1-5. Since Reid took over, they're 8-16 when losing or tying the turnover battle.

Smith is now in D.C., and the Chiefs have turned to 2017 No. 10 overall pick Pat Mahomes at quarterback. If we assume Mahomes performs at league average in interception rate (2.54%), he will nearly double Smith's pick rate over the last five years.

The Chiefs' 2018 Win Total is 8.5 games, or a full game worse than their pre-season Win Total last year. If we assume Kansas City will indeed be worse, Mahomes will throw more than Smith did. Smith reached 500 attempts twice in five seasons with Kansas City, including in 2017. If Mahomes throws 500 passes with a league-average INT rate, he will throw 13 picks. Smith threw five last year.

In a weak AFC, nine wins may very well be enough to make the playoffs. Last year, both AFC Wild Card teams went 9-7. All 9-7 NFC teams spent January on the couch. Throwing more interceptions on a 12- or 13-win team likely wouldn't ruin their playoff chances, and the same is true for a four- or five-win team. But for an eight- or nine-win team, throwing eight more picks could be the difference between making or missing the postseason.

One concerning fallout from added interceptions would be Kansas City's defense spending more time on the field. The Chiefs' defense isn't good enough to deal with more snaps or shorter fields. Last year's K.C. defense ranked 30th in efficiency and dead last in Early-Down Success Rate.

(cont'd - see KC-3)

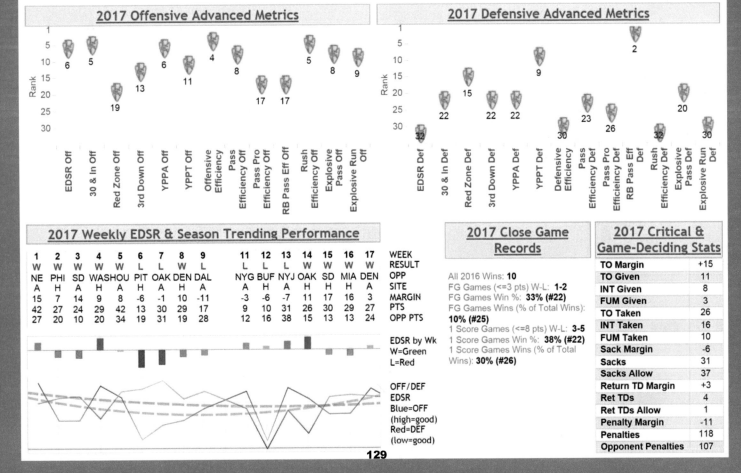

2017 Offensive Advanced Metrics

Metric	Rank
EDSR Off	6
30 & In Off	5
Red Zone Off	19
3rd Down Off	13
YPPA Off	6
YPPT Off	11
Offensive Efficiency	4
Pass Efficiency Off	8
Pass Pro Efficiency Off	17
RB Pass Eff Off	17
Rush Efficiency Off	5
Explosive Pass Off	8
Explosive Run Off	9

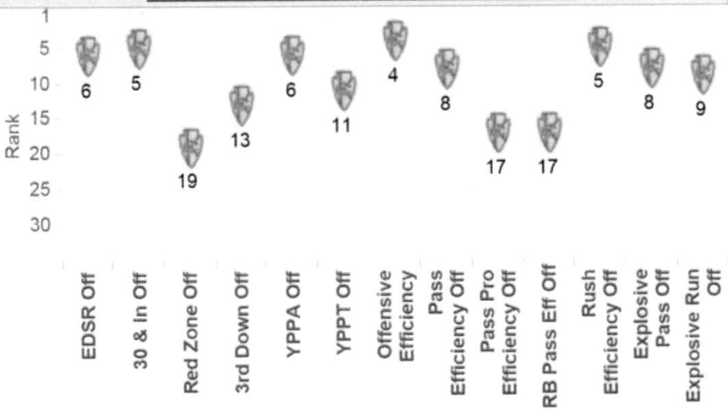

2017 Defensive Advanced Metrics

Metric	Rank
EDSR Def	32
30 & In Def	22
Red Zone Def	15
3rd Down Def	22
YPPA Def	22
YPPT Def	9
Defensive Efficiency	30
Pass Efficiency Def	23
Pass Pro Efficiency Def	26
RB Pass Eff Def	2
Rush Efficiency Def	32
Explosive Pass Def	20
Explosive Run Def	30

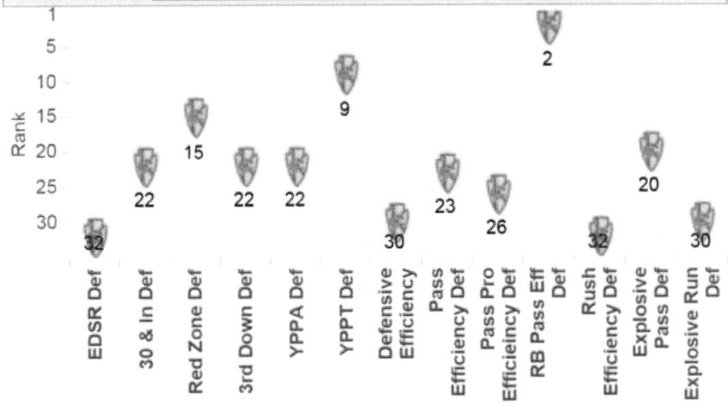

2017 Weekly EDSR & Season Trending Performance

WEEK	1	2	3	4	5	6	7	8	9	11	12	13	14	15	16	17
RESULT	W	W	W	W	W	L	L	W	L	L	L	L	W	W	W	W
OPP	NE	PHI	SD	WAS	HOU	PIT	OAK	DEN	DAL	NYG	BUF	NYJ	OAK	SD	MIA	DEN
SITE	A	H	A	H	A	H	A	H	A	A	H	A	H	H	H	A
MARGIN	15	7	14	9	8	-6	-1	10	-11	-3	-6	-7	11	17	16	3
PTS	42	27	24	29	42	13	30	29	17	9	10	31	26	30	29	27
OPP PTS	27	20	10	20	34	19	31	19	28	12	16	38	15	13	13	24

EDSR by Wk
W=Green
L=Red

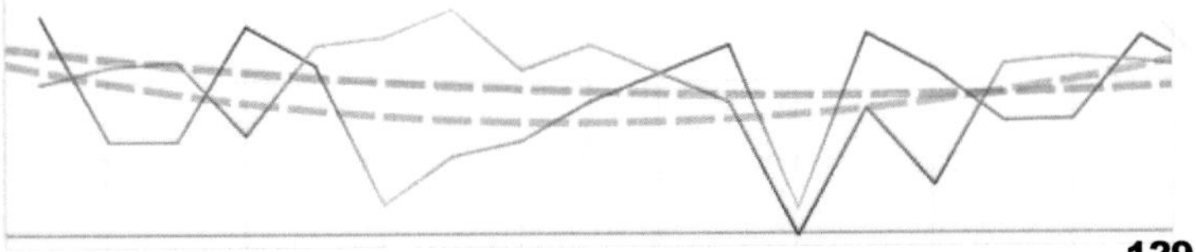

OFF/DEF EDSR
Blue=OFF (high=good)
Red=DEF (low=good)

2017 Close Game Records

All 2016 Wins: **10**
FG Games (<=3 pts) W-L: **1-2**
FG Games Win %: **33% (#22)**
FG Games Wins (% of Total Wins): **10% (#25)**
1 Score Games (<=8 pts) W-L: **3-5**
1 Score Games Win %: **38% (#22)**
1 Score Games Wins (% of Total Wins): **30% (#26)**

2017 Critical & Game-Deciding Stats

TO Margin	+15
TO Given	11
INT Given	8
FUM Given	3
TO Taken	26
INT Taken	16
FUM Taken	10
Sack Margin	-6
Sacks	31
Sacks Allow	37
Return TD Margin	+3
Ret TDs	4
Ret TDs Allow	1
Penalty Margin	-11
Penalties	118
Opponent Penalties	107

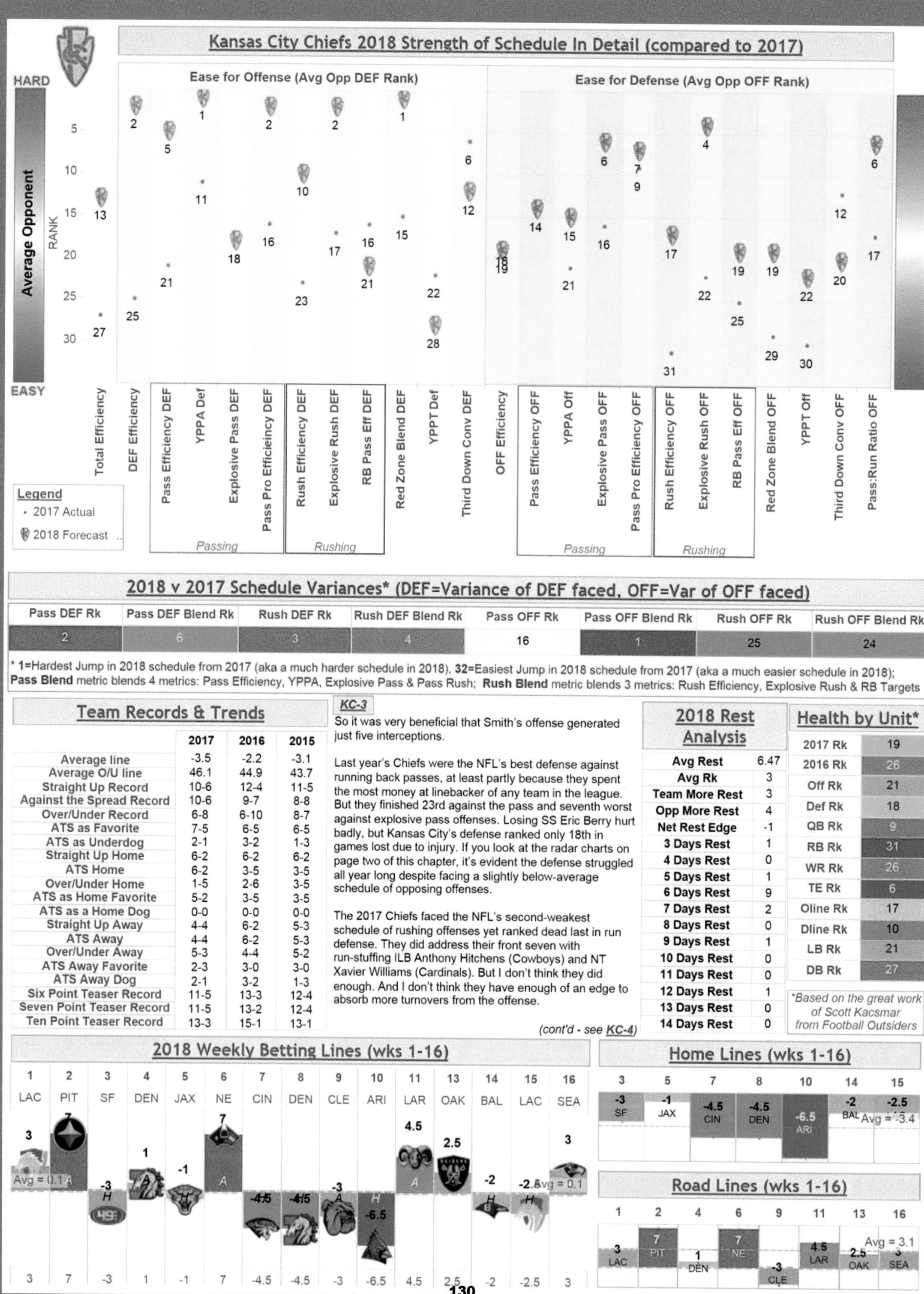

Kansas City Chiefs 2018 Strength of Schedule In Detail (compared to 2017)

2018 v 2017 Schedule Variances* (DEF=Variance of DEF faced, OFF=Var of OFF faced)

Pass DEF Rk	Pass DEF Blend Rk	Rush DEF Rk	Rush DEF Blend Rk	Pass OFF Rk	Pass OFF Blend Rk	Rush OFF Rk	Rush OFF Blend Rk
2	6	3	4	16	1	25	24

* **1**=Hardest Jump in 2018 schedule from 2017 (aka a much harder schedule in 2018), **32**=Easiest Jump in 2018 schedule from 2017 (aka a much easier schedule in 2018); **Pass Blend** metric blends 4 metrics: Pass Efficiency, YPPA, Explosive Pass & Pass Rush; **Rush Blend** metric blends 3 metrics: Rush Efficiency, Explosive Rush & RB Targets

Team Records & Trends

	2017	2016	2015
Average line	-3.5	-2.2	-3.1
Average O/U line	46.1	44.9	43.7
Straight Up Record	10-6	12-4	11-5
Against the Spread Record	10-6	9-7	8-8
Over/Under Record	6-8	6-10	8-7
ATS as Favorite	7-5	6-5	6-5
ATS as Underdog	2-1	3-2	1-3
Straight Up Home	6-2	6-2	6-2
ATS Home	6-2	3-5	3-5
Over/Under Home	1-5	2-6	3-5
ATS as Home Favorite	5-2	3-5	3-5
ATS as a Home Dog	0-0	0-0	0-0
Straight Up Away	4-4	6-2	5-3
ATS Away	4-4	6-2	5-3
Over/Under Away	5-3	4-4	5-2
ATS Away Favorite	2-3	3-0	3-0
ATS Away Dog	2-1	3-2	1-3
Six Point Teaser Record	11-5	13-3	12-4
Seven Point Teaser Record	11-5	13-2	12-4
Ten Point Teaser Record	13-3	15-1	13-1

KC-3

So it was very beneficial that Smith's offense generated just five interceptions.

Last year's Chiefs were the NFL's best defense against running back passes, at least partly because they spent the most money at linebacker of any team in the league. But they finished 23rd against the pass and seventh worst against explosive pass offenses. Losing SS Eric Berry hurt badly, but Kansas City's defense ranked only 18th in games lost due to injury. If you look at the radar charts on page two of this chapter, it's evident the defense struggled all year long despite facing a slightly below-average schedule of opposing offenses.

The 2017 Chiefs faced the NFL's second-weakest schedule of rushing offenses yet ranked dead last in run defense. They did address their front seven with run-stuffing ILB Anthony Hitchens (Cowboys) and NT Xavier Williams (Cardinals). But I don't think they did enough. And I don't think they have enough of an edge to absorb more turnovers from the offense.

(cont'd - see *KC-4*)

2018 Rest Analysis

Avg Rest	6.47
Avg Rk	3
Team More Rest	3
Opp More Rest	4
Net Rest Edge	-1
3 Days Rest	1
4 Days Rest	0
5 Days Rest	1
6 Days Rest	9
7 Days Rest	2
8 Days Rest	0
9 Days Rest	1
10 Days Rest	0
11 Days Rest	0
12 Days Rest	1
13 Days Rest	0
14 Days Rest	0

Health by Unit*

2017 Rk	19
2016 Rk	26
Off Rk	21
Def Rk	18
QB Rk	9
RB Rk	31
WR Rk	26
TE Rk	6
Oline Rk	17
Dline Rk	10
LB Rk	21
DB Rk	27

*Based on the great work of Scott Kacsmar from Football Outsiders

2018 Weekly Betting Lines (wks 1-16)

1	2	3	4	5	6	7	8	9	10	11	13	14	15	16
LAC	PIT	SF	DEN	JAX	NE	CIN	DEN	CLE	ARI	LAR	OAK	BAL	LAC	SEA
A	A	H	A	H	A	H	H	A	H	A	A	H	H	A
3	7	-3	1	-1	7	-4.5	-4.5	-3	-6.5	4.5	2.5	-2	-2.5	3

Avg = 0.1

Home Lines (wks 1-16)

3	5	7	8	10	14	15
SF	JAX	CIN	DEN	ARI	BAL	
-3	-1	-4.5	-4.5	-6.5	-2	-2.5

Avg = -3.4

Road Lines (wks 1-16)

1	2	4	6	9	11	13	16
LAC	PIT	DEN	NE	CLE	LAR	OAK	SEA
3	7	1	7	-3	4.5	2.5	3

Avg = 3.1

Kansas City Chiefs 2017 Play Analysis

2017 Play Tendencies

All Pass %	59%
All Pass Rk	14
All Rush %	41%
All Rush Rk	19
1 Score Pass %	60%
1 Score Pass Rk	5
2016 1 Score Pass %	57%
2016 1 Score Pass Rk	21
2017 Pass Increase %	4%
Pass Increase Rk	6
1 Score Rush %	40%
1 Score Rush Rk	27
Up Pass %	54%
Up Pass Rk	2
Up Rush %	46%
Up Rush Rk	31
Down Pass %	65%
Down Pass Rk	19
Down Rush %	35%
Down Rush Rk	14

2017 Down & Distance Tendencies

Down	Distance	Total Plays	Pass Rate	Run Rate	Play Success %
1	Short (1-3)	6	50%	50%	83%
	Med (4-7)	10	40%	60%	60%
	Long (8-10)	320	52%	48%	51%
	XL (11+)	14	57%	43%	43%
2	Short (1-3)	39	44%	56%	74%
	Med (4-7)	60	48%	52%	57%
	Long (8-10)	104	69%	31%	41%
	XL (11+)	41	73%	27%	20%
3	Short (1-3)	37	57%	43%	65%
	Med (4-7)	55	93%	7%	31%
	Long (8-10)	28	89%	11%	25%
	XL (11+)	32	88%	13%	34%
4	Short (1-3)	3	33%	67%	67%
	Med (4-7)	1	0%	100%	100%

Shotgun %:

Under Center	Shotgun
28%	72%
37%	*63%*

37% AVG 63%

Run Rate:

Under Center	Shotgun
69%	27%

68% AVG 23%

Pass Rate:

Under Center	Shotgun
31%	73%

32% AVG 77%

Short Yardage Intelligence:

2nd and Short Run

Run Freq	Run Rk	NFL Run Freq Avg	Run 1D Rate	Run NFL 1D Avg
48%	32	67%	83%	69%

2nd and Short Pass

Pass Freq	Pass Rk	NFL Pass Freq Avg	Pass 1D Rate	Pass NFL 1D Avg
52%	1	33%	92%	53%

Most Frequent Play

Down	Distance	Play Type	Player	Total Plays	Play Success %
1	Short (1-3)	RUSH	Kareem Hunt	3	100%
	Med (4-7)	RUSH	Kareem Hunt	3	67%
	Long (8-10)	RUSH	Kareem Hunt	115	40%
	XL (11+)	PASS	Albert Wilson	3	100%
		RUSH	Kareem Hunt	3	67%
2	Short (1-3)	RUSH	Kareem Hunt	14	71%
	Med (4-7)	RUSH	Kareem Hunt	24	63%
	Long (8-10)	PASS	Travis Kelce	22	50%
	XL (11+)	PASS	Kareem Hunt	8	25%
3	Short (1-3)	RUSH	Alex Smith	8	75%
	Med (4-7)	PASS	Travis Kelce	12	58%
	Long (8-10)	PASS	Travis Kelce	5	60%
	XL (11+)	PASS	Charcandrick West	6	0%

Most Successful Play*

Down	Distance	Play Type	Player	Total Plays	Play Success %
1	Long (8-10)	PASS	Demetrius Harris	10	90%
2	Short (1-3)	RUSH	Kareem Hunt	14	71%
	Med (4-7)	PASS	Tyreek Hill	8	88%
	Long (8-10)	PASS	Travis Kelce	22	50%
	XL (11+)	PASS	Travis Kelce	5	60%
3	Short (1-3)	RUSH	Kareem Hunt	7	86%
	Med (4-7)	PASS	Travis Kelce	12	58%
	Long (8-10)	PASS	Travis Kelce	5	60%
	XL (11+)	PASS	Tyreek Hill	5	60%

*Minimum 5 plays to qualify

2017 Snap Rates

Wk	Opp	Score	Travis Kelce	Tyreek Hill	Kareem Hunt	Demarcus Robinson	Albert Wilson	Demetrius Harris	Chris Conley	Ch. West	Anthony Sherman
1	NE	W 42-27	67 (99%)	50 (74%)	38 (56%)	5 (7%)	39 (57%)	25 (37%)	64 (94%)	23 (34%)	12 (18%)
2	PHI	W 27-20	51 (96%)	47 (89%)	39 (74%)	2 (4%)	34 (64%)	24 (45%)	46 (87%)	11 (21%)	1 (2%)
3	LAC	W 24-10	53 (100%)	39 (74%)	37 (70%)	9 (17%)	27 (51%)	22 (42%)	43 (81%)	14 (26%)	9 (17%)
4	WAS	W 29-20	71 (93%)	58 (76%)	50 (66%)	4 (5%)	43 (57%)	40 (53%)	71 (93%)	20 (26%)	12 (16%)
5	HOU	W 42-34	39 (51%)	48 (62%)	55 (71%)	12 (16%)	32 (42%)	55 (71%)	68 (88%)	21 (27%)	28 (36%)
6	PIT	L 19-13	52 (96%)	42 (78%)	42 (78%)	46 (85%)		18 (33%)		3 (6%)	9 (17%)
7	OAK	L 31-30	58 (94%)	40 (65%)	48 (77%)	61 (98%)	33 (53%)	31 (50%)			8 (13%)
8	DEN	W 29-19	57 (92%)	53 (85%)	46 (74%)	51 (82%)	16 (26%)	41 (66%)		12 (19%)	8 (13%)
9	DAL	L 28-17	54 (95%)	48 (84%)	31 (54%)	56 (98%)		20 (35%)		23 (40%)	3 (5%)
11	NYG	L 12-9	74 (99%)	64 (85%)	50 (67%)	72 (96%)		18 (24%)		19 (25%)	13 (17%)
12	BUF	L 16-10	56 (97%)	48 (83%)	38 (66%)	51 (88%)	46 (79%)	16 (28%)		16 (28%)	6 (10%)
13	NYJ	L 38-31	42 (91%)	42 (91%)	40 (87%)	29 (63%)	42 (91%)	19 (41%)			2 (4%)
14	OAK	W 26-15	69 (92%)	69 (92%)	51 (68%)	44 (59%)	66 (88%)	28 (37%)		20 (27%)	8 (11%)
15	LAC	W 30-13	59 (89%)	63 (95%)	43 (65%)	37 (56%)	62 (94%)	28 (42%)		17 (26%)	3 (5%)
16	MIA	W 29-13	72 (87%)	70 (84%)	58 (70%)	42 (51%)	69 (83%)	38 (46%)		23 (28%)	8 (10%)
17	DEN	W 27-24			5 (7%)	61 (91%)	28 (42%)	62 (93%)			53 (79%)
	Grand Total		874 (91%)	781 (81%)	671 (66%)	582 (57%)	537 (64%)	485 (46%)	292 (89%)	222 (26%)	183 (17%)

Personnel Groupings

Personnel	Team %	NFL Avg	Succ. %
1-1 [3WR]	54%	59%	48%
1-2 [2WR]	24%	19%	46%
2-1 [2WR]	6%	7%	48%
1-3 [1WR]	6%	5%	46%
2-2 [1WR]	6%	4%	41%

Grouping Tendencies

Personnel	Pass Rate	Pass Succ. %	Run Succ. %
1-1 [3WR]	64%	49%	45%
1-2 [2WR]	62%	44%	50%
2-1 [2WR]	54%	47%	48%
1-3 [1WR]	53%	48%	43%
2-2 [1WR]	14%	50%	39%

Red Zone Targets (min 3)

Receiver	All	Inside 5	6-10	11-20
Travis Kelce	21	1	2	18
Albert Wilson	12		2	10
Demarcus Robinson	9	2		7
Demetrius Harris	9	2	4	3
Kareem Hunt	9	2	1	6
Charcandrick West	8	1	1	6
Tyreek Hill	4	1		3

Red Zone Rushes (min 3)

Rusher	All	Inside 5	6-10	11-20
Kareem Hunt	39	11	9	19
Alex Smith	6	1	1	4
Anthony Sherman	4	2	1	1

Early Down Target Rate

RB	TE	WR
22%	32%	46%
23%	*21%* *NFL AVG*	*56%*

Overall Target Success %

RB	TE	WR
43% #19	51% #13	56% #2

Kansas City Chiefs 2017 Passing Recap & 2018 Outlook

The best part about watching the Mahomes era unfold is that I believe his immense talent will challenge Reid just as much as Reid will challenge Mahomes to keep getting better. I loved the decision to sit Mahomes for one year. Smith had a high floor but lower ceiling than the Chiefs' young new signal caller. And in the playoffs when facing great quarterbacks who protect the ball, the Chiefs couldn't count on a mediocre defense and winning the turnover battle to carry them. Kansas City needed more from the position.

But Reid needs to reduce the Chiefs' third-down passes to running backs. Charcandrick West posted a 53% Success Rate on early-down targets, but on third down his Success Rate fell to a dismal 18%. In fact, all Chiefs running back passes on third downs produced a horrible 15% Success Rate, less half the league-wide rate (32%). With Travis Kelce (63% third-down Success Rate) and two playmaker wideouts in Hill and Watkins, Reid must do away with inefficient third-down running back passes.

Alex Smith Rating All Downs

80
134
132
101
106
91

2017 Standard Passing Table

QB	Comp	Att	Comp %	Yds	YPA	TDs	INT	Sacks	Rating	Rk
Alex Smith	365	537	68%	4,306	8.0	28	5	39	106	2
Patrick Mahomes	22	35	63%	284	8.1	0	1	2	76	39
NFL Avg			62%		7.0				87.5	

Alex Smith Rating Early Downs

60
139
134
113
109
91

2017 Advanced Passing Table

QB	Success %	EDSR Passing Success %	20+ Yd Pass Gains	20+ Yd Pass %	30+ Yd Pass Gains	30+ Yd Pass %	Avg. Air Yds per Comp	Avg. YAC per Comp	20+ Air Yd Comp	20+ Air Yd %
Alex Smith	47%	52%	55	10.2%	30	5.6%	5.9	5.4	31	8%
Patrick Mahomes	51%	55%	2	5.7%	1	2.9%	5.2	7.0	1	5%
NFL Avg	44%	48%	27.7	8.8%	10.3	3.3%	6.0	4.7	11.7	6%

Interception Rates by Down

Yards to Go	1	2	3	4	Total
1 & 2	0.0%	0.0%	0.0%	0.0%	0.0%
3, 4, 5	0.0%	0.0%	0.0%	0.0%	0.0%
6 - 9	0.0%	0.0%	1.6%	33.3%	1.4%
10 - 14	0.5%	2.8%	0.0%		1.0%
15+	0.0%	0.0%	0.0%	0.0%	0.0%
Total	0.5%	1.0%	0.6%	14.3%	0.9%

3rd Down Passing - Short of Sticks Analysis

QB	Avg. Yds to Go	Avg. YIA (of Comp)	Avg Yds Short	Short of Sticks Rate	Short Rk
Alex Smith	7.7	7.3	-0.3	60%	14
NFL Avg	7.8	6.7	-1.1	60%	

Air Yds vs YAC

Air Yds %	YAC %	Rk
60%	40%	20
58%	42%	

2017 Receiving Recap & 2018 Outlook

Pairing 4.27 speedster Hill with strong-armed Mahomes is almost a dream come true, but consensus opinion seems too low on Watkins. It's likely because Watkins was inconsistent in Buffalo, and his 2017 numbers with the Rams underwhelmed. But keep in mind the Bills and Rams had prolific running games with very different-styled quarterbacks than Mahomes. Tyrod Taylor is a low-volume passer who shies away from risky contested throws. Goff's average Air Yards on completions was 6.0, right at league average. You can bet Mahomes is more of a believer in his own arm talent. And I believe Reid will scheme more production from Watkins.

Player *Min 50 Targets*	Targets	Comp %	YPA	Rating	TOARS	Success %	Success Rk	Missed YPA Rk	YAS % Rk	TDs
Travis Kelce	126	69%	8.8	110	5.3	58%	13	2	59	9
Tyreek Hill	116	71%	10.9	123	5.3	56%	19	33	12	7
Albert Wilson	66	67%	8.8	109	4.4	59%	6	20	49	3
Kareem Hunt	66	85%	7.0	111	4.3	49%	66	38	83	3

Directional Passer Rating Delivered

Receiver	Short Left	Short Middle	Short Right	Deep Left	Deep Middle	Deep Right	Player Total
Travis Kelce	120	79	112	145	75	95	110
Tyreek Hill	94	139	73	108	96	147	123
Albert Wilson	101	124	73	104	149	40	109
Kareem Hunt	112	95	93	96		158	111
Demarcus Robinson	81	59	102	119	0	76	65
Demetrius Harris	81	40	115	40	96	40	82
Charcandrick West	120	78	104			40	103
Chris Conley	108		97	65		110	105
De'Anthony Thomas	79	146	83	158	21		117
Team Total	106	101	94	135	74	133	108

2017 Rushing Recap & 2017 Outlook

Kareem Hunt burst onto the scene as a third-round rookie, leading the NFL in rushing yards and shining as a receiver. With Matt Nagy gone to Chicago, the Chiefs are turning to ex-RBs coach Eric Bienemy as offensive coordinator. Bienemy won't call plays, but he'll have a bigger game-planning role. Will Reid lean toward running more with Bienemy in the room? The Chiefs face a substantially more-difficult run-defense schedule, so this could be tough to execute if Mahomes experiences growing pains.

Player *Min 50 Rushes*	Rushes	YPC	Success %	Success Rk	Missed YPA Rk	YTS % Rk	YAS % Rk	Early Down Success %	Early Down Success Rk	TDs
Kareem Hunt	283	4.8	47%	30	29	65	14	45%	32	9

Yards per Carry by Direction

5.0
5.7
4.2
4.0
7.7
4.2
4.3
LT
LG
C
RG
RT

Directional Run Frequency

9%
7%
8%
42%
9%
13%
13%
LT
LG
C
RG
RT

KC-4

Far better on Reid and Smith's side of the ball, Kansas City finished No. 4 in offensive efficiency and No. 6 in Early-Down Success Rate.

'But context is king, and they produced those numbers against the league's eighth-softest schedule. Some modifications the Chiefs made tend to go overlooked but helped greatly.

The Chiefs shifted from using high rates of 21 and 13 personnel to more 11 and 12 packages. They went pass heavier in 11 and 12. Although Kansas City used 13 less, they passed far more often out of it. The 2016 Chiefs went 61% run out of 13 personnel, but managed a subpar 35% Success Rate. So in 2017, they passed on 53% of 13-personnel snaps.

Kansas City also had the NFL's seventh-most-injured receiver corps, primarily impacting their No. 2 wideout position. "X" receiver Chris Conley tore his Achilles' tendon in Week 5. Slot receiver Albert Wilson also got hurt in Week 5. The Chiefs turned to Demarcus Robinson, who struggled mightily with a 65 passer rating when targeted and anemic 6.3 yards-per-target average.

The Chiefs addressed wide receiver by making Sammy Watkins the NFL's fourth-highest-paid player at his position.

(cont'd - see KC-5)

Evan Silva's Fantasy Corner

All in on spread offense with Texas Tech alum Pat Mahomes at quarterback after leading the NFL in Run-Pass-Option (RPOs) percentage (18.1%) last year, the Chiefs aggressively made Sammy Watkins the league's fourth-highest-paid receiver at $16 million per year. Watkins never meshed with Jared Goff after the 2017 Rams acquired Watkins one month before Week 1, securing just 3-of-15 targets traveling 20-plus yards downfield despite dropping zero of those throws. (Watkins, in fact, didn't drop a pass all season.) He did score eight TDs, played 15 games for the first time since Watkins' 2014 rookie year, and showed up as exceptionally fast in Josh Hermsmeyer's Game Speed charts, particularly in the 10-23-yard and 35-plus-yard ranges. Whereas Watkins had to learn Sean McVay's offense on the fly, he gets a full offseason to build timing with Mahomes in K.C. Tyreek Hill is surer thing, but it's not crazy to suggest Watkins could equal or beat Hill in targets. Watkins is one of my favorite middle-round WR3/4 picks.

Division History: Season Wins & 2018 Projection

	2014 Wins	2015 Wins	2016 Wins	2017 Wins	Forecast 2018 Wins

Rank of 2018 Defensive Pass Efficiency Faced by Week

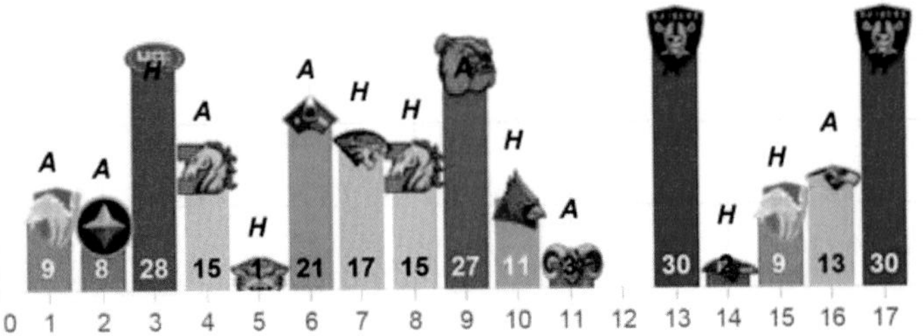

Rank of 2018 Defensive Rush Efficiency Faced by Week

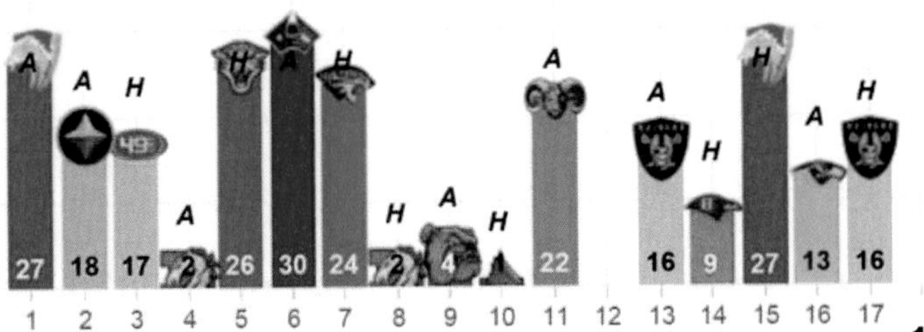

2017 Situational Usage by Player & Position

Usage Rate by Score

		Down Big (9-13)	One Score	Large Lead (9-13)	Blowout Lead (14+)	Grand Total
RUSH	Kareem Hunt	18%	30%	43%	38%	31%
	Tyreek Hill	2%	2%		1%	2%
	Travis Kelce		0%			0%
	Albert Wilson	1%	0%			0%
	Charcandrick West	1%	1%	3%	6%	2%
	Anthony Sherman		2%		3%	2%
	De'Anthony Thomas	1%				0%
	Akeem Hunt	2%	1%			1%
	C.J. Spiller		0%			0%
	Total	25%	38%	46%	48%	38%
PASS	Kareem Hunt	5%	8%	8%	5%	7%
	Tyreek Hill	12%	13%	13%	12%	13%
	Travis Kelce	20%	14%	11%	13%	14%
	Albert Wilson	7%	7%	7%	9%	7%
	Charcandrick West	9%	3%	5%	4%	4%
	Demarcus Robinson	5%	5%	4%	1%	5%
	Demetrius Harris	5%	4%	5%	4%	4%
	Anthony Sherman	1%	1%		1%	1%
	De'Anthony Thomas	4%	2%			2%
	Chris Conley	2%	2%			2%
	Akeem Hunt	2%	1%			1%
	Ross Travis		1%	1%	3%	1%
	C.J. Spiller		0%			0%
	Jehu Chesson	1%	0%			0%
	Orson Charles		0%			0%
	Total	75%	62%	54%	52%	62%

Positional Target Distribution vs NFL Average

		NFL Wide				Team Only			
		Left	Middle	Right	Total	Left	Middle	Right	Total
Deep	WR	962	499	966	2,427	24	10	21	55
	TE	178	136	175	489	14	14	13	41
	RB	37	9	40	86	2		2	4
	All	1,177	644	1,181	3,002	40	24	36	100
Short	WR	2,775	1,633	2,713	7,121	87	38	77	202
	TE	821	798	1,130	2,749	42	41	40	123
	RB	1,282	808	1,251	3,341	39	15	44	98
	All	4,878	3,239	5,094	13,211	168	94	161	423
Total		6,055	3,883	6,275	16,213	208	118	197	523

Positional Success Rates vs NFL Average

		NFL Wide				Team Only			
		Left	Middle	Right	Total	Left	Middle	Right	Total
Deep	WR	37%	45%	37%	39%	46%	40%	57%	49%
	TE	37%	51%	46%	44%	57%	64%	31%	51%
	RB	35%	56%	38%	38%	50%		50%	50%
	All	37%	47%	39%	40%	50%	54%	47%	50%
Short	WR	51%	57%	50%	52%	57%	68%	55%	58%
	TE	50%	56%	49%	51%	55%	54%	55%	54%
	RB	44%	51%	43%	45%	49%	47%	41%	45%
	All	49%	55%	48%	50%	55%	59%	51%	54%
Total		47%	54%	46%	48%	54%	58%	50%	53%

Successful Play Rate
0% 100%

Kansas City Chiefs - Success by Personnel Grouping & Play Type

Play Type	1-1 [3WR]	1-2 [2WR]	2-1 [2WR]	1-0 [4WR]	1-3 [1WR]	0-1 [4WR]	2-0 [3WR]	2-2 [1WR]	0-2 [3WR]	0-3 [2WR]	2-3 [0WR]	3-0 [2WR]	Grand Total
PASS	49% (342, 59%)	44% (147, 25%)	47% (34, 6%)	100% (1, 0%)	48% (31, 5%)	60% (5, 1%)	0% (1, 0%)	50% (8, 1%)	40% (5, 1%)	0% (4, 1%)	0% (2, 0%)		47% (580, 100%)
RUSH	45% (192, 47%)	50% (92, 23%)	48% (29, 7%)		43% (28, 7%)	0% (1, 0%)	100% (1, 0%)	39% (51, 13%)	100% (1, 0%)	0% (1, 0%)	50% (4, 1%)	0% (1, 0%)	45% (405, 100%)
TOTAL	48% (534, 54%)	46% (239, 24%)	48% (63, 6%)	100% (1, 0%)	46% (59, 6%)	50% (6, 1%)	50% (2, 0%)	41% (59, 6%)	50% (6, 1%)	0% (5, 1%)	33% (6, 1%)	0% (1, 0%)	46% (985, 100%)

Format Line 1: Success Rate Line 2: Total # of Plays, % of All Plays (by type)

KC-5

With Watkins and deep-threat Tyreek Hill on the field together, Travis Kelce dominating over the middle, and Kareem Hunt running efficiently, the Chiefs should be more dangerous in 12 personnel than they were last year. Will Reid be more conservative with a first-year starting quarterback? Reid has long been a pass-first coach, but his scheme decreases risk by drawing up shorter, easier completions with yards-after-catch upside.

It's hard to imagine a proven-winning coach like Reid discarding a productive, successful veteran like Smith unless he plans to unleash big-armed Mahomes. As seen in the graphics below, Tyreek Hill's 2017 Success Rate and yards per target suffered in 12 personnel last year without a productive running mate out wide. That's where Watkins comes in.

As excited as I am to see Mahomes, I remain concerned about a potential increase in interceptions and difficulty for the defense that would inevitably follow. Reid has a tough task to take on a freakishly gifted quarterback who believes he can make every throw and still keep Mahomes' INT rate low.

Receiving Success by Personnel Grouping

Position	Player	1-1 [3WR]	1-2 [2WR]	2-1 [2WR]	1-0 [4WR]	1-3 [1WR]	0-1 [4WR]	2-0 [3WR]	2-2 [1WR]	0-2 [3WR]	Total
RB	Kareem Hunt	52% 8.9 125.4 (31)	50% 5.5 89.4 (22)	50% 2.5 56.3 (2)		60% 5.2 127.9 (5)		0% 9.0 104.2 (1)	50% 8.5 102.1 (2)		51% 7.2 112.6 (63)
	Charcandrick West	39% 3.8 90.5 (23)	25% 5.6 90.1 (8)	0% 3.0 79.2 (1)		50% 7.0 135.4 (2)					35% 4.4 104.7 (34)
TE	Travis Kelce	56% 8.2 87.7 (68)	58% 8.8 134.0 (36)	67% 9.7 58.3 (6)		38% 9.9 124.5 (8)	0% 7.0 95.8 (1)		100% 10.0 108.3 (1)	50% 4.0 60.4 (2)	56% 8.5 105.8 (122)
WR	Tyreek Hill	63% 12.0 135.8 (65)	45% 8.9 105.1 (29)	75% 16.6 116.7 (8)		50% 2.0 56.3 (2)	100% 11.0 112.5 (1)				59% 11.3 126.8 (105)
	Albert Wilson	60% 9.6 110.3 (50)	50% 7.5 88.9 (6)	67% 6.3 132.6 (3)	100% 9.0 104.2 (1)		100% 3.0 79.2 (1)		0% 0.0 39.6 (1)		60% 8.9 111.9 (62)
	Demarcus Robinson	48% 6.3 75.1 (25)	56% 4.4 66.9 (9)	0% 0.0 0.0 (2)		100% 7.0 95.8 (1)	100% 7.0 95.8 (1)			0% 0.0 0.0 (1)	49% 5.4 48.2 (39)

Format Line 1: Success Rate Line 2: YPA Line 3: Passer Rating Line 4: Total # of Plays

Successful Play Rate
0% 100%

Rushing Success by Personnel Grouping

Position	Player	1-1 [3WR]	1-2 [2WR]	2-1 [2WR]	1-3 [1WR]	2-2 [1WR]	0-2 [3WR]	2-3 [0WR]	3-2 [0WR]	Total
QB	Alex Smith	53% 5.3 (32)	64% 12.3 (11)		100% 5.0 (3)	43% 0.3 (7)	100% 7.0 (1)	50% 0.0 (2)	0% -1.0 (4)	53% 5.4 (60)
RB	Kareem Hunt	47% 4.9 (122)	52% 4.6 (64)	44% 3.9 (25)	45% 6.3 (20)	38% 5.4 (39)		50% 3.0 (2)		46% 4.9 (272)
	Charcandrick West	20% 3.5 (10)	50% 3.0 (4)		0% 0.0 (1)	67% 8.3 (3)				33% 4.0 (18)

Format Line 1: Success Rate Line 2: YPC Line 3: Total # of Plays

Los Angeles Chargers

2018 Coaches

Head Coach:
Anthony Lynn (2nd yr)
Offensive Coordinator:
Ken Whisenhunt (3rd yr)
Defensive Coordinator:
Gus Bradley (2nd yr)

EASY HARD

2018 Forecast

Wins	Div Rank
9.5	#1

Past Records

2017: 9-7
2016: 5-11
2015: 4-12

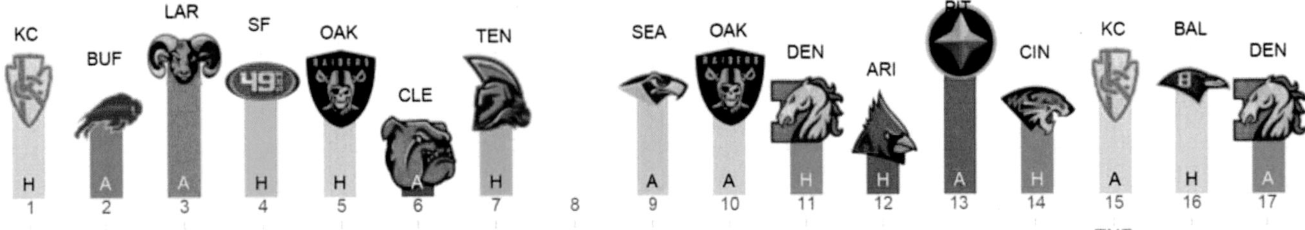

Key Players Lost

TXN	Player (POS)
Cut	Farrow, Kenneth RB
	Moore, Mike LB
	Rose, Nick K
Declared Free Agent	Attaochu, Jerry DE
	Boston, Tre S
	Burse, Isaiah WR
	Clemens, Kellen QB
	Cleveland, Asante TE
	Eulls, Kaleb DT
	Gates, Antonio TE
	Hairston, Chris T
	McCain, Chris DE
	McGrath, Sean TE
	Ola, Michael T
	Oliver, Branden RB
	Palepoi, Tenny DT
	Slauson, Matt C
	Toomer, Korey LB
	Wiggins, Kenny G
	Williams, Andre RB

Average Line	# Games Favored	# Games Underdog
-2.2	10	3

2018 Los Angeles Chargers Overview

The 2017 Chargers are a great testament to the impact of coaching on wins and losses, They made bad decisions to kick field goals and trusted an undrafted rookie kicker. They were run dominant on early downs in first halves of games. And they internally misevaluated what Antonio Gates had left.

These flaws were ultimately corrected, but not before it was too late. And they cost the Chargers a postseason berth. The Bolts eventually upgraded at kicker, but the latter two problems could only be uncovered by analytical study. Analytics allows us to recognize patterns early. Just a few weeks into the season, it became evident the Chargers were losing efficiency by running too often on early downs. And it was obvious Hunter Henry provided a significant edge in Success Rate and explosiveness over Gates. But the Bolts didn't pick up on either for months.

This is the problem when a team doesn't have an analytics department. It's safe to say most teams are understaffed from an analytics standpoint. Many have "a guy" studying statistics in some capacity, but are they the right statistics? And it takes more than one person to adequately review all data points, process them, and perform predictive studies to ensure teams operate at maximum efficiency. The other problem with the "we have a guy" approach is that most of these "guys" only study their specific team. They'll run opponent data and perhaps assist with game plans, but most don't look at league-wide trends. They don't look at what other teams are doing to succeed under modern NFL rules, or how the game has evolved. They have blinders on. But the Chargers took it to another level, because they didn't even have "a guy." They had no analytics department at all.

Chargers undrafted rookie kicker Younghoe Koo missed kicks in each of the first two games that caused Los Angeles to lose by three and two points. Coach Anthony Lynn understandably lost confidence in Koo, prompting the Chargers to make irrational decisions. In Week 3, they trailed by seven points at the Chiefs' 35-yard line with an entire fourth quarter to play. They ran the ball for a one-yard loss on first and ten.

(cont'd - see LAC2)

Key Free Agents/ Trades Added

- Aguayo, Roberto K
- Green, Virgil TE
- Pouncey, Mike C
- Smith, Geno QB
- Sturgis, Caleb K
- Watkins, Jaylen S

Drafted Players

Rd	Pk	Player (College)
1	17	S - Derwin James (Florida State)
2	48	LB - Uchenna Nwosu (USC)
3	84	DT - Justin Jones (NC State)
4	119	S - Kyzir White (West Virginia)
5	155	C - Scott Quessenberry (UCLA)
6	191	WR - Dylan Cantrell (Texas Tech)
7*	251	RB - Justin Jackson (Northwestern)

Regular Season Wins: Past & Current Proj

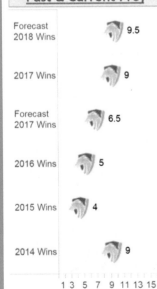

Forecast 2018 Wins	9.5
2017 Wins	9
Forecast 2017 Wins	6.5
2016 Wins	5
2015 Wins	4
2014 Wins	9

1 3 5 7 9 11 13 15

Lineup & Cap Hits

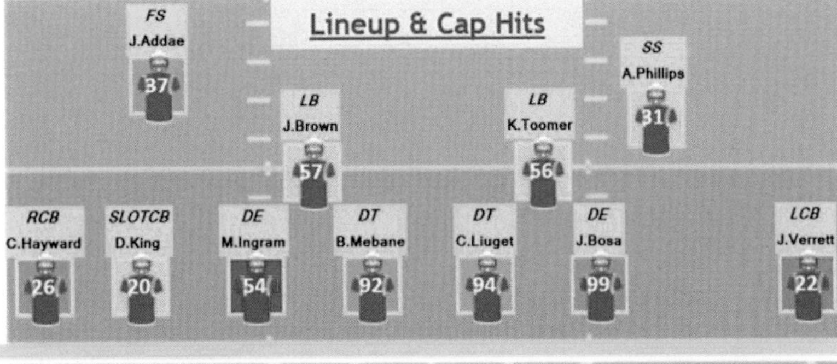

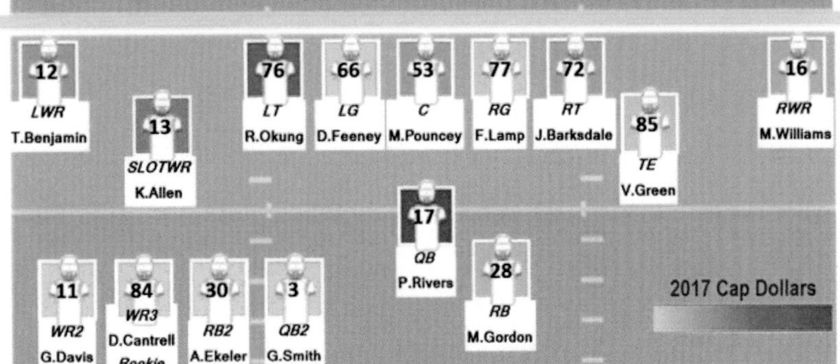

2018 Unit Spending

All DEF
All OFF

Positional Spending

	Rank	Total	2017 Rk
All OFF	12	$99.83M	12
QB	11	$24.11M	12
OL	12	$36.37M	29
RB	23	$5.48M	20
WR	6	$27.77M	7
TE	22	$6.09M	15
All DEF	17	$79.17M	21
DL	18	$24.57M	17
LB	13	$22.50M	12
CB	15	$20.27M	23
S	18	$11.82M	10

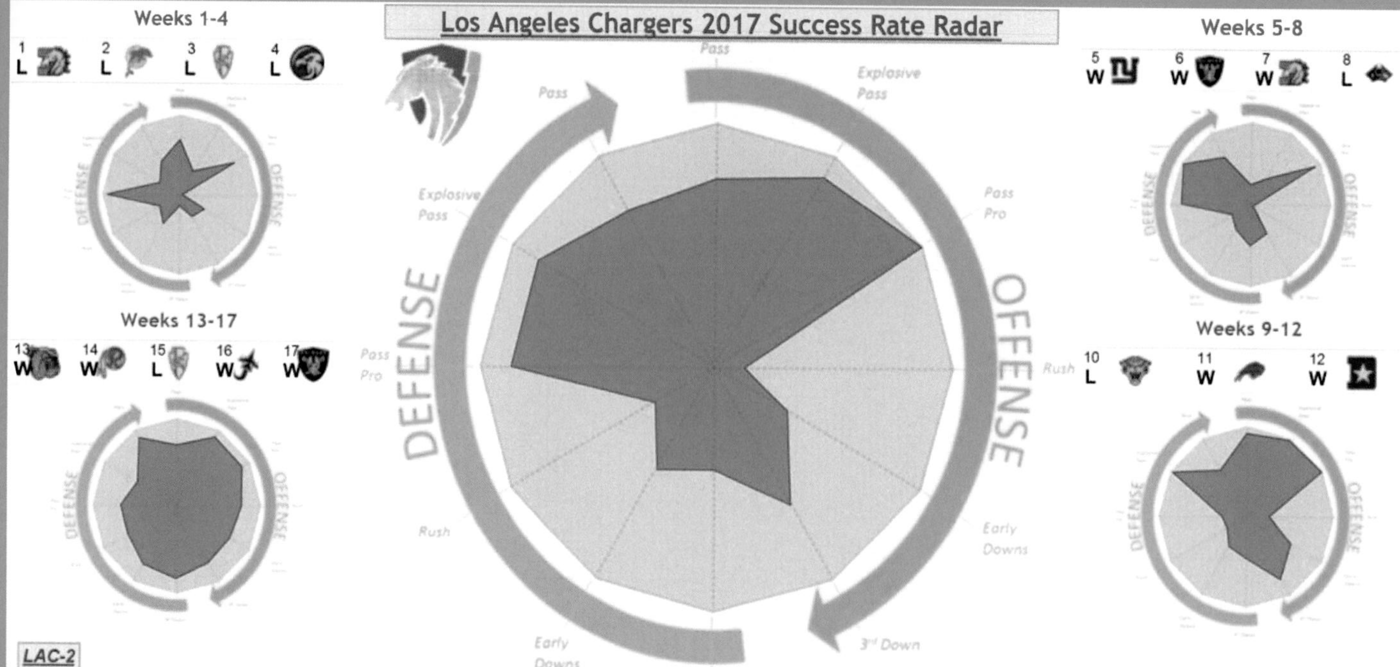

LAC-2

On second-and-11, they (ridiculously) ran again for one yard. Their third-and-ten pass failed. On fourth down, the Chargers took a delay-of-game penalty and punted instead of trying a 52-yard field goal. This critical AFC West game was lost not directly because of Koo, but because Koo's presence inspired such low confidence the coaches operated irrationally.

Over their first eight games, the Chargers ran on 52% of early downs in the first half, the sixth-highest rate in the league. They ran on 60% of first-down plays, the NFL's fourth-highest rate. Being predictable but successful is one thing. The Cowboys were a predictable first-down running team, but their Success Rate on such plays was 52%, fifth best in football. The 2017 Chargers ran on first down at the same rate as Dallas. But the Chargers' first-down rushing Success Rate was 26%, third worst in the league with a 2.9 yards-per-carry average.

The impact was enormous. The Chargers faced second and an average of 8.8 yards to go, fourth worst in the NFL. Yet their first-down passes were successful 46% of the time and averaged 7.0 yards per attempt. Their first-down running tendency lasted throughout Weeks 1-8, and the Chargers went 3-5 in those games.

After their Week 9 bye, the Chargers ran on only 46% of first-down plays, well below NFL average. They passed 54% of the time with a strong 57% Success Rate on first down, gaining 7.6 yards per attempt as opposed to 2.7 yards per carry on first-down runs in the second half of the year. This shift played a big role in the Chargers' Week 10 upset of Jacksonville. From that point on, the Chargers went 54% pass on first-half first-down plays, the NFL's seventh-highest rate after running at the sixth-highest rate on such plays in the first half of the year. The Chargers went 6-2 down the stretch, a huge improvement on their 3-5 start.

(cont'd - see LAC-3)

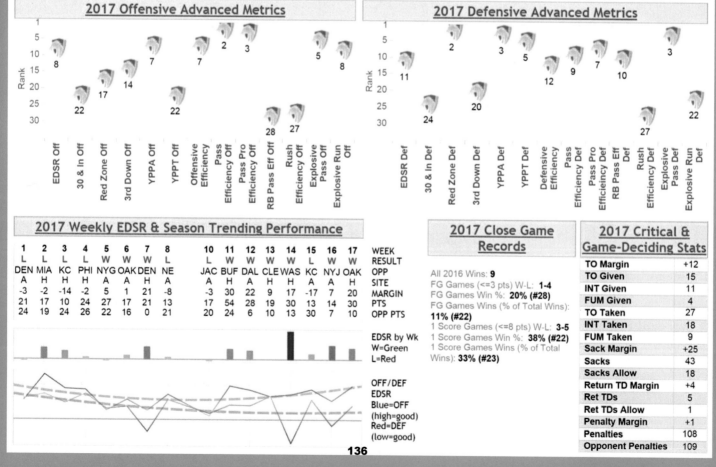

2017 Offensive Advanced Metrics

Metric	Rank
EDSR Off	8
30 & In Off	22
Red Zone Off	17
3rd Down Off	14
YPPA Off	7
YPPT Off	22
Offensive Efficiency	7
Pass Efficiency Off	2
Pass Pro Efficiency Off	3
RB Pass Eff Off	28
Rush Efficiency Off	27
Explosive Pass Off	5
Explosive Run Off	8

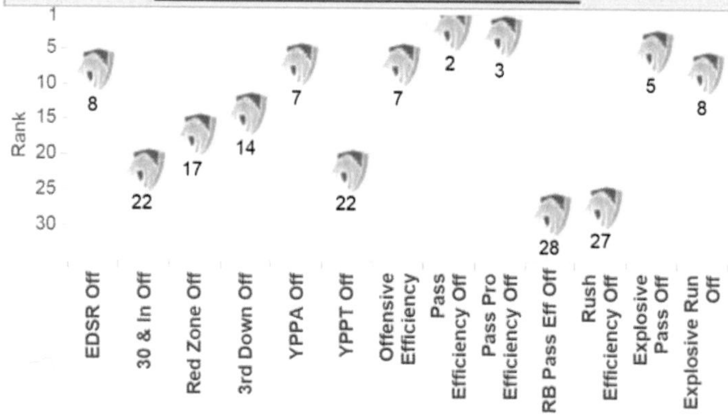

2017 Defensive Advanced Metrics

Metric	Rank
EDSR Def	11
30 & In Def	24
Red Zone Def	2
3rd Down Def	20
YPPA Def	3
YPPT Def	5
Defensive Efficiency	12
Pass Efficiency Def	9
Pass Pro Efficieincy Def	7
RB Pass Eff Def	10
Rush Efficiency Def	27
Explosive Pass Def	3
Explosive Run Def	22

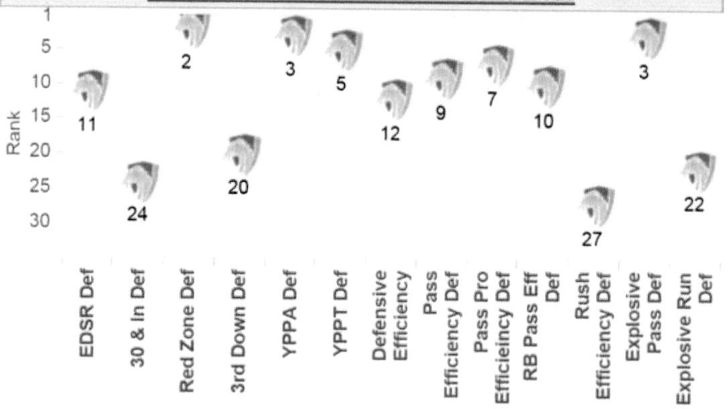

2017 Weekly EDSR & Season Trending Performance

WEEK	1	2	3	4	5	6	7	8	10	11	12	13	14	15	16	17
RESULT	L	L	L	L	W	W	W	L	L	W	W	W	W	L	W	W
OPP	DEN	MIA	KC	PHI	NYG	OAK	DEN	NE	JAC	BUF	DAL	CLE	WAS	KC	NYJ	OAK
SITE	A	H	H	H	A	A	H	A	A	H	A	H	H	A	A	H
MARGIN	-3	-2	-14	-2	5	1	21	-8	-3	30	22	9	17	-17	7	20
PTS	21	17	10	24	27	17	21	13	17	54	28	19	30	13	14	30
OPP PTS	24	19	24	26	22	16	0	21	20	24	6	10	13	30	7	10

EDSR by Wk
W=Green
L=Red

OFF/DEF EDSR
Blue=OFF (high=good)
Red=DEF (low=good)

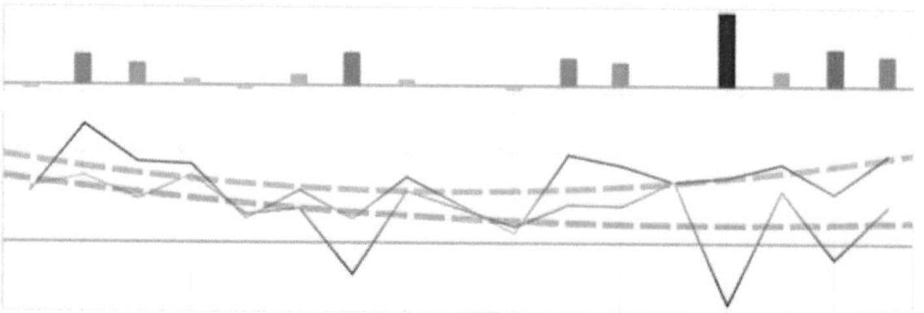

2017 Close Game Records

All 2016 Wins: **9**
FG Games (<=3 pts) W-L: **1-4**
FG Games Win %: **20% (#28)**
FG Games Wins (% of Total Wins): **11% (#22)**
1 Score Games (<=8 pts) W-L: **3-5**
1 Score Games Win %: **38% (#22)**
1 Score Games Wins (% of Total Wins): **33% (#23)**

2017 Critical & Game-Deciding Stats

TO Margin	+12
TO Given	15
INT Given	11
FUM Given	4
TO Taken	27
INT Taken	18
FUM Taken	9
Sack Margin	+25
Sacks	43
Sacks Allow	18
Return TD Margin	+4
Ret TDs	5
Ret TDs Allow	1
Penalty Margin	+1
Penalties	108
Opponent Penalties	109

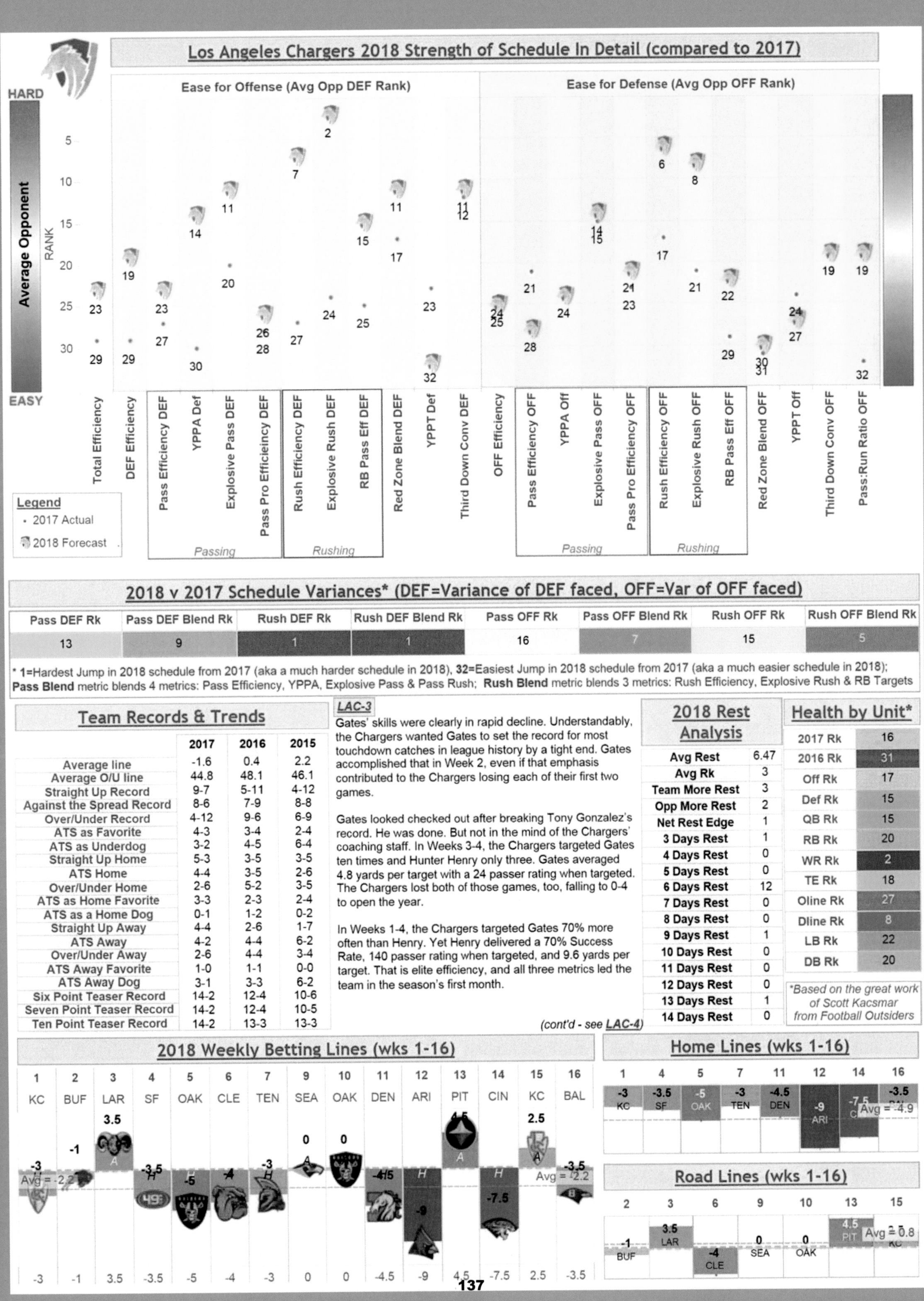

Los Angeles Chargers 2018 Strength of Schedule In Detail (compared to 2017)

2018 v 2017 Schedule Variances* (DEF=Variance of DEF faced, OFF=Var of OFF faced)

Pass DEF Rk	Pass DEF Blend Rk	Rush DEF Rk	Rush DEF Blend Rk	Pass OFF Rk	Pass OFF Blend Rk	Rush OFF Rk	Rush OFF Blend Rk
13	9	1	1	16	7	15	5

* **1**=Hardest Jump in 2018 schedule from 2017 (aka a much harder schedule in 2018), **32**=Easiest Jump in 2018 schedule from 2017 (aka a much easier schedule in 2018); **Pass Blend** metric blends 4 metrics: Pass Efficiency, YPPA, Explosive Pass & Pass Rush; **Rush Blend** metric blends 3 metrics: Rush Efficiency, Explosive Rush & RB Targets

Team Records & Trends

	2017	2016	2015
Average line	-1.6	0.4	2.2
Average O/U line	44.8	48.1	46.1
Straight Up Record	9-7	5-11	4-12
Against the Spread Record	8-6	7-9	8-8
Over/Under Record	4-12	9-6	6-9
ATS as Favorite	4-3	3-4	2-4
ATS as Underdog	3-2	4-5	6-4
Straight Up Home	5-3	3-5	3-5
ATS Home	4-4	3-5	2-6
Over/Under Home	2-6	5-2	3-5
ATS as Home Favorite	3-3	2-3	2-4
ATS as a Home Dog	0-1	1-2	0-2
Straight Up Away	4-4	2-6	1-7
ATS Away	4-2	4-4	6-2
Over/Under Away	2-6	4-4	3-4
ATS Away Favorite	1-0	1-1	0-0
ATS Away Dog	3-1	3-3	6-2
Six Point Teaser Record	14-2	12-4	10-6
Seven Point Teaser Record	14-2	12-4	10-5
Ten Point Teaser Record	14-2	13-3	13-3

LAC-3

Gates' skills were clearly in rapid decline. Understandably, the Chargers wanted Gates to set the record for most touchdown catches in league history by a tight end. Gates accomplished that in Week 2, even if that emphasis contributed to the Chargers losing each of their first two games.

Gates looked checked out after breaking Tony Gonzalez's record. He was done. But not in the mind of the Chargers' coaching staff. In Weeks 3-4, the Chargers targeted Gates ten times and Hunter Henry only three. Gates averaged 4.8 yards per target with a 24 passer rating when targeted. The Chargers lost both of those games, too, falling to 0-4 to open the year.

In Weeks 1-4, the Chargers targeted Gates 70% more often than Henry. Yet Henry delivered a 70% Success Rate, 140 passer rating when targeted, and 9.6 yards per target. That is elite efficiency, and all three metrics led the team in the season's first month.

*(cont'd - see **LAC-4**)*

2018 Rest Analysis

Avg Rest	6.47
Avg Rk	3
Team More Rest	3
Opp More Rest	2
Net Rest Edge	1
3 Days Rest	1
4 Days Rest	0
5 Days Rest	0
6 Days Rest	12
7 Days Rest	0
8 Days Rest	0
9 Days Rest	1
10 Days Rest	0
11 Days Rest	0
12 Days Rest	0
13 Days Rest	1
14 Days Rest	0

Health by Unit*

2017 Rk	16
2016 Rk	31
Off Rk	17
Def Rk	15
QB Rk	15
RB Rk	20
WR Rk	2
TE Rk	18
Oline Rk	27
Dline Rk	8
LB Rk	22
DB Rk	20

**Based on the great work of Scott Kacsmar from Football Outsiders*

2018 Weekly Betting Lines (wks 1-16)

1	2	3	4	5	6	7	9	10	11	12	13	14	15	16
KC	BUF	LAR	SF	OAK	CLE	TEN	SEA	OAK	DEN	ARI	PIT	CIN	KC	BAL
-3	-1	3.5	-3.5	-5	-4	-3	0	0	-4.5	-9	4.5	-7.5	2.5	-3.5

Home Lines (wks 1-16)

1	4	5	7	11	12	14	16
-3	-3.5	-5	-3	-4.5	-9	-7.5	-3.5
KC	SF	OAK	TEN	DEN	ARI	CIN	BAL

Road Lines (wks 1-16)

2	3	6	9	10	13	15
-1	3.5	-4	0	0	4.5	2.5
BUF	LAR	CLE	SEA	OAK	PIT	KC

Los Angeles Chargers 2017 Play Analysis

2017 Play Tendencies

All Pass %	59%
All Pass Rk	13
All Rush %	41%
All Rush Rk	20
1 Score Pass %	63%
1 Score Pass Rk	2
2016 1 Score Pass %	63%
2016 1 Score Pass Rk	4
2017 Pass Increase %	0%
Pass Increase Rk	13
1 Score Rush %	37%
1 Score Rush Rk	31
Up Pass %	52%
Up Pass Rk	7
Up Rush %	48%
Up Rush Rk	26
Down Pass %	67%
Down Pass Rk	12
Down Rush %	33%
Down Rush Rk	21

2017 Down & Distance Tendencies

Down	Distance	Total Plays	Pass Rate	Run Rate	Play Success %
1	Short (1-3)	7	29%	71%	57%
	Med (4-7)	12	67%	33%	25%
	Long (8-10)	317	46%	54%	43%
	XL (11+)	11	55%	45%	27%
2	Short (1-3)	25	28%	72%	60%
	Med (4-7)	60	62%	38%	55%
	Long (8-10)	106	74%	26%	51%
	XL (11+)	49	78%	22%	37%
3	Short (1-3)	44	64%	36%	55%
	Med (4-7)	40	95%	5%	43%
	Long (8-10)	40	100%	0%	40%
	XL (11+)	27	93%	7%	26%
4	Short (1-3)	3	33%	67%	33%
	Med (4-7)	1	100%	0%	100%
	XL (11+)	1	100%	0%	0%

Shotgun %:

Under Center	Shotgun
34%	66%
37%	*63%*

37% AVG 63%

Run Rate:

Under Center	Shotgun
74%	24%

68% AVG 23%

Pass Rate:

Under Center	Shotgun
26%	76%

32% AVG 77%

Short Yardage Intelligence:

2nd and Short Run

Run Freq	Run Rk	NFL Run Freq Avg	Run 1D Rate	Run NFL 1D Avg
71%	10	67%	50%	69%

2nd and Short Pass

Pass Freq	Pass Rk	NFL Pass Freq Avg	Pass 1D Rate	Pass NFL 1D Avg
29%	22	33%	100%	53%

Most Frequent Play

Down	Distance	Play Type	Player	Total Plays	Play Success %
1	Short (1-3)	RUSH	Melvin Gordon	3	67%
	Med (4-7)	RUSH	Melvin Gordon	3	0%
	Long (8-10)	RUSH	Melvin Gordon	127	31%
	XL (11+)	PASS	Melvin Gordon	3	0%
		RUSH	Melvin Gordon	3	67%
2	Short (1-3)	RUSH	Melvin Gordon	14	64%
	Med (4-7)	RUSH	Melvin Gordon	12	50%
	Long (8-10)	RUSH	Melvin Gordon	21	43%
	XL (11+)	PASS	Keenan Allen	11	64%
3	Short (1-3)	PASS	Keenan Allen	14	36%
	Med (4-7)	PASS	Keenan Allen	18	50%
	Long (8-10)	PASS	Keenan Allen	9	67%
	XL (11+)	PASS	Tyrell Williams	7	57%

Most Successful Play*

Down	Distance	Play Type	Player	Total Plays	Play Success %
1	Long (8-10)	PASS	Hunter Henry	18	83%
2	Short (1-3)	RUSH	Melvin Gordon	14	64%
	Med (4-7)	RUSH	Austin Ekeler	8	63%
	Long (8-10)	PASS	Hunter Henry	11	91%
	XL (11+)	PASS	Keenan Allen	11	64%
3	Short (1-3)	RUSH	Melvin Gordon	11	73%
	Med (4-7)	PASS	Hunter Henry	6	67%
	Long (8-10)	PASS	Keenan Allen	9	67%
	XL (11+)	PASS	Tyrell Williams	7	57%

**Minimum 5 plays to qualify*

2017 Snap Rates

Wk	Opp	Score	Keenan Allen	Tyrell Williams	Melvin Gordon	Hunter Henry	Travis Benjamin	Antonio Gates	Sean McGrath	Dontrelle Inman
1	DEN	L 24-21	53 (90%)	55 (93%)	44 (75%)	23 (39%)	39 (66%)	39 (66%)		
2	MIA	L 19-17	49 (84%)	52 (90%)	48 (83%)	33 (57%)	39 (67%)	32 (55%)	5 (9%)	13 (22%)
3	KC	L 24-10	61 (84%)	71 (97%)	33 (45%)	41 (56%)	44 (60%)	40 (55%)	10 (14%)	14 (19%)
4	PHI	L 26-24	49 (86%)	50 (88%)	42 (74%)	35 (61%)	37 (65%)	36 (63%)	6 (11%)	9 (16%)
5	NYG	W 27-22	71 (91%)	66 (85%)	65 (83%)	59 (76%)	46 (59%)	41 (53%)	20 (26%)	3 (4%)
6	OAK	W 17-16	55 (85%)	44 (68%)	58 (89%)	54 (83%)	21 (32%)	37 (57%)	25 (38%)	
7	DEN	W 21-0	47 (81%)	43 (74%)	40 (69%)	47 (81%)	22 (38%)	18 (31%)	23 (40%)	
8	NE	L 21-13	52 (93%)	46 (82%)	33 (59%)	35 (63%)	35 (63%)	25 (45%)	5 (9%)	
10	JAC	L 20-17	59 (86%)	43 (62%)	47 (68%)	45 (65%)	41 (59%)	26 (38%)	18 (26%)	
11	BUF	W 54-24	53 (72%)	61 (82%)	37 (50%)	44 (59%)	21 (28%)	15 (20%)	15 (20%)	
12	DAL	W 28-6	59 (87%)	60 (88%)	42 (62%)	52 (76%)	44 (65%)	18 (26%)	7 (10%)	
13	CLE	W 19-10	64 (91%)	51 (73%)	52 (74%)	50 (71%)	38 (54%)	27 (39%)	5 (7%)	
14	WAS	W 30-13	49 (68%)	51 (71%)	47 (65%)	42 (58%)	33 (46%)	19 (26%)	17 (24%)	
15	KC	L 30-13	47 (73%)	53 (83%)	53 (83%)	38 (59%)	36 (56%)	22 (34%)	11 (17%)	
16	NYJ	W 14-7	68 (93%)	57 (78%)	53 (73%)		31 (42%)	56 (77%)	28 (38%)	
17	OAK	W 30-10	63 (90%)	49 (70%)	55 (79%)		39 (56%)	49 (70%)	22 (31%)	
Grand Total			899 (85%)	852 (80%)	749 (71%)	598 (65%)	566 (54%)	500 (47%)	217 (21%)	39 (15%)

Personnel Groupings

Personnel	Team %	NFL Avg	Succ. %
1-1 [3WR]	56%	59%	47%
1-2 [2WR]	22%	19%	45%
2-1 [2WR]	8%	7%	38%
2-2 [1WR]	6%	4%	28%
1-3 [1WR]	5%	5%	37%

Grouping Tendencies

Personnel	Pass Rate	Pass Succ. %	Run Succ. %
1-1 [3WR]	73%	46%	51%
1-2 [2WR]	51%	46%	44%
2-1 [2WR]	32%	60%	28%
2-2 [1WR]	11%	29%	28%
1-3 [1WR]	37%	55%	26%

Red Zone Targets (min 3)

Receiver	All	Inside 5	6-10	11-20
Keenan Allen	24	7	8	9
Hunter Henry	12	2	7	3
Antonio Gates	11	3	7	1
Melvin Gordon	10		5	5
Austin Ekeler	5	1	1	3
Mike Williams	4		2	2
Travis Benjamin	2			2
Tyrell Williams	1			1

Red Zone Rushes (min 3)

Rusher	All	Inside 5	6-10	11-20
Melvin Gordon	49	14	13	22
Philip Rivers	7	4	1	2
Austin Ekeler	6	1	2	3

Early Down Target Rate

RB	TE	WR
24%	22%	54%
23%	*21% NFL AVG*	*56%*

Overall Target Success %

RB	TE	WR
40% #27	58% #1	48% #15

Los Angeles Chargers 2017 Passing Recap & 2018 Outlook

When Philip Rivers is dialed in, his passion for the game shows and he wears his emotions on his sleeve. But he's not the most trustworthy quarterback from a decision-making standpoint and tends to let isolated plays devolve into bad habits with inefficiency that can spiral out of control. Rivers' cause will be made tougher by losing Henry, particularly in the red zone. Henry scored ten touchdowns on red-zone targets over the past two years, most on the team. I would encourage the Chargers to throw more on first down, a longtime strength of Rivers. Last year, he averaged 8.4 yards per attempt with a 111 passer rating on first-down throws, second best in the NFL. Over the last two seasons, Rivers leads the league with a 115 rating on first-down passes. Yet he ranks 16th of 21 qualified quarterbacks in third-down passer rating over that span. This further accentuates the importance of early-down passing to generate larger gains and keep Rivers out of third-and-long trouble.

Philip Rivers Rating All Downs

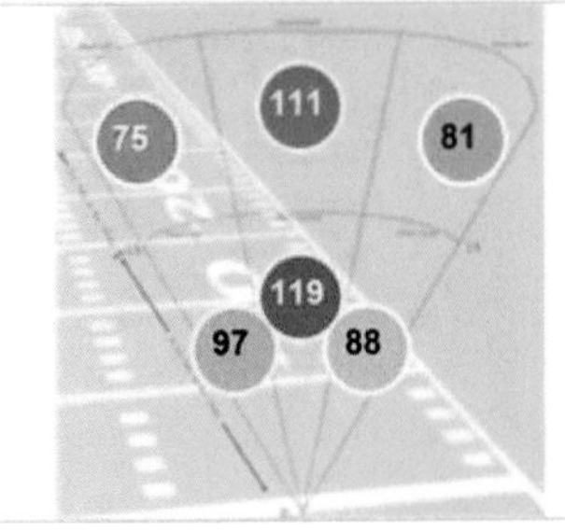

Philip Rivers Rating Early Downs

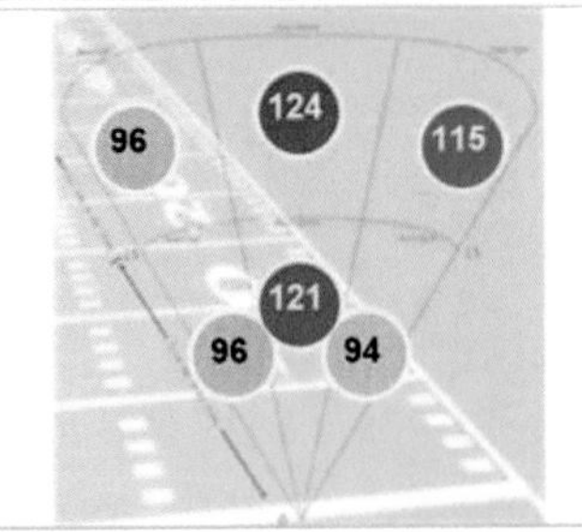

2017 Standard Passing Table

QB	Comp	Att	Comp %	Yds	YPA	TDs	INT	Sacks	Rating	Rk
Philip Rivers	360	576	63%	4,495	7.8	28	10	17	96	13
NFL Avg			62%		7.0				87.5	

2017 Advanced Passing Table

QB	Success %	EDSR Passing Success %	20+ Yd Pass Gains	20+ Yd Pass %	30+ Yd Pass Gains	30+ Yd Pass %	Avg. Air Yds per Comp	Avg. YAC per Comp	20+ Air Yd Comp	20+ Air Yd %
Philip Rivers	46%	49%	61	10.6%	22	3.8%	6.4	6.0	27	8%
NFL Avg	44%	48%	27.7	8.8%	10.3	3.3%	6.0	4.7	11.7	6%

Interception Rates by Down

Yards to Go	1	2	3	4	Total
1 & 2	0.0%	0.0%	0.0%	50.0%	4.0%
3, 4, 5	0.0%	0.0%	0.0%	0.0%	0.0%
6 - 9	0.0%	0.0%	7.5%		3.2%
10 - 14	0.0%	3.7%	0.0%	0.0%	1.0%
15+	0.0%	0.0%	7.7%		2.6%
Total	0.0%	1.5%	3.6%	20.0%	1.7%

3rd Down Passing - Short of Sticks Analysis

QB	Avg. Yds to Go	Avg. YIA (of Comp)	Avg Yds Short	Short of Sticks Rate	Short Rk
Philip Rivers	8.0	6.8	-1.1	56%	22
NFL Avg	7.8	6.7	-1.1	60%	

Air Yds vs YAC

Air Yds %	YAC %	Rk
53%	47%	33
58%	42%	

2017 Receiving Recap & 2018 Outlook

The Chargers have a deep, talented wideout corps but will be missing a top weapon. Over the last two years, Henry ranks No. 1 among tight ends in both Success Rate and yards per target. The Chargers won't get nearly the same production from blocker Virgil Green. I think they will use more three-receiver, 11-personnel formations with 2017 first-round pick Mike Williams back healthy. The Chargers also must target their running backs more in the passing game on early downs instead of waiting for third downs to throw to Melvin Gordon and Austin Ekeler.

Player *Min 50 Targets*	Targets	Comp %	YPA	Rating	TOARS	Success %	Success Rk	Missed YPA Rk	YAS % Rk	TDs
Keenan Allen	159	64%	8.8	99	5.5	56%	20	39	50	6
Melvin Gordon	83	70%	5.7	100	4.4	38%	119	68	115	4
Tyrell Williams	69	62%	10.6	105	4.2	47%	76	55	10	4
Travis Benjamin	65	52%	8.7	77	3.7	36%	125	119	15	4
Hunter Henry	62	73%	9.3	123	4.5	66%	2	6	52	4

Directional Passer Rating Delivered

Receiver	Short Left	Short Middle	Short Right	Deep Left	Deep Middle	Deep Right	Player Total
Keenan Allen	105	108	84	100	66	129	99
Melvin Gordon	84	127	104				100
Tyrell Williams	84	119	100	60	129	63	105
Travis Benjamin	112	40	92	55	119	69	77
Hunter Henry	94	132	120	156	40	117	123
Antonio Gates	121	118	0	119	40	52	79
Austin Ekeler	113	99	134	119			128
Dontrelle Inman	85		40	40			56
Team Total	99	119	91	78	111	88	100

2017 Rushing Recap & 2017 Outlook

Melvin Gordon became the first-ever running back to have his fifth-year option exercised as a former first-round pick. He has averaged fewer than four yards per carry in all three years of his career. And his 42% Success Rate on 538 carries the past two years ranked worst among all running backs with at least 425 carries. Last year, the Chargers ran Gordon on first down 161 times even though he was the worst first-down rusher in the league. Gordon did help me win a 2017 fantasy championship through volume and receiving ability, but not because he was efficient. It seems like Anthony Lynn's coaching staff views Gordon as a workhorse back, but Gordon isn't that type of player. The Chargers should target Gordon more in the passing game.

Player *Min 50 Rushes*	Rushes	YPC	Success %	Success Rk	Missed YPA Rk	YTS % Rk	YAS % Rk	Early Down Success %	Early Down Success Rk	TDs
Melvin Gordon	284	3.9	40%	62	50	50	24	39%	65	9

Yards per Carry by Direction

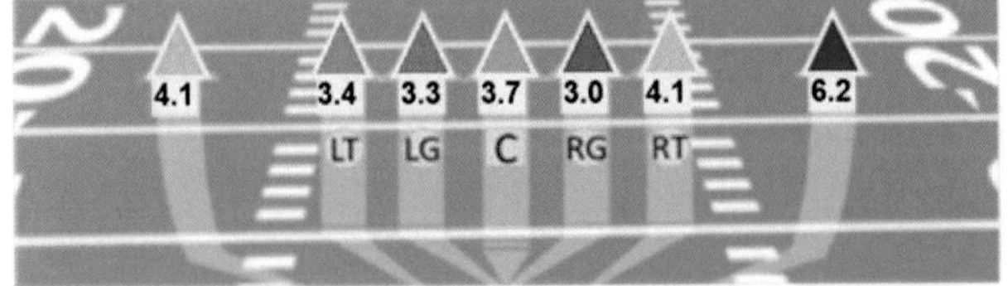

Directional Run Frequency

12% | 14% | 7% | 40% | 7% | 10% | 11%

LT | LG | C | RG | RT

But Henry's playing time didn't rise until Week 5, and it took until Week 7 for Gates' snap rate to fall below 50%, where it remained until Henry was lost for the season in Week 16. Henry's value was phenomenal, and his usage unmistakably correlated to wins. Through Week 13, the Chargers went 5-0 whenever Henry played at least 70% of the snaps. Otherwise, they were 1-6. When Henry drew five-plus targets, the Chargers went 7-1. Otherwise, 0-6.

This bad decision making put me on tilt. And I didn't even need complicated analytics or detailed support to back up my theories. The Chargers chose a bad kicker. They should have stopped running on first-and-ten sooner, and they should have transitioned fully from Gates to Henry. But because they didn't even have "a guy," they weren't aware until it was too late. In the modern age, that should be a crime. Players lose their jobs when teams miss the playoffs. Teams lose revenue.

Especially in a weak AFC, last year's Chargers should have been an 11- to 12-win team. They could have hosted a playoff game in their first year in Los Angeles. But the L.A. Rams captured the city with more optimal decision making. Fans don't want incompetence. When trying to convince a new city to buy into your team, it's impossible to justify ownership's unwillingness to provide an analytics staff for basic evaluations.

(cont'd - see LAC-5)

Evan Silva's Fantasy Corner

Keenan Allen overcame hard-luck injuries for his first-career 16-game season in 2017, capitalizing for top-five finishes in targets (159), catches (102), and yards (1,393) at his position. Allen scored only six TDs despite leading all NFL receivers in red-zone targets (24), hinting at forthcoming positive-touchdown regression; Allen hit pay dirt on just 5.9% of his catches after scoring on 7.2% of receptions in his first four years. Allen's early-career injuries were bad breaks: a broken collarbone, lacerated kidney, and non-contact knee ligament tear. Hunter Henry's ACL tear won't help the offense, but it further solidifies Allen as Rivers' go-to guy in scoring position with double-digit TDs well within his range of potential outcomes. Allen is my fantasy WR5 behind Antonio Brown, DeAndre Hopkins, Julio Jones, and Odell Beckham.

Division History: Season Wins & 2018 Projection

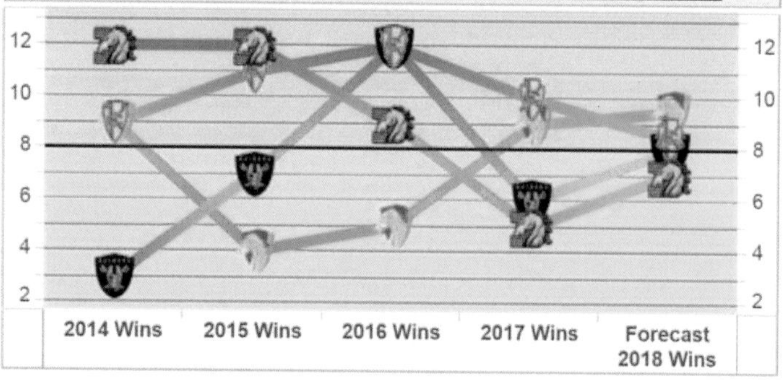

Rank of 2018 Defensive Pass Efficiency Faced by Week

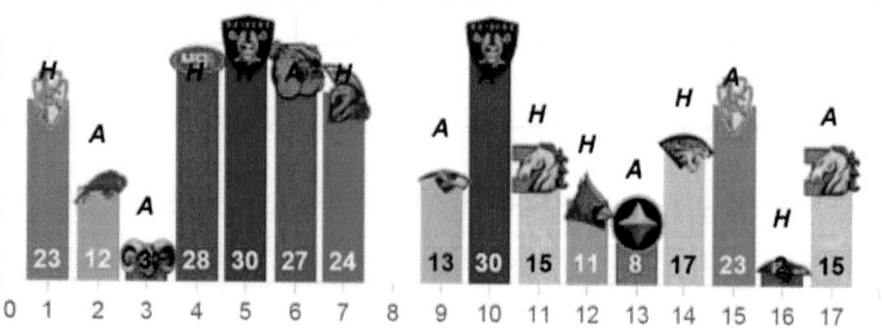

Rank of 2018 Defensive Rush Efficiency Faced by Week

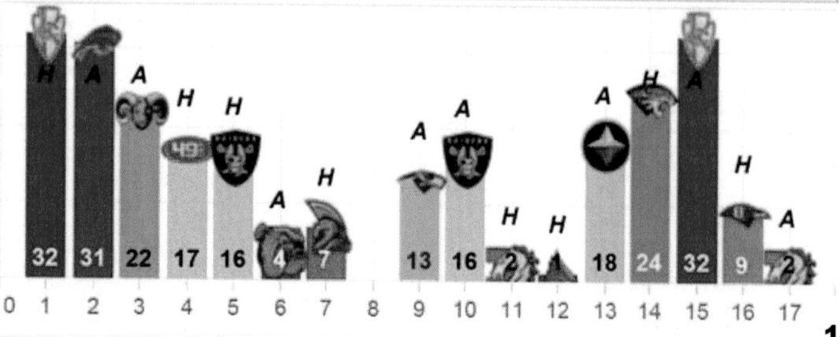

2017 Situational Usage by Player & Position

Usage Rate by Score

		Being Blown Out (14+)	Down Big (9-13)	One Score	Large Lead (9-13)	Blowout Lead (14+)	Grand Total
RUSH	Melvin Gordon	35%	24%	28%	34%	35%	29%
	Keenan Allen			0%			0%
	Austin Ekeler		3%	4%	2%	11%	5%
	Travis Benjamin			1%	2%	2%	1%
	Branden Oliver	2%	3%	4%	5%	1%	4%
	Andre Williams					6%	1%
	Derek Watt			0%		2%	1%
	Total	37%	29%	39%	42%	58%	41%
PASS	Melvin Gordon	9%	11%	9%	7%	4%	9%
	Keenan Allen	12%	16%	17%	25%	12%	16%
	Austin Ekeler	5%	3%	4%	2%	2%	4%
	Travis Benjamin	14%	11%	6%	5%	4%	7%
	Tyrell Williams	12%	16%	7%	7%	1%	7%
	Hunter Henry		3%	8%	3%	6%	6%
	Antonio Gates	5%	11%	6%	7%	1%	5%
	Branden Oliver	7%		1%			1%
	Mike Williams		1%	1%	2%	9%	2%
	Derek Watt			0%			0%
	Dontrelle Inman		1%	0%			0%
	Sean McGrath			0%		1%	0%
	Jeff Cumberland			0%		1%	0%
	Total	63%	71%	61%	58%	42%	59%

Positional Target Distribution vs NFL Average

		NFL Wide				Team Only			
		Left	Middle	Right	Total	Left	Middle	Right	Total
Deep	WR	955	483	964	2,402	31	26	23	80
	TE	185	148	181	514	7	2	7	16
	RB	38	9	42	89	1			1
	All	1,178	640	1,187	3,005	39	28	30	97
Short	WR	2,755	1,633	2,718	7,106	107	38	72	217
	TE	838	802	1,134	2,774	25	37	36	98
	RB	1,272	801	1,249	3,322	49	22	46	117
	All	4,865	3,236	5,101	13,202	181	97	154	432
Total		6,043	3,876	6,288	16,207	220	125	184	529

Positional Success Rates vs NFL Average

		NFL Wide				Team Only			
		Left	Middle	Right	Total	Left	Middle	Right	Total
Deep	WR	37%	45%	38%	39%	35%	46%	35%	39%
	TE	36%	53%	45%	44%	86%	0%	57%	63%
	RB	34%	56%	38%	38%	100%			100%
	All	37%	47%	39%	40%	46%	43%	40%	43%
Short	WR	51%	57%	50%	52%	57%	63%	40%	53%
	TE	50%	56%	49%	51%	60%	62%	53%	58%
	RB	45%	51%	43%	45%	27%	64%	46%	41%
	All	49%	55%	48%	50%	49%	63%	45%	51%
Total		47%	54%	46%	48%	49%	58%	44%	49%

Successful Play Rate
0% — 100%

Los Angeles Chargers - Success by Personnel Grouping & Play Type

Play Type	1-1 [3WR]	1-2 [2WR]	2-1 [2WR]	1-0 [4WR]	1-3 [1WR]	0-1 [4WR]	2-2 [1WR]	0-2 [3WR]	3-1 [1WR]	2-3 [0WR]	3-0 [2WR]	Grand Total
PASS	46% (417, 69%)	46% (112, 19%)	60% (25, 4%)	33% (3, 0%)	55% (20, 3%)	50% (8, 1%)	29% (7, 1%)	25% (8, 1%)	0% (1, 0%)			46% (601, 100%)
RUSH	51% (157, 37%)	44% (108, 26%)	28% (53, 13%)	0% (1, 0%)	26% (34, 8%)		28% (57, 14%)			25% (8, 2%)	0% (1, 0%)	40% (419, 100%)
TOTAL	47% (574, 56%)	45% (220, 22%)	38% (78, 8%)	25% (4, 0%)	37% (54, 5%)	50% (8, 1%)	28% (64, 6%)	25% (8, 1%)	0% (1, 0%)	25% (8, 1%)	0% (1, 0%)	44% (1,020, 100%)

Format Line 1: Success Rate Line 2: Total # of Plays, % of All Plays (by type)

LAC-5 Dean Spanos should be embarrassed. You can be anti-analytics all you want, Dean. But I'm here to say you are wrong. And it cost your team, and it cost your pocketbook.

The 2017 Chargers posted a +12 turnover margin, +25 sack margin, and +4 return-touchdown margin. Yet they went 1-4 in games decided by a field goal. Flip to page two of this chapter and you'll see they dominated Early-Down Success Rate on a weekly basis. Last year's Chargers were a very good team. And they should be very good again in 2018, even after Henry tore his ACL. They do face a slightly tougher schedule, but I love the defensive pieces they added in the draft. They are favored in ten of their first 15 games and are projected at 9.5 wins. They should have one of the NFL's top defenses, and their wideout corps is extremely deep.

But I'm down on the Chargers' strategy and philosophy, and lack confidence they'll be able to quickly fix issues that cost them games. I'd love to project the Chargers as clear AFC West favorites, But due to their coaching, Henry's loss, and lack of a true home-field advantage without a legitimate fanbase in Los Angeles, the Chargers are merely "in the mix," and not the i..

Receiving Success by Personnel Grouping

Position	Player	1-1 [3WR]	1-2 [2WR]	2-1 [2WR]	1-0 [4WR]	1-3 [1WR]	0-1 [4WR]	2-2 [1WR]	0-2 [3WR]	3-1 [1WR]	Total
RB	Melvin Gordon	40% 6.1 98.4 (60)	40% 4.8 122.8 (15)	33% 3.7 45.1 (3)		40% 5.2 73.8 (5)					40% 5.7 100.3 (83)
TE	Hunter Henry	75% 8.1 122.3 (28)	61% 9.3 113.3 (23)	100% 13.0 118.8 (4)		75% 20.5 156.3 (4)	0% 3.0 79.2 (1)	0% 0.0 39.6 (2)			68% 9.3 123.0 (62)
	Antonio Gates	45% 5.8 68.0 (42)	60% 3.6 67.1 (5)			67% 15.7 118.8 (3)	100% 7.0 135.4 (1)		0% 0.0 39.6 (1)		48% 6.1 78.7 (52)
WR	Keenan Allen	56% 8.6 100.3 (112)	53% 9.2 99.4 (34)	60% 10.4 95.4 (5)	100% 27.0 118.8 (1)		100% 9.0 104.2 (1)		40% 6.2 77.9 (5)	0% 0.0 39.6 (1)	55% 8.8 99.4 (159)
	Tyrell Williams	47% 8.1 82.0 (47)	36% 17.4 131.6 (11)	33% 18.7 121.5 (3)		75% 16.8 116.7 (4)	67% 10.7 102.1 (3)	0% 0.0 39.6 (1)			46% 10.6 105.2 (69)
	Travis Benjamin	40% 9.6 87.5 (53)	0% 1.6 47.9 (5)	100% 17.7 118.8 (3)			0% -0.5 56.3 (2)		0% 0.0 0.0 (2)		37% 8.7 76.9 (65)

Format Line 1: Success Rate Line 2: YPA Line 3: Passer Rating Line 4: Total # of Plays

Successful Play Rate
0% — 100%

Rushing Success by Personnel Grouping

Position	Player	1-1 [3WR]	1-2 [2WR]	2-1 [2WR]	1-0 [4WR]	1-3 [1WR]	2-2 [1WR]	2-3 [0WR]	3-0 [2WR]	Total
RB	Melvin Gordon	50% 5.3 (111)	40% 3.5 (70)	25% 3.4 (36)	0% 0.0 (1)	25% 2.3 (24)	37% 2.7 (35)	33% 0.3 (6)	0% 2.0 (1)	40% 3.9 (284)
	Austin Ekeler	55% 4.9 (22)	60% 7.1 (15)	75% 7.3 (4)		50% 4.0 (4)	0% 0.5 (2)			55% 5.5 (47)
	Branden Oliver	45% 3.8 (11)	42% 2.2 (12)	0% 0.7 (7)		25% 1.0 (4)	100% 6.0 (1)			34% 2.4 (35)

Format Line 1: Success Rate Line 2: YPC Line 3: Total # of Plays

2018 Coaches

Head Coach:
Sean McVay (2nd yr)
Offensive Coordinator:
(McVay calls plays) (1st yr)
Defensive Coordinator:
Wade Phillips (2nd yr)

Los Angeles Rams

2018 Forecast

Wins	Div Rank
9.5	#1

Past Records

2017: 11-5
2016: 4-12
2015: 7-9

EASY HARD

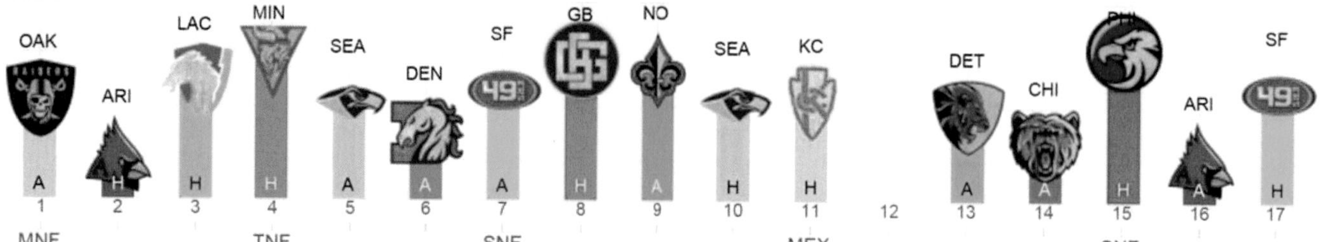

Key Players Lost

TXN	Player (POS)
Cut	Dunbar, Lance RB
	Sayles, Marcus CB
	Webster, Kayvon CB
Declared Free Agent	Barwin, Connor LB
	Carrier, Derek TE
	Davis, Cody S
	Easley, Dominique DT
	Johnson, Trumaine CB
	Laskey, Zach RB
	Lucas, Cornelius T
	Lynch, Cameron LB
	Robey-Coleman, Nickell CB
	Sullivan, John C
	Walker, Tyrunn DT
	Watkins, Sammy WR
	Williams, Darrell T

Average Line	# Games Favored	# Games Underdog
-3.0	14	1

Regular Season Wins: Past & Current Proj

Forecast 2018 Wins	9.5
2017 Wins	11
Forecast 2017 Wins	7
2016 Wins	4
2015 Wins	7
2014 Wins	6

1 3 5 7 9 11 13 15

2018 Los Angeles Rams Overview

Modern-day NFL arms races.

Is there anything more fun in the offseason than watching them unfold? In a salary-cap league, such arms races are not supposed to be as beneficial because of cost. Theoretically, it's hard to change an NFL team's fate in one offseason. In fact, we've historically seen a negative correlation between free agent spending and team success.

But in 2013, my eyes were opened while researching the Seahawks' dominance. The 2011 Collective Bargaining Agreement greatly reduced draft-pick salaries with slotted costs and fifth-year options for first-round picks. Quarterbacks were drafted No. 1 overall in 2009 (Matthew Stafford) and 2010 (Sam Bradford). Stafford signed a six-year, $72 million deal with $41.7 million guaranteed. Bradford landed a six-year, $78 million contract with $50 million guaranteed. Those were outrageously team-unfriendly deals for rookies who had never played an NFL snap.

After the 2011 CBA, Cam Newton and Andrew Luck were the next No. 1 overall picks. Newton's deal spanned four years for $22 million. Luck's slotted contract was almost identical. No six-year contracts. No $50 million in guarantees. No ridiculous cost escalation from one year to the next. Five years after Newton's deal, the Rams drafted Jared Goff at No. 1 overall and paid him $27.9 million over four seasons. Compare that to the nearly 40% five-year escalation between 2005 No. 1 overall pick Alex Smith's six-year, $56 million contract and Bradford's $78 million deal.

The new CBA created an instant advantage for teams hitting on rookie quarterbacks in the draft.

The Seahawks had an historically great 2012 draft, hitting on Bruce Irvin and Bobby Wagner in the first two rounds. But third-round pick Russell Wilson turned the franchise around. Still unsure of what they'd get in the draft that year, Seattle signed Matt Flynn to a three-year, $19.5 million deal. So they hadn't yet fully bottomed out their salary allocation at quarterback. But they cut Flynn the following offseason and re-signed Tarvaris Jackson to a one-year, $840,000 deal.

(cont'd - see LA2)

Key Free Agents/ Trades Added

- Cooks, Brandin WR
- Peters, Marcus CB
- Shields, Sam CB
- Suh, Ndamukong DT
- Talib, Aqib CB
- Wilson, Ramik LB

Drafted Players

Rd	Pk	Player (College)
3	89	OT - Joseph Noteboom (TCU)
4	111	C - Brian Allen (Michigan Sta..
4*	135	DE - John Franklin-Myers (St..
5	147	LB - Micah Kiser (Virginia)
	160	LB - Ogbonnia Okoronkwo (..
6	176	RB - John Kelly (Tennessee)
	192	OT - Jamil Demby (Maine)
	195	DT - Sebastian Joseph (Rutg..
	205	DE - Trevon Young (Louisville)
7	231	LB - Travin Howard (TCU)
	244	DE - Justin Lawler (SMU)

2018 Unit Spending

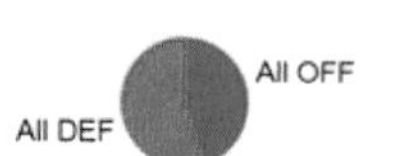

Lineup & Cap Hits

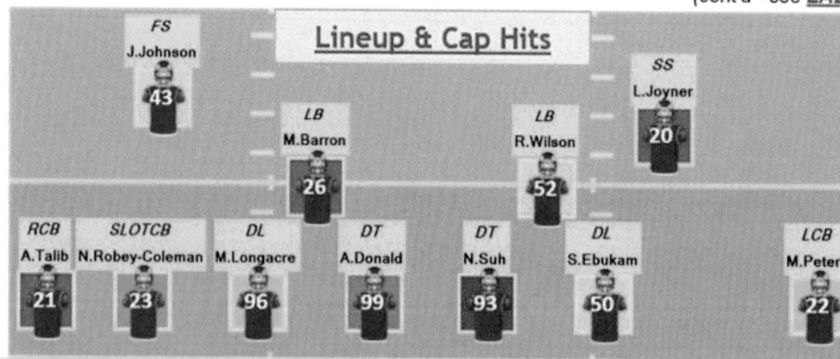

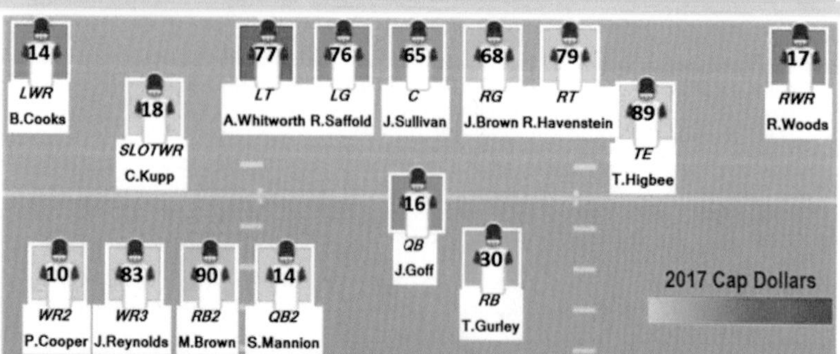

Positional Spending

	Rank	Total	2017 Rk
All OFF	30	$79.31M	22
QB	28	$9.76M	28
OL	15	$35.78M	15
RB	21	$7.03M	15
WR	15	$22.40M	5
TE	26	$4.34M	28
All DEF	4	$96.21M	2
DL	7	$39.32M	23
LB	20	$19.23M	2
CB	12	$22.34M	2
S	9	$15.32M	30

Los Angeles Rams 2017 Success Rate Radar

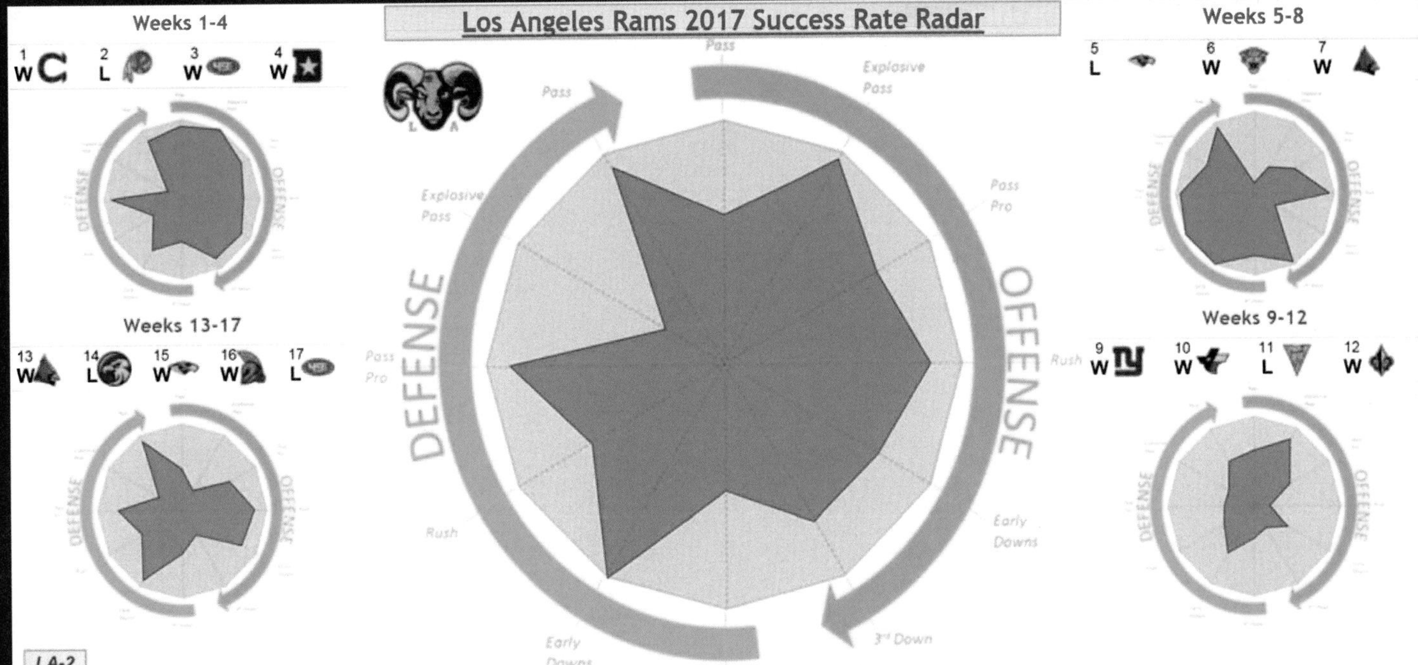

LA-2

And even that was more than they paid Wilson in his second season ($681,000). Combined, Seattle had starting and backup quarterbacks hitting the $123 million cap for $1.5 million. Their flexibility was immense, allowing GM John Schneider to sign DEs Michael Bennett and Cliff Avril in free agency.

With Irvin and Wagner on rookie deals, Seattle fielded the second-cheapest linebacker corps in the league. As FS Earl Thomas and CBs Richard Sherman and Byron Maxwell were also on rookie contracts, the Seahawks fielded the NFL's fifth-cheapest secondary. So they devoted high-dollar resources elsewhere, paying the most money in football to their tight ends, third-most money to their defensive line, and fifth most to wide receivers and running backs. This roster structure all-but won Seattle the Super Bowl in 2013.

Half of the last six Super Bowls were won by teams with quarterbacks on rookie deals. The other three were won by first-ballot Hall of Famers Tom Brady and Peyton Manning, both of whom sported below-market salaries. Thus, each of the last six Super Bowls were won by teams underpaying at quarterback, allowing them to build superior rosters for a sizable edge.

As the cap continues to increase, I don't doubt that a team paying high-end market value for a quarterback will eventually win the Lombardi Trophy. But the odds are against them. Today, 37.5% of NFL teams have projected starting quarterbacks on rookie deals.

And Brady is still only hitting the cap as the league's 11th-highest-paid quarterback. The writing is on the wall for Jameis Winston and Marcus Mariota; both will command massive contracts soon. With Goff and Carson Wentz each having three years left on their rookie deals, the Rams and Eagles are in win-now Super Bowl

(cont'd - see LA-3)

2017 Offensive Advanced Metrics

Metric	Rank
EDSR Off	13
30 & In Off	15
Red Zone Off	1
3rd Down Off	8
YPPA Off	3
YPPT Off	7
Offensive Efficiency	6
Pass Efficiency Off	7
Pass Pro Efficiency Off	9
RB Pass Eff Off	5
Rush Efficiency Off	9
Explosive Pass Off	3
Explosive Run Off	1

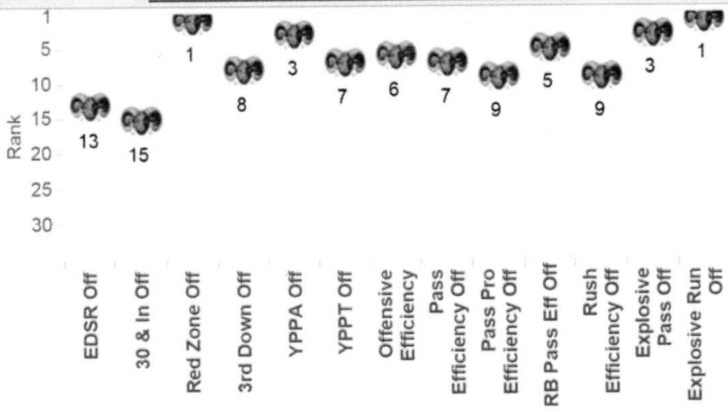

2017 Defensive Advanced Metrics

Metric	Rank
EDSR Def	8
30 & In Def	16
Red Zone Def	11
3rd Down Def	10
YPPA Def	5
YPPT Def	11
Defensive Efficiency	6
Pass Efficiency Def	3
Pass Pro Efficieincy Def	5
RB Pass Eff Def	3
Rush Efficiency Def	22
Explosive Pass Def	16
Explosive Run Def	25

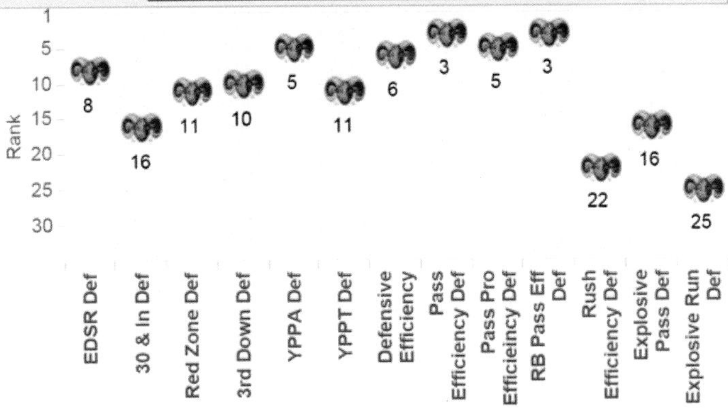

2017 Weekly EDSR & Season Trending Performance

WEEK	1	2	3	4	5	6	7	9	10	11	12	13	14	15	16	17
RESULT	W	L	W	W	L	W	W	W	W	L	W	W	L	W	W	L
OPP	IND	WAS	SF	DAL	SEA	JAC	ARI	NYG	HOU	MIN	NO	ARI	PHI	SEA	TEN	SF
SITE	H	H	A	A	H	A	N	A	H	A	H	A	H	A	A	H
MARGIN	37	-7	2	5	-6	10	33	34	26	-17	6	16	-8	35	4	-21
PTS	46	20	41	35	10	27	33	51	33	7	26	32	35	42	27	13
OPP PTS	9	27	39	30	16	17	0	17	7	24	20	16	43	7	23	34

EDSR by Wk
W=Green
L=Red

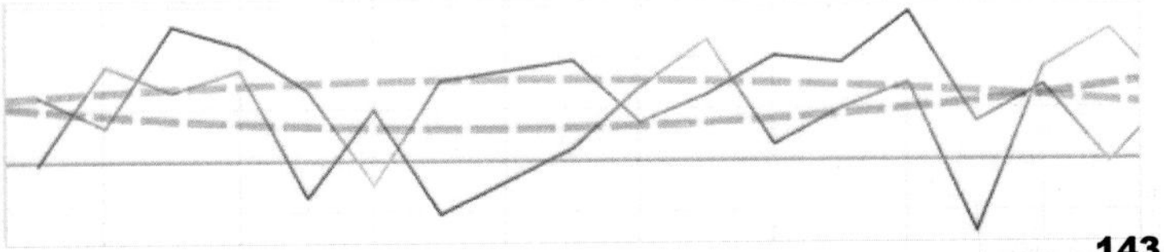

OFF/DEF EDSR
Blue=OFF (high=good)
Red=DEF (low=good)

2017 Close Game Records

All 2016 Wins: **11**
FG Games (<=3 pts) W-L: **1-0**
FG Games Win %: **100% (#1)**
FG Games Wins (% of Total Wins): **9% (#27)**
1 Score Games (<=8 pts) W-L: **4-3**
1 Score Games Win %: **57% (#12)**
1 Score Games Wins (% of Total Wins): **36% (#22)**

2017 Critical & Game-Deciding Stats

TO Margin	+7
TO Given	21
INT Given	7
FUM Given	14
TO Taken	28
INT Taken	18
FUM Taken	10
Sack Margin	+19
Sacks	47
Sacks Allow	28
Return TD Margin	+4
Ret TDs	6
Ret TDs Allow	2
Penalty Margin	-5
Penalties	107
Opponent Penalties	102

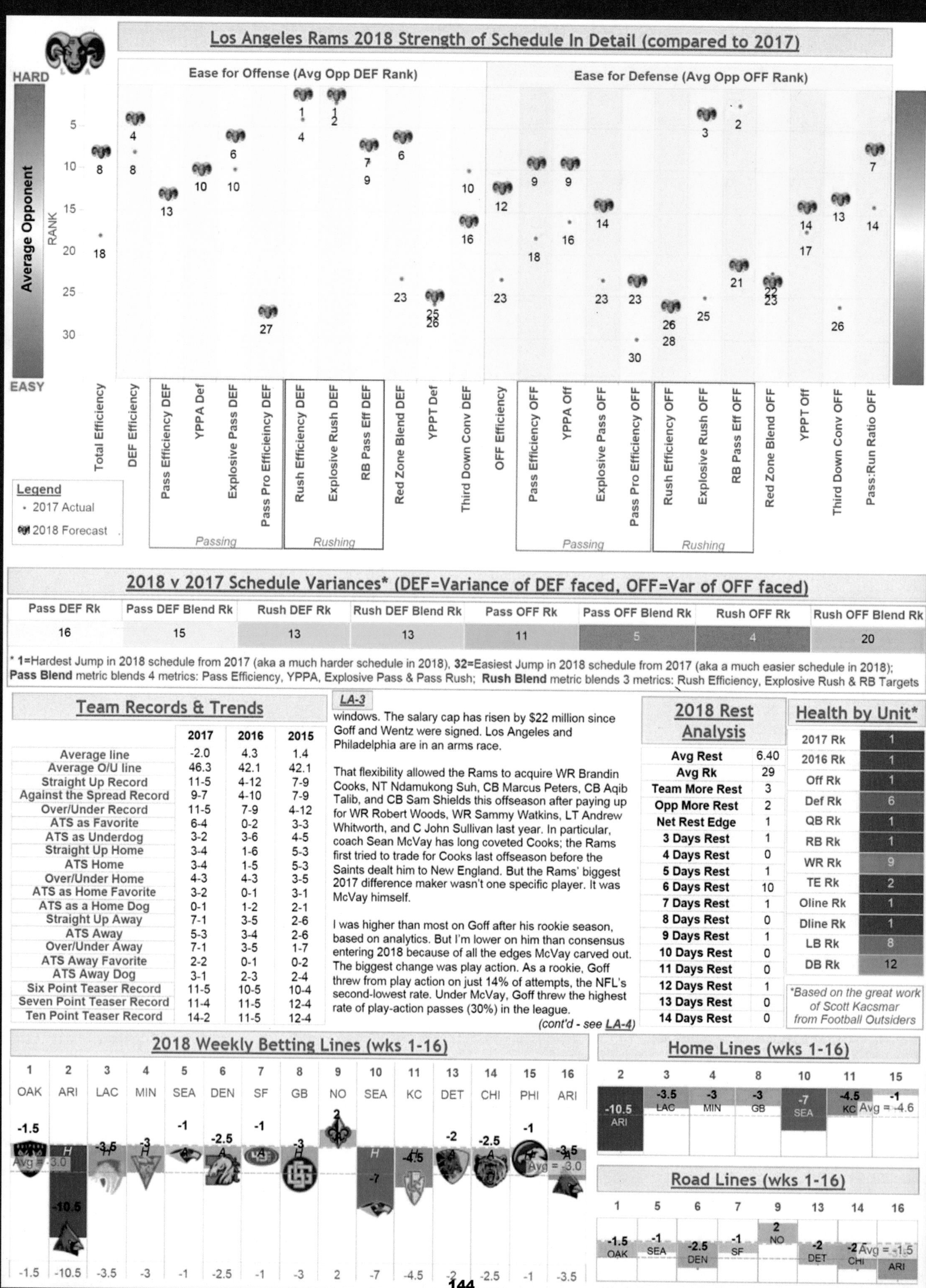

Los Angeles Rams 2018 Strength of Schedule In Detail (compared to 2017)

2018 v 2017 Schedule Variances* (DEF=Variance of DEF faced, OFF=Var of OFF faced)

Pass DEF Rk	Pass DEF Blend Rk	Rush DEF Rk	Rush DEF Blend Rk	Pass OFF Rk	Pass OFF Blend Rk	Rush OFF Rk	Rush OFF Blend Rk
16	15	13	13	11	5	4	20

* **1**=Hardest Jump in 2018 schedule from 2017 (aka a much harder schedule in 2018), **32**=Easiest Jump in 2018 schedule from 2017 (aka a much easier schedule in 2018); **Pass Blend** metric blends 4 metrics: Pass Efficiency, YPPA, Explosive Pass & Pass Rush; **Rush Blend** metric blends 3 metrics: Rush Efficiency, Explosive Rush & RB Targets

Team Records & Trends

	2017	2016	2015
Average line	-2.0	4.3	1.4
Average O/U line	46.3	42.1	42.1
Straight Up Record	11-5	4-12	7-9
Against the Spread Record	9-7	4-10	7-9
Over/Under Record	11-5	7-9	4-12
ATS as Favorite	6-4	0-2	3-3
ATS as Underdog	3-2	3-6	4-5
Straight Up Home	3-4	1-6	5-3
ATS Home	3-4	1-5	5-3
Over/Under Home	4-3	4-3	3-5
ATS as Home Favorite	3-2	0-1	3-1
ATS as a Home Dog	0-1	1-2	2-1
Straight Up Away	7-1	3-5	2-6
ATS Away	5-3	3-4	2-6
Over/Under Away	7-1	3-5	1-7
ATS Away Favorite	2-2	0-1	0-2
ATS Away Dog	3-1	2-3	2-4
Six Point Teaser Record	11-5	10-5	10-4
Seven Point Teaser Record	11-4	11-5	12-4
Ten Point Teaser Record	14-2	11-5	12-4

LA-3

windows. The salary cap has risen by $22 million since Goff and Wentz were signed. Los Angeles and Philadelphia are in an arms race.

That flexibility allowed the Rams to acquire WR Brandin Cooks, NT Ndamukong Suh, CB Marcus Peters, CB Aqib Talib, and CB Sam Shields this offseason after paying up for WR Robert Woods, WR Sammy Watkins, LT Andrew Whitworth, and C John Sullivan last year. In particular, coach Sean McVay has long coveted Cooks; the Rams first tried to trade for Cooks last offseason before the Saints dealt him to New England. But the Rams' biggest 2017 difference maker wasn't one specific player. It was McVay himself.

I was higher than most on Goff after his rookie season, based on analytics. But I'm lower on him than consensus entering 2018 because of all the edges McVay carved out. The biggest change was play action. As a rookie, Goff threw from play action on just 14% of attempts, the NFL's second-lowest rate. Under McVay, Goff threw the highest rate of play-action passes (30%) in the league.

(cont'd - see LA-4)

2018 Rest Analysis

Avg Rest	6.40
Avg Rk	29
Team More Rest	3
Opp More Rest	2
Net Rest Edge	1
3 Days Rest	1
4 Days Rest	0
5 Days Rest	1
6 Days Rest	10
7 Days Rest	1
8 Days Rest	0
9 Days Rest	1
10 Days Rest	0
11 Days Rest	0
12 Days Rest	1
13 Days Rest	0
14 Days Rest	0

Health by Unit*

2017 Rk	1
2016 Rk	1
Off Rk	1
Def Rk	6
QB Rk	1
RB Rk	1
WR Rk	9
TE Rk	2
Oline Rk	1
Dline Rk	1
LB Rk	8
DB Rk	12

**Based on the great work of Scott Kacsmar from Football Outsiders*

2018 Weekly Betting Lines (wks 1-16)

1	2	3	4	5	6	7	8	9	10	11	13	14	15	16
OAK	ARI	LAC	MIN	SEA	DEN	SF	GB	NO	SEA	KC	DET	CHI	PHI	ARI
-1.5	-10.5	-3.5	-3	-1	-2.5	-1	-3	2	-7	-4.5	-2	-2.5	-1	-3.5

Home Lines (wks 1-16)

2	3	4	8	10	11	15
ARI	LAC	MIN	GB	SEA	KC	
-10.5	-3.5	-3	-3	-7	-4.5	-1

Road Lines (wks 1-16)

1	5	6	7	9	13	14	16
OAK	SEA	DEN	SF	NO	DET	CHI	ARI
-1.5	-1	-2.5	-1	2	-2	-2	

Los Angeles Rams 2017 Play Analysis

2017 Play Tendencies

All Pass %	55%
All Pass Rk	24
All Rush %	45%
All Rush Rk	9
1 Score Pass %	60%
1 Score Pass Rk	8
2016 1 Score Pass %	58%
2016 1 Score Pass Rk	19
2017 Pass Increase %	2%
Pass Increase Rk	9
1 Score Rush %	40%
1 Score Rush Rk	25
Up Pass %	48%
Up Pass Rk	20
Up Rush %	52%
Up Rush Rk	13
Down Pass %	65%
Down Pass Rk	20
Down Rush %	35%
Down Rush Rk	13

2017 Down & Distance Tendencies

Down	Distance	Total Plays	Pass Rate	Run Rate	Play Success %
1	Short (1-3)	9	11%	89%	67%
	Med (4-7)	20	60%	40%	60%
	Long (8-10)	308	51%	49%	53%
	XL (11+)	10	40%	60%	40%
2	Short (1-3)	34	35%	65%	68%
	Med (4-7)	87	56%	44%	53%
	Long (8-10)	87	67%	33%	29%
	XL (11+)	38	68%	32%	37%
3	Short (1-3)	42	62%	38%	64%
	Med (4-7)	43	98%	2%	49%
	Long (8-10)	40	98%	3%	28%
	XL (11+)	31	81%	19%	16%
4	Short (1-3)	3	67%	33%	67%
	Med (4-7)	1	100%	0%	0%
	Long (8-10)	1	100%	0%	0%

Shotgun %:

Under Center	Shotgun
58%	42%
37%	*63%*

37% AVG 63%

Run Rate:

Under Center	Shotgun
66%	13%

68% AVG 23%

Pass Rate:

Under Center	Shotgun
34%	87%

32% AVG 77%

Short Yardage Intelligence:

2nd and Short Run

Run Freq	Run Rk	NFL Run Freq Avg	Run 1D Rate	Run NFL 1D Avg
76%	6	67%	59%	69%

2nd and Short Pass

Pass Freq	Pass Rk	NFL Pass Freq Avg	Pass 1D Rate	Pass NFL 1D Avg
24%	27	33%	71%	53%

Most Frequent Play

Down	Distance	Play Type	Player	Total Plays	Play Success %
1	Short (1-3)	RUSH	Todd Gurley	8	63%
	Med (4-7)	RUSH	Todd Gurley	5	40%
	Long (8-10)	RUSH	Todd Gurley	109	62%
	XL (11+)	RUSH	Todd Gurley	5	20%
2	Short (1-3)	RUSH	Todd Gurley	20	65%
	Med (4-7)	RUSH	Todd Gurley	30	63%
	Long (8-10)	RUSH	Todd Gurley	16	25%
	XL (11+)	PASS	Todd Gurley	8	25%
3	Short (1-3)	RUSH	Todd Gurley	12	50%
	Med (4-7)	PASS	Cooper Kupp	14	36%
	Long (8-10)	PASS	Robert Woods	7	29%
	XL (11+)	PASS	Todd Gurley	6	0%
			Robert Woods	6	33%

Most Successful Play*

Down	Distance	Play Type	Player	Total Plays	Play Success %
1	Short (1-3)	RUSH	Todd Gurley	8	63%
	Med (4-7)	RUSH	Todd Gurley	5	40%
	Long (8-10)	PASS	Cooper Kupp	16	69%
		RUSH	Tavon Austin	16	69%
	XL (11+)	RUSH	Todd Gurley	5	20%
2	Short (1-3)	RUSH	Todd Gurley	20	65%
	Med (4-7)	RUSH	Todd Gurley	30	63%
	Long (8-10)	PASS	Robert Woods	7	71%
	XL (11+)	PASS	Cooper Kupp	7	71%
3	Short (1-3)	PASS	Robert Woods	5	100%
	Med (4-7)	PASS	Robert Woods	5	100%
	Long (8-10)	PASS	Cooper Kupp	5	60%
	XL (11+)	PASS	Robert Woods	6	33%

**Minimum 5 plays to qualify*

2017 Snap Rates

Wk	Opp	Score	Todd Gurley	Sammy Watkins	Cooper Kupp	Tyler Higbee	Robert Woods	Gerald Everett	Tavon Austin	Pharoh Cooper
1	IND	W 46-9	48 (74%)	38 (58%)	39 (60%)	53 (82%)	43 (66%)	29 (45%)	7 (11%)	22 (34%)
2	WAS	L 27-20	44 (88%)	45 (90%)	30 (60%)	41 (82%)	45 (90%)	16 (32%)	9 (18%)	4 (8%)
3	SF	W 41-39	61 (94%)	42 (65%)	38 (58%)	59 (91%)	60 (92%)	11 (17%)	15 (23%)	9 (14%)
4	DAL	W 35-30	55 (80%)	60 (87%)	49 (71%)	47 (68%)	59 (86%)	21 (30%)	15 (22%)	9 (13%)
5	SEA	L 16-10	56 (76%)	59 (80%)	63 (85%)	48 (65%)	64 (86%)	26 (35%)	16 (22%)	12 (16%)
6	JAC	W 27-17	49 (83%)	48 (81%)	36 (61%)	46 (78%)	52 (88%)	18 (31%)	9 (15%)	4 (7%)
7	ARI	W 33-0	55 (69%)	67 (84%)	63 (79%)	54 (68%)	69 (86%)	18 (23%)	19 (24%)	12 (15%)
9	NYG	W 51-17	40 (63%)	33 (52%)	39 (61%)	50 (78%)	45 (70%)	15 (23%)	29 (45%)	13 (20%)
10	HOU	W 33-7	54 (82%)	50 (76%)	56 (85%)	54 (82%)	52 (79%)	20 (30%)	11 (17%)	10 (15%)
11	MIN	L 24-7	54 (92%)	49 (83%)	55 (93%)	44 (75%)	45 (76%)	19 (32%)	2 (3%)	5 (8%)
12	NO	W 26-20	69 (90%)	64 (83%)	61 (79%)	48 (62%)		24 (31%)	27 (35%)	11 (14%)
13	ARI	W 32-16	55 (95%)	58 (100%)	51 (88%)	38 (66%)		18 (31%)	11 (19%)	10 (17%)
14	PHI	L 43-35	45 (94%)	45 (94%)	45 (94%)	34 (71%)		12 (25%)	14 (29%)	7 (15%)
15	SEA	W 42-7	45 (63%)	52 (73%)	50 (70%)	50 (70%)	52 (73%)	8 (11%)	14 (20%)	16 (23%)
16	TEN	W 27-23	64 (93%)	66 (96%)	65 (94%)	55 (80%)	63 (91%)	11 (16%)	6 (9%)	1 (1%)
17	SF	L 34-13				12 (18%)		33 (51%)	24 (37%)	64 (98%)
	Grand Total		794 (82%)	776 (80%)	740 (76%)	733 (71%)	649 (82%)	299 (29%)	228 (22%)	209 (20%)

Personnel Groupings

Personnel	Team %	NFL Avg	Succ. %
1-1 [3WR]	81%	59%	47%
1-2 [2WR]	13%	19%	54%
0-1 [4WR]	3%	1%	26%
1-3 [1WR]	3%	5%	12%

Grouping Tendencies

Personnel	Pass Rate	Pass Succ. %	Run Succ. %
1-1 [3WR]	61%	45%	51%
1-2 [2WR]	33%	54%	54%
0-1 [4WR]	33%	11%	33%
1-3 [1WR]	12%	33%	9%

Red Zone Targets (min 3)

Receiver	All	Inside 5	6-10	11-20
Cooper Kupp	26	1	7	18
Todd Gurley	13	2	4	7
Robert Woods	12	3	2	7
Sammy Watkins	11	5	1	5
Gerald Everett	8	2	2	4
Josh Reynolds	8	4	1	3
Tyler Higbee	6	1	1	4
Tavon Austin	3		1	2

Red Zone Rushes (min 3)

Rusher	All	Inside 5	6-10	11-20
Todd Gurley	64	22	11	31
Malcolm Brown	9	1	4	4
Jared Goff	8	1	1	6
Tavon Austin	7		1	6

Early Down Target Rate

RB	TE	WR
21%	17%	62%
23%	*21% NFL AVG*	*56%*

Overall Target Success %

RB	TE	WR
45% #14	42% #31	49% #10

Los Angeles Rams 2017 Passing Recap & 2018 Outlook

Jared Goff was better than he looked in 2016 and worse than he looked last year. He must improve on passes to his right, especially on early downs. Goff managed a 44% Success Rate, 5.7 yards per attempt, and an 83 rating on right-side throws last year with even worse metrics on first and second down. To his left, Goff's Success Rate was 48% with an 8.6 YPA and 94 rating. Goff's right-versus-left splits were also apparent as a rookie, just in a smaller sample. Through two years, his right-side Success Rate on early downs is just 40% with a 5.2 YPA and 73 rating.

And Goff still throws too many third-down passes short of the sticks. He averaged 1.2 yards short of the sticks on third down as a rookie, and that number doubled (2.4) last year. McVay's play designs on third down did generate impressive YAC numbers, however. On third and 1-4 yards to go, the Rams converted a league-high 65% of passes into first downs. But on third and 7+ yards to go, the Rams ranked 20th in conversion rate and gained first downs on only 25% of passes.

Jared Goff Rating All Downs

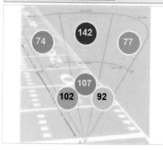

74 142 77
102 107 92

Jared Goff Rating Early Downs

93 151 78
93 109 83

2017 Standard Passing Table

QB	Comp	Att	Comp %	Yds	YPA	TDs	INT	Sacks	Rating	Rk
Jared Goff	321	524	61%	4,038	7.7	29	7	27	98	9
NFL Avg			62%		7.0				87.5	

2017 Advanced Passing Table

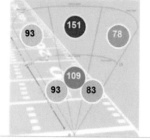

QB	Success %	EDSR Passing Success %	20+ Yd Pass Gains	20+ Yd Pass %	30+ Yd Pass Gains	30+ Yd Pass %	Avg. Air Yds per Comp	Avg. YAC per Comp	20+ Air Yd Comp	20+ Air Yd %
Jared Goff	45%	47%	57	10.9%	24	4.6%	6.0	6.3	20	6%
NFL Avg	44%	48%	27.7	8.8%	10.3	3.3%	6.0	4.7	11.7	6%

Interception Rates by Down

Yards to Go	1	2	3	4	Total
1 & 2		0.0%	0.0%	50.0%	4.3%
3, 4, 5	0.0%	0.0%	0.0%	0.0%	0.0%
6 - 9	0.0%	2.0%	0.0%	0.0%	1.0%
10 - 14	1.1%	1.6%	2.3%	0.0%	1.4%
15+	0.0%	0.0%	6.7%		2.4%
Total	**1.0%**	**1.1%**	**1.2%**	**14.3%**	**1.3%**

3rd Down Passing - Short of Sticks Analysis

QB	Avg. Yds to Go	Avg. YIA (of Comp)	Avg Yds Short	Short of Sticks Rate	Short Rk
Jared Goff	7.9	5.5	-2.4	60%	35
NFL Avg	7.8	6.7	-1.1	60%	

Air Yds vs YAC

Air Yds %	YAC %	Rk
48%	52%	39
58%	42%	

2017 Receiving Recap & 2018 Outlook

The Rams have a treasure trove at wide receiver. But they lack a strong tight end group, which is why they run so much three-wide 11 personnel. Brandin Cooks is an upgrade on Sammy Watkins (Chiefs), and Robert Woods is coming off a breakout year despite missing four games to a shoulder injury. Woods is also one of the NFL's top blocking receivers. Last year, Cooks' ranked eighth in the NFL in yards per target on early downs (10.4). Second-year slot WR Cooper Kupp drew all of his team-high 94 targets in 11 personnel and led the Rams in red-zone targets (23).

Player *Min 50 Targets	Targets	Comp %	YPA	Rating	TOARS	Success %	Success Rk	Missed YPA Rk	YAS % Rk	TDs
Cooper Kupp	107	65%	8.7	107	5.0	53%	37	78	36	6
Robert Woods	99	66%	9.3	112	4.9	53%	42	35	73	5
Todd Gurley	97	70%	8.2	103	4.7	46%	89	114	42	6
Sammy Watkins	74	54%	8.3	112	4.5	50%	58	64	2	8

Directional Passer Rating Delivered

Receiver	Short Left	Short Middle	Short Right	Deep Left	Deep Middle	Deep Right	Player Total
Cooper Kupp	94	83	142	119	85	102	107
Robert Woods	128	135	94	96	147	64	112
Todd Gurley	103	106	84	40	158		103
Sammy Watkins	117	129	129	9	141	43	112
Tyler Higbee	70	72	69	40	110	90	74
Gerald Everett	56	79	60	68	94	110	81
Tavon Austin	82	79	59	40		40	65
Pharoh Cooper	49	79	83		96	40	69
Michael Thomas	119		83	119		40	114
Lance Dunbar	40	40	79				42
Team Total	101	103	94	74	141	77	100

2017 Rushing Recap & 2017 Outlook

The best aspect of Gurley's usage is his passing-game involvement. Last year, Gurley drew 71 targets in 11 personnel – third most on the team – and recorded a 51% Success Rate, 9.3 yards per target, and a 118 passer rating when targeted. Excluding inefficient third- and fourth-down passing plays, Gurley's receiving Success Rate was 54% with a 9.9 yards-per-target average and 122 rating on early-down throws. The Rams targeted running backs on early downs at a below-average rate (21%), but because Gurley is their do-it-all back, he has a huge box-score advantage on lesser-targeted backs like Ezekiel Elliott and Leonard Fournette.

Player *Min 50 Rushes	Rushes	YPC	Success %	Success Rk	Missed YPA Rk	YTS % Rk	YAS % Rk	Early Down Success %	Early Down Success Rk	TDs
Todd Gurley	293	4.8	54%	9	33	29	15	55%	6	13
Malcolm Brown	65	4.0	32%	73	65	57	76	33%	72	1
Tavon Austin	58	4.6	50%	16	66	2	29	48%	20	1

Yards per Carry by Direction

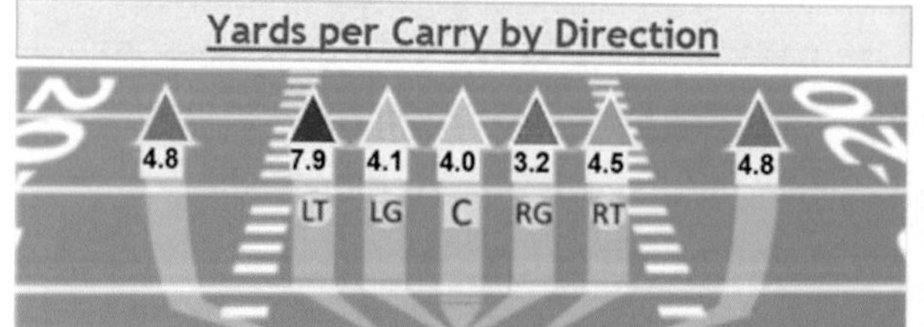

Directional Run Frequency

14% 12% 9% 32% 11% 11% 11%
LT LG C RG RT

LA-4

Goff threw from shotgun formations at the NFL's fifth-highest clip (87%). McVay called more run plays on second-and-short than the 2016 Rams, and Los Angeles improved its rushing Success Rate by 11%.

McVay also incorporated less-measurable elements such as quick tempo to the line of scrimmage without quick snaps so that McVay could read coverage and speak into Goff's headset for 5-10 seconds to audible. McVay used pre-snap motion with creative route designs. The Rams ran far more 11 personnel, upping their three-receiver usage from 66% under Jeff Fisher to a league-high 81%. Many teams reserve three-receiver personnel for obvious passing situations. But the Rams used it as a base offense and improved their record from 4-12 to 11-5.

The Rams' offensive focal point was still Todd Gurley. And boy did he deliver. On the fourth page of each chapter in this book, you can see teams' most-frequent play is usually a run with their No. 1 back. It's unusual that this play turns out to be their most successful play. But that was indeed the case with Gurley.

Last year's Rams didn't even have a great turnover margin (+7). Nor did they dominate one-score games (4-3). It was as impressive a coaching debut as you'll ever see. But McVay's club still needs work.

(cont'd - see LA-5)

Evan Silva's Fantasy Corner

Brandin Cooks' exact role and usage are murky as Sammy Watkins' replacement in a balanced Rams offense that doesn't generate a high volume of pass attempts. Despite turning in a rare healthy season, predecessor Watkins finished fourth on the team in 2017 targets behind Cooper Kupp, Todd Gurley, and Robert Woods. Watkins just barely stayed relevant with eight touchdowns, and failed to clear 600 yards. Watkins was mainly used as a clear-out route runner who ran deep patterns to create space for Gurley, Kupp, and Woods in the middle of the field. Cooks will inevitably mix in some big games, but his week-to-week consistency is a concern.

Division History: Season Wins & 2018 Projection

2014 Wins | 2015 Wins | 2016 Wins | 2017 Wins | Forecast 2018 Wins

Rank of 2018 Defensive Pass Efficiency Faced by Week

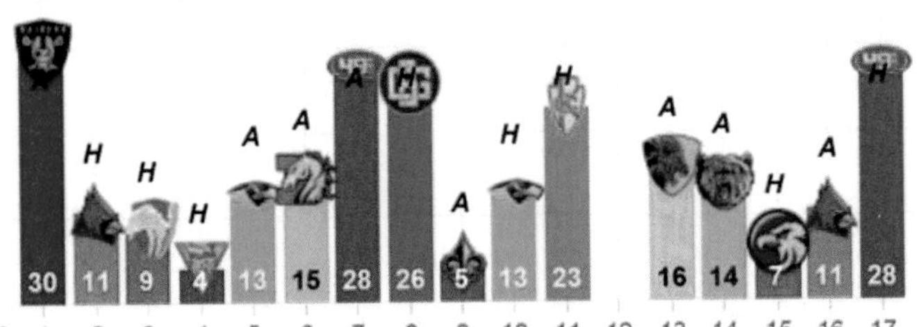

Rank of 2018 Defensive Rush Efficiency Faced by Week

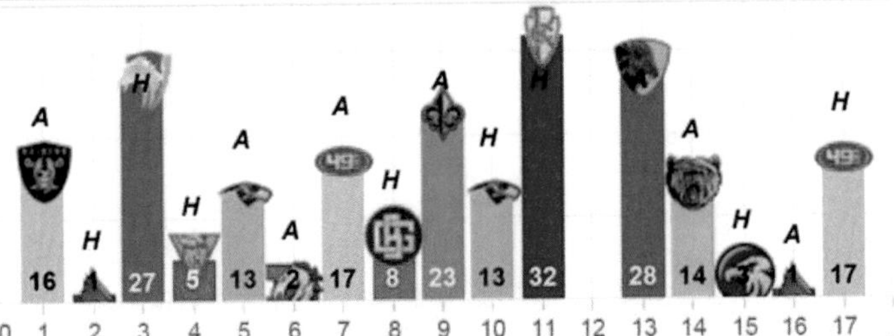

2017 Situational Usage by Player & Position

Usage Rate by Score

		Being Blown Out (14+)	Down Big (9-13)	One Score	Large Lead (9-13)	Blowout Lead (14+)	Grand Total
RUSH	Todd Gurley	4%	28%	33%	33%	27%	30%
	Robert Woods			0%		1%	0%
	Tavon Austin	6%	3%	5%	5%	9%	6%
	Malcolm Brown	19%	3%	1%	2%	24%	7%
	Gerald Everett					1%	0%
	Pharoh Cooper				1%		0%
	Lance Dunbar	6%	3%			3%	1%
	Justin Davis					1%	0%
	Total	33%	38%	39%	42%	65%	44%
PASS	Todd Gurley	4%	12%	12%	5%	7%	10%
	Cooper Kupp	11%	13%	12%	13%	6%	11%
	Robert Woods	4%	13%	11%	10%	8%	10%
	Tavon Austin	2%	2%	3%	2%	1%	2%
	Malcolm Brown	6%	1%	1%	1%	1%	1%
	Sammy Watkins		6%	8%	14%	5%	7%
	Tyler Higbee	2%	3%	6%	4%	3%	5%
	Gerald Everett	11%	4%	4%	2%	1%	3%
	Josh Reynolds	7%	3%	2%	3%	1%	2%
	Pharoh Cooper	9%		2%	1%	1%	2%
	Lance Dunbar	2%	1%		1%		0%
	Derek Carrier	4%		1%		3%	1%
	Michael Thomas	6%	1%	1%			1%
	Total	67%	62%	61%	58%	35%	56%

Positional Target Distribution vs NFL Average

		NFL Wide				Team Only			
		Left	Middle	Right	Total	Left	Middle	Right	Total
Deep	WR	960	487	959	2,406	26	22	28	76
	TE	186	145	178	509	6	5	10	21
	RB	38	8	42	88	1	1		2
	All	1,184	640	1,179	3,003	33	28	38	99
Short	WR	2,764	1,614	2,692	7,070	98	57	98	253
	TE	854	826	1,132	2,812	9	13	38	60
	RB	1,280	804	1,257	3,341	41	19	38	98
	All	4,898	3,244	5,081	13,223	148	89	174	411
Total		6,082	3,884	6,260	16,226	181	117	212	510

Positional Success Rates vs NFL Average

		NFL Wide				Team Only			
		Left	Middle	Right	Total	Left	Middle	Right	Total
Deep	WR	37%	45%	38%	39%	46%	50%	29%	41%
	TE	39%	52%	45%	45%	17%	60%	50%	43%
	RB	37%	50%	38%	39%	0%	100%		50%
	All	37%	47%	39%	40%	39%	54%	34%	41%
Short	WR	52%	57%	50%	52%	51%	60%	50%	53%
	TE	51%	56%	49%	52%	22%	46%	39%	38%
	RB	44%	51%	43%	45%	41%	58%	42%	45%
	All	50%	56%	48%	50%	47%	57%	46%	49%
Total		47%	54%	46%	49%	45%	56%	44%	47%

Successful Play Rate
0% 100%

Los Angeles Rams - Success by Personnel Grouping & Play Type

Play Type	1-1 [3WR]	1-2 [2WR]	1-0 [4WR]	1-3 [1WR]	0-1 [4WR]	2-0 [3WR]	2-2 [1WR]	0-2 [3WR]	Grand Total
PASS	45% (485, 89%)	54% (41, 8%)	50% (4, 1%)	33% (3, 1%)	11% (9, 2%)	0% (1, 0%)		0% (1, 0%)	45% (544, 100%)
RUSH	51% (314, 71%)	54% (84, 19%)		9% (22, 5%)	33% (18, 4%)		0% (5, 1%)		48% (443, 100%)
TOTAL	47% (799, 81%)	54% (125, 13%)	50% (4, 0%)	12% (25, 3%)	26% (27, 3%)	0% (1, 0%)	0% (5, 1%)	0% (1, 0%)	46% (987, 100%)

Format Line 1: Success Rate Line 2: Total # of Plays, % of All Plays (by type)

LA-5

The Rams ran the ball on 76% of second- and 1-2 yards to go plays, sixth most in the league. It's normally a smart strategy, but the Rams' Success Rate on such runs was 10% below league average. Gurley finished second on the team in red-zone targets, but his Success Rate (38%) was dismal there and far worse than passes to Robert Woods, Watkins, and Tyler Higbee. Goff rushed six times inside the red zone between the 11- and 20-yard line but produced a putrid 17% Success Rate. As the red zone is a compressed area, running the ball even on a broken play can lead to injury with so many defenders in close proximity. Ask Carson Wentz and Cam Newton. Goff needs to throw the ball away rather than absorb unnecessary red-zone hits.

No team experienced better injury fortune than the Rams over the past two years, a benefit that may be headed for regression. The Rams also face a tougher 2018 schedule on both offense and defense. They do draw their three hardest opponents (Eagles, Vikings, Packers) at home.

I love the Rams' talent, but I love their coaching even more with McVay running the offense and Wade Phillips controlling the defense. But in the Rams' five losses that mattered – including the playoffs and excluding Week 17 – common themes were losing the turnover battle, Goff playing poorly, and Goff taking at least two sacks. Gurley played well in three of the five losses, averaging 5.5 yards per carry or better with a 57% Success Rate. But passing efficiency more correlates to wins and losses, and McVay still needs more out of Goff.

You could certainly argue McVay ran the most quarterback-friendly offense in the league last year. The key 2018 question is whether defenses will find weaknesses in the scheme after offseason film study.

Receiving Success by Personnel Grouping

Position	Player	1-1 [3WR]	1-2 [2WR]	1-0 [4WR]	1-3 [1WR]	0-1 [4WR]	0-2 [3WR]	Total
RB	Todd Gurley	51% 9.5 113.4 (78)	60% 6.2 132.1 (5)		50% 5.0 64.6 (2)		0% 0.0 0.0 (1)	51% 9.1 109.8 (86)
TE	Tyler Higbee	51% 6.3 75.8 (35)	14% 4.9 47.3 (7)	100% 38.0 118.8 (1)		0% 2.0 56.3 (2)		44% 6.6 73.8 (45)
	Gerald Everett	29% 5.9 74.3 (28)	33% 23.7 109.7 (3)	100% 8.0 100.0 (1)				31% 7.6 83.3 (32)
WR	Cooper Kupp	57% 9.3 108.9 (93)				0% -6.0 79.2 (1)		56% 9.1 108.4 (94)
	Robert Woods	53% 9.1 121.0 (73)	50% 11.8 92.9 (10)	0% 0.0 39.6 (1)	0% 0.0 39.6 (1)			52% 9.2 114.9 (85)
	Sammy Watkins	50% 7.8 109.0 (64)	100% 18.2 158.3 (5)	0% 0.0 39.6 (1)				53% 8.5 116.0 (70)

Format Line 1: Success Rate Line 2: YPA Line 3: Passer Rating Line 4: Total # of Plays

Successful Play Rate
0% 100%

Rushing Success by Personnel Grouping

Position	Player	1-1 [3WR]	1-2 [2WR]	1-3 [1WR]	0-1 [4WR]	2-2 [1WR]	Total
QB	Jared Goff	46% 4.5 (13)	100% 6.0 (1)	0% -1.0 (9)		0% -1.0 (5)	25% 1.8 (28)
RB	Todd Gurley	53% 4.9 (210)	56% 4.0 (61)	25% 1.3 (4)			53% 4.6 (275)
	Malcolm Brown	37% 4.3 (41)	33% 2.7 (15)	0% 2.7 (3)	0% 0.0 (1)		33% 3.8 (60)

Format Line 1: Success Rate Line 2: YPC Line 3: Total # of Plays

Miami Dolphins

2018 Coaches

Head Coach:
Adam Gase (3rd yr)
Offensive Coordinator:
Dowell Loggains (CHI OC) (1st yr)
Defensive Coordinator:
Matt Burke (2nd yr)

2018 Forecast

Wins	Div Rank
6	#3

Past Records

2017: 6-10
2016: 10-6
2015: 6-10

EASY HARD

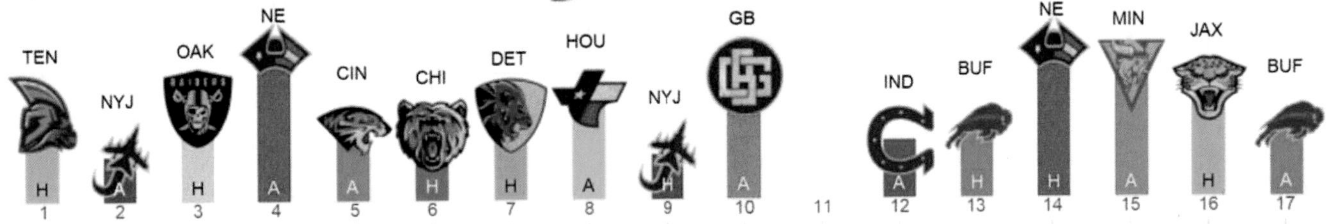

Key Players Lost

TXN	Player (POS)
Cut	Pouncey, Mike C
	Suh, Ndamukong DT
	Thomas, Julius TE
	Timmons, Lawrence LB
Declared Free Agent	Aikens, Walt CB
	Allen, Nate S
	Barrow, Lamin LB
	Bushrod, Jermon T
	Cutler, Jay QB
	Fales, David QB
	Fasano, Anthony TE
	Fede, Terrence DE
	Hewitt, Neville LB
	Misi, Koa LB
	Moore, Matt QB
	Smith, De'Veon RB
	Steen, Anthony C
	Verner, Alterraun CB
	Williams, Damien RB

Average Line	# Games Favored	# Games Underdog
3.1	5	10

Regular Season Wins: Past & Current Proj

Forecast 2018 Wins	6
2017 Wins	6
Forecast 2017 Wins	7
2016 Wins	10
2015 Wins	6
2014 Wins	8

1 3 5 7 9 11 13 15

2018 Miami Dolphins Overview

Knowing how much passing in today's NFL dictates wins and losses, let's play a blind resume game. How many games do you win given the following facts? You play the league's ninth-toughest schedule. Your defense allows the fourth-most points per game. One week into training camp, your quarterback tears his ACL. A week later, you lure Jay Cutler out of retirement for a one-year cash-grab contract at $10 million. You get 14 starts from Cutler and two from Matt Moore. Your offense ranks fifth worst in points per game. Your offensive line is second-most injured in the NFL. Overall, your team is third-most injured. You post a -14 turnover margin, -3 sack margin, -15 penalty margin, and -2 turnover margin.

Let's further stack the deck. Your Week 1 home game against the Bucs gets canceled due to a hurricane. You play Week 4 in London, and it counts as a home game. So you play only seven games in your own stadium. And you don't get a bye after your London game; you play the next week. And your bye isn't until Week 11, so there is no time to catch up on the extra travel. But because your Week 1 game was canceled, you don't get a bye at all. You play 16 games in a row. Remember that your quarterback wasn't signed until two weeks into camp.

Given all that adversity, it's remarkable last year's Dolphins won six games. Especially since they only went 1-3 against the Bills and Jets. Likewise remarkable were the Dolphins' wins. They beat three playoff teams in the Patriots, Falcons, and Titans, in addition to the Chargers.

Those difficulties would torpedo almost any team, especially one lacking leadership from a quarterback who was never "all in" from a team-building perspective. Cutler was a mercenary. Keep in mind Cutler never won more than six games in any of his prior four seasons. And in 2016, Cutler dealt with injuries to his throwing hand and throwing shoulder, the latter requiring surgery. He started five games for the '16 Bears, posting a dreadful 78 passer rating, 4:5 TD-to-INT ratio, and 59% completion rate.

(cont'd - see MIA2)

Lineup & Cap Hits

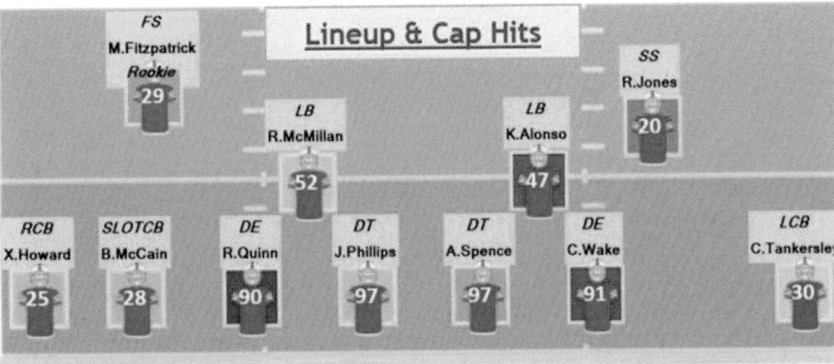

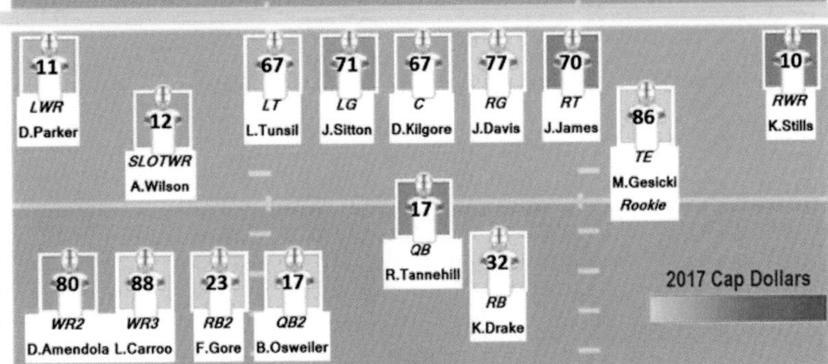

Key Free Agents/ Trades Added

Amendola, Danny WR
Escobar, Gavin TE
Gore, Frank RB
Kilgore, Daniel C
Osweiler, Brock QB
Petty, Bryce QB
Quinn, Robert LB
Sitton, Josh G
Spence, Akeem DT
Wilson, Albert WR

Drafted Players

Rd	Pk	Player (College)
1	11	S - Minkah Fitzpatrick (Alabama)
2	42	TE - Mike Gesicki (Penn State)
3	73	LB - Jerome Baker (Ohio State)
4	123	TE - Durham Smythe (Notre Dame)
	131	RB - Kalen Ballage (Arizona State)
6*	209	CB - Cornell Armstrong (Southern Miss)
7	227	LB - Quentin Poling (Ohio)
	229	K - Jason Sanders (New Mexico)

2018 Unit Spending

Positional Spending

	Rank	Total	2017 Rk
All OFF	28	$79.95M	24
QB	26	$10.82M	5
OL	20	$32.71M	24
RB	28	$4.23M	27
WR	5	$28.10M	30
TE	29	$4.08M	12
All DEF	13	$83.79M	7
DL	4	$46.76M	1
LB	25	$16.37M	28
CB	29	$7.80M	22
S	13	$12.87M	15

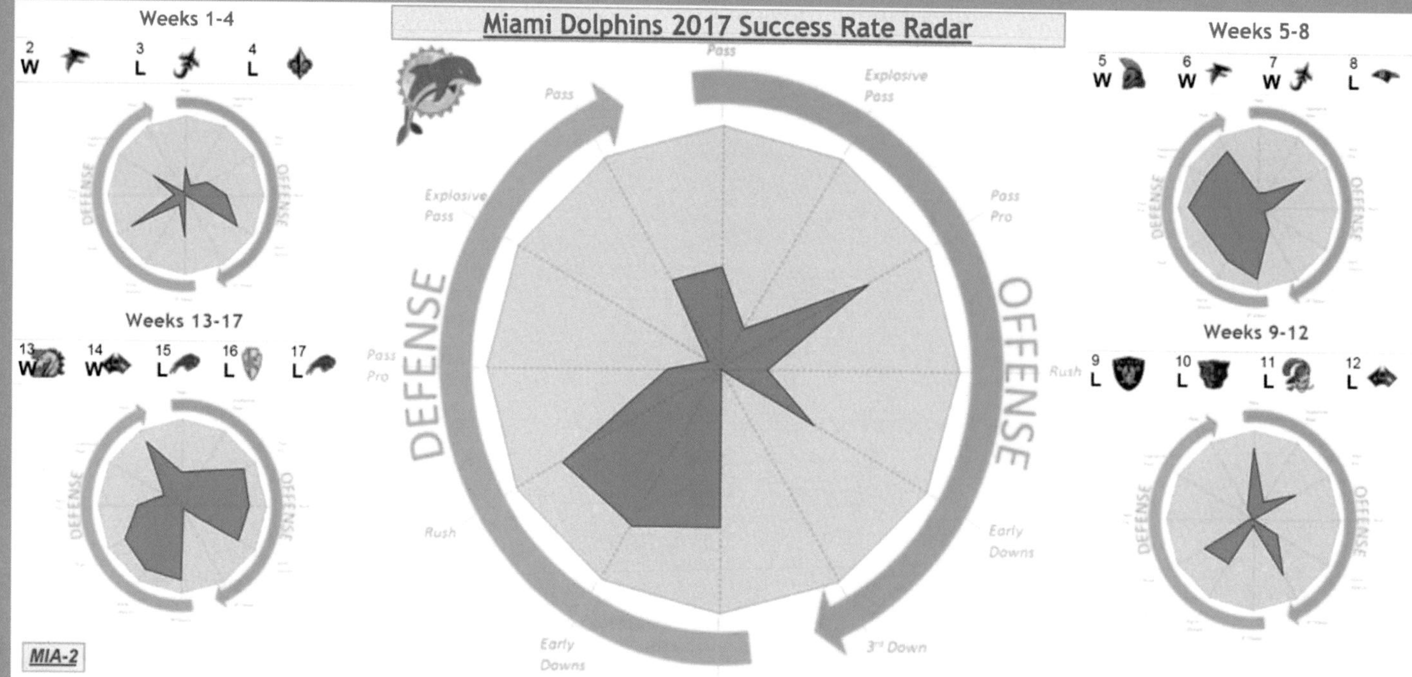

MIA-2

One interesting nugget: In neutral turnover-margin games, last year's Dolphins went 5-0. But they went 0-9 when they lost the turnover battle. Their only hope was a renaissance year from Cutler. The NFL average passer rating is 87. Cutler's passer rating exceeded 84 in just 4-of-14 games. When Cutler's passer rating was average or better, the Dolphins went 3-1. (Their lone loss was Cutler's best game of the year on Sunday Night Football against the Raiders, losing by three.) But Cutler beat the Jets, Patriots, and Chargers in the other three games.

The Dolphins were 3-7 when Cutler posted a below-average passer rating. Two of those three wins when Cutler didn't play well came in Weeks 5 and 6, rather than at the end of the season when the team was running on fumes with average to outright awful quarterback play.

The 2017 Dolphins were the NFL's pass-heaviest team, throwing on 64% of their offensive snaps. This meant even more dependency on Cutler and Matt Moore. In one-score games, Miami passed 58% of the time, 14th most in the league. But that was a big increase on 2016 with Ryan Tannehill, when the Dolphins passed in one-score games 52% of the time, fourth lowest in football. That passing increase in one-score games from 2016 to 2017 was the second-largest jump in the league. Adam Gase was in his third year as Dolphins coach last season. Logic would dictate Gase might run more with backup quarterbacks. But the run game was too unreliable.

Miami's 2017 rushing offense ranked 31st in efficiency. Jay Ajayi averaged 3.4 yards per carry with a 43% Success Rate, which ranked 49th in the league. But rushing success didn't come after Ajayi was shipped to Philadelphia.

(cont'd - see MIA-3)

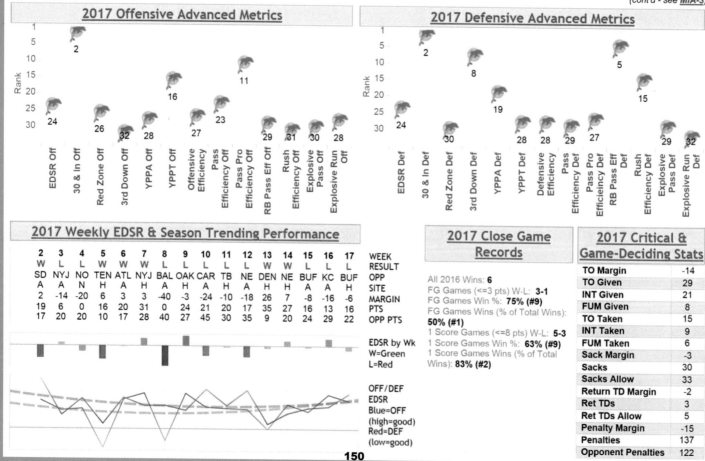

2017 Offensive Advanced Metrics

Metric	Rank
EDSR Off	24
30 & In Off	2
Red Zone Off	26
3rd Down Off	32
YPPA Off	28
YPPT Off	16
Offensive Efficiency	27
Pass Efficiency Off	23
Pass Pro Efficiency Off	11
RB Pass Eff Off	29
Rush Efficiency Off	31
Explosive Pass Off	30
Explosive Run Off	28

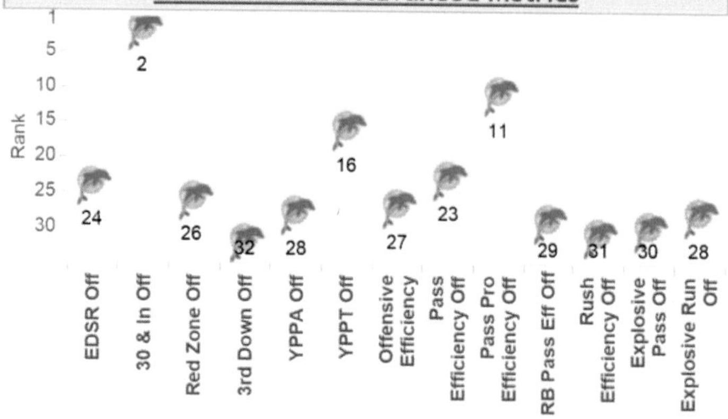

2017 Defensive Advanced Metrics

Metric	Rank
EDSR Def	24
30 & In Def	2
Red Zone Def	30
3rd Down Def	8
YPPA Def	19
YPPT Def	28
Defensive Efficiency	28
Pass Efficiency Def	29
Pass Pro Efficiency Def	27
RB Pass Eff Def	5
Rush Efficiency Def	15
Explosive Pass Def	29
Explosive Run Def	32

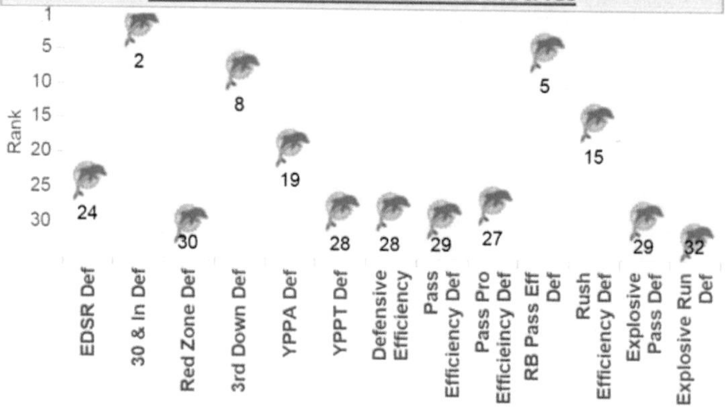

2017 Weekly EDSR & Season Trending Performance

WEEK	2	3	4	5	6	7	8	9	10	11	12	13	14	15	16	17
RESULT	W	L	L	W	W	W	L	L	L	L	L	W	W	L	L	L
OPP	SD	NYJ	NO	TEN	ATL	NYJ	BAL	OAK	CAR	TB	NE	DEN	NE	BUF	KC	BUF
SITE	A	A	N	H	A	H	A	H	A	H	A	H	H	A	A	H
MARGIN	2	-14	-20	6	3	3	-40	-3	-24	-10	-18	26	7	-8	-16	-6
PTS	19	6	0	16	20	31	0	24	21	20	17	35	27	16	13	16
OPP PTS	17	20	20	10	17	28	40	27	45	30	35	9	20	24	29	22

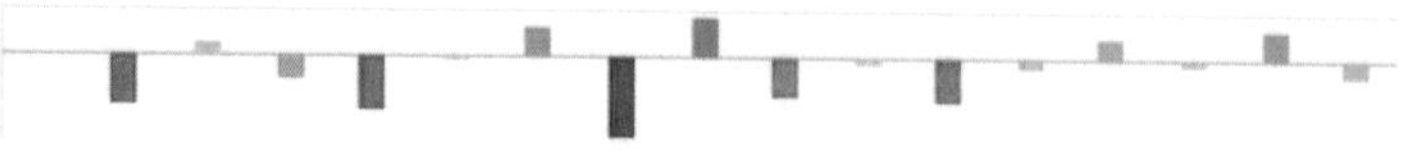

EDSR by Wk
W=Green
L=Red

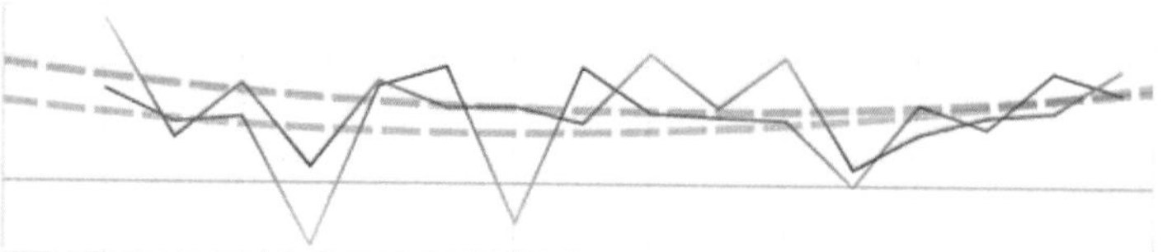

OFF/DEF EDSR
Blue=OFF (high=good)
Red=DEF (low=good)

2017 Close Game Records

All 2016 Wins: **6**
FG Games (<=3 pts) W-L: **3-1**
FG Games Win %: **75% (#9)**
FG Games Wins (% of Total Wins): **50% (#1)**
1 Score Games (<=8 pts) W-L: **5-3**
1 Score Games Win %: **63% (#9)**
1 Score Games Wins (% of Total Wins): **83% (#2)**

2017 Critical & Game-Deciding Stats

TO Margin	-14
TO Given	29
INT Given	21
FUM Given	8
TO Taken	15
INT Taken	9
FUM Taken	6
Sack Margin	-3
Sacks	30
Sacks Allow	33
Return TD Margin	-2
Ret TDs	3
Ret TDs Allow	5
Penalty Margin	-15
Penalties	137
Opponent Penalties	122

Miami Dolphins 2018 Strength of Schedule In Detail (compared to 2017)

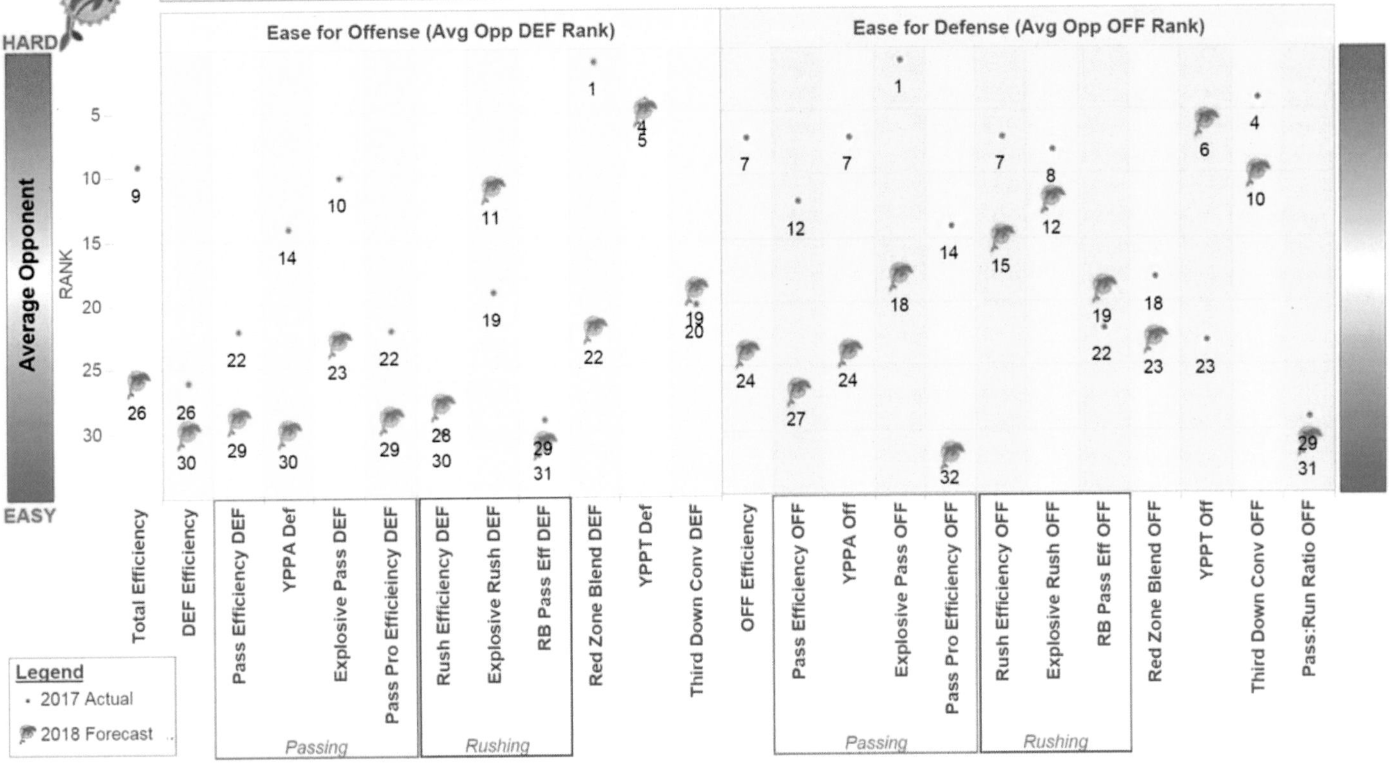

HARD / EASY — Average Opponent RANK

Ease for Offense (Avg Opp DEF Rank)

Metric	2017 Actual	2018 Forecast
Total Efficiency	9	26
DEF Efficiency	26	30
Pass Efficiency DEF (Passing)	22	29
YPPA Def (Passing)	14	30
Explosive Pass DEF (Passing)	10	23
Pass Pro Efficieincy DEF (Passing)	22	29
Rush Efficiency DEF (Rushing)	30	28
Explosive Rush DEF (Rushing)	19	11
RB Pass Eff DEF (Rushing)	29	31
Red Zone Blend DEF	1	22
YPPT Def	4	5
Third Down Conv DEF	20	19

Ease for Defense (Avg Opp OFF Rank)

Metric	2017 Actual	2018 Forecast
OFF Efficiency	7	24
Pass Efficiency OFF (Passing)	12	27
YPPA Off (Passing)	7	24
Explosive Pass OFF (Passing)	1	18
Pass Pro Efficiency OFF (Passing)	14	32
Rush Efficiency OFF (Rushing)	7	15
Explosive Rush OFF (Rushing)	8	12
RB Pass Eff OFF (Rushing)	22	19
Red Zone Blend OFF	18	23
YPPT Off	23	6
Third Down Conv OFF	4	10
Pass:Run Ratio OFF	29	31

Legend
- 2017 Actual
- 2018 Forecast

2018 v 2017 Schedule Variances* (DEF=Variance of DEF faced, OFF=Var of OFF faced)

Pass DEF Rk	Pass DEF Blend Rk	Rush DEF Rk	Rush DEF Blend Rk	Pass OFF Rk	Pass OFF Blend Rk	Rush OFF Rk	Rush OFF Blend Rk
24	27	15	12	28	30	23	23

* **1**=Hardest Jump in 2018 schedule from 2017 (aka a much harder schedule in 2018), **32**=Easiest Jump in 2018 schedule from 2017 (aka a much easier schedule in 2018); **Pass Blend** metric blends 4 metrics: Pass Efficiency, YPPA, Explosive Pass & Pass Rush; **Rush Blend** metric blends 3 metrics: Rush Efficiency, Explosive Rush & RB Targets

Team Records & Trends

	2017	2016	2015
Average line	4.6	1.8	1.2
Average O/U line	43.3	44.2	44.9
Straight Up Record	6-10	10-6	6-10
Against the Spread Record	5-9	9-7	5-11
Over/Under Record	8-8	12-4	7-9
ATS as Favorite	0-1	2-3	2-4
ATS as Underdog	4-8	6-4	3-6
Straight Up Home	4-3	6-2	3-5
ATS Home	3-2	4-4	2-6
Over/Under Home	4-3	7-1	3-5
ATS as Home Favorite	0-0	1-3	1-3
ATS as a Home Dog	2-2	3-1	1-2
Straight Up Away	2-6	4-4	3-5
ATS Away	2-6	5-3	3-5
Over/Under Away	4-4	5-3	4-4
ATS Away Favorite	0-1	1-0	1-1
ATS Away Dog	2-5	3-3	2-4
Six Point Teaser Record	11-5	12-4	6-10
Seven Point Teaser Record	11-5	12-4	6-9
Ten Point Teaser Record	12-4	13-3	10-6

MIA-3

Kenyan Drake managed a 44% Success Rate, which ranked 39th. Drake's biggest benefit was explosiveness, where he ranked fourth in the league. And his yards-per-carry average was 4.8 despite a low Success Rate. And Miami had the privilege of facing the NFL's third-softest schedule of run defenses.

Gone is Jarvis Landry, who led the team in 2017 targets (161). But while Landry's volume was tremendous, his production can be replaced. Landry caught 82 early-down passes to lead the NFL in 2017. But Landry averaged just 5.8 yards per target on early-down throws. And that was despite catching 69% of his early-down targets. Players with high catch rates typically have higher yards-per-target averages because they're hauling in so many completions and have fewer zeroes factoring in. But Landry had a high catch rate and bottom-barrel yards per target.

The Dolphins also fed Landry in scoring position, where only Julio Jones logged more targets inside the ten-yard line. Landry's catch rate there was a league-high 79%, way above average (52%). And Landry scored all nine of his touchdowns inside the ten. *(cont'd - see MIA-4)*

2018 Rest Analysis

Avg Rest	6.47
Avg Rk	3
Team More Rest	4
Opp More Rest	2
Net Rest Edge	2
3 Days Rest	1
4 Days Rest	0
5 Days Rest	0
6 Days Rest	12
7 Days Rest	0
8 Days Rest	0
9 Days Rest	1
10 Days Rest	0
11 Days Rest	0
12 Days Rest	0
13 Days Rest	1
14 Days Rest	0

Health by Unit*

2017 Rk	30
2016 Rk	28
Off Rk	29
Def Rk	29
QB Rk	32
RB Rk	19
WR Rk	13
TE Rk	15
Oline Rk	31
Dline Rk	17
LB Rk	29
DB Rk	32

*Based on the great work of Scott Kacsmar from Football Outsiders

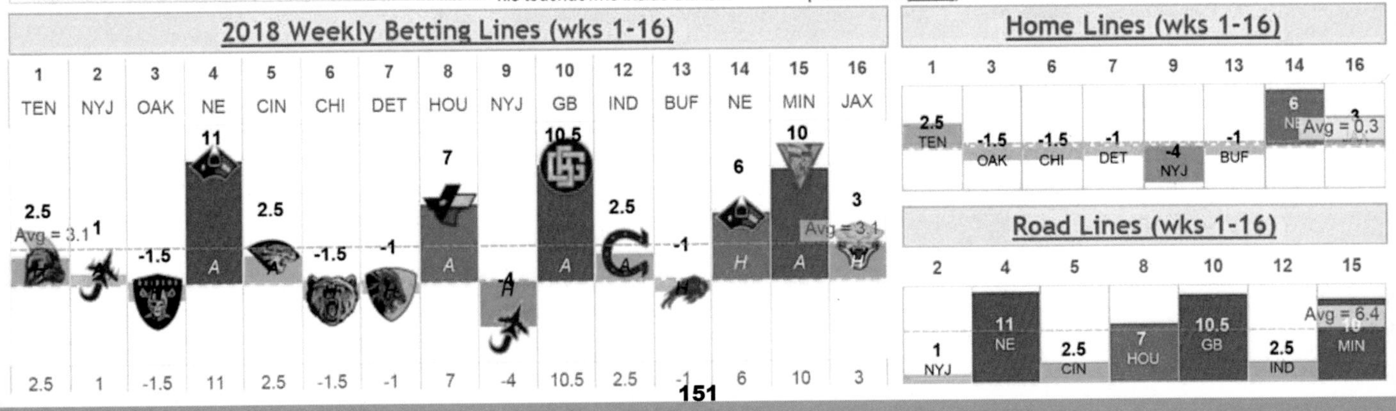

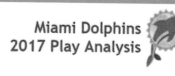

Miami Dolphins 2017 Play Analysis

2017 Play Tendencies

All Pass %	64%
All Pass Rk	1
All Rush %	36%
All Rush Rk	32
1 Score Pass %	58%
1 Score Pass Rk	14
2016 1 Score Pass %	52%
2016 1 Score Pass Rk	29
2017 Pass Increase %	6%
Pass Increase Rk	2
1 Score Rush %	42%
1 Score Rush Rk	19
Up Pass %	44%
Up Pass Rk	27
Up Rush %	56%
Up Rush Rk	6
Down Pass %	70%
Down Pass Rk	4
Down Rush %	30%
Down Rush Rk	29

2017 Down & Distance Tendencies

Down	Distance	Total Plays	Pass Rate	Run Rate	Play Success %
1	Short (1-3)	2	50%	50%	50%
	Med (4-7)	7	86%	14%	57%
	Long (8-10)	283	52%	48%	47%
	XL (11+)	16	56%	44%	31%
2	Short (1-3)	22	18%	82%	59%
	Med (4-7)	77	57%	43%	52%
	Long (8-10)	81	60%	40%	46%
	XL (11+)	51	59%	41%	24%
3	Short (1-3)	26	35%	65%	62%
	Med (4-7)	49	96%	4%	33%
	Long (8-10)	26	96%	4%	23%
	XL (11+)	38	84%	16%	8%
4	Short (1-3)	6	67%	33%	50%
	Med (4-7)	3	100%	0%	33%
	Long (8-10)	2	100%	0%	0%

Shotgun %:

Under Center	Shotgun
33%	67%
37% AVG	*63%*

Run Rate:

Under Center	Shotgun
63%	23%
68% AVG	*23%*

Pass Rate:

Under Center	Shotgun
37%	77%
32% AVG	*77%*

Short Yardage Intelligence:

2nd and Short Run

Run Freq	Run Rk	NFL Run Freq Avg	Run 1D Rate	Run NFL 1D Avg
74%	7	67%	70%	69%

2nd and Short Pass

Pass Freq	Pass Rk	NFL Pass Freq Avg	Pass 1D Rate	Pass NFL 1D Avg
26%	26	33%	43%	53%

Most Frequent Play

Down	Distance	Play Type	Player	Total Plays	Play Success %
1	Med (4-7)	PASS	Jarvis Landry	3	67%
	Long (8-10)	RUSH	Kenyan Drake	56	48%
	XL (11+)	PASS	Jarvis Landry	3	0%
2	Short (1-3)	RUSH	Kenyan Drake	7	43%
	Med (4-7)	PASS	Jarvis Landry	15	67%
		RUSH	Kenyan Drake	15	53%
	Long (8-10)	PASS	Jarvis Landry	17	53%
	XL (11+)	RUSH	Jay Ajayi	9	22%
3	Short (1-3)	RUSH	Jay Ajayi	6	83%
	Med (4-7)	PASS	Jarvis Landry	10	20%
	Long (8-10)	PASS	DeVante Parker	6	17%
	XL (11+)	PASS	Jarvis Landry	9	0%

Most Successful Play*

Down	Distance	Play Type	Player	Total Plays	Play Success %
1	Long (8-10)	PASS	Damien Williams	8	75%
2	Short (1-3)	RUSH	Jay Ajayi	6	67%
	Med (4-7)	PASS	Jarvis Landry	15	67%
	Long (8-10)	PASS	Julius Thomas	7	71%
	XL (11+)	PASS	Kenny Stills	5	80%
3	Short (1-3)	RUSH	Jay Ajayi	6	83%
	Med (4-7)	PASS	DeVante Parker	9	67%
	Long (8-10)	PASS	Jarvis Landry	5	60%
	XL (11+)	PASS	Kenny Stills	5	60%

**Minimum 5 plays to qualify*

2017 Snap Rates

Wk	Opp	Score	Kenny Stills	Jarvis Landry	DeVante Parker	Julius Thomas	Anthony Fasano	Kenyan Drake	Jay Ajayi	Damien Williams
2	LAC	W 19-17	60 (88%)	62 (91%)	63 (93%)	65 (96%)	15 (22%)	1 (1%)	64 (94%)	3 (4%)
3	NYJ	L 20-6	62 (98%)	60 (95%)	58 (92%)	37 (59%)	29 (46%)	20 (32%)	33 (52%)	10 (16%)
4	NO	L 20-0	47 (90%)	46 (88%)	47 (90%)	39 (75%)	18 (35%)	9 (17%)	32 (62%)	11 (21%)
5	TEN	W 16-10	51 (86%)	49 (83%)	3 (5%)	36 (61%)	44 (75%)	2 (3%)	46 (78%)	10 (17%)
6	ATL	W 20-17	60 (90%)	65 (97%)		54 (81%)	47 (70%)	1 (1%)	48 (72%)	18 (27%)
7	NYJ	W 31-28	72 (99%)	70 (96%)		39 (53%)	45 (62%)		51 (70%)	22 (30%)
8	BAL	L 40-0	64 (97%)	59 (89%)		36 (55%)	36 (55%)	12 (18%)	46 (70%)	8 (12%)
9	OAK	L 27-24	65 (97%)	66 (99%)	54 (81%)	49 (73%)	32 (48%)	37 (55%)		30 (45%)
10	CAR	L 45-21	57 (100%)	53 (93%)	51 (89%)	43 (75%)	19 (33%)	25 (44%)		32 (56%)
11	TB	L 30-20	57 (89%)	54 (84%)	57 (89%)	51 (80%)	28 (44%)	38 (59%)		27 (42%)
12	NE	L 35-17	56 (92%)	52 (85%)	56 (92%)	47 (77%)	17 (28%)	39 (64%)		24 (39%)
13	DEN	W 35-9	54 (81%)	53 (79%)	56 (84%)	42 (63%)	41 (61%)	53 (79%)		
14	NE	W 27-20	61 (84%)	66 (90%)	61 (84%)	43 (59%)	42 (58%)	66 (90%)		
15	BUF	L 24-16	64 (85%)	70 (93%)	64 (85%)	59 (79%)	25 (33%)	72 (96%)		
16	KC	L 29-13	49 (86%)	55 (96%)	45 (79%)		34 (60%)	54 (95%)		
17	BUF	L 22-16	63 (89%)	52 (73%)	63 (89%)		46 (65%)	48 (68%)		
	Grand Total		942 (91%)	932 (90%)	678 (81%)	640 (70%)	518 (50%)	477 (48%)	320 (71%)	195 (28%)

Personnel Groupings

Personnel	Team %	NFL Avg	Succ. %
1-1 [3WR]	73%	59%	42%
1-2 [2WR]	15%	19%	43%
1-3 [1WR]	7%	5%	39%
1-0 [4WR]	2%	2%	48%

Grouping Tendencies

Personnel	Pass Rate	Pass Succ. %	Run Succ. %
1-1 [3WR]	71%	43%	42%
1-2 [2WR]	45%	46%	41%
1-3 [1WR]	17%	18%	44%
1-0 [4WR]	86%	44%	67%

Red Zone Targets (min 3)

Receiver	All	Inside 5	6-10	11-20
Jarvis Landry	23	6	8	9
DeVante Parker	12	2	4	6
Julius Thomas	11	4	3	4
Kenny Stills	10	1		9
A.J. Derby	4		2	2
Damien Williams	3		2	1
Kenyan Drake	3		1	2

Red Zone Rushes (min 3)

Rusher	All	Inside 5	6-10	11-20
Kenyan Drake	14	4	1	9
Jay Ajayi	12	1	3	8

Early Down Target Rate

RB	TE	WR
17%	16%	67%
23%	*21% NFL AVG*	*56%*

Overall Target Success %

RB	TE	WR
39% #28	46% #25	48% #12

Miami Dolphins 2017 Passing Recap & 2018 Outlook

Ryan Tannehill's first year with Adam Gase was 2016. His season was cut short by injury, but Tannehill had his best-ever year, engineering an 8-5 record with career highs in yards per attempt, passer rating, completion rate, and TD percentage. I was impressed by Gase's play selection as exhibited on page four of this chapter, particularly on first- and second-down plays. But the Dolphins' third-down play selection and execution cost them. Last year, Gase used 11 personnel at a high frequency, but the Dolphins recorded a subpar 43% Success Rate on 11-personnel passes with Jay Cutler and Matt Moore. In 2016, Tannehill recorded a 46% Success Rate in 11 and a 54% Success Rate on early downs. The '16 Dolphins used 11 packages on 75% of early-down snaps, nearly 20% above league average and second most of any team. Miami used 11 personnel 76% of the time regardless of down, which was again second highest in the league. I expect to see a ton of 11 personnel this year and will be intrigued to watch athletic second-round tight end Mike Gesicki's progression.

Jay Cutler Rating All Downs

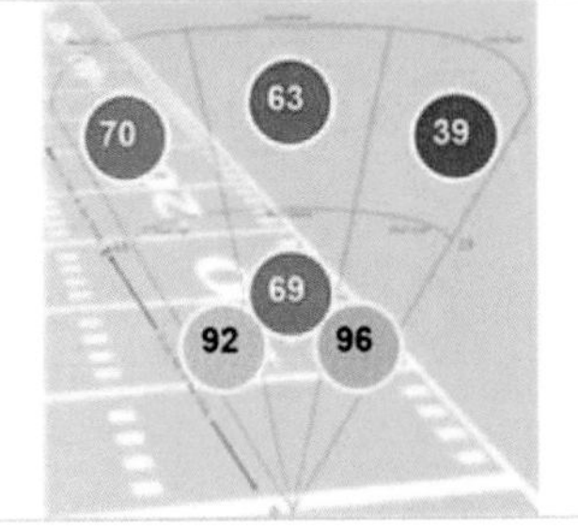

Jay Cutler Rating Early Downs

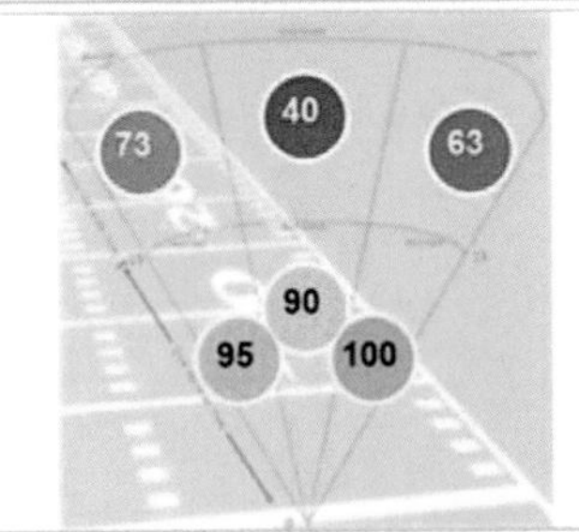

2017 Standard Passing Table

QB	Comp	Att	Comp %	Yds	YPA	TDs	INT	Sacks	Rating	Rk
Jay Cutler	266	430	62%	2,657	6.2	19	14	19	81	34
Matt Moore	78	127	61%	861	6.8	4	5	12	76	40
NFL Avg			62%		7.0				87.5	

2017 Advanced Passing Table

QB	Success %	EDSR Passing Success %	20+ Yd Pass Gains	20+ Yd Pass %	30+ Yd Pass Gains	30+ Yd Pass %	Avg. Air Yds per Comp	Avg. YAC per Comp	20+ Air Yd Comp	20+ Air Yd %
Jay Cutler	43%	50%	27	6.3%	7	1.6%	5.3	4.6	17	6%
Matt Moore	41%	44%	11	8.7%	3	2.4%	6.9	4.3	8	10%
NFL Avg	44%	48%	27.7	8.8%	10.3	3.3%	6.0	4.7	11.7	6%

Interception Rates by Down

Yards to Go	1	2	3	4	Total
1 & 2	0.0%	25.0%	11.1%	0.0%	11.1%
3, 4, 5	14.3%	0.0%	0.0%	0.0%	1.8%
6 - 9	0.0%	2.1%	4.5%	33.3%	4.0%
10 - 14	2.5%	0.0%	3.8%	0.0%	2.1%
15+	0.0%	13.3%	0.0%	0.0%	5.0%
Total	2.8%	3.0%	3.3%	7.7%	3.1%

3rd Down Passing - Short of Sticks Analysis

QB	Avg. Yds to Go	Avg. YIA (of Comp)	Avg Yds Short	Short of Sticks Rate	Short Rk
Jay Cutler	8.5	4.6	-3.9	76%	44
NFL Avg	7.8	6.7	-1.1	60%	

Air Yds vs YAC

Air Yds %	YAC %	Rk
46%	54%	43
58%	42%	

2017 Receiving Recap & 2018 Outlook

I expect this year's Dolphins to finish top two in 11-personnel usage featuring DeVante Parker, Kenny Stills, and Albert Wilson. And Gesicki was a tremendous college receiver at Penn State. Over the past two seasons, passing to tight ends in 11 personnel has generated a league-wide 51% Success Rate, 90 rating, and 7.0 yards per target. But when the Dolphins targeted their tight ends on early downs in 11, their Success Rate was much stronger (62%) with a 100 passer rating. Tannehill's Early-Down Success Rate passing to tight ends in 11 personnel was a whopping 78% with a 118 rating and 9.4 yards per attempt. But he targeted tight ends on early ..

Player *Min 50 Targets*	Targets	Comp %	YPA	Rating	TOARS	Success %	Success Rk	Missed YPA Rk	YAS % Rk	TDs
Jarvis Landry	161	70%	6.1	94	5.4	49%	67	49	120	9
DeVante Parker	96	59%	7.0	58	4.2	50%	58	66	58	1
Kenny Stills	105	55%	8.1	81	4.6	51%	49	44	53	6
Julius Thomas	62	66%	6.3	86	3.9	51%	51	24	116	3

Directional Passer Rating Delivered

Receiver	Short Left	Short Middle	Short Right	Deep Left	Deep Middle	Deep Right	Player Total
Jarvis Landry	109	75	102	63	79	71	94
Kenny Stills	52	113	85	102	55	92	81
DeVante Parker	64	57	99	7	119	42	58
Julius Thomas	67	150	92	50		58	86
Kenyan Drake	97	91	53	40		119	85
Damien Williams	83	91	113				97
Jay Ajayi	69	83	75				74
Anthony Fasano	79	90	95	56			74
A.J. Derby	40		65		40		40
MarQueis Gray	108		40	40			44
Team Total	82	85	92	40	68	68	81

2017 Rushing Recap & 2017 Outlook

It remains to be seen how Gase divvies touches between Kenyan Drake and Frank Gore, but I'm cautiously bullish on the former. I'd be even more bullish if not for Gase's reliance on wide receivers on early downs. In 2016 with Tannehill, the Dolphins threw to wide receivers on 68% of early-down targets. Running backs and tight ends managed target shares of 16% apiece, both well below league average. The 16% early-down running back target share was fourth lowest in the NFL. Even last year, Gase called only 17% of early-down passes to running backs, again below average (23%).

Player *Min 50 Rushes*	Rushes	YPC	Success %	Success Rk	Missed YPA Rk	YTS % Rk	YAS % Rk	Early Down Success %	Early Down Success Rk	TDs
Jay Ajayi	250	3.4	43%	49	67	4	55	41%	54	2
Kenyan Drake	133	4.8	44%	39	62	71	4	44%	38	3

Yards per Carry by Direction

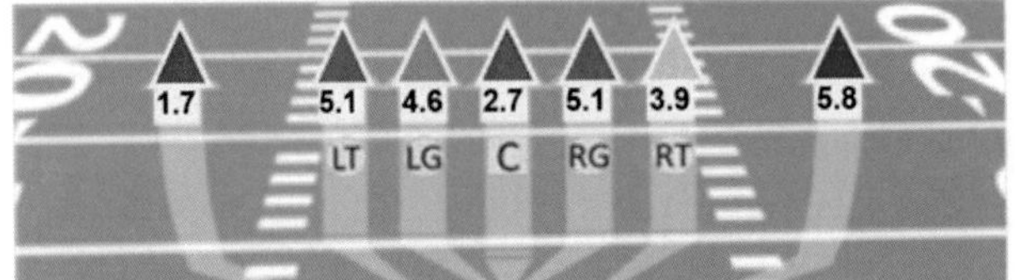

Directional Run Frequency

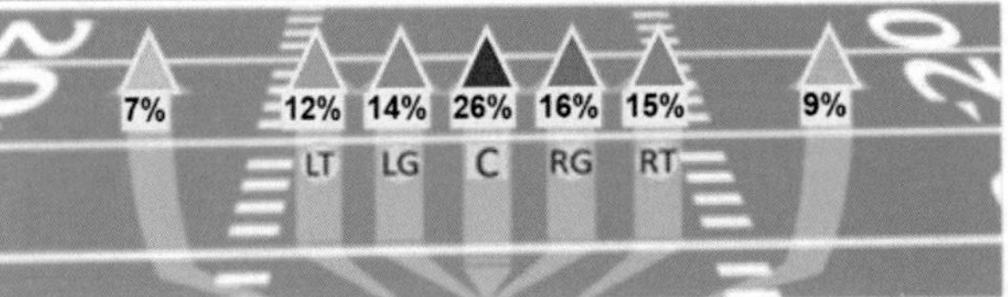

You can read this two ways; the Dolphins must replace a lot of red-zone TDs, or that Landry limited the offense by hogging open-field targets that had no chance to score. Landry offered a unique skill set and his ability to win quickly on pass routes produced a high completion rate, but his explosiveness was severely lacking.

Gase needs a slot receiver to fill this role, so the Dolphins signed ex-Chiefs slot WR Albert Wilson. On early downs the past two years, Wilson caught 75% of his 77 targets and averaged 8.3 yards per target with a 61% Success Rate. Landry's early-down catch rate was 71% with 7.0 yards per target and a 56% Success Rate. Wilson also showed more explosiveness with a YAS of 62%, far above Landry's 51%. Wilson's 2017 Early-Down Success Rate of 72% ranked No. 2 in the league, compared to Landry's No. 46 finish. I love how Gase designs red-zone pass plays and believe Wilson will succeed there in Miami.

But the Dolphins must reinvigorate their running game. They made offseason O-Line shakeups by jettisoning C Mike Pouncey and OG Jermon Bushrod in favor of Daniel Kilgore (49ers) and Josh Sitton (Bears). Pouncey had a miserable 2017 season; the Dolphins ran 26% of the time behind center for just 2.7 yards per carry, by far their worst YPC mark for any run direction. They averaged 2.3 YPC with an anemic 36% Success Rate when running behind Pouncey on first down.

(cont'd - see MIA-5)

Evan Silva's Fantasy Corner

As the Dolphins are missing the NFL's second-most targets from last year's team (290), opportunity abounds for a shaken-up pass-catcher corps with what should be improved quarterback play moving on from Jay Cutler and back to Ryan Tannehill. Rookie tight ends like Mike Gesicki historically struggle for first-year impact. DeVante Parker has shown no ability to beat press coverage, and Gase has shown no willingness to scheme him away from it. Albert Wilson and Danny Amendola are new faces in the slot. My pick to lead the 2018 Dolphins in receiving is Kenny Stills, who quietly drew a career-high 105 targets last season and offers the most-diverse skill set in Miami's wideout corps with speed to burn and slot capability. At his double-digit-round ADP, Stills will find himself on most of my fantasy rosters this year.

Division History: Season Wins & 2018 Projection

2014 Wins | 2015 Wins | 2016 Wins | 2017 Wins | Forecast 2018 Wins

Rank of 2018 Defensive Pass Efficiency Faced by Week

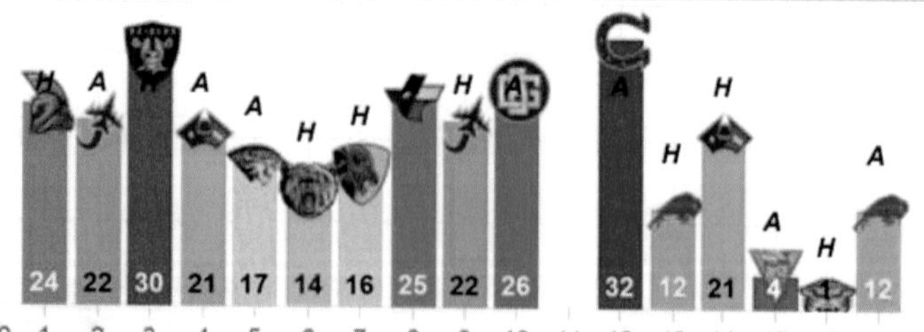

Rank of 2018 Defensive Rush Efficiency Faced by Week

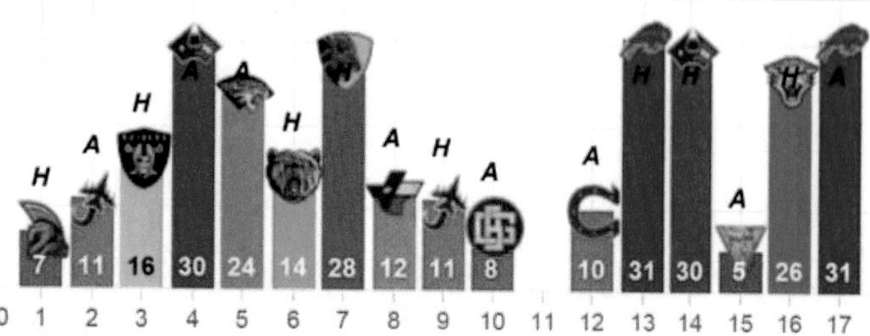

2017 Situational Usage by Player & Position

Usage Rate by Score

		Being Blown Out (14+)	Down Big (9-13)	One Score	Large Lead (9-13)	Blowout Lead (14+)	Grand Total
RUSH	Kenyan Drake	13%	10%	13%	49%	33%	14%
	Jarvis Landry			0%			0%
	Jay Ajayi	7%	10%	22%	5%		15%
	Damien Williams	4%	5%	6%			5%
	Jakeem Grant			0%		4%	0%
	Senorise Perry		1%	0%		21%	1%
	MarQueis Gray	0%	1%	1%			1%
	Total	24%	27%	42%	54%	58%	36%
PASS	Kenyan Drake	7%	9%	3%	5%	4%	5%
	Jarvis Landry	19%	21%	17%	12%	4%	17%
	Jay Ajayi	4%	1%	2%			2%
	Kenny Stills	17%	9%	9%	12%	21%	11%
	DeVante Parker	11%	12%	10%	7%	8%	10%
	Damien Williams	3%	3%	4%			3%
	Julius Thomas	6%	7%	8%	2%		7%
	Jakeem Grant	3%	4%	2%	5%		2%
	Anthony Fasano	1%	1%	2%	2%		2%
	Leonte Carroo	4%	1%	1%			2%
	A.J. Derby	1%	1%	1%			1%
	Senorise Perry		1%				0%
	MarQueis Gray			0%		4%	0%
	De'Veon Smith		2%				0%
	Total	76%	73%	58%	46%	42%	64%

Positional Target Distribution vs NFL Average

		NFL Wide				Team Only			
		Left	Middle	Right	Total	Left	Middle	Right	Total
Deep	WR	950	503	944	2,397	36	6	43	85
	TE	184	148	185	517	8	2	3	13
	RB	38	9	41	88	1		1	2
	All	1,172	660	1,170	3,002	45	8	47	100
Short	WR	2,765	1,599	2,682	7,046	97	72	108	277
	TE	827	829	1,139	2,795	36	10	31	77
	RB	1,271	811	1,263	3,345	50	12	32	94
	All	4,863	3,239	5,084	13,186	183	94	171	448
Total		6,035	3,899	6,254	16,188	228	102	218	548

Positional Success Rates vs NFL Average

		NFL Wide				Team Only			
		Left	Middle	Right	Total	Left	Middle	Right	Total
Deep	WR	37%	45%	38%	39%	31%	50%	37%	35%
	TE	39%	53%	45%	45%	25%	0%	33%	23%
	RB	37%	56%	37%	39%	0%		100%	50%
	All	37%	47%	39%	40%	29%	38%	38%	34%
Short	WR	52%	58%	50%	52%	51%	54%	56%	54%
	TE	51%	56%	49%	52%	42%	80%	48%	49%
	RB	44%	51%	43%	46%	38%	58%	31%	38%
	All	50%	56%	48%	50%	45%	57%	50%	50%
Total		47%	54%	46%	49%	42%	56%	48%	47%

Successful Play Rate
0% 100%

Miami Dolphins - Success by Personnel Grouping & Play Type

Play Type	1-1 [3WR]	1-2 [2WR]	2-1 [2WR]	1-0 [4WR]	1-3 [1WR]	0-1 [4WR]	2-0 [3WR]	2-2 [1WR]	0-0 [5WR]	0-2 [3WR]	0-3 [2WR]	2-3 [0WR]	Grand Total
PASS	43% (518, 82%)	46% (67, 11%)		44% (18, 3%)	18% (11, 2%)	56% (9, 1%)	100% (4, 1%)		20% (5, 1%)	33% (3, 0%)			43% (635, 100%)
RUSH	42% (207, 58%)	41% (81, 23%)	50% (2, 1%)	67% (3, 1%)	44% (55, 15%)	0% (3, 1%)		100% (1, 0%)			0% (1, 0%)	0% (5, 1%)	41% (359, 100%)
TOTAL	42% (725, 73%)	43% (148, 15%)	50% (2, 0%)	48% (21, 2%)	39% (66, 7%)	42% (12, 1%)	100% (4, 0%)	100% (1, 0%)	20% (5, 1%)	33% (3, 0%)	0% (1, 0%)	0% (5, 1%)	42% (994, 100%)

Format Line 1: Success Rate Line 2: Total # of Plays, % of All Plays (by type)

MIA-5 You can't begin analyzing the 2018 Dolphins without understanding how valuable rest, a real bye week, and easier schedule will be. The 2016 Dolphins faced the league's ninth-softest slate. Last year, I projected them to face the NFL's seventh-hardest schedule. It wound up ninth toughest. In 2018, I project Miami to face the league's ninth-easiest slate.

With an easy schedule, the 2016 Dolphins finished 10-6. With a hard schedule and overwhelming adversity, last year's Dolphins went 6-10. In 2018, they're back in the easy-schedule mix. The Dolphins' win projection is just 6.0 games, and they are favored in five. Yet they are favored by at least two points in just one game all year. Miami's worst 2018 stretch is Weeks 10-16, drawing the Packers, Vikings, Jaguars and Patriots. But it's certainly within the realm of possibility for the Dolphins to win enough pre-Week 14 games to beat its low win total.

Receiving Success by Personnel Grouping

Position	Player	1-1 [3WR]	1-2 [2WR]	1-0 [4WR]	1-3 [1WR]	0-1 [4WR]	2-0 [3WR]	0-0 [5WR]	0-2 [3WR]	Total
RB	Kenyan Drake	34% 5.0 87.5 (44)	50% 6.0 68.8 (2)	0% 2.5 56.3 (2)						33% 5.0 85.3 (48)
	Damien Williams	47% 4.7 74.2 (19)	60% 7.8 138.8 (5)	100% 10.0 108.3 (2)			100% 3.5 81.3 (2)			57% 5.5 96.6 (28)
TE	Julius Thomas	51% 6.0 87.5 (51)	67% 9.7 97.9 (6)	100% 20.0 118.8 (1)	0% 0.0 39.6 (3)	100% 5.0 87.5 (1)				52% 6.3 86.0 (62)
WR	Jarvis Landry	52% 6.5 93.5 (127)	46% 4.5 94.7 (26)	40% 5.6 90.0 (5)		0% 1.0 79.2 (1)	100% 14.0 118.8 (1)	0% 0.0 39.6 (1)		50% 6.1 93.9 (161)
	Kenny Stills	48% 8.0 80.9 (90)	63% 10.1 67.2 (8)	100% 29.0 158.3 (1)	0% 0.0 39.6 (3)	100% 6.0 91.7 (1)		50% 4.0 60.4 (2)		49% 8.1 80.9 (105)
	DeVante Parker	49% 7.3 56.2 (81)	43% 5.6 72.9 (7)	33% 4.3 47.9 (3)		100% 10.0 108.3 (1)	100% 5.0 87.5 (1)	0% 0.0 39.6 (1)	50% 5.5 66.7 (2)	49% 7.0 58.1 (96)

Format Line 1: Success Rate Line 2: YPA Line 3: Passer Rating Line 4: Total # of Plays

Successful Play Rate
0% 100%

Rushing Success by Personnel Grouping

Position	Player	1-1 [3WR]	1-2 [2WR]	2-1 [2WR]	1-0 [4WR]	1-3 [1WR]	2-2 [1WR]	Total
RB	Jay Ajayi	42% 3.1 (72)	42% 3.7 (45)		100% 6.0 (1)	42% 3.4 (19)	100% 3.0 (1)	43% 3.4 (138)
	Kenyan Drake	45% 4.6 (87)	43% 5.0 (23)		50% 2.5 (2)	38% 5.9 (21)		44% 4.8 (133)
	Damien Williams	25% 4.8 (28)	11% 2.6 (9)	50% 4.5 (2)		57% 2.1 (7)		28% 3.9 (46)

Format Line 1: Success Rate Line 2: YPC Line 3: Total # of Plays

2018 Coaches

Head Coach: Mike Zimmer (5th yr)
Offensive Coordinator: John DeFilippo (PHI QB) (1st yr)
Defensive Coordinator: George Edwards (5th yr)

Minnesota Vikings

2018 Forecast

Wins	Div Rank
10	#1

Past Records

2017: 13-3
2016: 8-8
2015: 11-5

EASY HARD

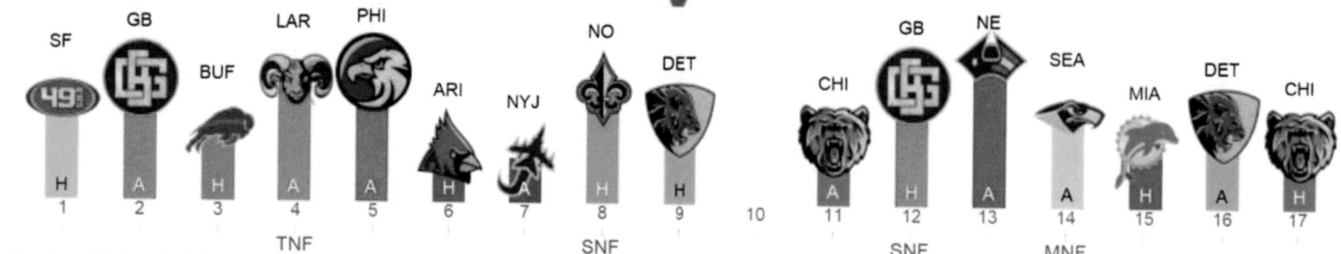

Key Players Lost

TXN	Player (POS)
Cut	Carter, Kyle TE
	Wright, Jarius WR
Declared Free Agent	Bradford, Sam QB
	Bridgewater, Teddy QB
	Brock, Tramaine CB
	Floyd, Michael WR
	Floyd, Sharrif DT
	Forbath, Kai K
	Johnson, Tom DT
	Keenum, Case QB
	Lamur, Emmanuel LB
	McKinnon, Jerick RB
	Newman, Terence CB
	Overbaugh, Jeff LB
	Sankey, Bishop RB
	Sherels, Marcus CB
	Sirles, Jeremiah G
	Stephen, Shamar DT
Retired	Berger, Joe G

Average Line	# Games Favored	# Games Underdog
-3.4	11	4

Regular Season Wins: Past & Current Proj

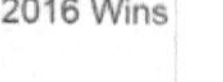

2018 Minnesota Vikings Overview

"The best-laid plans of mice and men go often askew." – Robert Burns.

Burns wasn't talking about the Vikings' quarterbacks in 1785, but he may as well have been. In back-to-back years, Mike Zimmer's Vikings lost their starting quarterback before Week 1 (Teddy Bridgewater, Sam Bradford) to year-ending knee injuries.

Bradford began last season by picking apart an elite Saints pass defense for 84% completions, 10.8 yards per attempt, 346 yards, and three touchdowns in Week 1. Bradford was one of only two quarterbacks in league history to open Week 1 with an 80% completion rate on 30-plus attempts, at least three touchdowns, and no picks. But that was the only game Bradford played all year. Minnesota turned to sixth-year journeyman Case Keenum, whom the Vikings took a cheap, $2 million flyer on for one season.

It might seem crazy given average salaries for starting NFL quarterbacks. But before the Vikings signed Kirk Cousins, Bradford was the lone quarterback on a Zimmer-coached team to ever hit the salary cap for more than $2 million since 2010. Yet Bradford's salary was only $7 million, and he was acquired via trade. In his entire 24-year NFL coaching career, Zimmer has never overseen a top-shelf quarterback in his prime. Zimmer spent one year apiece with Troy Aikman, Vinny Testaverde, and Drew Bledsoe, but for all three it was either their final full year or their last year as a starter.

Zimmer did spend Tony Romo's first year as a starter in Dallas, although Romo started only ten games that year. The closest Zimmer has ever gotten was Carson Palmer in 2009-2010. But those were bad years for Palmer; he never beat an 84 passer rating or 6.8 yards per attempt. Specific quarterbacks aside, Zimmer's teams have made the playoffs 100% of the time when they get a mere 86 passer rating and 7.0 yards per attempt from the other side of the ball.

In three years as Washington's starter, Cousins exceeded an 86 passer rating and 7.0 yards per attempt without fail. Cousins was the only healthy part of last year's Redskins.

(cont'd - see MIN2)

Lineup & Cap Hits

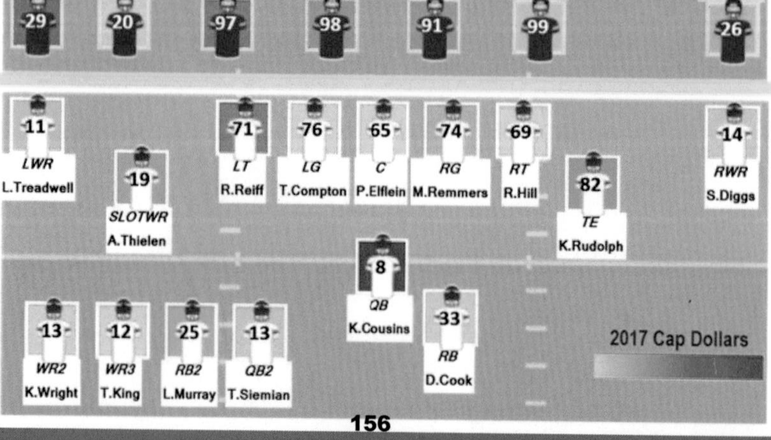

Key Free Agents/ Trades Added

Bradley, Dylan DT
Cliett, Reshard LB
Compton, Tom G
Cousins, Kirk QB
Dooley, Nick C
King, Tavarres WR
Price, Josiah TE
Richardson, Sheldon DT
Siemian, Trevor QB
Wright, Kendall WR

Drafted Players

Rd	Pk	Player (College)
1	30	CB - Mike Hughes (UCF)
2	62	OT - Brian O'Neill (Pittsburgh)
4	102	DE - Jalyn Holmes (Ohio State)
5	157	TE - Tyler Conklin (Central Michigan)
	167	K - Daniel Carlson (Auburn)
6*	213	G - Colby Gossett (Appalachian State)
	218	DE - Ade Aruna (Tulane)
7	225	LB - Devante Downs (California)

2018 Unit Spending

Positional Spending

	Rank	Total	2017 Rk
All OFF	20	$89.75M	16
QB	4	$26.94M	6
OL	27	$26.54M	13
RB	8	$9.27M	19
WR	28	$15.95M	25
TE	12	$11.04M	18
All DEF	5	$96.05M	9
DL	9	$36.46M	6
LB	17	$20.57M	29
CB	9	$23.22M	14
S	8	$15.81M	14

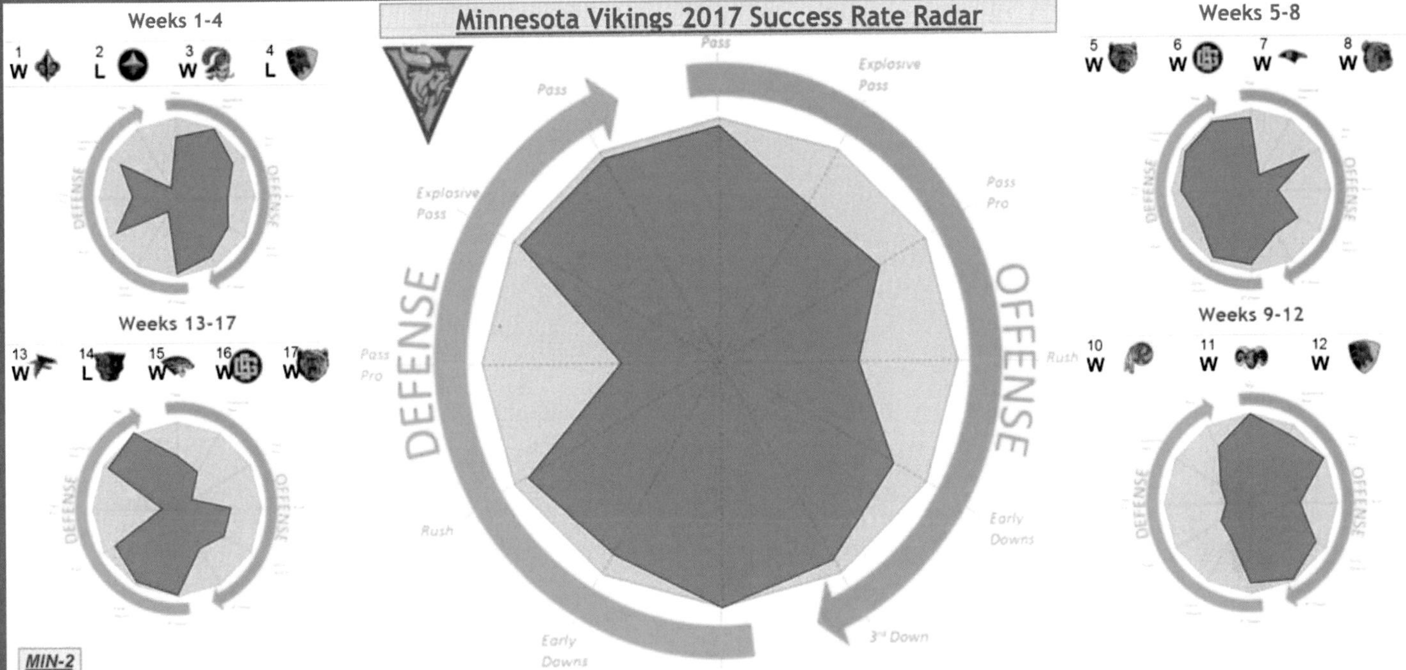

MIN-2

Flip to page three of Washington's chapter. The Redskins were the NFL's most-injured team, and second-most-injured offense. They had the league's third-most-injured offensive line, third-most-injured running backs, third-most-injured tight ends, and ninth-most-injured wide receivers.

Cousins still logged a 64% completion rate, 7.6 yards per attempt, and 94 passer rating. Only four other NFL quarterbacks accomplished those feats last year, and their names were Tom Brady, Drew Brees, Matthew Stafford, and Alex Smith. Only Brady, Brees, and Cousins were that efficient in each of the last three years.

Even more impressive was Cousins hitting those benchmarks against brutal opponents. In 2016, Cousins drew the NFL's second-toughest slate of pass defenses. Last year, Cousins drew the league's fourth-hardest pass-defense schedule.

No quarterback faced a tougher schedule of pass defenses in the last two years. Cousins played against 13 top-ten pass defenses in that two-year span.

In Minnesota, Cousins and Zimmer each get something they've never had before. Cousins gets to play on a team with a top-five defense on the other side of the ball. Zimmer gets a high-priced quarterback in the prime of his career who has played exceedingly well of late.

Last year, Zimmer's defense faced the NFL's fourth-hardest schedule of rushing offenses yet ranked top five in run defense. The Vikings signed difference-maker DT Sheldon Richardson to play alongside NT Linval Joseph. I also project this year's Vikings to face an easier schedule of run defenses. With a strong offense and great defense, opponents should be forced to pass against Minnesota frequently, especially in second halves of games.

(cont'd - see MIN-3)

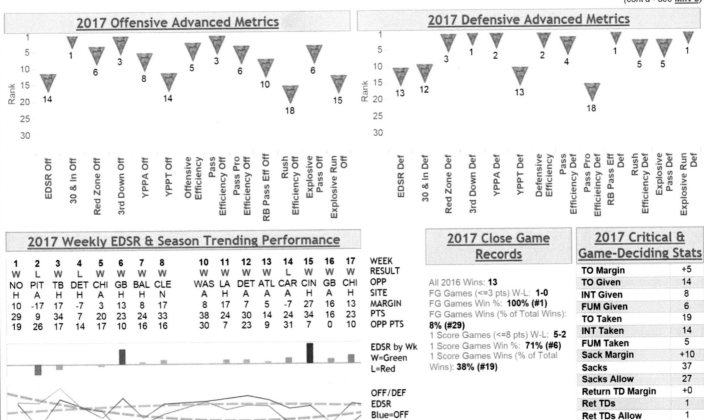

2017 Offensive Advanced Metrics

Metric	Rank
EDSR Off	14
30 & In Off	1
Red Zone Off	6
3rd Down Off	3
YPPA Off	8
YPPT Off	14
Offensive Efficiency	5
Pass Efficiency Off	3
Pass Pro Efficiency Off	6
RB Pass Eff Off	10
Rush Efficiency Off	18
Explosive Pass Off	6
Explosive Run Off	15

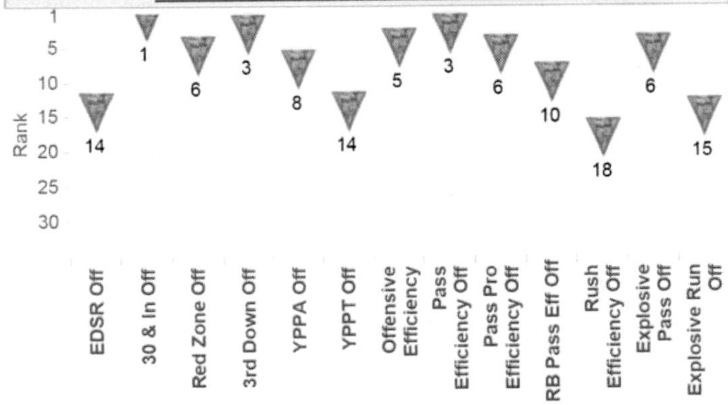

2017 Defensive Advanced Metrics

Metric	Rank
EDSR Def	13
30 & In Def	12
Red Zone Def	3
3rd Down Def	1
YPPA Def	2
YPPT Def	13
Defensive Efficiency	2
Pass Efficiency Def	4
Pass Pro Efficieincy Def	18
RB Pass Eff Def	1
Rush Efficiency Def	5
Explosive Pass Def	5
Explosive Run Def	1

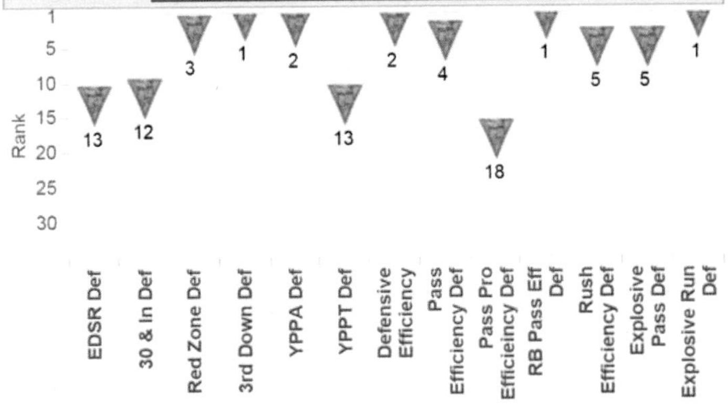

2017 Weekly EDSR & Season Trending Performance

WEEK	1	2	3	4	5	6	7	8	10	11	12	13	14	15	16	17
RESULT	W	L	W	L	W	W	W	W	W	W	W	W	L	W	W	W
OPP	NO	PIT	TB	DET	CHI	GB	BAL	CLE	WAS	LA	DET	ATL	CAR	CIN	GB	CHI
SITE	H	A	H	H	A	H	H	N	A	H	A	A	A	H	A	H
MARGIN	10	-17	17	-7	3	13	8	17	8	17	7	5	-7	27	16	13
PTS	29	9	34	7	20	23	24	33	38	24	30	14	24	34	16	23
OPP PTS	19	26	17	14	17	10	16	16	30	7	23	9	31	7	0	10

EDSR by Wk
W=Green
L=Red

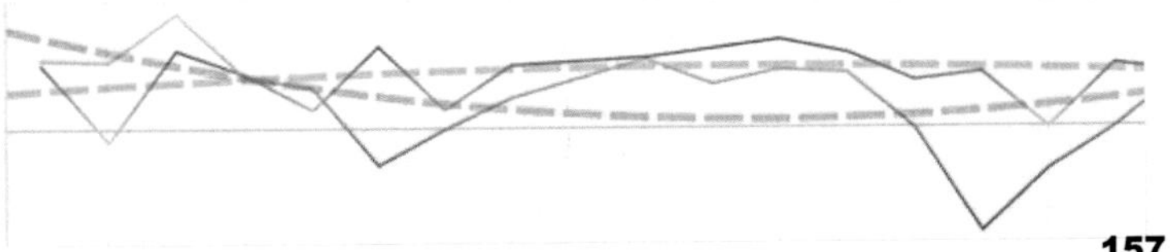

OFF/DEF EDSR
Blue=OFF (high=good)
Red=DEF (low=good)

2017 Close Game Records

All 2016 Wins: **13**
FG Games (<=3 pts) W-L: **1-0**
FG Games Win %: **100% (#1)**
FG Games Wins (% of Total Wins): **8% (#29)**
1 Score Games (<=8 pts) W-L: **5-2**
1 Score Games Win %: **71% (#6)**
1 Score Games Wins (% of Total Wins): **38% (#19)**

2017 Critical & Game-Deciding Stats

TO Margin	+5
TO Given	14
INT Given	8
FUM Given	6
TO Taken	19
INT Taken	14
FUM Taken	5
Sack Margin	+10
Sacks	37
Sacks Allow	27
Return TD Margin	+0
Ret TDs	1
Ret TDs Allow	1
Penalty Margin	+5
Penalties	100
Opponent Penalties	105

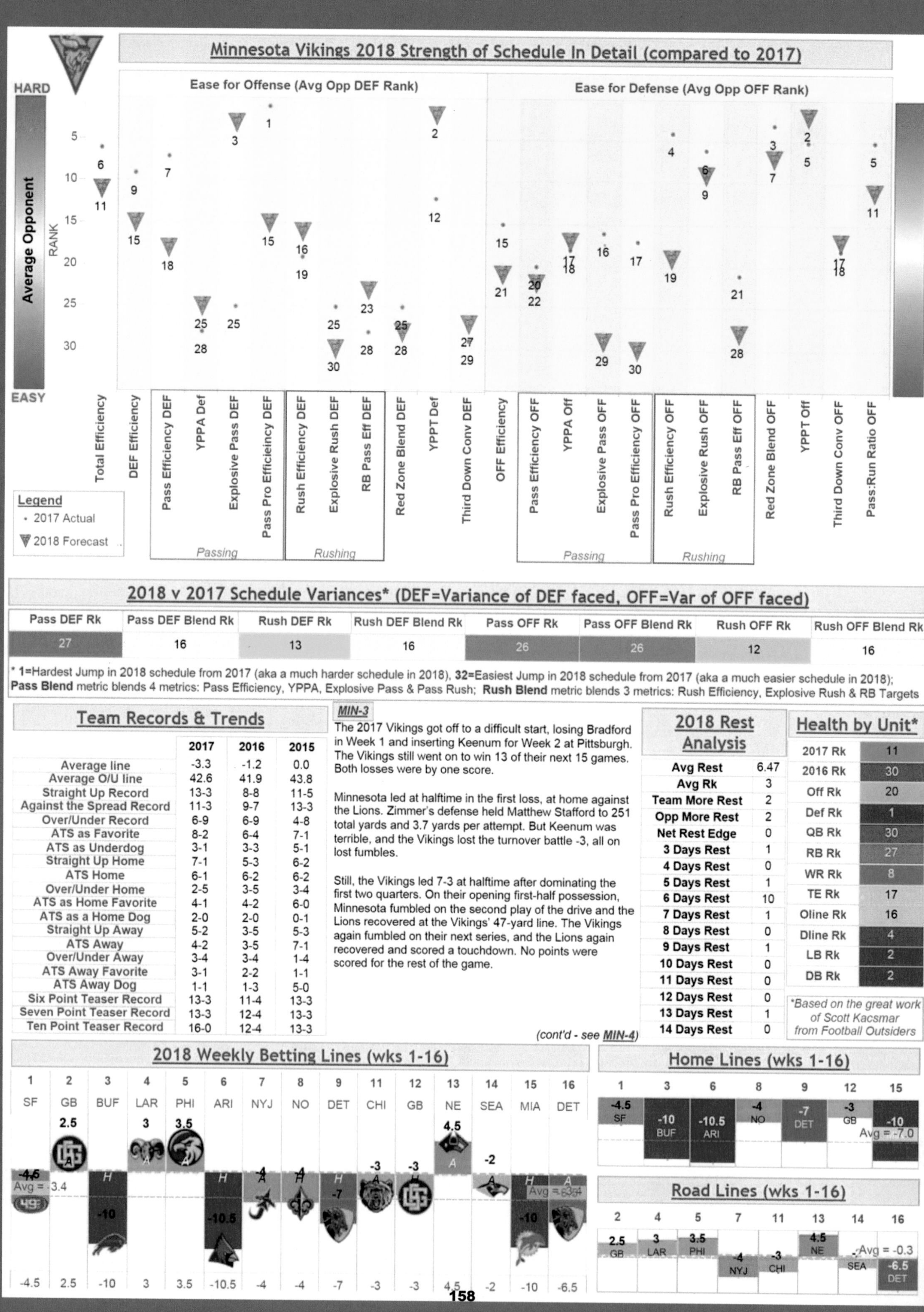

Minnesota Vikings 2018 Strength of Schedule In Detail (compared to 2017)

2018 v 2017 Schedule Variances* (DEF=Variance of DEF faced, OFF=Var of OFF faced)

Pass DEF Rk	Pass DEF Blend Rk	Rush DEF Rk	Rush DEF Blend Rk	Pass OFF Rk	Pass OFF Blend Rk	Rush OFF Rk	Rush OFF Blend Rk
27	16	13	16	26	26	12	16

* **1**=Hardest Jump in 2018 schedule from 2017 (aka a much harder schedule in 2018), **32**=Easiest Jump in 2018 schedule from 2017 (aka a much easier schedule in 2018); **Pass Blend** metric blends 4 metrics: Pass Efficiency, YPPA, Explosive Pass & Pass Rush; **Rush Blend** metric blends 3 metrics: Rush Efficiency, Explosive Rush & RB Targets

Team Records & Trends

	2017	2016	2015
Average line	-3.3	-1.2	0.0
Average O/U line	42.6	41.9	43.8
Straight Up Record	13-3	8-8	11-5
Against the Spread Record	11-3	9-7	13-3
Over/Under Record	6-9	6-9	4-8
ATS as Favorite	8-2	6-4	7-1
ATS as Underdog	3-1	3-3	5-1
Straight Up Home	7-1	5-3	6-2
ATS Home	6-1	6-2	6-2
Over/Under Home	2-5	3-5	3-4
ATS as Home Favorite	4-1	4-2	6-0
ATS as a Home Dog	2-0	2-0	0-1
Straight Up Away	5-2	3-5	5-3
ATS Away	4-2	3-5	7-1
Over/Under Away	3-4	3-4	1-4
ATS Away Favorite	3-1	2-2	1-1
ATS Away Dog	1-1	1-3	5-0
Six Point Teaser Record	13-3	11-4	13-3
Seven Point Teaser Record	13-3	12-4	13-3
Ten Point Teaser Record	16-0	12-4	13-3

MIN-3

The 2017 Vikings got off to a difficult start, losing Bradford in Week 1 and inserting Keenum for Week 2 at Pittsburgh. The Vikings still went on to win 13 of their next 15 games. Both losses were by one score.

Minnesota led at halftime in the first loss, at home against the Lions. Zimmer's defense held Matthew Stafford to 251 total yards and 3.7 yards per attempt. But Keenum was terrible, and the Vikings lost the turnover battle -3, all on lost fumbles.

Still, the Vikings led 7-3 at halftime after dominating the first two quarters. On their opening first-half possession, Minnesota fumbled on the second play of the drive and the Lions recovered at the Vikings' 47-yard line. The Vikings again fumbled on their next series, and the Lions again recovered and scored a touchdown. No points were scored for the rest of the game.

(cont'd - see ***MIN-4***)

2018 Rest Analysis

Avg Rest	6.47
Avg Rk	3
Team More Rest	2
Opp More Rest	2
Net Rest Edge	0
3 Days Rest	1
4 Days Rest	0
5 Days Rest	1
6 Days Rest	10
7 Days Rest	1
8 Days Rest	0
9 Days Rest	1
10 Days Rest	0
11 Days Rest	0
12 Days Rest	0
13 Days Rest	1
14 Days Rest	0

Health by Unit*

2017 Rk	11
2016 Rk	30
Off Rk	20
Def Rk	1
QB Rk	30
RB Rk	27
WR Rk	8
TE Rk	17
Oline Rk	16
Dline Rk	4
LB Rk	2
DB Rk	2

**Based on the great work of Scott Kacsmar from Football Outsiders*

2018 Weekly Betting Lines (wks 1-16)

1	2	3	4	5	6	7	8	9	11	12	13	14	15	16
SF	GB	BUF	LAR	PHI	ARI	NYJ	NO	DET	CHI	GB	NE	SEA	MIA	DET
H	A	H	A	A	H	A	H	H	A	H	A	A	H	A
-4.5	2.5	-10	3	3.5	-10.5	-4	-4	-7	-3	-3	4.5	-2	-10	-6.5

Avg = -3.4

Home Lines (wks 1-16)

1	3	6	8	9	12	15
SF	BUF	ARI	NO	DET	GB	
-4.5	-10	-10.5	-4	-7	-3	-10

Avg = -7.0

Road Lines (wks 1-16)

2	4	5	7	11	13	14	16
GB	LAR	PHI	NYJ	CHI	NE	SEA	DET
2.5	3	3.5	-4	-3	4.5	-2	-6.5

Avg = -0.3

Minnesota Vikings 2017 Play Analysis

2017 Play Tendencies

All Pass %	53%
All Pass Rk	28
All Rush %	47%
All Rush Rk	5
1 Score Pass %	56%
1 Score Pass Rk	19
2016 1 Score Pass %	62%
2016 1 Score Pass Rk	7
2017 Pass Increase %	-6%
Pass Increase Rk	26
1 Score Rush %	44%
1 Score Rush Rk	14
Up Pass %	47%
Up Pass Rk	24
Up Rush %	53%
Up Rush Rk	9
Down Pass %	61%
Down Pass Rk	30
Down Rush %	39%
Down Rush Rk	3

2017 Down & Distance Tendencies

Down	Distance	Total Plays	Pass Rate	Run Rate	Play Success %
1	Short (1-3)	13	15%	85%	77%
	Med (4-7)	16	44%	56%	38%
	Long (8-10)	358	42%	58%	49%
	XL (11+)	11	55%	45%	18%
2	Short (1-3)	47	26%	74%	64%
	Med (4-7)	99	57%	43%	58%
	Long (8-10)	112	59%	41%	53%
	XL (11+)	45	80%	20%	36%
	35	1	100%	0%	0%
3	Short (1-3)	58	76%	24%	66%
	Med (4-7)	63	97%	3%	54%
	Long (8-10)	29	100%	0%	28%
	XL (11+)	28	86%	14%	21%
	35	1	0%	100%	0%
4	Short (1-3)	1	0%	100%	100%
	Med (4-7)	2	100%	0%	0%
	XL (11+)	1	100%	0%	0%

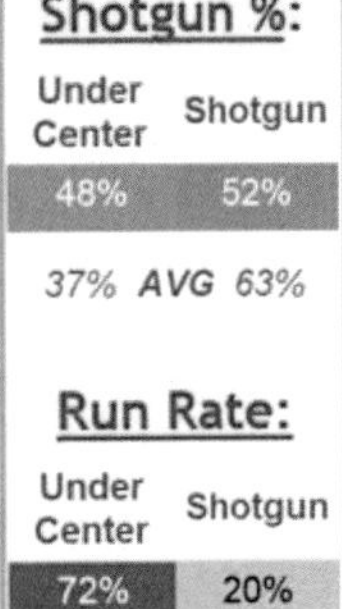

Shotgun %:

Under Center	Shotgun
48%	52%
37%	*63%* (*AVG*)

Run Rate:

Under Center	Shotgun
72%	20%
68%	*23%* (*AVG*)

Pass Rate:

Under Center	Shotgun
28%	80%
32%	*77%* (*AVG*)

Short Yardage Intelligence:

2nd and Short Run

Run Freq	Run Rk	NFL Run Freq Avg	Run 1D Rate	Run NFL 1D Avg
90%	1	67%	71%	69%

2nd and Short Pass

Pass Freq	Pass Rk	NFL Pass Freq Avg	Pass 1D Rate	Pass NFL 1D Avg
10%	32	33%	50%	53%

Most Frequent Play

Down	Distance	Play Type	Player	Total Plays	Play Success %
1	Short (1-3)	RUSH	Latavius Murray	7	86%
	Med (4-7)	RUSH	Latavius Murray	4	25%
			Jerick McKinnon	4	75%
	Long (8-10)	RUSH	Latavius Murray	104	39%
	XL (11+)	PASS	Jerick McKinnon	3	0%
		RUSH	Jerick McKinnon	3	0%
2	Short (1-3)	RUSH	Latavius Murray	20	55%
	Med (4-7)	RUSH	Latavius Murray	18	56%
	Long (8-10)	RUSH	Jerick McKinnon	19	47%
	XL (11+)	PASS	Jerick McKinnon	9	33%
3	Short (1-3)	PASS	Stefon Diggs	9	67%
	Med (4-7)	PASS	Adam Thielen	25	40%
	Long (8-10)	PASS	Adam Thielen	8	38%
	XL (11+)	PASS	Jerick McKinnon	6	0%

Most Successful Play*

Down	Distance	Play Type	Player	Total Plays	Play Success %
1	Short (1-3)	RUSH	Latavius Murray	7	86%
	Long (8-10)	PASS	Kyle Rudolph	21	76%
2	Short (1-3)	PASS	Kyle Rudolph	5	80%
	Med (4-7)	RUSH	Case Keenum	5	80%
	Long (8-10)	PASS	Michael Floyd	5	100%
	XL (11+)	PASS	Jerick McKinnon	9	33%
			Kyle Rudolph	6	33%
3	Short (1-3)	RUSH	Latavius Murray	7	86%
	Med (4-7)	PASS	Jerick McKinnon	6	83%
	Long (8-10)	PASS	Stefon Diggs	5	40%
	XL (11+)	PASS	Adam Thielen	5	60%

**Minimum 5 plays to qualify*

2017 Snap Rates

Wk	Opp	Score	Adam Thielen	Kyle Rudolph	Stefon Diggs	Jerick McKinnon	Laquon Treadwell	Latavius Murray	David Morgan	Jarius Wright
1	NO	W 29-19	65 (100%)	55 (85%)	58 (89%)	11 (17%)	36 (55%)	3 (5%)	18 (28%)	16 (25%)
2	PIT	L 26-9	62 (95%)	61 (94%)	60 (92%)	22 (34%)	50 (77%)	6 (9%)	7 (11%)	13 (20%)
3	TB	W 34-17	63 (85%)	68 (92%)	52 (70%)	14 (19%)	31 (42%)	8 (11%)	30 (41%)	18 (24%)
4	DET	L 14-7	55 (98%)	55 (98%)	48 (86%)	10 (18%)	25 (45%)	19 (34%)	18 (32%)	4 (7%)
5	CHI	W 20-17	68 (97%)	69 (99%)	49 (70%)	47 (67%)	42 (60%)	22 (31%)	12 (17%)	2 (3%)
6	GB	W 23-10	72 (94%)	75 (97%)		44 (57%)	44 (57%)	33 (43%)	16 (21%)	29 (38%)
7	BAL	W 24-16	65 (98%)	61 (92%)		35 (53%)	55 (83%)	31 (47%)	17 (26%)	39 (59%)
8	CLE	W 33-16	78 (92%)	82 (96%)	64 (75%)	54 (64%)	31 (36%)	31 (36%)	36 (42%)	14 (16%)
10	WAS	W 38-30	55 (90%)	53 (87%)	52 (85%)	31 (51%)	24 (39%)	30 (49%)	27 (44%)	15 (25%)
11	LA	W 24-7	73 (94%)	73 (94%)	53 (68%)	45 (58%)	16 (21%)	33 (42%)	40 (51%)	11 (14%)
12	DET	W 30-23	66 (90%)	65 (89%)	66 (90%)	33 (45%)	21 (29%)	40 (55%)	33 (45%)	16 (22%)
13	ATL	W 14-9	60 (91%)	64 (97%)	47 (71%)	35 (53%)	20 (30%)	30 (45%)	1 (2%)	13 (20%)
14	CAR	L 31-24	69 (93%)	55 (74%)	70 (95%)	42 (57%)	31 (42%)	32 (43%)		26 (35%)
15	CIN	W 34-7	56 (84%)	21 (31%)	46 (69%)	35 (52%)	24 (36%)	32 (48%)	50 (75%)	16 (24%)
16	GB	W 16-0	57 (88%)	35 (54%)	53 (82%)	25 (38%)	27 (42%)	40 (62%)	43 (66%)	12 (18%)
17	CHI	W 23-10	66 (88%)	32 (43%)	62 (83%)	44 (59%)	23 (31%)	31 (41%)	47 (63%)	12 (16%)
	Grand Total		1,030 (92%)	924 (83%)	780 (80%)	527 (46%)	500 (45%)	421 (38%)	395 (38%)	256 (23%)

Personnel Groupings

Personnel	Team %	NFL Avg	Succ. %
1-1 [3WR]	57%	59%	47%
1-2 [2WR]	22%	19%	51%
2-2 [1WR]	9%	4%	42%
2-1 [2WR]	5%	7%	57%
1-3 [1WR]	3%	5%	54%
2-0 [3WR]	2%	1%	33%

Grouping Tendencies

Personnel	Pass Rate	Pass Succ. %	Run Succ. %
1-1 [3WR]	66%	48%	43%
1-2 [2WR]	34%	57%	48%
2-2 [1WR]	19%	63%	38%
2-1 [2WR]	33%	63%	55%
1-3 [1WR]	39%	64%	47%
2-0 [3WR]	79%	32%	40%

Red Zone Targets (min 3)

Receiver	All	Inside 5	6-10	11-20
Adam Thielen	21	4	6	11
Kyle Rudolph	18	5	6	7
Stefon Diggs	15	3	4	8
Jerick McKinnon	8	1		7
Jarius Wright	5	1	2	2
Latavius Murray	2			2
Michael Floyd	1	1		

Red Zone Rushes (min 3)

Rusher	All	Inside 5	6-10	11-20
Latavius Murray	52	14	10	28
Jerick McKinnon	18	6	2	10
Dalvin Cook	10	3	2	5
Case Keenum	6	2	2	2
Sam Bradford	2			2

Early Down Target Rate

	RB	TE	WR
	24%	19%	57%
NFL AVG	*23%*	*21%*	*56%*

Overall Target Success %

RB	TE	WR
49% #10	57% #2	52% #7

Minnesota Vikings 2017 Passing Recap & 2018 Outlook

New OC John DeFilippo's only experience calling plays came in 2015 with Mike Pettine's Browns. Cleveland went 3-13 that year and ranked 27th in offensive efficiency, although they faced the NFL's toughest schedule. That year, first-round pick Johnny Manziel failed to beat out Josh McCown in training camp. Later, Manziel openly admitted he wasn't prepared to play in the NFL and didn't work hard enough.

We can surmise from DeFilippo's time in Philadelphia that he'll incorporate much of what helped the Eagles succeed into his Vikings offense. Over the last two years, Philadelphia ran the NFL's second-highest rate of two-tight end 12 personnel and second-highest rate of three-tight end 13 personnel. A league-high 27% of the Eagles' pass plays were thrown out of 12. Over that same span, Cousins has a strong 56% Success Rate and 101 passer rating in 12 formations, which ranks second best in the NFL behind Matt Ryan.

Case Keenum Rating All Downs

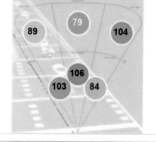

89 79 104
103 106 84

Case Keenum Rating Early Downs

111 82 87
112 112 82

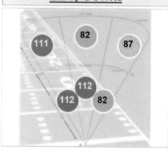

2017 Standard Passing Table

QB	Comp	Att	Comp %	Yds	YPA	TDs	INT	Sacks	Rating	Rk
Case Keenum	378	569	66%	4,136	7.3	24	10	25	95	16
Sam Bradford	32	43	74%	382	8.9	3	0	5	124	1
NFL Avg			62%		7.0				87.5	

2017 Advanced Passing Table

QB	Success %	EDSR Passing Success %	20+ Yd Pass Gains	20+ Yd Pass %	30+ Yd Pass Gains	30+ Yd Pass %	Avg. Air Yds per Comp	Avg. YAC per Comp	20+ Air Yd Comp	20+ Air Yd %
Case Keenum	49%	53%	53	9.3%	20	3.5%	5.2	4.9	17	4%
Sam Bradford	50%	55%	8	18.6%	3	7.0%	6.6	4.8	3	9%
NFL Avg	44%	48%	27.7	8.8%	10.3	3.3%	6.0	4.7	11.7	6%

Interception Rates by Down

Yards to Go	1	2	3	4	Total
1 & 2	0.0%	0.0%	0.0%	0.0%	0.0%
3, 4, 5	0.0%	0.0%	0.0%		0.0%
6 - 9	0.0%	1.4%	5.8%	0.0%	3.2%
10 - 14	1.7%	4.5%	0.0%	0.0%	2.2%
15+	0.0%	0.0%	0.0%	0.0%	0.0%
Total	1.5%	2.0%	1.6%	0.0%	1.7%

3rd Down Passing - Short of Sticks Analysis

QB	Avg. Yds to Go	Avg. YIA (of Comp)	Avg Yds Short	Short of Sticks Rate	Short Rk
Case Keenum	7.1	5.2	-1.9	66%	28
NFL Avg	7.8	6.7	-1.1	60%	

Air Yds vs YAC

Air Yds %	YAC %	Rk
48%	52%	40
58%	42%	

2017 Receiving Recap & 2018 Outlook

The Vikings are loaded at wide receiver with Stefon Diggs and Adam Thielen. Even without first-team practice reps in 2017 training camp with then-backup Case Keenum, Diggs and Thielen delivered absurd Success Rates. Add Kyle Rudolph and Dalvin Cook, and you have one of the NFL's youngest, most-dangerous skill-position corps. Thielen's 2017 emergence and a late-season high ankle sprain cut into Rudolph's target volume, but Rudolph still scored seven TDs and is a prime bounce-back candidate with DeFilippo calling plays. On red-zone passes alone, Rudolph delivered an 87% Success Rate, 6:0 TD-to-INT ratio, and 130 passer rating.

Player *Min 50 Targets	Targets	Comp %	YPA	Rating	TOARS	Success %	Success Rk	Missed YPA Rk	YAS % Rk	TDs
Adam Thielen	161	62%	8.6	90	5.3	51%	53	69	32	4
Stefon Diggs	117	67%	9.0	114	5.2	59%	7	19	28	9
Kyle Rudolph	93	68%	6.3	108	4.8	55%	29	17	111	9
Jerick McKinnon	84	77%	6.1	95	4.4	46%	88	127	92	2

Directional Passer Rating Delivered

Receiver	Short Left	Short Middle	Short Right	Deep Left	Deep Middle	Deep Right	Player Total
Adam Thielen	101	92	71	78	104	113	90
Stefon Diggs	118	118	79	70	88	127	114
Kyle Rudolph	127	110	85	80	96	85	108
Jerick McKinnon	91	49	113			40	95
Jarius Wright	93	108	92	119	40	71	109
Laquon Treadwell	56	78	73	74	40	0	48
Latavius Murray	101	70	85				92
Michael Floyd	84	75	21			56	43
Team Total	107	94	83	92	85	117	96

2017 Rushing Recap & 2017 Outlook

Dalvin Cook was on pace for 340 touches before tearing his ACL last Week 4. We can assume he'll be 100% by training camp. He should have lots of 2018 usage between the 20s. Inside the ten-yard line last year, the Vikings went 60% run featuring Latavius Murray, who delivered a rock-solid 55% Success Rate. Over the past two years, DeFilippo's Eagles offenses went 58% run in scoring position. That bodes well for DeFilippo's red-zone efficiency.

Yards per Carry by Direction

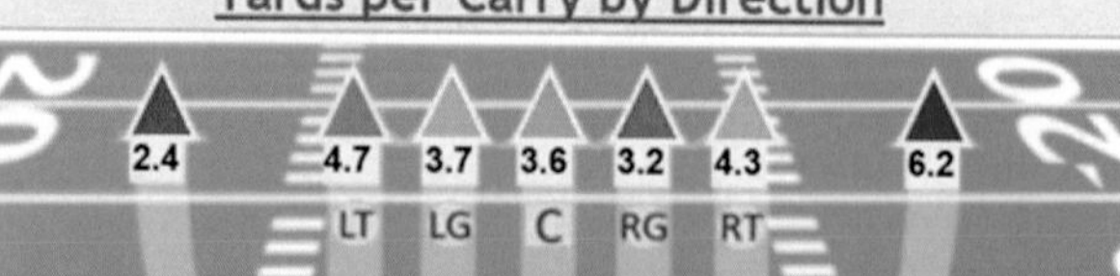

Player *Min 50 Rushes	Rushes	YPC	Success %	Success Rk	Missed YPA Rk	YTS % Rk	YAS % Rk	Early Down Success %	Early Down Success Rk	TDs
Latavius Murray	241	3.8	44%	36	22	44	32	43%	45	9
Jerick McKinnon	169	3.8	45%	33	69	14	43	46%	29	4
Dalvin Cook	74	4.8	54%	7	11	25	36	53%	10	2

Directional Run Frequency

9% 14% 17% 29% 12% 10% 9%
LT LG C RG RT

Minnesota's only other defeat the rest of the regular season came in Week 14 at Carolina. The Vikings did win the Early-Down Success Rate battle in Week 14. But this loss was on Keenum, who threw two picks. Coming out of halftime, Keenum was sacked and fumbled on the first play of the Vikings' initial third-quarter possession, giving Carolina the ball at Minnesota's 31-yard line and resulting in a field goal. The Vikings punted on their next series, then threw a pick after driving to the Panthers' 26. Although Minnesota's defense could have played better, this loss belonged to Keenum's offense.

More incredible was the fact that the Vikings lost against the spread just twice in 15 games with Keenum quarterbacking. Winning 13-of-15 games ATS is ridiculous. Linemakers set spreads based on Power Rankings and perception. Linemakers never catching up to the Vikings was a testament to how underrated Minnesota was by both the public and sportsbooks. Only 12 teams have covered over 75% of their games in the last 25 years. Two were coached by Zimmer: the 2015 and 2017 Vikings.

One reason for Minnesota's dominance was their ability to win Early-Down Success Rate. See page two of this chapter: The Vikings lost EDSR in just three games all year.

(cont'd - see MIN-5)

Evan Silva's Fantasy Corner

Stefon Diggs and Adam Thielen were outgoing quarterback Case Keenum's go-to guys, but Kyle Rudolph's volume is likely to grow with Kirk Cousins behind center. Cousins has long leaned heavily on tight ends, from healthy Jordan Reed to aging Vernon Davis and even situational TE/WR Niles Paul. Last year's Eagles targeted Zach Ertz, Trey Burton, or Brent Celek between 23% and 39% of the time in two-tight end 12-personnel packages. Rudolph drew targets on just 13% of 12-personnel snaps last year due to Thielen's breakout year and Rudolph's ankle sprain in 2017. Rudolph has 15 touchdowns over the last two seasons and is typically one of the final starting-caliber tight ends drafted in fantasy leagues. I'm targeting him in all of mine.

Division History: Season Wins & 2018 Projection

2014 Wins | 2015 Wins | 2016 Wins | 2017 Wins | Forecast 2018 Wins

Rank of 2018 Defensive Pass Efficiency Faced by Week

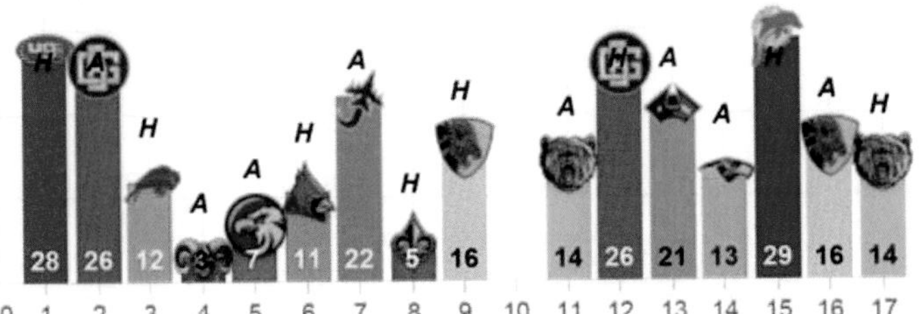

Rank of 2018 Defensive Rush Efficiency Faced by Week

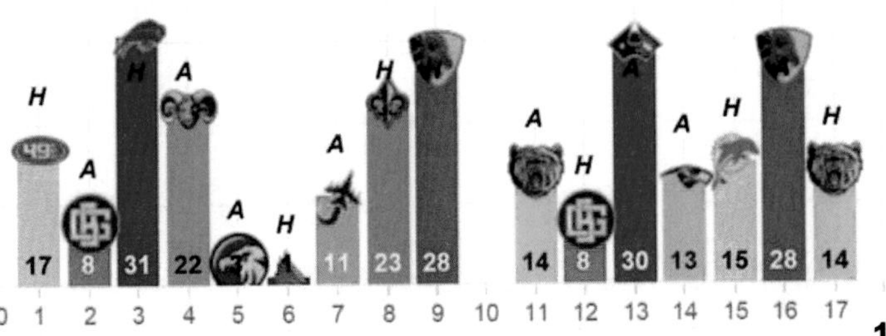

2017 Situational Usage by Player & Position

Usage Rate by Score

		Being Blown Out (14+)	Down Big (9-13)	One Score	Large Lead (9-13)	Blowout Lead (14+)	Grand Total
RUSH	Latavius Murray	5%	9%	22%	27%	26%	22%
	Jerick McKinnon	5%	2%	16%	17%	16%	15%
	Adam Thielen			0%			0%
	Stefon Diggs	2%		0%	2%	1%	1%
	Dalvin Cook	5%	14%	5%	7%	12%	7%
	Jarius Wright			0%			0%
	C.J. Ham	2%		1%		1%	1%
	Total	19%	26%	45%	53%	56%	45%
PASS	Latavius Murray	2%	2%	2%	1%	1%	2%
	Jerick McKinnon	19%	7%	7%	4%	8%	8%
	Adam Thielen	17%	12%	16%	15%	9%	15%
	Stefon Diggs	16%	14%	10%	11%	10%	11%
	Kyle Rudolph	7%	9%	10%	5%	6%	8%
	Dalvin Cook		5%	1%	1%	1%	1%
	Jarius Wright	14%	5%	2%	3%	4%	3%
	Laquon Treadwell	5%	9%	3%	3%	1%	3%
	Michael Floyd		5%	1%	2%	2%	2%
	C.J. Ham		2%	1%		1%	1%
	David Morgan	2%		1%	2%		1%
	Blake Bell		5%	0%			0%
	Stacy Coley			0%			0%
	Total	81%	74%	55%	47%	44%	55%

Positional Target Distribution vs NFL Average

		NFL Wide				Team Only			
		Left	Middle	Right	**Total**	Left	Middle	Right	**Total**
Deep	WR	949	495	943	**2,387**	37	14	44	**95**
	TE	185	148	183	**516**	7	2	5	**14**
	RB	39	9	41	**89**			1	**1**
	All	**1,173**	**652**	**1,167**	**2,992**	**44**	**16**	**50**	**110**
Short	WR	2,768	1,612	2,669	**7,049**	94	59	121	**274**
	TE	839	823	1,131	**2,793**	24	16	39	**79**
	RB	1,274	806	1,255	**3,335**	47	17	40	**104**
	All	**4,881**	**3,241**	**5,055**	**13,177**	**165**	**92**	**200**	**457**
Total		**6,054**	**3,893**	**6,222**	**16,169**	**209**	**108**	**250**	**567**

Positional Success Rates vs NFL Average

		NFL Wide				Team Only			
		Left	Middle	Right	**Total**	Left	Middle	Right	**Total**
Deep	WR	36%	45%	37%	**39%**	51%	36%	52%	**49%**
	TE	38%	53%	46%	**45%**	43%	50%	20%	**36%**
	RB	36%	56%	39%	**39%**			0%	**0%**
	All	**36%**	**47%**	**39%**	**40%**	**50%**	**38%**	**48%**	**47%**
Short	WR	51%	57%	50%	**52%**	60%	58%	46%	**53%**
	TE	50%	56%	49%	**51%**	58%	56%	62%	**59%**
	RB	44%	51%	43%	**45%**	55%	47%	43%	**49%**
	All	**49%**	**56%**	**48%**	**50%**	**58%**	**55%**	**49%**	**53%**
Total		**47%**	**54%**	**46%**	**48%**	**56%**	**53%**	**48%**	**52%**

Successful Play Rate
0% [color scale] 100%

Minnesota Vikings - Success by Personnel Grouping & Play Type

Play Type	1-1 [3WR]	1-2 [2WR]	2-1 [2WR]	1-0 [4WR]	1-3 [1WR]	0-1 [4WR]	2-0 [3WR]	2-2 [1WR]	2-3 [0WR]	Grand Total
PASS	48% (397, 72%)	57% (79, 14%)	63% (16, 3%)	27% (11, 2%)	64% (11, 2%)	100% (1, 0%)	32% (19, 3%)	63% (19, 3%)	100% (1, 0%)	50% (554, 100%)
RUSH	43% (203, 40%)	48% (156, 31%)	55% (33, 7%)	100% (2, 0%)	47% (17, 3%)		40% (5, 1%)	38% (80, 16%)	83% (6, 1%)	45% (502, 100%)
TOTAL	47% (600, 57%)	51% (235, 22%)	57% (49, 5%)	38% (13, 1%)	54% (28, 3%)	100% (1, 0%)	33% (24, 2%)	42% (99, 9%)	86% (7, 1%)	48% (1,056, 100%)

Format Line 1: Success Rate Line 2: Total # of Plays, % of All Plays (by type)

MIN-5 One was simply because they led the Buccaneers so dominantly that Minnesota played conservatively and Tampa Bay moved the ball successfully late in the game. Even in aforementioned losses to Carolina and Detroit, the 2017 Vikings won EDSR battles in those games

The 2017 Vikings led at halftime in 12-of-16 games and won 11 of them. Zimmer was terrific at second-half adjustments. Between 2015 and 2016, the Vikings recorded the NFL's second-best point differential in the third quarter, outscoring opponents by an average of 2.5 points. Only mastermind tactician Bill Belichick's Patriots were (slightly) better at 2.6 points.

In 2018, I'm excited to see how Dalvin Cook looks in his return from ACL surgery. With Jerick McKinnon (49ers) vacating a ton of running back touches, Cook's lone backup is pedestrian grinder Latavius Murray. Murray did record a passable 44% Success Rate off the bench last year, but he wasn't nearly as effective as Cook. Albeit against the NFL's fifth-softest schedule of run defenses in Weeks 1-4, Cook produced a 54% Success Rate and 53% Early-Down Success Rate. Those metrics ranked 10th and 11th in the league.

I'm also excited to see new OC John DeFilippo's scheme after he learned under Doug Pederson and Frank Reich in Philadelphia. As Eagles quarterbacks coach, DeFilippo had hands-on knowledge of Carson Wentz's year-two breakout and journeyman Nick Foles' magical postseason run. With DeFilippo's creativity, an elite supporting cast, and feeling he doesn't have to do everything himself because of Zimmer's stout defense, Cousins is set up for his most-productive year. Cousins' ceiling is especially high in the red zone, where Zimmer's defense will consistently get him short fields.

Receiving Success by Personnel Grouping

Position	Player	1-1 [3WR]	1-2 [2WR]	2-1 [2WR]	1-0 [4WR]	1-3 [1WR]	0-1 [4WR]	2-0 [3WR]	2-2 [1WR]	2-3 [0WR]	Total
RB	Jerick McKinnon	42% 6.0 80.5 (50)	57% 8.4 136.3 (7)		20% 0.2 79.2 (5)			33% 7.0 86.8 (3)	100% 13.0 158.3 (3)		44% 6.2 94.1 (68)
	Latavius Murray	57% 8.6 102.4 (7)	67% 5.2 88.2 (6)	0% 0.0 56.3 (2)					50% 5.5 89.6 (2)		53% 6.0 91.7 (17)
TE	Kyle Rudolph	57% 6.8 109.5 (60)	45% 3.1 52.8 (11)	100% 7.0 95.8 (2)		100% 14.3 118.8 (3)			75% 8.3 138.5 (4)	100% 1.0 118.8 (1)	59% 6.6 110.7 (81)
WR	Adam Thielen	48% 8.2 95.2 (106)	68% 11.3 145.5 (19)	67% 14.8 70.1 (6)		67% 18.3 109.7 (3)	100% 4.0 83.3 (1)	0% 0.0 39.6 (2)	50% 7.8 76.4 (6)		52% 8.9 98.7 (143)
	Stefon Diggs	59% 8.4 122.9 (69)	60% 9.0 110.2 (20)	67% 26.3 109.7 (3)				33% 3.3 43.8 (3)			59% 8.9 119.1 (95)
	Laquon Treadwell	48% 6.6 67.0 (29)	50% 4.0 20.8 (2)		0% 0.0 56.3 (2)			0% 0.0 39.6 (2)			43% 5.7 49.7 (35)

Format Line 1: Success Rate Line 2: YPA Line 3: Passer Rating Line 4: Total # of Plays

Successful Play Rate
0% [color scale] 100%

Rushing Success by Personnel Grouping

Position	Player	1-1 [3WR]	1-2 [2WR]	2-1 [2WR]	1-0 [4WR]	1-3 [1WR]	2-0 [3WR]	2-2 [1WR]	2-3 [0WR]	Total
RB	Latavius Murray	33% 3.6 (66)	48% 4.3 (80)	50% 2.9 (16)		50% 1.7 (6)		50% 4.4 (46)	100% 1.0 (2)	44% 3.9 (216)
	Jerick McKinnon	41% 4.3 (90)	44% 3.4 (36)	57% 4.3 (7)	100% 7.5 (2)	33% 1.0 (3)	40% 0.4 (5)	29% 2.0 (7)	100% 1.0 (1)	43% 3.8 (151)
	Dalvin Cook	52% 6.6 (27)	55% 4.2 (31)	50% 3.3 (6)		80% 3.4 (5)		33% 2.7 (3)	50% 0.5 (2)	54% 4.8 (74)

Format Line 1: Success Rate Line 2: YPC Line 3: Total # of Plays

New England Patriots

2018 Coaches

Head Coach:
Bill Belichick (19th yr)
Offensive Coordinator:
Josh Daniels (7th yr)
Defensive Coordinator:
Greg Schiano (Ohio St, DC) (1st yr)

2018 Forecast

Wins	Div Rank
11	#1

Past Records

2017: 13-3
2016: 14-2
2015: 12-4

EASY HARD

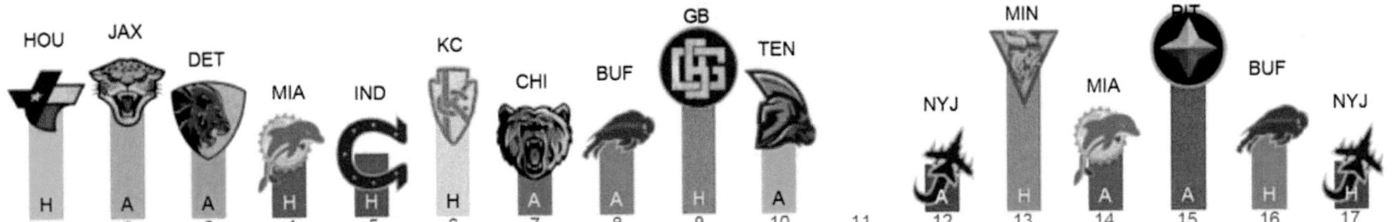

Key Players Lost

TXN	Player (POS)
Cut	Bennett, Martellus TE
	McClellin, Shea LB
Declared Free Agent	Amendola, Danny WR
	Bademosi, Johnson CB
	Branch, Alan DT
	Butler, Malcolm CB
	Farris, Chase G
	Fleming, Cameron T
	Flowers, Marquis LB
	Lewis, Dion RB
	Slater, Matthew WR
	Solder, Nate T
	Waddle, LaAdrian T
Retired	Harris, David LB
	Harrison, James LB

2018 New England Patriots Overview

Every NFL team can use analytics to improve. Some people think smart teams like the Patriots don't even need analytics because they're always operating at maximum output. But that isn't true. Even the Patriots can improve their efficiency, and they know it. They study what they did last week and the year before, and they adjust their decision making accordingly.

In last year's Football Preview, I wrote an article entitled "Front Office Plea: Increase Efficiency!" It detailed mistakes teams made and ways they could easily get better. They didn't need wholesale roster changes, or to swap out coaching staffs. They needed to open their minds and let data talk to them, and to not be so arrogant as to reject change.

The Patriots have made changes to improve efficiency. Last year, I shared research supporting the notion that teams should use less three-receiver 11 personnel and more light-receiver formations like 12 and 21. Another data-backed suggestion was running more in the red zone. The 2016 Patriots passed from 11 personnel on 69% of throws, exactly league average. The '17 Patriots passed from 11 personnel on 55% of throws while the NFL average stayed at 69%.

New England shifted 9% of its 11 groupings into 21 personnel, increasing their usage of 21 from 16% to 24% while dropping 11 usage from 53% to 44%. And the Patriots improved their 21-personnel Success Rate from 48% to 60% while their 11-personnel Success Rate stayed largely flat (47% in 2017, 49% in 2016). The 2016 Patriots threw from 21 personnel only 34% of the time, yet produced a strong 54% passing Success Rate. Their running Success Rate in 21 was 45%. In 2017, the Patriots passed from 21 personnel 50% of the time and increased their passing Success Rate to 61%. It was their most-successful passing formation last year.

Every Patriots pass catcher with at least 20 targets generated higher Success Rates from 21 personnel than 11, including Rob Gronkowski (71% vs. 49%), Danny Amendola (91% vs. 52%), Chris Hogan (56% vs. 43%), Brandin Cooks (48% vs. 47%), James White (56% vs. 53%), Dion Lewis (83% vs. 56%), Rex Burkhead (60% vs. 50%), and Dwayne Allen (67% vs. 0%).

(cont'd - see NE2)

Key Free Agents/ Trades Added

Brown, Trent G
Clayborn, Adrian DE
Hill, Jeremy RB
John, Ulrick T
Matthews, Jordan WR
McCourty, Jason CB
Niklas, Troy TE
Patterson, Cordarrelle WR
Shelton, Danny NT
Tobin, Matt T

Drafted Players

Rd	Pk	Player (College)
1	23	OT - Isaiah Wynn (Georgia)
	31	RB - Sony Michel (Georgia)
2	56	CB - Duke Dawson (Florida)
5	143	LB - Ja'Whaun Bentley (Purdue)
6	178	LB - Christian Sam (Arizona State)
6*	210	WR - Braxton Berrios (Miami (FL))
	219	QB - Danny Etling (LSU)
7	243	CB - Keion Crossen (Western Carolina)
	250	TE - Ryan Izzo (Florida State)

Average Line	# Games Favored	# Games Underdog
-6.0	14	1

Regular Season Wins: Past & Current Proj

Lineup & Cap Hits

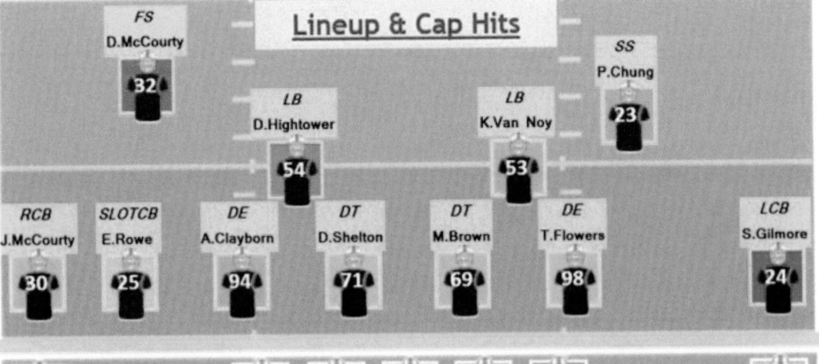

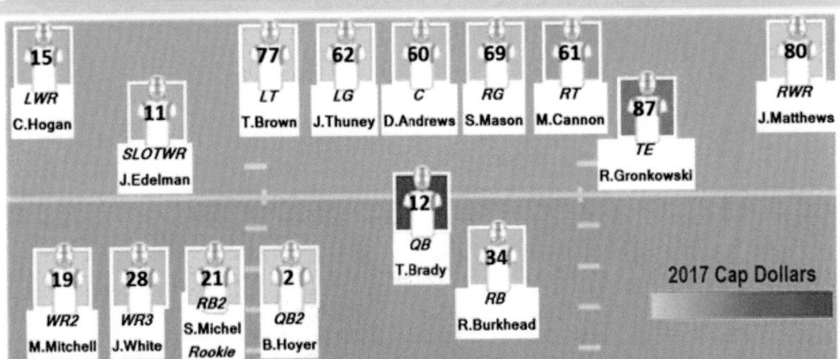

2018 Unit Spending

Positional Spending

	Rank	Total	2017 Rk
All OFF	16	$91.55M	11
QB	12	$23.42M	20
OL	32	$19.92M	21
RB	6	$9.94M	3
WR	21	$19.18M	18
TE	1	$19.09M	5
All DEF	14	$83.42M	23
DL	23	$20.22M	27
LB	23	$16.79M	26
CB	13	$21.58M	19
S	2	$24.83M	1

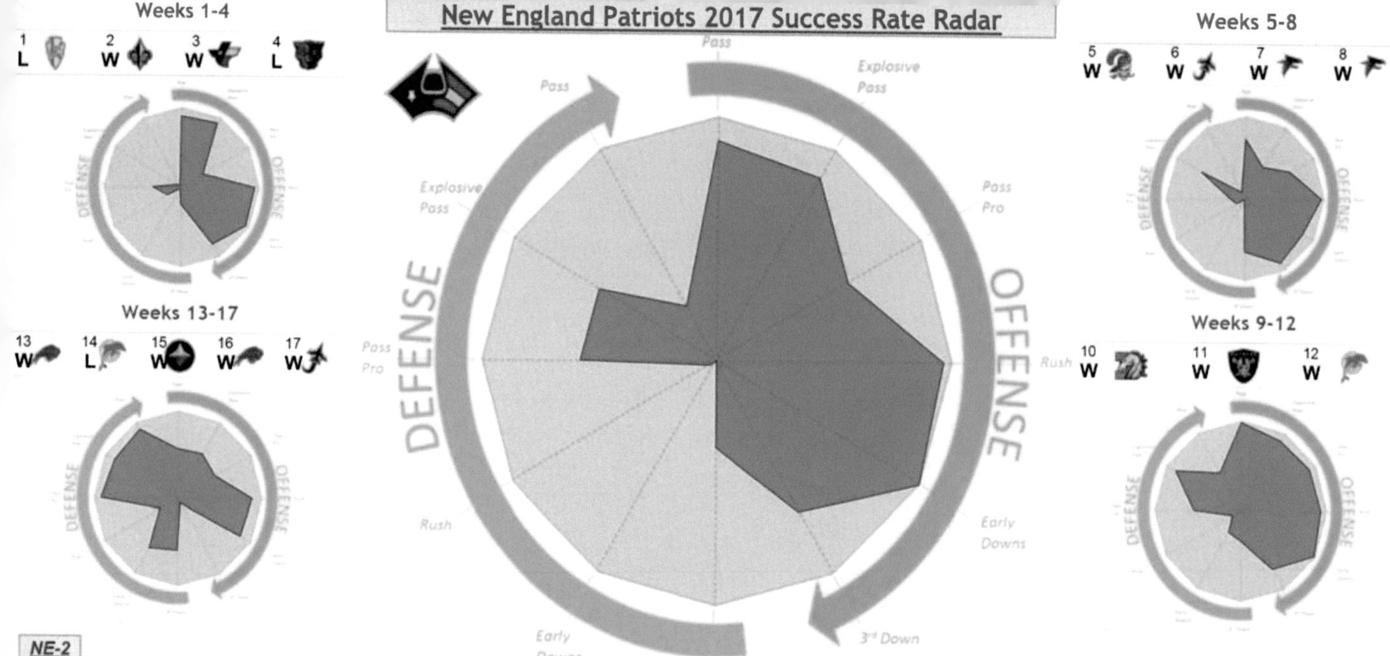

NE-2

But the Patriots were not the NFL's only offense to shift away from 11 personnel. The Saints went from 67% to 56% last season. The Falcons were on the low end (59-60%) the last two years. Same with Andy Reid's Chiefs. And Kyle Shanahan dropped the 49ers' 11-personnel usage from 83% to 62% last season.

My studies have shown red-zone rushing is most efficient. The 2016 Patriots with LeGarrette Blount were a run-first team inside the five-yard line; Blount had 32 carries inside the five, and no other Pats running back had more than four. When the Patriots passed, they used spread formations targeting Julian Edelman (5), Martellus Bennett (5), and Chris Hogan (4) in scoring position. They ranked sixth in the NFL in red-zone efficiency.

But all of that changed in 2017 with Rob Gronkowski healthy. The Patriots became a Gronk-first passing team inside the five, going 60% pass after leaning 67% run the year before. Gronk drew 12 targets inside the five-yard line. These targets produced a strong 58% Success Rate.

The Patriots still probably went too pass heavy at the goal line. Their goal-line passes produced a 51% Success Rate, including lower efficiencies from Hogan, Dion Lewis, and Rex Burkhead. All three recorded an exact 50% Success Rate on targets inside the five-yard line. On run plays inside the five, the Pats logged a 59% Success Rate with Burkhead (71%) leading the way. As Lewis (67%) and Mike Gillislee (63%) were also largely successful, New England left points on the board by not feeding their backs scoring-position carries.

Over the last two years, rushing inside the five-yard line produces a league-wide 58% Success Rate versus a 43% Success Rate when passing. Refer back to my opening chapter on NFL efficiency. Far too often, teams pass rather than run inside the five. And they don't even use optimal formations when passing.

(cont'd - see NE-3)

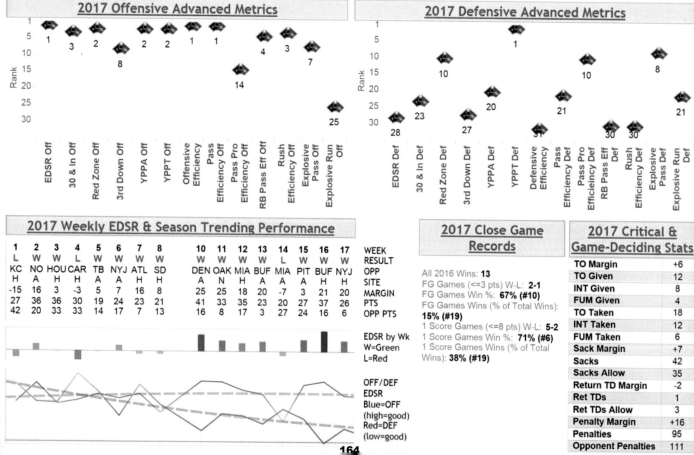

2017 Offensive Advanced Metrics

Metric	Rank
EDSR Off	1
30 & In Off	3
Red Zone Off	2
3rd Down Off	8
YPPA Off	2
YPPT Off	2
Offensive Efficiency	1
Pass Efficiency Off	1
Pass Pro Efficiency Off	14
RB Pass Eff Off	4
Rush Efficiency Off	3
Explosive Pass Off	7
Explosive Run Off	25

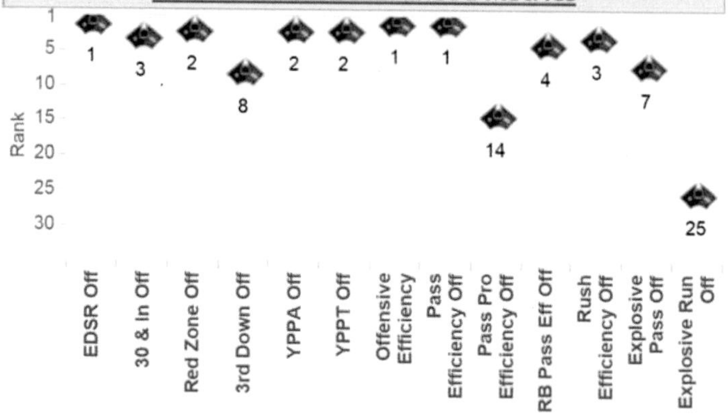

2017 Defensive Advanced Metrics

Metric	Rank
EDSR Def	28
30 & In Def	23
Red Zone Def	10
3rd Down Def	27
YPPA Def	20
YPPT Def	1
Defensive Efficiency	31
Pass Efficiency Def	21
Pass Pro Efficieincy Def	10
RB Pass Eff Def	30
Rush Efficiency Def	30
Explosive Pass Def	8
Explosive Run Def	21

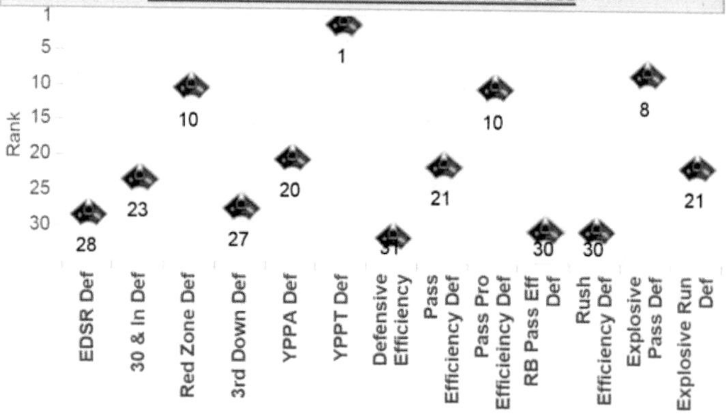

2017 Weekly EDSR & Season Trending Performance

1	2	3	4	5	6	7	8	10	11	12	13	14	15	16	17	WEEK
L	W	W	L	W	W	W	W	W	W	W	W	L	W	W	W	RESULT
KC	NO	HOU	CAR	TB	NYJ	ATL	SD	DEN	OAK	MIA	BUF	MIA	PIT	BUF	NYJ	OPP
H	A	H	H	A	A	H	H	A	N	H	A	A	A	H	H	SITE
-15	16	3	-3	5	7	16	8	25	25	18	20	-7	3	21	20	MARGIN
27	36	36	30	19	24	23	21	41	33	35	23	20	27	37	26	PTS
42	20	33	33	14	17	7	13	16	8	17	3	27	24	16	6	OPP PTS

EDSR by Wk
W=Green
L=Red

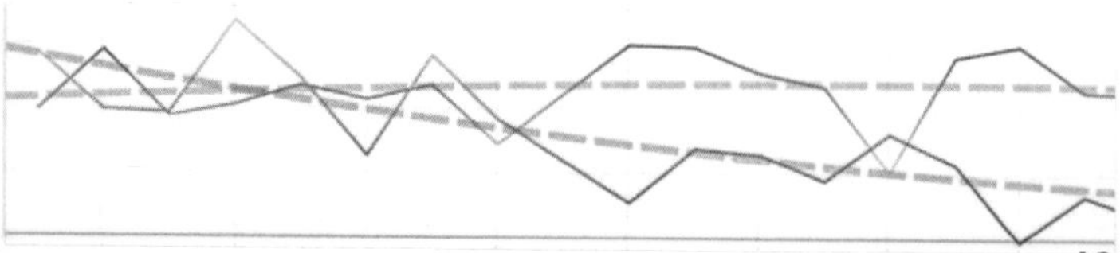

OFF/DEF
EDSR
Blue=OFF
(high=good)
Red=DEF
(low=good)

2017 Close Game Records

All 2016 Wins: **13**
FG Games (<=3 pts) W-L: **2-1**
FG Games Win %: **67% (#10)**
FG Games Wins (% of Total Wins): **15% (#19)**
1 Score Games (<=8 pts) W-L: **5-2**
1 Score Games Win %: **71% (#6)**
1 Score Games Wins (% of Total Wins): **38% (#19)**

2017 Critical & Game-Deciding Stats

TO Margin	+6
TO Given	12
INT Given	8
FUM Given	4
TO Taken	18
INT Taken	12
FUM Taken	6
Sack Margin	+7
Sacks	42
Sacks Allow	35
Return TD Margin	-2
Ret TDs	1
Ret TDs Allow	3
Penalty Margin	+16
Penalties	95
Opponent Penalties	111

New England Patriots 2018 Strength of Schedule In Detail (compared to 2017)

HARD — Average Opponent — EASY (RANK)

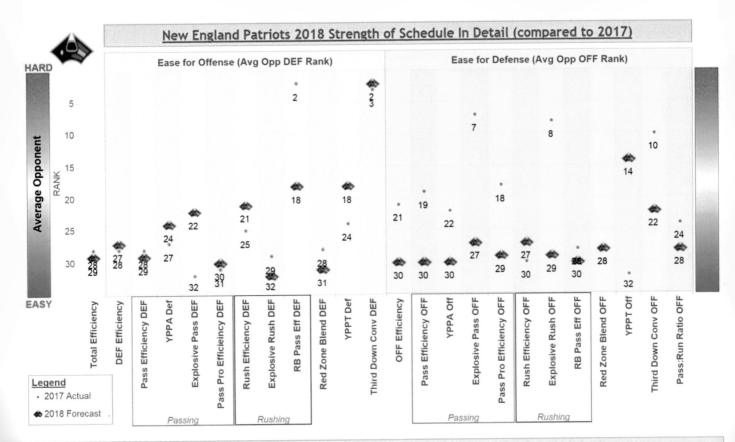

Ease for Offense (Avg Opp DEF Rank) | **Ease for Defense (Avg Opp OFF Rank)**

Category	Ranks shown
Total Efficiency	28, 29
DEF Efficiency	27, 28
Pass Efficiency DEF (Passing)	28, 29
YPPA Def (Passing)	24, 27
Explosive Pass DEF (Passing)	22, 32
Pass Pro Efficiency DEF (Passing)	30, 31
Rush Efficiency DEF (Rushing)	21, 25
Explosive Rush DEF (Rushing)	29, 32
RB Pass Eff DEF (Rushing)	2, 18
Red Zone Blend DEF	28, 31
YPPT Def	18, 24
Third Down Conv DEF	2, 3
OFF Efficiency	21, 30
Pass Efficiency OFF (Passing)	19, 30
YPPA Off (Passing)	22, 30
Explosive Pass OFF (Passing)	7, 27
Pass Pro Efficiency OFF (Passing)	18, 29
Rush Efficiency OFF (Rushing)	27, 30
Explosive Rush OFF (Rushing)	8, 29
RB Pass Eff OFF (Rushing)	28, 30
Red Zone Blend OFF	28
YPPT Off	14, 32
Third Down Conv OFF	10, 22
Pass:Run Ratio OFF	24, 28

Legend: • 2017 Actual; 2018 Forecast

2018 v 2017 Schedule Variances* (DEF=Variance of DEF faced, OFF=Var of OFF faced)

Pass DEF Rk	Pass DEF Blend Rk	Rush DEF Rk	Rush DEF Blend Rk	Pass OFF Rk	Pass OFF Blend Rk	Rush OFF Rk	Rush OFF Blend Rk
18	13	11	25	24	25	29	31

* 1=Hardest Jump in 2018 schedule from 2017 (aka a much harder schedule in 2018), 32=Easiest Jump in 2018 schedule from 2017 (aka a much easier schedule in 2018); **Pass Blend** metric blends 4 metrics: Pass Efficiency, YPPA, Explosive Pass & Pass Rush; **Rush Blend** metric blends 3 metrics: Rush Efficiency, Explosive Rush & RB Targets

Team Records & Trends

	2017	2016	2015
Average line	-8.9	-6.9	-7.8
Average O/U line	49.7	45.8	48.7
Straight Up Record	13-3	14-2	12-4
Against the Spread Record	10-5	12-3	8-7
Over/Under Record	6-9	6-10	8-8
ATS as Favorite	10-5	10-3	7-7
ATS as Underdog	0-0	1-0	0-0
Straight Up Home	6-2	6-2	7-1
ATS Home	5-3	6-2	5-2
Over/Under Home	5-3	4-4	4-4
ATS as Home Favorite	5-3	5-2	5-2
ATS as a Home Dog	0-0	0-0	0-0
Straight Up Away	6-1	8-0	5-3
ATS Away	4-2	6-1	3-5
Over/Under Away	1-5	2-6	4-4
ATS Away Favorite	4-2	5-1	2-5
ATS Away Dog	0-0	1-0	0-0
Six Point Teaser Record	12-4	14-2	11-4
Seven Point Teaser Record	12-4	14-2	12-4
Ten Point Teaser Record	12-4	14-2	14-2

NE-3

When the Patriots want to pass inside the five, they use three-receiver 11 personnel 82% of the time. And even though this maximizes dependency on Tom Brady – arguably the greatest player of all time – it remains less efficient near the goal line. Over the past two years, NFL teams have a lowly 42% Success Rate when passing from three-plus-receiver sets inside the five. In that span, the Patriots saw a Success Rate increase of 47% to 57% when running inside the five.

Inside the five-yard line, 64% of Patriots passes came from 11 personnel. 20% came from zero-receiver 23 personnel. But the Pats have a 47% passing Success Rate from 11 and 30% passing Success Rate from 23. League wide, optimal passing formations inside the five-yard line are 1-2 wide receiver sets, which the Patriots hardly use. But their Success Rate from such formations is 88% on those rare occasions, scoring seven TDs in eight attempts. The lone failure was an incomplete target to fullback James Develin.

(cont'd - see NE-4)

2018 Rest Analysis

Avg Rest	6.47
Avg Rk	3
Team More Rest	2
Opp More Rest	1
Net Rest Edge	1
3 Days Rest	1
4 Days Rest	0
5 Days Rest	1
6 Days Rest	10
7 Days Rest	1
8 Days Rest	0
9 Days Rest	1
10 Days Rest	0
11 Days Rest	0
12 Days Rest	0
13 Days Rest	1
14 Days Rest	0

Health by Unit*

2017 Rk	14
2016 Rk	8
Off Rk	18
Def Rk	10
QB Rk	14
RB Rk	15
WR Rk	29
TE Rk	8
Oline Rk	11
Dline Rk	13
LB Rk	25
DB Rk	7

*Based on the great work of Scott Kacsmar from Football Outsiders

2018 Weekly Betting Lines (wks 1-16)

Week	1	2	3	4	5	6	7	8	9	10	12	13	14	15	16
Opponent	HOU	JAX	DET	MIA	IND	KC	CHI	BUF	GB	TEN	NYJ	MIN	MIA	PIT	BUF
H/A	H	A	A	H	H	H	A	A	H	A	A	H	A	A	H
Line	-7	-2.5	-4	-11	-10.5	-7	-5	-4.5	-6	-3.5	-8.5	-4.5	-6	1	-10.5

Avg = -6.0

Home Lines (wks 1-16)

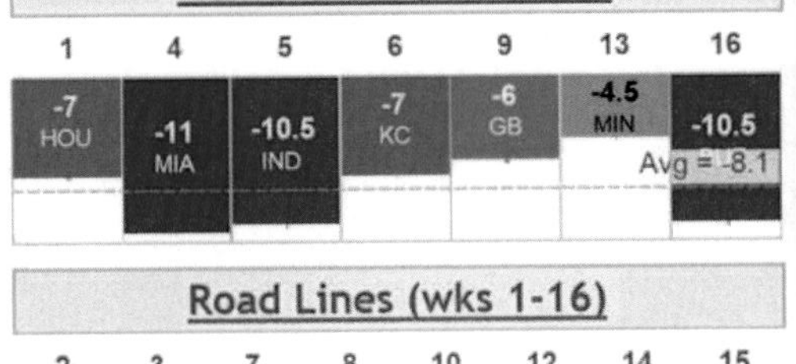

Road Lines (wks 1-16)

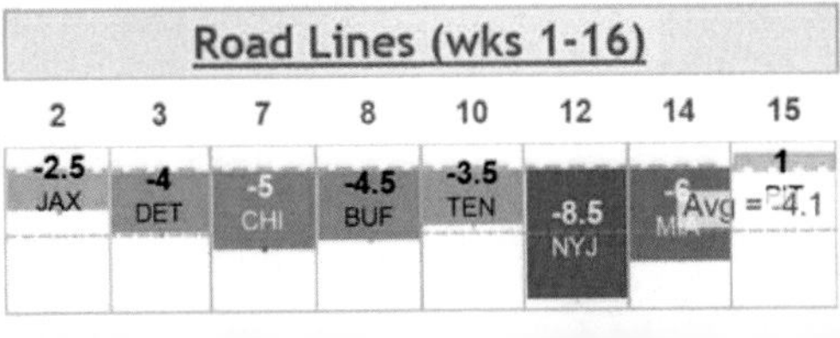

New England Patriots 2017 Play Analysis

2017 Play Tendencies

All Pass %	58%
All Pass Rk	16
All Rush %	42%
All Rush Rk	17
1 Score Pass %	61%
1 Score Pass Rk	4
2016 1 Score Pass %	57%
2016 1 Score Pass Rk	23
2017 Pass Increase %	4%
Pass Increase Rk	4
1 Score Rush %	39%
1 Score Rush Rk	29
Up Pass %	52%
Up Pass Rk	10
Up Rush %	48%
Up Rush Rk	23
Down Pass %	72%
Down Pass Rk	1
Down Rush %	28%
Down Rush Rk	32

2017 Down & Distance Tendencies

Down	Distance	Total Plays	Pass Rate	Run Rate	Play Success %
1	Short (1-3)	16	25%	75%	56%
	Med (4-7)	22	27%	73%	45%
	Long (8-10)	410	50%	50%	55%
	XL (11+)	9	89%	11%	44%
2	Short (1-3)	57	33%	67%	79%
	Med (4-7)	115	68%	32%	54%
	Long (8-10)	115	75%	25%	46%
	XL (11+)	36	83%	17%	42%
3	Short (1-3)	47	57%	43%	64%
	Med (4-7)	61	93%	7%	48%
	Long (8-10)	36	92%	8%	28%
	XL (11+)	28	93%	7%	32%
4	Short (1-3)	7	43%	57%	86%
	Med (4-7)	1	100%	0%	0%
	Long (8-10)	1	0%	100%	100%

Shotgun %:

Under Center	Shotgun
49%	51%
37%	*63%*

37% AVG 63%

Run Rate:

Under Center	Shotgun
67%	14%

68% AVG 23%

Pass Rate:

Under Center	Shotgun
33%	86%

32% AVG 77%

Short Yardage Intelligence:

2nd and Short Run

Run Freq	Run Rk	NFL Run Freq Avg	Run 1D Rate	Run NFL 1D Avg
66%	19	67%	90%	69%

2nd and Short Pass

Pass Freq	Pass Rk	NFL Pass Freq Avg	Pass 1D Rate	Pass NFL 1D Avg
34%	14	33%	47%	53%

Most Frequent Play

Down	Distance	Play Type	Player	Total Plays	Play Success %
1	Short (1-3)	RUSH	Rex Burkhead	4	50%
			Mike Gillislee	4	75%
	Med (4-7)	RUSH	Dion Lewis	8	50%
	Long (8-10)	RUSH	Dion Lewis	108	46%
	XL (11+)	PASS	James White	2	50%
			Rob Gronkowski	2	50%
2	Short (1-3)	RUSH	Mike Gillislee	15	80%
	Med (4-7)	RUSH	Dion Lewis	18	78%
	Long (8-10)	PASS	Danny Amendola	16	50%
	XL (11+)	PASS	Danny Amendola	7	43%
3	Short (1-3)	PASS	Danny Amendola	9	100%
	Med (4-7)	PASS	Danny Amendola	11	73%
	Long (8-10)	PASS	Rob Gronkowski	7	43%
			Danny Amendola	7	29%
	XL (11+)	PASS	Brandin Cooks	5	60%
			Rob Gronkowski	5	80%

Most Successful Play*

Down	Distance	Play Type	Player	Total Plays	Play Success %
1	Med (4-7)	RUSH	Dion Lewis	8	50%
	Long (8-10)	PASS	Phillip Dorsett	8	88%
2	Short (1-3)	RUSH	Rex Burkhead	7	100%
	Med (4-7)	PASS	Danny Amendola	10	80%
	Long (8-10)	PASS	Chris Hogan	8	75%
	XL (11+)	PASS	Rob Gronkowski	6	67%
3	Short (1-3)	PASS	Danny Amendola	9	100%
	Med (4-7)	PASS	Rob Gronkowski	9	78%
	Long (8-10)	PASS	Rob Gronkowski	7	43%
	XL (11+)	PASS	Rob Gronkowski	5	80%

Minimum 5 plays to qualify

2017 Snap Rates

Wk	Opp	Score	Brandin Cooks	Rob Gronkowski	Chris Hogan	Danny Amendola	Dwayne Allen	Dion Lewis	James White	Rex Burkhead
1	KC	L 42-27	67 (83%)	78 (96%)	73 (90%)	32 (40%)	27 (33%)	6 (7%)	43 (53%)	10 (12%)
2	NO	W 36-20	65 (86%)	46 (61%)	65 (86%)		46 (61%)	14 (18%)	30 (39%)	8 (11%)
3	HOU	W 36-33	58 (89%)	64 (98%)	59 (91%)	32 (49%)	17 (26%)	12 (18%)	32 (49%)	
4	CAR	L 33-30	64 (91%)	70 (100%)	68 (97%)	36 (51%)	9 (13%)	14 (20%)	43 (61%)	
5	TB	W 19-14	72 (97%)		74 (100%)	55 (74%)	50 (68%)	18 (24%)	35 (47%)	
6	NYJ	W 24-17	66 (97%)	63 (93%)	63 (93%)	29 (43%)	6 (9%)	29 (43%)	29 (43%)	
7	ATL	W 23-7	70 (95%)	70 (95%)	59 (80%)	38 (51%)	20 (27%)	26 (35%)	23 (31%)	13 (18%)
8	LAC	W 21-13	82 (95%)	86 (100%)	75 (87%)	32 (37%)	20 (23%)	30 (35%)	20 (23%)	27 (31%)
10	DEN	W 41-16	68 (97%)	61 (87%)		27 (39%)	20 (29%)	21 (30%)	11 (16%)	36 (51%)
11	OAK	W 33-8	56 (93%)	53 (88%)		35 (58%)	25 (42%)	26 (43%)	18 (30%)	19 (32%)
12	MIA	W 35-17	62 (89%)	65 (93%)		39 (56%)	38 (54%)	28 (40%)	18 (26%)	28 (40%)
13	BUF	W 23-3	68 (97%)	65 (93%)		32 (46%)	37 (53%)	26 (37%)	28 (40%)	22 (31%)
14	MIA	L 27-20	60 (98%)		55 (90%)	50 (82%)	56 (92%)	18 (30%)	35 (57%)	17 (28%)
15	PIT	W 27-24	57 (95%)	60 (100%)		37 (62%)	26 (43%)	30 (50%)	20 (33%)	16 (27%)
16	BUF	W 37-16	65 (92%)	66 (93%)		40 (56%)	44 (62%)	51 (72%)		
17	NYJ	W 26-6	78 (92%)	58 (68%)		55 (65%)	36 (42%)	52 (61%)		
Grand Total			1,058 (93%)	905 (90%)	591 (90%)	569 (54%)	477 (42%)	401 (35%)	385 (39%)	196 (28%)

Personnel Groupings

Personnel	Team %	NFL Avg	Succ. %
1-1 [3WR]	44%	59%	47%
2-1 [2WR]	24%	7%	60%
1-2 [2WR]	17%	19%	55%
2-2 [1WR]	6%	4%	49%
2-3 [0WR]	3%	1%	43%
1-3 [1WR]	2%	5%	48%

Grouping Tendencies

Personnel	Pass Rate	Pass Succ. %	Run Succ. %
1-1 [3WR]	73%	45%	52%
2-1 [2WR]	50%	61%	58%
1-2 [2WR]	48%	54%	55%
2-2 [1WR]	12%	13%	54%
2-3 [0WR]	20%	50%	42%
1-3 [1WR]	64%	56%	33%

Red Zone Targets (min 3)

Receiver	All	Inside 5	6-10	11-20
Rob Gronkowski	26	12	1	13
Danny Amendola	19	5	2	12
James White	15	4	3	8
Brandin Cooks	14	5	2	7
Chris Hogan	13	6	3	4
Dion Lewis	13	2	1	10
Rex Burkhead	6	2		4
Dwayne Allen	4	1		3

Red Zone Rushes (min 3)

Rusher	All	Inside 5	6-10	11-20
Dion Lewis	39	6	15	18
James White	25	5	8	12
Mike Gillislee	25	8	5	12
Rex Burkhead	16	7	2	7
Tom Brady	9		4	5
Brandin Cooks	3		1	2

Early Down Target Rate

RB	TE	WR
29%	25%	46%
23%	*21%* *NFL AVG*	*56%*

Overall Target Success %

RB	TE	WR
51% #6	55% #8	54% #3

New England Patriots 2017 Passing Recap & 2018 Outlook

The Patriots increased their early-down running back target rate from 25% in 2016 to 29% last season, third highest in football. This year, they moved on from Brandin Cooks and lost Julian Edelman to a four-game suspension. I'm expecting more 12 and 21 personnel from this year's Pats, which would increase their efficiency. But the byproduct would be even more running back targets than they threw last year. New England's running backs produced a 113 passer rating when targeted in 11 formations last season, plus a 62% Success Rate and 115 rating in 21 personnel. Wide receiver targets in 11 managed a 48% Success Rate and 88 passer rating. Wide receiver targets in 12 generated a 58% Success Rate and 97 rating. Calling more plays in 12 personnel allows an extra tight end to stay in to block while Rob Gronkowski runs routes, and the running back can release into a route as well. In 21 personnel, fullback James Develin operates as the blocking tight end and the tailback releases into a route. I'd much prefer to have six blockers – sixth being a blocking tight end or Develin – with Edelman, Hogan, Gronk, and James White or Burkhead as my four receivers rather than Brady playing with only five blockers.

Tom Brady Rating All Downs

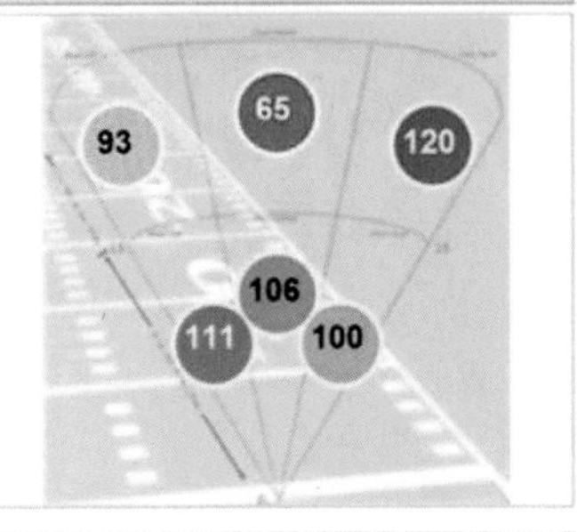

2017 Standard Passing Table

QB	Comp	Att	Comp %	Yds	YPA	TDs	INT	Sacks	Rating	Rk
Tom Brady	474	720	66%	5,708	7.9	40	8	39	104	3
NFL Avg			62%		7.0				87.5	

Tom Brady Rating Early Downs

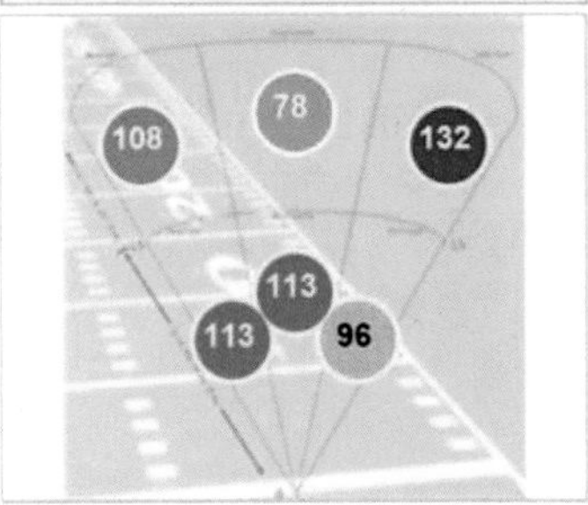

2017 Advanced Passing Table

QB	Success %	EDSR Passing Success %	20+ Yd Pass Gains	20+ Yd Pass %	30+ Yd Pass Gains	30+ Yd Pass %	Avg. Air Yds per Comp	Avg. YAC per Comp	20+ Air Yd Comp	20+ Air Yd %
Tom Brady	50%	53%	80	11.1%	27	3.8%	6.9	4.0	29	6%
NFL Avg	44%	48%	27.7	8.8%	10.3	3.3%	6.0	4.7	11.7	6%

Interception Rates by Down

Yards to Go	1	2	3	4	Total
1 & 2	0.0%	0.0%	4.2%	0.0%	2.0%
3, 4, 5	0.0%	0.0%	0.0%	0.0%	0.0%
6 - 9	0.0%	0.0%	5.7%		2.1%
10 - 14	0.4%	1.1%	2.3%	0.0%	0.8%
15+	0.0%	0.0%	9.1%		2.3%
Total	0.3%	0.4%	3.3%	0.0%	1.1%

3rd Down Passing - Short of Sticks Analysis

QB	Avg. Yds to Go	Avg. YIA (of Comp)	Avg Yds Short	Short of Sticks Rate	Short Rk
Tom Brady	7.3	7.8	0.0	59%	7
NFL Avg	7.8	6.7	-1.1	60%	

Air Yds vs YAC

Air Yds %	YAC %	Rk
62%	38%	15
58%	42%	

2017 Receiving Recap & 2018 Outlook

The Patriots' third-receiver battle carries intrigue on many fronts. The winner will open the season as New England's No. 2 wideout with Edelman missing the first four games. When Edelman returns, that receiver will continue to operate in three-wide 11 packages. Kenny Britt and Malcolm Mitchell are at the forefront of the competition. Britt benefited from learning the Patriots' system down the stretch last year. 2016 fourth-round pick Mitchell has battled persistent knee problems and skipped OTAs, so his playing time will surely come under coaching-staff scrutiny.

Player *Min 50 Targets	Targets	Comp %	YPA	Rating	TOARS	Success %	Success Rk	Missed YPA Rk	YAS % Rk	TDs
Brandin Cooks	133	56%	9.3	99	5.2	50%	58	51	4	7
Rob Gronkowski	132	64%	9.9	118	5.5	59%	8	10	24	11
Danny Amendola	119	73%	8.5	106	5.2	64%	3	14	86	4
James White	90	72%	5.6	100	4.6	46%	80	71	109	4
Chris Hogan	75	57%	7.9	108	4.4	45%	91	77	30	7
Dion Lewis	53	91%	6.1	111	4.0	55%	27	1	123	3

Directional Passer Rating Delivered

Receiver	Short Left	Short Middle	Short Right	Deep Left	Deep Middle	Deep Right	Player Total
Brandin Cooks	68	123	92	77	125	156	99
Rob Gronkowski	132	83	127	120	95	93	118
Danny Amendola	117	104	82	119	55	96	106
James White	102	118	88	94		94	100
Chris Hogan	118	121	92	70	49	103	108
Dion Lewis	110	90	125				111
Rex Burkhead	114	129	111	40		158	126
Dwayne Allen	62	83	97	40		40	71
Phillip Dorsett	106	98	111	110	0		86
Martellus Bennett	88	119					103
Kenny Britt	119	0	42				15
Team Total	113	108	102	93	67	119	106

2017 Rushing Recap & 2017 Outlook

Mike Gillislee drew more Weeks 1-2 usage than Rex Burkhead, out-snapping him 54 to 18. After the Patriots' Week 8 win over the Chargers and Week 9 bye, Gillislee was removed from the backfield equation. Gillislee may not even make the 53-man roster this year, facing competition from Jeremy Hill. The Patriots' most-intriguing running back battle pits Burkhead against surprise first-round pick Sony Michel from Georgia. Burkhead would have logged more 2017 touches if not for repeated injuries. With Dion Lewis gone to Nashville, the No. 1 running back position carries extreme value, especially if the Patriots smartly choose to become more run oriented inside the five-yard line.

Yards per Carry by Direction

	LT	LG	C	RG	RT	
5.1	3.8	4.3	4.3	4.2	4.7	6.0

Player *Min 50 Rushes	Rushes	YPC	Success %	Success Rk	Missed YPA Rk	YTS % Rk	YAS % Rk	Early Down Success %	Early Down Success Rk	TDs
Dion Lewis	213	4.8	55%	5	6	38	21	54%	7	6
Mike Gillislee	104	3.7	57%	3	4	7	42	59%	1	5
Rex Burkhead	68	4.2	54%	6	2	27	48	56%	5	5
James White	57	4.1	51%	14	43	8	72	58%	2	3

Directional Run Frequency

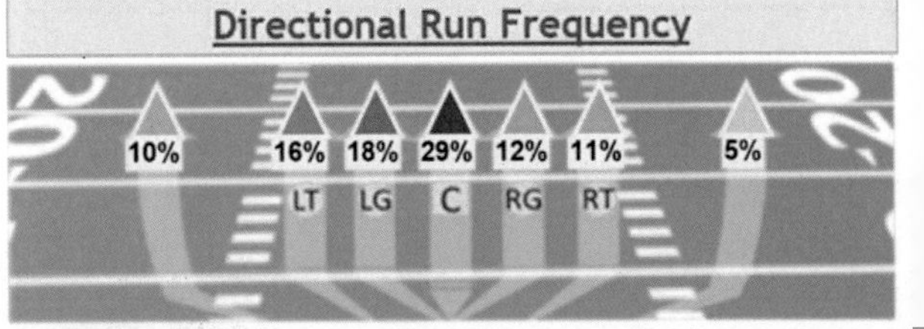

The Patriots' preferred grouping inside the five-yard line is zero-receiver 23 personnel, which vastly differs from league norms. All other teams use 23 on only 12% of snaps inside the five. The Patriots use it 40% of the time. And their Success Rate on 23-personnel runs inside the five is a sturdy 65%. This was the sweet-spot grouping for LeGarrette Blount in 2016, when he registered a 63% Success Rate and led the NFL in rushing TDs.

Brady is at least partly known for high-efficiency quarterback sneaks. But in 23 personnel, Brady has just one successful run in six attempts inside the five-yard line over the past two years. On QB sneaks inside the five, Brady's Success Rate is 100% in 11 personnel.

Critical to New England's two-decade greatness is their willingness to constantly evolve. The 2016 Patriots fielded a roster with the tenth-most-expensive offensive line. Last year, that cost dropped to 21st. The Patriots' 2018 line projects as cheapest in the league. This offensive-line savings allowed New England to spend more defensively on CB Jason McCourty, DE Adrian Clayborn, and NT Danny Shelton. New England will have carved out a competitive advantage if they can adequately protect Brady at such low cost.

(cont'd - see NE-5)

Evan Silva's Fantasy Corner

Having parted with Brandin Cooks, Dion Lewis, Danny Amendola, and Martellus Bennett, the Patriots are missing the NFL's fifth-most targets (240) from last year's team. A healthy Julian Edelman will soak up much of that opportunity once his four-game suspension ends, but Chris Hogan stands to benefit most. Before suffering a debilitating shoulder injury late last October, Hogan asserted himself as Tom Brady's second-most-trusted red-zone weapon behind Rob Gronkowski with five TDs in the first five games. Finally healthy in the Super Bowl, Hogan shredded the Eagles' secondary for six catches, 128 yards, and a touchdown on eight targets. Hogan is primed for a 2018 breakout as a middle-round upside pick.

Division History: Season Wins & 2018 Projection

2014 Wins | 2015 Wins | 2016 Wins | 2017 Wins | Forecast 2018 Wins

Rank of 2018 Defensive Pass Efficiency Faced by Week

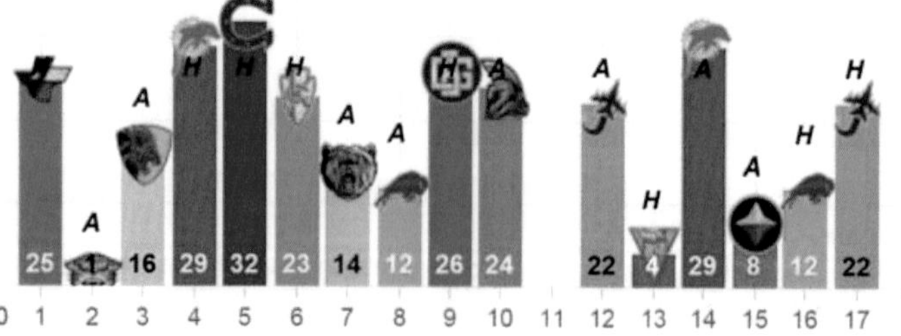

Rank of 2018 Defensive Rush Efficiency Faced by Week

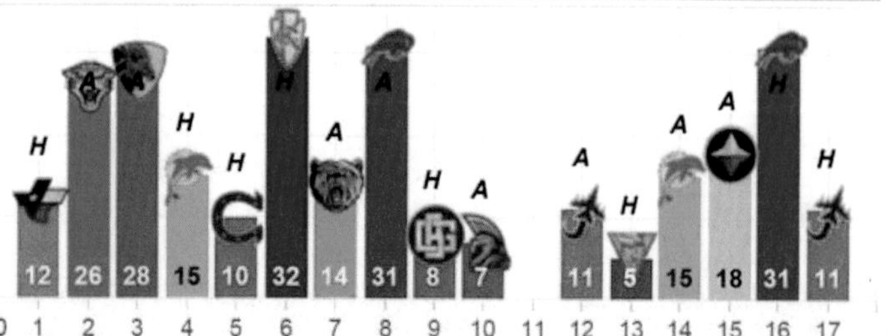

2017 Situational Usage by Player & Position

Usage Rate by Score

		Being Blown Out (14+)	Down Big (9-13)	One Score	Large Lead (9-13)	Blowout Lead (14+)	Grand Total
RUSH	Dion Lewis	22%	15%	17%	20%	20%	18%
	James White		6%	5%	5%	4%	5%
	Brandin Cooks			1%	1%	2%	1%
	Danny Amendola			0%			0%
	Rex Burkhead	3%		6%	5%	8%	6%
	Mike Gillislee			10%	10%	8%	9%
	Chris Hogan			1%			0%
	Phillip Dorsett				1%		0%
	Brandon Bolden				2%	7%	1%
	Jacob Hollister			0%			0%
	Total	25%	22%	39%	43%	49%	40%
PASS	Dion Lewis	3%	3%	5%	5%	4%	4%
	James White	22%	3%	8%	5%	7%	8%
	Brandin Cooks	6%	12%	11%	10%	11%	11%
	Rob Gronkowski	9%	15%	11%	12%	8%	11%
	Danny Amendola	19%	23%	10%	8%	7%	10%
	Rex Burkhead		3%	4%	5%	2%	3%
	Mike Gillislee			0%			0%
	Chris Hogan	9%	9%	7%	6%	4%	6%
	Dwayne Allen	3%	5%	2%	3%	1%	2%
	Phillip Dorsett	3%	3%	1%	4%	2%	2%
	Brandon Bolden			0%		1%	0%
	Jacob Hollister			1%		2%	1%
	James Develin		2%	1%	1%	1%	1%
	Martellus Bennett			1%		1%	1%
	Kenny Britt			1%		0%	0%
	Total	75%	78%	61%	57%	51%	60%

Positional Target Distribution vs NFL Average

		NFL Wide				Team Only			
		Left	Middle	Right	Total	Left	Middle	Right	Total
Deep	WR	936	477	967	2,380	50	32	20	102
	TE	176	144	170	490	16	6	18	40
	RB	36	9	39	84	3		3	6
	All	1,148	630	1,176	2,954	69	38	41	148
Short	WR	2,744	1,593	2,735	7,072	118	78	55	251
	TE	814	802	1,136	2,752	49	37	34	120
	RB	1,246	784	1,234	3,264	75	39	61	175
	All	4,804	3,179	5,105	13,088	242	154	150	546
Total		5,952	3,809	6,281	16,042	311	192	191	694

Positional Success Rates vs NFL Average

		NFL Wide				Team Only			
		Left	Middle	Right	Total	Left	Middle	Right	Total
Deep	WR	36%	46%	38%	39%	52%	38%	50%	47%
	TE	38%	53%	45%	44%	44%	50%	50%	48%
	RB	36%	56%	36%	38%	33%		67%	50%
	All	36%	47%	39%	40%	49%	39%	51%	47%
Short	WR	51%	57%	50%	52%	55%	63%	51%	57%
	TE	50%	56%	49%	51%	61%	59%	56%	59%
	RB	43%	51%	43%	45%	57%	54%	43%	51%
	All	49%	55%	48%	50%	57%	60%	49%	55%
Total		47%	54%	46%	48%	55%	56%	49%	54%

Successful Play Rate
0% 100%

New England Patriots - Success by Personnel Grouping & Play Type

Play Type	1-1 [3WR]	1-2 [2WR]	2-1 [2WR]	1-0 [4WR]	1-3 [1WR]	2-0 [3WR]	2-2 [1WR]	0-0 [5WR]	2-3 [0WR]	Grand Total
PASS	45% (339, 55%)	54% (85, 14%)	61% (128, 21%)	40% (20, 3%)	56% (16, 3%)	43% (7, 1%)	13% (8, 1%)	0% (1, 0%)	50% (6, 1%)	49% (611, 100%)
RUSH	52% (124, 28%)	55% (92, 21%)	58% (130, 29%)		33% (9, 2%)	67% (3, 1%)	54% (57, 13%)		42% (24, 5%)	54% (444, 100%)
TOTAL	47% (463, 44%)	55% (177, 17%)	60% (258, 24%)	40% (20, 2%)	48% (25, 2%)	50% (10, 1%)	49% (65, 6%)	0% (1, 0%)	43% (30, 3%)	51% (1,055, 100%)

Format Line 1: Success Rate Line 2: Total # of Plays, % of All Plays (by type)

NE-5

In three years prior to the 2018 NFL draft, the Patriots made just one top-50 pick. For perspective, the Saints made eight top-50 picks in that span. And it was evident the Patriots needed an infusion of youth on underpriced rookie deals. So in 2018, New England added two top-50 picks.

Part of the Patriots' beauty is balance. See their red-zone graphics on page four of this chapter. New England is the lone NFL team with at least six receivers in double digits for red-zone targets, with at least four different rushers at double-digit red-zone carries.

The Patriots used so many skill-position players on offense that I had to remove some from the snap rates on page four. They're the best-coached team in football with some of the best players in the league, and they're constantly looking for ways to innovate. The 2018 Pats face an easy schedule yet again, thanks to the incompetence of the AFC East and AFC in general. The Patriots' only obstacle would be injuries, but they've overcome those before.

Receiving Success by Personnel Grouping

Position	Player	1-1 [3WR]	1-2 [2WR]	2-1 [2WR]	1-0 [4WR]	1-3 [1WR]	2-0 [3WR]	2-2 [1WR]	0-0 [5WR]	2-3 [0WR]	3-2 [0WR]	Total
RB	James White	54% 6.4 112.0 (54)	0% 4.0 83.3 (1)	50% 6.4 93.3 (10)	25% 2.5 77.1 (4)		0% 1.0 79.2 (1)		0% 3.0 79.2 (1)			49% 6.0 105.9 (71)
	Dion Lewis	56% 5.3 125.9 (18)	40% 5.8 130.4 (5)	83% 8.5 102.1 (6)		80% 7.0 95.8 (5)	0% 3.0 79.2 (1)					60% 6.1 120.7 (35)
TE	Rob Gronkowski	50% 8.8 105.5 (50)	64% 11.1 111.6 (25)	74% 11.6 132.7 (19)		100% 19.5 118.8 (2)		0% 0.0 39.6 (1)		50% 1.0 95.8 (2)		59% 9.9 114.9 (99)
WR	Brandin Cooks	47% 10.1 83.7 (57)	65% 13.2 158.3 (17)	48% 8.4 85.8 (29)	0% 0.0 39.6 (3)	0% 1.0 56.3 (2)	100% 19.0 118.8 (1)	0% 0.0 39.6 (1)		100% 4.0 122.9 (1)	100% 7.0 95.8 (1)	49% 9.6 103.1 (112)
	Danny Amendola	50% 7.1 90.9 (62)	80% 7.8 99.2 (5)	92% 10.3 109.4 (12)	75% 8.0 97.9 (4)		100% 13.0 118.8 (1)	0% 0.0 39.6 (1)				59% 7.6 95.6 (85)
	Chris Hogan	43% 6.7 88.6 (37)		56% 10.0 135.4 (16)	40% 6.2 92.5 (5)		0% 0.0 39.6 (1)					46% 7.4 102.3 (59)

Format Line 1: Success Rate Line 2: YPA Line 3: Passer Rating Line 4: Total # of Plays

Successful Play Rate
0% 100%

Rushing Success by Personnel Grouping

Position	Player	1-1 [3WR]	1-2 [2WR]	2-1 [2WR]	1-3 [1WR]	2-0 [3WR]	2-2 [1WR]	2-3 [0WR]	Total
RB	Dion Lewis	55% 4.0 (47)	56% 4.9 (45)	61% 6.1 (64)	33% 1.0 (3)	50% 7.0 (2)	33% 4.0 (15)	100% 1.0 (1)	55% 4.9 (177)
	Mike Gillislee	67% 4.7 (12)	47% 2.8 (17)	61% 4.6 (36)	25% 3.0 (4)		58% 3.7 (26)	56% 0.7 (9)	57% 3.7 (104)
	Rex Burkhead	20% 3.2 (10)	56% 5.8 (16)	60% 3.7 (20)	0% 2.0 (1)		64% 5.1 (11)	67% 1.2 (6)	53% 4.1 (64)

Format Line 1: Success Rate Line 2: YPC Line 3: Total # of Plays

2018 Coaches

Head Coach:
Sean Payton (13th yr)

Offensive Coordinator:
Pete Carmichael (10th yr)

Defensive Coordinator:
Dennis Allen (4th yr)

New Orleans Saints

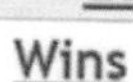

2018 Forecast

Wins	Div Rank
9.5	#1

Past Records

2017: 11-5
2016: 7-9
2015: 7-9

EASY HARD

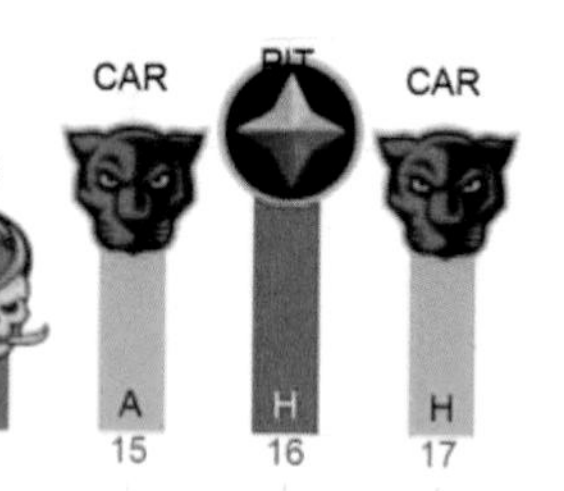

Week	Opponent	Site	Note
1	TB	H	
2	CLE	H	
3	ATL	A	
4	NYG	A	
5	WSH	H	MNF
6			
7	BAL	A	
8	MIN	A	SNF
9	LAR	H	
10	CIN	A	
11	PHI	H	
12	ATL	H	TKG
13	DAL	A	TNF
14	TB	A	
15	CAR	A	MNF
16	PIT	H	
17	CAR	H	

Key Players Lost

TXN	Player (POS)
Cut	Fairley, Nick DT
	Fleener, Coby TE
	Hodges, Gerald LB
	McDaniel, Tony DT
Declared Free Agent	Breaux, Delvin CB
	Bush, Rafael S
	Coleman, Brandon WR
	Daniel, Chase QB
	Freeny, Jonathan LB
	Harbor, Clay TE
	Hughes III, John DT
	Kelemete, Senio G
	Kuhn, John RB
	LeRibeus, Josh G
	Mauti, Michael LB
	Moore, Sterling CB
	Okafor, Alex DE
	Vaccaro, Kenny S
Retired	Strief, Zach T

Average Line	# Games Favored	# Games Underdog
-2.1	10	4

2018 New Orleans Saints Overview

Celebrate Greatness. That's the phrase I started using this offseason. As an analyst, it's often rewarding to highlight inefficiencies of a team, coaching staff, or play caller because we believe that if it's brought to light, it can be addressed and fixed and the team can ultimately improve. Personally, I hate watching inefficiency on Sundays. Anything I can do to help make the final product better while simultaneously giving coaches insight into areas they can improve or enhance is ideal. But this often means a ton of negativity and criticism. I believe it's healthy to move the other direction at times and celebrate true greatness in players, coaches, decision-making, and execution.

The reason is obvious: We don't know what the sport of football will look like 10 years from now. We have ideas, but what we know unequivocally is that it won't include the greats from the 2000s. And one of the most underrated of that bunch is QB Drew Brees.

Think about the journey Brees has taken. In 2001, Brees was projected to be a mid-first-round draft pick, but he slipped due to lack of height, a perceived lack of arm strength, supposed poor accuracy on deep passes, and the belief that the spread offense he ran at Purdue was the only reason he'd been successful in college. As such, he slipped to the second round. After two years with Brees as their starter, the Chargers felt so insecure about his future that they used the No. 1 overall pick in 2004 on a quarterback. Using that as motivation, Brees took the Chargers to a 12-4 record in 2004, posting the team's first winning record in nine seasons. The following season while playing under the franchise tag, Brees tore up the shoulder in his throwing arm. The Saints took a chance on Brees in free agency, and the rest was history.

With the Saints, Brees has always made the playoffs and always led the team to double digit-wins with an average of 11 wins per year so long as his defense ranked 25th or better. That's not a high bar, and for many years, the Saints had well below-average defenses, and Brees still carried them to the playoffs. But even in his worst years in New Orleans, when his defense was bottom-six in the league, he never won less than seven games. He averaged eight wins per season with bottom-six defenses.

(cont'd - see NO2)

Key Free Agents/ Trades Added

Bushrod, Jermon T
Coleman, Kurt S
Davis, Demario LB
Elliott, Jayrone LB
Huff, Josh WR
Meredith, Cameron WR
Robinson, Patrick CB
Savage, Tom QB
Theus, John T
Watson, Benjamin TE

Drafted Players

Rd	Pk	Player (College)
1	14	DE - Marcus Davenport (UTSA)
3	91	WR - Tre'Quan Smith (UCF)
4	127	OT - Rick Leonard (Florida State)
5	164	S - Natrell Jamerson (Wisconsin)
6	189	CB - Kamrin Moore (Boston College)
	201	RB - Boston Scott (Louisiana Tech)
7	245	C - Will Clapp (LSU)

Regular Season Wins: Past & Current Proj

Lineup & Cap Hits

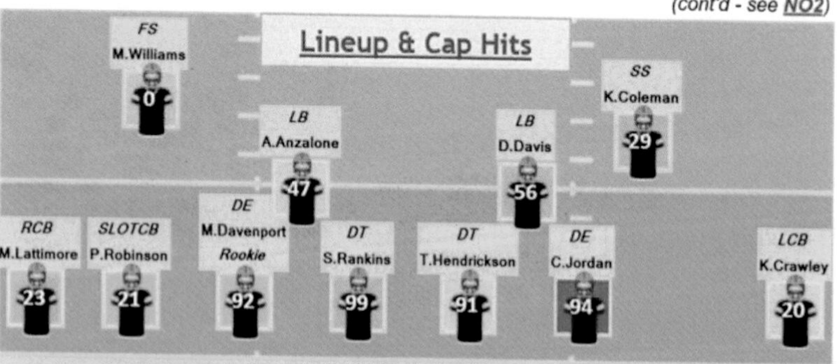

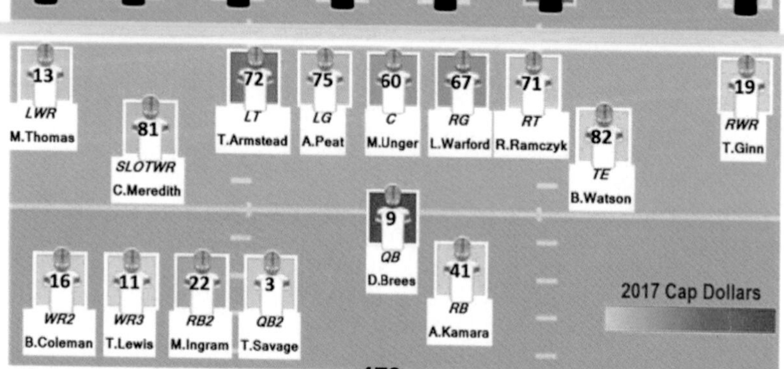

2018 Unit Spending

All DEF
All OFF

Positional Spending

	Rank	Total	2017 Rk
All OFF	7	$101.99M	9
QB	7	$26.49M	14
OL	4	$42.03M	7
RB	11	$8.95M	9
WR	29	$15.68M	31
TE	17	$8.84M	3
All DEF	28	$69.20M	31
DL	12	$31.12M	16
LB	18	$19.59M	18
CB	27	$9.48M	29
S	21	$9.01M	20

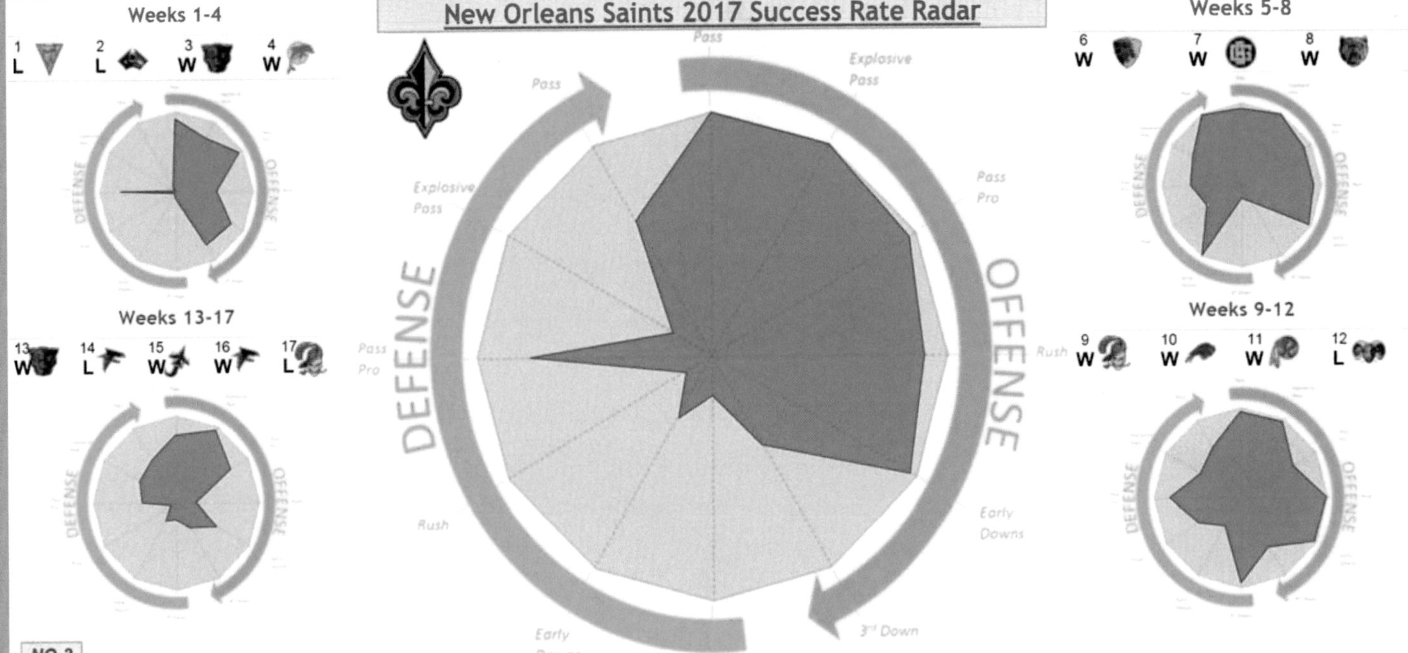

NO-2

While that's impressive, what's even more impressive is what this underdog quarterback has done from a production perspective. In NFL history, no quarterback has recorded more than four consecutive seasons with 7.5+ yards per attempt after turning 32 years old except for Brees, who has not five, not six, but seven consecutive 7.5+ YPA seasons since turning 32. And about that deep accuracy scouts were worried about? Brees owns the NFL's best YPA on deep passes (15.2) and the best completion percentage on deep passes (50.9%). These are numbers that a 6-foot quarterback shouldn't be able to produce, especially after tearing up his throwing shoulder a few years into his career. When we talk about quarterbacks, the focus nationally during the last decade seems to revolve around Tom Brady and Peyton Manning. On the edge of the conversation is Aaron Rodgers, and typically on the outside looking in at the "top three" is Brees.

How does this factor into 2018? Fewer people are talking about Brees heading into 2018 than at any time in recent memory, primarily due to his poor fantasy production in 2017.

The decreased production came as a result of his fewest attempts as a Saint (536), and he tossed only 23 touchdowns (11th in the league), which were also his fewest as a Saint. But Brees had a stellar 2017 season from a real football perspective. His 72.0% completion percentage set the NFL record. His 8.1 YPA was his best since 2011 and ranked No. 1 in the league. He led the league in completions (386) even though he ranked ninth in attempts. He ranked No. 2 in passer rating (103.9). His interception rate (1.5%) was the best of his career and fourth-best in the league.

Meanwhile, the biggest story coming out of New Orleans last year was either the run-game production (fueled by exciting rookie RB Alvin Kamara) or the great performance of a young defense. Once again, Brees and his tremendous season took a back seat, this time not league-wide, but in discussions of his own team's season.

(cont'd - see NO-3)

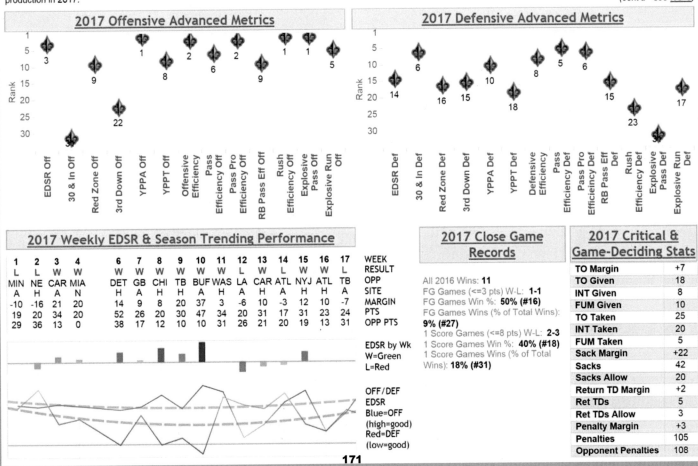

2017 Offensive Advanced Metrics

Metric	Rank
EDSR Off	3
30 & In Off	[illegible]
Red Zone Off	9
3rd Down Off	22
YPPA Off	1
YPPT Off	8
Offensive Efficiency	2
Pass Efficiency Off	6
Pass Pro Efficiency Off	2
RB Pass Eff Off	9
Rush Efficiency Off	1
Explosive Pass Off	1
Explosive Run Off	5

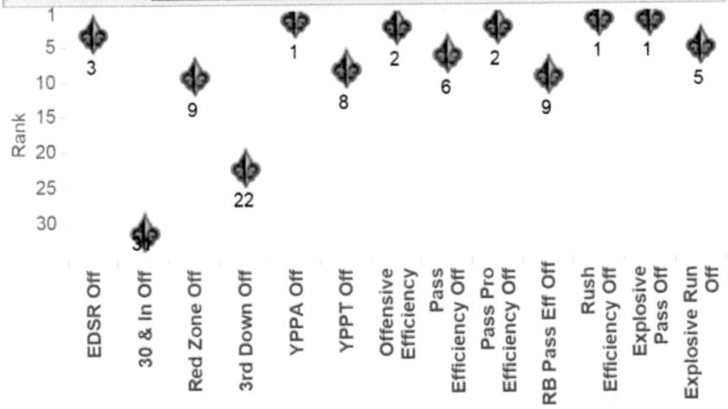

2017 Defensive Advanced Metrics

Metric	Rank
EDSR Def	14
30 & In Def	6
Red Zone Def	16
3rd Down Def	15
YPPA Def	10
YPPT Def	18
Defensive Efficiency	8
Pass Efficiency Def	5
Pass Pro Efficiency Def	6
RB Pass Eff Def	15
Rush Efficiency Def	23
Explosive Pass Def	[illegible]
Explosive Run Def	17

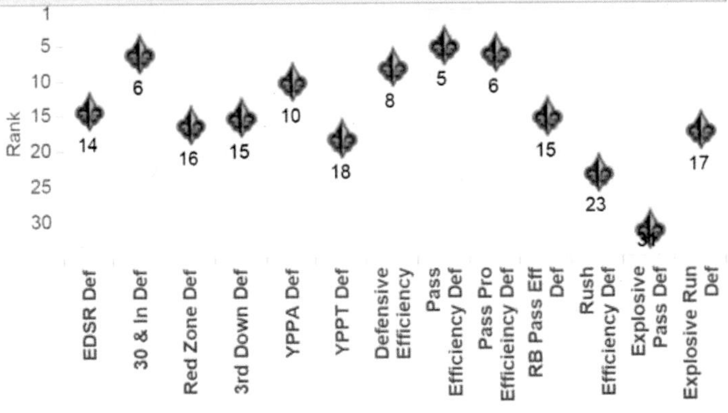

2017 Weekly EDSR & Season Trending Performance

WEEK	1	2	3	4	6	7	8	9	10	11	12	13	14	15	16	17
RESULT	L	L	W	W	W	W	W	W	W	W	L	W	L	W	W	L
OPP	MIN	NE	CAR	MIA	DET	GB	CHI	TB	BUF	WAS	LA	CAR	ATL	NYJ	ATL	TB
SITE	A	H	A	N	H	A	H	H	A	H	A	H	A	H	H	A
MARGIN	-10	-16	21	20	14	9	8	20	37	3	-6	10	-3	12	10	-7
PTS	19	20	34	20	52	26	20	30	47	34	20	31	17	31	23	24
OPP PTS	29	36	13	0	38	17	12	10	10	31	26	21	20	19	13	31

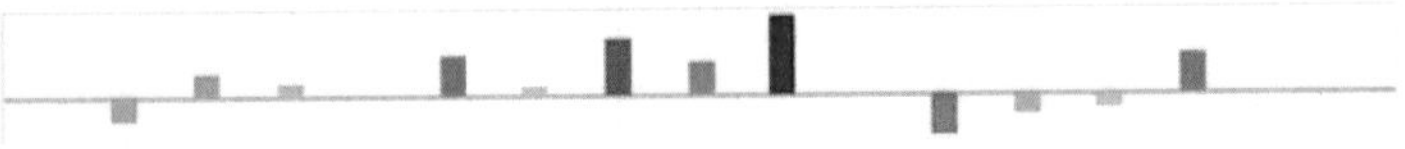

EDSR by Wk
W=Green
L=Red

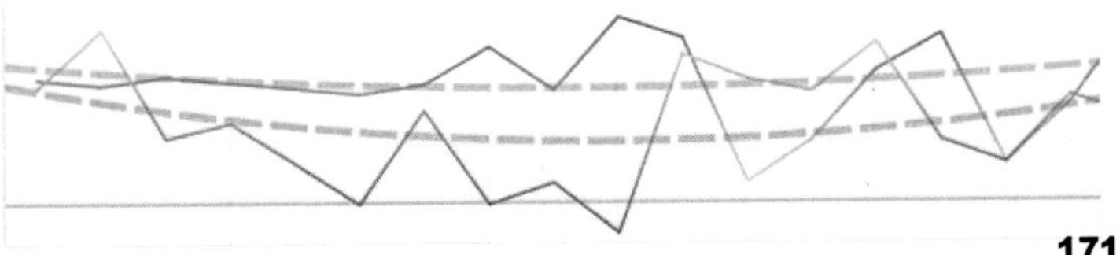

OFF/DEF EDSR
Blue=OFF (high=good)
Red=DEF (low=good)

2017 Close Game Records

All 2016 Wins: **11**
FG Games (<=3 pts) W-L: **1-1**
FG Games Win %: **50% (#16)**
FG Games Wins (% of Total Wins): **9% (#27)**
1 Score Games (<=8 pts) W-L: **2-3**
1 Score Games Win %: **40% (#18)**
1 Score Games Wins (% of Total Wins): **18% (#31)**

2017 Critical & Game-Deciding Stats

TO Margin	+7
TO Given	18
INT Given	8
FUM Given	10
TO Taken	25
INT Taken	20
FUM Taken	5
Sack Margin	+22
Sacks	42
Sacks Allow	20
Return TD Margin	+2
Ret TDs	5
Ret TDs Allow	3
Penalty Margin	+3
Penalties	105
Opponent Penalties	108

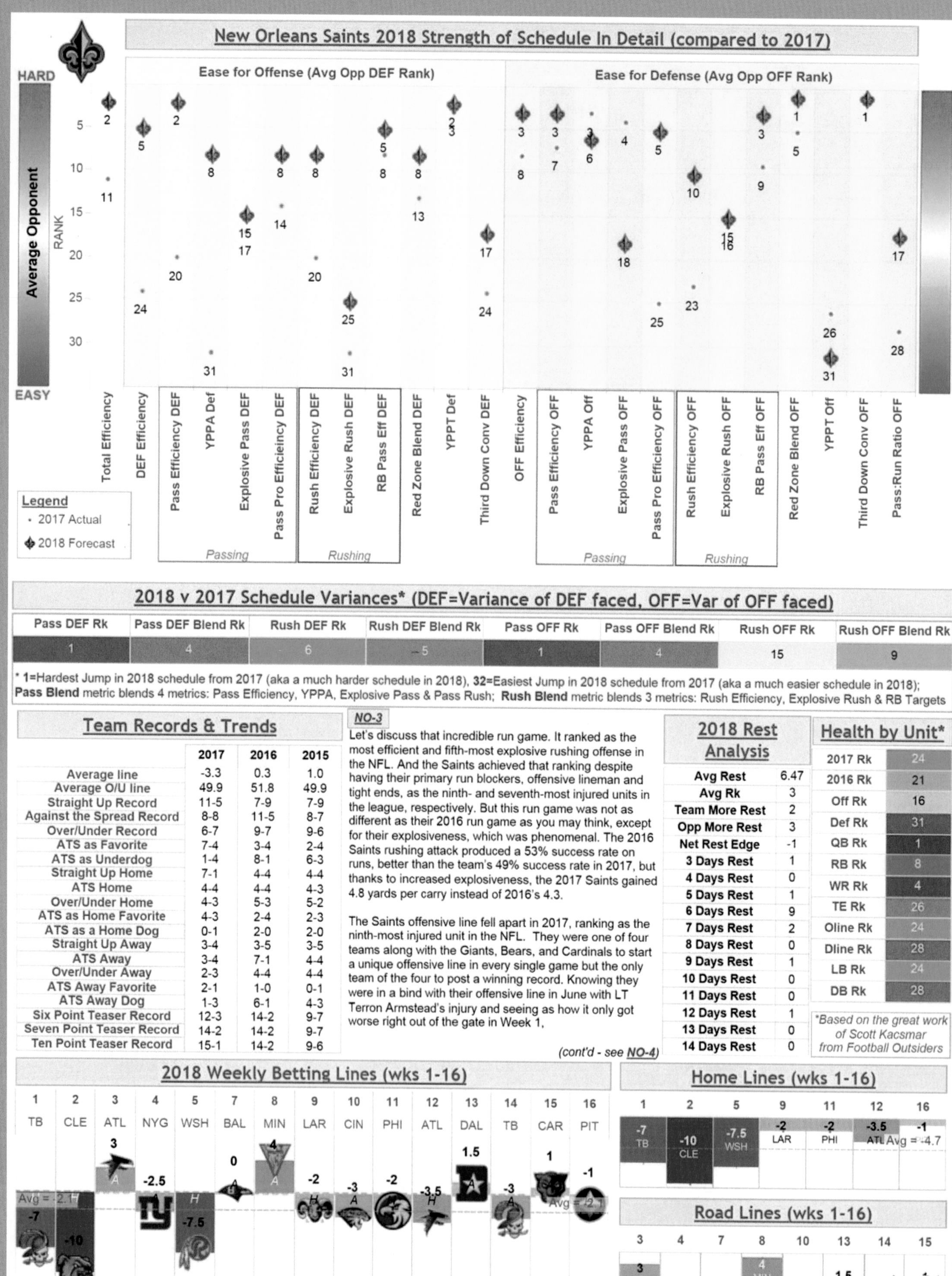

New Orleans Saints 2018 Strength of Schedule In Detail (compared to 2017)

2018 v 2017 Schedule Variances* (DEF=Variance of DEF faced, OFF=Var of OFF faced)

Pass DEF Rk	Pass DEF Blend Rk	Rush DEF Rk	Rush DEF Blend Rk	Pass OFF Rk	Pass OFF Blend Rk	Rush OFF Rk	Rush OFF Blend Rk
1	4	6	5	1	4	15	9

* **1**=Hardest Jump in 2018 schedule from 2017 (aka a much harder schedule in 2018), **32**=Easiest Jump in 2018 schedule from 2017 (aka a much easier schedule in 2018); **Pass Blend** metric blends 4 metrics: Pass Efficiency, YPPA, Explosive Pass & Pass Rush; **Rush Blend** metric blends 3 metrics: Rush Efficiency, Explosive Rush & RB Targets

Team Records & Trends

	2017	2016	2015
Average line	-3.3	0.3	1.0
Average O/U line	49.9	51.8	49.9
Straight Up Record	11-5	7-9	7-9
Against the Spread Record	8-8	11-5	8-7
Over/Under Record	6-7	9-7	9-6
ATS as Favorite	7-4	3-4	2-4
ATS as Underdog	1-4	8-1	6-3
Straight Up Home	7-1	4-4	4-4
ATS Home	4-4	4-4	4-3
Over/Under Home	4-3	5-3	5-2
ATS as Home Favorite	4-3	2-4	2-3
ATS as a Home Dog	0-1	2-0	2-0
Straight Up Away	3-4	3-5	3-5
ATS Away	3-4	7-1	4-4
Over/Under Away	2-3	4-4	4-4
ATS Away Favorite	2-1	1-0	0-1
ATS Away Dog	1-3	6-1	4-3
Six Point Teaser Record	12-3	14-2	9-7
Seven Point Teaser Record	14-2	14-2	9-7
Ten Point Teaser Record	15-1	14-2	9-6

NO-3

Let's discuss that incredible run game. It ranked as the most efficient and fifth-most explosive rushing offense in the NFL. And the Saints achieved that ranking despite having their primary run blockers, offensive lineman and tight ends, as the ninth- and seventh-most injured units in the league, respectively. But this run game was not as different as their 2016 run game as you may think, except for their explosiveness, which was phenomenal. The 2016 Saints rushing attack produced a 53% success rate on runs, better than the team's 49% success rate in 2017, but thanks to increased explosiveness, the 2017 Saints gained 4.8 yards per carry instead of 2016's 4.3.

The Saints offensive line fell apart in 2017, ranking as the ninth-most injured unit in the NFL. They were one of four teams along with the Giants, Bears, and Cardinals to start a unique offensive line in every single game but the only team of the four to post a winning record. Knowing they were in a bind with their offensive line in June with LT Terron Armstead's injury and seeing as how it only got worse right out of the gate in Week 1,

(cont'd - see NO-4)

2018 Rest Analysis

Avg Rest	6.47
Avg Rk	3
Team More Rest	2
Opp More Rest	3
Net Rest Edge	-1
3 Days Rest	1
4 Days Rest	0
5 Days Rest	1
6 Days Rest	9
7 Days Rest	2
8 Days Rest	0
9 Days Rest	1
10 Days Rest	0
11 Days Rest	0
12 Days Rest	1
13 Days Rest	0
14 Days Rest	0

Health by Unit*

2017 Rk	24
2016 Rk	21
Off Rk	16
Def Rk	31
QB Rk	1
RB Rk	8
WR Rk	4
TE Rk	26
Oline Rk	24
Dline Rk	28
LB Rk	24
DB Rk	28

*Based on the great work of Scott Kacsmar from Football Outsiders

2018 Weekly Betting Lines (wks 1-16)

1	2	3	4	5	7	8	9	10	11	12	13	14	15	16
TB	CLE	ATL	NYG	WSH	BAL	MIN	LAR	CIN	PHI	ATL	DAL	TB	CAR	PIT
-7	-10	3	-2.5	-7.5	0	4	-2	-3	-2	-3.5	1.5	-3	1	-1

Avg = -2.1

Home Lines (wks 1-16)

1	2	5	9	11	12	16
TB	CLE	WSH	LAR	PHI	ATL	
-7	-10	-7.5	-2	-2	-3.5	-1

Avg = -4.7

Road Lines (wks 1-16)

3	4	7	8	10	13	14	15
ATL	NYG	BAL	MIN	CIN	DAL	TB	CAR
3	-2.5	0	4	-3	1.5	-3	1

Avg = 0.1

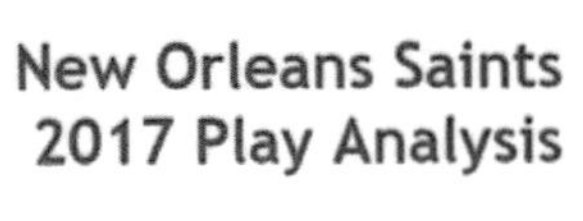

2017 Play Tendencies

All Pass %	56%
All Pass Rk	23
All Rush %	44%
All Rush Rk	10
1 Score Pass %	59%
1 Score Pass Rk	12
2016 1 Score Pass %	63%
2016 1 Score Pass Rk	3
2017 Pass Increase %	-4%
Pass Increase Rk	23
1 Score Rush %	41%
1 Score Rush Rk	21
Up Pass %	48%
Up Pass Rk	18
Up Rush %	52%
Up Rush Rk	15
Down Pass %	67%
Down Pass Rk	10
Down Rush %	33%
Down Rush Rk	23

2017 Down & Distance Tendencies

Down	Distance	Total Plays	Pass Rate	Run Rate	Play Success %
1	Short (1-3)	12	33%	67%	58%
	Med (4-7)	7	0%	100%	57%
	Long (8-10)	346	46%	54%	54%
	XL (11+)	11	73%	27%	27%
2	Short (1-3)	40	18%	83%	73%
	Med (4-7)	94	64%	36%	59%
	Long (8-10)	106	70%	30%	45%
	XL (11+)	30	87%	13%	23%
3	Short (1-3)	41	61%	39%	49%
	Med (4-7)	51	92%	8%	39%
	Long (8-10)	31	100%	0%	35%
	XL (11+)	23	96%	4%	26%
4	Short (1-3)	9	33%	67%	89%
	Med (4-7)	1	0%	100%	0%

Shotgun %:

Under Center	Shotgun
53%	47%
37% AVG	*63%*

Run Rate:

Under Center	Shotgun
73%	10%
68% AVG	*23%*

Pass Rate:

Under Center	Shotgun
27%	90%
32% AVG	*77%*

Short Yardage Intelligence:

2nd and Short Run

Run Freq	Run Rk	NFL Run Freq Avg	Run 1D Rate	Run NFL 1D Avg
78%	4	67%	76%	69%

2nd and Short Pass

Pass Freq	Pass Rk	NFL Pass Freq Avg	Pass 1D Rate	Pass NFL 1D Avg
22%	29	33%	63%	53%

Most Frequent Play

Down	Distance	Play Type	Player	Total Plays	Play Success %
1	Short (1-3)	RUSH	Mark Ingram	7	57%
	Med (4-7)	RUSH	Alvin Kamara	4	50%
	Long (8-10)	RUSH	Mark Ingram	108	49%
	XL (11+)	PASS	Michael Thomas	3	33%
			Ted Ginn	3	33%
2	Short (1-3)	RUSH	Mark Ingram	18	72%
	Med (4-7)	PASS	Michael Thomas	22	82%
	Long (8-10)	PASS	Alvin Kamara	18	56%
	XL (11+)	PASS	Mark Ingram	8	0%
3	Short (1-3)	PASS	Michael Thomas	9	78%
	Med (4-7)	PASS	Michael Thomas	15	33%
	Long (8-10)	PASS	Michael Thomas	8	75%
	XL (11+)	PASS	Mark Ingram	5	0%
			Michael Thomas	5	20%

Most Successful Play*

Down	Distance	Play Type	Player	Total Plays	Play Success %
1	Short (1-3)	RUSH	Mark Ingram	7	57%
	Long (8-10)	PASS	Ted Ginn	28	79%
2	Short (1-3)	RUSH	Alvin Kamara	5	80%
	Med (4-7)	PASS	Michael Thomas	22	82%
	Long (8-10)	PASS	Ted Ginn	8	63%
	XL (11+)	PASS	Alvin Kamara	5	60%
3	Short (1-3)	PASS	Michael Thomas	9	78%
	Med (4-7)	PASS	Ted Ginn	6	67%
	Long (8-10)	PASS	Michael Thomas	8	75%
	XL (11+)	PASS	Michael Thomas	5	20%

**Minimum 5 plays to qualify*

2017 Snap Rates

Wk	Opp	Score	Michael Thomas	Brandon Coleman	Ted Ginn	Josh Hill	Mark Ingram	Alvin Kamara	Coby Fleener	Willie Snead
1	MIN	L 29-19	58 (94%)	48 (77%)	42 (68%)	25 (40%)	26 (42%)	31 (50%)	32 (52%)	
2	NE	L 36-20	58 (89%)	58 (89%)	43 (66%)	26 (40%)	36 (55%)	16 (25%)	32 (49%)	
3	CAR	W 34-13	46 (79%)	46 (79%)	34 (59%)	37 (64%)	29 (50%)	17 (29%)	14 (24%)	
4	MIA	W 20-0	69 (93%)	54 (73%)	45 (61%)	8 (11%)	46 (62%)	26 (35%)	44 (59%)	
6	DET	W 52-38	59 (83%)	26 (37%)	37 (52%)	48 (68%)	47 (66%)	30 (42%)	18 (25%)	21 (30%)
7	GB	W 26-17	60 (79%)	54 (71%)	39 (51%)	41 (54%)	42 (55%)	37 (49%)	20 (26%)	
8	CHI	W 20-12	47 (77%)	48 (79%)	37 (61%)	40 (66%)	31 (51%)	31 (51%)	16 (26%)	4 (7%)
9	TB	W 30-10	48 (80%)	30 (50%)	37 (62%)	28 (47%)	36 (60%)	25 (42%)	22 (37%)	18 (30%)
10	BUF	W 47-10	56 (73%)	29 (38%)	50 (65%)	43 (56%)	37 (48%)	29 (38%)	17 (22%)	36 (47%)
11	WAS	W 34-31	56 (79%)	53 (75%)	53 (75%)	31 (44%)	28 (39%)	46 (65%)	36 (51%)	14 (20%)
12	LA	L 26-20	44 (77%)	27 (47%)	41 (72%)	38 (67%)	29 (51%)	32 (56%)	18 (32%)	19 (33%)
13	CAR	W 31-21	48 (75%)	33 (52%)	39 (61%)	43 (67%)	36 (56%)	37 (58%)		26 (41%)
14	ATL	L 20-17	45 (87%)	32 (62%)	35 (67%)	33 (63%)	42 (81%)	6 (12%)		22 (42%)
15	NYJ	W 31-19	63 (93%)	52 (76%)		45 (66%)	41 (60%)	33 (49%)		37 (54%)
16	ATL	W 23-13	38 (58%)	39 (60%)	45 (69%)	53 (82%)	32 (49%)	37 (57%)		38 (58%)
17	TB	L 31-24	53 (91%)	22 (38%)	37 (64%)	48 (83%)	33 (57%)	31 (53%)		27 (47%)
Grand Total			848 (82%)	651 (63%)	614 (63%)	587 (57%)	571 (55%)	464 (44%)	269 (37%)	262 (37%)

Personnel Groupings

Personnel	Team %	NFL Avg	Succ. %
1-1 [3WR]	48%	59%	51%
1-2 [2WR]	17%	19%	50%
2-1 [2WR]	12%	7%	55%
1-3 [1WR]	8%	5%	50%
2-2 [1WR]	5%	4%	43%
1-0 [4WR]	3%	2%	45%
2-0 [3WR]	3%	1%	33%

Grouping Tendencies

Personnel	Pass Rate	Pass Succ. %	Run Succ. %
1-1 [3WR]	67%	51%	52%
1-2 [2WR]	49%	54%	47%
2-1 [2WR]	44%	58%	53%
1-3 [1WR]	18%	53%	49%
2-2 [1WR]	26%	71%	33%
1-0 [4WR]	87%	44%	50%
2-0 [3WR]	90%	30%	67%

Red Zone Targets (min 3)

Receiver	All	Inside 5	6-10	11-20
Michael Thomas	21	7	3	11
Alvin Kamara	19		3	16
Mark Ingram	12	2	1	9
Brandon Coleman	8	1	3	4
Josh Hill	7	1	2	4
Ted Ginn	7		2	5
Coby Fleener	4	1	2	1
Willie Snead	4			4

Red Zone Rushes (min 3)

Rusher	All	Inside 5	6-10	11-20
Mark Ingram	35	16	3	16
Alvin Kamara	29	8	8	13
Drew Brees	7	2	2	3
Adrian Peterson	3	1	1	1
Ted Ginn	3		2	1

Early Down Target Rate

RB	TE	WR
33%	13%	54%
23%	*21% NFL AVG*	*56%*

Overall Target Success %

RB	TE	WR
50% #8	55% #7	58% #1

New Orleans Saints 2017 Passing Recap & 2018 Outlook

They said before the draft that Drew Brees lacks deep ball accuracy and arm strength. Then he went on to become the most prolific deep ball thrower in the game, dwarfing his peers during the best passing generation in NFL history. How's that for believing in yourself and sticking it to people who doubt what you will be able to become? If Cameron Meredith is fully healthy in Week 1 after undergoing ACL surgery last August, I expect the Saints passing offense to put up numbers that more closely resemble 2016 (when Brees was the fantasy QB3) and get there primarily using more 11 personnel. In 2016, the Saints used 11 personnel on 66% of their attempts and three or more wide receivers on 76% of their snaps. In 2017, due to reasons mentioned earlier in this chapter, those numbers dropped to 59% and 69%, respectively. In 2017, the Saints put up a 52% success rate in sets with three-plus wide receivers, a 5% decrease from 2016 (57%). But what Brees didn't have in 2016 was the ability to target Kamara, who was successful on 54% of his targets and recorded 8.1 yards per target. The Saints also (intelligently) targeted running backs more often in 2017 (34%) than 2016 (23%), and as a result, Brees had a record-breaking completion rate.

Drew Brees Rating All Downs

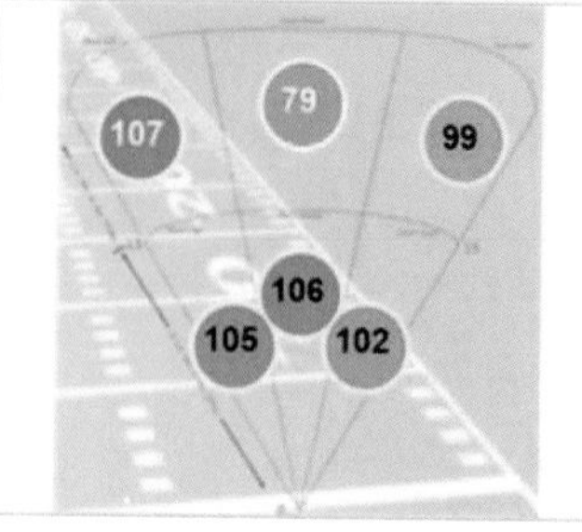

Drew Brees Rating Early Downs

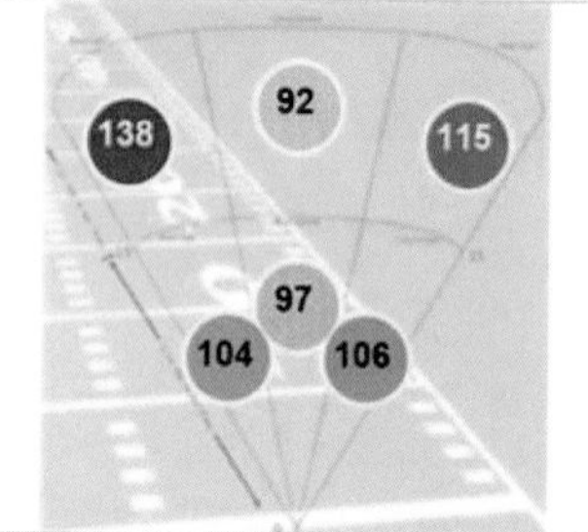

2017 Standard Passing Table

QB	Comp	Att	Comp %	Yds	YPA	TDs	INT	Sacks	Rating	Rk
Drew Brees	435	610	71%	5,008	8.2	28	11	23	104	4
NFL Avg			62%		7.0				87.5	

2017 Advanced Passing Table

QB	Success %	EDSR Passing Success %	20+ Yd Pass Gains	20+ Yd Pass %	30+ Yd Pass Gains	30+ Yd Pass %	Avg. Air Yds per Comp	Avg. YAC per Comp	20+ Air Yd Comp	20+ Air Yd %
Drew Brees	52%	58%	79	13.0%	25	4.1%	5.1	5.4	31	7%
NFL Avg	44%	48%	27.7	8.8%	10.3	3.3%	6.0	4.7	11.7	6%

Interception Rates by Down

Yards to Go	1	2	3	4	Total
1 & 2	0.0%	0.0%	0.0%	33.3%	2.9%
3, 4, 5	0.0%	0.0%	0.0%	0.0%	0.0%
6 - 9	0.0%	3.4%	1.8%		2.7%
10 - 14	0.9%	2.8%	0.0%	0.0%	1.3%
15+	10.0%	0.0%	6.7%		5.1%
Total	1.3%	2.2%	1.2%	14.3%	1.7%

3rd Down Passing - Short of Sticks Analysis

QB	Avg. Yds to Go	Avg. YIA (of Comp)	Avg Yds Short	Short of Sticks Rate	Short Rk
Drew Brees	7.5	4.2	-3.3	68%	43
NFL Avg	7.8	6.7	-1.1	60%	

Air Yds vs YAC

Air Yds %	YAC %	Rk
41%	59%	45
58%	42%	

2017 Receiving Recap & 2018 Outlook

The Saints love the run blocking they receive from Coleman, but at 6-foot-6, he has upside as a receiver as well. He was one of eight wide receivers last year to record over 9.5 yards per target and a success rate over 50%. He also was successful on 50% of his third-down targets, the second-best mark on the Saints. Coleman is great asset for the run and pass game. Meredith is ahead of schedule in his rehab from his ACL injury. We should all be excited at the prospect of Brees behind a healthy offensive line going three-wide with Kamara as a utility receiver out of the backfield and Watson as either a receiver or pass protector.

Player *Min 50 Targets	Targets	Comp %	YPA	Rating	TOARS	Success %	Success Rk	Missed YPA Rk	YAS % Rk	TDs
Michael Thomas	178	70%	8.7	100	5.7	61%	4	13	38	7
Alvin Kamara	111	78%	8.1	115	5.1	54%	31	30	85	6
Ted Ginn	87	75%	11.2	121	5.0	67%	1	3	9	5
Mark Ingram	73	82%	5.9	91	4.1	45%	90	103	79	0

Directional Passer Rating Delivered

Receiver	Short Left	Short Middle	Short Right	Deep Left	Deep Middle	Deep Right	Player Total
Michael Thomas	83	124	108	75	119	75	100
Alvin Kamara	114	144	111	82		50	115
Ted Ginn	120	3	96	129	107	129	121
Mark Ingram	90	88	94				91
Brandon Coleman	138	51	55	158	0	117	91
Josh Hill	125	108	112	40	53		97
Coby Fleener	129	133	85		119	119	126
Willie Snead	80	110	40	119		119	72
Tommylee Lewis	70		89	106		96	112
Team Total	106	109	100	109	82	98	105

2017 Rushing Recap & 2017 Outlook

I tried to paint my true impressions of what I think the 2018 Saints offense will look like, but I don't want any of my pro-Brees/passing slant to come across as if I'm not enthusiastic about the team's rushing attack in 2018. If the offensive line is healthier, the run game will be that much more dangerous. And if Brees continues to pass more on first down — as the metrics and common sense suggest he should — it will only help the Saints convert more first downs, which will inherently help their run game. Especially with Ingram suspended for the first four games of 2018, balance and health at the running back position will surely be one of Payton's more difficult-to-manage problems.

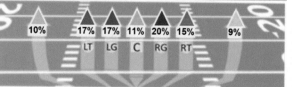

Player *Min 50 Rushes	Rushes	YPC	Success %	Success Rk	Missed YPA Rk	YTS % Rk	YAS % Rk	Early Down Success %	Early Down Success Rk	TDs
Mark Ingram	249	4.7	48%	23	9	69	17	48%	19	12
Alvin Kamara	141	5.6	53%	10	12	67	7	53%	9	9

Yards per Carry by Direction

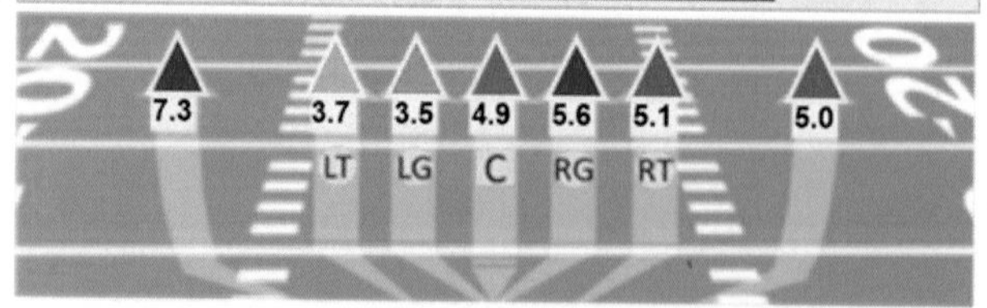

Directional Run Frequency

10% 17% 17% 11% 20% 15% 9%

LT LG C RG RT

it's understandable that the Saints wouldn't want to subject Brees to as many attempts as he had in prior years. In one-score games, the Saints moved from 63% passes in 2016 (second-most in the NFL) to 59% in 2017 (11th-most), but they were still above the league average of 57%.

Context is king in the NFL. It's imperative to know exactly what you're looking at. In 2017, the Saints led at halftime by double digits in six games. In 2016, they did so in just two games. So, let's look only at the first half when analyzing the biggest change in the Saints offense from 2016 to 2017. The biggest change in their pass rate was on first down. In the first half of games in 2016, the Saints passed on 56% of first downs (fourth-most), but in 2017 that number dropped to 48% (13th-most). On second down, they actually passed more often in 2017 (63%) than in 2016 (61%), and on third down, they passed much more often in 2017 (84%) than in 2016 (74%).

Why would a more run-dominant 2017 Saints pass more often on second down than their 2016 counterpart, and exceptionally more on third down? The answer is simple: Rushing gains fewer yards per play than passing. In 2017, a more run-heavy Saints team faced an average of 7.6 yards to go on second down. That number was 7.4 yards to go in 2016. And on third down, the 2017 Saints faced an average of 6.8 yards to go, a substantial increase from 6.2 in 2016.

(cont'd - see NO-5)

Chris Raybon's Fantasy Corner

Since 2002, only five running backs have averaged 5.0 yards per carry or more on at least 100 carries while scoring 10 or more total touchdowns in their rookie year: Ezekiel Elliott, Adrian Peterson, Maurice Jones-Drew, Clinton Portis and Alvin Kamara (and if you extend that back to 1989, Barry Sanders also joins that group). Kamara's 6.1 yards per carry is almost certain to regress, but there's no reason he can't repeat his 100 targets and double-digit touchdowns from 2017. He averaged 15.8 touches per game over the Saints' final five regular-season and playoff games, a fair (perhaps even conservative) expectation for 2018. And even if Kamara didn't improve on his 7.5 carries and 5.1 catches per game form the 2017 regular season and sees greatly reduced efficiency, he'd essentially have the numbers of 2017 Christian McCaffrey, who was a top-10 PPR back and a mid-range RB2 in standard formats. Combine that type of floor with a rookie season that put him in Hall of Fame company, and there's no doubt Kamara is a locked-in RB1.

Division History: Season Wins & 2018 Projection

2014 Wins | 2015 Wins | 2016 Wins | 2017 Wins | Forecast 2018 Wins

Rank of 2018 Defensive Pass Efficiency Faced by Week

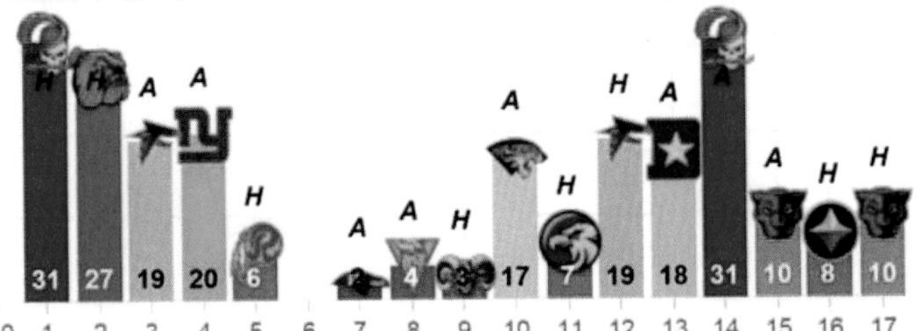

Rank of 2018 Defensive Rush Efficiency Faced by Week

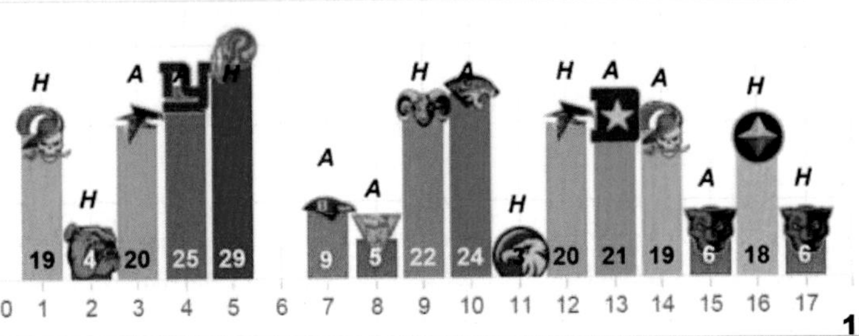

2017 Situational Usage by Player & Position

Usage Rate by Score

		Being Blown Out (14+)	Down Big (9-13)	One Score	Large Lead (9-13)	Blowout Lead (14+)	Grand Total
RUSH	Mark Ingram	8%	16%	23%	33%	35%	24%
	Alvin Kamara	10%	14%	13%	12%	18%	13%
	Ted Ginn			1%		1%	1%
	Josh Hill		2%				0%
	Adrian Peterson	7%	3%	2%	3%	3%	3%
	Tommylee Lewis			0%			0%
	Zach Line			1%	1%	1%	1%
	Trey Edmunds					6%	1%
	John Kuhn			0%			0%
	Total	25%	34%	41%	48%	65%	43%
PASS	Mark Ingram	8%	3%	8%	4%	6%	7%
	Alvin Kamara	11%	13%	11%	13%	4%	11%
	Michael Thomas	17%	20%	17%	13%	13%	16%
	Ted Ginn	12%	17%	8%	8%	2%	8%
	Brandon Coleman	7%	3%	4%	3%	3%	4%
	Josh Hill	6%	3%	3%	1%	1%	3%
	Adrian Peterson	1%		0%	1%		0%
	Coby Fleener	11%	2%	2%	3%		3%
	Willie Snead	2%	2%	2%	3%	2%	2%
	Tommylee Lewis		3%	2%	1%		1%
	Zach Line			1%		1%	1%
	Michael Hoomanawa..	1%		1%	3%	1%	1%
	Garrett Griffin			0%			0%
	Total	75%	66%	59%	53%	35%	57%

Positional Target Distribution vs NFL Average

		NFL Wide				Team Only			
		Left	Middle	Right	**Total**	Left	Middle	Right	**Total**
Deep	WR	946	495	961	**2,402**	40	14	26	**80**
	TE	191	143	187	**521**	1	7	1	**9**
	RB	36	9	35	**80**	3		7	**10**
	All	**1,173**	**647**	**1,183**	**3,003**	**44**	**21**	**34**	**99**
Short	WR	2,754	1,636	2,678	**7,068**	108	35	112	**255**
	TE	848	822	1,149	**2,819**	15	17	21	**53**
	RB	1,247	799	1,219	**3,265**	74	24	76	**174**
	All	**4,849**	**3,257**	**5,046**	**13,152**	**197**	**76**	**209**	**482**
Total		**6,022**	**3,904**	**6,229**	**16,155**	**241**	**97**	**243**	**581**

Positional Success Rates vs NFL Average

		NFL Wide				Team Only			
		Left	Middle	Right	**Total**	Left	Middle	Right	**Total**
Deep	WR	36%	45%	37%	**38%**	53%	57%	62%	**56%**
	TE	38%	52%	45%	**44%**	0%	71%	100%	**67%**
	RB	36%	56%	37%	**39%**	33%		43%	**40%**
	All	**36%**	**47%**	**38%**	**39%**	**50%**	**62%**	**59%**	**56%**
Short	WR	51%	57%	50%	**52%**	57%	69%	57%	**59%**
	TE	50%	56%	49%	**52%**	60%	71%	38%	**55%**
	RB	44%	51%	43%	**45%**	55%	54%	47%	**52%**
	All	**49%**	**55%**	**48%**	**50%**	**57%**	**64%**	**52%**	**56%**
Total		**47%**	**54%**	**46%**	**48%**	**56%**	**64%**	**53%**	**56%**

Successful Play Rate
0% ▭ 100%

New Orleans Saints - Success by Personnel Grouping & Play Type

Play Type	1-1 [3WR]	1-2 [2WR]	2-1 [2WR]	1-0 [4WR]	1-3 [1WR]	0-1 [4WR]	2-0 [3WR]	2-2 [1WR]	0-0 [5WR]	3-1 [1WR]	2-3 [0WR]	Grand Total
PASS	51% (324, 58%)	54% (84, 15%)	58% (55, 10%)	44% (27, 5%)	53% (15, 3%)	67% (3, 1%)	30% (27, 5%)	71% (14, 3%)	25% (4, 1%)	0% (1, 0%)	33% (3, 1%)	51% (557, 100%)
RUSH	52% (158, 36%)	47% (86, 19%)	53% (70, 16%)	50% (4, 1%)	49% (69, 16%)		67% (3, 1%)	33% (40, 9%)		0% (1, 0%)	50% (12, 3%)	49% (444, 100%)
TOTAL	51% (482, 48%)	50% (170, 17%)	55% (125, 12%)	45% (31, 3%)	50% (84, 8%)	67% (3, 0%)	33% (30, 3%)	43% (54, 5%)	25% (4, 0%)	0% (2, 0%)	47% (15, 1%)	50% (1,001, 100%)

Format Line 1: Success Rate Line 2: Total # of Plays, % of All Plays (by type)

NO-5 Essentially, Drew Brees is so good and so accurate a quarterback that even with as brilliant of a run game as the Saints had, they were that much less efficient with their productivity than when Brees dropped back to pass. While there are other benefits added for running the ball, the Saints offense gained fewer yards per play and thus had more yards to go. And guess what? This great offense of 2017 ranked just No. 22 in third-down conversion rate (37%) as opposed to No. 1 in 2016 (49%) because of having fewer yards to go (as well as having better receivers in 2016 than 2017, which I'll cover now).

In addition to the reasons just described in detail as to why the Saints ran the ball more often last season, another equally key reason was their receiving talent. The 2016 Saints featured a great threesome of wide receivers in Brandin Cooks, Michael Thomas, and Willie Snead. The team also had a healthy and moderately successful tight end in Coby Fleener. All four of these players played on at least 58% of the team's offensive snaps, drew at least 80 targets, and caught at least 50 passes. The team used 11 personnel (three wide receivers, one running back, one tight end) 62% of the time, and even though the 2016 Saints had a great run game (third-best in the NFL), they saw the value in passing the ball often thanks to Brees.

Last season, however, the receiving corps was significantly worse. Cooks was traded, Snead was suspended for 3 games and never re-entered the offense with efficiency, Fleener was injured in camp and likewise inefficient. As such, instead of having four wide receivers and/or tight ends drawing 80+ targets and catching 50+ passes like they did in 2016, the 2017 Saints had just one draw 80 targets (Thomas, 149) and two catch 50+ passes (Thomas, 104; Ginn, 53).

This offseason, the Saints had the excellent fortune of acquiring WR Cameron Meredith, formerly of the Bears. Meredith was the Bears' most successful wide receiver (56%) and delivered their highest yards per target (9.2). New Orleans also added back Ben Watson at tight end and kept Coleman, a tremendous run blocker and a huge, 6-foot-6 receiver. I see the Saints returning to more 11 personnel in 2018. In fact, I think there could be a substantial shift. As such, I'm higher on Brees than most. If the team's offensive line can stay healthier than 2017, the offense will be incredible. But they will need to be, as I have the Saints facing a top-five schedule of defenses, including the largest shift in difficulty from 2016 of any team. The defense is in for a tough go as well, facing a top-five schedule. I like the Saints' chances of taking the next step in 2018 but it won't be easy.

Receiving Success by Personnel Grouping

Position	Player	1-1 [3WR]	1-2 [2WR]	2-1 [2WR]	1-0 [4WR]	1-3 [1WR]	0-1 [4WR]	2-0 [3WR]	2-2 [1WR]	3-1 [1WR]	2-3 [0WR]	Total
RB	Alvin Kamara	54% 8.2 127.2 (63)	75% 15.0 118.8 (8)	80% 7.6 98.3 (10)	29% 3.7 53.3 (7)			33% 7.4 88.7 (9)	100% 7.3 97.2 (3)	0% 0.0 39.6 (1)		55% 8.2 117.2 (101)
	Mark Ingram	49% 6.6 94.3 (37)	20% 3.2 80.0 (5)	43% 5.0 87.5 (7)	50% 6.0 91.7 (2)	50% 6.2 83.3 (6)		33% 3.7 81.9 (9)	75% 9.5 106.3 (4)		0% 0.0 39.6 (1)	45% 5.9 91.1 (71)
TE	Coby Fleener	74% 10.4 139.1 (23)	33% 7.0 59.0 (3)	100% 10.0 108.3 (1)			0% 0.0 39.6 (1)		50% 12.0 93.8 (2)			67% 9.8 126.4 (30)
WR	Ted Ginn	67% 11.7 128.7 (46)	77% 13.1 144.4 (13)	50% 12.0 93.8 (4)	50% 7.5 97.9 (2)	100% 8.0 100.0 (2)		0% 0.0 39.6 (3)				66% 11.2 125.1 (70)
	Brandon Coleman	53% 13.0 106.8 (19)	40% 8.6 127.5 (5)	43% 4.9 69.9 (7)	50% 7.5 35.4 (2)	100% 20.0 118.8 (1)	100% 9.0 104.2 (1)	0% 0.0 0.0 (2)				49% 9.9 88.6 (37)
	Willie Snead	36% 5.2 69.1 (11)	100% 9.0 104.2 (1)		0% 0.0 39.6 (3)			100% 26.0 118.8 (1)				38% 5.8 67.7 (16)

Format Line 1: Success Rate Line 2: YPA Line 3: Passer Rating Line 4: Total # of Plays

Successful Play Rate
0% ▭ 100%

Rushing Success by Personnel Grouping

Position	Player	1-1 [3WR]	1-2 [2WR]	2-1 [2WR]	1-0 [4WR]	1-3 [1WR]	2-0 [3WR]	2-2 [1WR]	3-1 [1WR]	2-3 [0WR]	Total
RB	Mark Ingram	58% 5.3 (55)	38% 4.6 (52)	50% 6.5 (48)		53% 4.3 (51)		33% 3.1 (18)	0% 0.0 (1)	80% 0.8 (5)	49% 4.9 (230)
	Alvin Kamara	50% 5.0 (78)	61% 7.2 (18)	100% 7.0 (1)	50% 21.8 (4)	33% 4.3 (9)	100% 12.0 (1)	63% 7.5 (8)		0% 0.0 (1)	52% 6.1 (120)
	Adrian Peterson	25% 1.8 (8)	60% 3.3 (10)	50% 4.0 (2)		43% 3.7 (7)					44% 3.0 (27)

Format Line 1: Success Rate Line 2: YPC Line 3: Total # of Plays

New York Giants

2018 Coaches

Head Coach:
Pat Shurmur (MIN OC) (1st yr)
Offensive Coordinator:
Mike Shula (CAR OC) (1st yr)
Defensive Coordinator:
James Bettcher (ARI DC) (1st yr)

2018 Forecast

Wins	Div Rank
6.5	#3

Past Records

2017: 3-13
2016: 11-5
2015: 6-10

EASY HARD

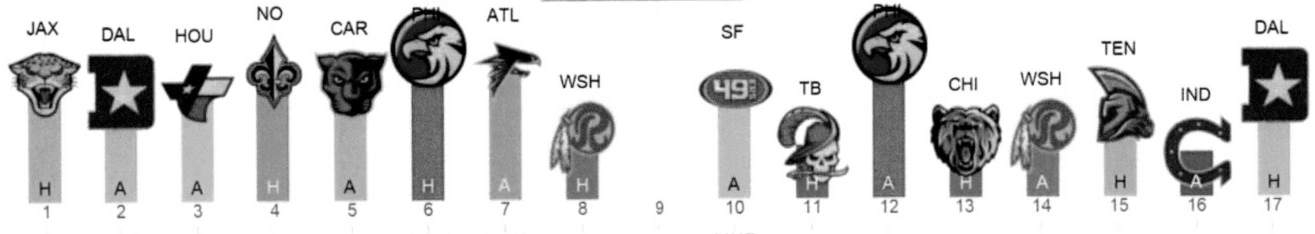

Key Players Lost

TXN	Player (POS)
Cut	Hart, Bobby T
	Marshall, Brandon WR
	Perkins, Paul RB
	Rodgers-Cromartie, Dominique C..
	Williams, Ishaq DE
Declared Free Agent	Ayers, Akeem LB
	Berhe, Nat S
	Casillas, Jonathan LB
	Darkwa, Orleans RB
	Fluker, D.J. G
	Grant, Curtis LB
	Kennard, Devon LB
	Morris, Darryl CB
	Pugh, Justin G
	Richburg, Weston C
	Robinson, Keenan LB
	Sheppard, Kelvin LB
	Smith, Geno QB
	Vereen, Shane RB

Average Line	# Games Favored	# Games Underdog
2.8	3	11

2018 New York Giants Overview

Coming off of an 11-win 2016 season, the Giants' 2017 win total was set at 8.5 games and they were projected to finish second in the NFC East. Their 2016 strength was their defense, which ranked first in EDSR and second in defensive efficiency. Their weakness was their offense, which ranked 22nd in efficiency and second-worst in EDSR. To remedy the latter, the team drafted TE Evan Engram 23rd overall and added WR Brandon Marshall along with G D.J. Fluker in free agency. There were positive expectations that the team could maintain its dominance on defense while taking a step forward offensively.

But heading into the 2017 season, I urged some caution with the offense. When it struggled in 2016, it did so against the fifth-easiest schedule of opposing defenses, and in 2017, I projected that it would face the ninth-most difficult schedule of opposing defenses, including the seventh-most difficult pass defenses. So while the Giants made moves to improve, they also would be facing a more difficult schedule.

And wouldn't you know it, out of the gates came an 0-5 start, which really should be broken up into an 0-2 whitewash followed by an 0-3 set of brutal, close losses. With the Giants scoring just three points and losing by 16 in Week 1, the hope was in their Week 2 home opener against the Lions, with Beckham Jr, the result would be different. It wasn't. Once again, the refrain was a lack of pass protection. Eli was sacked five times, and the Giants had just two explosive pass gains the entire game on 32 attempts. In the first half alone, Eli was sacked four times and threw an interception. The Giants ran the ball well, gaining 5.4 yards per carry and posting a 57% success rate, but due to the scoreboard they had to abandon the run in the second half. They lost 24-10.

Then came the three close losses — to the Eagles, Buccaneers and Chargers, all by five points or less — in which the Giants posted a 48% success rate on passes and 47% on runs (up from 44% and 33%, respectively). But they couldn't get into the win column, and then lost both Beckham Jr. and Marshall in the same game in Week 5 against the Chargers. Neither wideout would play again in 2017. In fact, the Giants' wide receiver corps was the second-most injured of any in 2017.

(cont'd - see NYG2)

Key Free Agents/ Trades Added

Gay, William CB
Latimer, Cody WR
Martin, Kareem LB
Mauro, Josh DE
Ogletree, Alec LB
Omameh, Patrick G
Solder, Nate T
Stewart, Jonathan RB
Thomas, Michael S
Webb, B.W. CB

Drafted Players

Rd	Pk	Player (College)
1	2	RB - Saquon Barkley (Penn State)
2	34	G - Will Hernandez (UTEP)
3	66	LB - Lorenzo Carter (Georgia)
	69	DT - B. J. Hill (NC State)
4	108	QB - Kyle Lauletta (Richmond)
5	139	DT - R. J. McIntosh (Miami (FL))

Regular Season Wins: Past & Current Proj

	Wins
Forecast 2018 Wins	6.5
2017 Wins	3
Forecast 2017 Wins	8
2016 Wins	11
2015 Wins	6
2014 Wins	6

1 3 5 7 9 11 13 15

Lineup & Cap Hits

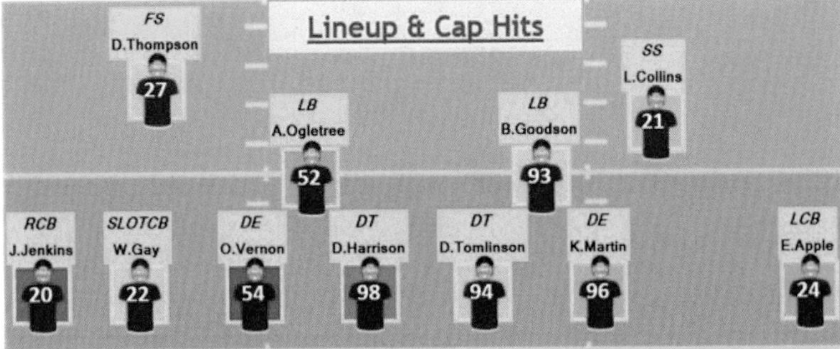

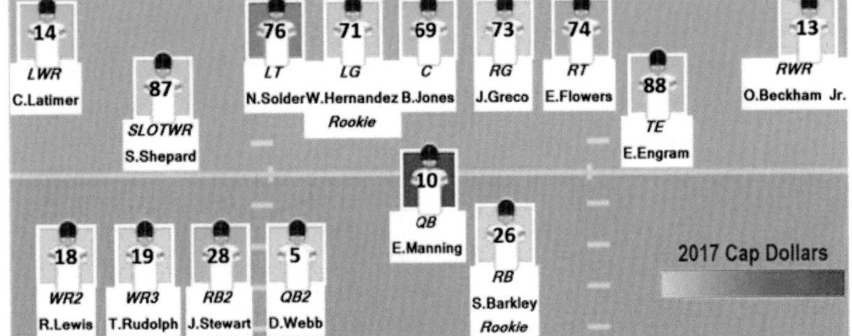

2018 Unit Spending

All DEF
All OFF

Positional Spending

	Rank	Total	2017 Rk
All OFF	21	$88.89M	23
QB	10	$24.23M	9
OL	24	$30.04M	27
RB	20	$7.27M	14
WR	23	$18.20M	19
TE	16	$9.15M	29
All DEF	19	$76.86M	3
DL	8	$39.00M	3
LB	31	$9.89M	21
CB	14	$20.88M	1
S	28	$7.09M	27

New York Giants 2017 Success Rate Radar

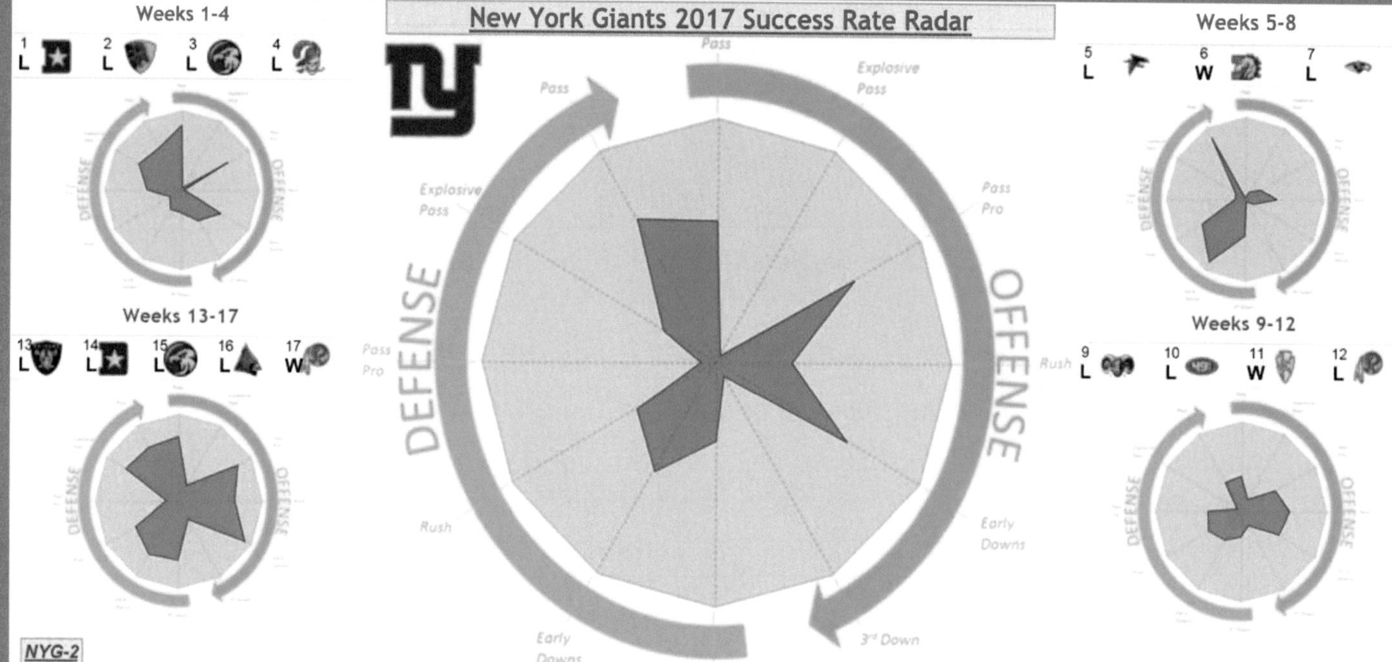

NYG-2

You may recall that in 2016, the Giants used 11 personnel on an incredible 92% of their offensive snaps, and three or more wide receivers on 94% of their snaps. Last year, under the same offensive scheme of Ben McAdoo, their wide receiving corps was so injured that they used 11 personnel on just 54% of snaps and three or more wide receivers on 73% of snaps. They used a lot more 12 personnel, with one running back, two tight ends, and two wide receivers. After using two or more tight ends on just 56 snaps in 2016, they used that package on 266 snaps last season. But instead of passing out of 12 proficiently, they attempted passes out of that grouping on only 33% of snaps. Even though 12 personnel sounds like a great formation to use with a bad offensive line and poor receiver depth, the Giants were not close to the league average in efficiency out of 12, nor did they receive the same bump from 11 to 12 which is commonly seen throughout the league.

The Giants fired head coach Ben McAdoo late in 2017, and after the season they hired Pat Shurmur to replace him. What I'm most excited to see out of Shurmur's offense is more diversity of personnel groupings.

Forty percent of Shurmur's snaps as Vikings offensive coordinator featured two or fewer wide receivers. In one-score games the past two seasons, that number was 38%. For the Giants the past two years under McAdoo, that number was 18%. And the Vikings saw tremendous efficiency in those sets, recording a 58% success rate and a 112 passer rating, whereas the Giants had only a 32% success rate and 69 passer rating. Additionally, the Giants didn't get too creative, primarily running 12 personnel when not in three-plus-wide-receiver sets, also sprinkling in some 21 (12%) along with less than 10% of other groupings. Meanwhile, Shurmur only used about 12 personnel about 50% of the time, and he ran a lot of 22 and 21.

In 2018, I anticipate the Giants using much less 11 personnel than they did in the past. I expect Engram to still receive plenty of targets from 11, but I think we'll see a lot more 12, 22, and 21 personnel groupings from the Shurmur-led Giants than we did from the McAdoo version.

(cont'd - see NYG-3)

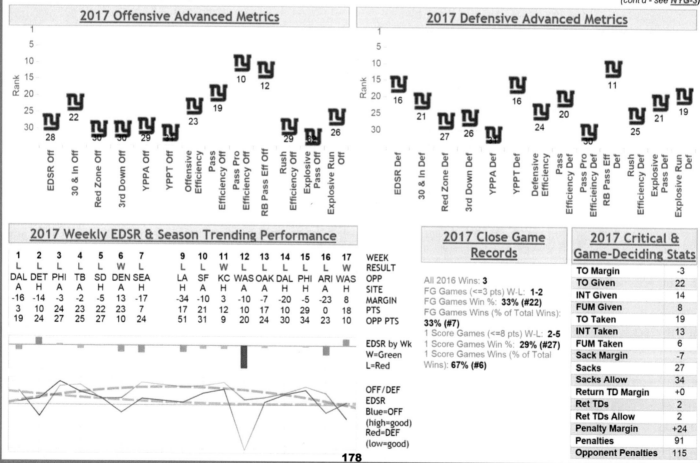

2017 Offensive Advanced Metrics

Metric	Rank
EDSR Off	28
30 & In Off	22
Red Zone Off	30
3rd Down Off	30
YPPA Off	29
YPPT Off	31
Offensive Efficiency	23
Pass Efficiency Off	19
Pass Pro Efficiency Off	10
RB Pass Eff Off	12
Rush Efficiency Off	29
Explosive Pass Off	32
Explosive Run Off	26

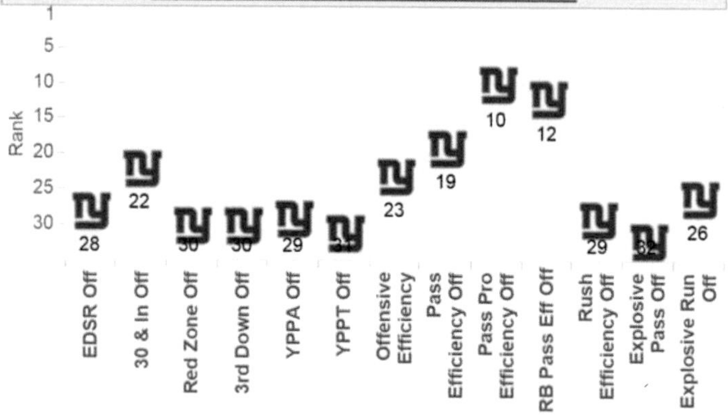

2017 Defensive Advanced Metrics

Metric	Rank
EDSR Def	16
30 & In Def	21
Red Zone Def	27
3rd Down Def	26
YPPA Def	31
YPPT Def	16
Defensive Efficiency	24
Pass Efficiency Def	20
Pass Pro Efficiency Def	30
RB Pass Eff Def	11
Rush Efficiency Def	25
Explosive Pass Def	21
Explosive Run Def	19

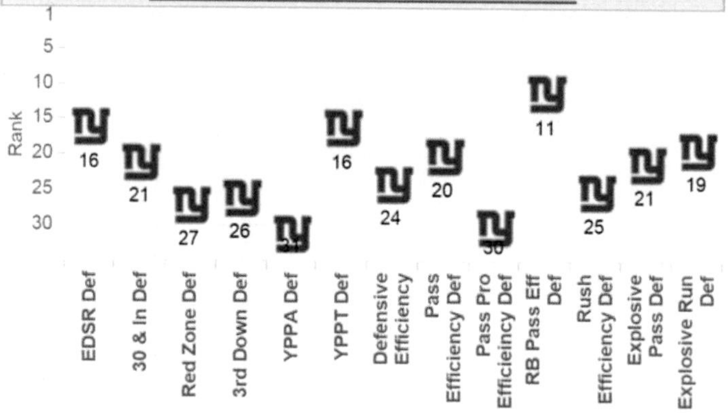

2017 Weekly EDSR & Season Trending Performance

WEEK	1	2	3	4	5	6	7	9	10	11	12	13	14	15	16	17
RESULT	L	L	L	L	L	W	L	L	L	W	L	L	L	L	L	W
OPP	DAL	DET	PHI	TB	SD	DEN	SEA	LA	SF	KC	WAS	OAK	DAL	PHI	ARI	WAS
SITE	A	H	A	A	H	A	H	H	A	H	A	A	H	H	A	H
MARGIN	-16	-14	-3	-2	-5	13	-17	-34	-10	3	-10	-7	-20	-5	-23	8
PTS	3	10	24	23	22	23	7	17	21	12	10	17	10	29	0	18
OPP PTS	19	24	27	25	27	10	24	51	31	9	20	24	30	34	23	10

EDSR by Wk
W=Green
L=Red

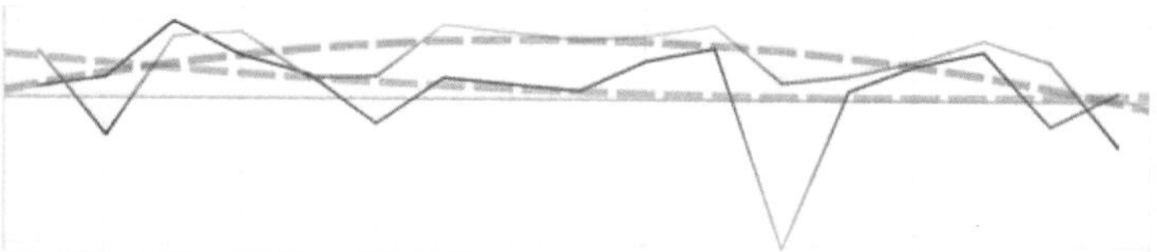

OFF/DEF EDSR
Blue=OFF (high=good)
Red=DEF (low=good)

2017 Close Game Records

All 2016 Wins: **3**
FG Games (<=3 pts) W-L: **1-2**
FG Games Win %: **33% (#22)**
FG Games Wins (% of Total Wins): **33% (#7)**
1 Score Games (<=8 pts) W-L: **2-5**
1 Score Games Win %: **29% (#27)**
1 Score Games Wins (% of Total Wins): **67% (#6)**

2017 Critical & Game-Deciding Stats

TO Margin	-3
TO Given	22
INT Given	14
FUM Given	8
TO Taken	19
INT Taken	13
FUM Taken	6
Sack Margin	-7
Sacks	27
Sacks Allow	34
Return TD Margin	+0
Ret TDs	2
Ret TDs Allow	2
Penalty Margin	+24
Penalties	91
Opponent Penalties	115

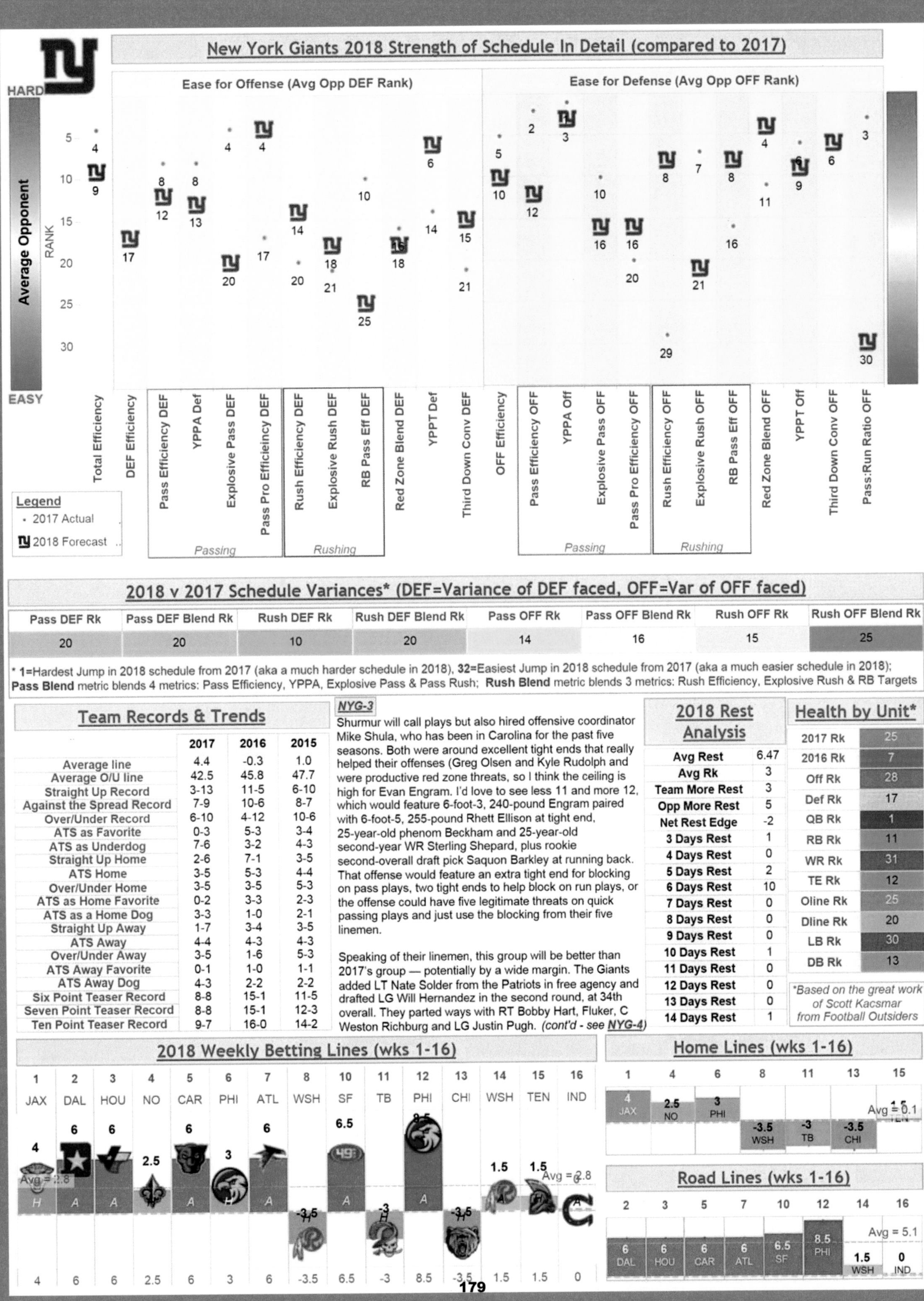

New York Giants 2018 Strength of Schedule In Detail (compared to 2017)

2018 v 2017 Schedule Variances* (DEF=Variance of DEF faced, OFF=Var of OFF faced)

Pass DEF Rk	Pass DEF Blend Rk	Rush DEF Rk	Rush DEF Blend Rk	Pass OFF Rk	Pass OFF Blend Rk	Rush OFF Rk	Rush OFF Blend Rk
20	20	10	20	14	16	15	25

* **1**=Hardest Jump in 2018 schedule from 2017 (aka a much harder schedule in 2018), **32**=Easiest Jump in 2018 schedule from 2017 (aka a much easier schedule in 2018); **Pass Blend** metric blends 4 metrics: Pass Efficiency, YPPA, Explosive Pass & Pass Rush; **Rush Blend** metric blends 3 metrics: Rush Efficiency, Explosive Rush & RB Targets

Team Records & Trends

	2017	2016	2015
Average line	4.4	-0.3	1.0
Average O/U line	42.5	45.8	47.7
Straight Up Record	3-13	11-5	6-10
Against the Spread Record	7-9	10-6	8-7
Over/Under Record	6-10	4-12	10-6
ATS as Favorite	0-3	5-3	3-4
ATS as Underdog	7-6	3-2	4-3
Straight Up Home	2-6	7-1	3-5
ATS Home	3-5	5-3	4-4
Over/Under Home	3-5	3-5	5-3
ATS as Home Favorite	0-2	3-3	2-3
ATS as a Home Dog	3-3	1-0	2-1
Straight Up Away	1-7	3-4	3-5
ATS Away	4-4	4-3	4-3
Over/Under Away	3-5	1-6	5-3
ATS Away Favorite	0-1	1-0	1-1
ATS Away Dog	4-3	2-2	2-2
Six Point Teaser Record	8-8	15-1	11-5
Seven Point Teaser Record	8-8	15-1	12-3
Ten Point Teaser Record	9-7	16-0	14-2

NYG-3

Shurmur will call plays but also hired offensive coordinator Mike Shula, who has been in Carolina for the past five seasons. Both were around excellent tight ends that really helped their offenses (Greg Olsen and Kyle Rudolph and were productive red zone threats, so I think the ceiling is high for Evan Engram. I'd love to see less 11 and more 12, which would feature 6-foot-3, 240-pound Engram paired with 6-foot-5, 255-pound Rhett Ellison at tight end, 25-year-old phenom Beckham and 25-year-old second-year WR Sterling Shepard, plus rookie second-overall draft pick Saquon Barkley at running back. That offense would feature an extra tight end for blocking on pass plays, two tight ends to help block on run plays, or the offense could have five legitimate threats on quick passing plays and just use the blocking from their five linemen.

Speaking of their linemen, this group will be better than 2017's group — potentially by a wide margin. The Giants added LT Nate Solder from the Patriots in free agency and drafted LG Will Hernandez in the second round, at 34th overall. They parted ways with RT Bobby Hart, Fluker, C Weston Richburg and LG Justin Pugh. *(cont'd - see **NYG-4**)*

2018 Rest Analysis

Avg Rest	6.47
Avg Rk	3
Team More Rest	3
Opp More Rest	5
Net Rest Edge	-2
3 Days Rest	1
4 Days Rest	0
5 Days Rest	2
6 Days Rest	10
7 Days Rest	0
8 Days Rest	0
9 Days Rest	0
10 Days Rest	1
11 Days Rest	0
12 Days Rest	0
13 Days Rest	0
14 Days Rest	1

Health by Unit*

2017 Rk	25
2016 Rk	7
Off Rk	28
Def Rk	17
QB Rk	1
RB Rk	11
WR Rk	31
TE Rk	12
Oline Rk	25
Dline Rk	20
LB Rk	30
DB Rk	13

*Based on the great work of Scott Kacsmar from Football Outsiders

2018 Weekly Betting Lines (wks 1-16)

1	2	3	4	5	6	7	8	10	11	12	13	14	15	16
JAX	DAL	HOU	NO	CAR	PHI	ATL	WSH	SF	TB	PHI	CHI	WSH	TEN	IND
H	A	A	H	A	H	A	H	A	H	A	H	A	H	A
4	6	6	2.5	6	3	6	-3.5	6.5	-3	8.5	-3.5	1.5	1.5	0

Avg = 2.8

Home Lines (wks 1-16)

1	4	6	8	11	13	15
JAX	NO	PHI	WSH	TB	CHI	TEN
4	2.5	3	-3.5	-3	-3.5	1.5

Avg = 0.1

Road Lines (wks 1-16)

2	3	5	7	10	12	14	16
DAL	HOU	CAR	ATL	SF	PHI	WSH	IND
6	6	6	6	6.5	8.5	1.5	0

Avg = 5.1

New York Giants 2017 Play Analysis

2017 Play Tendencies

All Pass %	62%
All Pass Rk	4
All Rush %	38%
All Rush Rk	29
1 Score Pass %	58%
1 Score Pass Rk	13
2016 1 Score Pass %	59%
2016 1 Score Pass Rk	17
2017 Pass Increase %	-1%
Pass Increase Rk	16
1 Score Rush %	42%
1 Score Rush Rk	20
Up Pass %	49%
Up Pass Rk	15
Up Rush %	51%
Up Rush Rk	18
Down Pass %	69%
Down Pass Rk	7
Down Rush %	31%
Down Rush Rk	26

2017 Down & Distance Tendencies

Down	Distance	Total Plays	Pass Rate	Run Rate	Play Success %
1	Short (1-3)	5	20%	80%	40%
	Med (4-7)	7	43%	57%	43%
	Long (8-10)	295	39%	61%	48%
	XL (11+)	10	90%	10%	30%
2	Short (1-3)	34	44%	56%	59%
	Med (4-7)	103	71%	29%	49%
	Long (8-10)	86	80%	20%	42%
	XL (11+)	32	59%	41%	19%
3	Short (1-3)	53	60%	40%	45%
	Med (4-7)	55	98%	2%	38%
	Long (8-10)	33	94%	6%	30%
	XL (11+)	23	78%	22%	9%
4	Short (1-3)	6	50%	50%	50%
	Med (4-7)	2	100%	0%	50%
	Long (8-10)	1	100%	0%	0%

Shotgun %:

Under Center	Shotgun
38%	62%
37%	*AVG 63%*

Run Rate:

Under Center	Shotgun
69%	20%
68%	*AVG 23%*

Pass Rate:

Under Center	Shotgun
31%	80%
32%	*AVG 77%*

Short Yardage Intelligence:

2nd and Short Run

Run Freq	Run Rk	NFL Run Freq Avg	Run 1D Rate	Run NFL 1D Avg
55%	28	67%	56%	69%

2nd and Short Pass

Pass Freq	Pass Rk	NFL Pass Freq Avg	Pass 1D Rate	Pass NFL 1D Avg
45%	5	33%	60%	53%

Most Frequent Play

Down	Distance	Play Type	Player	Total Plays	Play Success %
1	Short (1-3)	RUSH	Orleans Darkwa	3	67%
	Med (4-7)	RUSH	Wayne Gallman	3	33%
	Long (8-10)	RUSH	Orleans Darkwa	78	44%
	XL (11+)	PASS	Wayne Gallman	3	33%
			Sterling Shepard	3	67%
2	Short (1-3)	RUSH	Orleans Darkwa	11	45%
	Med (4-7)	PASS	Evan Engram	15	53%
	Long (8-10)	PASS	Evan Engram	15	53%
	XL (11+)	RUSH	Shane Vereen	6	0%
3	Short (1-3)	RUSH	Orleans Darkwa	11	55%
	Med (4-7)	PASS	Evan Engram	11	55%
	Long (8-10)	PASS	Roger Lewis	6	17%
	XL (11+)	PASS	Shane Vereen	5	0%

Most Successful Play*

Down	Distance	Play Type	Player	Total Plays	Play Success %
1	Long (8-10)	PASS	Rhett Ellison	6	100%
2	Short (1-3)	RUSH	Wayne Gallman	6	67%
	Med (4-7)	PASS	Sterling Shepard	6	83%
	Long (8-10)	PASS	Rhett Ellison	6	67%
	XL (11+)	PASS	Wayne Gallman	5	40%
3	Short (1-3)	PASS	Sterling Shepard	8	63%
	Med (4-7)	PASS	Odell Beckham Jr.	5	60%
	Long (8-10)	PASS	Evan Engram	5	40%
	XL (11+)	PASS	Shane Vereen	5	0%

**Minimum 5 plays to qualify*

2017 Snap Rates

Wk	Opp	Score	Evan Engram	Roger Lewis	Sterling Shepard	Rhett Ellison	Tavarres King	Shane Vereen	Brandon Marshall	Odell Beckham ..
1	DAL	L 19-3	48 (84%)	44 (77%)	57 (100%)	19 (33%)		31 (54%)	49 (86%)	
2	DET	L 24-10	43 (77%)	16 (29%)	56 (100%)	22 (39%)		17 (30%)	46 (82%)	34 (61%)
3	PHI	L 27-24	57 (83%)	11 (16%)	68 (99%)	19 (28%)		19 (28%)	65 (94%)	53 (77%)
4	TB	L 25-23	67 (84%)	14 (18%)	67 (84%)	31 (39%)		22 (28%)	66 (83%)	68 (85%)
5	LAC	L 27-22	57 (81%)	45 (64%)	24 (34%)	50 (71%)		23 (33%)	27 (39%)	55 (79%)
6	DEN	W 23-10	38 (70%)	48 (89%)		35 (65%)	46 (85%)	12 (22%)		
7	SEA	L 24-7	47 (80%)	50 (85%)		28 (47%)	59 (100%)	16 (27%)		
9	LA	L 51-17	58 (85%)	48 (71%)	63 (93%)	40 (59%)	35 (51%)	20 (29%)		
10	SF	L 31-21	52 (79%)	54 (82%)	66 (100%)	26 (39%)	53 (80%)	30 (45%)		
11	KC	W 12-9	58 (84%)	52 (75%)		47 (68%)	65 (94%)	23 (33%)		
12	WAS	L 20-10	49 (86%)	48 (84%)		28 (49%)	55 (96%)	15 (26%)		
13	OAK	L 24-17	53 (85%)	51 (82%)	61 (98%)	32 (52%)	37 (60%)	22 (35%)		
14	DAL	L 30-10	63 (79%)	75 (94%)	77 (96%)	39 (49%)		24 (30%)		
15	PHI	L 34-29	74 (84%)	81 (92%)	85 (97%)	26 (30%)	43 (49%)	31 (35%)		
16	ARI	L 23-0	13 (18%)	59 (83%)	64 (90%)	40 (56%)		6 (8%)		
17	WAS	W 18-10				55 (71%)		15 (19%)		
	Grand Total		777 (77%)	696 (69%)	688 (90%)	537 (50%)	393 (77%)	326 (30%)	253 (77%)	210 (75%)

Personnel Groupings

Personnel	Team %	NFL Avg	Succ. %
1-1 [3WR]	54%	59%	45%
1-2 [2WR]	19%	19%	46%
1-0 [4WR]	13%	2%	40%
2-1 [2WR]	4%	7%	36%
1-3 [1WR]	3%	5%	44%

Grouping Tendencies

Personnel	Pass Rate	Pass Succ. %	Run Succ. %
1-1 [3WR]	69%	45%	44%
1-2 [2WR]	36%	44%	48%
1-0 [4WR]	94%	41%	13%
2-1 [2WR]	26%	50%	31%
1-3 [1WR]	26%	43%	45%

Red Zone Targets (min 3)

Receiver	All	Inside 5	6-10	11-20
Evan Engram	11	3	5	3
Sterling Shepard	11	3	4	4
Roger Lewis	8		1	7
Odell Beckham Jr.	4	1	2	1
Tavarres King	3	1		2
Brandon Marshall	2			2

Red Zone Rushes (min 3)

Rusher	All	Inside 5	6-10	11-20
Orleans Darkwa	22	7	4	11
Wayne Gallman	14	3	5	6
Eli Manning	5	4		1
Shane Vereen	5			5
Paul Perkins	4	1		3

Early Down Target Rate

RB	TE	WR
26%	27%	47%
23%	*21% NFL AVG*	*56%*

Overall Target Success %

RB	TE	WR
45% #15	50% #18	47% #19

New York Giants 2017 Passing Recap & 2018 Outlook

Eli Manning struggled last year. That much is obvious. What's less obvious is the answer to the questions of to whom are those struggles attributable, and will a year-older Eli perform well enough for several seasons to make it worth not drafting a quarterback No. 2 overall? Those are difficult to answer. In last season's annual, I projected Eli would face the seventh-most difficult schedule of pass defenses in 2017, a year after he faced the sixth-easiest. When the dust settled, Eli played the eighth-most difficult schedule of pass defenses, nearly exactly what I projected. He did so with a weak offensive line and with a rash of injuries to his receivers, so it was only natural that Eli's performance dropped off from what it was in 2016, when he had the healthiest wide receiver unit in the league and the sixth-easiest pass-defense schedule. In 2017, one of the Giants' most glaring issues was its offense's inability to go downfield. After hitting 22 completions of 20+ air yards in 2016, that number was only 12 in 2017. Eli also had 23 passes that gained 30+ yards in 2016 but just 10 in 2017. The Giants need to do a better job of protecting for Eli, to give him time and confidence in the pocket to execute the downfield passing offense better.

Eli Manning Rating All Downs

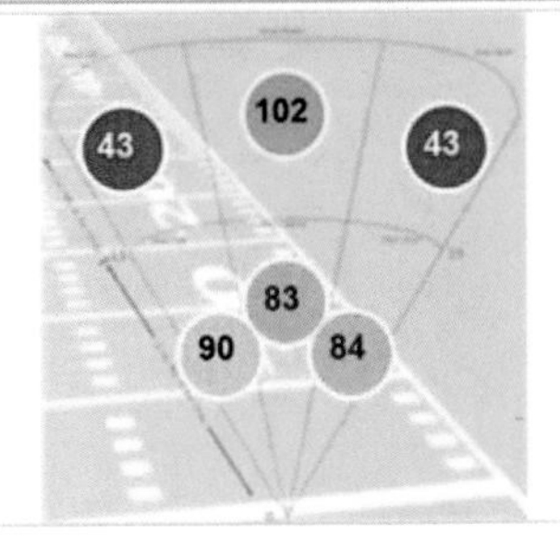

Eli Manning Rating Early Downs

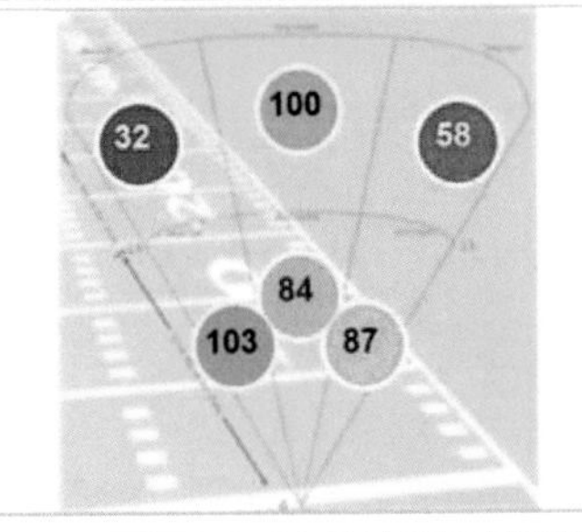

2017 Standard Passing Table

QB	Comp	Att	Comp %	Yds	YPA	TDs	INT	Sacks	Rating	Rk
Eli Manning	350	569	62%	3,461	6.1	19	13	31	80	35
NFL Avg			62%		7.0				87.5	

2017 Advanced Passing Table

QB	Success %	EDSR Passing Success %	20+ Yd Pass Gains	20+ Yd Pass %	30+ Yd Pass Gains	30+ Yd Pass %	Avg. Air Yds per Comp	Avg. YAC per Comp	20+ Air Yd Comp	20+ Air Yd %
Eli Manning	45%	51%	30	5.3%	10	1.8%	5.2	4.7	12	3%
NFL Avg	44%	48%	27.7	8.8%	10.3	3.3%	6.0	4.7	11.7	6%

Interception Rates by Down

Yards to Go	1	2	3	4	Total
1 & 2		0.0%	0.0%	0.0%	0.0%
3, 4, 5	0.0%	0.0%	2.0%	0.0%	0.9%
6 - 9	0.0%	2.4%	2.1%	0.0%	2.3%
10 - 14	2.3%	1.6%	5.7%	33.3%	3.0%
15+	9.1%	0.0%	0.0%		2.7%
Total	2.7%	1.3%	2.3%	5.9%	2.2%

3rd Down Passing - Short of Sticks Analysis

QB	Avg. Yds to Go	Avg. YIA (of Comp)	Avg Yds Short	Short of Sticks Rate	Short Rk
Eli Manning	6.9	6.8	-0.1	54%	12
NFL Avg	7.8	6.7	-1.1	60%	

Air Yds vs YAC

Air Yds %	YAC %	Rk
63%	37%	11
58%	42%	

2017 Receiving Recap & 2018 Outlook

I am extremely excited to see what Shurmur does with a passing offense, which, even in a healthy 2016 season, was a true mess under McAdoo. Shurmur's offense should be suited to flourish in '12' personnel and he a true game changer like Beckham, who often requires double teams. I'm intrigued to see if Shurmur chooses to send Beckham on deeper routes than McAdoo. Of Beckham's 221 targets, only 23% have come on deep passes, averaging a 73 rating and a 31% completion rate. The Giants need improve Beckham's depth of target numbers in order to open up things further in the run game and the shorter passes to Engram and Barkley.

Player *Min 50 Targets*	Targets	Comp %	YPA	Rating	TOARS	Success %	Success Rk	Missed YPA Rk	YAS % Rk	TDs
Evan Engram	114	55%	6.3	77	4.6	42%	107	61	71	6
Sterling Shepard	84	70%	8.7	105	4.6	58%	11	4	19	2
Roger Lewis	72	50%	5.8	48	3.5	41%	109	97	74	2

Directional Passer Rating Delivered

Receiver	Short Left	Short Middle	Short Right	Deep Left	Deep Middle	Deep Right	Player Total
Evan Engram	117	75	79	0	156	20	77
Sterling Shepard	97	127	77	96	77	52	105
Roger Lewis	73	18	55	146	0	70	48
Shane Vereen	82	86	92	40			87
Wayne Gallman	68	89	75			40	76
Odell Beckham Jr.	119	106	76	40	96	117	98
Tavarres King	142	79	98	40	110	47	97
Brandon Marshall	83	92	67	0		40	54
Rhett Ellison	81	110	127	96			116
Orleans Darkwa	85	73	68				76
Jerell Adams	89	80	67			119	98
Paul Perkins	97	56	83				86
Team Total	95	88	84	41	85	48	83

2017 Rushing Recap & 2017 Outlook

The Giants play the fourth-hardest overall schedule, but they play the most brutal schedule in the league the first seven weeks of the season. It features zero bottom-10 opponents and four top-10 opponents, plenty of whom are playoff hopefuls like the Eagles, Jaguars, Saints, Falcons, Texans, Panthers and Cowboys. This means there shouldn't be much "garbage time" rushing for Barkley. He'll have to contribute against good teams with good pass defenses. If he struggles, the team could become too one-dimensional while trying to keep pace with those opposing offenses. Barkley has the chance to be a special player in the league, and if he starts quick against tall odds, it could be a special season for the Giants.

Player *Min 50 Rushes*	Rushes	YPC	Success %	Success Rk	Missed YPA Rk	YTS % Rk	YAS % Rk	Early Down Success %	Early Down Success Rk	TDs
Orleans Darkwa	171	4.4	46%	32	13	54	31	44%	37	5
Wayne Gallman	111	4.3	50%	17	17	16	45	51%	13	0

Yards per Carry by Direction

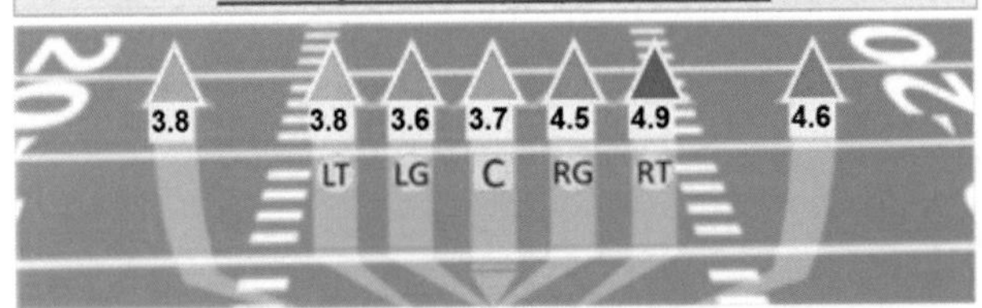

Directional Run Frequency

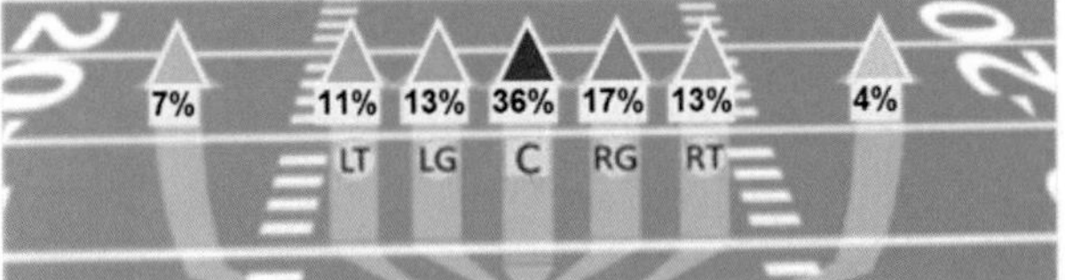

NYG-4

Another way to help protect Manning is with a strong running back. And the Giants surely believe they now have one, thanks to the drafting of Barkley second overall. But they better be more than sure. They better be absolutely 100% correct, or they burned a valuable draft pick on a replaceable position. We know that passing correlates more to wins than does rushing. It's not even a little more correlated. It's not just twice as correlated. It's many times more correlated. We also know that drafted players are essentially given slotted salaries based on draft position. So the salary the Giants are paying to rookie RB Saquan Barkley is far above most other RBs in the league. He's expected to sign a four-year deal with $31 million guaranteed and a signing bonus of just over $20 million. It will be the second-most lucrative deal for any running back in NFL history. And he hasn't played a single snap. The contract would be the same if the Giants had drafted a more valuable position, such as quarterback or an edge rusher. So not only are the Giants paying a ton for a running back without any NFL experience, but they also sacrificed a huge opportunity cost by not drafting a player who would have contributed more the passing aspect of games, which is the far more important side of the offense toward winning games.

Whether general manager Dave Gettleman refuses to believe the running back position has been devalued or not, the facts are the facts. As a result primarily of rule changes from 2010 along with teams getting more analytically informed, most teams are no longer jumping to (cont'd - see NYG-5)

Chris Raybon's Fantasy Corner

Taking a rookie in the first round of your fantasy draft — even one as polished as NCAA award-winning, Penn State record-breaking, NFL Combine destroying Saquon Barkley — isn't for the faint of heart. But Barkley should be well worth the pick. The Giants offensive line allowed the likes of Orleans Darkwa and Wayne Gallman to combine for 282 carries for 1,227 yards in 2017, with both averaging 4.3+ yards per carry, and Pat Shurmur has brought in larger (and better) reinforcements in Nate Solder and Patrick Omameh and second-round rookie Will Hernandez, who are well suited to run Shurmur's inside zone scheme, one that Barkley is familiar with from his Penn State days. Add in Barkley's 102-catch, 11.7 yard-per-catch college receiving pedigree, and you're looking at a back that could challenge for fantasy's overall RB1 if he stays healthy.

Division History: Season Wins & 2018 Projection

2014 Wins | 2015 Wins | 2016 Wins | 2017 Wins | Forecast 2018 Wins

Rank of 2018 Defensive Pass Efficiency Faced by Week

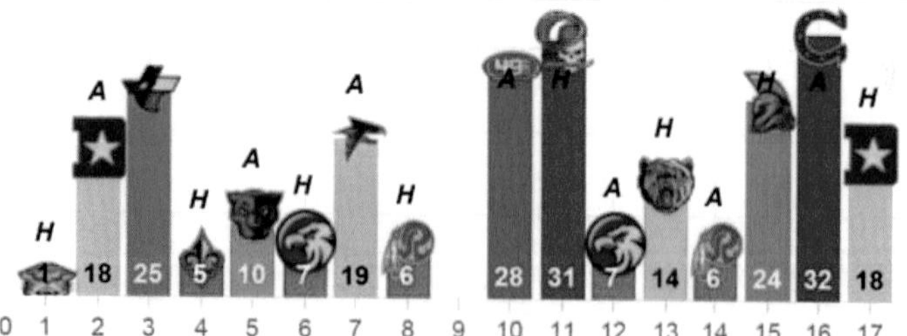

Rank of 2018 Defensive Rush Efficiency Faced by Week

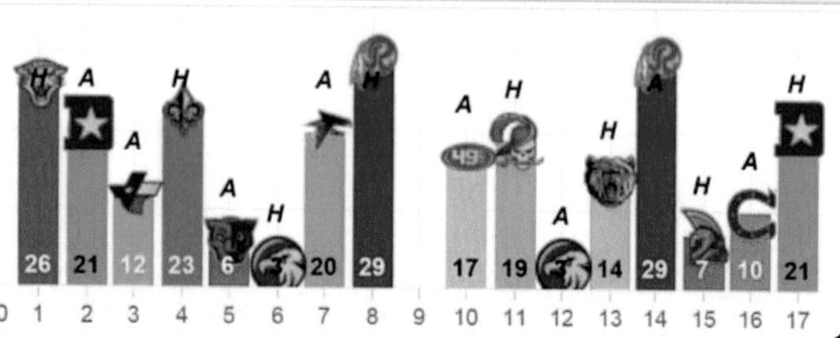

2017 Situational Usage by Player & Position

Usage Rate by Score

		Being Blown Out (14+)	Down Big (9-13)	One Score	Large Lead (9-13)	Blowout Lead (14+)	Grand Total
RUSH	Orleans Darkwa	4%	10%	20%	25%	53%	17%
	Wayne Gallman	4%	1%	14%	30%	11%	11%
	Evan Engram				5%		0%
	Shane Vereen	4%	5%	5%			5%
	Sterling Shepard	1%	1%	0%			0%
	Paul Perkins	8%	5%	3%			4%
	Odell Beckham Jr.			0%			0%
	Tavarres King			0%			0%
	Kalif Raymond			0%			0%
	Total	22%	22%	43%	60%	63%	39%
PASS	Orleans Darkwa	2%	2%	3%	5%		3%
	Wayne Gallman	4%	1%	5%	10%	5%	5%
	Evan Engram	10%	15%	12%		16%	12%
	Shane Vereen	10%	9%	4%			5%
	Sterling Shepard	17%	15%	6%			9%
	Roger Lewis	9%	7%	7%	5%	5%	7%
	Paul Perkins	1%		1%			1%
	Odell Beckham Jr.	4%	7%	4%			4%
	Tavarres King	3%	5%	4%	5%	11%	4%
	Brandon Marshall	4%	10%	3%			3%
	Rhett Ellison	5%	4%	3%	5%		3%
	Travis Rudolph	4%	1%	2%	5%		2%
	Jerell Adams	2%	1%	1%			1%
	Hunter Sharp	1%		1%	5%		1%
	Darius Powe		1%	0%			0%
	Marquis Bundy			0%			0%
	Kalif Raymond			0%			0%
	Ed Eagan	1%					0%
	Matt LaCosse			0%			0%
	Total	78%	78%	57%	40%	37%	61%

Positional Target Distribution vs NFL Average

		NFL Wide				Team Only			
		Left	Middle	Right	Total	Left	Middle	Right	Total
Deep	WR	961	500	971	2,432	25	9	16	50
	TE	182	146	177	505	10	4	11	25
	RB	38	9	41	88	1		1	2
	All	1,181	655	1,189	3,025	36	13	28	77
Short	WR	2,777	1,608	2,721	7,106	85	63	69	217
	TE	828	793	1,119	2,740	35	46	51	132
	RB	1,279	782	1,242	3,303	42	41	53	136
	All	4,884	3,183	5,082	13,149	162	150	173	485
Total		6,065	3,838	6,271	16,174	198	163	201	562

Positional Success Rates vs NFL Average

		NFL Wide				Team Only			
		Left	Middle	Right	Total	Left	Middle	Right	Total
Deep	WR	37%	45%	38%	39%	32%	44%	31%	34%
	TE	40%	52%	46%	45%	10%	75%	36%	32%
	RB	37%	56%	39%	40%	0%		0%	0%
	All	37%	47%	39%	40%	25%	54%	32%	32%
Short	WR	52%	57%	50%	52%	54%	57%	46%	53%
	TE	50%	56%	49%	51%	60%	52%	51%	54%
	RB	44%	51%	43%	45%	43%	49%	45%	46%
	All	49%	56%	48%	50%	52%	53%	47%	51%
Total		47%	54%	46%	48%	47%	53%	45%	48%

Successful Play Rate
0% — 100%

New York Giants - Success by Personnel Grouping & Play Type

Play Type	1-1 [3WR]	1-2 [2WR]	2-1 [2WR]	1-0 [4WR]	1-3 [1WR]	0-1 [4WR]	2-0 [3WR]	2-2 [1WR]	0-0 [5WR]	0-2 [3WR]	0-3 [2WR]	2-3 [0WR]	Grand Total
PASS	45% (385, 60%)	44% (73, 11%)	50% (10, 2%)	41% (126, 20%)	43% (7, 1%)	60% (10, 2%)	60% (10, 2%)	0% (3, 0%)	38% (8, 1%)	25% (4, 1%)	0% (1, 0%)	67% (3, 0%)	44% (640, 100%)
RUSH	44% (175, 44%)	48% (128, 32%)	31% (29, 7%)	13% (8, 2%)	45% (20, 5%)		14% (7, 2%)	50% (16, 4%)				80% (5, 1%)	43% (394, 100%)
TOTAL	45% (560, 54%)	46% (201, 19%)	36% (39, 4%)	40% (134, 13%)	44% (27, 3%)	60% (10, 1%)	41% (17, 2%)	42% (19, 2%)	38% (8, 1%)	25% (4, 0%)	0% (1, 0%)	75% (8, 1%)	44% (1,034, 100%)

Format Line 1: Success Rate Line 2: Total # of Plays, % of All Plays (by type)

NYG-5 break the bank on running backs. Even five years ago, the top-10 most expensive running backs hit the cap for $8.36 million. Today that number is $7.54 million. Compare that to quarterbacks, who hit the cap for $15.2 million in 2013 and now $25.5 million in 2018. The story is the same for WRs, LTs, CBs or DEs. Teams spending in the passing game. In 2016, the Giants ranked No. 32 in rushing success vs. the No. 14 strength of schedule. Their worst element was early-down running back runs. So heading into 2017, they made some small dollar roster moves to help improve their run game. And it worked. The 2017 Giants ranked No. 14 in early-down running back runs vs. the No. 20 strength of schedule. They improved their early-down success from 27th (42%) to eighth (47%) in one-score games., behind a terrible line and with a neutered passing game that was obliterated by injuries. If I told you they drafted Saquon Barkely No. 2 overall heading into 2017, you likely would correlate his arrival with that improvement. But the Giants didn't spend a No. 2 overall pick to see their run game take an astronomical leap. They simply cut aging veteran RB Rashad Jennings and drafted RB Wayne Gallman in the fourth round at No. 140 overall. They gave more carries to RB Orleans Darkwa than in 2016 (171 vs. 30) and gave Gallman 111 carries.

The moral of the story is, there are other ways to improve rushing efficiency aside from taking a running back in the top two picks of the draft. The Giants did, so now they better get their money's worth. And they can accomplish two huge objectives in terms of getting their money's worth by doing one thing offensively: throwing him the ball more often on early downs. This would enhance Barkley's contribution to the offense in terms of total efficiency provided and would keep him healthier and extend his career. As this book mentions earlier, throwing the ball to a running back on third down is the worst pass a quarterback can make. But on early downs, it's a huge matchup edge. Running backs are more likely to be injured when running through the offensive and defensive line, with 300-plus-pound linemen falling all around their lower extremities, than when catching the ball in space, where they have more time to see who is looking to hit them and facing defenders who are sized similarly, such as defensive backs or coverage linebackers. This is a legitimately smart move for a team to make if they want to add a "life extension" element to their run game as well as improve efficiency. Barkley is a freak. He's the only running back ever to weigh over 225 pounds at the combine and record a sub-4.5 forty-yard dash and at least a 38-inch vertical. Get him a significant portion of his total touches as passes in space and let him create offense and destroy defenders.

Receiving Success by Personnel Grouping

Position	Player	1-1 [3WR]	1-2 [2WR]	2-1 [2WR]	1-0 [4WR]	1-3 [1WR]	0-1 [4WR]	2-0 [3WR]	2-2 [1WR]	0-0 [5WR]	0-2 [3WR]	0-3 [2WR]	2-3 [0WR]	Total
RB	Shane Vereen	46% 5.0 87.5 (28)	67% 6.0 82.6 (3)	0% 2.0 79.2 (1)	42% 4.6 85.7 (19)					100% 7.0 95.8 (1)				46% 4.9 87.0 (52)
TE	Evan Engram	54% 7.8 107.3 (63)	44% 6.3 49.2 (16)	75% 11.5 112.5 (4)	23% 2.9 25.9 (22)	33% 2.7 109.7 (3)	0% 1.7 42.4 (3)		0% 0.0 0.0 (1)			0% 0.0 39.6 (1)	0% 0.0 39.6 (1)	44% 6.3 77.2 (114)
	Rhett Ellison	53% 6.6 88.6 (17)	78% 10.2 109.3 (9)		100% 9.0 104.2 (1)		100% 13.0 118.8 (1)			0% 0.0 39.6 (1)	100% 5.0 87.5 (1)		100% 1.5 118.8 (2)	66% 7.3 116.0 (32)
WR	Sterling Shepard	57% 9.3 115.9 (51)	60% 10.2 94.6 (5)	100% 6.0 91.7 (1)	65% 10.3 108.7 (17)	0% 0.0 39.6 (1)	67% 5.3 79.9 (3)	0% 0.0 39.6 (1)		67% 3.3 71.5 (3)	0% 0.0 39.6 (2)			57% 8.7 104.8 (84)
	Roger Lewis	44% 5.9 64.9 (48)	33% 3.0 42.4 (3)		33% 4.9 29.4 (18)			50% 17.0 95.8 (2)		0% 0.0 0.0 (1)				40% 5.8 48.1 (72)
	Odell Beckham Jr.	42% 7.3 99.8 (26)	50% 6.0 68.8 (6)		86% 8.4 101.8 (7)		100% 4.0 83.3 (1)	100% 13.0 118.8 (1)						54% 7.4 97.8 (41)

Format Line 1: Success Rate Line 2: YPA Line 3: Passer Rating Line 4: Total # of Plays

Successful Play Rate
0% — 100%

Rushing Success by Personnel Grouping

Position	Player	1-1 [3WR]	1-2 [2WR]	2-1 [2WR]	1-0 [4WR]	1-3 [1WR]	2-0 [3WR]	2-2 [1WR]	2-3 [0WR]	Total
RB	Orleans Darkwa	46% 5.8 (46)	49% 4.5 (70)	18% 1.6 (17)	0% -4.0 (1)	47% 3.0 (17)	33% 4.0 (3)	58% 6.6 (12)	80% 1.0 (5)	46% 4.4 (171)
	Wayne Gallman	48% 4.3 (60)	56% 4.8 (41)	67% 4.3 (3)	0% 1.0 (1)	0% 2.5 (2)	0% -1.0 (1)	33% 0.3 (3)		50% 4.3 (111)
	Shane Vereen	49% 4.0 (37)	33% 0.7 (3)		0% 4.0 (3)		0% 0.5 (2)			42% 3.6 (45)

Format Line 1: Success Rate Line 2: YPC Line 3: Total # of Plays

2018 Coaches

Head Coach:
Todd Bowles (4th yr)

Offensive Coordinator:
Jeremy Bates (NYJ QB) (1st yr)

Defensive Coordinator:
Kacy Rodgers (3rd yr)

EASY HARD

2018 Forecast

Wins	Div Rank
6	#4

Past Records

2017: 5-11
2016: 5-11
2015: 10-6

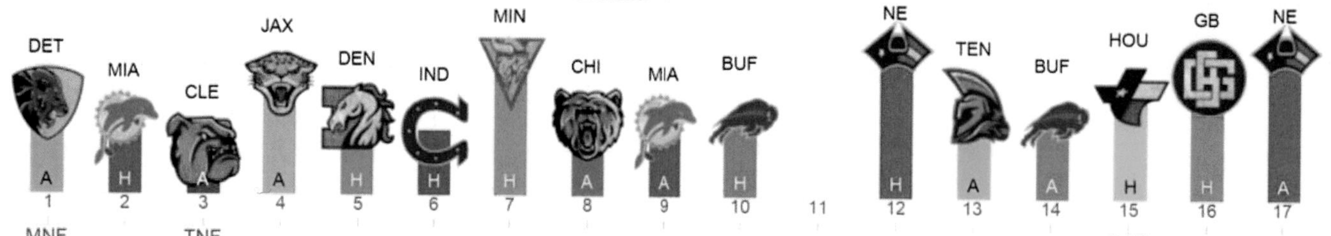

Key Players Lost

TXN	Player (POS)
Cut	Langford, Jeremy RB
	Marshall, Jalin WR
	Petty, Bryce QB
	Wilkerson, Muhammad DE
Declared Free Agent	Bass, David LB
	Brooks, Terrence S
	Carter, Bruce LB
	Claiborne, Morris CB
	Cooper, Xavier DE
	Davis, Demario LB
	Dozier, Dakota G
	Ealy, Kony DE
	Harrison, Jonotthan C
	Johnson, Wesley C
	Pennel, Mike DT
	Seferian-Jenkins, Austin TE
	Stanford, Julian LB
Retired	Forte, Matt RB
	Mangold, Nick C

Average Line	# Games Favored	# Games Underdog
3.6	4	11

Regular Season Wins: Past & Current Proj

2018 New York Jets Overview

One problem for the Jets last season was their inability to hold onto leads coupled with their inability to mount comebacks. The Jets trailed at halftime in only seven of their 16 games last year. But they never lost by fewer points than they were down at halftime. They were unable to mount comebacks of any kind. Routinely, one-point halftime deficits grew to nine-point losses, or 11-point halftime deficits grew to 25-point losses. The glass-half-full way to look at their halftime margins was that in nine of their 16 games they didn't trail at halftime. Yet they lost four of the nine games, including multiple blown halftime leads.

In the first half of games, the Jets produced a 45% passing success rate (13th) and a 35% rushing success rate (31st). In the second half, their passing success dropped to 38% (28th) while their rushing success increased slightly to 41% (26th), as it is easier to run the football when trailing and the opponent is playing pass. Defensively, the Jets' pass defense was their biggest problem in these second halves. They held opponents to a 41% passing success rate (8th) in the first half, but that dropped to 47% (25th) in the second half. Their rushing defense improved, from 44% success allowed in the first half to 40% (6th) in the second half.

What was happening on both sides of the ball to cause the Jets to become unable to mount comebacks and hold onto leads in the second half of games? If you want to ensure you lose a game you're trailing, take some notes from what the Jets did in 2017. Despite trailing, the Jets went run on nearly 50% of their first downs (47%) and produced a 36% success rate when doing so. The NFL average when trailing in the second half was 63% pass. But, more importantly, no team ran the ball more with anywhere near the terrible 36% success rate like the Jets produced. The Falcons and Rams ran it slightly more than the Jets, but they produced 55% and 66% success rates when running, respectively. Meanwhile, the Jets were successful on 54% of their first-down passes and produced 7.2 YPA (versus 3.7 YPC), so their efficiency was really stunted by this decision.

The result of such terrible first-down decision-making was that the Jets were successful on just 34% of their second-down plays in these second-half situations, the third-worst success rate in the NFL.

(cont'd - see NYJ2)

Key Free Agents/ Trades Added

Anderson, Henry DT
Bridgewater, Teddy QB
Crowell, Isaiah RB
Hewitt, Neville LB
Johnson, Trumaine CB
Minter, Kevin LB
Pryor Sr., Terrelle WR
Rawls, Thomas RB
Roberts, Andre WR
Swanson, Travis C

Drafted Players

Rd	Pk	Player (College)
1	3	QB - Sam Darnold (USC)
3	72	DT - Nathan Shepherd (Fort Hays State)
4	107	TE - Chris Herndon (Miami (FL))
	179	CB - Parry Nickerson (Tulane)
6	180	DT - Folorunso Fatukasi (Connecticut)
	204	RB - Trenton Cannon (Virginia State)

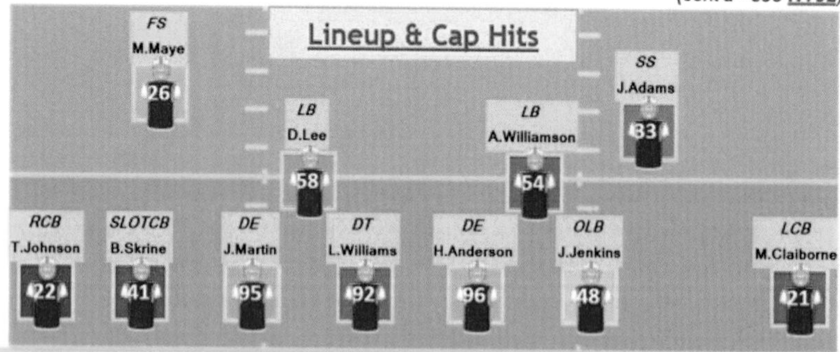

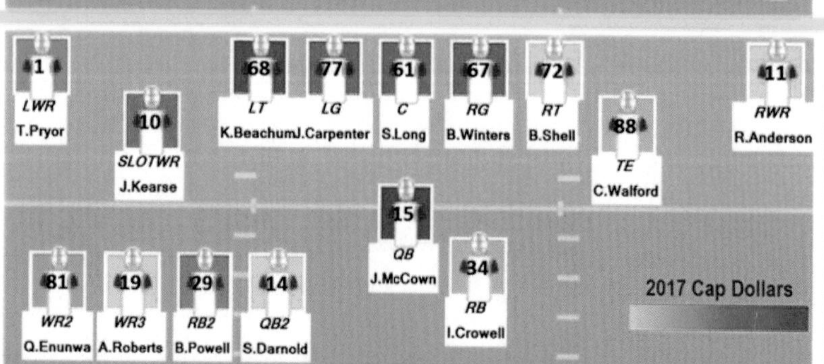

2018 Unit Spending

All DEF
All OFF

Positional Spending

	Rank	Total	2017 Rk
All OFF	14	$94.14M	27
QB	21	$16.48M	25
OL	7	$40.38M	8
RB	13	$8.70M	7
WR	14	$23.78M	16
TE	25	$4.81M	31
All DEF	15	$81.64M	16
DL	24	$19.89M	7
LB	19	$19.40M	23
CB	2	$30.26M	15
S	17	$12.09M	32

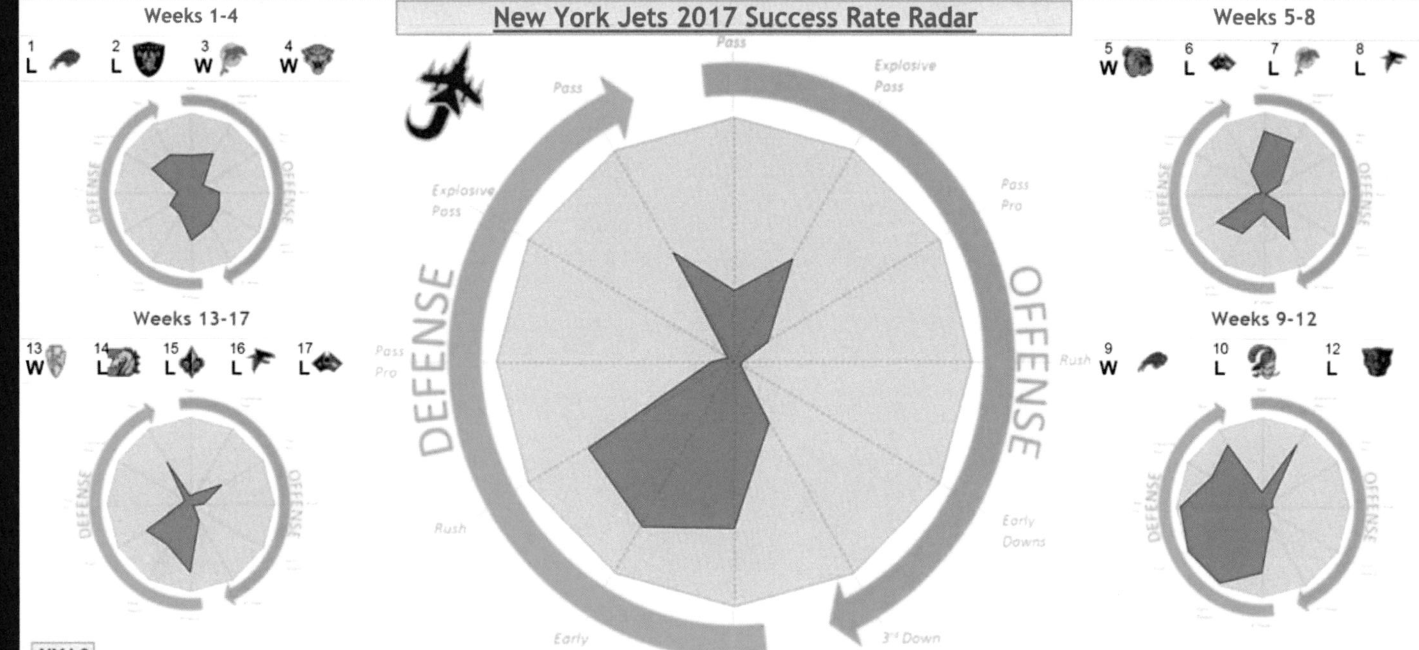

NYJ-2

And thus, on third down, except for a couple passes from 12 personnel, the Jets went 11 personnel on over 91% of their snaps and produced a 24% success rate. While the Jets trailed at halftime in just seven games, they led the league in punts when trailing in the second half. That's not a stat you want to lead the league in. The Jets had 31 punts in the second half of games when trailing, more than the 0-16 Browns. This was because of their terrible play-calling and execution in the second half when trailing. Of their 61 drives when trailing in the second half, nearly 75 of them ended with a punt, turnover, by the clock running out, on downs, or by a safety. Further, the Jets lost a lot of leads because of their predictability. They called run plays on first down on 83% of their plays, the second-most in the league. As a result, they had 8.4 yards to go on average on second down. The Jets' success rate on those second downs with a lead was only 26%, worst in the NFL and well below the 41% league average. Part of the reason was the Jets running way more than league average on second down following a first-down run; those second-down rushes were successful just 23% of the time, the worst in the NFL. They tried to burn the clock, but it was woefully unsuccessful. And it put them in a big hole on third down. As such, the Jets need to be much more intelligent with their second-half play-calling, with or without a lead, under new OC Jeremy Bates. While the Jets suggest that third overall selection Sam Darnold is third on the depth chart, I would be shocked if he doesn't work his way up to No. 1 by the start of the season. Will he be a "better" QB than Josh McCown in their Week 1 game against Detroit? Likely not. But this is where the team-building philosophy must kick in.

Since the 2011 CBA introduced fifth-year options, as well as a slotted salary making it easier to sign and pay rookies a more universally consistent amount, the teams winning Super Bowls are those with QBs on rookie deals or other QBs taking far less than their true market value. Look at the past six Super Bowls: Carson Wentz, Russell Wilson, and Joe Flacco were all QBs who led their team to the Super Bowl despite being on their rookie deals.

(cont'd - see NYJ-3)

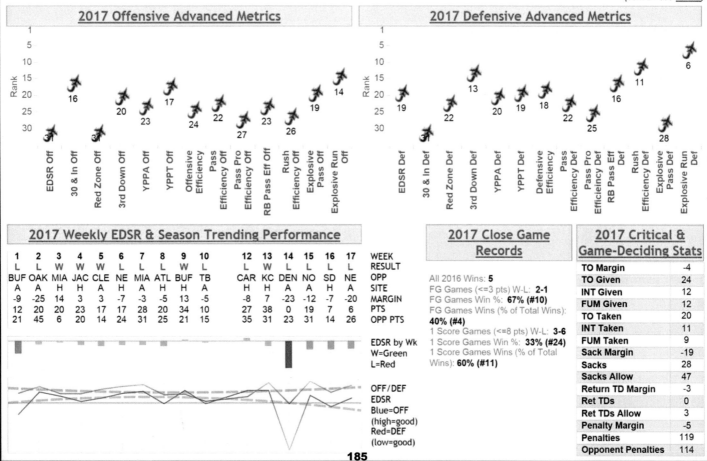

2017 Offensive Advanced Metrics

Metric	Rank
EDSR Off	3[illegible]
30 & In Off	16
Red Zone Off	3[illegible]
3rd Down Off	20
YPPA Off	23
YPPT Off	17
Offensive Efficiency	24
Pass Efficiency Off	22
Pass Pro Efficiency Off	27
RB Pass Eff Off	23
Rush Efficiency Off	26
Explosive Pass Off	19
Explosive Run Off	14

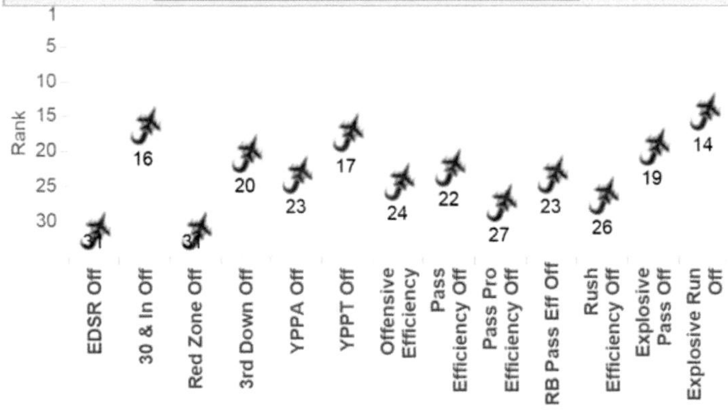

2017 Defensive Advanced Metrics

Metric	Rank
EDSR Def	19
30 & In Def	3[illegible]
Red Zone Def	22
3rd Down Def	13
YPPA Def	20
YPPT Def	19
Defensive Efficiency	18
Pass Efficiency Def	22
Pass Pro Efficieincy Def	25
RB Pass Eff Def	16
Rush Efficiency Def	11
Explosive Pass Def	28
Explosive Run Def	6

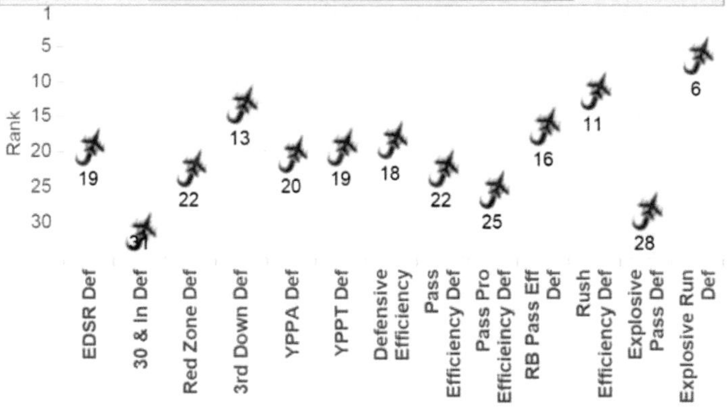

2017 Weekly EDSR & Season Trending Performance

WEEK	1	2	3	4	5	6	7	8	9	10	12	13	14	15	16	17
RESULT	L	L	W	W	W	L	L	L	W	L	L	W	L	L	L	L
OPP	BUF	OAK	MIA	JAC	CLE	NE	MIA	ATL	BUF	TB	CAR	KC	DEN	NO	SD	NE
SITE	A	A	H	H	A	H	A	H	H	A	H	H	A	A	H	A
MARGIN	-9	-25	14	3	3	-7	-3	-5	13	-5	-8	7	-23	-12	-7	-20
PTS	12	20	20	23	17	17	28	20	34	10	27	38	0	19	7	6
OPP PTS	21	45	6	20	14	24	31	25	21	15	35	31	23	31	14	26

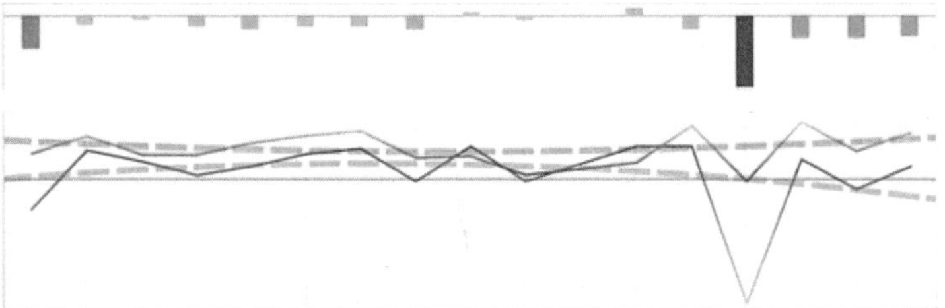

EDSR by Wk
W=Green
L=Red

OFF/DEF EDSR
Blue=OFF (high=good)
Red=DEF (low=good)

2017 Close Game Records

All 2016 Wins: **5**
FG Games (<=3 pts) W-L: **2-1**
FG Games Win %: **67% (#10)**
FG Games Wins (% of Total Wins): **40% (#4)**
1 Score Games (<=8 pts) W-L: **3-6**
1 Score Games Win %: **33% (#24)**
1 Score Games Wins (% of Total Wins): **60% (#11)**

2017 Critical & Game-Deciding Stats

TO Margin	-4
TO Given	24
INT Given	12
FUM Given	12
TO Taken	20
INT Taken	11
FUM Taken	9
Sack Margin	-19
Sacks	28
Sacks Allow	47
Return TD Margin	-3
Ret TDs	0
Ret TDs Allow	3
Penalty Margin	-5
Penalties	119
Opponent Penalties	114

New York Jets 2018 Strength of Schedule In Detail (compared to 2017)

HARD / EASY — Average Opponent RANK

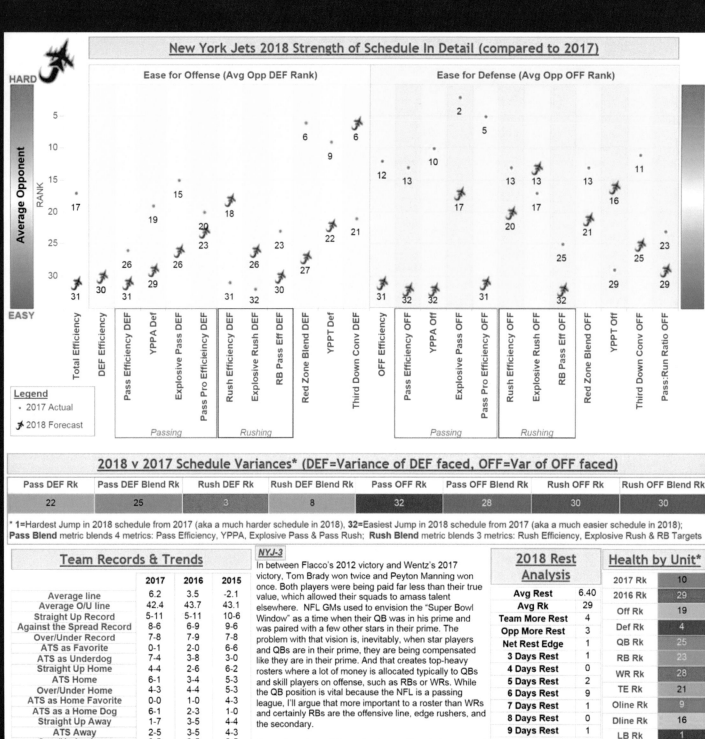

Ease for Offense (Avg Opp DEF Rank)

Metric	Group	2017 Actual	2018 Forecast
Total Efficiency		17	31
DEF Efficiency			30
Pass Efficiency DEF	Passing	26	31
YPPA Def	Passing	19	29
Explosive Pass DEF	Passing	15	26
Pass Pro Efficiency DEF	Passing	20	23
Rush Efficiency DEF	Rushing	31	18
Explosive Rush DEF	Rushing	32	26
RB Pass Eff DEF	Rushing	23	30
Red Zone Blend DEF		6	27
YPPT Def		9	22
Third Down Conv DEF		21	6

Ease for Defense (Avg Opp OFF Rank)

Metric	Group	2017 Actual	2018 Forecast
OFF Efficiency		12	31
Pass Efficiency OFF	Passing	13	32
YPPA Off	Passing	10	32
Explosive Pass OFF	Passing	2	17
Pass Pro Efficiency OFF	Passing	5	31
Rush Efficiency OFF	Rushing	13	20
Explosive Rush OFF	Rushing	17	13
RB Pass Eff OFF	Rushing	25	32
Red Zone Blend OFF		13	21
YPPT Off		29	16
Third Down Conv OFF		11	25
Pass:Run Ratio OFF		23	29

Legend
- 2017 Actual
- 2018 Forecast

2018 v 2017 Schedule Variances* (DEF=Variance of DEF faced, OFF=Var of OFF faced)

Pass DEF Rk	Pass DEF Blend Rk	Rush DEF Rk	Rush DEF Blend Rk	Pass OFF Rk	Pass OFF Blend Rk	Rush OFF Rk	Rush OFF Blend Rk
22	25	3	8	32	28	30	30

* **1**=Hardest Jump in 2018 schedule from 2017 (aka a much harder schedule in 2018), **32**=Easiest Jump in 2018 schedule from 2017 (aka a much easier schedule in 2018); **Pass Blend** metric blends 4 metrics: Pass Efficiency, YPPA, Explosive Pass & Pass Rush; **Rush Blend** metric blends 3 metrics: Rush Efficiency, Explosive Rush & RB Targets

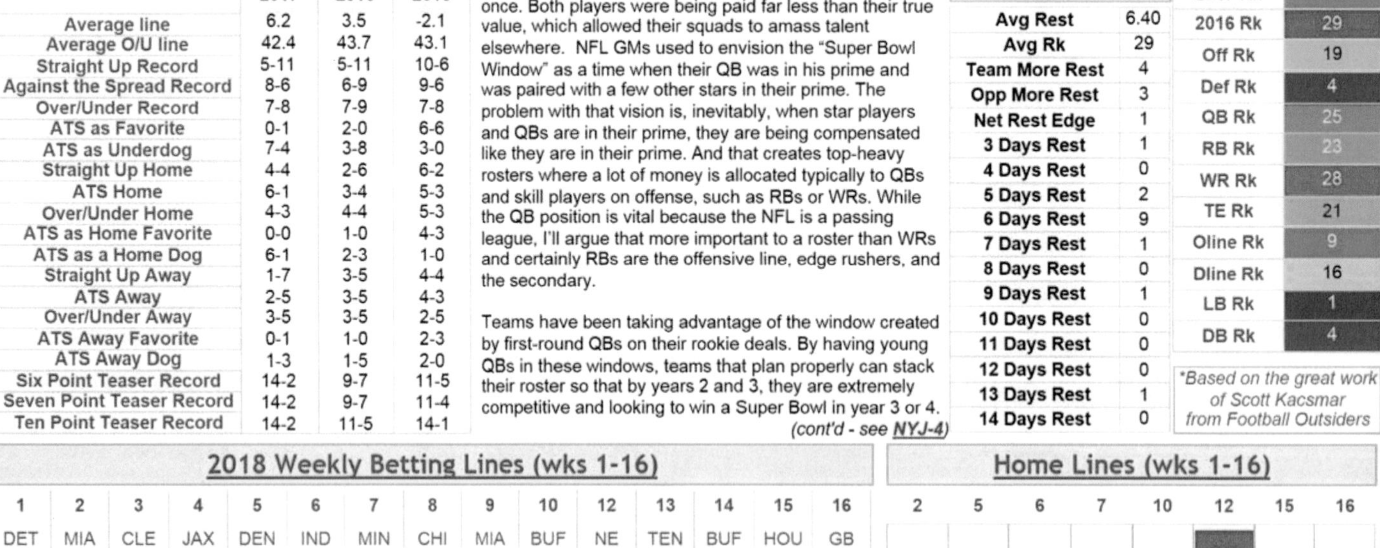

Team Records & Trends

	2017	2016	2015
Average line	6.2	3.5	-2.1
Average O/U line	42.4	43.7	43.1
Straight Up Record	5-11	5-11	10-6
Against the Spread Record	8-6	6-9	9-6
Over/Under Record	7-8	7-9	7-8
ATS as Favorite	0-1	2-0	6-6
ATS as Underdog	7-4	3-8	3-0
Straight Up Home	4-4	2-6	6-2
ATS Home	6-1	3-4	5-3
Over/Under Home	4-3	4-4	5-3
ATS as Home Favorite	0-0	1-0	4-3
ATS as a Home Dog	6-1	2-3	1-0
Straight Up Away	1-7	3-5	4-4
ATS Away	2-5	3-5	4-3
Over/Under Away	3-5	3-5	2-5
ATS Away Favorite	0-1	1-0	2-3
ATS Away Dog	1-3	1-5	2-0
Six Point Teaser Record	14-2	9-7	11-5
Seven Point Teaser Record	14-2	9-7	11-4
Ten Point Teaser Record	14-2	11-5	14-1

NYJ-3

In between Flacco's 2012 victory and Wentz's 2017 victory, Tom Brady won twice and Peyton Manning won once. Both players were being paid far less than their true value, which allowed their squads to amass talent elsewhere. NFL GMs used to envision the "Super Bowl Window" as a time when their QB was in his prime and was paired with a few other stars in their prime. The problem with that vision is, inevitably, when star players and QBs are in their prime, they are being compensated like they are in their prime. And that creates top-heavy rosters where a lot of money is allocated typically to QBs and skill players on offense, such as RBs or WRs. While the QB position is vital because the NFL is a passing league, I'll argue that more important to a roster than WRs and certainly RBs are the offensive line, edge rushers, and the secondary.

Teams have been taking advantage of the window created by first-round QBs on their rookie deals. By having young QBs in these windows, teams that plan properly can stack their roster so that by years 2 and 3, they are extremely competitive and looking to win a Super Bowl in year 3 or 4.

(cont'd - see NYJ-4)

2018 Rest Analysis

Avg Rest	6.40
Avg Rk	29
Team More Rest	4
Opp More Rest	3
Net Rest Edge	1
3 Days Rest	1
4 Days Rest	0
5 Days Rest	2
6 Days Rest	9
7 Days Rest	1
8 Days Rest	0
9 Days Rest	1
10 Days Rest	0
11 Days Rest	0
12 Days Rest	0
13 Days Rest	1
14 Days Rest	0

Health by Unit*

2017 Rk	10
2016 Rk	29
Off Rk	19
Def Rk	4
QB Rk	25
RB Rk	23
WR Rk	28
TE Rk	21
Oline Rk	9
Dline Rk	16
LB Rk	1
DB Rk	4

*Based on the great work of Scott Kacsmar from Football Outsiders

2018 Weekly Betting Lines (wks 1-16)

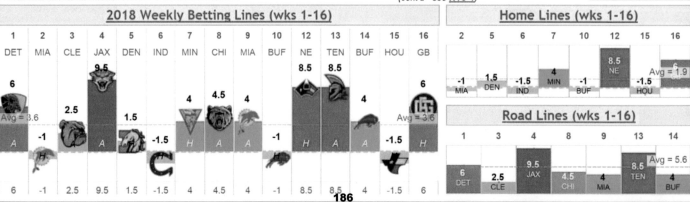

Week	1	2	3	4	5	6	7	8	9	10	12	13	14	15	16
Opponent	DET	MIA	CLE	JAX	DEN	IND	MIN	CHI	MIA	BUF	NE	TEN	BUF	HOU	GB
Site	A	H	A	A	H	H	H	A	A	H	H	A	A	H	H
Line	6	-1	2.5	9.5	1.5	-1.5	4	4.5	4	-1	8.5	8.5	4	-1.5	6

Avg = 3.6

Home Lines (wks 1-16)

Week	2	5	6	7	10	12	15	16
Opponent	MIA	DEN	IND	MIN	BUF	NE	HOU	GB
Line	-1	1.5	-1.5	4	-1	8.5	-1.5	6

Avg = 1.9

Road Lines (wks 1-16)

Week	1	3	4	8	9	13	14
Opponent	DET	CLE	JAX	CHI	MIA	TEN	BUF
Line	6	2.5	9.5	4.5	4	8.5	4

Avg = 5.6

New York Jets 2017 Play Analysis

2017 Play Tendencies

All Pass %	57%
All Pass Rk	18
All Rush %	43%
All Rush Rk	15
1 Score Pass %	56%
1 Score Pass Rk	20
2016 1 Score Pass %	54%
2016 1 Score Pass Rk	26
2017 Pass Increase %	2%
Pass Increase Rk	8
1 Score Rush %	44%
1 Score Rush Rk	13
Up Pass %	44%
Up Pass Rk	28
Up Rush %	56%
Up Rush Rk	5
Down Pass %	62%
Down Pass Rk	28
Down Rush %	38%
Down Rush Rk	5

2017 Down & Distance Tendencies

Down	Distance	Total Plays	Pass Rate	Run Rate	Play Success %
1	Short (1-3)	4	25%	75%	50%
	Med (4-7)	3	0%	100%	33%
	Long (8-10)	282	39%	61%	44%
	XL (11+)	15	47%	53%	20%
2	Short (1-3)	33	39%	61%	58%
	Med (4-7)	63	54%	46%	40%
	Long (8-10)	95	63%	37%	40%
	XL (11+)	47	66%	34%	36%
3	Short (1-3)	42	64%	36%	40%
	Med (4-7)	49	86%	14%	51%
	Long (8-10)	37	89%	11%	24%
	XL (11+)	36	72%	28%	25%
4	Short (1-3)	4	50%	50%	50%
	XL (11+)	1	100%	0%	100%

Shotgun %:

Under Center	Shotgun
45%	55%
37% AVG	*63%*

Run Rate:

Under Center	Shotgun
69%	23%
68% AVG	*23%*

Pass Rate:

Under Center	Shotgun
31%	77%
32% AVG	*77%*

Short Yardage Intelligence:

2nd and Short Run

Run Freq	Run Rk	NFL Run Freq Avg	Run 1D Rate	Run NFL 1D Avg
53%	29	67%	56%	69%

2nd and Short Pass

Pass Freq	Pass Rk	NFL Pass Freq Avg	Pass 1D Rate	Pass NFL 1D Avg
47%	4	33%	43%	53%

Most Frequent Play

Down	Distance	Play Type	Player	Total Plays	Play Success %
1	Med (4-7)	RUSH	Matt Forte	2	50%
	XL (11+)	RUSH	Elijah McGuire	3	0%
2	Short (1-3)	RUSH	Matt Forte	6	67%
	XL (11+)	PASS	Robby Anderson	8	50%
		RUSH	Matt Forte	8	25%
3	Long (8-10)	PASS	Robby Anderson	9	22%

Most Successful Play*

Down	Distance	Play Type	Player	Total Plays	Play Success %
1	Long (8-10)	PASS	Elijah McGuire	5	80%
2	Short (1-3)	RUSH	Elijah McGuire	5	80%
	Med (4-7)	PASS	Robby Anderson	7	71%
	Long (8-10)	PASS	Robby Anderson	17	53%
	XL (11+)	PASS	Jermaine Kearse	8	75%
3	Short (1-3)	RUSH	Bilal Powell	10	50%
	Med (4-7)	PASS	Jeremy Kerley	8	75%
	Long (8-10)	PASS	Austin Seferian-Jenkins	5	40%
	XL (11+)	PASS	Robby Anderson	5	40%

*Minimum 5 plays to qualify

2017 Snap Rates

Wk	Opp	Score	Jermaine Kearse	Robby Anderson	Austin Seferian-J..	Eric Tomlinson	Bilal Powell	Matt Forte	Chad Hansen	Jeremy Kerley
1	BUF	L 21-12	55 (95%)	57 (98%)		13 (22%)	30 (52%)	35 (60%)	12 (21%)	
2	OAK	L 45-20	49 (88%)	44 (79%)			18 (32%)	27 (48%)	2 (4%)	44 (79%)
3	MIA	W 20-6	44 (70%)	49 (78%)	48 (76%)		28 (44%)	23 (37%)		34 (54%)
4	JAC	W 23-20	67 (96%)	55 (79%)	54 (77%)	29 (41%)	46 (66%)		1 (1%)	46 (66%)
5	CLE	W 17-14	47 (89%)	39 (74%)	44 (83%)	20 (38%)	17 (32%)		2 (4%)	36 (68%)
6	NE	L 24-17	61 (80%)	58 (76%)	58 (76%)	33 (43%)		44 (58%)	11 (14%)	47 (62%)
7	MIA	L 31-28	51 (91%)	45 (80%)	42 (75%)	34 (61%)	21 (38%)	28 (50%)	6 (11%)	29 (52%)
8	ATL	L 25-20	52 (85%)	54 (89%)	55 (90%)	27 (44%)	29 (48%)	29 (48%)	9 (15%)	35 (57%)
9	BUF	W 34-21	56 (84%)	50 (75%)	44 (66%)	45 (67%)	15 (22%)	32 (48%)	32 (48%)	6 (9%)
10	TB	L 15-10	66 (96%)	56 (81%)	58 (84%)	20 (29%)	33 (48%)		48 (70%)	
12	CAR	L 35-27	58 (83%)	57 (81%)	59 (84%)	28 (40%)	23 (33%)	29 (41%)	27 (39%)	
13	KC	W 38-31	74 (81%)	62 (68%)	58 (64%)	43 (47%)	37 (41%)	35 (38%)	48 (53%)	
14	DEN	L 23-0	44 (88%)	34 (68%)	35 (70%)	17 (34%)	23 (46%)	26 (52%)	35 (70%)	
15	NO	L 31-19	48 (65%)	59 (80%)	57 (77%)	30 (41%)	24 (32%)	28 (38%)	35 (47%)	
16	LAC	L 14-7	57 (88%)	61 (94%)	43 (66%)	38 (58%)	27 (42%)	27 (42%)	26 (40%)	
17	NE	L 26-6	49 (83%)	33 (56%)		32 (54%)	30 (51%)		47 (80%)	
Grand Total			878 (85%)	813 (78%)	655 (76%)	409 (44%)	401 (42%)	363 (47%)	341 (34%)	277 (56%)

Personnel Groupings

Personnel	Team %	NFL Avg	Succ. %
1-1 [3WR]	63%	59%	41%
1-2 [2WR]	17%	19%	46%
2-1 [2WR]	6%	7%	37%
2-2 [1WR]	6%	4%	23%
1-3 [1WR]	5%	5%	26%

Grouping Tendencies

Personnel	Pass Rate	Pass Succ. %	Run Succ. %
1-1 [3WR]	67%	40%	43%
1-2 [2WR]	47%	56%	37%
2-1 [2WR]	37%	43%	33%
2-2 [1WR]	24%	33%	19%
1-3 [1WR]	28%	8%	32%

Red Zone Targets (min 3)

Receiver	All	Inside 5	6-10	11-20
Austin Seferian-Jenki..	11	6	2	3
Robby Anderson	10	1	4	5
Jermaine Kearse	8	2	1	5
Bilal Powell	6	1	3	2
Matt Forte	5	1	1	3

Red Zone Rushes (min 3)

Rusher	All	Inside 5	6-10	11-20
Bilal Powell	20	9	4	7
Matt Forte	11	4	3	4
Josh McCown	8	4	2	2
Elijah McGuire	7	1	2	4

Early Down Target Rate

RB	TE	WR
21%	21%	57%
23%	*21% NFL AVG*	*56%*

Overall Target Success %

RB	TE	WR
42% #23	45% #27	48% #14

New York Jets 2017 Passing Recap & 2018 Outlook

Considering the challenges he faced, including WR injuries, poor line protection, and subpar play-calling, Josh McCown did a great job with the Jets. They exceeded expectations heading into the season, as their five wins pushed on the opening win total but won as the total was bet down to 4.5 and ultimately four. They were favored in just one game to start the season. McCown exceeded the NFL average in YPA, passer rating, completion rate, and percentage of passes that gained 20-plus yards. And he was deadly down the deep right sideline, whether it was to Jermaine Kearse (5/9, 19.4 YPA, 3:0 TD:INT) or Robby Anderson (8/17, 16.8 YPA, 6:1 TD:INT). Unfortunately, the Jets didn't make any hay throwing deep middle or deep left. Their 2018 schedule features worse pass rushes and worse pass defenses, so things could come easier. I'm hoping Darnold makes an early appearance into the starting lineup, but that's no knock on McCown. The main thing Darnold needs to focus on is his decision-making. Whether it's interceptions or ball security in the pocket, it seemed like Darnold was thinking two steps ahead and relying on his talent, rather than taking a pragmatic approach with more attention to what the defense was doing.

Josh McCown Rating All Downs

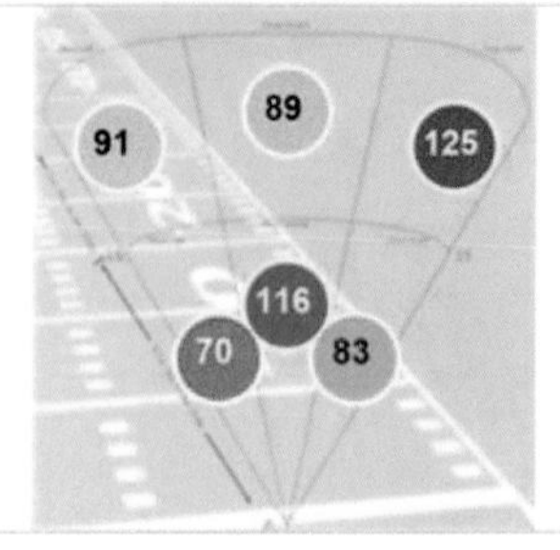

Josh McCown Rating Early Downs

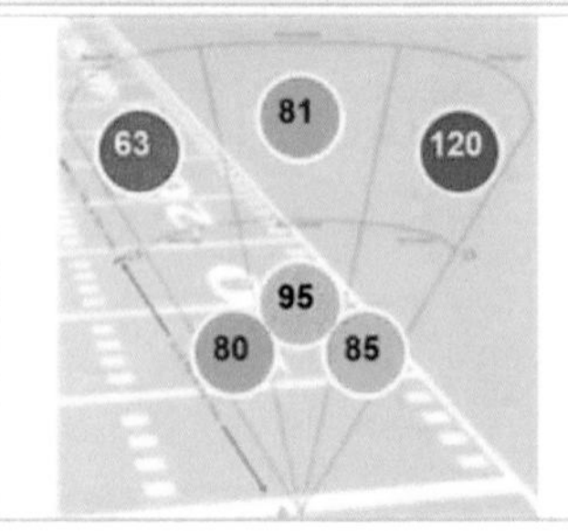

2017 Standard Passing Table

QB	Comp	Att	Comp %	Yds	YPA	TDs	INT	Sacks	Rating	Rk
Josh McCown	262	393	67%	2,886	7.3	18	9	38	94	17
Bryce Petty	54	109	50%	539	4.9	1	3	8	56	56
NFL Avg			62%		7.0				87.5	

2017 Advanced Passing Table

QB	Success %	EDSR Passing Success %	20+ Yd Pass Gains	20+ Yd Pass %	30+ Yd Pass Gains	30+ Yd Pass %	Avg. Air Yds per Comp	Avg. YAC per Comp	20+ Air Yd Comp	20+ Air Yd %
Josh McCown	44%	47%	40	10.1%	17	4.3%	5.8	4.8	18	7%
Bryce Petty	31%	42%	5	4.5%	3	2.7%	5.0	4.4	3	5%
NFL Avg	44%	48%	27.7	8.8%	10.3	3.3%	6.0	4.7	11.7	6%

Interception Rates by Down

Yards to Go	1	2	3	4	Total
1 & 2	0.0%	0.0%	0.0%	100.0%	3.3%
3, 4, 5	0.0%	0.0%	2.7%	0.0%	1.6%
6 - 9	0.0%	2.1%	4.9%	0.0%	3.3%
10 - 14	1.6%	1.8%	0.0%	0.0%	1.4%
15+	0.0%	6.3%	0.0%	0.0%	2.6%
Total	1.4%	2.0%	2.2%	16.7%	2.1%

3rd Down Passing - Short of Sticks Analysis

QB	Avg. Yds to Go	Avg. YIA (of Comp)	Avg Yds Short	Short of Sticks Rate	Short Rk
Josh McCown	7.6	6.6	-1.0	62%	20
NFL Avg	7.8	6.7	-1.1	60%	

Air Yds vs YAC

Air Yds %	YAC %	Rk
56%	44%	26
58%	42%	

2017 Receiving Recap & 2018 Outlook

Jermaine Kearse had the best success rate on the team (51%), and Robby Anderson showed explosion with his 8.3 YPA. But neither player was imposing enough to cause a defense to adjust or worry too much about the Jets' approach to their attack. Both players are back, and no new talent is really going to contend for a starter position. Quincy Enunwa is attempting a comeback after missing the entire 2017 season with a neck injury. Clive Walford is a new addition but was very unproductive in Oakland in his three years there. There is little quality depth behind Walford, however, so he'll have a big opportunity to contribute.

Player *Min 50 Targets*	Targets	Comp %	YPA	Rating	TOARS	Success %	Success Rk	Missed YPA Rk	YAS % Rk	TDs
Robby Anderson	114	55%	8.3	85	4.7	43%	100	82	27	7
Jermaine Kearse	102	64%	7.9	92	4.7	51%	49	31	88	5
Austin Seferian-Jenkins	74	68%	4.8	92	4.1	44%	97	48	127	3

Directional Passer Rating Delivered

Receiver	Short Left	Short Middle	Short Right	Deep Left	Deep Middle	Deep Right	Player Total
Robby Anderson	51	95	57	91	91	108	85
Jermaine Kearse	74	123	95	6	0	140	92
Austin Seferian-Jenki..	83	96	95	40	110	96	92
Matt Forte	92	147	72	40			100
Bilal Powell	51	65	104	40			67
Jeremy Kerley	92	107	86	158		72	114
Elijah McGuire	75	116	92			96	98
Neal Sterling	69	104	62		96		79
Charone Peake		79					79
Team Total	76	113	79	75	58	122	91

2017 Rushing Recap & 2017 Outlook

With Matt Forte gone, it appears that Bilal Powell, the leading rusher in 2017, will be bypassed by acquisition Isaiah Crowell. For a second straight year, Crowell was more of a hit-or-miss rusher who would occasionally break off big chunk rushes to elevate his YAC. But out of the 22 rushers with 200-plus carries, Crowell ranked second-worst in success rate in 2017 (40%). This was very similar to his 2016 season, where he was successful on just 39% of his rushes, ranking last out of 27 RBs with 150 carries. But because he was second-best in YAS% (explosiveness), he was able to post an impressive 4.8 YPC. The problem with such a rushing style is it's not dependable, making it valuable only when rushing in +EV situations.

Player *Min 50 Rushes*	Rushes	YPC	Success %	Success Rk	Missed YPA Rk	YTS % Rk	YAS % Rk	Early Down Success %	Early Down Success Rk	TDs
Bilal Powell	178	4.3	35%	69	71	74	5	34%	69	5
Matt Forte	103	3.7	41%	56	52	22	69	42%	49	2
Elijah McGuire	88	3.6	33%	72	75	61	18	32%	73	1

Yards per Carry by Direction

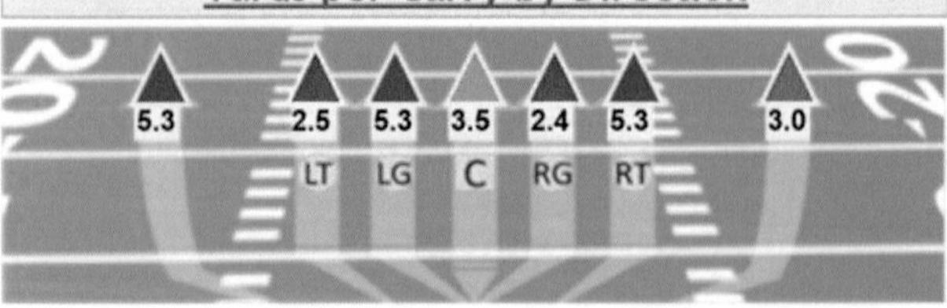

Directional Run Frequency

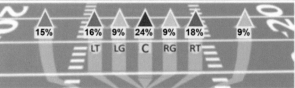

15% | 16% | 9% | 24% | 9% | 18% | 9%

LT LG C RG RT

NYJ-4

We saw Russell Wilson and Carson Wentz outperform their windows and win Super Bowls for their cities in year 2. We saw Jared Goff struggle tremendously in year 1, make the playoffs in year 2, and now is headed toward Super Bowl contention in year 3 with the Rams. The same situation should happen in New York with Sam Darnold. As much as I like Josh McCown and think he's underrated as a backup QB, he will be 39 years old this season; he's not the future. He's also not leading this Jets team to the Super Bowl. The priority for the Jets should be getting as much experience for Darnold as possible. Anyone on the coaching staff who uses the line that "McCown gives the Jets the best chance to win" doesn't understand the future plan. The only game(s) in 2018 Darnold should not start are games he's not ready for. If he doesn't know the playbook or can get himself hurt on the field because he's not yet shown aptitude for the protection schemes, route timing, and other fundamentals of the offense, then he shouldn't start. Once he gets those fundamentals down, he needs to be learning as the Jets' starting QB.

One supporting (yet big) reason the Jets should feel comfortable getting Darnold in the lineup right away is their schedule. Whether you take the season by the first three weeks, the first six weeks, or the first 10 weeks, the Jets boast the NFL's easiest strength of schedule. Through the first 10 weeks, the Jets play six teams that rank bottom 10 -- the most in the league and twice as many as most teams. The schedule is particularly favorable regarding opposing pass defenses.

(cont'd - see NYJ-5)

Bryan Mears' Fantasy Corner

Robby Anderson's 2017 campaign is likely a bit underrated, mostly because the sample includes four weeks of atrocious QB play from Bryce Petty. During the first 13 weeks of the season, Anderson ranked top 10 among wide receivers in standard scoring. Per FantasyLabs' Ian Hartitz, only Tyreek Hill created a higher average rate of separation than Anderson among WRs with 100-plus targets last season. The talent is clearly there. Regardless of whether it's Josh McCown or Sam Darnold starting, Anderson will receive better QB play than what he saw in the final month of 2017. He looks to be the Jets' clear No. 1 option and should receive heavy volume throughout the season given how often New York is likely to be behind.

Division History: Season Wins & 2018 Projection

2014 Wins | 2015 Wins | 2016 Wins | 2017 Wins | Forecast 2018 Wins

Rank of 2018 Defensive Pass Efficiency Faced by Week

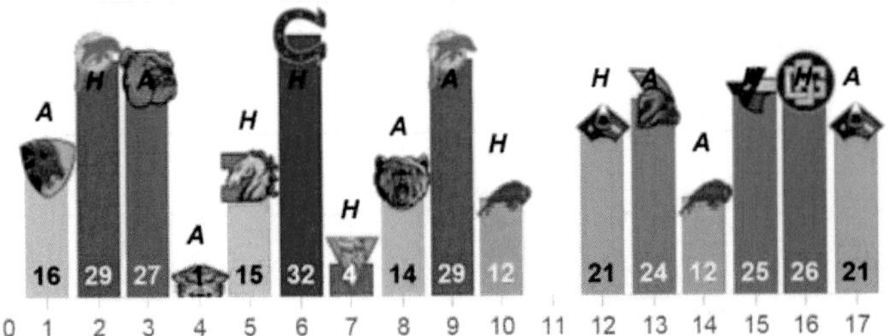

Rank of 2018 Defensive Rush Efficiency Faced by Week

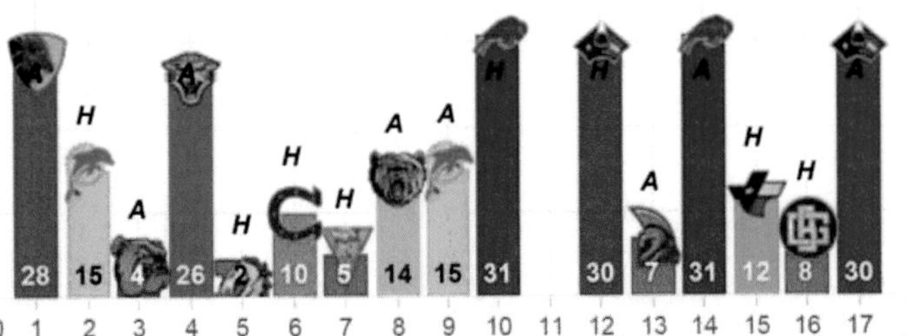

2017 Situational Usage by Player & Position

Usage Rate by Score

		Being Blown Out (14+)	Down Big (9-13)	One Score	Large Lead (9-13)	Blowout Lead (14+)	Grand Total
RUSH	Bilal Powell	18%	15%	21%	17%	32%	21%
	Matt Forte	7%	8%	13%	17%	14%	12%
	Robby Anderson		1%	0%			0%
	Elijah McGuire	9%	10%	9%	30%	27%	10%
	ArDarius Stewart		1%	1%			1%
	JoJo Natson			0%			0%
	Travaris Cadet			0%			0%
	Total	34%	34%	45%	65%	73%	44%
PASS	Bilal Powell	2%	3%	4%			4%
	Matt Forte	6%	8%	5%	4%	3%	5%
	Robby Anderson	10%	20%	13%	9%	5%	13%
	Elijah McGuire	4%	3%	3%		3%	3%
	Jermaine Kearse	17%	11%	12%	4%	3%	12%
	Austin Seferian-Jenki..	2%	10%	9%	9%	11%	9%
	Jeremy Kerley	2%	1%	3%	9%	3%	3%
	ArDarius Stewart	2%	3%	1%			1%
	Chad Hansen	5%	4%	1%			2%
	Eric Tomlinson	2%		1%			1%
	Neal Sterling	9%		1%			1%
	JoJo Natson	1%	2%	0%			1%
	Will Tye	2%		1%			1%
	Travaris Cadet			0%			0%
	Charone Peake			0%			0%
	Total	66%	66%	55%	35%	27%	56%

Positional Target Distribution vs NFL Average

		NFL Wide				Team Only			
		Left	Middle	Right	Total	Left	Middle	Right	Total
Deep	WR	971	497	958	2,426	15	12	29	56
	TE	191	145	186	522	1	5	2	8
	RB	37	9	40	86	2		2	4
	All	1,199	651	1,184	3,034	18	17	33	68
Short	WR	2,787	1,636	2,712	7,135	75	35	78	188
	TE	837	819	1,133	2,789	26	20	37	83
	RB	1,282	797	1,257	3,336	39	26	38	103
	All	4,906	3,252	5,102	13,260	140	81	153	374
Total		6,105	3,903	6,286	16,294	158	98	186	442

Positional Success Rates vs NFL Average

		NFL Wide				Team Only			
		Left	Middle	Right	Total	Left	Middle	Right	Total
Deep	WR	37%	45%	37%	39%	47%	33%	48%	45%
	TE	38%	52%	45%	45%	0%	60%	50%	50%
	RB	38%	56%	38%	40%	0%		50%	25%
	All	37%	47%	39%	40%	39%	41%	48%	44%
Short	WR	52%	57%	50%	52%	48%	74%	47%	53%
	TE	51%	57%	49%	52%	46%	40%	46%	45%
	RB	44%	51%	43%	45%	36%	54%	42%	43%
	All	50%	55%	48%	50%	44%	59%	46%	48%
Total		47%	54%	46%	48%	44%	56%	46%	48%

Successful Play Rate
0% — 100%

New York Jets - Success by Personnel Grouping & Play Type

Play Type	1-1 [3WR]	1-2 [2WR]	2-1 [2WR]	1-0 [4WR]	1-3 [1WR]	0-1 [4WR]	2-0 [3WR]	2-2 [1WR]	2-3 [0WR]	Grand Total
PASS	40% (415, 75%)	56% (77, 14%)	43% (23, 4%)	50% (2, 0%)	8% (13, 2%)	100% (1, 0%)	33% (6, 1%)	33% (15, 3%)	50% (4, 1%)	42% (556, 100%)
RUSH	43% (209, 49%)	37% (86, 20%)	33% (40, 9%)		32% (34, 8%)			19% (47, 11%)	45% (11, 3%)	37% (427, 100%)
TOTAL	41% (624, 63%)	46% (163, 17%)	37% (63, 6%)	50% (2, 0%)	26% (47, 5%)	100% (1, 0%)	33% (6, 1%)	23% (62, 6%)	47% (15, 2%)	40% (983, 100%)

Format Line 1: Success Rate Line 2: Total # of Plays, % of All Plays (by type)

NYJ-5 That said, the obvious downside is that if Darnold isn't starting the first month of the season, he won't be taking starter reps in training camp or during the weeks leading up to their final preseason games. Even if the Jets don't want Darnold to start the first month of the season (like the Bears did with Trubisky) they would be wise to leave it as an "open competition" all the way until Week 1 so that Darnold gets his share of starter reps in camp.

One thing the Jets need to work on in preparation for a less-experienced QB is fixing their offensive line. They ranked sixth-worst in the league last year, and the only piece they acquired who is likely to start is C Spencer Long. They face a near equivalent schedule of pass rushing defenses in 2018 as they did in 2017. They will face the third-easiest schedule of opposing defenses. But the problem is they faced the very same third-easiest schedule of opposing defenses in 2017 and were terrible. The 2017 Jets were a bad team, but some of it can be explained by injuries: They had the most-injured WR corps and the 12th most-injured TE corps. Their defense should face a nice boost from a much easier schedule. They go from facing above average offenses in 2017 to the NFL's second-easiest schedule in 2018. It's the biggest positive jump any team will see from last season.

A much better schedule of offenses should allow their defense to play better. And if the defense plays better, there won't be as much required out of the offense. That's ideal for a rookie QB, as he may not be put in as many situations where he would need to pass the ball 35-plus times. I'm interested to see what new OC Jeremy Bates implements and what he does with largely the same team from last season apart from the QB. The Jets added a few new faces on their roster via free agency, the primary being RB Isaiah Crowell. The other additions are likely to be backups, and the team had limited draft capital this year, with just three picks taken prior to the sixth round.

While the Jets were 10-6 in 2015, they are a couple of years away from really competing to win the AFC East. The good news for them is the AFC East is very fragile apart from the Patriots. That said, it's a terrible strategy long-term to hope to finish second and land a Wild Card spot. The Jets are not close to truly competing, and thus their goal in 2018 should be to indoctrinate Darnold and allow him to learn in the QB room from Josh McCown, who should be a great teacher. If they don't have a successful year, that means they will have better draft picks in 2019, which should be their secondary goal.

Receiving Success by Personnel Grouping

Position	Player	1-1 [3WR]	1-2 [2WR]	2-1 [2WR]	1-0 [4WR]	1-3 [1WR]	2-0 [3WR]	2-2 [1WR]	2-3 [0WR]	Total
RB	Matt Forte	52% 7.3 107.2 (33)	33% 4.8 86.6 (9)			0% 0.0 39.6 (2)	50% 4.5 62.5 (2)			46% 6.4 100.5 (46)
	Bilal Powell	37% 5.8 72.5 (27)	0% 0.0 56.3 (2)			0% 0.0 39.6 (1)	0% 1.0 56.3 (2)			31% 4.9 66.9 (32)
TE	Austin Seferian-Jenkins	39% 5.3 87.7 (51)	55% 5.3 84.7 (11)	50% 3.5 58.3 (4)		50% 3.5 58.3 (2)		50% 3.5 81.3 (2)	50% 0.8 95.8 (4)	43% 4.8 92.0 (74)
WR	Robby Anderson	42% 8.5 94.3 (78)	68% 9.9 77.5 (22)	50% 6.5 70.8 (4)		0% 0.0 39.6 (5)	100% 11.0 112.5 (1)	25% 5.0 47.9 (4)		46% 8.3 84.7 (114)
	Jermaine Kearse	55% 8.2 95.0 (75)	56% 9.0 122.9 (16)	57% 7.1 91.4 (7)	50% 2.0 16.7 (2)	0% 0.0 39.6 (1)		0% 0.0 39.6 (1)		54% 7.9 92.4 (102)
	Jeremy Kerley	59% 8.3 113.7 (27)								59% 8.3 113.7 (27)

Format Line 1: Success Rate Line 2: YPA Line 3: Passer Rating Line 4: Total # of Plays

Successful Play Rate
0% — 100%

Rushing Success by Personnel Grouping

Position	Player	1-1 [3WR]	1-2 [2WR]	2-1 [2WR]	1-3 [1WR]	2-2 [1WR]	2-3 [0WR]	Total
RB	Bilal Powell	34% 4.7 (79)	48% 5.0 (27)	19% 3.7 (21)	37% 3.4 (19)	28% 4.7 (25)	57% 0.3 (7)	35% 4.3 (178)
	Matt Forte	44% 4.4 (57)	33% 3.3 (30)	80% 3.8 (5)	40% 0.6 (5)	25% 2.5 (4)	0% -0.5 (2)	41% 3.7 (103)
	Elijah McGuire	37% 5.3 (43)	33% 2.6 (21)	31% 1.7 (13)	33% 3.0 (3)	14% 0.0 (7)	0% 0.0 (1)	33% 3.6 (88)

Format Line 1: Success Rate Line 2: YPC Line 3: Total # of Plays

2018 Coaches

Head Coach:
Jon Gruden (1st yr)
Offensive Coordinator:
Greg Olson (LAR QB) (1st yr)
Defensive Coordinator:
Paul Guenther (CIN DC) (1st yr)

Oakland Raiders

2018 Forecast

Wins	Div Rank
8	#2

Past Records

2017: 6-10
2016: 12-4
2015: 7-9

EASY HARD

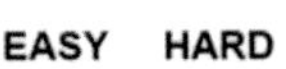

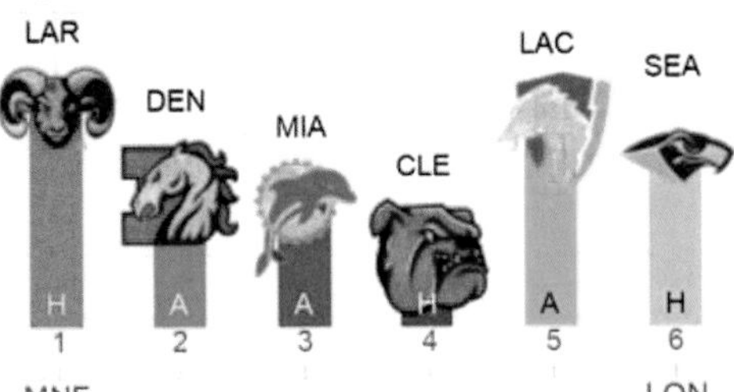

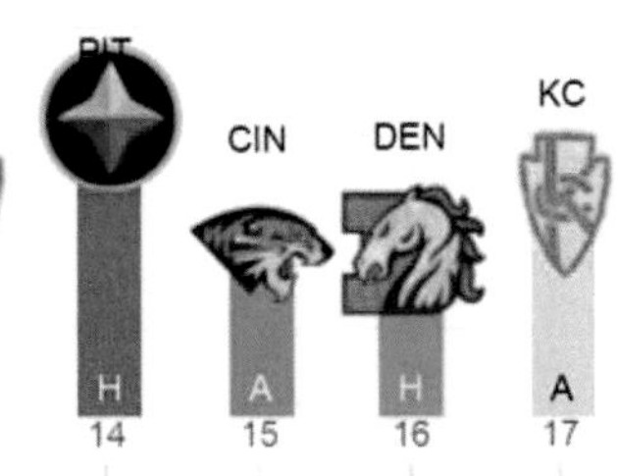

Key Players Lost

TXN	Player (POS)
Cut	Amerson, David CB
	Bryant, Armonty DE
	Crabtree, Michael WR
	King, Marquette P
	Newhouse, Marshall T
	Northnagel, Bradley C
	Smith, Aldon LB
	Smith, Sean CB
	Walford, Clive TE
Declared Free Agent	Autry, Denico DE
	Bowman, NaVorro LB
	Carrie, TJ CB
	Condo, Jon LB
	Janikowski, Sebastian K
	Manuel, EJ QB
	McGill, Keith CB
	Nelson, Reggie S
	Smith, Lee TE

Average Line	# Games Favored	# Games Underdog
-0.2	7	7

2018 Oakland Raiders Overview

The Raiders are an interesting study into what happens when a team pays its rookie-deal quarterback. In 2016, Derek Carr hit the cap for $1.465M and the team won 12 games. Not wanting Carr, a second-round draft pick and not eligible for a fifth-year option, to hit free agency, the Raiders signed him to a 5-year, $125M contract after just three NFL seasons under his belt. His inexpensive rookie-deal salary in 2016 allowed the Raiders to have the most-expensive offensive line and the 10th most-expensive defense. Not only was Carr cheap, they had the second-lowest QB cap hit in the entire league. Compare that to his $25M hit this year, which is the third-highest mark in the league.

The Raiders didn't want to rebuild with head coach Jon Gruden taking over in his first season, so instead of taking a more measured approach to the roster, the Raiders got ultra-aggressive. They let go of many of their high-priced veterans, including franchise mainstays like Sebastian Janikowski and Marquette King, so that they could afford to sign offensive players Gruden liked. These weren't the blue chip free agents other teams just couldn't sign. Rather, they were over-the-hill players Gruden saw play well while he was announcing on Monday Night Football.

Some examples are 36-year-old Derrick Johnson, 34-year-old Jordy Nelson, 34-year-old Leon Hall, 33-year-old Breno Giacomini, 31-year-old Shareece Wright, and 29-year-old Doug Martin. If you wanted to put a positive spin on it, you could say Gruden values veteran leadership. But the reality is the Raiders had the eighth-oldest roster according to snap-weighted age in 2017, and that roster will be considerably older in 2018. The Raiders have "made it work" with these vets by paying them cheaper money for short deals. Filling out a roster with one-year deals on aging vets in a new system could be considered aggressive. It could also be considered wishful thinking. And, unfortunately, racking up one-year contracts of aging vets has given the Raiders the most-expensive offense in 2018 in terms of cap allocation, but the eighth-cheapest defense.

While Gruden is clearly not a young, up-and-coming coach, his strategy hasn't been that dissimilar from the recent young offensive coaches who got first time head coaching jobs like Kyle Shanahan and Sean McVay.

(cont'd - see OAK2)

Key Free Agents/ Trades Added

Bryant, Martavis WR
Carradine, Tank DE
Carrier, Derek TE
Hall, Leon CB
Lamur, Emmanuel LB
Martin, Doug RB
Nelson, Jordy WR
Switzer, Ryan WR
Whitehead, Tahir LB
Wright, Shareece CB

Drafted Players

Rd	Pk	Player (College)
1	15	OT - Kolton Miller (UCLA)
2	57	DT - P. J. Hall (Sam Houston State)
3	65	OT - Brandon Parker (North Carolina A&T)
	87	DE - Arden Key (LSU)
4	110	CB - Nick Nelson (Wisconsin)
5	140	DT - Maurice Hurst (Michigan)
5*	173	P - Johnny Townsend (Florida)
6*	216	LB - Azeem Victor (Washington)
7	228	WR - Marcell Ateman (Oklahoma State)

Regular Season Wins: Past & Current Proj

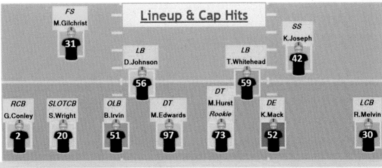

Lineup & Cap Hits

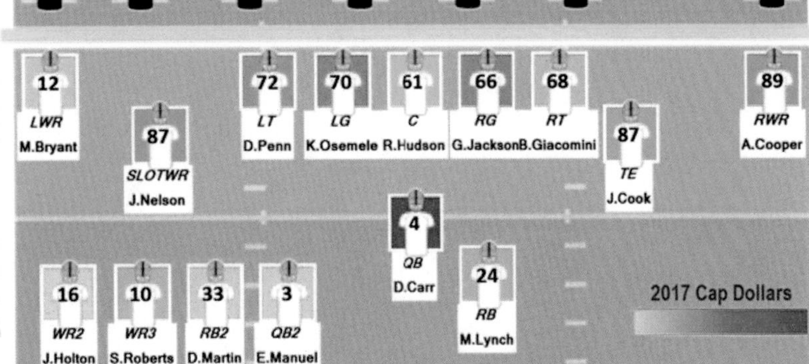

2018 Unit Spending

All DEF
All OFF

Positional Spending

	Rank	Total	2017 Rk
All OFF	1	$116.77M	14
QB	6	$26.78M	31
OL	2	$44.39M	3
RB	16	$7.74M	25
WR	10	$25.49M	11
TE	6	$12.37M	8
All DEF	25	$73.22M	27
DL	17	$25.47M	28
LB	14	$22.02M	25
CB	22	$12.78M	8
S	12	$12.95M	16

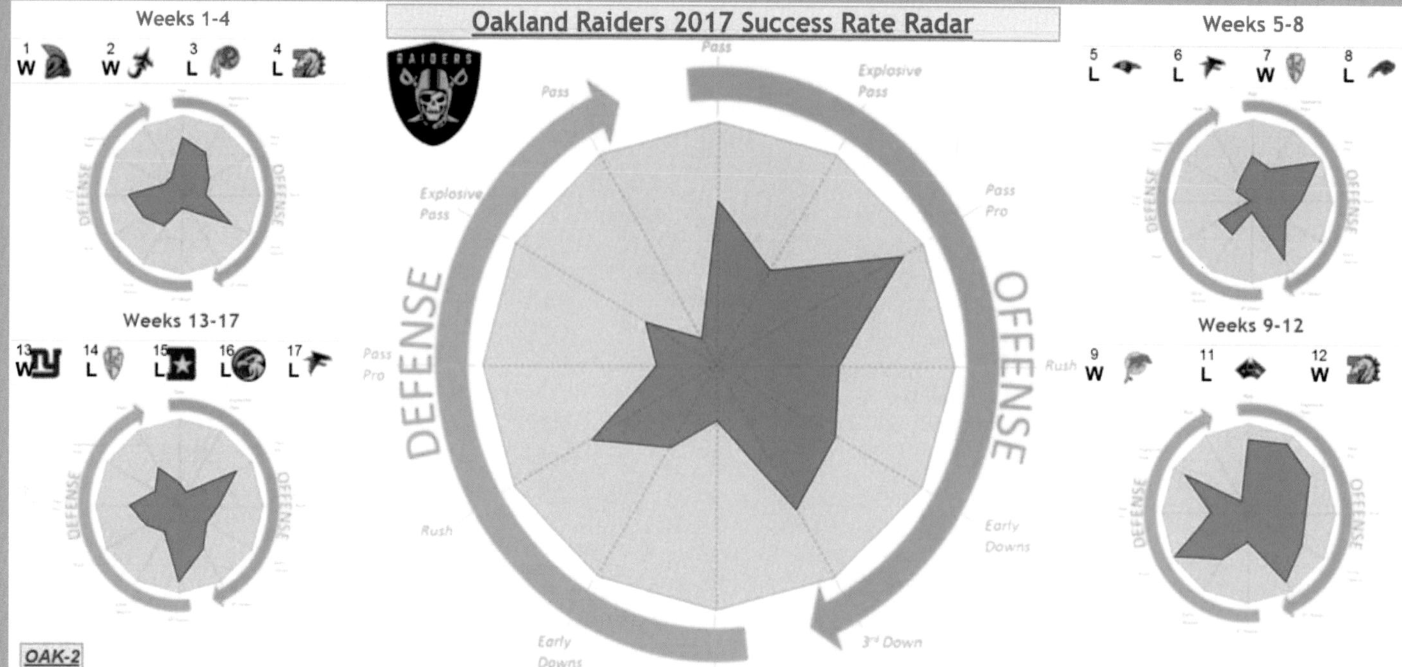

OAK-2

These guys know that, ultimately, as the play callers on offense, they will be judged on how well their offense performs. Both Shanahan and McVay were ultra-aggressive in acquiring players they liked and thought would work in their system, both in the draft and in free agency. While Gruden is more established in the league, he has a ton to prove thanks to a 10-year, $100M contract. And if his offense struggles, as the signal caller, head coach, and key voice in personnel decisions, he'll have no one to blame but himself.

Offensively, a lot needs to change from a strategical perspective, but it's a big question whether Gruden will implement those changes. The NFL is much different than the last time he called plays. Gruden came from a time where running the football was far more popular. The modern game is built around a well-designed passing scheme. And it must be able to defeat good pass defenses.

Last year, the Raiders faced an average schedule of pass defenses. But their splits were stark: Against units ranked 18th or better, they went 1-8 on the season. In the other games they went 5-2. And even the games against the tougher defenses weren't that challenging: That sample includes the Redskins, Broncos, Bills, Ravens, and Cowboys. And still Carr's numbers against these teams were catastrophic. He produced a 78.6 rating, a 41% success rate, and 6.3 YPA. The total Raiders points in those eight losses were 10, 10, 10, 10, 14, 16, 17, and 17. It's nearly impossible to win in the NFL with that level of quarterback play.

The passing game is going to look a lot different in 2018. For starters, Gruden wants to empower Carr more at the line of scrimmage to run up-tempo and to audible.

*(cont'd - see **OAK-3**)*

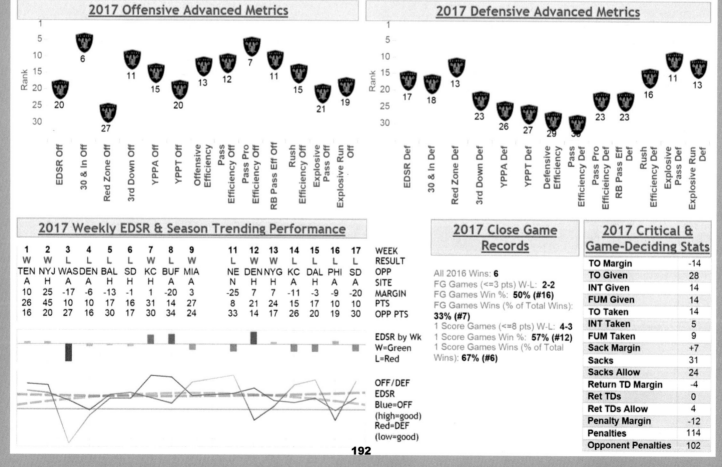

2017 Offensive Advanced Metrics

Metric	Rank
EDSR Off	20
30 & In Off	6
Red Zone Off	27
3rd Down Off	11
YPPA Off	15
YPPT Off	20
Offensive Efficiency	13
Pass Efficiency Off	12
Pass Pro Efficiency Off	7
RB Pass Eff Off	11
Rush Efficiency Off	15
Explosive Pass Off	21
Explosive Run Off	19

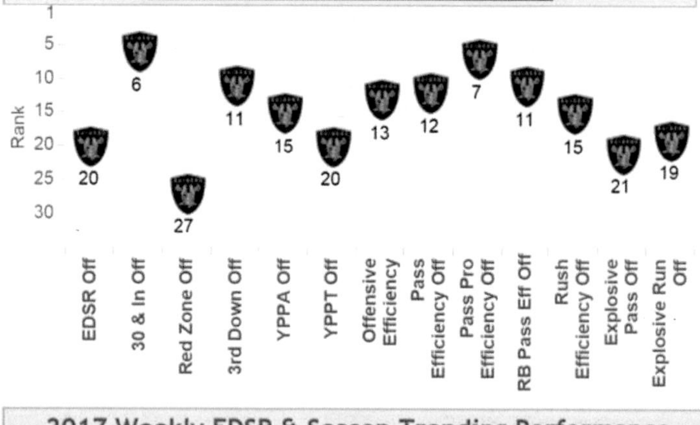

2017 Defensive Advanced Metrics

Metric	Rank
EDSR Def	17
30 & In Def	18
Red Zone Def	13
3rd Down Def	23
YPPA Def	26
YPPT Def	27
Defensive Efficiency	29
Pass Efficiency Def	30
Pass Pro Efficiency Def	23
RB Pass Eff Def	23
Rush Efficiency Def	16
Explosive Pass Def	11
Explosive Run Def	13

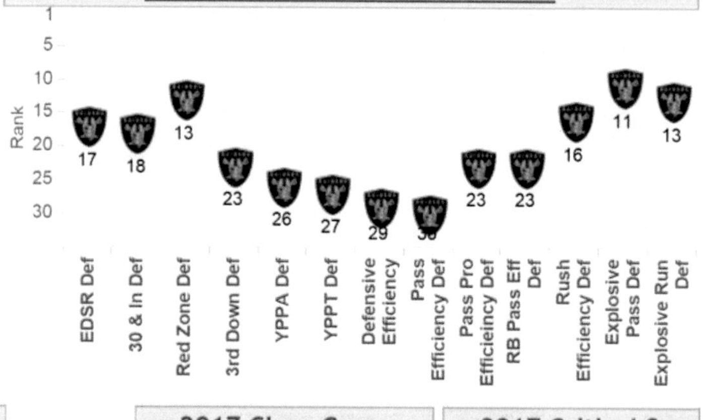

2017 Weekly EDSR & Season Trending Performance

WEEK	1	2	3	4	5	6	7	8	9	11	12	13	14	15	16	17
RESULT	W	W	L	L	L	L	W	L	W	L	W	W	L	L	L	L
OPP	TEN	NYJ	WAS	DEN	BAL	SD	KC	BUF	MIA	NE	DEN	NYG	KC	DAL	PHI	SD
SITE	A	H	A	A	H	H	H	A	A	N	H	H	A	H	A	A
MARGIN	10	25	-17	-6	-13	-1	1	-20	3	-25	7	7	-11	-3	-9	-20
PTS	26	45	10	10	17	16	31	14	27	8	21	24	15	17	10	10
OPP PTS	16	20	27	16	30	17	30	34	24	33	14	17	26	20	19	30

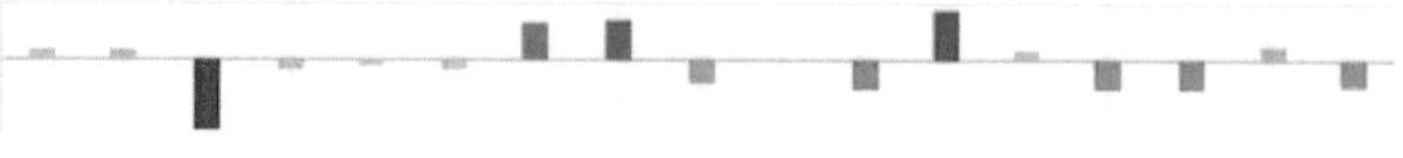

EDSR by Wk
W=Green
L=Red

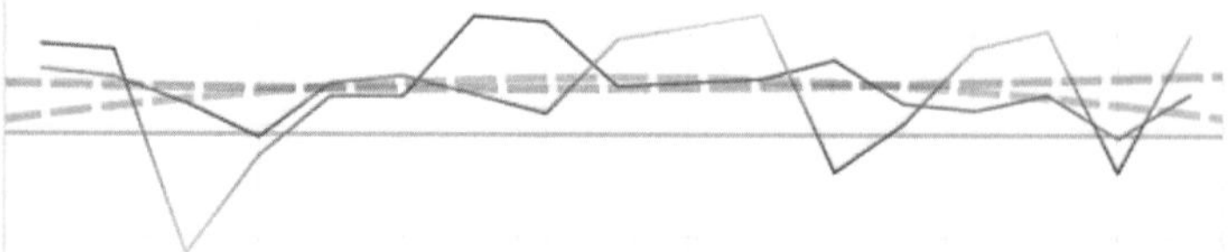

OFF/DEF
EDSR
Blue=OFF
(high=good)
Red=DEF
(low=good)

2017 Close Game Records

All 2016 Wins: **6**
FG Games (<=3 pts) W-L: **2-2**
FG Games Win %: **50% (#16)**
FG Games Wins (% of Total Wins): **33% (#7)**
1 Score Games (<=8 pts) W-L: **4-3**
1 Score Games Win %: **57% (#12)**
1 Score Games Wins (% of Total Wins): **67% (#6)**

2017 Critical & Game-Deciding Stats

TO Margin	-14
TO Given	28
INT Given	14
FUM Given	14
TO Taken	14
INT Taken	5
FUM Taken	9
Sack Margin	+7
Sacks	31
Sacks Allow	24
Return TD Margin	-4
Ret TDs	0
Ret TDs Allow	4
Penalty Margin	-12
Penalties	114
Opponent Penalties	102

Oakland Raiders 2018 Strength of Schedule In Detail (compared to 2017)

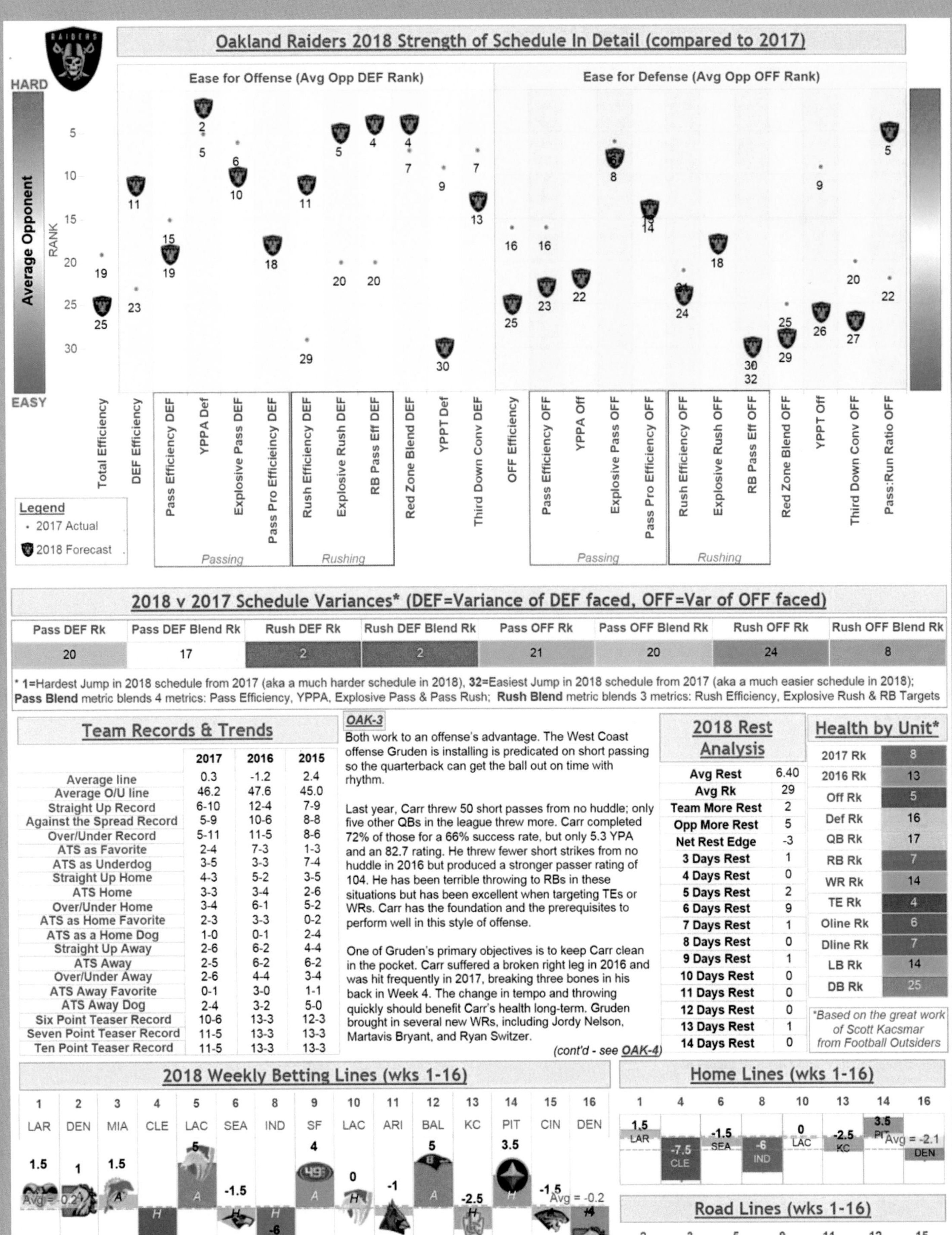

2018 v 2017 Schedule Variances* (DEF=Variance of DEF faced, OFF=Var of OFF faced)

Pass DEF Rk	Pass DEF Blend Rk	Rush DEF Rk	Rush DEF Blend Rk	Pass OFF Rk	Pass OFF Blend Rk	Rush OFF Rk	Rush OFF Blend Rk
20	17	2	2	21	20	24	8

* **1**=Hardest Jump in 2018 schedule from 2017 (aka a much harder schedule in 2018), **32**=Easiest Jump in 2018 schedule from 2017 (aka a much easier schedule in 2018); **Pass Blend** metric blends 4 metrics: Pass Efficiency, YPPA, Explosive Pass & Pass Rush; **Rush Blend** metric blends 3 metrics: Rush Efficiency, Explosive Rush & RB Targets

Team Records & Trends

	2017	2016	2015
Average line	0.3	-1.2	2.4
Average O/U line	46.2	47.6	45.0
Straight Up Record	6-10	12-4	7-9
Against the Spread Record	5-9	10-6	8-8
Over/Under Record	5-11	11-5	8-6
ATS as Favorite	2-4	7-3	1-3
ATS as Underdog	3-5	3-3	7-4
Straight Up Home	4-3	5-2	3-5
ATS Home	3-3	3-4	2-6
Over/Under Home	3-4	6-1	5-2
ATS as Home Favorite	2-3	3-3	0-2
ATS as a Home Dog	1-0	0-1	2-4
Straight Up Away	2-6	6-2	4-4
ATS Away	2-5	6-2	6-2
Over/Under Away	2-6	4-4	3-4
ATS Away Favorite	0-1	3-0	1-1
ATS Away Dog	2-4	3-2	5-0
Six Point Teaser Record	10-6	13-3	12-3
Seven Point Teaser Record	11-5	13-3	13-3
Ten Point Teaser Record	11-5	13-3	13-3

OAK-3

Both work to an offense's advantage. The West Coast offense Gruden is installing is predicated on short passing so the quarterback can get the ball out on time with rhythm.

Last year, Carr threw 50 short passes from no huddle; only five other QBs in the league threw more. Carr completed 72% of those for a 66% success rate, but only 5.3 YPA and an 82.7 rating. He threw fewer short strikes from no huddle in 2016 but produced a stronger passer rating of 104. He has been terrible throwing to RBs in these situations but has been excellent when targeting TEs or WRs. Carr has the foundation and the prerequisites to perform well in this style of offense.

One of Gruden's primary objectives is to keep Carr clean in the pocket. Carr suffered a broken right leg in 2016 and was hit frequently in 2017, breaking three bones in his back in Week 4. The change in tempo and throwing quickly should benefit Carr's health long-term. Gruden brought in several new WRs, including Jordy Nelson, Martavis Bryant, and Ryan Switzer.

(cont'd - see OAK-4)

2018 Rest Analysis

Avg Rest	6.40
Avg Rk	29
Team More Rest	2
Opp More Rest	5
Net Rest Edge	-3
3 Days Rest	1
4 Days Rest	0
5 Days Rest	2
6 Days Rest	9
7 Days Rest	1
8 Days Rest	0
9 Days Rest	1
10 Days Rest	0
11 Days Rest	0
12 Days Rest	0
13 Days Rest	1
14 Days Rest	0

Health by Unit*

2017 Rk	8
2016 Rk	13
Off Rk	5
Def Rk	16
QB Rk	17
RB Rk	7
WR Rk	14
TE Rk	4
Oline Rk	6
Dline Rk	7
LB Rk	14
DB Rk	25

**Based on the great work of Scott Kacsmar from Football Outsiders*

2018 Weekly Betting Lines (wks 1-16)

1	2	3	4	5	6	8	9	10	11	12	13	14	15	16
LAR	DEN	MIA	CLE	LAC	SEA	IND	SF	LAC	ARI	BAL	KC	PIT	CIN	DEN
1.5	1	1.5	-7.5	5	-1.5	-6	4	0	-1	5	-2.5	3.5	-1.5	-4

Avg = -0.2

Home Lines (wks 1-16)

1	4	6	8	10	13	14	16
LAR	CLE	SEA	IND	LAC	KC	PIT	DEN
1.5	-7.5	-1.5	-6	0	-2.5	3.5	

Avg = -2.1

Road Lines (wks 1-16)

2	3	5	9	11	12	15
DEN	MIA	LAC	SF	ARI	BAL	CIN
1	1.5	5	4	-1	5	-1.5

Avg = 2.0

Oakland Raiders 2017 Play Analysis

2017 Play Tendencies

All Pass %	61%
All Pass Rk	9
All Rush %	39%
All Rush Rk	24
1 Score Pass %	57%
1 Score Pass Rk	17
2016 1 Score Pass %	60%
2016 1 Score Pass Rk	13
2017 Pass Increase %	-3%
Pass Increase Rk	22
1 Score Rush %	43%
1 Score Rush Rk	16
Up Pass %	52%
Up Pass Rk	8
Up Rush %	48%
Up Rush Rk	25
Down Pass %	70%
Down Pass Rk	2
Down Rush %	30%
Down Rush Rk	31

2017 Down & Distance Tendencies

Down	Distance	Total Plays	Pass Rate	Run Rate	Play Success %
1	Short (1-3)	6	83%	17%	50%
	Med (4-7)	5	60%	40%	60%
	Long (8-10)	263	48%	52%	45%
	XL (11+)	15	93%	7%	47%
2	Short (1-3)	25	36%	64%	52%
	Med (4-7)	69	48%	52%	61%
	Long (8-10)	91	51%	49%	42%
	XL (11+)	33	76%	24%	24%
3	Short (1-3)	41	39%	61%	51%
	Med (4-7)	42	93%	7%	60%
	Long (8-10)	26	96%	4%	31%
	XL (11+)	35	94%	6%	9%
4	Short (1-3)	9	22%	78%	33%
	Med (4-7)	1	0%	100%	0%
	XL (11+)	1	0%	100%	0%

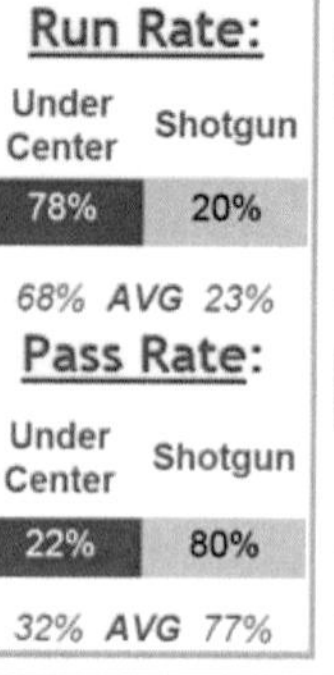

Shotgun %:

Under Center	Shotgun
32%	68%
37% *AVG*	63%

Run Rate:

Under Center	Shotgun
78%	20%
68% *AVG*	23%

Pass Rate:

Under Center	Shotgun
22%	80%
32% *AVG*	77%

Short Yardage Intelligence:

2nd and Short Run

Run Freq	Run Rk	NFL Run Freq Avg	Run 1D Rate	Run NFL 1D Avg
58%	26	67%	53%	69%

2nd and Short Pass

Pass Freq	Pass Rk	NFL Pass Freq Avg	Pass 1D Rate	Pass NFL 1D Avg
42%	7	33%	55%	53%

Most Frequent Play

Down	Distance	Play Type	Player	Total Plays	Play Success %
1	Short (1-3)	PASS	Michael Crabtree	3	67%
	Med (4-7)	RUSH	Marshawn Lynch	2	50%
	Long (8-10)	RUSH	Marshawn Lynch	78	47%
	XL (11+)	PASS	Jared Cook	3	67%
2	Short (1-3)	RUSH	Marshawn Lynch	9	44%
	Med (4-7)	RUSH	Marshawn Lynch	21	62%
	Long (8-10)	RUSH	Marshawn Lynch	26	38%
	XL (11+)	PASS	Amari Cooper	4	0%
			Jared Cook	4	25%
3	Short (1-3)	RUSH	Marshawn Lynch	17	71%
	Med (4-7)	PASS	Michael Crabtree	9	78%
	Long (8-10)	PASS	Amari Cooper	6	17%
	XL (11+)	PASS	Jalen Richard	5	0%

Most Successful Play*

Down	Distance	Play Type	Player	Total Plays	Play Success %
1	Long (8-10)	PASS	Lee Smith	5	80%
2	Short (1-3)	RUSH	Marshawn Lynch	9	44%
	Med (4-7)	PASS	Jared Cook	7	71%
	Long (8-10)	PASS	Jared Cook	7	100%
3	Short (1-3)	RUSH	Marshawn Lynch	17	71%
	Med (4-7)	PASS	Michael Crabtree	9	78%
	Long (8-10)	PASS	Jared Cook	5	60%
	XL (11+)	PASS	Jalen Richard	5	0%
4	Short (1-3)	RUSH	Marshawn Lynch	5	40%

*Minimum 5 plays to qualify

2017 Snap Rates

Wk	Opp	Score	Jared Cook	Seth Roberts	Amari Cooper	Michael Crabtree	Marshawn Lynch	Cordarrelle Patterson	DeAndre Washington
1	TEN	W 26-16	47 (71%)	55 (83%)	61 (92%)	48 (73%)	32 (48%)	22 (33%)	15 (23%)
2	NYJ	W 45-20	45 (79%)	34 (60%)	48 (84%)	35 (61%)	23 (40%)	27 (47%)	13 (23%)
3	WAS	L 27-10	41 (80%)	45 (88%)	44 (86%)	31 (61%)	16 (31%)	26 (51%)	16 (31%)
4	DEN	L 16-10	48 (89%)	50 (93%)	53 (98%)		23 (43%)	32 (59%)	6 (11%)
5	BAL	L 30-17	34 (61%)	52 (93%)	55 (98%)	36 (64%)	27 (48%)	19 (34%)	
6	LAC	L 17-16	46 (79%)	42 (72%)	55 (95%)	49 (84%)	30 (52%)	17 (29%)	5 (9%)
7	KC	W 31-30	67 (82%)	72 (88%)	78 (95%)	72 (88%)	10 (12%)	18 (22%)	25 (30%)
8	BUF	L 34-14	46 (71%)		63 (97%)	55 (85%)		57 (88%)	32 (49%)
9	MIA	W 27-24	53 (84%)	35 (56%)	57 (90%)	51 (81%)	37 (59%)	6 (10%)	9 (14%)
11	NE	L 33-8	54 (73%)	59 (80%)	67 (91%)	58 (78%)	21 (28%)	25 (34%)	24 (32%)
12	DEN	W 21-14	59 (87%)	57 (84%)	28 (41%)	5 (7%)	47 (69%)	37 (54%)	14 (21%)
13	NYG	W 24-17	50 (77%)	46 (71%)			32 (49%)	34 (52%)	14 (22%)
14	KC	L 26-15	54 (89%)	55 (90%)	15 (25%)	54 (89%)	28 (46%)	27 (44%)	14 (23%)
15	DAL	L 20-17	60 (86%)	66 (94%)		61 (87%)	51 (73%)	45 (64%)	11 (16%)
16	PHI	L 19-10	51 (74%)	52 (75%)	44 (64%)	31 (45%)	44 (64%)	13 (19%)	17 (25%)
17	LAC	L 30-10	41 (76%)	34 (63%)	42 (78%)	17 (31%)	41 (76%)	25 (46%)	7 (13%)
Grand Total			796 (79%)	754 (79%)	710 (81%)	603 (67%)	462 (49%)	430 (43%)	222 (23%)

Personnel Groupings

Personnel	Team %	NFL Avg	Succ. %
1-1 [3WR]	71%	59%	48%
1-2 [2WR]	12%	19%	36%
1-3 [1WR]	7%	5%	39%
0-1 [4WR]	5%	1%	30%

Grouping Tendencies

Personnel	Pass Rate	Pass Succ. %	Run Succ. %
1-1 [3WR]	68%	47%	50%
1-2 [2WR]	46%	44%	28%
1-3 [1WR]	13%	11%	43%
0-1 [4WR]	84%	28%	43%

Red Zone Targets (min 3)

Receiver	All	Inside 5	6-10	11-20
Michael Crabtree	14	7	4	3
Amari Cooper	10	5	3	2
Jared Cook	9	2	1	6
Cordarrelle Patterson	4	1	1	2
DeAndre Washington	4	1		3
Seth Roberts	4		1	3

Red Zone Rushes (min 3)

Rusher	All	Inside 5	6-10	11-20
Marshawn Lynch	24	10	3	11
Jalen Richard	4			4
DeAndre Washington	3	1	1	1

Early Down Target Rate

RB	TE	WR
24%	19%	56%
23%	21% NFL AVG	56%

Overall Target Success %

RB	TE	WR
45% #13	52% #11	46% #21

Oakland Raiders 2017 Passing Recap & 2018 Outlook

How much of Carr's 2017 regression can we blame on his Week 4 injury and the lack of quality pass protection from his offensive line? Jon Gruden hopes the answer is a lot. When Carr targeted players out of three-plus WR formations, he recorded 6.6 YPA, a 47% success rate, and an 86 rating. A ridiculous 89% of his total passes came in three-plus WR formations. But in 12 personnel -- the only other formation used at least 10 times -- Carr produced 9.3 YPA, a 45% success rate, and a 91 rating.

I hope Gruden gets more creative offensively from a personnel grouping standpoint and brings more diversity into the Raiders' passing attack. The Raiders didn't even attempt a pass out of 21 personnel last year. Gruden's focus in the passing game, apart from installing his WCO fundamentals, appears to be on the health of Carr and his QB's ability to freelance more at the line of scrimmage. Neither of these are bad goals at all. And the team appears to be strongly buying in to what Gruden is selling, at least at this early point in the season.

Derek Carr Rating All Downs

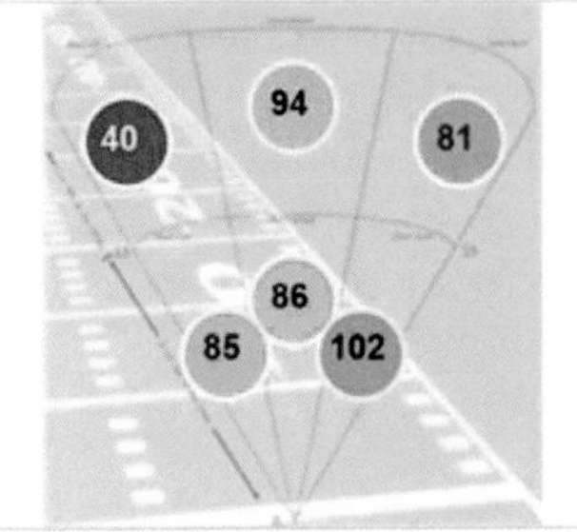

Derek Carr Rating Early Downs

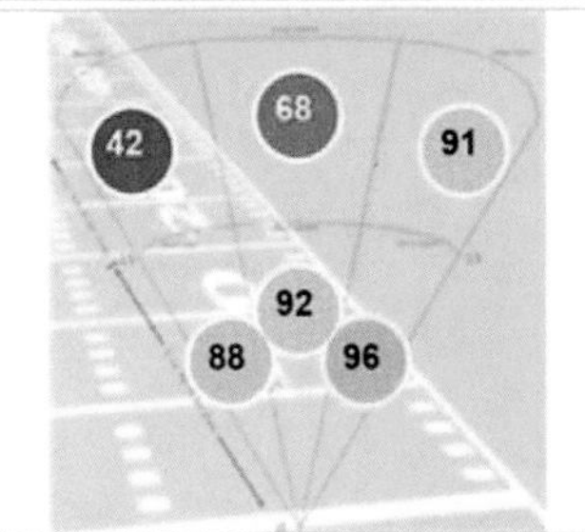

2017 Standard Passing Table

QB	Comp	Att	Comp %	Yds	YPA	TDs	INT	Sacks	Rating	Rk
Derek Carr	323	515	63%	3,502	6.8	22	13	20	86	24
E.J. Manuel	24	43	56%	265	6.2	1	1	4	72	45
NFL Avg			62%		7.0				87.5	

2017 Advanced Passing Table

QB	Success %	EDSR Passing Success %	20+ Yd Pass Gains	20+ Yd Pass %	30+ Yd Pass Gains	30+ Yd Pass %	Avg. Air Yds per Comp	Avg. YAC per Comp	20+ Air Yd Comp	20+ Air Yd %
Derek Carr	45%	50%	43	8.3%	13	2.5%	5.7	5.2	17	5%
E.J. Manuel	38%	41%	4	9.3%	1	2.3%	7.4	3.7	1	4%
NFL Avg	44%	48%	27.7	8.8%	10.3	3.3%	6.0	4.7	11.7	6%

Interception Rates by Down

Yards to Go	1	2	3	4	Total
1 & 2	0.0%	0.0%	11.1%	0.0%	3.6%
3, 4, 5	0.0%	3.8%	2.5%	0.0%	2.7%
6 - 9	0.0%	3.6%	2.1%	0.0%	2.8%
10 - 14	1.7%	3.5%	4.7%	0.0%	2.5%
15+	0.0%	0.0%	0.0%	0.0%	0.0%
Total	1.5%	3.0%	3.3%	0.0%	2.4%

3rd Down Passing - Short of Sticks Analysis

QB	Avg. Yds to Go	Avg. YIA (of Comp)	Avg Yds Short	Short of Sticks Rate	Short Rk
Derek Carr	8.2	6.8	-1.4	63%	24
NFL Avg	7.8	6.7	-1.1	60%	

Air Yds vs YAC

Air Yds %	YAC %	Rk
58%	42%	21
58%	42%	

2017 Receiving Recap & 2018 Outlook

I was definitely intrigued by the Nelson signing and will be interested in his usage, as the biggest "drop-off" came via Brett Hundley: In 2016 with Rodgers, Jordy posted a 59% success rate (#4 in NFL) and 8.2 YPA (#11). In 2017, through Week 5 (with Rodgers), Jordy posted a 64% success rate (#2) and once again 8.2 YPA (#22). But after Week 5 (with Hundley), Nelson posted a 48% success rate (#39) and only 4.5 YPA (#55). If Gruden uses Jordy more in the slot, it will emphasize his shorter route running, which was a strength with Rodgers. The plan also is to move Amari Cooper around the offense a lot to prevent No. 1 DBs from locking down on him.

Player *Min 50 Targets*	Targets	Comp %	YPA	Rating	TOARS	Success %	Success Rk	Missed YPA Rk	YAS % Rk	TDs
Michael Crabtree	101	57%	6.1	89	4.6	49%	70	22	72	8
Amari Cooper	96	50%	7.1	76	4.3	40%	115	121	22	7
Jared Cook	86	63%	8.0	95	4.5	57%	18	18	90	2
Seth Roberts	65	66%	7.0	79	3.9	53%	41	86	110	1

Directional Passer Rating Delivered

Receiver	Short Left	Short Middle	Short Right	Deep Left	Deep Middle	Deep Right	Player Total
Michael Crabtree	93	83	111	55	19	88	89
Amari Cooper	57	60	122	37	144	60	76
Jared Cook	91	98	86	106	135	40	95
Seth Roberts	77	62	94	79	82	95	79
DeAndre Washington	75	87	123			40	91
Cordarrelle Patterson	103	79	79	40	119	60	94
Jalen Richard	135	88	90				105
Marshawn Lynch	70	26	88				63
Clive Walford	40	107	82	40	96	40	85
Jamize Olawale	79	56	94				86
Team Total	84	80	104	39	113	67	86

2017 Rushing Recap & 2017 Outlook

If Carr regains his positive form from 2016, the element of the Raiders offense that concerns me most is their run blocking. Lynch is another year older, and unless Gruden is serving bottled water from the Fountain of Youth, Doug Martin isn't going to be of much use. The Raiders face an easier-than-average schedule of run defenses, and Gruden seems intent on using a fullback at times. Lynch was out of the league in 2016, and when he came back to Oakland in 2017 the team didn't even utilize a FB. Gruden signed FB Keith Smith in March. Time will tell how much he will use Smith and how creative they will get with play action when Smith is in the game.

Player *Min 50 Rushes*	Rushes	YPC	Success %	Success Rk	Missed YPA Rk	YTS % Rk	YAS % Rk	Early Down Success %	Early Down Success Rk	TDs
Marshawn Lynch	207	4.3	49%	20	14	37	35	47%	26	7
DeAndre Washington	57	2.7	40%	59	61	1	71	39%	62	2
Jalen Richard	56	4.9	36%	68	56	76	20	35%	68	1

Yards per Carry by Direction

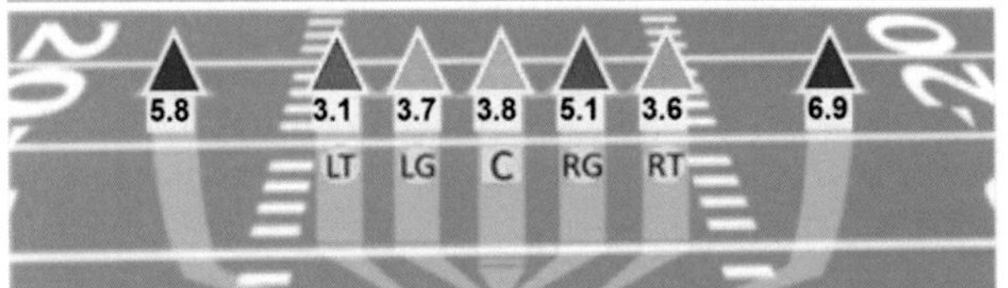

Directional Run Frequency

7%
15%
14%
35%
10%
13%
7%
LT
LG
C
RG
RT

<u>OAK-4</u>

The WCO should benefit Nelson, as he's lost some of his long-range speed. Over the past two years, he's ranked third in success rate (66%) and fourth in passer rating delivered (114) on short routes. Bryant could make big plays happen if Gruden opens up the WCO to the deep passing attack with max protections. That said, Bryant was successful on just 32% of his deep targets and produced a 63 passer rating on those, which ranked 45th out of 61 qualified receivers.

Next comes the run game. It's mostly the same as 2017 except for the addition of new offensive line coach Tom Cable. He brings an affinity for pure zone blocking, which is also a function of the modern WCO. That said, the Raiders offensive line, at least the 2017 version, was far more proficient using power blocking. Gruden drafted two new tackles in his first three picks of the draft and commented that the Raiders struggled too much at the tackle position last year. The elephant in the room is whether Cable will teach a bad outside zone team to become better or if he and Gruden will adapt a more Pro Style WCO and allow his linemen to do what they do best.

Overall last year, Marshawn Lynch was productive, especially on first downs, recording a 48% success rate that ranked eighth out of 32 RBs with 75-plus carries.

(cont'd - see OAK-5)

Bryan Mears' Fantasy Corner

Amari Cooper had a tumultuous 2017 campaign, mostly thanks to nagging health concerns and some poor luck in the red zone. Of course, some of it was his fault: Cooper has dropped a league-high 32 passes since entering the league in 2015. Still, things are looking up for 2018, especially if Gruden is willing to move him around. Per Pro Football Focus, Cooper averaged 2.21 yards per route from the slot last season compared to 1.54 when lined up outside. If Gruden indeed establishes an up-tempo West Coast offense predicated on short throws, Cooper could blossom in the offense.

Division History: Season Wins & 2018 Projection

2014 Wins | 2015 Wins | 2016 Wins | 2017 Wins | Forecast 2018 Wins

Rank of 2018 Defensive Pass Efficiency Faced by Week

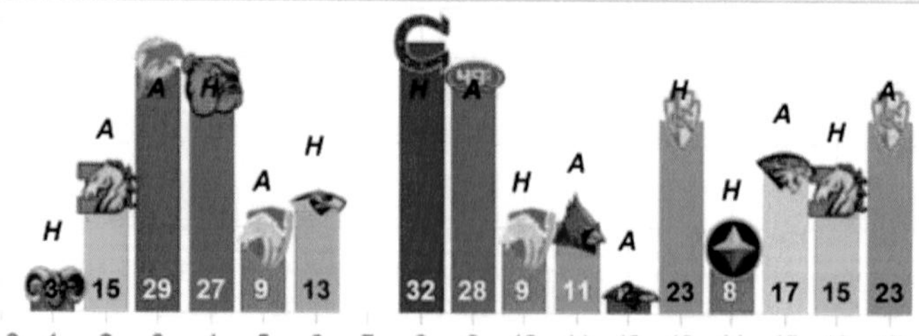

Rank of 2018 Defensive Rush Efficiency Faced by Week

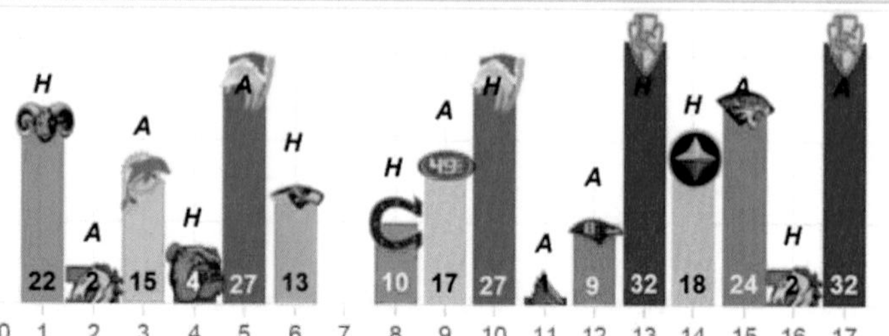

2017 Situational Usage by Player & Position

Usage Rate by Score

		Being Blown Out (14+)	Down Big (9-13)	One Score	Large Lead (9-13)	Blowout Lead (14+)	Grand Total
RUSH	Marshawn Lynch	14%	18%	26%	44%	28%	23%
	DeAndre Washington	2%	8%	7%	11%	12%	6%
	Amari Cooper			0%			0%
	Jalen Richard	9%	2%	6%		12%	6%
	Cordarrelle Patterson	1%	2%	2%			1%
	Jamize Olawale	3%		1%			1%
	Total	28%	29%	42%	56%	51%	38%
PASS	Marshawn Lynch	4%	3%	3%		5%	3%
	DeAndre Washington	10%	2%	4%	11%	9%	5%
	Michael Crabtree	16%	12%	11%		2%	11%
	Amari Cooper	7%	13%	12%	33%	2%	11%
	Jalen Richard	3%	7%	4%		7%	4%
	Jared Cook	10%	12%	9%		7%	10%
	Seth Roberts	12%	8%	6%			7%
	Cordarrelle Patterson	6%	8%	3%		9%	5%
	Johnny Holton	2%	3%	2%		5%	2%
	Jamize Olawale	1%		1%			1%
	Clive Walford	2%	2%	1%			1%
	Lee Smith		3%	1%		2%	1%
	Isaac Whitney			0%			0%
	Total	72%	71%	58%	44%	49%	62%

Positional Target Distribution vs NFL Average

		NFL Wide				Team Only			
		Left	Middle	Right	Total	Left	Middle	Right	Total
Deep	WR	953	496	965	2,414	33	13	22	68
	TE	183	146	184	513	9	4	4	17
	RB	39	9	41	89			1	1
	All	1,175	651	1,190	3,016	42	17	27	86
Short	WR	2,757	1,639	2,691	7,087	105	32	99	236
	TE	833	817	1,140	2,790	30	22	30	82
	RB	1,285	776	1,260	3,321	36	47	35	118
	All	4,875	3,232	5,091	13,198	171	101	164	436
Total		6,050	3,883	6,281	16,214	213	118	191	522

Positional Success Rates vs NFL Average

		NFL Wide				Team Only			
		Left	Middle	Right	Total	Left	Middle	Right	Total
Deep	WR	37%	45%	38%	39%	24%	54%	32%	32%
	TE	37%	53%	46%	45%	56%	50%	0%	41%
	RB	36%	56%	39%	39%			0%	0%
	All	37%	47%	39%	40%	31%	53%	26%	34%
Short	WR	52%	58%	50%	52%	47%	47%	58%	51%
	TE	51%	56%	49%	52%	47%	64%	57%	55%
	RB	44%	51%	43%	45%	39%	49%	49%	46%
	All	50%	56%	48%	50%	45%	51%	55%	50%
Total		47%	54%	46%	48%	42%	52%	51%	48%

Successful Play Rate
0% [color scale] 100%

Oakland Raiders - Success by Personnel Grouping & Play Type

Play Type	1-1 [3WR]	1-2 [2WR]	1-0 [4WR]	1-3 [1WR]	0-1 [4WR]	2-0 [3WR]	2-2 [1WR]	0-0 [5WR]	0-2 [3WR]	3-1 [1WR]	2-3 [0WR]	1-4 [0WR]	3-0 [2WR]	Grand Total
PASS	47% (462, 79%)	44% (54, 9%)	20% (5, 1%)	11% (9, 2%)	28% (36, 6%)		100% (4, 1%)	0% (1, 0%)	56% (9, 2%)	100% (1, 0%)	0% (1, 0%)			45% (582, 100%)
RUSH	50% (215, 58%)	28% (64, 17%)	0% (1, 0%)	43% (60, 16%)	43% (7, 2%)	0% (1, 0%)	69% (13, 4%)		100% (1, 0%)		67% (3, 1%)	0% (4, 1%)	0% (1, 0%)	45% (370, 100%)
TOTAL	48% (677, 71%)	36% (118, 12%)	17% (6, 1%)	39% (69, 7%)	30% (43, 5%)	0% (1, 0%)	76% (17, 2%)	0% (1, 0%)	60% (10, 1%)	100% (1, 0%)	50% (4, 0%)	0% (4, 0%)	0% (1, 0%)	45% (952, 100%)

Format Line 1: Success Rate Line 2: Total # of Plays, % of All Plays (by type)

OAK-5 But that came against the fourth-easiest schedule of opposing run defenses, and 2018 looks to be much more difficult. The fact that Gruden signed Doug Martin thinking he could be helpful was curious: Out of 40 RBs with 200-plus carries over the past two years, Martin ranks 40th in success rate (38%), 40th in YPC (2.9), 40th in percentage of runs that gained three or fewer yards (65%), and 40th in percentage of runs that gained five-plus yards (25%).

After being projected to finish in first place in the AFC West with 9.5 wins, the Raiders are projected to finish in second place this year, but with only eight wins. On paper, the Raiders' offensive depth looks old. I have serious questions about their defense, as they made almost no improvements to a unit that faced merely an average schedule of opposing offenses, was extremely healthy apart from their DBs, and still ranked as the fourth-worst defense in the league. For the Raiders to post a winning season, either Derek Carr is going to need to be really special in this Gruden offense, or the defense is going to have to play lights out and hope the new QBs in the AFC West don't live up to expectations.

Receiving Success by Personnel Grouping

Position	Player	1-1 [3WR]	1-2 [2WR]	1-0 [4WR]	1-3 [1WR]	0-1 [4WR]	2-2 [1WR]	0-0 [5WR]	0-2 [3WR]	3-1 [1WR]	2-3 [0WR]	Total
RB	DeAndre Washington	41% 4.5 92.7 (44)				0% 0.0 39.6 (1)						40% 4.4 90.7 (45)
	Jalen Richard	48% 6.5 101.7 (31)	100% 22.0 118.8 (2)	0% 0.0 39.6 (1)			100% 10.5 110.4 (2)					53% 7.4 104.6 (36)
TE	Jared Cook	57% 8.5 93.4 (67)	30% 5.0 81.3 (10)		0% 0.0 39.6 (1)	80% 7.2 96.7 (5)	100% 4.0 83.3 (1)		100% 29.0 158.3 (1)		0% 0.0 39.6 (1)	55% 8.0 95.4 (86)
WR	Michael Crabtree	48% 5.4 77.9 (86)	40% 9.1 106.7 (10)	100% 23.0 158.3 (1)		100% 13.3 158.3 (3)			0% 0.0 39.6 (1)			49% 6.1 89.5 (101)
	Amari Cooper	45% 8.4 91.8 (73)	33% 5.3 12.5 (3)	0% 0.0 39.6 (1)	0% 0.0 39.6 (3)	15% 2.5 46.6 (13)	100% 6.0 91.7 (1)	0% 0.0 39.6 (1)		100% 14.0 118.8 (1)		40% 7.1 75.9 (96)
	Seth Roberts	57% 7.3 80.1 (58)	100% 7.0 95.8 (1)	0% 0.0 39.6 (1)		0% 2.7 42.4 (3)			100% 7.0 95.8 (2)			55% 7.0 78.7 (65)

Format Line 1: Success Rate Line 2: YPA Line 3: Passer Rating Line 4: Total # of Plays

Successful Play Rate
0% [color scale] 100%

Rushing Success by Personnel Grouping

Position	Player	1-1 [3WR]	1-2 [2WR]	1-3 [1WR]	2-0 [3WR]	2-2 [1WR]	2-3 [0WR]	1-4 [0WR]	Total
RB	Marshawn Lynch	53% 4.9 (112)	33% 2.8 (40)	51% 3.3 (43)	0% 0.0 (1)	75% 11.4 (8)	50% 0.5 (2)	0% 0.0 (1)	49% 4.3 (207)
	DeAndre Washington	46% 3.1 (41)	10% 1.6 (10)	40% 1.2 (5)		100% 2.0 (1)			40% 2.7 (57)
	Jalen Richard	36% 4.7 (42)	33% 3.4 (9)	40% 9.4 (5)					36% 4.9 (56)

Format Line 1: Success Rate Line 2: YPC Line 3: Total # of Plays

Philadelphia Eagles

2018 Coaches

Head Coach:
Doug Pederson (3rd yr)

Offensive Coordinator:
Doug Pederson will call plays (1st yr)

Defensive Coordinator:
Jim Schwartz (2nd yr)

2018 Forecast

Wins	Div Rank
10.5	#1

Past Records

2017: 13-3
2016: 7-9
2015: 7-9

EASY HARD

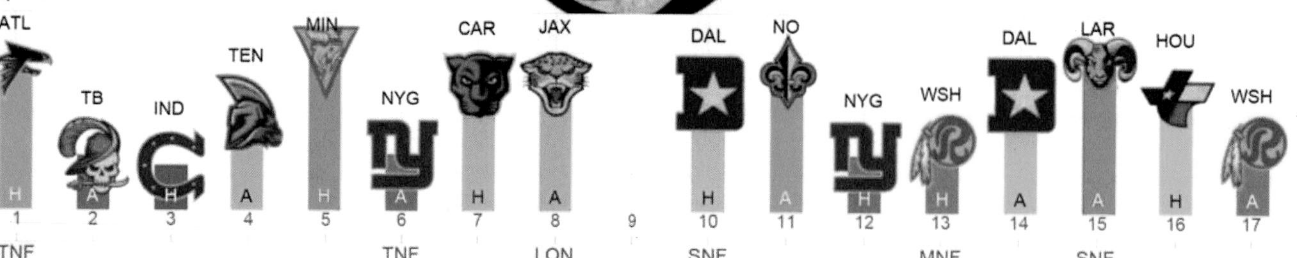

Key Players Lost

TXN	Player (POS)
Cut	Bouka, Elie CB
	Celek, Brent TE
	Curry, Vinny DE
	Williams, Dom WR
	Worley, Daryl CB
Declared Free Agent	Allen, Beau DT
	Barner, Kenjon RB
	Beatty, Will T
	Blount, LeGarrette RB
	Braman, Bryan LB
	Burton, Trey TE
	Ellerbe, Dannell LB
	Goode, Najee LB
	Graham, Corey S
	Robinson, Patrick CB
	Sproles, Darren RB
	Sturgis, Caleb K
	Watkins, Jaylen S
Retired	Jones, Donnie P

Average Line	# Games Favored	# Games Underdog
-3.7	11	2

Regular Season Wins: Past & Current Proj

Forecast 2018 Wins: 10.5

2017 Wins: 13

Forecast 2017 Wins: 7

2016 Wins: 7

2015 Wins: 7

2014 Wins: 10

2018 Philadelphia Eagles Overview

The Eagles are in peak Super Bowl mode. They have Carson Wentz on a cheap rookie deal for three more years (2+1 option). The salary cap has risen by $22 million since he was signed, and, unlike most teams, the Eagles don't have to spend that on a starting QB. And they clearly have a good enough roster and coaching staff to win now. For the Eagles, in competing with difficult NFC teams, it's an arms race at this point. Not that they will, but the Eagles cannot afford to rest on any laurels; the NFC is coming for them, and it's going to take more innovation and execution to succeed in their quest for back-to-back titles.

In 2017, the Eagles were a top-10 team that tapped into analytics just enough to overcome any personnel deficiencies they had and game-planned better than most of their competition. We shouldn't make the mistake of putting this team on a pedestal of being the most talented in 2017 or one of the best champions we've seen in recent years. That's not to take anything away from them: They were tremendous, but they still had glaring weaknesses at times.

Like most teams, the Eagles thrived when winning the turnover battle and struggled when losing it. In games with a positive turnover differential, they were 11-0; in the others, they were 2-3. Referencing page 2 of this chapter, the Eagles were top 10 in most advanced metrics but certainly not all, and there were issues on both sides of the ball they struggled with to varying degrees.

Looking at their weekly EDSR performance, the Eagles were good but not great, save for a few games with outstanding performances. Even down the stretch, from Weeks 13-16, they were not uber-impressive from an efficiency standpoint. They lost the turnover battle -2 to the Seahawks, and Carson Wentz's 45-pass attempt performance was not efficient enough to prevent a blowout loss to Seattle, 24-10. They earned narrow victories the next three weeks against the Rams, Giants, and Raiders, but they won the EDSR battle in only one game. Two of their three playoff wins were one-score affairs that could have gone either way.

Simply put, the coaching staff and players put themselves into great positions to see success in these games, and the chips fell in their favor.

(cont'd - see PHI2)

Lineup & Cap Hits

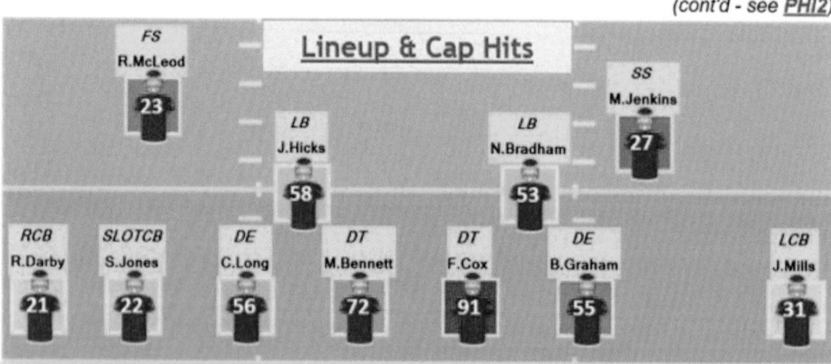

Key Free Agents/ Trades Added

Bennett, Michael DE
Jones, Matt RB
Nelson, Corey LB
Ngata, Haloti DT
Rodgers, Richard TE
Wallace, Mike WR
Wheaton, Markus WR
Worley, Daryl CB
Worrilow, Paul LB

Drafted Players

Rd	Pk	Player (College)
2	49	TE - Dallas Goedert (South Dakota State)
4	125	CB - Avonte Maddox (Pittsburgh)
	130	DE - Josh Sweat (Florida State)
6	206	OT - Matt Pryor (TCU)
7	233	OT - Jordan Mailata ((from Australia))

2018 Unit Spending

All DEF
All OFF

Positional Spending

	Rank	Total	2017 Rk
All OFF	19	$90.76M	2
QB	17	$22.14M	26
OL	9	$37.81M	2
RB	22	$6.40M	6
WR	26	$16.21M	9
TE	18	$8.21M	10
All DEF	9	$90.24M	20
DL	3	$51.23M	8
LB	32	$9.74M	22
CB	31	$6.85M	30
S	3	$22.43M	9

Philadelphia Eagles 2017 Success Rate Radar

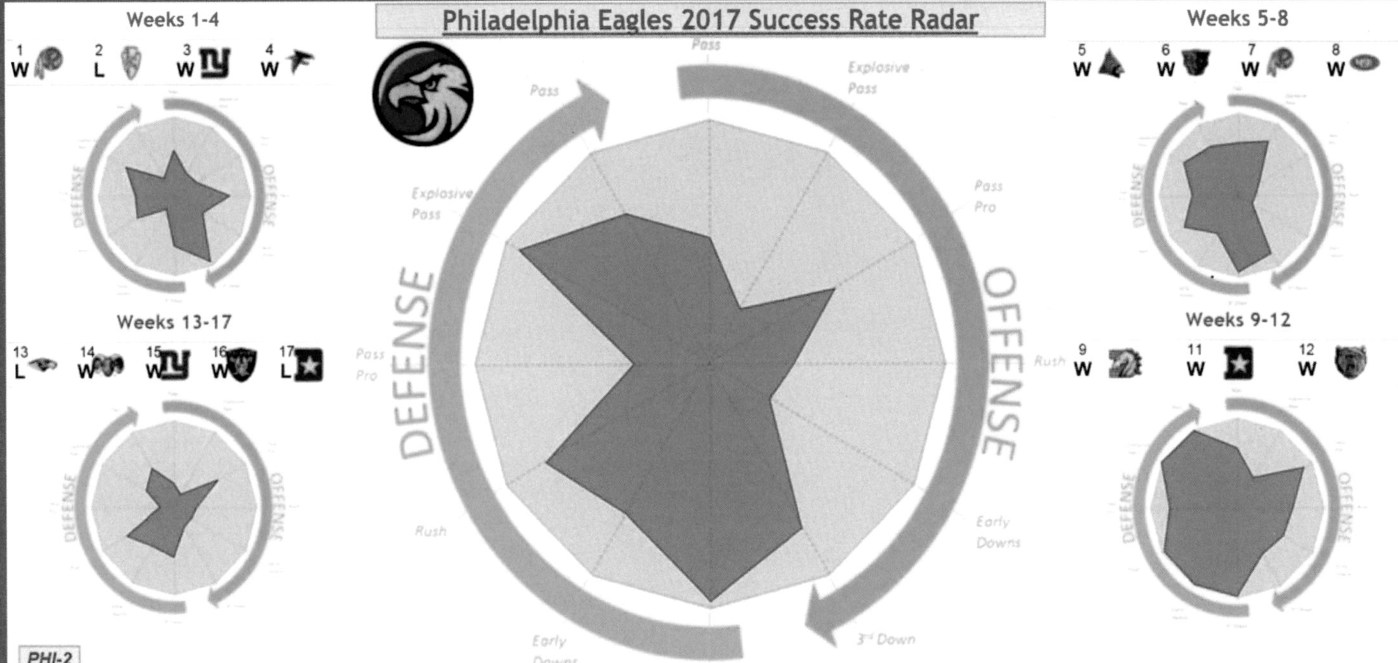

PHI-2

But on a deeper level, the Eagles put themselves in a position of success because of their usage of analytics. And I don't just mean fourth-down decision-making, although that is what grabs the headlines because it is the easiest to distinguish that they "did something different" than most teams. But it certainly wasn't the only thing they did nor was it even the largest contributor to their analytical success in 2017.

The Eagles' success last year was in large part thanks to analytical decisions they made apart from fourth-down "kick-or-go" decisions. On first-and-10 in the first three quarters of games, the Eagles passed the ball on 58% of their plays, just ahead of the Steelers (55%) for the most in the NFL. That was 12% above the league average. League-wide, the success rate on first-and-10 passes in the first three quarters was 52%. Run success rates were only 44%, for reference. One might think this would cause teams to be more pass-oriented, but the league average was 54% run. By spurning the traditional run-first philosophy, the Eagles helped maximize their overall efficiency.

Another opportunity to increase efficiency came on second-and-short. The league went 67% run in these situations, but the average first down conversion rate was 69% on run plays versus just 53% on pass plays. It's not quite to the extent of taking a layup versus pulling up at the free throw line for a transition jumper, but it's close.

The Eagles ran the ball on 77% of their second-and-short plays -- the fifth-most run-heavy team in the league. In the playoffs, they fully embraced analytics: The Eagles had seven plays on second-and-short in the playoffs and ran the ball 100% of the time. [Note: The run rate on other teams with multiple second-and-short plays in the playoffs was 100% for the Saints and Vikings, 75% run for the Jaguars, and 71% run for the Patriots. All those teams ran the ball above the league average (67% run). The only playoff team that completely ignored analytics was, unsurprisingly, the Titans, who went 100% pass on their four attempts and produced a mere 50% success rate.]

(cont'd - see PHI-3)

2017 Offensive Advanced Metrics

Metric	Rank
EDSR Off	10
30 & In Off	8
Red Zone Off	3
3rd Down Off	5
YPPA Off	13
YPPT Off	1
Offensive Efficiency	8
Pass Efficiency Off	5
Pass Pro Efficiency Off	12
RB Pass Eff Off	16
Rush Efficiency Off	17
Explosive Pass Off	23
Explosive Run Off	3

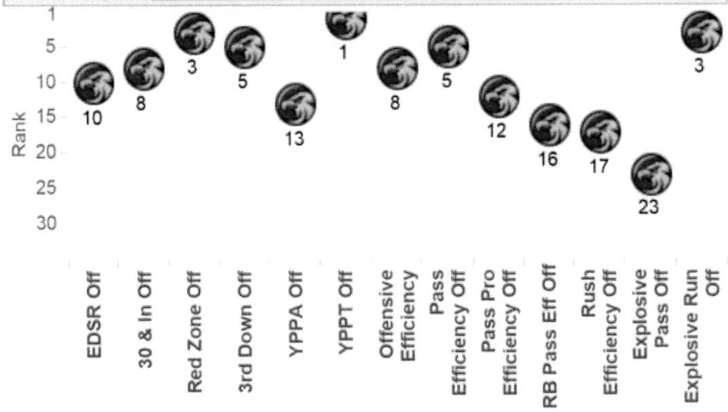

2017 Defensive Advanced Metrics

Metric	Rank
EDSR Def	9
30 & In Def	12
Red Zone Def	14
3rd Down Def	3
YPPA Def	4
YPPT Def	7
Defensive Efficiency	5
Pass Efficiency Def	7
Pass Pro Efficiency Def	19
RB Pass Eff Def	13
Rush Efficiency Def	3
Explosive Pass Def	6
Explosive Run Def	11

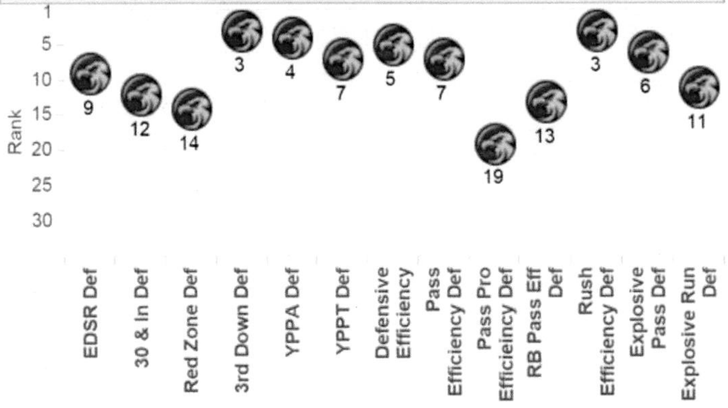

2017 Weekly EDSR & Season Trending Performance

WEEK	1	2	3	4	5	6	7	8	9	11	12	13	14	15	16	17
RESULT	W	L	W	W	W	W	W	W	W	W	W	L	W	W	W	L
OPP	WAS	KC	NYG	SD	ARI	CAR	WAS	SF	DEN	DAL	CHI	SEA	LA	NYG	OAK	DAL
SITE	A	A	H	A	H	A	H	H	H	A	H	A	A	A	H	H
MARGIN	13	-7	3	2	27	5	10	23	28	28	28	-14	8	5	9	-6
PTS	30	20	27	26	34	28	34	33	51	37	31	10	43	34	19	0
OPP PTS	17	27	24	24	7	23	24	10	23	9	3	24	35	29	10	6

EDSR by Wk
W=Green
L=Red

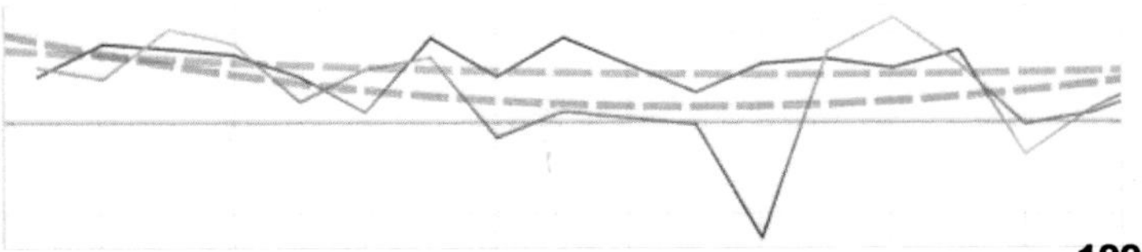

OFF/DEF EDSR
Blue=OFF (high=good)
Red=DEF (low=good)

2017 Close Game Records

All 2016 Wins: **13**
FG Games (<=3 pts) W-L: **2-0**
FG Games Win %: **100% (#1)**
FG Games Wins (% of Total Wins): **15% (#19)**
1 Score Games (<=8 pts) W-L: **5-2**
1 Score Games Win %: **71% (#6)**
1 Score Games Wins (% of Total Wins): **38% (#19)**

2017 Critical & Game-Deciding Stats

TO Margin	+11
TO Given	20
INT Given	9
FUM Given	11
TO Taken	31
INT Taken	19
FUM Taken	12
Sack Margin	+2
Sacks	38
Sacks Allow	36
Return TD Margin	+3
Ret TDs	6
Ret TDs Allow	3
Penalty Margin	-15
Penalties	116
Opponent Penalties	101

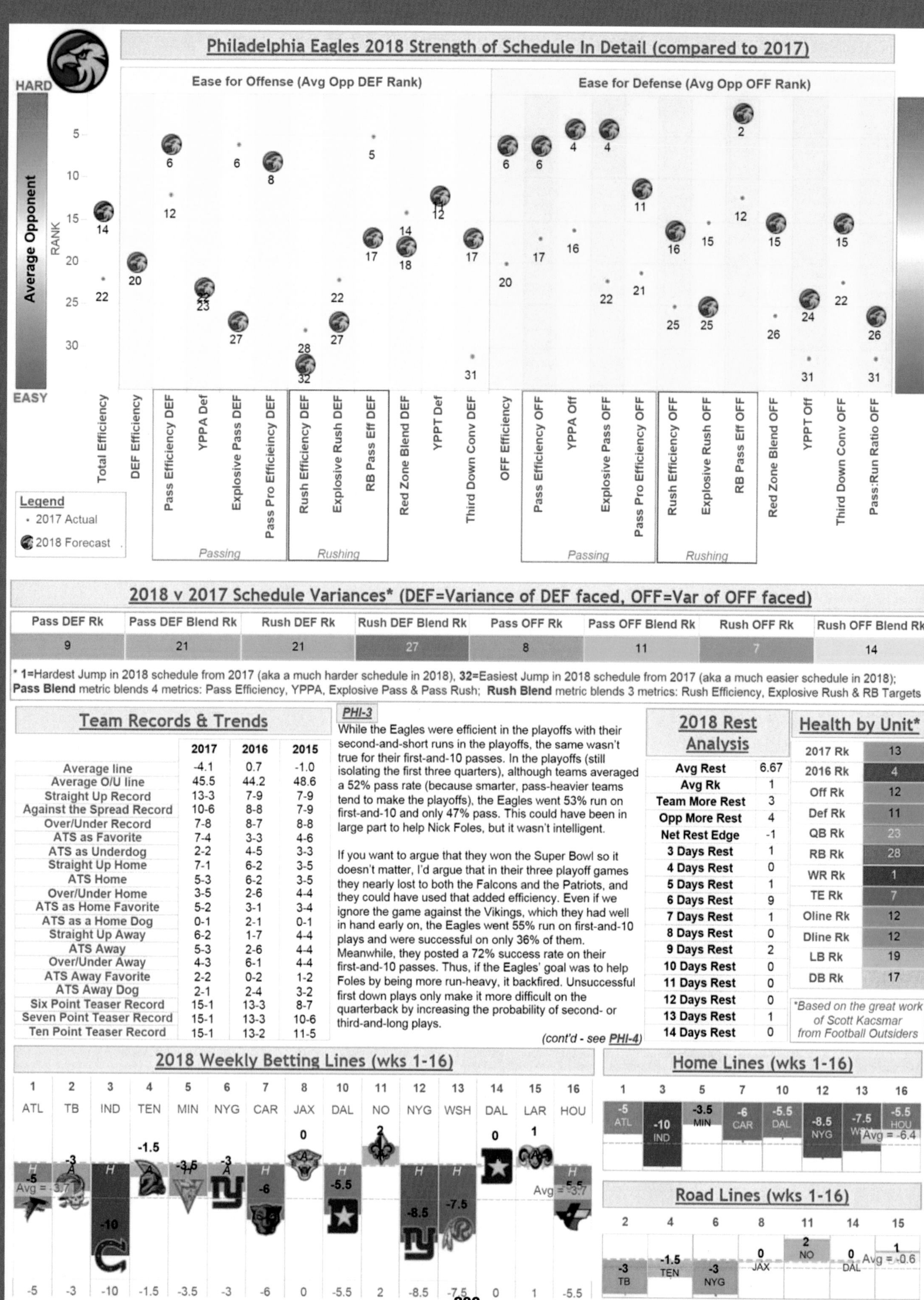

Philadelphia Eagles 2018 Strength of Schedule In Detail (compared to 2017)

2018 v 2017 Schedule Variances* (DEF=Variance of DEF faced, OFF=Var of OFF faced)

Pass DEF Rk	Pass DEF Blend Rk	Rush DEF Rk	Rush DEF Blend Rk	Pass OFF Rk	Pass OFF Blend Rk	Rush OFF Rk	Rush OFF Blend Rk
9	21	21	27	8	11	7	14

* **1**=Hardest Jump in 2018 schedule from 2017 (aka a much harder schedule in 2018), **32**=Easiest Jump in 2018 schedule from 2017 (aka a much easier schedule in 2018); **Pass Blend** metric blends 4 metrics: Pass Efficiency, YPPA, Explosive Pass & Pass Rush; **Rush Blend** metric blends 3 metrics: Rush Efficiency, Explosive Rush & RB Targets

Team Records & Trends

	2017	2016	2015
Average line	-4.1	0.7	-1.0
Average O/U line	45.5	44.2	48.6
Straight Up Record	13-3	7-9	7-9
Against the Spread Record	10-6	8-8	7-9
Over/Under Record	7-8	8-7	8-8
ATS as Favorite	7-4	3-3	4-6
ATS as Underdog	2-2	4-5	3-3
Straight Up Home	7-1	6-2	3-5
ATS Home	5-3	6-2	3-5
Over/Under Home	3-5	2-6	4-4
ATS as Home Favorite	5-2	3-1	3-4
ATS as a Home Dog	0-1	2-1	0-1
Straight Up Away	6-2	1-7	4-4
ATS Away	5-3	2-6	4-4
Over/Under Away	4-3	6-1	4-4
ATS Away Favorite	2-2	0-2	1-2
ATS Away Dog	2-1	2-4	3-2
Six Point Teaser Record	15-1	13-3	8-7
Seven Point Teaser Record	15-1	13-3	10-6
Ten Point Teaser Record	15-1	13-2	11-5

PHI-3

While the Eagles were efficient in the playoffs with their second-and-short runs in the playoffs, the same wasn't true for their first-and-10 passes. In the playoffs (still isolating the first three quarters), although teams averaged a 52% pass rate (because smarter, pass-heavier teams tend to make the playoffs), the Eagles went 53% run on first-and-10 and only 47% pass. This could have been in large part to help Nick Foles, but it wasn't intelligent.

If you want to argue that they won the Super Bowl so it doesn't matter, I'd argue that in their three playoff games they nearly lost to both the Falcons and the Patriots, and they could have used that added efficiency. Even if we ignore the game against the Vikings, which they had well in hand early on, the Eagles went 55% run on first-and-10 plays and were successful on only 36% of them. Meanwhile, they posted a 72% success rate on their first-and-10 passes. Thus, if the Eagles' goal was to help Foles by being more run-heavy, it backfired. Unsuccessful first down plays only make it more difficult on the quarterback by increasing the probability of second- or third-and-long plays.

(cont'd - see PHI-4)

2018 Rest Analysis

Avg Rest	6.67
Avg Rk	1
Team More Rest	3
Opp More Rest	4
Net Rest Edge	-1
3 Days Rest	1
4 Days Rest	0
5 Days Rest	1
6 Days Rest	9
7 Days Rest	1
8 Days Rest	0
9 Days Rest	2
10 Days Rest	0
11 Days Rest	0
12 Days Rest	0
13 Days Rest	1
14 Days Rest	0

Health by Unit*

2017 Rk	13
2016 Rk	4
Off Rk	12
Def Rk	11
QB Rk	23
RB Rk	28
WR Rk	1
TE Rk	7
Oline Rk	12
Dline Rk	12
LB Rk	19
DB Rk	17

*Based on the great work of Scott Kacsmar from Football Outsiders

2018 Weekly Betting Lines (wks 1-16)

1	2	3	4	5	6	7	8	10	11	12	13	14	15	16
ATL	TB	IND	TEN	MIN	NYG	CAR	JAX	DAL	NO	NYG	WSH	DAL	LAR	HOU
-5	-3	-10	-1.5	-3.5	-3	-6	0	-5.5	2	-8.5	-7.5	0	1	-5.5

Avg = -3.7

Home Lines (wks 1-16)

1	3	5	7	10	12	13	16
ATL	IND	MIN	CAR	DAL	NYG	WSH	HOU
-5	-10	-3.5	-6	-5.5	-8.5	-7.5	-5.5

Avg = -6.4

Road Lines (wks 1-16)

2	4	6	8	11	14	15
TB	TEN	NYG	JAX	NO	DAL	
-3	-1.5	-3	0	2	0	1

Avg = -0.6

Philadelphia Eagles 2017 Play Analysis

2017 Play Tendencies

All Pass %	56%
All Pass Rk	22
All Rush %	44%
All Rush Rk	11
1 Score Pass %	59%
1 Score Pass Rk	11
2016 1 Score Pass %	60%
2016 1 Score Pass Rk	14
2017 Pass Increase %	-1%
Pass Increase Rk	14
1 Score Rush %	41%
1 Score Rush Rk	22
Up Pass %	49%
Up Pass Rk	16
Up Rush %	51%
Up Rush Rk	17
Down Pass %	64%
Down Pass Rk	23
Down Rush %	36%
Down Rush Rk	10

2017 Down & Distance Tendencies

Down	Distance	Total Plays	Pass Rate	Run Rate	Play Success %
1	Short (1-3)	9	22%	78%	33%
	Med (4-7)	9	11%	89%	67%
	Long (8-10)	393	56%	44%	49%
	XL (11+)	17	29%	71%	24%
2	Short (1-3)	43	30%	70%	53%
	Med (4-7)	70	56%	44%	50%
	Long (8-10)	132	54%	46%	36%
	XL (11+)	58	64%	36%	28%
3	Short (1-3)	50	46%	54%	68%
	Med (4-7)	68	93%	7%	43%
	Long (8-10)	43	81%	19%	42%
	XL (11+)	36	89%	11%	25%
4	Short (1-3)	17	35%	65%	88%
	Med (4-7)	3	100%	0%	0%
	Long (8-10)	1	100%	0%	0%

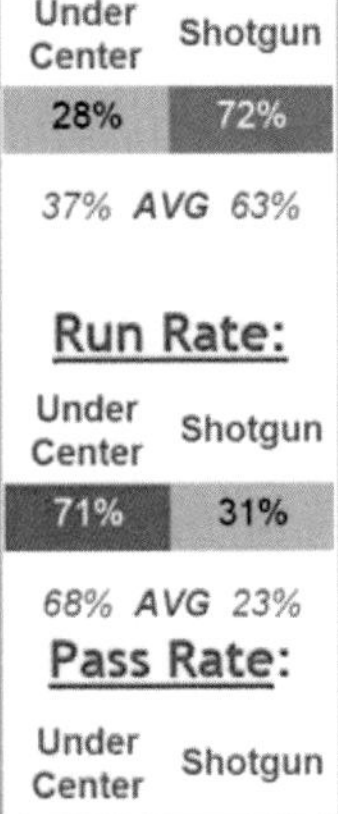

Shotgun %:

Under Center	Shotgun
28%	72%
37%	63%

37% AVG 63%

Run Rate:

Under Center	Shotgun
71%	31%

68% AVG 23%

Pass Rate:

Under Center	Shotgun
29%	69%

32% AVG 77%

Short Yardage Intelligence:

2nd and Short Run

Run Freq	Run Rk	NFL Run Freq Avg	Run 1D Rate	Run NFL 1D Avg
77%	5	67%	65%	69%

2nd and Short Pass

Pass Freq	Pass Rk	NFL Pass Freq Avg	Pass 1D Rate	Pass NFL 1D Avg
23%	28	33%	57%	53%

Most Frequent Play

Down	Distance	Play Type	Player	Total Plays	Play Success %
1	Short (1-3)	RUSH	LeGarrette Blount	5	20%
	Med (4-7)	RUSH	LeGarrette Blount	4	50%
	Long (8-10)	RUSH	LeGarrette Blount	68	49%
	XL (11+)	RUSH	LeGarrette Blount	4	25%
2	Short (1-3)	RUSH	LeGarrette Blount	12	58%
	Med (4-7)	RUSH	LeGarrette Blount	17	47%
	Long (8-10)	RUSH	LeGarrette Blount	19	16%
	XL (11+)	PASS	Alshon Jeffery	7	14%
			Torrey Smith	7	14%
3	Short (1-3)	RUSH	LeGarrette Blount	9	44%
	Med (4-7)	PASS	Alshon Jeffery	14	43%
	Long (8-10)	PASS	Alshon Jeffery	12	42%
	XL (11+)	PASS	Nelson Agholor	9	33%

Most Successful Play*

Down	Distance	Play Type	Player	Total Plays	Play Success %
1	Short (1-3)	RUSH	LeGarrette Blount	5	20%
	Long (8-10)	RUSH	Carson Wentz	10	70%
2	Short (1-3)	RUSH	Jay Ajayi	7	71%
	Med (4-7)	PASS	Zach Ertz	7	71%
	Long (8-10)	PASS	Nelson Agholor	9	67%
	XL (11+)	PASS	Zach Ertz	5	60%
3	Short (1-3)	RUSH	Carson Wentz	8	100%
	Med (4-7)	PASS	Torrey Smith	8	63%
	Long (8-10)	PASS	Zach Ertz	9	44%
	XL (11+)	PASS	Nelson Agholor	9	33%
4	Short (1-3)	RUSH	Carson Wentz	7	100%

*Minimum 5 plays to qualify

2017 Snap Rates

Wk	Opp	Score	Alshon Jeffery	Nelson Agholor	Zach Ertz	Torrey Smith	Brent Celek	LeGarrette Blount	Trey Burton	Corey Clement	Jay Ajayi
1	WAS	W 30-17	60 (88%)	42 (62%)	60 (88%)	48 (71%)	25 (37%)	23 (34%)	14 (21%)		
2	KC	L 27-20	61 (85%)	55 (76%)	60 (83%)	62 (86%)	17 (24%)	6 (8%)	14 (19%)	1 (1%)	
3	NYG	W 27-24	69 (91%)	45 (59%)	75 (99%)	58 (76%)	20 (26%)	22 (29%)	19 (25%)	7 (9%)	
4	LAC	W 26-24	68 (86%)	61 (77%)	60 (76%)	57 (72%)	34 (43%)	26 (33%)	9 (11%)	18 (23%)	
5	ARI	W 34-7	53 (79%)	47 (70%)	57 (85%)	42 (63%)	26 (39%)	26 (39%)	16 (24%)	23 (34%)	
6	CAR	W 28-23	56 (90%)	48 (77%)	49 (79%)	35 (56%)	24 (39%)	30 (48%)	13 (21%)	10 (16%)	
7	WAS	W 34-24	53 (82%)	47 (72%)	53 (82%)	41 (63%)	33 (51%)	25 (38%)	16 (25%)	12 (18%)	
8	SF	W 33-10	48 (69%)	36 (51%)	64 (91%)	32 (46%)	30 (43%)	35 (50%)	21 (30%)	19 (27%)	
9	DEN	W 51-23	49 (71%)	42 (61%)		31 (45%)	54 (78%)	16 (23%)	47 (68%)	28 (41%)	17 (25%)
11	DAL	W 37-9	47 (73%)	47 (73%)	60 (94%)	42 (66%)	23 (36%)	30 (47%)	13 (20%)	19 (30%)	13 (20%)
12	CHI	W 31-3	67 (86%)	65 (83%)	65 (83%)	41 (53%)	30 (38%)	37 (47%)		15 (19%)	22 (28%)
13	SEA	L 24-10	70 (93%)	66 (88%)	45 (60%)	58 (77%)	23 (31%)	14 (19%)	21 (28%)	28 (37%)	31 (41%)
14	LA	W 43-35	86 (95%)	77 (85%)		67 (74%)	47 (52%)	15 (16%)	48 (53%)	27 (30%)	43 (47%)
15	NYG	W 34-29	61 (90%)	49 (72%)	60 (88%)	51 (75%)	23 (34%)	17 (25%)	11 (16%)	10 (15%)	35 (51%)
16	OAK	W 19-10	63 (93%)	58 (85%)	56 (82%)	55 (81%)	20 (29%)	13 (19%)	10 (15%)	27 (40%)	28 (41%)
17	DAL	L 6-0	18 (31%)	30 (51%)	14 (24%)	15 (25%)	35 (59%)	19 (32%)	28 (47%)	11 (19%)	
	Grand Total		929 (81%)	815 (72%)	778 (80%)	735 (64%)	464 (41%)	354 (32%)	300 (28%)	255 (24%)	189 (36%)

Personnel Groupings

Personnel	Team %	NFL Avg	Succ. %
1-1 [3WR]	65%	59%	44%
1-2 [2WR]	23%	19%	43%
1-3 [1WR]	10%	5%	42%

Grouping Tendencies

Personnel	Pass Rate	Pass Succ. %	Run Succ. %
1-1 [3WR]	59%	42%	48%
1-2 [2WR]	57%	49%	35%
1-3 [1WR]	28%	48%	39%

Red Zone Targets (min 3)

Receiver	All	Inside 5	6-10	11-20
Alshon Jeffery	20	6	5	9
Nelson Agholor	20	4	6	10
Zach Ertz	20	6	2	12
Trey Burton	7			7
Torrey Smith	5	1		4
Corey Clement	4	1	1	2

Red Zone Rushes (min 3)

Rusher	All	Inside 5	6-10	11-20
LeGarrette Blount	40	16	3	21
Corey Clement	15	6	1	8
Jay Ajayi	13	2	2	9
Carson Wentz	8	2	3	3
Nick Foles	4	1		3
Wendell Smallwood	3	1	1	1

Early Down Target Rate

	RB	TE	WR
	15%	25%	60%
NFL AVG	23%	21%	56%

Overall Target Success %

RB	TE	WR
50%	56%	48%
#7	#5	#16

Philadelphia Eagles 2017 Passing Recap & 2018 Outlook

One of my favorite elements of the 2017 Eagles was the way in which they coached their QBs. Wentz improved so much from 2016 to 2017, and even when he went down with an ACL injury, the coaching staff coached up Nick Foles to the point he was shredding playoff defenses a few weeks later. My favorite Wentz stat is what he did on third-and-long: On third downs with 8-10 yards to go last year, the Eagles converted an unheard-of 48% of passes into first downs. That was nearly 20% above the NFL average. Wentz completed 68% of his passes (NFL average was 54%), he averaged 9.0 YPA (NFL average was 7.1), and he posted a 136 passer rating (NFL average was 72). Hopefully the Eagles won't be in as many third-and-long situations in 2018, but they'll feel better about it if they do, although those numbers are so insane they are sure to regress. Wentz improved his YPA from 6.2 to 7.5, his TD:INT ratio from 16:14 to 32:7, his passer rating from 71 to 101, and his explosiveness: His completions averaged 7.6 air yards compared to 5.1 air yards in 2016. These aren't "baby steps" of improvement; these are massive.

Carson Wentz Rating All Downs

115	106	89
94	123	95

Carson Wentz Rating Early Downs

76	46	98
92	112	85

2017 Standard Passing Table

QB	Comp	Att	Comp %	Yds	YPA	TDs	INT	Sacks	Rating	Rk
Carson Wentz	264	439	60%	3,280	7.5	32	7	28	101	6
Nick Foles	134	207	65%	1,508	7.3	11	3	7	98	10
NFL Avg			62%		7.0				87.5	

2017 Advanced Passing Table

QB	Success %	EDSR Passing Success %	20+ Yd Pass Gains	20+ Yd Pass %	30+ Yd Pass Gains	30+ Yd Pass %	Avg. Air Yds per Comp	Avg. YAC per Comp	20+ Air Yd Comp	20+ Air Yd %
Carson Wentz	45%	44%	40	9.1%	15	3.4%	7.6	4.8	21	8%
Nick Foles	50%	53%	15	7.2%	9	4.3%	5.0	1.9	2	1%
NFL Avg	44%	48%	27.7	8.8%	10.3	3.3%	6.0	4.7	11.7	6%

Interception Rates by Down

Yards to Go	1	2	3	4	Total
1 & 2	0.0%	0.0%	0.0%	0.0%	0.0%
3, 4, 5	0.0%	0.0%	3.1%	0.0%	1.6%
6 - 9	0.0%	0.0%	0.0%	0.0%	0.0%
10 - 14	0.5%	3.3%	6.1%		1.8%
15+	0.0%	8.3%	0.0%		3.7%
Total	0.5%	2.2%	2.3%	0.0%	1.5%

3rd Down Passing - Short of Sticks Analysis

QB	Avg. Yds to Go	Avg. YIA (of Comp)	Avg Yds Short	Short of Sticks Rate	Short Rk
Carson Wentz	7.9	9.2	0.0	44%	4
NFL Avg	7.8	6.7	-1.1	60%	

Air Yds vs YAC

Air Yds %	YAC %	Rk
63%	37%	10
58%	42%	

2017 Receiving Recap & 2018 Outlook

What I love most about the Eagles offense is they have the X-factors of great receiving TEs and RBs. As much as the NFL has moved in an 11 personnel direction, I'd much rather have both Zach Ertz and either Corey Clement/Darren Sproles out in a route rather than putting Mike Wallace on the field. Using both a TE and an RB on the same route allows for so many more matchup advantages. Torrey Smith's 40% success rate was the worst of any major receiver, so his loss won't be felt, although it might be if Wallace plays a big role. After the Eagles played the sixth-hardest schedule of explosive pass defenses last year, 2018 projections look easier.

Player *Min 50 Targets*	Targets	Comp %	YPA	Rating	TOARS	Success %	Success Rk	Missed YPA Rk	YAS % Rk	TDs
Alshon Jeffery	137	50%	7.2	94	5.1	46%	87	90	39	11
Zach Ertz	132	70%	7.7	109	5.4	58%	14	9	96	9
Nelson Agholor	113	68%	8.3	110	5.1	50%	56	54	51	8
Torrey Smith	88	56%	6.7	83	4.2	40%	112	94	93	3

Directional Passer Rating Delivered

Receiver	Short Left	Short Middle	Short Right	Deep Left	Deep Middle	Deep Right	Player Total
Alshon Jeffery	91	128	92	88	85	67	94
Zach Ertz	98	124	88	70	138	149	109
Nelson Agholor	100	125	94	131	40	66	110
Torrey Smith	89	131	79	94	85	40	83
Trey Burton	116	106	125	107		105	130
Brent Celek	72	51	110	40			82
Corey Clement	102	79	146	158			147
Mack Hollins	92	100	101	52	119	96	98
Jay Ajayi	133		50				108
Wendell Smallwood	89	56	85				86
Darren Sproles	40	115	43				41
LeGarrette Blount	115	83	119				132
Team Total	100	125	94	116	99	82	103

2017 Rushing Recap & 2017 Outlook

Last year, Jay Ajayi was great from shotgun. When leading, the Eagles ran from shotgun on 61 out of 120 attempts. Ajayi had 28 carries in shotgun for 8.6 YPC and was their shotgun workhorse. When tied or trailing, the Eagles ran from shotgun on 79 of 125 attempts (63%), and Ajayi was again their shotgun workhorse, averaging 4.6 YPC on 41 carries. Ajayi was terrible under center with 3.6 YPC when leading and 2.6 YPC when tied or trailing. The Eagles are a shotgun offense, using 77% shotgun in the first half of games on early downs. It's a perfect offense for Ajayi to see success. Without Blount, more red zone rushing attempts will be up for grabs, but Ajayi better improve efficiency if he wants to keep them.

Player *Min 50 Rushes*	Rushes	YPC	Success %	Success Rk	Missed YPA Rk	YTS % Rk	YAS % Rk	Early Down Success %	Early Down Success Rk	TDs
LeGarrette Blount	202	4.4	43%	45	28	68	22	44%	40	5
Jay Ajayi	250	5.3	43%	47	37	73	10	43%	42	2
Corey Clement	80	4.5	51%	13	47	17	23	48%	17	4

Yards per Carry by Direction

	LT	LG	C	RG	RT	
5.2	4.8	4.3	4.5	2.7	4.6	4.2

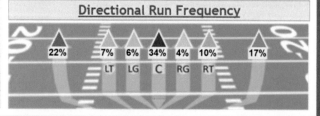

Directional Run Frequency

	LT	LG	C	RG	RT	
22%	7%	6%	34%	4%	10%	17%

<u>PHI-4</u>

It was evident by studying the data that Doug Pederson started implementing analytical decision-making in 2017 rather than in 2016. In his first year in Philadelphia, he was far less analytically inclined to maximize efficiency. Yes, it was Wentz's rookie year, but on first-and-10, the Eagles were 50/50 run/pass despite passes producing a 5% more successful outcome (55%) than runs (50%). It wasn't until 2017 that Pederson's Eagles went 58% pass. And on second-and-short, instead of going 77% run as they did in 2017, the Eagles went 65% run. They produced first downs at a 79% rate (instead of 54% with passes), and I suggested in last year's publication the Eagles go more run-heavy in 2017. They did just that.

And they still have ways to improve their analytical decision-making in 2018. One easy thing is targeting RBs more often on early downs. In 2016, the Eagles targeted their RBs on 20% of early-down passes. But in 2017, that number dipped to 15%, well below the league average. The Eagles' early-down RB passes generated a 49% success rate and 6.9 YPA. These were as successful as WR passes on early downs (49%), and the RB passes posted a better YPA than WR passes (6.6 YPA). In the playoffs, the Eagles turned to their secret weapon -- the RB with the best combination of early-down receiving success (50%) and YPA (7.5), Corey Clement. Clement's 83% success rate on early-down passes in the playoffs led the team, and his 8.0 YPA was right behind Alshon Jeffery's and Zach Ertz's marks.

(cont'd - see PHI-5)

Bryan Mears' Fantasy Corner

Jay Ajayi averaged just 13.8 carries and 2.5 targets per game over the last six games of 2017, but that could increase with LeGarrette Blount out of town. Blount was clearly the guy in the red zone last year, and Ajayi made it through the entire 2017 season without getting a touch inside the 5-yard line either with the Dolphins or Eagles. Wendell Smallwood was a scratch for all but one of Ajayi's games in an Eagles uniform, and other backs Darren Sproles and Corey Clement are unlikely to get short-down carries. Per FantasyLabs' Ian Hartitz, Ajayi converted 5-of-9 (56%) goal line rushes into touchdowns in 2015-16; the league average over the past three seasons was 44%. With increased usage, especially in the red zone, Ajayi could be an under-the-radar mid-round steal.

Division History: Season Wins & 2018 Projection

2014 Wins | 2015 Wins | 2016 Wins | 2017 Wins | Forecast 2018 Wins

Rank of 2018 Defensive Pass Efficiency Faced by Week

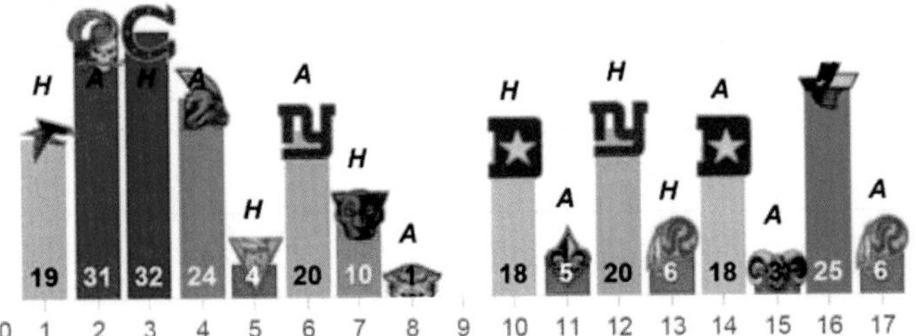

Rank of 2018 Defensive Rush Efficiency Faced by Week

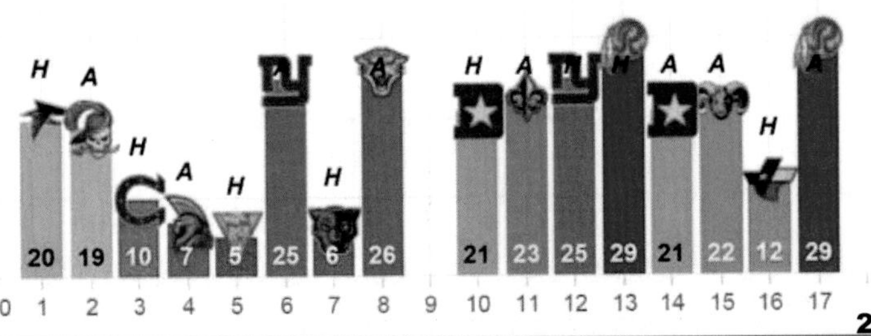

2017 Situational Usage by Player & Position

Usage Rate by Score

		Being Blown Out (14+)	Down Big (9-13)	One Score	Large Lead (9-13)	Blowout Lead (14+)	Grand Total
RUSH	LeGarrette Blount		17%	17%	25%	22%	18%
	Jay Ajayi	3%	24%	9%	3%	12%	10%
	Nelson Agholor			1%			0%
	Corey Clement	3%	10%	5%	9%	15%	7%
	Torrey Smith					0%	0%
	Wendell Smallwood			5%	3%	3%	4%
	Darren Sproles			2%			1%
	Kenjon Barner			1%		2%	1%
	Total	5%	52%	40%	41%	55%	42%
PASS	LeGarrette Blount			1%		0%	1%
	Alshon Jeffery	18%	3%	12%	16%	10%	12%
	Jay Ajayi	5%	7%	2%		1%	2%
	Zach Ertz	5%	17%	12%	3%	12%	12%
	Nelson Agholor	21%	10%	10%	9%	7%	10%
	Corey Clement	5%	3%	2%	3%	1%	2%
	Torrey Smith	8%	7%	8%	9%	6%	8%
	Wendell Smallwood			2%	6%	1%	2%
	Trey Burton	21%		3%	3%	1%	3%
	Darren Sproles	5%		1%	3%		1%
	Brent Celek			2%	6%	2%	2%
	Kenjon Barner	3%		1%		0%	1%
	Mack Hollins	3%		2%		1%	2%
	Marcus Johnson			1%		1%	1%
	Shelton Gibson			0%			0%
	Total	95%	48%	60%	59%	45%	58%

Positional Target Distribution vs NFL Average

		NFL Wide				Team Only			
		Left	Middle	Right	Total	Left	Middle	Right	Total
Deep	WR	946	488	935	**2,369**	40	21	52	**113**
	TE	184	145	185	**514**	8	5	3	**16**
	RB	38	9	42	**89**	1			**1**
	All	**1,168**	**642**	**1,162**	**2,972**	**49**	**26**	**55**	**130**
Short	WR	2,759	1,617	2,663	**7,039**	103	54	127	**284**
	TE	817	795	1,118	**2,730**	46	44	52	**142**
	RB	1,277	816	1,261	**3,354**	44	7	34	**85**
	All	**4,853**	**3,228**	**5,042**	**13,123**	**193**	**105**	**213**	**511**
Total		**6,021**	**3,870**	**6,204**	**16,095**	**242**	**131**	**268**	**641**

Positional Success Rates vs NFL Average

		NFL Wide				Team Only			
		Left	Middle	Right	Total	Left	Middle	Right	Total
Deep	WR	37%	46%	38%	**39%**	33%	33%	33%	**33%**
	TE	38%	52%	45%	**44%**	50%	60%	67%	**56%**
	RB	34%	56%	38%	**38%**	100%			**100%**
	All	**37%**	**47%**	**39%**	**40%**	**37%**	**38%**	**35%**	**36%**
Short	WR	52%	57%	50%	**52%**	47%	70%	53%	**54%**
	TE	50%	56%	49%	**51%**	52%	64%	52%	**56%**
	RB	44%	51%	43%	**45%**	57%	71%	41%	**52%**
	All	**49%**	**55%**	**48%**	**50%**	**50%**	**68%**	**51%**	**54%**
Total		**47%**	**54%**	**46%**	**48%**	**48%**	**62%**	**47%**	**50%**

Successful Play Rate
0% 100%

Philadelphia Eagles - Success by Personnel Grouping & Play Type

Play Type	1-1 [3WR]	1-2 [2WR]	2-1 [2WR]	1-0 [4WR]	1-3 [1WR]	2-0 [3WR]	0-2 [3WR]	2-3 [0WR]	1-4 [0WR]	Grand Total
PASS	42% (410, 68%)	49% (140, 23%)	33% (3, 1%)	25% (12, 2%)	48% (29, 5%)	100% (1, 0%)	0% (2, 0%)	100% (1, 0%)	100% (1, 0%)	44% (599, 100%)
RUSH	48% (284, 60%)	35% (104, 22%)	50% (2, 0%)	57% (7, 1%)	39% (74, 16%)				0% (2, 0%)	43% (473, 100%)
TOTAL	44% (694, 65%)	43% (244, 23%)	40% (5, 0%)	37% (19, 2%)	42% (103, 10%)	100% (1, 0%)	0% (2, 0%)	100% (1, 0%)	33% (3, 0%)	44% (1,072, 100%)

Format Line 1: Success Rate Line 2: Total # of Plays, % of All Plays (by type)

PHI-5 The Eagles are rich with talent in positions that truly matter, and they have multiple excellent receiving backs, as Darren Sproles is set to return (newly signed to a one-year contract) and join the budding Clement. Given those talented options, the Eagles cannot afford to target RBs as little as they did in 2017. If the Eagles continue to turn over every stone through analytics looking for efficiency edges, a key focus in 2018 will be more RB passes on early downs. They targeted WRs 60% of the time on early downs, well above the NFL average of 56%, despite those being their least-efficient targets. I'd be in favor of the 2018 Eagles shifting 9% of those targets to the RBs and producing a 24/25/51 rate between RB/TE/WRs instead of the 15/25/60 they employed in 2017.

One of the beautiful elements of the Eagles offense in 2017 was their red zone offense. It ranked third in the league, and they converted TDs at a rate that bested the individual defense's average by 12%. It was the best rate in the NFL. And still, they can also optimize efficiency on these plays. On first downs in the red zone, the Eagles produced successful passes on just 26% of attempts, which was the second-worst rate in the NFL. They focused on Nelson Agholor in 11 personnel on these first-down passes.

Fortunately for the Eagles, their success on third-down passes was 50%, the second-best rate in the NFL. Wide receiver targets were still terrible on third down, with a collective 33% success rate. One difference on third down was fewer passes to WRs: On first down, they targeted WRs on 56% of attempts; on third down, it was only 44%. They targeted TEs more, and those targets produced a 78% success rate; RB targets produced a 67% success rate. If the Eagles can improve their red zone play-calling on first down and either find better route concepts to use for their WRs or simply throw to TEs and RBs more often on 12 and 13 personnel, they will score far more often in the red zone in 2018 and become that much more dangerous. The Eagles made several moves to ensure they will continue their strong production despite losing some talent via free agency. At 32 years old, DE Michael Bennett is one of only 28 NFL DEs (since 1988) to record at least five sacks and 20 tackles in each of their prior four years leading up to their 10th NFL season. They beefed up their TE corps and added NT Haloti Ngata, WR Mike Wallace, and drafted DE Josh Sweat. The fact that the Eagles won the Super Bowl in the 2017 season and overcame so many injuries in the process, largely thanks to analytics and coaching, warms my heart. But they are going to need to redouble their efforts to maximize all edges possible if they want to return to the promised land in 2018.

Receiving Success by Personnel Grouping

Position	Player	1-1 [3WR]	1-2 [2WR]	2-1 [2WR]	1-0 [4WR]	1-3 [1WR]	0-2 [3WR]	2-3 [0WR]	Total
RB	Corey Clement	55% 8.9 92.2 (11)	50% 6.3 130.2 (4)						53% 8.2 131.4 (15)
TE	Zach Ertz	52% 7.6 79.4 (73)	64% 8.1 138.7 (25)	100% 10.0 108.3 (1)		56% 5.8 121.3 (9)	0% 5.0 87.5 (1)	100% 1.0 118.8 (1)	55% 7.5 106.0 (110)
WR	Alshon Jeffery	41% 7.0 87.9 (85)	46% 5.4 78.3 (28)		0% 0.0 39.6 (2)	75% 7.5 135.4 (4)			43% 6.5 87.3 (119)
	Nelson Agholor	46% 8.3 111.9 (81)	64% 7.3 97.0 (11)		33% 4.3 75.7 (3)				47% 8.1 109.5 (95)
	Torrey Smith	31% 6.1 76.6 (51)	38% 6.2 66.2 (13)		50% 9.5 104.2 (4)				34% 6.3 76.2 (68)
	Trey Burton	69% 9.1 142.2 (16)	50% 6.4 124.0 (12)			100% 12.0 116.7 (2)	0% 1.0 79.2 (1)		61% 8.0 136.8 (31)

Format Line 1: Success Rate Line 2: YPA Line 3: Passer Rating Line 4: Total # of Plays

Successful Play Rate
0% 100%

Rushing Success by Personnel Grouping

Position	Player	1-1 [3WR]	1-2 [2WR]	1-0 [4WR]	1-3 [1WR]	1-4 [0WR]	Total
QB	Carson Wentz	65% 6.3 (40)	78% 5.9 (9)	0% 5.0 (1)	7% -0.7 (14)		53% 4.7 (64)
RB	LeGarrette Blount	44% 5.2 (99)	30% 3.4 (37)		51% 3.6 (35)	0% -2.0 (2)	42% 4.4 (173)
	Jay Ajayi	44% 7.2 (43)	22% 2.6 (18)	80% 8.0 (5)	50% 2.5 (4)		41% 5.8 (70)

Format Line 1: Success Rate Line 2: YPC Line 3: Total # of Plays

Pittsburgh Steelers

2018 Coaches

Head Coach:
Mike Tomlin (12th yr)

Offensive Coordinator:
Randy Fichtner (PIT QB) (1st yr)

Defensive Coordinator:
Keith Butler (3rd yr)

EASY HARD

2018 Forecast

Wins	Div Rank
10.5	#1

Past Records

2017: 13-3
2016: 11-5
2015: 10-6

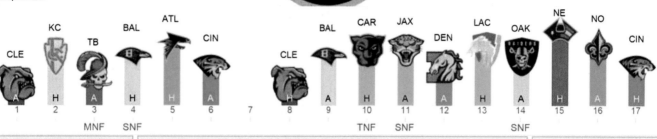

Week	1	2	3	4	5	6	7	8	9	10	11	12	13	14	15	16	17
Opponent	CLE	KC	TB	BAL	ATL	CIN		CLE	BAL	CAR	JAX	DEN	LAC	OAK	NE	NO	CIN
H/A	A	H	A	H	H	A		H	A	H	A	A	H	A	H	A	H
			MNF	SNF						TNF	SNF			SNF			

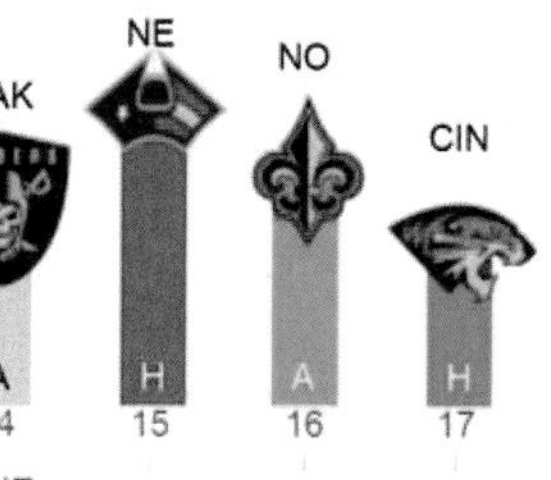

Key Players Lost

TXN	Player (POS)
Cut	Crawford, Antonio CB
	Gay, William CB
	Golden, Robert S
	Mitchell, Mike S
	Wilcox, J.J. S
Declared Free Agent	Ducre, Greg CB
	Hubbard, Chris C
	Hunter, Justin WR
	Matthews, Mike C
	McCullers, Daniel DT
	Moats, Arthur LB
	Ridley, Stevan RB
	Rogers, Eli WR
	Spence, Sean LB
	Toussaint, Fitzgerald RB

Average Line	# Games Favored	# Games Underdog
-4.1	13	1

2018 Pittsburgh Steelers Overview

Success in the NFL often gets taken for granted. Of the 32 teams, only five have double-digit wins in over half of the past four seasons. Only two have won double-digit games in each of the past four years: The Steelers and Patriots. It's been a tremendous run for the Steelers, but unlike the Patriots, who have three Super Bowl appearances and two Lombardi trophies in those four years, the Steelers have appeared in just one Conference Championship, which they lost to the Patriots.

Since 2014, the Steelers have been jettisoned from the playoffs with a home loss to the Jaguars (2017), road loss to the Patriots (2016, without running back Le'Veon Bell for most of the game), road loss to the Peyton Manning-led Broncos (2015, without Bell and wide receiver Antonio Brown), and home loss to the Ravens (2014, without Bell). In most of those games the absence of the dynamic Bell forced more of the workload onto Ben Roethlisberger, and regardless of how underrated Big Ben may be it's not ideal to take away a key weapon and put the game on his shoulders.

This offseason the Steelers decided not to renew the contract of six-year offensive coordinator Todd Haley and instead promoted quarterbacks coach Randy Fichtner to coordinator. Fichtner, who turns 55 this season, hasn't called plays at the NFL level. The last time he called plays was in the college ranks at Memphis in 2006, using an up-tempo spread system before it was en vogue, but that was a long time ago. So what are Fichtner's plans?

Roethlisberger says the offense is completely new. Haley is now with the Browns, whom the Steelers play in Week 1, so the terminology should be new, but how will the offense vary from Haley's? Although little has been discussed, that the Steelers promoted their QB coach (who has a close relationship with Roethlisberger and no NFL play-calling experience) suggests that Fichtner could be a Big Ben yes man. And considering how Roethlisberger and Haley clashed, we can expect that what Roethlisberger unsuccessfully lobbied for in the past will be a priority under the Fichtner regime. We should specifically expect to see more tempo and no-huddle offense. Haley didn't use as much no-huddle as Roethlisberger wanted.

(cont'd - see PIT2)

Key Free Agents/ Trades Added

Berhe, Nat S
Bostic, Jon LB
Burnett, Morgan S
Cheek, Joseph T
Collins, Parker C
Graham, Larson T
Rodgers, Jake T

Drafted Players

Rd	Pk	Player (College)
1	28	S - Terrell Edmunds (Virginia Tech)
2	60	WR - James Washington (Oklahoma State)
3	76	QB - Mason Rudolph (Oklahoma State)
	92	OT - Chukwuma Okorafor (Western Michigan)
5	148	S - Marcus Allen (Penn State)
	165	FB - Jaylen Samuels (NC State)
7	246	DT - Joshua Frazier (Alabama)

Regular Season Wins: Past & Current Proj

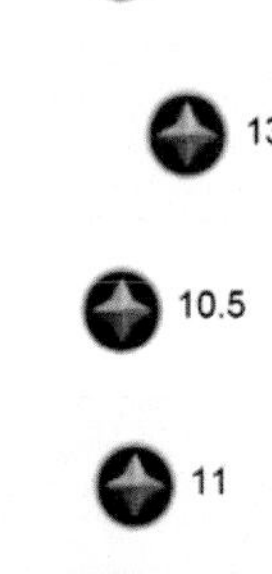

Lineup & Cap Hits

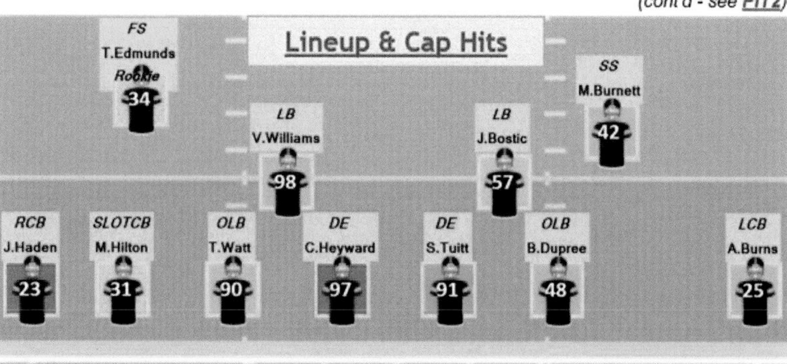

2018 Unit Spending

All DEF
All OFF

Positional Spending

	Rank	Total	2017 Rk
All OFF	4	$106.14M	1
QB	5	$26.81M	13
OL	8	$37.90M	4
RB	1	$17.52M	1
WR	30	$14.65M	15
TE	15	$9.26M	30
All DEF	18	$77.11M	32
DL	16	$27.21M	26
LB	11	$23.91M	17
CB	16	$19.67M	24
S	30	$6.32M	12

Pittsburgh Steelers 2017 Success Rate Radar

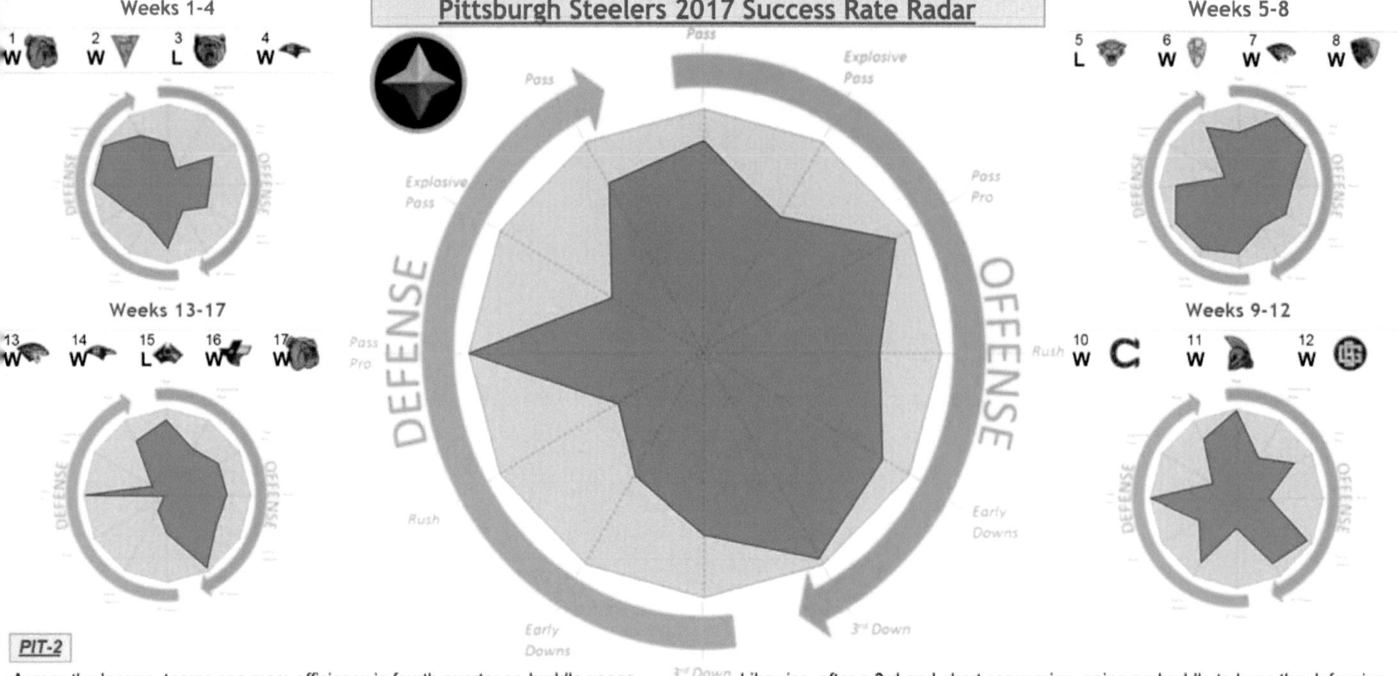

PIT-2

Across the league, teams see more efficiency in fourth-quarter no-huddle usage, but that primarily occurs when teams are down, the clock is an issue, and defenses are playing prevent. Considering just first-half usage, the Steelers have not been substantially better in the no-huddle over the past two years. With first-half huddling, Roethlisberger had a 49% Success Rate, 7.3 YPA, and 95 passer rating. In first-half no-huddle, Roethlisberger had a 51% Success Rate, 6.5 YPA, and 72 passer rating. Situationally, the biggest no-huddle edge for the Steelers was third-down running, where they produced a 67% Success Rate (vs. 50% when huddling). But on early downs and third-down passing, there was no measurable difference between huddling and not huddling.

It's probably best not to use tempo and no-huddle just to use them, but situational usage is important. There are tremendous edges to be gained by hustling to the line of scrimmage after a nice first-down gain to convert an easy 2nd-and-short run while the defense has its 1st-and-10 personnel on the field.

Likewise, after a 3rd-and-short conversion, going no-huddle to keep the defensive short-yardage package on the field for a 1st-and-10 play is intelligent. It's also beneficial for a quarterback to get to the line of scrimmage quickly so he can use pre-snap motion to diagnose coverage and then audible as needed. In these instances, the goal of using tempo is put the defense at a disadvantage. Being uptempo for uptempo's sake is ridiculous, but there's also no benefit to sitting in the huddle for half the play clock.

But we don't know what to expect from Fichtner. In up-tempo situations experienced play callers will have a play ready to call in so the quarterback can go no-huddle more easily. If it takes Fichtner time to figure out the play he wants, either Roethlisberger will call some of the plays in no-huddle or there will be fewer no-huddle options. To this point in his career, Roethlisberger hasn't exhibited a Peyton Manning-like ability to be a high-level play caller as well as quarterback.

(cont'd - see PIT-3)

2017 Offensive Advanced Metrics

2017 Defensive Advanced Metrics

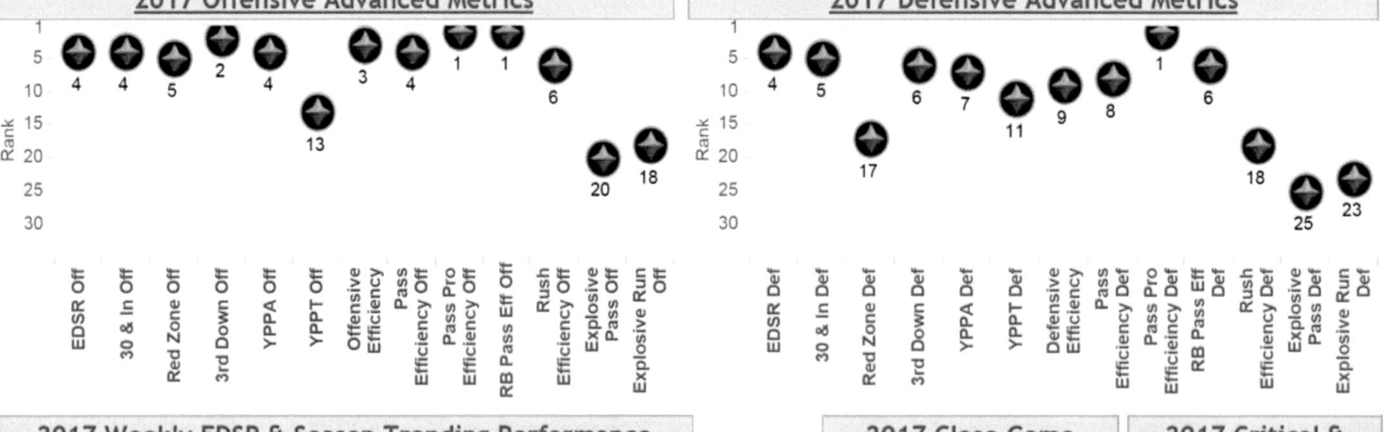

2017 Weekly EDSR & Season Trending Performance

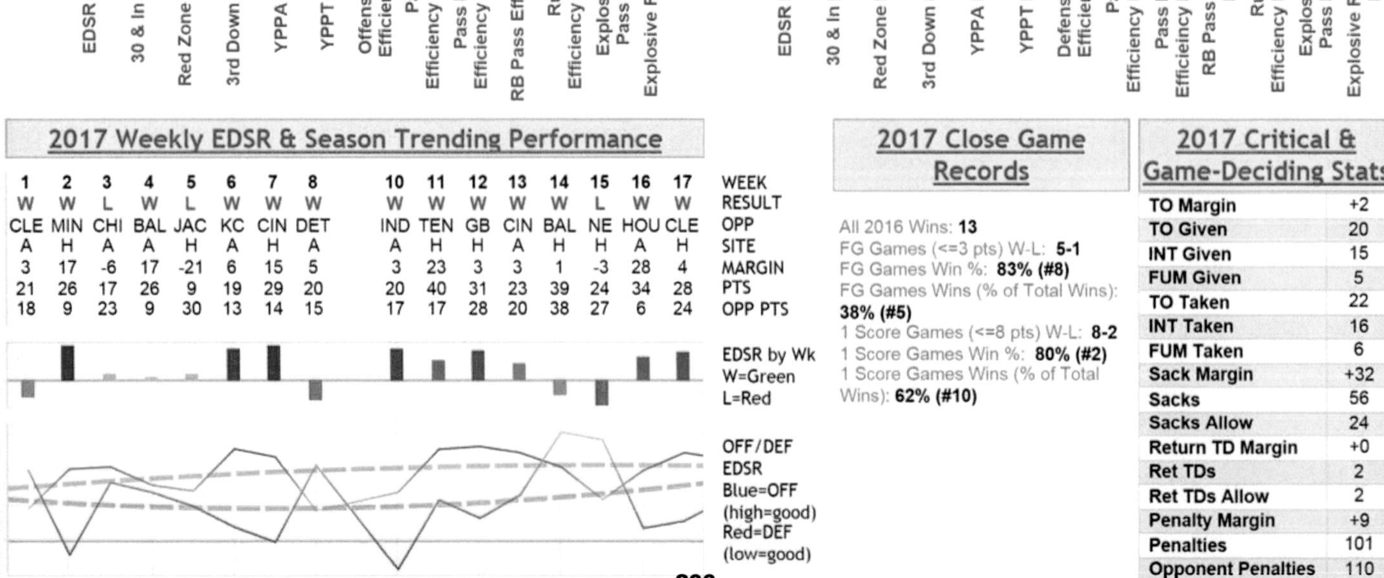

WEEK	1	2	3	4	5	6	7	8	10	11	12	13	14	15	16	17
RESULT	W	W	L	W	L	W	W	W	W	W	W	W	W	L	W	W
OPP	CLE	MIN	CHI	BAL	JAC	KC	CIN	DET	IND	TEN	GB	CIN	BAL	NE	HOU	CLE
SITE	A	H	A	A	H	A	H	A	A	H	H	A	H	H	A	H
MARGIN	3	17	-6	17	-21	6	15	5	3	23	3	3	1	-3	28	4
PTS	21	26	17	26	9	19	29	20	20	40	31	23	39	24	34	28
OPP PTS	18	9	23	9	30	13	14	15	17	17	28	20	38	27	6	24

2017 Close Game Records

All 2016 Wins: **13**
FG Games (<=3 pts) W-L: **5-1**
FG Games Win %: **83% (#8)**
FG Games Wins (% of Total Wins): **38% (#5)**
1 Score Games (<=8 pts) W-L: **8-2**
1 Score Games Win %: **80% (#2)**
1 Score Games Wins (% of Total Wins): **62% (#10)**

2017 Critical & Game-Deciding Stats

TO Margin	+2
TO Given	20
INT Given	15
FUM Given	5
TO Taken	22
INT Taken	16
FUM Taken	6
Sack Margin	+32
Sacks	56
Sacks Allow	24
Return TD Margin	+0
Ret TDs	2
Ret TDs Allow	2
Penalty Margin	+9
Penalties	101
Opponent Penalties	110

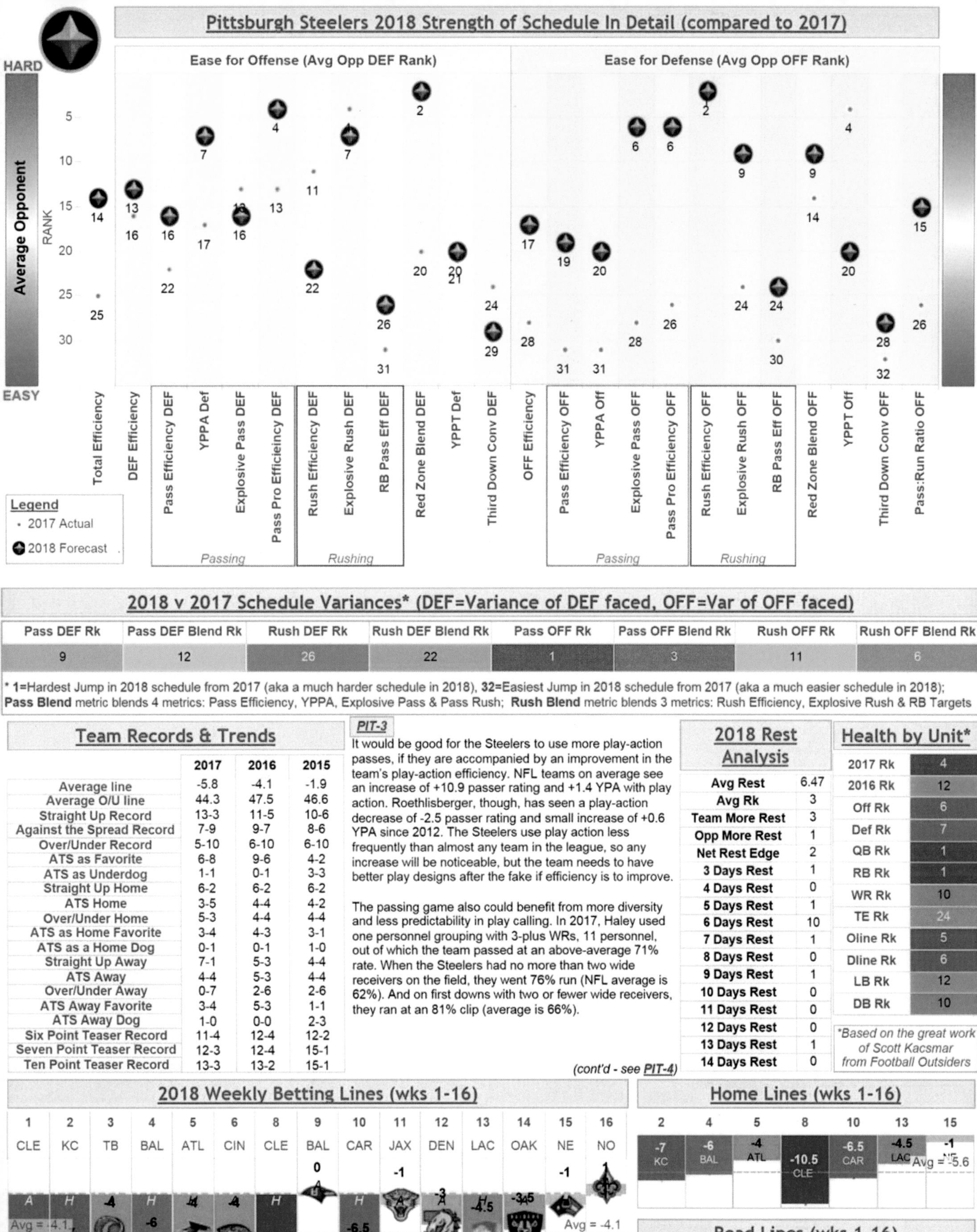

2018 v 2017 Schedule Variances* (DEF=Variance of DEF faced, OFF=Var of OFF faced)

Pass DEF Rk	Pass DEF Blend Rk	Rush DEF Rk	Rush DEF Blend Rk	Pass OFF Rk	Pass OFF Blend Rk	Rush OFF Rk	Rush OFF Blend Rk
9	12	26	22	1	3	11	6

* **1**=Hardest Jump in 2018 schedule from 2017 (aka a much harder schedule in 2018), **32**=Easiest Jump in 2018 schedule from 2017 (aka a much easier schedule in 2018); **Pass Blend** metric blends 4 metrics: Pass Efficiency, YPPA, Explosive Pass & Pass Rush; **Rush Blend** metric blends 3 metrics: Rush Efficiency, Explosive Rush & RB Targets

Team Records & Trends

	2017	2016	2015
Average line	-5.8	-4.1	-1.9
Average O/U line	44.3	47.5	46.6
Straight Up Record	13-3	11-5	10-6
Against the Spread Record	7-9	9-7	8-6
Over/Under Record	5-10	6-10	6-10
ATS as Favorite	6-8	9-6	4-2
ATS as Underdog	1-1	0-1	3-3
Straight Up Home	6-2	6-2	6-2
ATS Home	3-5	4-4	4-2
Over/Under Home	5-3	4-4	4-4
ATS as Home Favorite	3-4	4-3	3-1
ATS as a Home Dog	0-1	0-1	1-0
Straight Up Away	7-1	5-3	4-4
ATS Away	4-4	5-3	4-4
Over/Under Away	0-7	2-6	2-6
ATS Away Favorite	3-4	5-3	1-1
ATS Away Dog	1-0	0-0	2-3
Six Point Teaser Record	11-4	12-4	12-2
Seven Point Teaser Record	12-3	12-4	15-1
Ten Point Teaser Record	13-3	13-2	15-1

PIT-3

It would be good for the Steelers to use more play-action passes, if they are accompanied by an improvement in the team's play-action efficiency. NFL teams on average see an increase of +10.9 passer rating and +1.4 YPA with play action. Roethlisberger, though, has seen a play-action decrease of -2.5 passer rating and small increase of +0.6 YPA since 2012. The Steelers use play action less frequently than almost any team in the league, so any increase will be noticeable, but the team needs to have better play designs after the fake if efficiency is to improve.

The passing game also could benefit from more diversity and less predictability in play calling. In 2017, Haley used one personnel grouping with 3-plus WRs, 11 personnel, out of which the team passed at an above-average 71% rate. When the Steelers had no more than two wide receivers on the field, they went 76% run (NFL average is 62%). And on first downs with two or fewer wide receivers, they ran at an 81% clip (average is 66%).

(cont'd - see PIT-4)

2018 Rest Analysis

Avg Rest	6.47
Avg Rk	3
Team More Rest	3
Opp More Rest	1
Net Rest Edge	2
3 Days Rest	1
4 Days Rest	0
5 Days Rest	1
6 Days Rest	10
7 Days Rest	1
8 Days Rest	0
9 Days Rest	1
10 Days Rest	0
11 Days Rest	0
12 Days Rest	0
13 Days Rest	1
14 Days Rest	0

Health by Unit*

2017 Rk	4
2016 Rk	12
Off Rk	6
Def Rk	7
QB Rk	1
RB Rk	1
WR Rk	10
TE Rk	24
Oline Rk	5
Dline Rk	6
LB Rk	12
DB Rk	10

**Based on the great work of Scott Kacsmar from Football Outsiders*

2018 Weekly Betting Lines (wks 1-16)

1	2	3	4	5	6	8	9	10	11	12	13	14	15	16
CLE	KC	TB	BAL	ATL	CIN	CLE	BAL	CAR	JAX	DEN	LAC	OAK	NE	NO
A	H	A	H	H	A	H	A	H	A	A	H	A	H	A
-7	-7	-4	-6	-4	-4	-10.5	0	-6.5	-1	-3	-4.5	-3.5	-1	1

Avg = -4.1

Home Lines (wks 1-16)

2	4	5	8	10	13	15
KC	BAL	ATL	CLE	CAR	LAC	NE
-7	-6	-4	-10.5	-6.5	-4.5	-1

Avg = -5.6

Road Lines (wks 1-16)

1	3	6	9	11	12	14	16
CLE	TB	CIN	BAL	JAX	DEN	OAK	NO
-7	-4	-4	0	-1	-3	-3.5	1

Avg = -2.7

Pittsburgh Steelers 2017 Play Analysis

2017 Play Tendencies

All Pass %	58%
All Pass Rk	15
All Rush %	42%
All Rush Rk	18
1 Score Pass %	60%
1 Score Pass Rk	7
2016 1 Score Pass %	60%
2016 1 Score Pass Rk	15
2017 Pass Increase %	0%
Pass Increase Rk	12
1 Score Rush %	40%
1 Score Rush Rk	26
Up Pass %	53%
Up Pass Rk	4
Up Rush %	47%
Up Rush Rk	29
Down Pass %	70%
Down Pass Rk	3
Down Rush %	30%
Down Rush Rk	30

2017 Down & Distance Tendencies

Down	Distance	Total Plays	Pass Rate	Run Rate	Play Success %
1	Short (1-3)	7	29%	71%	86%
	Med (4-7)	13	62%	38%	54%
	Long (8-10)	343	56%	44%	48%
	XL (11+)	12	58%	42%	25%
2	Short (1-3)	40	40%	60%	65%
	Med (4-7)	79	56%	44%	49%
	Long (8-10)	107	50%	50%	44%
	XL (11+)	45	71%	29%	31%
3	Short (1-3)	44	66%	34%	66%
	Med (4-7)	50	94%	6%	56%
	Long (8-10)	33	91%	9%	36%
	XL (11+)	31	94%	6%	19%
4	Short (1-3)	3	33%	67%	33%
	XL (11+)	1	100%	0%	100%

Shotgun %:

Under Center	Shotgun
29%	71%
37%	*63%*

AVG

Run Rate:

Under Center	Shotgun
78%	24%
68%	*23%*

AVG

Pass Rate:

Under Center	Shotgun
22%	76%
32%	*77%*

AVG

Short Yardage Intelligence:

2nd and Short Run

Run Freq	Run Rk	NFL Run Freq Avg	Run 1D Rate	Run NFL 1D Avg
58%	25	67%	73%	69%

2nd and Short Pass

Pass Freq	Pass Rk	NFL Pass Freq Avg	Pass 1D Rate	Pass NFL 1D Avg
42%	8	33%	44%	53%

Most Frequent Play

Down	Distance	Play Type	Player	Total Plays	Play Success %
1	Short (1-3)	RUSH	Le'Veon Bell	4	100%
	Med (4-7)	PASS	Juju Smith-Schuster	3	33%
		RUSH	Le'Veon Bell	3	67%
	Long (8-10)	RUSH	Le'Veon Bell	119	41%
	XL (11+)	RUSH	Le'Veon Bell	5	0%
2	Short (1-3)	RUSH	Le'Veon Bell	22	82%
	Med (4-7)	RUSH	Le'Veon Bell	30	53%
	Long (8-10)	RUSH	Le'Veon Bell	46	37%
	XL (11+)	PASS	Antonio Brown	12	33%
3	Short (1-3)	PASS	Antonio Brown	10	60%
	Med (4-7)	PASS	Antonio Brown	10	40%
	Long (8-10)	PASS	Antonio Brown	5	60%
			Martavis Bryant	5	60%
			Juju Smith-Schuster	5	60%
			Eli Rogers	5	0%
	XL (11+)	PASS	Antonio Brown	9	22%

Most Successful Play*

Down	Distance	Play Type	Player	Total Plays	Play Success %
1	Long (8-10)	PASS	Le'Veon Bell	39	64%
	XL (11+)	RUSH	Le'Veon Bell	5	0%
2	Short (1-3)	RUSH	Le'Veon Bell	22	82%
	Med (4-7)	PASS	Antonio Brown	10	70%
	Long (8-10)	PASS	Vance McDonald	5	80%
	XL (11+)	PASS	Le'Veon Bell	5	40%
3	Short (1-3)	PASS	Le'Veon Bell	6	83%
	Med (4-7)	PASS	Martavis Bryant	7	71%
	Long (8-10)	PASS	Antonio Brown	5	60%
			Martavis Bryant	5	60%
			Juju Smith-Schuster	5	60%
	XL (11+)	PASS	Antonio Brown	9	22%

*Minimum 5 plays to qualify

2017 Snap Rates

Wk	Opp	Score	Le'Veon Bell	Jesse James	Antonio Brown	Juju Smith-Schuster	Martavis Bryant	Eli Rogers	Vance McDonald	Roosevelt Nix
1	CLE	W 21-18	43 (72%)	54 (90%)	51 (85%)	25 (42%)	50 (83%)	39 (65%)	18 (30%)	10 (17%)
2	MIN	W 26-9	68 (92%)	71 (96%)	70 (95%)	38 (51%)	47 (64%)	37 (50%)		11 (15%)
3	CHI	L 23-17	62 (97%)	46 (72%)	64 (100%)	51 (80%)	45 (70%)	22 (34%)	16 (25%)	4 (6%)
4	BAL	W 26-9	69 (91%)	58 (76%)	68 (89%)	54 (71%)	48 (63%)		30 (39%)	13 (17%)
5	JAC	L 30-9	73 (92%)	72 (91%)	75 (95%)	65 (82%)	61 (77%)		15 (19%)	13 (16%)
6	KC	W 19-13	58 (91%)	55 (86%)	57 (89%)	44 (69%)	33 (52%)	13 (20%)	31 (48%)	17 (27%)
7	CIN	W 29-14	61 (88%)	50 (72%)	64 (93%)	31 (45%)	36 (52%)	11 (16%)	29 (42%)	22 (32%)
8	DET	W 20-15	60 (94%)	58 (91%)	59 (92%)	51 (80%)		19 (30%)		18 (28%)
10	IND	W 20-17	65 (98%)	45 (68%)	63 (95%)	53 (80%)	37 (56%)	18 (27%)	30 (45%)	9 (14%)
11	TEN	W 40-17	68 (89%)	74 (97%)	70 (92%)	67 (88%)	45 (59%)	26 (34%)		5 (7%)
12	GB	W 31-28	72 (97%)	64 (86%)	74 (100%)		58 (78%)	55 (74%)		5 (7%)
13	CIN	W 23-20	63 (95%)	58 (88%)	66 (100%)	54 (82%)	40 (61%)	17 (26%)		5 (8%)
14	BAL	W 39-38	80 (90%)	71 (80%)	86 (97%)		71 (80%)	52 (58%)	35 (39%)	10 (11%)
15	NE	L 27-24	57 (85%)	60 (90%)	21 (31%)	66 (99%)	36 (54%)	25 (37%)		7 (10%)
16	HOU	W 34-6	46 (75%)	32 (52%)		52 (85%)	44 (72%)	27 (44%)	29 (48%)	16 (26%)
17	CLE	W 28-24		37 (63%)		56 (95%)	33 (56%)	26 (44%)	37 (63%)	17 (29%)
Grand Total			945 (90%)	905 (81%)	888 (90%)	707 (75%)	684 (65%)	387 (40%)	270 (40%)	182 (17%)

Personnel Groupings

Personnel	Team %	NFL Avg	Succ. %
1-1 [3WR]	71%	59%	49%
2-2 [1WR]	12%	4%	39%
1-2 [2WR]	11%	19%	55%
2-1 [2WR]	2%	7%	28%

Grouping Tendencies

Personnel	Pass Rate	Pass Succ. %	Run Succ. %
1-1 [3WR]	72%	49%	49%
2-2 [1WR]	12%	47%	38%
1-2 [2WR]	36%	49%	59%
2-1 [2WR]	44%	55%	7%

Red Zone Targets (min 3)

Receiver	All	Inside 5	6-10	11-20
Antonio Brown	23	4	6	13
Le'Veon Bell	17	2	4	11
Juju Smith-Schuster	16	3	4	9
Jesse James	12	3	5	4
Eli Rogers	9		2	7
Martavis Bryant	9	1	2	6
Vance McDonald	5	2	1	2

Red Zone Rushes (min 3)

Rusher	All	Inside 5	6-10	11-20
Le'Veon Bell	65	10	18	37
Ben Roethlisberger	5		1	4
Stevan Ridley	5	2		3
James Conner	4			4

Early Down Target Rate

RB	TE	WR
22%	17%	61%
23%	*21%*	*56%*

NFL AVG

Overall Target Success %

RB	TE	WR
53% #2	50% #17	52% #8

Pittsburgh Steelers 2017 Passing Recap & 2018 Outlook

It's easy to point the finger at Roethlisberger when he does something dumb, but the national media and public probably focus too much on his most glaring errors, which leads them to overlook his brilliance. Last year his YPA and passer rating were better than they were in 2016. Roethlisberger naturally won't have the high air-yard numbers of some other quarterbacks, but that's because he throws so many passes to Bell. This year his wide receivers will be a lot younger. Gone are veterans Martavius Bryant and Eli Rogers, and starting alongside Brown in 11 personnel will be the second-year JuJu Smith-Schuster and second-rounder James Washington. The Steelers also added the diverse fifth-round H-back Jaylen Samuels, whose usage I'll track in the preseason. Getting diverse weapons on the field together could be an edge that Fichtner uses in an up-tempo offense, and a promising 12 personnel grouping would be Brown and Smith-Schuster at receiver, Bell as the back, Vance McDonald as a pass-catching tight end, and Samuels as a move player who could line up at tight end, lead block, split out wide, or play at running back with Bell split out wide. However, based on head coach Mike Tomlin's traditional usage of rookies, this grouping isn't likely to see much action.

Ben Roethlisberger Rating All Downs

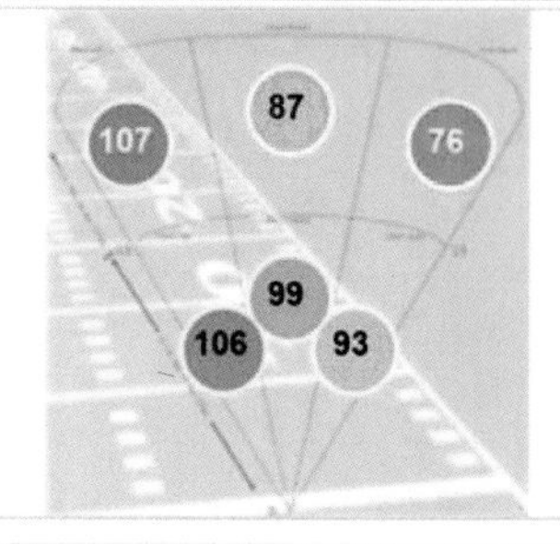

Ben Roethlisberger Rating Early Downs

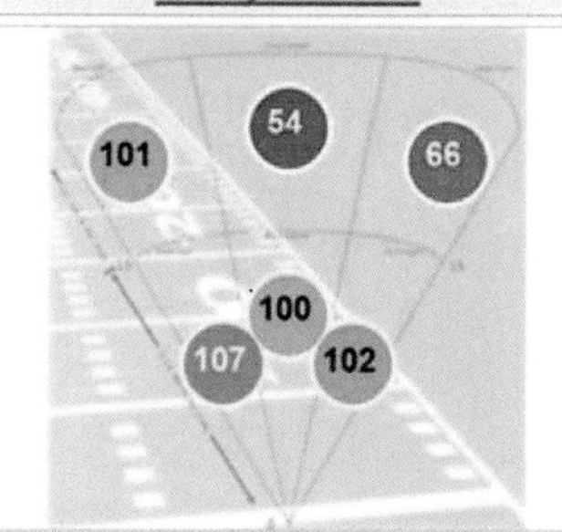

2017 Standard Passing Table

QB	Comp	Att	Comp %	Yds	YPA	TDs	INT	Sacks	Rating	Rk
Ben Roethlisberger	397	619	64%	4,720	7.6	33	15	23	95	15
Landry Jones	23	28	82%	239	8.5	1	1	3	99	7
NFL Avg			62%		7.0				87.5	

2017 Advanced Passing Table

QB	Success %	EDSR Passing Success %	20+ Yd Pass Gains	20+ Yd Pass %	30+ Yd Pass Gains	30+ Yd Pass %	Avg. Air Yds per Comp	Avg. YAC per Comp	20+ Air Yd Comp	20+ Air Yd %
Ben Roethlisberger	49%	51%	59	9.5%	29	4.7%	6.3	4.9	24	6%
Landry Jones	45%	48%	3	10.7%	2	7.1%	6.7	3.7	1	4%
NFL Avg	44%	48%	27.7	8.8%	10.3	3.3%	6.0	4.7	11.7	6%

Interception Rates by Down

Yards to Go	1	2	3	4	Total
1 & 2	0.0%	0.0%	0.0%	0.0%	0.0%
3, 4, 5	0.0%	2.8%	2.0%	0.0%	2.2%
6 - 9	0.0%	0.0%	9.1%		4.0%
10 - 14	0.4%	4.9%	6.1%	0.0%	1.8%
15+	0.0%	4.0%	5.9%		4.0%
Total	0.4%	2.5%	5.1%	0.0%	2.3%

3rd Down Passing - Short of Sticks Analysis

QB	Avg. Yds to Go	Avg. YIA (of Comp)	Avg Yds Short	Short of Sticks Rate	Short Rk
Ben Roethlisberger	7.4	7.4	0.0	55%	10
NFL Avg	7.8	6.7	-1.1	60%	

Air Yds vs YAC

Air Yds %	YAC %	Rk
57%	43%	23
58%	42%	

2017 Receiving Recap & 2018 Outlook

The Steelers traded Bryant during the draft, but they could have used him this year: He has physical attributes that the current Steelers receivers don't have. Bryant is 6'4" and fast. Brown is 5'10," Smith-Schuster is 6'1," Washington is 5'11," and none of them has Bryant's speed. Years ago Roethlisberger complained after losing his tall target in Plaxico Burress, and he could miss Bryant in 2018, but the Steelers had no plans to re-sign him, and he was entering the final year of his contract. In that context, trading him away was understandable. Additionally, Bryant's height didn't help him last year in the red zone, where he had a team-low 22% Success Rate.

Player *Min 50 Targets*	Targets	Comp %	YPA	Rating	TOARS	Success %	Success Rk	Missed YPA Rk	YAS % Rk	TDs
Antonio Brown	173	62%	9.6	101	5.6	55%	26	46	7	11
Le'Veon Bell	119	79%	6.2	98	5.0	55%	28	27	99	3
Martavis Bryant	88	59%	7.7	89	4.4	48%	73	93	34	4
Juju Smith-Schuster	84	73%	11.0	135	5.0	57%	16	11	6	8
Jesse James	65	68%	5.9	98	4.1	52%	44	40	121	3

Directional Passer Rating Delivered

Receiver	Short Left	Short Middle	Short Right	Deep Left	Deep Middle	Deep Right	Player Total
Antonio Brown	105	106	103	114	53	92	101
Le'Veon Bell	101	89	85			158	98
Martavis Bryant	109	100	99	91	0	81	89
Juju Smith-Schuster	115	142	83	96	100	141	135
Jesse James	85	115	96	40			98
Eli Rogers	70	49	96	77	40	40	56
Vance McDonald	106	61	81	96	70		71
Xavier Grimble		78	56			40	51
Team Total	103	101	93	108	84	98	98

2017 Rushing Recap & 2017 Outlook

The biggest edge Fichtner can bring to the rushing game is a smarter usage of Bell so that he can stay healthy longer, because the Steelers cannot advance in the playoffs without him. They need to stop using inefficient run plays, or at least stop using Bell on them. They need to give Bell a higher rate of receptions to rushes, since backs are less likely to suffer injuries on pass plays. If the Steelers are ahead in a game, they should have other backs spell Bell more often in the second half, but they could still reward him with goal-line carries to keep him hungry and focused on both short- and long-term goals. Bell is the only back in NFL history with three seasons of 1,200 rushing yds, 600 receiving yds, and nine touchdowns by the age of 25.

Player *Min 50 Rushes*	Rushes	YPC	Success %	Success Rk	Missed YPA Rk	YTS % Rk	YAS % Rk	Early Down Success %	Early Down Success Rk	TDs
Le'Veon Bell	337	4.0	48%	26	32	20	47	48%	22	9

Yards per Carry by Direction

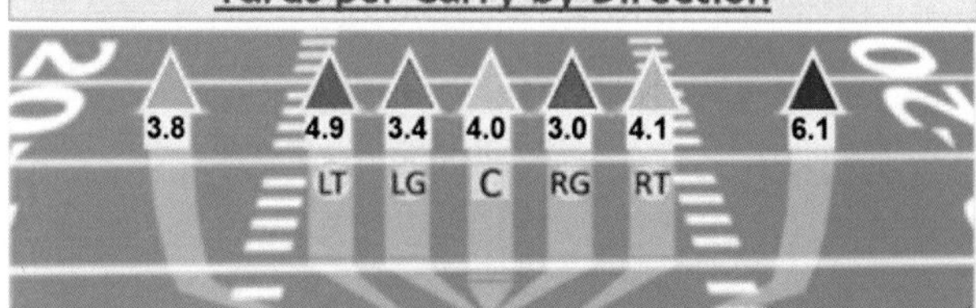

Directional Run Frequency

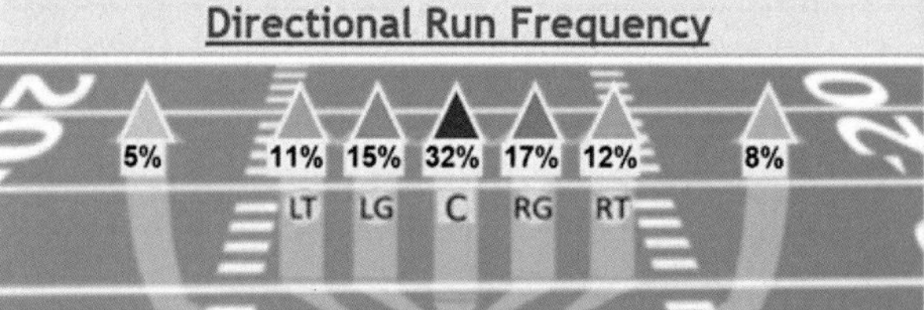

Despite this predictability, the Steelers were successful from 12 personnel, rushing a more reasonable 69% of the time with a 57% Success Rate and 4.5 YPC. And when they passed from 12 personnel, they had a 65% Success Rate and 10.8 YPA. But for some reason Haley used 22 personnel more often and with disastrous effect. The Steelers ran the ball a predictable 93% of the time with just a 37% Success Rate and 3.8 YPC.

The team was similarly split on third down. The Steelers ran from 12 personnel a balanced 50% of the time and had an incredible 83% Success Rate. But they had more third-down runs in 22 personnel, from which they ran at a predictable 78% rate with a 14% Success Rate.

As a play caller, Haley had confounding run-game tendencies. On all downs, when the Steelers ran out of 12 personnel they had a 59% Success Rate and 4.3 YPC. From all other groupings, they had a 34% Success Rate and 3.2 YPC. Yet the Steelers chose to run out of 12 personnel on only 33% of their non-11 personnel runs. The remaining 67% of such runs were inefficient and forced the Steelers into longer to-go distances than they should have had. And it wasn't just Bell who was better in 12 vs. 22 personnel. Every Steelers back was better in 12 groupings.

(cont'd - see PIT-5)

Matthew Freedman's Fantasy Corner

Bell has led all running backs with an average of 23.3 PPR points per game over the past four years and is locked in as a top-three fantasy back by average draft position, but there is room for pessimism in his evaluation. He started last season slowly due to his training-camp holdout, and he reportedly intends to skip camp this year. Additionally, the offense could suffer or shift more toward the pass with the change at coordinator, which might reduce Bell's efficiency or opportunity. Finally, Bell might have less upside than some of the other top backs due to his scoring deficiencies. Whereas Davis Johnson (1.0), Ezekiel Elliott (1.0), Alvin Kamara (0.88), and Todd Gurley (0.80) all have a significant number of touchdowns per game, Bell (0.69) has lagged as a scorer even as he's been a perennial Pro-Bowler. If other areas of his game regress and he continues to score at a mediocre rate, he could finish the season outside of the top-five backs.

Division History: Season Wins & 2018 Projection

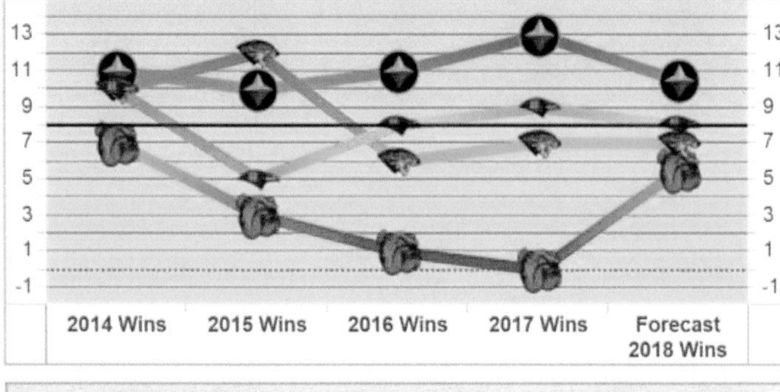

Rank of 2018 Defensive Pass Efficiency Faced by Week

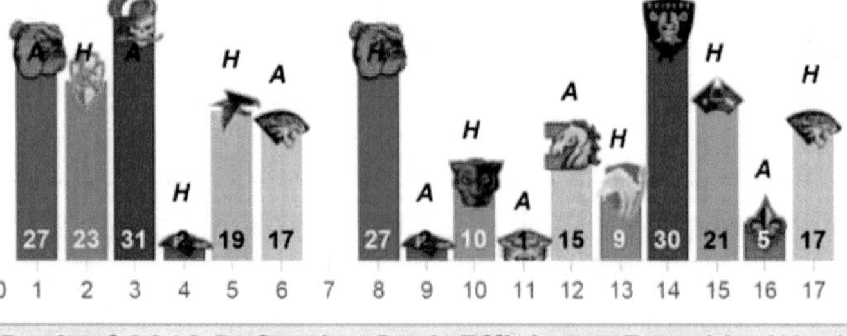

Rank of 2018 Defensive Rush Efficiency Faced by Week

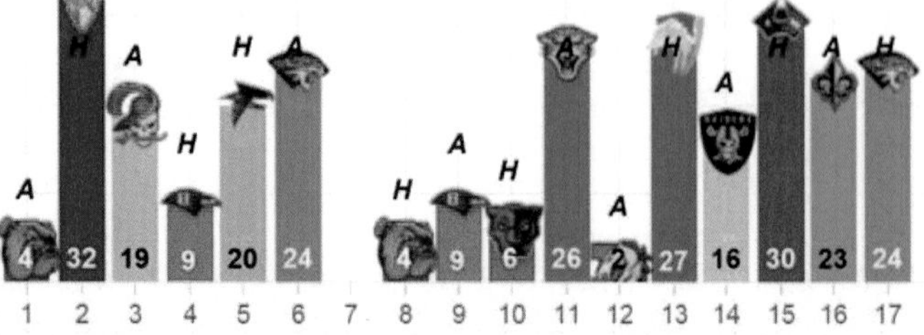

2017 Situational Usage by Player & Position

Usage Rate by Score

		Being Blown Out (14+)	Down Big (9-13)	One Score	Large Lead (9-13)	Blowout Lead (14+)	Grand Total
RUSH	Le'Veon Bell	23%	17%	33%	40%	34%	32%
	Martavis Bryant		1%	1%		2%	1%
	James Conner	4%	4%	2%	2%	11%	3%
	Stevan Ridley			2%	1%	13%	2%
	Fitzgerald Toussaint			1%			1%
	Darrius Heyward-Bey			0%		2%	0%
	Roosevelt Nix			0%	1%		0%
	Terrell Watson			0%	1%	2%	0%
	Total	27%	22%	40%	46%	64%	39%
PASS	Le'Veon Bell	17%	11%	11%	10%	13%	11%
	Antonio Brown	21%	24%	15%	18%	4%	16%
	Martavis Bryant	5%	12%	9%	7%	2%	8%
	Juju Smith-Schuster	7%	7%	8%	5%	11%	8%
	Jesse James	2%	10%	7%	5%	2%	6%
	Eli Rogers	5%	4%	4%	5%	4%	4%
	Vance McDonald	12%	5%	3%	1%		4%
	James Conner			0%			0%
	Justin Hunter	2%	1%	1%	1%		1%
	Xavier Grimble		4%	1%	1%		1%
	Fitzgerald Toussaint			0%			0%
	Darrius Heyward-Bey		1%	0%	1%		0%
	Roosevelt Nix			0%			0%
	Total	73%	78%	60%	54%	36%	61%

Positional Target Distribution vs NFL Average

		NFL Wide				Team Only			
		Left	Middle	Right	**Total**	Left	Middle	Right	**Total**
Deep	WR	944	481	932	**2,357**	42	28	55	**125**
	TE	187	147	186	**520**	5	3	2	**10**
	RB	39	9	41	**89**			1	**1**
	All	**1,170**	**637**	**1,159**	**2,966**	**47**	**31**	**58**	**136**
Short	WR	2,771	1,598	2,693	**7,062**	91	73	97	**261**
	TE	843	787	1,137	**2,767**	20	52	33	**105**
	RB	1,276	787	1,258	**3,321**	45	36	37	**118**
	All	**4,890**	**3,172**	**5,088**	**13,150**	**156**	**161**	**167**	**484**
Total		**6,060**	**3,809**	**6,247**	**16,116**	**203**	**192**	**225**	**620**

Positional Success Rates vs NFL Average

		NFL Wide				Team Only			
		Left	Middle	Right	**Total**	Left	Middle	Right	**Total**
Deep	WR	37%	45%	38%	**39%**	40%	43%	38%	**40%**
	TE	39%	52%	46%	**45%**	20%	67%	0%	**30%**
	RB	36%	56%	37%	**38%**			100%	**100%**
	All	**37%**	**47%**	**39%**	**40%**	**38%**	**45%**	**38%**	**40%**
Short	WR	51%	57%	50%	**52%**	58%	62%	58%	**59%**
	TE	50%	57%	49%	**52%**	55%	50%	55%	**52%**
	RB	44%	51%	43%	**45%**	51%	61%	51%	**54%**
	All	**49%**	**55%**	**48%**	**50%**	**56%**	**58%**	**56%**	**56%**
Total		**47%**	**54%**	**46%**	**48%**	**52%**	**56%**	**51%**	**53%**

Successful Play Rate
0% 100%

Pittsburgh Steelers - Success by Personnel Grouping & Play Type

Play Type	1-1 [3WR]	1-2 [2WR]	2-1 [2WR]	1-3 [1WR]	2-2 [1WR]	2-3 [0WR]	Grand Total
PASS	49% (528, 87%)	49% (43, 7%)	55% (11, 2%)	43% (7, 1%)	47% (15, 2%)	100% (2, 0%)	49% (606, 100%)
RUSH	49% (203, 47%)	59% (75, 17%)	7% (14, 3%)	42% (12, 3%)	38% (113, 26%)	25% (12, 3%)	46% (429, 100%)
TOTAL	49% (731, 71%)	55% (118, 11%)	28% (25, 2%)	42% (19, 2%)	39% (128, 12%)	36% (14, 1%)	48% (1,035, 100%)

Format Line 1: Success Rate Line 2: Total # of Plays, % of All Plays (by type)

PIT-5

Haley evidently didn't study these trends, and he lacked the sixth sense to recognize that the team underperformed when running from non-12 personnel. Fichtner probably won't look at these analytics on a progressive basis, but he might be better able to intuit which groupings result in inferior production.

Haley's biggest problem with the Steelers was his ego. He was a cocky play caller. Unless Bell or Brown were out, the Steelers offense was almost always more talented than the opposing defense. As a result, Haley relied on the talents of his players more than the possibilities of a well-crafted game plan. He didn't often enough attack week-to-week matchup deficiencies. He simply planned to have his players outmatch their opponents, and they often did. But that strategy doesn't work in the playoffs, when the level of competition is elevated and teams tend to be more complete.

Defensively, the Steelers were weak against the run last year, ranking 18th in efficiency, but they had the league's toughest run-offense schedule, so it's natural that they would struggle. The problem is that this year they have the second-toughest run-offense schedule. Last year they also ranked 23rd in explosive-run defense and 25th in explosive-pass defense, which is a problem since this year they are facing teams considerably more explosive than their 2017 opponents. Because of their defensive liabilities, it's even more vital for the Steelers to control the ball with the run game by using optimal personnel groupings.

Last year the Steelers were 8-2 in one-score games and 5-1 in field-goal games. They were +32 in sack margin and +2 in turnover margin. Despite the common thought that stats like these naturally regress, that's not necessarily true for teams better than the mean. The Steelers and Patriots are the two most consistent, winning teams of the past four years. In 2014-16, they together went 8-4 in field-goal games and 28-15 in one-score games. Some regression is probable, but to expect the Steelers to drop to 8-8 simply because "regression is due" is ill-founded. They are favored in 13 of their Weeks 1-16 contests. Hitting their 10.5-win total won't be easy, but it will be achievable if Fichtner is better as a play caller than Haley was, which isn't guaranteed.

Receiving Success by Personnel Grouping

Position	Player	1-1 [3WR]	1-2 [2WR]	2-1 [2WR]	1-3 [1WR]	2-2 [1WR]	2-3 [0WR]	Total
RB	Le'Veon Bell	52% 5.6 92.8 (92)	71% 12.4 118.5 (7)	100% 4.7 86.1 (3)	50% 8.5 102.1 (2)	100% 7.0 95.8 (1)		55% 6.1 94.5 (105)
TE	Jesse James	53% 6.2 96.5 (57)	100% 8.5 102.1 (2)		0% 2.0 79.2 (1)	0% 0.0 39.6 (1)	100% 1.0 118.8 (1)	53% 6.0 101.0 (62)
	Vance McDonald	50% 8.0 108.3 (16)	75% 8.5 100.0 (4)		0% 0.0 0.0 (2)	50% 13.0 95.8 (2)		50% 7.8 79.9 (24)
WR	Antonio Brown	57% 9.7 99.4 (142)	36% 11.0 93.4 (11)	25% 1.0 39.6 (4)		67% 9.3 96.5 (3)		55% 9.6 97.1 (160)
	Martavis Bryant	47% 7.2 85.4 (72)	50% 6.8 65.8 (10)		100% 10.0 108.3 (1)			48% 7.2 83.3 (83)
	Juju Smith-Schuster	58% 10.6 140.8 (67)	25% 5.3 26.0 (4)	100% 5.0 87.5 (1)	100% 46.0 118.8 (1)	75% 12.3 117.7 (4)		58% 10.8 132.5 (77)

Format Line 1: Success Rate Line 2: YPA Line 3: Passer Rating Line 4: Total # of Plays

Successful Play Rate
0% 100%

Rushing Success by Personnel Grouping

Position	Player	1-1 [3WR]	1-2 [2WR]	2-1 [2WR]	1-3 [1WR]	2-2 [1WR]	2-3 [0WR]	Total
RB	Le'Veon Bell	49% 3.8 (164)	55% 4.4 (56)	8% 1.8 (13)	60% 4.4 (5)	46% 4.4 (74)	100% 1.0 (2)	48% 3.9 (314)
	James Conner	57% 3.7 (14)	67% 5.0 (6)		50% 4.5 (2)	40% 5.3 (10)		53% 4.5 (32)
	Stevan Ridley	25% 3.0 (4)	75% 6.8 (4)		25% 0.5 (4)	36% 4.8 (14)		38% 4.2 (26)

Format Line 1: Success Rate Line 2: YPC Line 3: Total # of Plays

Seattle Seahawks

2018 Coaches

Head Coach:
Pete Carroll (9th yr)
Offensive Coordinator:
Brian Schottenheimer (IND QB) (1st yr)
Defensive Coordinator:
Ken Norton (SF DC) (1st yr)

2018 Forecast

Wins	Div Rank
8	#3

Past Records

2017: 9-7
2016: 10-5-1
2015: 10-6

EASY HARD

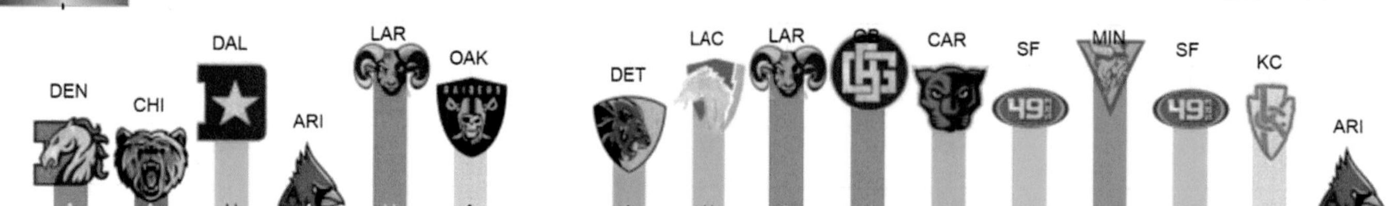

Key Players Lost

TXN	Player (POS)
Cut	Avril, Cliff DE
	Lane, Jeremy CB
	Shead, Deshawn CB
	Sherman, Richard CB
Declared Free Agent	Aboushi, Oday G
	Davis, Mike RB
	Dawson, P.J. LB
	Forrest, Josh LB
	Graham, Jimmy TE
	Joeckel, Luke G
	Lacy, Eddie RB
	Maxwell, Byron CB
	Rawls, Thomas RB
	Richardson Jr., Paul WR
	Richardson, Sheldon DT
	Smith II, Marcus DE
	Walsh, Blair K
	Wilhoite, Michael LB
	Willson, Luke TE

Average Line	# Games Favored	# Games Underdog
1.1	3	9

2018 Seattle Seahawks Overview

While the 2017 Seahawks had a winning record, they weren't the team they've historically been since drafting Russell Wilson, even though they had the 14th-easiest schedule. They were +8 in turnover margin (vs. just +1 in 2016), but Seattle couldn't win without that edge, going 0-4 when losing the turnover battle and 6-1 when winning it. Before last season, Seattle in the Wilson era was a remarkable 11-8 (58%) with a negative turnover differential. Although teams should win only 20% of games in such situations — only one other team had a win rate above 41% in 2012-16 (Patriots) — the Seahawks didn't have a single season with a sub-.500 record when losing the turnover battle in Wilson's first five years. But last season, for the first time in his career, Wilson didn't have the support he needed to carry the team in suboptimal circumstances.

What went wrong with Seattle? The defense was a clear problem, but let's start with the offense. Last year's passing game was similar to that of the previous year: The Seahawks ranked 16th in efficiency both seasons. They had wide receiver Doug Baldwin and tight end Jimmy Graham as their top options, and in the preseason they intelligently traded away wide receiver Jermaine Kearse and replaced him on the depth chart with Paul Richardson, who delivered a team-best 8.8 YPA and 104 rating.

But even though the 2016 and 2017 Seahawks ranked identically in pass-game efficiency, they were different in a key way. Last year, yards after the catch (YAC) was a big issue for Seattle. Wilson's 2017 air yardage was as good as (if not slightly better than) it was the prior year, but only 33% of his total yardage came through YAC (vs. 50% in 2016). While that could be construed as a positive development since YAC is less dependable than air yardage, the Seahawks gave Wilson just 4.4 YAC per completion, down from 4.8 in 2016 and below the 4.7 NFL average. With less YAC, the team had fewer big gains. After recording 31 completions of 30-plus yards in 2016, Wilson had 19 in 2017. Big pass plays change games, and the Seahawks needed these plays (especially because their run game was inept), but they struggled to get splash gains through the air.

But as disappointing as the passing game was, the running game was worse.

(cont'd - see SEA2)

Key Free Agents/ Trades Added

Alexander, Maurice S
Brown, Jaron WR
Dickson, Ed TE
Fluker, D.J. G
Janikowski, Sebastian K
Johnson, Dontae CB
King, Akeem CB
Mingo, Barkevious LB
Stephen, Shamar DT

Drafted Players

Rd	Pk	Player (College)
1	27	RB - Rashaad Penny (San Diego State)
3	79	DE - Rasheem Green (USC)
4	120	TE - Will Dissly (Washington)
5	141	LB - Shaquem Griffin (UCF)
	146	S - Tre Flowers (Oklahoma State)
	149	P - Michael Dickson (Texas)
	168	OT - Jamarco Jones (Ohio State)
6	186	LB - Jacob Martin (Temple)
7	220	QB - Alex McGough (Florida International)

Regular Season Wins: Past & Current Proj

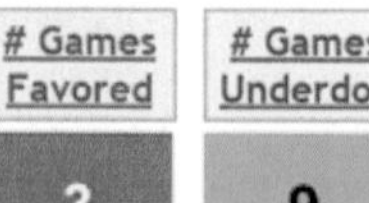

	Wins
Forecast 2018 Wins	8
2017 Wins	9
Forecast 2017 Wins	11
2016 Wins	10
2015 Wins	10
2014 Wins	12

1 3 5 7 9 11 13 15

Lineup & Cap Hits

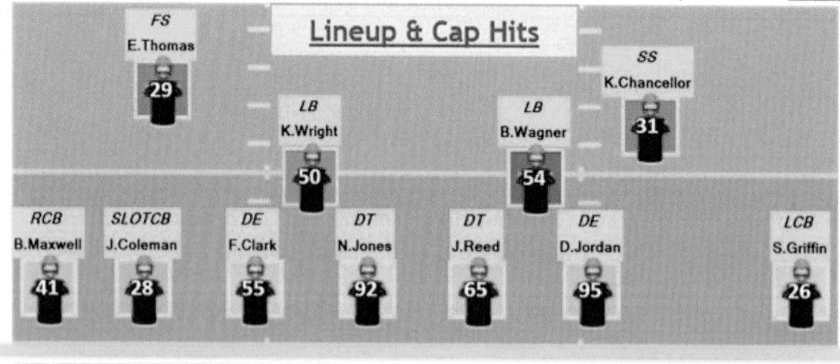

2018 Unit Spending

Positional Spending

	Rank	Total	2017 Rk
All OFF	23	$82.31M	21
QB	9	$25.01M	15
OL	28	$26.42M	32
RB	25	$5.23M	17
WR	19	$21.37M	13
TE	28	$4.29M	4
All DEF	16	$81.40M	4
DL	30	$15.58M	14
LB	6	$27.54M	14
CB	25	$10.61M	7
S	1	$27.67M	2

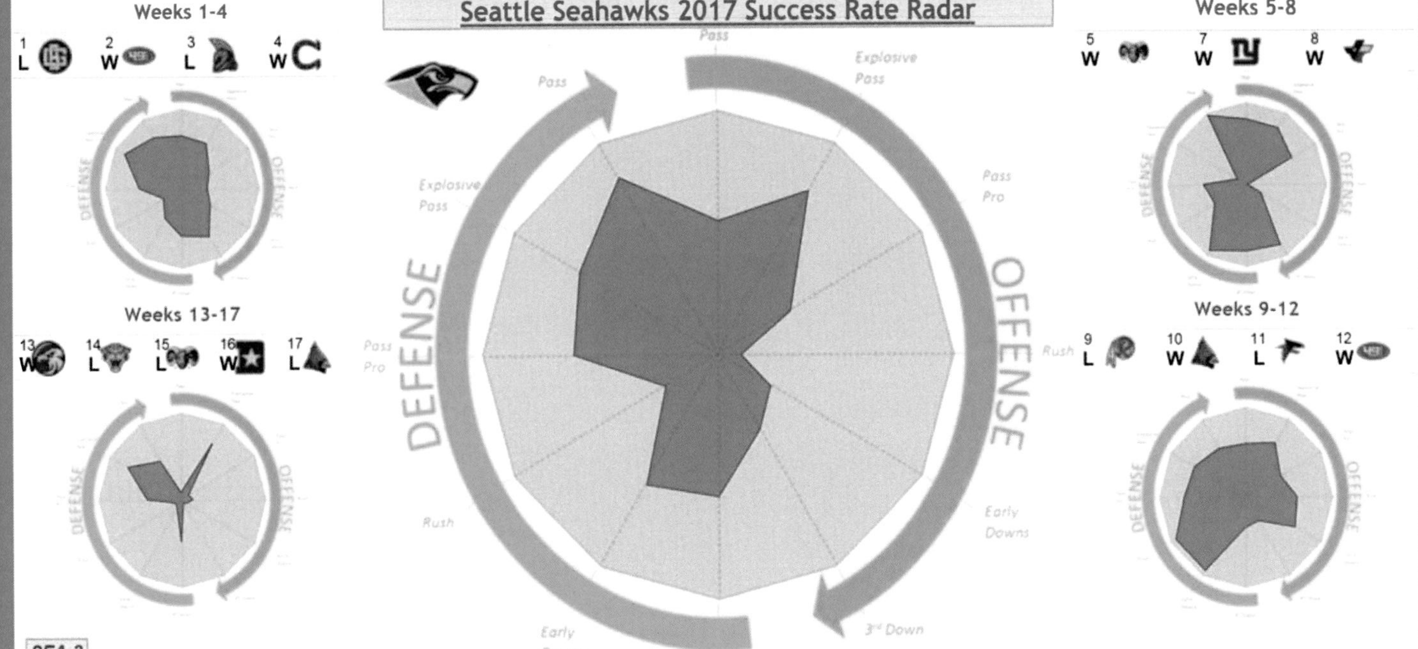

SEA-2

While both Thomas Rawls and Christine Michael had over 45% Success Rates and 3.7 YPC in 2016, none of Seattle's 2017 backs with 50-plus carries had anything better than a 31% Success Rate or 3.3 YPC. Seattle's early-down run game was terrible with a 31% Success Rate, which was the league's worst rate and 13% below average.

Despite their early-down rushing inability, the Seahawks called run plays within 2% of the NFL average, which inevitably put them in difficult positions on third down, where they had the league's fourth-worst to-go average at 7.9 yards. On third-down pass plays, they had 8.4 yards to go. Behind a below-average offensive line, Wilson underperformed in this situation. Although he had the fifth-best early-down passer rating (101) with a 48% Success Rate and 7.7 YPA, he struggled on third down, ranking 27th in passer rating (76) with a 34% Success Rate as well as 5.7 YPA (35th in NFL).

Instead of running behind a subpar offensive line, the Seahawks could have used their backs more efficiently by throwing to them, but over the last two years (under former offensive coordinator Darrell Bevell) the Seahawks targeted backs at a league-low early-down 14% rate (vs. 21% NFL average). What makes this especially egregious is that when they did throw to backs they ranked second in YPA (7.5 vs. 6.0 NFL average) and third in Success Rate (58% vs. 49% average). And on early-down under-center pass attempts to backs, Wilson had a league-leading performance with an 84% Success Rate, 12.1 YPA, 152 rating, and 2:0 TD:INT, but he threw just 19 such attempts in two years.

Early-down passing to running backs is one of the modern NFL's great efficiency edges. Last year, quarterbacks were more successful on early-down passes to running backs (54% Success Rate) than to wide receivers. Over the past two years, first-down passes to backs have had a 57% Success Rate. In 2017, the Seahawks had the league's second-best mark at 72%, but they threw an NFL-low 9% of their first-down passes to backs (vs. 22% average).

(cont'd - see SEA-3)

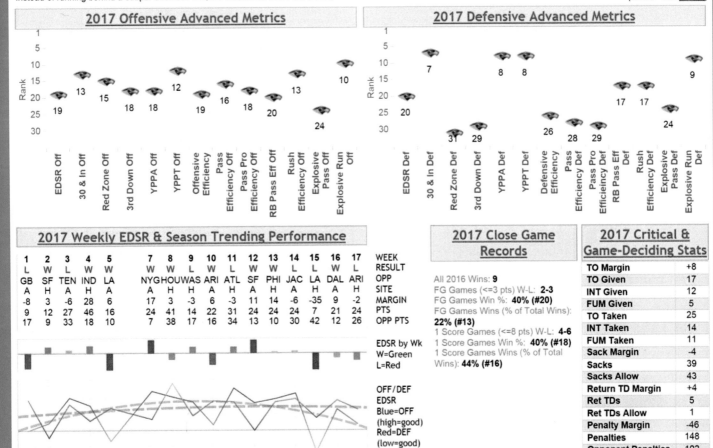

2017 Offensive Advanced Metrics

Metric	Rank
EDSR Off	19
30 & In Off	13
Red Zone Off	15
3rd Down Off	18
YPPA Off	18
YPPT Off	12
Offensive Efficiency	19
Pass Efficiency Off	16
Pass Pro Efficiency Off	18
RB Pass Eff Off	20
Rush Efficiency Off	13
Explosive Pass Off	24
Explosive Run Off	10

2017 Defensive Advanced Metrics

Metric	Rank
EDSR Def	20
30 & In Def	7
Red Zone Def	31
3rd Down Def	29
YPPA Def	8
YPPT Def	8
Defensive Efficiency	26
Pass Efficiency Def	28
Pass Pro Efficieincy Def	29
RB Pass Eff Def	17
Rush Efficiency Def	17
Explosive Pass Def	24
Explosive Run Def	9

2017 Weekly EDSR & Season Trending Performance

WEEK	1	2	3	4	5	7	8	9	10	11	12	13	14	15	16	17
RESULT	L	W	L	W	W	W	W	L	W	L	W	W	L	L	W	L
OPP	GB	SF	TEN	IND	LA	NYG	HOU	WAS	ARI	ATL	SF	PHI	JAC	LA	DAL	ARI
SITE	A	H	A	H	A	A	H	H	A	H	A	H	A	H	A	H
MARGIN	-8	3	-6	28	6	17	3	-3	6	-3	11	14	-6	-35	9	-2
PTS	9	12	27	46	16	24	41	14	22	31	24	24	24	7	21	24
OPP PTS	17	9	33	18	10	7	38	17	16	34	13	10	30	42	12	26

EDSR by Wk
W=Green
L=Red

OFF/DEF EDSR
Blue=OFF (high=good)
Red=DEF (low=good)

2017 Close Game Records

All 2016 Wins: **9**
FG Games (<=3 pts) W-L: **2-3**
FG Games Win %: **40% (#20)**
FG Games Wins (% of Total Wins): **22% (#13)**
1 Score Games (<=8 pts) W-L: **4-6**
1 Score Games Win %: **40% (#18)**
1 Score Games Wins (% of Total Wins): **44% (#16)**

2017 Critical & Game-Deciding Stats

TO Margin	+8
TO Given	17
INT Given	12
FUM Given	5
TO Taken	25
INT Taken	14
FUM Taken	11
Sack Margin	-4
Sacks	39
Sacks Allow	43
Return TD Margin	+4
Ret TDs	5
Ret TDs Allow	1
Penalty Margin	-46
Penalties	148
Opponent Penalties	102

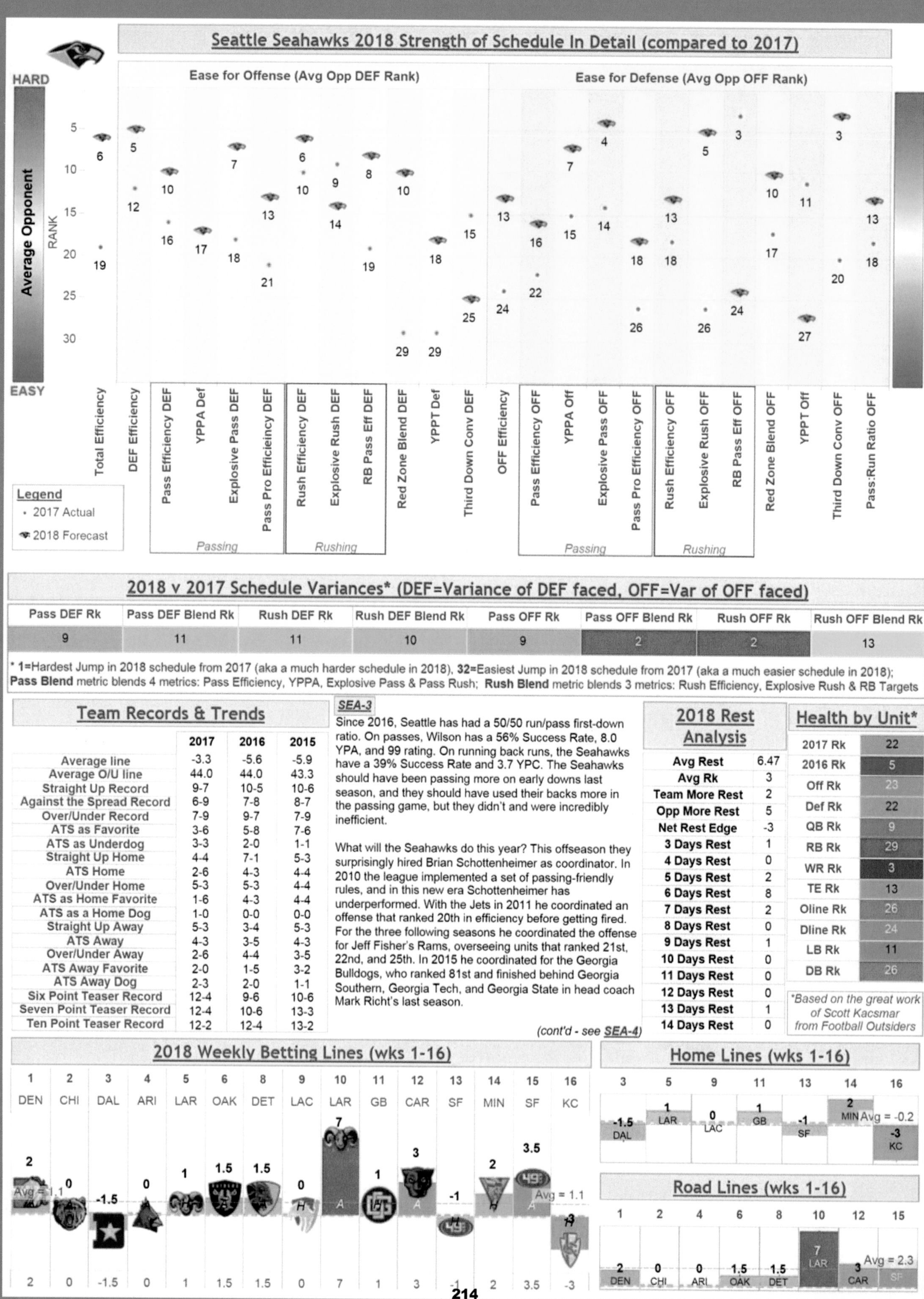

Seattle Seahawks 2018 Strength of Schedule In Detail (compared to 2017)

2018 v 2017 Schedule Variances* (DEF=Variance of DEF faced, OFF=Var of OFF faced)

Pass DEF Rk	Pass DEF Blend Rk	Rush DEF Rk	Rush DEF Blend Rk	Pass OFF Rk	Pass OFF Blend Rk	Rush OFF Rk	Rush OFF Blend Rk
9	11	11	10	9	2	2	13

* **1**=Hardest Jump in 2018 schedule from 2017 (aka a much harder schedule in 2018), **32**=Easiest Jump in 2018 schedule from 2017 (aka a much easier schedule in 2018); **Pass Blend** metric blends 4 metrics: Pass Efficiency, YPPA, Explosive Pass & Pass Rush; **Rush Blend** metric blends 3 metrics: Rush Efficiency, Explosive Rush & RB Targets

Team Records & Trends

	2017	2016	2015
Average line	-3.3	-5.6	-5.9
Average O/U line	44.0	44.0	43.3
Straight Up Record	9-7	10-5	10-6
Against the Spread Record	6-9	7-8	8-7
Over/Under Record	7-9	9-7	7-9
ATS as Favorite	3-6	5-8	7-6
ATS as Underdog	3-3	2-0	1-1
Straight Up Home	4-4	7-1	5-3
ATS Home	2-6	4-3	4-4
Over/Under Home	5-3	5-3	4-4
ATS as Home Favorite	1-6	4-3	4-4
ATS as a Home Dog	1-0	0-0	0-0
Straight Up Away	5-3	3-4	5-3
ATS Away	4-3	3-5	4-3
Over/Under Away	2-6	4-4	3-5
ATS Away Favorite	2-0	1-5	3-2
ATS Away Dog	2-3	2-0	1-1
Six Point Teaser Record	12-4	9-6	10-6
Seven Point Teaser Record	12-4	10-6	13-3
Ten Point Teaser Record	12-2	12-4	13-2

SEA-3

Since 2016, Seattle has had a 50/50 run/pass first-down ratio. On passes, Wilson has a 56% Success Rate, 8.0 YPA, and 99 rating. On running back runs, the Seahawks have a 39% Success Rate and 3.7 YPC. The Seahawks should have been passing more on early downs last season, and they should have used their backs more in the passing game, but they didn't and were incredibly inefficient.

What will the Seahawks do this year? This offseason they surprisingly hired Brian Schottenheimer as coordinator. In 2010 the league implemented a set of passing-friendly rules, and in this new era Schottenheimer has underperformed. With the Jets in 2011 he coordinated an offense that ranked 20th in efficiency before getting fired. For the three following seasons he coordinated the offense for Jeff Fisher's Rams, overseeing units that ranked 21st, 22nd, and 25th. In 2015 he coordinated for the Georgia Bulldogs, who ranked 81st and finished behind Georgia Southern, Georgia Tech, and Georgia State in head coach Mark Richt's last season.

(cont'd - see ***SEA-4***)

2018 Rest Analysis

Avg Rest	6.47
Avg Rk	3
Team More Rest	2
Opp More Rest	5
Net Rest Edge	-3
3 Days Rest	1
4 Days Rest	0
5 Days Rest	2
6 Days Rest	8
7 Days Rest	2
8 Days Rest	0
9 Days Rest	1
10 Days Rest	0
11 Days Rest	0
12 Days Rest	0
13 Days Rest	1
14 Days Rest	0

Health by Unit*

2017 Rk	22
2016 Rk	5
Off Rk	23
Def Rk	22
QB Rk	9
RB Rk	29
WR Rk	3
TE Rk	13
Oline Rk	26
Dline Rk	24
LB Rk	11
DB Rk	26

*Based on the great work of Scott Kacsmar from Football Outsiders

2018 Weekly Betting Lines (wks 1-16)

1	2	3	4	5	6	8	9	10	11	12	13	14	15	16
DEN	CHI	DAL	ARI	LAR	OAK	DET	LAC	LAR	GB	CAR	SF	MIN	SF	KC
2	0	-1.5	0	1	1.5	1.5	0	7	1	3	-1	2	3.5	-3

Home Lines (wks 1-16)

3	5	9	11	13	14	16
DAL	LAR	LAC	GB	SF	MIN	KC
-1.5	1	0	1	-1	2	-3

Road Lines (wks 1-16)

1	2	4	6	8	10	12	15
DEN	CHI	ARI	OAK	DET	LAR	CAR	SF
2	0	0	1.5	1.5	7	3	

Seattle Seahawks 2017 Play Analysis

2017 Play Tendencies

All Pass %	59%
All Pass Rk	12
All Rush %	41%
All Rush Rk	21
1 Score Pass %	59%
1 Score Pass Rk	9
2016 1 Score Pass %	61%
2016 1 Score Pass Rk	10
2017 Pass Increase %	-1%
Pass Increase Rk	17
1 Score Rush %	41%
1 Score Rush Rk	24
Up Pass %	51%
Up Pass Rk	11
Up Rush %	49%
Up Rush Rk	22
Down Pass %	66%
Down Pass Rk	15
Down Rush %	34%
Down Rush Rk	18

2017 Down & Distance Tendencies

Down	Distance	Total Plays	Pass Rate	Run Rate	Play Success %
1	Short (1-3)	7	29%	71%	14%
	Med (4-7)	9	33%	67%	22%
	Long (8-10)	308	49%	51%	41%
	XL (11+)	12	75%	25%	25%
2	Short (1-3)	26	50%	50%	54%
	Med (4-7)	67	54%	46%	51%
	Long (8-10)	100	58%	42%	39%
	XL (11+)	58	83%	17%	29%
3	Short (1-3)	41	56%	44%	61%
	Med (4-7)	47	91%	9%	43%
	Long (8-10)	31	87%	13%	32%
	XL (11+)	46	85%	15%	9%
4	Short (1-3)	4	50%	50%	50%
	Med (4-7)	1	100%	0%	100%

Shotgun %:

Under Center	Shotgun
41%	59%
37%	*63%*

37% AVG 63%

Run Rate:

Under Center	Shotgun
63%	19%

68% AVG 23%

Pass Rate:

Under Center	Shotgun
37%	81%

32% AVG 77%

Short Yardage Intelligence:

2nd and Short Run

Run Freq	Run Rk	NFL Run Freq Avg	Run 1D Rate	Run NFL 1D Avg
67%	17	67%	50%	69%

2nd and Short Pass

Pass Freq	Pass Rk	NFL Pass Freq Avg	Pass 1D Rate	Pass NFL 1D Avg
33%	16	33%	56%	53%

Most Frequent Play

Down	Distance	Play Type	Player	Total Plays	Play Success %
1	Short (1-3)	RUSH	Russell Wilson	2	50%
	Med (4-7)	RUSH	Thomas Rawls	4	0%
	Long (8-10)	RUSH	Eddie Lacy	34	26%
	XL (11+)	PASS	Doug Baldwin	2	0%
			Tyler Lockett	2	50%
		RUSH	Russell Wilson	2	50%
2	Short (1-3)	PASS	Jimmy Graham	6	67%
	Med (4-7)	PASS	Doug Baldwin	8	38%
	Long (8-10)	PASS	Paul Richardson	15	53%
	XL (11+)	PASS	Doug Baldwin	16	44%
3	Short (1-3)	PASS	Tyler Lockett	6	100%
	Med (4-7)	PASS	Doug Baldwin	13	62%
	Long (8-10)	PASS	Paul Richardson	7	29%
	XL (11+)	PASS	Tyler Lockett	7	0%

Most Successful Play*

Down	Distance	Play Type	Player	Total Plays	Play Success %
1	Long (8-10)	PASS	Nick Vannett	7	71%
2	Short (1-3)	PASS	Jimmy Graham	6	67%
	Med (4-7)	RUSH	Russell Wilson	5	100%
	Long (8-10)	PASS	Jimmy Graham	6	67%
	XL (11+)	PASS	Doug Baldwin	16	44%
3	Short (1-3)	PASS	Tyler Lockett	6	100%
	Med (4-7)	PASS	Doug Baldwin	13	62%
	Long (8-10)	PASS	Doug Baldwin	6	67%
	XL (11+)	PASS	Jimmy Graham	6	17%
		RUSH	Russell Wilson	6	17%

*Minimum 5 plays to qualify

2017 Snap Rates

Wk	Opp	Score	Doug Baldwin	Paul Richardson	Jimmy Graham	Tyler Lockett	Luke Willson	J.D. McKissic	Thomas Rawls	Eddie Lacy
1	GB	L 17-9	43 (88%)	41 (84%)	40 (82%)	26 (53%)	17 (35%)			7 (14%)
2	SF	W 12-9	81 (99%)	39 (48%)	53 (65%)	61 (74%)	37 (45%)		16 (20%)	
3	TEN	L 33-27	51 (70%)	61 (84%)	48 (66%)	66 (90%)	25 (34%)		1 (1%)	
4	IND	W 46-18	46 (68%)	50 (74%)	46 (68%)	50 (74%)	22 (32%)	10 (15%)		23 (34%)
5	LA	W 16-10	49 (72%)	47 (69%)	42 (62%)	38 (56%)	26 (38%)	18 (26%)	32 (47%)	19 (28%)
7	NYG	W 24-7	50 (66%)	49 (64%)	49 (64%)	41 (54%)	30 (39%)	23 (30%)	30 (39%)	21 (28%)
8	HOU	W 41-38	49 (71%)	55 (80%)	49 (71%)	39 (57%)	19 (28%)	16 (23%)	41 (59%)	12 (17%)
9	WAS	L 17-14	70 (84%)	68 (82%)	57 (69%)	55 (66%)	24 (29%)	30 (36%)	42 (51%)	11 (13%)
10	ARI	W 22-16	49 (78%)	33 (52%)	44 (70%)	44 (70%)	24 (38%)	20 (32%)	29 (46%)	
11	ATL	L 34-31	60 (81%)	61 (82%)	48 (65%)	47 (64%)	33 (45%)	50 (68%)		6 (8%)
12	SF	W 24-13	53 (79%)	56 (84%)	46 (69%)	46 (69%)	5 (7%)	29 (43%)	1 (1%)	35 (52%)
13	PHI	W 24-10	43 (69%)	52 (84%)	42 (68%)	29 (47%)	20 (32%)	9 (15%)	3 (5%)	3 (5%)
14	JAC	L 30-24	59 (95%)	58 (94%)	38 (61%)	39 (63%)	20 (32%)	31 (50%)	1 (2%)	
15	LA	L 42-7	48 (84%)	47 (82%)	46 (81%)	41 (72%)	19 (33%)	36 (63%)		
16	DAL	W 21-12	46 (81%)	47 (82%)	40 (70%)	35 (61%)	27 (47%)	2 (4%)	10 (18%)	
17	ARI	L 26-24	56 (97%)	51 (88%)	42 (72%)	36 (62%)	29 (50%)	22 (38%)	14 (24%)	
	Grand Total		853 (80%)	815 (77%)	730 (69%)	693 (64%)	377 (35%)	296 (34%)	220 (26%)	137 (22%)

Personnel Groupings

Personnel	Team %	NFL Avg	Succ. %
1-1 [3WR]	66%	59%	43%
1-2 [2WR]	18%	19%	43%
1-3 [1WR]	8%	5%	42%
2-1 [2WR]	3%	7%	41%

Grouping Tendencies

Personnel	Pass Rate	Pass Succ. %	Run Succ. %
1-1 [3WR]	64%	45%	41%
1-2 [2WR]	57%	49%	36%
1-3 [1WR]	28%	41%	42%
2-1 [2WR]	47%	38%	44%

Red Zone Targets (min 3)

Receiver	All	Inside 5	6-10	11-20
Jimmy Graham	26	14	2	10
Paul Richardson	11	1	4	6
Doug Baldwin	8	2	3	3
Tyler Lockett	8	1	3	4
Luke Willson	5		2	3
J.D. McKissic	3		2	1

Red Zone Rushes (min 3)

Rusher	All	Inside 5	6-10	11-20
Thomas Rawls	14	6	5	3
Eddie Lacy	7	4		3
J.D. McKissic	7	1	1	5
Mike Davis	6	1	1	4
Russell Wilson	6	3		3
Tyler Lockett	3			3

Early Down Target Rate

	RB	TE	WR
	12%	25%	63%
NFL AVG	*23%*	*21%*	*56%*

Overall Target Success %

RB	TE	WR
52%	52%	49%
#4	#12	#11

Seattle Seahawks 2017 Passing Recap & 2018 Outlook

Wilson will be tested to the extreme in 2018, and it will be up to Schottenheimer to design an offense that can achieve some of the passing goals the team failed to hit last year. For starters, the passing game needs to be more successful on deep passes to non-wide receivers. Seattle had an above-average 42% Success Rate on deep wide-receiver passes last year, and Wilson had the league's fourth-best pass rating at 118. However on his 22 deep tight-end targets Wilson had a 32% Success Rate, 59.5 rating, and a 3:4 TD:INT ratio, with three of those interceptions coming on early downs. Seattle also needs better wide-receiver efficiency in the short middle of the field, where a high Success Rate is usually the easiest to achieve. Seattle's lone wide receiver with a passer rating above 75 in that area of the field was the departed Richardson. Amazingly, Baldwin (the most targeted receiver) posted a 38% Success Rate and a 37.5 rating in the short middle.

Russell Wilson Rating All Downs

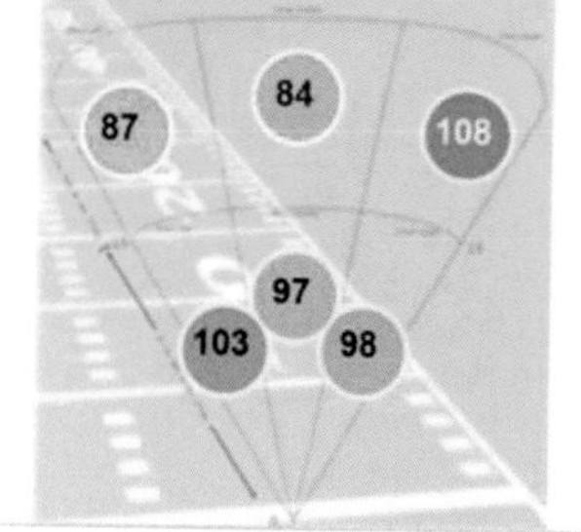

Russell Wilson Rating Early Downs

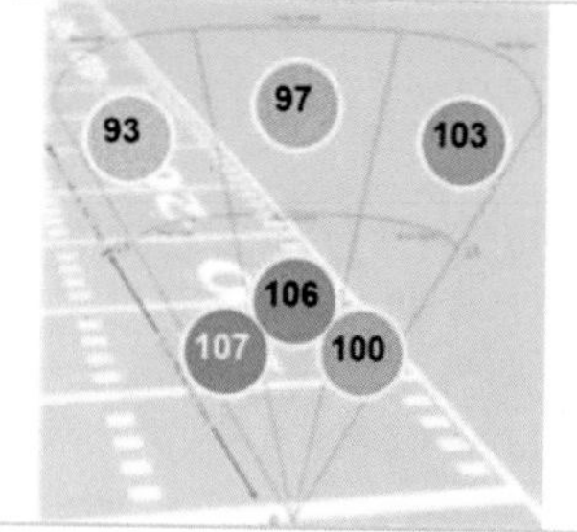

2017 Standard Passing Table

QB	Comp	Att	Comp %	Yds	YPA	TDs	INT	Sacks	Rating	Rk
Russell Wilson	339	553	61%	3,986	7.2	34	11	43	95	14
NFL Avg			62%		7.0				87.5	

2017 Advanced Passing Table

QB	Success %	EDSR Passing Success %	20+ Yd Pass Gains	20+ Yd Pass %	30+ Yd Pass Gains	30+ Yd Pass %	Avg. Air Yds per Comp	Avg. YAC per Comp	20+ Air Yd Comp	20+ Air Yd %
Russell Wilson	44%	48%	59	10.7%	19	3.4%	7.2	4.4	31	9%
NFL Avg	44%	48%	27.7	8.8%	10.3	3.3%	6.0	4.7	11.7	6%

Interception Rates by Down

Yards to Go	1	2	3	4	Total
1 & 2	0.0%	11.1%	0.0%	0.0%	3.7%
3, 4, 5	0.0%	0.0%	2.5%	0.0%	1.4%
6 - 9	0.0%	2.0%	1.9%	0.0%	1.8%
10 - 14	2.4%	0.0%	0.0%		1.5%
15+	0.0%	7.7%	0.0%	0.0%	3.6%
Total	**2.2%**	**2.0%**	**1.2%**	**0.0%**	**1.8%**

3rd Down Passing - Short of Sticks Analysis

QB	Avg. Yds to Go	Avg. YIA (of Comp)	Avg Yds Short	Short of Sticks Rate	Short Rk
Russell Wilson	8.4	6.6	-1.8	56%	27
NFL Avg	7.8	6.7	-1.1	60%	

Air Yds vs YAC

Air Yds %	YAC %	Rk
67%	33%	5
58%	42%	

2017 Receiving Recap & 2018 Outlook

Richardson's loss creates an offensive void, particularly on deep passes and explosive plays, as he ranked 21st in YAS% (Yards Above Successful, an explosiveness quotient). The Seahawks have a more difficult schedule in 2018 and will face units with better explosive-pass defense. The Seahawks have suggested that they want to get Penny involved as a third-down receiver, but passing to backs on that down is highly inefficient. If he's to be a part of the passing game, Penny should ideally get his workload on the early downs.

Player **Min 50 Targets*	Targets	Comp %	YPA	Rating	TOARS	Success %	Success Rk	Missed YPA Rk	YAS % Rk	TDs
Doug Baldwin	116	65%	8.5	100	5.0	52%	48	47	64	8
Jimmy Graham	95	60%	5.5	92	4.6	51%	55	87	84	10
Paul Richardson	80	55%	8.8	104	4.5	48%	74	124	21	6
Tyler Lockett	71	63%	7.8	91	4.1	45%	92	112	56	2

Directional Passer Rating Delivered

Receiver	Short Left	Short Middle	Short Right	Deep Left	Deep Middle	Deep Right	Player Total
Doug Baldwin	85	38	104	102	51	142	100
Jimmy Graham	103	144	111	31	2	0	92
Paul Richardson	95	104	89	84	140	88	104
Tyler Lockett	111	55	94	96	56	117	91
J.D. McKissic	100	74	88	110	40	96	93
Luke Willson	137	70	90	40	135	158	109
Mike Davis	111	111	56				97
Nick Vannett	79		97		119	158	123
Thomas Rawls	119	94	48				90
C.J. Prosise	61	40	100	96		40	80
Team Total	103	90	98	88	84	91	99

2017 Rushing Recap & 2017 Outlook

While Seattle has historically been more efficient passing than rushing, last year the Seahawks' rushing efficiency (13th) ranked higher than their passing efficiency (16th), which speaks to the drop in pass production. With Thomas Rawls and Eddie Lacy now gone, the team has a massive void. The current veteran backs on the roster were terrible at running behind the entirety of the offensive line last year except for directly behind center Justin Britt. The Seahawks don't need a great or even dominant run game thanks to Wilson's presence, but they need something more than the miserable league-low 32% Success Rate and 3.1 YPC the team's backs gave them last year.

Player **Min 50 Rushes*	Rushes	YPC	Success %	Success Rk	Missed YPA Rk	YTS % Rk	YAS % Rk	Early Down Success %	Early Down Success Rk	TDs
Eddie Lacy	69	2.6	29%	75	54	39	75	26%	76	0
Mike Davis	68	3.3	28%	76	76	75	1	31%	74	0
Thomas Rawls	58	2.7	31%	74	63	66	38	28%	75	0

Yards per Carry by Direction

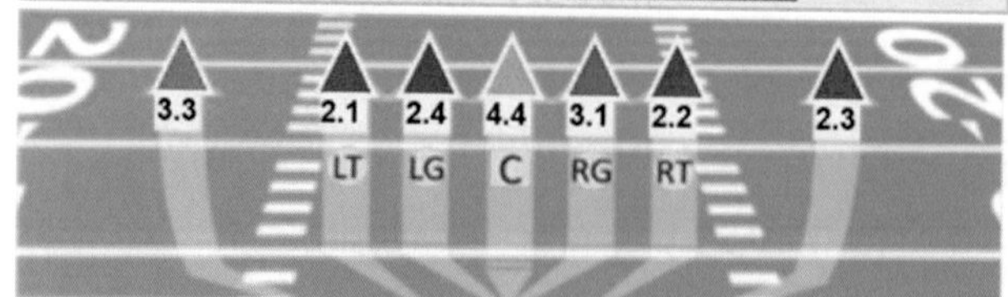

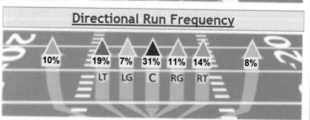

Directional Run Frequency

10%
19%
7%
31%
11%
14%
8%
LT
LG
C
RG
RT

Schottenheimer hasn't called plays since then, serving as the Colts quarterbacks coach under Chuck Pagano and Rob Chudzinski for the past two years. There's little reason to expect him to be better than he has been to this point.

Seattle this offseason hasn't made substantial upgrades along the offensive line aside from adding guard DJ Fluker, but there is hope that midseason addition left tackle Duane Brown will anchor the line and improve the run game. The team drafted first-round rookie running back Rashaad Penny, who seemed like a reach (but not as much of a reach as Schottenheimer as coordinator). Penny could be a tremendous NFL back, but his pass-protection skills are limited, and he didn't have much receiving experience in college. The Seahawks are already talking about throwing to Penny on third downs, but they'd be better served by targeting him on early downs.

With Richardson and Graham now gone, the Seahawks are looking to account for their 16 departed receiving touchdowns by using Tyler Lockett and Amara Darboh as the Nos. 2-3 wide receivers and Ed Dickson at tight end. The receiving talent will be worse in 2018 than it was in 2017.

Last year the Seahawks played the second-easiest schedule. In 2018 they'll face the third hardest with a weaker receiving corps, unproven offensive line, and Schottenheimer calling plays.

(cont'd - see SEA-5)

Matthew Freedman's Fantasy Corner

Although Schottenheimer is the modern equivalent of a caveman coordinator, in his nine years as a play caller his lead backs have averaged 249 carries and 39.9 targets per season. The Seahawks perhaps misjudged the market in selecting Penny at No. 27 overall, but he has lead back size (5'11" and 220 lbs.), plus athleticism (4.46-second 40-yard dash), and elite college production (nation-leading 2,248 yards rushing as a senior). He has the long-term potential to return value at his NFL draft position. If Schottenheimer uses Penny the way he's used his previous lead backs, the rookie will likely exceed expectations as the current RB18 by average draft position.

Division History: Season Wins & 2018 Projection

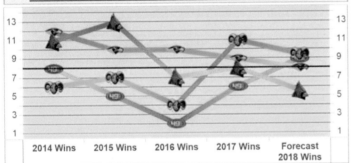

2014 Wins | 2015 Wins | 2016 Wins | 2017 Wins | Forecast 2018 Wins

Rank of 2018 Defensive Pass Efficiency Faced by Week

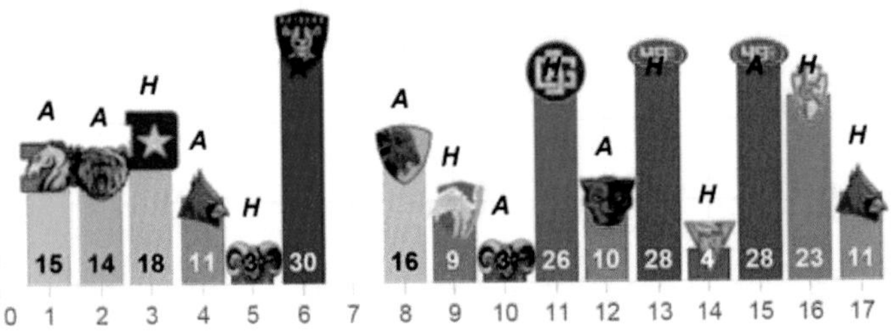

Rank of 2018 Defensive Rush Efficiency Faced by Week

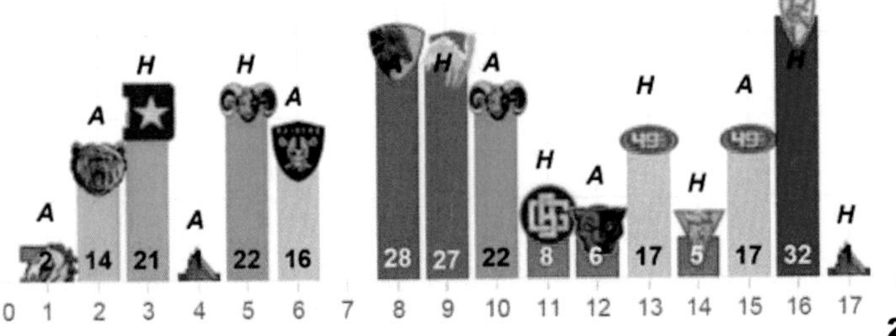

2017 Situational Usage by Player & Position

Usage Rate by Score

		Being Blown Out (14+)	Down Big (9-13)	One Score	Large Lead (9-13)	Blowout Lead (14+)	Grand Total
RUSH	Doug Baldwin			0%			0%
	J.D. McKissic	16%	7%	4%	18%	8%	5%
	Mike Davis	9%	12%	7%	14%	13%	8%
	Tyler Lockett		2%	1%			1%
	Eddie Lacy	2%	3%	9%		31%	8%
	Thomas Rawls		4%	8%	27%	3%	7%
	Chris Carson		1%	7%		8%	6%
	C.J. Prosise	2%		2%			1%
	Total	29%	29%	37%	59%	62%	37%
PASS	Doug Baldwin	15%	10%	15%	5%	8%	14%
	Jimmy Graham	9%	18%	11%	9%	8%	11%
	J.D. McKissic	7%	6%	5%	9%	5%	5%
	Mike Davis	5%	1%	2%		3%	2%
	Tyler Lockett	11%	9%	9%	9%	3%	8%
	Paul Richardson	16%	14%	9%	5%	5%	10%
	Eddie Lacy			1%		3%	1%
	Thomas Rawls		3%	2%			2%
	Chris Carson		1%	1%			1%
	C.J. Prosise		1%	2%			1%
	Luke Willson	5%	6%	2%	5%	3%	3%
	Nick Vannett		1%	2%			2%
	Amara Darboh	2%	2%	2%			2%
	Tanner McEvoy			1%		3%	1%
	Tre Madden			0%			0%
	Total	71%	71%	63%	41%	38%	63%

Positional Target Distribution vs NFL Average

		NFL Wide				Team Only			
		Left	Middle	Right	**Total**	Left	Middle	Right	**Total**
Deep	WR	946	484	960	**2,390**	40	25	27	**92**
	TE	184	141	183	**508**	8	9	5	**22**
	RB	37	9	41	**87**	2		1	**3**
	All	**1,167**	**634**	**1,184**	**2,985**	**50**	**34**	**33**	**117**
Short	WR	2,764	1,627	2,711	**7,102**	98	44	79	**221**
	TE	833	814	1,115	**2,762**	30	25	55	**110**
	RB	1,307	812	1,281	**3,400**	14	11	14	**39**
	All	**4,904**	**3,253**	**5,107**	**13,264**	**142**	**80**	**148**	**370**
Total		**6,071**	**3,887**	**6,291**	**16,249**	**192**	**114**	**181**	**487**

Positional Success Rates vs NFL Average

		NFL Wide				Team Only			
		Left	Middle	Right	**Total**	Left	Middle	Right	**Total**
Deep	WR	36%	46%	38%	**39%**	48%	32%	44%	**42%**
	TE	39%	54%	45%	**45%**	25%	33%	40%	**32%**
	RB	35%	56%	39%	**39%**	50%		0%	**33%**
	All	**37%**	**48%**	**39%**	**40%**	**44%**	**32%**	**42%**	**40%**
Short	WR	52%	58%	50%	**52%**	50%	52%	54%	**52%**
	TE	51%	56%	49%	**51%**	37%	72%	58%	**55%**
	RB	44%	51%	43%	**45%**	57%	64%	29%	**49%**
	All	**50%**	**55%**	**48%**	**50%**	**48%**	**60%**	**53%**	**53%**
Total		**47%**	**54%**	**46%**	**48%**	**47%**	**52%**	**51%**	**50%**

Successful Play Rate
0% 100%

Seattle Seahawks - Success by Personnel Grouping & Play Type

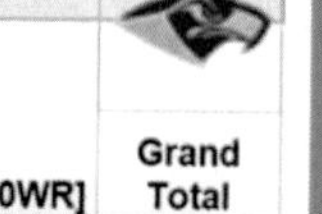

Play Type	1-1 [3WR]	1-2 [2WR]	2-1 [2WR]	1-0 [4WR]	1-3 [1WR]	0-1 [4WR]	2-0 [3WR]	2-2 [1WR]	0-0 [5WR]	0-2 [3WR]	0-3 [2WR]	2-3 [0WR]	1-4 [0WR]	Grand Total
PASS	45% (417, 71%)	49% (101, 17%)	38% (16, 3%)	33% (6, 1%)	41% (22, 4%)	27% (11, 2%)	0% (2, 0%)	100% (1, 0%)	0% (2, 0%)	50% (2, 0%)	0% (1, 0%)	50% (2, 0%)	0% (1, 0%)	44% (584, 100%)
RUSH	41% (234, 58%)	36% (75, 19%)	44% (18, 4%)	33% (3, 1%)	42% (57, 14%)		17% (6, 1%)	33% (6, 1%)				0% (2, 0%)	100% (1, 0%)	39% (403, 100%)
TOTAL	43% (651, 66%)	43% (176, 18%)	41% (34, 3%)	33% (9, 1%)	42% (79, 8%)	27% (11, 1%)	13% (8, 1%)	43% (7, 1%)	0% (2, 0%)	50% (2, 0%)	0% (1, 0%)	25% (4, 0%)	50% (2, 0%)	42% (987, 100%)

Format Line 1: Success Rate Line 2: Total # of Plays, % of All Plays (by type)

SEA-5 They will have to pass more because of worse game script, which will put Wilson in an even more difficult position than he faced in 2017. The best part about the Seahawks is Wilson, but not much will come easy for this offense in 2018.

Defensively, the Seahawks last year were a shell of their 2016 selves, primarily due to injury. After ranking as the fourth-healthiest defense in 2016, Seattle ranked 22nd in 2017, losing key secondary players in cornerback Richard Sherman and safety Kam Chancellor, who each played only nine games. A once reliable defense moved from No. 5 overall in 2016 to No. 26 in 2017. They dropped from No. 2 against the run to No. 17 and from No. 13 against the pass to No. 28. Without Sherman, defensive tackle Sheldon Richardson, defensive ends Michael Bennett and Cliff Avril, and maybe Chancellor, the unit that last year had the fourth-highest cap figure will have an approximately league-average allocation this year. Entering a new era, this defense will be tested. While the first month will be manageable, the Seahawks will face one of the most difficult schedules of opposing offenses starting in Week 5, with two games apiece against the Rams and 49ers, one-offs with the Packers, Vikings, Chiefs, and Chargers.

It could be a foreign feeling for Wilson not to have the support blanket of a strong defense, although he got a sense of what it's like last year. In the second half of 2017, when the defense was without numerous key players, the Seahawks lost the turnover battle in four games (after not losing it in a single game in the first half). The Seahawks lost all four games. With Schottenheimer and without the defensive support blanket, Wilson will need to be Superman. Although the Seahawks are projected to be a .500 team, for the first time since Wilson was drafted they are not favored in at least nine games. In fact, they are favored in just three according to the early Weeks 1-16 odds and aren't favored to win any game by more than three points. Compare that to 2013-14, when they were favored by over three points in 13 games, or 12 games in 2015, 11 games in 2016, and then eight games last year.

The market's lack of confidence in Seattle has a lot to do with the schedule, defense, Schottenheimer, and lack of a solid offensive line. But the Seahawks are also at their best when they can play up the underdog role. Head coach Pete Carroll thrives in that motivational environment. If the defense and offensive line don't improve enough to help Wilson, the Seahawks could have a lot of "motivation" this year.

Receiving Success by Personnel Grouping

Position	Player	1-1 [3WR]	1-2 [2WR]	2-1 [2WR]	1-0 [4WR]	1-3 [1WR]	0-1 [4WR]	2-0 [3WR]	0-0 [5WR]	0-2 [3WR]	2-3 [0WR]	1-4 [0WR]	Total
RB	Thomas Rawls	50% 5.9 76.7 (10)	67% 11.7 115.3 (3)										54% 7.2 89.9 (13)
TE	Jimmy Graham	55% 6.2 96.4 (67)	50% 3.6 77.6 (16)	50% 16.5 95.8 (2)		17% 1.8 39.6 (6)	0% 0.0 39.6 (1)				100% 1.0 118.8 (1)	0% 0.0 39.6 (1)	51% 5.5 93.4 (94)
WR	Doug Baldwin	55% 9.2 95.1 (85)	44% 7.4 124.7 (16)	33% 7.2 73.6 (6)	100% 10.0 108.3 (1)	50% 10.0 108.3 (2)	67% 6.0 82.6 (3)	0% 3.0 79.2 (1)	0% 0.0 39.6 (1)				52% 8.6 101.0 (115)
	Paul Richardson	49% 9.4 119.0 (59)	53% 9.1 106.8 (15)	0% 0.0 0.0 (1)	0% 0.0 39.6 (1)		0% 0.0 39.6 (1)			100% 10.0 108.3 (1)			49% 9.0 106.9 (78)
	Tyler Lockett	52% 8.6 103.6 (56)	33% 7.4 67.6 (9)	0% 0.0 39.6 (1)	0% 0.0 39.6 (2)		0% 0.0 39.6 (1)						46% 8.0 92.1 (69)
	J.D. McKissic	48% 4.8 85.3 (33)	60% 7.2 130.0 (10)	0% 0.0 0.0 (1)		100% 9.0 104.2 (1)							51% 5.3 91.0 (45)

Format Line 1: Success Rate Line 2: YPA Line 3: Passer Rating Line 4: Total # of Plays

Successful Play Rate
0% 100%

Rushing Success by Personnel Grouping

Position	Player	1-1 [3WR]	1-2 [2WR]	2-1 [2WR]	1-0 [4WR]	1-3 [1WR]	2-0 [3WR]	2-2 [1WR]	2-3 [0WR]	1-4 [0WR]	3-2 [0WR]	Total
QB	Russell Wilson	61% 7.8 (66)	50% 6.0 (6)	100% 7.0 (2)	0% 1.0 (1)	29% 1.8 (14)	0% 1.0 (1)	0% -1.0 (2)	0% -1.0 (1)	100% 1.0 (1)	0% -1.0 (1)	53% 6.2 (95)
RB	Eddie Lacy	21% 2.4 (34)	43% 2.9 (14)	0% -0.2 (5)	0% 3.0 (1)	54% 4.3 (13)	0% -2.0 (1)	0% 0.0 (1)				29% 2.6 (69)
	Mike Davis	29% 3.6 (45)	20% 1.4 (15)			33% 7.7 (3)			0% 0.0 (1)			27% 3.2 (64)

Format Line 1: Success Rate Line 2: YPC Line 3: Total # of Plays

San Francisco 49ers

2018 Coaches

Head Coach:
Kyle Shanahan (2nd yr)
Offensive Coordinator:
(Shanahan calls plays) (1st yr)
Defensive Coordinator:
Robert Saleh (1st yr)

2018 Forecast

Wins	Div Rank
9	#2

Past Records

2017: 6-10
2016: 2-14
2015: 5-11

EASY HARD

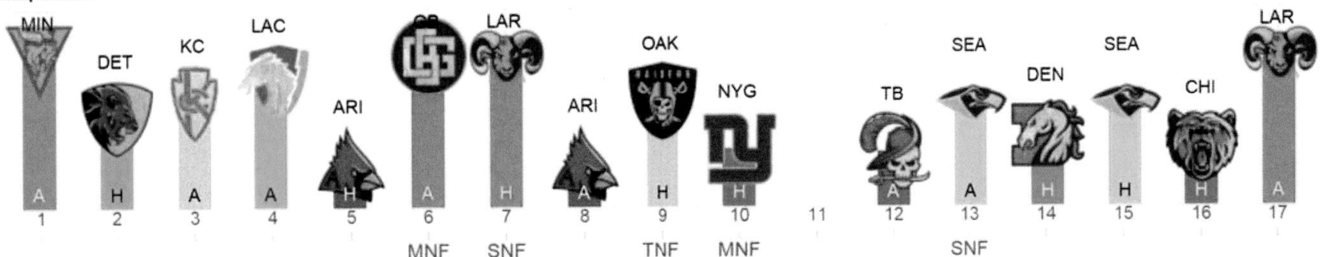

Key Players Lost

TXN	Player (POS)
Cut	Beadles, Zane G
	Gilbert, Jimmie LB
	McCoil, Dexter S
	Newsom, Donavin LB
Declared Free Agent	Barnes, Tim C
	Carradine, Tank DE
	Coyle, Brock LB
	Douzable, Leger DE
	Dumervil, Elvis LB
	Exum Jr., Antone S
	Fusco, Brandon G
	Hall, Leon CB
	Hyde, Carlos RB
	Jackson, Asa CB
	Johnson, Dontae CB
	Jones, Chris DT
	Lynch, Aaron LB
	Murphy, Louis WR
	Paulsen, Logan TE
	Reid, Eric S

Average Line	# Games Favored	# Games Underdog
-1.4	9	6

2018 San Francisco 49ers Overview

The 49ers enter the season as the league's second-hottest team. The energy coming out of San Francisco is tangible. Once Jimmy Garoppolo won his first game against the Bears, hope was born. He followed it up with another great performance in which he averaged 10.1 YPA, and then hope turned into belief when Garoppolo closed the season by defeating three straight playoff teams en route to a 5-0 record. Outside of the Super Bowl-winning Eagles, no team has a better vibe heading into 2018 than the 49ers.

It's difficult to find a franchise quarterback, and the 49ers have found theirs in Garoppolo, although this offseason they paid dearly to keep him, giving him a five-year, $137.5 million contract. Three of the last six teams to win a Super Bowl were captained by rookie-deal quarterbacks, and the other three were led by quarterbacks (Tom Brady and Peyton Manning) who took below-market compensation so their teams could add talent to their rosters. Fortunately for the 49ers they had one of the best salary-cap situations when extending Garoppolo, so they could afford to frontload his contract. He has an immense cap hit of $37 million in 2018 but an average of just $25 million per year over the next four years. To put that into perspective: Of the starting quarterbacks with non-rookie deals, the cheapest will have a cap hit of $16 million in 2019, and Garoppolo will have the second-cheapest cap hit at $20 million. Although his deal is massive, Garoppolo has a team-friendly contract, and the salary cap will continue to increase each year, so the 49ers should be able to build around their quarterback.

When it comes to building the team, the 49ers are giving head coach Kyle Shanahan great freedom to implement his grand design. In Shanahan's first draft with the team, there was only one quarterback he reportedly wanted: Not Mitchell Trubisky, Patrick Mahomes, or Deshaun Watson but C.J. Beathard of Iowa. The 49ers traded fourth- and seventh-round picks to Minnesota in exchange for the Vikings' third-rounder (No. 104 overall), which they used to draft Beathard, whom many draftniks viewed as a reach, especially since the team traded two picks to acquire him, but Shanahan wanted him because he thought he was similar to Kirk Cousins, and the team obliged.

In the same draft, general manager John Lynch's big board did not include running back Joe

(cont'd - see SF2)

Key Free Agents/ Trades Added

Attaochu, Jerry DE
Cooper, Jonathan G
Johnson, Malcolm RB
Locke, Jeff P
McKinnon, Jerick RB
Person, Mike C
Richburg, Weston C
Sherman, Richard CB
Toomer, Korey LB

Drafted Players

Rd	Pk	Player (College)
1	9	OT - Mike McGlinchey (Notre Dame)
2	44	WR - Dante Pettis (Washington)
3	70	LB - Fred Warner (BYU)
	95	S - Tarvarius Moore (Southern Miss)
4	128	DE - Kentavius Street (NC State)
5	142	CB - D. J. Reed (Kansas State)
6	184	S - Marcell Harris (Florida)
7	223	DT - Jullian Taylor (Temple)
	240	WR - Richie James (Middle Tennessee)

Regular Season Wins: Past & Current Proj

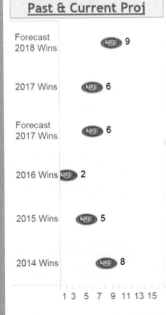

Forecast 2018 Wins: 9
2017 Wins: 6
Forecast 2017 Wins: 6
2016 Wins: 2
2015 Wins: 5
2014 Wins: 8

1 3 5 7 9 11 13 15

Lineup & Cap Hits

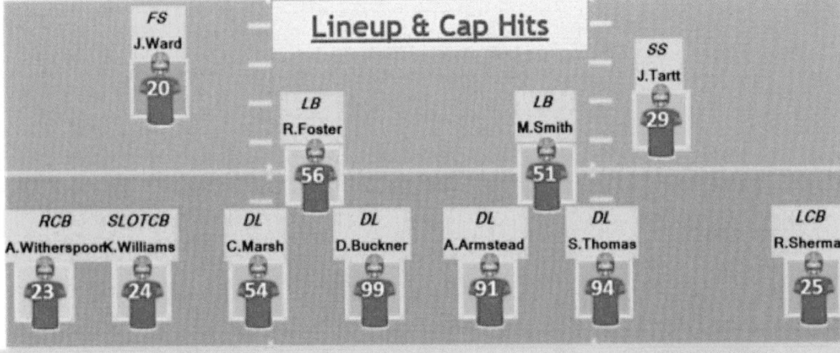

11 LWR M.Goodwin
81 SLOTWR T.Taylor
74 LT J.Staley
75 LG L.Tomlinson
70 C W.Richburg
65 RG J.Garnett
69 RT M.McGlinchey Rookie
89 TE V.McDonald
15 RWR P.Garcon
10 QB J.Garoppolo
21 RB J.McKinnon
18 WR2 D.Pettis Rookie
19 WR3 A.Robinson
22 RB2 M.Breida
3 QB2 C.Beathard

2017 Cap Dollars

2018 Unit Spending

Positional Spending

	Rank	Total	2017 Rk
All OFF	2	$112.15M	30
QB	1	$39.32M	27
OL	11	$36.81M	16
RB	12	$8.94M	29
WR	17	$21.56M	17
TE	24	$5.52M	13
All DEF	24	$73.33M	29
DL	15	$28.65M	24
LB	26	$15.37M	10
CB	23	$12.03M	28
S	6	$17.28M	18

SF-2

Williams, but Shanahan craved Williams above all other players. On the morning of Day 3 of the draft, Shanahan reportedly told Peter King: "I'm telling you right now: If we don't get him, I'll be sick. I will be contemplating Joe Williams all night." So the 49ers traded fourth- and fifth-round picks to the Colts in order to move up to No. 121 and draft Williams. The 49ers actually spent more draft capital in the trade to acquire Williams than they did to acquire Beathard, even though Williams was selected with the lower pick. The 49ers spared no expense to give Shanahan what he wanted.

Unfortunately for the 49ers, neither of these moves has paid off so far. Beathard started five games for the 49ers (Weeks 6-12), recording a 37% Success Rate, 69 passer rating, and 6.4 YPA. The 49ers went 1-4 in those games. Meanwhile, Williams missed the entire season after an up-and-down preseason, ending up on Injured Reserve as the 49ers cut the roster down to 53 players. Both draft moves (made by Lynch to appease Shanahan) cost the 49ers substantial capital, and both had as much 2017 success as a lead balloon.

The moves that did pay off last year came in free agency and the trade market. First was the signing of free agent fullback Kyle Juszczyk (although the 49ers still likely overpaid him). Juszczyk was given a four-year, $21 million deal with $7 million guaranteed, which is massive. The only other top fullback who signed in the 2017 free-agent class was Patrick DiMarco, who received just $8.4 million over four years in the second-most lucrative deal at the position. Why did the 49ers pay Juszczyk so much? Because the coach wanted him. Shanahan identified several "must-have" offensive players, and the 49ers paid to get them, including wide receivers Pierre Garcon (five-year, $47.5 million deal, $17 million guaranteed) and Marquise Goodwin (three-year, $19.25 million deal, $7.7M guaranteed). The 49ers had the money and cap space, so overpaying the players hasn't created a huge problem yet, but the dynamic of Shanahan asking and Lynch listening and paying could be an issue later.

The moves continued into the season, when the 49ers pulled of the huge

(cont'd - see SF-3)

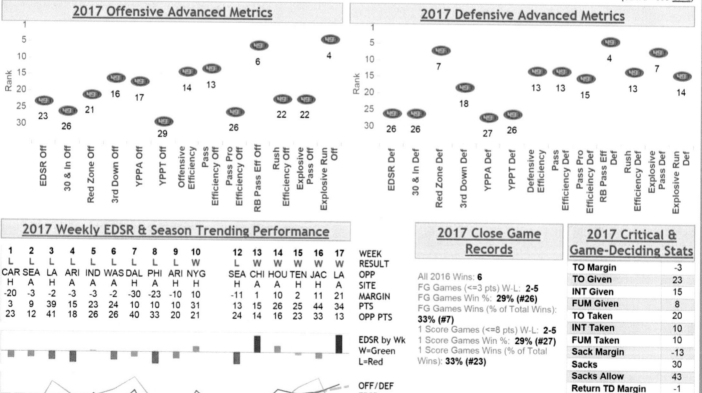

2017 Offensive Advanced Metrics

Metric	Rank
EDSR Off	23
30 & In Off	26
Red Zone Off	21
3rd Down Off	16
YPPA Off	17
YPPT Off	29
Offensive Efficiency	14
Pass Efficiency Off	13
Pass Pro Efficiency Off	26
RB Pass Eff Off	6
Rush Efficiency Off	22
Explosive Pass Off	22
Explosive Run Off	4

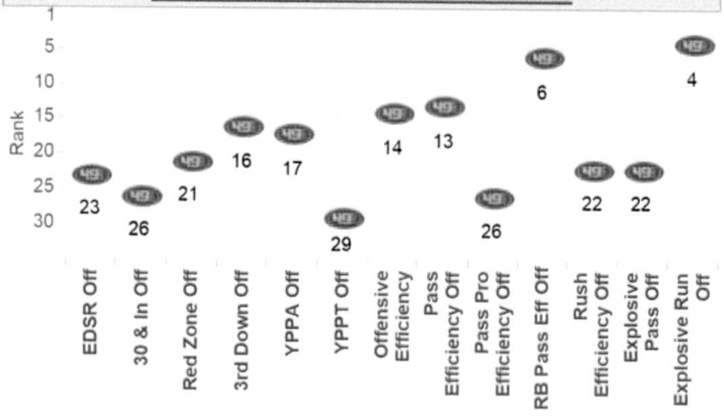

2017 Defensive Advanced Metrics

Metric	Rank
EDSR Def	26
30 & In Def	26
Red Zone Def	7
3rd Down Def	18
YPPA Def	27
YPPT Def	26
Defensive Efficiency	13
Pass Efficiency Def	13
Pass Pro Efficiency Def	15
RB Pass Eff Def	4
Rush Efficiency Def	13
Explosive Pass Def	7
Explosive Run Def	14

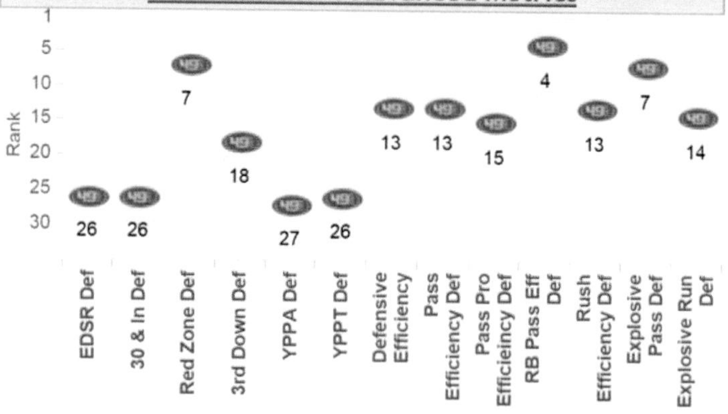

2017 Weekly EDSR & Season Trending Performance

WEEK	1	2	3	4	5	6	7	8	9	10	12	13	14	15	16	17
RESULT	L	L	L	L	L	L	L	L	L	W	L	W	W	W	W	W
OPP	CAR	SEA	LA	ARI	IND	WAS	DAL	PHI	ARI	NYG	SEA	CHI	HOU	TEN	JAC	LA
SITE	H	A	H	A	A	A	H	A	H	H	H	A	A	H	H	A
MARGIN	-20	-3	-2	-3	-3	-2	-30	-23	-10	10	-11	1	10	2	11	21
PTS	3	9	39	15	23	24	10	10	10	31	13	15	26	25	44	34
OPP PTS	23	12	41	18	26	26	40	33	20	21	24	14	16	23	33	13

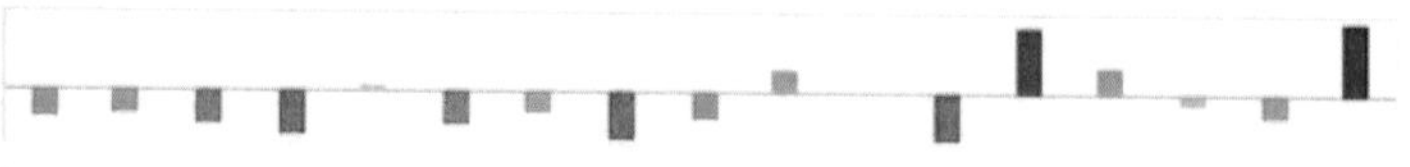

EDSR by Wk
W=Green
L=Red

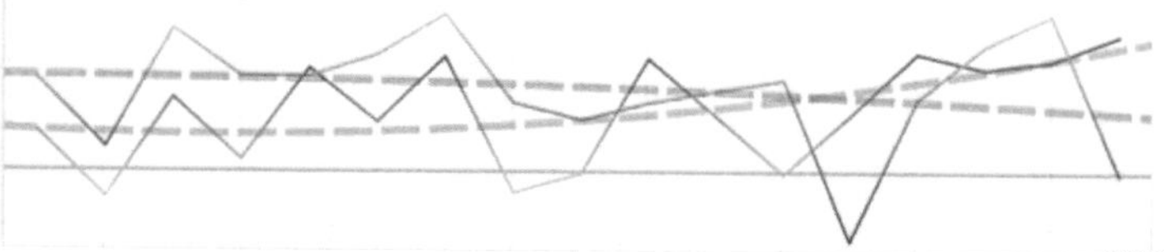

OFF/DEF EDSR
Blue=OFF (high=good)
Red=DEF (low=good)

2017 Close Game Records

All 2016 Wins: **6**
FG Games (<=3 pts) W-L: **2-5**
FG Games Win %: **29% (#26)**
FG Games Wins (% of Total Wins): **33% (#7)**
1 Score Games (<=8 pts) W-L: **2-5**
1 Score Games Win %: **29% (#27)**
1 Score Games Wins (% of Total Wins): **33% (#23)**

2017 Critical & Game-Deciding Stats

TO Margin	-3
TO Given	23
INT Given	15
FUM Given	8
TO Taken	20
INT Taken	10
FUM Taken	10
Sack Margin	-13
Sacks	30
Sacks Allow	43
Return TD Margin	-1
Ret TDs	1
Ret TDs Allow	2
Penalty Margin	-26
Penalties	123
Opponent Penalties	97

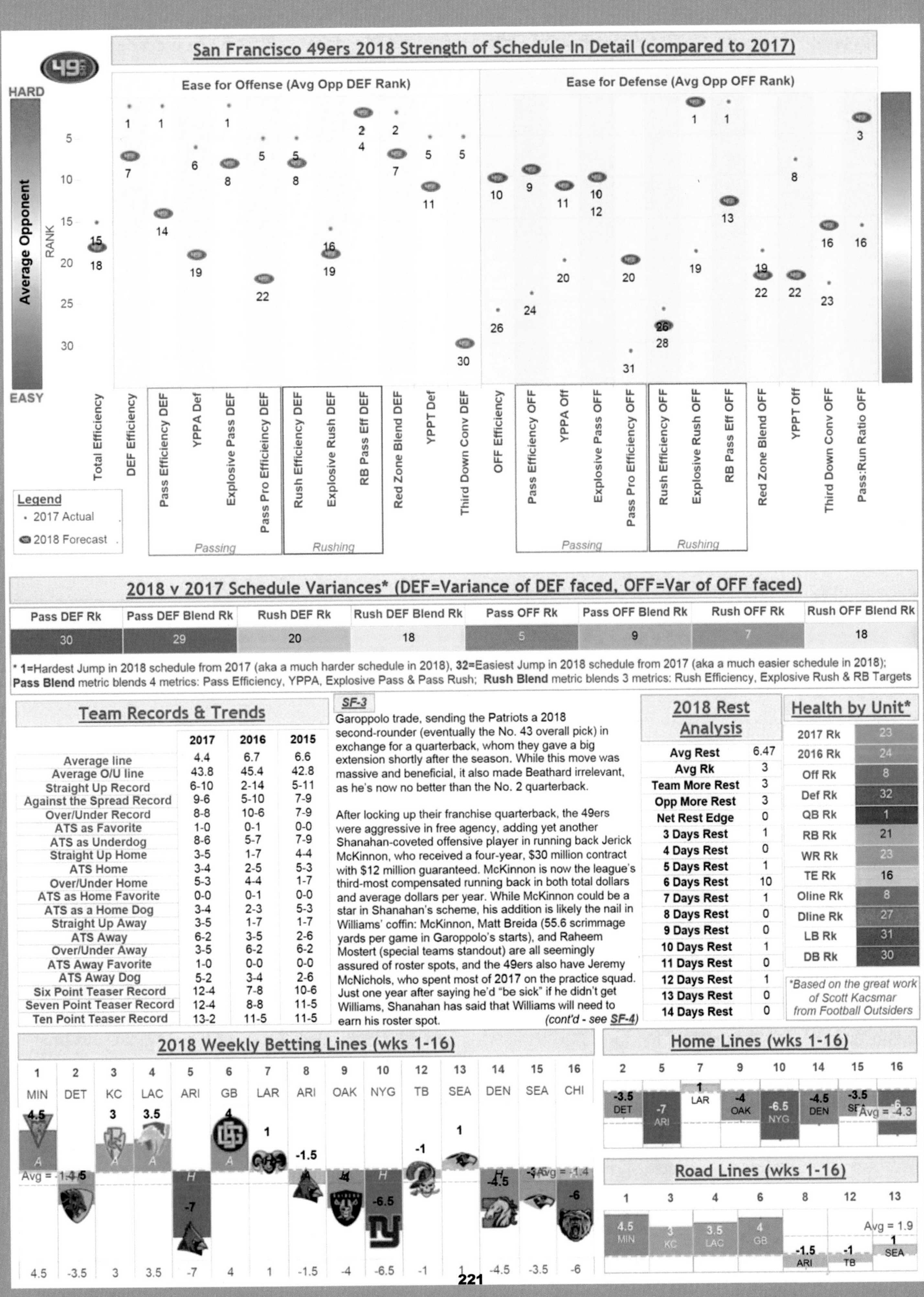

San Francisco 49ers 2018 Strength of Schedule In Detail (compared to 2017)

2018 v 2017 Schedule Variances* (DEF=Variance of DEF faced, OFF=Var of OFF faced)

Pass DEF Rk	Pass DEF Blend Rk	Rush DEF Rk	Rush DEF Blend Rk	Pass OFF Rk	Pass OFF Blend Rk	Rush OFF Rk	Rush OFF Blend Rk
30	29	20	18	5	9	7	18

* **1**=Hardest Jump in 2018 schedule from 2017 (aka a much harder schedule in 2018), **32**=Easiest Jump in 2018 schedule from 2017 (aka a much easier schedule in 2018); **Pass Blend** metric blends 4 metrics: Pass Efficiency, YPPA, Explosive Pass & Pass Rush; **Rush Blend** metric blends 3 metrics: Rush Efficiency, Explosive Rush & RB Targets

Team Records & Trends

	2017	2016	2015
Average line	4.4	6.7	6.6
Average O/U line	43.8	45.4	42.8
Straight Up Record	6-10	2-14	5-11
Against the Spread Record	9-6	5-10	7-9
Over/Under Record	8-8	10-6	7-9
ATS as Favorite	1-0	0-1	0-0
ATS as Underdog	8-6	5-7	7-9
Straight Up Home	3-5	1-7	4-4
ATS Home	3-4	2-5	5-3
Over/Under Home	5-3	4-4	1-7
ATS as Home Favorite	0-0	0-1	0-0
ATS as a Home Dog	3-4	2-3	5-3
Straight Up Away	3-5	1-7	1-7
ATS Away	6-2	3-5	2-6
Over/Under Away	3-5	6-2	6-2
ATS Away Favorite	1-0	0-0	0-0
ATS Away Dog	5-2	3-4	2-6
Six Point Teaser Record	12-4	7-8	10-6
Seven Point Teaser Record	12-4	8-8	11-5
Ten Point Teaser Record	13-2	11-5	11-5

SF-3

Garoppolo trade, sending the Patriots a 2018 second-rounder (eventually the No. 43 overall pick) in exchange for a quarterback, whom they gave a big extension shortly after the season. While this move was massive and beneficial, it also made Beathard irrelevant, as he's now no better than the No. 2 quarterback.

After locking up their franchise quarterback, the 49ers were aggressive in free agency, adding yet another Shanahan-coveted offensive player in running back Jerick McKinnon, who received a four-year, $30 million contract with $12 million guaranteed. McKinnon is now the league's third-most compensated running back in both total dollars and average dollars per year. While McKinnon could be a star in Shanahan's scheme, his addition is likely the nail in Williams' coffin: McKinnon, Matt Breida (55.6 scrimmage yards per game in Garoppolo's starts), and Raheem Mostert (special teams standout) are all seemingly assured of roster spots, and the 49ers also have Jeremy McNichols, who spent most of 2017 on the practice squad. Just one year after saying he'd "be sick" if he didn't get Williams, Shanahan has said that Williams will need to earn his roster spot. *(cont'd - see SF-4)*

2018 Rest Analysis

Avg Rest	6.47
Avg Rk	3
Team More Rest	3
Opp More Rest	3
Net Rest Edge	0
3 Days Rest	1
4 Days Rest	0
5 Days Rest	1
6 Days Rest	10
7 Days Rest	1
8 Days Rest	0
9 Days Rest	0
10 Days Rest	1
11 Days Rest	0
12 Days Rest	1
13 Days Rest	0
14 Days Rest	0

Health by Unit*

2017 Rk	23
2016 Rk	24
Off Rk	8
Def Rk	32
QB Rk	1
RB Rk	21
WR Rk	23
TE Rk	16
Oline Rk	8
Dline Rk	27
LB Rk	31
DB Rk	30

*Based on the great work of Scott Kacsmar from Football Outsiders

2018 Weekly Betting Lines (wks 1-16)

1	2	3	4	5	6	7	8	9	10	12	13	14	15	16
MIN	DET	KC	LAC	ARI	GB	LAR	ARI	OAK	NYG	TB	SEA	DEN	SEA	CHI
4.5	-3.5	3	3.5	-7	4	1	-1.5	-4	-6.5	-1	1	-4.5	-3.5	-6

Avg = -1.4

Home Lines (wks 1-16)

2	5	7	9	10	14	15	16
DET	ARI	LAR	OAK	NYG	DEN	SEA	CHI
-3.5	-7	1	-4	-6.5	-4.5	-3.5	-6

Avg = -4.3

Road Lines (wks 1-16)

1	3	4	6	8	12	13
MIN	KC	LAC	GB	ARI	TB	SEA
4.5	3	3.5	4	-1.5	-1	1

Avg = 1.9

San Francisco 49ers 2017 Play Analysis

2017 Play Tendencies

All Pass %	61%
All Pass Rk	6
All Rush %	39%
All Rush Rk	27
1 Score Pass %	59%
1 Score Pass Rk	10
2016 1 Score Pass %	47%
2016 1 Score Pass Rk	32
2017 Pass Increase %	13%
Pass Increase Rk	1
1 Score Rush %	41%
1 Score Rush Rk	23
Up Pass %	47%
Up Pass Rk	22
Up Rush %	53%
Up Rush Rk	11
Down Pass %	67%
Down Pass Rk	11
Down Rush %	33%
Down Rush Rk	22

2017 Down & Distance Tendencies

Down	Distance	Total Plays	Pass Rate	Run Rate	Play Success %
1	Short (1-3)	2	0%	100%	100%
	Med (4-7)	11	18%	82%	64%
	Long (8-10)	329	49%	51%	49%
	XL (11+)	17	71%	29%	35%
2	Short (1-3)	30	37%	63%	53%
	Med (4-7)	73	53%	47%	44%
	Long (8-10)	103	65%	35%	39%
	XL (11+)	46	80%	20%	17%
3	Short (1-3)	42	57%	43%	55%
	Med (4-7)	55	91%	9%	45%
	Long (8-10)	37	100%	0%	35%
	XL (11+)	36	83%	17%	14%
4	Short (1-3)	6	17%	83%	67%
	Med (4-7)	2	100%	0%	0%

Shotgun %:

Under Center	Shotgun
55%	45%
37%	*63%*

37% AVG 63%

Run Rate:

Under Center	Shotgun
56%	15%

68% AVG 23%

Pass Rate:

Under Center	Shotgun
44%	85%

32% AVG 77%

Short Yardage Intelligence:

2nd and Short Run

Run Freq	Run Rk	NFL Run Freq Avg	Run 1D Rate	Run NFL 1D Avg
74%	8	67%	47%	69%

2nd and Short Pass

Pass Freq	Pass Rk	NFL Pass Freq Avg	Pass 1D Rate	Pass NFL 1D Avg
26%	25	33%	50%	53%

Most Frequent Play

Down	Distance	Play Type	Player	Total Plays	Play Success %
1	Med (4-7)	RUSH	Carlos Hyde	7	71%
	Long (8-10)	RUSH	Carlos Hyde	109	40%
	XL (11+)	PASS	Carlos Hyde	4	0%
2	Short (1-3)	RUSH	Carlos Hyde	11	55%
	Med (4-7)	RUSH	Carlos Hyde	18	56%
	Long (8-10)	RUSH	Carlos Hyde	22	27%
	XL (11+)	PASS	Carlos Hyde	7	0%
3	Short (1-3)	RUSH	Carlos Hyde	9	56%
	Med (4-7)	PASS	Trent Taylor	9	56%
	Long (8-10)	PASS	Trent Taylor	7	29%
	XL (11+)	PASS	Carlos Hyde	6	0%
			Trent Taylor	6	0%

Most Successful Play*

Down	Distance	Play Type	Player	Total Plays	Play Success %
1	Med (4-7)	RUSH	Carlos Hyde	7	71%
	Long (8-10)	PASS	Trent Taylor	8	88%
2	Short (1-3)	RUSH	Carlos Hyde	11	55%
	Med (4-7)	RUSH	Carlos Hyde	18	56%
	Long (8-10)	PASS	Kyle Juszczyk	8	75%
	XL (11+)	PASS	Marquise Goodwin	6	50%
3	Short (1-3)	PASS	Trent Taylor	6	83%
	Med (4-7)	PASS	Marquise Goodwin	6	67%
	Long (8-10)	PASS	Marquise Goodwin	6	67%
	XL (11+)	PASS	Carlos Hyde	6	0%
			Matt Breida	5	0%
			Trent Taylor	6	0%

**Minimum 5 plays to qualify*

2017 Snap Rates

Wk	Opp	Score	Carlos Hyde	Marquise Goodwin	George Kittle	Garrett Celek	Trent Taylor	Pierre Garcon	Kyle Juszczyk	Matt Breida	Logan Paulsen
1	CAR	L 23-3	45 (79%)	50 (88%)	54 (95%)	14 (25%)	24 (42%)	50 (88%)	19 (33%)	10 (18%)	3 (5%)
2	SEA	L 12-9	40 (82%)	42 (86%)	43 (88%)	16 (33%)	21 (43%)	39 (80%)	17 (35%)	9 (18%)	5 (10%)
3	LA	L 41-39	58 (73%)	57 (72%)	37 (47%)	36 (46%)	37 (47%)	66 (84%)	25 (32%)	16 (20%)	28 (35%)
4	ARI	L 18-15	58 (69%)	9 (11%)	75 (89%)	21 (25%)	47 (56%)	74 (88%)	24 (29%)	26 (31%)	1 (1%)
5	IND	L 26-23	33 (46%)	55 (76%)	40 (56%)	32 (44%)	35 (49%)	63 (88%)	35 (49%)	35 (49%)	3 (4%)
6	WAS	L 26-24	56 (78%)	61 (85%)	65 (90%)	30 (42%)	44 (61%)	60 (83%)		17 (24%)	3 (4%)
7	DAL	L 40-10	51 (77%)	39 (59%)	32 (48%)	20 (30%)	46 (70%)	46 (70%)		15 (23%)	11 (17%)
8	PHI	L 33-10	44 (67%)	43 (65%)	41 (62%)	26 (39%)	39 (59%)	32 (48%)	20 (30%)	21 (32%)	
9	ARI	L 20-10	56 (76%)	67 (91%)	33 (45%)	55 (74%)	15 (20%)		17 (23%)	17 (23%)	
10	NYG	W 31-21	46 (75%)	48 (79%)		56 (92%)			38 (62%)	17 (28%)	12 (20%)
12	SEA	L 24-13	64 (90%)	54 (76%)	25 (35%)	48 (68%)	47 (66%)		16 (23%)	7 (10%)	6 (8%)
13	CHI	W 15-14	50 (67%)	58 (77%)	27 (36%)	52 (69%)	31 (41%)		40 (53%)	24 (32%)	8 (11%)
14	HOU	W 26-16	41 (56%)	52 (71%)	20 (27%)	61 (84%)	31 (42%)		37 (51%)	32 (44%)	6 (8%)
15	TEN	W 25-23	51 (73%)	63 (90%)	28 (40%)	46 (66%)	34 (49%)		32 (46%)	19 (27%)	9 (13%)
16	JAC	W 44-33	44 (65%)	50 (74%)	35 (51%)	17 (25%)	25 (37%)		39 (57%)	23 (34%)	30 (44%)
17	LA	W 34-13	45 (70%)	21 (33%)	36 (56%)	34 (53%)	15 (23%)		39 (61%)	20 (31%)	23 (36%)
Grand Total			782 (71%)	769 (71%)	591 (58%)	564 (51%)	491 (47%)	430 (78%)	398 (42%)	308 (28%)	148 (16%)

Personnel Groupings

Personnel	Team %	NFL Avg	Succ. %
1-1 [3WR]	50%	59%	41%
2-1 [2WR]	28%	7%	46%
1-2 [2WR]	13%	19%	50%
2-2 [1WR]	3%	4%	41%

Grouping Tendencies

Personnel	Pass Rate	Pass Succ. %	Run Succ. %
1-1 [3WR]	75%	39%	45%
2-1 [2WR]	46%	49%	44%
1-2 [2WR]	50%	41%	58%
2-2 [1WR]	24%	75%	31%

Red Zone Targets (min 3)

Receiver	All	Inside 5	6-10	11-20
George Kittle	16	1	6	9
Marquise Goodwin	15	3	6	6
Carlos Hyde	11		2	9
Kendrick Bourne	8		5	3
Trent Taylor	7	2	1	4
Garrett Celek	6	3	3	
Kyle Juszczyk	6		1	5
Pierre Garcon	5			5
Aldrick Robinson	4			4

Red Zone Rushes (min 3)

Rusher	All	Inside 5	6-10	11-20
Carlos Hyde	41	18	10	13
Matt Breida	13	1	1	11
C.J. Beathard	5	2	2	1
Jimmy Garoppolo	4	2		2

Early Down Target Rate

RB	TE	WR
32%	15%	54%
23%	*21%* *NFL AVG*	*56%*

Overall Target Success %

RB	TE	WR
43% #20	51% #16	46% #22

San Francisco 49ers 2017 Passing Recap & 2018 Outlook

Last year I was concerned with Brian Hoyer's ability to complete the deep ball. He simply hadn't shown aptitude to push the ball downfield, and explosive plays are important to Shanahan's system. Unsurprisingly, Hoyer had just a 77.6 rating, 44% Success Rate, and 12.7 YPA on passes of 15-plus air yards. Beathard, however, had surprising production. He underperformed from a win-loss perspective, but he recorded a 109 passer rating, 44% Success Rate, and 16.1 YPA on deep passes. Of all quarterbacks with 30-plus deep passes, Beathard ranked No. 4 in passer rating and No. 2 in YPA. Garoppolo was also surprising, but not in a good way. He posted a 34.8 rating on deep passes with a 0:3 TD:INT ratio, ranking 39th out of 40 QBs with 30-plus attempts. He had only a 38% Success Rate and 9.7 YPA. Perhaps Garoppolo struggled with his timing on the deep routes because he joined the team late in the season. The extra time in the system should improve his 2018 numbers, but Shanahan will need to ensure that Garoppolo can take advantage of the opportunities available through the deep passing game.

Jimmy Garoppolo Rating All Downs

27 | 70 | 34

98 | 124 | 113

Jimmy Garoppolo Rating Early Downs

27 | 67 | 65

117 | 114 | 100

2017 Standard Passing Table

QB	Comp	Att	Comp %	Yds	YPA	TDs	INT	Sacks	Rating	Rk
Jimmy Garoppolo	120	178	67%	1,560	8.8	7	5	8	96	12
C.J. Beathard	123	224	55%	1,430	6.4	4	6	19	69	51
NFL Avg			62%		7.0				87.5	

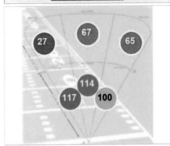

2017 Advanced Passing Table

QB	Success %	EDSR Passing Success %	20+ Yd Pass Gains	20+ Yd Pass %	30+ Yd Pass Gains	30+ Yd Pass %	Avg. Air Yds per Comp	Avg. YAC per Comp	20+ Air Yd Comp	20+ Air Yd %
Jimmy Garoppolo	54%	56%	20	11.2%	10	5.6%	7.2	5.5	4	3%
C.J. Beathard	37%	39%	16	7.1%	8	3.6%	6.1	5.5	10	8%
NFL Avg	44%	48%	27.7	8.8%	10.3	3.3%	6.0	4.7	11.7	6%

Interception Rates by Down

Yards to Go	1	2	3	4	Total
1 & 2		0.0%	0.0%		0.0%
3, 4, 5		0.0%	0.0%	0.0%	0.0%
6 - 9	0.0%	0.0%	10.5%		4.8%
10 - 14	3.0%	0.0%	0.0%		2.2%
15+	25.0%	0.0%	0.0%		6.7%
Total	4.1%	0.0%	3.6%	0.0%	2.7%

3rd Down Passing - Short of Sticks Analysis

QB	Avg. Yds to Go	Avg. YIA (of Comp)	Avg Yds Short	Short of Sticks Rate	Short Rk
Jimmy Garoppolo	7.4	8.1	0.0	33%	6
NFL Avg	7.8	6.7	-1.1	60%	

Air Yds vs YAC

Air Yds %	YAC %	Rk
56%	44%	25
58%	42%	

2017 Receiving Recap & 2018 Outlook

Garcon was expected to have a good first year with Shanahan, given their prior history together and Garcon's target load in Washington the previous season. Garcon saw double-digit targets in four of the first six games, but he eclipsed 100 yards just once and did not score a touchdown. Unfortunately for Garcon, he was injured and played in just eight games, missing all of Garoppolo's starts. Goodwin was the biggest beneficiary and saw 105 targets and a tremendous 9.2 YPA. Watch out for the tight ends in 2018: When targeting tight ends, Garoppolo had a 140 rating and 11.9 YPA (vs. 79.8 rating and 7.9 YPA with wide receivers).

Player *Min 50 Targets	Targets	Comp %	YPA	Rating	TOARS	Success %	Success Rk	Missed YPA Rk	YAS % Rk	TDs
Marquise Goodwin	105	53%	9.2	83	4.6	46%	81	56	3	2
Carlos Hyde	88	67%	4.0	70	4.1	40%	113	101	131	0
Pierre Garcon	67	60%	7.5	77	3.9	49%	65	100	67	0
George Kittle	63	68%	8.2	90	3.9	47%	78	76	17	2
Trent Taylor	60	72%	7.2	82	3.8	46%	82	120	122	2

Directional Passer Rating Delivered

Receiver	Short Left	Short Middle	Short Right	Deep Left	Deep Middle	Deep Right	Player Total
Marquise Goodwin	74	85	73	43	104	91	83
Carlos Hyde	79	43	80		40	40	70
Pierre Garcon	83	101	55	88			77
George Kittle	61	117	102	67	119	47	90
Trent Taylor	79	108	113	0	96	40	82
Aldrick Robinson	21	129	48	52	40	127	63
Kyle Juszczyk	92	128	83	117			106
Matt Breida	32	158	85				69
Kendrick Bourne	20	92	76	58		25	48
Garrett Celek	109	74	117	149	90	96	124
Team Total	66	99	84	64	100	63	81

2017 Rushing Recap & 2017 Outlook

I'm excited about McKinnon. The aggressiveness that Shanahan displayed in free agency to acquire McKinnon suggests that he has big plans for the back. When Shanahan traded up for Williams in 2017, Williams was comped to McKinnon. In essence, Shanahan liked McKinnon enough to demand that the 49ers take a knockoff McKinnon or he'd "be sick." As soon as McKinnon became available, Shanahan overpaid to acquire him. Offensive play callers sit around all hours of the night sketching up concepts, watching film, and dreaming of players and plays. I think McKinnon is someone Shanahan has thought long and hard about. He should have a major role in 2018.

Yards per Carry by Direction

Player *Min 50 Rushes	Rushes	YPC	Success %	Success Rk	Missed YPA Rk	YTS % Rk	YAS % Rk	Early Down Success %	Early Down Success Rk	TDs
Carlos Hyde	240	3.9	43%	41	53	33	30	44%	41	8
Matt Breida	105	4.4	47%	29	48	31	40	47%	28	2

Directional Run Frequency

13% | 14% | 10% | 27% | 11% | 9% | 16%

LT | LG | C | RG | RT

SF-4

Based on the moves the 49ers have made since drafting Beathard and Williams, the aggressiveness with which they pursued both players seems to have been unwarranted and reckless. The team's roster-building missteps haven't resulted in catastrophe, but the 49ers have a clear issue: They lack discipline when it comes to capital allocation.

In the 2018 draft, Shanahan and the 49ers were once again aggressive. They traded second- and third-round selections to the Redskins for their second- and fifth-rounders, using the first of those to select wide receiver and punt returner Dante Pettis. Projected to be drafted no earlier than the third round, Pettis admitted after the draft that even he was surprised by his second-round selection. Obviously, Shanahan and Lynch are optimistic on Pettis, but it remains to be seen if this trade-up will pay off or blow up like their 2017 offensive draft moves.

Clearly the 49ers are hellbent on letting Shanahan exercise his offensive aggressiveness from a personnel perspective. In 2018, we could see Shanahan's aggressiveness also manifest in his play calling. When coordinating the league-leading 2016 Falcons offense, Shanahan employed a "Blitzkrieg" attack in the first half. The Falcons averaged 19 first-half points per game, second in NFL history to only the 2007 Patriots.

(cont'd - see SF-5)

Matthew Freedman's Fantasy Corner

Without a true No. 1 receiver last year, Shanahan's offense gave 166 targets to running backs and fullbacks, with 88 of them going to a relatively stone-handed Hyde. Many of those targets figure this year to go to McKinnon, who has captured a high 33.9% of his 2,902 career scrimmage yards via the passing game. In each of the past three seasons, Shanahan's lead back has finished top-12 in PPR per-game scoring: Hyde (2017, No. 12) and Devonta Freeman twice (2016, No. 7; 2015, No. 1). Physically talented, slated to lead the 49ers in carries, and available as the RB14 by average draft position, McKinnon has top-three fantasy upside.

Division History: Season Wins & 2018 Projection

2014 Wins | 2015 Wins | 2016 Wins | 2017 Wins | Forecast 2018 Wins

Rank of 2018 Defensive Pass Efficiency Faced by Week

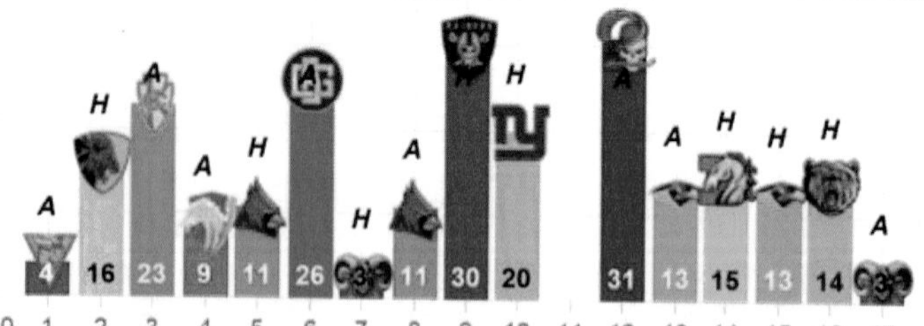

Rank of 2018 Defensive Rush Efficiency Faced by Week

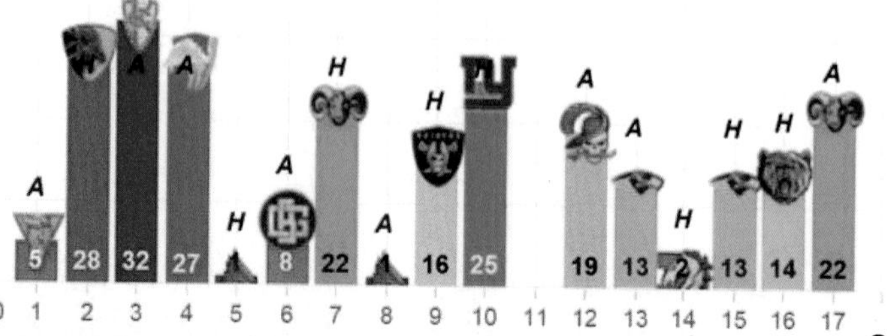

2017 Situational Usage by Player & Position

Usage Rate by Score

	49ers	Being Blown Out (14+)	Down Big (9-13)	One Score	Large Lead (9-13)	Blowout Lead (14+)	Grand Total
RUSH	Carlos Hyde	18%	15%	27%	31%	38%	25%
	Matt Breida	6%	8%	12%	28%	18%	11%
	Marquise Goodwin			1%			0%
	Kyle Juszczyk		2%	1%			1%
	Raheem Mostert		1%	1%			1%
	Total	24%	26%	41%	59%	56%	38%
PASS	Carlos Hyde	15%	13%	8%		6%	9%
	Matt Breida	5%	9%	3%		3%	4%
	Marquise Goodwin	11%	9%	12%	7%		11%
	Pierre Garcon	11%	10%	6%			7%
	George Kittle	9%	7%	6%	3%	6%	7%
	Trent Taylor	8%	4%	6%	7%		6%
	Kyle Juszczyk	2%	2%	5%	3%	9%	4%
	Aldrick Robinson	7%	10%	4%		6%	5%
	Kendrick Bourne	3%	7%	3%	10%	9%	4%
	Garrett Celek	2%	4%	4%		3%	3%
	Louis Murphy	2%		2%	7%	3%	2%
	Cole Hikutini	2%					0%
	Logan Paulsen			0%	3%		0%
	Total	76%	74%	59%	41%	44%	62%

Positional Target Distribution vs NFL Average

		NFL Wide				Team Only			
		Left	Middle	Right	Total	Left	Middle	Right	Total
Deep	WR	954	491	968	2,413	32	18	19	69
	TE	186	147	182	515	6	3	6	15
	RB	35	8	41	84	4	1	1	6
	All	1,175	646	1,191	3,012	42	22	26	90
Short	WR	2,776	1,610	2,692	7,078	86	61	98	245
	TE	835	813	1,143	2,791	28	26	27	81
	RB	1,245	797	1,237	3,279	76	26	58	160
	All	4,856	3,220	5,072	13,148	190	113	183	486
Total		6,031	3,866	6,263	16,160	232	135	209	576

Positional Success Rates vs NFL Average

		NFL Wide				Team Only			
		Left	Middle	Right	Total	Left	Middle	Right	Total
Deep	WR	37%	45%	38%	39%	28%	61%	37%	39%
	TE	38%	52%	45%	44%	50%	67%	50%	53%
	RB	31%	63%	39%	38%	75%	0%	0%	50%
	All	37%	47%	39%	40%	36%	59%	38%	42%
Short	WR	52%	57%	50%	52%	41%	59%	50%	49%
	TE	51%	56%	49%	52%	39%	62%	48%	49%
	RB	44%	51%	43%	45%	43%	46%	40%	43%
	All	50%	56%	48%	51%	42%	57%	46%	47%
Total		47%	54%	46%	49%	41%	57%	45%	46%

Successful Play Rate
0% [color scale] 100%

San Francisco 49ers - Success by Personnel Grouping & Play Type

Play Type	1-1 [3WR]	1-2 [2WR]	2-1 [2WR]	1-0 [4WR]	1-3 [1WR]	0-1 [4WR]	2-0 [3WR]	2-2 [1WR]	0-0 [5WR]	0-3 [2WR]	2-3 [0WR]	Grand Total
PASS	39% (396, 62%)	41% (70, 11%)	49% (136, 21%)	33% (3, 0%)	33% (9, 1%)	25% (12, 2%)	33% (6, 1%)	75% (8, 1%)		0% (1, 0%)		41% (641, 100%)
RUSH	45% (130, 32%)	58% (71, 18%)	44% (157, 39%)	50% (2, 0%)	60% (5, 1%)	0% (1, 0%)	50% (6, 1%)	31% (26, 6%)	0% (1, 0%)		50% (4, 1%)	46% (404, 100%)
TOTAL	41% (526, 50%)	50% (141, 13%)	46% (293, 28%)	40% (5, 0%)	43% (14, 1%)	23% (13, 1%)	42% (12, 1%)	41% (34, 3%)	0% (1, 0%)	0% (1, 0%)	50% (4, 0%)	43% (1,045, 100%)

Format Line 1: Success Rate Line 2: Total # of Plays, % of All Plays (by type)

SF-5 Shanahan said that "all plays are designed with the goal of making the defense defend everybody. Each play should get the defense to think about and account for the run, the pass, the screen game, play-action bootlegs, and drop backs." In 2017, the 49ers were too deficient in talent to allow Shanahan to execute this style of offense. He specifically was reluctant to use Garoppolo behind the offensive line, which allowed 35 sacks in 11 games before Garoppolo's first start. In all aspects, the pre-Garoppolo offense was lacking. Not a single receiver had an 80 passer rating or 50% Success Rate before Garoppolo started, and no running back exceeded a 47% success rate. Lead back Carlos Hyde had just 3.9 YPC.

All of that should change in 2018, partly because of the schedule. Last year the 49ers offense played the No. 1 most difficult schedule of opposing defenses. In 2018, the in-division defenses (and especially secondaries) of the Seahawks and Cardinals won't be as strong. Also, the team has finally given Shanahan a talented roster of dynamic offensive chess pieces to deploy. The 49ers now have the league's highest paid fullback and third-highest paid running back. A coach like Shanahan wouldn't pay those players unless he planned use them both heavily as dual threats.

The 49ers may not have a true No. 1 wide receiver, but they have enough talent and versatility to be proficient. They have some reliable guys, some burners, and some high-agility guys. They don't have a Julio Jones-style guy as Shanahan did in Atlanta, but the receivers should be good enough to make defensive coordinators worry about the offense. Where Shanahan could improve the passing game is with his play calling after a 1st-and-10 incompletion on his side of the field. Last year Shanahan called runs 63% of the time in this situation (10% above league average). These runs were successful just 35% of the time and averaged 3.2 YPC, setting up 3rd and long. With Garoppolo, they went 100% run (in a smaller sample). In 2018, Shanahan needs to be more aggressive in 2nd-and-long situations.

Even though the team went 6-10 last year, their Garoppolo-led five-game winning streak to close the season has elevated expectations. After finishing dead last in the NFC West for three straight years and not once amassing more than six wins, the 49ers are projected to win nine games. This offense is substantially better, especially the passing game, and this is a passing league. In each place where he's worked with the same quarterback for two seasons, Shanahan's second year has been better than the first.

Receiving Success by Personnel Grouping

Position	Player	1-1 [3WR]	1-2 [2WR]	2-1 [2WR]	1-3 [1WR]	0-1 [4WR]	2-0 [3WR]	2-2 [1WR]	Total
RB	Carlos Hyde	37% 4.0 75.9 (67)	33% 0.3 70.1 (3)	36% 5.0 68.4 (11)	100% 7.0 95.8 (1)	0% 4.0 20.8 (2)	0% 0.0 39.6 (1)	100% 3.0 79.2 (2)	38% 4.0 69.3 (87)
	Kyle Juszczyk	50% 4.3 61.5 (4)		53% 7.8 108.8 (34)	100% 7.0 95.8 (1)			50% 9.0 104.2 (2)	54% 7.5 105.9 (41)
TE	George Kittle	44% 7.1 80.6 (39)	50% 7.1 90.0 (10)	57% 12.6 113.7 (7)	0% 2.0 70.1 (3)	100% 13.0 118.8 (1)		100% 19.0 118.8 (1)	46% 7.7 87.6 (61)
WR	Marquise Goodwin	45% 8.6 87.1 (51)	50% 10.3 82.2 (18)	58% 9.5 76.7 (31)		0% 0.0 39.6 (1)		0% 0.0 39.6 (1)	49% 9.0 81.4 (102)
	Pierre Garcon	42% 6.0 64.1 (45)	70% 12.7 112.5 (10)	60% 8.8 88.8 (10)		50% 7.5 97.9 (2)			49% 7.5 76.7 (67)
	Trent Taylor	49% 7.0 78.6 (51)	100% 13.0 118.8 (2)	50% 8.5 79.2 (2)		33% 5.7 81.3 (3)	100% 6.0 91.7 (1)		51% 7.2 81.4 (59)

Format Line 1: Success Rate Line 2: YPA Line 3: Passer Rating Line 4: Total # of Plays

Successful Play Rate
0% [color scale] 100%

Rushing Success by Personnel Grouping

Position	Player	1-1 [3WR]	1-2 [2WR]	2-1 [2WR]	1-0 [4WR]	1-3 [1WR]	0-1 [4WR]	2-0 [3WR]	2-2 [1WR]	0-0 [5WR]	2-3 [0WR]	3-2 [0WR]	Total
QB	C.J. Beathard	67% 6.1 (15)	100% 5.3 (4)	67% 7.3 (3)	100% 4.0 (1)				0% -1.0 (3)				65% 5.2 (26)
RB	Carlos Hyde	43% 5.0 (77)	55% 4.2 (49)	41% 3.5 (86)	0% -2.0 (1)	50% 1.3 (4)	0% 1.0 (1)	25% 2.3 (4)	40% 2.8 (10)	0% 0.0 (1)	33% -0.7 (3)	0% 2.0 (1)	43% 3.9 (237)
	Matt Breida	38% 4.3 (29)	50% 3.4 (16)	49% 4.8 (53)		100% 2.0 (1)		100% 5.0 (2)	33% 5.3 (3)				47% 4.5 (104)

Format Line 1: Success Rate Line 2: YPC Line 3: Total # of Plays

Tampa Bay Buccaneers

2018 Coaches

Head Coach:
Dirk Koetter (3rd yr)
Offensive Coordinator:
Todd Monken (3rd yr)
Defensive Coordinator:
Mike Smith (2nd yr)

2018 Forecast

Wins	Div Rank
6.5	#4

Past Records

2017: 5-11
2016: 9-7
2015: 6-10

EASY HARD

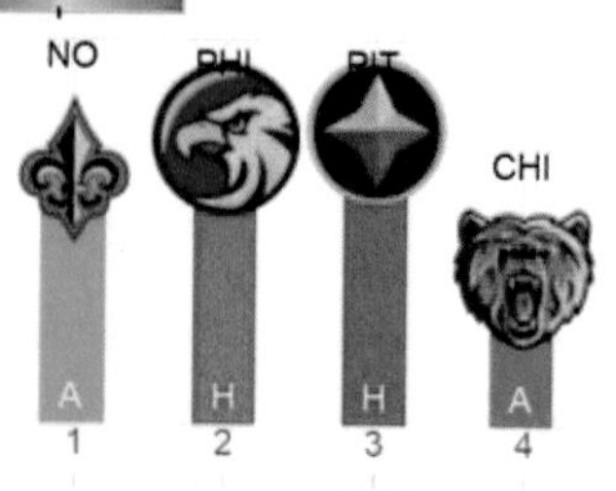

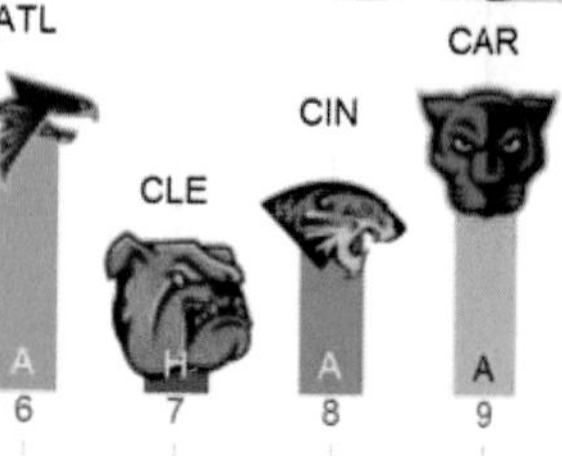
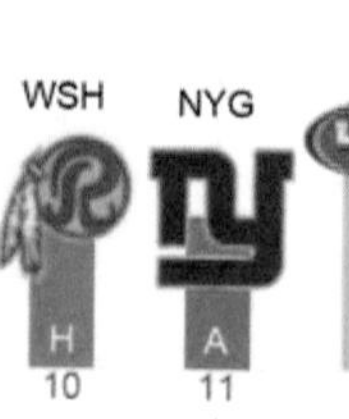
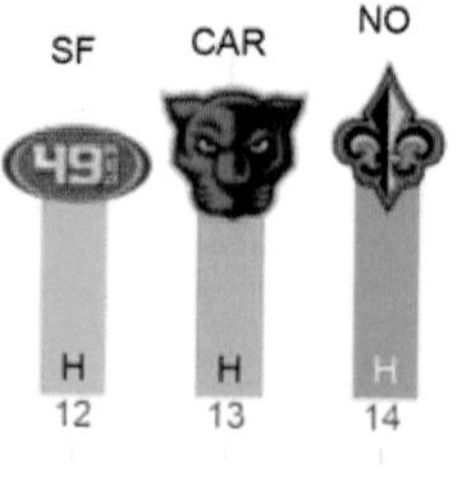
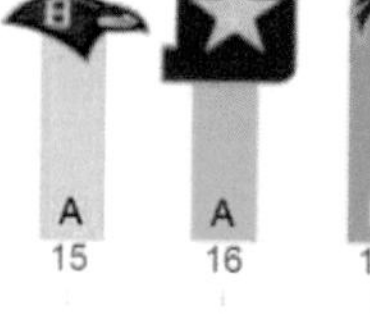

Week	Opponent	H/A
1	NO	A
2	PHI	H
3 (MNF)	PIT	H
4	CHI	A
5		
6	ATL	A
7	CLE	H
8	CIN	A
9	CAR	A
10	WSH	H
11	NYG	A
12	SF	H
13	CAR	H
14	NO	H
15	BAL	A
16	DAL	A
17	ATL	H

Key Players Lost

TXN	Player (POS)
Cut	Ayers Jr., Robert DE
	Baker, Chris DT
	Folk, Nick K
	Martin, Doug RB
	Young, Avery G
Declared Free Agent	Adjei-Barimah, Jude CB
	Clarke, Will DE
	Gettis, Adam T
	Grimes, Brent CB
	Hawley, Joe C
	McClain, Robert CB
	McDonald, Clinton DT
	Murray, Patrick K
	Pamphile, Kevin G
	Sanborn, Garrison LB
	Siliga, Sealver DT
	Sims, Charles RB
	Smith, Evan G
	Trattou, Justin DE
	Ward, T.J. S

Average Line	# Games Favored	# Games Underdog
2.6	3	12

2018 Tampa Bay Buccaneers Overview

Worst to first: That's been a reality in the NFC East for multiple years in a row, but not in the NFC South, where the Buccaneers have been bottom-dwellers for most of the past decade. For five years in a row (2011-15), the Bucs finished fourth in division. The coaching staff turned over multiple times during that span, from Raheem Morris to Greg Schiano to Lovie Smith. Then suddenly hope was on the horizon. In Jameis Winston's second season he was paired with first-year head coach Dirk Koetter, and the Bucs earned their first winning record (9-7) in a half decade, finishing second in the NFC South. But then in 2017, like a college grad without a well-paying job, the Bucs moved back into their parents' basement. They didn't just finish fourth: They weren't even close. While every other team in the division had a winning record and made the playoffs, the Bucs went 5-11.

What happened to Tampa Bay in 2017? Despite having a similar year-over-year strength of schedule, the Bucs had worse metrics nearly across the board, especially on defense, where they moved from 13th in efficiency to 32nd. They had bottom-two marks in metrics that matter: Pass defense, pass rush, and third down. As a result, they struggled immensely.

One problem was that in the games in which they won the turnover battle — games that typically result in an 80% win rate — they won just 50%. And in the games with a negative turnover differential they went 0-6 through the first 16 weeks (they beat the playoff-bound Saints in Week 17).

In some respects, though, the team played better than its five-win record, ranking No. 2 in the league in early-down Success Rate. On top of that, the Bucs lost the EDSR battle in just two games, and four of their games with negative turnover margins they lost by just three points. In one-score games, they went 3-7. In games decided by a field goal, the Buccaneers went 3-0 in 2016. In 2017, they went 1-4.

A strange problem for the Bucs was their ridiculously horrendous second-quarter offensive performances, especially since they were top-10 in Success Rate in every other quarter: Q1, No. 7 (48%); Q2, No. 30 (40%); Q3, No. 6 (49%); and Q4, No. 3 (51%).

(cont'd - see TB2)

Key Free Agents/ Trades Added

- Allen, Beau DT
- Catanzaro, Chandler K
- Curry, Vinny DE
- Jensen, Ryan C
- Lynch, Cameron LB
- Pierre-Paul, Jason DE
- Unrein, Mitch DE

Drafted Players

Rd	Pk	Player (College)
1	12	DT - Vita Vea (Washington)
2	38	RB - Ronald Jones (USC)
	53	CB - M. J. Stewart (North Carolina)
	63	CB - Carlton Davis (Auburn)
3	94	OT - Alex Cappa (Humboldt State)
4	117	S - Jordan Whitehead (Pittsburgh)
5	144	WR - Justin Watson (Penn)
6	202	LB - Jack Cichy (Wisconsin)

Regular Season Wins: Past & Current Proj

Forecast 2018 Wins  6.5
2017 Wins  5
Forecast 2017 Wins  7
2016 Wins  9
2015 Wins 6
2014 Wins  2

1 3 5 7 9 11 13 15

Lineup & Cap Hits

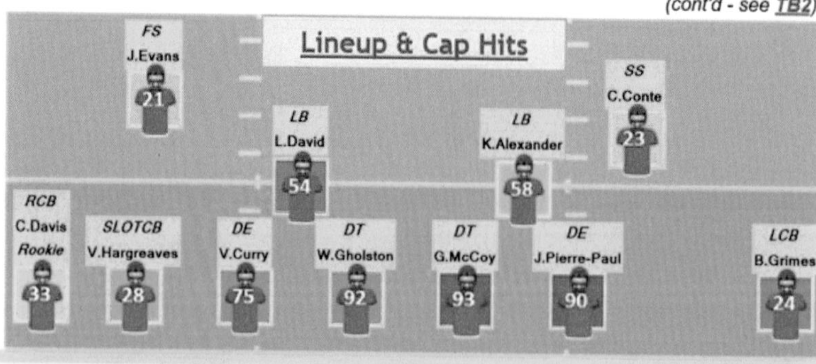

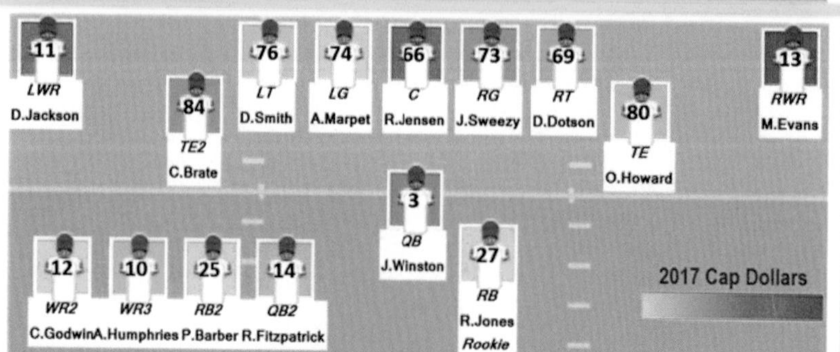

2018 Unit Spending

All DEF
All OFF

Positional Spending

	Rank	Total	2017 Rk
All OFF	9	$101.05M	25
QB	23	$13.22M	24
OL	18	$34.17M	23
RB	24	$5.30M	4
WR	1	$36.84M	10
TE	10	$11.52M	26
All DEF	3	$96.48M	11
DL	2	$54.51M	2
LB	24	$16.52M	31
CB	19	$17.53M	17
S	27	$7.91M	23

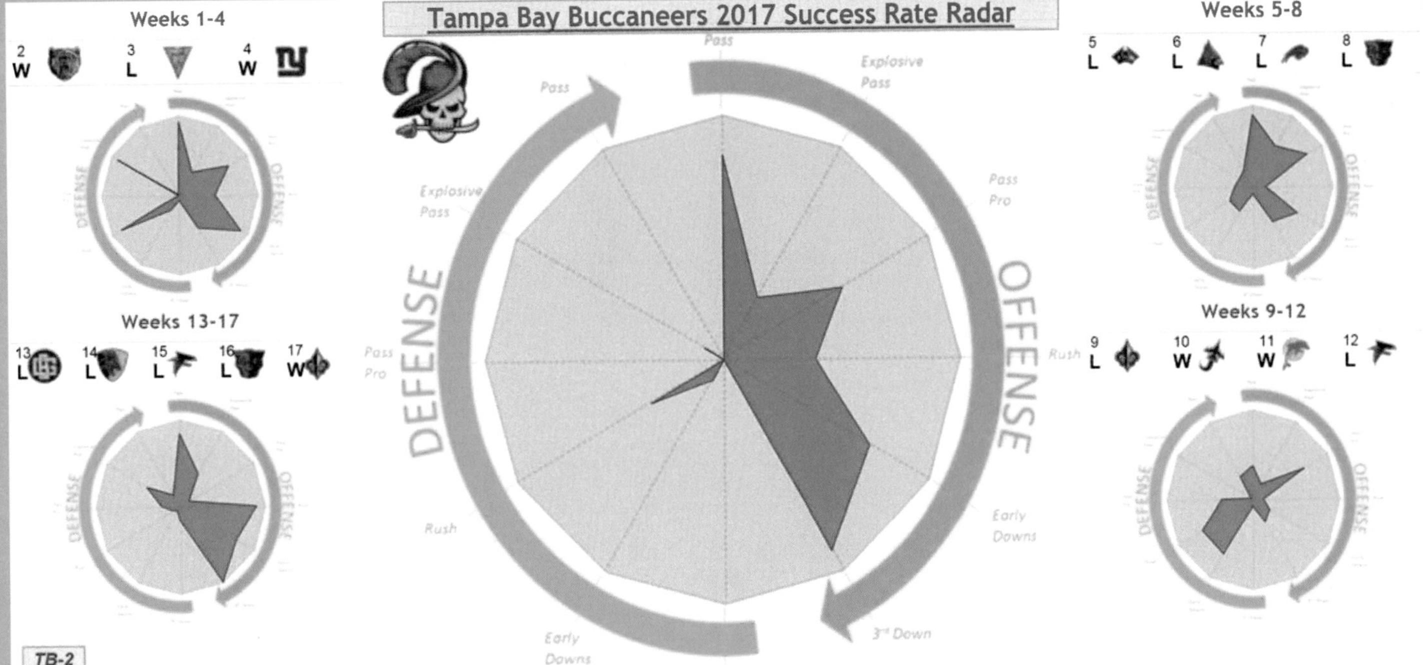

TB-2

The Buccaneers specifically struggled with second-quarter passing efficiency: Q1, No. 3 (52%); Q2, No. 27 (38%); Q3, No. 3 (48%); and Q4, No. 3 (55%). Without the second quarter, the Bucs had the league's top passing offense (52% Success Rate), just ahead of the vaunted Saints, Steelers, Falcons, and Patriots.

This problem persisted even when the Bucs went no huddle. In the second quarter, the team had a 36% no-huddle passing Success Rate. In all other quarters, they had a league-high Success Rate, finishing with marks of at least 60% in each quarter, something no other team achieved.

What was the source of the second-quarter problems? Play calling and predictability. In the first quarter, the Bucs ran on first down 62% of the time (vs. 59% league average) with a 39% Success Rate, which significantly trailed their league-best first-down 71% passing Success Rate. Even so, in the first quarter the Bucs often ran the ball on first down, probably attempting to establish the ground game.

Presumably having realized that their earlier first-down attempts to run the ball had been futile, the Bucs usually shifted to a pass-heavy attack after the first quarter, going from a 62% first-down rush rate to a 57% first-down pass rate in the second quarter (No. 4 in NFL). It seems that they realized after 15 minutes of play that pounding into a brick wall on first down wasn't helping them score points.

The problem, though, was that their pass-heavy second-quarter attack suffered from the byproduct of predictability. On first-quarter first downs, the Bucs used 11 personnel 38% of the time; 12 personnel, 46%; 13 personnel, 10%; and 21 personnel, 5%. They used many of the groupings on scripted plays and showed variety. On first-down pass plays within the first quarter, the Bucs had a 128 passer rating and 11.2 YPA. In the second quarter, though, when the scripted plays had been used, the team lost its creativity as it shifted to the passing game: On second-quarter first downs, the Bucs used 11 personnel on 75% of their passes and 12 personnel on 25%.

(cont'd - see TB-3)

2017 Offensive Advanced Metrics

Metric	Rank
EDSR Off	2
30 & In Off	21
Red Zone Off	13
3rd Down Off	10
YPPA Off	9
YPPT Off	28
Offensive Efficiency	11
Pass Efficiency Off	9
Pass Pro Efficiency Off	16
RB Pass Eff Off	19
Rush Efficiency Off	25
Explosive Pass Off	25
Explosive Run Off	27

2017 Defensive Advanced Metrics

Metric	Rank
EDSR Def	21
30 & In Def	30
Red Zone Def	23
3rd Down Def	32
YPPA Def	30
YPPT Def	15
Defensive Efficiency	32
Pass Efficiency Def	31
Pass Pro Efficiency Def	32
RB Pass Eff Def	21
Rush Efficiency Def	19
Explosive Pass Def	26
Explosive Run Def	26

2017 Weekly EDSR & Season Trending Performance

WEEK	2	3	4	5	6	7	8	9	10	11	12	13	14	15	16	17
RESULT	W	L	W	L	L	L	L	L	W	W	L	L	L	L	L	W
OPP	CHI	MIN	NYG	NE	ARI	BUF	CAR	NO	NYJ	MIA	ATL	GB	DET	ATL	CAR	NO
SITE	H	A	H	H	A	A	H	A	H	A	A	A	H	H	A	H
MARGIN	22	-17	2	-5	-5	-3	-14	-20	5	10	-14	-6	-3	-3	-3	7
PTS	29	17	25	14	33	27	3	10	15	30	20	20	21	21	19	31
OPP PTS	7	34	23	19	38	30	17	30	10	20	34	26	24	24	22	24

EDSR by Wk
W=Green
L=Red

OFF/DEF
EDSR
Blue=OFF
(high=good)
Red=DEF
(low=good)

2017 Close Game Records

All 2016 Wins: **5**
FG Games (<=3 pts) W-L: **1-4**
FG Games Win %: **20% (#28)**
FG Games Wins (% of Total Wins): **20% (#16)**
1 Score Games (<=8 pts) W-L: **3-7**
1 Score Games Win %: **30% (#26)**
1 Score Games Wins (% of Total Wins): **60% (#11)**

2017 Critical & Game-Deciding Stats

TO Margin	-1
TO Given	27
INT Given	14
FUM Given	13
TO Taken	26
INT Taken	13
FUM Taken	13
Sack Margin	-17
Sacks	22
Sacks Allow	39
Return TD Margin	-1
Ret TDs	4
Ret TDs Allow	5
Penalty Margin	+5
Penalties	104
Opponent Penalties	109

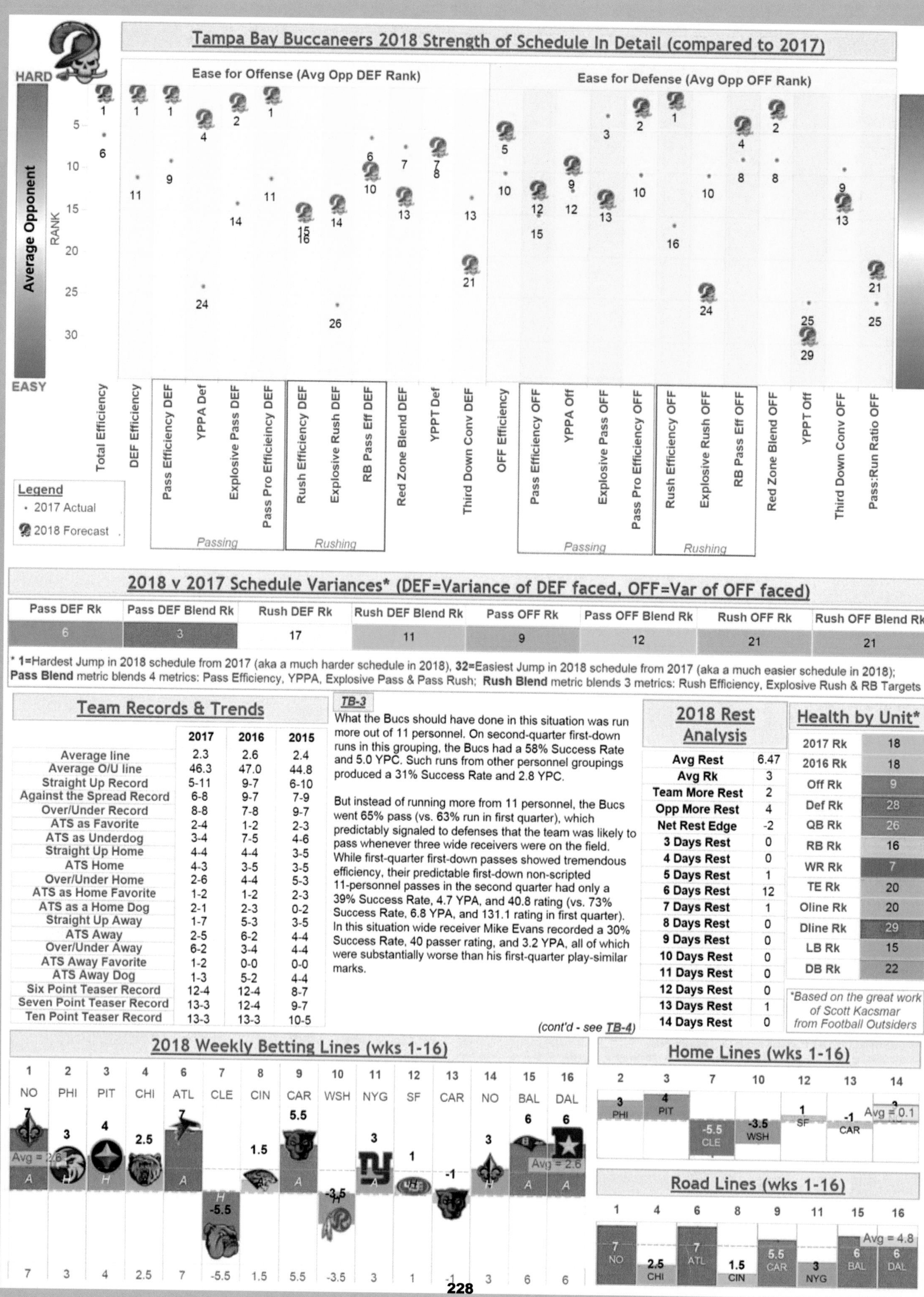

Tampa Bay Buccaneers 2018 Strength of Schedule In Detail (compared to 2017)

2018 v 2017 Schedule Variances* (DEF=Variance of DEF faced, OFF=Var of OFF faced)

Pass DEF Rk	Pass DEF Blend Rk	Rush DEF Rk	Rush DEF Blend Rk	Pass OFF Rk	Pass OFF Blend Rk	Rush OFF Rk	Rush OFF Blend Rk
6	3	17	11	9	12	21	21

* **1**=Hardest Jump in 2018 schedule from 2017 (aka a much harder schedule in 2018), **32**=Easiest Jump in 2018 schedule from 2017 (aka a much easier schedule in 2018); **Pass Blend** metric blends 4 metrics: Pass Efficiency, YPPA, Explosive Pass & Pass Rush; **Rush Blend** metric blends 3 metrics: Rush Efficiency, Explosive Rush & RB Targets

Team Records & Trends

	2017	2016	2015
Average line	2.3	2.6	2.4
Average O/U line	46.3	47.0	44.8
Straight Up Record	5-11	9-7	6-10
Against the Spread Record	6-8	9-7	7-9
Over/Under Record	8-8	7-8	9-7
ATS as Favorite	2-4	1-2	2-3
ATS as Underdog	3-4	7-5	4-6
Straight Up Home	4-4	4-4	3-5
ATS Home	4-3	3-5	3-5
Over/Under Home	2-6	4-4	5-3
ATS as Home Favorite	1-2	1-2	2-3
ATS as a Home Dog	2-1	2-3	0-2
Straight Up Away	1-7	5-3	3-5
ATS Away	2-5	6-2	4-4
Over/Under Away	6-2	3-4	4-4
ATS Away Favorite	1-2	0-0	0-0
ATS Away Dog	1-3	5-2	4-4
Six Point Teaser Record	12-4	12-4	8-7
Seven Point Teaser Record	13-3	12-4	9-7
Ten Point Teaser Record	13-3	13-3	10-5

TB-3

What the Bucs should have done in this situation was run more out of 11 personnel. On second-quarter first-down runs in this grouping, the Bucs had a 58% Success Rate and 5.0 YPC. Such runs from other personnel groupings produced a 31% Success Rate and 2.8 YPC.

But instead of running more from 11 personnel, the Bucs went 65% pass (vs. 63% run in first quarter), which predictably signaled to defenses that the team was likely to pass whenever three wide receivers were on the field. While first-quarter first-down passes showed tremendous efficiency, their predictable first-down non-scripted 11-personnel passes in the second quarter had only a 39% Success Rate, 4.7 YPA, and 40.8 rating (vs. 73% Success Rate, 6.8 YPA, and 131.1 rating in first quarter). In this situation wide receiver Mike Evans recorded a 30% Success Rate, 40 passer rating, and 3.2 YPA, all of which were substantially worse than his first-quarter play-similar marks.

(cont'd - see TB-4)

2018 Rest Analysis

Avg Rest	6.47
Avg Rk	3
Team More Rest	2
Opp More Rest	4
Net Rest Edge	-2
3 Days Rest	0
4 Days Rest	0
5 Days Rest	1
6 Days Rest	12
7 Days Rest	1
8 Days Rest	0
9 Days Rest	0
10 Days Rest	0
11 Days Rest	0
12 Days Rest	0
13 Days Rest	1
14 Days Rest	0

Health by Unit*

2017 Rk	18
2016 Rk	18
Off Rk	9
Def Rk	28
QB Rk	26
RB Rk	16
WR Rk	7
TE Rk	20
Oline Rk	20
Dline Rk	29
LB Rk	15
DB Rk	22

Based on the great work of Scott Kacsmar from Football Outsiders

2018 Weekly Betting Lines (wks 1-16)

1	2	3	4	6	7	8	9	10	11	12	13	14	15	16
NO	PHI	PIT	CHI	ATL	CLE	CIN	CAR	WSH	NYG	SF	CAR	NO	BAL	DAL
A	H	H	A	A	H	A	A	H	A	H	H	H	A	A
7	3	4	2.5	7	-5.5	1.5	5.5	-3.5	3	1	-1	3	6	6

Avg = 2.6

Home Lines (wks 1-16)

2	3	7	10	12	13	14
PHI	PIT	CLE	WSH	SF	CAR	NO
3	4	-5.5	-3.5	1	-1	3

Avg = 0.1

Road Lines (wks 1-16)

1	4	6	8	9	11	15	16
NO	CHI	ATL	CIN	CAR	NYG	BAL	DAL
7	2.5	7	1.5	5.5	3	6	6

Avg = 4.8

2017 Play Tendencies

All Pass %	62%
All Pass Rk	3
All Rush %	38%
All Rush Rk	30
1 Score Pass %	61%
1 Score Pass Rk	3
2016 1 Score Pass %	55%
2016 1 Score Pass Rk	25
2017 Pass Increase %	6%
Pass Increase Rk	3
1 Score Rush %	39%
1 Score Rush Rk	30
Up Pass %	57%
Up Pass Rk	1
Up Rush %	43%
Up Rush Rk	32
Down Pass %	67%
Down Pass Rk	13
Down Rush %	33%
Down Rush Rk	20

2017 Down & Distance Tendencies

Down	Distance	Total Plays	Pass Rate	Run Rate	Play Success %
1	Short (1-3)	6	17%	83%	50%
	Med (4-7)	13	46%	54%	38%
	Long (8-10)	325	46%	54%	50%
	XL (11+)	10	60%	40%	40%
2	Short (1-3)	28	25%	75%	46%
	Med (4-7)	83	64%	36%	47%
	Long (8-10)	106	64%	36%	38%
	XL (11+)	35	91%	9%	26%
3	Short (1-3)	33	58%	42%	58%
	Med (4-7)	58	93%	7%	53%
	Long (8-10)	35	100%	0%	26%
	XL (11+)	22	91%	9%	23%
4	Med (4-7)	2	100%	0%	50%

Shotgun %:

Under Center	Shotgun
54%	46%
37% AVG	*63%*

Run Rate:

Under Center	Shotgun
59%	10%
68% AVG	*23%*

Pass Rate:

Under Center	Shotgun
41%	90%
32% AVG	*77%*

Tampa Bay Buccaneers 2017 Play Analysis

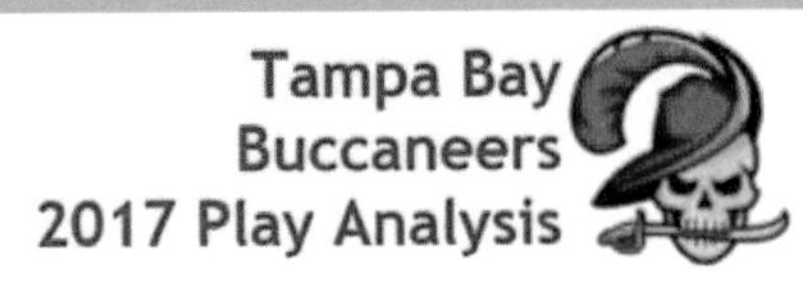

Short Yardage Intelligence:

2nd and Short Run

Run Freq	Run Rk	NFL Run Freq Avg	Run 1D Rate	Run NFL 1D Avg
64%	23	67%	57%	69%

2nd and Short Pass

Pass Freq	Pass Rk	NFL Pass Freq Avg	Pass 1D Rate	Pass NFL 1D Avg
36%	10	33%	31%	53%

Most Frequent Play

Down	Distance	Play Type	Player	Total Plays	Play Success %
1	Short (1-3)	RUSH	Peyton Barber	2	50%
			Jacquizz Rodgers	2	50%
	Med (4-7)	RUSH	Doug Martin	3	0%
	Long (8-10)	RUSH	Doug Martin	67	40%
	XL (11+)	PASS	Adam Humphries	2	50%
2	Short (1-3)	RUSH	Peyton Barber	10	60%
	Med (4-7)	PASS	Mike Evans	12	25%
	Long (8-10)	PASS	DeSean Jackson	17	47%
	XL (11+)	PASS	DeSean Jackson	8	38%
3	Short (1-3)	RUSH	Doug Martin	4	50%
			Peyton Barber	4	100%
	Med (4-7)	PASS	Mike Evans	11	45%
			Cameron Brate	11	64%
	Long (8-10)	PASS	Mike Evans	9	22%
	XL (11+)	PASS	Cameron Brate	6	50%

Most Successful Play*

Down	Distance	Play Type	Player	Total Plays	Play Success %
1	Long (8-10)	PASS	Chris Godwin	11	82%
2	Short (1-3)	RUSH	Doug Martin	6	67%
	Med (4-7)	RUSH	Jacquizz Rodgers	7	71%
	Long (8-10)	PASS	Mike Evans	11	73%
	XL (11+)	PASS	DeSean Jackson	8	38%
3	Med (4-7)	PASS	Adam Humphries	10	80%
	Long (8-10)	PASS	Adam Humphries	6	33%
			Cameron Brate	6	33%
	XL (11+)	PASS	Cameron Brate	6	50%

**Minimum 5 plays to qualify*

2017 Snap Rates

Wk	Opp	Score	Mike Evans	Adam Humphries	DeSean Jackson	O.J. Howard	Cameron Brate	Chris Godwin	Charles Sims	Doug Martin	Peyton Barber	Jacquizz Rodgers
2	CHI	W 29-7	55 (77%)	41 (58%)	36 (51%)	46 (65%)	38 (54%)	29 (41%)	21 (30%)		16 (23%)	34 (48%)
3	MIN	L 34-17	47 (89%)	39 (74%)	43 (81%)	34 (64%)	26 (49%)	11 (21%)	26 (49%)			25 (47%)
4	NYG	W 25-23	59 (92%)	43 (67%)	45 (70%)	42 (66%)	35 (55%)	9 (14%)	22 (34%)		4 (6%)	38 (59%)
5	NE	L 19-14	68 (94%)	52 (72%)	52 (72%)	41 (57%)	49 (68%)	17 (24%)	31 (43%)	26 (36%)		13 (18%)
6	ARI	L 38-33	64 (91%)	48 (69%)	53 (76%)	45 (64%)	44 (63%)	14 (20%)	27 (39%)	37 (53%)		6 (9%)
7	BUF	L 30-27	63 (88%)	52 (72%)	52 (72%)	51 (71%)	38 (53%)	22 (31%)	24 (33%)	43 (60%)	1 (1%)	2 (3%)
8	CAR	L 17-3	62 (93%)	39 (58%)	50 (75%)	39 (58%)	40 (60%)	13 (19%)	19 (28%)	39 (58%)	3 (4%)	6 (9%)
9	NO	L 30-10	51 (86%)	34 (58%)	39 (66%)	37 (63%)	34 (58%)	18 (31%)	18 (31%)	18 (31%)	23 (39%)	
10	NYJ	W 15-10		46 (65%)	54 (76%)	50 (70%)	33 (46%)	69 (97%)	22 (31%)	36 (51%)	7 (10%)	6 (8%)
11	MIA	W 30-20	55 (83%)	33 (50%)	40 (61%)	46 (70%)	41 (62%)	22 (33%)	23 (35%)	37 (56%)	3 (5%)	2 (3%)
12	ATL	L 34-20	61 (86%)	43 (61%)	44 (62%)	53 (75%)	34 (48%)	19 (27%)	26 (37%)	13 (18%)	10 (14%)	25 (35%)
13	GB	L 26-20	66 (87%)	42 (55%)	47 (62%)	55 (72%)	32 (42%)	17 (22%)	19 (25%)		52 (68%)	5 (7%)
14	DET	L 24-21	58 (82%)	38 (54%)	30 (42%)	56 (79%)	25 (35%)	40 (56%)	20 (28%)	19 (27%)	31 (44%)	
15	ATL	L 24-21	51 (84%)	40 (66%)	23 (38%)	13 (21%)	29 (48%)	35 (57%)	28 (46%)		32 (52%)	2 (3%)
16	CAR	L 22-19	52 (78%)	36 (54%)			45 (67%)	53 (79%)	24 (36%)	17 (25%)	25 (37%)	2 (3%)
17	NO	W 31-24	70 (84%)	58 (70%)			43 (52%)	58 (70%)	32 (39%)	4 (5%)	45 (54%)	2 (2%)
	Grand Total		882 (86%)	684 (63%)	608 (65%)	608 (64%)	586 (54%)	446 (40%)	382 (35%)	289 (38%)	252 (28%)	168 (18%)

Personnel Groupings

Personnel	Team %	NFL Avg	Succ. %
1-1 [3WR]	62%	59%	49%
1-2 [2WR]	24%	19%	44%
1-3 [1WR]	9%	5%	43%

Grouping Tendencies

Personnel	Pass Rate	Pass Succ. %	Run Succ. %
1-1 [3WR]	75%	47%	56%
1-2 [2WR]	45%	55%	34%
1-3 [1WR]	26%	52%	40%

Red Zone Targets (min 3)

Receiver	All	Inside 5	6-10	11-20
Mike Evans	19	4	5	10
Cameron Brate	13	1	3	9
Chris Godwin	8	3	2	3
Charles Sims	6		1	5
DeSean Jackson	6	2		4
O.J. Howard	6	2	2	2
Adam Humphries	5			5
Doug Martin	3		1	2

Red Zone Rushes (min 3)

Rusher	All	Inside 5	6-10	11-20
Peyton Barber	21	9	4	8
Doug Martin	20	5	2	13
Jacquizz Rodgers	12	3	3	6
Jameis Winston	12	3	4	5
Ryan Fitzpatrick	3		2	1

Early Down Target Rate

RB	TE	WR
16%	19%	64%
23%	*21% NFL AVG*	*56%*

Overall Target Success %

RB	TE	WR
43% #17	57% #3	53% #5

Tampa Bay Buccaneers 2017 Passing Recap & 2018 Outlook

In 2016, Winston struggled to his deep right, recording a 72 rating with only 8.4 YPA, but to the deep left (minus a few 3rd/4th-and-long desperation tosses) Winston posted a 102 rating with 11.5 YPA. With the 2017 addition of wide receiver DeSean Jackson, Winston's deep-right efficiency improved. When specifically targeting Jackson on the deep right, Winston completed 7-of-15 passes for 11.1 YPA and a 109 passer rating (similar to his 2016 deep-left passing). On all passes to the deep right, Winston delivered 9.3 YPA and a 105 passer rating, ranking ninth in the league. However, his productivity to the deep left faltered, save for passes to tight end O.J. Howard, on which Winston went 3-of-3 for 36 YPA, two touchdowns, and a perfect 158.3 passer rating. To all other players, Winston had an 8.3 YPA, 32% Success Rate, and 60.7 passer rating.

Jameis Winston Rating All Downs

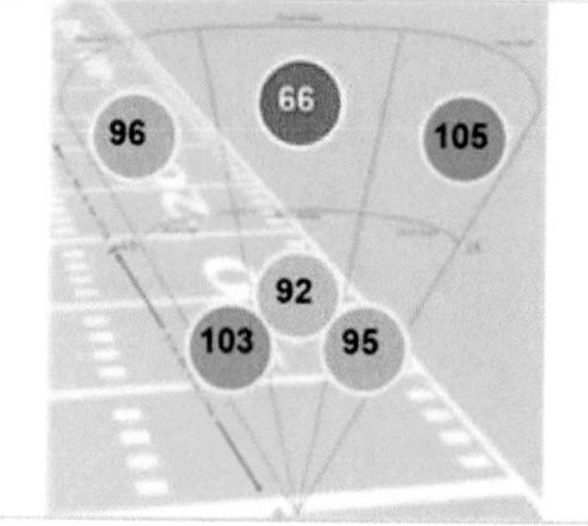

Jameis Winston Rating Early Downs

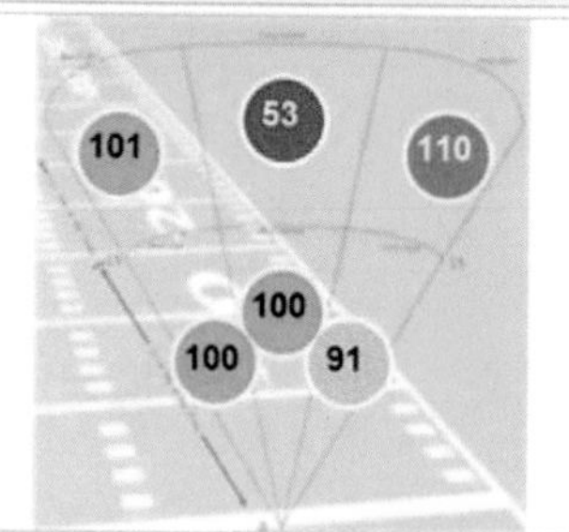

2017 Standard Passing Table

QB	Comp	Att	Comp %	Yds	YPA	TDs	INT	Sacks	Rating	Rk
Jameis Winston	281	441	64%	3,508	8.0	18	11	33	92	20
Ryan Fitzpatrick	96	163	59%	1,103	6.8	7	3	6	86	25
NFL Avg			62%		7.0				87.5	

2017 Advanced Passing Table

QB	Success %	EDSR Passing Success %	20+ Yd Pass Gains	20+ Yd Pass %	30+ Yd Pass Gains	30+ Yd Pass %	Avg. Air Yds per Comp	Avg. YAC per Comp	20+ Air Yd Comp	20+ Air Yd %
Jameis Winston	49%	52%	32	7.2%	16	3.6%	7.7	4.6	17	6%
Ryan Fitzpatrick	46%	49%	15	9.2%	2	1.2%	7.1	4.1	7	7%
NFL Avg	44%	48%	27.7	8.8%	10.3	3.3%	6.0	4.7	11.7	6%

Interception Rates by Down

Yards to Go	1	2	3	4	Total
1 & 2	0.0%	0.0%	0.0%	0.0%	0.0%
3, 4, 5	0.0%	8.7%	0.0%		3.5%
6 - 9	0.0%	3.1%	2.5%		2.8%
10 - 14	1.8%	1.7%	7.4%	0.0%	2.3%
15+	0.0%	0.0%	0.0%		0.0%
Total	1.6%	3.0%	2.6%	0.0%	2.3%

3rd Down Passing - Short of Sticks Analysis

QB	Avg. Yds to Go	Avg. YIA (of Comp)	Avg Yds Short	Short of Sticks Rate	Short Rk
Jameis Winston	7.4	8.5	0.0	47%	5
NFL Avg	7.8	6.7	-1.1	60%	

Air Yds vs YAC

Air Yds %	YAC %	Rk
64%	36%	8
58%	42%	

2017 Receiving Recap & 2018 Outlook

At 21 years old, wide receiver Chris Godwin posted an early-down 10.7 YPA (No. 5 in NFL) and was one of eight wide receivers with at least a 9.5 YPA and 50% Success Rate as well as the team's most efficient receiver, finishing No. 1 in YPA, Success Rate, and passer rating delivered. He more than proved himself. The Bucs are flush with receiving talent. They were more productive last year in 12 personnel than 11, but part of that is due to their second-quarter issues. The Bucs should continue to work Godwin into the rotation.

Player *Min 50 Targets*	Targets	Comp %	YPA	Rating	TOARS	Success %	Success Rk	Missed YPA Rk	YAS % Rk	TDs
Mike Evans	136	52%	7.4	76	4.9	51%	52	58	33	5
DeSean Jackson	90	56%	7.4	72	4.2	49%	64	41	41	3
Adam Humphries	83	73%	7.6	99	4.5	56%	21	15	108	1
Cameron Brate	77	62%	7.7	101	4.4	55%	25	73	117	6
Chris Godwin	55	62%	9.5	92	3.9	58%	11	65	5	1

Directional Passer Rating Delivered

Receiver	Short Left	Short Middle	Short Right	Deep Left	Deep Middle	Deep Right	Player Total
Mike Evans	71	84	95	25	56	109	76
DeSean Jackson	94	149	73	0	20	109	72
Adam Humphries	91	111	90	104	119	83	99
Cameron Brate	105	93	87		102	117	101
Chris Godwin	112	87	118	58	18	101	92
Charles Sims	96	88	105	40		40	94
O.J. Howard	155	79	133	158	5	119	133
Peyton Barber	56	89	86				70
Doug Martin	68	97	42				63
Jacquizz Rodgers	76	103	113				95
Team Total	93	97	94	56	55	114	90

2017 Rushing Recap & 2017 Outlook

Of the 40 backs with 200-plus carries over the last two years, Martin ranked dead last in Success Rate (38%), YPC (2.8), percentage of runs with no more than three yards (65%), and percentage of runs with five-plus yards (25%). It made perfect sense for the Bucs to move on and draft a second-round running back this year. While Barber has little name recognition, he was the top Bucs back last year and should play a major role in the backfield. The team would be wise to focus touches on Jones and Barber and stop rotating backs as often as it did in 2017.

Player *Min 50 Rushes*	Rushes	YPC	Success %	Success Rk	Missed YPA Rk	YTS % Rk	YAS % Rk	Early Down Success %	Early Down Success Rk	TDs
Doug Martin	138	2.9	35%	70	57	23	60	34%	71	3
Peyton Barber	108	3.9	56%	4	3	6	51	54%	7	3
Jacquizz Rodgers	64	3.8	41%	57	18	58	54	40%	59	1

Yards per Carry by Direction

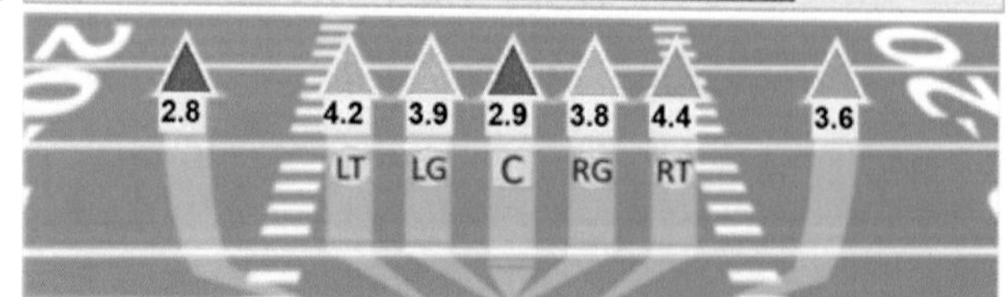

Directional Run Frequency

TB-4

As a result, even though the Bucs passed significantly more on first downs in the second quarter — and even though passes gain more yards than rushes on average — the Bucs gained nearly 1.5 more first-down yards per play in the first quarter. That's almost unbelievable.

Their second-quarter predictability problems extended to and were compounded by second-down play calling. After first-down pass attempts that resulted in no yards, the Bucs called running plays 50% of the time on 2nd and 10, making them the league's fifth-most run-heavy team in this situation, but their run Success Rate was only 27%, which set them up for disadvantageous 3rd-and-long downs.

The horrendous mistake of rushing after failed first-down passes was debilitating for the Bucs. After first-half first-down pass attempts of no gain, the Bucs ran the ball 61% of the time. Only the Bills predictably ran it more often. In this situation the Bucs averaged just a 29% running Success Rate and 4.1 YPC. The average NFL Success Rate is 29% in this scenario for a run vs. 45% for a pass. It will be a long year for the Bucs if they don't shift to a pass-heavy strategy in 2nd-and-long situations.

(cont'd - see TB-5)

Matthew Freedman's Fantasy Corner

One of just three players in NFL history to open his career with four straight 1,000-yard receiving campaigns (the other two are Randy Moss and A.J. Green), Evans is coming off a down year in which he ranked 20th with 13.5 PPR points per game. In 2016, however, Evans was third with 19.0 PPR points per game, and he has No. 1 positional upside. In 2018 he should progress from last year's 3.7% touchdown rate to his 5.5% career average, and since entering the league in 2014 he's been No. 5 overall with 579 targets. The likely Winston suspension isn't ideal, but in 17 career games Evans has actually done better without Winston (16.1 PPR points per game) than with him (15.6). Available as the No. 7 wide receiver by average draft position, Evans is a risk-seeking fantasy option with league-winning potential.

Division History: Season Wins & 2018 Projection

2014 Wins | 2015 Wins | 2016 Wins | 2017 Wins | Forecast 2018 Wins

Rank of 2018 Defensive Pass Efficiency Faced by Week

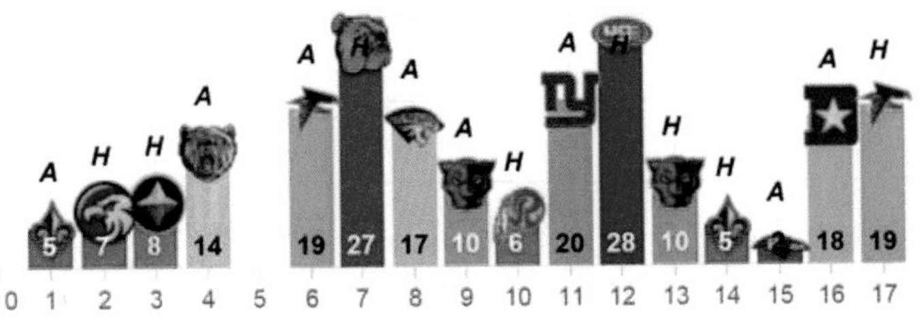

Rank of 2018 Defensive Rush Efficiency Faced by Week

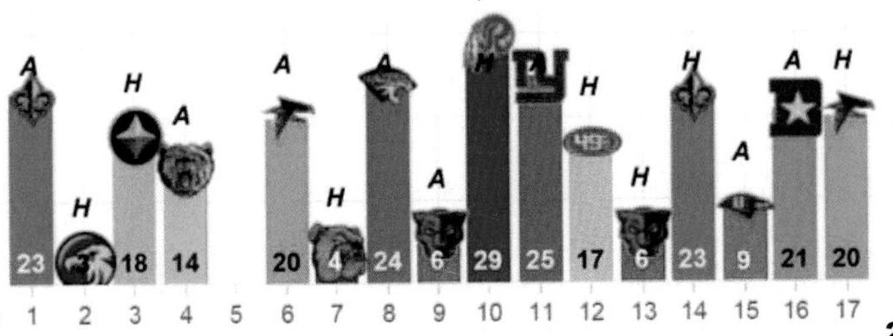

2017 Situational Usage by Player & Position

Usage Rate by Score

		Being Blown Out (14+)	Down Big (9-13)	One Score	Large Lead (9-13)	Blowout Lead (14+)	Grand Total
RUSH	Doug Martin	8%	18%	17%	12%		15%
	Peyton Barber	9%	8%	12%	4%	26%	12%
	DeSean Jackson	1%	1%	0%			0%
	Adam Humphries			0%			0%
	Jacquizz Rodgers	6%	4%	5%	32%	23%	7%
	Charles Sims	1%	1%	3%	4%		2%
	Bernard Reedy	1%		0%			0%
	Bobo Wilson			0%			0%
	Total	27%	32%	38%	52%	49%	36%
PASS	Doug Martin	1%	3%	2%			2%
	Mike Evans	16%	18%	13%	20%	13%	15%
	Peyton Barber	3%	4%	2%			2%
	DeSean Jackson	11%	11%	9%	8%	8%	10%
	Adam Humphries	12%	9%	8%		8%	9%
	Cameron Brate	9%	12%	8%	4%	8%	8%
	Jacquizz Rodgers	1%	1%	1%			1%
	Charles Sims	6%	5%	4%	8%	8%	5%
	Chris Godwin	5%	3%	7%		3%	6%
	O.J. Howard	6%	3%	4%	8%	5%	4%
	Alan Cross	1%	1%	1%			1%
	Freddie Martino			1%			1%
	Bernard Reedy	1%					0%
	Bobo Wilson			0%			0%
	Luke Stocker	2%					0%
	Antony Auclair			0%			0%
	Total	73%	68%	62%	48%	51%	64%

Positional Target Distribution vs NFL Average

		NFL Wide				Team Only			
		Left	Middle	Right	Total	Left	Middle	Right	Total
Deep	WR	950	483	946	2,379	36	26	41	103
	TE	189	138	179	506	3	12	9	24
	RB	37	9	41	87	2		1	3
	All	1,176	630	1,166	2,972	41	38	51	130
Short	WR	2,757	1,614	2,691	7,062	105	57	99	261
	TE	833	813	1,134	2,780	30	26	36	92
	RB	1,282	802	1,263	3,347	39	21	32	92
	All	4,872	3,229	5,088	13,189	174	104	167	445
Total		6,048	3,859	6,254	16,161	215	142	218	575

Positional Success Rates vs NFL Average

		NFL Wide				Team Only			
		Left	Middle	Right	Total	Left	Middle	Right	Total
Deep	WR	37%	45%	38%	39%	25%	42%	37%	34%
	TE	37%	54%	44%	44%	100%	42%	67%	58%
	RB	38%	56%	39%	40%	0%		0%	0%
	All	37%	47%	39%	40%	29%	42%	41%	38%
Short	WR	51%	57%	50%	52%	56%	65%	61%	60%
	TE	50%	57%	49%	52%	67%	46%	47%	53%
	RB	44%	50%	43%	45%	38%	71%	34%	45%
	All	49%	55%	48%	50%	54%	62%	53%	55%
Total		47%	54%	46%	48%	49%	56%	50%	51%

Successful Play Rate
0% [color scale] 100%

Tampa Bay Buccaneers - Success by Personnel Grouping & Play Type

Play Type	1-1 [3WR]	1-2 [2WR]	2-1 [2WR]	1-0 [4WR]	1-3 [1WR]	0-1 [4WR]	2-0 [3WR]	2-2 [1WR]	0-0 [5WR]	0-2 [3WR]	3-1 [1WR]	2-3 [0WR]	1-4 [0WR]	Grand Total
PASS	47% (477, 74%)	55% (110, 17%)	71% (7, 1%)	27% (11, 2%)	52% (23, 4%)	63% (8, 1%)	0% (1, 0%)	100% (1, 0%)	100% (1, 0%)	0% (3, 0%)			100% (2, 0%)	48% (644, 100%)
RUSH	56% (162, 42%)	34% (133, 34%)	25% (12, 3%)		40% (65, 17%)	100% (1, 0%)		0% (4, 1%)			0% (2, 1%)	0% (2, 1%)	67% (9, 2%)	44% (390, 100%)
TOTAL	49% (639, 62%)	44% (243, 24%)	42% (19, 2%)	27% (11, 1%)	43% (88, 9%)	67% (9, 1%)	0% (1, 0%)	20% (5, 0%)	100% (1, 0%)	0% (3, 0%)	0% (2, 0%)	0% (2, 0%)	73% (11, 1%)	#######

Format Line 1: Success Rate Line 2: Total # of Plays, % of All Plays (by type)

TB-5 Because of their second-quarter play-calling predictability and lack of intelligence, the Bucs were outscored in the second quarter 121-31 outside of their two games against backup (or backup-caliber) quarterbacks. In the remaining 14 representative games, they scored just two second-quarter touchdowns.

The reality is that, even if they had performed better in the second quarter, won more three-point games, or won more games in which they were up in the turnover battle, they still wouldn't have done well because they had some major issues, starting with the passing game: They need to improve at protecting Winston and sacking the opposing quarterback. Winning the sack battle has historically resulted in a 71% win rate (as well as a corresponding 29% loss rate for the opposing team). In 10 games the Buccaneers lost the sack battle last year, winning just two (20%) of them. This offseason the Bucs added center Ryan Jensen to solidify the line and shifted Ali Marpet from center to left guard. They also beefed up their defensive line by acquiring defensive end Vinny Curry from the Eagles and drafting defensive tackle Vita Vea at No. 12 overall. These additions might assist with the pass rush on both sides of the ball.

To improve one of the NFL's worst rushing offenses for years, the Bucs drafted USC running back Ronald Jones at No. 38 overall after releasing the run-down Doug Martin. Jones should start ahead of Peyton Barber, who was by far the Bucs most successful rusher last year, ranking fourth in Success Rate and third in missed YPA out of the 76 backs with 50-plus carries.

Most importantly, to improve the team needs to alter its decision-making process, perhaps by consulting analytics experts, because they made some fundamental mistakes last year. The Bucs are better than last year's 5-11 record, but their 2018 schedule is outrageously difficult: They have the second-toughest overall schedule and the most difficult schedule of opposing offenses. This team should perform better in 2018, win more games, and do well against the spread if the defense improves, but a winning record and playoff appearance seem optimistic.

Receiving Success by Personnel Grouping

Position	Player	1-1 [3WR]	1-2 [2WR]	2-1 [2WR]	1-0 [4WR]	1-3 [1WR]	0-1 [4WR]	2-2 [1WR]	0-0 [5WR]	0-2 [3WR]	1-4 [0WR]	Total
TE	Cameron Brate	54% 7.7 101.0 (61)	60% 9.5 133.3 (10)			33% 4.7 49.3 (6)						53% 7.7 101.2 (77)
	O.J. Howard	50% 9.4 87.1 (20)	55% 10.4 145.5 (11)	100% 7.0 135.4 (1)		75% 26.0 156.3 (4)	100% 17.0 118.8 (1)			0% 0.0 39.6 (1)	100% 2.0 118.8 (1)	56% 11.1 132.7 (39)
WR	Mike Evans	47% 6.9 78.3 (91)	45% 5.9 49.6 (29)	67% 9.3 96.5 (3)	50% 2.0 56.3 (2)	83% 19.5 158.3 (6)	67% 9.3 56.9 (3)	100% 19.0 118.8 (1)	100% 12.0 116.7 (1)			50% 7.4 76.3 (136)
	DeSean Jackson	46% 7.2 62.1 (61)	60% 8.9 102.4 (25)		50% 4.0 60.4 (2)	0% 0.0 39.6 (1)				0% 0.0 39.6 (1)		49% 7.4 71.9 (90)
	Adam Humphries	58% 7.8 102.1 (78)	0% 0.0 39.6 (2)		50% 5.0 64.6 (2)		100% 9.0 104.2 (1)					57% 7.6 99.0 (83)
	Chris Godwin	55% 9.2 87.6 (44)	75% 11.4 112.0 (8)	100% 18.0 118.8 (1)	0% 0.0 39.6 (1)	100% 13.0 118.8 (1)						58% 9.5 91.9 (55)

Format Line 1: Success Rate Line 2: YPA Line 3: Passer Rating Line 4: Total # of Plays

Successful Play Rate
0% [color scale] 100%

Rushing Success by Personnel Grouping

Position	Player	1-1 [3WR]	1-2 [2WR]	2-1 [2WR]	1-3 [1WR]	2-2 [1WR]	1-4 [0WR]	Total
RB	Doug Martin	50% 4.8 (46)	27% 2.4 (70)		24% 0.6 (21)		100% 1.0 (1)	35% 2.9 (138)
	Peyton Barber	66% 4.0 (41)	50% 3.5 (30)	0% 3.0 (1)	50% 4.7 (30)	0% 2.0 (1)	80% 1.0 (5)	56% 3.9 (108)
	Jacquizz Rodgers	54% 5.4 (28)	22% 2.4 (18)	33% 2.4 (9)	80% 4.4 (5)	0% 2.0 (3)	0% -1.0 (1)	41% 3.8 (64)

Format Line 1: Success Rate Line 2: YPC Line 3: Total # of Plays

2018 Coaches

Head Coach:
Mike Vrabel (HOU DC) (1st yr)

Offensive Coordinator:
Matt LaFleur (LAR OC) (1st yr)

Defensive Coordinator:
Dean Pees (BAL DC) (1st yr)

Tennessee Titans

2018 Forecast

Wins	Div Rank
8	#3

Past Records

2017: 9-7
2016: 9-7
2015: 3-13

EASY HARD

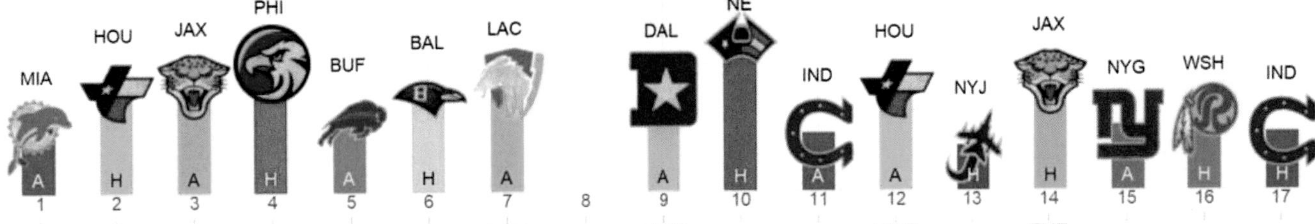

LON MNF MNF TNF

Key Players Lost

TXN	Player (POS)
Cut	Cassel, Matt QB
	Klug, Karl DT
	Maxey, Johnny DE
	Muhammad, Khalfani RB
	Murray, DeMarco RB
	Ochi, Victor LB
	Searcy, Da'Norris S
	Tanney, Alex QB
	Williams, Sylvester NT
Declared Free Agent	Decker, Eric WR
	Douglas, Harry WR
	Jones, DaQuan DE
	McCain, Brice CB
	Riley, Curtis CB
	Schwenke, Brian C
	Walden, Erik LB
	Weeden, Brandon QB
	Williamson, Avery LB
Retired	Griffin, Michael S

Average Line	# Games Favored	# Games Underdog
-0.2	7	6

2018 Tennessee Titans Overview

The exotic smashmouth is dead. RIP. Did it work? It landed the Titans back-to-back winning records for the first time in nine years and took them to the playoffs, but teams are more than their records and postseason appearances. There's a grey area in the NFL, and most of the game's meaningful elements are found in that murky expanse.

When you hear "exotic smashmouth," you think of a hard-nosed team that can grind out the hard yards and move the chains, but the Titans weren't that. If we ignore fourth-quarter game-theory play calling, the Titans were a below-average short-yardage team. On 3rd/4th and 1-2 yards to go, the Titans last year had a 55% rushing Success Rate and gained 1.7 YPC. The NFL averages were 70% and 3.6 YPC.

Outside of short-yardage situations, the Titans' more "exotic" groupings were different but not better. They were worse than the league averages across the board. On running back carries, the Titans used 12% more 13-personnel rushing (20%) than the league average (8%) but had a 38% Success Rate vs. the 44% league average. They used 5% more 12 personnel than the league average, but their 38% Success Rate was 5% worse than average (43%). They used 3% more 21 personnel than the league, but their 39% Success Rate was 4% worse than average. The only formation in which they were above average in usage and success was 22 personnel. They used it 3% more than the league, but their 52% Success Rate was similar to the 51% average.

The running game ironically was best with not a smashmouth style but 11 personnel. Over the last two years, the Titans produced a 52% Success Rate and gained 5.1 YPC (again, not counting sample-skewing fourth-quarter runs). They used 11 personnel on only 24% of their rushes (league average is 47%), but 25% of those were by quarterback Marcus Mariota on either designed read options or scrambles, and he had an incredible 86% Success Rate and 8.8 YPC. Running backs, though, had only a 42% Success Rate and 4.0 YPC on 11-personnel attempts, well below the 45% and 4.4 YPC league averages.

(cont'd - see *TEN2*)

Key Free Agents/ Trades Added

Butler, Malcolm CB
Campanaro, Michael WR
Compton, Will LB
Gabbert, Blaine QB
Lewis, Dion RB
Lewis, Kendrick S
Logan, Bennie DT
Pamphile, Kevin G
President, Gimel LB
Su'a-Filo, Xavier G

Drafted Players

Rd	Pk	Player (College)
1	22	LB - Rashaan Evans (Alabama)
2	41	LB - Harold Landry (Boston College)
5	152	CB - Dane Cruikshank (Arizona)
6	199	QB - Luke Falk (Washington State)

Regular Season Wins: Past & Current Proj

Forecast 2018 Wins  8

2017 Wins  9

Forecast 2017 Wins  5.5

2016 Wins  9

2015 Wins 3

2014 Wins  2

1 3 5 7 9 11 13 15

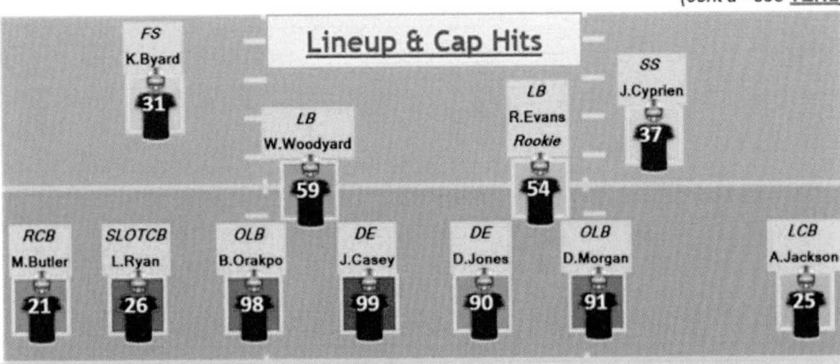

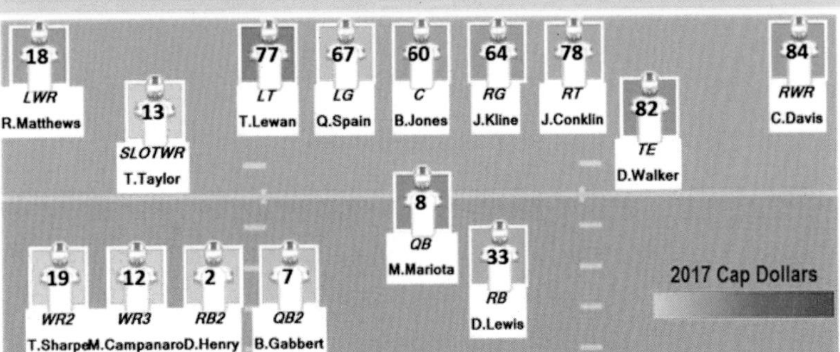

2018 Unit Spending

Positional Spending

	Rank	Total	2017 Rk
All OFF	24	$82.26M	32
QB	27	$10.22M	23
OL	16	$35.31M	30
RB	19	$7.38M	10
WR	25	$17.18M	23
TE	7	$12.17M	16
All DEF	2	$99.67M	10
DL	14	$29.07M	19
LB	3	$35.33M	5
CB	10	$23.17M	21
S	16	$12.10M	8

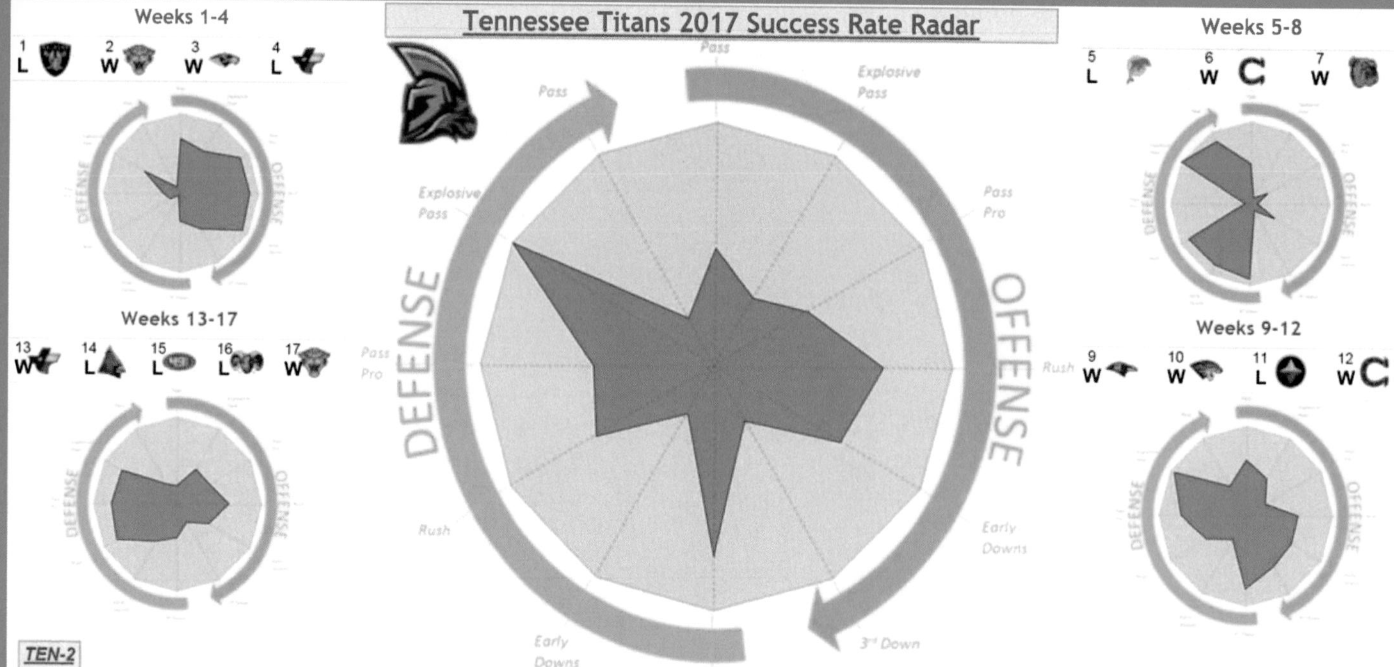

TEN-2

While the Titans ranked eighth in rushing efficiency and 12th in Success Rate in the regular season, their numbers were inflated by quarterback rushes. On their running back carries the Titans ranked 19th in Success Rate (43%), below the 45% league average.

From 2016 to 2017, the Titans rushing attack dropped off significantly. Two years ago, when it was the sixth-most efficient rushing attack and DeMarco Murray and Derrick Henry each had at least a 51% Success Rate, the Titans had the NFL's easiest run-defense schedule. They didn't face a single top-10 run defense, and they played against bottom-10 units six times.

Last year, the Titans played the ninth-toughest run-defense schedule with five games against top-10 run defenses and just three against the bottom 10. Only five games were against below-average run units. The enhanced difficulty in schedule had a tangible effect on the coaching staff as well Murray, who is no longer with the team. The Titans' 2017 run game was worse than perceived. The exotic smashmouth was a failure. For 2018 at least the Titans have a new offensive scheme and the league's largest improvement in year-over-year projected run-defense schedule.

But the run game wasn't the Titans' only problem last year. After ranking as the ninth-most efficient pass offense in 2016, the Titans added three wide receivers in Corey Davis (No. 5 overall pick), Taywan Taylor (third-rounder), and Eric Decker (free agent) to go along with wide receiver Rishard Matthews and tight end Delanie Walker, their top 2016 targets.

(cont'd - see TEN-3)

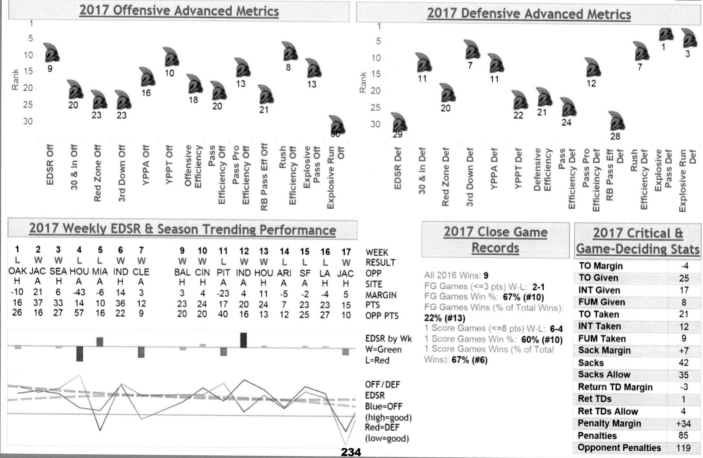

2017 Offensive Advanced Metrics

Metric	Rank
EDSR Off	9
30 & In Off	20
Red Zone Off	23
3rd Down Off	23
YPPA Off	16
YPPT Off	10
Offensive Efficiency	18
Pass Efficiency Off	20
Pass Pro Efficiency Off	13
RB Pass Eff Off	21
Rush Efficiency Off	8
Explosive Pass Off	13
Explosive Run Off	30

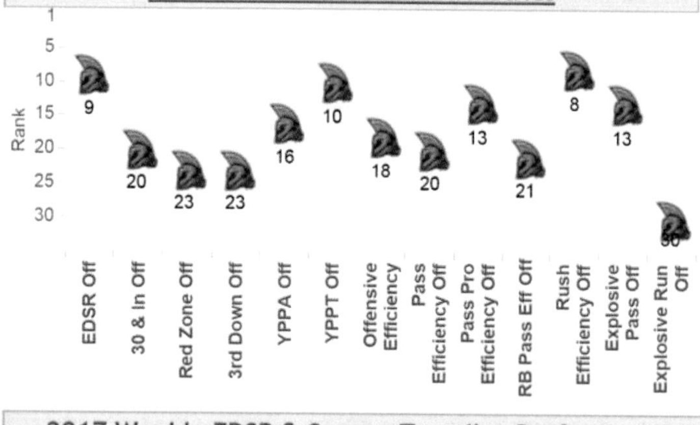

2017 Defensive Advanced Metrics

Metric	Rank
EDSR Def	29
30 & In Def	11
Red Zone Def	20
3rd Down Def	7
YPPA Def	11
YPPT Def	22
Defensive Efficiency	21
Pass Efficiency Def	24
Pass Pro Efficieincy Def	12
RB Pass Eff Def	28
Rush Efficiency Def	7
Explosive Pass Def	1
Explosive Run Def	3

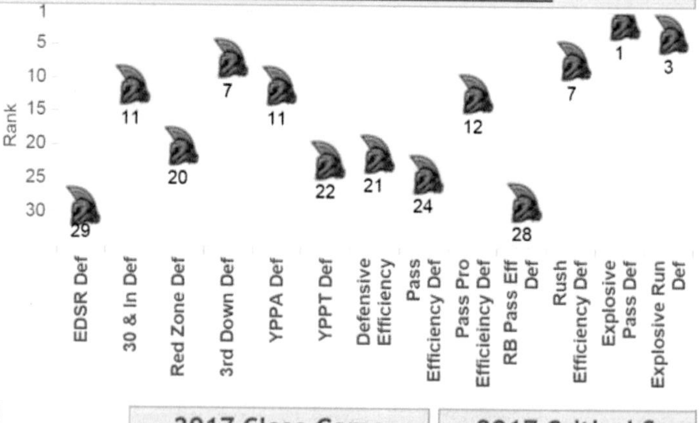

2017 Weekly EDSR & Season Trending Performance

WEEK	1	2	3	4	5	6	7	9	10	11	12	13	14	15	16	17
RESULT	L	W	W	L	L	W	W	W	W	L	W	W	L	L	L	W
OPP	OAK	JAC	SEA	HOU	MIA	IND	CLE	BAL	CIN	PIT	IND	HOU	ARI	SF	LA	JAC
SITE	H	A	H	A	A	H	A	H	H	A	A	H	A	A	H	H
MARGIN	-10	21	6	-43	-6	14	3	3	4	-23	4	11	-5	-2	-4	5
PTS	16	37	33	14	10	36	12	23	24	17	20	24	7	23	23	15
OPP PTS	26	16	27	57	16	22	9	20	20	40	16	13	12	25	27	10

EDSR by Wk
W=Green
L=Red

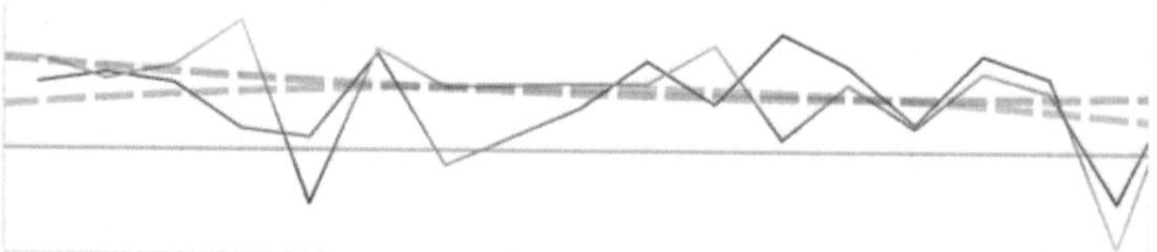

OFF/DEF EDSR
Blue=OFF (high=good)
Red=DEF (low=good)

2017 Close Game Records

All 2016 Wins: **9**
FG Games (<=3 pts) W-L: **2-1**
FG Games Win %: **67% (#10)**
FG Games Wins (% of Total Wins): **22% (#13)**
1 Score Games (<=8 pts) W-L: **6-4**
1 Score Games Win %: **60% (#10)**
1 Score Games Wins (% of Total Wins): **67% (#6)**

2017 Critical & Game-Deciding Stats

TO Margin	-4
TO Given	25
INT Given	17
FUM Given	8
TO Taken	21
INT Taken	12
FUM Taken	9
Sack Margin	+7
Sacks	42
Sacks Allow	35
Return TD Margin	-3
Ret TDs	1
Ret TDs Allow	4
Penalty Margin	+34
Penalties	85
Opponent Penalties	119

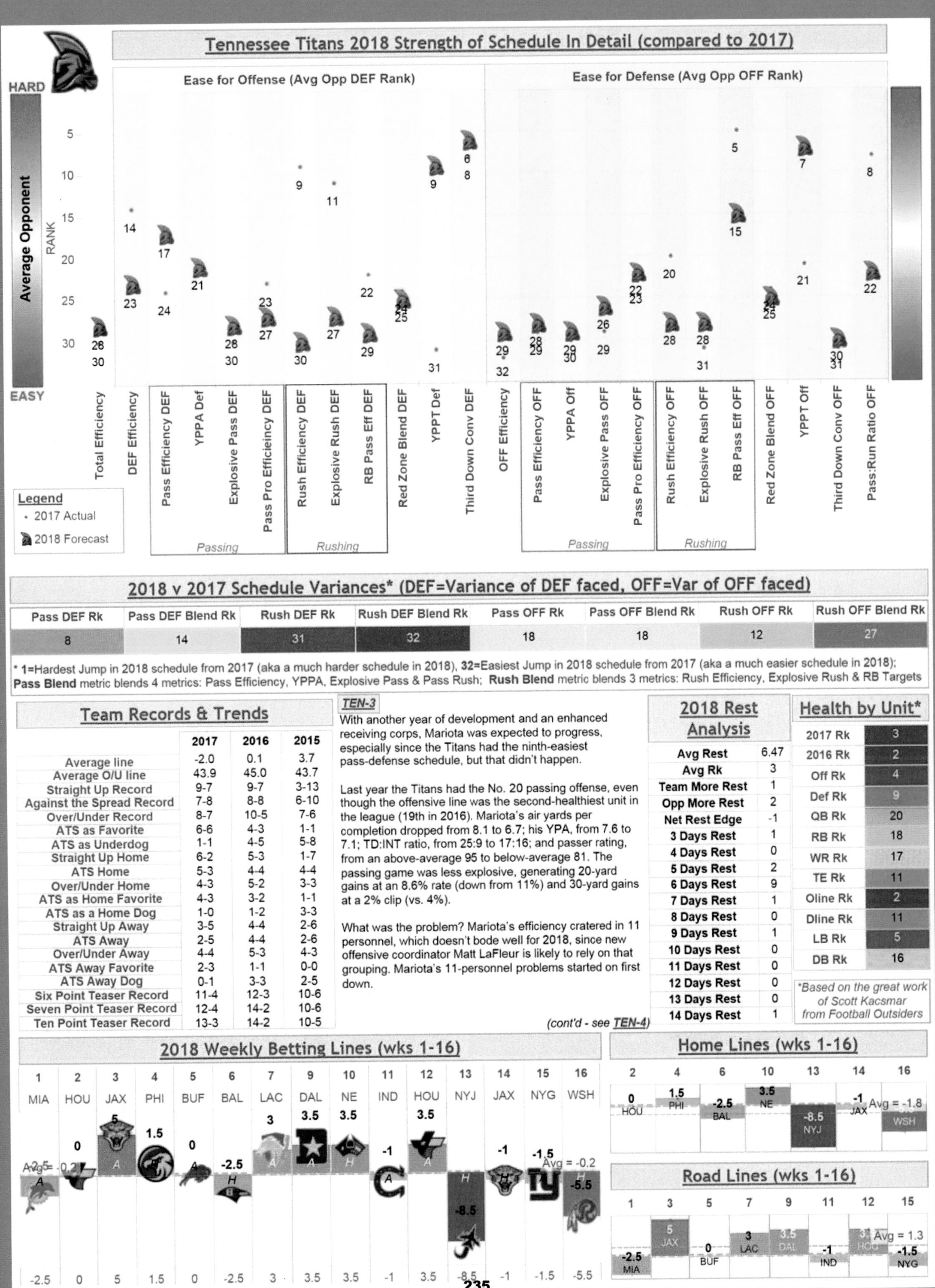

Tennessee Titans 2018 Strength of Schedule In Detail (compared to 2017)

2018 v 2017 Schedule Variances* (DEF=Variance of DEF faced, OFF=Var of OFF faced)

Pass DEF Rk	Pass DEF Blend Rk	Rush DEF Rk	Rush DEF Blend Rk	Pass OFF Rk	Pass OFF Blend Rk	Rush OFF Rk	Rush OFF Blend Rk
8	14	31	32	18	18	12	27

* **1**=Hardest Jump in 2018 schedule from 2017 (aka a much harder schedule in 2018), **32**=Easiest Jump in 2018 schedule from 2017 (aka a much easier schedule in 2018); **Pass Blend** metric blends 4 metrics: Pass Efficiency, YPPA, Explosive Pass & Pass Rush; **Rush Blend** metric blends 3 metrics: Rush Efficiency, Explosive Rush & RB Targets

Team Records & Trends

	2017	2016	2015
Average line	-2.0	0.1	3.7
Average O/U line	43.9	45.0	43.7
Straight Up Record	9-7	9-7	3-13
Against the Spread Record	7-8	8-8	6-10
Over/Under Record	8-7	10-5	7-6
ATS as Favorite	6-6	4-3	1-1
ATS as Underdog	1-1	4-5	5-8
Straight Up Home	6-2	5-3	1-7
ATS Home	5-3	4-4	4-4
Over/Under Home	4-3	5-2	3-3
ATS as Home Favorite	4-3	3-2	1-1
ATS as a Home Dog	1-0	1-2	3-3
Straight Up Away	3-5	4-4	2-6
ATS Away	2-5	4-4	2-6
Over/Under Away	4-4	5-3	4-3
ATS Away Favorite	2-3	1-1	0-0
ATS Away Dog	0-1	3-3	2-5
Six Point Teaser Record	11-4	12-3	10-6
Seven Point Teaser Record	12-4	14-2	10-6
Ten Point Teaser Record	13-3	14-2	10-5

TEN-3

With another year of development and an enhanced receiving corps, Mariota was expected to progress, especially since the Titans had the ninth-easiest pass-defense schedule, but that didn't happen.

Last year the Titans had the No. 20 passing offense, even though the offensive line was the second-healthiest unit in the league (19th in 2016). Mariota's air yards per completion dropped from 8.1 to 6.7; his YPA, from 7.6 to 7.1; TD:INT ratio, from 25:9 to 17:16; and passer rating, from an above-average 95 to below-average 81. The passing game was less explosive, generating 20-yard gains at an 8.6% rate (down from 11%) and 30-yard gains at a 2% clip (vs. 4%).

What was the problem? Mariota's efficiency cratered in 11 personnel, which doesn't bode well for 2018, since new offensive coordinator Matt LaFleur is likely to rely on that grouping. Mariota's 11-personnel problems started on first down.

(cont'd - see TEN-4)

2018 Rest Analysis

Avg Rest	6.47
Avg Rk	3
Team More Rest	1
Opp More Rest	2
Net Rest Edge	-1
3 Days Rest	1
4 Days Rest	0
5 Days Rest	2
6 Days Rest	9
7 Days Rest	1
8 Days Rest	0
9 Days Rest	1
10 Days Rest	0
11 Days Rest	0
12 Days Rest	0
13 Days Rest	0
14 Days Rest	1

Health by Unit*

2017 Rk	3
2016 Rk	2
Off Rk	4
Def Rk	9
QB Rk	20
RB Rk	18
WR Rk	17
TE Rk	11
Oline Rk	2
Dline Rk	11
LB Rk	5
DB Rk	16

*Based on the great work of Scott Kacsmar from Football Outsiders

2018 Weekly Betting Lines (wks 1-16)

1	2	3	4	5	6	7	9	10	11	12	13	14	15	16
MIA	HOU	JAX	PHI	BUF	BAL	LAC	DAL	NE	IND	HOU	NYJ	JAX	NYG	WSH
A	A	A	A	A	H	A	A	H	A	A	H	H	H	H
-2.5	0	5	1.5	0	-2.5	3	3.5	3.5	-1	3.5	-8.5	-1	-1.5	-5.5

Avg = -0.2

Home Lines (wks 1-16)

2	4	6	10	13	14	16
HOU	PHI	BAL	NE	NYJ	JAX	WSH
0	1.5	-2.5	3.5	-8.5	-1	-5.5

Avg = -1.8

Road Lines (wks 1-16)

1	3	5	7	9	11	12	15
MIA	JAX	BUF	LAC	DAL	IND	HOU	NYG
-2.5	5	0	3	3.5	-1	3.5	-1.5

Avg = 1.3

Tennessee Titans 2017 Play Analysis

2017 Play Tendencies

All Pass %	55%
All Pass Rk	25
All Rush %	45%
All Rush Rk	8
1 Score Pass %	54%
1 Score Pass Rk	25
2016 1 Score Pass %	51%
2016 1 Score Pass Rk	30
2017 Pass Increase %	2%
Pass Increase Rk	7
1 Score Rush %	46%
1 Score Rush Rk	8
Up Pass %	45%
Up Pass Rk	25
Up Rush %	55%
Up Rush Rk	8
Down Pass %	63%
Down Pass Rk	26
Down Rush %	37%
Down Rush Rk	7

2017 Down & Distance Tendencies

Down	Distance	Total Plays	Pass Rate	Run Rate	Play Success %
1	Short (1-3)	4	25%	75%	75%
	Med (4-7)	14	50%	50%	71%
	Long (8-10)	325	48%	52%	48%
	XL (11+)	14	93%	7%	29%
2	Short (1-3)	38	39%	61%	71%
	Med (4-7)	91	45%	55%	46%
	Long (8-10)	92	40%	60%	38%
	XL (11+)	46	70%	30%	20%
3	Short (1-3)	41	54%	46%	54%
	Med (4-7)	70	93%	7%	39%
	Long (8-10)	27	89%	11%	37%
	XL (11+)	29	93%	7%	7%
4	Short (1-3)	5	0%	100%	40%

Shotgun %:

Under Center	Shotgun
44%	56%
37%	*63%*

37% AVG 63%

Run Rate:

Under Center	Shotgun
72%	20%

68% AVG 23%

Pass Rate:

Under Center	Shotgun
28%	80%

32% AVG 77%

Short Yardage Intelligence:

2nd and Short Run

Run Freq	Run Rk	NFL Run Freq Avg	Run 1D Rate	Run NFL 1D Avg
72%	9	67%	71%	69%

2nd and Short Pass

Pass Freq	Pass Rk	NFL Pass Freq Avg	Pass 1D Rate	Pass NFL 1D Avg
28%	24	33%	63%	53%

Most Frequent Play

Down	Distance	Play Type	Player	Total Plays	Play Success %
1	Short (1-3)	RUSH	DeMarco Murray	2	50%
	Med (4-7)	RUSH	Derrick Henry	5	80%
	Long (8-10)	RUSH	DeMarco Murray	80	40%
	XL (11+)	PASS	Rishard Matthews	3	67%
2	Short (1-3)	RUSH	DeMarco Murray	12	83%
	Med (4-7)	RUSH	DeMarco Murray	25	28%
	Long (8-10)	RUSH	DeMarco Murray	23	9%
	XL (11+)	PASS	Rishard Matthews	6	33%
		RUSH	DeMarco Murray	6	0%
3	Short (1-3)	RUSH	Derrick Henry	12	58%
	Med (4-7)	PASS	Delanie Walker	15	33%
	Long (8-10)	PASS	Rishard Matthews	9	33%
	XL (11+)	PASS	DeMarco Murray	6	0%
			Delanie Walker	6	17%

Most Successful Play*

Down	Distance	Play Type	Player	Total Plays	Play Success %
1	Med (4-7)	RUSH	Derrick Henry	5	80%
	Long (8-10)	PASS	DeMarco Murray	13	69%
2	Short (1-3)	RUSH	DeMarco Murray	12	83%
	Med (4-7)	RUSH	Marcus Mariota	5	100%
	Long (8-10)	RUSH	Marcus Mariota	10	70%
	XL (11+)	PASS	Jonnu Smith	5	40%
3	Short (1-3)	PASS	Rishard Matthews	9	67%
	Med (4-7)	PASS	Rishard Matthews	9	56%
	Long (8-10)	PASS	Delanie Walker	6	50%
	XL (11+)	PASS	Delanie Walker	6	17%

**Minimum 5 plays to qualify*

2017 Snap Rates

Wk	Opp	Score	Rishard Matthews	Delanie Walker	Eric Decker	DeMarco Murray	Jonnu Smith	Corey Davis	Derrick Henry	Phillip Supernaw	Luke Stocker
1	OAK	L 26-16	52 (81%)	53 (83%)	60 (94%)	47 (73%)	24 (38%)	44 (69%)	18 (28%)	9 (14%)	
2	JAC	W 37-16	48 (71%)	56 (82%)	44 (65%)	37 (54%)	37 (54%)	23 (34%)	30 (44%)	25 (37%)	
3	SEA	W 33-27	62 (85%)	50 (68%)	61 (84%)	48 (66%)	48 (66%)		30 (41%)	10 (14%)	
4	HOU	L 57-14	34 (83%)	31 (76%)	34 (83%)	23 (56%)	22 (54%)		18 (44%)	3 (7%)	
5	MIA	L 16-10	50 (85%)	46 (78%)	49 (83%)	49 (83%)	36 (61%)		11 (19%)	14 (24%)	
6	IND	W 36-22	53 (76%)	44 (63%)	58 (83%)	38 (54%)	43 (61%)		40 (57%)	18 (26%)	
7	CLE	W 12-9	57 (79%)	38 (53%)	66 (92%)	43 (60%)	49 (68%)		30 (42%)	18 (25%)	
9	BAL	W 23-20	42 (81%)	32 (62%)	23 (44%)	37 (71%)	30 (58%)	39 (75%)	19 (37%)	16 (31%)	
10	CIN	W 24-20	78 (87%)	67 (74%)	34 (38%)	67 (74%)	47 (52%)	78 (87%)	29 (32%)	14 (16%)	
11	PIT	L 40-17	52 (80%)	47 (72%)	22 (34%)	52 (80%)	38 (58%)	54 (83%)	16 (25%)	15 (23%)	
12	IND	W 20-16		43 (74%)	48 (83%)	31 (53%)	34 (59%)	42 (72%)	32 (55%)	22 (38%)	
13	HOU	W 24-13		35 (65%)	48 (89%)	32 (59%)	35 (65%)	43 (80%)	24 (44%)	15 (28%)	
14	ARI	L 12-7	46 (77%)	50 (83%)	44 (73%)	47 (78%)	29 (48%)	45 (75%)	13 (22%)	17 (28%)	
15	SF	L 25-23	57 (89%)	56 (88%)	55 (86%)	48 (75%)	17 (27%)	54 (84%)	16 (25%)		11 (17%)
16	LA	L 27-23	64 (93%)	62 (90%)	49 (71%)	48 (70%)	26 (38%)	54 (78%)	21 (30%)		15 (22%)
17	JAC	W 15-10	51 (78%)	34 (52%)	41 (63%)		41 (63%)	42 (65%)	63 (97%)	7 (11%)	34 (52%)
	Grand Total		746 (82%)	744 (73%)	736 (73%)	647 (67%)	556 (54%)	518 (73%)	410 (40%)	203 (23%)	60 (30%)

Personnel Groupings

Personnel	Team %	NFL Avg	Succ. %
1-1 [3WR]	44%	59%	42%
1-2 [2WR]	24%	19%	44%
1-3 [1WR]	13%	5%	48%
2-1 [2WR]	9%	7%	48%
2-2 [1WR]	5%	4%	46%

Grouping Tendencies

Personnel	Pass Rate	Pass Succ. %	Run Succ. %
1-1 [3WR]	74%	40%	46%
1-2 [2WR]	46%	49%	41%
1-3 [1WR]	31%	48%	49%
2-1 [2WR]	50%	54%	41%
2-2 [1WR]	12%	33%	48%

Red Zone Targets (min 3)

Receiver	All	Inside 5	6-10	11-20
Delanie Walker	12	5	3	4
Eric Decker	11	1	4	6
Rishard Matthews	9		2	7
Corey Davis	7			7
Derrick Henry	5			5
DeMarco Murray	2		1	1

Red Zone Rushes (min 3)

Rusher	All	Inside 5	6-10	11-20
Derrick Henry	29	8	7	14
DeMarco Murray	20	7	5	8
Marcus Mariota	16	1	7	8

Early Down Target Rate

RB	TE	WR
12%	33%	56%
23%	*21% NFL AVG*	*56%*

Overall Target Success %

RB	TE	WR
42% #22	49% #20	47% #18

Tennessee Titans 2017 Passing Recap & 2018 Outlook

It's hard to know how much of Mariota's 2017 struggles were due to an antiquated scheme vs. personal shortcomings. We saw how much better Jared Goff looked in Year 1 with Sean McVay and LaFleur, so Mariota could improve in 2018, although his improvement might come more from "edges" (such as more running back passes) than true progression. Mariota's 2016 deep passing (particularly to the right) was near the bottom of the league with a 26% Success Rate, 8.5 YPA, and 58 passer rating. In 2017 he was even worse with a 38% Success Rate, 9.7 YPA, and 59 passer rating. I'll be fascinated to see how LaFleur uses Mariota's wide receivers in 11 personnel and how efficient they are. If Mariota can improve just his interception rate, the team will be off to a great start. Only DeShone Kizer threw more early-down interceptions and had a higher interception rate than Mariota (11, 3.6%).

Marcus Mariota Rating All Downs

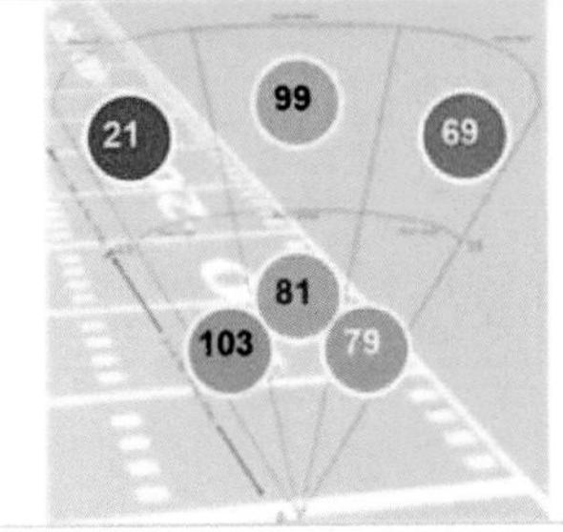

Marcus Mariota Rating Early Downs

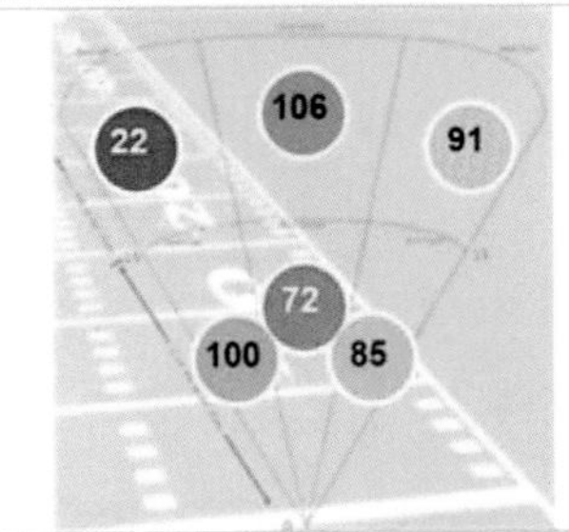

2017 Standard Passing Table

QB	Comp	Att	Comp %	Yds	YPA	TDs	INT	Sacks	Rating	Rk
Marcus Mariota	322	520	62%	3,691	7.1	17	16	37	81	33
NFL Avg			62%		7.0				87.5	

2017 Advanced Passing Table

QB	Success %	EDSR Passing Success %	20+ Yd Pass Gains	20+ Yd Pass %	30+ Yd Pass Gains	30+ Yd Pass %	Avg. Air Yds per Comp	Avg. YAC per Comp	20+ Air Yd Comp	20+ Air Yd %
Marcus Mariota	44%	48%	45	8.6%	10	1.9%	6.7	3.9	18	6%
NFL Avg	44%	48%	27.7	8.8%	10.3	3.3%	6.0	4.7	11.7	6%

Interception Rates by Down

Yards to Go	1	2	3	4	Total
1 & 2	0.0%	0.0%	0.0%		0.0%
3, 4, 5	0.0%	3.7%	2.0%	0.0%	2.4%
6 - 9	0.0%	5.0%	3.8%	50.0%	5.1%
10 - 14	3.6%	3.2%	0.0%	0.0%	3.1%
15+	0.0%	0.0%	0.0%		0.0%
Total	3.2%	3.1%	1.8%	20.0%	2.9%

3rd Down Passing - Short of Sticks Analysis

QB	Avg. Yds to Go	Avg. YIA (of Comp)	Avg Yds Short	Short of Sticks Rate	Short Rk
Marcus Mariota	7.7	7.4	-0.3	59%	13
NFL Avg	7.8	6.7	-1.1	60%	

Air Yds vs YAC

Air Yds %	YAC %	Rk
69%	31%	2
58%	42%	

2017 Receiving Recap & 2018 Outlook

The receiver under the biggest microscope in 2018 is Davis. Being drafted No. 5 overall presents challenges for any player, particularly one who can't do his job unless he's targeted, but he disappointed in a big way in 2017, and only part of that was due to the time he missed with an injury. His 42% Success Rate was more than 10% worse than that of any other Titan with 50-plus targets. His 5.9 YPA was over 1.0 YPA worse as well. With a new offensive system that should be built around maximizing Davis' athleticism, he has an opportunity to lead the team in receiving and maybe to the playoffs.

Player *Min 50 Targets*	Targets	Comp %	YPA	Rating	TOARS	Success %	Success Rk	Missed YPA Rk	YAS % Rk	TDs
Delanie Walker	125	66%	7.4	80	4.9	53%	43	28	95	3
Rishard Matthews	97	59%	8.6	75	4.4	53%	40	70	37	4
Eric Decker	95	65%	7.0	93	4.6	54%	32	25	100	2
Corey Davis	80	54%	5.9	64	3.9	42%	104	53	87	2

Directional Passer Rating Delivered

Receiver	Short Left	Short Middle	Short Right	Deep Left	Deep Middle	Deep Right	Player Total
Delanie Walker	99	54	75	27	129	114	80
Rishard Matthews	114	153	81	0	104	12	75
Eric Decker	106	77	88	97	129	48	93
Corey Davis	81	92	55	46	65	62	64
DeMarco Murray	102	86	89				97
Jonnu Smith	72	14	119	40		133	80
Taywan Taylor	75	101	56	56	40	122	78
Derrick Henry	148	81	87				109
Harry Douglas	40		100			0	3
Team Total	100	76	83	16	97	66	81

2017 Rushing Recap & 2017 Outlook

Dion Lewis is a fantastically efficient player and could have success with a rushing quarterback like Mariota. Over the past two years, Lewis is second among all running backs in Success Rate (54%) and fourth in Missed YPA (yds/play on unsuccessful plays, min. 125 touches). Out of 49 backs with at least 175 carries since 2016, only two recorded at least a 53% Success Rate and 4.5 YPC: Ezekiel Elliott and Lewis. He is versatile with great success in 11 personnel (4.1 YPC, 55% Success Rate), 12 (4.7 YPC, 55%), and 21 (5.3 YPC, 60%). His overall Success Rate (56%) was 7% better than the collective mark of all the other Patriots running backs.

Player *Min 50 Rushes*	Rushes	YPC	Success %	Success Rk	Missed YPA Rk	YTS % Rk	YAS % Rk	Early Down Success %	Early Down Success Rk	TDs
Derrick Henry	211	4.4	48%	24	46	35	9	47%	24	6
DeMarco Murray	184	3.6	39%	65	45	62	39	39%	63	6

Yards per Carry by Direction

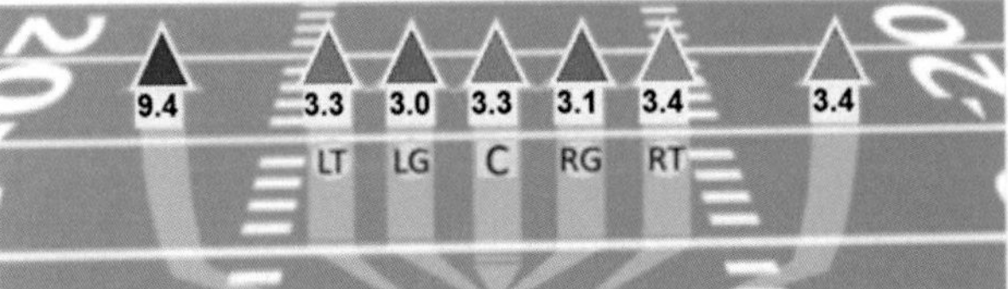

Directional Run Frequency

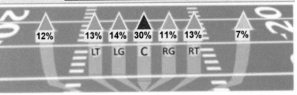

12% 13% 14% 30% 11% 13% 7%

LT LG C RG RT

TEN-4

With two or fewer wide receivers, Mariota had an astronomical 69% first-down Success Rate, 10.6 YPA, 121 passer rating, and 7:3 TD:INT ratio. But with three or more wide receivers, Mariota had a poor 46% first-down Success Rate, 5.1 YPA, 47 passer rating, and 0:5 TD:INT ratio, much worse than he had done in 2016, when he had a 58% first-down Success Rate, 7.1 YPA, 84 passer rating, and 1:1 TD:INT ratio. While Decker (50% Success Rate) and Matthews (59% Success Rate) were acceptable as his top first-down options, Davis was targeted almost as frequently, and he sabotaged Mariota with a 13% Success Rate, 1.8 YPA, 0 passer rating, and 0:2 TD:INT ratio.

Mariota's struggles weren't limited to the early downs. With three-plus wide receivers and at least four yards to go on third down, Mariota dropped from a 44% Success Rate, 7.5 YPA, 103 passer rating, and 6:1 TD:INT ratio to a 31% Success Rate, 5.2 YPA, 58 passer rating, and 1:3 TD:INT ratio. Mariota's most-targeted option was Matthews, but he underwhelmed with a 39% Success Rate, 5.9 YPA, 23 passer rating, and 0:2 TD:INT. Decker was the most successful receiver in this situation (44% Success Rate), but the wide receivers generally failed on third down. Mariota's backfield also didn't help him out. In 2016 he had a 50% Success Rate when targeting backs on third down from 11 personnel. In 2017, that number dropped to 7%.

(cont'd - see TEN-5)

Matthew Freedman's Fantasy Corner

Last year Mariota was the QB24 with 14.0 fantasy points per game thanks primarily to a career-low 2.9% touchdown rate and career-high 3.3% interception rate, which were bottom-six marks. He should experience natural progression in both metrics, and the addition of Lewis as a pass-catching back and development of Davis, Taylor, and even tight end Jonnu Smith as second-year players should increase his odds of enjoying a bounceback campaign. Blessed with high-end dual-threat capability and finally operating within a modern offense, Mariota has top-five positional upside and is worth rostering as the QB14 by average draft position.

Division History: Season Wins & 2018 Projection

2014 Wins | 2015 Wins | 2016 Wins | 2017 Wins | Forecast 2018 Wins

Rank of 2018 Defensive Pass Efficiency Faced by Week

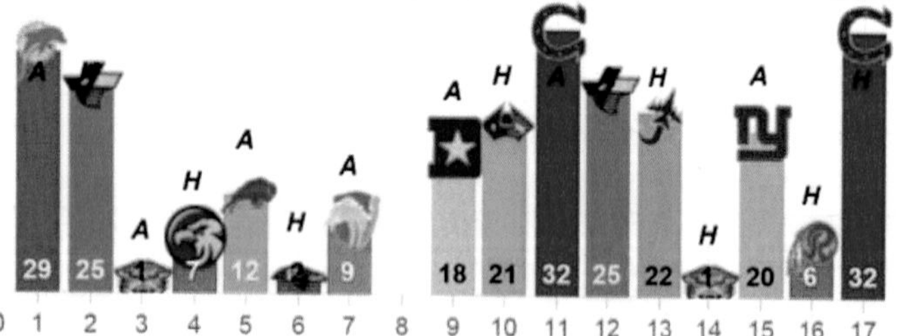

Rank of 2018 Defensive Rush Efficiency Faced by Week

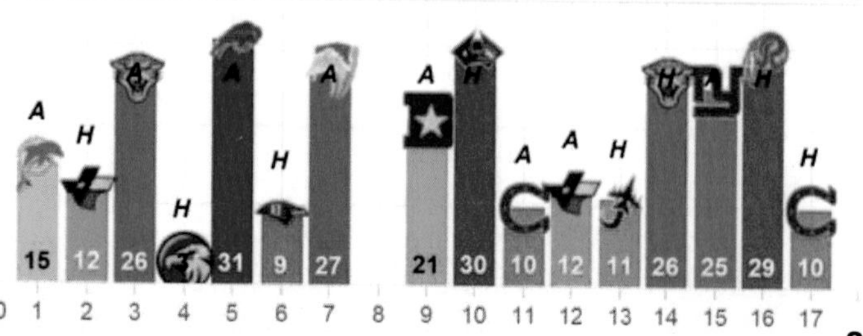

2017 Situational Usage by Player & Position

Usage Rate by Score

		Being Blown Out (14+)	Down Big (9-13)	One Score	Large Lead (9-13)	Blowout Lead (14+)	Grand Total
RUSH	Derrick Henry	21%	11%	22%	29%	63%	22%
	DeMarco Murray	4%	18%	22%	19%		19%
	Delanie Walker			0%	2%		0%
	Rishard Matthews			0%			0%
	Taywan Taylor	1%		1%			1%
	David Fluellen	1%				19%	0%
	Eric Weems			0%			0%
	Jalston Fowler			0%		6%	0%
	Total	27%	29%	45%	50%	88%	43%
PASS	Derrick Henry	6%	1%	2%	2%		2%
	DeMarco Murray	4%	6%	5%	2%		5%
	Delanie Walker	19%	20%	12%	12%	6%	13%
	Rishard Matthews	18%	9%	9%	14%		10%
	Eric Decker	9%	11%	10%	14%		10%
	Corey Davis	12%	14%	8%	2%		8%
	Taywan Taylor	4%	1%	4%	2%		3%
	Jonnu Smith	1%	5%	4%		6%	4%
	Phillip Supernaw			1%			1%
	David Fluellen			0%			0%
	Eric Weems			0%			0%
	Harry Douglas		1%	0%			0%
	Jalston Fowler			0%			0%
	Luke Stocker			0%			0%
	Null		1%				0%
	Total	73%	71%	55%	50%	13%	57%

Positional Target Distribution vs NFL Average

		NFL Wide				Team Only			
		Left	Middle	Right	**Total**	Left	Middle	Right	**Total**
Deep	WR	954	492	962	**2,408**	32	17	25	**74**
	TE	180	140	179	**499**	12	10	9	**31**
	RB	39	9	42	**90**				
	All	**1,173**	**641**	**1,183**	**2,997**	**44**	**27**	**34**	**105**
Short	WR	2,774	1,643	2,705	**7,122**	88	28	85	**201**
	TE	819	802	1,122	**2,743**	44	37	48	**129**
	RB	1,285	809	1,275	**3,369**	36	14	20	**70**
	All	**4,878**	**3,254**	**5,102**	**13,234**	**168**	**79**	**153**	**400**
Total		**6,051**	**3,895**	**6,285**	**16,231**	**212**	**106**	**187**	**505**

Positional Success Rates vs NFL Average

		NFL Wide				Team Only			
		Left	Middle	Right	**Total**	Left	Middle	Right	**Total**
Deep	WR	37%	45%	38%	**39%**	25%	59%	28%	**34%**
	TE	39%	53%	44%	**45%**	25%	50%	67%	**45%**
	RB	36%	56%	38%	**39%**				
	All	**37%**	**47%**	**39%**	**40%**	**25%**	**56%**	**38%**	**37%**
Short	WR	52%	58%	50%	**52%**	53%	54%	55%	**54%**
	TE	50%	57%	49%	**52%**	57%	43%	50%	**50%**
	RB	44%	51%	43%	**45%**	36%	43%	55%	**43%**
	All	**49%**	**56%**	**48%**	**50%**	**51%**	**47%**	**54%**	**51%**
Total		**47%**	**54%**	**46%**	**48%**	**45%**	**49%**	**51%**	**48%**

Successful Play Rate
0% ▬ 100%

Tennessee Titans - Success by Personnel Grouping & Play Type

Play Type	1-1 [3WR]	1-2 [2WR]	2-1 [2WR]	1-0 [4WR]	1-3 [1WR]	0-1 [4WR]	2-0 [3WR]	2-2 [1WR]	0-2 [3WR]	3-1 [1WR]	2-3 [0WR]	1-4 [0WR]	Grand Total
PASS	40% (312, 59%)	49% (105, 20%)	54% (41, 8%)	50% (2, 0%)	48% (40, 8%)	40% (5, 1%)	25% (4, 1%)	33% (6, 1%)	38% (8, 2%)		50% (2, 0%)		43% (525, 100%)
RUSH	46% (110, 25%)	41% (125, 29%)	41% (41, 9%)	50% (2, 0%)	49% (88, 20%)	33% (3, 1%)	50% (2, 0%)	48% (44, 10%)	0% (1, 0%)	50% (2, 0%)	82% (11, 3%)	25% (4, 1%)	45% (433, 100%)
TOTAL	42% (422, 44%)	44% (230, 24%)	48% (82, 9%)	50% (4, 0%)	48% (128, 13%)	38% (8, 1%)	33% (6, 1%)	46% (50, 5%)	33% (9, 1%)	50% (2, 0%)	77% (13, 1%)	25% (4, 0%)	44% (958, 100%)

Format Line 1: Success Rate Line 2: Total # of Plays, % of All Plays (by type)

TEN-5 I'm excited about the new coaching staff, but they have their work cut out for them. Last year the Titans ran a league-low 43% of their snaps from 11 personnel (average is 59%) while LaFleur's Rams were the league's most 11-heavy team with an 81% snap rate. Of the Rams' 544 pass attempts last year, 500 (92%) were with at least three wide receivers on the field. But just because the Terry Robiskie-designed 2017 offense was bad in 11 personnel does not mean LaFleur's 2018 offense will be. For one, we're likely to see more early-down passes to backs. In the first half of games last year, the Rams targeted running backs at an above-average 25% rate on early downs, whereas the Titans had a league-low 8% (average is 23%). On just first down, the Rams threw 26% of targets to backs while the Titans were last at 6%. The Rams were most efficient on first-down passing when targeting backs, generating a 55% Success Rate (vs. 52% with tight ends and 46% with wide receivers). Amazingly, the Titans were one of the few teams with an even better efficiency mark on first-down running back passes with a 57% Success Rate, yet they hardly targeted their backs at all.

On the other side of the ball, the Titans were 24th in pass defense even though they had the fourth-easiest pass-offense schedule. When they faced competent pass offenses they were exploited, allowing 57 points to Deshaun Watson (114 rating, 62% Success Rate, 9.8 YPA), 40 to Ben Roethlisberger (115 rating, 54% Success Rate, 4:0 TD:INT), 25 to Jimmy Garoppolo (107 rating, 57% Success Rate, 8.9 YPA), 27 to Jared Goff (114 rating, 51% Success Rate, 4:0 TD:INT), 21 in the first half to Alex Smith (138 rating, 56% Success Rate, 10 YPA), and 35 to Tom Brady (102 rating, 58% success rate, 3:0 TD:INT). The Titans had the fourth-worst defense in EDSR and fifth worst at defensing running back passes, but the unit has some talent, and head Coach Mike Vrabel and defensive coordinator Dean Pees can get the Titans back on track. The team selected defensive players with their first three picks in the draft and added defensive tackle Bennie Logan and cornerback Malcom Butler in free agency. LaFleur should be more unpredictable and successful than Robiskie was. Flip to the fourth page of this chapter, and you'll see that the most frequent play for the Titans (outside of 3rd and medium/long) were predictable and inefficient runs, mostly by Murray. The Titans were healthy last year and had the third-easiest schedule (based on efficiency), yet six of their nine wins were by one score. The AFC South should be even tougher this year. If the Titans hope to win the division, they will need continued injury luck, improvement from Mariota, and a quick payoff from the new coaching staff.

Receiving Success by Personnel Grouping

Position	Player	1-1 [3WR]	1-2 [2WR]	2-1 [2WR]	1-3 [1WR]	0-1 [4WR]	2-0 [3WR]	2-2 [1WR]	0-2 [3WR]	2-3 [0WR]	Total
RB	DeMarco Murray	33% 4.5 96.4 (30)	70% 7.6 98.3 (10)	60% 9.4 105.8 (5)	100% 4.0 83.3 (1)		0% 5.0 87.5 (1)				45% 5.7 97.3 (47)
	Derrick Henry	33% 2.7 60.9 (9)	67% 28.0 158.3 (3)	33% 4.7 77.1 (3)	50% 7.0 72.9 (2)						41% 8.0 108.9 (17)
TE	Delanie Walker	58% 6.4 71.1 (65)	41% 6.6 83.7 (17)	44% 8.0 100.0 (9)	57% 12.9 101.8 (14)			33% 7.3 88.2 (3)		50% 1.0 95.8 (2)	54% 7.3 82.7 (110)
WR	Rishard Matthews	46% 5.9 31.2 (56)	50% 13.8 128.2 (18)	100% 18.5 118.8 (6)	100% 15.0 158.3 (3)	50% 10.0 85.4 (2)	100% 20.0 118.8 (1)	100% 19.0 118.8 (1)			54% 9.1 77.5 (87)
	Eric Decker	50% 6.3 87.5 (52)	64% 5.1 82.7 (14)	56% 10.9 103.0 (9)	100% 16.0 118.8 (1)	100% 8.0 100.0 (1)		0% 0.0 39.6 (1)	33% 4.7 49.3 (3)		53% 6.6 87.1 (81)
	Corey Davis	31% 4.8 34.1 (48)	60% 9.6 106.7 (10)	33% 9.0 95.1 (3)	0% 0.0 39.6 (1)		0% 0.0 39.6 (1)				35% 5.6 47.9 (63)

Format Line 1: Success Rate Line 2: YPA Line 3: Passer Rating Line 4: Total # of Plays

Successful Play Rate
0% ▬ 100%

Rushing Success by Personnel Grouping

Position	Player	1-1 [3WR]	1-2 [2WR]	2-1 [2WR]	1-3 [1WR]	0-1 [4WR]	2-0 [3WR]	2-2 [1WR]	0-2 [3WR]	3-1 [1WR]	2-3 [0WR]	1-4 [0WR]	Total
QB	Marcus Mariota	83% 8.0 (24)	50% 5.5 (14)	50% 7.5 (2)	40% 3.4 (5)	50% 2.0 (2)		18% -0.1 (11)	0% 6.0 (1)		100% 2.0 (1)		57% 5.2 (60)
RB	DeMarco Murray	35% 3.7 (51)	34% 3.4 (70)	38% 4.8 (24)	29% 2.8 (17)			71% 3.7 (7)		0% 3.0 (1)	67% 1.2 (6)		37% 3.5 (176)
	Derrick Henry	33% 2.1 (27)	49% 3.1 (39)	47% 3.6 (15)	52% 6.6 (63)		0% 1.0 (1)	52% 3.0 (23)		100% 11.0 (1)	100% 1.0 (1)	25% 3.3 (4)	48% 4.3 (174)

Format Line 1: Success Rate Line 2: YPC Line 3: Total # of Plays

Washington Redskins

2018 Coaches

Head Coach:
Jay Gruden (5th yr)
Offensive Coordinator:
Matt Cavanaugh (2nd yr)
Defensive Coordinator:
Greg Manusky (2nd yr)

2018 Forecast

Wins	Div Rank
7	#4

Past Records

2017: 7-9
2016: 8-7-1
2015: 9-7

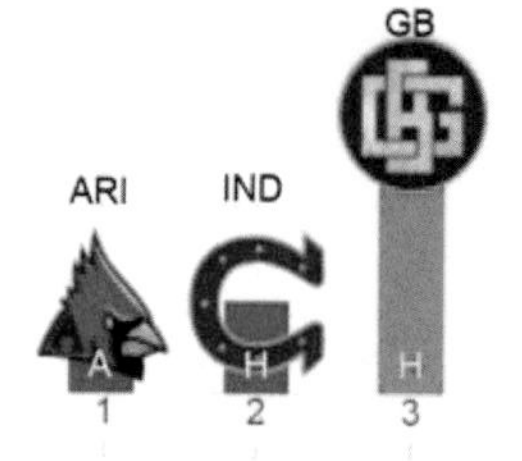

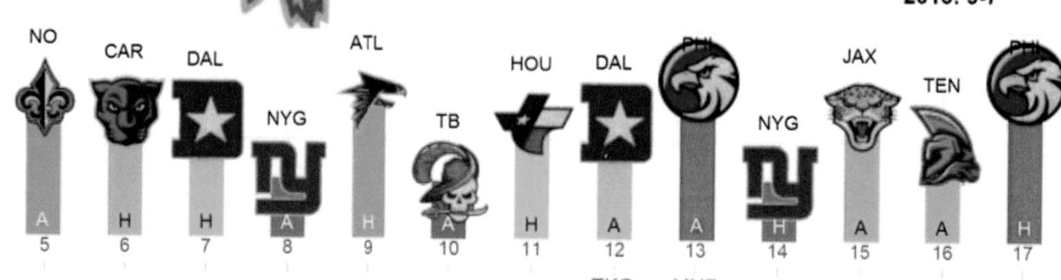

Key Players Lost

TXN	Player (POS)
Cut	Bowen, Kevin T
	Hilliard, Kenny RB
	McClain, Terrell DT
Declared Free Agent	Breeland, Bashaud CB
	Brown, Zach LB
	Compton, Will LB
	Cousins, Kirk QB
	Galette, Junior LB
	Grant, Ryan WR
	Hall, DeAngelo S
	Jones, Arthur DT
	Lauvao, Shawn G
	Long, Spencer C
	Murphy, Trent DE
	Paul, Niles TE
	Pryor Sr., Terrelle WR
	Quick, Brian WR
	Taylor Sr., Phil NT
Retired	Franklin, Orlando G

Average Line	# Games Favored	# Games Underdog
3.0	4	11

2018 Washington Redskins Overview

For the past few seasons Washington's quarterback situation reminded me of Eeyore. A rain cloud hovered over the Redskins and prevented too much joy at any time because there was always the question about Kirk Cousins' future. The Redskins were Robert Griffin III's team in 2012, and they made the playoffs. In 2013, Griffin was still the quarterback, but he went on Injured Reserve in December, and Cousins went 0-3 as the fill-in with a 4:7 TD:INT ratio. The Shanahans were fired after the season, and new head coach Jay Gruden cycled through Griffin, Cousins, and even Colt McCoy in his first year with the team, benching Cousins for the rest of the season at halftime of Week 7. Although he finished 1-4, Cousins was once again named the starter in 2015 and finally had a breakout season, going 9-7 with a 69.8% completion rate and 29:11 TD:INT ratio in the final year of his rookie deal. And then the saga began.

The Redskins couldn't reach an agreement with Cousins after the season, so they franchised him, making him prove his worth in 2016 against the toughest schedule in the league. And he proved it with another strong season. But once again the rain cloud did not disappear. The Redskins couldn't come to terms with Cousins in the offseason, and they franchised him again for 2017 amid constant rumors in the media about the relationship between Cousins and the team.

Heading into last season, I projected the Redskins for the toughest schedule of pass defenses. They ended up with the fourth toughest, and Cousins finally struggled, but it wasn't all his fault. His top wide receivers from the previous season in Pierre Garcon and DeSean Jackson both left in free agency, and the Redskins had the second-most injured offense during the year. It's hard to win games in that situation, and yet the Redskins were still one win away from 8-8.

In the offseason the Redskins decided to let Cousins leave. He signed a guaranteed three-year, $84-million contract with the Vikings, and the Redskins traded for Alex Smith, giving him a four-year, $94-million contract with $55 million guaranteed. While Jay Gruden says the team upgraded "without a doubt," Cousins and Smith are different types of players. Smith is coming off his best season, but much of his success was due to his teammates and the aggressive coaching.

(cont'd - see WAS2)

Key Free Agents/ Trades Added

Hogan, Kevin QB
Irwin-Hill, Sam P
McPhee, Pernell LB
Richardson Jr., Paul WR
Scandrick, Orlando CB
Smith, Alex QB

Drafted Players

Rd	Pk	Player (College)
1	13	DT - Da'Ron Payne (Alabama)
2	59	RB - Derrius Guice (LSU)
3	74	OT - Geron Christian (Louisville)
4	109	S - Troy Apke (Penn State)
5	163	DT - Tim Settle (Virginia Tech)
6	197	LB - Shaun Dion Hamilton (Alabama)
7	241	CB - Greg Stroman (Virginia Tech)
7*	256	WR - Trey Quinn (SMU)

Regular Season Wins: Past & Current Proj

Forecast 2018 Wins  7

2017 Wins  7

Forecast 2017 Wins  7

2016 Wins  8

2015 Wins  9

2014 Wins  4

1 3 5 7 9 11 13 15

Lineup & Cap Hits

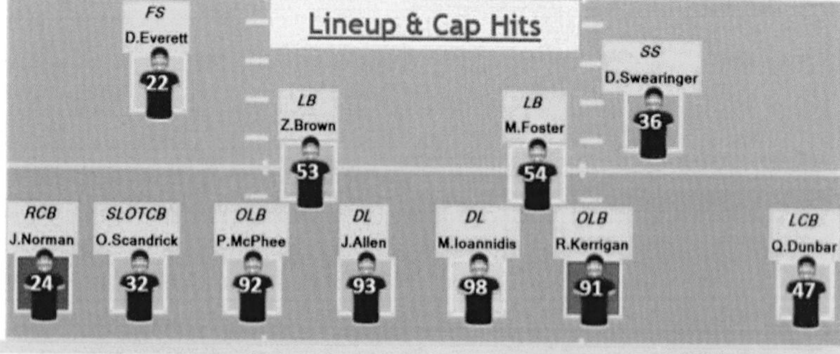

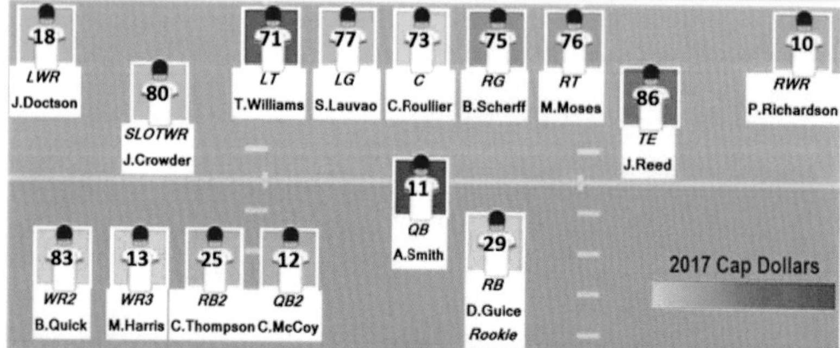

2018 Unit Spending

Positional Spending

	Rank	Total	2017 Rk
All OFF	8	$101.30M	4
QB	15	$22.63M	3
OL	6	$40.39M	6
RB	18	$7.64M	24
WR	32	$13.11M	27
TE	2	$17.54M	6
All DEF	22	$73.87M	14
DL	29	$15.80M	29
LB	9	$25.64M	8
CB	8	$24.11M	4
S	24	$8.32M	11

Washington Redskins 2017 Success Rate Radar

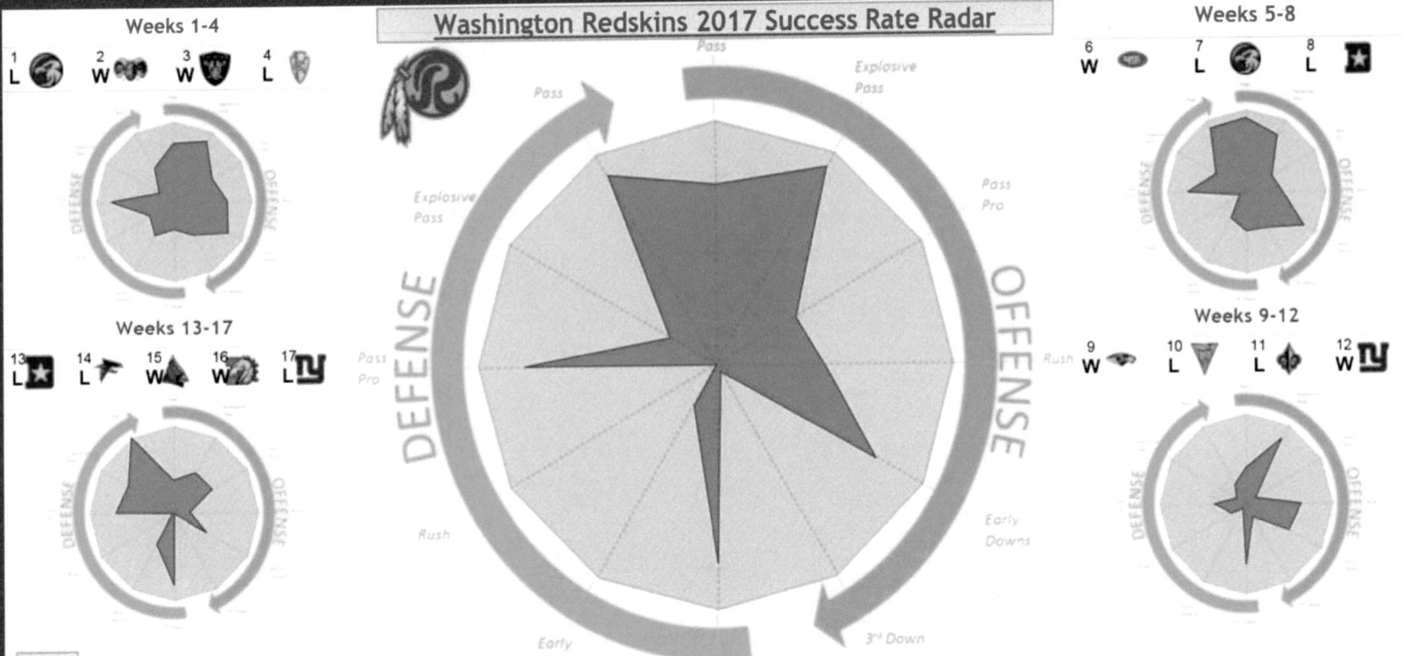

WAS-2

Smith's performance improved as the Chiefs used Tyreek Hill as more of a downfield threat. He also had an elite tight end in Travis Kelce, who didn't miss a start. Meanwhile, Cousins didn't have a reliable deep threat or a healthy playmaking tight end. Smith was tremendous on deep passes, highly accurate, and careful with the ball (26:5 TD:INT), but he also had the 12th-easiest pass-defense schedule. If Smith had been beset by Cousins' circumstances last year, he probably wouldn't have had such a strong season.

Gruden may not use Smith the way he deployed Cousins, but we can learn more about Smith's 2018 prospects by studying Cousins and the 2017 Redskins. One thing that stands out is Cousins' failure to lead the Redskins back from halftime deficits. Washington went 0-7 when trailing at halftime, and five of these games were in division. In contrast, in 2016 the Redskins won four games they trailed at halftime, with victories against the Eagles and Giants.

They specifically struggled in the second half. In the first half of games, the Redskins offense ranked 11th and 13th in passing and rushing success, but in the second half they were 14th and 22nd. After halftime they were respectable on early downs, but on third down they were below average in passing and 32nd in rushing. Whereas the league averaged a 46% Success Rate on second-half third-down rushes, the Redskins averaged 22%. Everyone on the team was terrible in this situation, but Samaje Perine was particularly bad, turning his team-leading six carries into one first down with 0.7 YPC. And the team's third-down problems weren't limited to the second half: The Redskins need to overhaul their third-down play calling if Smith is to have success. In 2016 the Redskins were successful on 73% of their third-down runs (No. 1 in the NFL) and 40% of their third-down passes (No. 10). They had the fifth-best third-down offense, but in 2017 everything changed: They had the second-worst third-down offense with Success Rates of 33% on runs (No. 32) and 32% on passes (No. 26).

(cont'd - see **WAS-3**)

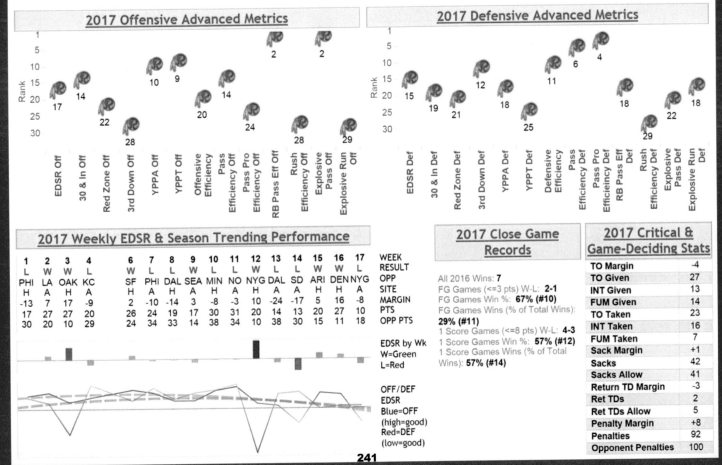

2017 Offensive Advanced Metrics

Metric	Rank
EDSR Off	17
30 & In Off	14
Red Zone Off	22
3rd Down Off	28
YPPA Off	10
YPPT Off	9
Offensive Efficiency	20
Pass Efficiency Off	14
Pass Pro Efficiency Off	24
RB Pass Eff Off	2
Rush Efficiency Off	28
Explosive Pass Off	2
Explosive Run Off	29

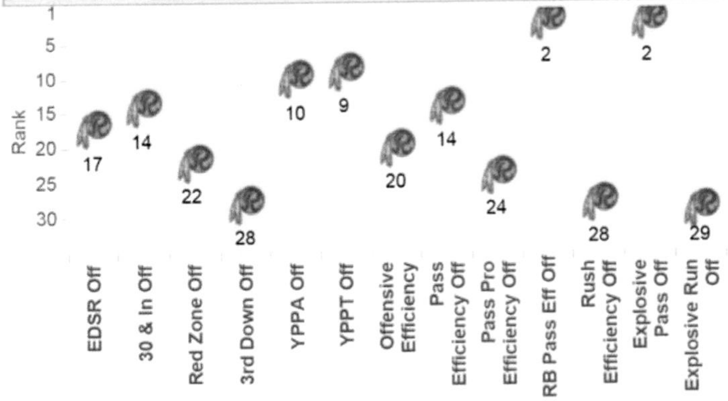

2017 Defensive Advanced Metrics

Metric	Rank
EDSR Def	15
30 & In Def	19
Red Zone Def	21
3rd Down Def	12
YPPA Def	18
YPPT Def	25
Defensive Efficiency	11
Pass Efficiency Def	6
Pass Pro Efficiency Def	4
RB Pass Eff Def	18
Rush Efficiency Def	29
Explosive Pass Def	22
Explosive Run Def	18

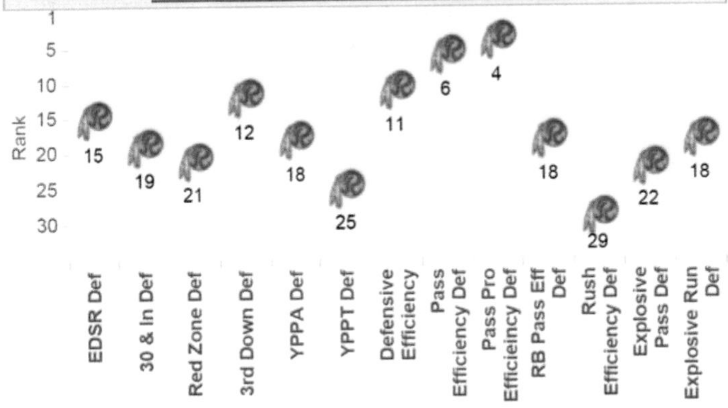

2017 Weekly EDSR & Season Trending Performance

WEEK	1	2	3	4	6	7	8	9	10	11	12	13	14	15	16	17
RESULT	L	W	W	L	W	L	L	W	L	L	W	L	L	W	W	L
OPP	PHI	LA	OAK	KC	SF	PHI	DAL	SEA	MIN	NO	NYG	DAL	SD	ARI	DEN	NYG
SITE	H	A	H	A	H	A	H	A	H	A	H	A	A	H	H	A
MARGIN	-13	7	17	-9	2	-10	-14	3	-8	-3	10	-24	-17	5	16	-8
PTS	17	27	27	20	26	24	19	17	30	31	20	14	13	20	27	10
OPP PTS	30	20	10	29	24	34	33	14	38	34	10	38	30	15	11	18

EDSR by Wk
W=Green
L=Red

OFF/DEF
EDSR
Blue=OFF
(high=good)
Red=DEF
(low=good)

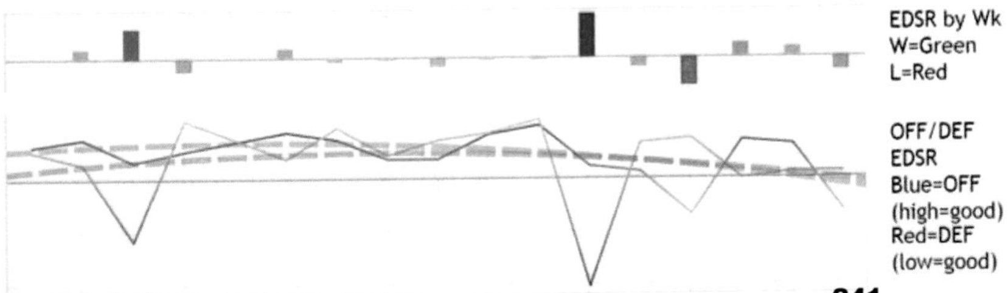

2017 Close Game Records

All 2016 Wins: **7**
FG Games (<=3 pts) W-L: **2-1**
FG Games Win %: **67% (#10)**
FG Games Wins (% of Total Wins): **29% (#11)**
1 Score Games (<=8 pts) W-L: **4-3**
1 Score Games Win %: **57% (#12)**
1 Score Games Wins (% of Total Wins): **57% (#14)**

2017 Critical & Game-Deciding Stats

TO Margin	-4
TO Given	27
INT Given	13
FUM Given	14
TO Taken	23
INT Taken	16
FUM Taken	7
Sack Margin	+1
Sacks	42
Sacks Allow	41
Return TD Margin	-3
Ret TDs	2
Ret TDs Allow	5
Penalty Margin	+8
Penalties	92
Opponent Penalties	100

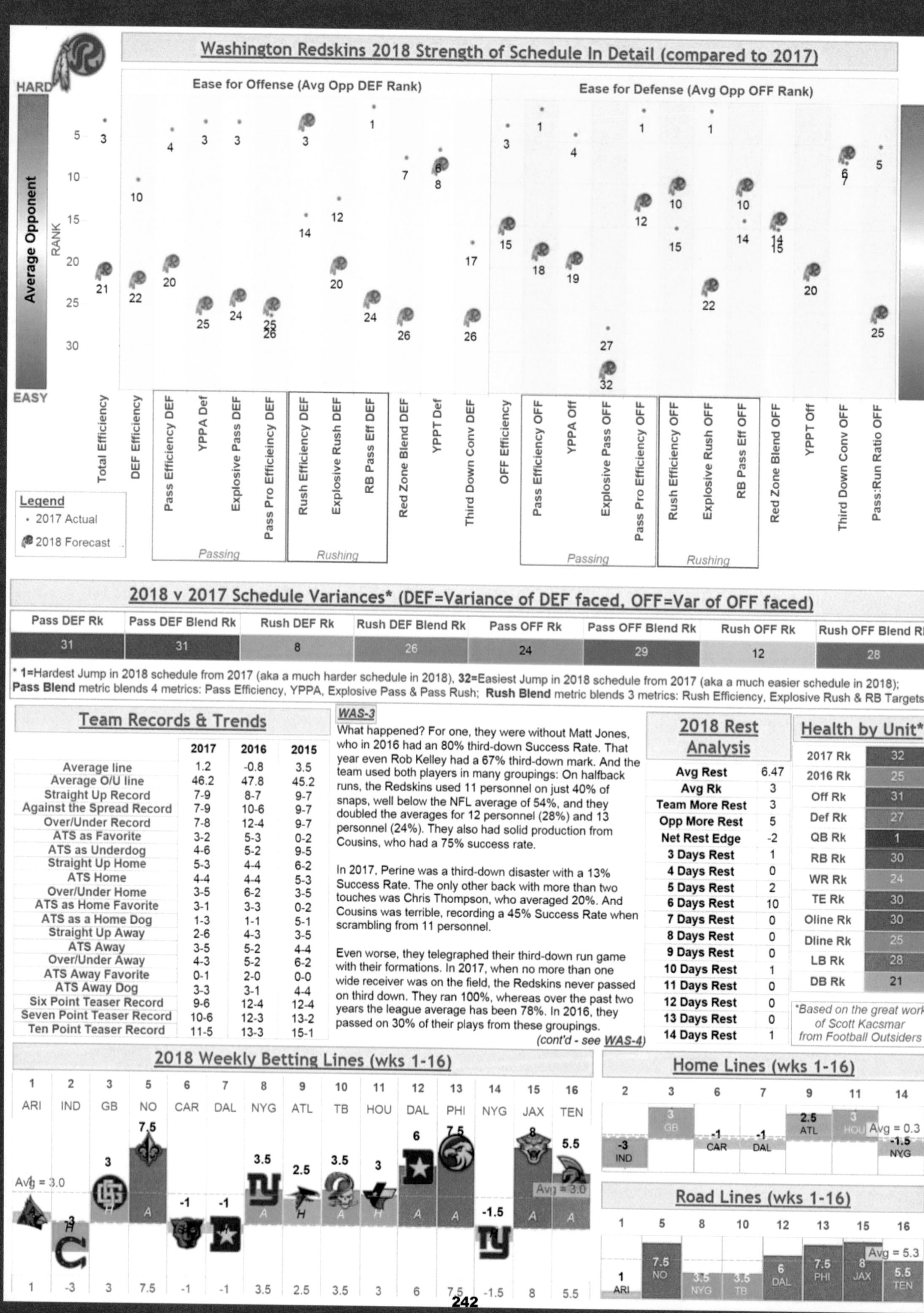

Washington Redskins 2018 Strength of Schedule In Detail (compared to 2017)

2018 v 2017 Schedule Variances* (DEF=Variance of DEF faced, OFF=Var of OFF faced)

Pass DEF Rk	Pass DEF Blend Rk	Rush DEF Rk	Rush DEF Blend Rk	Pass OFF Rk	Pass OFF Blend Rk	Rush OFF Rk	Rush OFF Blend Rk
31	31	8	26	24	29	12	28

* **1**=Hardest Jump in 2018 schedule from 2017 (aka a much harder schedule in 2018), **32**=Easiest Jump in 2018 schedule from 2017 (aka a much easier schedule in 2018); **Pass Blend** metric blends 4 metrics: Pass Efficiency, YPPA, Explosive Pass & Pass Rush; **Rush Blend** metric blends 3 metrics: Rush Efficiency, Explosive Rush & RB Targets

Team Records & Trends

	2017	2016	2015
Average line	1.2	-0.8	3.5
Average O/U line	46.2	47.8	45.2
Straight Up Record	7-9	8-7	9-7
Against the Spread Record	7-9	10-6	9-7
Over/Under Record	7-8	12-4	9-7
ATS as Favorite	3-2	5-3	0-2
ATS as Underdog	4-6	5-2	9-5
Straight Up Home	5-3	4-4	6-2
ATS Home	4-4	4-4	5-3
Over/Under Home	3-5	6-2	3-5
ATS as Home Favorite	3-1	3-3	0-2
ATS as a Home Dog	1-3	1-1	5-1
Straight Up Away	2-6	4-3	3-5
ATS Away	3-5	5-2	4-4
Over/Under Away	4-3	5-2	6-2
ATS Away Favorite	0-1	2-0	0-0
ATS Away Dog	3-3	3-1	4-4
Six Point Teaser Record	9-6	12-4	12-4
Seven Point Teaser Record	10-6	12-3	13-2
Ten Point Teaser Record	11-5	13-3	15-1

WAS-3

What happened? For one, they were without Matt Jones, who in 2016 had an 80% third-down Success Rate. That year even Rob Kelley had a 67% third-down mark. And the team used both players in many groupings: On halfback runs, the Redskins used 11 personnel on just 40% of snaps, well below the NFL average of 54%, and they doubled the averages for 12 personnel (28%) and 13 personnel (24%). They also had solid production from Cousins, who had a 75% success rate.

In 2017, Perine was a third-down disaster with a 13% Success Rate. The only other back with more than two touches was Chris Thompson, who averaged 20%. And Cousins was terrible, recording a 45% Success Rate when scrambling from 11 personnel.

Even worse, they telegraphed their third-down run game with their formations. In 2017, when no more than one wide receiver was on the field, the Redskins never passed on third down. They ran 100%, whereas over the past two years the league average has been 78%. In 2016, they passed on 30% of their plays from these groupings.

(cont'd - see ***WAS-4***)

2018 Rest Analysis

Avg Rest	6.47
Avg Rk	3
Team More Rest	3
Opp More Rest	5
Net Rest Edge	-2
3 Days Rest	1
4 Days Rest	0
5 Days Rest	2
6 Days Rest	10
7 Days Rest	0
8 Days Rest	0
9 Days Rest	0
10 Days Rest	1
11 Days Rest	0
12 Days Rest	0
13 Days Rest	0
14 Days Rest	1

Health by Unit*

2017 Rk	32
2016 Rk	25
Off Rk	31
Def Rk	27
QB Rk	1
RB Rk	30
WR Rk	24
TE Rk	30
Oline Rk	30
Dline Rk	25
LB Rk	28
DB Rk	21

*Based on the great work of Scott Kacsmar from Football Outsiders

2018 Weekly Betting Lines (wks 1-16)

Week	1	2	3	5	6	7	8	9	10	11	12	13	14	15	16
Opp	ARI	IND	GB	NO	CAR	DAL	NYG	ATL	TB	HOU	DAL	PHI	NYG	JAX	TEN
H/A	A	H	H	A	H	H	A	H	A	H	A	A	H	A	A
Line	1	-3	3	7.5	-1	-1	3.5	2.5	3.5	3	6	7.5	-1.5	8	5.5

Home Lines (wks 1-16)

Week	2	3	6	7	9	11	14
Opp	IND	GB	CAR	DAL	ATL	HOU	NYG
Line	-3	3	-1	-1	2.5	3	-1.5

Road Lines (wks 1-16)

Week	1	5	8	10	12	13	15	16
Opp	ARI	NO	NYG	TB	DAL	PHI	JAX	TEN
Line	1	7.5	3.5	3.5	6	7.5	8	5.5

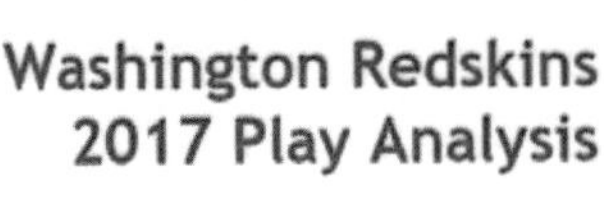

Washington Redskins 2017 Play Analysis

2017 Play Tendencies

All Pass %	59%
All Pass Rk	10
All Rush %	41%
All Rush Rk	23
1 Score Pass %	55%
1 Score Pass Rk	23
2016 1 Score Pass %	61%
2016 1 Score Pass Rk	11
2017 Pass Increase %	-6%
Pass Increase Rk	27
1 Score Rush %	45%
1 Score Rush Rk	10
Up Pass %	52%
Up Pass Rk	9
Up Rush %	48%
Up Rush Rk	24
Down Pass %	69%
Down Pass Rk	6
Down Rush %	31%
Down Rush Rk	27

2017 Down & Distance Tendencies

Down	Distance	Total Plays	Pass Rate	Run Rate	Play Success %
1	Short (1-3)	4	50%	50%	25%
	Med (4-7)	11	9%	91%	64%
	Long (8-10)	285	38%	62%	45%
	XL (11+)	10	70%	30%	60%
2	Short (1-3)	32	34%	66%	63%
	Med (4-7)	87	69%	31%	51%
	Long (8-10)	84	70%	30%	45%
	XL (11+)	44	84%	16%	36%
3	Short (1-3)	36	69%	31%	42%
	Med (4-7)	54	91%	9%	41%
	Long (8-10)	30	97%	3%	20%
	XL (11+)	32	94%	6%	25%
4	Short (1-3)	7	43%	57%	86%
	Med (4-7)	3	100%	0%	33%

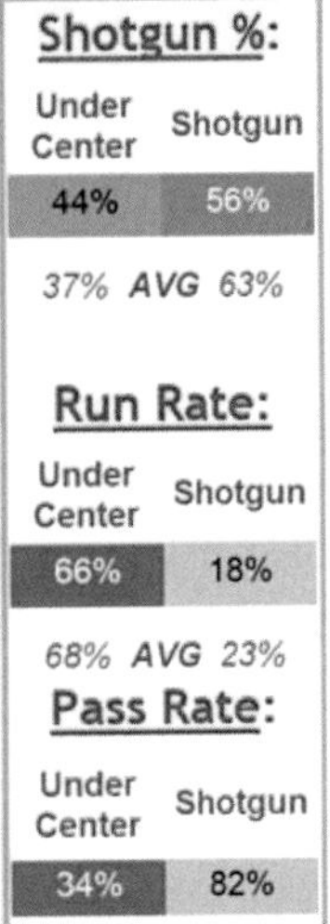

Shotgun %:

Under Center	Shotgun
44%	56%
37% AVG	63%

Run Rate:

Under Center	Shotgun
66%	18%
68% AVG	23%

Pass Rate:

Under Center	Shotgun
34%	82%
32% AVG	77%

Short Yardage Intelligence:

2nd and Short Run

Run Freq	Run Rk	NFL Run Freq Avg	Run 1D Rate	Run NFL 1D Avg
66%	20	67%	57%	69%

2nd and Short Pass

Pass Freq	Pass Rk	NFL Pass Freq Avg	Pass 1D Rate	Pass NFL 1D Avg
34%	13	33%	55%	53%

Most Frequent Play

Down	Distance	Play Type	Player	Total Plays	Play Success %
1	Med (4-7)	RUSH	Rob Kelley	5	60%
	Long (8-10)	RUSH	Samaje Perine	83	35%
	XL (11+)	PASS	Niles Paul	2	50%
		RUSH	Chris Thompson	2	50%
2	Short (1-3)	RUSH	Samaje Perine	14	57%
	Med (4-7)	PASS	Jamison Crowder	11	45%
			Josh Doctson	11	55%
	Long (8-10)	PASS	Josh Doctson	14	29%
	XL (11+)	PASS	Chris Thompson	7	43%
3	Short (1-3)	RUSH	Kirk Cousins	5	60%
	Med (4-7)	PASS	Jamison Crowder	14	36%
	Long (8-10)	PASS	Ryan Grant	6	0%
	XL (11+)	PASS	Jamison Crowder	6	33%

Most Successful Play*

Down	Distance	Play Type	Player	Total Plays	Play Success %
1	Med (4-7)	RUSH	Rob Kelley	5	60%
	Long (8-10)	PASS	Chris Thompson	7	100%
2	Short (1-3)	RUSH	Samaje Perine	14	57%
	Med (4-7)	PASS	Chris Thompson	6	67%
	Long (8-10)	PASS	Jamison Crowder	13	62%
	XL (11+)	PASS	Chris Thompson	7	43%
3	Short (1-3)	RUSH	Kirk Cousins	5	60%
	Med (4-7)	PASS	Vernon Davis	5	60%
		RUSH	Kirk Cousins	5	60%
	Long (8-10)	PASS	Jamison Crowder	5	20%
	XL (11+)	PASS	Jamison Crowder	6	33%

*Minimum 5 plays to qualify

2017 Snap Rates

Wk	Opp	Score	Vernon Davis	Josh Doctson	Jamison Crowder	Ryan Grant	Samaje Perine	Chris Thompson	Jordan Reed	Rob Kelley
1	PHI	L 30-17	27 (43%)	20 (32%)	49 (78%)	37 (59%)		30 (48%)	55 (87%)	33 (52%)
2	LA	W 27-20	55 (77%)	29 (41%)	38 (54%)	30 (42%)	26 (37%)	29 (41%)	40 (56%)	16 (23%)
3	OAK	W 27-10	56 (82%)	36 (53%)	48 (71%)	34 (50%)	30 (44%)	28 (41%)		
4	KC	L 29-20	35 (70%)	17 (34%)	36 (72%)	22 (44%)	12 (24%)	26 (52%)	13 (26%)	12 (24%)
6	SF	W 26-24	48 (65%)	19 (26%)	53 (72%)	40 (54%)	25 (34%)	45 (61%)	54 (73%)	
7	PHI	L 34-24	29 (45%)	54 (84%)	58 (91%)	26 (41%)		37 (58%)	50 (78%)	27 (42%)
8	DAL	L 33-19	49 (83%)	47 (80%)	56 (95%)	40 (68%)		47 (80%)	21 (36%)	12 (20%)
9	SEA	W 17-14	47 (75%)	56 (89%)		59 (94%)	6 (10%)	33 (52%)		26 (41%)
10	MIN	L 38-30	64 (85%)	69 (92%)	60 (80%)	9 (12%)	20 (27%)	45 (60%)		10 (13%)
11	NO	L 34-31	62 (90%)	60 (87%)	41 (59%)	53 (77%)	48 (70%)	18 (26%)		
12	NYG	W 20-10	65 (92%)	71 (100%)	37 (52%)	49 (69%)	50 (70%)			
13	DAL	L 38-14	54 (90%)	60 (100%)	49 (82%)	53 (88%)	34 (57%)			
14	LAC	L 30-13	42 (84%)	47 (94%)	41 (82%)	30 (60%)	40 (80%)			
15	ARI	W 20-15	49 (92%)	52 (98%)	38 (72%)	45 (85%)	33 (62%)			
16	DEN	W 27-11	67 (97%)	69 (100%)	31 (45%)	44 (64%)	34 (49%)			
17	NYG	L 18-10	55 (96%)	51 (89%)	39 (68%)	44 (77%)	2 (4%)			
Grand Total			804 (79%)	757 (75%)	674 (71%)	615 (61%)	360 (44%)	338 (52%)	233 (59%)	136 (31%)

Personnel Groupings

Personnel	Team %	NFL Avg	Succ. %
1-1 [3WR]	66%	59%	45%
1-2 [2WR]	23%	19%	47%
1-3 [1WR]	8%	5%	38%

Grouping Tendencies

Personnel	Pass Rate	Pass Succ. %	Run Succ. %
1-1 [3WR]	69%	44%	45%
1-2 [2WR]	46%	50%	45%
1-3 [1WR]	30%	42%	36%

Red Zone Targets (min 3)

Receiver	All	Inside 5	6-10	11-20
Josh Doctson	16	4	3	9
Jamison Crowder	14	5		9
Ryan Grant	9	1	2	6
Vernon Davis	9	1	1	7
Chris Thompson	6	1	3	2
Jordan Reed	4	1		3
Terrelle Pryor	4	1		3
Brian Quick	1			1

Red Zone Rushes (min 3)

Rusher	All	Inside 5	6-10	11-20
Samaje Perine	24	4	7	13
Rob Kelley	13	7	5	1
Chris Thompson	10		2	8
Kirk Cousins	10	4	2	4

Early Down Target Rate

RB	TE	WR
20%	25%	54%
23%	21% NFL AVG	56%

Overall Target Success %

RB	TE	WR
53% #3	50% #18	47% #17

Washington Redskins 2017 Passing Recap & 2018 Outlook

When the Redskins passed last year, they did so from 11 personnel on 65% of their first downs, 70% of second downs, and 97% of third downs. Last year Smith's Chiefs averaged 57%, 57%, and 63%, all well below the NFL average. The lack of grouping diversity may be a detriment to Smith. Last year Cousins ranked 30th on third downs short of the sticks: His completions fell an average of 2.1 yards short of the line to gain. Smith has also struggled on third down, but he improved last year, ranking 14th and falling only 0.3 yards short of the sticks on average. If the team can maintain its early-down passing productivity, and if Gruden can make third-down adjustments that cater to Smith's strengths, the Redskins will see an efficiency boost.

Kirk Cousins Rating All Downs

91
61
106
80
107
90

Kirk Cousins Rating Early Downs

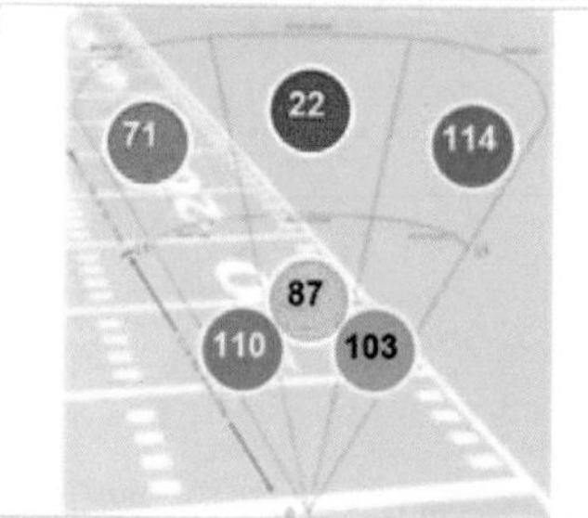

2017 Standard Passing Table

QB	Comp	Att	Comp %	Yds	YPA	TDs	INT	Sacks	Rating	Rk
Kirk Cousins	347	540	64%	4,093	7.6	27	13	41	94	18
NFL Avg			62%		7.0				87.5	

2017 Advanced Passing Table

QB	Success %	EDSR Passing Success %	20+ Yd Pass Gains	20+ Yd Pass %	30+ Yd Pass Gains	30+ Yd Pass %	Avg. Air Yds per Comp	Avg. YAC per Comp	20+ Air Yd Comp	20+ Air Yd %
Kirk Cousins	45%	51%	59	10.9%	28	5.2%	5.6	6.1	21	6%
NFL Avg	44%	48%	27.7	8.8%	10.3	3.3%	6.0	4.7	11.7	6%

Interception Rates by Down

Yards to Go	1	2	3	4	Total
1 & 2	0.0%	0.0%	0.0%	0.0%	0.0%
3, 4, 5	0.0%	0.0%	0.0%	0.0%	0.0%
6 - 9		3.1%	4.6%	0.0%	3.7%
10 - 14	1.8%	1.7%	3.0%	33.3%	2.3%
15+	0.0%	0.0%	5.9%		2.1%
Total	1.7%	1.8%	2.9%	9.1%	2.2%

3rd Down Passing - Short of Sticks Analysis

QB	Avg. Yds to Go	Avg. YIA (of Comp)	Avg Yds Short	Short of Sticks Rate	Short Rk
Kirk Cousins	7.7	5.6	-2.1	64%	30
NFL Avg	7.8	6.7	-1.1	60%	

Air Yds vs YAC

Air Yds %	YAC %	Rk
48%	52%	41
58%	42%	

2017 Receiving Recap & 2018 Outlook

The Redskins have a great receiving back in Thompson, but he's not immune to third-down inefficiency. Washington threw to running backs at an above-average rate on third downs with a below-average 30% Success Rate. Conversely, on early downs they targeted backs at a below-average rate, but they had a league-best 62% Success Rate, which is better than the marks they got from their wide receivers and tight ends. They still lack an adequate replacement for Garcon, and last year Crowder was inefficient. For the past two years Richardson ranked as the No. 2 wide receiver in early-down deep passing with a 127 rating and 16.3 YPA.

Player *Min 50 Targets*	Targets	Comp %	YPA	Rating	TOARS	Success %	Success Rk	Missed YPA Rk	YAS % Rk	TDs
Jamison Crowder	103	64%	7.7	81	4.5	43%	102	91	89	3
Josh Doctson	78	45%	6.4	81	4.1	40%	114	88	11	6
Vernon Davis	68	63%	9.5	97	4.1	47%	76	37	35	3
Ryan Grant	65	69%	8.8	98	4.1	52%	47	62	46	4
Chris Thompson	60	73%	9.9	120	4.3	56%	22	113	68	4

Directional Passer Rating Delivered

Receiver	Short Left	Short Middle	Short Right	Deep Left	Deep Middle	Deep Right	Player Total
Jamison Crowder	57	68	101	54	96	110	81
Josh Doctson	111	73	73	80	0	122	81
Vernon Davis	78	96	89	89	134	102	97
Ryan Grant	123	91	65	147	104	60	98
Chris Thompson	154	68	93	40		149	119
Terrelle Pryor	84	100	58	40	40	113	83
Jordan Reed	127	95	111		85	40	111
Samaje Perine	141	95	97				112
Niles Paul	56	70	81	119		40	76
Kapri Bibbs	85	56	155				118
Brian Quick	104	104	63			119	104
Rob Kelley	79		57				62
Team Total	109	80	91	91	61	104	95

2017 Rushing Recap & 2017 Outlook

If the offensive line stays healthy, they could be much better on the ground. In 2016 they faced the fifth-toughest run-defense schedule and ranked fourth in efficiency. Kelley and Jones combined for nine rushing touchdowns and both had Success Rates above 48%. The fourth-rounder Perine struggled last year, but this year Guice should be a better player as a second-round pick. With a more mobile quarterback in Smith, the offense could have even more wrinkles.

Player *Min 50 Rushes*	Rushes	YPC	Success %	Success Rk	Missed YPA Rk	YTS % Rk	YAS % Rk	Early Down Success %	Early Down Success Rk	TDs
Samaje Perine	175	3.4	43%	47	19	12	67	44%	39	1
Chris Thompson	64	4.6	42%	54	72	63	33	45%	34	2
Rob Kelley	62	3.1	48%	21	26	3	58	48%	23	3

Yards per Carry by Direction

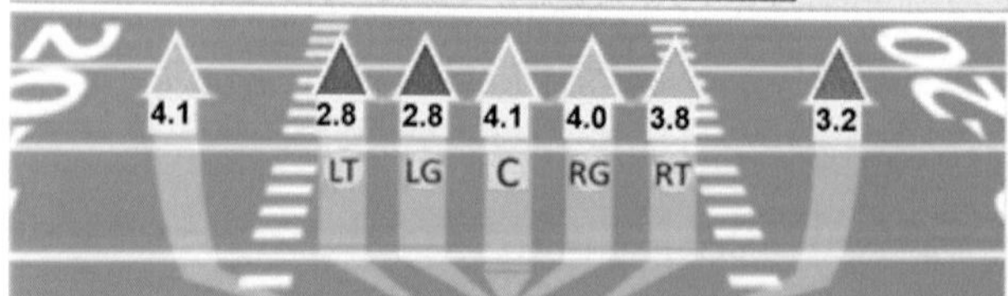

Directional Run Frequency

18%
10%
11%
23%
12%
13%
15%
LT
LG
C
RG
RT

WAS-4

By going 100% run in 2017 they allowed defenses to sell out to stop the run, and they did: In 2016 the Redskins gained first downs on 71% of such runs. Last year, they averaged 20%. When leading, they almost exclusively ran with Perine out of big sets with one wide receiver and two-plus tight ends with a 10% Success Rate and 0.4 YPC. And when trailing they ran only out of 11 personnel, usually with Thompson, for a 33% Success Rate.

In the passing game, it's easy to pinpoint last year's problems. In 2016, Garcon was tremendous with a 54% Success Rate and 10.3 YPA on third down. The tight ends were solid as well with marks of 54% and 10.1 YPA. The rest of the team, though, was terrible: All other receivers combined for a 38% Success Rate and 7.6 YPA. In 2017, Garcon's replacements failed to replicate his production and the tight ends declined. It's that simple. Jamison Crowder has had poor third-down Success Rates each of the past two years (39% in 2016 and 32% in 2017). Ryan Grant and Terrelle Pryor led the team last year, but neither averaged even 44%, and Pryor had a disastrous 3.6 YPA. But by far the worst wide receiver was Josh Doctson, who recorded an 11% Success Rate and 2.7 YPA. And the tight ends combined for a 42% Success Rate and 8.3 YPA.

(cont'd - see WAS-5)

Matthew Freedman's Fantasy Corner

Thompson's not a starter, but no Washington running back had more than his 123 receptions, 1,965 scrimmage yards, and 13 touchdowns in Cousins' three years as a starter. Since 2015, Thompson has averaged a viable 10.0 fantasy points per game in point-per-reception (PPR) scoring across 39 contests, and last year he was the fantasy RB11 with 15.1 PPR points per game. He's a locked-in part of the offense with 35-plus receptions in each of the past three years, and he's available outside of the top 36 players at the position with an average draft position in the 120s. Given the team's dearth of receiving options, Gruden might choose to use Thompson in something of a Tyreek-esque playmaker role.

Division History: Season Wins & 2018 Projection

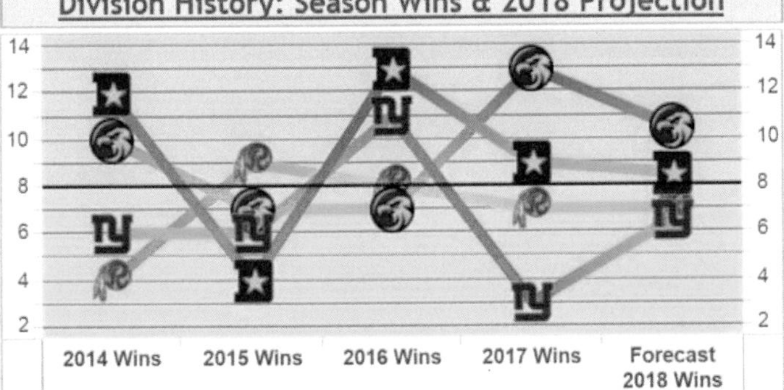

Rank of 2018 Defensive Pass Efficiency Faced by Week

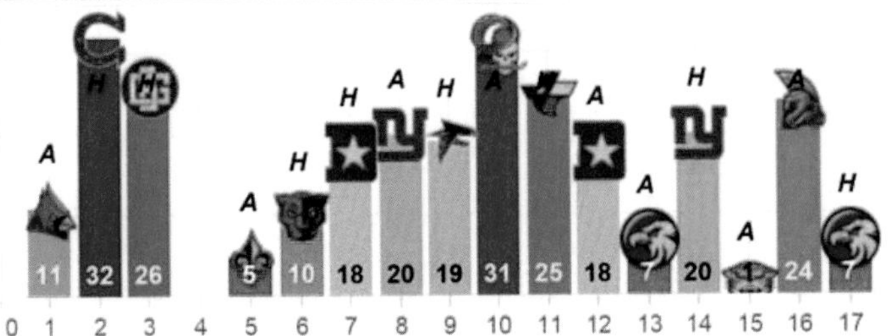

Rank of 2018 Defensive Rush Efficiency Faced by Week

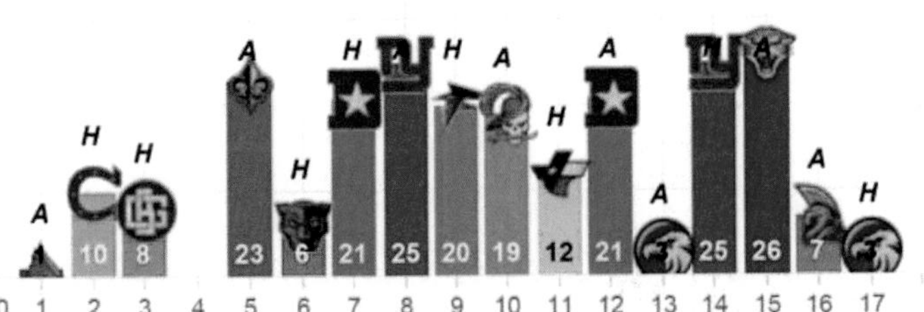

2017 Situational Usage by Player & Position

Usage Rate by Score

		Being Blown Out (14+)	Down Big (9-13)	One Score	Large Lead (9-13)	Blowout Lead (14+)	Grand Total
RUSH	Samaje Perine	13%	12%	21%	31%	20%	20%
	Chris Thompson	3%	7%	7%	3%	17%	7%
	Jamison Crowder	1%		1%			1%
	Josh Doctson			0%			0%
	Rob Kelley	3%	4%	9%	3%		7%
	Kapri Bibbs		1%	3%		6%	2%
	Niles Paul			0%			0%
	Byron Marshall	4%		1%	3%		1%
	Mack Brown			0%		13%	1%
	LeShun Daniels Jr.	2%		0%			0%
	Total	27%	24%	42%	41%	56%	40%
PASS	Samaje Perine	8%		3%			3%
	Chris Thompson	2%	12%	5%	10%	13%	6%
	Jamison Crowder	21%	15%	11%	3%	6%	12%
	Josh Doctson	12%	8%	9%	7%	7%	9%
	Rob Kelley	2%		1%			1%
	Vernon Davis	6%	17%	7%	3%	6%	8%
	Ryan Grant	5%	8%	8%	7%	6%	7%
	Kapri Bibbs		1%	3%			2%
	Terrelle Pryor	4%		5%	3%	4%	4%
	Jordan Reed	7%	4%	3%	17%	2%	4%
	Niles Paul	1%	4%	2%	3%		2%
	Byron Marshall	1%	4%	1%			1%
	Mack Brown					2%	0%
	Brian Quick	2%		1%			1%
	Maurice Harris	1%	3%	0%			1%
	Jeremy Sprinkle			0%	3%		0%
	Total	73%	76%	58%	59%	44%	60%

Positional Target Distribution vs NFL Average

		NFL Wide				Team Only			
		Left	Middle	Right	**Total**	Left	Middle	Right	**Total**
Deep	WR	970	491	965	**2,426**	16	18	22	**56**
	TE	182	144	179	**505**	10	6	9	**25**
	RB	38	9	39	**86**	1		3	**4**
	All	**1,190**	**644**	**1,183**	**3,017**	**27**	**24**	**34**	**85**
Short	WR	2,786	1,602	2,700	**7,088**	76	69	90	**235**
	TE	835	812	1,127	**2,774**	28	27	43	**98**
	RB	1,291	799	1,251	**3,341**	30	24	44	**98**
	All	**4,912**	**3,213**	**5,078**	**13,203**	**134**	**120**	**177**	**431**
Total		**6,102**	**3,857**	**6,261**	**16,220**	**161**	**144**	**211**	**516**

Positional Success Rates vs NFL Average

		NFL Wide				Team Only			
		Left	Middle	Right	**Total**	Left	Middle	Right	**Total**
Deep	WR	37%	46%	38%	**39%**	38%	28%	36%	**34%**
	TE	37%	53%	45%	**45%**	50%	50%	44%	**48%**
	RB	37%	56%	36%	**38%**	0%		67%	**50%**
	All	**37%**	**48%**	**39%**	**40%**	**41%**	**33%**	**41%**	**39%**
Short	WR	51%	58%	50%	**52%**	57%	55%	42%	**51%**
	TE	51%	56%	49%	**52%**	46%	52%	51%	**50%**
	RB	44%	51%	42%	**45%**	67%	46%	57%	**57%**
	All	**49%**	**56%**	**48%**	**50%**	**57%**	**53%**	**48%**	**52%**
Total		**47%**	**54%**	**46%**	**48%**	**54%**	**49%**	**47%**	**50%**

Successful Play Rate
0% 100%

Washington Redskins - Success by Personnel Grouping & Play Type

Play Type	1-1 [3WR]	1-2 [2WR]	2-1 [2WR]	1-0 [4WR]	1-3 [1WR]	0-1 [4WR]	2-0 [3WR]	2-2 [1WR]	0-0 [5WR]	2-3 [0WR]	1-4 [0WR]	Grand Total
PASS	44% (445, 77%)	50% (105, 18%)	100% (1, 0%)	100% (1, 0%)	42% (24, 4%)	50% (2, 0%)		100% (1, 0%)	0% (1, 0%)	0% (1, 0%)		45% (581, 100%)
RUSH	45% (201, 50%)	45% (121, 30%)		100% (1, 0%)	36% (55, 14%)		50% (2, 0%)	100% (2, 0%)		35% (17, 4%)	50% (2, 0%)	44% (401, 100%)
TOTAL	45% (646, 66%)	47% (226, 23%)	100% (1, 0%)	100% (2, 0%)	38% (79, 8%)	50% (2, 0%)	50% (2, 0%)	100% (3, 0%)	0% (1, 0%)	33% (18, 2%)	50% (2, 0%)	45% (982, 100%)

Format Line 1: Success Rate Line 2: Total # of Plays, % of All Plays (by type)

WAS-5

How can the Redskins improve in 2018? They should be better on the ground, where they'll get an immediate third-down boost thanks to Smith's rushing ability. Last year he had a 53% third-down Success Rate and is a better runner than Cousins. They should also improve thanks to the rookie Derrius Guice, who should take over as the lead and short-yardage back.

In the passing game, their best hope is an easier pass-defense schedule. They also will need to hope that Smith plays better than Cousins, Gruden fixes their third-down woes, and the offensive line stays healthy. They added Paul Richardson, who should play frequently in 11 personnel, but in Seattle he was successful on just 43% of his third-down targets. Gruden needs to get more creative with his personnel groupings, if only to force opposing defenses to strategize more than they've had to the last two years.

Third downs are important to the Redskins partially because they have been so good on early downs. They ranked eighth in early-down Success Rate last year and were particularly great when passing, recording a 51% Success Rate (No. 6).

The Redskins are not bad on offense. They were just abhorrent last year on third down. They can fix that if they study their tendencies and improve their play calling. And if that happens, their entire offense will perform much better.

Defensively the Redskins were tremendous against the pass, allowing just 40% of passes to grade as successful (No. 2), but they allowed a horrible 53% Success Rate on rushes (No. 32), which contributed to their inability to overcome second-half deficits: Opposing offenses could run down the clock. Unfortunately for the Redskins, they play a more difficult rushing-offense schedule this year, so they'll need their defensive line to be healthy and play better. The addition of No. 13 overall pick nose tackle Da'Ron Payne should help.

The Redskins and their fans hope that with Cousins gone the rain cloud has left the DC skyline, but 2018 might not go swimmingly. Washington is favored in just four games and is scheduled to do no better than Cousins' worst starting record (7-9). I'm cautiously optimistic that Smith will fit in well with the offense, but I'm still concerned about the third-down play calling and wide receiver production.

Receiving Success by Personnel Grouping

Position	Player	1-1 [3WR]	1-2 [2WR]	1-3 [1WR]	0-1 [4WR]	2-2 [1WR]	2-3 [0WR]	Total
RB	Rob Kelley	75% 4.8 84.4 (4)	0% -0.3 42.4 (3)					43% 2.6 62.2 (7)
TE	Vernon Davis	49% 9.4 99.0 (49)	47% 10.4 95.4 (15)	0% 0.5 56.3 (2)	100% 31.0 118.8 (1)		0% 0.0 39.6 (1)	47% 9.5 96.9 (68)
	Jordan Reed	52% 5.8 103.1 (25)	80% 6.5 127.1 (10)					60% 6.0 110.5 (35)
WR	Jamison Crowder	45% 7.3 80.1 (95)	38% 11.4 91.1 (8)					45% 7.7 80.9 (103)
	Josh Doctson	42% 5.9 83.4 (50)	35% 8.7 67.8 (17)	44% 6.0 101.2 (9)	0% 0.0 39.6 (1)	100% 4.0 83.3 (1)		41% 6.4 81.3 (78)
	Ryan Grant	52% 8.9 98.6 (56)	56% 8.4 99.3 (9)					52% 8.8 97.8 (65)

Format Line 1: Success Rate Line 2: YPA Line 3: Passer Rating Line 4: Total # of Plays

Successful Play Rate
0% 100%

Rushing Success by Personnel Grouping

Position	Player	1-1 [3WR]	1-2 [2WR]	1-0 [4WR]	1-3 [1WR]	2-0 [3WR]	2-2 [1WR]	2-3 [0WR]	1-4 [0WR]	Total
RB	Samaje Perine	51% 3.7 (69)	43% 4.1 (67)		28% 2.2 (36)		100% 2.0 (1)	0% 0.0 (1)	0% -1.0 (1)	43% 3.4 (175)
	Chris Thompson	41% 4.7 (56)	33% 3.2 (6)		100% 5.0 (2)					42% 4.6 (64)
	Rob Kelley	37% 2.4 (19)	42% 3.3 (26)	100% 3.0 (1)	63% 4.5 (8)	50% 3.0 (2)	100% 4.0 (1)	75% 3.5 (4)	100% 1.0 (1)	48% 3.1 (62)

Format Line 1: Success Rate Line 2: YPC Line 3: Total # of Plays

Made in the USA
Middletown, DE
14 July 2018